Simply Java™ Programming

H. M. Deitel
Deitel & Associates, Inc.

P. J. Deitel
Deitel & Associates, Inc.

J. A. Listfield
Deitel & Associates, Inc.

C. H. Yaeger
Deitel & Associates, Inc.

S. Zhang
Deitel & Associates, Inc.

PEARSON

Prentice Hall

Upper Saddle River, NJ 07458

Library of Congress Cataloging-in-Publication Data

On file

Vice President and Editorial Director: *Marcia Horton*

Senior Acquisitions Editor: *Kate Hargett*

Assistant Editor: *Sarah Parker*

Editorial Assistant: *Michael Giacobbe*

Vice President and Director of Production and Manufacturing, ESM: *David W. Riccardi*

Executive Managing Editor: *Vince O'Brien*

Managing Editor: *Tom Manshreck*

Production Editors: *Chirag Thakkar, John Lovell*

Director of Creative Services: *Paul Belfanti*

Creative Director: *Carole Anson*

Art Director: *Geoff Cassar*

Chapter Opener and Cover Designer: *Dr. Harvey Deitel and David Merrell*

Manufacturing Manager: *Trudy Pisciotti*

Manufacturing Buyer: *Lisa McDowell*

Marketing Manager: *Pamela Shaffer*

Marketing Assistant: *Barrie Reinhold*

 © 2004 by Pearson Education, Inc.
Upper Saddle River, New Jersey 07458

Printed in the United States of America

10 9 8 7 6 5 4 3 2 1

ISBN 0-13-142648-6

Pearson Education Ltd., *London*

Pearson Education Australia Pty. Ltd., *Sydney*

Pearson Education Singapore, Pte. Ltd.

Pearson Education North Asia Ltd., *Hong Kong*

Pearson Education Canada, Inc., *Toronto*

Pearson Educación de Mexico, S.A. de C.V.

Pearson Education–Japan, *Tokyo*

Pearson Education Malaysia, Pte. Ltd.

Pearson Education, Inc., *Upper Saddle River, New Jersey*

Simply Java™ Programming

Deitel Books, Cyber Classrooms, Complete Training Courses and Web-Based Training Courses Published by Prentice Hall

Simply Series

Simply C#®: An Application-Driven Tutorial Approach

Simply Visual Basic® .NET: An Application Driven Tutorial Approach (Visual Studio .NET 2002 Edition)

Simply Java™ Programming: An Application-Driven Tutorial Approach

Simply Visual Basic® .NET: An Application Driven Tutorial Approach (Visual Studio .NET 2003 Edition)

How to Program Series

Advanced Java™ 2 Platform How to Program
C How to Program, 4/E
C++ How to Program, 4/E
C#® How to Program
e-Business and e-Commerce How to Program
Internet and World Wide Web How to Program, 2/E
Java™ How to Program, 5/E
Perl How to Program
Python How to Program
Visual Basic® 6 How to Program
Visual Basic® .NET How to Program, 2/E
Visual C++® .NET How to Program
Wireless Internet & Mobile Business How to Program
XML How to Program

.NET How to Program Series

C#® How to Program
Visual Basic® .NET How to Program, 2/E
Visual C++® .NET How to Program

Visual Studio Series

C#® How to Program
Getting Started with Microsoft® Visual C++® 6 with an Introduction to MFC
Simply C#®: An Application-Driven Tutorial Approach
Simply Visual Basic® .NET: An Application- Driven Tutorial Approach (Visual Studio .NET 2002 Edition)
Simply Visual Basic® .NET: An Application- Driven Tutorial Approach (Visual Studio .NET 2003 Edition)
Visual Basic® 6 How to Program
Visual Basic® .NET How to Program, 2/E
Visual C++® .NET How to Program

CS1 Programming Series

Java™ Software Design

For Managers Series

e-Business and e-Commerce for Managers

DEITEL® Developer Series

Java™ Web Services for Experienced Programmers
Web Services A Technical Introduction

Multimedia Cyber Classroom Series

C++ Multimedia Cyber Classroom, 4/E
C# Multimedia Cyber Classroom
e-Business and e-Commerce Multimedia Cyber Classroom
Internet and World Wide Web Multimedia Cyber Classroom, 2/E
Java™ 2 Multimedia Cyber Classroom, 5/E
Perl Multimedia Cyber Classroom
Python Multimedia Cyber Classroom
Visual Basic® 6 Multimedia Cyber Classroom
Visual Basic® .NET Multimedia Cyber Classroom, 2/E
Wireless Internet & Mobile Business Programming Multimedia Cyber Classroom
XML Multimedia Cyber Classroom

The Complete Training Course Series

The Complete C++ Training Course, 4/E
The Complete C#® Training Course
The Complete e-Business and e-Commerce Programming Training Course
The Complete Internet and World Wide Web Programming Training Course, 2/E
The Complete Java™ 2 Training Course, 5/E
The Complete Perl Training Course
The Complete Python Training Course
The Complete Visual Basic® 6 Training Course
The Complete Visual Basic® .NET Training Course, 2/E
The Complete Wireless Internet & Mobile Business Programming Training Course
The Complete XML Programming Training Course

Computer Science Series

Operating Systems, 3/E

To communicate with the authors, send e-mail to:

deitel@deitel.com

For information on corporate on-site seminars and public seminars offered by Deitel & Associates, Inc. worldwide, visit:

www.deitel.com

For continuing updates on Prentice Hall and Deitel publications visit:

www.deitel.com,
www.prenhall.com/deitel or
www.InformIT.com/deitel

To Barbara Deitel:

Thank you for coining the name "Simply Series" for these books that work so hard to teach complex topics in a straightforward and engaging manner.

Harvey and Paul

To all my grandparents:

Maurice and Gertrude Fogel, and Sol and Sylvia Listfield.

Jeff

To Perry, Susan, Lauren, Gary and Dana:

You have given me holidays full of wonderful memories. Thank you.

Cheryl

To my mom and sister:

Your support is abundant and your love is nourishing.

Su

Trademarks:

Brief Table of Contents

CONTENTS

PREFACE

Welcome to Java, the Internet and World-Wide-Web programming! This book, the second in our new *Simply* series, was a joy to create. Our goal was to write a book that focuses on core concepts and features of Java while keeping the discussion of this highly technical subject as simple as possible.

To achieve these goals, we implemented an innovative teaching methodology. We present the core concepts of leading-edge computing technologies using the tutorial-based, APPLICATION-DRIVEN approach, combined with the DEITEL® signature LIVE-CODE approach of teaching programming using complete, working, real-world applications. We merged the notion of a lab manual with that of a conventional textbook, creating a book that works well in a traditional classroom setting or with students sitting at computers and building each example application as they read the tutorials.

As students work through the tutorials, they learn about Java and its fundamental features, such as graphical-user-interface (GUI) components, multimedia (audio, images, animation and video), file processing, database processing and Internet and World-Wide-Web-based client/server networking. At the end of most sections, we provide self-review questions with answers so that students receive immediate feedback on their understanding of the material. Hundreds of additional self-review questions with answers are available on this book's Companion Web Site.

Features in Simply Java Programming

This book is loaded with pedagogic features, including:

- **APPLICATION-DRIVEN *Tutorial Approach.*** Each tutorial uses a contemporary, real-world application to teach programming concepts. The examples and exercises are up-to-the-minute with Internet/Web-related examples and with popular applications, such as game playing, graphics, multimedia and even a three-tier Web-based bookstore. Most examples have a business focus. At the beginning of each tutorial, students "test-drive" the completed application so they can see how it works. Then, they build the application by following step-by-step instructions. The book concentrates on the principles of good software design and stresses program clarity.

- ***LIVE-CODE Approach.*** This book uses LIVE-CODE examples. Each tutorial ends with the complete, working application code and the students can run the application that they just created. We call this method of teaching and writing the ***LIVE-CODE Approach.*** We feel that this approach is more effective than presenting only snippets of code out of the context of a complete application.

- ***Real-World Technologies.*** This text incorporates today's technologies to develop useful applications. For example, we use the Unified Modeling Language™ (UML) to replace flowcharts—an older standard. The UML has become the preferred graphical modeling language for designing object-oriented applications. In *Simply Java*, we use UML to show the flow of control

for several applications, so students gain practice reading the type of diagrams that are used in industry.

■ *Graphical User Interface (GUI) Programming.* From the first tutorial, we immerse students in GUI programming techniques and modifying Java GUIs. Students who learn these techniques can create graphical applications quickly and easily. The early tutorials provide students with a foundation for designing GUIs—concepts that they will apply throughout the book as we teach core programming concepts. Many tutorials contain *GUI Design Tips* that are summarized at the end of the tutorials for easy reference. Additionally, Appendix C, GUI Design Guidelines, compiles these tips to help students as they prepare for exams.

■ *Full-Color Presentation.* This book is in full color so that students can see sample outputs as they would appear on a monitor. Also, we syntax color the Java code, similar to the way Java integrated development environments (IDEs) color the code in their editor windows. This way, students can match what they see in the book with what they see on their screens. Our syntax-coloring conventions are as follows:

```
comments appear in green
keywords appear in dark blue
literal values and constants appear in light blue
text, class, method and variable names appear in black
errors appear in red
```

■ *Graphics and Multimedia.* Graphics and multimedia make applications fun to create and use. In our introduction to graphics, Tutorial 20, we discuss basic concepts and features of graphics. Part of Java's initial appeal was that it supported graphics, enabling Java programmers to visually enhance their applications. You will learn several of Java's capabilities for drawing two-dimensional shapes and controlling colors. In Tutorial 27, we expand our discussion of graphics by introducing additional methods of the `Graphics` class to outline and fill in different types of shapes. In Tutorial 28, you will explore the Java Speech API, which produces synthetic speech from text inputs. You will create a phone book application in which the user selects a name and the application speaks the corresponding phone number.

■ *Databases.* Databases are crucial to businesses today, and we use real-world applications to teach the fundamentals of database programming. Tutorial 26 and Tutorial 31 familiarize students with databases, presented in the context of two applications—an ATM and a three-tier Web-based bookstore. In Tutorial 26, you will learn how to connect to a database and retrieve information from a database using the JDBC API.

■ *Case Study.* This book concludes with a sequence of four tutorials in which the student builds a Web-based bookstore application. In Tutorial 29, you will learn the multi-tier architecture that is used to create Web applications. You will learn about Web servers and install the Apache Tomcat Web server, which you will need to run your bookstore application. In Tutorial 30, you will use HTML to create the client tier (also called the top tier)—the user interface of your application. In Tutorial 31, you will create the application's information tier and create the connections with your database as well as use SQL statements to obtain information from the database. Finally in Tutorial 32, you will create the middle tier of the Web-based bookstore and complete the application.

■ *Object-Oriented Programming.* Object-oriented programming is the most widely employed technique for developing robust, reusable software, and Java offers advanced object-oriented programming features. This book intro-

duces students to declaring classes and using objects, laying a solid foundation for future programming courses.

■ *Java Debugger.* The Java 2 Software Development Kit (J2SDK) provides software called a debugger, which allows you to analyze the behavior of your applications to locate logic errors. At the ends of several tutorials, we provide *Using the Debugger* sections in which you will learn to detect and remove logic errors by using the Java debugger.

Notes to the Instructor

Focus of the Book

Our goal was clear: Produce a Java textbook for introductory-level courses in computer programming for students with little or no programming experience. This book teaches computer programming principles and the Java language, including data types, control statements, object-oriented programming, classes, GUI concepts, event-driven programming, graphics, database, Web-applications development and more. After mastering the material in this book, students will be able to program in Java and to employ its cross-platform capabilities.

Lab Setup

Before you can compile and run the applications in this book, the Java 2 Software Development Kit (J2SDK), or an appropriate Java development tool, must be installed. We discuss installing the J2SDK in the *Before You Begin* section that follows the Preface. For computer labs in which students are not allowed to install software, instructors and system administrators must ensure that appropriate Java software is installed on the lab computers in advance of the course. Several tutorials require additional software. Tutorial 26 requires IBM's Cloudscape database software, which is included on the CD that accompanies this book. The Cloudscape installation instructions appear in Tutorial 26. Tutorial 28 uses speech synthesis software, which must be installed to run and develop the **Phone Book** application. Download and installation instructions for this software appear in Tutorial 28. Configuring and executing the **Bookstore** case study in Tutorials 29–32 require IBM's Cloudscape database software and Apache Tomcat software, which is also included on the CD that accompanies this book. Installation instructions for Apache Tomcat appear in Tutorial 29. [*Note:* For instructors and students who prefer to use Microsoft Access for the database applications, we will post instructions at www.deitel.com/books/simplyJava1/index.html.]

Note Regarding the Platform We Used to Develop the Book

We assume that students are using Windows platform computers (Windows 2000 or Windows XP, in particular), so all directory names, instructions and sample screen captures appear in Windows format. However, the instructions and concepts presented work well on most computer platforms. [*Note:* All windows that show source code were created in Sun™ ONE Studio 4 Community Edition. © Copyright 2003 Sun Microsystems, Inc. All rights reserved. Used by permission.]

Note Regarding Terminology Used for Event Handlers in the Book

Each event handler in this book calls another method, which actually contains the code that processes the event. For a JButton named calculateJButton, for example, the event handler actionPerformed calls method calculateJButtonActionPerformed to process the event. We implemented the code in this manner so that our code would be similar to the code that is generated by the GUI designers provided with many of today's popular Java IDEs. In the early chapters, we refer to methods such as calculateJButtonActionPerformed as "event handlers." Chapter 13 presents a more thorough introduction to event handling. At that point, we refer to methods like calculateJButtonActionPerformed as "methods" and use the term "event handler" only for those methods that are declared by event-listener interfaces.

Objectives

Each tutorial begins with objectives that inform students of what to expect and give them an opportunity, after reading the tutorial, to determine whether they have met the intended goals.

Outline

The tutorial outline enables students to approach the material in top-down fashion. Along with the tutorial objectives, the outline helps students anticipate future topics and set a comfortable and effective learning pace.

Example Applications (with Application Outputs)

We present Java features in the context of complete, working Java applications. We call this our LIVE-CODE approach. All examples are available on the CD that accompanies the book or as downloads from our Web site, www.deitel.com/books/simplyJava1/index.html.

Illustrations/Figures

An abundance of charts, line drawings and application outputs are included. The discussion of control statements, for example, features carefully drawn UML activity diagrams. [*Note:* We do not teach UML diagramming as a program-development tool, but we do use UML diagrams to explain the precise operation of many of Java's control statements.]

Programming Tips

Hundreds of programming tips help students focus on important aspects of application development. These tips and practices represent the best the authors have gleaned from a combined seven decades of programming and teaching experience.

Good Programming Practices

Good Programming Practices highlight techniques that help students write applications that are clearer, more understandable and more maintainable.

Common Programming Errors

Students learning a language—especially in their first programming course—frequently make errors. Pointing out these *Common Programming Errors* in the text reduces the likelihood that students will make the same mistakes.

Error Prevention Tips

These tips describe aspects of Java that prevent errors from getting into applications in the first place, which simplifies the testing and debugging process.

GUI Design Tips

The *GUI Design Tips* highlight graphical-user-interface conventions to help students design attractive, user-friendly GUIs and use GUI features.

Performance Tips

Teaching students to write clear and understandable applications is the most important goal for a first programming course. But students want to write applications that run the fastest, use the least memory, require the smallest number of keystrokes, etc. *Performance Tips* highlight opportunities for improving application performance.

 **Portability Tips**

The *Portability Tips* provide insights on how Java achieves its high degree of portability among different platforms.

Software Design Tips

The *Software Design Tips* highlight architectural and design issues that affect the construction of object-oriented software systems.

Skills Summary

Each tutorial includes a bullet-list-style summary of the new programming concepts presented. This reinforces key actions taken to build the application in each tutorial.

Key Terms

Each tutorial includes a list of important terms defined in the tutorial. These terms also appear in the index and in a book-wide glossary, so the student can locate terms and their definitions quickly.

240 Self-Review Questions and Answers

Self-review multiple-choice questions and answers are included after most sections to build students' confidence with the material and prepare them for the regular exercises. Students should be encouraged to attempt all the self-review exercises and check their answers.

506 Exercises (Solutions in Instructor's Manual)

Each tutorial concludes with exercises. Typical exercises include 10 multiple-choice questions, a "What does this code do?" exercise, a "What's wrong with this code?" exercise, three regular programming exercises and a programming challenge. [*Note:* In the "What does this code do?" and "What's wrong with this code?" exercises, we show only portions of the code in the text, but the instructor's manual contains full applications with outputs.] Several tutorials also include exercises that require students to use the Java debugger to locate and fix logic errors in applications.

The questions involve simple recall of important terminology and concepts, writing individual Java statements, writing small portions of Java applications and writing complete Java methods, classes and applications. Every programming exercise uses a step-by-step methodology to guide the student. The solutions for the exercises are *available only to instructors* through their Prentice-Hall representatives. [***NOTE:*** **Please do not write to us requesting the instructor's manual. Distribution of this publication is strictly limited to instructors teaching from the book. Instructors may obtain the solutions manual only from their regular Prentice Hall representatives. We regret that we cannot provide the solutions to professionals.**]

GUI Design Guidelines

Consistent and proper graphical user interface design is crucial to visual programming. In each tutorial, we summarize the GUI design guidelines that were introduced. Appendix C, GUI Design Guidelines, presents a cumulative list of these GUI design guidelines for easy reference.

Java Library Reference Summaries

Each tutorial includes a summary of the components, classes, methods and other Java Library objects discussed in the tutorial. The summary includes a picture of each component, shows the component "in action" and lists the component's properties, events and methods that were discussed up to and including that tutorial. In addition, Appendix D groups the controls by tutorial for easy reference.

Index

The extensive index includes important terms both under main headings and as separate entries so that students can search for any term or concept by keyword. The code examples and the exercises are also included in the index. For every Java source code application in the book, we indexed it both under the appropriate application and as a subindex item under "applications." We have also double-indexed features such as components, methods and classes. This makes it easier to find examples using particular features.

Simply Java Ancillary Package

Simply Java is accompanied by extensive ancillary materials for instructors, including the following:

- *Instructor's Resource CD (IRCD)* which contains the
    - *Instructor's Manual* with solutions to the end-of-tutorial exercises
    - *Test-Item File* of multiple-choice questions (approximately two per tutorial section).
- *Customizable PowerPoint® Slides* containing all the code and figures in the text, and bulleted items that summarize the key points in the text. The slides are downloadable from www.deitel.com/books/simplyJava1/index.html and are available as part of Prentice Hall's *Companion Web Site* for *Simply Java Programming*, which offers resources for both instructors and students. The *Companion Web Site* is located at www.prenhall.com/deitel.

Companion Web Site

For instructors, the *Companion Web Site* offers a *Syllabus Manager*, which helps instructors plan courses interactively and create online syllabi. Students also benefit from the functionality of the *Companion Web Site*. Book-specific resources for students include:

- PowerPoint® slides
- Example source code
- Reference materials from the book appendices
- Tutorial objectives
- Tutorial summaries
- Tutorial outlines
- Programming tips from each tutorial
- Online Study Guide—contains additional short-answer self-review exercises with answers
- Students can track their results and course performance on quizzes using the *Student Profile* feature, which records and manages all feedback and results from tests taken on the *Companion Web Site*. To access the *Companion Web Site* for *Simply Java Programming*, visit www.prenhall.com/deitel.

Course Management Systems

Selected content from *Simply Java Programming* and other Deitel texts, is available to integrate into various Course Management Systems, including CourseCompass, Blackboard and WebCT. Course Management Systems help faculty create, manage and use sophisticated Web-based educational tools and programs. Blackboard, CourseCompass and WebCT offer:

- Features to create and customize an online course
- Communication tools
- Flexible testing tools
- Support materials

In addition to the tools found in Blackboard and WebCT, CourseCompass from Prentice Hall includes:

■ **CourseCompass course home page**, which makes the course as easy to navigate as a book.

■ **Hosting on Prentice Hall's centralized servers**, which allows course administrators to avoid separate licensing fees or server-space issues.

■ **"How Do I" online-support sections** are available for users who need help personalizing course sites.

■ **Instructor Quick Start Guide**

Acknowledgments

One of the great pleasures of writing a textbook is acknowledging the efforts of many people whose names may not appear on the cover, but whose hard work, cooperation, friendship and understanding were crucial to the production of the book. Many people at Deitel & Associates, Inc., devoted long hours to this project.

■ Abbey Deitel, President

■ Barbara Deitel, Chief Financial Officer

■ Christi Kelsey, Director of Business Development

We would also like to thank several of the participants in the Deitel & Associates, Inc., College Internship Program: Adam Burke, Connor Dutson, Nathan Larson, Brian O'Connor, Mike Oliver and Nick Cassie.[1]

We are fortunate to have been able to work on this project with the talented and dedicated team of publishing professionals at Prentice Hall. We especially appreciate the extraordinary efforts of our Computer Science Editor, Kate Hargett and her boss and our mentor in publishing—Marcia Horton, Editorial Director of Prentice-Hall's Engineering and Computer Science Division. Tom Manshreck and Vince O'Brien did a marvelous job managing the production of the book. Chirag Thakkar and John Lovell served as production editors and Sarah Parker handled editorial responsibilities on the book's extensive ancillary package.

We wish to acknowledge the efforts of our reviewers and to thank Carole Snyder of Prentice Hall, who managed the review process. The 37 reviewers from colleges, industry and Sun Microsystems helped us to get this book "right." Adhering to a tight time schedule, these reviewers scrutinized the text and the applications, providing countless suggestions for improving the accuracy and completeness of the presentation. It is a privilege to have the guidance of such talented and busy professionals.

Simply Java Programming *reviewers:*
Alireza Fazelpour (Palm Beach Community College)
Amardeep Kahlon (Austin Community College)
Andrea Shelly (Florida International University)
Andy Mortensen (Southern Connecticut State University)
Annette Schoenberger (St. Cloud State University)
Ayad Boudiab (Georgia Perimeter College)
Balaji Janamanchi (Texas Tech University)
Brian Larson (Modesto Junior College)

---

1. The Deitel & Associates, Inc. College Internship Program offers a limited number of salaried positions to college students majoring in Computer Science, Information Technology, Marketing and English. Students work at our corporate headquarters in Maynard, Massachusetts full-time in the summers and (for those attending college in the Boston area) part-time during the academic year. We also offer full-time internship positions for students interested in taking a semester off from school to gain industry experience. Regular full-time positions are available to college graduates. For more information, please contact Abbey Deitel at deitel@deitel.com, visit our Web site, www.deitel.com and subscribe to our free e-mail newsletter at www.deitel.com/newsletter/subscribe.html.

Carol Buse (Amarillo College)
Catherine Wyman (DeVry University)
Charles Cadenhead (Brookhaven College)
Charles Lake (Faulkner State College)
Christopher Crane (Cisco Systems, Inc.)
Clint Bickmore (Front Range Community College)
Craig Slinkman (University of Texas at Arlington)
Darrel Karbginsky (Chemeketa Community College)
David Zeng (DeVry Institute of Technology, Calgary)
Deborah Shapiro (Cittone Institute)
Doug Kohlert (Sun Microsystems)
Edmund Weihrauch (Community College of Allegheny County)
Elizabeth Branca (Westchester Community College)
Gavin Osborne (Saskatchewan Institute)
Hong Lin (DeVry University)
James Huddleston (Independent Consultant)
Judith Ashworth (Orillion USA, Inc.)
Kristin Enders (Grand Rapids Community College)
Loran Walker (Lawrence Technological University)
Manu Gupta (Patni Computer Systems)
Merrill Parker (Chattanooga State Technical Community College)
Michael Newby (California State University, Fullerton)
Paul McLachlan (Compuware Corporation)
Rama Roberts (Sun Microsystems)
Rekha Bhowmik (Winona State University)
Sachin Korgaonkar (Idealake Technologies Ltd.)
Sergio Davalos (University of Washington- Tacoma)
Susan Fry (Boise State University)
Terry Hull (Sun Certified Architect, Rational Qualified Practitioner)

We would sincerely appreciate your comments, criticisms, corrections and suggestions for improving this textbook. Please address all correspondence to:

`deitel@deitel.com`

We will respond promptly.

Well, that's it for now. Welcome to the exciting world of Java programming. We hope you enjoy this look at leading-edge computer applications development. Good luck!

Dr. Harvey M. Deitel
Paul J. Deitel
Jeff A. Listfield
Cheryl H. Yaeger
Su Zhang

About the Authors

Dr. Harvey M. Deitel, Chairman of Deitel & Associates, Inc., has 42 years experience in the computing field, including extensive industry and academic experience. Dr. Deitel earned B.S. and M.S. degrees from the Massachusetts Institute of Technology and a Ph.D. from Boston University. He worked on the pioneering virtual-memory operating-systems projects at IBM and MIT that developed techniques now widely implemented in systems such as UNIX, Linux and Windows XP. He has 20 years of college teaching experience and served as the Chairman of the Computer Science Department at Boston College before founding Deitel & Associates, Inc., with his son, Paul J. Deitel. He is the author or co-author of several dozen books and multimedia packages. With translations published in numerous foreign languages, Dr. Deitel's texts have earned international recognition. Dr. Deitel has

delivered professional seminars to major corporations, government organizations and various branches of the military.

Paul J. Deitel, CEO and Chief Technical Officer of Deitel & Associates, Inc., is a graduate of the Massachusetts Institute of Technology's Sloan School of Management, where he studied information technology. Through Deitel & Associates, Inc., he has delivered professional seminars to numerous industry and government clients and has lectured on C++ and Java for the Boston Chapter of the Association for Computing Machinery. He and his father, Dr. Harvey M. Deitel, are the world's best-selling Computer Science textbook authors.

Jeff A. Listfield is a Computer Science graduate of Harvard University. His coursework included classes in computer graphics, networks and computational theory and he has programming experience in several languages. Jeff has co-authored *C# How to Program*, *C# A Programmer's Introduction* and *C# for Experienced Programmers*, and contributed to *Perl How to Program* and *Java How to Program, 5/e*.

Cheryl H. Yaeger, Director of Microsoft Software Publications with Deitel & Associates, Inc., graduated from Boston University in three years with a bachelor's degree in Computer Science. Cheryl has co-authored various Deitel & Associates, Inc. publications, including *C# How to Program*, *C#: A Programmer's Introduction*, *C# for Experienced Programmers* and *Visual Basic.NET for Experienced Programmers*. Cheryl has also contributed to other Deitel & Associates publications including *Perl How to Program*, *Wireless Internet and Mobile Business How to Program*, *Internet and World Wide Web How to Program, 2/e*, *Visual Basic .NET How to Program, 2/e* and *Simply Visual Basic .NET*.

Su Zhang holds B.Sc. and M.Sc. degrees in Computer Science from McGill University. Her graduate research included modeling and simulation, real-time systems and Java technology. She worked on Java and Web-technologies-related projects prior to joining Deitel. She has contributed to several Deitel Publications including *Advanced Java 2 Platform How to Program*, *Python How to Program*, *Java How to Program, 5/e* and she co-authored *Java Web Services for Experienced Programmers*.

About Deitel & Associates, Inc.

Deitel & Associates, Inc., is an internationally recognized corporate-training and content-creation organization specializing in computer programming languages education, object technology and Internet/World Wide Web software technology. Through its 27-year publishing partnership with Prentice Hall, Deitel & Associates, Inc. publishes leading-edge programming textbooks, professional books, interactive CD-ROM-based multimedia *Cyber Classrooms*, *Complete Training Courses* and course management systems e-content. To learn more about Deitel & Associates, Inc., its publications and its worldwide corporate on-site curriculum, visit:

www.deitel.com

Individuals wishing to purchase Deitel books, *Cyber Classrooms* and *Complete Training Courses* can do so through bookstores, or online booksellers and:

www.deitel.com
www.prenhall.com/deitel
www.InformIT.com/deitel

Bulk orders by corporations and academic institutions should be placed directly with Prentice Hall. For ordering information, please visit:

www.prenhall.com/deitel

The Deitel® Buzz Online e-Mail Newsletter

Our free e-mail newsletter includes commentary on industry trends and developments, links to articles and resources from our published books and upcoming publications, information on future publications, product-release schedules and more. For quick opt-in registration, visit www.deitel.com/newsletter/subscribe.html.

BEFORE YOU BEGIN

P lease follow the instructions in this section to ensure that your computer is set up properly before you begin using this book.

Font and Naming Conventions

We use fonts to distinguish between GUI components (such as menu names and menu items) and Java code. Our convention is to emphasize GUI components in a sans-serif bold **Helvetica** font (for example, **File** menu) and to emphasize program text in a sans-serif `Lucida` font (for example, `Math.random()`). We use *italics* to emphasize GUI component properties, such as the *bounds* and *text* properties.

Software and Other Resources on the CD That Accompanies *Simply Java Programming*

- Java 2 Software Development Kit (version 1.4.1_02) for Windows/Linux
- Sun One Studio 4 (update 1) for Windows/Linux
- IBM Cloudscape (version 5.1.3) for Windows/Linux
- Apache Tomcat (version 4.1.24) for Windows/Linux
- jGRASP (version 1.5.3) and handbook, for Windows/Linux
- jEdit (version 4.1) for Windows/Linux
- JCreatorLite (version 2.50 build 8) for Windows only
- *Java How to Program, 5/E* Applets Chapter
- *Internet & World Wide Web How to Program, 2/E* XHTML Chapters

Hardware and Software Requirements to Run the Java 2 Software Development Kit (J2SDK)

To install and run the J2SDK, Sun recommends that PCs have these minimum requirements:

- Pentium III processor
- 500 MHz 256 MB RAM
- 100 MB free space

[*Note:* the J2SDK is available for Windows, Linux and Solaris Operating Systems.]

Theme Settings for Windows XP Users

If you are using Windows XP, we assume that your theme is set to Windows Classic Style. Follow these steps to set Windows XP to display the Windows Classic theme:

1. Open the **Control Panel,** then double click **Display.**

2. Click the **Themes** tab. Select **Windows Classic** from the **Theme:** drop-down list.

3. Click **OK** to save the settings.

Copying and Organizing Files

All of the examples for *Simply Java Programming* are included on the CD that accompanies this textbook. Follow the steps in the box, *Copying the Book Examples from the CD*, to copy the examples directory from the CD onto your hard drive. We suggest that you work from your hard drive rather than your CD drive for two reasons: You cannot save your applications to the book's CD (the CD is read-only), and files can be accessed faster from a hard drive than from a CD. The examples from the book are also available for download from:

```
www.deitel.com
www.prenhall.com/deitel
```

Screen shots in the box might differ slightly from what you see on your computer, depending on whether you are using Windows 2000 or Windows XP, or your version of Internet Explorer.

Copying the Book Examples from the CD

1. ***Inserting the CD.*** Insert the CD that accompanies *Simply Java Programming* into your computer's CD drive. The window displayed in Fig. 1 should appear. If the page appears, proceed to *Step 3* of this box. If the page does not appear, proceed to *Step 2*.

Click the **Browse CD Contents** link to access the CD's contents

Figure 1 Welcome page for *Simply Java Programming* CD.

(cont.)   2. ***Opening the CD directory using My Computer.*** If the page shown in Fig. 1
              does not appear, double click the **My Computer** icon on your desktop. In the
              My Computer window, double click your CD-ROM drive (Fig. 2) to access
              the CD's contents. Proceed to *Step 4.*

Figure 2   Locating the CD-ROM drive.

3. ***Opening the CD-ROM directory.*** If the page in Fig. 1 does appear, click the
    Browse CD Contents link (Fig. 1) to access the CD's contents.

4. ***Copying the examples directory.*** Right click the `examples` directory
    (Fig. 3), then select **Copy**. Next, go to **My Computer** and double click the `C:`
    drive. Select the **Edit** menu and select **Paste** to copy the directory and its
    contents from the CD to your `C:` drive.

    [*Note*: We save the examples to the `C:` drive and refer to this drive
    throughout the text. You may choose to save your files to a different drive
    based on your lab setup or personal preferences. If you are working in a
    computer lab, please see your instructor for more information to confirm
    where the examples should be saved.]

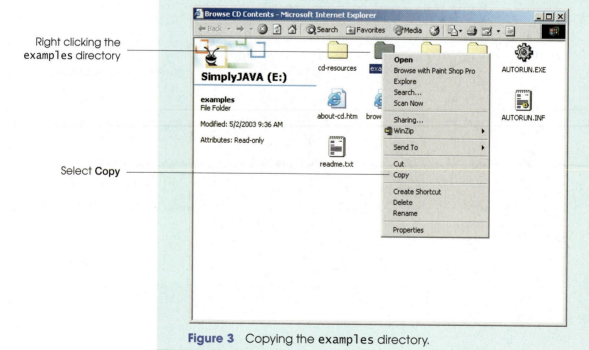

Figure 3   Copying the `examples` directory.

The book example files you copied onto your computer from the CD are read-only. Next, you will remove the read-only property so you can modify and run the examples.

Changing the Read-Only Property of Files

1. *Opening the Properties dialog.* Right click the examples directory and select **Properties** from the menu. The examples **Properties** dialog appears (Fig. 4).

2. *Changing the read-only property.* In the **Attributes** section of this dialog, click the box next to **Read-only** to remove the check mark. Click **Apply** to apply the changes.

Uncheck the **Read-only** attribute

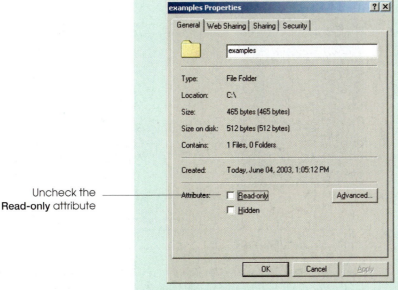

Figure 4   Removing the check in the **Read-only** check box.

3. *Changing the property for all files.* Clicking **Apply** will display the **Confirm Attribute Changes** window (Fig. 5). In this window, click the radio button next to **Apply changes to this folder, subfolders and files** and click **OK** to remove the read-only property for all of the files and directories in the examples directory.

Click this radio button to remove the **Read-only** property for all the files

Figure 5   Removing read-only for all the files in the examples directory.

Before you can run the applications in *Simply Java Programming* or build your own applications, you must install the Java 2 Software Development Kit (J2SDK) or another Java development tool. The following box describes how to install the J2SDK.

Installing the Java 2 Software Development Kit

1. *Locating the J2SDK installer.* On the CD, locate the directory `software\windows\sun`. In this directory, you will find the installer program named `j2sdk-1_4_1_02-windows-i586.exe`.

2. *Starting installation of the J2SDK.* Double click the installer program to begin installing the J2SDK. When the **InstallShield Wizard** window (Fig. 6) is displayed, select the **Next >** button to begin installation.

Figure 6   InstallShield Wizard for the J2SDK.

3. *Accepting the license agreement.* Carefully read the license agreement. Select **Yes** to agree to the terms (Fig. 7). [*Note:* If you choose not to accept the license agreement, the software will not install and you will not be able to execute or create Java applications.]

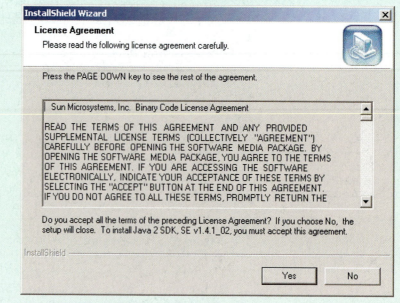

Figure 7   J2SDK license agreement.

(cont.)   4. ***Choosing the installation directory for the J2SDK***. Select the directory in which you want the J2SDK to be installed (Fig. 8). If you change the default installation directory, be sure to remember the exact name and location of the directory you choose, as you will need this information later in the installation process. After you have selected a directory, click the **Next >** button.

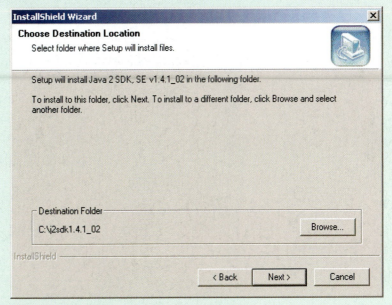

Figure 8   Choosing the destination location.

5. ***Selecting components to be installed***. Select all the components of the Java 2 SDK (Fig. 9). After you have selected the desired components, click the **Next >** button.

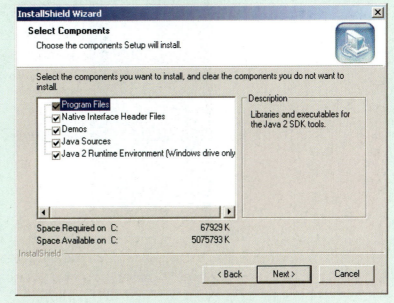

Figure 9   Selecting the components of the J2SDK to install.

(cont.)

6. ***Selecting browsers.*** As part of the installation, you have the option of making the Java plug-in the default Java runtime environment for Java programs that run in Web browsers (Fig. 10). After you have selected the desired browsers click the **Next >** button.

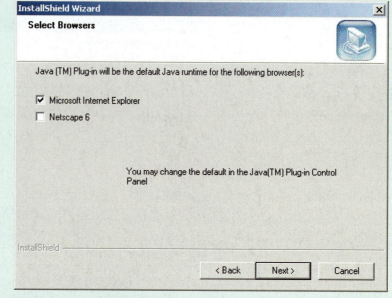

Figure 10   Selecting browsers.

7. ***Finishing the installation.*** The program will now install the J2SDK. Click the **Finish** button to complete the installation process (Fig. 11).

Figure 11   Completing the installation.

The PATH environment variable on your computer designates which directories the computer searches when looking for applications, such as the applications that enable you to compile and run your Java applications (called `javac.exe` and `java.exe`, respectively). You will now learn how to set the PATH environment variable on your computer.

Setting the PATH Variable

1. ***Opening the System Properties dialog.*** Right click on the **My Computer** icon on your desktop and select **Properties** from the menu. The **System Properties** dialog (Fig. 12) appears. [*Note*: Your **System Properties** dialog may appear different than the one shown in Fig. 12, depending on your version of Microsoft Windows. This particular dialog is from a computer running Microsoft Windows 2000. Your dialog might display different information.]

Figure 12   **System Properties** dialog.

2. ***Opening the Environment Variables dialog.*** Select the **Advanced** tab at the top of the **System Properties** dialog (Fig. 13). Click the **Environment Variables** button to display the **Environment Variables** dialog (Fig. 14).

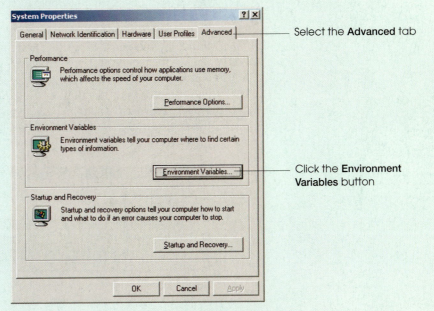

Select the **Advanced** tab

Click the **Environment Variables** button

Figure 13   **Advanced** tab of **System Properties** dialog.

(cont.)

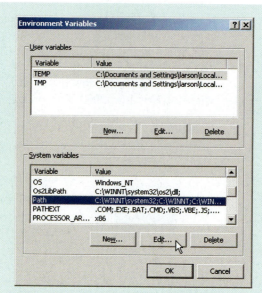

Figure 14 **Environment Variables** dialog.

3. ***Editing the PATH variable.*** Scroll down inside the **System variables** box to select the PATH variable. Click the **Edit** button. This will cause the **Edit System Variable** dialog to appear (Fig. 15).

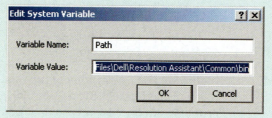

Figure 15 Edit **System Variable** dialog.

4. ***Changing the contents of the PATH variable.*** Place the cursor inside the **Variable Value** field. Use the left-arrow key to move the cursor to the beginning of the list. At the beginning of the list, add the name of the directory in which you placed the J2SDK (Fig. 8) followed by `\bin;` (Fig. 16). If you chose the default installation directory in *Step 4* of the box *Installing the Java 2 Software Development Kit*, you will add `c:\j2sdk1.4.1_02\bin;` to the PATH variable here. Click the **OK** button to complete the modification of the PATH variable.

Figure 16 Editing the PATH variable.

As you work through this book, you will be developing your own applications. Now, you will create a directory on your C: drive in which you will save all of your applications.

Creating Your Working Directory

1. ***Selecting the drive.*** Double click the **My Computer** icon on your desktop to access a list of your computer drives (Fig. 17), then double click the **C:** drive. The contents of the **C:** drive are displayed.

Local disk ——

Figure 17 Computer drives listed under **My Computer**.

2. ***Creating a new directory.*** Select the **File** menu and under the **New** submenu, select **Folder** (Fig. 18). [*Note:* A folder is another name for a directory. Throughout this book we will refer to it as a directory.] A new, empty directory appears in your **C:** directory (Fig. 19). [*Note:* From this point onward, we use the **>** character to indicate the selection of a menu command. For example, we use the notation **File > New > Folder** to indicate the selection of the **Folder** command from the **New** submenu of the **File** menu.]

New folder option (selected) ——

Figure 18 Creating a new directory.

New directory ——

Figure 19 New directory appears on the **C:** drive.

(cont.)

3. ***Naming the directory.*** Enter SimplyJava as the directory name (Fig. 20). The instructions throughout the book assume that you are working in the directory C:\SimplyJava and will instruct you to place your applications and your exercise solutions here.

Newly created work directory

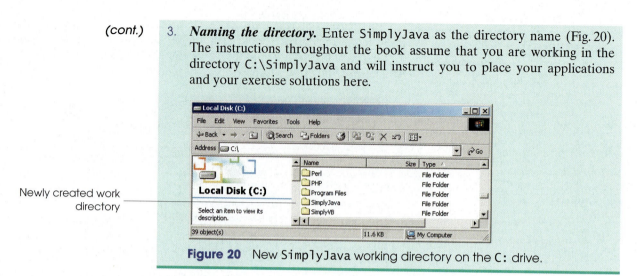

Figure 20 New SimplyJava working directory on the C: drive.

You are now ready to begin your Java studies with *Simply Java Programming.* We hope you enjoy the book! You can reach us easily at deitel@deitel.com.

Moving Shapes Application

Introducing Computers, the Internet and Java Programming

Objectives

In this tutorial, you will learn:
- The units into which typical computers are divided.
- To identify the characteristics of low-level and high-level programming languages.
- About the history of high-level programming languages.
- What objects are and why object technology is important.
- The evolution of the Internet and the World Wide Web.
- How to run your first Java application.
- How to locate additional Java information using the Internet.

Outline

Welcome to Java! This book uses a straightforward, step-by-step tutorial approach to teach Java programming fundamentals. We hope that you will be informed and entertained as you learn how to program in Java.

The core of the book teaches Java using our application-driven approach, which provides step-by-step instructions for creating and interacting with useful, real-world computer applications. We combine this approach with our signature live-code approach, which shows dozens of complete, working Java applications and depicts their outputs to help you learn the basic skills that are the foundation of good programming. You can also study bonus tutorials on graphics, multimedia, database and Web programming. All of the book's examples are available on the accompanying CD-ROM and on our Web site, www.deitel.com.

Computer use is increasing in almost every field. In an era of rising costs, computing costs are actually decreasing dramatically because of rapid developments in both hardware and software technology. Silicon chip technology has made computing so economical that hundreds of millions of general-purpose computers are in use worldwide, helping people in business, industry, government and their personal lives.

Reading this text will start you on a challenging and rewarding educational path. If you'd like to communicate with us, send an e-mail to deitel@deitel.com, and we will respond promptly. For more information, visit our Web sites at www.deitel.com and www.prenhall.com/deitel.

1.1 What Is a Computer?

A **computer** is a device capable of performing computations and making logical decisions at speeds millions and even billions of times faster than humans can. For example, many of today's most powerful personal computers can perform billions of calculations per second. A person operating a desk calculator might require a lifetime to complete the same number of calculations that a powerful personal computer can perform in one second. Today's fastest **supercomputers** can perform hundreds of billions of calculations per second. Trillion-instruction-per-second computers are already functioning in research laboratories!

Computers process **data**, using sets of instructions called **computer programs**. These programs guide computers through orderly sets of actions that are specified by people known as **computer programmers**. **Object-oriented programming (OOP)** (which models real-world objects with software counterparts), available in Java and other programming languages, is a significant breakthrough that can greatly enhance programmers' productivity. In this book, we generally use the term "application" instead of the term "program." An **application** is a program that performs a useful task. Most tutorials in this book present five object-oriented applications—one in the main example and four in the exercises. There are 145 applications in the book.

A computer is composed of various devices (such as the keyboard, screen, mouse, hard drive, memory, CD-ROM drive and processing units) that are known as **hardware**. The programs that run on a computer are referred to as **software**.

SELF-REVIEW

1. Computers process data, using sets of instructions called _____.
   - a) hardware
   - b) computer programs
   - c) processing units
   - d) programmers

2. The devices that make up a computer are called _____.
   - a) hardware
   - b) software
   - c) programs
   - d) applications

Answers: 1) b. 2) a.

1.2 Computer Organization

Computers can be thought of as being divided into six units:

1. **Input unit**. This "receiving" section of the computer obtains information (data and computer programs) from various **input devices**, such as the keyboard and the mouse. Other input devices include microphones (for recording speech to the computer), scanners (for scanning images) and digital cameras (for taking photographs and making videos).

2. **Output unit**. This "shipping" section of the computer takes information that the computer has processed and places it on various **output devices**, making the information available for use outside the computer. Output can be displayed on screens, played on audio/video devices, printed on paper and sent over a computer network (such as the Internet), among other things. Output also can be used to control other devices, such as robots used in manufacturing.

3. **Memory unit**. This rapid-access, relatively low-capacity "warehouse" section of the computer stores data temporarily while an application is running. The memory unit retains information that has been entered through input devices, so the information is immediately available for processing. To be executed, computer programs must be in memory. The memory unit also retains processed information until the information can be sent to output devices, on which it is made available to users. Often, the memory unit is called either **memory** or **primary memory**. **Random access memory (RAM)** is an example of primary memory. Primary memory is usually **volatile**, which means that it is erased when the computer is turned off.

4. **Arithmetic and logic unit (ALU)**. The ALU is the "manufacturing" section of the computer. It performs calculations such as addition, subtraction, multiplication and division. It also makes decisions, allowing the computer to perform tasks such as determining whether two items stored in memory are equal.

5. **Central processing unit (CPU).** The CPU serves as the "administrative" section of the computer, supervising the operation of the other sections. The CPU alerts the input unit when information should be read into the memory unit, instructs the ALU when to use information from the memory unit in calculations and tells the output unit when to send information from the memory unit to various output devices.

6. **Secondary storage unit.** This unit is the long-term, high-capacity "warehouse" section of the computer. Secondary storage devices, such as hard drives, DVD drives, CD-ROM drives, Zip® drives and floppy disk drives, normally hold programs and data that other units are not actively using; the computer then can retrieve this information when it is needed—hours, days, months or even years later. Information in secondary storage takes much longer to access than information in primary memory. However, secondary storage is much less expensive than primary memory. Secondary storage is also **nonvolatile**, retaining information even when the computer is turned off.

SELF-REVIEW

1. The _____ is responsible for performing calculations and contains decision-making mechanisms.
   a) central processing unit
   b) memory unit
   c) arithmetic and logic unit
   d) output unit

2. Information stored in _____ is normally erased when the computer is turned off.
   a) primary memory
   b) secondary storage
   c) CD-ROM drives
   d) hard drives

Answers: 1) c. 2) a.

1.3 Machine Languages, Assembly Languages and High-Level Languages

Programmers write computer instructions in various programming languages, some of which are directly understandable by computers and others require intermediate translation steps. Although hundreds of computer languages are in use today, the diverse offerings can be divided into three general types:

1. Machine languages

2. Assembly languages

3. High-level languages

A computer can directly understand only its own **machine language**. As the "natural language" of a particular computer, machine language is defined by the computer's hardware design. Machine languages (also called **first generation languages**) generally consist of streams of numbers (ultimately reduced to 1s and 0s) that instruct computers how to perform their most elementary operations. Machine languages are **machine dependent**, which means that a particular machine language can be used on only one type of CPU. The following section of a machine-language program, which adds *overtime pay* to *base pay* and stores the result in *gross pay*, demonstrates the incomprehensibility of machine language to humans:

```
+1300042774
+1400593419
+1200274027
```

Machine-language programming tends to be slow and error prone. Instead of using strings of numbers that computers can directly understand, programmers can use English-like abbreviations to represent the basic operations of the computer. These abbreviations form the basis of **assembly languages** (also called **second gener-**

ation languages). **Translator programs** called **assemblers** convert assembly-language programs to machine language at computer speeds. The following section of an assembly-language program also adds *overtime pay* to *base pay* and stores the result in *gross pay*, but presents the steps somewhat more clearly to human readers than the machine-language example:

```
LOAD    BASEPAY
ADD     OVERTIMEPAY
STORE   GROSSPAY
```

This assembly-language code is clearer to humans, but computers cannot understand it until the code is translated into machine language by an assembler.

Although assembly languages enable programmers to write programs much more quickly than machine languages, assembly languages still require many instructions to accomplish even the simplest tasks. To speed up the programming process, programmers primarily use **high-level languages** (also called **third generation languages**), in which single program statements accomplish more substantial tasks. Translator programs called **compilers** convert high-level-language programs into machine language. High-level languages enable programmers to write instructions that look almost like everyday English and that contain common mathematical notations. For example, a payroll application written in a high-level language might contain a statement such as

```
grossPay = basePay + overTimePay
```

From these examples, it is clear why programmers prefer high-level languages to either machine languages or assembly languages. Java is one of the most popular high-level programming languages in the world. In the next section, you will learn about the origins and benefits of Java.

The process of compiling a high-level language program into machine language can take a considerable amount of computer time. **Interpreter** programs were developed to execute high-level language programs directly without the need for compiling those programs into machine language. Although compiled programs execute much faster than interpreted programs, interpreters are popular in program-development environments in which programs are recompiled frequently as new features are added and errors are corrected. Once a program is developed, a compiled version can be produced to run most efficiently.

Some languages in use today, called **fourth generation languages** (**4GL**s), are even closer to natural languages like English. Fourth generation languages are primarily used to manipulate information that is stored in organized collections of data called **databases**. For example, an automated teller machine (ATM) application that uses a fourth generation language might contain a statement such as

```
SELECT balance
    FROM AccountInformation
    WHERE accountNumber = "123456"
```

to obtain the balance for a specified account number, or a statement such as

```
UPDATE AccountInformation
    SET balance = 365.74
    WHERE accountNumber = "123456"
```

to update the balance for a specified account number. You will learn more about databases and the 4GL shown here (called **SQL**) in Tutorial 26.

SELF-REVIEW   1. The only programming language that a computer's CPU can directly understand is its own _____.

        a) high-level language   b) assembly language

        c) machine language   d) English

2. Programs that translate high-level language programs into machine language are called
_____.

a) assemblers   b) compilers
c) programmers   d) converters

Answers: 1) c. 2) b.

1.4 Java

The Java language was created in 1991 by James Gosling as part of a corporate research project at Sun Microsystems. This project, code-named Green, began in response to predictions that **microprocessors**—the chips that make computers work—would have a profound impact on intelligent consumer electronic devices. The Java programming language is based on C++, a widely used programming language that provides capabilities for object-oriented programming.

The marketplace for intelligent consumer electronic devices did not develop as quickly as Sun had anticipated; as a result, the Green project suffered some initial difficulties. By sheer good fortune, the World Wide Web exploded in popularity in 1993, and Sun saw an immediate potential for using Java to create **dynamic content** (animated and interactive content) for Web pages. Sun introduced a mechanism for building Java programs called **applets** that could execute in Web pages that were viewed in Web browsers.

Sun formally announced Java at a conference in May 1995. Ordinarily, an event like this would not have generated much attention. However, Java generated immediate excitement in the business community because of the phenomenal interest in the Web. Developers now use Java to create dynamic Web pages, to build large-scale enterprise applications, to enhance the functionality of Web servers (computers that provide the content that is distributed to your Web browser when you browse Web sites), to provide applications for consumer devices (such as cell phones, pagers and PDAs) and for many other purposes. Java is no longer a language used simply to make Web pages "come alive." Java has become the preferred language for meeting many organizations' programming needs.

There are several reasons why so many programmers prefer Java to other languages. First, Java is fully **object oriented**. **Objects** are reusable software **components** that model items in the real world. Object-oriented programs are often easier to understand, correct and modify than programs developed with previous techniques.

Second, Java programs consist of pieces called **classes**, which are used to define objects. Classes include **methods**, which perform tasks and return information when they complete those tasks. You can create each piece you need to form a Java program. However, most Java programmers take advantage of the rich collection of existing classes in the **Java class library**, which is also known as the **Java API (Application Programming Interface)**. Thus, there are really two pieces to learning the Java "world." The first is the Java language itself, so that you can program your own classes and methods; the second is the Java class library, which provides an extensive set of reusable classes. Throughout this book, we discuss many library classes. You will use some of them to create applications that contain **graphical user interfaces (GUIs)**—the visual part of the application with which users interact. You will also use library classes to make your GUIs **event driven**, meaning that they will respond to user-initiated events, such as mouse clicks and keystrokes.

Finally, many programmers favor using Java because it is **platform independent**, meaning that Java applications can be created and run on a variety of **computer platforms** (that is, different types of computers running different operating systems such as Windows and Linux). This concept of "write once, run anywhere" allows for a truly portable experience—one application can be given to people on several different computer platforms, regardless of the computer platform on which the application was created. Java achieves its portability and good performance with a clever combination of compilation and interpretation of Java programs.

Java has become the language of choice for implementing Internet-based applications, as well as software for devices that communicate over a network. Don't be surprised when your new stereo and other devices in your home become networked together by Java technology! Even today, wireless devices, like cell phones, pagers and personal digital assistants (PDAs), communicate over the so-called Wireless Internet using the kind of Java-based networking applications that you will learn in this book.

SELF-REVIEW

1. The Java language was created in 1991 by James Gosling at _____.

   a) Apple
   b) IBM
   c) Microsoft
   d) Sun Microsystems

2. A(n) _____ language is one in which applications can be created then run on many different computer platforms running different operating systems.

   a) GUI driven
   b) event driven
   c) platform independent
   d) platform dependent

Answers: 1) d. 2) c.

1.5 Other High-Level Languages

Although hundreds of high-level languages have been developed, only a few have achieved broad acceptance. IBM Corporation developed **FORTRAN** (FORmula TRANslator) in the mid-1950s to create scientific and engineering applications that require complex mathematical computations. FORTRAN is still widely used in the engineering community.

COBOL (COmmon Business Oriented Language) was developed in the late 1950s by a group of computer manufacturers in conjunction with government and industrial computer users. COBOL is used primarily for business applications that manipulate large amounts of data. A considerable portion of today's business software is still programmed in COBOL.

The **C** language, which Dennis Ritchie developed at Bell Laboratories in the early 1970s, gained widespread recognition as a development language of the UNIX operating system. **C++**, an extension of C, was developed by Bjarne Stroustrup in the early 1980s at Bell Laboratories. C++ provides capabilities for object-oriented programming. Many of today's major operating systems are written in C or C++.

The **BASIC** (Beginner's All-Purpose Symbolic Instruction Code) programming language was developed in the mid-1960s by Professors John Kemeny and Thomas Kurtz of Dartmouth College as a language for writing simple programs. BASIC's primary purpose was to familiarize novices with programming techniques. **Visual Basic** was introduced by Microsoft in 1991 to simplify the process of developing Microsoft Windows applications.

Visual Basic .NET is designed for Microsoft's new **.NET** (pronounced "dot-net") framework. Visual Basic .NET offers full object orientation and makes use of .NET's powerful library of reusable software components called the **Framework Class Library** (FCL). This library is shared among Visual Basic .NET, Visual C++ .NET, C# (Microsoft's new language) and many other languages that Microsoft and other software vendors are making available for .NET.

Microsoft's **C#** (pronounced "C Sharp") programming language was designed specifically for the .NET framework. It has roots in C, C++ and Java. C#, Java and Visual Basic .NET have comparable capabilities, so learning Java may create many opportunities for you.

SELF-REVIEW

1. _____ is an extension of C and offers object-oriented capabilities.

   a) Visual Basic
   b) C++
   c) assembly language
   d) Windows

2. _____ is a programming language originally developed for Microsoft's .NET framework.
   a) C#
   b) Java
   c) C++
   d) Visual Basic

3. _____, developed in the late 1950s, is still used to produce a considerable portion of today's business software.
   a) COBOL
   b) FORTRAN
   c) Java
   d) C

4. _____, developed in the 1950s, is still used to create scientific and engineering applications that require complex mathematical computations.
   a) Visual Basic
   b) FORTRAN
   c) COBOL
   d) C#

Answers: 1) b. 2) a. 3) a. 4) b.

1.6 Structured Programming

During the 1960s, software development efforts often ran behind schedule, costs greatly exceeded budgets and the finished products were unreliable. People began to realize that software development was a far more complex activity than they had imagined. Research activity intended to address these issues resulted in the evolution of **structured programming**—a disciplined approach to the creation of programs that are clear, correct and easy to modify.

One of the results of this research was the development of the **Pascal** programming language in 1971. Pascal, named after the 17th-century mathematician and philosopher Blaise Pascal, was designed for teaching structured programming and rapidly became the preferred introductory programming language in most colleges. Unfortunately, the language lacked many features needed to make it useful in commercial, industrial and government applications. By contrast, C, which also arose from research on structured programming, did not have the limitations of Pascal, and professional programmers quickly adopted it.

The **Ada** programming language was developed under the sponsorship of the U.S. Department of Defense (DOD) during the 1970s and early 1980s. The language was named after **Lady Ada Lovelace**, daughter of the poet Lord Byron. Lady Lovelace is generally credited as being the world's first computer programmer because of an application she wrote in the early 1800s for the Analytical Engine mechanical computing device designed by Charles Babbage.

SELF-REVIEW

1. _____ was designed to teach structured programming in academic environments.
   a) C++
   b) C
   c) Java
   d) Pascal

2. _____ is generally credited as being the world's first computer programmer.
   a) Lord Byron
   b) Dennis Ritchie
   c) Lady Ada Lovelace
   d) Charles Babbage

Answers: 1) d. 2) c.

1.7 Key Software Trend: Object Technology

As the benefits of structured programming were realized in the 1970s, improved software technology began to appear. However, it was not until object-oriented programming became widely used in the 1980s and 1990s that software developers finally felt they had the necessary tools to improve the software development process dramatically.

What are objects, and why are they special? **Object technology** is a packaging scheme for creating meaningful software units. There are date objects, time objects, paycheck objects, invoice objects, automobile objects, people objects, audio objects, video objects, file objects, record objects and so on. In fact, almost any noun can be reasonably represented as a software object. Objects have **attributes** (also called **properties**), such as color, size and weight; and perform **actions** (also called **behaviors** or **methods**), such as moving, sleeping or drawing. Classes are types of similar objects. For example, all cars belong to the "car" class, even though individual cars may vary in make, model, color and options packages. A class specifies the general form of its objects, and the properties and actions available to an object depend on its class. An object is related to its class in much the same way as a building is related to its blueprint.

Before object-oriented languages appeared, **procedural programming languages** (such as FORTRAN, Pascal, BASIC and C) focused on actions (verbs) rather than objects (nouns). Using today's popular object-oriented languages, such as Java, Visual Basic .NET, C++ and C#, programmers can program in an object-oriented manner that more naturally reflects the way in which they perceive the world.

With object technology, properly designed classes can be reused on future projects. Using libraries of classes can greatly reduce the amount of effort required to implement new applications. Some organizations report that such software reusability is not, in fact, the key benefit of object-oriented programming. Rather, they indicate that object-oriented programming tends to produce software that is more understandable because it is better organized and has fewer maintenance requirements.

Object orientation allows the programmer to focus on the "big picture." Instead of worrying about the minute details of how reusable objects are implemented, the programmer can focus on the behaviors and interactions of objects. A road map that showed every tree, house and driveway would be difficult, if not impossible, to read. When such details are removed and only the essential information (roads) remains, the map becomes easier to understand. In the same way, an application that is divided into objects is easy to understand, modify and update because it hides much of the detail. It is clear that object-oriented programming will be the key programming methodology for at least the next decade. Java is one of the world's most widely used object-oriented languages.

SELF-REVIEW   1. _____ focuses on actions (verbs) rather than things (nouns).

     a) C#   b) Object-oriented programming

     c) Java   d) Procedural programming

2. In object-oriented programming, _____, which are in a sense like blueprints, are types of similar objects.

     a) classes   b) attributes

     c) behaviors   d) properties

Answers: 1) d. 2) a.

1.8 The Internet and the World Wide Web

In the late 1960s, ARPA—the Advanced Research Projects Agency of the Department of Defense—rolled out blueprints for networking the main computer systems of approximately a dozen ARPA-funded universities and research institutions. The computers were to be connected with communications lines operating at a then-stunning 56 Kbps (1 Kbps is equal to 1,024 bits per second), at a time when most people (of the few who even had networking access) were connecting over telephone lines to computers at a rate of 110 bits per second. Academic research was

about to take a giant leap forward. ARPA proceeded to implement what quickly became called the **ARPAnet**, the grandparent of today's **Internet**.

Things worked out differently from the original plan. Although the ARPAnet enabled researchers to network their computers, its main benefit proved to be the capability for quick and easy communication via what came to be known as **electronic mail (e-mail)**. This is true even on today's Internet, with e-mail, instant messaging and file transfer allowing hundreds of millions of people worldwide to communicate with each other.

The protocol (in other words, the set of rules) for communicating over the ARPAnet became known as the **Transmission Control Protocol (TCP)**. TCP ensured that messages, consisting of pieces called "packets," were properly routed from sender to receiver and that those messages arrived intact.

In parallel with the early evolution of the Internet, organizations worldwide were implementing their own networks for both intraorganization (that is, within an organization) and interorganization (that is, between organizations) communication. A huge variety of networking hardware and software appeared. One challenge was to enable these different networks to communicate with each other. ARPA accomplished this by developing the **Internet Protocol (IP)**—which created a true "network of networks"—the current architecture of the Internet. The combined set of protocols is now commonly called **TCP/IP**.

Businesses rapidly realized that, by using the Internet, they could improve their operations and offer new and better services to their clients. Companies started spending large amounts of money to develop and enhance their Internet presence. This generated fierce competition among communications carriers and hardware and software suppliers to meet the increased infrastructure demand. As a result, **bandwidth**—the information-carrying capacity of communications lines—on the Internet has increased tremendously, while hardware costs have plummeted.

The **World Wide Web** (**WWW**) is a collection of hardware and software associated with the Internet that allows computer users to locate and view multimedia-based documents (documents with various combinations of text, graphics, animations, audios and videos) on almost any subject. Even though the Internet was developed more than three decades ago, the introduction of the World Wide Web was a relatively recent event. In 1989, Tim Berners-Lee of CERN (the European Organization for Nuclear Research) began to develop a technology for sharing information by using "hyperlinked" text documents. Berners-Lee called his invention the **HyperText Markup Language (HTML)**. He also wrote communication protocols to form the backbone of his new hypertext information system, which he referred to as the World Wide Web.

In October 1994, Berners-Lee founded an organization, called the **World Wide Web Consortium** (**W3C**, `www.w3.org`), devoted to developing technologies for the World Wide Web. One of the W3C's primary goals is to make the Web universally accessible—regardless of a person's disabilities, language or culture.

The Internet and the World Wide Web will surely be listed among the most important creations of humankind. In the past, most computer applications ran on "stand-alone" computers (computers that were not connected to one another). Today's applications can be written with the aim of communicating among the world's hundreds of millions of computers. The Internet and World Wide Web enable even individuals and small businesses to achieve worldwide exposure. They are profoundly changing the way we do business and conduct our personal lives. To highlight the importance of Internet and Web programming, we include four tutorials at the end of the book in which you will actually build and run a Web-based bookstore application. It is interesting to note that Java's platform-independent nature came about as the result of the early focus on using Java for Web development.

1. Today's Internet evolved from the _____, which was a Department of Defense project.

    a) ARPAnet   b) HTML

    c) CERN   d) WWW

2. The combined set of protocols for communicating over the Internet is now commonly called _____.

    a) HTML   b) TCP/IP

    c) ARPA   d) TCP

Answers: 1) a. 2) b.

1.9 The Java Runtime Environment (JRE)

In this book's *For Students and Instructors: Important Information Before You Begin* section (which appeared before this tutorial), you installed the Java 2 Software Development Kit (J2SDK). In this section, you will learn about the **Java Runtime Environment (JRE)**, a portion of the J2SDK that enables you to execute (that is, run) Java applications. Throughout most of this text, you will focus on two types of files—`.java` and `.class` files. Files with the extension `.java` (called **source code files**) store Java statements written by you, the programmer. These statements indicate actions you would like your applications to perform. You learned in Section 1.3 that such statements are not understood by the computer. To execute the application, the statements stored in the `.java` file must be converted into statements that the JRE can understand. The process of converting statements from a high-level language into statements of a machine language is known as **compilation**. In Tutorial 2, you will learn how to compile a `.java` file into a `.class` file. The statements contained in a `.class` file, although unreadable by the programmer, can be executed by the JRE. In the next section, you will execute a `.class` file.

    The **Command Prompt** is a Windows program that lets you give the computer instructions by typing text at a prompt (**C:\>** in Fig. 1.1). Whereas in a graphical user interface, like Windows, you might double click the **Notepad** icon to launch the **Notepad** text editor, using a **Command Prompt** you would type the name "Notepad" and press the *Enter* key to launch the program.

    Figure 1.1 shows a **Command Prompt** window on a computer running Windows 2000. You can access the Windows 2000 **Command Prompt** window in the **Start > Programs > Accessories** menu. When the **Command Prompt** window is started, the beginning directory is `C:\`.

Beginning directory for Windows 2000 —————

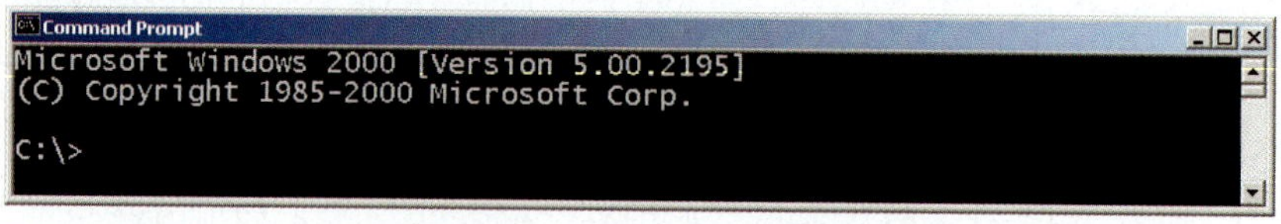

```
Command Prompt                                                    _□×
Microsoft Windows 2000 [Version 5.00.2195]
(C) Copyright 1985-2000 Microsoft Corp.

C:\>
```

Figure 1.1 A **Command Prompt** window in Windows 2000.

    Figure 1.2 shows a **Command Prompt** window on a computer running Windows XP. You can access the Windows XP **Command Prompt** window in the **Start > All Programs > Accessories** menu. When the **Command Prompt** window is started, the beginning directory is `C:\Documents and Settings\Administrator`. `Administrator` is the user name on our computer. On your computer, `Administrator` will be replaced with your user name.

Beginning directory
for Windows XP

Figure 1.2 A **Command Prompt** window in Windows XP.

If you are running Windows 98 or Windows ME, your **Command Prompt** will be called the **MS-DOS Prompt** and your beginning directory may be different.

SELF-REVIEW

1. A _____ file contains the Java statements written by you.
   a) .java   b) .jre
   c) .exe   d) .class

2. The Java Runtime Environment can recognize only _____ files.
   a) .java   b) .jre
   c) .exe   d) .class

Answers: 1) a. 2) d.

1.10 Test-Driving the Moving Shapes Application

In this section, you will be introduced to a Java application, using our application-driven approach. In each tutorial, you will begin by "test-driving" an application. You will actually run and interact with the completed application. Then you will learn the Java features you need to build the application. Finally, you will "put it all together" and create your own working version of the application. You will begin here in Tutorial 1 by running a "painting" application that allows you to draw various shapes that, once drawn, will move about the screen. You will actually build a similar application in Tutorial 27.

We created the **Moving Shapes** application to demonstrate a fully graphical and interactive application. In the following box, *Test-Driving the Java **Moving Shapes** Application*, you will run the application and add your own moving shapes. The elements and functionality you see in this application are typical of what you will learn to program in this text. [*Note*: We use fonts to distinguish between features you see on a GUI (such as menu names) and elements that are not directly related to a GUI. Our convention is to emphasize GUI features (such as the **File** menu) in a semibold **sans-serif Helvetica** font and to emphasize non-GUI elements, such as file names (for example, `ProgramName.java`) in a `sans-serif Lucida` font. As you have already noticed, each term that is defined is set in heavy bold.]

---

*Test-Driving the Java
Moving Shapes
Application*

1. ***Checking your setup.*** Read the *For Students and Instructors: Important Information Before You Begin* section to confirm that you have set up Java properly on your computer and that you have copied the book's examples to your hard drive.

2. ***Locating the completed application.*** Open a **Command Prompt** window by selecting **Start > Programs > Accessories > Command Prompt**. Change to your completed **Moving Shapes** application directory by typing `cd C:\Examples\Tutorial01\MovingShapes`, then pressing *Enter* (Fig. 1.3). The command `cd` is used to change directories.

(cont.)

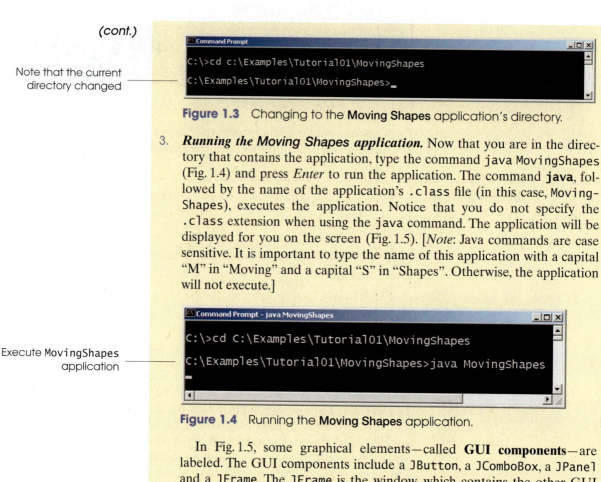

Note that the current directory changed

Figure 1.3 Changing to the **Moving Shapes** application's directory.

3. ***Running the Moving Shapes application.*** Now that you are in the directory that contains the application, type the command `java MovingShapes` (Fig. 1.4) and press *Enter* to run the application. The command **java**, followed by the name of the application's `.class` file (in this case, `Moving-Shapes`), executes the application. Notice that you do not specify the `.class` extension when using the `java` command. The application will be displayed for you on the screen (Fig. 1.5). [*Note:* Java commands are case sensitive. It is important to type the name of this application with a capital "M" in "Moving" and a capital "S" in "Shapes". Otherwise, the application will not execute.]

Execute `MovingShapes` application

Figure 1.4 Running the **Moving Shapes** application.

In Fig. 1.5, some graphical elements—called **GUI components**—are labeled. The GUI components include a `JButton`, a `JComboBox`, a `JPanel` and a `JFrame`. The `JFrame` is the window, which contains the other GUI components and displays the application. You can use the GUI components in this application to specify the type of shape to draw (chosen using the `JComboBox`) and the color of the shape (chosen using the `JButton`).

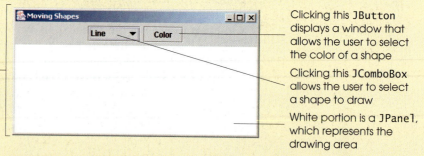

Application displays in a `JFrame` (that is, a window)

Clicking this `JButton` displays a window that allows the user to select the color of a shape

Clicking this `JComboBox` allows the user to select a shape to draw

White portion is a `JPanel`, which represents the drawing area

Figure 1.5 **Moving Shapes** Java application with an interactive GUI.

Because you can use existing GUI components—which are objects—you can get powerful applications running in Java much faster than if you had to write all the code yourself. In this text, you will learn how to use many pre-existing GUI components, as well as how to write your own application code to customize your applications.

When the application begins executing, the shape displayed in the JComboBox is **Line** and the drawing color is gray (represented by the background color of the **Color** JButton). These values are known as **default** values—that is, the initial values you see when you first run the application. These default values indicate that, if the user were to begin drawing without selecting a shape or a color, a gray line will be drawn. You will now interact with the application by choosing the type and color of the shape to draw.

(cont.)   4. ***Changing the type of the shape to draw.*** Click the **Line** JComboBox. A list of
options will be displayed (Fig. 1.6). Move the mouse cursor over the various
options and notice that each option is highlighted as the mouse cursor passes
over it. Click the **Rectangle** option. The text displayed on the JComboBox
will change to display **Rectangle** (Fig. 1.7).

Rectangle option
highlighted

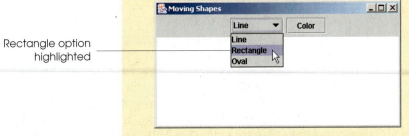

Figure 1.6 JComboBox displaying options.

5. ***Displaying the Select a Color dialog.*** Click the **Color** JButton (Fig. 1.7). A
dialog will appear (Fig. 1.8). A dialog is a window used to display a message
to the user or display various options from which the user can choose. This
particular dialog is predefined by Java so that you can use it in your applications to allow the users of those applications to choose colors.

Figure 1.7 Clicking the **Color** JButton.

Palette of color swatches

Select a color by
clicking the mouse

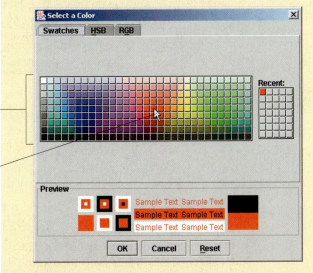

Figure 1.8 **Select a Color** dialog.

6. ***Changing the color of the shape to be drawn.*** Select a color from the **palette**
(series of colors) by clicking one of the colored squares (also called
swatches). Once you have selected a color, click the **OK** button. The dialog
will close, and the **Color** JButton's background color will change to reflect
the selected color (Fig. 1.9).

(cont.)

JButton with changed
background color

Figure 1.9 Application once color has been modified.

7. ***Drawing a rectangle.*** Shapes are drawn by **dragging the mouse** over the drawing area. Once a shape is drawn, that shape will move around the JPanel continuously. Place the mouse in the drawing area, then drag the mouse to draw a rectangle (Fig. 1.10). To drag the mouse, press and hold the left mouse button and move the mouse. Release the mouse button. The rectangle will begin to move around the drawing area (Fig. 1.11). The direction and speed of the shape are chosen randomly by the application. The rectangle will move continuously until you close the application in *Step 10*.

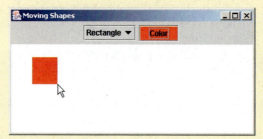

Figure 1.10 Drawing a rectangle.

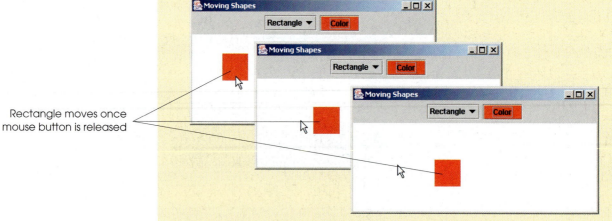

Rectangle moves once
mouse button is released

Figure 1.11 Moving rectangle after mouse button is released.

8. ***Drawing an oval.*** While the rectangle moves, you can draw more shapes that will move about the window. Click the JComboBox at the top and select **Oval** (Fig. 1.12). Then click the **Color** JButton and select a new color for your next shape. Now drag the mouse over a portion of the drawing area to draw an oval. After you release the mouse button, the oval will also move around the window (Fig. 1.13).

(cont.)

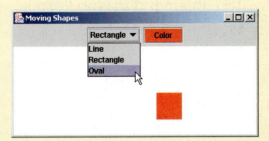

Figure 1.12   Selecting **Oval** as the shape to draw.

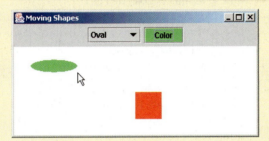

Figure 1.13   Drawing an oval.

9. ***Drawing additional shapes.*** Create several more shapes on your own. You can continue to draw rectangles and ovals, and you can also draw lines by selecting the **Line** option from the `JComboBox`. Each shape that you draw will move about the `JPanel`. Notice that when two shapes move across the same space, one shape overlaps the other, with the most recently drawn shape appearing on top (Fig. 1.14).

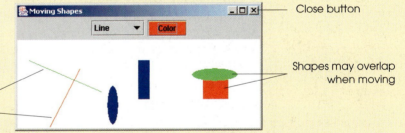

Close button

Shapes may overlap when moving

Lines may be drawn as well as rectangles and ovals

Figure 1.14   **Moving Shapes** application with several shapes drawn.

10. ***Closing the application.*** Close the application by clicking its **close** button, ⊠. You will be returned to the **Command Prompt** window.

11. ***Closing the Command Prompt.*** Close the **Command Prompt** window by clicking its close button.

The components that allow you to interact with this application (`JButton`, `JComboBox`, `JPanel` and `JFrame`) have already been defined as part of the Java API. You can customize these components for your own purposes. For example, the `JComboBox` in this application was customized to provide three options—**Line**, **Rectangle** and **Oval**. The `JButton` was customized to display the text **Color**. You did not need to define the general look and feel of these components. This is an excellent example of **software reuse**. Sun provides these components—which the company no doubt spent a considerable amount of time and money creating—so millions of programmers worldwide like you can use the components to prepare professional-quality GUIs without having to do much programming at all!

1.11 Internet and Web Resources

The Internet and Web are extraordinary resources. This section includes interesting and informative Web sites. Links to all these sites are provided on the CD included with this text and at www.deitel.com. Reference sections like this one are included throughout the book where appropriate.

www.deitel.com
Visit this site for updates, corrections and additional resources for Deitel & Associates publications, including *Simply Java Programming* errata, frequently asked questions (FAQs), links, code downloads and PowerPoint® slide downloads.

www.prenhall.com/deitel
The Deitel & Associates page on the Prentice Hall Web site contains information about our publications, code downloads and PowerPoint slides for this book.

www.softlord.com/comp
Visit this site to learn more about the history of computers.

www.elsop.com/wrc/h_comput.htm
This site presents the history of computing. It discusses famous people in the computer field, the evolution of programming languages and the development of operating systems.

www.w3.org/History.html
Visit this site for the history of the World Wide Web.

www.netvalley.com/intval.html
This site presents the history of the Internet.

java.sun.com
The Sun Microsystems, Inc. Java Web site contains the J2SDK (as well as other software useful in Java development), code samples, access to documentation for the Java APIs and links to tutorials that readers can use to learn Java.

developer.java.sun.com/developer/onlineTraining/new2java
The *New to Java™ Programming Center* site provides a collection of resources including articles, tutorials and code downloads, as well as quizzes and puzzles to test what you've learned.

1.12 Wrap-Up

In this tutorial, you learned about how computers are organized. You studied the levels of programming languages and which kinds of languages, including Java, require translators. You became familiar with some of the most popular programming languages. You learned the importance of structured programming and object-oriented programming. You studied a brief history of the Internet and the World Wide Web and learned the history of the Java programming language.

You took a working Java application out for a "test-drive." In the process of doing this, you learned that Java provides many preexisting GUI components that perform useful functions and that, by familiarizing yourself with the capabilities of these components, you can develop powerful applications much faster than if you tried to build them completely yourself. You were encouraged to explore several Web sites with additional information on this book, computers, the Internet, the Web and Java.

In the next tutorial, you will learn how to use some pre-existing Java components—namely the JLabel and the JFrame. You will use the JLabel component to display text and images on the JFrame. This will help you prepare to create your own Java applications. You will continue to learn with our application-driven approach, in which you will see all Java features in useful applications and in which you will

1. study the user requirements for an application,

2. test-drive a working version of the application,

3. learn the technologies you'll need to build the application yourself and

4. build your own version of the application.

As you work through the book, if you have any questions about Java, just send an e-mail to `deitel@deitel.com`, and we will respond promptly. We sincerely hope you enjoy learning Java—one of the most widely used programming languages in the world—with *Simply Java Programming*. Good luck!

KEY TERMS

Ada—A programming language, named after Lady Ada Lovelace, that was developed under the sponsorship of the U.S. Department of Defense (DOD) in the 1970s and early 1980s.

arithmetic and logic unit (ALU)—The "manufacturing" section of the computer. The ALU performs calculations and makes decisions.

assembly language—A type of programming language that uses English-like abbreviations to represent the fundamental operations of the computer.

attribute—Another name for a property of an object.

bandwidth—The information-carrying capacity of communications lines.

BASIC (Beginner's All-Purpose Symbolic Instruction Code)—A programming language that was developed in the mid-1960s by Professors John Kemeny and Thomas Kurtz of Dartmouth College as a language for writing simple programs and its primary purpose was to familiarize novices with programming techniques.

central processing unit (CPU)—The part of the computer's hardware that is responsible for supervising the operation of the other units of the computer.

class—The type of a group of similar objects. A class specifies the general format of its objects; the properties and actions available to an object depend on its class. An object is to its class much as a house is to its blueprint.

.class file—A file that contains statements converted from Java to a form that can be recognized by the Java Runtime Environment (JRE).

COBOL (COmmon Business Oriented Language)—A programming language that was developed in the late 1950s by a group of computer manufacturers in conjunction with government and industrial computer users. This language is used primarily for business applications that manipulate large amounts of data.

compiler—A translator program that converts high-level-language programs into machine language.

computer—A device capable of performing computations and making logical decisions at speeds millions and even billions of times faster than the speeds at which human beings carry out those same tasks.

computer program—A set of instructions that guides a computer through an orderly series of actions.

computer programmer—A person who writes computer programs in programming languages.

database—An organized collection of information.

dialog—A window used to display a message to the user or display various options from which the user can choose.

dragging the mouse—Moving the mouse while holding down the mouse button.

dynamic content—A type of content that is animated or interactive.

first generation language—Another name for a machine language.

FORTRAN (FORmula TRANslator)—A programming language developed by IBM Corporation in the mid-1950s to create scientific and engineering applications that require complex mathematical computations.

fourth generation language (4GL)—A programming language similar to a natural language like English and is primarily used to manipulate information that is stored in databases.

Framework Class Library (FCL)—A powerful library of reusable software components developed for Microsoft's .NET platform. The FCL provides similar capabilities to the Java class library.

graphical user interface (GUI)—The visual part of an application with which users interact.

GUI component—A reusable component, such as a `JButton` or `JComboBox`, that enables the user to interact with an application.

hardware—The various devices that make up a computer, including the keyboard, screen, mouse, hard drive, memory, CD-ROM and DVD drives and processing units.

high-level language—A type of programming language in which a single program statement accomplishes a substantial task. High-level language instructions look almost like everyday English and contain common mathematical notations.

HyperText Markup Language (HTML)—A language for marking up information to share over the World Wide Web via hyperlinked text documents.

input unit—The "receiving" section of the computer that obtains information (data and computer programs) from various input devices, such as the keyboard and the mouse.

Internet—A worldwide computer network. Most people today access the Internet through the World Wide Web.

interpreter—A program that executes high-level language programs directly without the need for compiling those programs into machine language.

.java file—A file that contains Java source code.

Java API (Application Programming Interface)—Collection of existing classes provided as part of the Java programming language.

Java class library—See Java API.

Java Runtime Environment (JRE)—A portion of the J2SDK that executes (that is, runs) Java programs.

Lady Ada Lovelace—The person credited with being the world's first computer programmer, for work she did in the early 1800s.

machine dependent—Only one computer platform supports a machine-dependent technology.

machine language—A computer's "natural" language, generally consisting of streams of numbers (1s and 0s) that tell the computer how to perform its most elementary operations.

memory unit—The rapid-access, relatively low-capacity "warehouse" section of the computer, which stores data temporarily while an application is running.

method—A portion of a Java class that performs a task and possibly returns information when it completes that task.

microprocessor—The chip that makes a computer work (that is, the "brain" of the computer).

object—A reusable software component that models a real world entity.

object technology—A packaging scheme for creating meaningful software units that are focused on particular application areas. Examples of objects include date objects, time objects, paycheck objects and file objects.

output device—A device to which information that is processed by the computer can be sent.

output unit—The section of the computer that takes information the computer has processed and places it on various output devices, making the information available for use outside the computer.

palette—A set of colors.

Pascal—A programming language named after the 17th-century mathematician and philosopher Blaise Pascal. This language was designed for teaching structured programming.

platform independent—Not dependent on a specific computer system. The Java programming language is platform independent, because Java programs can be created and run on various systems.

procedural programming language—A programming language (such as FORTRAN, Pascal, BASIC and C) that focuses on actions (verbs) rather than things or objects (nouns).

property—An object attribute, such as size, color or weight.

second generation language—Another name for an assembly language.

secondary storage unit—The long-term, high-capacity "warehouse" section of the computer.

software—The programs that run on computers.

software reuse—An approach to software development that enables programmers to develop new applications faster, through the reuse of existing software components.

source code file—A file with the extension `.java` that stores Java code written by a programmer.

structured programming—A disciplined approach to creating programs that are clear, correct and easy to modify.

supercomputer—A computer that can perform hundreds of billions of calculations per second.

third generation language—Another name for a high-level language.

Transmission Control Protocol/Internet Protocol (TCP/IP)—The combined set of communications protocols for the Internet.

World Wide Web Consortium (W3C)—A forum through which individuals and companies cooperate to develop and recommend technologies for the World Wide Web.

World Wide Web (WWW)—A collection of hardware and software associated with the Internet that allows computer users to locate and view multimedia-based documents (such as documents with text, graphics, animations, audios and videos).

MULTIPLE-CHOICE QUESTIONS

1.1 The World Wide Web was developed _____.
a) by ARPA
b) at CERN by Tim Berners-Lee
c) before the Internet
d) as a replacement for the Internet

1.2 Files with the extension _____ store Java source code written by programmers.
a) `.java`
b) `.class`
c) `.exe`
d) `.jre`

1.3 `JComboBoxes`, `JButtons` and `JPanels` are examples of _____.
a) platforms
b) high-level languages
c) methods
d) GUI components

1.4 _____ is an example of primary memory.
a) TCP
b) RAM
c) ALU
d) CD-ROM

1.5 Java is an example of a(n) _____ language, in which single program statements accomplish more substantial tasks.
a) machine
b) assembly
c) high-level
d) None of the above.

1.6 The protocol is primarily intended to create a "network of networks." _____
a) TCP
b) IP
c) OOP
d) FCL

1.7 The _____ programming language is not object oriented.
a) C
b) C++
c) Java
d) Visual Basic .NET

1.8 The visual part of the application with which users interact is known as the _____.
a) event
b) platform
c) GUI
d) library

1.9 The information-carrying capacity of communications lines is called _____.
a) networking
b) secondary storage
c) traffic
d) bandwidth

1.10 The Java programming language provides _____ that can be used by developers, rather than every application having to be created from scratch.

a) preexisting classes
b) TCP
c) assembly code
d) secondary storage

EXERCISES

1.11 Categorize each of the following items as either hardware or software:

a) CPU
b) Compiler
c) Input unit
d) A word-processor program
e) A Java program

1.12 Translator programs, such as assemblers and compilers, convert programs from one language (referred to as the source language) to another language (referred to as the target language). Determine which of the following statements are *true* and which are *false* (if the answer is *false*, explain why):

a) A compiler translates high-level-language programs into target-language programs.

b) An assembler translates source-language programs into machine-language programs.

c) A compiler translates source-language programs into target-language programs.

d) High-level languages are generally machine dependent.

e) A machine-language program requires translation before it can be run on a computer.

1.13 Computers can be thought of as being divided into six units.

a) Which unit can be thought of as "the boss" of the other units?

b) Which unit is the high-capacity "warehouse" and retains information even when the computer is powered off?

c) Which unit might determine whether two items stored in memory are identical?

d) Which unit obtains information from devices like the keyboard and mouse?

1.14 Expand each of the following acronyms:

a) W3C
b) TCP/IP
c) OOP
d) JRE
e) HTML

1.15 What are the advantages to using object-oriented programming techniques?

Welcome Application

Introduction to Graphical User Interface Programming

Today, users prefer software with interactive graphical user interfaces (GUIs) that respond to actions such as button clicks and data input. As a result, the vast majority of applications are GUI based. With Java, you can create graphical applications that input and output information in a variety of ways, which you will learn throughout the book.

In this tutorial, you will use GUI programming to create a **Welcome** application. You will build your application's GUI by placing two components—a JLabel with text and a JLabel with an image—on the window. You will customize the appearance of the window and the JLabels by setting their properties. You will set many property values including the window's background color, one JLabel's text ("Welcome to Java Programming!") and the other JLabel's image (a picture of the Deitel bug character).

2.1 Test-Driving the Welcome Application

The last tutorial introduced you to Java. In this tutorial, you will use Java to build the **Welcome** application. Your application must meet the following requirements:

Application Requirements

*A software company (Deitel & Associates) has asked you to develop a simple **Welcome** application that includes the greeting "Welcome to Java Programming!" and a picture of the company's bug mascot.*

You begin by test-driving the completed application. Then, you will learn the additional Java technologies you will need to create your own version of this application.

*Test-Driving the Welcome
Application*

1. ***Locating the completed application.*** Open the **Command Prompt** window by selecting **Start > Programs > Accessories > Command Prompt**. Change to your completed **Welcome** application directory by typing cd C:\Examples\Tutorial02\CompletedApplication\Welcome, then pressing the *Enter* key (Fig. 2.1).

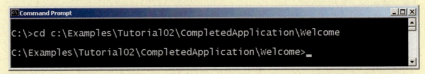

Figure 2.1   Locating the completed **Welcome** application.

2. ***Running the Welcome application.*** Type java Welcome in the **Command Prompt** window and press the *Enter* key to run the application (Fig. 2.2). Remember that Java commands are case sensitive, so Welcome must be capitalized; otherwise, the application will not execute. Figure 2.3 displays the executing application.

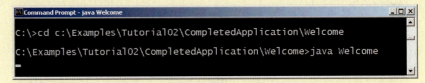

Figure 2.2   Running the completed **Welcome** application.

close
button

Figure 2.3   **Welcome** application executing.

3. ***Closing the running application.*** Close the running application by clicking its close button, ⊠. This returns you to the **Command Prompt** window.

4. ***Closing the Command Prompt window.*** Close the **Command Prompt** window by clicking its close button.

2.2 Compiling and Running the Template Welcome Application

In Tutorial 1, you learned that the Java Runtime Environment (JRE) can run only files with the .class extension. A **.class file** is created by **compiling** a Java source code file (a file with the .java extension) that contains your application's code. Next, you will learn how to compile the **Welcome** application.

Compiling the Welcome Application

1. ***Copying the template to your working directory.*** Copy the `C:\Examples\Tutorial02\TemplateApplication\Welcome` directory to your `C:\SimplyJava` directory.

2. ***Locating the template application.*** Open the **Command Prompt** window by selecting **Start > Programs > Accessories > Command Prompt**. Change directories to your working directory, `Welcome`, by typing `cd C:\SimplyJava\Welcome`, then pressing the *Enter* key. Type **`dir`**, then press *Enter* to list the contents of the directory (Fig. 2.4). Inside this directory should be a `Welcome.java` file, but no `Welcome.class` file.

Change directories

Display a directory listing

No `.class` file

```
Command Prompt
C:\>cd C:\SimplyJava\Welcome

C:\SimplyJava\Welcome>dir
 Volume in drive C has no label.
 Volume Serial Number is 4803-E3B8

 Directory of C:\SimplyJava\Welcome

02/14/2003  03:46p      <DIR>          .
02/14/2003  03:46p      <DIR>          ..
10/29/2001  11:25a              30,644 bug.png
02/12/2003  04:46p               2,256 Welcome.java
               2 File(s)         32,900 bytes
               2 Dir(s)  21,427,941,376 bytes free

C:\SimplyJava\Welcome>_
```

Figure 2.4 Locating the template **Welcome** application.

3. ***Compiling the application.*** In the **Command Prompt** window, type

    ```
    javac Welcome.java
    ```

    and press *Enter*. The ***`javac`*** command will compile the Java source code file and create a `Welcome.class` file in the directory. Type `dir` and press *Enter* again to see that the directory now contains the `Welcome.class` file (Fig. 2.5).

Compile `Welcome.java`

Display a directory listing

`.class` file was created

```
Command Prompt
C:\SimplyJava\Welcome>javac Welcome.java

C:\SimplyJava\Welcome>dir
 Volume in drive C has no label.
 Volume Serial Number is 4803-E3B8

 Directory of C:\SimplyJava\Welcome

02/11/2003  10:19a      <DIR>          .
02/11/2003  10:19a      <DIR>          ..
10/29/2001  11:25a              30,644 bug.png
02/11/2003  10:19a                 931 Welcome.class
02/07/2003  12:10p               2,286 Welcome.java
               3 File(s)         33,861 bytes
               2 Dir(s)  21,094,977,536 bytes free

C:\SimplyJava\Welcome>_
```

Figure 2.5 Compiling the template **Welcome** application.

4. Once you have created the `.class` file, you run the application by typing

    ```
    java Welcome
    ```

    and pressing *Enter*. At this point, the application is a blank **`JFrame`** (Fig. 2.6)—that is, a blank window. Each application you will create will be displayed in its own `JFrame`. We typically call this the "window" or "application window." In the rest of the tutorial you will customize the two `JLabel` components that will be displayed on the `JFrame` as shown in Fig. 2.3.

(cont.)

Figure 2.6 Running the template **Welcome** application.

5. *Closing the application.* Close the running application by clicking its close button, ⊠. This returns you to the **Command Prompt** window.

6. *Closing the Command Prompt window.* Close the **Command Prompt** window by clicking its close button.

SELF-REVIEW

1. A source code file has the _____ extension.

   a) .class   b) .source

   c) .java   d) None of the above.

2. The _____ converts a .java file to a .class file.

   a) debugger   b) compiler

   c) converter   d) JRE

Answers: 1) c. 2) b.

2.3 Constructing the Welcome Application

In this section, you develop your **Welcome** application. The application consists of a single JFrame that uses two JLabel components. A JLabel component displays text that the user cannot change or an image that the user cannot change. Recalling our discussions of Section 1.4 and Section 1.7, the name JLabel represents a Java class—the two JLabel components you will create in this example are objects of the JLabel class. You will now begin constructing the **Welcome** application.

Changing the *JFrame's* Title Bar Text

1. *Opening the Welcome application's template file.* Locate the C:\Simply-Java\Welcome directory where the application is saved. Find the Welcome.java file and open it in your text editor or integrated development environment (IDE). The code should look similar to Fig. 2.7, though each text editor and IDE will be different. [*Note:* As you look at the application code in your editor, please keep in mind that you are seeing only a portion of the code. Also, to help you along in the early tutorials, we will provide most of the code for you, and we will ask you to insert or modify only some of the code in each application.]

2. *Setting the text in the JFrame's title bar.* Insert line 33 of Fig. 2.8 into your application. This line sets the *title* property of our application to "Welcome". The *title* property contains the text that is shown in the JFrame's **title bar** (the top portion of the window that contains the window's title; see the word **Welcome** at the top of Fig. 2.3). JFrame titles should be short, descriptive names that use **book-title capitalization**, where the first letter of each significant word in the text is capitalized and the title does not end with any punctuation (for example, *Capitalization in a Book Title*).

(cont.)

```
Source Editor [Welcome]                                    _ □ ×
 1  // Tutorial 2: Welcome.java
 2  // This application welcomes the user to Java programming.
 3  import java.awt.*;
 4  import javax.swing.*;
 5
 6  public class Welcome extends JFrame
 7  {
 8      private JLabel textJLabel;    // label that displays text
 9      private JLabel pictureJLabel; // label that displays an image
10
11      // no-argument constructor
12      public Welcome()
13      {
14          createUserInterface();
15      }
16
17      // create and position GUI components; register event handlers
18      private void createUserInterface()
19      {
20          // get content pane and set layout to null
21          Container contentPane = getContentPane();
22          contentPane.setLayout( null );
```

Figure 2.7   **Welcome** application's Java source code in an editor window. (*Note:* All windows that show source code like the one in this figure were created in Sun™ ONE Studio 4 Community Edition. © Copyright 2003 Sun Microsystems, Inc. All rights reserved. Used by permission.)

Set title bar text ——————

```
Source Editor [Welcome *]                                  _ □ ×
32          // set properties application's window
33          setTitle( "Welcome" ); // set JFrame's title bar string
34          setSize( 100, 100 );   // set width and height of JFrame
35          setVisible( true );    // display JFrame on screen
```

Figure 2.8   Setting the text in the `JFrame`'s title bar.

Take a closer look at the line of code you just inserted:

```
setTitle( "Welcome" );
```

This is an executable Java **statement** that performs an action. Statements end when the **semicolon** (**;**) character is reached. This statement will *set* the *title* property of the `JFrame` to the value `"Welcome"`.

Text that is enclosed in double quotes is called a **String** or a **String literal**. In this case, the `String` represents text you wish to display in the `JFrame`'s title bar. `String` is also a class in Java.

Java code is **case sensitive**. This means that uppercase and lowercase letters are treated differently. For example, `settitle` and `setTitle` are considered to be different identifiers.

3. *Saving the application.* Save your modified source code file. In most editors, this can be done by selecting **File > Save**.

4. *Opening the Command Prompt window and changing directories.* Open the **Command Prompt** window by selecting **Start > Programs > Accessories > Command Prompt**. Change to your working directory, `Welcome`, by typing `cd C:\SimplyJava\Welcome` (Fig. 2.9), then pressing *Enter*.

5. *Compiling the application.* Compile your application by typing the command `javac Welcome.java` (Fig. 2.9), then pressing *Enter*. If the application does not compile correctly, error messages will be displayed in the **Command Prompt** window. If your application does not compile correctly, check that you typed line 33 exactly as in Fig. 2.8.

(cont.)

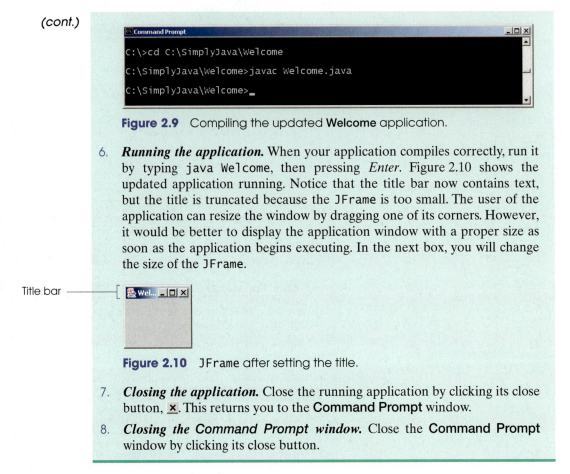

Figure 2.9 Compiling the updated **Welcome** application.

6. *Running the application.* When your application compiles correctly, run it by typing `java Welcome`, then pressing *Enter*. Figure 2.10 shows the updated application running. Notice that the title bar now contains text, but the title is truncated because the `JFrame` is too small. The user of the application can resize the window by dragging one of its corners. However, it would be better to display the application window with a proper size as soon as the application begins executing. In the next box, you will change the size of the `JFrame`.

Title bar

Figure 2.10 `JFrame` after setting the title.

7. *Closing the application.* Close the running application by clicking its close button, **×**. This returns you to the **Command Prompt** window.

8. *Closing the Command Prompt window.* Close the **Command Prompt** window by clicking its close button.

A `JFrame` can be resized by setting its *size* property, which specifies the `JFrame`'s width and height in units called **pixels** (*pic*ture *el*ements). A pixel is a tiny point on your computer screen that displays a color. The height of a `JFrame` includes its title bar. You learn how to set the `JFrame`'s width and height in the box, *Setting the `JFrame`'s* size *Property*.

Setting the *JFrame*'s size Property

1. *Setting the JFrame's width and height.* Modify the `setSize` statement (line 34) in your application as shown in Fig. 2.11. The first value in the parentheses (608) represents the width of the `JFrame` in pixels, and the second value (413) represents the height of the `JFrame` in pixels.

 You should notice that the form of this statement follows that of the previous example of setting a property. You wrote `set`, then the name of the property with a capitalized first letter (that is, `Size`), then the value of the property enclosed by parentheses and finally a semicolon.

Change the JFrame's width and height

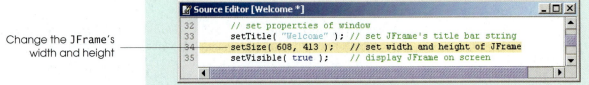

```
32      // set properties of window
33      setTitle( "Welcome" ); // set JFrame's title bar string
34      setSize( 608, 413 );   // set width and height of JFrame
35      setVisible( true );    // display JFrame on screen
```

Figure 2.11 The *size* property controls the width and height of the `JFrame`.

2. *Saving the application.* Save your modified source code file. In most editors, this can be done by selecting **File > Save**.

(cont.)

3. ***Opening the Command Prompt window and changing directories.*** Open the **Command Prompt** window by selecting **Start > Programs > Accessories > Command Prompt**. Change to your working directory, Welcome, by typing cd C:\SimplyJava\Welcome (Fig. 2.12), then pressing *Enter*.

4. ***Compiling the application.*** Compile your application by typing the command javac Welcome.java (Fig. 2.12), then pressing *Enter*. If your application does not compile correctly, check that you typed line 34 exactly as in Fig. 2.11.

Figure 2.12 Compiling the updated **Welcome** application.

5. ***Running the application.*** When your application compiles correctly, run the updated application by typing java Welcome, then pressing *Enter*. Figure 2.13 shows the updated application running. Notice that you now can see the complete title in the title bar, but the JFrame is still empty.

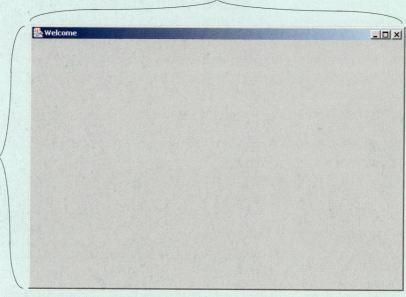

Figure 2.13 JFrame after setting its *title* and *size* properties.

6. ***Closing the application.*** Close the running application by clicking its close button, ⊠. This returns you to the **Command Prompt** window.

7. ***Closing the Command Prompt window.*** Close the **Command Prompt** window by clicking its close button.

Now that you have set the JFrame's size, you will customize your application window further by changing its background color from gray to yellow. Every screen color is created by combining red, green and blue values. Together these are called **RGB values**. All three RGB values are whole numbers in the range from 0 to 255. The first RGB value specifies the amount of red, the second specifies the amount of green and the third specifies the amount of blue. The larger the RGB value, the greater the amount of that particular color. So 0, 0, 0 is black; 255, 255, 255 is white; and 255, 0, 0 is red. Java provides you with 13 predefined colors, which are

listed in Fig. 2.14. Later in the book, you will learn how to create `Color` objects in which you specify the RGB values. At that point, you might find it interesting to experiment with the 16.7 million colors that you can create.

Constant	RGB value	Constant	RGB value
Color.BLACK	0, 0, 0	Color.MAGENTA	255, 0, 255
Color.BLUE	0, 0, 255	Color.ORANGE	255, 200, 0
Color.CYAN	0, 255, 255	Color.PINK	255, 175, 175
Color.DARK_GRAY	64, 64, 64	Color.RED	255, 0, 0
Color.GRAY	128, 128, 128	Color.WHITE	255, 255, 255
Color.GREEN	0, 255, 0	Color.YELLOW	255, 255, 0
Color.LIGHT_GRAY	192, 192, 192		

Figure 2.14 Predefined colors and their RGB values.

Every `JFrame` has a container object called a **content pane**. The purpose of this container is to provide a visual area in which to place GUI components like `JLabels`. The content pane occupies the entire visible area inside the borders of the `JFrame`. It starts just below the `JFrame`'s title bar and extends to the bottom, left and right edges of the `JFrame` (Fig. 2.15).

The dashed box represents the area of the content pane

Figure 2.15 `JFrame` with highlighted content pane.

Next, you will use the content pane's *background* property to control the color that will appear in the background of the window. You will change the background of the content pane from gray to yellow.

Setting the Window's Background Color

1. **Changing the window's background color.** Insert line 22 of Fig. 2.16 into your application. This line sets the *background* property of the content pane to the predefined color yellow (`Color.YELLOW`). This color corresponds to the RGB value 255, 255, 0. This line of code has a slightly different format than the previous lines you have seen. Because you are manipulating only a part of the `JFrame` (its content pane), you must first specify which part, then specify the property of the part that you wish to change. The dot separates the part from the property. This notation will be fully explained in Tutorial 4.

(cont.)

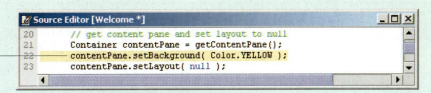

Figure 2.16 Setting the JFrame's *background* property to yellow.

Change the background color

GUI Design Tip

Use colors in your applications, but not to the point of distracting the user.

2. *Saving the application.* Save your modified source code file.

3. *Opening the Command Prompt window and changing directories.* Open the **Command Prompt** by selecting **Start > Programs > Accessories > Command Prompt**. Change to your working directory, Welcome, by typing cd C:\SimplyJava\Welcome (Fig. 2.17), then pressing *Enter*.

4. *Compiling the application.* Compile your application by typing the command javac Welcome.java (Fig. 2.17), then pressing *Enter*. If your application does not compile correctly, check that you typed line 22 exactly as in Fig. 2.16.

Figure 2.17 Compiling the updated **Welcome** application.

5. *Running the application.* When your application compiles correctly, run it by typing java Welcome, then pressing *Enter*. Figure 2.18 shows the updated application running.

Figure 2.18 JFrame after setting the title, size and background color.

6. *Closing the application.* Close the running application by clicking its close button, **x**. This returns you to the **Command Prompt** window.

7. *Closing the Command Prompt window.* Close the **Command Prompt** window by clicking its close button.

Now that you have finished customizing the JFrame and its content pane, you will customize a JLabel component that will display a text greeting on the JFrame.

Customizing a JLabel
on the content pane

1. ***Customizing a* JLabel*'s appearance.*** Insert line 27 of Fig. 2.19 into your code. This line sets the ***text*** property of the JLabel to "Welcome to Java Programming!". When a JLabel is displayed, its *text* property will be displayed on the JLabel inside the JFrame.

Setting the *text* property ————

```
Source Editor [Welcome *]                                    _ |□| X|
25        // set up textJLabel
26        textJLabel = new JLabel();
27        textJLabel.setText( "Welcome to Java Programming!" );
28        contentPane.add( textJLabel );
```

Figure 2.19   Setting the *text* property of the JLabel.

GUI Design Tip

Use JLabels to display text that users cannot change.

2. ***Setting the* location *property.*** Insert line 28 of Fig. 2.20 to set the ***location*** property of the JLabel.

```
Source Editor [Welcome *]                                    _ |□| X|
25        // set up textJLabel
26        textJLabel = new JLabel();
27        textJLabel.setText( "Welcome to Java Programming!" );
28        textJLabel.setLocation( 35, 0 );
29        contentPane.add( textJLabel );
```

Setting the location of the JLabel ————

Figure 2.20   Setting the *location* property of the JLabel.

The JLabel's *location* property specifies the position of the upper-left corner of the component in the content pane. Java assigns the value 0, 0 to the top-left corner of the content pane (which is located just below the title bar of the window). A component's *location* property is set according to its distance from that point in the content pane. As the first number of the *location* property increases, the component moves to the right along the *x* axis. As the second number of the *location* property increases, the component moves toward the bottom of the content pane along the *y* axis. In this case, the value of 35, 0 indicates that the JLabel is placed 35 pixels to the right of the top-left corner of the content pane and 0 pixels down from the top-left corner of the content pane. A value of 35, 48 would indicate that the JLabel has been placed 35 pixels to the right of the top-left corner of the content pane and 48 pixels down from the top-left corner of the content pane.

GUI Design Tip

Ensure that all JLabel components are large enough to display their text.

3. ***Setting the* size *property.*** Insert line 29 of Fig. 2.21 to set the *size* property of the JLabel. The *size* property of a JLabel specifies its width and height in pixels, just like the *size* property of the JFrame. In fact, many Java components have identical properties. This makes the components easier to learn and use.

```
Source Editor [Welcome *]                                    _ |□| X|
25        // set up textJLabel
26        textJLabel = new JLabel();
27        textJLabel.setText( "Welcome to Java Programming!" );
28        textJLabel.setLocation( 35, 0 );
29        textJLabel.setSize( 550, 88 );
30        contentPane.add( textJLabel );
```

Setting the size of the JLabel ————

Figure 2.21   Setting the *size* property of the JLabel.

(cont.)   4. ***Setting the* font *property of the* JLabel.** Insert line 30 of Fig. 2.22 to set the
JLabel's font name, style and size. Setting the ***font*** property of a JLabel
allows you to set the font name (Times, Courier, etc.), font style (plain, bold,
italic, etc.) and font size (16, 18, etc.) in points (one point equals 1/72 of an
inch). This statement sets the font name to "SansSerif", the style to
Font.PLAIN and the size to 36 points. The "SansSerif" font name actually
describes a related group of fonts that includes Arial and Helvetica. If the
JLabel's text is larger than the JLabel, the text will be truncated.

Setting the font of the JLabel ⎯⎯⎯

```
Source Editor [Welcome *]                                    _ |□| x|
25        // set up textJLabel
26        textJLabel = new JLabel();
27        textJLabel.setText( "Welcome to Java Programming!" );
28        textJLabel.setLocation( 35, 0 );
29        textJLabel.setSize( 550, 88 );
30        textJLabel.setFont( new Font( "SansSerif", Font.PLAIN, 36 ) );
31        contentPane.add( textJLabel );
```

Figure 2.22   Changing the JLabel's font size to 36 points.

5. ***Aligning the* JLabel*'s text.*** To align text inside a JLabel, you will set the
JLabel's ***horizontalAlignment*** property. This property allows you to align
the text to the right, center or left of the JLabel. Insert line 31 of Fig. 2.23
into your application. The text will now be centered (JLabel.CENTER) on
the JLabel. Text on a JLabel also can be left justified (JLabel.LEFT, the
default) or right justified (JLabel.RIGHT).

Centering the text in the JLabel ⎯⎯⎯

```
Source Editor [Welcome *]                                    _ |□| x|
25        // set up textJLabel
26        textJLabel = new JLabel();
27        textJLabel.setText( "Welcome to Java Programming!" );
28        textJLabel.setLocation( 35, 0 );
29        textJLabel.setSize( 550, 88 );
30        textJLabel.setFont( new Font( "SansSerif", Font.PLAIN, 36 ) );
31        textJLabel.setHorizontalAlignment( JLabel.CENTER );
32        contentPane.add( textJLabel );
```

Figure 2.23   Centering the JLabel's text.

6. ***Saving the application.*** Save your modified source code file.

7. ***Opening the* Command Prompt *window and changing directories.*** Open
the **Command Prompt** window by selecting **Start > Programs > Accessories > Command Prompt**. Change to your working directory, Welcome, by
typing cd C:\SimplyJava\Welcome (Fig. 2.24), then pressing *Enter*.

8. ***Compiling the application.*** Compile your application by typing the command javac Welcome.java (Fig. 2.24), then pressing *Enter*. If your application does not compile correctly, check that you typed lines 27–31 exactly as
in Fig. 2.23.

```
Command Prompt                                              _ |□| x|
C:\>cd C:\SimplyJava\Welcome

C:\SimplyJava\Welcome>javac Welcome.java

C:\SimplyJava\Welcome>_
```

Figure 2.24   Compiling the updated **Welcome** application.

9. ***Running the application.*** When your application compiles correctly, run it
by typing java Welcome, then pressing *Enter*. Figure 2.25 shows the updated
application running.

(cont.)

(0, 0) coordinate of content pane

JLabel component with text

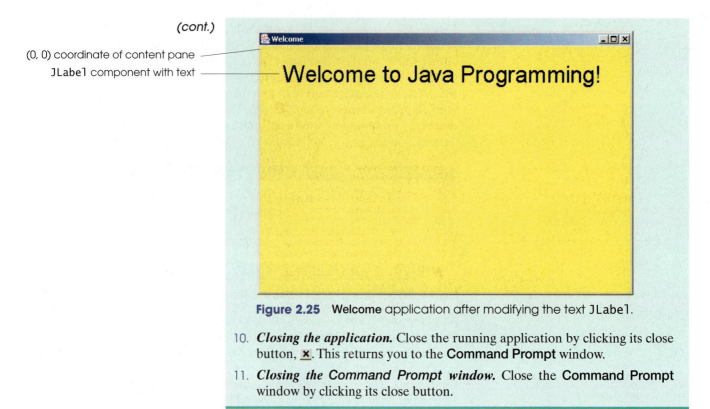

Figure 2.25 **Welcome** application after modifying the text JLabel.

10. ***Closing the application.*** Close the running application by clicking its close button, **✕**. This returns you to the **Command Prompt** window.

11. ***Closing the Command Prompt window.*** Close the **Command Prompt** window by clicking its close button.

The box, *Inserting an Image and Running the **Welcome** Application*, will guide you through the process of customizing a JLabel component to display an image to complete your first Java application.

Inserting an Image and Running the Welcome Application

1. ***Setting the* icon *property of a* JLabel.** When the *icon* property of the JLabel is set, an image is displayed in the JLabel. Insert line 36 of Fig. 2.26 into your application. This line will cause the image in the file "bug.png" to be displayed in the JLabel. Unless the string you specify in this statement includes the full path to the image (for instance, "C:\SimplyJava\Welcome\bug.png"), this statement assumes that the image is in the same directory as the application (as it does here).

Displaying an image

```
34        // set up pictureJLabel
35        pictureJLabel = new JLabel();
36        pictureJLabel.setIcon( new ImageIcon( "bug.png" ) );
37        contentPane.add( pictureJLabel );
```

Figure 2.26 Setting the *icon* property to display an image on a JLabel.

You can display any of several popular image formats, including

GUI Design Tip

Use JLabels with images to enhance GUIs with graphics that users cannot change.

- *PNG (Portable Network Graphics)*
- *GIF (Graphics Interchange Format)*
- *JPEG (Joint Photographic Experts Group)*
- *BMP (Windows Bitmap).*

(cont.)

You will use a PNG-format image in this application. Creating new images requires image-editing software, such as Jasc® Paint Shop Pro™ (www.jasc.com), Adobe® Photoshop™ (www.adobe.com), Microsoft Picture It!® (photos.msn.com) or Microsoft Paint (provided with Windows). You will not create images in this book; instead, you will be provided with all the images you will need.

2. ***Setting the* bounds *property for the* JLabel.** Insert line 37 of Fig. 2.27. This line sets the ***bounds*** property of the JLabel. The *bounds* property controls both the size and the location of the JLabel. The first two numbers set the location of the component's upper-left corner (54, 120). The last two numbers set the width and height of the component (500, 250).

GUI Design Tip

Ensure that all JLabel components are large enough to display their images.

Setting the bounds (size and location) of the JLabel

```
 Source Editor [Welcome *]                                    _ □ ×
34        // set up pictureJLabel
35        pictureJLabel = new JLabel();
36        pictureJLabel.setIcon( new ImageIcon( "bug.png" ) );
37        pictureJLabel.setBounds( 54, 120, 500, 250 );
38        contentPane.add( pictureJLabel );
```

Figure 2.27   Using the *bounds* property to set the size and location.

3. ***Setting the* horizontalAlignment *property.*** Insert line 38 of Figure 2.28 into your application to center the image in the JLabel. The *horizontalAlignment* property of the JLabel controls the alignment of the JLabel's contents. In this case, we use the predefined alignment constant JLabel.CENTER to center the image in the JLabel. Note that the image also can be left justified (JLabel.LEFT, the default) or right justified (JLabel.RIGHT).

Centering the image

```
 Source Editor [Welcome *]                                    _ □ ×
34        // set up pictureJLabel
35        pictureJLabel = new JLabel();
36        pictureJLabel.setIcon( new ImageIcon( "bug.png" ) );
37        pictureJLabel.setBounds( 54, 120, 500, 250 );
38        pictureJLabel.setHorizontalAlignment( JLabel.CENTER );
39        contentPane.add( pictureJLabel );
```

Figure 2.28   Setting the *horizontalAlignment* property of the JLabel.

4. ***Saving the application.*** Save your modified source code file.

5. ***Opening the* Command Prompt *window and changing directories.*** Open the **Command Prompt** window by selecting **Start > Programs > Accessories > Command Prompt**. Change to your working directory, Welcome, by typing cd C:\SimplyJava\Welcome (Fig. 2.29), then pressing *Enter*.

6. ***Compiling the application.*** Compile your completed application by typing javac Welcome.java (Fig. 2.29), then pressing *Enter*. If your application does not compile correctly, check that you typed lines 36–38 exactly as in Fig. 2.28.

```
 Command Prompt                                               _ □ ×
C:\>cd C:\SimplyJava\Welcome

C:\SimplyJava\Welcome>javac Welcome.java

C:\SimplyJava\Welcome>_
```

Figure 2.29   Compiling the updated **Welcome** application.

(cont.)

7. ***Running the application.*** When your application compiles correctly, run it by typing `java Welcome`, then pressing *Enter*. Figure 2.30 shows the completed application running.

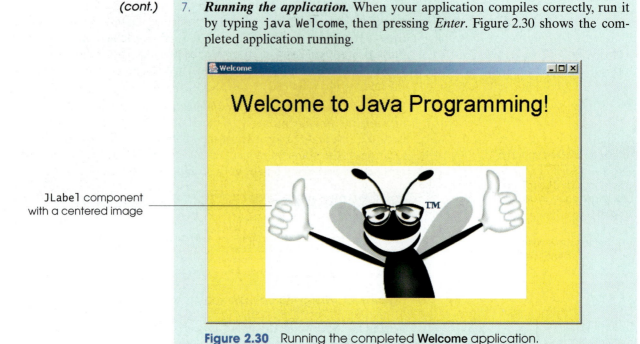

JLabel component with a centered image

Figure 2.30　Running the completed **Welcome** application.

8. ***Closing the application.*** Close the running application by clicking its close button, ⊠. This returns you to the **Command Prompt** window.

9. ***Closing the Command Prompt window.*** Close the **Command Prompt** window by clicking its close button.

Figure 2.31 presents the source code for the **Welcome** application. The lines of code that you added, viewed or modified in this tutorial are highlighted.

```
1   // Tutorial 2: Welcome.java
2   // This application welcomes the user to Java programming.
3   import java.awt.*;
4   import javax.swing.*;
5
6   public class Welcome extends JFrame
7   {
8      private JLabel textJLabel;    // JLabel that displays text
9      private JLabel pictureJLabel; // JLabel that displays an image
10
11     // no-argument constructor
12     public Welcome()
13     {
14        createUserInterface();
15     }
16
17     // create and position GUI components; register event handlers
18     private void createUserInterface()
19     {
20        // get content pane and set layout to null
21        Container contentPane = getContentPane();
22        contentPane.setBackground( Color.YELLOW );
23        contentPane.setLayout( null );
24
```

Setting the background color of the content pane to yellow

Figure 2.31 Code for the **Welcome** application. (Part 1 of 2.)

```
25        // set up textJLabel
26        textJLabel = new JLabel();
27        textJLabel.setText( "Welcome to Java Programming!" );
28        textJLabel.setLocation( 35, 0 );
29        textJLabel.setSize( 550, 88 );
30        textJLabel.setFont( new Font( "SanSerif", Font.PLAIN, 36 ) );
31        textJLabel.setHorizontalAlignment( JLabel.CENTER );
32        contentPane.add( textJLabel );
33
34        // set up pictureJLabel
35        pictureJLabel = new JLabel();
36        pictureJLabel.setIcon( new ImageIcon( "bug.png" ) );
37        pictureJLabel.setBounds( 54, 120, 500, 250 );
38        pictureJLabel.setHorizontalAlignment( JLabel.CENTER );
39        contentPane.add( pictureJLabel );
40
41        // set properties of application's window
42        setTitle( "Welcome" ); // set JFrame's title bar string
43        setSize( 608, 413 );   // set width and height of JFrame
44        setVisible( true );    // display JFrame on screen
45
46     } // end method createUserInterface
47
48     // main method
49     public static void main( String[] args )
50     {
51        Welcome application = new Welcome();
52        application.setDefaultCloseOperation( JFrame.EXIT_ON_CLOSE );
53
54     } // end method main
55
56  } // end class Welcome
```

Customize `textJLabel`'s properties

Customize `pictureJLabel`'s properties

Set the `JFrame`'s title and size

Figure 2.31 Code for the **Welcome** application. (Part 2 of 2.)

SELF-REVIEW

1. Use _____ to set the text that appears on a JFrame's title bar.

   a) setText   b) setTitle
   c) setTitleBar   d) setName

2. Use _____ to specify the image to display on a JLabel.

   a) setIcon   b) setPicture
   c) setImage   d) setGraphic

Answers: 1) b. 2) a.

2.4 Syntax Errors

In this tutorial, you learned to compile the **Welcome** application by typing javac Welcome.java in the **Command Prompt** window. If you do not write your code correctly, your application will not compile and errors will appear in the **Command Prompt** window. Even after an application compiles correctly, it may still contain errors. **Debugging** is the process of fixing errors in an application. There are two types of errors—syntax errors and logic errors.

   Syntax errors (also called **compilation errors** or **compile-time errors**) occur when code statements violate the grammatical rules of the programming language. Examples of such errors include misspelling a word that is special to Java and not placing a semicolon at the end of each statement you added to your application in this tutorial. An application cannot be executed until all of its syntax errors are corrected—that is, until it compiles correctly.

Logic errors do not prevent your application from compiling successfully, but do cause your application to produce erroneous results when it runs. The Java 2 Software Development Kit provides software called a **debugger**, which allows you to analyze the behavior of your application to locate logic errors.

During the compilation of a Java application, any syntax errors appear in the **Command Prompt** window, along with a description of each error. Figure 2.32 displays the error message that appears when the semicolon character is omitted from the end of line 37 of Fig. 2.31. You would then insert the semicolon and recompile.

Missing semicolon at the end of this line

```
C:\SimplyJava\Welcome>javac Welcome.java
Welcome.java:37: ';' expected
        pictureJLabel.setBounds( 54, 120, 500, 250 )
                                                    ^
1 error

C:\SimplyJava\Welcome>
```

Figure 2.32   **Command Prompt** window listing syntax errors.

At the ends of several tutorials, we provide *Using the Debugger* sections in which you will learn to detect and remove logic errors by using the Java debugger. In the box, *Using the Debugger: Syntax Errors*, you will create some syntax errors, view the error messages from the compiler and fix the errors. In later *Using the Debugger* sections, you will actually use the debugger.

Using the Debugger: Syntax Errors

1. ***Opening the application.*** If the **Welcome** application source code is not currently open, locate the `Welcome.java` file and open it in your text editor or IDE.

2. ***Creating your own syntax errors.*** You will now create your own syntax errors, for demonstration purposes. Add the letter "`s`" to the end of `textJLabel` in line 27 and delete the right parenthesis at the end of the statement in line 28. Figure 2.33 shows the two modified (incorrect) lines.

Two syntax errors

Figure 2.33   Introducing two syntax errors into your code.

3. ***Saving the application.*** Save your modified source code file.

4. ***Opening the Command Prompt window and changing directories.*** Open the **Command Prompt** window by selecting **Start > Programs > Accessories > Command Prompt**. Change to your working directory, `Welcome`, by typing `cd C:\SimplyJava\Welcome`, then pressing *Enter*.

5. ***Compiling the application.*** Compile your application by typing the command `javac Welcome.java`, then pressing *Enter*. Figure 2.34 shows the error messages generated by the compiler.

6. ***Locating the syntax errors.*** Each error that the compiler finds is accompanied by the file name (`Welcome.java`), the line number, a description of the error and the actual line of source code that produced that error. In this case, the compiler notified you that it found errors on line 27 and 28.

(cont.)

File name and line number ——

Explanation of the error ——

Line of code ——

Number of errors ——

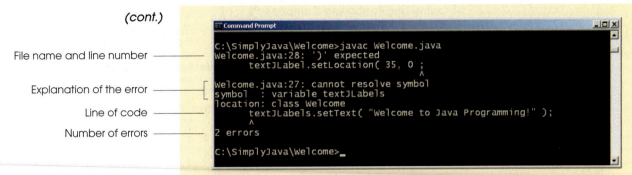

Figure 2.34 Two error messages about syntax errors generated by the compiler.

7. *Fixing the syntax errors.* Now that the compiler has told you where the syntax errors are located, go back to the source code and correct the two errors you created in *Step 2*. Save the file and return once more to the **Command Prompt** window. Recompile your application, which should now compile correctly.

8. *Closing the Command Prompt window.* Close the **Command Prompt** window by clicking its close button. [Note: You do not need to close the application, because you did not execute it. You were just compiling to experiment with finding syntax errors.]

SELF-REVIEW

1. Upon finding a syntax error in an application, the compiler will notify the user of an error by giving the user _____.

   a) the line number of the error   b) the correct code to fix the error

   c) a brief description of the error   d) Both a and c.

2. Syntax errors occur for many reasons, such as when a(n) _____.

   a) application terminates unexpectedly   b) parenthesis is omitted

   c) word is spelled incorrectly   d) Both b and c.

Answers: 1) d. 2) d.

2.5 Wrap-Up

This tutorial introduced you to programming in Java. You learned how to customize the graphical user interface portion of an application by changing the properties of various Java components.

In creating your **Welcome** application, you set the JFrame's title bar text and size (width and height) using the *title* and *size* properties, respectively. You set the background color of the JFrame's content pane by using its *background* property. You learned that JLabels are components that can display text and images. You displayed text in a JLabel by setting its *text*, *font* and *horizontalAlignment* properties, and you displayed an image by setting a JLabel's *icon* and *horizontalAlignment* properties. You arranged JLabels on your JFrame by setting their *size* and *location* properties, or alternatively by setting their *bounds* property.

In the next tutorial, you will continue learning how to create graphical applications. In particular, you will create an application with GUI components designed to accept user input.

SKILLS SUMMARY   **Creating GUIs Quickly and Efficiently**

■ Use predefined graphical user interface components like JLabels.

Sizing and Positioning Components

■ Use setSize and setLocation to set the *size* and *location* properties or setBounds to set the *bounds* property, which sizes and positions components.

Setting the Dimensions of a JFrame or JLabel by Using Property *size*

■ Use setSize to set the width and height in pixels of the JFrame or JLabel.

Setting the Content Pane's Background Color

■ Use setBackground to set the content pane's *background* property. Some predefined colors include Color.RED, Color.GREEN and Color.BLUE. A complete list of predefined colors is in Fig. 2.14.

Setting a JLabel's *text* Property

■ Use setText to set the JLabel's *text* property to display information.

Setting a JLabel's *font* Property

■ Use setFont to set the JLabel's *font* property, which changes the font of the displayed text. You can specify the font name (for example, SansSerif, Times, Courier, etc.), the font style (for instance, Font.PLAIN) and the font size in points.

Aligning Text in a JLabel

■ Use setHorizontalAlignment to set the JLabel's *horizontalAlignment* property. Possible values for the *horizontalAlignment* property are JLabel.LEFT (the default), JLabel.CENTER and JLabel.RIGHT.

Adding an Image to the JFrame

■ Use a JLabel to display the image.
■ Use setIcon to set the JLabel's *icon* property to display the image.

KEY TERMS

background **property**—Property that specifies the background color of a content pane or component.

book-title capitalization—A style that capitalizes the first letter of each significant word in the text (for example, **Calculate the Total**).

bounds **property**—The property that specifies both the location and size of a component.

case sensitive—Distinguishes between uppercase and lowercase letters in code.

.class file—The type of file that is executed by the Java Runtime Environment (JRE). A .class file is created by compiling the application's .java file.

compiling—The process that converts a source code file (.java) into a .class file.

content pane—The portion of a JFrame that contains the GUI components.

debugging—The process of locating and removing errors in an application.

dir command—Command typed in a **Command Prompt** window to list the directory contents.

font **property**—The property that specifies the font name (for example, SansSerif, Times, Courier, etc.), style (for instance, Font.PLAIN) and font size in points (for example, 12, 18, 36, etc.) of any displayed text in a JFrame or one of its components.

horizontalAlignment **property**—The property that specifies how text is aligned within a JLabel.

icon **property**—The property that specifies the file name of the image displayed in a JLabel.

javac command—The command that compiles a source code file (.java) into a .class file.

.java file—The type of file in which programmers write the Java code for an application.

JLabel—The component that displays text or an image that the user cannot modify.

location **property**—The property that specifies where a component's upper-left corner appears on the JFrame.

logic error—An error that does not prevent your application from compiling successfully, but does cause your application to produce erroneous results.

pixel—A point on your computer screen. Pixel is short for "picture element."

RGB value—The amount of red, green and blue needed to create a color.

semicolon (;)—The character used to indicate the end of a Java statement.

***size* property**—Property that specifies the width and height, in pixels, of a component.

source code file—A file with a `.java` extension. These files are editable by the programmer, but are not executable.

statement—Code that instructs the computer to perform a task. Every statement ends with a semicolon (;) character. Most applications consist of many statements.

String—A sequence of characters that represents text information.

String literal—A sequence of characters within double quotes.

syntax error—An error that occurs when code violates the grammatical rules of a programming language.

***text* property**—The property that specifies the text displayed by a `JLabel`.

title bar—The area at the top of a `JFrame` where its title appears.

GUI DESIGN GUIDELINES

Overall Design

■ Use colors in your applications, but not to the point of distracting the user.

JFrames

■ Choose short, descriptive `JFrame` titles.

■ `JFrame` titles should use book-title capitalization, in which the first letter of each significant word is capitalized and the title does not end with any punctuation.

JLabels

■ Use `JLabels` to display text that users cannot change.

■ Ensure that all `JLabel` components are large enough to display their text.

■ Use `JLabels` with images to enhance GUIs with graphics that users cannot change.

■ Ensure that all `JLabel` components are large enough to display their images.

JAVA LIBRARY REFERENCE

JFrame This component enables a Java application to appear in its own window. All other components in an application are displayed within the application's window.

■ *In action*

■ *Methods*

`setBackground`—Sets the background color of the `JFrame`'s content pane (or of other components). For example, if the content pane of the `JFrame` is called `contentPane`, then the statement `contentPane.setBackground( Color.YELLOW );` sets the background color of the content pane to yellow.

`setSize`—Sets the size (in pixels) of the `JFrame`.

`setTitle`—Sets the text displayed in the title bar of the `JFrame`.

JLabel This component displays text or an image that the user cannot modify.

■ *In action*

Welcome to Java Programming!

■ *Methods*

`setBounds`—Specifies the size and location in the `JLabel`.

`setFont`—Specifies the font name, style and size of the text displayed in the `JLabel`.

setHorizontalAlignment—Determines how the text is aligned in the JLabel.

setIcon—Specifies the file name and path of the image in the JLabel.

setSize—Specifies the height and width (in pixels) in the JLabel.

setText—Specifies the text displayed in the JLabel.

MULTIPLE-CHOICE QUESTIONS

2.1 Use _____ to specify the content pane's background color.

    a) setBackground   b) setBackColor

    c) setRGB   d) setColor

2.2 To compile an application, type the command _____ followed by the name of the file.

    a) build   b) compile

    c) javac   d) create

2.3 The *font* property controls the _____ of the font displayed by a JLabel.

    a) size   b) style

    c) name   d) All of the above.

2.4 Syntax errors are found by the _____.

    a) JRE   b) compiler

    c) **Command Prompt**   d) application

2.5 Java source code files have the extension _____.

    a) .class   b) .java

    c) .javac   d) .source

2.6 The *bounds* property controls the _____.

    a) size of the text   b) location of a component

    c) size of a component   d) Both b and c

2.7 A JLabel component displays the text specified by _____.

    a) setCaption   b) setData

    c) setText   d) setName

2.8 Use _____ to align the text inside a JLabel.

    a) setAlignment   b) setCenter

    c) setRight   d) setHorizontalAlignment

2.9 RGB values specify the _____.

    a) size of a JLabel   b) components of a color

    c) size of the window   d) components in a JFrame

2.10 Pixels are _____.

    a) picture elements   b) a font size measurement

    c) a set of fonts   d) properties that determine the location of a component

EXERCISES

In Exercises 2.11–2.16, you will use the GUI programming techniques presented in this tutorial to customize a variety of GUIs. The applications you customize here will not respond to user interactions. You will learn how to make your applications fully operational in later tutorials.

2.11 *(Calculator GUI)* Many components have the same kinds of properties as JLabels. For instance, JButtons also have *size*, *location* and *text* properties. In this exercise, you will customize the plus (**+**) JButton in the **Calculator** GUI shown in Fig. 2.35.

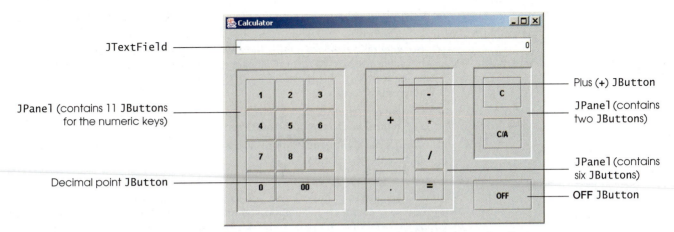

Figure 2.35 **Calculator** GUI for completed application.

a) *Copying the template to your working directory.* Copy the C:\Examples\ Tutorial02\Exercises\Calculator directory to your C:\SimplyJava directory.

b) *Opening the Command Prompt window and changing directories.* Open the **Command Prompt** by selecting **Start > Programs > Accessories > Command Prompt**. Change to your working directory by typing cd C:\SimplyJava\Calculator, then pressing *Enter*.

c) *Compiling the template application.* Compile your application by typing the command javac Calculator.java, then pressing *Enter*.

d) *Running the template application.* Run the application by typing java Calculator. The GUI of the **Calculator** template application should appear as shown in Fig. 2.36. Notice that the plus (**+**) JButton is missing. The template application creates the plus (**+**) JButton, but the JButton's default width and height are both zero, so it does not appear on the screen. You will customize the plus (**+**) JButton's *text* and *bounds* properties to make it appear as in Fig. 2.35.

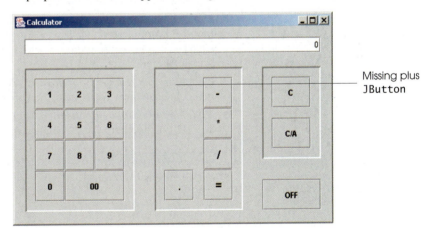

Figure 2.36 **Calculator** GUI with missing plus (**+**) button.

e) *Closing the application.* Close the running application by clicking its close button. This returns you to the **Command Prompt** window.

f) *Opening the template file.* Open the Calculator.java file in your text editor.

g) *Customizing the plus JButton on the center JPanel.* When a GUI component is placed on a JPanel, the component is positioned from the top-left corner of the JPanel, which has the position *(0, 0)*. Customize the JButton for the plus function. The name of this JButton is plusJButton. After line 122 in the template code, insert a statement to set plusJButton's *text* property to "+". On the next line, insert a statement to set plusJButton's *bounds* property to 16, 16, 48, 128.

h) *Saving the application.* Save your modified source code file.

i) *Compiling the completed application.* In the **Command Prompt** window, compile your application by typing javac Calculator.java, then pressing *Enter*.

j) *Running the completed application.* When your application compiles correctly, run it by typing java Calculator. Compare the GUI of your completed **Calculator** application with the GUI shown in Fig. 2.35 to ensure that you customized the plus (**+**) JButton correctly.

k) *Closing the application.* Close the running application by clicking its close button. This returns you to the **Command Prompt** window.

l) *Closing the Command Prompt window.* Close the **Command Prompt** window by clicking its close button.

2.12 *(Alarm Clock GUI)* As you saw in Exercise 2.11, JButtons have some properties in common with JLabels. In this exercise, you will customize the properties of the **AM** and **PM** JRadioButton components. In addition, you will customize the JPanel that displays the time by setting its *background* property to black and setting its *foreground* property to white (by using setForeground). When you complete your modifications, the **Alarm Clock** GUI will appear as in Fig. 2.37.

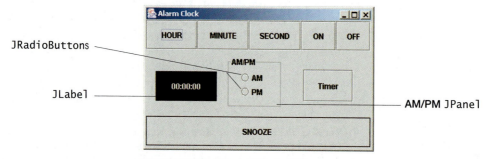

Figure 2.37 **Alarm Clock** GUI.

a) *Copying the template to your working directory.* Copy the C:\Examples\ Tutorial02\Exercises\AlarmClock directory to your C:\SimplyJava directory.

b) *Opening the Command Prompt window and changing directories.* Open the Command Prompt by selecting **Start > Programs > Accessories > Command Prompt**. Change to your working directory by typing cd C:\SimplyJava\AlarmClock, then pressing *Enter*.

c) *Compiling the template application.* Compile your application by typing the command javac AlarmClock.java, then pressing *Enter*.

d) *Running the template application.* Run the application by typing java AlarmClock. The GUI of the **Alarm Clock** template application should appear as shown in Fig. 2.38.

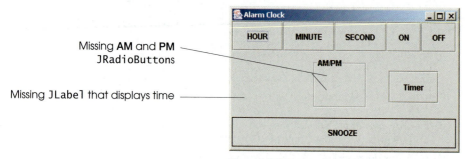

Figure 2.38 **Alarm Clock** GUI with missing JLabel and JRadioButtons.

e) *Closing the application.* Close the running application by clicking its close button. This returns you to the **Command Prompt** window.

f) *Opening the template file.* Open the AlarmClock.java file in your text editor.

g) *Customizing the time JLabel.* When a GUI component is placed on the JFrame's content pane, the component is positioned from the top-left corner of the content pane, which has the position *(0, 0)*. Customize the JLabel that displays the time. The

name of this JLabel is timeJLabel. After line 60 in the template code, insert a statement to set timeJLabel's *text* property to "00:00:00". On the next line, insert a statement to set timeJLabel's *bounds* property to 16, 80, 100, 46. On the next line, insert a statement to set timeJLabel's *foreground* property to Color.WHITE by using setForeground. On the next line, insert a statement to set timeJLabel's *background* property to Color.BLACK. [Note: Most GUI components have *foreground* and *background* properties.]

h) *Customizing the AM JRadioButton on the AM/PM JPanel.* In Exercise 2.11, you learned that a GUI component on a JPanel is positioned from the top-left corner of the JPanel, which has the position *(0, 0)*. Customize the JRadioButton for the **AM** selection. Name it amJRadioButton. After line 78 in the template code, insert a statement to set amJRadioButton's *text* property to "AM". On the next line, insert a statement to set amJRadioButton's *bounds* property to 20, 18, 50, 30.

i) *Customizing the PM JRadioButton on the AM/PM JPanel.* Customize the JRadioButton for the **PM** selection. The name of this JRadioButton is pmJRadioButton. After line 84 in the template code, insert a statement to set pmJRadioButton's *text* property to "PM". On the next line, insert a statement to set pmJRadioButton's *bounds* property to 20, 40, 50, 30.

j) *Saving the application.* Save your modified source code file.

k) *Compiling the completed application.* In the **Command Prompt** window, compile your application by typing javac AlarmClock.java, then pressing *Enter*.

l) *Running the completed application.* When your application compiles correctly, run it by typing java AlarmClock. Compare the GUI of your completed **Alarm Clock** application with the GUI shown in Fig. 2.37 to ensure that you customized the JLabel and JRadioButtons correctly.

m) *Closing the application.* Close the running application by clicking its close button. This returns you to the **Command Prompt** window.

n) *Closing the Command Prompt window.* Close the **Command Prompt** window by clicking its close button.

2.13 *(Microwave Oven GUI)* JPanels, like other GUI components, have *bounds* and *background* properties. In this exercise, you will customize the *bounds* and *background* properties of the JPanel that represents a microwave oven's door. The completed GUI is shown in Fig. 2.39.

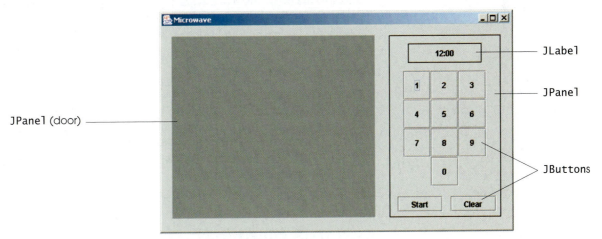

Figure 2.39 Microwave Oven GUI.

a) *Copying the template to your working directory.* Copy the C:\Examples\Tutorial02\Exercises\MicrowaveOven directory to your C:\SimplyJava directory.

b) *Opening the Command Prompt window and changing directories.* Open the **Command Prompt** by selecting **Start > Programs > Accessories > Command Prompt**. Change to your working directory by typing cd C:\SimplyJava\MicrowaveOven, then pressing *Enter*.

c) *Compiling the template application.* Compile your application by typing the command javac Microwave.java, then pressing *Enter.*

d) *Running the template application.* Run the application by typing java Microwave-Oven. The GUI of the **Microwave** template application should appear as shown in Fig. 2.40.

Missing JPanel (door)

Figure 2.40   **Microwave Oven** GUI with missing door JPanel.

e) *Closing the application.* Close the running application by clicking its close button. This returns you to the **Command Prompt** window.

f) *Opening the template file.* Open the Microwave.java file in your text editor.

g) *Customizing the door JPanel on the content pane.* Customize the JPanel to display the microwave door. The name of this JPanel is doorJPanel. After line 31, insert a statement to set doorJPanel's *bounds* property to 16, 16, 328, 284. On the next line, insert a statement to set doorJPanel's *background* property to Color.GRAY.

h) *Saving the application.* Save your modified source code file.

i) *Compiling the completed application.* In the **Command Prompt** window, compile your application by typing javac Microwave.java, then pressing *Enter.*

j) *Running the completed application.* When your application compiles correctly, run it by typing java Microwave. Compare the GUI of your completed **Microwave** application with the GUI shown in Fig. 2.39 to ensure that you customized the JPanel correctly.

k) *(Optional) Changing the door JPanel's background color to yellow.* In a later tutorial, you will modify the **Microwave** application to simulate a real microwave. When you start cooking, the light inside the microwave will turn on. Change the background color of the microwave door to yellow to simulate the running microwave.

l) *Closing the application.* Close the running application by clicking its close button. This returns you to the **Command Prompt** window.

m) *Closing the Command Prompt window.* Close the **Command Prompt** window by clicking its close button.

2.14 *(Cell Phone GUI)* In this exercise, you will adjust the size of the cell phone's numeric keypad and the position of the keypad buttons so that they appear as shown in Fig. 2.41.

a) *Copying the template to your working directory.* Copy the C:\Examples\ Tutorial02\Exercises\Phone directory to your C:\SimplyJava directory.

b) *Opening the Command Prompt window and changing directories.* Open the **Command Prompt** by selecting **Start > Programs > Accessories > Command Prompt**. Change to your working directory by typing cd C:\SimplyJava\Phone, then pressing *Enter.*

c) *Compiling the template application.* Compile your application by typing the command javac Phone.java, then pressing *Enter.*

d) *Running the template application.* Run the application by typing java Phone. The GUI of the **Phone** template application should appear as shown in Fig. 2.42.

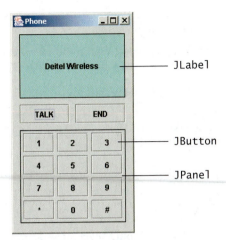

Figure 2.41 Cell **Phone** GUI.

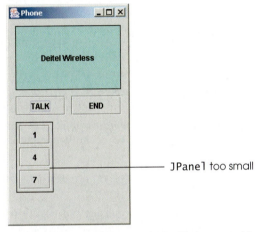

Figure 2.42 Cell **Phone** GUI with incorrect keypad format.

e) *Closing the application.* Close the running application by clicking its close button. This returns you to the **Command Prompt** window.

f) *Opening the template file.* Open the Phone.java file in your text editor.

g) *Customizing the keypad JPanel.* The keypad JPanel is too small for all the keypad buttons. You must resize the JPanel. The name of this JPanel is numberJPanel. In line 54, modify the statement that sets numberJPanel's *bounds* property such that the width of the JPanel is 170 and the height is 145.

h) *Customizing the keypad JButtons.* Lines 59–129 contain the statements that specify the properties of the keypad JButtons. Locate the statement that sets the *bounds* property of each JButton and modify the statement to position the JButton correctly. The *x*-coordinate of each JButton in the left column should be 5. The *x*-coordinate of each JButton in the center column should be 60. The *x*-coordinate of each JButton in the right column should be 115. The *y*-coordinate of each JButton in the first row should be 5. The *y*-coordinate of each JButton in the second row should be 40. The *y*-coordinate of each JButton in the third row should be 75. The *y*-coordinate of each JButton in the fourth row should be 110.

i) *Saving the application.* Save your modified source code file.

j) *Compiling the completed application.* In the **Command Prompt** window, compile your application by typing javac Phone.java, then pressing *Enter*.

k) *Running the completed application.* When your application compiles correctly, run it by typing java Phone. Compare the GUI of your completed **Phone** application with Fig. 2.41 to ensure that you customized the JPanel and JButtons correctly.

l) *Closing the application.* Close the running application by clicking its close button. This returns you to the **Command Prompt** window.

m) *Closing the Command Prompt window.* Close the **Command Prompt** window by clicking its close button.

2.15 *(Vending Machine GUI)* In this exercise, you will customize the properties of several JLabels that display images (as shown in Fig. 2.43).

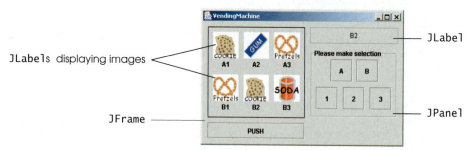

Figure 2.43   Vending Machine GUI.

a) *Copying the template to your working directory.* Copy the C:\Examples\Tutorial02\Exercises\VendingMachine directory to the C:\SimplyJava directory.

b) *Opening the Command Prompt window and changing directories.* Open the **Command Prompt** by selecting **Start > Programs > Accessories > Command Prompt**. Change to your working directory by typing cd C:\SimplyJava\VendingMachine, then pressing *Enter*.

c) *Compiling the template application.* Compile your application by typing the command javac VendingMachine.java, then pressing *Enter*.

d) *Running the template application.* Run the application by typing java VendingMachine. The GUI of the **VendingMachine** template application should appear as shown in Fig. 2.44.

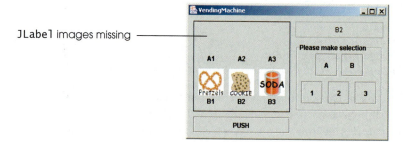

Figure 2.44   Vending Machine GUI with three missing images.

e) *Closing the application.* Close the running application by clicking its close button. This returns you to the **Command Prompt** window.

f) *Opening the template file.* Open the VendingMachine.java file in your text editor.

g) *Customizing a JLabel's icon.* You must specify the icon for the JLabel above **A1** on the GUI. The name of this JLabel is a1IconJLabel. After line 39, insert a statement that sets a1IconJLabel's *icon* property to "images/cookie.png". [Hint: Use a statement like line 36 of Fig. 2.31.]

h) *Customizing the icons for the JLabels above A2 and A3.* You must also specify the icons for the JLabels above **A2** and **A3** on the GUI. The names of these JLabels are a2IconJLabel and a3IconJLabel, respectively. After line 52, insert a statement that sets a2IconJLabel's *icon* property to "images/gum.png". After line 65, insert a statement that sets a3IconJLabel's *icon* property to "images/pretzel.png".

i) *Saving the application.* Save your modified source code file.

j) *Compiling the completed application.* In the **Command Prompt** window, compile your application by typing javac VendingMachine.java, then pressing *Enter*.

k) *Running the completed application.* When your application compiles correctly, run it by typing java VendingMachine. Compare the completed **VendingMachine** GUI with the GUI shown in Fig. 2.43 to ensure that you customized the JLabels correctly.

l) *Closing the application.* Close the running application by clicking its close button. This returns you to the **Command Prompt** window.

m) *Closing the Command Prompt window.* Close the **Command Prompt** window by clicking its close button.

Programming Challenge ▶   **2.16** *(Radio GUI)* An important part of GUI design is color selection. The **Radio** GUI shown in Fig. 2.45 uses colors that some people find unattractive. Using the predefined Color values from the table of Fig. 2.14, modify the colors in this GUI to make it more attractive. For instance, the **Radio** GUI shown in Fig. 2.46 replaces all orange with cyan and replaces all pink with light gray. You should try several possibilities.

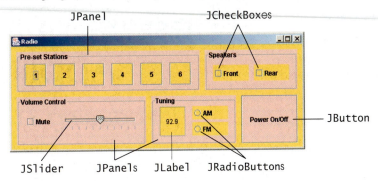

Figure 2.45 **Radio** GUI.

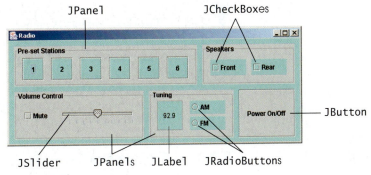

Figure 2.46 **Radio** GUI with different colors

a) *Copying the template to your working directory.* Copy the C:\Examples\ Tutorial02\Exercises\Radio directory to your C:\SimplyJava directory.

b) *Opening the template file.* Open the Radio.java file in your text editor.

c) *Customizing colors.* In the template code, locate every occurrence of Color.ORANGE and replace it with Color.CYAN. Then, locate every occurrence of Color.PINK and replace it with Color.LIGHT_GRAY.

d) *Saving the application.* Save your modified source code file.

e) *Opening the Command Prompt window and changing directories.* Open the **Command Prompt** by selecting **Start > Programs > Accessories > Command Prompt**. Change to your working directory by typing cd C:\SimplyJava\Radio, then pressing *Enter*.

f) *Compiling the completed application.* In the **Command Prompt** window, compile your application by typing javac Radio.java, then pressing *Enter*.

g) *Running the completed application.* When your application compiles correctly, run it by typing java Radio. Compare the GUI of your completed **Radio** application with the GUI shown in Fig. 2.46 to ensure that you customized the colors correctly.

h) *(Optional) Customizing the colors of each GUI component.* Experiment with other colors from Fig. 2.14 to customize the GUI components to your liking.

T U T O R I A L

3

Objectives

In this tutorial, you will learn to:
- Use graphical user interface design guidelines to create a useful GUI.
- Customize `JLabel`s, `JTextField`s and a `JButton` in an application window.
- Align text horizontally in a `JTextField`.
- Specify that a `JTextField` is uneditable.

Outline

Designing the Inventory Application

Introducing JTextFields and JButtons

This tutorial introduces you to additional GUI components and begins to discuss GUI design. You will design the GUI for a simple inventory application. Through each set of steps, you will enhance the application's user interface by customizing components. You will learn new properties for `JLabel`s, and you will customize `JTextField`s and a `JButton`. Once again, all of these components will appear in a `JFrame`. At the end of the tutorial, you will find a list of new GUI design guidelines to help you create appealing and easy-to-use graphical user interfaces. The book's GUI design guidelines are summarized in Appendix C.

3.1 Test-Driving the Inventory Application

In this tutorial, you will create the graphical user interface for an inventory application that calculates the number of textbooks received by a college bookstore. This application must meet the following requirements:

Application Requirements

A college bookstore receives cartons of textbooks. In each shipment, each carton contains the same number of textbooks. The inventory manager wants to use a computer to calculate the total number of textbooks arriving at the bookstore for each shipment. The inventory manager will enter the number of cartons received and the fixed number of textbooks in each carton of the shipment; the application should then calculate and display the total number of textbooks in the shipment.

This application performs a simple calculation. The user (the inventory manager) inputs into `JTextField`s the number of cartons and number of items in each carton. The user then clicks a `JButton`, which causes the application to multiply the two numbers and display in a `JTextField` the total number of textbooks received. In this tutorial, you will customize `JTextField`s and a `JButton` in a `JFrame`. In Tutorial 4, you will complete the **Inventory** application by adding the code that executes when the user clicks the `JButton`. You begin by test-driving the completed application. Then, you will learn the additional Java technologies you will need to create your own version of this application.

Test-Driving the
Completed Inventory
Application

1. **Locating the completed application.** Open the **Command Prompt** window by selecting **Start > Programs > Accessories > Command Prompt**. Change to the completed **Inventory** application directory by typing cd C:\Examples\Tutorial03\CompletedApplication\Inventory, then pressing *Enter*.

2. **Running the Inventory application.** Type java Inventory in the **Command Prompt** window and press *Enter* to run the application (Fig. 3.1). Remember that Java is case sensitive so the first letter of Inventory must be capitalized; otherwise, the application will not execute.

   Notice that this application introduces two component types that you did not use in the **Welcome** application—JTextFields and a JButton. A **JTextField** enables a user to input data from the keyboard. It can also display data as output to the user. A **JButton** is a component that the user can click to cause the application to perform an action.

Input JTextFields ———— 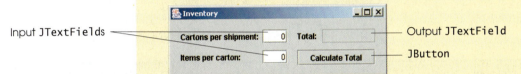 ———— Output JTextField
                                                      JButton

Figure 3.1 Inventory application JFrame with default data displayed in the input JTextFields.

3. **Entering quantities in the application.** Notice that the application uses **descriptive JLabel**s, a JLabel placed next to each JTextField to describe its purpose. In our discussions, we will refer to each JTextField component by the text displayed in the corresponding JLabel. For example, in Fig. 3.2, the **Cartons per shipment:** JLabel describes the JTextField to its right, which is referred to this as the **Cartons per shipment:** JTextField. Enter 3 in the **Cartons per shipment:** JTextField. Enter 15 in the **Items per carton:** JTextField. Figure 3.2 shows the JFrame after these values have been entered.

Descriptive JLabels ————

Figure 3.2 Inventory application after you enter new quantities.

4. **Calculating the total number of items received.** Click the **Calculate Total** JButton. The application will multiply the two numbers you entered and display the result (45) in the **Total:** JTextField (Fig. 3.3). Notice that the **Total:** JTextField has a different appearance than the **Cartons per shipment:** and **Items per carton:** JTextFields. The **Total:** JTextField is an **uneditable JTextField**—you cannot type values in the JTextField. Such JTextFields are often used to display results of calculations.

Result of calculation displayed in an uneditable JTextField

Figure 3.3 Calculating the total number of items received.

(cont.)

5. ***Closing the application.*** Close your running application by clicking its close button.

6. ***Closing the Command Prompt window.*** Close the **Command Prompt** window by clicking its close button.

3.2 Customizing JLabels in the Inventory Application

GUI Design Tip

Use JLabels to identify other GUI components.

Now you will develop your own version of the **Inventory** application, which contains three JLabels (Fig. 3.4). As the component name indicates, a JLabel is often used to identify (or label) another component in a window.

Descriptive JLabels ——

Figure 3.4   JLabels in the **Inventory** application.

Customizing a JLabel

GUI Design Tip

Descriptive JLabels should use sentence-style capitalization and end with a colon.

GUI Design Tip

Place each descriptive JLabel either above or to the left of the component (for example, a JTextField) that it identifies.

Set the text and bounds of the cartonsJLabel ——

1. ***Copying the template to your working directory.*** Copy the C:\Examples\ Tutorial03\TemplateApplication\Inventory directory to your C:\SimplyJava directory. You will begin with an empty content pane.

2. ***Opening the Inventory application's template file.*** Open the template file Inventory.java in your text editor.

3. ***Setting the JLabel's text, size and location.*** Insert lines 40–41 of Fig. 3.5 into your application. Line 40 uses setText to set cartonsJLabel's *text* property to "Cartons per shipment:". When specifying the value for a JLabel's *text* property, you should use **sentence-style capitalization**, in which you capitalize only the first letter of the first word in the text and the first letter of each proper noun (for example, **Sales for January:**).

   Line 41 sets the cartonsJLabel's *bounds* property to position the JLabel in the JFrame's content pane. Recall from Tutorial 2 that setBounds sets the location and size of a component. This JLabel's location will be 16, 16 and its width and height will be 130, 21. You can also set a component's location and size using setLocation and setSize, respectively.

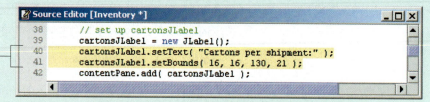

Figure 3.5   Setting the **Cartons per shipment:** JLabel's text and bounds.

4. ***Saving the application.*** Save your modified source code file.

5. ***Opening the Command Prompt window and changing directories.*** Open the **Command Prompt** window by selecting **Start > Programs > Accessories > Command Prompt**. Change to your working directory by typing cd C:\SimplyJava\Inventory, then pressing *Enter*.

6. ***Compiling the application.*** Compile your application by typing javac Inventory.java, then pressing *Enter*. If there are no compilation errors, proceed to *Step 7*. Otherwise, fix the errors in your code and repeat this step.

(cont.)

7. ***Running the application.*** When your application compiles correctly, run it by typing `java Inventory`, then pressing *Enter*. Figure 3.6 shows the updated application running.

Upper-left corner of
`JLabel` appears at 16, 16

Figure 3.6   Updated application with **Cartons per shipment:** `JLabel`.

8. ***Closing the application.*** Close your running application by clicking its close button.

9. ***Closing the Command Prompt window.*** Close the **Command Prompt** window by clicking its close button.

Now, you will configure the remaining `JLabels` to help the user understand what inputs to provide and interpret the application's output. Later in this tutorial, you will customize the components that these `JLabels` identify.

Customizing Additional JLabels

1. ***Customizing a second descriptive `JLabel`.*** Insert lines 46–47 of Fig. 3.7. Line 46 sets `itemsJLabel`'s text to `"Items per carton:"`. Line 47 sets `items-JLabel`'s bounds to 16, 48, 104, 21. Note that both the **Items per carton:** and **Cartons per shipment:** `JLabels` are the same distance (16 pixels) from the left edge of the window. This causes the `JLabels` to align vertically.

Set the text and bounds
of the `itemsJLabel`

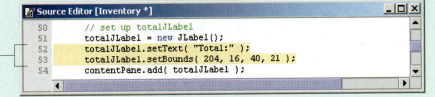

Figure 3.7   Setting the **Items per carton:** `JLabel`'s text and bounds.

 **GUI Design Tip**

Align the left sides of a group of descriptive `JLabels` if the `JLabels` are arranged vertically.

2. ***Customizing a third descriptive `JLabel`.*** Insert lines 52–53 of Fig. 3.8. Line 52 sets `totalJLabel`'s text to `"Total:"`. Line 53 sets `totalJLabel`'s bounds to 204, 16, 40, 21.

Set the text and bounds
of the `totalJLabel`

Figure 3.8   Setting the **Total:** `JLabel`'s text and bounds.

3. ***Saving the application.*** Save your modified source code file.

4. ***Opening the Command Prompt window and changing directories.*** Open the **Command Prompt** window by selecting **Start > Programs > Accessories > Command Prompt**. Change to your working directory by typing `cd C:\SimplyJava\Inventory`, then pressing *Enter*.

(cont.)

5. *Compiling the application.* Compile your application by typing `javac Inventory.java`, then pressing *Enter*. If there are no compilation errors, proceed to *Step 6*. Otherwise, fix the errors in your code and repeat this step.

6. *Running the application.* When your application compiles correctly, run it by typing `java Inventory`, then pressing *Enter*. Figure 3.9 shows the updated application running. You will soon add the missing components.

Figure 3.9 Running **Inventory** application with three customized `JLabel`s.

7. *Closing the application.* Close your running application by clicking its close button.

8. *Closing the Command Prompt window.* Close the **Command Prompt** window by clicking its close button.

SELF-REVIEW

1. The text on a `JLabel` is specified with _____.
   a) `setLabel`
   b) `changeLabel`
   c) `setText`
   d) `changeText`

2. The location and size of a `JLabel` can be specified with _____.
   a) `setSizeAndLocation`
   b) `setBounds`
   c) Neither of the above.
   d) Both of the above.

Answers: 1) c. 2) b.

3.3 Customizing `JTextFields` and a `JButton` in the Inventory Application

GUI Design Tip

Use `JTextFields` to input data from the keyboard.

The **Inventory** application requires input from the user to calculate the total number of textbooks in a shipment. Specifically, the user types in the number of cartons and the number of books per carton. You use `JTextField` components to input this data from the keyboard. Next, you will learn how to customize `JTextFields`.

Customizing JTextFields

GUI Design Tip

Each `JTextField` should have a descriptive `JLabel` indicating the `JTextField`'s purpose.

1. *Customizing a JTextField.* Setting the properties of a `JTextField` is similar to setting the properties of a `JLabel`. Return to your text editor. In your code, insert lines 58–60 of Fig. 3.10. Line 58 uses `setText` to set the *text* property of the **Cartons per shipment:** `JTextField` to `"0"`. This will display a default value in the `JTextField` when you run the application. Line 59 uses `setBounds` to set the *bounds* property to `148, 16, 40, 21`. These location and size values align the top of the `JTextField` with the top of the **Cartons per shipment:** `JLabel` that describes it. (The value 16 indicates the vertical position of the `JTextField`.) Line 60 uses **`setHorizontalAlignment`** to set the *horizontalAlignment* property of the `JTextField` to **`JTextField.RIGHT`**, which right aligns the text in the `JTextField`. Text in a `JTextField` also can be left aligned (**`JTextField.LEFT`**) or centered (**`JTextField.CENTER`**).

(cont.)

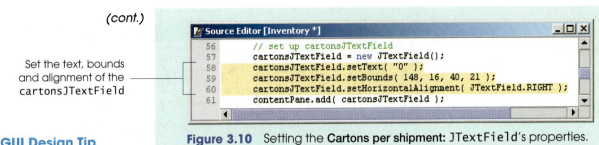

Figure 3.10 Setting the **Cartons per shipment:** JTextField's properties.

Set the text, bounds and alignment of the `cartonsJTextField`

GUI Design Tip

Make JTextFields wide enough for their expected inputs, if possible. Otherwise, the text will scroll as the user types and only part of the text will be visible.

GUI Design Tip

Align the left sides of JTextFields that are arranged vertically.

2. **Customizing a second *JTextField.*** Insert lines 65–67 of Fig. 3.11 into your code. Lines 65 sets the text in the **Items per carton:** JTextField to "0", which will be displayed in the JTextField when the application begins executing. Line 66 sets the bounds of the JTextField to 148, 48, 40, 21. These values ensure that the left sides of the **Cartons per shipment:** and the **Items per carton:** JTextFields align. These values also ensure that the tops of the **Items per carton:** JLabel and the **Items per carton:** JTextField align. Line 67 right aligns the text in the JTextField.

Figure 3.11 Setting the **Items per carton:** JTextField's properties.

Set the text, bounds and alignment of the `itemsJTextField`

GUI Design Tip

In general, numeric values in JTextFields should be right aligned.

3. **Customizing the output *JTextField.*** Insert lines 72–74 of Fig. 3.12 into your application. Line 72 sets the bounds of the JTextField to 244, 16, 86, 21. The statement in lines 73–74 right aligns the text in the JTextField. We do not set any default text (that is, text that appears when the JTextField is displayed) for the output JTextField, so it will initially be blank.

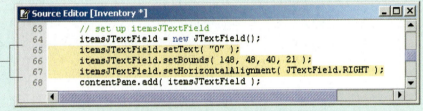

Figure 3.12 Setting the **Total:** JTextField's bounds and horizontal alignment.

Set the bounds and alignment of the `totalResultJTextField`

4. **Making the output *JTextField* uneditable.** Insert line 75 of Fig. 3.13 into your application. This line uses **setEditable** to set the *editable* property of the **Total:** JTextField to false. When the *editable* property is false, the JTextField turns gray to indicate that the user cannot edit any existing text or type any new text in the JTextField. You use uneditable JTextFields to display information to the user. Although an uneditable JTextField cannot be changed by the user, the application can change the value displayed in the JTextField. For text that will not be changed after it is displayed, use a JLabel.

GUI Design Tip

Place an application's output components below and/or to the right of the application's input components.

(cont.)

Set the *editable* property of the
`totalResultJTextField` to
`false` to prevent the user
from modifying it

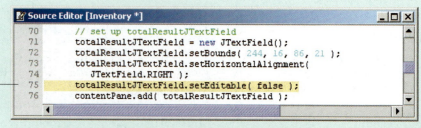

Figure 3.13 Changing the *editable* property of the **Total:** `JTextField`.

5. *Saving the application.* Save your modified source code file.

6. *Opening the Command Prompt window and changing directories.* Open the **Command Prompt** window by selecting **Start > Programs > Accessories > Command Prompt**. Change to your working directory by typing `cd C:\SimplyJava\Inventory`, then pressing *Enter*.

7. *Compiling the application.* Compile your application by typing `javac Inventory.java`, then pressing *Enter*. If there are no compilation errors, proceed to *Step 8*. Otherwise, fix the errors in your code and repeat this step.

8. *Running the application.* When your application compiles correctly, run it by typing `java Inventory`, then pressing *Enter*. Figure 3.14 shows the updated application running.

Figure 3.14 Running **Inventory** application with customized `JTextField`s.

9. *Closing the application.* Close your running application by clicking its close button.

10. *Closing the Command Prompt window.* Close the **Command Prompt** window by clicking its close button.

GUI Design Tip

Output `JTextField`s should be distinguishable from those used for input. Setting the *editable* property of an output `JTextField` to `false` prevents the user from typing in the `JTextField` and causes the `JTextField` to appear with a gray background in the user interface.

GUI Design Tip

A descriptive `JLabel` should have the same height as the component it describes if the components are arranged horizontally (see Fig. 3.14).

GUI Design Tip

A descriptive `JLabel` and the component it identifies should be top aligned if they are arranged horizontally.

GUI Design Tip

A descriptive `JLabel` and the component it identifies should be left aligned if they are arranged vertically.

In Fig. 3.14, notice that your components align horizontally and vertically. In general, you should place each descriptive `JLabel` above or to the left of the component it describes (for instance, a `JTextField`). If you arrange your components horizontally (that is, on the same line), the descriptive `JLabel` and the component it describes should be the same height. If you arrange your components vertically (that is, one above the other), the `JLabel` should be placed above the component it describes and the left sides of the components should align. Also, leave some space between each group of components in your `JFrame`. Following these simple guidelines will make your applications more visually appealing and easier to use.

You have now customized all of the `JTextField`s in your application. Two of these are **input `JTextField`s**, for gathering data from the user. The third is an **output `JTextField`**, for displaying information to the user.

Now that the user can enter data using a `JTextField`, you need a way for the user to command the application to perform the multiplication calculation. The most common way for a user to do this is by clicking a `JButton`. Next, you will customize the `JButton` in your **Inventory** application.

Customizing a *JButton*

GUI Design Tip

JButtons are labeled by using their *text* property. JButton text should use book-title capitalization and be as short as possible while still being meaningful to the user.

Set the text and bounds of the calculateJButton

GUI Design Tip

JButtons should be stacked vertically downward from the top right of the JFrame or arranged horizontally on the same line starting from the bottom right of the JFrame.

1. ***Customizing a JButton.*** Insert lines 80–81 of Fig. 3.15 in your code. Line 80 uses `setText` to set the JButton's *text* property to `"Calculate Total"`. The JButton's *text* property displays its value on the face of the JButton. You should use book-title capitalization in a JButton's *text* property—that is, capitalize the first letter of the each significant word in the text (as in, **Calculate Total**). When labeling JButtons, keep the text as short as possible while still clearly indicating the JButton's function. Line 81 uses `setBounds` to set the *bounds* property for the JButton to 204, 48, 126, 24. These values will cause the left and right sides of the JButton to align below the **Total:** JLabel and the **Total:** JTextField.

```
78        // set up calculateJButton
79        calculateJButton = new JButton();
80        calculateJButton.setText( "Calculate Total" );
81        calculateJButton.setBounds( 204, 48, 126, 24 );
82        contentPane.add( calculateJButton );
```

Figure 3.15   Customizing the **Calculate Total** JButton.

2. ***Saving the application.*** Save your modified source code file.

3. ***Opening the Command Prompt window and changing directories.*** Open the **Command Prompt** window by selecting **Start > Programs > Accessories > Command Prompt**. Change to your working directory by typing `cd C:\SimplyJava\Inventory`, then pressing *Enter*.

4. ***Compiling the application.*** Compile your application by typing `javac Inventory.java`, then pressing *Enter*. If there are no compilation errors, proceed to *Step 5*. Otherwise, fix the errors in your code and repeat this step.

5. ***Running the application.*** When your application compiles correctly, run it by typing `java Inventory`, then pressing *Enter*. Figure 3.16 shows the updated application running. Notice that no action occurs if you click the **Calculate Total** JButton. This is because you have not yet written code to tell the application how to respond to clicking the JButton. In Tutorial 4, you will complete your **Inventory** application by writing code that, when the user clicks the JButton, displays in the **Total:** JTextField the total number of books in the shipment.

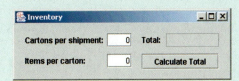

Figure 3.16   Running the application after customizing the **Calculate Total** JButton.

6. ***Closing the application.*** Close your running application by clicking its close button.

7. ***Closing the Command Prompt window.*** Close the **Command Prompt** window by clicking its close button.

Figure 3.17 presents the source code of the **Inventory** application. The lines of code that you added, viewed or modified in this tutorial are highlighted.

```java
1   // Tutorial 3: Inventory.java
2   // Calculates the number of items in a shipment based on the number
3   // of cartons received and the number of items per carton.
4   import java.awt.*;
5   import java.awt.event.*;
6   import javax.swing.*;
7
8   public class Inventory extends JFrame
9   {
10     // JLabel and JTextField for cartons per shipment
11     private JLabel cartonsJLabel;
12     private JTextField cartonsJTextField;
13
14     // JLabel and JTextField for items per carton
15     private JLabel itemsJLabel;
16     private JTextField itemsJTextField;
17
18     // JLabel and JTextField for total items per shipment
19     private JLabel totalJLabel;
20     private JTextField totalResultJTextField;
21
22     // JButton to initiate calculation of total items per shipment
23     private JButton calculateJButton;
24
25     // no-argument constructor
26     public Inventory()
27     {
28        createUserInterface();
29     }
30
31     // create and position GUI components; register event handlers
32     public void createUserInterface()
33     {
34        // get content pane and set layout to null
35        Container contentPane = getContentPane();
36        contentPane.setLayout( null );
37
38        // set up cartonsJLabel
39        cartonsJLabel = new JLabel();
40        cartonsJLabel.setText( "Cartons per shipment:" );
41        cartonsJLabel.setBounds( 16, 16, 130, 21 );
42        contentPane.add( cartonsJLabel );
43
44        // set up itemsJLabel
45        itemsJLabel = new JLabel();
46        itemsJLabel.setText( "Items per carton:" );
47        itemsJLabel.setBounds( 16, 48, 104, 21 );
48        contentPane.add( itemsJLabel );
49
50        // set up totalJLabel
51        totalJLabel = new JLabel();
52        totalJLabel.setText( "Total:" );
53        totalJLabel.setBounds( 204, 16, 40, 21 );
54        contentPane.add( totalJLabel );
55
```

Set the text and bounds of the cartonsJLabel → (lines 40–41)

Set the text and bounds of the itemsJLabel → (lines 46–47)

Set the text and bounds of the totalJLabel → (lines 52–53)

Figure 3.17 **Inventory** application code. (Part 1 of 2.)

```
56          // set up cartonsJTextField
57          cartonsJTextField = new JTextField();
58          cartonsJTextField.setText( "0" );
59          cartonsJTextField.setBounds( 148, 16, 40, 21 );
60          cartonsJTextField.setHorizontalAlignment( JTextField.RIGHT );
61          contentPane.add( cartonsJTextField );
62
63          // set up itemsJTextField
64          itemsJTextField = new JTextField();
65          itemsJTextField.setText( "0" );
66          itemsJTextField.setBounds( 148, 48, 40, 21 );
67          itemsJTextField.setHorizontalAlignment( JTextField.RIGHT );
68          contentPane.add( itemsJTextField );
69
70          // set up totalResultJTextField
71          totalResultJTextField = new JTextField();
72          totalResultJTextField.setBounds( 244, 16, 86, 21 );
73          totalResultJTextField.setHorizontalAlignment(
74             JTextField.RIGHT );
75          totalResultJTextField.setEditable( false );
76          contentPane.add( totalResultJTextField );
77
78          // set up calculateJButton
79          calculateJButton = new JButton();
80          calculateJButton.setText( "Calculate Total" );
81          calculateJButton.setBounds( 204, 48, 126, 24 );
82          contentPane.add( calculateJButton );
83
84          // set properties of application's window
85          setTitle( "Inventory" ); // set title bar text
86          setSize( 354, 112 );     // set window size
87          setVisible( true );      // display window
88
89       } // end method createUserInterface
90
91       // main method
92       public static void main( String[] args )
93       {
94          Inventory application = new Inventory();
95          application.setDefaultCloseOperation( JFrame.EXIT_ON_CLOSE );
96
97       } // end method main
98
99    } // end class Inventory
```

Set the text, bounds and alignment of the cartonsJTextField

Set the text, bounds and alignment of the itemsJTextField

Set the bounds, alignment and editability of the totalResultJTextField

Set the text and bounds of the calculateJButton

Figure 3.17   Inventory application code. (Part 2 of 2.)

SELF-REVIEW

1. Use _____ to set the text on the face of a JButton.

   a) setName   b) setText

   c) setTitle   d) setFace

2. JButtons should use _____ capitalization.

   a) book-title   b) sentence-style

   c) button-style   d) None of the above.

Answers: 1) b. 2) a.

3.4 Wrap-Up

In this tutorial, you began constructing your **Inventory** application by designing its graphical user interface. You learned how to use JLabels to describe components. Then, you customized JTextFields to allow the user to input data from the keyboard and to output results to the user. You learned to set a JTextField's *editable* property to false to specify that the JTextField is to be used only for output. Finally, you customized a JButton on the **Inventory** application to allow a user to signal the application to perform an action (in this case, to multiply the two numbers from the JTextFields and display the result). As you customized components in the JFrame, you learned some GUI design guidelines to help you create appealing and intuitive graphical user interfaces.

The next tutorial teaches you to program code in Java to run when the user clicks the **Calculate Total** JButton. When the JButton is clicked, the application receives a signal called an event. You will learn how to program your application to respond to that event by performing the multiplication calculation and displaying the result.

SKILLS SUMMARY

Customizing a Descriptive JLabel

■ Customize a JLabel by setting its *text* property (using setText) and by setting its *bounds* property (using setBounds) such that the JLabel aligns with another component.

Customizing a JTextField

■ Customize a JTextField by setting its *text* property (using setText), by setting its *bounds* property (using setBounds) such that the JTextField aligns with another component and by setting its *horizontalAlignment* property (using setHorizontalAlignment with options JTextField.LEFT, JTextField.CENTER or JTextField.RIGHT).

Customizing an Output JTextField

■ Customize an output JTextField by setting the *editable* property to false (using setEditable).

Customizing a JButton

■ Customize a JButton by setting the *text* property (using setText) and by setting its *bounds* property (using setBounds) such that the JButton aligns with another component.

KEY TERMS

editable **property**—The property that specifies the appearance and behavior of a JTextField, which allows you to distinguish an input JTextField (*editable* property is true) from an output JTextField (*editable* property is false).

horizontalAlignment **property**—The property that specifies the text alignment in a JTextField (JTextField.LEFT, JTextField.CENTER or JTextField.RIGHT).

input JTextField—A JTextField used to get user input. The *editable* property of an input JTextField is set to true, which is the default.

JButton component—A component that, when clicked, commands the application to perform an action.

JLabel component—A component used to describe another component. This helps users understand a component's purpose.

JTextField component—A component that can accept user input from the keyboard or display output to the user.

JTextField.CENTER—Used with setHorizontalAlignment to center align the text in a JTextField.

JTextField.LEFT—Used with setHorizontalAlignment to left align the text in a JTextField.

JTextField.RIGHT—Used with setHorizontalAlignment to right align the text in a JTextField.

output JTextField—A JTextField used to display calculation results. The *editable* property of an output JTextField is set to false with setEditable.

sentence-style capitalization—A style that capitalizes the first letter of the first word in the text (for example, **Cartons per shipment**); other letters in the text are lowercase, unless they are the first letters of proper nouns.

uneditable `JTextField`—A `JTextField` in which the user cannot type values or edit existing text. Such `JTextField`s are often used to display the results of calculations.

GUI DESIGN GUIDELINES

JButton

- `JButton`s are labeled by using their *text* property. `JButton` text should use book-title capitalization and be as short as possible while still being meaningful to the user.
- `JButton`s should be stacked vertically downward from the top right of the `JFrame` or arranged horizontally on the same line starting from the bottom right of the `JFrame`.

JFrame

- Place an application's output components below and/or to the right of the application's input components.

JLabel

- Use `JLabel`s to identify other GUI components.
- Descriptive `JLabel`s should use sentence-style capitalization and end with a colon.
- Place each descriptive `JLabel` either above or to the left of the component (for example, a `JTextField`) that it identifies.
- Align the left sides of a group of descriptive `JLabel`s if the `JLabel`s are arranged vertically.
- A descriptive `JLabel` should have the same height as the component it describes if the components are arranged horizontally.
- A descriptive `JLabel` and the component it identifies should be top aligned if they are arranged horizontally.
- A descriptive `JLabel` and the component it identifies should be left aligned if they are arranged vertically.

JTextField

- Use editable `JTextField`s to input data from the keyboard. `JTextField`s are editable by default
- Each `JTextField` should have a descriptive `JLabel` indicating the `JTextField`'s purpose.
- Make `JTextField`s wide enough for their expected inputs, if possible. Otherwise, the text will scroll as the user types and only part of the text will be visible.
- Align the left sides of `JTextField`s that are arranged vertically.
- In general, numeric values in `JTextField`s should be right aligned.
- Output `JTextField`s should be distinguishable from those used for input. Setting the *editable* property of an output `JTextField` to `false` prevents the user from typing in the `JTextField` and causes the `JTextField` to appear with a gray background in the user interface.

JAVA LIBRARY REFERENCE

JButton   This component allows the user to command the application to perform an action.

- ***In action***

- ***Methods***

    `setBounds`—Sets the *bounds* property, which specifies the location and size of the `JButton`.

    `setText`—Sets the *text* property of the `JButton`.

JLabel This component displays text that the user cannot modify.

- *In action*

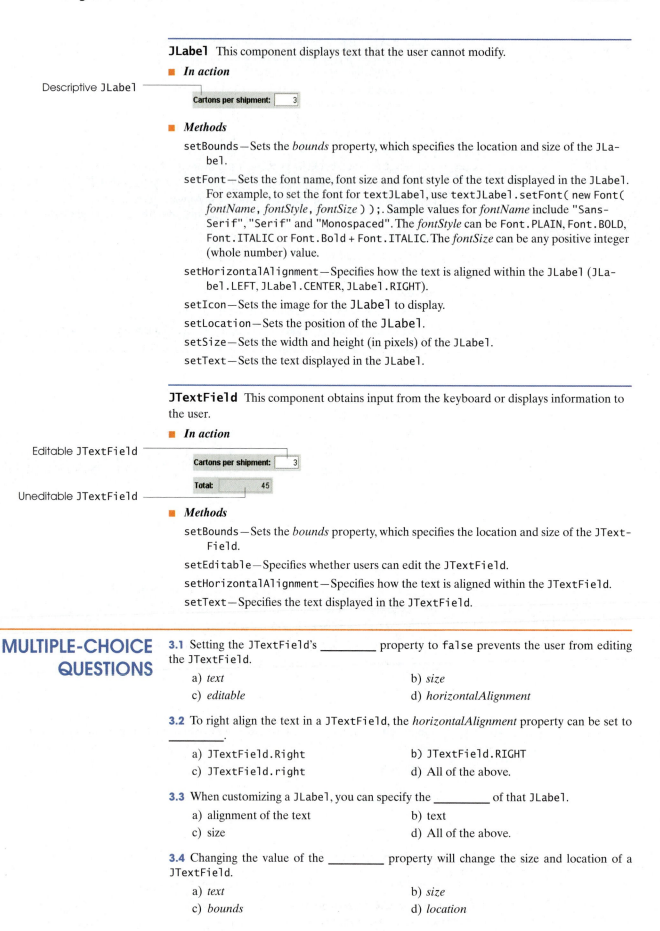

Descriptive `JLabel`

- *Methods*

  `setBounds`—Sets the *bounds* property, which specifies the location and size of the `JLabel`.

  `setFont`—Sets the font name, font size and font style of the text displayed in the `JLabel`. For example, to set the font for `textJLabel`, use `textJLabel.setFont( new Font(` *fontName*, *fontStyle*, *fontSize* `) );`. Sample values for *fontName* include `"Sans-Serif"`, `"Serif"` and `"Monospaced"`. The *fontStyle* can be `Font.PLAIN`, `Font.BOLD`, `Font.ITALIC` or `Font.Bold + Font.ITALIC`. The *fontSize* can be any positive integer (whole number) value.

  `setHorizontalAlignment`—Specifies how the text is aligned within the `JLabel` (`JLabel.LEFT`, `JLabel.CENTER`, `JLabel.RIGHT`).

  `setIcon`—Sets the image for the `JLabel` to display.

  `setLocation`—Sets the position of the `JLabel`.

  `setSize`—Sets the width and height (in pixels) of the `JLabel`.

  `setText`—Sets the text displayed in the `JLabel`.

JTextField This component obtains input from the keyboard or displays information to the user.

- *In action*

Editable `JTextField`

Uneditable `JTextField`

- *Methods*

  `setBounds`—Sets the *bounds* property, which specifies the location and size of the `JTextField`.

  `setEditable`—Specifies whether users can edit the `JTextField`.

  `setHorizontalAlignment`—Specifies how the text is aligned within the `JTextField`.

  `setText`—Specifies the text displayed in the `JTextField`.

MULTIPLE-CHOICE QUESTIONS

3.1 Setting the `JTextField`'s _____ property to `false` prevents the user from editing the `JTextField`.

a) *text*　　　　　　　　　　　b) *size*

c) *editable*　　　　　　　　　d) *horizontalAlignment*

3.2 To right align the text in a `JTextField`, the *horizontalAlignment* property can be set to _____.

a) `JTextField.Right`　　　　　b) `JTextField.RIGHT`

c) `JTextField.right`　　　　　d) All of the above.

3.3 When customizing a `JLabel`, you can specify the _____ of that `JLabel`.

a) alignment of the text　　　b) text

c) size　　　　　　　　　　　d) All of the above.

3.4 Changing the value of the _____ property will change the size and location of a `JTextField`.

a) *text*　　　　　　　　　　　b) *size*

c) *bounds*　　　　　　　　　d) *location*

3.5 The position of the text in a `JTextField` can be set by _____.

a) `setAlignmentProperty`   b) `setAlignment`

c) `setHorizontalAlignment`   d) None of the above.

3.6 A _____ helps the user understand a component's purpose.

a) `JButton`   b) descriptive `JLabel`

c) `JTextField`   d) title bar

3.7 A _____ is a component in which the user can enter data from a keyboard.

a) `JButton`   b) `JTextField`

c) `JLabel`   d) None of the above.

3.8 A descriptive `JLabel` should use _____.

a) sentence-style capitalization   b) book-title capitalization

c) a colon at the end of its text   d) Both a and c.

3.9 You should use _____ to set the text on a `JButton`.

a) `setText`   b) `setButtonText`

c) `setJButtonText`   d) `setTEXT`

3.10 You should use _____ for a `JButton`'s *text* property.

a) book-title capitalization   b) sentence-style capitalization

c) a colon at the end of its text   d) Both a and c.

EXERCISES

For Exercises 3.11–3.14, you are asked to customize a portion of the GUI shown in each exercise. You will use the GUI programming techniques presented in this tutorial to customize a variety of GUIs. Because you are customizing only GUIs, your applications will not be fully operational. (You will make them fully functional later in the text.)

3.11 (***Address Book GUI***) In this exercise, you apply the GUI design guidelines you have learned to a graphical user interface for an address book (Fig. 3.18). You will set the bounds of the **Address:** `JLabel` and `JTextField` such that they align properly with the other GUI components.

Figure 3.18 **Address Book** application.

a) ***Copying the template to your working directory.*** Copy the `C:\Examples\Tutorial03\Exercises\AddressBook` directory to your `C:\SimplyJava` directory.

b) ***Opening the Command Prompt window and changing directories.*** Open the **Command Prompt** by selecting **Start > Programs > Accessories > Command Prompt**. Change to your working directory by typing `cd C:\SimplyJava\AddressBook`, then pressing *Enter*.

c) ***Compiling the template application.*** Compile your application by typing `javac AddressBook.java`, then pressing *Enter*.

d) ***Running the template application.*** Run the application by typing `java Address-Book`. The GUI of the **Address Book** template application should appear as shown in Fig. 3.19. Note the differences from Fig. 3.18.

Figure 3.19   **Address Book** template application.

e) *Closing the application.* Close your running application by clicking its close button.

f) *Opening the template file.* Open the AddressBook.java file in your text editor.

g) *Customizing the Address: JLabel and JTextField.* Using Fig. 3.18 and the template code as a guide, you will set the *bounds* property of addressJLabel and addressJTextField such that addressJLabel is left aligned with firstNameJLabel (see line 68 in the template code) and addressJTextField is left aligned with firstNameJTextField (see line 74 in the template code). After line 91, insert a statement that sets the *bounds* property of addressJLabel such that its *y*-coordinate is 56 and its *x*-coordinate, width and height are identical to the *x*-coordinate, width and height of firstNameJLabel. After line 97, insert a statement that sets the *bounds* property of addressJTextField such that its *y*-coordinate is 56, its width is 360, and its *x*-coordinate and height are identical to the *x*-coordinate and height of firstNameJTextField.

h) *Saving the application.* Save your modified source code file.

i) *Compiling the completed application.* In the **Command Prompt** window, compile your application by typing javac AddressBook.java, then pressing *Enter.*

j) *Running the completed application.* When your application compiles correctly, run it by typing java AddressBook. Compare the GUI of your completed **AddressBook** application with the GUI shown in Fig. 3.18 to ensure that you customized the JLabel and JTextField correctly.

k) *Closing the application.* Close your running application by clicking its close button.

l) *Closing the Command Prompt window.* Close the **Command Prompt** window by clicking its close button.

3.12 *(Mortgage Calculator GUI)* In this exercise, you apply the GUI design guidelines you have learned to a graphical user interface for a mortgage calculator (Fig. 3.20). You will set the bounds of the **Loan amount:** JLabel and JTextField such that they align properly with the other GUI components.

Figure 3.20   **Mortgage Calculator** application.

a) *Copying the template to your working directory.* Copy the `C:\Examples\Tutorial03\Exercises\MortgageCalculator` directory to your `C:\SimplyJava` directory.

b) *Opening the Command Prompt window and changing directories.* Open the **Command Prompt** by selecting **Start > Programs > Accessories > Command Prompt**. Change to your working directory by typing `cd C:\SimplyJava\MortgageCalculator`, then pressing *Enter*.

c) *Compiling the template application.* Compile your application by typing `javac MortgageCalculator.java`, then pressing *Enter*.

d) *Running the template application.* Run the application by typing `java MortgageCalculator`, then pressing *Enter*. The GUI of the **Mortgage Calculator** template application should appear as shown in Fig. 3.21.

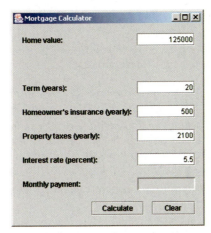

Figure 3.21 **Mortgage Calculator** template application.

e) *Closing the application.* Close your running application by clicking its close button.

f) *Opening the template file.* Open the `MortgageCalculator.java` file in your text editor.

g) *Customizing the Loan amount: JLabel and JTextField.* Using Fig. 3.20 and the template code as a guide, you will set the *bounds* property of the `loanAmountJLabel` and the `loanAmountJTextField` such that the `loanAmountJLabel` is left aligned with the `homeValueJLabel` (see line 57 in the template code) and the `loanAmountJTextField` is left aligned with the `homeValueJTextField` (see line 63 in the template code). After line 69, insert a statement that sets the *bounds* property of the `loanAmountJLabel` such that its *y*-coordinate is 56 and its *x*-coordinate, width and height are identical to the *x*-coordinate, width and height of the `homeValueJLabel`. After line 75, insert a statement that sets the *bounds* property of the `loanAmountJTextField` such that its *y*-coordinate is 56 and its *x*-coordinate, width and height are identical to the *x*-coordinate, width and height of the `homeValueJTextField`.

h) *Saving the application.* Save your modified source code file.

i) *Compiling the completed application.* In the **Command Prompt** window, compile your application by typing `javac MortgageCalculator.java`, then pressing *Enter*.

j) *Running the completed application.* When your application compiles correctly, run it by typing `java MortgageCalculator`. Compare the GUI of your completed **Mortgage Calculator** application with the GUI shown in Fig. 3.20 to ensure that you customized the `JLabel` and `JTextField` correctly.

k) *Closing the application.* Close your running application by clicking its close button.

l) *Closing the Command Prompt window.* Close the **Command Prompt** window by clicking its close button.

3.13 *(Password GUI)* In this exercise, you apply the GUI design guidelines you have learned to a graphical user interface for a password-protected message application (Fig. 3.22). You will set the bounds of the **Enter your secret message:** `JTextArea` such that

it is left aligned with the **Enter your secret message:** `JLabel` and right aligned with the **Log In** `JButton`.

Figure 3.22 **Password** application.

a) *Copying the template to your working directory.* Copy the `C:\Examples\Tutorial03\Exercises\Password` directory to your `C:\SimplyJava` directory.

b) *Opening the Command Prompt window and changing directories.* Open the **Command Prompt** by selecting **Start > Programs > Accessories > Command Prompt**. Change to your working directory by typing `cd C:\SimplyJava\Password`, then pressing *Enter*.

c) *Compiling the template application.* Compile your application by typing `javac Password.java`, then pressing *Enter*.

d) *Running the template application.* Run the application by typing `java Password`. The GUI of the **Password** template application should appear as shown in Fig. 3.23. Notice the differences from Fig. 3.22.

Figure 3.23 **Password** template application.

e) *Closing the application.* Close your running application by clicking its close button.

f) *Opening the template file.* Open the `Password.java` file in your text editor.

g) *Customizing the Enter your secret message: JTextArea.* Using Fig. 3.22 and the template code as a guide, you will set the *bounds* property of `messageJTextArea` such that `messageJTextArea` is left aligned with `messageJLabel` (see line 90 in the template code) and right aligned with `logInJButton` (see line 84 in the template code). After line 95, insert a statement that sets the *bounds* property of `messageJTextArea`—the *x*-coordinate should be identical to `messageJLabel`'s *x*-coordinate; the *y*-coordinate should be 160; calculate the width based on the bounds of the `messageJLabel` and the `logInJButton`; the height should be 72.

h) *Saving the application.* Save your modified source code file.

i) *Compiling the completed application.* In the **Command Prompt** window, compile your application by typing javac Password.java, then pressing *Enter*.

j) *Running the completed application.* When your application compiles correctly, run it by typing java Password. Compare the GUI of your completed **Password** application with the GUI shown in Fig. 3.22 to ensure that you customized the JTextArea correctly. Later in the text you will make your applications fully functional.

k) *Closing the application.* Close your running application by clicking its close button.

l) *Closing the Command Prompt window.* Close the **Command Prompt** window by clicking its close button.

Programming Challenge ▶ **3.14** *(Computer Monitor Invoice GUI)* In this exercise, you apply the GUI design guidelines you have learned to a graphical user interface for an invoicing application (Fig. 3.24). You will specify the bounds of the JTextFields in the rows of the GUI that begin with the **15"**, **17"** and **19"** JLabels.

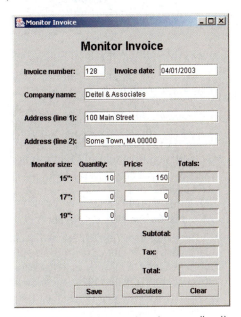

Figure 3.24 **Monitor Invoice** application.

a) *Copying the template to your working directory.* Copy the C:\Examples\ Tutorial03\Exercises\MonitorInvoice directory to your C:\SimplyJava directory.

b) *Opening the Command Prompt window and changing directories.* Open the **Command Prompt** by selecting **Start > Programs > Accessories > Command Prompt**. Change to your working directory by typing cd C:\SimplyJava\MonitorInvoice, then pressing *Enter*.

c) *Compiling the template application.* Compile your application by typing javac MonitorInvoice.java, then pressing *Enter*.

d) *Running the template application.* Run the application by typing java MonitorInvoice. The GUI of the **Monitor Invoice** template application should appear as shown in Fig. 3.25.

e) *Closing the application.* Close your running application by clicking its close button.

f) *Opening the template file.* Open the MonitorInvoice.java file in your text editor.

Figure 3.25 Monitor Invoice template application.

g) *Customizing the JTextFields below the Quantity: JLabel.* Using Fig. 3.24 and the template code as a guide, set the *bounds* property of `quantity15JTextField`, `quantity17JTextField` and `quantity19JTextField` such that they all left align with the `quantityJLabel` (see line 136 in the template code) and align vertically with their corresponding JLabels: `fifteenJLabel` (see line 154 in the template code), `seventeenJLabel` (see line 161 in the template code) and `nineteenJLabel` (see line 168 in the template code), respectively. The width and height of these `JTextFields` should be 64 and 21, respectively.

h) *Customizing the JTextFields below the Price: JLabel.* Using Fig. 3.24 and the template code as a guide, set the *bounds* property of `price15JTextField`, `price-17JTextField` and `price19JTextField` such that they all left align with the `priceJLabel` (see line 142 in the template code) and align vertically with their corresponding JLabels: `fifteenJLabel` (see line 154 in the template code), `seventeenJLabel` (see line 161 in the template code) and `nineteenJLabel` (see line 168 in the template code), respectively. The width and height of these `JTextFields` should be 80 and 21, respectively.

i) *Customizing the JTextFields below the Totals: JLabel.* Using Fig. 3.24 and the template code as a guide, set the *bounds* property of `totals15JTextField`, `totals-17JTextField` and `totals19JTextField` such that they all left align with the `totalJLabel` (see line 187 in the template code) and align vertically with their corresponding JLabels: `fifteenJLabel` (see line 154 in the template code), `seventeenJLabel` (see line 161 in the template code) and `nineteenJLabel` (see line 168 in the template code), respectively. The width and height of these `JTextFields` should be 72 and 21, respectively.

j) *Saving the application.* Save your modified source code file.

k) *Compiling the completed application.* In the **Command Prompt** window, compile your application by typing `javac MonitorInvoice.java`, then pressing *Enter*.

l) *Running the completed application.* When your application compiles correctly, run it by typing `java MonitorInvoice`. Compare the GUI of your completed **Monitor Invoice** application with the GUI shown in Fig. 3.24 to ensure that you customized the `JTextFields` correctly.

m) *Closing the application.* Close your running application by clicking its close button.

n) *Closing the Command Prompt window.* Close the **Command Prompt** window by clicking its close button.

Objectives

In this tutorial, you will learn to:
- Enable your applications to perform actions in response to `JButton` clicks.
- Use the multiplication operator.
- Use method `Integer.parseInt` to convert a `String` to an `int`.
- Use method `String.valueOf` to convert a numeric value to a `String`.

Outline

Completing the Inventory Application

Introducing Programming

This tutorial introduces fundamentals of Java programming to create an application with which users can interact. You will learn programming concepts as you add functionality (with Java code) to the **Inventory** application you designed in Tutorial 3. The term **functionality** describes the tasks an application can perform. In this tutorial, you will examine **events**, which represent user actions such as clicking a `JButton` or altering a value in a `JTextField`, and **event handlers**, which are code segments that are executed (called) when such events occur. You will learn why events and event handlers are crucial to programming GUI applications.

4.1 Test-Driving the Inventory Application

In this tutorial, you will complete the **Inventory** application you began in Tutorial 3. Recall that the application must meet the following requirements:

Application Requirements

A college bookstore receives cartons of textbooks. In each shipment, each carton contains the same number of textbooks. The inventory manager wants to use a computer to calculate the total number of textbooks arriving at the bookstore for each shipment. The inventory manager will enter the number of cartons received in a shipment and the fixed number of textbooks per carton of the shipment; the application should then calculate and display the total number of textbooks in the shipment.

The inventory manager has reviewed and approved your design. Now you must add code that, when the user clicks a `JButton`, will make the application multiply the number of cartons by the number of textbooks per carton and display the result—that is, the total number of textbooks received. You begin by test-driving the completed application. Then, you will learn the additional Java technologies you will need to create your own version of this application.

1. ***Locating the completed application.*** Open the **Command Prompt** window by selecting **Start > Programs > Accessories > Command Prompt**. Change to your **Inventory** application directory by typing cd C:\Examples\ Tutorial04\CompletedApplication\Inventory2, then pressing *Enter*. [*Note:* From this point forward, we will no longer tell you to press *Enter* after each command you type in the **Command Prompt** window.]

2. ***Running the Inventory application.*** Type java Inventory in the **Command Prompt** window to run the application. Enter 3 in the **Cartons per shipment:** JTextField and enter 15 in the **Items per carton:** JTextField (Fig. 4.1).

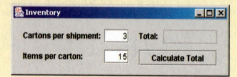

Figure 4.1 **Inventory** application with quantities entered.

3. ***Calculating the total number of items received.*** Click the **Calculate Total** JButton. The application multiplies the two numbers you entered and displays the result (45) in the **Total:** JTextField (Fig. 4.2).

Result of calculation

Figure 4.2 Calculating the total in the **Inventory** application.

4. ***Closing the application.*** Close your running application by clicking its close button.

5. ***Closing the Command Prompt window.*** Close the **Command Prompt** window by clicking its close button.

4.2 Introduction to Java Code

In Tutorials 2 and 3, you learned basic Java statements that are used primarily to customize an application's GUI. In this section, you will study other aspects of Java programming and use this new knowledge to enhance your **Inventory** application.

GUI programming is fun and creates visually appealing applications, but GUI programming alone is insufficient to complete the vast majority of applications. So far, as the programmer of the **Inventory** application, you've been performing tasks such as setting the text on a JLabel or setting the location of a JButton. However, your application should be able to perform actions based on the user's input. For example, your application needs to be programmed to perform an action when the JButton is clicked. The key is to develop the right mix of GUI components and functionality for each application. In the box, *Introducing Java Code*, you will take your first peek at using Java code to add functionality to an application.

Introducing Java Code

1. ***Copying the template to your work directory.*** Copy the C:\Examples\ Tutorial04\TemplateApplication\Inventory2 directory to your C:\SimplyJava directory. This directory contains a template based on the application you created in Tutorial 3.

(cont.)

2. ***Opening the Inventory application's template file.*** Open the template Inventory.java in your text editor (Fig. 4.3).

Beginning of class declaration ———

```
Source Editor [Inventory]                           _ □ ×
 1  // Tutorial 4: Inventory.java
 2  // Calculates the number of items in a shipment based on the number
 3  // of cartons received and the number of items per carton.
 4  import java.awt.*;
 5  import java.awt.event.*;
 6  import javax.swing.*;
 7
 8  public class Inventory extends JFrame
 9  {
10     // JLabel and JTextField for cartons per shipment
11     private JLabel cartonsJLabel;
12     private JTextField cartonsJTextField;
13
14     // JLabel and JTextField for items per carton
15     private JLabel itemsJLabel;
16     private JTextField itemsJTextField;
17
18     // JLabel and JTextField for total items per shipment
19     private JLabel totalJLabel;
20     private JTextField totalResultJTextField;
21
22     // JButton to initiate calculation of total items per shipment
23     private JButton calculateJButton;
```

Figure 4.3 Text editor showing a portion of the code for the **Inventory** application.

All Java applications consist of pieces called **classes**, which simplify application organization, and those classes include pieces called **methods**. Methods contain groups of code statements (generally referred to as **blocks** of code) that perform tasks and the methods often return information when the tasks are completed. The template code in the c file defines your **Inventory** application class. (Lines 8–118 of Fig. 4.3 collectively are called a **class declaration**.) Most Java applications consist of a combination of code written by programmers (like you) and pre-existing classes written and provided by Sun Microsystems and others in the Java API. A key to successful Java application development is achieving the right mix of the two. You will learn how to use both techniques in your applications.

3. ***Examining class declarations.*** Line 8 of Fig. 4.3 begins the class declaration. The **class keyword** introduces a class declaration in Java and is immediately followed by the **class name** (Inventory in this application). Every application in Java consists of at least one class declaration that is defined by you—the programmer. By convention, all class names in Java begin with a capital letter and begin every new word in the class name with a capital letter (for instance, SampleClassName). The name of the class is specified by an **identifier**, which is a sequence of characters consisting of letters, digits, underscores (_) and dollar signs ($). Identifiers cannot begin with a digit and cannot contain spaces. Examples of valid identifiers are Welcome1, $value1, label_Value, exitJButton and _total. The sequence of characters 7welcome is not a valid identifier because it begins with a digit, and input field is not a valid identifier because it contains a space. Recall that Java is **case sensitive**—that is, uppercase and lowercase letters are distinct—so a1 and A1 are different (but both valid) identifiers.

Keywords (or **reserved words**) are reserved for use by Java, so you can't use keywords to create your own identifiers. Appendix 16 includes a complete list of Java keywords. You will learn most of Java's keywords in this text.

Good Programming Practice

Capitalize the first letter in each word of a class identifier, as in the identifier SampleClassName.

Common Programming Error

Using uppercase letters in Java keywords results in syntax errors when you compile your applications.

(cont.)

When you save your class declaration in a file, the file name must be the class name followed by the ".java" file name extension. For our application, the file name is Inventory.java. All Java class declarations are stored in files ending with the file name extension ".java."

A **left brace** (at line 9 of Fig. 4.3), {, begins the **body** of every class declaration. A corresponding **right brace** (at line 118 in the template), }, must end each class declaration. The code for our **Inventory** application makes up the body of the Inventory class. We will talk more about elements of the template code in this tutorial and Tutorial 5.

Common Programming Error

Omitting either or both of the required curly braces in a class declaration is a syntax error.

4. ***Understanding inheriting from class JFrame.*** Every GUI application consists of at least one class that **inherits** from class JFrame (Fig. 4.3, line 8) in the Java API (Java's library of predefined classes). The **extends** keyword indicates that the class Inventory inherits members from another class (this is also called **extending a class**). By using **inheritance** to extend JFrame, your application uses class JFrame as a "template." A key benefit of inheriting from class JFrame is that the Java API previously defined "what it means to be a JFrame." The windows you see on your screen have certain capabilities. However, because class JFrame already provides those capabilities, programmers do not need to "reinvent the wheel" by defining all those capabilities themselves. Extending class JFrame enables you to create GUIs quickly and easily.

In the previous box, we examined the class declaration in the template code. The code inside the class declaration creates and customizes the other GUI components that appear in the JFrame when the application executes.

SELF-REVIEW

1. Identifiers _____.

   a) can begin with any character, but cannot contain spaces

   b) must begin with a digit, but cannot contain spaces

   c) cannot begin with a digit and cannot contain spaces

   d) cannot begin with a digit, but can contain spaces

2. The keyword _____ indicates that a new class inherits from an existing class.

   a) inherits   b) extends

   c) reuses   d) None of the above

Answers: 1) c. 2) b.

4.3 Placing Code in an Event Handler

Now you will modify your application to respond to user input. Most of the Java applications in this book provide such functionality in the form of event handlers. Recall that an event handler executes when an event occurs, such as when you click a JButton.

Viewing a JButton's actionPerformed Event Handler

1. ***Viewing the event handler.*** We have provided you with a template for the event handler in this application. Lines 105–108 in Fig. 4.4 show the event handler for the calculateJButton's actionPerformed event.

   This event handler will contain the code that will execute when the **Inventory** application's user clicks the **Calculate Total** JButton. More specifically, clicking the **Calculate Total** JButton generates an **actionPerformed** event, which in turn will cause the event handler on lines 105–108 to execute.

(cont.)

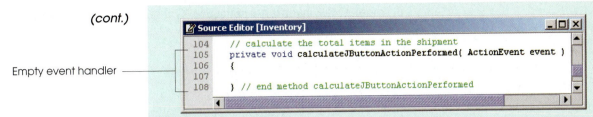

Empty event handler

Figure 4.4 Empty event handler `calculateJButtonActionPerformed` before you add your application code.

Note that the name `calculateJButtonActionPerformed` is used for the event handler that will respond to the **Calculate Total** `JButton`'s `actionPerformed` event. Our naming convention for event handlers is to combine the GUI component name (`calculateJButton`) with the event that occurs (`actionPerformed`) when the user interacts with the component. We use this convention for readability and to match the event handler with the corresponding GUI component. For example, if the application contained another `JButton` named `submitJButton`, its event handler would be `submitJButtonActionPerformed`.

2. ***Opening the*** **Command Prompt** ***window and changing directories.*** Open the **Command Prompt** window by selecting **Start > Programs > Accessories > Command Prompt**. Change to your working directory by typing `cd C:\SimplyJava\Inventory2`.

3. ***Compiling the application.*** Compile your application by typing `javac Inventory.java`.

4. ***Running the application.*** When your application compiles correctly, run it by typing `java Inventory`. Figure 4.5 shows the running application. Click the **Calculate Total** `JButton`. Notice that, although the code contains an event handler for the **Calculate Total** `JButton`'s `actionPerformed` event, no action occurs when you click the **Calculate Total** `JButton` because you haven't added any code to the event handler yet. In the next box, you will add code that executes when the user clicks the **Calculate Total** `JButton`. The code will calculate the total number of items in the shipment.

Figure 4.5 Running the application before adding functionality to the event handler.

5. ***Closing the application.*** Close your running application by clicking its close button.

6. ***Closing the*** **Command Prompt** ***window.*** Close the **Command Prompt** window by clicking its close button.

Now that you have viewed the template code for the **Calculate Total** `JButton`'s event handler, you will insert code in the event handler that, when a user clicks the **Calculate Total** `JButton`, multiplies two integers and displays the results in the **Total:** `JTextField` (`totalResultJTextField`). So that we can demonstrate how to display a numeric result in a `JTextField`, the calculation performed in the following box will always use the integers 3 and 15, regardless of the values the user types in the **Cartons per shipment:** and **Items per carton:** `JTextFields`. Thus, the calculation will always produce 45. After performing the tasks in the following box, you

will complete the **Inventory** application by inserting code that performs the correct calculation.

<table>
<tr><td>

Adding Code to an Empty Event Handler

</td><td>

1. *Opening the Inventory application's template file.* Open the template Inventory.java in your text editor.

2. *Adding code to the event handler.* Scroll to the JButton's event handler in line 105 and insert lines 107–108 of Fig. 4.6.

</td></tr>
</table>

Event handler for
Calculate Total JButton

Type this code

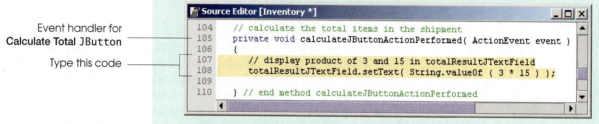

Figure 4.6 Code added to the **Calculate Total** JButton's event handler.

Line 107 of Fig. 4.6 begins with two **forward-slash** characters (//), indicating that the remainder of the line is a **comment**. You insert comments in your applications to improve the readability of your code. These comments explain the code so that you (and possibly other programmers) can understand your code more easily. Comments also help you understand your code later when you haven't looked at your code for a while.

Comments can be placed either in their own lines (these are called "**full-line comments**") or at the end of a line of code (these are called "**end-of-line comments**"). Comments appear in green when displayed in many text editors. [*Note:* The comment on line 107 is not in green because the editor we are using unfortunately removes coloring when we highlight lines of code.]

The Java compiler ignores comments, so comments do not cause the computer to perform any actions when your applications run. The comment in line 107 simply describes the task performed by the statement in line 108. Notice the comment in line 110 of Fig. 4.6, indicating that the closing curly brace (}) is the end of our event handler.

You have already seen lines similar to line 108 in Tutorials 2 and 3. You will now learn about the code in more detail. Line 108 of Fig. 4.6 is an executable **statement** that performs an action. Each statement ends when the **semicolon** (;) character is reached, as at the end of line 108. This statement sets the *text* property of totalResultJTextField.

Let's study the statement in more detail. Normally, to set the *text* property of a component, you use the **setText** method. For instance, you can write

    componentName.setText("*text to set*");

which causes the component called *componentName* to display "*text to set*" on the screen. For example, if the statement on line 108 read

    totalResultJTextField.setText("100");

the statement would set totalResultJTextField's *text* property to "100", which would then be displayed in the JTextField.

 Good Programming Practice

Comments written at the end of a line of code should be preceded by one or more spaces, to enhance program readability.

 Good Programming Practice

Place a blank line above a comment that is on a line by itself. The blank line makes the comment stand out and improves program readability.

 **Common Programming Error**

Forgetting the semicolon at the end of a statement results in a syntax error when you compile your application.

(cont.)

The preceding statement uses a so-called method (setText) to modify the value of totalResultJTextField's *text* property. A method is a piece of code that performs a task or action when it is called (executed). Sometimes a method **returns** a value to the location from which it was called. You call a method by typing its name followed by parentheses. Any values inside the parentheses (for example, "100" in the previous statement) are the method's **arguments**. Arguments are inputs to a method that provide information that the method needs to perform its task. Method setText requires one argument, which specifies the value you want to use to modify a component's *text* property. You will learn how to create your own methods in Tutorial 12.

You can access a component's property by specifying the component's name followed by a dot (.) and the name of the method that accesses the property. The dot is known as the **dot separator**.

In line 108, the setText method's argument is

```
String.valueOf( 3 * 15 )
```

which calls the **String.valueOf** method to convert a numeric value to text. Calculations are performed using numeric values. Unfortunately, a JTextField can display only a text value. So, a numeric value (such as the result of a calculation) needs to be converted into text before it is used to set a component's *text* property. The String.valueOf method takes the number you supply as its argument and returns a corresponding text value. For instance, if you pass the value 35 as an argument, this method returns the String "35". In line 108, the String returned by the String.valueOf method becomes the argument to totalResultJTextField's setText method and is displayed in totalResultJTextField.

The argument of the String.valueOf method in line 108 is the expression 3 * 15. The asterisk (*) is known as the **multiplication operator**. It multiplies two numeric values and returns their product. In algebra, you would typically represent multiplication with the middle dot operator as in $3 \cdot 15$. However, the middle dot operator is not available on computer keyboards, so most programming languages use the asterisk character (*) instead. The expressions on either side of the multiplication operator are its **operands**. This operator multiplies the value on the left of the operator (the **left operand**) and the value on the right of the operator (the **right operand**). The multiplication operator is known as a **binary operator**, because it has two operands. In this case, the operands are the integer values 3 and 15. [*Note:* You can perform addition, subtraction and division with the +, - and / operators, respectively.]

When the user clicks the **Calculate Total** JButton, the event handler in lines 105–110 (Fig. 4.6) will execute, displaying the value of the expression 3 * 15 (that is, 45). Clearly, this is not the correct result for all possible values the user can type in the **Cartons per shipment:** and **Items per carton:** JTextFields—the correct result is the number of items per carton times the number of cartons per shipment. In the next box, you will learn how to correct this error.

3. *Saving the application.* Save your modified source code file.

4. *Opening the Command Prompt window and changing directories.* Open the **Command Prompt** window by selecting **Start > Programs > Accessories > Command Prompt**. Change to your working directory by typing cd C:\SimplyJava\Inventory2.

(cont.)

5. ***Compiling the application.*** Compile your application by typing javac Inventory.java. If there are no compilation errors, proceed to *Step 6*. Otherwise, fix the errors in your code and repeat this step.

6. ***Running the application.*** When your application compiles correctly, run it by typing java Inventory. Figure 4.7 shows the running application. Type 5 into the **Cartons per shipment:** JTextField and 10 into the **Items per carton:** JTextField, then click the **Calculate Total** JButton. Notice that the totalResultJTextField still displays 45, which is the correct result based on the calculation performed at line 108. However, the result that should be displayed based on the numbers in the **Cartons per shipment:** and **Items per carton:** JTextFields is 50. Again, you will fix this in the next section by performing the calculation with the actual values in the **Cartons per shipment:** and **Items per carton:** JTextFields.

Result of clicking **Calculate Total** JButton

Figure 4.7 Execution of application with an event handler.

7. ***Closing the application.*** Close your running application by clicking its close button.

8. ***Closing the Command Prompt window.*** Close the **Command Prompt** window by clicking its close button.

SELF-REVIEW

1. Method _____ converts a numeric value to text.
   a) Integer.valueOf
   b) Integer.parseInt
   c) String.parseInt
   d) String.valueOf

2. The expressions on either side of the multiplication operator are referred to as its _____.
   a) operator values
   b) results
   c) operands
   d) arguments

Answers: 1) d. 2) c.

4.4 Performing a Calculation and Displaying the Result

Now that you are familiar with displaying output in a JTextField, you will complete the **Inventory** application by calculating and displaying the product of the number of cartons per shipment and the number of items per carton.

Completing the Inventory Application

1. ***Opening the Inventory application's template file.*** Open the template Inventory.java in your text editor.

2. ***Adding a multiline statement.*** Scroll to the event handler for the calculateJButton in line 105 of Fig. 4.6. Replace lines 107–108 of calculateJButtonActionPerformed with lines 107–110 of Fig. 4.8.

(cont.)

Read the values from
cartonsJTextField and
itemsJTextField, convert them
to integers, multiply the integer
values and display the result in
totalResultJTextField

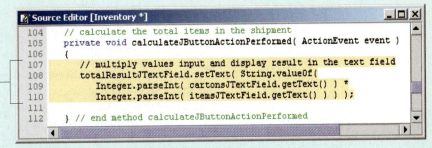

Figure 4.8 Using multiplication in the **Inventory** application.

Good Programming Practice

A lengthy statement may be spread over several lines. If a single statement must be split across lines, choose breaking points that make sense, such as after an operator. If a statement is split across two or more lines, indent all subsequent lines with one "level" of indentation.

Common Programming Error

Splitting a statement in the middle of a String literal is a syntax error.

Recall from the previous box, *Adding Code to an Empty Event Handler*, that a Java statement ends with a semicolon. Notice in lines 108–110 that only line 110 ends with a semicolon. In this case, lines 108–110 represent one **multiline statement**. A single statement can be spread across many lines, because Java ignores the extra spaces, tabs and **newline** characters in your code. Newlines characters are inserted when you press *Enter*. Together spaces, tabs and newlines are called **white space**. [*Note:* White space is not ignored inside the double quotes of a String literal.] A programmer typically splits long statements into multiple lines to make the code more readable. Also, notice that lines 109–110 of the statement are indented. The indentation is a visual indication that the statement continues from the previous line.

Lines 108–110 perform the multiplication calculation and use setText to set totalResultJTextField's *text* property. As in the previous box, *Adding Code to an Empty Event Handler*, the argument to setText is the result of the call to the String.valueOf method, which converts a numeric value to text.

In lines 108–110, the String.valueOf method receives as its argument the result of the following Java code (lines 109–110):

```
Integer.parseInt( cartonsJTextField.getText() ) *
Integer.parseInt( itemsJTextField.getText() )
```

which performs the multiplication calculation using the values in the **Cartons per shipment:** and **Items per carton:** JTextFields. Just as a numeric value needs to be converted into text to be displayed, text read from a JTextField needs to be converted into a numeric value to be used in a calculation (such as multiplication). Lines 109 and 110 each call the conversion method **Integer.parseInt**, which takes a text value as an argument and returns an equivalent integer value. The text values are obtained from the *text* properties of the **Cartons per shipment:** and **Items per carton:** JTextFields.

(cont.)

It is possible to get the *text* property of a component by using its **getText** method, as in

> *componentName*.getText()

which will get the text that is displayed by the component on the screen. In the **Inventory** application, if you enter 5 in the **Cartons per shipment:** JTextField in Fig. 4.7, then cartonsJTextField.getText() in line 109 of Fig. 4.8 will get the **Cartons per shipment:** JTextField's *text* property, which is the String containing 5. Because cartonsJTextField.get-Text() appears inside the parentheses of the Integer.parseInt method call, the result of the call to cartonsJTextField.getText() (that is, the String containing 5) is used as the argument to the Integer.parseInt method. The text in the **Cartons per shipment:** JTextField's *text* property is converted to an integer for use as the left operand in the multiplication calculation. Similarly, on line 110, the result of itemsJTextField.get-Text() is passed as the argument to Integer.parseInt to get the number of items per carton for use as the right operand in the multiplication calculation.

You should be careful when using Integer.parseInt. If the text you pass to the method does not represent an integer value, an exception occurs. Java uses exceptions to indicate when problems occur during application execution. By default, the exception information will be output to the **Command Prompt** window. You will learn how to write code that processes exceptions in Tutorial 24.

3. *Saving the application.* Save your modified source code file.

4. *Opening the Command Prompt window and changing directories.* Open the **Command Prompt** window by selecting **Start > Programs > Accessories > Command Prompt**. Change to your working directory by typing cd C:\SimplyJava\Inventory2.

5. *Compiling the application.* Compile your application by typing javac Inventory.java. If there are no compilation errors, proceed to *Step 6*. Otherwise, fix the errors in your code and repeat this step.

6. *Running the application.* When your application compiles correctly, run it by typing java Inventory. Figure 4.9 shows the running application. Now when you enter data in both JTextFields (use 5 and 10, respectively) and click the **Calculate Total** JButton, the application will correctly multiply the two numbers entered and display the result (50) in totalResultJText-Field.

Figure 4.9 Execution of the completed **Inventory** application.

7. *Closing the application.* Close your running application by clicking its close button.

8. *Closing the Command Prompt window.* Close the running application by clicking the window's close button.

Figure 4.10 presents the source code for the **Inventory** application. The lines of code that you added, viewed or modified in this tutorial are highlighted.

```
1    // Tutorial 4: Inventory.java
2    // Calculates the number of items in a shipment based on the number
3    // of cartons received and the number of items per carton.
4    import java.awt.*;
5    import java.awt.event.*;
6    import javax.swing.*;
7
8    public class Inventory extends JFrame
9    {
10      // JLabel and JTextField for cartons per shipment
11      private JLabel cartonsJLabel;
12      private JTextField cartonsJTextField;
13
14      // JLabel and JTextField for items per carton
15      private JLabel itemsJLabel;
16      private JTextField itemsJTextField;
17
18      // JLabel and JTextField for total items per shipment
19      private JLabel totalJLabel;
20      private JTextField totalResultJTextField;
21
22      // JButton to initiate calculation of total items per shipment
23      private JButton calculateJButton;
24
25      // no-argument constructor
26      public Inventory()
27      {
28         createUserInterface();
29      }
30
31      // create and position GUI components; register event handlers
32      public void createUserInterface()
33      {
34         // get content pane and set layout to null
35         Container contentPane = getContentPane();
36         contentPane.setLayout( null );
37
38         // set up cartonsJLabel
39         cartonsJLabel = new JLabel();
40         cartonsJLabel.setText( "Cartons per shipment:" );
41         cartonsJLabel.setBounds( 16, 16, 130, 21 );
42         contentPane.add( cartonsJLabel );
43
44         // set up itemsJLabel
45         itemsJLabel = new JLabel();
46         itemsJLabel.setText( "Items per carton:" );
47         itemsJLabel.setBounds( 16, 48, 104, 21 );
48         contentPane.add( itemsJLabel );
49
50         // set up totalJLabel
51         totalJLabel = new JLabel();
52         totalJLabel.setText( "Total:" );
53         totalJLabel.setBounds( 204, 16, 40, 21 );
54         contentPane.add( totalJLabel );
55
56         // set up cartonsJTextField
57         cartonsJTextField = new JTextField();
58         cartonsJTextField.setText( "0" );
```

Figure 4.10 **Inventory** application code. (Part 1 of 3.)

```
59    cartonsJTextField.setBounds( 148, 16, 40, 21 );
60    cartonsJTextField.setHorizontalAlignment( JTextField.RIGHT );
61    contentPane.add( cartonsJTextField );
62
63    // set up itemsJTextField
64    itemsJTextField = new JTextField();
65    itemsJTextField.setText( "0" );
66    itemsJTextField.setBounds( 148, 48, 40, 21 );
67    itemsJTextField.setHorizontalAlignment( JTextField.RIGHT );
68    contentPane.add( itemsJTextField );
69
70    // set up totalResultJTextField
71    totalResultJTextField = new JTextField();
72    totalResultJTextField.setBounds( 244, 16, 86, 21 );
73    totalResultJTextField.setHorizontalAlignment(
74       JTextField.RIGHT );
75    totalResultJTextField.setEditable( false );
76    contentPane.add( totalResultJTextField );
77
78    // set up calculateJButton
79    calculateJButton = new JButton();
80    calculateJButton.setText( "Calculate Total" );
81    calculateJButton.setBounds( 204, 48, 126, 24 );
82    contentPane.add( calculateJButton );
83    calculateJButton.addActionListener(
84
85       new ActionListener() // anonymous inner class
86       {
87          // event handler called when calculateJButton is pressed
88          public void actionPerformed( ActionEvent event )
89          {
90             calculateJButtonActionPerformed( event );
91          }
92
93       } // end anonymous inner class
94
95    ); // end call to addActionListener
96
97    // set properties of application's window
98    setTitle( "Inventory" ); // set title bar text
99    setSize( 354, 112 );    // set window size
100   setVisible( true );      // display window
101
102 } // end method createUserInterface
103
104 // calculate the total items in the shipment
105 private void calculateJButtonActionPerformed( ActionEvent event )
106 {
107    // multiply values input and display result in the text field
108    totalResultJTextField.setText( String.valueOf(
109       Integer.parseInt( cartonsJTextField.getText() ) *
110       Integer.parseInt( itemsJTextField.getText() ) ) );
111
112 } // end method calculateJButtonActionPerformed
113
114 // main method
115 public static void main( String[] args )
116 {
```

Read the values from cartonsJTextField and itemsJTextField, convert them to integers, multiply the integer values and display the result in totalResultJTextField

Figure 4.10   Inventory application code. (Part 2 of 3.)

```
117            Inventory application = new Inventory();
118            application.setDefaultCloseOperation( JFrame.EXIT_ON_CLOSE );
119
120      } // end method main
121
122 } // end class Inventory
```

Figure 4.10   **Inventory** application code. (Part 3 of 3.)

1. The method `Integer.parseInt` _____.

   a) converts an integer to text

   b) converts text to an integer

   c) performs the same task as `String.valueOf`

   d) None of the above.

2. If `totalJTextField` is a `JTextField`, you can use _____ to get the *text* property of the `totalJTextField`.

   a) `totalJTextField.gettext()`

   b) `totalJTextField.setText()`

   c) `totalJTextField.getText()`

   d) `totalJTextField.text()`

Answers: 1) b. 2) c.

4.5 Wrap-Up

In this tutorial, you learned how to use a `JTextField` component to allow users to input data and how to use a `JButton` component to tell your running application to perform a particular action. You were introduced to some of the code in the class declaration that creates an application's GUI. Though you are not yet expected to understand such code, you learned that a key to good programming is to achieve the right balance between employing GUI components and writing code that adds functionality to your GUIs.

After learning briefly about methods and operators in Java, you inserted code in an event handler to perform a simple multiplication calculation and display the result to the user. You also used comments to improve the readability of your code. You learned that placing code in an event handler allows an application to respond to an event, such as the click of a `JButton`.

In the next tutorial, you will continue to enhance your **Inventory** application by creating variables that will enable your application to store information for use later in the application. You will also enhance your **Inventory** application by using the `keyPressed` event, which occurs when the user changes the value in a `JText-Field`. After applying your knowledge of variables, you will use the debugger while an application runs to remove a logic error from that application.

SKILLS SUMMARY

Accessing a Component's Property Values

■ Place the name of the method that modifies or accesses the value after the component name and the dot separator (.). For example, to get the *text* property of a `JTextField` named `cartonsJTextField`, use `cartonsJTextField.getText()` and, to set the *text* property of that `JTextField`, use `cartonsJTextField.setText( "value" )`.

Inserting Comments in Code

■ Begin the comment with two forward-slash characters (`//`). Then, insert text that describes what is happening in the code so you can understand the code better. A comment can be placed either on its own line or at the end of a line of code.

Naming an Event Handler

■ Use the format *componentNameEventName* for the name of an event handler, where *componentName* is the name of the component that the event is related to and *eventName*

is the name of the event. For instance, `calculateJButtonActionPerformed` would be the event handler for `calculateJButton`'s `actionPerformed` event.

Using the Multiplication Operator

■ Use an asterisk (*) between the two numeric operands to be multiplied. The multiplication operator multiplies its left and right numeric operands. [*Note:* You can also use +, – and / to perform addition, subtraction and division, respectively.]

Obtaining an Integer Value from a `JTextField` and Converting It to an Integer

■ Access the `JTextField`'s *text* property, using method `getText`, and provide the result as an argument to method `Integer.parseInt`. For example, the following expression converts the text in `itemsJTextField` to an integer:

```
Integer.parseInt( itemsJTextField.getText() )
```

Converting a Numeric Value to a Text Value for Display in a `JTextField`

■ Provide the numeric value as an argument to method `String.valueOf`, which returns a `String` containing an equivalent text value. Pass the result to the `JTextField`'s `setText` method. For example, the following statement converts the number 100 to a text value and displays the text in `totalResultsJTextField`:

```
totalResultsJTextField.setText( String.valueOf( 100 ) );
```

KEY TERMS

actionPerformed event—The kind of event that occurs when a `JButton` is clicked.

argument—A value that is passed to a method by being placed in the parentheses that follow the method name in a method call.

block—A group of code statements that are enclosed in curly braces ({ and }).

body—A set of statements that is enclosed in curly braces ({ and }). This is also called a block.

binary operator—An operator that requires two operands.

case sensitive—Identifiers with identical spelling are treated differently if the capitalization of the identifiers differs.

class declaration—The code that defines a class, beginning with the `class` keyword.

class name—The identifier used as the name of a class.

class keyword—The keyword used to begin a class declaration.

comment (//)—Explanatory text that is inserted to improve an application's readability.

dot separator—Allows programmers to call methods of a particular class or object.

end-of-line comment—A comment that appears at the end of a code line.

event—An action that can trigger an event handler.

event handler—Code that executes when a certain event occurs.

extending a class—Creating a new class based on an existing class (also called inheritance).

extends keyword—The keyword the specifies that a class inherits data and functionality from an existing class.

forward-slash characters—A comment begins with two forward slashes (//).

full-line comment—A comment that appears on a line by itself in source code.

functionality—The tasks or actions an application can execute.

getText method—A method that accesses (or gets) the *text* property of a component such as a `JLabel`, `JTextField` or a `JButton`.

identifier—A series of characters consisting of letters, digits and underscores used to name application units such as classes and GUI components.

inheritance—Creating a new class based on an existing class (also called extending a class).

Integer.parseInt method—Returns the integer equivalent of its `String` argument.

keyword—A word that is reserved by Java. These words cannot be used as identifiers.

left brace ({)—Denotes the beginning of a block of code.

left operand—An expression that appears on the left side of a binary operator.

method—An application segment containing statements that perform a task. A method often returns information after performing its task.

multiline statement—A statement that is spread over multiple lines of code for readability.

multiplication operator—The asterisk (*) used to multiply its two numeric operands, calculating their product as a result.

newline—A character that is inserted in code when you press *Enter*.

operand—An expression that is combined with an operator (and possibly other expressions) to perform a task (such as multiplication).

reserved word—A word that is reserved for use by Java and cannot be used to create your own identifiers. See also "keyword."

return a value from a method—Some methods, when called, return a value to the statement in the application that called the method. The returned value can then be used in that statement.

right brace (})—Denotes the end of a block of code.

right operand—An expression that appears on the right side of a binary operator.

semicolon (;)—Character used to terminate each statement in an application.

setText method—A method that sets the *text* property of a component, such as a `JLabel`, `JTextField` or `JButton`.

statement—A unit of code that performs an action and ends with a semicolon.

`String.valueOf` method—A method that converts a numeric value into text.

white space—A tab, space or newline.

JAVA LIBRARY REFERENCE

Integer The `Integer` class contains methods that process integer values.

■ *Method*

parseInt—Returns the integer equivalent of its `String` argument.

JButton This component allows the user to cause an event by pressing a button in an application's graphical user interface.

■ *In action*

■ *Event*

actionPerformed—Occurs when the user clicks the `JButton`.

■ *Methods*

setBounds—Sets the location and size of the `JButton`.

setText—Sets the *text* property of the `JButton`.

JTextField This component allows the user to input information and can be used to display results to the user.

■ *In action*

Editable `JTextField` ——————

Uneditable `JTextField` ——————

■ *Methods*

getText—Returns the text displayed in the `JTextField`.

setBounds—Sets the location and size of the `JTextField`.

setEditable—Specifies whether users can edit the `JTextField`. A `true` value (the default) means the `JTextField` is an editable input `JTextField` and a `false` value means the `JTextField` is an uneditable output `JTextField`.

setHorizontalAlignment—Specifies how the text is aligned within the `JTextField` (`JTextField.LEFT`, `JTextField.CENTER` or `JTextField.RIGHT`).

setText—Specifies the text displayed in the `JTextField`.

String The String class stores and manipulates text data.

■ *Method*

valueOf—Returns the String equivalent of its argument.

MULTIPLE-CHOICE QUESTIONS

4.1 A(n) _____ represents a user action, such as clicking a JButton.
   a) statement   b) event
   c) application   d) function

4.2 The _____ character is the multiplication operator.
   a) asterisk (*)   b) forward-slash (/)
   c) semicolon (;)   d) None of the above.

4.3 A _____ operator has two operands.
   a) comment   b) text
   c) binary   d) None of the above.

4.4 Comments _____.
   a) help improve application readability   b) are preceded by two forward slashes
   c) are ignored by the compiler   d) All of the above.

4.5 Java statements end when (the) _____ is (are) reached.
   a) forward-slash (/) character   b) semicolon (;) character
   c) two forward-slash (//) characters d) asterisk (*)

4.6 Method _____ is used to modify the *text* property of a JTextField.
   a) changeText   b) getText
   c) setText   d) modifyText

4.7 A portion of code that performs a specific task and may return a value is known as a(n) _____.
   a) variable   b) method
   c) operand   d) identifier

4.8 Java keywords are _____.
   a) identifiers   b) reserved for use by Java
   c) case sensitive   d) Both b and c.

4.9 Class declarations end with a _____.
   a) right brace (})   b) semicolon (;)
   c) end keyword   d) class keyword

4.10 The method _____ converts text into numeric values.
   a) Integer.getInt   b) String.valueOf
   c) Integer.parseInt   d) String.value

EXERCISES

4.11 *(Inventory Application Enhancement)* Enhance the **Inventory** application to include a JTextField in which the user can enter the number of shipments received in a week (Fig. 4.11). Assume every shipment has the same number of cartons (each of which has the same number of items), and modify the code so that the **Inventory** application uses the number of shipments in its calculation.

   a) *Copying the template to your working directory.* Copy the directory C:\Examples\Tutorial04\Exercises\Inventory2Enhancement to your C:\SimplyJava directory.

Figure 4.11 Enhanced **Inventory** application.

b) *Opening the Command Prompt window and changing directories.* Open the **Command Prompt** window by selecting **Start > Programs > Accessories > Command Prompt**. Change to your working directory by typing `cd C:\SimplyJava\Inventory2Enhancement`.

c) *Compiling the template application.* Compile your application by typing `javac Inventory.java`.

d) *Running the template application.* Run the enhanced **Inventory** template application by typing `java Inventory`. The GUI of the **Address Book** template application should appear as shown in Fig. 4.12. Note the differences from Fig. 4.11.

Figure 4.12 Enhanced **Inventory** template application.

e) *Opening the template file.* Open the `Inventory.java` file in your text editor.

f) *Customizing the Shipments this week: JLabel.* After line 70, insert a statement that sets the *text* property of `shipmentsJLabel` to `"Shipments this week:"`. On the next line, insert a statement that sets the *bounds* property of `shipmentsJLabel` such that its *y*-coordinate is 80 and its *x*-coordinate, width and height are identical to the *x*-coordinate, width and height of `itemsJLabel` (see line 59 in the template code).

g) *Customizing the Shipments this week: JTextField.* After line 76, insert a statement that sets the *text* property of `shipmentsJTextField` to `"0"`. On the next line, insert a statement that sets the *bounds* property of `shipmentsJTextField` such that its *y*-coordinate is 80 and its *x*-coordinate, width and height are identical to the *x*-coordinate, width and height of `itemsJTextField` (see line 65 in the template code). On the next line, insert a statement that sets the *horizontalAlignment* property of `shipmentsJTextField` so that the text is right justified (`JTextField.RIGHT`).

h) *Repositioning the Calculate Total JButton.* Modify the statement in line 99 that sets the *bounds* property of `calculateJButton` such that the top of the JButton aligns with the top of `shipmentsJTextField`.

i) *Modifying the event-handling code.* Modify the `calculateJButtonActionPerformed` event handler (lines 122–131) so that the statement in lines 126–129 multiplies the number of shipments per week with the product of the number of cartons in a shipment and the number of items in a carton.

j) *Saving the application.* Save your modified source code file.

k) *Compiling the completed application.* Compile your application by typing `javac Inventory.java`.

l) *Running the completed application.* When your application compiles correctly, run it by typing `java Inventory`. Compare the GUI of your completed **Inventory** application with the GUI shown in Fig. 4.11 to ensure that you customized the GUI components and event handler correctly.

4.12 *(Counter Application)* Create a **Counter** application (Fig. 4.13). Your **Counter** application's GUI will consist of a `JTextField` and a `JButton`. The `JTextField` initially displays 0, but each time a user clicks the `JButton`, the value in the `JTextField` increases by 1.

Figure 4.13 **Counter** application.

a) *Copying the template to your working directory.* Copy the C:\Examples\Tutorial04\Exercises\Counter directory to your C:\SimplyJava directory.

b) *Opening the Command Prompt window and changing directories.* Open the **Command Prompt** window by selecting **Start > Programs > Accessories > Command Prompt**. Change to your working directory by typing cd C:\SimplyJava\Counter.

c) *Compiling the template application.* Compile your application by typing javac Counter.java.

d) *Running the template application.* Run the **Counter** template application by typing java Counter. The GUI of the **Counter** template application should appear as shown in Fig. 4.14. Note the differences from Fig. 4.13.

Figure 4.14 **Counter** template application.

e) *Opening the template file.* Open the Counter.java file in your text editor.

f) *Customizing countJTextField.* After line 30, insert a statement that sets the *text* property of countJTextField to "0". On the next line, insert a statement that sets the *horizontalAlignment* property of countJTextField so that the text is centered (JTextField.CENTER) in the JTextField.

g) *Customizing countJButton.* After line 38, insert a statement that sets the *text* property of countJButton to the text "Count".

h) *Inserting code in the event handler.* In line 66 in the body of the event handler countJButtonActionPerformed (lines 63–67), insert a statement that increments the value in countJTextField by one each time the user clicks the **Count** JButton, then uses the new value to set the *text* property of countJTextField. To do this, you will use the addition operator (+), which adds its two numeric operands. Use the expression 1 + Integer.parseInt(countJTextField.getText()) to calculate the new value to display. The result of the preceding expression must be converted to text with String.valueOf before it can be displayed in countJTextField.

i) *Saving the application.* Save your modified source code file.

j) *Compiling the completed application.* Compile your application by typing javac Counter.java.

k) *Running the completed application.* When your application compiles correctly, run it by typing java Counter. Compare the GUI of your completed **Counter** application with the GUI shown in Fig. 4.13 to ensure that you customized the GUI components and event handler correctly.

4.13 *(Bank Account Information Application)* Create an application that allows a user to input a deposit amount (Fig. 4.15). Each time the user clicks the **Enter** JButton, the application adds the deposit amount entered by the user in the **Deposit amount:** JTextField to the balance that is currently displayed in the **Balance:** JTextField, then displays the new result in the **Balance:** JTextField. [*Note:* This application displays Sue Purple as a default client name and 12345 as a default account number.]

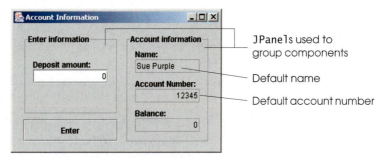

Figure 4.15   **Account Information** application.

a) *Copying the template to your working directory.* Copy the C:\Examples\ Tutorial04\Exercises\AccountInformation directory to your C:\SimplyJava directory.

b) *Opening the Command Prompt window and changing directories.* Open the **Command Prompt** window by selecting **Start > Programs > Accessories > Command Prompt.** Change to your working directory by typing cd C:\SimplyJava\ AccountInformation.

c) *Compiling the template application.* Compile your application by typing javac AccountInformation.java.

d) *Running the template application.* Run the **Bank Account Information** template application by typing java AccountInformation. Type 100 in the **Deposit amount:** JTextField. When you press the **Enter** JButton, notice that the deposit amount is not added to the balance because you have not added code to the **Enter** JButton's event handler yet.

e) *Opening the template file.* Open the AccountInformation.java file in your text editor.

f) *Inserting code in the event handler.* In your editor, scroll to the event handler enter-JButtonActionPerformed (lines 145–149). In line 148 in the body of the event handler, insert a statement that obtains the numeric values of the text in the **Deposit amount:** JTextField (depositJTextField) and the **Balance:** JTextField (balanceJTextField), then adds the values and displays the result in the **Balance:** JTextField. Use techniques similar to lines 108–110 of Fig. 4.10. On the next line, insert a statement that sets the *text* property of the **Deposit amount:** JTextField to "0".

g) *Saving the application.* Save your modified source code file.

h) *Compiling the completed application.* Compile your application by typing javac AccountInformation.java.

i) *Running the completed application.* When your application compiles correctly, run it by typing java AccountInformation.

j) *Testing the application.* Type 100 in the **Deposit amount:** JTextField, then press the **Enter** JButton. The **Balance:** JTextField should now contain 100 and the **Deposit amount:** JTextField should now contain 0. Type 50 in the **Deposit amount:** JTextField, then press the **Enter** JButton. The **Balance:** JTextField should now contain 150, and the **Deposit amount:** JTextField should now contain 0.

What does this code do? ▶   **4.14** After entering 2 in the priceJTextField and 14 in the hammersJTextField, a user clicks the JButton named calculateJButton to calculate the total price for the specified number of hammers. What is the result of the click, given the following code?

```
1   private void calculateJButtonActionPerformed( ActionEvent event )
2   {
3      totalPriceJTextField.setText( String.valueOf(
4         Integer.parseInt( priceJTextField.getText() ) *
5         Integer.parseInt( hammersJTextField.getText() ) ) );
6
7   } // calculateJButtonActionPerformed
```

What's wrong with this code? ▶ **4.15** The following event handler should execute when the user clicks a **Multiply** JButton. Assume that each of the JTextFields contains text that represents an integer value. Identify the error(s) in the code.

```
1    private void multiplyJButtonActionPerformed( ActionEvent event )
2    {
3       resultJTextField.setText( leftOperandJTextField.getText() *
4          rightOperandJTextField.getText() );
5
6    } // multiplyJButtonActionPerformed
```

Remove errors from this code. ▶ **4.16** *(Bank Account Information Debugging Exercise)* Copy the C:\Examples\ Tutorial04\Exercises\DebuggingExercise directory to the C:\SimplyJava directory. Compile and run the **Bank Account Information** application. Remove any syntax errors and logic errors, so that the application runs correctly. [*Hint:* All the syntax and logic errors appear in the event handler code (lines 146–156 of the application).]

Programming Challenge ▶ **4.17** *(Enhanced Bank Account Information Application)* Modify Exercise 4.13 to enable the user to input both a withdrawal amount and a deposit amount (Fig. 4.16). When the **Enter** JButton is clicked, the balance is updated appropriately.

Figure 4.16 Enhanced **Bank Account Information** application.

a) *Copying the template to your working directory.* Copy the C:\Examples\ Tutorial04\Exercises\AccountInformationEnhancement directory to your C:\SimplyJava directory.

b) *Opening the Command Prompt window and changing directories.* Open the **Command Prompt** window by selecting **Start > Programs > Accessories > Command Prompt**. Change to your working directory by typing cd C:\SimplyJava\ AccountInformationEnhancement.

c) *Compiling the template application.* Compile your application by typing javac AccountInformation.java.

d) *Running the template application.* Run the enhanced **Bank Account Information** template application by typing java AccountInformation. Type 50 in the **Withdrawal amount:** JTextField and type 100 in the **Deposit amount:** JTextField. When you press the **Enter** JButton, notice that the balance does not change because you have not added code to the **Enter** JButton's event handler yet.

e) *Opening the template file.* Open the AccountInformation.java file in your text editor.

f) *Inserting code in the event handler.* In your editor, scroll to the event handler enter-JButtonActionPerformed (lines 163–167). At line 166 in the body of the event handler, insert a statement that obtains the numeric values of the text in the **Withdrawal amount:** JTextField (withdrawalJTextField), the **Deposit amount:** JTextField (depositJTextField) and the **Balance:** JTextField (balanceJTextField), then performs the calculation *balance + deposit amount – withdrawal amount* and displays the result in the **Balance:** JTextField. Use techniques similar to lines 108–110 of

Fig. 4.10. Insert two additional statements in the event handler that set the *text* properties of the **Withdrawal amount:** JTextField and **Deposit amount:** JTextField to "0".

g) ***Saving the application.*** Save your modified source code file.

h) ***Compiling the completed application.*** Compile your application by typing javac AccountInformation.java.

i) ***Running the completed application.*** When your application compiles correctly, run it by typing java AccountInformation.

j) ***Testing the application.*** Type 50 in the **Withdrawal amount:** JTextField and type 100 in the **Deposit amount:** JTextField, then press the **Enter** JButton. The **Balance:** JTextField should now contain 50 and the **Withdrawal amount:** and **Deposit amount:** JTextFields should now contain 0. Type 50 in the **Deposit amount:** JTextField, then press the **Enter** JButton. The **Balance:** JTextField should now contain 100, and the **Deposit amount:** JTextField should now contain 0.

Objectives

In this tutorial, you will learn to:
- Declare variables.
- Handle the `keyPressed` event for a `JTextField`.
- Apply basic memory concepts using variables.
- Use the precedence rules of arithmetic operators.
- Set breakpoints to debug applications.
- Use the debugger's `run`, `stop`, `cont` and `print` commands.

Outline

Enhancing the Inventory Application

Introducing Variables, Memory Concepts, Arithmetic and Keyboard Events

In the previous tutorial, you developed an **Inventory** application that multiplied the number of cartons received by the number of items per carton to calculate the total number of items received by a company. You used `JTextFields` to read user input from the keyboard and to display outputs. You also added a `JButton` to the `JFrame` and programmed that `JButton` to respond to a user's click. In this tutorial, you will enhance your **Inventory** application using additional programming concepts, including variables, keyboard events and arithmetic.

5.1 Test-Driving the Enhanced Inventory Application

In this tutorial, you will enhance the previous tutorial's **Inventory** application by using variables to perform arithmetic calculations. You will study memory concepts to help you understand how applications run on computers. Recall that your **Inventory** application from Tutorial 4 calculated the number of items received based on information supplied by the user—the number of cartons and the number of textbooks per carton. The enhanced application must meet the following requirements:

Application Requirements

*The inventory manager notices a flaw in your **Inventory** application. Although the application calculates the correct result, that result continues to display even after new data is entered. The only time the output changes is when the inventory manager clicks the **Calculate** JButton again. You should alter the **Inventory** application to clear the result as soon as the user enters new information into either of the JTextFields, to avoid any confusion over the accuracy of your calculated result.*

You begin by test-driving the completed application. Then, you learn the additional Java technologies you will need to create your own version of this application.

***Test-Driving the
Enhanced Inventory
Application***

1. ***Locating the completed application.*** Open the **Command Prompt** window by selecting **Start > Programs > Accessories > Command Prompt**. Change to your completed **Inventory** application directory by typing `cd C:\Examples\Tutorial05\CompletedApplication\Inventory3`.

2. ***Running the Inventory application.*** Type `java Inventory` in the **Command Prompt** window to run the application (Fig. 5.1).

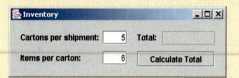

Figure 5.1   Running the enhanced **Inventory** application.

3. ***Calculating the number of items in the shipment.*** Enter 5 in the **Cartons per shipment:** JTextField and 6 in the **Items per carton:** JTextField. Click the **Calculate Total** JButton. The result will be displayed in the **Total:** output JTextField (Fig. 5.2).

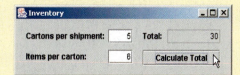

Figure 5.2   Calculating the number of items in the shipment.

4. ***Entering new quantities.*** The result displayed in the **Total:** JTextField will be removed when the user enters a new quantity in either of the other JTextFields. Enter 13 as the new number of cartons. Notice that when you type 1 the last calculation's result is cleared (Fig. 5.3). The Java technique for doing this will be explained later in this tutorial.

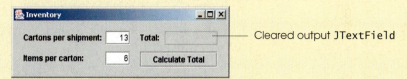

Cleared output JTextField

Figure 5.3   Enhanced **Inventory** application clears output JTextField (to avoid confusion) after new input.

5. ***Closing the application.*** Close your running application by clicking its close button.

6. ***Closing the Command Prompt.*** Close the **Command Prompt** window by clicking its close button.

5.2 Variables

Good Programming Practice

Typically, variable names begin with a lowercase letter. Every word in the name after the first word should begin with a capital letter (for example, `firstNumber`).

A **variable** is a storage location that holds data, much as the *text* property of a JLabel holds the text to be displayed to the user. Unlike the *text* property of a JLabel, variables allow you to store and manipulate data without necessarily showing the data to the user. Variables also allow you to store data without using GUI components. Variables store data such as numbers, dates, times and the like. However, each variable used in Java corresponds to exactly one type of information. For example, a variable that stores a number cannot be used to store a name (or any other text).

In Java, all variables must be **declared** before they are used in the application. All variable **declarations** include the variable's **type**, which specifies the type of data a variable stores, and an optional **initialization value**, which specifies the beginning value stored in the variable. In this tutorial, you study type `int`, which you use to declare integer variables—that is, variables whose values must be whole numbers.

Good Programming Practice

Use only letters and digits in your variable names.

Next, you will learn to program with variables. A variable name must be a valid identifier, which, as you learned in Tutorial 4, is a sequence of characters consisting of letters, digits, underscores (_) and dollar signs ($), and is not a keyword. Identifiers cannot begin with a digit and cannot contain spaces.

Using Variables in the Inventory Application

1. *Copying the template to your working directory.* Copy the `C:\Examples\Tutorial05\TemplateApplication\Inventory3` directory to your `C:\SimplyJava` directory.

2. *Opening the Inventory application's template file.* Open the template file `Inventory.java` in your text editor.

3. *Adding variable declarations to event handler `calculateJButtonAction-Performed`.* Add lines 135–138 of Fig. 5.4 to the `calculateJButtonActionPerformed` event handler. Lines 136–138 are declarations, which begin with each variable's type—in this case, **int**. The `int` keyword indicates that the variable being declared will store only integer values (whole numbers such as 919, 0 and –11). The words `cartons`, `items` and `result` are the variables' names.

```
Source Editor [Inventory *]
132      // calculate the total items in the shipment
133      private void calculateJButtonActionPerformed( ActionEvent event )
134      {
135         // declare variables
136         int cartons; // stores number of cartons in shipment
137         int items;   // stores number of items per carton
138         int result;  // stores product of cartons and items
139
140      } // end method calculateJButtonActionPerformed
```

Variable declarations ⎯⎯⎯ (lines 136–138)

Figure 5.4   Declaring variables in event handler `calculateJButton-ActionPerformed`.

4. *Retrieving input from `JTextFields`.* Insert lines 140–142 of Fig. 5.5 into your code. The numbers that the user enters are found in the *text* properties of the `JTextFields`. These numbers must be converted to numerical values using `Integer.parseInt`, and the resulting integers must be assigned to variables `cartons` (line 141) and `items` (line 142) using the **assignment operator**, `=`. The assignment operator copies the value of the expression on its right side into the variable on its left side. Line 141 actually performs three actions in sequence. First, it gets the *text* property of `cartonsJTextField` by calling the `getText` method. Then, `Integer.parseInt` converts that value from a `String` to an `int`. Finally, that integer value is placed in the variable `cartons`. Line 141 is read as "`cartons` *is assigned* the integer value returned by `Integer.parseInt( cartonsJTextField.getText() )`." Line 142 assigns the integer value of `itemsJTextField`'s *text* property to the variable `items`.

(cont.)

Assigning user input to variables ——

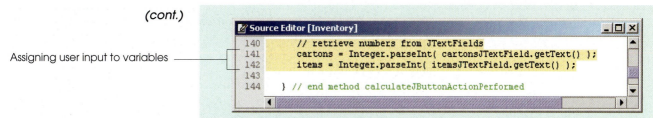

Figure 5.5 Retrieving numerical input from `JTextField`s in event handler `calculateJButtonActionPerformed`.

5. *Saving the application.* Save your modified source code file.

6. *Opening the Command Prompt window and changing directories.* Open the **Command Prompt** window by selecting **Start > Programs > Accessories > Command Prompt**. Change to your working directory by typing `cd C:\SimplyJava\Inventory3`.

7. *Compiling the application.* Compile your application by typing `javac Inventory.java`.

8. *Running the application.* When your application compiles correctly, run it by typing `java Inventory`. Figure 5.6 shows the updated application running. Enter the values 5 and 6 in the two `JTextField`s and press the **Calculate Total** `JButton`. The total will not be displayed in the **Total:** `JTextField` since that code has not been added to your application yet; you will add that code in the following box.

Figure 5.6 Updated **Inventory** application.

9. *Closing the application.* Close your running application by clicking its close button.

10. *Closing the Command Prompt window.* Close the **Command Prompt** window by clicking its close button.

You just learned that variables of type `int` are whole numbers. Variables of type **double** store numbers with a decimal point. These are called **floating-point numbers** and they hold values such as `2.3456`, `0.0` and `-845.4680`. Variables of type `double` can hold much larger (and much smaller) values than variables of type `int`. Types already defined in Java, such as `int`, are known as **primitive types**. Primitive type names are also keywords. The eight primitive types are listed in Fig. 5.7. Recall that keywords are reserved for use by Java, so keywords cannot be used as identifiers. (A complete list of Java keywords is presented in Appendix 16.)

Primitive types

boolean	byte	char	short
int	long	float	double

Figure 5.7 Java primitive types.

Lines 141 and 142 (Fig. 5.5) convert the two values typed by the user into the `JTextField`s to `int`s and assign them to the `cartons` and `items` variables. Now you will use these variables to calculate the number of textbooks received.

Using Variables in a Calculation

1. ***Performing the multiplication operation.*** In your text editor, add a blank line after the end of the last statement you inserted in the previous box (line 142). Then, insert lines 144–145 of Fig. 5.8. The statement in line 145 multiplies the value of the `int` variable `cartons` by the value of the `int` variable `items` and assigns the result to variable `result`, using the assignment operator, `=`. The statement is read as "`result` *is assigned* the value of `cartons * items`." (Most calculations are performed in assignment statements.) When a variable appears in a calculation, the current value of that variable is used in the calculation. This calculation does not modify `cartons` or `items`.

Multiply `cartons` and `items`, then assign the result to the variable `result`

```
143
144          // multiply values input
145          result = cartons * items;
146
147      } // end method calculateJButtonActionPerformed
```

Figure 5.8 Multiplying two variables in an assignment statement.

2. ***Displaying the result.*** Add lines 147–148 of Fig. 5.9 to the `calculateJButtonActionPerformed` event handler. After the calculation is completed, line 148 will display the result of the multiplication operation by setting the *text* property of the output `JTextField`, `totalResultJTextField`. Recall from Tutorial 4 that `String.valueOf` converts a number into a `String` that can be displayed in a `JTextField`.

Display result of calculation in `totalResultJTextField`

```
146
147          // display result in totalResultJTextField
148          totalResultJTextField.setText( String.valueOf( result ) );
149
150      } // end method calculateJButtonActionPerformed
```

Figure 5.9 Displaying the result of the calculation.

3. ***Saving the application.*** Save your modified source code file.

4. ***Opening the Command Prompt window and changing directories.*** Open the **Command Prompt** window by selecting **Start > Programs > Accessories > Command Prompt**. Change to your working directory by typing `cd C:\SimplyJava\Inventory3`.

5. ***Compiling the application.*** Compile your application by typing `javac Inventory.java`.

6. ***Running the application.*** When your application compiles correctly, run it by typing `java Inventory`. Figure 5.10 shows the updated application running. Type 5 in the **Cartons per shipment:** `JTextField` and type 6 in the **Items per carton:** `JTextField`. When you press the **Calculate Total** JButton, the **Total:** `JTextField` displays the result, 30.

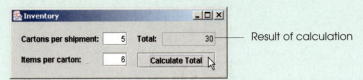

Result of calculation

Figure 5.10 Displaying the multiplication result.

(cont.)

7. ***Closing the application.*** Close your running application by clicking its close button.

8. ***Closing the Command Prompt window.*** Close the **Command Prompt** window by clicking its close button.

SELF-REVIEW

1. The name of a variable must be a _____.
   a) keyword
   b) valid identifier
   c) Both of the above.
   d) None of the above.

2. Types already defined in Java, such as `int`, are known as _____ types.
   a) built up
   b) existing
   c) defined
   d) primitive

Answers: 1) b. 2) d.

5.3 Handling the keyPressed event for a JTextField

You might have noticed that the flaw, or **bug**, mentioned in the application requirements at the beginning of this tutorial remains in your application. Although the `totalResultJTextField` displays the current result, once you enter a new number into either or both of the input `JTextFields`, that result is no longer valid. The result displayed does not become valid again until you click the **Calculate Total** `JButton`, potentially confusing anyone using the application.

Handling the keyPressed Event

1. ***Adding an event handler for the cartonsJTextField's keyPressed event.*** Insert line 155 of Fig. 5.11 into your code. According to the application requirements for this tutorial, the application should clear the value in `totalResultJTextField` every time users change the text in either input `JTextField`. The **keyPressed event** is triggered any time a key is pressed in a `JTextField`. Line 155 uses `setText` to clear the value in `totalResultJ-TextField`. The notation `""` (side-by-side double quotes) in line 155 is called an **empty string**, which is a string value that does not contain any characters. This empty string replaces whatever is stored in `totalResultJText-Field`'s *text* property, thus clearing the result on the screen.

keyPressed event handler ————

Clear totalResultJTextField ————

```
Source Editor [Inventory]
152       // clear totalResultJTextField because the value is now invalid
153       private void cartonsJTextFieldKeyPressed( KeyEvent event )
154       {
155          totalResultJTextField.setText( "" ); // clear output JTextField
156
157       } // end method cartonsJTextFieldKeyPressed
```

Figure 5.11   keyPressed event handler for **Cartons per shipment:** JText-Field.

2. ***Adding an event handler for the itemsJTextField's keyPressed event.*** Since the result should be cleared regardless of which input `JTextField` is changed first, you will also handle the keyPressed event of `items-JTextField`. Insert line 162 of Fig. 5.12 into the new event handler. Notice that this line performs the same task as line 155 of Fig. 5.11. This is because you want the same action, namely the clearing of a `JTextField`, to occur.

(cont.)

Clear `totalResultJTextField` —

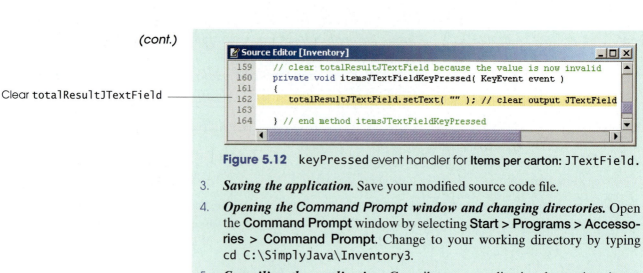

Figure 5.12 keyPressed event handler for **Items per carton:** JTextField.

3. *Saving the application.* Save your modified source code file.

4. *Opening the Command Prompt window and changing directories.* Open the **Command Prompt** window by selecting **Start > Programs > Accessories > Command Prompt.** Change to your working directory by typing `cd C:\SimplyJava\Inventory3`.

5. *Compiling the application.* Compile your application by typing `javac Inventory.java`.

6. *Running the application.* When your application compiles correctly, run it by typing `java Inventory`. Figure 5.13 shows the completed application running. To test the application, enter 8 in the **Cartons per shipment:** JTextField and enter 7 in the **Items per carton:** JTextField. When you click the **Calculate Total** JButton, the number 56 should appear in the output JTextField. Then enter 9 in the **Items per carton:** JTextField to ensure that the keyPressed event handler clears the output JTextField (as shown in Fig. 5.13). Click **Calculate Total** to calculate the new result (72), then change the value in the **Cartons per shipment:** JTextField to ensure that doing so will clear the output JTextField.

output JTextField clears when the value in either input JTextField is changed

Figure 5.13 Testing the completed **Inventory** application.

7. *Closing the application.* Close your running application by clicking its close button.

8. *Closing the Command Prompt window.* Close the **Command Prompt** window by clicking its close button.

Figure 5.14 presents the source code for the enhanced **Inventory** application. The lines of code that you added, viewed or modified in this tutorial are highlighted.

```
1   // Tutorial 5: Inventory.java
2   // Calculates the number of items in a shipment based on the number
3   // of cartons received and the number of items per carton.
4   import java.awt.*;
5   import java.awt.event.*;
6   import javax.swing.*;
7
8   public class Inventory extends JFrame
9   {
10     // JLabel and JTextField for cartons per shipment
11     private JLabel cartonsJLabel;
12     private JTextField cartonsJTextField;
```

Figure 5.14 **Inventory** application code. (Part 1 of 4.)

```
13
14       // JLabel and JTextField for items per carton
15       private JLabel itemsJLabel;
16       private JTextField itemsJTextField;
17
18       // JLabel and JTextField for total items per shipment
19       private JLabel totalJLabel;
20       private JTextField totalResultJTextField;
21
22       // JButton to initiate calculation of total items per shipment
23       private JButton calculateJButton;
24
25       // no-argument constructor
26       public Inventory()
27       {
28          createUserInterface();
29       }
30
31       // create and position GUI components; register event handlers
32       public void createUserInterface()
33       {
34          // get content pane for attaching GUI components
35          Container contentPane = getContentPane();
36
37          // enable explicit positioning of GUI components
38          contentPane.setLayout( null );
39
40          // set up cartonsJLabel
41          cartonsJLabel = new JLabel();
42          cartonsJLabel.setText( "Cartons per shipment:" );
43          cartonsJLabel.setBounds( 16, 16, 130, 21 );
44          contentPane.add( cartonsJLabel );
45
46          // set up cartonsJTextField
47          cartonsJTextField = new JTextField();
48          cartonsJTextField.setText( "0" );
49          cartonsJTextField.setBounds( 148, 16, 40, 21 );
50          cartonsJTextField.setHorizontalAlignment( JTextField.RIGHT );
51          contentPane.add( cartonsJTextField );
52          cartonsJTextField.addKeyListener(
53
54             new KeyAdapter() // anonymous inner class
55             {
56                // method called when user types in cartonsJTextField
57                public void keyPressed( KeyEvent event )
58                {
59                   cartonsJTextFieldKeyPressed( event );
60                }
61
62             } // end anonymous inner class
63
64          ); // end call to addKeyListener
65
66          // set up itemsJLabel
67          itemsJLabel = new JLabel();
68          itemsJLabel.setText( "Items per carton:" );
69          itemsJLabel.setBounds( 16, 48, 104, 21 );
70          contentPane.add( itemsJLabel );
71
```

Figure 5.14   **Inventory** application code. (Part 2 of 4.)

```
72          // set up itemsJTextField
73          itemsJTextField = new JTextField();
74          itemsJTextField.setText( "0" );
75          itemsJTextField.setBounds( 148, 48, 40, 21 );
76          itemsJTextField.setHorizontalAlignment( JTextField.RIGHT );
77          contentPane.add( itemsJTextField );
78          itemsJTextField.addKeyListener(
79
80             new KeyAdapter() // anonymous inner class
81             {
82                // method called when user types in itemsJTextField
83                public void keyPressed( KeyEvent event )
84                {
85                   itemsJTextFieldKeyPressed( event );
86                }
87
88             } // end anonymous inner class
89
90          ); // end call to addKeyListener
91
92          // set up totalJLabel
93          totalJLabel = new JLabel();
94          totalJLabel.setText( "Total:" );
95          totalJLabel.setBounds( 204, 16, 40, 21 );
96          contentPane.add( totalJLabel );
97
98          // set up totalResultJTextField
99          totalResultJTextField = new JTextField();
100         totalResultJTextField.setBounds( 244, 16, 86, 21 );
101         totalResultJTextField.setHorizontalAlignment(
102            JTextField.RIGHT );
103         totalResultJTextField.setEditable( false ); // output only
104         contentPane.add( totalResultJTextField );
105
106         // set up calculateJButton
107         calculateJButton = new JButton();
108         calculateJButton.setText( "Calculate Total" );
109         calculateJButton.setBounds( 204, 48, 126, 24 );
110         contentPane.add( calculateJButton );
111         calculateJButton.addActionListener(
112
113            new ActionListener() // anonymous inner class
114            {
115               // method called when calculateJButton is pressed
116               public void actionPerformed( ActionEvent event )
117               {
118                  calculateJButtonActionPerformed( event );
119               }
120
121            } // end anonymous inner class
122
123         ); // end call to addActionListener
124
125         // set properties of application's window
126         setTitle( "Inventory" ); // set title bar text
127         setSize( 354, 112 );     // set window size
128         setVisible( true );      // display window
129
130      } // end method createUserInterface
```

Figure 5.14 **Inventory** application code. (Part 3 of 4.)

Use keyword **int** to declare variables inside an event handler

Assigning a value to a variable

Calculating a result

Displaying a variable's value

Setting a JTextField's *text* property to the empty string

Setting a JTextField's *text* property to the empty string

```
131
132        // calculate the total items in the shipment
133        private void calculateJButtonActionPerformed( ActionEvent event )
134        {
135            // declare variables
136            int cartons; // stores number of cartons in shipment
137            int items;   // stores number of items per carton
138            int result;  // stores product of cartons and items
139
140            // retrieve numbers from JTextFields
141            cartons = Integer.parseInt( cartonsJTextField.getText() );
142            items = Integer.parseInt( itemsJTextField.getText() );
143
144            // multiply values input
145            result = cartons * items;
146
147            // display result in totalResultJTextField
148            totalResultJTextField.setText( String.valueOf( result ) );
149
150        } // end method calculateJButtonActionPerformed
151
152        // clear totalResultJTextField because the value is now invalid
153        private void cartonsJTextFieldKeyPressed( KeyEvent event )
154        {
155            totalResultJTextField.setText( "" ); // clear output JTextField
156
157        } // end method cartonsJTextFieldKeyPressed
158
159        // clear totalResultJTextField because the value is now invalid
160        private void itemsJTextFieldKeyPressed( KeyEvent event )
161        {
162            totalResultJTextField.setText( "" ); // clear output JTextField
163
164        } // end method itemsJTextFieldKeyPressed
165
166        // main method
167        public static void main( String[] args )
168        {
169            Inventory application = new Inventory();
170            application.setDefaultCloseOperation( JFrame.EXIT_ON_CLOSE );
171
172        } // end method main
173
174    } // end class Inventory
```

Figure 5.14 **Inventory** application code. (Part 4 of 4.)

SELF-REVIEW

1. The _____ is represented by "" in Java.

   a) empty character

   b) empty string

   c) empty value

   d) None of the above.

2. Use the _____ method to clear any text displayed in a JTextField.

   a) clearText

   b) removeText

   c) resetText

   d) setText

Answers: 1) b. 2) d.

5.4 Memory Concepts

Variable names—such as `cartons`, `items` and `result`—correspond to actual locations in the computer's memory. Every variable has a **name**, **type**, **size** and **value**. In the **Inventory** application code listing in Fig. 5.14, when the assignment statement (line 141)

```
cartons = Integer.parseInt( cartonsJTextField.getText() );
```

executes, the user input stored in `cartonsJTextField` is converted to a value of type `int`. This `int` value is placed into the memory location to which the name `cartons` has been assigned. Suppose that the user enters 12 in the **Cartons per shipment:** `JTextField`. This input is stored (in the *text* property) in `cartonsJTextField`. When the user clicks **Calculate Total**, this JButton's event handler executes, making method `Integer.parseInt` convert the user input to an `int` and placing this `int` value into location `cartons`, as shown in Fig. 5.15.

Figure 5.15   Memory location showing name and value of variable `cartons`.

Whenever a value is placed in a memory location, this value replaces the value previously stored in that location. The previous value is overwritten (lost). So the process of writing to a memory location is said to be **destructive**.

Each primitive type in Fig. 5.7 has a size—that is, a number of bytes in memory used to store a value of that type. For instance, an `int` is stored in four bytes of memory and is capable of representing values in the range –2,147,483,648 to +2,147,483,647. For some applications, this range is too small. In such cases, you might use type `long`, which is stored in eight bytes of memory and is capable of representing whole number values in the range –9,223,372,036,854,775,808 to +9,223,372,036,854,775,807. Appendix 17 summarizes each primitive type, its size in bytes and the range of values that can be stored in a variable of that type.

Suppose the user enters 10 in the **Items per carton:** `JTextField` and clicks **Calculate Total**, causing this JButton's event handler to execute. line 142 of Fig. 5.14

```
items = Integer.parseInt( itemsJTextField.getText() );
```

then converts the string stored in `itemsJTextField` to an `int` and places the `int` value 10 into location `items`. Memory then appears as shown in Fig. 5.16.

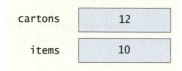

Figure 5.16   Memory locations after assigning values to `cartons` and `items`.

When the **Calculate Total** JButton is clicked, its event handler executes, causing line 145 to multiply these values and place their total into the `result` variable. The statement

```
result = cartons * items;
```

performs the multiplication and replaces (that is, overwrites) `result`'s previous value. After `result` is calculated, the memory appears as shown in Fig. 5.17. Note that the values of `cartons` and `items` appear exactly as they did before they were used in the calculation of `result`. Although these values were used when the computer performed the calculation, they were not overwritten. This illustrates that,

when a value is read from a memory location, the process is **nondestructive** (meaning that the value is not changed).

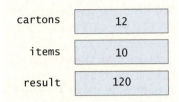

cartons	12
items	10
result	120

Figure 5.17   Memory locations after a multiplication operation.

1. When a value is placed into a memory location, the value _____ the previous value in that location.

   a) copies   b) replaces
   c) adds itself to   d) moves

2. When a value is read from memory, that value is _____.

   a) overwritten   b) replaced with a new value
   c) moved to a new location in memory   d) not changed

Answers: 1) b. 2) d.

5.5 Arithmetic

Most applications perform arithmetic calculations. In the last tutorial, you performed the arithmetic multiplication operation by using the multiplication operator (*). The **arithmetic operators** are summarized in Fig. 5.18. Note the use of various special symbols that are not used in algebra. For example, the **asterisk** (*) indicates multiplication, the **percent sign** (%) represents the **remainder operator** which will be explained shortly, and the **forward slash** (/) represents division.

All arithmetic operators in Fig. 5.18 are binary operators, each requiring two operands. For example, the expression sum + value contains the binary operator + and the two operands sum and value. Java also provides **unary operators**, which are operators that take only one operand. For example, unary versions of plus (+) and minus (–) are provided so that programmers can write expressions such as +9 (a positive number) and –19 (a negative number). [*Note:* Unary plus is rarely used because numbers are positive by default.]

Java operation	Arithmetic operator	Algebraic expression	Java expression
Addition	+	$f + 7$	f + 7
Subtraction	–	$p - c$	p - c
Multiplication	*	bm	b * m
Division	/	x / y or $\frac{x}{y}$ or $x \div y$	x / y
Remainder	%	$r \bmod s$	r % s

Figure 5.18   Arithmetic operators.

Integer division takes two integer (int) operands and yields an integer quotient. For example, the expression 7 / 4 evaluates to 1, and the expression 17 / 5 evaluates to 3. Note that any fractional part of the integer division result is discarded (this is called **truncating**)—no rounding occurs. When floating-point numbers (numbers with decimal points) are used with the division operator, the result is

a floating-point number. For example, the expression 7.0 / 4.0 evaluates to 1.75 and the expression 17.0 / 5.0 evaluates to 3.4.

The remainder operator, %, yields the remainder after division. For example, the expression x % y yields the remainder after x is divided by y. Thus, 7 % 4 yields 3 and 17 % 5 yields 2. This operator is used most commonly with int operands, but it also can be used with other types. The remainder operator can be applied to several interesting problems, such as discovering whether one number is a multiple of another. For example, if a and b are numbers, a % b yields 0 if a is a multiple of b. 8 % 3 yields 2, so 8 is not a multiple of 3. But 8 % 2 and 8 % 4 each yield 0, because 8 is a multiple of both 2 and 4.

Arithmetic expressions in Java must be written in **straight-line form** so that you can type them into a computer. For example, the division of 7.1 by 4.3 is not written

$$\frac{7.1}{4.3}$$

but is written in straight-line form as 7.1 / 4.3.

Parentheses are used in Java expressions in the same manner as in algebraic expressions. For example, to multiply *a* times the quantity *b* + *c*, you write

    a * (b + c)

Java applies the operators in arithmetic expressions in a precise sequence determined by its **rules of operator precedence,** which are generally the same as those followed in algebra. These rules enable Java to apply operators in the correct order. Figure 5.19 lists these rules in order.

Rules of operator precedence

1. ***Unary plus (+) and minus (–) are applied first***. If an expression contains several unary plus and minus operators, these operators are applied from right to left.

2. ***Multiplication (*), division (/) and remainder (%) are applied next***. If an expression contains several multiplication, division and remainder operations, these operators are applied from left to right.

3. ***Addition (+) and subtraction (–) are applied last***. If an expression contains several addition and subtraction operations, these operators are applied from left to right.

Figure 5.19 Rules of operator precedence.

Let's consider several expressions in light of the rules of operator precedence. Each example lists an algebraic expression and its Java equivalent.

The following calculates the average of three numbers:

Algebra: $m = \dfrac{(a+b+c)}{3}$

Java: m = (a + b + c) / 3

As in algebra, parentheses can be used to group expressions for evaluation purposes. The parentheses in the preceding expression are required, because division has higher precedence than addition. The entire quantity (a + b + c) is to be divided by 3. If the parentheses are omitted, you obtain a + b + c / 3, which evaluates as

$$a + b + \frac{c}{3}$$

producing an incorrect result (this is an example of a logic error). Also note that assignment to the variable m occurs last, after the addition.

The following is the equation of a straight line:

Algebra: $y = mx + b$

Java: y = m * x + b

No parentheses are required. The multiplication is applied first, because multiplication has a higher precedence than addition. The assignment occurs last because it has a lower precedence than multiplication and addition. Note that

$$y = mx + b$$

would be a logic error, because mx in java is a valid name for a single variable—mx does not mean "m times x" as it does in algebra.

To develop a better understanding of the rules of operator precedence, consider how the expression $y = ax^2 + bx + c$ is evaluated:

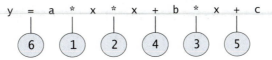

The circled numbers under the statement indicate the order in which Java applies the operators. In Java, x^2 is represented as x * x, because there is no exponentiation operator. Also, note that the assignment operator is applied last because it has a lower precedence than any of the arithmetic operators.

As in algebra, it is acceptable to place unnecessary parentheses in an expression to make the expression easier to read—these parentheses are called **redundant parentheses**. For example, the preceding assignment statement might use redundant parentheses to emphasize terms:

```
y = ( a * x * x ) + ( b * x ) + c
```

Good Programming Practice

The use of redundant parentheses in complex arithmetic expressions can make the expressions easier to read.

SELF-REVIEW

1. Arithmetic expressions in Java must be written _____ to facilitate entering expressions into the computer.

   a) using parentheses   b) on multiple lines
   c) in straight-line form   d) None of the above.

2. The expression to the right of the assignment operator (=) is always evaluated _____ the assignment occurs.

   a) before   b) after
   c) at the same time   d) None of the above.

Answers: 1) c. 2) a.

5.6 Using the Debugger: Breakpoints and the run, stop, cont and print Commands

In Section 2.4, you learned that there are two types of errors—syntax errors and logic errors—and you learned how to eliminate syntax errors from your code.

Logic errors do not prevent the application from compiling successfully, but do cause the application to produce erroneous results when it runs. The Java SDK includes software called a **debugger**, which allows you to monitor the execution of your applications to locate and remove logic errors.

The debugger will be one of your most important application development tools. You begin your study of the debugger by learning about **breakpoints**, which are markers that can be set at any executable line of code. When application execution reaches a breakpoint, execution pauses, allowing you to examine the values of variables and ensure that there are no logic errors. For example, you can examine the value of a variable that stores the result of a calculation to ensure that the calculation was performed correctly. Note that setting a breakpoint at a line of code that is not executable (such as a comment) causes the debugger to display an error message. You will use breakpoints and various debugger commands to examine the values of the variables declared in the event handler calculateJButtonActionPerformed.

Using the Debugger: Breakpoints and the run, stop, cont, clear and print Commands

1. **Opening the Command Prompt *window and changing directories.*** Open the **Command Prompt** window by selecting **Start > Programs > Accessories > Command Prompt**. Change to your working directory by typing `cd C:\SimplyJava\Inventory3`.

2. **Compiling the Inventory application.** The Java debugger works only with `.class` files that were compiled with the **-g** compiler option, which generates debugging information that is used by the debugger to help you debug your applications. Compile the **Inventory** application with the -g command-line option by typing `javac -g Inventory.java`.

3. **Starting the debugger.** In the **Command Prompt**, type **jdb** (Fig. 5.20). This command will start the Java debugger and enable you to use the debugger's features.

Start the Java debugger ——

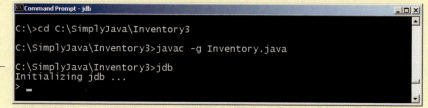

Figure 5.20 Starting the Java debugger.

4. **Running an application in the debugger.** Run the **Inventory** application through the debugger by typing **run** Inventory (Fig. 5.21). When you do not set any breakpoints before running your application in the debugger, the application will run just as it would using the `java` command.

Run the **Inventory** application ——

Inventory application ——

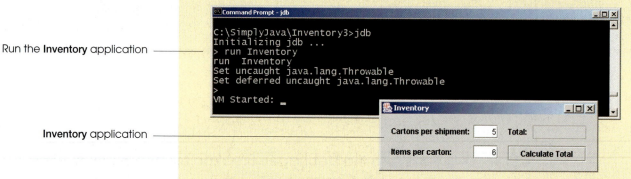

Figure 5.21 Running the **Inventory** application through the debugger.

5. **Closing the running application and restarting the debugger.** To make proper use of the debugger, you normally set at least one breakpoint before running the application. Terminate your running application by clicking the its close button, then restart the debugger by typing jdb (Fig. 5.22).

Restart the debugger ——

Figure 5.22 Restarting the debugger.

(cont.)

6. ***Inserting breakpoints in Java.*** You set a breakpoint at a specific line of code in your application. The line numbers used in these steps are from the source code in Fig. 5.14. Set a breakpoint at line 145 in the source code by typing `stop at Inventory:145` (Fig. 5.23). The **stop command** inserts a breakpoint at the line number specified after the command. You can set as many breakpoints as necessary. Set another breakpoint at line 148 of your code by typing `stop at Inventory:148` (Fig. 5.23). When the application runs, it suspends execution at any line that contains a breakpoint. The application is said to be in **break mode** when the debugger pauses the application's execution. Breakpoints can be set even after the debugger has started.

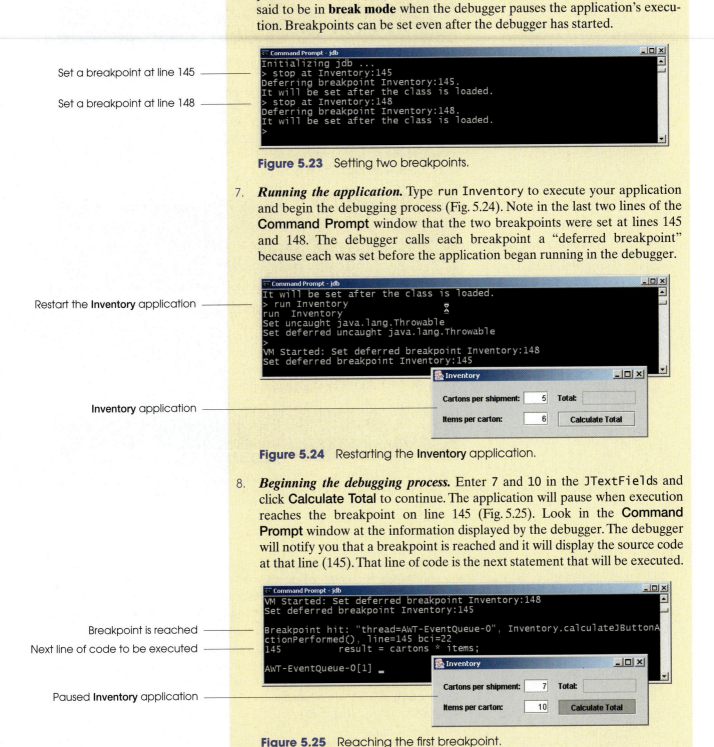

Figure 5.23   Setting two breakpoints.

7. ***Running the application.*** Type `run Inventory` to execute your application and begin the debugging process (Fig. 5.24). Note in the last two lines of the **Command Prompt** window that the two breakpoints were set at lines 145 and 148. The debugger calls each breakpoint a "deferred breakpoint" because each was set before the application began running in the debugger.

Figure 5.24   Restarting the **Inventory** application.

8. ***Beginning the debugging process.*** Enter 7 and 10 in the `JTextFields` and click **Calculate Total** to continue. The application will pause when execution reaches the breakpoint on line 145 (Fig. 5.25). Look in the **Command Prompt** window at the information displayed by the debugger. The debugger will notify you that a breakpoint is reached and it will display the source code at that line (145). That line of code is the next statement that will be executed.

Figure 5.25   Reaching the first breakpoint.

(cont.)

9. ***Using the cont command to resume execution.*** Type **cont**. The application will continue running until the next breakpoint is reached (line 148) at which point the **Command Prompt** window will notify you (Fig. 5.26).

Another breakpoint is reached

```
ᴄˣ Command Prompt - jdb                                              _|□|x|

AWT-EventQueue-0[1] cont
>
Breakpoint hit: "thread=AWT-EventQueue-0", Inventory.calculateJButtonAc
tionPerformed(), line=148 bci=27
148              totalResultJTextField.setText( String.valueOf( result ) );

AWT-EventQueue-0[1]
```

Figure 5.26 Execution reaches the second breakpoint.

10. ***Examining a variable's value.*** Type **print** cartons. The current value stored in the cartons variable will be displayed (Fig. 5.27). The print command allows you to peek inside the computer at the value of one of your variables. This command will help you find and eliminate logic errors in your code. Use the print command to output the values stored in variables cartons, items and result (Fig. 5.27).

The value in cartons

The value in items

The value in result

```
ᴄˣ Command Prompt - jdb                                              _|□|x|

AWT-EventQueue-0[1] print cartons
 cartons = 7
AWT-EventQueue-0[1] print items
 items = 10
AWT-EventQueue-0[1] print result
 result = 70
AWT-EventQueue-0[1]
```

Figure 5.27 Examine the values of three variables.

11. ***Continuing application execution.*** Type cont to continue the application's execution. There are no more breakpoints, so the application continues executing and displays the output in the **Total:** JTextField (Fig. 5.28). At this point, the application is no longer in break mode.

Execution resumes

```
ᴄˣ Command Prompt - jdb                                              _|□|x|
 result = 70
AWT-EventQueue-0[1] cont
> ▮
```

```
🐾 Inventory                                    _|□|x|

Cartons per shipment:    7    Total:         70

Items per carton:       10    Calculate Total
```

Figure 5.28 Continue application execution.

12. ***Removing a breakpoint.*** You can display a list of all of the breakpoints in the application by typing **clear** (Fig. 5.29). Remove the first breakpoint by typing clear Inventory:145. Remove the second breakpoint (line 148) as well. Now type clear to list the remaining breakpoints in the application. The debugger should indicate that no breakpoints are set (Fig. 5.29).

13. ***Executing the application without breakpoints.*** Enter the values 4 and 9 in the two JTextFields of your running **Inventory** application and press the **Calculate Total** JButton. If the two breakpoints were removed successfully, the new output (36) will be displayed in the output JTextField without the application halting (Fig. 5.30).

(cont.)

Two breakpoints are set ⎯⎯⎯⎯⎯

Clear breakpoint at line 145 ⎯⎯⎯⎯⎯

Clear breakpoint at line 148 ⎯⎯⎯⎯⎯

Both breakpoints are removed ⎯⎯⎯⎯⎯

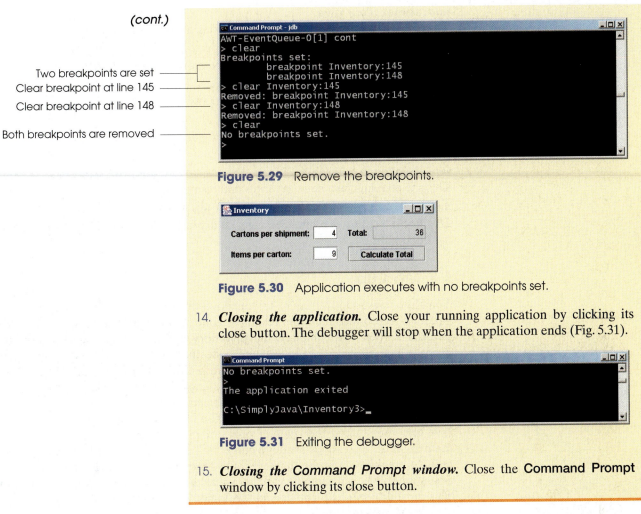

Figure 5.29   Remove the breakpoints.

Figure 5.30   Application executes with no breakpoints set.

14. ***Closing the application.*** Close your running application by clicking its close button. The debugger will stop when the application ends (Fig. 5.31).

Figure 5.31   Exiting the debugger.

15. ***Closing the Command Prompt window.*** Close the **Command Prompt** window by clicking its close button.

In this section, you learned how to enable the debugger and set breakpoints so that you can examine variables with the `print` command while an application is running. You also learned how to use the `cont` command to continue execution after an application suspends execution at a breakpoint and how to use the `clear` command to remove breakpoints.

SELF-REVIEW

1. A breakpoint cannot be set at a(n) _____.

    a) comment

    b) executable line of code

    c) assignment statement

    d) arithmetic statement

2. When application execution suspends at a breakpoint, the next statement to be executed is the statement _____ the breakpoint.

    a) before

    b) after

    c) at

    d) None of the above.

Answers: 1) a. 2) c.

5.7 Internet and Web Resources

Please take a moment to visit each of these Web sites.

java.sun.com/j2se
This site contains information about the Java 2 Platform, Standard Edition (J2SE). This book uses J2SE version 1.4.1. The site contains an overview of all of the features of J2SE and includes links to articles, news and related technologies.

www.aewnet.com/java
This site includes links to training, directories, articles and Java sites.

www.java.ittoolbox.com
This site contains Java news, technical discussions, code and tutorials.

java.sun.com/search
This site offers a search engine designed to answer your Java questions.

www.ibiblio.org/javafaq
This site offers Java news, frequently asked questions on commonly used APIs and other Java resources.

www.developer.com/java
This site contains Java news, tutorials and resources.

java.sun.com/products/jpda/doc/soljdb.html
This site describes the Java debugger and presents additional information about how to use it.

5.8 Wrap-Up

You have now added variables to your **Inventory** application. You began by using variables to produce the same results as your previous **Inventory** application from Tutorial 4. Then you enhanced the **Inventory** application, using the keyPressed event, which allowed you to execute code that cleared the value in the output JTextField when the user changed a value in either of the two input JTextFields.

You learned about memory concepts, including how variables are read and written. You will apply these concepts to the applications that you will build in later tutorials, which rely heavily on variables. You learned how to perform arithmetic in Java and you studied the rules of operator precedence to help ensure that your mathematical expressions evaluate correctly. Finally, you learned how to insert and remove breakpoints in the debugger. Breakpoints allow you to pause application execution so you can examine variable values with the debugger's print command. This capability will help you find and fix logic errors in your applications.

In the next tutorial, you will design a graphical user interface and write code to create a wage calculator. You will learn pseudocode, an informal language that can help you design your applications. You will use the debugger's print command to evaluate Java expressions, and you will learn to use the debugger's set command to change the values of variables in your application.

SKILLS SUMMARY

Declaring a Variable

- Specify a variable type, such as int, for each variable.
- Use a valid identifier as a variable name.

Handling a JTextField's keyPressed Event

- Insert code into the JTextField's event handler, which executes when the user types in a JTextField.

Reading a Value from a Memory Location

- Use the variable's name on the right side of an assignment statement or in an expression.

Replacing a Value in a Memory Location

- Use the variable name, followed by the assignment operator (=), followed by an expression giving the new value.

Representing Positive and Negative Numbers

- Use the unary versions of plus (+) and minus (-).

Performing Arithmetic Operations

- Write arithmetic expressions in Java in straight-line form.

- Use the rules of operator precedence to determine the order in which operators will be applied.
- Use operator + to perform addition.
- Use operator – to perform subtraction.
- Use operator * to perform multiplication.
- Use operator / to perform division.
- Use operator % to calculate the remainder after division.
- Use operator = to assign the results of a calculation to a variable.
- Use parentheses, (), to group expressions for evaluation purposes.

Running the Debugger

- From a **Command Prompt**, type jdb to start the debugger.

Running an Application through the Debugger

- While running the debugger, type the run command and specify the class name of the application to run.

Setting a Breakpoint

- While running the debugger, use the stop command and specify the class name followed by a colon and the line number at which to set a breakpoint.

Resuming Application Execution after Entering Break Mode

- While running the Java debugger, use the cont command to resume execution.

Examining a Variable While at a Breakpoint

- While at a breakpoint, use the print command followed by the name of the variable whose contents you wish to view.

Viewing a List of an Application's Breakpoints

- While running the debugger, use the clear command to list the breakpoints.

Removing a Breakpoint

- While running the debugger, use the clear command and specify the class name followed by a colon and the line number to remove a breakpoint.

KEY TERMS   **arithmetic operators**—The operators +, -, *, / and % used for performing calculations.

assignment operator—The assignment operator, =, copies the value of the expression on its right side into the variable on its left side.

asterisk (*)—An arithmetic operator that indicates multiplication.

break mode—Debugger mode the application is in when execution stops at a breakpoint.

breakpoint—A marker that can be set in the debugger at any executable line of source code, causing the application to pause when it reaches the specified line of code. One reason to set a breakpoint is to be able to examine the values of variables at that point in the application's execution.

bug—A flaw in an application that prevents the application from executing correctly.

clear debugger command—Command that removes a breakpoint.

cont debugger command—Command that resumes program execution after a breakpoint is reached while debugging.

debugger—Software that allows you to monitor the execution of your applications to locate and remove logic errors.

declare a variable—Specify the type and name of a variable to be used in an application.

declaration—Code that specifies the name and type of a variable.

destructive—The process of writing to a memory location in which the previous value is overwritten or lost.

double—Type that is used to store floating-point numbers.

empty string ("")—A string that does not contain any characters.

forward slash (/)—An arithmetic operator that indicates division.

floating-point number—A number with a decimal point such as 2.3456, 0.0 and –845.4680.

-g compiler option—Causes the compiler to generates debugging information that is used by the debugger to help you debug your applications.

initialization value—The beginning value of a variable.

integer—A whole number, such as 919, –11 or 0.

int type—The type that stores integer values.

jdb—Starts the Java debugger when typed at the **Command Prompt**.

keyPressed event—The event that occurs when any key is pressed in a JTextField.

logic error—An error that does not prevent the application from compiling successfully, but does cause the application to produce erroneous results when it runs.

name of a variable—The identifier used in an application to access or modify a variable's value.

nondestructive—The process of reading from a memory location, which does not modify the value in that location.

% (remainder operator)—This operator yields the remainder after division.

primitive type—A type already defined in Java. The primitive types are boolean, byte, char, short, int, long, float and double.

print debugger command—Command that displays the value of a variable when an application is stopped at a breakpoint during execution in the debugger.

redundant parentheses—Extra parentheses used in calculations to clarify the order in which calculations are performed. Such parentheses can be removed without affecting the results of the calculations.

remainder operator (%)—An arithmetic operator that calculates the remainder of a division.

rules of operator precedence—Rules that determine the precise order in which operators are applied in an expression.

run debugger command—Command to begin executing an application with the Java debugger.

size of a variable—The number of bytes required to store a value of the variable's type. For example, an int is stored in four bytes of memory and a double is stored in eight bytes.

stop debugger command—Command that sets a breakpoint at the specified line of executable code.

straight-line form—The manner in which arithmetic expressions must be written so they can be typed in Java code.

truncating in integer division—Any fractional part of an integer division result is discarded.

type of a variable—Specifies the kind of data that can be stored in a variable and the range of values that can be stored. For instance, a int variable can store only whole numbers in the range –2,147,483,648 to +2,147,483,647.

unary operator—An operator with only one operand (such as unary + or unary -).

value of a variable—The piece of data that is stored in a variable's location in memory.

variable—A location in the computer's memory where a value can be stored for use by an application.

JAVA LIBRARY REFERENCE

JTextField This component allows the user to input information and can be used to display results to the user.

■ *In action*

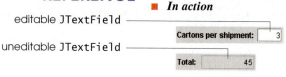

editable JTextField
uneditable JTextField

■ *Events*

keyPressed—Raised when any key is pressed in the JTextField.

■ *Methods*

getText—Returns the text displayed in the JTextField.

setBounds—Sets the location and size of the JTextField.

setEditable—Specifies whether users can edit the JTextField. A true value (the default) means the JTextField is an editable input JTextField and a false value means the JTextField is an uneditable output JTextField.

setHorizontalAlignment—Specifies how the text is aligned within the JTextField.

setText—Specifies the text displayed in the JTextField.

MULTIPLE-CHOICE QUESTIONS

5.1 Parentheses that are added to an expression simply to make it easier to read are known as _____ parentheses.

a) necessary

b) redundant

c) embedded

d) nested

5.2 The _____ operator performs division.

a) /

b) \

c) %

d) *

5.3 Every variable has a _____.

a) name

b) type

c) Both of the above.

d) Neither of the above.

5.4 In Java, use _____ to force the order of evaluation of operators.

a) parentheses

b) variables

c) the debugger

d) memory

5.5 If an expression contains several multiplication, division and remainder operators, they are performed from _____.

a) right to left

b) left to right

c) Both of the above.

d) Neither of the above.

5.6 Reading a value from a variable is a _____ process.

a) destructive

b) nondestructive

c) overwriting

d) None of the above.

5.7 Pressing a key in a JTextField raises the _____ event.

a) textTyped

b) valueChanged

c) pressedKey

d) keyPressed

5.8 The debugger command _____ sets a breakpoint at an executable line of source code in an application.

a) stop

b) run

c) print

d) clear

5.9 Variables used to store integer values should be declared with keyword _____.

a) integer

b) int

c) intVariable

d) Int

5.10 The debugger command _____ allows you to "peek into the computer" and look at the value of a variable.

a) value

b) variable

c) print

d) peek

EXERCISES

5.11 *(Simple Encryption Application)* This application uses a simple technique to encrypt a number. Encryption is the process of modifying data so that only those intended to receive the data can undo the changes and view the original data. The user inputs in a JTextField the number to be encrypted—this is often called the "plain text" value. The application then multiplies the number by 7 and adds 5 to encrypt the original number—this new value is often called the "cypher text" value. The application displays the encrypted number in an

uneditable JTextField as shown in Fig. 5.32. A user who receives the encrypted number and who knows the encryption algorithm could determine the original number (25) by subtracting 5 from 180 (to get 175) and dividing by 7 to get 25. Reconstructing the original number from the encrypted number is called decryption.

Figure 5.32 Result of completed **Simple Encryption** application.

a) *Copying the template to your working directory.* Copy the directory C:\Examples\ Tutorial05\Exercises\SimpleEncryption to your C:\SimplyJava directory.

b) *Opening the template file.* Open the SimpleEncryption.java file in your text editor.

c) *Coding the encryptJButtonActionPerformed event handler.* Scroll to the event handler encryptJButtonActionPerformed (lines 98–101). Insert a statement that gets the number in the enterJTextField, converts the number to an int and assigns the value to int variable plainText. Next, insert a statement that multiplies the number stored in variable plainText by 7 and adds 5, then stores the result in int variable cypherText. Finally, insert a statement that displays the value of cypherText in encryptedJTextField.

d) *Clearing the result when a new value is input by the user.* Locate the event handler enterJTextFieldKeyPressed (it appears immediately after the event handler encryptJButtonActionPerformed) in the template source code. In the body of the event handler, insert a statement that clears the **Encrypted number:** JTextField (named encryptedJTextField) whenever the user enters new input.

e) *Saving the application.* Save your modified source code file.

f) *Opening the Command Prompt window and changing directories.* Open the **Command Prompt** window by selecting **Start > Programs > Accessories > Command Prompt**. Change to your working directory by typing cd C:\SimplyJava\Simple-Encryption.

g) *Compiling the completed application.* Compile your application by typing javac SimpleEncryption.java.

h) *Running the completed application.* When your application compiles correctly, run it by typing java SimpleEncryption. Type 25 in the **Enter number to encrypt:** JTextField, then press the **Encrypt** JButton. Ensure that the encrypted value 180 appears in the **Encrypted number:** JTextField.

5.12 *(Temperature Conversion Application)* Write an application that converts a Celsius temperature, *C*, to its equivalent Fahrenheit temperature, *F*. Figure 5.33 displays the completed application. Use the following formula:

$$F = \frac{9}{5}C + 32$$

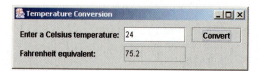

Figure 5.33 Completed **Temperature Conversion** application.

a) *Copying the template to your working directory.* Copy the directory C:\Examples\ Tutorial05\Exercises\TemperatureConversion to your C:\SimplyJava directory.

b) *Opening the template file.* Open the TemperatureConversion.java file in your text editor.

c) *Clearing the result when a new value is input by the user.* Scroll to the event handler celsiusJTextFieldKeyPressed (lines 99–102). In the body of the event handler,

insert a statement that clears the **Fahrenheit equivalent:** JTextField (named fahr-enheitJTextField) whenever the user enters new input.

d) ***Coding the convertJButtonActionPerformed event handler.*** Locate the event handler convertJButtonActionPerformed (immediately after the event handler celsiusJTextFieldKeyPressed). In its body, insert a statement that gets the number in the celsiusJTextField, converts the number to an int and assigns the value to int variable celsius. Next, insert a statement that performs the conversion calculation and assigns the result to the double variable fahrenheit as follows:

```
double fahrenheit = 9.0 / 5.0 * celsius + 32;
```

Finally, insert a statement that displays the value of fahrenheit in fahrenheit-JTextField.

e) ***Saving the application.*** Save your modified source code file.

f) ***Opening the Command Prompt window and changing directories.*** Open the **Command Prompt** window by selecting **Start > Programs > Accessories > Command Prompt**. Change to your working directory by typing cd C:\SimplyJava\TemperatureConversion.

g) ***Compiling the completed application.*** Compile your application by typing javac TemperatureConversion.java.

h) ***Running the completed application.*** When your application compiles correctly, run it by typing java TemperatureConversion. Type 24 in the **Enter a Celsius temperature:** JTextField, then press the **Convert** JButton. Ensure that the converted value 75.2 appears in the **Fahrenheit equivalent:** JTextField.

5.13 *(Simple Calculator Application)* In this exercise, you will add functionality to a simple calculator application. The calculator will allow a user to enter two numbers in the input JTextFields. There will be four JButtons, labeled +, -, / and *. When the user clicks the JButton labeled as + (addition), - (subtraction), * (multiplication) or / (division), the application will perform that operation on the numbers in the **Enter first number:** and **Enter second number:** input JTextFields and display the resulting the **Result:** output JTextField. Figure 5.34 displays the completed calculator.

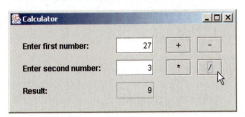

Figure 5.34   Result of **Calculator** application.

a) ***Copying the template to your working directory.*** Copy the directory C:\Examples\ Tutorial05\Exercises\SimpleCalculator to your C:\SimplyJava directory.

b) ***Opening the template file.*** Open the SimpleCalculator.java file in your text editor.

c) ***Code the + JButton event handler.*** Scroll to the addJButtonActionPerformed event handler (lines 215–218). After line 216 insert statements that obtain the user input from firstNumberJTextField and secondNumberJTextField, convert those numbers to int values and assign the numbers to int variables number1 and number2, respectively. Next, insert a statement that adds the numbers and assigns the result to int variable result. Finally, insert a statement that displays the value of result in resultJTextField.

d) ***Code the - JButton event handler.*** Locate the subtractJButtonActionPerformed event handler (immediately following addJButtonActionPerformed). In the body of the event handler, insert statements that obtain the user input from firstNumber-JTextField and secondNumberJTextField, convert those numbers to int values and assign the numbers to int variables number1 and number2, respectively. Next, insert a statement that subtracts the second number from the first number and assigns the result to int variable result. Finally, insert a statement that displays the value of result in resultJTextField.

e) *Code the * JButton event handler.* Locate the multiplyJButtonActionPerformed event handler (immediately following subtractJButtonActionPerformed). In the body of the event handler, insert statements that obtain the user input from first-NumberJTextField and secondNumberJTextField, convert those numbers to int values and assign the numbers to int variables number1 and number2, respectively. Next, insert a statement that multiplies the numbers and assigns the result to int variable result. Finally, insert a statement that displays the value of result in resultJTextField.

f) *Code the / JButton event handler.* Locate the divideJButtonActionPerformed event handler (immediately following multiplyJButtonActionPerformed). In the body of the event handler, insert statements that obtain the user input from first-NumberJTextField and secondNumberJTextField, convert those numbers to int values and assign the numbers to int variables number1 and number2, respectively. Next, insert a statement that divides the first number by the second number and assigns the result to int variable result. Finally, insert a statement that displays the value of result in resultJTextField.

g) *Saving the application.* Save your modified source code file.

h) *Opening the Command Prompt window and changing directories.* Open the **Command Prompt** window by selecting **Start > Programs > Accessories > Command Prompt**. Change to your working directory by typing cd C:\SimplyJava\Simple-Calculator.

i) *Compiling the completed application.* Compile your application by typing javac SimpleCalculator.java.

j) *Running the completed application.* When your application compiles correctly, run it by typing java SimpleCalculator. Test each calculation to ensure that you implemented the event handlers properly.

What does this code do? ▶ 5.14 This code modifies values number1, number2 and result. What are the final values of these variables?

```
1   int number1;
2   int number2;
3   int result;
4
5   number1 = 5 * ( 4 + 6 );
6   number2 = 2 * 2;
7   result = number1 / number2;
```

What's wrong with this code? ▶ 5.15 Find the error(s) in the following code, which uses variables to perform a calculation.

```
1   int number1;
2   int number2;
3   int result;
4
5   number1 = (4 * 6 - 4) / (10 % 4 - 2);
6   number2 = (16 / 3) - 2 * 6 + 1;
7   result = number1 - number2;
```

Using the Debugger ▶ 5.16 *(Average Three Numbers)* You have just written an application that takes three numbers as input in JTextFields, stores the three numbers in variables and then finds the average of the numbers. The output is displayed in an uneditable JTextField (see Fig. 5.35, which displays the incorrect output). You soon realize, however, that the number displayed in the **Average is:** JTextField is not the average, but rather a number that does not make sense given the input. Use the debugger to help locate and remove this error.

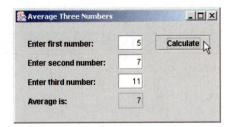

Figure 5.35 Average Three Numbers application.

a) *Copying the template to your working directory.* Copy the directory C:\Examples\Tutorial05\Exercises\AverageDebugging to your C:\SimplyJava directory.

b) *Opening the Command Prompt window and changing directories.* Open the **Command Prompt** window by selecting **Start > Programs > Accessories > Command Prompt**. Change to your working directory by typing cd C:\SimplyJava\AverageDebugging.

c) *Running the application.* Run the **Average Three Numbers** application by typing java Average. Type 5, 7 and 11 in the three input JTextFields. View the output to observe that it is incorrect. The average of these three numbers should be 7 in integer arithmetic. (Recall from Section 5.5 that integer division yields an integer result.)

d) *Compiling with the -g option.* Compile your application for use in the debugger by typing javac -g Average.java.

e) *Starting the debugger.* Close the application and start the debugger by typing jdb.

f) *Setting breakpoints.* Set breakpoints in the calculateJButtonActionPerformed event handler at lines 137 and 140. Remember, breakpoints are set by typing stop at Average: followed immediately by the line number. Run the application again, and use the debugger to help find the logic error(s). Type 5, 7 and 11 in the three input JTextFields, then press the **Calculate** JButton. The program will stop executing at the first breakpoint. Use the cont command to continue execution until the next breakpoint. Then, inspect the values of the variables number1, number2, number3 and result.

g) *Finding and correcting the error(s).* Once you have found the logic error(s) in calculateJButtonActionPerformed (lines 126–142), open Average.java in your text editor. Modify the code in calculateJButtonActionPerformed so that it correctly calculates the average of three numbers and test the application again.

Programming Challenge ▶

5.17 *(Digit Extraction)* Complete an application that allows the user to enter a five-digit number into a JTextField. Your application should then separate the number into its individual digits and display each digit in five uneditable JTextFields (Fig. 5.36). All of the code you need to write should go inside the enterJButtonActionPerformed event handler. This event handler is declared in lines 124–127 of the template file DigitExtractor.java. Before you begin, copy the C:\Examples\Tutorial04\Exercises\DigitExtractor directory to your C:\SimplyJava directory. You should start writing your code at line 126 in the file. Obtain the number input by the user in enterNumberJTextField, convert it to an int and store it in int variable number. [*Hint:* You can use the % operator to extract the ones digit from a number. For instance, 12345 % 10 is 5. You can use division (/) to "peel off" digits from a number. For instance, 12345 / 10 is 1234. This allows you to treat the 4 in 12345 as a ones digit. Now you can isolate the 4 by using the % operator. Apply this technique to the rest of the digits.]

Figure 5.36 Digit Extractor application GUI.

TUTORIAL

6

Wage Calculator Application

Introducing Algorithms, Pseudocode and Program Control

Before you write an application, it is essential to have a thorough understanding of the problem you need to solve. This will help you carefully plan your approach to finding a solution. When writing an application, it is equally important to recognize the types of building blocks that are available and to use proven application-construction principles. In this tutorial, you will learn the theory and principles of **structured programming**. Structured programming is a technique for organizing program control to help you develop applications that are easy to understand, debug and modify. The techniques presented are applicable to most high-level languages, including Java.

6.1 Test-Driving the Wage Calculator Application

In this tutorial, you will build a **Wage Calculator** application that enables you to input an employee's hourly wage and hours worked to calculate the employee's wages for a week. This application must meet the following requirements:

> ### Application Requirements
>
> *A company needs an application that calculates the gross wages per week for each of its employees. Each employee's weekly salary is based on the employee's number of hours worked and hourly wage. A standard work week is 40 hours. Any time worked over 40 hours in a week is considered "overtime," and employees earn time-and-a-half for the extra hours. Create an application that accepts one employee's number of hours worked and hourly wage, and calculates the employee's total (gross) wages for the week.*

This application calculates gross wages from an employee's hourly wage and hours worked per week. If an employee has worked 40 or fewer hours, the employee is paid regular wages. The calculation differs if the employee has worked more than the standard 40-hour work week. In this tutorial, you will learn a programming tool known as a **control statement** that allows you to make this distinction and perform different calculations based on different user inputs. You begin by test-driving the completed **Wage Calculator** application. Then, you will learn the additional Java technologies you will need to create your own version of this application.

Test-Driving the Wage Calculator Application

1. *Locating the completed application.* Open the **Command Prompt** window by selecting **Start > Programs > Accessories > Command Prompt.** Change to your completed **Wage Calculator** application directory by typing cd C:\Examples\Tutorial06\CompletedApplication\WageCalculator.

2. *Running the Wage Calculator application.* Type java WageCalculator in the **Command Prompt** window to run the application (Fig. 6.1).

Figure 6.1　Running the **Wage Calculator** application.

3. *Enter the employee's hourly wage.* Enter **10** in the **Hourly wage:** JTextField.

4. *Enter the number of hours the employee worked.* Enter **45** in the **Hours worked:** JTextField.

5. *Calculate the employee's gross earnings.* Click the **Calculate** JButton. The result (**$475.00**) is displayed in the **Gross wages:** output JTextField (Fig. 6.2). Notice that the employee's wages for one week are the sum of the wages for the standard 40-hour work week (40 * 10) and the overtime pay (5 * 10 * 1.5).

Figure 6.2　Calculating wages by clicking the **Calculate** JButton.

6. *Closing the application.* Close your running application by clicking its close button.

7. *Closing the Command Prompt window.* Close the **Command Prompt** window by clicking its close button.

6.2 Algorithms

Computing problems can be solved by executing a series of actions in a specific order. A procedure for solving a problem, in terms of:

1. the **actions** to be executed and

2. the **order** in which these actions are to be executed

is called an **algorithm**. The following example demonstrates the importance of correctly specifying the order in which the actions are to be executed. Consider the "rise-and-shine algorithm" followed by one junior executive for getting out of bed and going to work: (1) get out of bed, (2) take off pajamas, (3) take a shower, (4) get

dressed, (5) eat breakfast and (6) carpool to work. This routine prepares the executive for a productive day at the office.

However, suppose that the executive performs the same steps in a slightly different order: (1) get out of bed, (2) take off pajamas, (3) get dressed, (4) take a shower, (5) eat breakfast and (6) carpool to work. In this case, our junior executive shows up for work soaking wet.

Program control refers to the task of executing an application's statements in the correct order. In this tutorial, you will begin to investigate Java's program-control capabilities.

SELF-REVIEW

1. _____ refer(s) to the task of executing an application's statements in the correct order.

   a) Actions   b) Program control

   c) Control statements   d) GUI design

2. A(n) _____ is a procedure for solving a problem in terms of the actions to be executed and the order in which these actions are to be executed.

   a) chart   b) control statement

   c) algorithm   d) ordered list

Answers: 1) b. 2) c.

6.3 Pseudocode

Pseudocode is an informal language that helps you develop algorithms. The pseudocode you will learn is particularly useful in the development of algorithms that will be converted to structured programming portions of Java applications. Pseudocode resembles everyday English; it is convenient and user-friendly, but it is not an actual computer programming language.

Pseudocode statements are not executed on computers. Rather, pseudocode helps you "think out" an application before attempting to write it in a programming language, such as Java. In this tutorial, you will see several examples of pseudocode.

The style of pseudocode that you will learn consists solely of characters, so you can create and modify pseudocode conveniently by using your text editor. A carefully prepared pseudocode program can be converted easily to a corresponding Java application. Much of this conversion is as simple as replacing pseudocode statements with their Java equivalents. Now let's look at an example of a pseudocode statement:

   Assign 0 to the counter

This pseudocode statement specifies an easy to understand task. You can put several such statements together to form an algorithm that can be used to meet application requirements. When the pseudocode algorithm has been completed, you can then convert pseudocode statements to their equivalent Java statements. The pseudocode statement above, for instance, can be converted to the following Java statement:

```
counter = 0;
```

Pseudocode normally describes only **executable statements**, which are the actions that are performed when the corresponding Java application is run. An example of a programming statement that is not executable is a declaration. The declaration

```
int counter;
```

informs the compiler of `counter`'s type and instructs the compiler to reserve space in memory for this variable. The declaration does not cause any action (such as

Software Design Tip

Pseudocode helps you conceptualize an application during the application design process. Pseudocode statements can be converted to Java at a later point.

input, output or a calculation) to occur when the application executes, so you would not include this information in the pseudocode even though each variable must be declared before it is used in an application.

SELF-REVIEW

1. _____ is an artificial and informal language that helps programmers develop algorithms.

   a) Pseudocode   b) Java-Speak

   c) Notation   d) Executable

2. Pseudocode _____.

   a) usually describes only declarations   b) is executed on computers

   c) usually describes only executable lines   d) usually describes declarations and
       of code   executable lines of code

Answers: 1) a. 2) c.

6.4 Control Statements

Normally, statements in an application are executed one after another in the order in which they are written. This is called **sequential execution**. However, Java allows you to specify that the next statement to be executed might not be the next one in sequence. A **transfer of control** occurs when the next statement to be executed does not come immediately after the currently executing statement. This is common in computer applications.

All applications can be written in terms of only three forms of control: **sequence**, **selection** and **repetition**. Unless directed to act otherwise, the computer executes Java statements sequentially—that is, one after the other in the order in which they appear in the application. The **activity diagram** in Fig. 6.3 illustrates two statements that execute in sequence. In this case, two calculations are performed in order. The activity diagram presents a graphical representation of the algorithm.

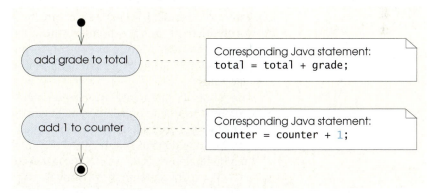

Figure 6.3 Sequence statement activity diagram.

Activity diagrams are part of the **Unified Modeling Language (UML)**—an industry standard for modeling software systems. An activity diagram models the **activity** (also called the **workflow**) of a portion of a software system. An activity might include a portion of an algorithm, such as the sequence of two statements in Fig. 6.3. Activity diagrams are composed of special-purpose symbols, such as **action-state symbols** (rectangles with their left and right sides replaced with arcs curving outward), **diamonds** and **small circles**. These symbols are connected by **transition arrows**, which represent the flow of the activity. Figure 6.3 does not include any diamond symbols—these will be used in later activity diagrams.

Like pseudocode, activity diagrams help programmers develop and represent algorithms. Activity diagrams clearly show how control statements operate.

Consider the activity diagram for the sequence statement in Fig. 6.3. The activity diagram contains two **action states**, which represent actions to perform. Each action state contains an **action expression**—for example, "add grade to total" or "add 1 to counter"—which specifies a particular action to perform. Action expressions are similar to pseudocode. The arrows in the activity diagram, called transition arrows, represent **transitions**, which indicate the order in which the actions represented by the action states occur. The application that implements the activities illustrated by Fig. 6.3 first adds grade to total, then adds 1 to counter.

The **solid circle** located at the top of the activity diagram represents the activity's **initial state**—the beginning of the workflow, before the application performs the activities. The solid circle surrounded by a hollow circle that appears at the bottom of the activity diagram represents the **final state**—the end of the workflow, after the application performs its activities.

Notice, in Fig. 6.3, the rectangles with the upper-right corners folded over. These look like sheets of paper and are called **notes** in the UML. Notes are like comments in Java applications—they are explanatory remarks that describe the purpose of symbols in the diagram. Figure 6.3 uses UML notes to show the Java code that the programmer might associate with each action state in the activity diagram. A **dotted line** connects each note to the element that the note describes. Activity diagrams normally do not show the Java code that implements the activity, but we use notes here to show you how the diagram relates to Java code.

Java provides three types of **selection statements**, which you will learn in this tutorial and in Tutorial 11. The if statement is a **single-selection statement** because it selects or ignores a single action to execute. The if...else statement is called a **double-selection statement** because it selects between two different actions. The switch statement (discussed in Tutorial 11) is called a **multiple-selection statement** because it selects among many different actions or sequences of actions.

Java provides three types of **repetition statements**—while, do...while and for—to execute statements in an application repeatedly. The while repetition statement is covered in Tutorial 8, do...while is covered in Tutorial 9 and for is covered in Tutorial 10. The words if, else, switch, while, do and for are all Java keywords—Appendix E includes a complete list of Java keywords. Most of Java's keywords and their uses are discussed throughout this book.

So, Java has three forms of control—sequence, selection and repetition. Each Java application is formed by combining as many of each type of control statement as is necessary.

Java control statements are **single-entry/single-exit control statements**—each has one entry point and one exit point. Such control statements make it easy to build applications—the control statements are attached to one another by connecting the exit point of one control statement to the entry point of the next. This is similar to stacking building blocks, so we call it **control-statement stacking**. The only other way to connect control statements is through **control-statement nesting**, whereby one control statement is placed inside another. Thus, algorithms in Java applications are constructed from only three forms of control (sequence, selection and repetition) combined in only two ways (stacking and nesting). This is a model of simplicity.

SELF-REVIEW

1. All Java applications can be written in terms of _____ types of program control.

   a) one   b) two
   c) three   d) four

2. The process of application statements executing one after another in the order in which they are written is called _____.

   a) transfer of control   b) sequential execution
   c) workflow   d) None of the above.

Answers: 1) c. 2) b.

6.5 if Selection Statement

A selection statement chooses among alternative courses of action in an application. The **if** selection statement performs (selects) an action based on a condition. A **condition** is an expression with a true or false value that is used to make a decision. A condition is evaluated (that is, tested) to determine whether its value is true or false. These values are of type **boolean** and are specified in Java code by using the keywords **true** and **false**. Sometimes a condition is referred to as a **boolean expression**. If the condition evaluates to true, the action specified by the if statement will execute. If the condition evaluates to false, the action specified by the if statement will be skipped. For example, suppose that the passing grade on a test is 60 (out of 100). The pseudocode statement

> If student's grade is greater than or equal to 60
>   Display "Passed"

determines whether the condition "student's grade is greater than or equal to 60" is true or false. If the condition is true, then "Passed" is displayed, and the next pseudocode statement in order is "performed." (Remember that pseudocode is not a real programming language, so pseudocode "programs" do not actually execute on computers.) If the condition is false, the display statement is ignored, and the next pseudocode statement in order is performed.

The preceding pseudocode *if* statement may be written in Java as

```
if ( studentGrade >= 60 )
{
    gradeDisplayJLabel.setText( "Passed" );
}
```

Good Programming Practice

Always using braces in an if statement helps prevent their accidental omission when the if statement's body contains more than one statement.

Notice that the Java code corresponds closely to the pseudocode, demonstrating the usefulness of pseudocode as a program-development tool. The body (sometimes called a **block**) of the if statement contains a statement that displays the string "Passed" in a JLabel. The left brace symbol "{" begins the body of an if statement, and the right brace symbol "}" closes the body of an if statement. The body of an if statement can specify a single action or a sequence of actions (that is, many statements). The braces are required only when the body of an if statement contains more than one statement. We suggest, however, that you always use braces to delimit the body of an if statement. To avoid omitting one or both of the braces, some programmers type the beginning and ending braces of a block even before typing the individual statements in the braces.

Good Programming Practice

Indent the body of if statements to improve readability.

Notice the indentation of the statement in the body of the if statement. Such indentation makes it easier for you and others to read your application code. The Java compiler ignores white space, such as spaces, tabs and newlines used for indentation and vertical spacing, unless the white space is contained in strings.

The condition in the parentheses after keyword if determines whether the statement(s) in the body of the if statement will execute. If the condition is true, the body of the if statement executes. If the condition is false, the body does not execute. Conditions in if statements can be formed by using the **equality operators** and **relational operators**, which are summarized in Fig. 6.4. The relational and equality operators all have the same level of precedence. Appendix A contains the complete operator precedence chart.

Common Programming Error

It is a syntax error to add spaces between the symbols in the operators !=, >= and <= (as in ! =, > =, < =).

Common Programming Error

Reversal of the symbols in the operators !=, >= and <= (as in =!, =>, =<) is a syntax error.

Common Programming Error

Using the assignment operator, =, when the equality operator, ==, is intended is a syntax error (unless the the operands are type `boolean`).

Algebraic equality or relational operators	Java equality or relational operators	Example of Java condition	Meaning of Java condition
Relational operators			
>	>	x > y	x is greater than y
<	<	x < y	x is less than y
≥	>=	x >= y	x is greater than or equal to y
≤	<=	x <= y	x is less than or equal to y
Equality operators			
=	==	x == y	x is equal to y
≠	!=	x != y	x is not equal to y

Figure 6.4 Equality and relational operators.

Figure 6.5 uses a UML activity diagram to illustrate the single-selection `if` statement. This diagram contains what is perhaps the most important symbol in an activity diagram—the diamond, or **decision symbol**, which indicates that a decision is to be made. Note the two expressions in square brackets above or next to the arrows leading from the decision symbol—these are called **guard conditions**. Each transition arrow emerging from a decision symbol has a guard condition. If a particular guard condition is true, the workflow enters the action state to which that transition arrow points. For example, in Fig. 6.5, if the grade is greater than or equal to 60, the application displays "Passed", then transitions to the final state of this activity. If the grade is less than 60, the application immediately transitions to the final state without displaying a message (because the grade was a failing grade—59 or less). Only one guard condition associated with a particular decision symbol can be true at once.

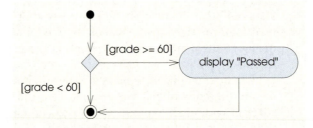

Figure 6.5 `if` single-selection statement UML activity diagram.

Note that the `if` statement diagrammed in Fig. 6.5, is a single-entry/single-exit statement. The UML activity diagrams for the remaining control statements also contain (aside from small circle symbols and transition arrows) only action-state symbols, indicating actions to be performed, and diamond symbols. Representing control statements in this way emphasizes the **action/decision model of programming**. To understand the process of structured programming better, you can envision bins, each containing many copies of different types of control statements in the form of UML activity diagrams. The UML activity diagrams in each bin are empty, meaning that nothing is written in the action-state symbols and no guard conditions are written next to the decision symbols. Your task is to assemble an application, using as many appropriate UML activity diagrams as the algorithm demands, combining the control statements in only two possible ways (stacking or nesting) and filling in the actions and decisions (with the decisions' guard conditions) in a manner appropriate to the algorithm. Again, each particular UML activity diagram is implemented in Java as a control statement.

1. Which of the following `if` statements correctly displays that a student received an A on an exam if the score was 90 or above?

    a) ```
       if (studentGrade != 90)
       {
           displayJLabel.setText("Student received an A");
       }
       ```

    b) ```
       if ( studentGrade > 90 )
       {
           displayJLabel.setText( "Student received an A" );
       }
       ```

    c) ```
       if (studentGrade <= 90)
       {
           displayJLabel.setText("Student received an A");
       }
       ```

    d) ```
       if ( studentGrade >= 90 )
       {
           displayJLabel.setText( "Student received an A" );
       }
       ```

2. The symbol _____ is not a Java operator.

    a) `*`   b) `!=`

    c) `<>`   d) `%`

Answers: 1) d. 2) c.

6.6 `if...else` Selection Statement

As you have learned, the `if` selection statement performs an indicated action (or sequence of actions) only when the condition evaluates to true; otherwise, the action (or sequence of actions) is skipped. The **`if...else`** selection statement performs an action (or sequence of actions) if a condition is true and performs a different action (or sequence of actions) if the condition is false. For this reason, `if...else` is known as a double-selection statement. For example, the pseudocode statement

> If student's grade is greater than or equal to 60
>   Display "Passed"
> else
>   Display "Failed"

displays "*Passed*" if the student's grade is greater than or equal to 60, but displays "*Failed*" if the student's grade is less than 60. In either case, after output occurs, the next pseudocode statement in sequence is "performed."

The preceding pseudocode *If...else* statement may be written in Java as

```
if ( studentGrade >= 60 )
{
    displayJLabel.setText( "Passed" );
}
else
{
    displayJLabel.setText( "Failed" );
}
```

Good Programming Practice

Apply a standard indentation convention consistently throughout your applications to enhance readability.

Good Programming Practice

Indent both body statements of an `if...else` statement to improve readability.

Note that the body of the **else** clause is indented so that it lines up with the indented body of the `if` clause. A standard indentation convention should be applied consistently throughout your applications. It is difficult to read code that does not use uniform spacing conventions. The `if...else` selection statement follows the same general syntax as the `if` statement. The `else` keyword and any related statements are placed following the end of the `if` statement's body.

Figure 6.6 uses a UML activity diagram to illustrate the flow of control in the `if...else` double-selection statement. Once again, note that (besides the initial state, transition arrows and final state) the only symbols in the activity diagram rep-

resent action states and decisions. In this example, the grade is either less than 60 or greater than or equal to 60. If the grade is less than 60, the application displays "Failed". If the grade is greater than or equal to 60, the application displays "Passed". We continue to emphasize this action/decision model of computing. Imagine again a deep bin containing as many empty UML activity diagrams representing double-selection statements as might be needed to build any Java application. Your job as a programmer is to assemble these double-selection statements (by stacking and nesting) with any other control statements required by the algorithm. You fill in the action states and decision symbols with action expressions and guard conditions appropriate to the algorithm.

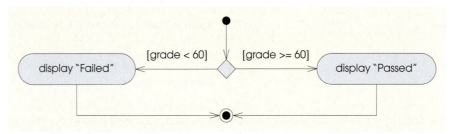

Figure 6.6 if...else double-selection statement UML activity diagram.

Good Programming Practice

If there are several levels of indentation, each level should be indented further to the right by the same amount of space.

Nested if...else statements test for multiple conditions by placing if...else statements inside other if...else statements. For example, the pseudocode in Fig. 6.7 will display "A" for exam grades greater than or equal to 90, "B" for grades in the range 80–89, "C" for grades in the range 70–79, "D" for grades in the range 60–69 and "F" for all other grades.

```
if student's grade is greater than or equal to 90
    Display "A"
else
    If student's grade is greater than or equal to 80
        Display "B"
    else
        If student's grade is greater than or equal to 70
            Display "C"
        else
            If student's grade is greater than or equal to 60
                Display "D"
            else
                Display "F"
```

Figure 6.7 Pseudocode for an application that displays a student's grades.

Common Programming Error

Following an else clause with another else or else if clause is a syntax error.

The pseudocode in Fig. 6.7 may be written in Java as shown in Fig. 6.8. If studentGrade is greater than or equal to 90, the first condition evaluates to true and the statement displayJLabel.setText("A"); is executed. Notice that, with a value for studentGrade greater than or equal to 90, the remaining three conditions would also evaluate to true. These conditions, however, are never evaluated, because they are placed within the else portion of the outer if...else statement. Because the first condition is true, all statements within the else clause are skipped. Now assume studentGrade contains the value 75. The first condition evaluates to false, so the program will execute the statements within the else clause. This else clause also contains an if...else statement, with the condition studentGrade >= 80. This condition evaluates to false, causing the statements in the following else clause to execute. This else clause contains yet another if...else statement, with the condition studentGrade >= 70. This condition is true, causing the statement displayJLabel.setText("C"); to execute. The else clause of this if...else statement is then skipped.

```
if ( studentGrade >= 90 )
{
   displayJLabel.setText( "A" );
}
else
   if ( studentGrade >= 80 )
   {
      displayJLabel.setText( "B" );
   }
   else
      if ( studentGrade >= 70 )
      {
         displayJLabel.setText( "C" );
      }
      else
         if ( studentGrade >= 60 )
         {
            displayJLabel.setText( "D" );
         }
         else
         {
            displayJLabel.setText( "F" );
         }
```

Figure 6.8　Java code converted from the pseudocode in Fig. 6.7.

Java programmers, when writing nested if...else statements such as the one in Fig. 6.8, often use the format shown in Fig. 6.9.

```
if ( studentGrade >= 90 )
{
   displayJLabel.setText( "A" );
}
else if ( studentGrade >= 80 )
{
   displayJLabel.setText( "B" );
}
else if ( studentGrade >= 70 )
{
   displayJLabel.setText( "C" );
}
else if ( studentGrade >= 60 )
{
   displayJLabel.setText( "D" );
}
else
{
   displayJLabel.setText( "F" );
}
```

Figure 6.9　Nested if...else statements with alternative indentation.

The nested if...else statements in Fig. 6.8 and Fig. 6.9 are equivalent, but the latter statement is preferred by some programmers because it avoids deep indentation of the code. Such deep indentation often leaves little room on a line, forcing statements to be split and decreasing code readability. Some programmers feel that the code in Fig. 6.8 better emphasizes the nesting of the if...else statements.

SELF-REVIEW　　1. if...else is a _____-selection statement.

　　　　a) single　　　　　　　　　　　　b) double
　　　　c) triple　　　　　　　　　　　　d) nested

2. Placing an if...else statement inside another if...else statement is an example of
_____.

     a) nesting if...else statements   b) stacking if...else statements

     c) creating sequential if...else statements   d) None of the above.

Answers: 1) b. 2) a.

6.7 Constructing the Wage Calculator Application

Now you will build your **Wage Calculator** application by using the if...else statement, which will allow you to calculate only regular wages or to include overtime pay based on the number of hours worked. The following pseudocode describes the basic operation of the **Wage Calculator** application that calculates and displays the employee's pay when the user clicks the **Calculate** JButton.

> When the user clicks the Calculate JButton:
>   Input the hourly wage
>   Input the number of hours worked
>
>   If the number of hours worked is less than or equal to 40 hours
>   Gross wages equals hours worked times hourly wage
>   else
>   Gross wages equals 40 times hourly wage plus
>   hours above 40 times hourly wage times 1.5
>
>   Display gross wages

This book teaches programming by using an application-driven approach in which all topics are presented in graphical user interface (GUI) applications. Users interact with GUI applications by clicking JButtons, changing text in JTextFields, pressing keys on the keyboard and the like. Each of these user interactions generates an event in Java on a particular GUI component. For instance, clicking a JButton generates an actionPerformed event for that JButton. This style of programming is referred to as **object-oriented, event-driven (OOED) programming**—events happen on components (objects) and cause actions. The way you program these applications is by placing your code within methods that handle events. In this way, the desired results of the code occur in response to specific events.

Before developing each application, you take it for a test drive. Here you interact with the application's GUI and begin to understand the purpose of the application. You also learn the GUI components that will be required to obtain user input and display results. Frequently, when determining the requirements of an application, you will design a prototype of the application's GUI. As you develop each application for the remainder of this textbook, you will use two application development aids—pseudocode and **Action/Component/Event (ACE) tables**. Pseudocode describes the algorithm—that is, the actions to be performed and the order in which those actions should be performed. As you read the pseudocode, you will see that there are specific actions to perform, such as "Calculate gross wages," "Input the hourly wage" and "Display gross wages." An ACE table helps relate the events that occur on GUI components with the actions that should be performed in response to those events.

Figure 6.10 presents the Action/Component/Event (ACE) table for the **Wage Calculator** application. Sometimes, when creating an ACE table, actions in the pseudocode can be lifted and inserted directly in the left column of the table—for instance, "Display gross wages." In other cases, one action might be represented with a substantial amount of pseudocode—for instance, calculating an employee's gross wages requires most of the pseudocode that describes the **Wage Calculator** application. It would be tedious to list all this pseudocode in the table. In such cases, you might use a shorthand representation of the action, such as "Calculate gross wages." The left column sometimes includes actions that are not represented in the pseudocode at all. For example, the action "Label the application's components" is

not part of the pseudocode, but is an important part of constructing this application. The middle column specifies the GUI component or class associated with the action. The right column specifies the event that initiates the action.

*Action/Component/
Event (ACE) Table for the
Wage Calculator
Application*

Action	Component	Event
Label the application's components	`hourlyWageJLabel` `hoursWorkedJLabel` `grossWagesJLabel`	Application is run
	`calculateJButton`	User clicks **Calculate** `JButton`
Input the hourly wage	`hourlyWageJTextField`	
Input the number of hours worked	`hoursWorkedJTextField`	
If the number of hours worked is less than or equal to 40 hours Gross wages equals hours worked times hourly wage else Gross wages equals 40 times hourly wage plus hours above 40 times hourly wage times 1.5		
Display gross wages	`grossWagesJTextField`	

Figure 6.10   ACE table for the **Wage Calculator** application.

The `JLabel`s in the first row of Fig. 6.10 label the application's components for the user. The `setText` method will be used with each `JLabel` to specify the text displayed on the `JLabel`. In the second row, the user clicks `calculateJButton` to calculate the gross wages for an employee. In the third column of this row, the phrase "User clicks **Calculate** `JButton`" indicates the event that initiates the calculation. The `JTextField`s in the third and fourth rows will obtain input from the user. For each `JTextField`, the `getText` method will be used to obtain the input from the `JTextField`. The second to last row shows the `if...else` statement that determines the gross wages. The `setText` method of the component in the last row, `grossWagesJTextField`, displays the gross wages.

You will now use the pseudocode and the ACE table to complete your own version of this application. The following box will guide you through the process of declaring the variables you'll need to calculate the employee's wages in the **Calculate** `JButton`'s event handler (`calculateJButtonActionPerformed`). You will use the variables to store input from the user. Then, you will use those variables in an `if...else` statement to compute the employee's gross wages. Finally, you will display the gross wages. If you forget to add code for this `actionPerformed` event, the application will not respond when the user clicks the **Calculate** `JButton`.

*Implementing the
Calculate JButton's
actionPerformed
Event Handler*

1. ***Copying the template to your working directory.*** Copy the `C:\Examples\Tutorial06\TemplateApplication\WageCalculator` directory to your `C:\SimplyJava` directory.

2. ***Opening the Wage Calculator application's template file.*** Open the template file `WageCalculator.java` in your text editor.

3. ***Locating the `calculateJButtonActionPerformed` event handler.*** In this example, the event handler calculates the gross wages when the user clicks the **Calculate** `JButton`. Lines 109–112 of Fig. 6.11 show the initially empty event handler. Next, you will write the code for this event handler so that your application will indeed calculate and display the gross wages.

(cont.)

Calculate JButton event handler ——

```
Source Editor [WageCalculator]                                    _ □ ×
108    // method called when user presses calculateJButton
109    private void calculateJButtonActionPerformed( ActionEvent event )
110    {
111
112    } // end method calculateJButtonActionPerformed
```

Figure 6.11 `calculateJButtonActionPerformed` event handler (initially empty).

Notice the comments on lines 108 and 112. In lines 110 and 112, the "{" and "}" symbols indicate the body of the event handler `calculateJButtonActionPerformed`. The comment after the "}" symbol documents the end of the event handler.

4. ***Declaring variables and obtaining inputs from the JTextFields.*** This application uses primitive type `double`. As you learned in Tutorial 5, type **double** is used to represent floating-point numbers (that is, numbers with decimal points). Because an employee's hourly wage and hours worked are often fractional numbers, the data type `int` is not appropriate for this application. Insert lines 111–117 of Fig. 6.12 into `calculateJButtonActionPerformed`. The statement in lines 112–113 declares `double` variable `hourlyWage` and assigns to it the `double` value of the `hourlyWageJTextField`'s *text* property. The statement in lines 116–117 declares `double` variable `hoursWorked` and assigns to it the `double` value of the `hoursWorkedJTextField`'s *text* property. Notice that lines 113 and 117 both use the **Double.parseDouble** method to convert a `String` to a `double` value.

Declare variable `hourlyWage` and assign it the user input from `hourlyWageJTextField` ——

Declare variable `hoursWorked` and assign it the user input from `hoursWorkedJTextField` ——

```
Source Editor [WageCalculator *]                                    _ □ ×
108    // method called when user presses calculateJButton
109    private void calculateJButtonActionPerformed( ActionEvent event )
110    {
111        // get hourly wage
112        double hourlyWage =
113            Double.parseDouble( hourlyWageJTextField.getText() );
114
115        // get number of hours worked this week
116        double hoursWorked =
117            Double.parseDouble( hoursWorkedJTextField.getText() );
118
119    } // end method calculateJButtonActionPerformed
```

Figure 6.12 Assigning user input to variables.

5. ***Declaring a constant.*** Add lines 119–121 of Fig. 6.13 in the event handler `calculateJButtonActionPerformed`. Line 121 contains a **constant**—a variable whose value cannot be changed after its initial declaration. Constants are declared by preceding the data type with the keyword **final**. In this case, you assign to the constant `HOUR_LIMIT` the maximum number of hours worked before mandatory overtime pay (`40.0`). Notice that you capitalize the constant's name to emphasize that it is a constant.

Good Programming Practice

Capitalize all letters in a constant's name to make the constant stand out in the application. Separate each word in the name of a constant with an underscore to make the identifier easier to read.

Constant declaration ——

```
Source Editor [WageCalculator *]                                    _ □ ×
119        // constant for maximum hours employee can
120        // work before being paid for overtime
121        final double HOUR_LIMIT = 40.0;
```

Figure 6.13 Creating a constant.

(cont.)

6. ***Declaring a variable to store the gross wages.*** Add lines 123–124 of Fig. 6.14 to calculateJButtonActionPerformed. Line 124 contains a variable declaration for the variable wages, which you will use to store the employee's gross wages for the week.

Declare **double** variable wages ———

```
Source Editor [WageCalculator *]                          _ □ ×
119        // constant for maximum hours employee can
120        // work before being paid for overtime
121        final double HOUR_LIMIT = 40.0;
122
123        // gross wages for week; calculated in if...else statement
124        double wages;
```

Figure 6.14   Declaring a variable of type **double**.

7. ***Determining wages based on hours worked.*** Add lines 126–140 of Fig. 6.15 in the event handler calculateJButtonActionPerformed. This if...else statement determines whether the employee worked overtime and calculates the gross wages accordingly.

if...else statement to calculate wages ———

```
Source Editor [WageCalculator *]                          _ □ ×
123        // gross wages for week; calculated in if...else statement
124        double wages;
125
126        // determine gross wages
127        if ( hoursWorked <= HOUR_LIMIT )
128        {
129            // regular wages for HOUR_LIMIT (40) hours or less
130            wages = ( hoursWorked * hourlyWage );
131        }
132        else // worked more than HOUR_LIMIT (40) hours
133        {
134            // wages for first HOUR_LIMIT (40) hours
135            wages = HOUR_LIMIT * hourlyWage;
136
137            // add time-and-a-half for overtime hours
138            wages = wages +
139                ( hoursWorked - HOUR_LIMIT ) * ( 1.5 * hourlyWage );
140        }
141
```

Figure 6.15   if...else statement that calculates gross wages.

Line 127 determines whether the value stored in hoursWorked is less than or equal to HOUR_LIMIT (40.0, specified in line 121). If it is, then line 130 calculates the product of hoursWorked and hourlyWage and assigns the result to wages.

If, on the other hand, hoursWorked is greater than HOUR_LIMIT, then execution proceeds to the else clause in lines 132–140. Line 135 computes the wages for the hours worked up to the limit set by HOUR_LIMIT (that is, 40.0) and assigns the result to wages. Lines 138–139 calculate the user's overtime pay and add it to the wages calculated in line 135. The expression in line 139 first determines the user's overtime hours (by using the calculation hoursWorked - HOUR_LIMIT), then multiplies the overtime hours by the product of 1.5 times the user's hourly wage. The overtime pay is then added to the value of wages, and the result is assigned to wages.

8. ***Displaying the result.*** Insert lines 142–143 of Fig. 6.16 in calculate-JButtonActionPerformed. Line 143 converts the value in the variable wages to a String and uses that String to set the *text* property of the grossWagesJTextField.

9. ***Saving the application.*** Save your modified source code file.

(cont.)

Displaying output

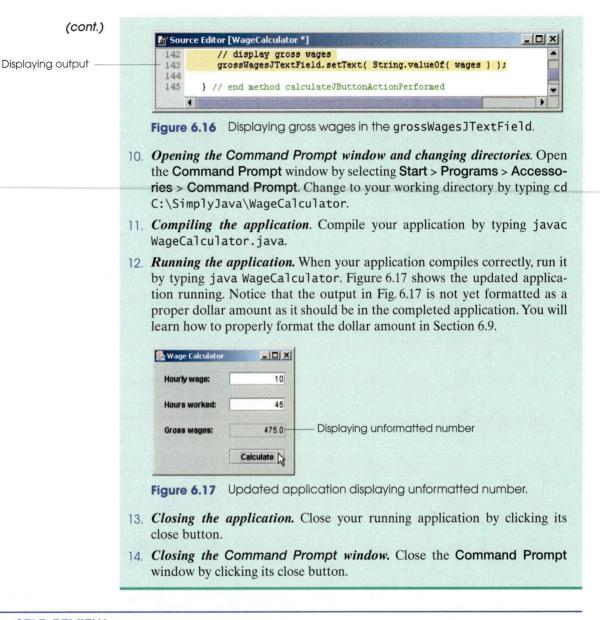

Figure 6.16 Displaying gross wages in the `grossWagesJTextField`.

10. ***Opening the Command Prompt window and changing directories.*** Open the **Command Prompt** window by selecting **Start > Programs > Accessories > Command Prompt**. Change to your working directory by typing cd `C:\SimplyJava\WageCalculator`.

11. ***Compiling the application.*** Compile your application by typing javac `WageCalculator.java`.

12. ***Running the application.*** When your application compiles correctly, run it by typing java `WageCalculator`. Figure 6.17 shows the updated application running. Notice that the output in Fig. 6.17 is not yet formatted as a proper dollar amount as it should be in the completed application. You will learn how to properly format the dollar amount in Section 6.9.

Displaying unformatted number

Figure 6.17 Updated application displaying unformatted number.

13. ***Closing the application.*** Close your running application by clicking its close button.

14. ***Closing the Command Prompt window.*** Close the **Command Prompt** window by clicking its close button.

SELF-REVIEW

1. The double type can be used to store _____.
   a) letters and digits   b) numbers with decimal points
   c) strings   d) None of the above.

2. Constants are declared with the keyword _____.
   a) fixed   b) constant
   c) final   d) const

Answers: 1) b. 2) c.

6.8 Assignment Operators

Java provides several **assignment operators** for abbreviating assignment statements. For example, the statement

```
value = value + 3;
```

which adds 3 to the value in the variable value, can be abbreviated with the addition assignment operator += as

```
value += 3;
```

The **addition assignment (+=) operator** adds the value of its right operand to the current value of its left operand and stores the result in the left operand. Java provides assignment operators for several binary operators, including +, -, *, / and %. When an addition assignment statement is evaluated, the expression to the right of the operator is always evaluated first, then added to the variable on the left. Figure 6.18 includes the arithmetic assignment operators, sample expressions using these operators and explanations.

Assignment operators	Sample expression	Explanation	Assigns to c
Assume c = 4			
+=	c += 7	c = c + 7	11
-=	c -= 3	c = c - 3	1
*=	c *= 4	c = c * 4	16
/=	c /= 2	c = c / 2	2
%=	c %= 3	c = c % 3	1

Figure 6.18 Arithmetic assignment operators.

Next, you will learn how to abbreviate your overtime wages calculation with the += operator. When you run the application again, you will notice that the application runs the same as before.

Using the Addition Assignment Operator

1. ***Opening the Wage Calculator application's template file.*** Open the template file WageCalculator.java in your text editor.

2. ***Using the addition assignment operator.*** Replace lines 138–139 of Fig. 6.15 with lines 138–139 of Fig. 6.19. The new statement uses the addition assignment operator, making it unnecessary to include the wages variable in both the left and right operands of the assignment. The statement still performs the same action—the overtime pay for the employee is calculated and added to the regular wages earned.

Addition assignment operator

```
 Source Editor [WageCalculator *]                                  _ □ ×
137              // add time-and-a-half for hours above HOUR_LIMIT (40)
138          wages +=
139              ( hoursWorked - HOUR_LIMIT ) * ( 1.5 * hourlyWage );
140       }
141
142      } // end method calculateJButtonActionPerformed
```

Figure 6.19   Using the addition assignment operator in a calculation.

3. ***Saving the application.*** Save your modified source code file.

4. ***Opening the Command Prompt window and changing directories.*** Open the **Command Prompt** window by selecting **Start > Programs > Accessories > Command Prompt**. Change to your working directory by typing cd C:\SimplyJava\WageCalculator.

5. ***Compiling the application.*** Compile your application by typing javac WageCalculator.java.

6. ***Running the application.*** When your application compiles correctly, run it by typing java WageCalculator. Notice that the application executes as it did in the previous box. Once you have finished testing the application, close it.

7. ***Closing the application.*** Close your running application by clicking its close button.

1. The *= operator _____.

a) adds the value of its right operand to the value of its left operand and stores the result in its left operand

b) creates a new variable and assigns the value of the right operand to that variable

c) multiplies the value of its left operand by the value of its right operand and stores the result in its left operand

d) None of the above.

2. If the variable x contains the value 5, what value will x contain after the expression x -= 3 is executed?

a) 3   b) 5

c) 7   d) 2

Answers: 1) c. 2) d.

6.9 Formatting Text

There are several ways to format output in Java. In this section, you will use class **DecimalFormat**'s method **format** to control how text displays. Modifying the appearance of text for display purposes is known as text **formatting**. DecimalFormat is a class that is used to format decimal numbers. Method format of DecimalFormat takes a double argument and returns a String that contains formatted double values.

Recall that your **Wage Calculator** application does not display the result of its calculation with the appropriate decimal places and dollar sign that you saw when test-driving the application. Next, you will learn how to apply currency formatting to the value in the **Gross wages:** JTextField.

Formatting the Gross Wages

1. ***Opening the Wage Calculator application's template file.*** Open the template file WageCalculator.java in your text editor.

2. ***Modifying the Calculate JButton's actionPerformed event.*** Replace lines 142–143 of Fig. 6.16 with lines 142–146 of Fig. 6.20. Line 143 creates the DecimalFormat variable dollars, which is initialized with the pattern "$0.00". Each 0 specifies a required digit position in the formatted floating-point number. This particular format indicates that every number formatted with dollars will have a dollar sign followed by at least one digit to the left of the decimal point and exactly two digits to the right of the decimal point. In line 146, the expression dollars.format(wages) formats the value of variable wages. The resulting String is used as the value of grossWagesJTextField's *text* property. The formatted number is rounded to the nearest hundredth.

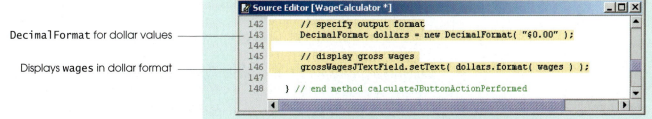

DecimalFormat for dollar values ——

Displays wages in dollar format ——

Figure 6.20   Using the format method of DecimalFormat to display the gross wages as currency.

3. ***Saving the application.*** Save your modified source code file.

(cont.)

4. ***Opening a Command Prompt window and changing directories.*** Open the **Command Prompt** window by selecting **Start > Programs > Accessories > Command Prompt**. Change to your working directory by typing `cd C:\SimplyJava\WageCalculator`.

5. ***Compiling the application.*** Compile your application by typing `javac WageCalculator.java`.

6. ***Running the application.*** When your application compiles correctly, run it by typing `java WageCalculator`. Figure 6.21 shows the completed application running with a properly formatted number.

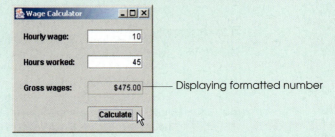

Figure 6.21 Completed application displaying formatted wages.

7. ***Closing the application.*** Close your running application by clicking its close button.

8. ***Closing the Command Prompt window.*** Close the **Command Prompt** window by clicking its close button.

Good Programming Practice

Place a blank line above and below each `if...else` statement to help make your applications more readable. In general, do this for all control statements.

Figure 6.22 shows the completed source code of the **Wage Calculator** application. The lines of code that you added, viewed or modified in this tutorial are highlighted. In lines 125–141, notice the use of blank lines above and below the `if...else` statement. Such vertical spacing makes your applications easier to read.

```java
1   // Tutorial 6: WageCalculator.java
2   // This application inputs the hourly wage and number of hours
3   // worked for an employee, then calculates the employee's gross
4   // wages (with overtime for hours worked over 40 hours).
5   import java.awt.*;
6   import java.awt.event.*;
7   import javax.swing.*;
8   import java.text.*;
9
10  public class WageCalculator extends JFrame
11  {
12     // JLabel and JTextField for wage per hour
13     private JLabel hourlyWageJLabel;
14     private JTextField hourlyWageJTextField;
15
16     // JLabel and JTextField for hours worked in a week
17     private JLabel hoursWorkedJLabel;
18     private JTextField hoursWorkedJTextField;
19
20     // JLabel and JTextField for gross wages
21     private JLabel grossWagesJLabel;
22     private JTextField grossWagesJTextField;
23
24     // JButton to initiate wage calculation
25     private JButton calculateJButton;
```

Figure 6.22 **Wage Calculator** application completed source code. (Part 1 of 4.)

```
26
27        // no-argument constructor
28        public WageCalculator()
29        {
30           createUserInterface();
31        }
32
33        // create and position GUI components; register event handlers
34        public void createUserInterface()
35        {
36           // get content pane for attaching GUI components
37           Container contentPane = getContentPane();
38
39           // enable explicit positioning of GUI components
40           contentPane.setLayout( null );
41
42           // set up hourlyWageJLabel
43           hourlyWageJLabel = new JLabel();
44           hourlyWageJLabel.setBounds( 16, 16, 90, 21 );
45           hourlyWageJLabel.setText( "Hourly wage:" );
46           contentPane.add( hourlyWageJLabel );
47
48           // set up hourlyWageJTextField
49           hourlyWageJTextField = new JTextField();
50           hourlyWageJTextField.setBounds( 120, 16, 90, 21 );
51           hourlyWageJTextField.setHorizontalAlignment(
52              JTextField.RIGHT );
53           contentPane.add( hourlyWageJTextField );
54
55           // set up hoursWorkedJLabel
56           hoursWorkedJLabel = new JLabel();
57           hoursWorkedJLabel.setBounds( 16, 56, 90, 21 );
58           hoursWorkedJLabel.setText( "Hours worked:" );
59           contentPane.add( hoursWorkedJLabel );
60
61           // set up hoursWorkedJTextField
62           hoursWorkedJTextField = new JTextField();
63           hoursWorkedJTextField.setBounds( 120, 56, 90, 21 );
64           hoursWorkedJTextField.setHorizontalAlignment(
65              JTextField.RIGHT );
66           contentPane.add( hoursWorkedJTextField );
67
68           // set up grossWagesJLabel
69           grossWagesJLabel = new JLabel();
70           grossWagesJLabel.setBounds( 16, 96, 90, 21 );
71           grossWagesJLabel.setText( "Gross wages:" );
72           contentPane.add( grossWagesJLabel );
73
74           // set up grossWagesJTextField
75           grossWagesJTextField = new JTextField();
76           grossWagesJTextField.setBounds( 120, 96, 90, 21 );
77           grossWagesJTextField.setHorizontalAlignment(
78              JTextField.RIGHT );
79           grossWagesJTextField.setEditable( false );
80           contentPane.add( grossWagesJTextField );
81
82           // set up calculateJButton
83           calculateJButton = new JButton();
```

Figure 6.22 **Wage Calculator** application completed source code. (Part 2 of 4.)

```
84        calculateJButton.setBounds( 120, 136, 90, 24 );
85        calculateJButton.setText( "Calculate" );
86        contentPane.add( calculateJButton );
87        calculateJButton.addActionListener(
88
89           new ActionListener() // anonymous inner class
90           {
91              // event handler called when calculateJButton is pressed
92              public void actionPerformed ( ActionEvent event )
93              {
94                 calculateJButtonActionPerformed( event );
95              }
96
97           } // end anonymous inner class
98
99        ); // end call to addActionListener
100
101       // set properties of application's window
102       setTitle( "Wage Calculator" ); // set title bar text
103       setSize( 230, 200 );            // set window size
104       setVisible( true );             // display window
105
106    } // end method createUserInterface
107
108    // method called when user presses calculateJButton
109    private void calculateJButtonActionPerformed( ActionEvent event )
110    {
111       // get hourly wage
112       double hourlyWage =
113          Double.parseDouble( hourlyWageJTextField.getText() );
114
115       // get number of hours worked this week
116       double hoursWorked =
117          Double.parseDouble( hoursWorkedJTextField.getText() );
118
119       // constant for maximum hours employee can
120       // work before being paid for overtime
121       final double HOUR_LIMIT = 40.0;
122
123       // gross wages for week; calculated in if...else statement
124       double wages;
125
126       // determine gross wages
127       if ( hoursWorked <= HOUR_LIMIT )
128       {
129          // regular wages for HOUR_LIMIT (40) hours or less
130          wages = ( hoursWorked * hourlyWage );
131       }
132       else // worked more than HOUR_LIMIT (40) hours
133       {
134          // wages for first HOUR_LIMIT (40) hours
135          wages = HOUR_LIMIT * hourlyWage;
136
137          // add time-and-a-half for overtime hours
138          wages +=
139             ( hoursWorked - HOUR_LIMIT ) * ( 1.5 * hourlyWage );
140       }
141
```

Convert hourly wage to **double** by using **Double.parseDouble** — (lines 112)

Convert hours worked to **double** by using **Double.parseDouble** — (lines 116)

Keyword **final** specifies that **HOUR_LIMIT** is a constant — (line 121)

Variable to store gross wages — (line 124)

Begin **if...else** statement — (line 127)

End **if** part of **if...else** statement and begin **else** part; **else** body executes when condition in line 127 evalues to **false** — (line 132)

Assign to left operand the result of adding left and right operands — (line 138)

End **else** part of **if...else** — (line 140)

Figure 6.22 **Wage Calculator** application completed source code. (Part 3 of 4.)

Format result as a dollar amount

```
142        // specify output format
143        DecimalFormat dollars = new DecimalFormat( "$0.00" );
144
145        // display gross wages
146        grossWagesJTextField.setText( dollars.format( wages ) );
147
148     } // end method calculateJButtonActionPerformed
149
150     // main method
151     public static void main( String[] args )
152     {
153        WageCalculator application = new WageCalculator();
154        application.setDefaultCloseOperation( JFrame.EXIT_ON_CLOSE );
155
156     } // end method main
157
158  } // end class WageCalculator
```

Figure 6.22 **Wage Calculator** application completed source code. (Part 4 of 4.)

SELF-REVIEW

1. Class DecimalFormat is used to _____.
   a) create constant variables
   b) format Java statements
   c) control how decimal numbers are formatted as text
   d) All of the above.

2. Method _____ of DecimalFormat can display double values in a special format, such as with two digits to the right of the decimal point.
   a) format
   b) getFormat
   c) formatDouble
   d) setHundred

Answers: 1) c. 2) a.

6.10 Using the Debugger: The print and set Commands

Java includes several debugging commands that are accessible from the command-line debugger. As you learned in Section 5.6, the print command allows you to examine the value of a variable. In this section, you will learn how to use the print command to examine the value of more complex expressions. The set command allows the programmer to assign new values to variables.

Using the Debugger: The print and set commands

1. **Opening the Command Prompt window and changing directories**. Open the **Command Prompt** window by selecting **Start > Programs > Accessories > Command Prompt**. Change to your working directory by typing cd C:\SimplyJava\WageCalculator.

2. **Compiling the application for debugging**. Compile the application with the -g command-line option by typing javac -g WageCalculator.java. As you learned in Section 5.6, the Java debugger works only with .class files compiled with the -g compiler option.

3. **Starting debugging.** In the **Command Prompt**, type jdb. This command will start the Java debugger.

4. **Inserting breakpoints.** Set a breakpoint at line 116 in the source code by typing stop at WageCalculator:116 (Fig. 6.23). Set another breakpoint at line 130 of the code by typing stop at WageCalculator:130.

(cont.)

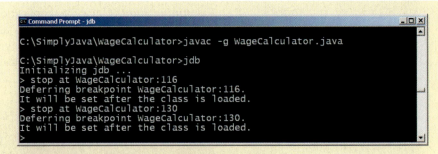

Figure 6.23 Setting breakpoints at lines 116 and 130.

5. ***Running the application***. Type run WageCalculator to begin the debugging process. Type 12 in the **Hourly wage:** JTextField and type 40 in the **Hours worked:** JTextField (Fig. 6.24).

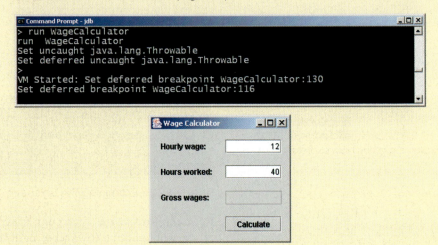

Figure 6.24 Suspended application execution.

6. ***Suspending application execution***. Click the **Calculate** JButton. This will cause event handler calculateJButtonActionPerformed to execute until the breakpoint at line 116 is reached. This suspends application execution and switches the application into break mode (Fig. 6.25). At this point, the statement in lines 112–113 (Fig. 6.22) has assigned the hourly wage input by the user (12) to variable hourlyWage, and the statement in lines 116–117 is the next statement that will be executed.

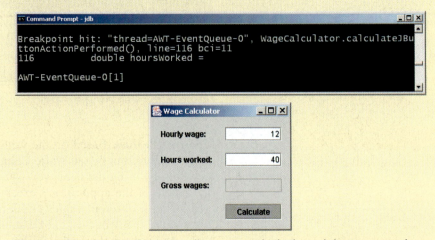

Figure 6.25 Application execution suspended when debugger reaches the breakpoint at line 116.

(cont.)

7. ***Examining data.*** Once the application has entered break mode, you can explore the values of your variables using the debugger's **print** command. In the **Command Prompt** window, type `print hourlyWage`. The value will be displayed (Fig. 6.26). Notice that this value is `12.0`—the value assigned to `hourlyWage` in line 112.

Value of variable `hourlyWage` —

```
Command Prompt - jdb                                    _|□|x|
AWT-EventQueue-0[1] print hourlyWage
 hourlyWage = 12.0
AWT-EventQueue-0[1]
```

Figure 6.26 Examining variable `hourlyWage`.

8. ***Evaluating arithmetic and boolean expressions.*** In the **Command Prompt** window, type `print (hourlyWage + 3) * 5`. Notice that the `print` command can evaluate arithmetic expressions. In this case, it returns the value `75.0` (Fig. 6.27). In the **Command Prompt** window, type `print hourlyWage == 3`. Expressions containing the `==` symbol are treated as `boolean` expressions. The value returned is `false` (Fig. 6.27), because `hourlyWage` does not currently contain the value 3.

Evaluating an arithmetic expression —
Evaluating a `boolean` expression —

```
Command Prompt - jdb                                    _|□|x|
 hourlyWage = 12.0
AWT-EventQueue-0[1] print (hourlyWage + 3) * 5
 (hourlyWage + 3) * 5 = 75.0
AWT-EventQueue-0[1] print hourlyWage == 3
 hourlyWage == 3 = false
AWT-EventQueue-0[1]
```

Figure 6.27 Examining the values of expressions.

9. ***Resuming execution.*** Type `cont` to resume execution (Fig. 6.28). The application will continue to execute until the next breakpoint, at line 130. Lines 116–117 (Fig. 6.22) execute, assigning the hours worked value (40) to `hoursWorked`. Line 121 declares constant `HOUR_LIMIT` and assigns it an initial value (`40.0`). Line 124 declares variable `wages` to store the gross wages. The `if` condition in line 127 evaluates to `true`, so the `if` statement's body executes and the application is once again suspended at line 130. Type `print hoursWorked` (Fig. 6.28). The `hoursWorked` value will be displayed.

Resume execution —

Display value of variable `hoursWorked` —

```
Command Prompt - jdb                                    _|□|x|
 hourlyWage == 3 = false
AWT-EventQueue-0[1] cont
>
Breakpoint hit: "thread=AWT-EventQueue-0", WageCalculator.calculateJBu
ttonActionPerformed(), line=130 bci=37
130                wages = ( hoursWorked * hourlyWage );

AWT-EventQueue-0[1] print hoursWorked
 hoursWorked = 40.0
AWT-EventQueue-0[1]
```

Figure 6.28 Resuming execution and displaying the value of the variable `hoursWorked`.

10. ***Modifying values.*** Based on the values input by the user (12 and 40), the gross wages output by the **Wage Calculator** application should be `$480.00`. However, by using the debugger, you can change the values of variables in the middle of the application's execution. This can be valuable for experimenting with different values and for locating logic errors in applications. You can use the debugger's **set** command to change the value of a variable. Type `set hoursWorked = 10.0`. The debugger changes the value of `hoursWorked` and displays its new value (Fig. 6.29).

(cont.)

Value modified in the debugger ——————

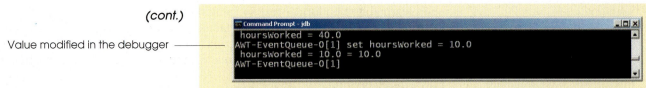

Figure 6.29   Modifying values.

11. ***Viewing the application result.*** Type cont to continue application execution. Method calculateJButtonActionPerformed finishes execution and
displays the result in the **Gross wages:** JTextField. Notice that the result
is $120.00 (Fig. 6.30). This shows that the previous step changed the value
of hoursWorked from the user input value (40) to 10.0. The **Hours**
worked: JTextField still displays the value **40**, because you changed the
value of hoursWorked, but not the *text* property of the **Hours worked:**
JTextField. Once the event handler finishes executing, the final results
are displayed in the **Wage Calculator** window.

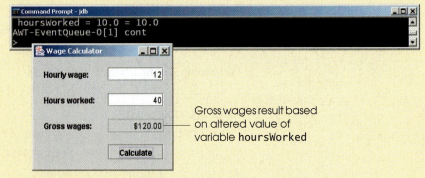

Gross wages result based
on altered value of
variable hoursWorked

Figure 6.30   Output displayed after the debugging process.

12. ***Closing the application.*** Close your running application by clicking its
close button.

13. ***Closing the Command Prompt window.*** Close the **Command Prompt**
window by clicking its close button.

SELF-REVIEW   1. You can examine the value of an expression by using the debugger's _____ command.

    a) run   b) set

    c) print   d) stop

2. You can modify the value of a variable by using the debugger's _____ command.

    a) run   b) set

    c) print   d) stop

Answers: 1) c. 2) b.

6.11 Wrap-Up

In this tutorial, you learned techniques for solving programming problems. You
were introduced to algorithms, pseudocode, the UML and control statements. You
learned different types of control statements and when each might be used.

    You began by test-driving an application that used an if...else statement to
determine an employee's gross wages. You learned the if and if...else control
statements and studied UML activity diagrams that showed the decision-making
processes of these statements.

You learned how to format text by using the `DecimalFormat` method `format` and how to abbreviate mathematical statements by using the arithmetic assignment operators. In the *Using the Debugger* section, you learned how to use the `print` command to examine the value of an expression and how to use the `set` command to change the value of a variable.

In the next tutorial, you will learn how to use message dialogs to display information to the user. You will study the logical operators, which give you more expressive power for forming the conditions in your control statements. You will use the `JCheckBox` component to allow the user to select from various options in an application.

SKILLS SUMMARY

Choosing Among Alternate Courses of Action

- Use the `if`, `if`...`else` or nested `if`...`else` control statements.

Conceptualizing the Application Before Using Java

- Use pseudocode.
- Create an Action/Component/Event (ACE) table.

Understanding the Flow of Control in Control Statements

- View the control statement's corresponding UML activity diagram.

Performing Comparisons in Conditions

- Use the equality (`==` and `!=`) and relational (`<`, `<=`, `>` and `>=`) operators.

Creating a Constant

- Use the `final` keyword at the beginning of the variable's declaration.
- Assign a value to the constant in the declaration.

Abbreviating Assignment Expressions

- Use the assignment operators `+=`, `-=`, `*=`, `/=` and `%=`.

Formatting a Decimal Value

- Use method `format` of class `DecimalFormat` to format decimal numbers.

Examining Expression Values During Application Execution

- Use the debugger to set a breakpoint, and examine expressions using the `print` command.

Modifying Data During Application Execution

- Use the debugger to set a breakpoint, and modify variable values using the `set` command.

KEY TERMS

ACE table—A program development tool you can use to relate GUI events with the actions that should be performed in response to those events.

action/decision model of programming—Representing control statements as UML activity diagrams with action-state symbols, indicating *actions* to be performed, and diamond symbols, indicating *decisions* to be made.

action expression (in the UML)—Used in an action state within a UML activity diagram to specify a particular action to perform.

action state (in the UML)—An action (represented by an action-state symbol) to perform in a UML activity diagram.

action-state symbol (in the UML)—A rectangle with its left and right sides replaced with arcs curving outward that represents an action to perform in a UML activity diagram.

activity diagram (in the UML)—A UML diagram that models the activity (also called the workflow) of a portion of a software system.

algorithm—A procedure for solving a problem, specifying the actions to be executed and the order in which these actions are to be executed.

block—A set of statements that is enclosed in curly braces ({ and }).

boolean type—A type that represents the values `true` and `false`.

condition— A boolean expression with a true or false value that is used to make a decision.

constant—A variable whose value cannot be changed after its initial declaration.

control statement—A program statement (such as if, if...else, switch, while, do...while or for) that specifies the flow of control (that is, the order in which statements execute).

control-statement nesting—Placing one control statement in the body of another control statement.

control-statement stacking—A set of control statements in sequence. The exit point of one control statement is connected to the entry point of the next control statement in sequence.

DecimalFormat—The class used to format floating-point numbers (that is, numbers with decimal points).

decision symbol (in the UML)—The diamond-shaped symbol in a UML activity diagram that indicates a decision is to be made.

diamond (in the UML)—The symbol (also known as the decision symbol) in a UML activity diagram that indicates a decision is to be made. [*Note:* In a later tutorial, you will learn that this symbol serves two purposes in the UML.]

dotted line (in the UML)—A UML activity diagram symbol that connects each UML-style note with the element that the note describes.

Double.parseDouble method—A method that converts a String containing a floating-point number into a double value.

double type—A type that can represent numbers with decimal points.

double-selection statement—A statement, such as if...else, that selects between two different actions or sequences of actions.

equality operators—Operators == (is equal to) and != (is not equal to) that compare two values.

executable statement—An action that is performed when the corresponding Java application is run.

false—One of the two possible values for a boolean type; the other is true.

final keyword—Precedes the data type in a declaration of a constant.

final state (in the UML)—A solid circle surrounded by a hollow circle (a "bullseye") in a UML activity diagram. It represents the end of the workflow after an application performs its activities.

format method of DecimalFormat—Method that returns a String containing a formatted number.

formatting—Modifying the appearance of text for display purposes.

guard condition (in the UML)—A condition contained in square brackets that must be associated with a transition arrow leading from a decision symbol in a UML activity diagram. The guard condition associated with a particular transition determines whether workflow continues along that path.

if statement—The if single-selection statement performs an action (or sequence of actions) based on a condition.

if...else statement—The if...else double-selection statement performs an action (or sequence of actions) if a condition is true and performs a different action (or sequence of actions) if the condition is false.

initial state (in the UML)—The beginning of the workflow in a UML activity diagram before the application performs the activities.

multiple-selection statement—A statement that selects from among many different actions or sequences of actions, such as the switch statement.

nested statement—A statement that is placed inside another control statement.

note (in the UML)—An explanatory remark (represented by a rectangle with a folded upper-right corner) describing the purpose of a symbol in a UML activity diagram.

object-oriented, event-driven programming (OOED)—Using objects, such as GUI components, to enable users to interact with an application. Each interaction generates an event, which causes the application to perform an action.

print command (in the debugger)—A debugger command that is used to examine the values of variables and expressions.

program control—The task of executing an application's statements in the correct order.

pseudocode—An informal language that helps programmers develop algorithms.

relational operators—Operators < (less than), > (greater than), <= (less than or equal to) and >= (greater than or eqaul to) that compare two values.

repetition statement—A control statement that might cause an application to execute statements multiple times.

selection statement—A control statement that selects among alternative courses of action.

set command (in the debugger)—A debugger command that is used to change the value of a variable.

single-entry/single-exit control statement—Each control statement has one entry point and one exit point.

single-selection statement—A statement, such as the `if` statement, that selects or ignores a single action or sequence of actions.

small circles (in the UML)—The solid circle in an activity diagram represents the activity's initial state and the solid circle surrounded by a hollow circle represents the activity's final state.

solid circle (in the UML)—A UML activity diagram symbol that represents the activity's initial state.

structured programming—A technique for organizing program control to help you develop applications that are easy to understand, debug and modify.

transition (in the UML)—A change from one action state to another that is represented by transition arrows in a UML activity diagram.

true—One of the two possible values for a `boolean` type; the other is `false`.

UML (Unified Modeling Language)—An industry standard for modeling software systems graphically.

workflow—The activity of a portion of a software system.

JAVA LIBRARY REFERENCE

DecimalFormat Class `DecimalFormat` is used to format floating-point numbers (that is, numbers with decimal points).

■ *Methods*

`format`—Converts a `double` value into a specified format.

MULTIPLE-CHOICE QUESTIONS

6.1 The _____ operator returns `false` if the left operand is greater than the right operand.

    a) `==`   b) `<`

    c) `<=`   d) All of the above.

6.2 A _____ occurs when an executed statement does not directly follow the previously executed statement in the written application.

    a) transition   b) flow

    c) logical error   d) transfer of control

6.3 A variable or an expression can be examined by the _____ debugger command.

    a) `print`   b) `get`

    c) `display`   d) `examine`

6.4 The `if` statement is called a _____ statement because it selects or ignores one action (or sequence of actions).

    a) single-selection   b) multiple-selection

    c) double-selection   d) repetition

6.5 The three types of program control are sequence, selection and _____.

    a) reduction   b) decision

    c) branching   d) repetition

6.6 In an activity diagram, a rectangle with curved sides represents _____.

    a) a complete algorithm   b) a comment

    c) an action   d) the termination of the application

6.7 The body of an `if` statement that contains multiple statements is placed in _____.

    a) `()`   b) `[]`

    c) `<>`   d) `{}`

6.8 A variable of type `boolean` can be assigned the values _____ and _____.

    a) `true`, `false`   b) `off`, `on`

    c) `one`, `zero`   d) `yes`, `no`

6.9 A variable whose value cannot be changed after its initial declaration is called a _____.

    a) `double`   b) `constant`

    c) `standard`   d) `boolean`

6.10 The _____ operator assigns to the left operand the result of adding the left and right operands.

    a) `+`   b) `=+`

    c) `+=`   d) `+ =`

EXERCISES

6.11 *(Currency Converter Application)* Develop an application that functions as a currency converter as shown in Fig. 6.31. The user provides a number in the **Dollars to convert:** `JTextField` and a currency name (as text) in the **Convert from dollars to:** `JTextField`. Clicking the **Convert** `JButton` will convert the specified amount into the indicated currency and display it in a `JLabel`. Your application should be able to convert currency amounts from dollars to euros, yen and pesos, using the following exchange rates: 1 Dollar = 1.02 Euros, 120 Yen and 10 Pesos. [*Note:* Currency exchange rates are constantly changing. There are many online sites where you can view current exchange rates, including `finance.yahoo.com/m3`, `www.x-rates.com` and `www.rubicon.com/passport/currency/currency.html`.]

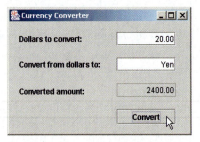

Figure 6.31 Currency Converter GUI.

    a) *Copying the template to your working directory.* Copy the directory `C:\Examples\Tutorial06\Exercises\CurrencyConverter` to your `C:\SimplyJava` directory.

    b) *Opening the template file.* Open the `CurrencyConverter.java` file in your text editor.

    c) *Obtaining the user input.* In the `convertJButtonActionPerformed` event handler (lines 105–108), insert a statement that uses method `Double.parseDouble` to convert the user input from the `dollarJTextField` to a `double` and assigns the result to `double` variable `amount`.

    d) *Obtaining the currency name.* Add a statement that obtains the currency name from the `typeJTextField` and assigns it to `String` variable `currencyName`.

    e) *Performing the currency conversion.* Next, you will use a nested `if...else` statement to determine which currency the user entered, then perform the appropriate conversion. To compare `currencyName` with another `String`, you will use `String` method `equals`—as in the expression `currencyName.equals( "Euros" )`. `String` method `equals` performs a case sensitive comparison and returns `true` if the `String` to the left of the dot (`.`) is identical to the `String` in parentheses; otherwise, the method

returns `false`. Insert a nested `if...else` statement with three conditions. In the first condition, use the expression `currencyName.equals( "Euros" )`, which evaluates to true if `currencyName` contains `"Euros"`—the spelling, including uppercase and lowercase letters, must be indentical. If this condition is true, the body of this `if` statement should convert the dollars to euros by multiplying `amount` by `1.02` and storing the result in `amount`. Otherwise, in the nested `if` statement, test the condition `currencyName.equals( "Yen" )`. If this condition is true, the body of this `if` statement will convert the dollars to yen by multiplying `amount` by `120` and storing the result in `amount`. Finally, if the first two conditions are false, the third nested `if` statement should test the condition `currencyName.equals( "Pesos" )`. If this condition is true, the body of this `if` statement should convert the dollars to pesos by multiplying the amount by `10` and storing the result in `amount`.

f) *Displaying the result.* Insert a statement that creates a `DecimalFormat` as you did in the **Wage Calculator** application (Fig. 6.20, line 143), but without the "$" sign. Finally, display the formatted result in `convertedJTextField`.

g) *Opening the Command Prompt window and changing directories.* Open the **Command Prompt** window by selecting **Start > Programs > Accessories > Command Prompt**. Change to your working directory by typing cd `C:\SimplyJava\Currency-Converter`.

h) *Saving the application.* Save your modified source code file.

i) *Compiling the application.* Compile your application by typing javac `Currency-Converter.java`.

j) *Running the completed application.* When your application compiles correctly, run it by typing java CurrencyConverter. Type `20.00` in the **Dollars to convert:** JTextField and type Yen in the **Convert from dollars to:** JTextField, then press the **Convert** JButton. Ensure that the converted value `2400.00` appears in the **Converted amount:** JTextField. Type Euros in the **Convert from dollars to:** JTextField, then press the **Convert** JButton. Ensure that the converted value `20.40` appears in the **Converted amount:** JTextField. Type Pesos in the **Convert from dollars to:** JTextField, then press the **Convert** JButton. Ensure that the converted value `200.00` appears in the **Converted amount:** JTextField. Finally, type anything else in the **Convert from dollars to:** JTextField, then press the **Convert** JButton. Notice that the application simply displays the dollar amount if an incorrect type is entered.

k) *Closing the application.* Close your running application by clicking its close button.

l) *Closing the Command Prompt window.* Close the **Command Prompt** window by clicking its close button.

6.12 *(Expanded Wage Calculator that Performs Tax Calculations)* Develop an application that calculates an employee's wages as shown in Fig. 6.32. The user enters the hourly wage and number of hours worked per week. When the **Calculate** JButton is clicked, the gross wages of the user should display in the **Gross wages:** JTextField. The **Federal taxes:** JTextField should display the amount deducted for Federal taxes, and the **Net wages:** JTextField should display the difference between the gross wages and the Federal tax amount. Assume overtime wages are `1.5` times the hourly wage and Federal withholding taxes are 15% of gross earnings.

a) *Copying the template to your working directory.* Copy the directory `C:\Examples\Tutorial06\Exercises\ExpandedWageCalculator` to your `C:\SimplyJava` directory.

b) *Opening the template file.* Open the `WageCalculator.java` file in your text editor.

c) *Modifying the Calculate JButton's ActionPerformed event handler.* Add the code for *Steps d* and *e* to `calculateJButtonActionPerformed` (lines 192–231).

Figure 6.32 Expanded **Wage Calculator** GUI.

d) *Calculating and displaying the Federal taxes deducted.* After line 230, insert a statement that declares a constant double variable—TAX_RATE—and assigns it 0.15, which represents 15%. On the next line, insert a statement that declares double variable federalTaxes and assigns it the product of wages and TAX_RATE. The result is the amount that will be deducted for Federal taxes from the gross wages. Insert a statement that displays this value in federalTaxesJTextField, using method format of DecimalFormat dollars that you created earlier (see Fig. 6.20 for the basic syntax of this statement).

e) *Calculating and displaying the employee's net wages.* Insert a statement that subtracts federalTaxes from wages to calculate the employee's net wages. Display this value in netWagesJTextField, using method format of DecimalFormat dollars.

f) *Opening the Command Prompt window and changing directories.* Open the **Command Prompt** window by selecting **Start > Programs > Accessories > Command Prompt**. Change to your working directory by typing cd C:\SimplyJava\Expanded-WageCalculator.

g) *Saving the application.* Save your modified source code file.

h) *Compiling the application.* Compile your application by typing javac WageCalculator.java.

i) *Running the completed application.* When your application compiles correctly, run it by typing java WageCalculator. Type 10 in the **Hourly wage:** JTextField and type 45 in the **Hours worked:** JTextField, then press the **Calculate** JButton. Ensure that the results appear as shown in Fig. 6.32.

j) *Closing the application.* Close your running application by clicking its close button.

k) *Closing the Command Prompt window.* Close the **Command Prompt** window by clicking its close button.

6.13 *(Credit Checker Application)* Develop an application (as shown in Fig. 6.33) that a credit manager can use to determine whether a department store customer has exceeded the credit limit on a charge account. For each customer, the credit manager enters an account number (an int), a balance at the beginning of the month (a double), the total of all items charged this month (a double), the total of all credits applied to the customer's account this month (a double) and the customer's allowed credit limit (a double). The application should input each of these facts, calculate the new balance (= *beginning balance + charges – credits*), display the new balance and determine whether the new balance exceeds the customer's credit limit. If the customer's credit limit is exceeded, the application should display a message (in an output JTextField at the bottom of the JFrame) informing the of this fact.

a) *Copying the template to your working directory.* Copy the directory C:\Examples\Tutorial06\Exercises\CreditChecker to your C:\SimplyJava directory.

b) *Opening the template file.* Open the CreditChecker.java file in your text editor.

c) *Coding the Calculate Balance JButton's ActionPerformed event handler.* Add the code for *Steps d* through *f* to event handler calculateJButtonActionPerformed (lines 196–199).

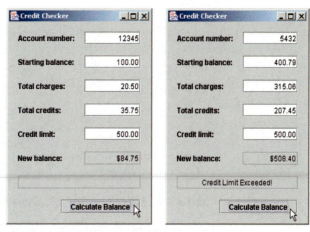

Figure 6.33 Credit Checker GUI.

d) *Declaring variables.* Starting in line 198, insert statements that declare four double variables—startBalance, totalCharges, totalCredits and creditLimit. Assign to each of these variables the value from the corresponding JTextField (start-BalanceJTextField, totalChargesJTextField, totalCreditsJTextField and creditLimitJTextField, respectively) converted to type double.

e) *Calculating and displaying the new balance.* Declare a fifth double variable called newBalance to store the new balance in the account after the charges and credits have been applied. Calculate the new balance by adding the total charges to the starting balance and subtracting the credits. Assign the result to newBalance. Declare a DecimalFormat dollarFormat, as you did in Fig. 6.20. Format the newBalance using dollarFormat and display the formatted number in newBalanceJtextField.

f) *Determining if the credit limit has been exceeded.* Insert an if statement that determines whether the new balance exceeds the specified credit limit. If so, display "Credit Limit Exceeded!" in errorJTextField. Otherwise, clear the contents of errorJTextField.

g) *Opening the Command Prompt window and changing directories.* Open the **Command Prompt** window by selecting **Start > Programs > Accessories > Command Prompt**. Change to your working directory by typing cd C:\SimplyJava\Credit-Checker.

h) *Saving the application.* Save your modified source code file.

i) *Compiling the application.* Compile your application by typing javac Credit-Checker.java.

j) *Running the completed application.* When your application compiles correctly, run it by typing java CreditChecker. Use the values shown in the two sample outputs of Fig. 6.33 to ensure that your application performs the credit check correctly.

k) *Closing the application.* Close your running application by clicking its close button.

l) *Closing the Command Prompt window.* Close the **Command Prompt** window by clicking its close button.

What does this code do? ▶

6.14 Assume that the user has entered the value 27 into ageJTextField. Determine what is displayed in outputJTextField by the following code:

```
1   int age = Integer.parseInt( ageJTextField.getText() );
2
3   if ( age < 0 )
4   {
5       outputJTextField.setText(
6           "Enter a value greater than or equal to zero." );
7   }
```

(continued on next page)

```
 8   else if ( age < 13 )                    (continued from previous page)
 9   {
10      outputJTextField.setText( "Child" );
11   }
12   else if ( age < 20 )
13   {
14      outputJTextField.setText( "Teenager" );
15   }
16   else if ( age < 30 )
17   {
18      outputJTextField.setText( "Young Adult" );
19   }
20   else if ( age < 65 )
21   {
22      outputJTextField.setText( "Adult" );
23   }
24   else
25   {
26      outputJTextField.setText( "Senior Citizen" );
27   }
```

What's wrong with this code? ▶ **6.15** The following code segment should display "AM" in ampmJLabel if the hour is a value in the range 0–11 and should display "PM" in ampmJLabel if the hour is a value in the range 12–23. For any other hour value, the code segment should display "Time Error" in ampmJLabel. Find the error(s) in the following code:

```
 1   int hour = 14;
 2
 3   if ( hour >= 0 )
 4   {
 5      if ( hour < 12 )
 6      {
 7         ampmJLabel.setText( "AM" );
 8      }
 9   }
10   else
11   {
12      ampmJLabel.setText( "Time Error." );
13   }
14   else if ( hour >= 12 )
15   {
16      if ( hour < 24 )
17      {
18         ampmJLabel.setText( "PM" );
19      }
20   }
```

Using the Debugger ▶ **6.16** *(Grade Converter Application)* The **Grade Converter** application is supposed to input an integer grade between 0 and 100 from the user and display the corresponding letter grade. For values 90–100 the application should display **A**; for 80–89 the application should display **B**; for 70–79 the application should display **C**; for 60–69 the application should display **D**; and for grades from 0–59, the application should display **F**. However, when you run the application you will notice that the application incorrectly displays **B** for all values in the range 90–100; the application should display **A** for these values. Follow the steps below to locate and fix the logic error. Figure 6.34 shows the incorrect output when the value 95 is input.

Figure 6.34   Incorrect output for **Grade Converter** application.

a) *Copying the template to your working directory.* Copy the directory C:\Examples\
   Tutorial06\Exercises\Debugger\GradeConverter to your C:\SimplyJava
   directory.

b) *Opening the Command Prompt window and changing directories.* Open the **Command Prompt** by selecting **Start > Programs > Accessories > Command Prompt**.
   Change to your working directory by typing cd C:\SimplyJava\GradeConverter.

c) *Compiling the application for debugging.* Compile the application with the -g command-line option by typing javac -g GradeConverter.java.

d) *Starting debugging.* In the **Command Prompt**, type jdb. This command will start the
   Java debugger.

e) *Setting breakpoints.* Use the stop command to set breakpoints at lines 95 and 99.

f) *Running the application in the debugger.* Run the **Grade Converter** application in
   the debugger by typing run GradeConverter. Type 95 in the **Enter grade (0-100):**
   JTextField, then press the **Convert** JButton.

g) *Locating the logic error.* Use the debugger's print and cont commands to help you
   locate the logic error. When you continue execution from the breakpoint at line 95,
   notice that execution continues to line 99, which is in the next if statement. If the
   application logic is implemented correctly, the convertJButtonActionPerformed
   event handler should terminate after line 95 executes. Open GradeConverter.java
   in your text editor and scroll to lines 95–99 in the application and fix the logic error.

h) *Saving the application.* Save your modified source code file.

i) *Compiling the completed application.* Compile your application by typing javac
   GradeConverter.java.

j) *Running the application.* When your application compiles correctly, run it by typing
   java GradeConverter. Test the application again with the value 95 to ensure that the
   application displays the correct letter grade (**A**).

k) *Closing the application.* Close your running application by clicking its close button.

l) *Closing the Command Prompt window.* Close the **Command Prompt** window by
   clicking its close button.

Programming Challenge ▶

6.17 *(Encryption Application)* A company that transmits data over the telephone is concerned that its phones could be tapped. All its data is transmitted as four-digit int values. The
company has asked you to write an application that encrypts its data so that the data may be
transmitted more securely. Encryption is the process of transforming data for security reasons. Your application should read a four-digit integer input by the user in a JTextField and
encrypt the information as described in the steps of this exercise when the user clicks the
Encrypt JButton (Fig. 6.35).

Figure 6.35   **Encryption** application.

a) *Copying the template to your working directory.* Copy the directory C:\Examples\
   Tutorial06\Exercises\Encryption to your C:\SimplyJava directory.

b) *Opening the template file.* Open the Encryption.java file in your text editor.

c) *Coding the Encrypt JButton's ActionPerformed event handler.* Add the code for *Steps d* through *f* to event handler encryptJButtonActionPerformed (lines 139–142).

d) *Obtaining the user input.* In line 141, insert a statement that obtains the user input from numberJTextField, converts it to an int and assigns the value to int variable number.

e) *Extracting the digits from the user input.* Use the programming techniques you used to solve Exercise 5.17 to insert statements that extract the digits from int variable number. Store the digits of number in the int variables digit1, digit2, digit3 and digit4, respectively.

f) *Encrypt each digit and display the encrypted results.* Replace each digit by performing the calculation *(the sum of that digit plus 7) modulo 10.* We use the term **modulo** (**mod**, for short) to indicate that you are to use the remainder (%) operator. Swap the first digit with the third, and swap the second digit with the fourth. Display the encrypted numbers in the corresponding JTextFields: encryptedDigit1-JTextField, encryptedDigit2JTextField, encryptedDigit3JTextField and encryptedDigit4JTextField. [*Note:* Once a number is encrypted, it will need to be decrypted in the future. You might consider how to write an application that will decrypt these values.]

g) *Opening the Command Prompt window and changing directories.* Open the **Command Prompt** window by selecting **Start > Programs > Accessories > Command Prompt**. Change to your working directory by typing cd C:\SimplyJava\Encryption.

h) *Saving the application.* Save your modified source code file.

i) *Compiling the completed application.* Compile your application by typing javac Encryption.java.

j) *Running the application.* When your application compiles correctly, run it by typing java Encryption. Use the values shown in the sample output of Fig. 6.35 to ensure that your application performs the encryption correctly.

k) *Closing the application.* Close your running application by clicking its close button.

l) *Closing the Command Prompt window.* Close the **Command Prompt** window by clicking its close button.

TUTORIAL 7

Dental Payment Application

Introducing JCheckBoxes, Message Dialogs and Logical Operators

M any Java applications use **dialogs**, or windows, that display and retrieve information. You encounter many dialogs while using a computer, from those that instruct you to select files or enter passwords to others that notify you of problems while using an application. There are different types of dialogs. In this tutorial, you will learn how to use a **message dialog** to display a message to the user.

JTextFields allow users to enter any textual value as input. In some cases, you may want to use components that provide users with a limited set of predefined options. One way to do this is by providing JCheckBoxes in your application. You also will learn about **logical operators**, which you can use in your applications to make more complex decisions.

7.1 Test-Driving the Dental Payment Application

Dentists perform many different procedures on their patients, and they frequently use computers to prepare their bills. In this tutorial, you will develop the **Dental Payment** application. This application must meet the following requirements:

> ### Application Requirements
>
> *A dentist has asked you to create an application that employees can use to bill patients. Your application must allow the user to enter the patient's name and specify which services were performed during the visit. Your application must then calculate the total charges. If a user attempts to calculate the total of a bill before any services are specified or before the patient's name is entered, an error message should be displayed.*

You begin by test-driving the completed application. Then, you will learn the additional Java technologies you will need to create your own version of this application.

**Test-Driving the
Completed Dental
Payment Application**

1. *Locating the completed application.* Open the **Command Prompt** window by selecting **Start > Programs > Accessories > Command Prompt**. Change to the completed **Dental Payment** application directory by typing `cd C:\Examples\Tutorial07\CompletedApplication\DentalPayment`.

2. *Running the Dental Payment application.* Type `java DentalPayment` in the **Command Prompt** window to run the application (Fig. 7.1). Notice that there are three square-shaped components in the left column. These are **JCheckBox** components. A JCheckBox is a small gray square that either is blank or contains a check mark. When a JCheckBox is selected, a black check mark appears in the box (☑). A JCheckBox can be selected by simply clicking within the JCheckBox's small gray square or by clicking on the text of the JCheckBox (such as **Cleaning**, **Cavity Filling** and **X-Ray** in Fig. 7.1). A selected JCheckBox can be deselected in the same way. You will learn how to customize JCheckBox components shortly.

JCheckBox components
(unchecked)

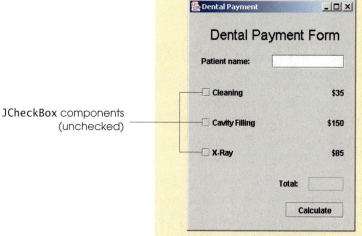

Figure 7.1   **Dental Payment** application without input entered.

3. *Attempting to calculate a total without entering input.* Leave the **Patient name:** JTextField blank and deselect any JCheckBoxes that you have selected. Click the **Calculate** JButton. Notice that a message dialog appears, indicating that you must enter data (Fig. 7.2). Close this dialog by clicking its **OK** JButton.

Message dialog

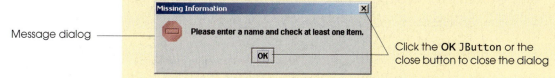

Click the **OK** JButton or the
close button to close the dialog

Figure 7.2   Message dialog appears when no name is entered and/or no JCheckBoxes are selected.

4. *Entering a name and selecting services.* The **Dental Payment** application is still displayed. Type Bob Jones in the **Patient name:** JTextField. Select all three JCheckBoxes by single clicking each one. Notice that a check mark appears in each JCheckBox.

5. *Deselecting the Cavity Filling JCheckBox.* Click the **Cavity Filling** JCheckBox to remove its check mark. Only the **Cleaning** and **X-Ray** JCheckBoxes should now be selected.

(cont.)

6. ***Determining the bill.*** Click the **Calculate** JButton. This causes the application to calculate the total price of the services performed during the dentist visit. The result is displayed in the **Total:** JTextField (Fig. 7.3).

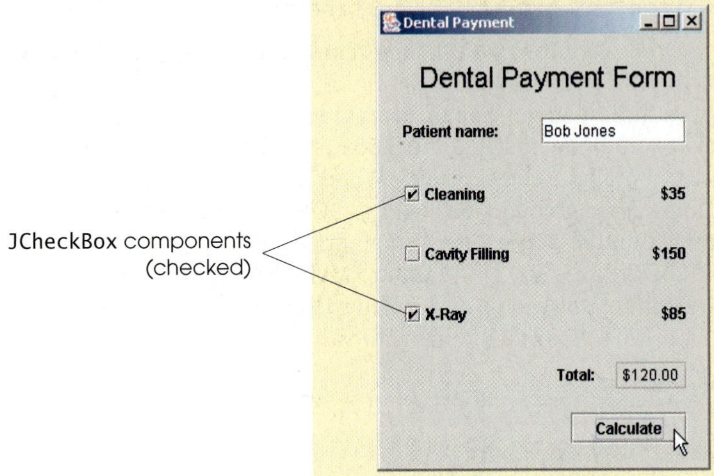

JCheckBox components (checked)

Figure 7.3 **Dental Payment** application with input entered and total price of services displayed.

7. ***Closing the running application.*** Close the running application by clicking its close button.

8. ***Closing the Command Prompt window.*** Close the **Command Prompt** window by clicking its close button.

7.2 Constructing the Dental Payment Application

Now you will build your **Dental Payment** application by using JCheckBoxes and message dialogs. The following pseudocode describes the basic operation of the **Dental Payment** application, which executes when the user clicks the **Calculate** JButton. Recall that pseudocode is an informal language that helps programmers develop algorithms. The pseudocode is as follows:

```
When the user clicks the Calculate JButton:
    Obtain patient name from JTextField

    If user has not entered a patient name or has not selected any JCheckBoxes
        Display error message in dialog
    Else

        If Cleaning JCheckBox is selected
            Add cost of cleaning to total

        If Cavity Filling JCheckBox is selected
            Add cost of cavity filling to total

        If X-Ray JCheckBox is selected
            Add cost of x-ray to total

    Display total price of services rendered in dollar format
```

It is a good practice to place a blank line above and below if statements, as we have done in the above pseudocode. Now that you have test-driven the **Dental Payment** application and studied its pseudocode representation, you will use an ACE table to help you convert the pseudocode to Java. Figure 7.4 lists the actions, components and events that will help you complete your own version of this application.

*Action/Component/
Event (ACE) Table for the
Dental Payment
Application*

Action	Component/Class/Object	Event
Label the application's components	dentalPaymentFormJLabel, patientNameJLabel, totalJLabel, cleaningPriceJLabel, cavityFillingPriceJLabel, xRayPriceJLabel, cleaningJCheckBox, cavityFillingJCheckBox, xRayJCheckBox	Application is run
	calculateJButton	User clicks **Calculate** JButton
Obtain patient name from JTextField	patientNameJTextField	
If user has not entered a name or has not selected any JCheckBoxes	cleaningJCheckBox, cavityFillingJCheckBox, xRayJCheckBox	
Display error message in dialog	JOptionPane	
Else If Cleaning JCheckBox is selected Add cost of cleaning to total	cleaningJCheckBox	
If Cavity Filling JCheckBox is selected Add cost of cavity filling to total	cavityFillingJCheckBox	
If X-Ray JCheckBox selected Add cost of an x-ray to total	xRayJCheckBox	
Display total price of services rendered in dollar format	totalJTextField, dollars (DecimalFormat)	

Figure 7.4   ACE table for **Dental Payment** application.

Data is input via patientNameJTextField and cleaningJCheckBox, cavity-FillingJCheckBox and xRayJCheckBox. Output is displayed in totalJTextField when calculateJButton is clicked. Note that JCheckBoxes label themselves, so it is not necessary to place a JLabel next to a JCheckBox, although these JCheckBoxes have corresponding priceJLabels to indicate the price of each service.

7.3 Using JCheckBoxes

GUI Design Tip

A JCheckBox's text should be descriptive and as short as possible. A JCheckBox's text should use book-title capitalization.

As mentioned earlier, a JCheckBox is a small gray square that either is blank or contains a check mark. A JCheckBox is known as a **state button**, because it can be in the on/off (true/false) state. When a JCheckBox is selected, a black check mark appears in the box. Any number of JCheckBoxes can be selected at a time, including none at all. The text that appears alongside a JCheckBox is called the **JCheck-Box text**.

You can determine whether a JCheckBox is on (that is, selected) by getting the value of the JCheckBox's *selected* property, using JCheckBox method **isSelected**. For example, if you selected the **Cleaning** JCheckBox in Fig. 7.3, the expression cleaningJCheckBox.isSelected() returns true; otherwise, it returns false. In general, if a component's property is a boolean value, simply write *component-Name*.is*PropertyName*() to get the boolean value of that property.

You will now create the **Dental Payment** application from the template provided. The application you will build in the next two boxes will not display a dialog if the JTextField is empty or all the JCheckBoxes are deselected when you click the **Calculate** JButton. You will learn how to display that dialog later in the tutorial.

Customizing
JCheckBoxes

1. *Copying the template to your working directory.* Copy the C:\Examples\ Tutorial07\TemplateApplication\DentalPayment directory to your C:\SimplyJava directory.

2. *Opening the Dental Payment application's template file.* Open the template file DentalPayment.java in your text editor.

3. *Customizing the first JCheckBox.* For this application, you will modify the *bounds* and *text* properties of each JCheckBox. Add lines 75–76 of Fig. 7.5. Line 75 sets the *bounds* property of cleaningJCheckBox to 16, 112, 122, 24. Line 76 sets the *text* property of cleaningJCheckBox to "Cleaning".

```
Source Editor [DentalPayment]
73        // set up cleaningJCheckBox
74        cleaningJCheckBox = new JCheckBox();
75        cleaningJCheckBox.setBounds( 16, 112, 122, 24 );
76        cleaningJCheckBox.setText( "Cleaning" );
77        contentPane.add( cleaningJCheckBox );
```

Figure 7.5 Changing the *text* and *bounds* properties of cleaning-JCheckBox.

4. *Customizing the second JCheckBox.* Add lines 88–89 of Fig. 7.6. Line 88 sets the *bounds* property of cavityFillingJCheckBox to 16, 159, 122, 24. Line 89 sets the *text* property of cavityFillingJCheckBox to "Cavity Filling".

```
Source Editor [DentalPayment]
86        // set up cavityFillingJCheckBox
87        cavityFillingJCheckBox = new JCheckBox();
88        cavityFillingJCheckBox.setBounds( 16, 159, 122, 24 );
89        cavityFillingJCheckBox.setText( "Cavity Filling" );
90        contentPane.add( cavityFillingJCheckBox );
```

Figure 7.6 Changing the *text* and *bounds* properties of cavityFilling-JCheckBox.

GUI Design Tip

Align groups of JCheckBoxes either horizontally or vertically.

5. *Customizing the third JCheckBox.* Add lines 102–103 of Fig. 7.7. Line 102 sets the *bounds* property of xRayJCheckBox to 16, 206, 122, 24. Line 103 sets the *text* property of xRayJCheckBox to "X-Ray".

```
Source Editor [DentalPayment *]
100       // set up xRayJCheckBox
101       xRayJCheckBox = new JCheckBox();
102       xRayJCheckBox.setBounds( 16, 206, 122, 24 );
103       xRayJCheckBox.setText( "X-Ray" );
104       contentPane.add( xRayJCheckBox );
```

Figure 7.7 Changing the *text* and *bounds* properties of xRayJCheckBox.

6. *Saving the application.* Save your modified source code file.

7. *Opening the Command Prompt window and changing directories.* Open the **Command Prompt** window by selecting **Start > Programs > Accessories > Command Prompt**. Change to your working directory by typing cd C:\SimplyJava\DentalPayment.

(cont.)

8. ***Compiling the application.*** Compile your application by typing `javac DentalPayment.java`.

9. ***Running the application.*** When your application compiles correctly, run it by typing `java DentalPayment`. Figure 7.8 shows the updated application running. Notice that the application displays three `JCheckBox`es. You can select and deselect the `JCheckBox`es, but no action occurs when the **Calculate** `JButton` is clicked. You will begin adding the functionality for this `JButton` in the following box.

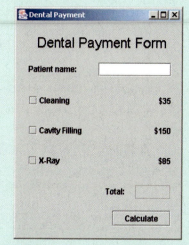

Figure 7.8   Application running after customizing three `JCheckBox`es.

10. ***Closing the running application.*** Close your running application by clicking its close button.

11. ***Closing the Command Prompt window.*** Close the **Command Prompt** window by clicking its close button.

Now that you have customized the `JCheckBox`es, you need to add code that will execute when the **Calculate** `JButton` is pressed.

Adding Code for the Calculate `JButton`

1. ***Adding `if` statements to calculate the patient's bill.*** Add lines 155–179 of Fig. 7.9 to your application. Be sure to include all blank lines and comments as shown in Fig. 7.9 to improve code readability and to ensure that your line numbers are correct. Line 155 declares variable `total`, which stores the total charges for the patient as a `double`. This variable is initialized to `0.0`. Lines 157–173 define three `if` statements that determine which of the `JCheckBox`es have been selected. Each `if` statement's condition uses the `JCheckBox` method `isSelected` to determine whether the `JCheckBox` is selected (`true`) or not selected (`false`). For each `if` statement, the dollar value of the service is added to `total` if the service's `JCheckBox` is selected. For example, the first `if` statement (lines 158–161) adds 35 to `total` (line 160) if `cleaningJCheckBox` is selected (line 158). Notice that the numeric values added to `total` correspond to the monetary values displayed on the `JLabel` to the right of each service.

2. ***Saving the application.*** Save your modified source code file.

3. ***Opening the Command Prompt window and changing directories.*** Open the **Command Prompt** window by selecting **Start > Programs > Accessories > Command Prompt**. Change to your working directory by typing `cd C:\SimplyJava\DentalPayment`.

(cont.)

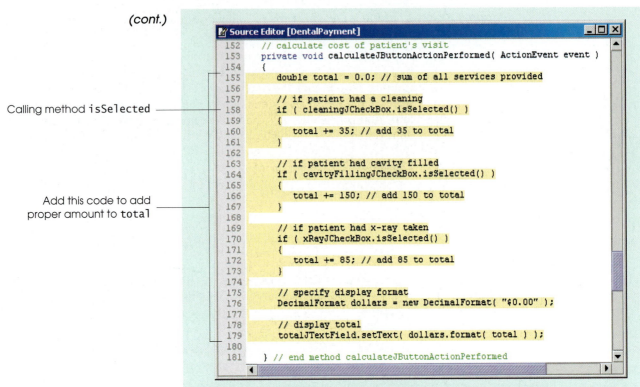

Calling method `isSelected`

Add this code to add proper amount to `total`

```
152    // calculate cost of patient's visit
153    private void calculateJButtonActionPerformed( ActionEvent event )
154    {
155        double total = 0.0; // sum of all services provided
156
157        // if patient had a cleaning
158        if ( cleaningJCheckBox.isSelected() )
159        {
160            total += 35; // add 35 to total
161        }
162
163        // if patient had cavity filled
164        if ( cavityFillingJCheckBox.isSelected() )
165        {
166            total += 150; // add 150 to total
167        }
168
169        // if patient had x-ray taken
170        if ( xRayJCheckBox.isSelected() )
171        {
172            total += 85; // add 85 to total
173        }
174
175        // specify display format
176        DecimalFormat dollars = new DecimalFormat( "$0.00" );
177
178        // display total
179        totalJTextField.setText( dollars.format( total ) );
180
181    } // end method calculateJButtonActionPerformed
```

Figure 7.9 Determining if a **JCheckBox** has been selected.

4. *Compiling the application.* Compile your application by typing `javac DentalPayment.java`.

5. *Running the application.* When your application compiles correctly, run it by typing `java DentalPayment`. Figure 7.10 shows the updated application running. Notice that the user is not required to enter a name or select any JCheckBoxes before clicking the **Calculate** JButton. If no JCheckBoxes are selected, the bill displays the value **$0.00**.

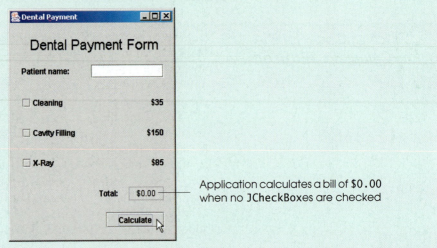

Application calculates a bill of $0.00 when no JCheckBoxes are checked

Figure 7.10 Application running without input.

6. *Selecting and deselecting the JCheckBoxes* Select the **Cleaning** JCheckBox and click the **Calculate** JButton. Notice that the **Total:** field now displays **$35.00** (Fig. 7.11). Select different combinations of JCheckBoxes and click **Calculate** to see the different totals.

(cont.)

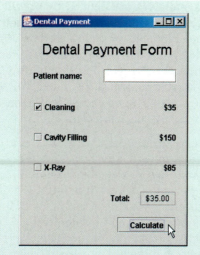

Figure 7.11 Application running with services selected, but no patient name entered.

7. ***Closing the running application***. Close your running application by clicking its close button.

8. ***Closing the Command Prompt window***. Close the **Command Prompt** window by clicking its close button.

SELF-REVIEW

1. The _____ method sets a JCheckBox's text.

   a) `setText`   b) `setValue`

   c) `setLabel`   d) `setChecked`

2. The _____ method determines whether a JCheckBox is checked.

   a) `isChecked`   b) `isSelected`

   c) `isClicked`   d) `getClicked`

Answers: 1.) a. 2.) b.

7.4 Using a Dialog to Display a Message

In the completed application, a message is displayed in a dialog if the user attempts to calculate the total charges without entering a patient name or without specifying which services were performed. In this section, you will learn how to display a dialog when a patient name is not input. Later in this tutorial, you will learn how to determine whether at least one JCheckBox is selected. When the dialog is closed, you can continue entering input in your application window. The message dialog used in the completed application is displayed in Fig. 7.12.

Title bar

Icon indicates the tone of the message

OK JButton allows the user to close the dialog

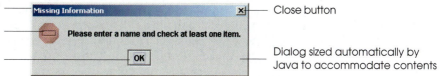

Close button

Dialog sized automatically by Java to accommodate contents

Figure 7.12 Message dialog displayed by the application.

Notice that the message dialog contains a title bar, a close button, a message (**Please enter a name and check at least one item.**), an **OK** JButton and an icon that indicates the tone of the message (in this case, the red stop sign, 🛑, notifies the user of an error). You can click either the close button or the **OK** JButton to **dismiss** (close) the dialog (which you must do to proceed).

GUI Design Tip

Text displayed in a message dialog should be descriptive and as short as possible.

Message dialogs are defined by class **JOptionPane** and can be displayed by using method **JOptionPane.showMessageDialog**. The message dialog is customized by the arguments passed to method JOptionPane.showMessageDialog. You will now learn how to display a message dialog based on a condition. Remember that, for now, your application should display the message dialog only if the user has not entered a patient name. Later, you will modify your application to display the message dialog when the patient name has not been entered or none of the JCheckBoxes have been selected.

Displaying a Message Dialog

1. **Adding an if statement to the calculateJButtonActionPerformed method.** The message dialog should display only if the user does not enter the patient's name. Add lines 155–162 of Fig. 7.13 to the calculateJButtonActionPerformed method. Be sure to include a blank line after the closing brace of the if statement.

   Line 156 gets the value of patientNameJTextField's *text* property and assigns that value to variable patient. If patientNameJTextField is empty, the getText method returns the empty string (""). Line 159 tests whether data was entered in the **Patient name:** JTextField. If no data has been entered, the expression patient.equals("") evaluates to true. The **equals** method returns true when the string (patient) contains the same text as the argument to method equals, which in this case is an empty string (""). This is necessary because a String is an object and the == operator cannot be used with objects—only primitives. You will add the body of this if statement in *Step 2*.

Add this code to verify that a patient name was entered

```
152    // calculate cost of patient's visit
153    private void calculateJButtonActionPerformed( ActionEvent event )
154    {
155        // get patient's name
156        String patient = patientNameJTextField.getText();
157
158        // display error message if no name entered
159        if ( patient.equals( "" ) )
160        {
161
162        }
163
164        double total = 0.0; // sum of all services provided
```

Figure 7.13 Adding an if statement to method calculateJButton-ActionPerformed.

2. **Adding code to display a message dialog.** Add lines 161–164 of Fig. 7.14 in the body of the if statement you created in the previous step. Lines 162–164 call method JOptionPane.showMessageDialog using four arguments, separated by commas. The first argument (line 162) uses keyword null to indicate that the message dialog should appear in the middle of your screen. You learn more about this argument in Tutorial 22. The second argument (line 163) specifies the text ("Please enter a name.") that displays in the dialog. The third argument (line 164) specifies the text ("Missing Information") that appears in the message dialog's title bar. The fourth argument (JOptionPane.ERROR_MESSAGE at line 164) indicates what type of message icon is displayed. You will learn about the fourth argument shortly.

(cont.)

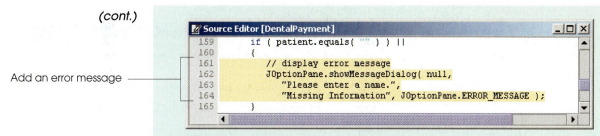

Add an error message

Figure 7.14 Message dialog code that displays a message to users.

3. ***Adding an `else` part to the `if` statement.*** If the condition in line 159 of Fig. 7.14 is `true` (that is, the user has omitted some required information), then the method should not execute the code that calculates the bill. You can prevent that code from executing by changing the `if` statement in lines 159–165 of Fig. 7.14 into an `if...else` statement. Add lines 166–167 and line 194 of Fig. 7.15 into the method. Also, lines 168–192, which are now in the body of the `else`, should be indented one more level to the right for readability (remember that the compiler ignores this indentation, so your application runs the same regardless of how it's indented). The body of the `else` will now execute only if the user enters a name in the **Patient name:** `JTextField`.

Add an `else` statement

Add the right brace to end the `else` statement

```
164            "Missing information", JOptionPane.ERROR_MESSAGE );
165      }
166      else // otherwise, do calculations
167      {
168          double total = 0.0; // sum of all services provided
169
170          // if patient had a cleaning
171          if ( cleaningJCheckBox.isSelected() )
172          {
173              total += 35; // add 35 to total
174          }
175
176          // if patient had cavity filled
177          if ( cavityFillingJCheckBox.isSelected() )
178          {
179              total += 150; // add 150 to total
180          }
181
182          // if patient had x-ray taken
183          if ( xRayJCheckBox.isSelected() )
184          {
185              total += 85; // add 85 to total
186          }
187
188          // specify display format
189          DecimalFormat dollars = new DecimalFormat( "$0.00" );
190
191          // display total
192          totalJTextField.setText( dollars.format( total ) );
193
194      } // end else
195
196    } // end method calculateJButtonActionPerformed
```

Figure 7.15 Adding an `else` part to an `if` statement.

Figure 7.16 displays the entire method `calculateJButtonActionPerformed` after the new code has been added. Compare this code to your own to ensure that you have added the new code correctly. Once again, note the syntax coloring used in Fig. 7.16. In this text, comments appear in green, keywords in blue and constants (such as numbers and text) in cyan. The same code may appear in different colors on your screen, based on the text editor used.

(cont.)

```
Source Editor [DentalPayment]
152     // calculate cost of patient's visit
153     private void calculateJButtonActionPerformed( ActionEvent event )
154     {
155         // get patient's name
156         String patient = patientNameJTextField.getText();
157
158         // display error message if no name entered
159         if ( patient.equals( "" ) )
160         {
161             // display error message
162             JOptionPane.showMessageDialog( null,
163                 "Please enter a name.",
164                 "Missing information", JOptionPane.ERROR_MESSAGE );
165         }
166         else // otherwise, do calculations
167         {
168             double total = 0.0; // sum of all services provided
169
170             // if patient had a cleaning
171             if ( cleaningJCheckBox.isSelected() )
172             {
173                 total += 35; // add 35 to total
174             }
175
176             // if patient had cavity filled
177             if ( cavityFillingJCheckBox.isSelected() )
178             {
179                 total += 150; // add 150 to total
180             }
181
182             // if patient had x-ray taken
183             if ( xRayJCheckBox.isSelected() )
184             {
185                 total += 85; // add 85 to total
186             }
187
188             // specify display format
189             DecimalFormat dollars = new DecimalFormat( "$0.00" );
190
191             // display total
192             totalJTextField.setText( dollars.format( total ) );
193
194         } // end else
195
196     } // end method calculateJButtonActionPerformed
```

Figure 7.16 Completed `calculateJButtonActionPerformed` method.

4. *Saving the application.* Save your modified source code file.

5. *Opening the Command Prompt window and changing directories.* Open the **Command Prompt** window by selecting **Start > Programs > Accessories > Command Prompt**. Change to your working directory by typing cd C:\SimplyJava\DentalPayment.

6. *Compiling the application.* Compile your application by typing javac DentalPayment.java.

7. *Running the application.* When your application compiles correctly, run it by typing java DentalPayment. Figure 7.17 shows the updated application running. Notice that you do not have to select any JCheckBoxes before clicking the **Calculate** JButton, but you must enter a name in the **Patient name:** JTextField. If you do not enter a name, the message dialog in Fig. 7.17 displays. If none of the JCheckBoxes is selected but a name is entered, the bill will contain the value **$0.00** (Fig. 7.18). In the following section, you will modify the code to test whether the user has selected any JCheckBoxes.

(cont.)

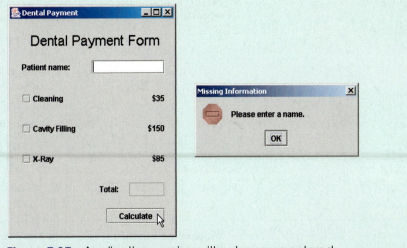

Figure 7.17   Application running without a name entered.

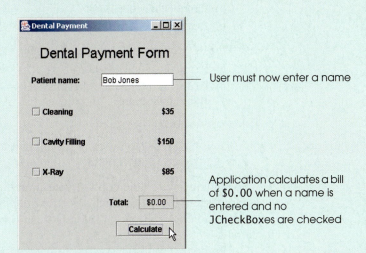

User must now enter a name

Application calculates a bill of **$0.00** when a name is entered and no **JCheckBoxes** are checked

Figure 7.18   Application running with a name entered, but without any **JCheckBoxes** selected.

8. ***Closing the running application.*** Close your running application by clicking its close button.

9. ***Closing the Command Prompt window.*** Close the **Command Prompt** window by clicking its close button.

Lines 162–164 of Fig. 7.14 passed four arguments to method JOption-Pane.showMessageDialog. The first argument is used to determine the position of the message dialog on the screen (null centers the dialog on the screen). The second and third arguments indicate the text of the dialog's message ("Please enter a name.") and the text of the dialog's title bar ("Missing Information"), respectively. The fourth argument (JOptionPane.ERROR_MESSAGE) specifies the icon that will be displayed in the dialog. This icon sets the tone for the dialog. The available icon constants are shown in Fig. 7.19.

JOptionPane Constants	Icon	Description
JOptionPane. ERROR_MESSAGE		Icon containing a stop sign. Typically used to alert the user of errors or critical situations.

Figure 7.19   JOptionPane dialog icon constants. (Part 1 of 2.)

JOptionPane Constants	Icon	Description
JOptionPane. INFORMATION_MESSAGE		Icon containing the letter "i." Typically used to display information about the state of the application.
JOptionPane. QUESTION_MESSAGE		Icon containing a question mark. Typically used to ask the user a question.
JOptionPane. WARNING_MESSAGE		Icon containing an exclamation point. Typically used to caution the user against potential problems.
JOptionPane. PLAIN_MESSAGE	no icon	Displays a dialog that simply contains a message, with no icon.

Figure 7.19 **JOptionPane** dialog icon constants. (Part 2 of 2.)

SELF-REVIEW

1. Which constant, when passed to method JOptionPane.showMessageDialog, indicates that a question is being asked?

   a) JOptionPane.QUESTION   b) JOptionPane.QUESTION_MESSAGE
   c) JOptionPaneIcon.QUESTION_MESSAGE d) JOptionPaneIcon.QUESTION

2. What is the message dialog icon containing the letter "i" typically used for?

   a) To ask the user a question.   b) To alert the user to critical situations.
   c) To display information about the state d) To caution the user against potential
      of the application.   problems.

Answers: 1.) b. 2.) c.

7.5 Logical Operators

So far, you have studied only **simple conditions**, such as count <= 10, total > 1000, and number != value. Each selection statement that you have used evaluated only one condition with one of the relational (or comparison) operators <, >, <=, >=, == or !=.

To handle multiple conditions more efficiently, Java provides logical operators that can be used to form **complex conditions**, or conditions that combine multiple simple conditions. The logical operators are **&& (conditional AND)**, **|| (conditional OR)**, **∧ (boolean logical exclusive OR)** and **! (logical negation)**. After you learn about logical operators, you will use them to create a complex condition in your **Dental Payment** application to confirm JCheckBox entries.

Using Conditional AND (&&)

Suppose that you wish to ensure that two conditions are *both* true in an application before choosing a certain path of execution. In that case, you can use the conditional && operator as follows:

```
if ( gender.equals( "Female" ) && age >= 65 )
{
    seniorFemales += 1;
}
```

This if statement contains two simple conditions. The condition gender.equals("Female") determines whether a person is female, and the condition age >= 65 determines whether a person is a senior citizen. The if statement then considers the combined condition

```
gender.equals( "Female" ) && age >= 65
```

This condition is true *if and only if* both of the simple conditions are true, meaning that gender contains the value "Female" and age contains a value greater than or

Error-Prevention Tip

Always write the simplest condition possible by limiting the number of logical operators used. Conditions with many logical operators can be hard to read and can introduce subtle bugs into your applications.

equal to 65. When this combined condition is true, the count of `seniorFemales` is incremented by 1. However, if either or both of the simple conditions are false, the application skips the increment and proceeds to the statement following the `if` statement. The readability of the preceding combined condition can be improved by adding redundant (that is, unnecessary) parentheses:

```
( gender.equals( "Female" ) ) && ( age >= 65 )
```

Figure 7.20 illustrates the outcome of using the `&&` operator with two `boolean` expressions. The table lists all four possible combinations of `true` and `false` values for *expression1* and *expression2*, which represent the left operand and the right operand, respectively. Such tables are called **truth tables**. Java evaluates to `true` or `false` expressions with relational operators, equality operators and logical operators.

expression1	expression2	expression1 && expression2
false	false	false
false	true	false
true	false	false
true	true	true

Figure 7.20   Truth table for the `&&` operator.

Using Conditional OR (||)

Now let's consider the `||` operator. Suppose that you wish to ensure that *either or both* of two conditions are true before you choose a certain path of execution. You would use the `||` operator as in the following `if` statement:

```
if ( semesterAverage >= 90 || finalExam >= 90 )
{
   JOptionPane.showMessageDialog( null, "Student grade is A.",
      "Student Grade", JOptionPane.INFORMATION_MESSAGE );
}
```

This statement also contains two simple conditions. The condition `semesterAverage >= 90` is evaluated to determine whether the student deserves an "A" in the course because of an outstanding performance throughout the semester. The condition `finalExam >= 90` is evaluated to determine whether the student deserves an "A" in the course because of an outstanding performance on the final exam. The `if` statement then considers the combined condition

```
( semesterAverage >= 90 || finalExam >= 90 )
```

and awards the student an "A" if either or both of the conditions are true, meaning that the student performed well during the semester, performed well on the final exam or both. Note that the text `"Student grade is A."` is displayed in a message dialog unless both of the conditions are false. Figure 7.21 provides a truth table for the `||` operator. Note in Appendix A that the `&&` operator has a higher precedence than the `||` operator.

expression1	expression2	expression1 || expression2
false	false	false
false	true	true
true	false	true
true	true	true

Figure 7.21   Truth table for the `||` operator.

An expression containing operator **&&** is evaluated only until it is known whether the condition is true or false. For example, evaluation of the expression

```
( gender.equals( "Female" ) && age >= 65 )
```

stops immediately if **gender** is not equal to **"Female"** (which would mean the entire expression is false). In this case, the evaluation of the second expression is irrelevant—once the first expression is known to be false, the whole expression must be false. Evaluation of the second expression occurs if and only if **gender** is equal to **"Female"** (which would mean that the entire expression could still be true if the condition **age >= 65** is true).

Similarly, an expression containing **||** is evaluated only until it is known whether the condition is true or false. For example, evaluation of the expression

```
if ( semesterAverage >= 90 || finalExam >= 90 )
```

stops immediately if **semesterAverage** is greater than or equal to 90 (which would mean the entire expression is true). In this case, the evaluation of the second expression is irrelevant—once the first expression is known to be true, the whole expression must be true.

This way of evaluating logical expressions can require fewer operations, therefore taking less time. This performance feature for the evaluation of **&&** and **||** expressions is called **short-circuit evaluation**. [Note that Java also provides the **&** (boolean logical AND) and **|** (boolean logical inclusive OR) operators, which are identical to **&&** and **||**, but do not perform short-circuit evaluation. They always evaluate their right operand regardless of whether their left operand is known to be true or false.]

Error-Prevention Tip

When writing conditions that contain combinations of **&&** and **||** operators, use parentheses to ensure that the conditions evaluate properly. Otherwise, logic errors could occur, because **&&** has higher precedence than **||**.

Using Boolean Logical Exclusive OR (∧)

A condition containing the boolean logical exclusive OR (∧) operator is true *if and only if* one of its operands results in a true value and the other results in a false value. If both operands are true or both are false, the entire condition is false. Figure 7.22 presents a truth table for the boolean logical exclusive OR operator (∧). This operator always evaluates both of its operands (that is, there is no short-circuit evaluation).

expression1	expression2	expression1 ∧ expression2
false	false	false
false	true	true
true	false	true
true	true	false

Figure 7.22 Truth table for the boolean logical exclusive OR (∧) operator.

Using Logical Negation (!)

Java's **!** (logical negation, also called logical NOT or logical complement) operator enables a programmer to "reverse" the meaning of a condition. Unlike the logical operators **&&**, **||** and **∧**, each of which combines two expressions (that is, these are all binary operators), the logical negation operator is a unary operator, requiring only one operand. The logical negation operator is placed before a condition to choose a path of execution if the original condition (without the logical negation operator) is false. The logical negation operator is demonstrated by the following **if** statement:

```
if ( !( grade == value ) )
{
   displayLabel.setText( "They are not equal!" );
}
```

In this case, the body of the if executes if grade is not equal to value. The parentheses around the condition grade == value are necessary, because the logical negation operator (!) has a higher precedence than the equality operator. For clarity, most programmers prefer to write

```
!( grade == value )
```

as

```
( grade != value )
```

Figure 7.23 provides a truth table for the logical negation operator. Next, you will modify your **Dental Payment** application to use a complex logical expression to determine whether any of the JCheckBoxes are selected.

expression	! expression
false	true
true	false

Figure 7.23 Truth table for the ! (logical negation) operator.

Using Logical Operators in Complex Expressions

1. ***Inserting a complex expression into the calculateJButtonActionPerformed method.*** Replace line 159 of Fig. 7.13 with lines 159–162 of Fig. 7.24.

Inserting a complex expression

```
 Source Editor [DentalPayment]
156          String patient = patientNameJTextField.getText();
157
158          // display error message if no name entered
159          if ( ( patient.equals( "" ) ) ||
160             ( !cleaningJCheckBox.isSelected() &&
161             !cavityFillingJCheckBox.isSelected() &&
162             !xRayJCheckBox.isSelected() ) )
163          {
164             // display error message
```

Figure 7.24 Using the && and || logical operators.

Lines 159–162 define a more complex logical expression than those you have used so far in this book. Notice the use of || and &&. If the patient's name is blank or if no JCheckBox is selected, a dialog should appear. After the original expression patient.equals(""), you use || to indicate that either the expression on the left (patient.equals("")) or the expression on the right (which determines if no JCheckBox has been selected) needs to be true for the entire expression to evaluate to true. The body of the if statement is executed only if the entire expression evaluates to true. The complex expression on the right uses && twice to determine if all of the JCheckBoxes are deselected. If a JCheckBox is deselected, the isSelected method will return false and the ! operator will reverse that condition, yielding true. For example, if cleaningJCheckBox is not selected, the expression cleaningJCheckBox.isSelected() will return false and the expression !cleaningJCheckBox.isSelected() will return true.

2. ***Modifying the message dialog.*** Modify lines 158–159 and 167 to appear as shown in Fig. 7.25. Now that your application tests whether a JCheckBox has been selected, you should update the if...else statement's comment (line 158–159) as well as the message displayed in the message dialog (line 167).

(cont.)

```
Source Editor [DentalPayment *]                                   _ □ ×
156        String patient = patientNameJTextField.getText();
157
158        // display error message if no name entered or
159        // no JCheckBox is selected
160        if ( ( patient.equals( "" ) ) ||
161             ( !cleaningJCheckBox.isSelected() &&
162               !cavityFillingJCheckBox.isSelected() &&
163               !xRayJCheckBox.isSelected() ) )
164        {
165             // display error message
166             JOptionPane.showMessageDialog( null,
167                "Please enter a name and check at least one item.",
168                "Missing Information", JOptionPane.ERROR_MESSAGE );
```

Figure 7.25 Message dialog displayed if no name is entered and no JCheckBoxes are selected.

3. **Saving the application.** Save your modified source code file.

4. **Opening the Command Prompt window and changing directories.** Open the **Command Prompt** window by selecting **Start > Programs > Accessories > Command Prompt**. Change to your working directory by typing cd C:\SimplyJava\DentalPayment.

5. **Compiling the application.** Compile your application by typing javac DentalPayment.java.

6. **Running the application.** When your application compiles correctly, run it by typing java DentalPayment. Figure 7.26 shows the completed application running. Notice that the user must enter a name and select at least one JCheckBox before clicking the **Calculate** JButton. Otherwise, a message dialog is displayed. The application appears the same as in the test-drive. (You have finally corrected the weakness from your earlier implementation of the **Dental Payment** application.) Figure 7.27 shows the completed application running with correct input.

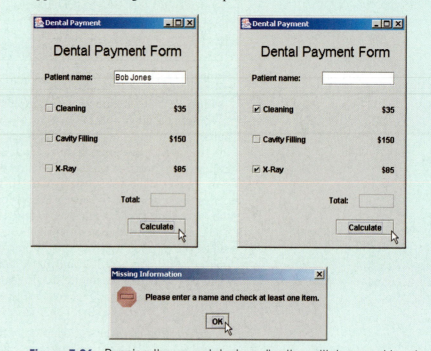

Figure 7.26 Running the completed application with incorrect input.

(cont.)

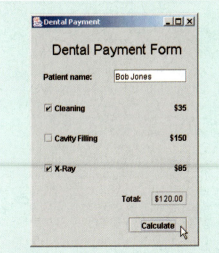

Figure 7.27 Running the completed application with correct input.

7. ***Closing the running application.*** Close your running application by clicking its close button.

8. ***Closing the Command Prompt window.*** Close the **Command Prompt** window by clicking its close button.

Figure 7.28 presents the source code for the **Dental Payment** application. The lines of code that you added, viewed or modified in this tutorial are highlighted.

```
1   // Tutorial 7: DentalPayment.java
2   // This application calculates the total cost of the bill for a
3   // patient at a dental office.
4   import java.awt.*;
5   import java.awt.event.*;
6   import java.text.*;
7   import javax.swing.*;
8
9   public class DentalPayment extends JFrame
10  {
11     // JLabel that displays header on application window
12     private JLabel dentalPaymentFormJLabel;
13
14     // JLabel and JTextField for patient name
15     private JLabel patientNameJLabel;
16     private JTextField patientNameJTextField;
17
18     // JCheckBox and JLabel for cleaning
19     private JCheckBox cleaningJCheckBox;
20     private JLabel cleaningPriceJLabel;
21
22     // JCheckBox and JLabel for cavity filling
23     private JCheckBox cavityFillingJCheckBox;
24     private JLabel cavityFillingPriceJLabel;
25
26     // JCheckBox and JLabel for X-Ray
27     private JCheckBox xRayJCheckBox;
28     private JLabel xRayPriceJLabel;
29
```

Figure 7.28 Code for the **Dental Payment** application. (Part 1 of 5.)

```
30      // JLabel and JTextField for total fee
31      private JLabel totalJLabel;
32      private JTextField totalJTextField;
33
34      // JButton to initiate calculation of fee
35      private JButton calculateJButton;
36
37      // no-argument constructor
38      public DentalPayment()
39      {
40         createUserInterface();
41      }
42
43      // create and position GUI components; register event handlers
44      private void createUserInterface()
45      {
46         // get content pane for attaching GUI components
47         Container contentPane = getContentPane();
48
49         // enable explicit positioning of GUI components
50         contentPane.setLayout( null );
51
52         // set up dentalPaymentFormJLabel
53         dentalPaymentFormJLabel = new JLabel();
54         dentalPaymentFormJLabel.setBounds( 19, 19, 235, 28 );
55         dentalPaymentFormJLabel.setText( "Dental Payment Form" );
56         dentalPaymentFormJLabel.setFont(
57            new Font( "Default", Font.PLAIN, 22 ) );
58         dentalPaymentFormJLabel.setHorizontalAlignment(
59            JLabel.CENTER );
60         contentPane.add( dentalPaymentFormJLabel );
61
62         // set up patientNameJLabel
63         patientNameJLabel = new JLabel();
64         patientNameJLabel.setBounds( 19, 65, 91, 21 );
65         patientNameJLabel.setText( "Patient name:" );
66         contentPane.add( patientNameJLabel );
67
68         // set up patientNameJTextField
69         patientNameJTextField = new JTextField();
70         patientNameJTextField.setBounds( 132, 65, 117, 21 );
71         contentPane.add( patientNameJTextField );
72
73         // set up cleaningJCheckBox
74         cleaningJCheckBox = new JCheckBox();
75         cleaningJCheckBox.setBounds( 16, 112, 122, 24 );
76         cleaningJCheckBox.setText( "Cleaning" );
77         contentPane.add( cleaningJCheckBox );
78
79         // set up cleaningPriceJLabel
80         cleaningPriceJLabel = new JLabel();
81         cleaningPriceJLabel.setBounds( 211, 112, 38, 24 );
82         cleaningPriceJLabel.setText( "$35" );
83         cleaningPriceJLabel.setHorizontalAlignment( JLabel.RIGHT );
84         contentPane.add( cleaningPriceJLabel );
85
86         // set up cavityFillingJCheckBox
87         cavityFillingJCheckBox = new JCheckBox();
```

Customizing `cleaningJCheckBox`

Figure 7.28 Code for the **Dental Payment** application. (Part 2 of 5.)

```
Customizing          88    cavityFillingJCheckBox.setBounds( 16, 159, 122, 24 );
cavityFillingJCheckBox 89   cavityFillingJCheckBox.setText( "Cavity Filling" );
                     90    contentPane.add( cavityFillingJCheckBox );
                     91
                     92    // set up cavityFillingPriceJLabel
                     93    cavityFillingPriceJLabel = new JLabel();
                     94    cavityFillingPriceJLabel.setBounds( 211, 159, 38, 24 );
                     95    cavityFillingPriceJLabel.setText( "$150" );
                     96    cavityFillingPriceJLabel.setHorizontalAlignment(
                     97       JLabel.RIGHT );
                     98    contentPane.add( cavityFillingPriceJLabel );
                     99
                    100    // set up xRayJCheckBox
                    101    xRayJCheckBox = new JCheckBox();
Customizing xRayJCheckBox 102  xRayJCheckBox.setBounds( 16, 206, 122, 24 );
                    103    xRayJCheckBox.setText( "X-Ray" );
                    104    contentPane.add( xRayJCheckBox );
                    105
                    106    // set up xRayPriceJLabel
                    107    xRayPriceJLabel = new JLabel();
                    108    xRayPriceJLabel.setBounds( 211, 206, 38, 24 );
                    109    xRayPriceJLabel.setText( "$85" );
                    110    xRayPriceJLabel.setHorizontalAlignment( JLabel.RIGHT );
                    111    contentPane.add( xRayPriceJLabel );
                    112
                    113    // set up totalJLabel
                    114    totalJLabel = new JLabel();
                    115    totalJLabel.setBounds( 144, 256, 41, 21 );
                    116    totalJLabel.setText( "Total:" );
                    117    contentPane.add( totalJLabel );
                    118
                    119    // set up totalJTextField
                    120    totalJTextField = new JTextField();
                    121    totalJTextField.setBounds( 192, 256, 56, 21 );
                    122    totalJTextField.setEditable( false );
                    123    totalJTextField.setHorizontalAlignment( JTextField.CENTER );
                    124    contentPane.add( totalJTextField );
                    125
                    126    // set up calculateJButton
                    127    calculateJButton = new JButton();
                    128    calculateJButton.setBounds( 155, 296, 94, 24 );
                    129    calculateJButton.setText( "Calculate" );
                    130    contentPane.add( calculateJButton );
                    131    calculateJButton.addActionListener(
                    132
                    133       new ActionListener() // anonymous inner class
                    134       {
                    135          // event handler called when user clicks calculateJButton
                    136          public void actionPerformed( ActionEvent event )
                    137          {
                    138             calculateJButtonActionPerformed( event );
                    139          }
                    140
                    141       } // end anonymous inner class
                    142
                    143    ); // end call to addActionListener
                    144
```

Figure 7.28 Code for the **Dental Payment** application. (Part 3 of 5.)

```
145        // set properties of application's window
146        setTitle( "Dental Payment" ); // set title bar string
147        setSize( 272, 364 );          // set window size
148        setVisible( true );           // display window
149
150     } // end method createUserInterface
151
152     // calculate cost of patient's visit
153     private void calculateJButtonActionPerformed( ActionEvent event )
154     {
155        // get patient's name
156        String patient = patientNameJTextField.getText();
157
158        // display error message if no name entered or no box selected
159        if ( ( patient.equals( "" ) ) ||
160           ( !cleaningJCheckBox.isSelected() &&
161           !cavityFillingJCheckBox.isSelected() &&
162           !xRayJCheckBox.isSelected() ) )
163        {
164           // display error message
165           JOptionPane.showMessageDialog( null,
166              "Please enter a name and check at least one item.",
167              "Missing Information", JOptionPane.ERROR_MESSAGE );
168        }
169        else // otherwise, do calculations
170        {
171           double total = 0.0; // sum of all services provided
172
173           // if patient had a cleaning
174           if ( cleaningJCheckBox.isSelected() )
175           {
176              total += 35; // add 35 to total
177           }
178
179           // if patient had cavity filled
180           if ( cavityFillingJCheckBox.isSelected() )
181           {
182              total += 150; // add 150 to total
183           }
184
185           // if patient had x-ray taken
186           if ( xRayJCheckBox.isSelected() )
187           {
188              total += 85; // add 85 to total
189           }
190
191           // specify display format
192           DecimalFormat dollars = new DecimalFormat( "$0.00" );
193
194           // display total
195           totalJTextField.setText( dollars.format( total ) );
196
197        } // end else
198
199     } // end method calculateJButtonActionPerformed
200
```

Annotations (left margin, top to bottom):
- Obtaining patient name → (line 156)
- Using logical operators and JCheckBox method isSelected → (lines 159–162)
- Displaying a JOptionPane message dialog → (lines 165–167)
- Examining the *selected* property of cleaningJCheckBox → (line 174)
- Examining the *selected* property of cavityFillingJCheckBox → (line 180)
- Examining the *selected* property of xRayJCheckBox → (line 186)
- Format and display total → (line 195)

Figure 7.28 Code for the **Dental Payment** application. (Part 4 of 5.)

```
201    // main method
202    public static void main( String[] args )
203    {
204        DentalPayment application = new DentalPayment();
205        application.setDefaultCloseOperation( JFrame.EXIT_ON_CLOSE );
206
207    } // end method main
208
209 } // end class DentalPayment
```

Figure 7.28   Code for the **Dental Payment** application. (Part 5 of 5.)

SELF-REVIEW

1. A unary operator _____.
   a) requires exactly one operand   b) requires two operands
   c) must use **&&**   d) can have no operands

2. The _____ operator is used to ensure that two conditions are both true.
   a) ^   b) **&&**
   c) and   d) ||

Answers: 1.) a. 2.) b.

7.6 Wrap-Up

In this tutorial, you used JCheckBox components to provide a series of choices to users in your **Dental Payment** application. JCheckBoxes provide options that can be selected and deselected by clicking them. When a JCheckBox is selected, its gray square contains a check mark. You can determine whether a JCheckBox is selected in your code by accessing its *selected* property with method isSelected.

You used a message dialog to display a message to the user when information was not entered appropriately. To implement dialogs in your application, you used the JOptionPane class, which provides methods and constants necessary to display a dialog containing a JButton and an icon. You used several if statements nested in an if...else statement to calculate the cost of the dental visit or display a message dialog if the user was missing input.

You learned to use the conditional AND (&&) operator when both conditions must be true for the overall condition to be true—if either condition is false, the overall condition is false. You also learned that the conditional OR (||) operator requires at least one of its conditions to be true for the overall condition to be true—if both conditions are false, the overall condition is false. The boolean logical exclusive OR (^) operator requires exactly one of its conditions to be true for the overall condition to be true—if both conditions are false or if both conditions are true, the overall condition is false. The logical NOT (!) operator reverses the boolean result of a condition—true becomes false, and false becomes true. You used the && and || operators to form a complex expression.

In the next tutorial, you will learn more about Java's control statements. In particular, you will use **repetition statements**, which allow the programmer to specify that an action or a group of actions should be performed many times.

SKILLS SUMMARY

Selecting a JCheckBox
- Click the JCheckBox, and a check mark will appear in the gray box.

Deselecting a JCheckBox
- Click a selected JCheckBox to remove its check mark.

Determining Whether a JCheckBox is Selected

- Access the JCheckBox's *selected* property with method isSelected.

Displaying a Message Dialog

- Use method JOptionPane.showMessageDialog.
- Use null as the first argument to center the dialog on the screen.
- Specify the text of the dialog's message as the second argument.
- Specify the text of the dialog's title bar as the third argument.
- Specify the icon that will be displayed in the dialog as the fourth argument.

Combining Multiple Conditions

- Use the logical operators to form complex conditions by combining simple ones.

KEY TERMS

boolean logical exclusive OR (^) operator—A logical operator that evaluates to true if and only if one of its operands is true and the other is false.

complex condition—A condition that combines multiple simple conditions.

conditional AND (&&) operator—A logical operator used to ensure that two conditions are both true before choosing a path of execution. Performs short-circuit evaluation.

conditional OR (||) operator—A logical operator used to ensure that either or both of two conditions are true before a path of execution is chosen. Performs short-circuit evaluation.

dialog—A window that displays and/or retrieves information.

dismiss—A synonym for closing a dialog.

equals method of class String—Returns true when String contains the same text as the argument to method equals.

isSelected method of class JCheckBox—Specifies whether the JCheckBox is selected (true) or deselected (false).

JCheckBox component—A small gray square GUI element that either is blank or contains a check mark. This component includes the text displayed beside the square.

JCheckBox text—The text that appears alongside a JCheckBox.

JOptionPane class—Provides a method for displaying message dialogs and constants for displaying icons in those dialogs.

logical operators—The operators (&&, ||, &, |, ^ and !) that can be used to form complex conditions by combining simple ones.

logical negation (!) operator—A logical operator that enables a programmer to reverse the meaning of a condition: A true condition, when logically negated, becomes false, and a false condition, when logically negated, becomes true.

message dialog—A dialog that displays messages to users.

***selected* property**—Defines if a component has been selected.

short-circuit evaluation—The evaluation of the right operand in && and || expressions occurs only if the left condition is true in an expression containing && or false in an expression containing ||.

showMessageDialog method of class JOptionPane—Used to display a message dialog.

simple condition—A condition that contains one expression.

state button—A button that can be in the on/off (true/false) state.

truth table—A table that displays the truth value of a logical operator for all possible combinations of true and false values of its operand(s).

GUI DESIGN GUIDELINES

JCheckBoxes

- A JCheckBox's text should be descriptive and as short as possible. When a JCheckBox's text contains more than one word, use book-title capitalization.
- Align groups of JCheckBoxes either horizontally or vertically.

Message Dialogs

- Text displayed in a message dialog should be descriptive and as short as possible.

JAVA LIBRARY REFERENCE

JCheckBox   This component allows the user to select an option. If an application contains several JCheckBoxes, any number of them (including zero or all) can be selected at once).

■ *In action*

■ *Methods*

isSelected—Returns true if a JCheckBox is selected.

setBounds—Sets the location and size of a JCheckBox component.

setText—Sets the text displayed alongside a JCheckBox.

JOptionPane   This class allows the user to display dialogs.

■ *Methods*

showMessageDialog—Displays a message dialog, taking four arguments. The first argument (null in the examples so far) specifies the position of the message dialog on the screen. The second and third arguments indicate the text of the dialog's message and the text of the dialog's title bar, respectively. The fourth argument (one of the constants defined in class JOptionPane) specifies the icon that will be displayed in the dialog.

■ *Constants*

ERROR_MESSAGE ( )—Icon containing a stop sign. Typically used to alert the user of errors or critical situations.

INFORMATION_MESSAGE ( )—Icon containing the letter "i." Typically used to display information about the state of the application.

PLAIN_MESSAGE—Displays a dialog that simply contains a message, with no icon.

QUESTION_MESSAGE ( )—Icon containing a question mark. Typically used to ask the user a question.

WARNING_MESSAGE ( )—Icon containing an exclamation point. Typically used to caution the user against potential problems.

String   This class is used to manipulate textual data.

■ *Methods*

equals—Returns true when String contains the same text as the String argument to method equals.

MULTIPLE-CHOICE QUESTIONS

7.1 How many JCheckBoxes in a GUI can be selected at once?

    a) 0   b) 1

    c) 4   d) any number

7.2 The text that appears alongside a JCheckBox is referred to as the _____.

    a) JCheckBox value   b) JCheckBox name

    c) JCheckBox text   d) JCheckBox data

7.3 The second argument passed to method JOptionPane.showMessageDialog is _____.

    a) the text displayed in the dialog's title bar

    b) a constant representing the JButtons displayed in the dialog

    c) the message displayed by the dialog

    d) a constant representing the icon that appears in the dialog

7.4 The _____ constant can be used to display an error message in a message dialog.

    a) JOptionPane.ERROR_MESSAGE   b) JOptionPane.ERROR_ICON

    c) JOptionPane.ERROR   d) JOptionPane.ERROR_IMAGE

7.5 The JOptionPane dialog icon typically used to caution the user against potential problems is the _____.

a) stop sign   b) exclamation point
c) letter i   d) question mark

7.6 Operator && _____.

a) performs short-circuit evaluation   b) is a comparison operator
c) evaluates to false if both operands are true
d) None of the above.

7.7 A JCheckBox is selected when its isSelected method returns _____.

a) on   b) true
c) selected   d) checked

7.8 The condition *expression1* && *expression2* evaluates to true when _____.

a) *expression1* is true and *expression2* is false
b) *expression1* is false and *expression2* is true
c) both *expression1* and *expression2* are true
d) both *expression1* and *expression2* are false

7.9 The condition *expression1* || *expression2* evaluates to false when _____.

a) *expression1* is true and *expression2* is false
b) *expression1* is false and *expression2* is true
c) both *expression1* and *expression2* are true
d) both *expression1* and *expression2* are false

7.10 The condition *expression1* ^ *expression2* evaluates to true when _____.

a) *expression1* is true and *expression2* is false
b) *expression1* is false and *expression2* is true
c) both *expression1* and *expression2* are true
d) Both a and b.

EXERCISES

7.11 (***Enhanced Dental Payment Application***) Modify the **Dental Payment** application from this tutorial to include additional services as shown in Fig. 7.29. Add the proper functionality (using if statements) to determine whether any of the new JCheckBoxes are selected and, if so, add the price of the service to the total bill. As in the original application, a message dialog should be displayed if the patient's name is missing or if none of the JCheckBoxes is selected.

Figure 7.29 Enhanced **Dental Payment** application.

a) ***Copying the template to your working directory.*** Copy the directory C:\Examples\ Tutorial07\Exercises\DentalPaymentEnhanced to your C:\SimplyJava directory.

b) ***Opening the template file.*** Open the DentalPayment.java file in your text editor.

c) ***Customizing the Fluoride JCheckBox and its price JLabel.*** In line 128 set the *bounds* property of fluorideJCheckBox to 16, 210, 140, 24. In line 129 set the *text* property of fluorideJCheckBox to "Fluoride". The price for a fluoride treatment is $50. In line 135 set the *text* property of fluoridePriceJLabel to "$50".

d) ***Customizing the Root Canal JCheckBox and its price JLabel.*** In line 141 set the *bounds* property of rootCanalJCheckBox to 16, 242, 140, 24. In line 142 set the *text* property of rootCanalJCheckBox to "Root Canal". The price for a root canal treatment is $225. In line 148 set the *text* property of rootCanalJPriceLabel to "$225".

e) ***Customizing the Other JCheckBox, its price JLabel and a JTextField for the user to input a price.*** In line 154 set the *bounds* property of otherJCheckBox to 16, 274, 140, 24. In line 155 set the *text* property of otherJCheckBox to "Other". In line 160 set the *bounds* property of otherPriceJLabel to 206, 274, 32, 24. In line 161 set the *text* property of otherPriceJLabel to "$". In lines 166–168, you need to set the *bounds* (with values 214, 274, 34, 24) and *horizontalAlignment* (with value JTextField.RIGHT) properties of the otherPriceJTextField so that the text will be displayed right justified in the JTextField and the JTextField will be placed on the right hand side of otherPriceJLabel (Fig. 7.29). Use two lines to set the *horizontalAlignment* property to increase readability.

f) ***Modifying the calculateJButtonActionPerformed method.*** Modify the if statement that starts in line 217 to check if the user has not entered a name and/or selected any JCheckBoxes. Also add code to the calculateJButtonActionPerformed method (starting in line 252) that determines whether the new JCheckBoxes have been selected. This can be done using if statements that are similar to the ones already in the method. Use the if statements to update the bill amount. The bill amount should be displayed in the totalPriceJTextField with the format "$0.00".

g) ***Saving the application.*** Save your modified source code file.

h) ***Opening the Command Prompt window and changing directories.*** Open the **Command Prompt** window by selecting **Start > Programs > Accessories > Command Prompt**. Change to your working directory by typing cd C:\SimplyJava\Dental-PaymentEnhanced.

i) ***Compiling the application.*** Compile your application by typing javac DentalPayment.java.

j) ***Running the completed application.*** When your application compiles correctly, run it by typing java DentalPayment. Test each calculation to ensure that you implemented the method properly. Make sure the functionality for each of the JCheckBoxes works properly, both the existing JCheckBoxes and the JCheckBoxes customized in the tutorial.

k) ***Closing the completed application.*** Close your running application by clicking its close button.

l) ***Closing the Command Prompt window.*** Close the **Command Prompt** window by clicking its close button.

7.12 (*Fuzzy Dice Order Form Application*) Write an application that allows users to process orders for fuzzy dice as shown in Fig. 7.30. The application should calculate the total price of the order, including tax. JTextFields for inputting the order number, the customer name and the shipping address are provided. Initially, these fields contain text that describes their purpose. If the user does not modify this text, a message dialog is displayed. Provide JCheckBoxes for selecting the fuzzy dice color and JTextFields for inputting the quantities of fuzzy dice to order. If the user does not select any of the fuzzy dice JCheckBoxes, a message dialog is displayed. The application should also contain a JButton that, when clicked, calculates the subtotals for each type of fuzzy dice ordered and the total of the entire order (including tax). Use 5% for the tax rate.

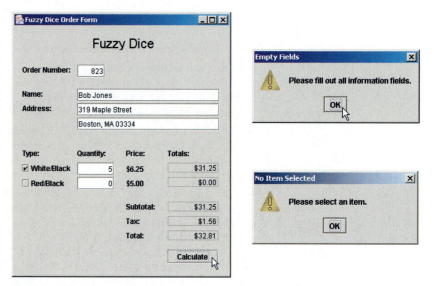

Figure 7.30 Fuzzy Dice Order Form application.

a) *Copying the template to your working directory.* Copy the directory C:\Examples\ Tutorial07\Exercises\FuzzyDiceOrderForm to your C:\SimplyJava directory.

b) *Opening the template file.* Open FuzzyDiceOrderForm.java in your text editor.

c) *Customizing the JCheckBoxes.* In line 137 set the *bounds* (10, 227, 93, 21) and *text* (White/Black) properties of whiteTypeJCheckBox. In line 143 set the *bounds* (10, 252, 88, 21) and *text* (Red/Black) properties of redTypeJCheckBox.

d) *Coding the calculateJButtonActionPerformed method.* Code should be placed in the calculateJButtonActionPerformed method, which begins in line 283. In line 298, replace the keyword true with an expression that will return true if white-TypeJCheckBox has been selected. On line 305 replace keyword true with an expression that will return true if redTypeJCheckBox has been selected. These if statements should now calculate subtotals for each type of dice if that type of dice has been selected. Beginning in line 312, replace keyword true with a complex expression that returns true if the user has not entered shipping data. In the body of this if statement, display a message dialog informing the user that they must fill out all information fields. In the else if portion that follows, replace keyword true with an expression that returns true if neither JCheckBox is selected. In the body of this else if portion of code, display a message dialog asking the user to select an item and enter a quantity.

e) *Saving the application.* Save your modified source code file.

f) *Opening the Command Prompt window and changing directories.* Open the **Command Prompt** window by selecting **Start > Programs > Accessories > Command Prompt**. Change to your working directory by typing cd C:\SimplyJava\FuzzyDiceOrderForm.

g) *Compiling the application.* Compile your application by typing javac FuzzyDiceOrderForm.java.

h) *Running the completed application.* When your application compiles correctly, run it by typing java FuzzyDiceOrderForm. Test each calculation to ensure that you implemented the method properly. Test the application by providing quantities for checked items. For example, ensure that your application is calculating 5% sales tax. Also, determine whether your code containing the logical operators works correctly by clicking the **Calculate** JButton when the shipping information has not been entered and/or none of the JCheckBoxes is selected.

i) *Closing the completed application.* Close your running application by clicking its close button.

j) *Closing the Command Prompt window.* Close the **Command Prompt** window by clicking its close button.

7.13 (*Modified Fuzzy Dice Order Form Application*) Modify the **Fuzzy Dice Order Form** application from Exercise 7.12 to determine whether a customer should receive a 7% discount for ordering more than $50 (before tax) in fuzzy dice. The discount amount should be displayed as a negative value, because the amount will be subtracted from the user's total (Fig. 7.31).

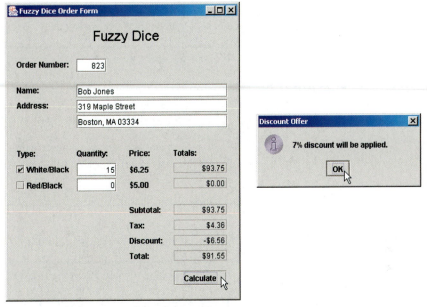

Figure 7.31   Modified **Fuzzy Dice Order Form** application.

a) *Copying the template to your working directory.* Copy the directory C:\Examples\ Tutorial07\Exercises\FuzzyDiceOrderFormModified to your C:\SimplyJava directory.

b) *Opening the template file.* Open the FuzzyDiceOrderForm.java file in your text editor.

c) *Determining whether the total cost is over $50.* In the calculateJButton-ActionPerformed method, add an if statement to determine if the amount ordered is greater than $50. [*Hint*: This if statement can be added after the code that calculates the subtotal cost and before the code that calculates the tax.]

d) *Displaying the discount and subtracting the discount from the total.* If a customer orders more than $50, display a message dialog as shown in Fig. 7.31 that informs the user that the customer is entitled to a 7% discount. The message dialog should contain an INFORMATION_MESSAGE icon. Calculate 7% of the total amount, and display the discount amount as a negative value in discountJTextField, which is uneditable. Subtract this amount from the total and update totalJTextField.

e) *Adding an else statement.* If a customer does not order more than $50, the customer gets no discount. Add an else statement to the if statement you created in *Step c*. The body of this statement should output "$0.00" in discountJTextField.

f) *Saving the application.* Save your modified source code file.

g) *Opening the Command Prompt window and changing directories.* Open the **Command Prompt** window by selecting **Start > Programs > Accessories > Command Prompt**. Change to your working directory by typing cd C:\SimplyJava\Fuzzy-DiceOrderFormModified.

h) *Compiling the application.* Compile your application by typing javac FuzzyDice-OrderForm.java.

i) *Running the completed application.* When your application compiles correctly, run it by typing java FuzzyDiceOrderForm. Test each calculation to ensure that you implemented the method properly. Perform the same checks as you did in the previous exercise. Also test that the discount is applied only when ordering $50 or more of fuzzy dice.

j) *Closing the completed application.* Close your running application by clicking its close button.

k) *Closing the Command Prompt window.* Close the **Command Prompt** window by clicking its close button.

What does this code do? ▶

7.14 Assume that nameJTextField is a JTextField and that otherJCheckBox is a JCheck-Box next to which is a JTextField otherJTextField. What does this code segment do?

```
1    String name = nameJTextField.getText();
2    String other = otherJTextField.getText();
3
4    if ( name.equals( "" ) ||
5       ( otherJCheckBox.isSelected() && other.equals( "" ) ) )
6    {
7       JOptionPane.showMessageDialog( null,
8          "Mystery Message", "Input Error",
9          JOptionPane.WARNING_MESSAGE )
10   }
```

What's wrong with this code? ▶

7.15 Assume that nameJTextField is a JTextField. Find the error(s) in the following code:

```
1    String name = nameJTextField.getText();
2
3    if name.equals( "John Doe" )
4    {
5       JOptionPane.showMessageDialog( "Welcome, John!",
6          JOptionPane.INFORMATION_MESSAGE );
7    }
```

Using the Debugger ▶

7.16 (*Sibling Survey Application*) The **Sibling Survey** application displays the siblings selected by the user in a dialog. If the user checks either the **Brother(s)** or **Sister(s)** JCheck-Box, and the **No Siblings** JCheckBox, the user is asked to verify the selection. Otherwise, the user's selection is displayed in a JOptionPane message dialog. While testing this application, you noticed that it does not execute properly. Use the debugger jdb to find and correct the logic error(s) in the code. Figure 7.32 shows the correct output for the application.

a) *Copying the template to your working directory.* Copy the directory C:\Examples\ Tutorial07\Exercises\Debugger\SiblingSurvey to your C:\SimplyJava directory.

b) *Opening the Command Prompt window and changing directories.* Open the **Command Prompt** window by selecting **Start > Programs > Accessories > Command Prompt**. Change to your working directory by typing cd C:\SimplyJava\Debugger\ SiblingSurvey.

c) *Running the application.* Run the **Sibling Survey** application by typing java Sib-lingSurvey. Test the different options. Notice that when you select either the **Brother(s)** or the **Sister(s)** JCheckBox, the desired result is not performed. Also, notice that when you select the **No Siblings** JCheckBox as well as one of the other JCheckBoxes, the desired result is not performed.

d) *Compiling the application for debugging.* Compile the application with the -g com-mand-line option by typing javac -g SiblingSurvey.java.

e) *Starting the debugger.* Start the debugger by typing jdb.

f) *Opening the template file.* Open the SiblingSurvey.java file in your text editor.

g) *Finding and correcting the error(s).* Use the debugging skills learned in previous tuto-rials to determine where the application's logic errors exist. Set breakpoints in the method submitServeyJButtonActionPerformed and follow the program logic to locate the errors. Modify the application so that it displays the correct message dialogs.

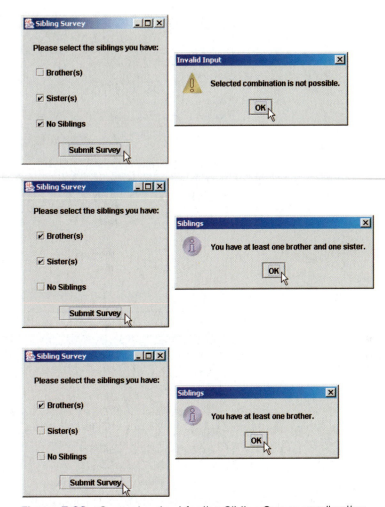

Figure 7.32 Correct output for the **Sibling Survey** application.

h) *Saving the application.* Save your modified source code file.

i) *Compiling the application.* Compile your application by typing javac SiblingSurvey.java.

j) *Running the corrected application.* When your application compiles correctly, run it by typing java SiblingSurvey. Test the different user options, including the options that worked correctly in the template. Ensure that all options work correctly.

k) *Closing the corrected application.* Close your running application by clicking its close button.

l) *Closing the Command Prompt window.* Close the **Command Prompt** window by clicking its close button.

Programming Challenge ▶   **7.17** (*Enhanced Fuzzy Dice Order Form Application*) Enhance the **Fuzzy Dice Order Form** application from Exercise 7.13 so that when a JCheckBox is deselected, its corresponding quantity JTextField is made uneditable and the quantity value is reset to 0 (Fig. 7.33). All the monetary values should also be reset to $0.00. When a JCheckBox is selected, its corresponding quantity JTextField should then be made editable. Again, all the monetary values should be reset to $0.00. To solve this exercise, you will need to use methods for the JCheckBoxes. Empty methods are provided for you. The steps below will walk you through adding the proper code to these methods.

a) *Copying the template to your working directory.* Copy the directory C:\Examples\Tutorial07\Exercises\FuzzyDiceOrderFormEnhanced to your C:\SimplyJava directory.

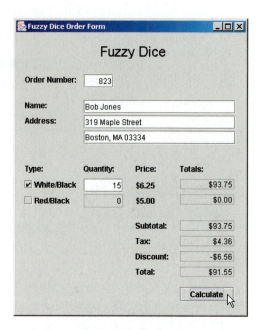

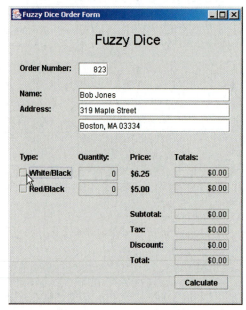

Figure 7.33 Enhanced **Fuzzy Dice Order Form** application.

b) *Opening the template file.* Open the FuzzyDiceOrderForm.java file in your text editor.

c) *Customizing the application's components.* Set the *editable* property of whiteQuan-tityJTextField and redQuantityJTextField to false. You want both JText-Fields to be uneditable at the start of the application. On lines 189 and 198, set the *editable* property of each JTextField to false after the code that sets each JText-Field *text* property to "0".

d) *Coding the whiteTypeJCheckBoxActionPerformed method.* In the whiteType-JCheckBoxActionPerformed method (which is right after the calculateJButton-ActionPerformed method), test whether whiteTypeJCheckBox has been selected. If it has, set whiteQuantityJTextField's *editable* property to true. If the JCheckBox has not been selected, set whiteQuantityJTextField's *editable* property to false, set whiteQuantityJTextField's *text* property to 0 and call method clearResults. Method clearResults, provided in the application's template, resets the application's output components.

e) *Coding the redTypeJCheckBoxActionPerformed method.* In the redTypeJCheck-BoxActionPerformed method (which is right after the whiteTypeJCheckBox-ActionPerformed method), test whether redTypeJCheckBox has been selected. If it has, set redQuantityJTextField's *editable* property to true. If the JCheckBox has not been selected, set redQuantityJTextField's *editable* property to false, set redQuantityJTextField's *text* property to 0 and call method clearResults.

f) *Saving the application.* Save your modified source code file.

g) *Opening the Command Prompt window and changing directories.* Open the **Command Prompt** window by selecting **Start > Programs > Accessories > Command Prompt**. Change to your working directory by typing cd C:\SimplyJava\Fuzzy-DiceOrderFormEnhanced.

h) *Compiling the application.* Compile your application by typing javac FuzzyDice-OrderForm.java.

i) *Running the completed application.* When your application compiles correctly, run it by typing java FuzzyDiceOrderForm. Test each calculation to ensure that you implemented the methods properly. Perform checks to test the functionality added in Exercise 7.12 and Exercise 7.13. Also select and deselect the application's JCheck-Boxes to ensure that the application is updated appropriately.

j) *Closing the completed application.* Close your running application by clicking its close button.

k) *Closing the Command Prompt window.* Close the **Command Prompt** window by clicking its close button.

TUTORIAL 8

Objectives

In this tutorial, you will learn to:
- Use the `while` repetition statement to execute statements in an application repeatedly.
- Use counter-controlled repetition.
- Use the increment and decrement operators.
- Display information in `JTextArea`s.

Outline

Car Payment Calculator Application

Introducing the *while Repetition Statement and JTextAreas*

This tutorial continues the discussion of control statements that began in Tutorial 6. You will learn to use repetition statements, which are control statements that repeat actions while a condition remains true. In your daily life, you perform many repetitive tasks based on conditions. For example, each time you turn a page in this book (while there are more pages to read), you are repeating the simple task of turning a page, based on the condition that there are more pages to read.

The ability to perform tasks repeatedly is an important part of application development. Repetition statements are used in many types of applications. In this tutorial, you will learn to use the `while` repetition statement. You will include a repetition statement in the **Car Payment Calculator** application that you build. Later tutorials will introduce additional repetition statements.

8.1 Test-Driving the Car Payment Calculator Application

In this tutorial, you will build a **Car Payment Calculator** application that displays monthly payments for loan lengths of two, three, four and five years. The following problem statement indicates that the application must repeat a calculation four times—a repetition statement will be needed to solve this problem. This application must meet the following requirements:

Application Requirements

Typically, banks offer car loans for periods ranging from two to five years (24 to 60 months). Borrowers repay the loans in fixed monthly payments. The amount of each monthly payment is based on the length of the loan, the amount borrowed and the interest rate. Create an application that allows the customer to enter the price of a car, the down payment amount and the annual interest rate of the loan. Your application should display the loan's duration in months and the monthly payments for two-, three-, four- and five-year loans.

You begin by test-driving the completed application. Then, you will learn the additional Java technologies you will need to create your own version of this application.

180

1. *Locating the completed application.* Open the **Command Prompt** window by selecting **Start > Programs > Accessories > Command Prompt**. Change to your completed **Car Payment Calculator** application directory by typing `cd C:\Examples\Tutorial08\CompletedApplication\CarPayment`.

2. *Running the Car Payment Calculator application.* Type `java CarPayment` in the **Command Prompt** window to run the application (Fig. 8.1). Notice a new GUI component—the **JTextArea** component, which allows users to view multiline output (Fig. 8.3). The JTextArea can accept keyboard input, but users can add or delete text only if the JTextArea's *editable* property is `true`. This JTextArea is uneditable because it is used only to display, not enter, information. You will need to add code to your application to add or remove text from a JTextArea.

JTextArea component ——

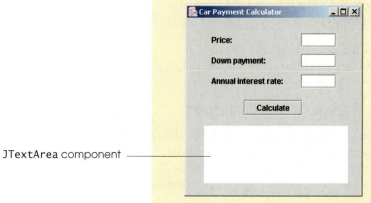

Figure 8.1 **Car Payment Calculator** application before data has been entered.

3. *Entering quantities in the application.* Enter 16900 in the **Price:** JTextField. Enter 6000 in the **Down payment:** JTextField. Enter 7.5 in the **Annual interest rate:** JTextField. The application appears as in Fig. 8.2.

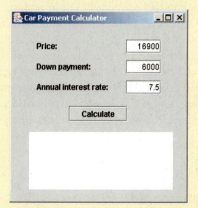

Figure 8.2 **Car Payment Calculator** application after data has been entered.

4. *Calculating the monthly payment amounts.* Click the **Calculate** JButton. The application displays the monthly payment amounts in the JTextArea (Fig. 8.3). The information is organized in tabular format. You will use a `while` repetition statement to produce the output shown in the JTextArea.

5. *Closing the running application.* Close your running application by clicking its close button.

(cont.)

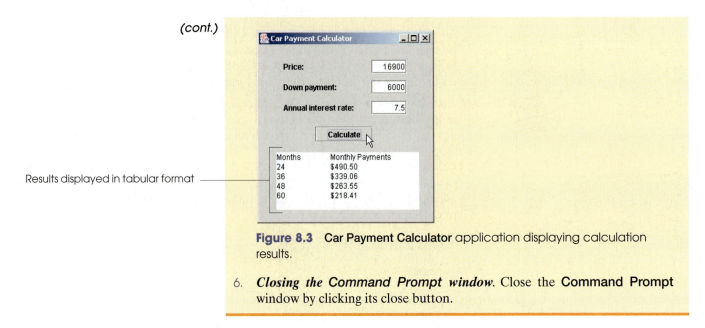

Results displayed in tabular format ——————

Figure 8.3 **Car Payment Calculator** application displaying calculation results.

6. ***Closing the Command Prompt window***. Close the **Command Prompt** window by clicking its close button.

8.2 `while` Repetition Statement

A **repetition statement** repeats actions, depending on the value of a condition (which can be either true or false). For example, if you go to the grocery store with a list of items to purchase, you go through the list until you have each item. This process is described by the following pseudocode statements:

> While there are still items on my shopping list
> > Add an item to my shopping cart
> > Cross it off my list

These statements describe the repetitive actions that occur during a shopping trip. The condition, "there are still items on my shopping list" can be true or false. If it is true, then the actions, "Add an item to my shopping cart" and "Cross it off my list" are performed in sequence. These actions execute repeatedly while the condition remains true. The statement(s) indented in this repetition statement constitute its body. When the last item on the shopping list has been purchased and crossed off the list, the condition becomes false. At this point, the repetition terminates, and the first statement after the repetition statement executes. In the shopping example, you would proceed to the checkout station.

As an example of a `while` repetition statement, consider an application segment designed to find the first power of 3 greater than 50.

```
int product = 3;

while ( product <= 50 )
{
    product *= 3;
}
```

Common Programming Error

Provide in the body of every `while` statement an action that eventually causes the loop-continuation condition to become false. If you do not, the repetition statement never terminates, causing an error called an **infinite loop**. (*Note:* To terminate an application containing an infinite loop, click in the **Command Prompt** window, hold the *ctrl* key and press the letter *C*.)

The application segment initializes variable `product` to 3. The condition in the `while` statement, `product <= 50`, is referred to as the **loop-continuation condition**. While the loop-continuation condition remains `true`, the `while` statement executes its body repeatedly. When the loop-continuation condition becomes `false`, the `while` statement finishes executing, and `product` contains the first power of 3 larger than 50. Let's examine the execution of the preceding code in detail.

When the flow of control enters the `while` statement, the value of `product` is 3. Each time the loop executes, `product` is multiplied by 3, successively taking on the values 3, 9, 27 and 81. When `product` becomes 81, the condition in the `while` state-

ment, product <= 50, evaluates to `false`. When the repetition ends, the final value of product is 81, which is indeed the first power of 3 greater than 50. Application execution continues with the next statement after the repetition statement. Note that, if a `while` statement's condition is initially `false`, the body statements are not performed and your application simply continues executing with the next statement after the right curly brace that ends the body of the `while` loop. The following box describes each step as the above repetition statement executes.

Executing the** while* ***Repetition Statement	1. The application declares variable product and sets its value to 3.
	2. The application enters the `while` repetition statement.
	3. The loop-continuation condition is checked. The condition evaluates to `true` (product is 3, which is less than or equal to 50), so the application will execute the `while` loop's body.
	4. The number (currently 3) stored in product is multiplied by 3 and the result is assigned to product; product now contains 9.
	5. The loop-continuation condition is checked. The condition evaluates to `true` (product is 9, which is still less than or equal to 50), so the application will execute the `while` loop's body.
	6. The number (currently 9) stored in product is multiplied by 3 and the result is assigned to product; product now contains 27.
	7. The loop-continuation condition is checked. The condition evaluates to `true` (product is 27, which is still less than or equal to 50), so the application will execute the `while` loop's body.
	8. The number (currently 27) stored in product is multiplied by 3 and the result is assigned to product; product now contains 81.
	9. The loop-continuation condition is checked. The condition evaluates to `false` (product is now 81, which is not less than or equal to 50), so the application exits the `while` statement and the application continues execution at the first statement after the right curly brace that ends the body of the `while` loop.

Let's use a UML activity diagram to illustrate the flow of control in the preceding `while` repetition statement. In the UML activity diagram in Fig. 8.4, the action state represents the action in which the value of product is multiplied by 3.

Figure 8.4 introduces the UML's **merge symbol**. The UML **diamond symbol** is used as both the merge symbol and the decision symbol. The merge symbol joins two flows of activity into one flow of activity. In this diagram, the merge symbol joins the transitions from the initial state and from the action state, so they both flow into the decision that determines whether the loop's body statement should execute. In this case, the UML diagram enters its action state when the loop-continuation guard condition product <= 50 is true.

Although the UML represents both the decision and the merge symbols with the diamond shape, the symbols can be distinguished by the number of "incoming" and "outgoing" transition arrows. A decision symbol has one transition arrow pointing to the diamond and two (or more) transition arrows pointing from the diamond to indicate possible transitions from that point. In addition, each transition arrow pointing from a decision symbol has a guard condition next to it. A merge symbol has two (or more) transition arrows pointing to the diamond and only one transition arrow pointing from the diamond, to indicate multiple activity flows merging to continue the activity. None of the transition arrows associated with a merge have guard conditions.

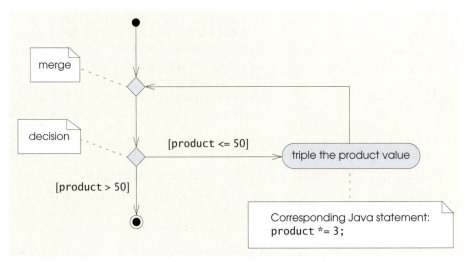

Figure 8.4 `while` repetition statement UML activity diagram.

The activity diagram in Fig. 8.4 clearly shows the repetition. The transition arrow emerging from the action state points back to the merge from which the activity transitions into the decision, creating a loop. The guard conditions are tested each time the loop iterates (executes its body) until the guard condition `product > 50` eventually becomes true. At this point, the `while` loop terminates, and control passes to the next statement in the application following the loop.

SELF-REVIEW

1. The body of a `while` statement executes _____.

   a) at least once   b) never

   c) if its condition is true   d) if its condition is false

2. The UML represents both the merge symbol and the decision symbol as _____.

   a) rectangles with rounded sides   b) diamonds

   c) small black circles   d) ovals

Answers: 1) c. 2) b.

8.3 Increment and Decrement Operators

The process of **incrementing** a variable (increasing it by one) is so common in computer applications that Java has a specific operator for this purpose, `++`. Similarly, Java provides an operator, `--`, to subtract one from a variable, which is called **decrementing** a variable. The names of these operators are the **unary increment operator** (`++`) and the **unary decrement operator** (`--`), respectively. These operators are summarized in Fig. 8.5. An application can increment the value of a variable called `counter` by 1 using the increment operator, `++`, rather than the expressions

```
counter = counter + 1
counter += 1
```

An increment or decrement operator that is prefixed to (placed before) a variable is referred to as the preincrement or predecrement operator. An increment or decrement operator that is postfixed to (placed after) a variable is referred to as the postincrement or postdecrement operator.

Operator	Called	Sample Expression	Explanation
++	preincrement	++counter	Increment counter by 1, then use the new value of counter in the expression in which counter resides.
++	postincrement	counter++	Use the current value of counter in the expression in which counter resides, then increment counter by 1.
--	predecrement	--counter	Decrement counter by 1, then use the new value of counter in the expression in which counter resides.
--	postdecrement	counter--	Use the current value of counter in the expression in which counter resides, then decrement counter by 1.

Figure 8.5   Increment and decrement operators.

Good Programming Practice

Unary operators should be placed next to their operands, with no intervening spaces.

Preincrementing (or predecrementing) a variable causes the variable to be incremented (decremented) by 1, after which the new value of the variable is used in the expression in which it appears. For example, if counter is 5, the statement

```
textJLabel.setText( String.valueOf( ++counter ) );
```

adds one to counter and stores the result (6) in counter, then displays the new value of counter (6) on textJLabel.

Postincrementing (or postdecrementing) the variable causes the current value of the variable to be used in the expression in which it appears, after which the variable value is incremented (decremented) by 1. For example, if counter is 5, the statement

```
textJLabel.setText( String.valueOf( counter++ ) );
```

displays the current value of counter (5) on textJLabel, then adds one to counter and stores the result (6) in counter.

It is important to note that when incrementing or decrementing a variable in a statement by itself, as in

```
++counter;
```

or

```
counter++;
```

the preincrement and postincrement (and similarly the predecrement and postdecrement) forms have the same effect. It is only when a variable appears in the context of a larger expression that preincrementing and postincrementing (and similarly predecrementing and postdecrementing) the variable have different effects.

SELF-REVIEW

1. Assuming a = 3, the values of variables a and b after the assignment b = a-- are _____.

   a) 3, 3   b) 2, 3
   c) 3, 2   d) 2, 2

2. Assuming c = 5, the value of variable d after the assignment d = c * ++c is _____.

   a) 25   b) 30
   c) 36   d) None of the above.

Answers: 1) b. 2) b.

8.4 Constructing the Car Payment Calculator Application

Now that you have learned the `while` repetition statement, you are ready to construct your **Car Payment Calculator** application.

The following pseudocode describes the basic operations of the **Car Payment Calculator** application whenever a user enters information and clicks the **Calculate JButton**:

> When the user clicks the Calculate JButton:
>> Initialize loan length to two years
>> Clear the JTextArea of any previous text
>> Get car price, down payment and annual interest rate
>> Calculate loan amount
>> Calculate monthly interest rate
>>
>> While loan length is less than or equal to five years
>>> Calculate number of months
>>> Calculate monthly payment based on loan amount, monthly interest rate
>>>> and loan length in months
>>> Display result
>>> Increment loan length by one year

Now that you have test-driven the **Car Payment Calculator** application and studied its pseudocode representation, you will use an ACE table to help you convert the pseudocode to Java. Figure 8.6 lists the actions, components and events that will help you complete your own version of this application.

Action/Component/Event (ACE) Table for the Car Payment Calculator

Action	Component	Event
Label all the application's components	`priceJLabel`, `downPaymentJLabel`, `interestJLabel`	Application is run
	`calculateJButton`	User clicks **Calculate JButton**
Initialize loan length to two years		
Clear the JTextArea of any previous text	`paymentsJTextArea`	
Get car price, down payment and annual interest rate	`priceJTextField`, `downPaymentJTextField`, `interestJTextField`	
Calculate loan amount		
Calculate monthly interest rate		
While loan length is less than or equal to five years		
Calculate number of months		
Calculate monthly payment based on loan amount, monthly interest rate and loan length in months		
Display result	`paymentsJTextArea`	
Increment loan length by one year		

Figure 8.6 **Car Payment Calculator** application ACE table.

Notice in the pseudocode that retrieving the user input and calculating the loan amount and the monthly interest rate occur before the repetition statement because they need to be performed only once. The statements that have different results in each iteration (repetition) are included in the repetition statement. The repetition statement's body includes converting loan length in years to loan length in months, calculating the monthly payment amount, displaying the calculation's result and

incrementing the loan length in years. The application displays the calculation results in a JTextArea. Next, you will customize the JTextArea that displays the results.

Customizing the
JTextArea **of the** *Car*
Payment Calculator
Application

1. *Copying the template to your working directory.* Copy the directory C:\Examples\Tutorial08\TemplateApplication\CarPayment to your C:\SimplyJava directory.

2. *Opening the Car Payment Calulator application's template file.* Open the template file CarPayment.java in your text editor.

3. *Customizing a JTextArea component in the JFrame.* Insert lines 99–100 (Fig. 8.7) to set the *bounds* property to 28, 168, 232, 90 and to set the *editable* property to false.

Customizing paymentsJTextArea ——

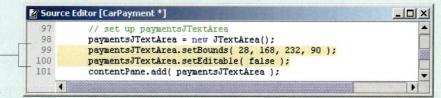

```
97        // set up paymentsJTextArea
98        paymentsJTextArea = new JTextArea();
99        paymentsJTextArea.setBounds( 28, 168, 232, 90 );
100       paymentsJTextArea.setEditable( false );
101       contentPane.add( paymentsJTextArea );
```

Figure 8.7   Customize a JTextArea component.

4. *Saving the application.* Save your modified source code file.

5. *Opening the Command Prompt window and changing directories.* Open the **Command Prompt** window by selecting **Start > Programs > Accessories > Command Prompt**. Change to your working directory by typing cd C:\SimplyJava\CarPayment.

6. *Compiling the application.* Compile your application by typing javac CarPayment.java.

7. *Running the application.* When your application compiles correctly, run it by typing java CarPayment. Figure 8.8 shows the updated application running with the JTextArea component added to the JFrame.

JTextArea component ——

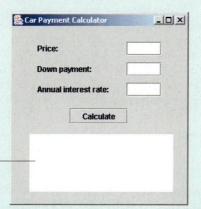

Figure 8.8   JTextArea in **Car Payment Calculator** application's JFrame.

8. *Closing the application.* Close your running application by clicking its close button.

9. *Closing the Command Prompt window.* Close the **Command Prompt** window by clicking its close button.

After adding the JTextArea, you must write event handling code, so the application can respond to the user clicking the **Calculate** JButton. The event handler calculateJButtonActionPerformed calculates the various payment amounts and displays them in the JTextArea.

Using Code to Change a *JTextArea's* Contents

1. *Clearing the **JTextArea** component.* Insert lines 113–114 of Fig. 8.9 into the event handler `calculateJButtonActionPerformed`. Each time the user clicks the **Calculate** JButton, any content previously displayed in the JTextArea should be removed by calling the **JTextArea**'s **setText** method (line 114) with an empty string (`""`) as the argument. The `setText` method replaces the text in a JTextArea with the contents of the `String` argument passed to `setText`.

```
Source Editor [CarPayment *]                                        _ □ ×
110      // method called when user clicks calculateJButton
111      private void calculateJButtonActionPerformed( ActionEvent event )
112      {
113          // clear paymentsJTextArea
114          paymentsJTextArea.setText( "" );
115
116      } // end method calculateJButtonActionPerformed
```

Set JTextArea's text ⎯⎯ (points to lines 113–114)

Figure 8.9 Clearing the contents of a JTextArea.

2. *Adding content to the **JTextArea** component.* The JTextArea will display the number of monthly payments and the amount per payment. For clarity, you will add line of text at the top of the JTextArea—called a **header**—that introduces the information being displayed. Add lines 116–117 of Fig. 8.10 to the event handler `calculateJButtonActionPerformed`. The JTextArea's **append** method (line 117) adds more text to the JTextArea's *text* property—in this case, a header that consists of the column headings `"Months"` and `"Monthly Payment"`.

GUI Design Tip

Use headers in a JTextArea to improve readability when you are displaying tabular data.

```
Source Editor [CarPayment *]                                        _ □ ×
114      paymentsJTextArea.setText( "" );
115
116          // add header to paymentsJTextArea
117          paymentsJTextArea.append( "Months\tMonthly Payments" );
118
119      } // end method calculateJButtonActionPerformed
```

Append text to JTextArea ⎯⎯ (points to lines 116–117)

Figure 8.10 Adding a header to a JTextArea.

In line 117, the header is created by joining the values "Months" and "Monthly Payments" with the characters `\t`. The backslash (`\`) is called an **escape character**. When a backslash appears in a string of characters, Java combines the next character with the backslash to form an **escape sequence**. The escape sequence **\t** represents the tab character. The application uses one tab character of separation between columns (Fig. 8.3).

3. *Saving the application.* Save your modified source code file.

4. *Opening the **Command Prompt** window and changing directories.* Open the **Command Prompt** window by selecting **Start > Programs > Accessories > Command Prompt**. Change to your working directory by typing `cd C:\SimplyJava\CarPayment`.

5. *Compiling the application.* Compile your application by typing `javac CarPayment.java`.

6. *Running the application.* When your application compiles correctly, run it by typing `java CarPayment`. Figure 8.11 shows the updated application running. Notice that the application displays a header in the JTextArea when you click the **Calculate** JButton.

(cont.)

Figure 8.11   Header displayed in the `paymentsJTextArea`.

7. *Closing the application.* Close your running application by clicking its close button.

8. *Closing the Command Prompt window.* Close the **Command Prompt** window by clicking its close button.

Now that you have learned how to change a `JTextArea`'s contents, you need to declare variables and obtain user input for the calculation. The following box shows you how to initialize the **Car Payment Calculator** application's variables. The box also guides you through converting the annual interest rate to the monthly interest rate and shows you how to calculate the amount of the loan.

Declaring Variables and Receiving User Input

1. *Declaring variables.* Add lines 113–115 of Fig. 8.12 to the event handler `calculateJButtonActionPerformed` (above the code you added in the previous box). Variables `years` and `months` store the length of the loan in years and in months, respectively. The calculation requires the length in months, but the loop-continuation condition will use the number of years. Variable `monthlyPayment` stores the calculation result.

Declaring variables to store the length of the loan and result

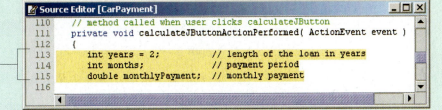

Figure 8.12   Variables for the **Car Payment Calculator** application.

2. *Retrieving user input needed for the calculation.* Add lines 123–128 of Fig. 8.13 to the end of event handler `calculateJButtonActionPerformed`. Lines 124–128 declare variables `price`, `downPayment` and `interest` to store the user input from the `JTextFields`. Lines 124–125 indicate that the variables `price` and `downPayment` are type `int`, so the car price and downpayment must be entered as whole number values.

(cont.)

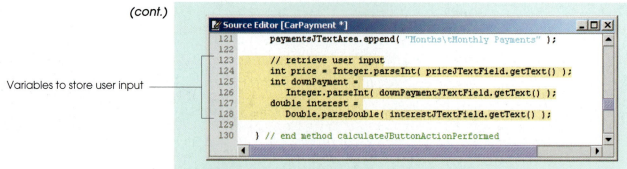

```
121        paymentsJTextArea.append( "Months\tMonthly Payments" );
122
123        // retrieve user input
124        int price = Integer.parseInt( priceJTextField.getText() );
125        int downPayment =
126           Integer.parseInt( downPaymentJTextField.getText() );
127        double interest =
128           Double.parseDouble( interestJTextField.getText() );
129
130     } // end method calculateJButtonActionPerformed
```

Variables to store user input

Figure 8.13   Retrieving input in the **Car Payment Calculator** application.

3. *Calculating the loan amount and the monthly interest.* The application computes the loan amount by subtracting the down payment from the price. Add lines 130–132 of Fig. 8.14 to the end of event handler `calculateJButtonActionPerformed` to calculate the amount borrowed (line 131) and the monthly interest rate (line 132). Notice that line 132 divides the interest rate by 1200 to obtain the floating-point equivalent of monthly interest. This is equivalent to taking the interest rate percentage as input by the user and dividing it by 100 to get the equivalent floating-point value, then dividing by 12 to obtain the monthly interest rate. For example, if the annual interest rate is 5%, dividing 5 by 100 produces the floating-point equivalent (0.05) of the annual interest rate, then dividing the floating-point value of the annual interest rate by 12 produces the monthly interest rate. Because these calculations occur only once, they are placed before the `while` statement. Variables `loanAmount` and `monthlyInterest` will be used in the calculation of monthly payments, which you will add to your application shortly.

```
128           Double.parseDouble( interestJTextField.getText() );
129
130        // calculate loan amount and monthly interest
131        int loanAmount = price - downPayment;
132        double monthlyInterest = interest / 1200;
133
134     } // end method calculateJButtonActionPerformed
```

Calculate loan amount and monthly interest

Figure 8.14   Determining amount borrowed and monthly interest rate.

4. *Declaring DecimalFormat for displaying results.* The application formats the results using `DecimalFormat`. Add lines 134–135 of Fig. 8.15 to the end of event handler `calculateJButtonActionPerformed` to define the format for displaying the monthly payment.

```
132        double monthlyInterest = interest / 1200;
133
134        // format to display monthlyPayment in currency format
135        DecimalFormat currency = new DecimalFormat( "$0.00" );
136
137     } // end method calculateJButtonActionPerformed
```

Create `DecimalFormat` for dollar amounts

Figure 8.15   Declaring `DecimalFormat currency` for displaying the result in currency format.

5. *Saving the application.* Save your modified source code file.

(cont.) 6. ***Opening the Command Prompt window and changing directories***. Open the **Command Prompt** window by selecting **Start > Programs > Accessories > Command Prompt**. Change to your working directory by typing `cd C:\SimplyJava\CarPayment`.

7. ***Compiling the application***. Compile your application by typing `javac CarPayment.java`. Ensure that your application compiles correctly. [*Note:* There is no need to run your application here because the application will appear to execute as it did in Fig. 8.11.]

8. ***Closing the Command Prompt window***. Close the **Command Prompt** window by clicking its close button.

The following box adds a `while` statement to the application to calculate the monthly payments for loans of two, three, four and five years.

Calculating the Monthly Payment Amounts with a *while* Repetition Statement

1. ***Setting the loop-continuation condition***. Add lines 137–141 of Fig. 8.16 to the end of event handler `calculateJButtonActionPerformed`.

Insert `while` statement ⎯⎯⎯⎯

```
☑ Source Editor [CarPayment *]                                    _ □ ×
     135        DecimalFormat currency = new DecimalFormat( "$0.00" );
     136
     137        // while years is less than or equal to five years
     138        while ( years <= 5 )
     139        {
     140
     141        } // end while
     142
     143     } // end method calculateJButtonActionPerformed
```

Figure 8.16 Adding the `while` statement.

Recall that the shortest loan in this application lasts two years, so you initialized `years` to 2 in line 113 (Fig. 8.12). The loop-continuation condition (`years <= 5`) in line 138 of Fig. 8.16 specifies that the `while` statement executes while `years` remains less than or equal to the maximum length of the loan (5). This loop is an example of **counter-controlled repetition**. This technique uses a variable called a **counter** (`years`) to control the number of times that a set of statements will execute. Counter-controlled repetition also is called **definite repetition**, because the number of repetitions is known before the loop begins executing. In this example, repetition terminates when the counter (`years`) exceeds 5.

2. ***Calculating the payment period***. Add lines 140–141 of Fig. 8.17 to the body of the `while` repetition statement to calculate the number of payments (that is, the length of the loan in months). The number of months changes as the length of the payment period changes, so the calculation result changes with each iteration of the loop. Variable `months` will have the values 24, 36, 48 and 60, on successive iterations of the loop.

Determine the number of months in a loan period ⎯⎯⎯⎯

```
☑ Source Editor [CarPayment *]                                    _ □ ×
     137        // while years is less than or equal to five years
     138        while ( years <= 5 )
     139        {
     140           // calculate payment period
     141           months = 12 * years;
     142
     143        } // end while
```

Figure 8.17 Converting the loan duration from years to months.

(cont.)   3.   ***Getting the monthly payment.*** Add lines 143–145 of Fig. 8.18 to the `while` repetition statement immediately after the code you just entered. Lines 144–145 use method `calculateMonthlyPayment` to calculate the user's monthly payment. This method is provided for you in the template code. The method returns a `double` value that specifies the monthly payment amount on a loan for a constant interest rate (`monthlyInterest`), a given time period (`months`) and a given loan amount (`loanAmount`). Lines 144–145 pass to `calculate-MonthlyPayment` the interest rate, the number of months and the amount borrowed.

Calculate the monthly payment ⎯⎯⎯

```
Source Editor [CarPayment *]                                    _ □ ×
141            months = 12 * years;
142
143            // get monthlyPayment
144            monthlyPayment = calculateMonthlyPayment(
145                monthlyInterest, months, loanAmount );
146
147        } // end while
```

Figure 8.18   Method `calculateMonthlyPayment` returns monthly payment.

4.   ***Displaying the monthly payment amount.*** Add lines 147–149 of Fig. 8.19 to the `while` repetition statement immediately after the code you just entered. The number of monthly payments and the monthly payment amounts are displayed beneath the header. To add this content to the `JTextArea`, call method **append** (lines 148–149 of Fig. 8.19). The plus sign (+) can also be used as a **string-concatenation operator**. This operator concatenates its two operands into one `String`. When one of the operands of the plus operator is a `String`, the operator converts the other operand to a `String` and performs string concatenation. Like `\t`, which you saw in Fig. 8.10, the two characters `\` and `n` form an escape sequence (`\n`), which represents the newline character. This character is used in this example to begin placing text on a new line in the `paymentsJTextArea`. Line 149 uses method `currency.format` to format `monthlyPayment` as a dollar amount. Notice that the tab character ensures that the monthly payment amount is placed in the second column.

Display monthly payment ⎯⎯⎯

```
Source Editor [CarPayment *]                                    _ □ ×
145                monthlyInterest, months, loanAmount );
146
147            // insert result into paymentsJTextArea
148            paymentsJTextArea.append( "\n" + months + "\t" +
149                currency.format( monthlyPayment ) );
150
151        } // end while
```

Figure 8.19   Displaying the number of months and the amount of each monthly payment.

5.   ***Incrementing the counter variable.*** Add line 151 of Fig. 8.20 before the closing brace of the `while` repetition statement. Line 151 uses operator ++ to increment the counter variable (`years`). Variable `years` will be incremented until it equals 6. Then, the loop-continuation condition (`years <= 5`) will evaluate to `false` and the repetition will end.

(cont.)

Increment the `years` counter ————

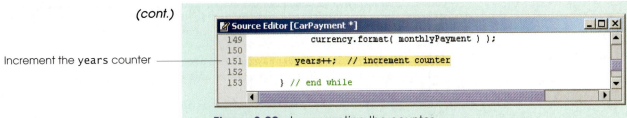

Figure 8.20 Incrementing the counter.

6. ***Saving the application***. Save your modified source code file.

7. ***Opening the Command Prompt window and changing directories***. Open the **Command Prompt** window by selecting **Start > Programs > Accessories > Command Prompt**. Change to your working directory by typing `cd C:\SimplyJava\CarPayment`.

8. ***Compiling the application***. Compile your application by typing `javac CarPayment.java`.

9. ***Running the application***. When your application compiles correctly, run it by typing `java CarPayment`. Figure 8.21 shows the executing application.

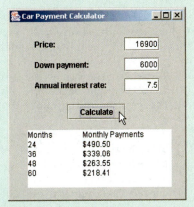

Figure 8.21 Running the completed application.

10. ***Closing the application***. Close the running application by clicking the window's close button.

11. ***Closing the Command Prompt window***. Close the **Command Prompt** window by clicking its close button.

Figure 8.22 presents the source code for the **Car Payment Calculator** application. The lines of code that you added, viewed or modified in this tutorial are highlighted.

```
1   // Tutorial 8: CarPayment.java
2   // Calculate different billing plans for a car loan.
3   import java.awt.*;
4   import java.awt.event.*;
5   import javax.swing.*;
6   import java.text.DecimalFormat;
7
8   public class CarPayment extends JFrame
9   {
10      // JLabel and JTextField for price
11      private JLabel priceJLabel;
```

Figure 8.22 **Car Payment Calculator** application code. (Part 1 of 4.)

```
12      private JTextField priceJTextField;
13
14      // JLabel and JTextField for down payment
15      private JLabel downPaymentJLabel;
16      private JTextField downPaymentJTextField;
17
18      // JLabel and JTextField for interest
19      private JLabel interestJLabel;
20      private JTextField interestJTextField;
21
22      // JButton to initiate calculation
23      private JButton calculateJButton;
24
25      // JTextArea to display results
26      private JTextArea paymentsJTextArea;
27
28      // no-argument constructor
29      public CarPayment()
30      {
31         createUserInterface();
32      }
33
34      // create and position GUI components; register event handlers
35      private void createUserInterface()
36      {
37         // get content pane and set layout to null
38         Container contentPane = getContentPane();
39         contentPane.setLayout( null );
40
41         // set up priceJLabel
42         priceJLabel = new JLabel();
43         priceJLabel.setBounds( 40, 24, 80, 21 );
44         priceJLabel.setText( "Price:" );
45         contentPane.add( priceJLabel );
46
47         // set up priceJTextField
48         priceJTextField = new JTextField();
49         priceJTextField.setBounds( 184, 24, 56, 21 );
50         priceJTextField.setHorizontalAlignment( JTextField.RIGHT );
51         contentPane.add( priceJTextField );
52
53         // set up downPaymentJLabel
54         downPaymentJLabel = new JLabel();
55         downPaymentJLabel.setBounds( 40, 56, 96, 21 );
56         downPaymentJLabel.setText( "Down payment:" );
57         contentPane.add( downPaymentJLabel );
58
59         // set up downPaymentJTextField
60         downPaymentJTextField = new JTextField();
61         downPaymentJTextField.setBounds( 184, 56, 56, 21 );
62         downPaymentJTextField.setHorizontalAlignment(
63            JTextField.RIGHT );
64         contentPane.add( downPaymentJTextField );
65
66         // set up interestJLabel
67         interestJLabel = new JLabel();
68         interestJLabel.setBounds( 40, 88, 120, 21 );
69         interestJLabel.setText( "Annual interest rate:" );
70         contentPane.add( interestJLabel );
```

Figure 8.22 **Car Payment Calculator** application code. (Part 2 of 4.)

```
71
72       // set up interestJTextField
73       interestJTextField = new JTextField();
74       interestJTextField.setBounds( 184, 88, 56, 21 );
75       interestJTextField.setHorizontalAlignment( JTextField.RIGHT );
76       contentPane.add( interestJTextField );
77
78       // set up calculateJButton and register its event handler
79       calculateJButton = new JButton();
80       calculateJButton.setBounds( 92, 128, 94, 24 );
81       calculateJButton.setText( "Calculate" );
82       contentPane.add( calculateJButton );
83       calculateJButton.addActionListener(
84
85          new ActionListener() // anonymous inner class
86          {
87             // event handler called when user clicks calculateJButton
88             public void actionPerformed( ActionEvent event )
89             {
90                calculateJButtonActionPerformed( event );
91             }
92
93          } // end anonymous inner class
94
95       ); // end call to addActionListener
96
97       // set up paymentsJTextArea
98       paymentsJTextArea = new JTextArea();
99       paymentsJTextArea.setBounds( 28, 168, 232, 90 );
100      paymentsJTextArea.setEditable( false );
101      contentPane.add( paymentsJTextArea );
102
103      // set properties of window application's
104      setTitle( "Car Payment Calculator" ); // set title bar text
105      setSize( 288, 302 );                  // set window's size
106      setVisible( true );                   // display window
107
108   } // end method createUserInterface
109
110   // method called when user clicks calculateJButton
111   private void calculateJButtonActionPerformed( ActionEvent event )
112   {
113      int years = 2;          // repetition counter
114      int months;             // payment period
115      double monthlyPayment;  // monthly payment
116
117      // clear paymentsJTextArea
118      paymentsJTextArea.setText( "" );
119
120      // add header to paymentsJTextArea
121      paymentsJTextArea.append( "Months\tMonthly Payments" );
122
123      // retrieve user input
124      int price = Integer.parseInt( priceJTextField.getText() );
125      int downPayment =
126         Integer.parseInt( downPaymentJTextField.getText() );
127      double interest =
128         Double.parseDouble( interestJTextField.getText() );
```

Customizing the **JTextArea** — (lines 99–100)

Declaring variables — (lines 113–115)

Clearing the **paymentsJTextArea** — (line 118)

Adding a header to the **paymentsJTextArea** — (line 121)

Obtaining the user input — (lines 124–128)

Figure 8.22   Car Payment Calculator application code. (Part 3 of 4.)

```
129
130       // calculate loan amount and monthly interest
131       int loanAmount = price - downPayment;
132       double monthlyInterest = interest / 1200;
133
134       // format to display monthlyPayment in currency format
135       DecimalFormat currency = new DecimalFormat( "$0.00" );
136
137       // while years is less than or equal to five years
138       while ( years <= 5 )
139       {
140          // calculate payment period
141          months = 12 * years;
142
143          // get monthlyPayment
144          monthlyPayment = calculateMonthlyPayment(
145             monthlyInterest, months, loanAmount );
146
147          // insert result into JTextArea
148          paymentsJTextArea.append( "\n" + months + "\t" +
149             currency.format( monthlyPayment ) );
150
151          years++;   // increment counter
152
153       } // end while
154
155    } // end method calculateJButtonActionPerformed
156
157    // calculate monthlyPayment
158    private double calculateMonthlyPayment( double monthlyInterest,
159       int months, int loanAmount )
160    {
161       double base = Math.pow( 1 + monthlyInterest, months );
162       return loanAmount * monthlyInterest / ( 1 - ( 1 / base ) );
163    }
164
165    // main method
166    public static void main( String[] args )
167    {
168       CarPayment application = new CarPayment();
169       application.setDefaultCloseOperation( JFrame.EXIT_ON_CLOSE );
170
171    } // end method main
172
173 } // end class CarPayment
```

Labels (left margin):
- Calculating the loan amount and monthly interest → lines 131–132
- Declaring the `DecimalFormat` → line 135
- Calling the method `calculateMonthlyPayment` to get the monthly payment → lines 144–145
- Displaying the monthly payment → lines 148–149
- Incrementing the counter → line 151

Figure 8.22 **Car Payment Calculator** application code. (Part 4 of 4.)

SELF-REVIEW

1. Counter-controlled repetition is also called _____ because the number of repetitions is known before the loop begins executing.

   a) definite repetition   b) known repetition

   c) sequential repetition   d) counter repetition

2. The line of text that is added to a `JTextArea` to clarify the information that will be displayed in tabular format is called a _____.

   a) title   b) starter

   c) header   d) clarifier

Answers: 1) a. 2) c.

8.5 Wrap-Up

In this tutorial, you began using repetition statements. You used the `while` statement to repeat actions in an application, depending on a loop-continuation condition. The `while` repetition statement executes as long as its loop-continuation condition is true. When the loop-continuation condition becomes false, the repetition terminates. An infinite loop occurs if this condition never becomes false.

You learned about counter-controlled repetition, in which a repetition statement uses a counter variable to precisely count the number of iterations. You used a repetition statement to develop your **Car Payment Calculator** application, in which you calculated the monthly payments for a given loan amount and a given interest rate for loan durations of two, three, four and five years.

In your **Car Payment Calculator** application, you used the `JTextArea` component to display several payment options on a car loan. You learned about the `JTextArea` component, which you used to display multiline text. Text is added to a `JTextArea` by invoking method append or replaced by invoking method `setText`.

You also learned that the plus operator (+) can be for string concatenation. If one of the operands of the plus operator is a `String`, the other operand is converted to a `String` and the two operands are concatenated. You also learned how to add newlines and tabs to a `String` using the escape sequences (\n) and (\t), respectively.

In the next tutorial, you will learn the do…`while` repetition statement and continue exploring counter-controlled repetition. The **Car Payment Calculator** application demonstrated one common use of repetition statements—performing a calculation for several different values. The next application introduces another common application of repetition statements—summing and averaging a series of numbers.

SKILLS SUMMARY

Displaying Values in a JTextArea

- Invoke method append to add text to the `JTextArea` component.

Clearing a JTextArea's Contents

- Invoke method `setText` with an empty string to delete (clear) all the text in the `JTextArea`.

Repeating Actions in an Application

- Use a repetition statement (such as the `while` statement) that depends on the `true` or `false` value of a loop-continuation condition.

Executing a Repetition Statement for a Known Number of Repetitions

- Use counter-controlled repetition with a counter variable to determine the number of times that a set of statements will execute.

Using the `while` Repetition Statement

- This repetition statement executes while its loop-continuation condition is `true`.
- An infinite loop occurs if the condition never becomes `false`.

KEY TERMS

append method of `JTextArea`—Adds text to a `JTextArea` component.

counter—A variable often used to determine the number of times a block of statements in a loop will execute.

counter-controlled repetition—A technique that uses a counter variable to determine the number of times that a block of statements will execute. Also called definite repetition.

decrementing—The process of subtracting one from an integer variable.

definite repetition—See counter-controlled repetition.

diamond symbol (in the UML)—The UML symbol that represents the decision symbol or the merge symbol, depending on how it is used.

escape character—The backslash (\\) character that is used to form escape sequences.

escape sequence—The backslash (\\) and the character next to it, when used within a string, form an escape sequence to represent a special character such as a newline (\\n) or a tab (\\t).

header—A line of text at the top of a JTextArea that clarifies the information being displayed.

incrementing—The process of adding one to an integer variable.

infinite loop—A logical error in which a repetition statement never terminates.

JTextArea component—Allows the user to view multiline text.

loop—Another name for a repetition statement.

loop-continuation condition—The condition used in a repetition statement (such as while) that enables repetition to continue while the condition is true, but that causes repetition to terminate when the condition becomes false.

merge symbol—A symbol in the UML that joins two flows of activity into one flow of activity.

repetition statement—Allows the programmer to specify that an action or actions should be repeated, depending on the value of a condition.

setEditable method of JTextArea—Sets the *editable* property of the JTextArea component to specify whether or not the user can edit the text in the JTextArea.

setText method of JTextArea—Sets the *text* property of the JTextArea component.

string-concatenation operator—A version of the plus (+) operator that combines its two operands into a single String.

unary decrement operator (--)—Subtracts one from an integer variable.

unary increment operator (++)—Adds one to an integer variable.

while repetition statement—A control statement that executes a set of body statements while its loop-continuation condition is true.

GUI DESIGN GUIDELINES

JTextArea

■ Use headers in a JTextArea to improve readability when you are displaying tabular data.

JAVA LIBRARY REFERENCE

JTextArea   This component allows the user to view multiline text in a JTextArea.

■ *In action*

Months	Monthly Payments
24	$490.50
36	$339.06
48	$263.55
60	$218.41

■ *Methods*

append—Adds text to a JTextArea.

setBounds—Sets the *x*-coordinate, *y*-coordinate, width and height of a JTextArea.

setEditable—Specifies whether a JTextArea is editable. If the setEditable is false, then the JTextArea is not able to receive input from the keyboard.

setText—Sets the *text* property of a JTextArea.

MULTIPLE-CHOICE QUESTIONS

8.1 Users cannot edit the text in a JTextArea if its _____ property is set to false.

a) *editable*   b) *isEditable*

c) *edit*   d) *canEdit*

8.2 The _____ statement executes until its loop-continuation condition becomes false.

a) while   b) if

c) until   d) if...else

8.3 A(n) _____ loop occurs when a condition in a `while` statement never becomes `false`.

    a) indefinite   b) undefined

    c) nested   d) infinite

8.4 A _____ is a variable that helps control the number of times that a set of statements will execute.

    a) repeater   b) counter

    c) loop   d) repetition control statement

8.5 The _____ component allows users to add and view multiline text.

    a) `JMultiArea`   b) `JArea`

    c) `JTextArea`   d) `JMultiLineArea`

8.6 In a UML activity diagram, a(n) _____ symbol joins two flows of activity into one flow of activity.

    a) merge   b) combine

    c) action state   d) decision

8.7 The UML decision and merge symbols can be distinguished by _____.

    a) the number of flowlines entering or exiting the symbol   b) whether or not the flowlines have guard conditions

    c) Both of the above.   d) Neither of the above.

8.8 `JTextArea` method _____, when called with an empty string, can be used to delete all the text in a `JTextArea`.

    a) `clear`   b) `append`

    c) `setText`   d) `delete`

8.9 `JTextArea` method _____ adds text to a `JTextArea`.

    a) `include`   b) `append`

    c) `add`   d) `insert`

8.10 Counter-controlled repetition also is called _____.

    a) infinite repetition   b) unlimited repetition

    c) limited repetition   d) definite repetition

EXERCISES

8.11 *(Table of Powers Application)* Write an application that displays a table of numbers from 1 to an upper limit, along with the square and cube each number. The user should specify the upper limit, and the results should be displayed in a `JTextArea` as in Fig. 8.23.

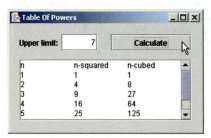

Figure 8.23 Table of Powers application.

    a) *Copying the template to your working directory.* Copy the directory `C:\Examples\Tutorial08\Exercises\TableOfPowers` to your `C:\SimplyJava` directory.

    b) *Opening the template file.* Open the `TableOfPowers.java` file in your text editor.

    c) *Handling the keyPressed event for the Upper limit: JTextField.* Add code to the `limitJTextFieldKeyPressed` event handler (which begins in line 97) to clear `outputJTextArea`.

d) ***Adding code to the Calculate JButton event handler.*** Add the code specified in steps *e* through *j* to the `calculateJButtonActionPerformed` event handler, which immediately follows the `limitJTextFieldKeyPressed` event handler.

e) ***Declaring a variable to store the loop counter.*** In the `calculateJButtonAction-Performed` event handler, declare `int` variable `counter` and initialize its value to 1.

f) ***Clearing outputJTextArea.*** Add a statement to `calculateJButtonActionPer-formed` that uses JTextArea method `setText` to clear any previous output in `outputJTextArea`.

g) ***Adding a header to outputJTextArea.*** Add a statement to `calculateJButton-ActionPerformed` that uses JTextArea method `append` to insert a header in the `outputJTextArea`. The header should label three columns n, n-squared and n-cubed. Column headings should be separated by tab characters.

h) ***Obtaining the upper limit supplied by the user.*** Add a statement to `calculate-JButtonActionPerformed` that declares `int` variable `limit` and assigns it the value entered by the user in the **Upper limit:** JTextField (`limitJTextField`).

i) ***Calculating the powers from 1 to the specified upper limit.*** Add a `while` statement to `calculateJButtonActionPerformed` that calculates the square and the cube of each number from 1 to the `limit`, inclusive. Use JTextArea method `append` to add to `outputJTextArea` a line of text containing the current `counter` value, its square and its cube.

j) ***Incrementing counter in the while statement.*** Remember to increment the `counter` each time through the loop.

k) ***Saving the application.*** Save your modified source code file.

l) ***Opening the Command Prompt window and changing directories.*** Open the **Command Prompt** window by selecting **Start > Programs > Accessories > Command Prompt**. Change to your working directory by typing cd `C:\SimplyJava\TableOf-Powers`.

m) ***Compiling the application.*** Compile your application by typing javac `TableOf-Powers.java`.

n) ***Running the completed application.*** When your application compiles correctly, run it by typing java `TableOfPowers`. Type an integer value in the **Upper limit:** JText-Field, then press the **Calculate** JButton to test your application.

8.12 *(Mortgage Calculator Application)* A bank offers mortgages that can be repaid in 10, 15, 20, 25 or 30 years. Write an application that allows a user to enter the amount of the mortgage and the annual interest rate. When the user clicks a JButton, the application displays a table of the mortgage length in years together with the monthly payment as shown in Fig. 8.24.

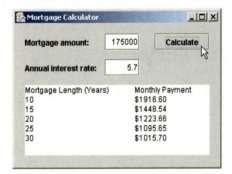

Figure 8.24 **Mortgage Calculator** application.

a) ***Copying the template to your working directory.*** Copy the directory `C:\Examples\Tutorial08\Exercises\MortgageCalculator2` to your `C:\SimplyJava` directory.

b) ***Opening the template file.*** Open the `MortgageCalculator.java` file in your text editor.

c) ***Customizing a JTextArea.*** After line 109, insert a statement that sets the *bounds* property of `outputJTextArea` to 16, 96, 298, 110. On the next line, add a statement that sets the *editable* property of `outputJTextArea` to `false`.

d) *Adding code to the Calculate JButton event handler.* Add the code specified in *Steps e–m* to the calculateJButtonActionPerformed event handler, which begins at line 134.

e) *Declaring variables required to determine monthly payments.* In calculateJButtonActionPerformed, declare int variable years and initialize its value to 10. Also, declare int variable months and double variable monthlyPayment.

f) *Obtaining the user input and converting the annual interest rate to the monthly interest rate.* Add a statement to calculateJButtonActionPerformed that declares int variable amount, gets the mortgage amount from amountJTextField, converts it to an int and assigns the value to amount. Add another statement that declares double variable monthlyRate, gets the annual interest rate from interestJTextField, converts it to a double and assigns the value to monthlyRate. To convert the annual interest rate from a percent value into its double equivalent, divide the annual rate by 100. Then, divide the annual rate by 12 to obtain the monthly rate.

g) *Creating a DecimalFormat to format dollar amounts.* Add a statement to calculateJButtonActionPerformed that creates a DecimalFormat called currency that will format floating point values with "$0.00".

h) *Clearing the JTextArea and displaying a header.* Add a statement to calculateJButtonActionPerformed that uses method setText to replace any text that appears in outputJTextArea with the column headers "Mortgage Length (Years)" and "Monthly Payment", separated by a tab character.

i) *Using a while repetition statement.* Add a while statement to calculateJButtonActionPerformed that calculates five monthly payment options for the user's mortgage. Each option has a different number of years that the mortgage can last. For this exercise, the while statement will iterate over the following sequence of values: 10, 15, 20, 25 and 30.

j) *Converting the length of the mortgage from years to months.* In the while statement, add a statement that converts the number of years to months (by multiplying years by 12).

k) *Calculating the monthly payments for five different mortgages.* On the next line in the while statement, call the calculateMonthlyPayment method (provided in the template) to compute the monthly payments. Pass to the method the monthly interest rate, the number of months in the mortgage and the mortgage amount. Assign the result of the method call to monthlyPayment.

l) *Displaying the results.* Use JTextArea method append to display the length of the mortgage in years and the monthly payment in outputJTextArea. You will need to use two tab characters to ensure that the monthly payment appears in the second column (because of the lengthy header in the first column).

m) *Incrementing counter in the while statement.* Remember to increment the years by 5 each time through the loop.

n) *Saving the application.* Save your modified source code file.

o) *Opening the Command Prompt window and changing directories.* Open the **Command Prompt** window by selecting **Start > Programs > Accessories > Command Prompt**. Change to your working directory by typing cd C:\SimplyJava\ MortgageCalculator2.

p) *Compiling the application.* Compile the application by typing javac MortgageCalculator.java.

q) *Running the completed application.* When your application compiles correctly, run it by typing java MortgageCalculator. Use the values in Fig. 8.24 to test your application.

8.13 *(Office Supplies Application)* Create an application that allows a user to make a list of office supplies to buy as shown in Fig. 8.25. The user should enter the supply in a JTextField, then click the **Buy** JButton to add it to the JTextArea. The **Clear** JButton removes all the items from the JTextArea.

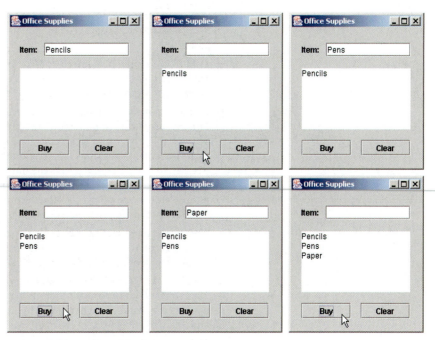

Figure 8.25 **Office Supplies** application.

a) *Copying the template to your working directory.* Copy the directory `C:\Examples\Tutorial08\Exercises\OfficeSupplies` to your `C:\SimplyJava` directory.

b) *Opening the template file.* Open the `OfficeSupplies.java` file in your text editor.

c) *Adding code to the event handler for the Buy JButton.* Add a statement to the `buyJButtonActionPerformed` event handler (which begins in line 105) that obtains the user input from `itemJTextField`, then appends the user input to `outputJTextArea`. Add another statement that clears the `itemJTextField`.

d) *Adding code to the event handler for the Clear JButton.* Add a statement to the `clearJButtonActionPerformed` event handler (immediately after the `buyJButtonActionPerformed` event handler) that uses `JTextArea` method `setText` to clear `outputJTextArea`.

e) *Saving the application.* Save your modified source code file.

f) *Opening the Command Prompt window and changing directories.* Open the **Command Prompt** window by selecting **Start > Programs > Accessories > Command Prompt**. Change to your working directory by typing `cd C:\SimplyJava\OfficeSupplies`.

g) *Compiling the application.* Compile your application by typing `javac OfficeSupplies.java`.

h) *Running the completed application.* When your application compiles correctly, run it by typing `java OfficeSupplies`. Use the values in Fig. 8.25 to test your application.

What does this code do? ▶   **8.14** What is the result of the following code?

```
1   int x = 1;
2   int mysteryValue = 1;
3
4   while ( x < 6 )
5   {
6      mysteryValue *= x;
7      x++;
8   }
9
10  displayJLabel.setText( String.valueOf( mysteryValue ) );
```

What's wrong with this code? ▶   **8.15** Find the error(s) in the following code:

a) Assume that the variable `counter` is declared and initialized to 1. The loop should sum the numbers from 1 to 100.

```
1   while ( counter <= 100 )
2   {
3      total += counter;
4   }
5
6   counter++;
```

b) Assume that the variable `counter` is declared and initialized to 1000. The loop should iterate from 1000 to 1.

```
1   while ( counter > 0 )
2   {
3      displayJLabel.setText( String.valueOf( counter ) );
4      counter++;
5   }
```

c) Assume that the variable `counter` is declared and initialized to 1. The loop should execute five times, appending the numbers 1–5 to a `JTextArea`.

```
1   while ( counter < 5 )
2   {
3      numbersJTextArea.append( String.valueOf( counter ) );
4      counter++;
5   }
```

Using the Debugger ▶   **8.16** (*Odd Numbers Application*) The **Odd Numbers** application should display all of the odd integers from one through the number input by the user. Figure 8.26 displays the correct output for the application. In this exercise, you will use the debugger to find and fix the error(s) in the application.

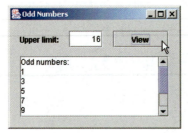

Figure 8.26   Correct output for the **Odd Numbers** application.

a) *Copying the template to your working directory.* Copy the directory `C:\Examples\Tutorial08\Exercises\Debugger\OddNumbers` to your `C:\SimplyJava` directory.

b) *Opening the Command Prompt window and changing directories.* Open the **Command Prompt** window by selecting **Start > Programs > Accessories > Command Prompt**. Change to your working directory by typing `cd C:\SimplyJava\OddNumbers`.

c) *Running the application.* Run the application by typing `java OddNumbers`. Enter a value into the **Upper limit:** `JTextField`, then click the **View** `JButton`. Notice that the `JButton` remains pressed and no output occurs. This is because the application contains an infinite loop in the `viewJButtonActionPerformed` event handler.

d) *Closing the running application.* Close the running application by clicking in the **Command Prompt** window, holding the *ctrl* key and pressing *C*.

e) *Compiling the application for debugging.* Compile the application with the -g command-line option by typing javac -g OddNumbers.java.

f) *Starting the debugger.* In the **Command Prompt**, type jdb.

g) *Setting breakpoints.* Setting a breakpoint at line 94 in method viewJButtonAction-Performed by typing stop at OddNumbers:94.

h) *Running the application in the debugger.* Run the **Odd Numbers** application in the debugger by typing run OddNumbers. Type 10 in the **Upper limit:** JTextField and click the **View** JButton. The application will enter break mode at line 94.

i) *Locating the logic error.* Use the debugger's print command to examine the values of variables counter and limit. The values should be 1 and 10, respectively. Use the cont command to continue execution from the breakpoint at line 94. This causes one iteration of the loop to be performed, then the application enters break mode again at line 94. Use the debugger's print command to examine the values of variables counter and limit again. The values should be 2 and 10, respectively. However, the value of counter is still 1 and the value of limit is now 11. If necessary, use cont and print several more times to determine the problem in the code.

j) *Opening the template file and fixing the error in the code.* Open the OddNumbers.java file in your text editor, scroll to lines 92–101, locate the error in the code and fix the error.

k) *Saving the application.* Save your modified source code file.

l) *Compiling the application.* Compile your application by typing javac OddNumbers.java.

m) *Running the completed application.* When your application compiles correctly, run it by typing java OddNumbers. Test the application again by entering an integer in the **Upper limit:** JTextField, then clicking the **View** JButton.

n) *Closing the application.* Close your running application by clicking its close button.

o) *Closing the Command Prompt window.* Close the **Command Prompt** window by clicking its close button.

Programming Challenge ▶ **8.17** *(To-Do List Application)* Use a JTextArea as a to-do list. Enter each item in a JTextField, and add it to the JTextArea by clicking a JButton. The item should be displayed in a numbered list as in Fig. 8.27. To do this, you will need JTextArea method getLineCount, which returns the number of lines in a JTextArea. The following statement assigns the number of lines displayed in the outputJTextArea to int variable counter:

```
int counter = outputJTextArea.getLineCount();
```

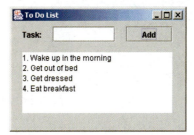

Figure 8.27 **To-Do List** application.

a) *Copying the template to your working directory.* Copy the directory C:\Examples\Tutorial08\Exercises\ToDoList to your C:\SimplyJava directory.

b) *Opening the template file.* Open the ToDoList.java file in your text editor.

c) *Adding code to the event handler for the Add JButton.* Add code to the addJButtonActionPerformed event handler (which begins in line 82) to obtain the number of lines displayed in the outputJTextArea. Get the user input from taskJText-

Field append it the `outputJTextArea` with a line number in front of it. After the input is added to the `outputJTextArea`, clear the `taskJTextField`.

d) *Saving the application.* Save your modified source code file.

e) *Opening the Command Prompt window and changing directories.* Open the **Command Prompt** window by selecting **Start > Programs > Accessories > Command Prompt**. Change to your working directory by typing cd `C:\SimplyJava\ToDoList`.

f) *Compiling the application.* Compile your application by typing javac `ToDoList.java`.

g) *Running the completed application.* When your application compiles correctly, run it by typing java `ToDoList`. Use the values in Fig. 8.27 to test your application.

Objectives

In this tutorial, you will learn to:
- Use the **do...while** statement.
- Understand counter-controlled repetition.
- Display an input dialog.
- Enable and disable **JButtons**.

Outline

Class Average Application

Introducing the do...while Repetition Statement

This tutorial continues our discussion of repetition statements. In the previous tutorial, you examined the **while** repetition statement, which tests a loop-continuation condition before performing the statement(s) in the body of the loop. This tutorial introduces an additional repetition statement, **do...while**, which performs its test after performing the loop body statements. As a result, these statements are performed at least once.

You will also learn how to disable and enable components. When a component, such as a **JButton**, is disabled, it will no longer respond to user interactions. This can help prevent errors in your applications. This tutorial also introduces **input dialogs**, which allow applications to wait for the user to input data and process that data.

9.1 Test-Driving the Class Average Application

The **Class Average** application must meet the following requirements:

> **Application Requirements**
>
> *A teacher gives quizzes to a class of 10 students. The grades on these quizzes are integers in the range from 0 to 100, inclusive (0 and 100 are each valid grades). The teacher would like you to develop an application that computes the class average for a quiz. Your application should use an input dialog to enable the teacher to enter the grades.*

The class average is equal to the sum of the grades divided by the number of students who took the quiz. The algorithm for solving this problem on a computer is to input each of the grades, total the grades, perform the averaging calculation and display the result.

You begin by test-driving the completed application. Then, you will learn the additional Java technologies you will need to create your own version of this application.

Test-Driving the Class Average Application

GUI Design Tip

Most JTextAreas should have a descriptive JLabel, indicating what output is expected to be displayed. Use sentence-style capitalization for such a JLabel.

1. ***Locating the completed application.*** Open the **Command Prompt** window by selecting **Start > Programs > Accessories > Command Prompt.** Change to your completed **Class Average** application directory by typing cd C:\Examples\Tutorial09\CompletedApplication\ClassAverage.

2. ***Running the Class Average application.*** Type java ClassAverage in the **Command Prompt** window to run the application (Fig. 9.1). The **Get Grades** JButton causes the application to display a series of input dialogs in which the user can enter grades. The **Average** JButton causes the application to calculate the average of those grades. The grades are displayed in the **Grade list:** JTextArea, and the average is displayed in the **Class average:** JTextField. Notice that the **Average** JButton is **disabled** when the application begins executing—the color of its text is gray, and clicking it does not invoke its event handler. This is because users should not be able to calculate an average before grades have been entered. The JTextArea is large enough to easily display 10 lines, one for each grade. Also a JLabel indicates what information will be displayed in the JTextArea.

JTextArea ——

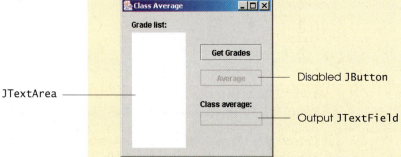

Disabled JButton

Output JTextField

Figure 9.1   Running the completed **Class Average** application.

3. ***Entering quiz grades.*** Click the **Get Grades** JButton. This will display an input dialog in which you will enter one grade at a time (Fig. 9.2). Notice that an input dialog is similar to a message dialog, but includes a JTextField, allowing you to enter data. Enter 85 as the first quiz grade in the input dialog, and click the **OK** JButton. Clicking the **OK** JButton causes the dialog to be dismissed (removed from the screen). The value entered (85), can be accessed by the application and used in the average calculation. The application displays the input dialog from a loop. So, as you enter a grade and press the **OK** button, the application displays another input dialog in which you can enter the next grade. This continues until the loop terminates.

JTextField of input dialog ——

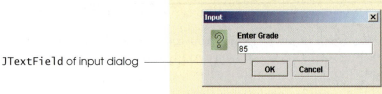

Figure 9.2   Entering grades in the **Class Average** application.

(cont.)

4. **Repeat** Step 3 *nine times*. Enter the nine other grades shown in Fig. 9.3 and click the **OK** JButton after each entry. When you are finished, all 10 grades will be displayed in the JTextArea (Fig. 9.3). At this point, the application enables the **Average** JButton, so you can click it to calculate and display the average. Notice that the **Average** JButton also has a thin blue rectangle around its text, indicating that this component has been selected and enabled. When a component is selected, it is said to have the **focus** of the application. This rectangle helps focus the user's attention on the component that should be used next. An important part of GUI design is to help users understand which components they need to interact with in the application. You will learn how to set the focus of a component later in this tutorial. When a JButton has the focus, you can either click the JButton using the mouse or press the *Space Bar* to cause its action to be performed.

Ten quiz grades entered ———

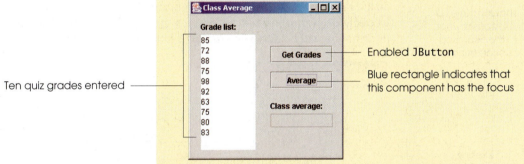

Enabled JButton

Blue rectangle indicates that this component has the focus

Figure 9.3   **Class Average** application after 10 grades have been entered.

5. **Calculating the average.** Select the **Average** JButton by pressing the *Space Bar*. The average of the 10 grades will be displayed in the **Class average:** JTextField (Fig. 9.4).

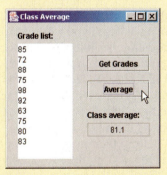

Figure 9.4   **Class Average** application after calculating the average.

6. **Entering another set of grades.** You can calculate the class average for another set of 10 grades without restarting the application. Click the **Get Grades** JButton to make the input dialog reappear.

7. **Closing the running application.** Close your running application by clicking its close button.

8. **Closing the Command Prompt window.** Close the **Command Prompt** window by clicking its close button.

9.2 do...while Repetition Statement

The **do...while** repetition statement is similar to the while statement—each statement iterates while its loop-continuation condition is true. In the while statement, the loop-continuation condition is tested at the beginning of the loop, before the

body of the loop is performed. The do...while statement evaluates the loop-continuation condition *after* the loop body is performed. Therefore, in a do...while statement, the loop body always executes at least once. Recall that a while statement executes only if its loop-continuation condition is true, so it is possible that the body of a while statement will never execute. When a do...while statement terminates, execution continues with the first statement after the do...while statement.

To illustrate the do...while repetition style, consider the example of packing a suitcase: Before you begin packing, the suitcase is empty. You will always pack at least one item in the suitcase. You place an item in the suitcase, then determine whether the suitcase is full. As long as the suitcase is not full, you continue to put items in the suitcase. (Assume for the purpose of this example that you are packing more items than the suitcase will hold.) For an example of a do...while statement, look at the following application segment designed to display the numbers 1 through 3 in a JTextArea:

```
int counter = 1;

do
{
    displayJTextArea.append( counter + "\n" );
    counter++;
}
while ( counter <= 3 );
```

The application segment initializes the counter to 1. The loop-continuation condition in the do...while statement is counter <= 3. The do...while statement executes its body once, then loops (executing repeatedly) while the loop-continuation condition is true. The do...while contains a block comprised of two statements. The first calls JTextArea method append to append the value of the counter (and a newline) to displayJTextArea. The second statement increments the value of counter. When the loop-continuation condition becomes false (that is, when counter becomes greater than 3), the do...while statement finishes executing and displayJTextArea contains the numbers 1 through 3, each on a separate line. The following box describes each step as the preceding repetition statement executes.

Common Programming Error

An infinite loop occurs when the loop-continuation condition in a do...while repetition statement never becomes false.

Error-Prevention Tip

Make sure each do...while loop body contains code that eventually makes the loop-continuation condition become false.

Executing the do...while Repetition Statement

1. The application declares variable counter and sets its value to 1.
2. The application enters the do...while repetition statement.
3. The number stored in counter (currently 1) is appended to displayJText-Area (along with a newline).
4. The value of counter is increased by 1; counter now contains 2.
5. The loop-continuation condition is checked. The condition evaluates to true (counter is less than or equal to 3), so the application executes the statement contained in the do...while statement.
6. The number stored in counter (currently 2) is appended to displayJText-Area (along with a newline).
7. The value of counter is increased by 1; counter now contains 3.
8. The loop-continuation condition is checked. The condition evaluates to true (counter is less than or equal to 3), so the application executes the statement contained in the do...while statement. The number stored in counter (currently 3) is appended to displayJTextArea (along with a newline).
9. The value of counter is increased by 1; counter now contains 4.
10. The loop-continuation condition is checked. The condition evaluates to false (counter is not less than or equal to 3), so the application exits the do...while statement.
11. Execution continues with the next statement after the do...while statement.

An **off-by-one error** (a type of logic error) occurs when a loop executes for one more or one fewer iteration than is necessary. Such logic errors are introduced into applications when you provide incorrect loop-continuation conditions. For example, the do...while statement discussed in this section should loop three times. If the condition is incorrectly stated as counter < 3 or counter <= 2, the JTextArea would display only 1 and 2. The most frequent causes of off-by-one errors are including an incorrect relational operator (such as the less than sign in counter < 3) or an incorrect final value for a loop counter (such as the 2 in counter <= 2) in the condition of any repetition statement.

Figure 9.5 illustrates the UML activity diagram for the preceding do...while statement. This diagram makes it clear that the loop-continuation guard condition ([counter <= 3]) is not checked until after the loop enters the action state at least once. Recall that action states can include one or more Java statements executed one after the other (sequentially) as in the preceding example. When you use do...while statements in building your applications, you will provide the appropriate action states and guard conditions for your application.

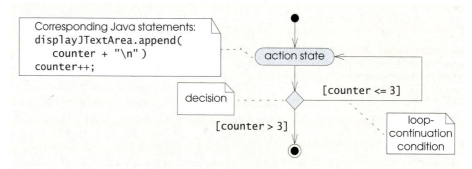

Figure 9.5 do...while repetition statement UML activity diagram.

SELF-REVIEW

1. The do...while statement tests the loop-continuation condition _____.
   - a) after the loop body executes
   - b) before the loop body executes
   - c) Both of the above.
   - d) Neither of the above.

2. An infinite loop occurs when the loop-continuation condition in a do...while statement _____.
   - a) never becomes true
   - b) never becomes false
   - c) is false
   - d) is tested repeatedly

Answers: 1) a. 2) b.

9.3 Creating the Class Average Application

Now that you have learned the do...while statement, you can begin to develop your **Class Average** application. First, you will study pseudocode that lists the actions to be performed and indicates the order in which those actions should be performed. You will then use counter-controlled repetition to input the grades one at a time. Recall that this technique uses a variable called a counter to determine the number of times a set of statements executes. In this example, repetition terminates when the counter exceeds 10. The following is a pseudocode algorithm for the **Class Average** application:

When the user clicks the Get Grades JButton:
  Set total to zero
  Set grade counter to one
  Clear the JTextArea
  Clear the output JTextField

> Do
>> Get the next grade from the input dialog
>> Append the grade to the JTextArea
>> Add the grade to the total
>> Add one to the grade counter
> While the grade counter is less than or equal to 10
>
> Enable Average JButton
> Give focus to Average JButton
>
> When the user clicks the Average JButton:
>> Calculate the class average by dividing the total by 10
>> Display the class average in the output JTextField
>> Disable Average JButton
>> Give focus to Get Grades JButton

Now that you have test-driven the **Class Average** application and studied its pseudocode representation, you will use an ACE table to help you convert the pseudocode to Java. Figure 9.6 lists the actions, components and events that will help you complete your own version of this application.

Action/Component/ Event (ACE) Table for the Class Average Application

Action	Component/Class	Event
Label the application's components	gradeListJLabel, classAverageJLabel	Application is run
	getGradesJButton	User clicks **Get Grades** JButton
Set total to zero		
Set grade counter to one		
Clear the JTextArea	gradeListJTextArea	
Clear the output JTextField	classAverageJTextField	
Do		
Get the next grade from the input dialog	JOptionPane	
Append the grade to the JTextArea	gradeListJTextArea	
Add the grade to the total		
Add one to the grade counter		
While the grade counter is less than or equal to 10		
Enable Average JButton	averageJButton	
Give focus to Average JButton	averageJButton	
	averageJButton	User clicks **Average** JButton
Calculate the class average by dividing the total by 10		
Display the class average in the output JTextField	classAverageJTextField	
Disable Average JButton	averageJButton	
Give focus to Get Grades JButton	getGradesJButton	

Figure 9.6   ACE table for the **Class Average** application.

The application's GUI is labeled using JLabels classAverageJLabel and gradeListJLabel. The user clicks the getGradesJButton to enter grades. The JButton's actionPerformed event handler displays input dialogs that enable the user to enter grades. The grades are added to a total and displayed in the

gradeListJTextArea as they are entered. When the user has entered 10 grades, the averageJButton is enabled. This JButton, when clicked, computes the class average by dividing the total by 10. The class average then will be displayed in classAverageJTextField.

Now that you have formulated an algorithm for solving the **Class Average** problem, you can begin adding functionality to the template application. The following box guides you through adding functionality to the **Get Grades** JButton's event handler to display an input dialog.

Entering a Grade in the Class Average Application	1. **Copying the template to your working directory.** Copy the C:\Examples\Tutorial09\TemplateApplication\ClassAverage directory to your C:\SimplyJava directory.
	2. **Opening the Class Average application's template file.** Open the template file ClassAverage.java in your text editor.
	3. **Viewing the total variable.** Look at the declaration in line 23 in the template code (Fig. 9.7). Variable total has been declared and initialized to 0. This variable stores the total of the grades, and will be used in the class average calculation. You have already learned about variables and have declared variables within an event handler method. Variables declared in a method are known as **local variables**, and can only be used in the body of the method in which they are declared. Once a method finishes executing, its local variables no longer can be used. In previous applications, the local variables were not needed after the method in which they were declared finished executing. Variable total, however, will be used in both the event handler method for the **Get Grades** JButton and the event handler method for the **Average** JButton. To preserve total's value between JButton clicks, this variable will need to be declared as an **instance variable**. An instance variable is defined within a class, but outside any methods. By declaring variable total outside the event handler methods, we are making total an instance variable that can be accessed in any of the class's methods, including the event handlers for the **Get Grades** and **Average** JButtons. The private keyword is an "access specifier" which indicates that the variable total can be used only by methods in this class. Local variables and instance variables will be discussed further in Tutorial 14. You will learn about the private keyword in Tutorial 18.

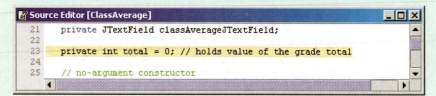

Figure 9.7 Variable **total** declared outside a method.

4. **Declaring variables used in the class-average calculation.** Insert lines 114–117 of Fig. 9.8 in the getGradesJButtonActionPerformed event handler, which begins in line 112. Line 114 sets the value of the total instance variable to 0, clearing any previous totals. Line 115 declares and initializes the integer local variable counter, which will be used as the counter in our repetition statement. It is important that variables used as totals and counters have appropriate initial values before they are used. Otherwise, errors may occur. The variable input (declared in line 116) will be used to store the input entered by the user into the input dialog. You will need to convert the input into an integer, which will be stored in the grade local variable (line 117).

Error-Prevention Tip

Initialize counters and totals before they are used to help prevent compiler errors and logic errors.

(cont.)

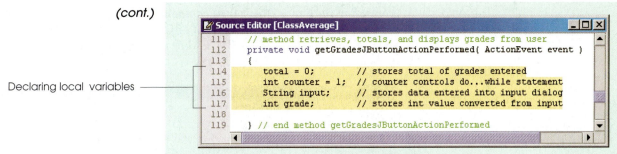

```
Source Editor [ClassAverage]                                    _ □ ×
111       // method retrieves, totals, and displays grades from user
112       private void getGradesJButtonActionPerformed( ActionEvent event )
113       {
114           total = 0;        // stores total of grades entered
115           int counter = 1;  // counter controls do...while statement
116           String input;     // stores data entered into input dialog
117           int grade;        // stores int value converted from input
118
119       } // end method getGradesJButtonActionPerformed
```

Declaring local variables

Figure 9.8   Initializing your application's variables.

5. ***Clearing the Grade list: JTextArea and Class Average: JTextField of
   any output from a previous calculation.*** Insert lines 119–121 of Fig. 9.9 in
   the getGradesJButtonActionPerformed event handler, which executes
   when the **Get Grades** JButton is clicked. Any text in the JTextArea and
   the JTextField should be deleted before the next calculation. Lines 120–
   121 clear the *text* property of both components, using the setText method.

```
Source Editor [ClassAverage]                                    _ □ ×
117           int grade;         // stores int value converted from input
118
119           // clear previous grades and calculation result
120           gradeListJTextArea.setText( "" );
121           classAverageJTextField.setText( "" );
122
123       } // end method getGradesJButtonActionPerformed
```

Clearing the grade list
and class average

Figure 9.9   Clearing the output components.

6. ***Displaying and retrieving data from an input dialog.*** Add lines 123–125
   of Fig. 9.10 to the getGradesJButtonActionPerformed event handler.
   Line 124 displays an input dialog by calling the **JOptionPane.showInput-
   Dialog** method, which displays an input dialog (as you have seen in the
   test-drive) and returns the data entered by the user into the input dialog's
   JTextField. The first argument to showInputDialog, null, indicates that
   the dialog should appear in the middle of your screen. The second argument specifies the text (sometimes called a prompt) that will appear above
   the JTextField in the input dialog. When the dialog is dismissed by clicking the **OK** JButton, the data entered into the dialog's JTextField is
   returned as a String. Line 125 calls the Integer.parseInt method to
   convert the data entered into the input dialog into an integer. The final
   result is stored in int variable grade.

```
Source Editor [ClassAverage]                                    _ □ ×
121           classAverageJTextField.setText( "" );
122
123           // get user input
124           input = JOptionPane.showInputDialog( null, "Enter Grade" );
125           grade = Integer.parseInt( input );
126
127       } // end method getGradesJButtonActionPerformed
```

Retrieving data from
an input dialog

Figure 9.10   Getting the grade input using an input dialog.

(cont.)

7. ***Appending data to a JTextArea component.*** Add lines 127–128 of Fig. 9.11 to the `getGradesJButtonActionPerformed` event handler. Line 128 appends the grade entered and a newline character to `gradeListJTextArea` by using `JTextArea` method append.

Appending the input value to the `gradeListJTextArea`

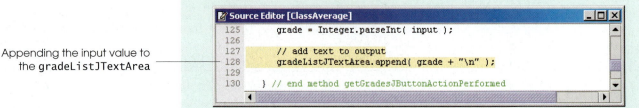

```
125          grade = Integer.parseInt( input );
126
127          // add text to output
128          gradeListJTextArea.append( grade + "\n" );
129
130       } // end method getGradesJButtonActionPerformed
```

Figure 9.11   Adding the grade input to the `gradeListJTextArea`.

8. ***Saving the application.*** Save your modified source code file.

9. ***Opening the Command Prompt window and changing directories.*** Open the **Command Prompt** window by selecting **Start > Programs > Accessories > Command Prompt**. Change to your working directory by typing `cd C:\SimplyJava\ClassAverage`.

10. ***Compiling the application.*** Compile your application by typing `javac ClassAverage.java`.

11. ***Running the application.*** When your application compiles correctly, run it by typing `java ClassAverage`. Figure 9.12 shows the updated application running. Your application can now input one grade (using an input dialog) each time the **Get Grades** JButton is clicked. Click the **Get Grades** JButton to display an input dialog. In this dialog, enter the value 78 and click the **OK** JButton. You will be returned to your application's JFrame, with the value 78 displayed in the JTextArea. Notice that if you press the **Get Grades** JButton again and enter a new value, that value will replace (or overwrite) 78. Remember that if there is already data in the JTextArea, that text is cleared at the beginning of the event handler. Notice that the **Average** JButton is disabled.

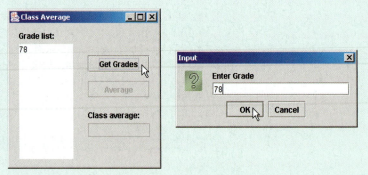

Figure 9.12   Running the updated application.

12. ***Closing the running application.*** Close your running application by clicking its close button.

13. ***Closing the Command Prompt window.*** Close the **Command Prompt** window by clicking its close button.

You have added the code to display a single grade entered in an input dialog in the JTextArea when the user clicks the **Get Grades** JButton. Next, you will use a do...while loop to input multiple grades.

Inputting Multiple Grades

1. *Creating a do...while loop to input 10 grades.* Your application should accept exactly 10 grades when the user clicks the **Get Grades** JButton, then enable the **Average** JButton so the user can click it to calculate the class average. If the user enters 10 grades and presses the **Get Grades** JButton again, the existing 10 grades will be cleared and 10 new grades will be accepted. The input dialog should be displayed exactly 10 times each time the **Get Grades** JButton is clicked. Add lines 123–124 of Fig. 9.13 to event handler getGradesJButtonActionPerformed, directly after gradeListJTextArea and classAverageJTextField are cleared.

   Add lines 132–134 of Fig. 9.13 to the end of event handler getGradesJButtonActionPerformed. Indent lines 125–130 three more spaces (one level of indentation). You have now defined a do...while loop. Line 132 increments the counter variable, which ensures that the do...while loop will eventually terminate. Line 134 determines whether counter is less than or equal to 10. After the tenth grade is entered, line 132 will increment counter to 11 and the do...while statement will terminate.

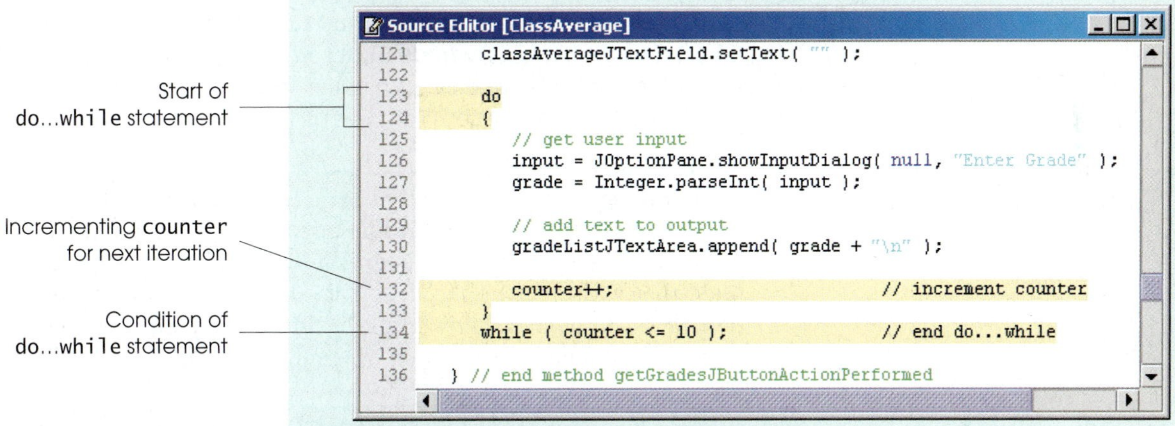

```
Source Editor [ClassAverage]
121         classAverageJTextField.setText( "" );
122
123         do
124         {
125            // get user input
126            input = JOptionPane.showInputDialog( null, "Enter Grade" );
127            grade = Integer.parseInt( input );
128
129            // add text to output
130            gradeListJTextArea.append( grade + "\n" );
131
132            counter++;                              // increment counter
133         }
134         while ( counter <= 10 );                  // end do...while
135
136      } // end method getGradesJButtonActionPerformed
```

Start of do...while statement — lines 123–124
Incrementing counter for next iteration — line 132
Condition of do...while statement — line 134

Figure 9.13 Defining the do...while loop.

2. *Saving the application.* Save your modified source code file.

3. *Opening the Command Prompt window and changing directories.* Open the **Command Prompt** window by selecting **Start > Programs > Accessories > Command Prompt**. Change to your working directory by typing cd C:\SimplyJava\ClassAverage.

4. *Compiling the application.* Compile your application by typing javac ClassAverage.java.

5. *Running the application.* When your application compiles correctly, run it by typing java ClassAverage. Figure 9.14 shows the updated application running. Click the **Get Grades** JButton and enter a value into the input dialog that is displayed. Notice that after you enter a value and press the **OK** JButton, the value is added to the gradeListJTextArea and another dialog immediately appears. The do...while loop causes these actions to occur a total of 10 times. Enter nine more values, which will all be displayed in the gradeListJTextArea. Notice, however, that the class average is still not displayed when the **Average** JButton is clicked. You will add this portion of your application's functionality shortly.

6. *Closing the running application.* Close your running application by clicking its close button.

7. *Closing the Command Prompt window.* Close the **Command Prompt** window by clicking its close button.

(cont.)

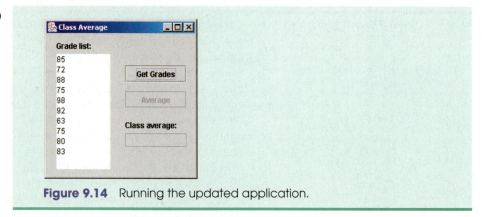

Figure 9.14   Running the updated application.

While the user enters grades, your application should total the grades for use in the average calculation. After 10 grades have been entered and displayed in the gradeListJTextArea, your application should enable the **Average** JButton, so the user can click it to calculate and display the average of the 10 grades. Next, you will modify the repetition statement to total the grades as they are input. You will then add code to enable the **Average** JButton and you will add code to the `averageJButtonActionPerformed` event handler to calculate the average and display the results in the **Class average:** JTextField.

Calculating the Class Average

1. ***Summing the grades displayed in the JTextArea.*** Add line 131 of Fig. 9.15 to the `getGradesJButtonActionPerformed` event handler, before the statement that increments counter. Line 131 adds to variable total the last grade that was input by the user. This statement occurs in the do...while loop, so it will be executed 10 times. When the do...while loop terminates, total will contain the sum of the 10 grades entered.

Add input to total

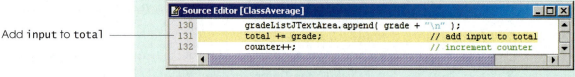

```
130          gradeListJTextArea.append( grade + "\n" );
131          total += grade;                    // add input to total
132          counter++;                         // increment counter
```

Figure 9.15   Summing the grades.

2. ***Viewing the Average JButton's initial state.*** Scroll to line 74 (Fig. 9.16) of your source code file. Your application should not allow users to calculate an average before all 10 grades have been entered. To prevent the **Average** JButton's event-handling method from executing before grades have been entered, line 74 uses the **setEnabled** method to set the JButton's *enabled* property to false, which disables the JButton. With the **Average** JButton disabled at the start of your application, no code will be executed when this JButton is clicked. In the next step, you will enable the **Average** JButton by setting its *enabled* property to true.

GUI Design Tip

Disable a JButton when its function should not be available to the user.

Use method setEnabled to enable or disable a JButton

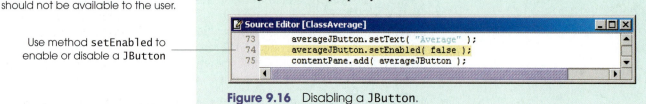

```
73          averageJButton.setText( "Average" );
74          averageJButton.setEnabled( false );
75          contentPane.add( averageJButton );
```

Figure 9.16   Disabling a JButton.

(cont.)

3. ***Enabling the Average JButton.*** Add line 136 of Fig. 9.17 to getGrades-JButtonActionPerformed. Once the 10 grades have been entered, the user should be able to click the **Average** JButton. Line 136 calls the setEnabled method and passes the argument true to enable the averageJButton.

To enable a JButton or other GUI component, pass true to the setEnabled method

```
 Source Editor [ClassAverage]                                      _ □ ✕
134        while ( counter <= 10 );              // end do...while
135
136        averageJButton.setEnabled( true );    // enable averageJButton
137
138    } // end method getGradesJButtonActionPerformed
```

Figure 9.17   Enabling a JButton.

4. ***Transferring the focus to the Average JButton.*** Add line 137 of Fig. 9.18 to getGradesJButtonActionPerformed. The user will most likely want to click the **Average** JButton once it is enabled, so you want to set your application's focus (in other words, **transfer the focus**) to averageJButton at this time. To do this, call the JButton's **requestFocusInWindow** method.

Transfer focus to a GUI component by using method requestFocusInWindow

```
 Source Editor [ClassAverage]                                      _ □ ✕
136        averageJButton.setEnabled( true );      // enable averageJButton
137        averageJButton.requestFocusInWindow(); // transfer focus
138
139    } // end method getGradesJButtonActionPerformed
```

Figure 9.18   Transferring focus to a JButton.

5. ***Calculating the average of ten grades.*** Add lines 144–145 of Fig. 9.19 to averageJButtonActionPerformed, which executes when the **Average** JButton is clicked. Line 144 calculates the average by dividing the sum of the grades entered by 10. Recall from Section 5.5 that integer division yields integer results—any fractional part is truncated. In this case, you would like a more accurate floating-point result (such as 81.1 in Fig. 9.4). To achieve this result, precede the division operation with (double). Often in Java programming, type names will be placed in parentheses, as we have done here. This is known as a **cast operator**, and is used to convert the operand (in this case total) to the type placed within the parentheses of the cast. The floating-point result of the division in line 144 is stored as a double in local variable average. You will learn more about casts in Tutorial 14. Line 145 displays the value of variable average in classAverageJTextField.

Calculating and displaying the class average

```
 Source Editor [ClassAverage]                                      _ □ ✕
141    // method calculates average of grades entered
142    private void averageJButtonActionPerformed( ActionEvent event )
143    {
144        double average = ( double ) total / 10; // calculate average
145        classAverageJTextField.setText( String.valueOf( average ) );
146
147    } // end method averageJButtonActionPerformed
```

Figure 9.19   Calculating and displaying the class average.

6. ***Saving the application.*** Save your modified source code file.

7. ***Opening the Command Prompt window and changing directories.*** Open the **Command Prompt** window by selecting **Start > Programs > Accessories > Command Prompt**. Change to your working directory by typing cd C:\SimplyJava\ClassAverage.

(cont.)

8. ***Compiling the application***. Compile your application by typing javac ClassAverage.java.

9. ***Running the application.*** When your application compiles correctly, run it by typing java ClassAverage. Figure 9.20 shows the completed application running. The application should now run as it did in the test-drive.

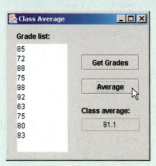

Figure 9.20 Completed **Class Average** application.

10. ***Closing the running application***. Close your running application by clicking its close button.

11. ***Closing the Command Prompt window***. Close the **Command Prompt** window by clicking its close button.

Figure 9.21 presents the source code for the **Class Average** application. The lines of code that you added, viewed or modified in this tutorial are highlighted.

```
1   // Tutorial 9: ClassAverage.java
2   // Application enables user to have the average of grades calculated.
3   import java.awt.*;
4   import java.awt.event.*;
5   import javax.swing.*;
6
7   public class ClassAverage extends JFrame
8   {
9      // JLabel and JTextArea for list of grades
10     private JLabel gradeListJLabel;
11     private JTextArea gradeListJTextArea;
12
13     // JButton initiates retrieving grades
14     private JButton getGradesJButton;
15
16     // JButton initiates calculating average
17     private JButton averageJButton;
18
19     // JLabel and JTextField used to display average
20     private JLabel classAverageJLabel;
21     private JTextField classAverageJTextField;
22
23     private int total = 0; // holds value of the grade total
24
25     // no-argument constructor
26     public ClassAverage()
27     {
28        createUserInterface();
29     }
30
```

Declaring an instance variable ——— 23

Figure 9.21 **Class Average** application code. (Part 1 of 4.)

```
31      // create and position GUI components; register event handlers
32      private void createUserInterface()
33      {
34         // get content pane for attaching GUI components
35         Container contentPane = getContentPane();
36
37         // enable explicit positioning of GUI components
38         contentPane.setLayout( null );
39
40         // set up gradeListJLabel
41         gradeListJLabel = new JLabel();
42         gradeListJLabel.setBounds( 16, 8, 70, 23 );
43         gradeListJLabel.setText( "Grade list:" );
44         contentPane.add( gradeListJLabel );
45
46         // set up gradeListJTextArea
47         gradeListJTextArea = new JTextArea();
48         gradeListJTextArea.setBounds( 16, 32, 88, 180 );
49         contentPane.add( gradeListJTextArea );
50
51         // set up getGradesJButton
52         getGradesJButton = new JButton();
53         getGradesJButton.setBounds( 128, 50, 100, 26 );
54         getGradesJButton.setText( "Get Grades" );
55         contentPane.add( getGradesJButton );
56         getGradesJButton.addActionListener(
57
58            new ActionListener() // anonymous inner class
59            {
60               // event handler called when getGradesJButton is clicked
61               public void actionPerformed( ActionEvent event )
62               {
63                  getGradesJButtonActionPerformed( event );
64               }
65
66            } // end anonymous inner class
67
68         ); // end call to addActionListener
69
70         // set up averageJButton
71         averageJButton = new JButton();
72         averageJButton.setBounds( 128, 90, 100, 26 );
73         averageJButton.setText( "Average" );
74         averageJButton.setEnabled( false );
75         contentPane.add( averageJButton );
76         averageJButton.addActionListener(
77
78            new ActionListener() // anonymous inner class
79            {
80               // event handler called when averageJButton is clicked
81               public void actionPerformed( ActionEvent event )
82               {
83                  averageJButtonActionPerformed( event );
84               }
85
86            } // end anonymous inner class
87
88         ); // end call to addActionListener
```

Disabling the **Average** JButton —— 74

Figure 9.21　**Class Average** application code. (Part 2 of 4.)

```
89
90            // set up classAverageJLabel
91            classAverageJLabel = new JLabel();
92            classAverageJLabel.setBounds( 128, 132, 90, 23 );
93            classAverageJLabel.setText( "Class average:" );
94            contentPane.add( classAverageJLabel );
95
96            // set up classAverageJTextField
97            classAverageJTextField = new JTextField();
98            classAverageJTextField.setBounds( 128, 156, 100, 21 );
99            classAverageJTextField.setEditable( false );
100           classAverageJTextField.setHorizontalAlignment(
101              JTextField.CENTER );
102           contentPane.add( classAverageJTextField );
103
104           // set properties of application's window
105           setTitle( "Class Average" ); // set title bar text
106           setSize( 250, 250 );          // set window size
107           setVisible( true );           // display window
108
109        } // end method createUserInterface
110
111        // method retrieves, totals and displays grades from user
112        private void getGradesJButtonActionPerformed( ActionEvent event )
113        {
114           total = 0;          // stores total of grades entered
115           int counter = 1;   // counter controls do...while statement
116           String input;       // stores data entered into input dialog
117           int grade;          // stores int value converted from input
118
119           // clear previous grades and calculation result
120           gradeListJTextArea.setText( "" );
121           classAverageJTextField.setText( "" );
122
123           do
124           {
125              // get user input
126              input = JOptionPane.showInputDialog( null, "Enter Grade" );
127              grade = Integer.parseInt( input );
128
129              // add text to output
130              gradeListJTextArea.append( grade + "\n" );
131              total += grade;                 // add input to total
132              counter++;                      // increment counter
133           }
134           while ( counter <= 10 );            // end do...while
135
136           averageJButton.setEnabled( true );     // enable averageJButton
137           averageJButton.requestFocusInWindow(); // transfer focus
138
139        } // end method getGradesJButtonActionPerformed
140
141        // method calculates average of grades entered
142        private void averageJButtonActionPerformed( ActionEvent event )
143        {
144           double average = ( double ) total / 10; // calculate average
145           classAverageJTextField.setText( String.valueOf( average ) );
146
147        } // end method averageJButtonActionPerformed
```

Labels (left margin):
- Declaring local variables (lines 114–117)
- Clearing a JTextArea and JTextField (lines 120–121)
- Using a do...while statement to calculate the class average (lines 123–134)
- Enabling the **Average** JButton and giving it the focus (lines 136–137)
- Calculating and displaying class average (lines 144–145)

Figure 9.21   **Class Average** application code. (Part 3 of 4.)

```
148
149      // main method
150      public static void main( String[] args )
151      {
152         ClassAverage application = new ClassAverage();
153         application.setDefaultCloseOperation( JFrame.EXIT_ON_CLOSE );
154
155      } // end method main
156
157   } // end class ClassAverage
```

Figure 9.21   Class Average application code. (Part 4 of 4.)

SELF-REVIEW

1. The _____ operator converts its operand to the type specified in parentheses.

   a) type   b) converter

   c) convert   d) cast

2. Call JOptionPane's _____ method to display an input dialog.

   a) showInput   b) showMessageDialog

   c) showInputDialog   d) None of the above.

Answers: 1) d. 2) c.

9.4 Wrap-Up

In this tutorial, you learned how to use the do...while repetition statement. You studied a UML activity diagram that explained how this statement executes. You used the do...while statement in your **Class Average** application. You learned how to use an instance variable to store information that is required by multiple methods of your class.

The do...while repetition statement executes as long as its loop-continuation condition is true. This repetition statement always executes its body at least once. When the loop-continuation condition becomes false, the repetition terminates. An infinite loop occurs if the loop-continuation condition never becomes false.

You also learned how to use input dialogs to retrieve data from the user. You learned how to enable and disable a JButton, and how to transfer the focus of the application to a JButton. In addition, you learned how to convert between numeric types by using a cast operator. In the next tutorial, you will continue studying repetition statements. You will learn how to use the for repetition statement, which is particularly useful for counter-controlled repetition.

SKILLS SUMMARY

Looping with the do...while Repetition Statement

■ Insert a do...while statement in your code and place the statements that you want to execute at least once in its body. The loop will iterate while its loop-continuation condition remains true.

■ Place the loop-continuation condition in the parentheses after while at the end of the loop body.

■ Place a semicolon (;) after the closing right parenthesis of the condition.

Displaying an Input Dialog

■ Call the JOptionPane.showInputDialog method.

■ Use null as the first argument to center the dialog on the screen.

■ Specify the text (prompt) to be displayed in the dialog as the second argument.

Retrieving Input from an Input Dialog

■ Input from an input dialog is returned from the `JOptionPane.showInputDialog` method as a `String`.

Disabling a `JButton`

■ Call the `setEnabled` method, and pass the argument `false`.

Enabling a `JButton`

■ Call the `setEnabled` method, and pass the argument `true`.

Transferring the Focus to a Component

■ Call the component's `requestFocusInWindow` method.

Declaring an Instance Variable

■ Declare the variable within the application's class, but outside of any methods.

Converting an `int` Variable's Value to a `double`

■ Place the cast operator (`double`) before the integer variable's name.

KEY TERMS

cast operator—Converts its operand to the type placed within the parentheses of the cast.

disabled—A component that has its *enabled* property set to `false`. Such components do not respond to user interactions.

do...while repetition statement—A control statement that executes a set of body statements while the loop-continuation condition is `true`. The condition is tested after the loop body executes, so the body statements always execute at least once.

enabled **property**—Specifies whether a component, such as a `JButton`, appears enabled (`true`) or disabled (`false`).

focus—When a component is selected, it is said to have the focus of the application. Focus is used to help bring attention to the component that should be used next.

input dialog—Causes the application to wait for the user to input data. The dialog contains a `JTextField` designed to retrieve user input.

instance variable—A variable defined in a class but outside any of that class's methods. An instance variable's value is preserved between method calls, and the variable can be used in multiple methods of the class.

JOptionPane.showInputDialog method—Displays an input dialog.

local variable—A variable that can be used only in the method in which it is declared.

off-by-one error—The kind of logic error that occurs when a loop executes for one more or one fewer iterations than is intended.

requestFocusInWindow method—The method that sets the component to have the focus, attracting the user's attention.

setEnabled method—Sets the *enabled* property of a component to `true` or `false`. Set the *enabled* property to `true` if the component should react to user interactions. Set the *enabled* property to `false` if the component should not react to user interactions.

transferring the focus—Setting a component to have the application's focus. This is implemented by calling the component's `requestFocusInWindow` method.

GUI DESIGN GUIDELINES

`JButton`

■ Disable a `JButton` when its function should not be available to the user.

■ Enable a `JButton` when its function should be available to the user.

`JTextArea`

■ Most `JTextArea`s should have a descriptive `JLabel`, indicating what output is expected to be displayed. Use sentence-style capitalization for such a `JLabel`.

JAVA LIBRARY REFERENCE

JButton This class is used to display message and input dialogs.

■ *In action*

── Enabled `JButton`

── Enabled `JButton` with focus

── Disabled `JButton`

■ *Methods*

`requestFocusInWindow`—Sets the `JButton` to have the focus.
`setBounds`—Sets the bounds of the `JButton`, which determines its location and size.
`setEnabled`—Sets the *enabled* property of the `JButton` to `true` or `false`.
`setText`—Sets the *text* property of a `JButton`.

JOptionPane This class is used to display message and input dialogs.

■ *Methods*

`showInputDialog`—Displays an input dialog.
`showMessageDialog`—Displays a message dialog.

MULTIPLE-CHOICE QUESTIONS

9.1 A(n) _____ occurs when a loop-continuation condition in a do…while never becomes `false`.

    a) infinite loop
    b) counter-controlled loop
    c) control statement
    d) nested control statement

9.2 The _____ statement executes its body at least once and continues executing until its loop-termination condition becomes `false`.

    a) `while`
    b) `if`
    c) `do…while`
    d) `if…else`

9.3 The _____ argument of the `JOptionPane.showInputDialog` method specifies the prompt that appears above an input dialog's `JTextField`.

    a) first
    b) second
    c) third
    d) fourth

9.4 A(n) _____ occurs when a loop executes for one more or one less iteration than is intended.

    a) infinite loop
    b) counter-controlled loop
    c) off-by-one error
    d) nested control statement

9.5 If its loop-continuation condition is `false` the first time it is evaluated, a do…while repetition statement _____.

    a) executes its body until the condition becomes `true`
    b) executes its body while the condition is `false`
    c) never executes
    d) has executed its body only once

9.6 The input dialog displayed by method `showInputDialog` contains a _____ component that enables the user to enter input.

    a) `JTextArea`
    b) `JTextField`
    c) `JLabel`
    d) title bar

9.7 You can use method _____ to enable a `JButton` component.

    a) `enable`
    b) `requestEnabled`
    c) `setEnabled`
    d) `requestFocusInWindow`

9.8 When a JButton has the application's focus, you can either click the JButton or press the _____ to perform the JButton's action.

a) *Space Bar*

b) *Tab* key

c) *Enter* key

d) None of the above.

9.9 Method showInputDialog returns _____.

a) the value in the dialog's JTextField

b) true if the value entered is greater than 0, false otherwise

c) nothing

d) 0 if the user clicked the **OK** JButton, 1 otherwise

9.10 In a do...while statement, the keyword while appears _____.

a) after the do keyword, but before the do...while body

b) after the do keyword, as the last statement in the body of the do...while

c) before the do keyword

d) after the do keyword and after the do...while body

EXERCISES

9.11 (*Modified Class Average Application*) The **Class Average** application of Fig. 9.21 has a deficiency. The **Average** JButton is never disabled after the average is calculated the first time. Modify the **Class Average** application as in Fig. 9.22, so that the **Get Grades** JButton is disabled after the user enters 10 grades. The user's only option then will be to click the **Average** JButton to display the average. Once the average is displayed, have the application disable the **Average** JButton, enable the **Get Grades** JButton and give the **Get Grades** JButton the application's focus, so that the user may enter 10 new grades.

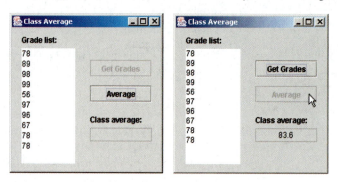

Figure 9.22　Modified **Class Average** application.

a) *Copying the template to your working directory.* Copy the directory C:\Examples\Tutorial09\Exercises\ModifiedClassAverage to your C:\SimplyJava directory.

b) *Opening the template file.* Open the ClassAverage.java file in your text editor.

c) *Modifying the getGradesJButtonActionPerformed event handler.* Add code in lines 139–140 to disable the **Get Grades** JButton. Use line 139 for a comment and line 140 to perform the disabling.

d) *Modifying the averageJButtonActionPerformed event handler.* Add code starting in line 150 that will disable the **Average** JButton, enable the **Get Grades** JButton and give the application's focus to the **Get Grades** JButton.

e) *Saving the application.* Save your modified source code file.

f) *Opening the Command Prompt window and changing directories.* Open the **Command Prompt** window by selecting **Start > Programs > Accessories > Command Prompt**. Change to your working directory by typing cd C:\SimplyJava\ModifiedClassAverage.

g) *Compiling the application.* Compile your application by typing javac ClassAverage.java.

h) *Running the completed application.* When your application compiles correctly, run it by typing java ClassAverage. Test the application by clicking the **Get Grades** JButton and entering 10 grades. Make sure that once 10 grades are entered, the **Get**

Grades JButton is disabled and the **Average** JButton is enabled. The **Average** JButton should have the focus. Press the *Space Bar* to calculate the average. Make sure that the average is correct. The **Average** JButton should now be disabled and the **Get Grades** JButton should be enabled and have the focus.

i) *Closing the application.* Close your running application by clicking its close button.

j) *Closing the Command Prompt window.* Close the **Command Prompt** window by clicking its close button.

9.12 *(Class Average Application That Handles Any Number of Grades)* Modify the original **Class Average** application to handle any number of grades, as in Fig. 9.23. When the user clicks the **Get Grades** JButton, an input dialog will ask the user to input the number of grades to be entered. The application should execute as it did in the test-drive (Section 9.1), except that each time the **Get Grades** JButton is clicked the input dialog will appear as many times as the number of grades the user wishes to enter.

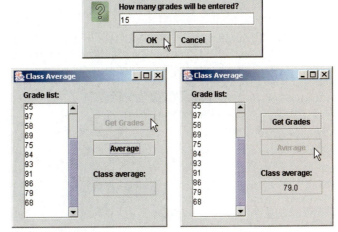

Figure 9.23 Modified **Class Average** application handling an arbitrary number of grades.

a) *Copying the template to your working directory.* Copy the directory C:\Examples\ Tutorial09\Exercises\ClassAverageAnyNumberOfGrades to your C:\SimplyJava directory.

b) *Opening the template file.* Open the ClassAverage.java file in your text editor.

c) *Declaring an instance variable.* Add code in line 26 that declares int variable limit. This variable will store the number of grades the user wishes to enter.

d) *Modifying the getGradesJButtonActionPerformed event handler.* Add code in lines 130–131 (before the do...while statement) that will display an input dialog for the user. Use two lines for readability. Set the text displayed in the input dialog to "How many grades will be entered?". Assign the result of this input dialog to variable input. Add code in line 132 that will convert the value of input to an integer, and assign the result to the instance variable limit.

e) *Modifying the do...while statement in getGradesJButtonActionPerformed.* Modify the condition of the do...while statement (line 145) so that the repetition statement will loop the amount of times entered by the user. In the condition, use the limit instance variable to determine when the loop should terminate.

f) *Calculating the class average.* Modify the code in the averageJButtonActionPerformed event handler (lines 156–170) so that line 158 calculates the average by using the instance variable limit rather than the value 10.

g) *Saving the application.* Save your modified source code file.

h) *Opening the Command Prompt window and changing directories.* Open the **Command Prompt** window by selecting **Start > Programs > Accessories > Command Prompt**. Change to your working directory by typing cd C:\SimplyJava\Class-AverageAnyNumberOfGrades.

i) *Compiling the application.* Compile your application by typing `javac ClassAverage.java`.

j) *Running the completed application.* When your application compiles correctly, run it by typing `java ClassAverage`. Test the application by pressing the **Get Grades** JButton. In the first input dialog, enter the amount of grades you would like to enter. The input dialog should appear as many time as the number of grades you have decided to enter. When all your grades have been entered, the **Average** JButton should be enabled and have the focus. Press the *Space Bar* to calculate the average and make sure the average calculated is correct.

k) *Closing the application.* Close your running application by clicking its close button.

l) *Closing the Command Prompt window.* Close the **Command Prompt** window by clicking its close button.

9.13 *(Arithmetic Calculator Application)* Write an application that allows users to enter two numbers that can then be added or multiplied (Fig. 9.24). Users should enter each number in an input dialog, displayed when the **Enter Operands** JButton is clicked. Each number should be appended to the **Operands:** JTextArea. The **Add** and **Multiply** JButtons are initially disabled, but they should be enabled after the two operands are input. Once a result is calculated using the **Add** JButton, this JButton should be disabled until two new numbers are added. Once a result is calculated using the **Multiply** JButton, this JButton should be disabled until two new numbers are added.

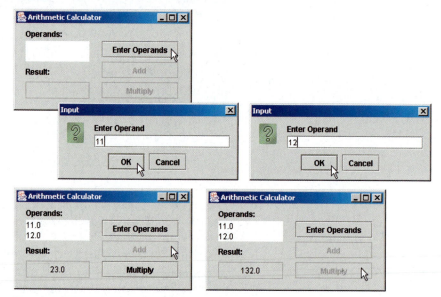

Figure 9.24 Arithmetic Calculator application.

a) *Copying the template to your working directory.* Copy the directory `C:\Examples\Tutorial09\Exercises\ArithmeticCalculator` to your `C:\SimplyJava` directory.

b) *Opening the template file.* Open the `ArithmeticCalculator.java` file in your text editor. Lines 25–26 in the template already declare two instance variables of type double—`value1` and `value2`—that you will need in this application. Variable `value1` will store the first value entered by the user, and `value2` will store the second value entered by the user. Each variable is initialized to 0.

c) *Displaying an input dialog.* The template contains a do...while statement in the `enterOperandsJButtonActionPerformed` event handler, beginning in line 145. Add code in lines 147–148 (within the do...while statement) to display an input dialog that asks the user to enter an operand. Use two lines to increase readability. Store the value the user enters in the input dialog in the variable `input` (which is declared in line 139).

d) *Retrieving input from the user.* After the code you added to display an input dialog, there is an empty if...else statement. The if portion executes when counter contains the value 1 (that is, the user has entered the first operand). Add a line of code to

the body of the `if` to convert the value of `input` to type `double` and assign the value to instance variable `value1`. The `else` portion executes when the user has entered the second operand. Add a line of code to the body of the `else` portion to convert the value of `input` to type `double` and assign the value to instance variable `value2`.

e) ***Incrementing the loop counter and modifying the do...while statement condition.*** Add code in line 160 (within the do...while statement) to increment the value of `counter`. Modify the repetition statement's condition in line 162 so that the do...while statement executes twice.

f) ***Transferring the focus to the Add JButton.*** Add code in lines 171–172 to transfer the focus to the **Add** JButton. Line 171 should be a comment.

g) ***Modifying the addJButtonActionPerformed event handler.*** This method already adds `value1` and `value2`, assigns the result to `result` and displays the result in `resultJTextField`. You now need to disable the **Add** JButton. Add code to do this in lines 182–183. Use line 182 for a comment and line 183 to disable the JButton.

h) ***Modifying the multiplyJButtonActionPerformed event handler.*** This method already multiplies `value1` and `value2`, assigns the result to `result` and displays the result in `resultJTextField`. You now need to disable the **Multiply** JButton. Add code to do this in lines 193–194. Use line 193 for a comment and line 194 to disable the JButton.

i) ***Saving the application.*** Save your modified source code file.

j) ***Opening the Command Prompt window and changing directories.*** Open the **Command Prompt** window by selecting **Start > Programs > Accessories > Command Prompt**. Change to your working directory by typing `cd C:\SimplyJava\ArithmeticCalculator`.

k) ***Compiling the application.*** Compile your application by typing `javac ArithmeticCalculator.java`.

l) ***Running the completed application.*** When your application compiles correctly, run it by typing `java ArithmeticCalculator`. Test the application by entering two inputs and pressing the **Add** and **Multiply** JButtons. Make sure that the **Add** JButton has the focus after the numbers are entered. Also make sure that when either the **Add** or **Multiply** JButtons are clicked, the addition or multiplication is performed and the JButton clicked is disabled.

m) ***Closing the application.*** Close your running application by clicking its close button.

n) ***Closing the Command Prompt window.*** Close the **Command Prompt** window by clicking its close button.

What does this code do? ▶

9.14 What is the result of the following code? Assume that there is no text in `displayJTextArea` when this code begins executing.

```
1   int y;
2   int x = 1;
3
4   do {
5      y = x * x;
6      displayJTextArea.append( y + "\n" );
7      x += 1;
8   } while ( x <= 10 );
```

What's wrong with this code? ▶

9.15 Find the error(s) in the following code. This code should append the numbers from 10 down to 1 to outputJTextArea.

```
1   int counter = 10;
2
3   do
4   {
5      outputJTextArea.append( counter + "\n" );
6   }
7   while ( counter >= 10 );
8
9   --counter;
```

Using the Debugger ▶

9.16 (*Factorial Application*) The **Factorial** application calculates the factorial of an integer input by the user. The factorial of an integer is the product of each integer from one to that integer. For example, the factorial of 3—represented in mathematics as 3!— is 6 ($1 \times 2 \times 3$). While testing the application, you notice that it does not execute correctly. Use the debugger to find and correct the logic error(s) in the application. Figure 9.25 displays the correct output for the **Factorial** application.

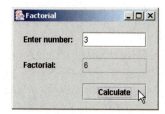

Figure 9.25 Correct output for the **Factorial** application.

a) *Copying the template to your working directory.* Copy the C:\Examples\Tutorial09\Exercises\Debugger\Factorial directory to your C:\SimplyJava directory.

b) *Opening the Command Prompt window and changing directories.* Open the **Command Prompt** window by selecting **Start > Programs > Accessories > Command Prompt**. Change to your working directory by typing cd C:\SimplyJava\Debugger\Factorial.

c) *Running the application.* Run the **Factorial** application by typing java Factorial. Enter the value 3 into the **Enter number:** JTextField and press the **Calculate** JButton. Notice that the result displayed in the **Factorial:** JTextField (0) is not the correct value (6).

d) *Closing the application.* Close your running application by clicking its close button.

e) *Compiling with the -g option.* For debugging, compile the application by typing javac -g Factorial.java.

f) *Starting the debugger.* Start the debugger by typing jdb.

g) *Opening the template file.* Open the Factorial.java file in your text editor.

h) *Finding and correcting the error(s).* Use the debugging skills learned in previous tutorials to locate the logic error(s) in the calculateJButtonActionPerformed event handler (lines 85–104 in the template file). Set a breakpoint in the do...while statement that enables you to examine the value of variable counter, then use the debugger's print command to examine variable counter during each iteration of the loop. After you locate the logic error, modify the code in calculateJButtonActionPerformed so it displays the correct results.

i) *Saving the application.* Save your modified source code file.

j) *Compiling the application.* Compile your application by typing javac Factorial.java.

k) ***Running the completed application.*** When your application compiles correctly, run it by typing `java Factorial`. Test the application using several different inputs to ensure the resulting factorial output is correct for each input value.

l) ***Closing the application.*** Close your running application by clicking its close button.

m) ***Closing the Command Prompt window.*** Close the **Command Prompt** window by clicking its close button.

Programming Challenge ▶

9.17 (*Restaurant Bill Application*) Develop an application that calculates a restaurant bill (Fig. 9.26). When the user clicks the **Add Items** JButton, the user should be able to enter the item ordered, the quantity of the item ordered and the price of the item. To do this, three input dialogs will be displayed per item. The user can enter exactly three items. Once all three items have been entered, your application should display the number ordered, the item ordered and the price per unit in three JTextAreas. The event handler should then calculate and display the total price. For each set of input, the item's information will be appended to the JTextAreas. Display all prices with dollar formats (that is, preceded by a dollar sign and with two digits to the right of the decimal point). Notice that the text in each input dialog displays the current item number for the user.

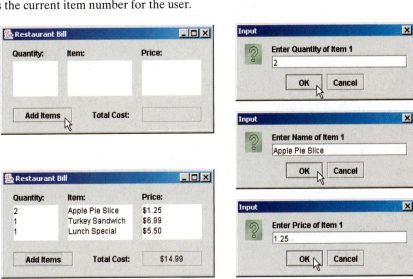

Figure 9.26   **Restaurant Bill** application.

a) ***Copying the template to your working directory.*** Copy the directory `C:\Examples\Tutorial09\Exercises\RestaurantBill` to your `C:\SimplyJava` directory.

b) ***Opening the template file.*** Open the `RestaurantBill.java` file in your text editor.

c) ***Adding the do...while loop to the addJButtonActionPerformed event handler.*** Beginning in line 130, add a do...while statement that will loop three times. Use an `int` variable called `counter` to control the loop.

d) ***Adding code to the do...while loop.*** Within the do...while loop, write three statements that display input dialogs (using the `JOptionPane.showInputDialog` method) to retrieve the quantity, name and price of an item, respectively. Use the value of variable `counter` in the input dialog prompts to indicate that the user is inputting information for the first, second or third item. Convert the result of the quantity input dialog to type `int` and the result of the price input dialog to type `double`. Use JTextArea method `append` to append the results of each input dialog to the appropriate JTextArea. Then calculate the `total` by multiplying the current item's quantity and price, then adding the result to `total`. Be sure to increment `counter` before the end of the do...while loop.

e) ***Saving the application.*** Save your modified source code file.

f) ***Opening the Command Prompt window and changing directories.*** Open the **Command Prompt** window by selecting **Start > Programs > Accessories > Command Prompt**. Change to your working directory by typing `cd C:\SimplyJava\RestaurantBill`.

g) *Compiling the application.* Compile your application by typing `javac Restaurant-Bill.java`.

h) *Running the completed application.* When your application compiles correctly, run it by typing `java RestaurantBill`. Test the application using several different inputs, and make sure each resulting total is correct. Also make sure that the input is displayed in the correct `JTextAreas`.

i) *Closing the application.* Close your running application by clicking its close button.

j) *Closing the Command Prompt window.* Close the **Command Prompt** window by clicking its close button.

Objectives

In this tutorial, you will learn to:
- Execute statements repeatedly with the **for** repetition statement.
- Use the **JSpinner** component to obtain input within a specified range of values.
- Add scrollbars to a **JTextArea** by placing the component inside a **JScrollPane**.

Outline

Interest Calculator Application

Introducing the for Repetition Statement

A s you learned in Tutorials 8 and 9, applications are often required to repeat actions. Using a `while` or a `do...while` statement allows you to specify a loop-continuation condition and test that condition either before entering the loop or after executing the body of the loop. In the **Car Payment Calculator** application and the **Class Average** application, a counter was used to determine the number of times the loop should iterate. Counter-controlled repetition is so common in applications that Java provides an additional control statement specially designed for such cases—the `for` repetition statement. In this tutorial, you will use the `for` repetition statement to create an **Interest Calculator** application.

10.1 Test-Driving the Interest Calculator Application

The **Interest Calculator** application calculates the amount of money in your savings account based on the initial amount of money in the account, the interest rate and the number of years the money remains on deposit. Users specify the principal amount (the initial amount of money in the account), the annual interest rate and the number of years for which interest will be calculated. The application then displays the amount of money you will have on deposit at the end of each year of that time. This application must meet the following requirements:

Application Requirements

You are considering investing $1000.00 in a savings account that yields 5% interest, and you want to forecast how your investment will grow. Assuming that you will leave all interest on deposit, develop an application that will calculate and print the amount of money in your account at the end of each year over a period of n years. To compute these amounts, use the following formula:

$$a = p(1 + r)^n$$

where

p is the original amount of money invested (the principal)
r is the annual interest rate
n is the number of years
a is the amount on deposit at the end of the nth year.

[*Note:* Percentages need to be divided by 100 to be used correctly in calculations. For instance, 5% will appear as .05 in our interest calculations. The user will enter an interest rate such as 5 or 7.5 and your application will divide this value by 100 to obtain the value used in the interest rate calculations .05 or .075.]

You begin by test-driving the completed application. Then, you will learn the additional Java technologies you will need to create your own version of this application.

Test-Driving the Interest Calculator Application

1. ***Locating the completed application.*** Open the **Command Prompt** window by selecting **Start > Programs > Accessories > Command Prompt**. Change to your **Interest Calculator** application directory by typing cd C:\Examples\ Tutorial10\CompletedApplication\InterestCalculator.

2. ***Running the Interest Calculator application.*** Type java InterestCalculator in the **Command Prompt** window to run the application (Fig. 10.1). The user is provided with JTextFields to enter the principal invested and the annual interest rate. A JSpinner component is used to enter the number of years. The **JSpinner** component limits a user's choices to a specific range of values—in this case, 1 through 10, inclusive. The initial value is 1, and users can click the up and down arrows to increase or decrease the value in the JSpinner. Click the up and down arrows to test this functionality. Once the user enters the principal amount, interest rate and number of years, the **Calculate** JButton can be clicked, causing the amount on deposit for each year to be displayed in the JTextArea at the bottom of the application's GUI.

JSpinner component ——

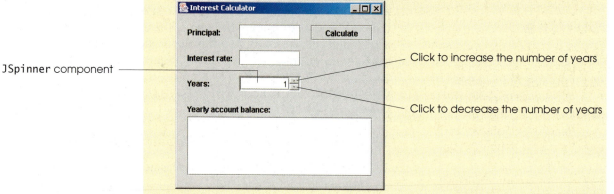

Click to increase the number of years

Click to decrease the number of years

Figure 10.1   Running the completed **Interest Calculator** application.

3. ***Entering a principal value.*** Once the application is running, enter a value in the **Principal:** JTextField. Input 1000 as specified in the application requirements.

4. ***Entering an interest-rate value.*** Next, enter a value in the **Interest rate:** JTextField. The specified interest rate was 5% in the problem statement, so enter 5 in the **Interest rate:** JTextField.

5. ***Selecting the duration of the investment.*** Now you should choose the number of years for which you want to calculate the amount in the savings account. In this case, select 10 by clicking the up arrow in the **Years:** JSpinner repeatedly until the value reads 10.

6. ***Calculating the amount.*** Click the **Calculate** JButton. The amount of money in your account at the end of each year during a period of 10 years will be displayed in the JTextArea with a scrollbar (Fig. 10.2), so that the user may view all the output data. Notice that the scrollbar automatically scrolls to the bottom of the JTextArea's text. Use the mouse to drag the scrollbar up, and view the data not initially displayed (Fig. 10.3).

(cont.)

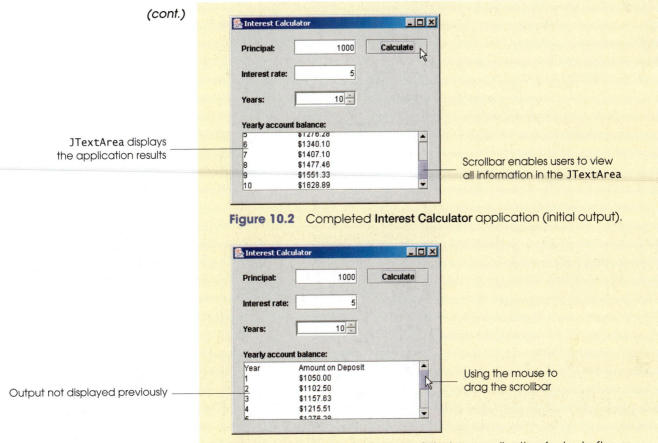

Figure 10.2 Completed **Interest Calculator** application (initial output).

JTextArea displays the application results

Scrollbar enables users to view all information in the JTextArea

Output not displayed previously

Using the mouse to drag the scrollbar

Figure 10.3 Completed **Interest Calculator** application (output after scrolling up).

7. ***Examining the JSpinner more closely.*** Click the down arrow repeatedly until the value in the JSpinner is 1. Click the down arrow again. Notice that the value of the JSpinner does not change. Now, click the up arrow repeatedly until the value in the JSpinner is 10. Click the up arrow again. Notice again that the value of the JSpinner does not change. If the JSpinner contains the lowest value in the range (in this case, 1), clicking the down arrow will have no effect on the value of the JSpinner. Likewise, if the JSpinner contains the highest value in the range (in this case, 10), clicking the up arrow will have no effect on the value of the JSpinner. Use the keyboard to enter valid input (an integer between 1 and 10) directly into the JSpinner's text area and click the **Calculate** JButton (Fig. 10.4). Notice that the application works properly.

Use the keyboard to enter an invalid value (that is, a numeric value not between the values 1 and 10, or a string of text such as `"hello"`), then try to click the up and down arrows (Figures 10.5 and 10.6). Notice that when invalid data is entered, the up and down arrows make a beep sound, but do not modify the text of the JSpinner. Click the **Calculate** JButton. The value in the JSpinner is changed back to the most recent valid value, and the application calculates the proper amounts (that is, clicking the **Calculate** JButton for the input of figures 10.5 and 10.6 provides the output of Fig. 10.4, and resets the value in the JSpinner). A JSpinner will reset invalid data values when it loses the focus—for example, when another GUI component is clicked.

GUI Design Tip

Use a JSpinner when you would use a JTextField, but when you want the user to enter input values only within a specified range. The JSpinner prevents invalid input by rejecting values that either are of the wrong type or are out-of-range values. When invalid data is rejected, the previous value in the JSpinner is restored.

(cont.)

Valid input directly entered by typing in the **JSpinner**

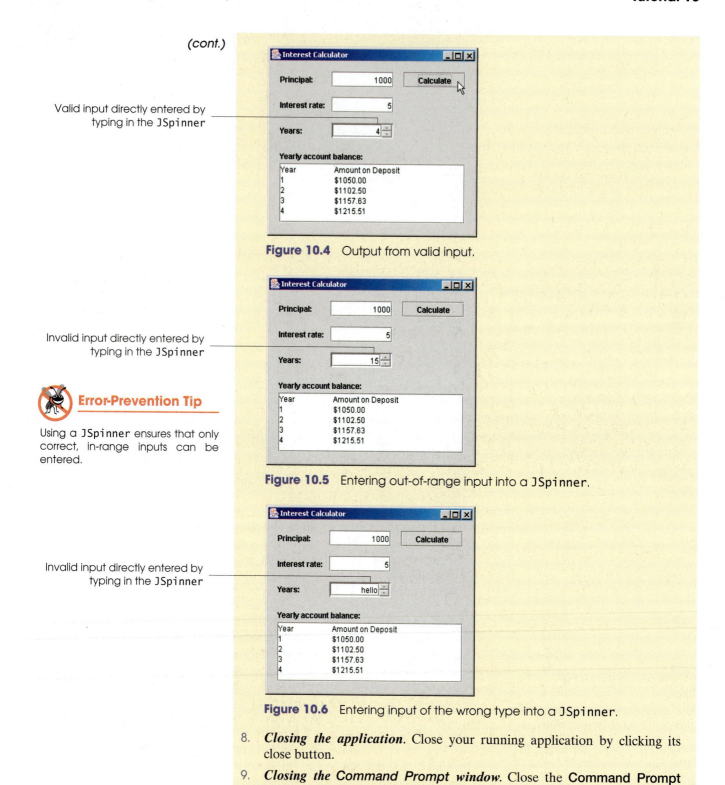

Figure 10.4 Output from valid input.

Invalid input directly entered by typing in the **JSpinner**

![Error-Prevention Tip icon] **Error-Prevention Tip**

Using a **JSpinner** ensures that only correct, in-range inputs can be entered.

Figure 10.5 Entering out-of-range input into a **JSpinner**.

Invalid input directly entered by typing in the **JSpinner**

Figure 10.6 Entering input of the wrong type into a **JSpinner**.

8. *Closing the application*. Close your running application by clicking its close button.

9. *Closing the Command Prompt window*. Close the **Command Prompt** window by clicking its close button.

10.2 Essentials of Counter-Controlled Repetition

This section uses the while repetition statement introduced in Tutorial 8 to formalize the elements required to perform counter-controlled repetition. There are four essential elements of counter-controlled repetition. They are

1. the **name** of the **control variable** (or loop counter) that is used to determine whether the loop continues to iterate.

2. the **initial value** of the control variable.

3. the **increment** (or **decrement**) by which the control variable is modified during each iteration of the loop (that is, each time the loop is performed).

4. the condition that tests for the **final value** of the control variable (to determine whether looping should continue).

Figure 10.7 contains the while repetition statement from Tutorial 8's completed application. The counter for that while statement was represented by variable years; for simplicity, we call the variable counter in this figure.

```
1    int counter = 2; // repetition counter
2
3    while ( counter <= 5 )
4    {
5       months = 12 * counter; // calculate payment period
6
7       // get monthly payment
8       monthlyPayment = calculateMonthlyPayment(
9          monthlyInterest, months, loanAmount );
10
11      // insert result into paymentsJTextArea
12      paymentsJTextArea.append( "\n" + months + "\t" +
13         currency.format( monthlyPayment ) );
14
15      counter++; // increment counter
16
17   } // end while
```

Figure 10.7   Counter-controlled repetition example.

This example uses the four elements of counter-controlled repetition. Recall that the **Car Payment Calculator** application calculates and displays monthly car payments over periods of two through five years. The declaration in line 1 names the control variable (counter), indicating that it is of data type int. This declaration also includes an initialization, which sets the variable to an initial value of 2.

Consider the while statement (lines 3–17). Line 5 uses the counter variable to calculate the number of months over which car payments are to be made. Lines 8–9 call the calculateMonthlyPayment method provided in your application from Tutorial 8 to determine the monthly payment for the car. This method takes as arguments the interest rate, the duration of the payment period in months and the car's price. Lines 12–13 display the amount in a JTextArea. Line 15 increments the control variable counter by 1 for each iteration of the loop. The condition in the while statement (line 3) tests whether the value of the control variable is less than or equal to 5, meaning that 5 is the final value for which the condition is true. The body of this while is performed even when the control variable is 5. The loop terminates when the control variable exceeds 5 (that is, when counter has a value of 6).

1. The control variable's _____ is one of the four essential elements of counter-controlled repetition.

   a) final value
   b) initial value
   c) increment (or decrement)
   d) All of the above.

2. What element of counter-controlled repetition determines how the control variable is modified during each iteration of the loop?

   a) name
   b) initial value
   c) increment (or decrement)
   d) final value

Answers: 1) d. 2) c.

10.3 Introducing the for Repetition Statement

The **for** repetition statement makes it easier for you to write code to perform counter-controlled repetition. This statement conveniently specifies all four elements essential to counter-controlled repetition. To help solidify your understanding of this new repetition statement, you will now learn how the `while` statement of Fig. 10.7 can be replaced by an equivalent `for` statement. The converted code is shown in Fig. 10.8.

```
1   for ( int counter = 2; counter <= 5; counter += 1 )
2   {
3      months = 12 * counter; // calculate payment period
4
5      // get monthly payment
6      monthlyPayment = calculateMonthlyPayment(
7         monthlyInterest, months, loanAmount );
8
9      // insert result into paymentsJTextArea
10     paymentsJTextArea.append( "\n" + months + "\t" +
11        currency.format( monthlyPayment ) );
12
13  } // end for
```

Figure 10.8   Code segment for the **Car Payment Calculator** application that demonstrates the **for** statement.

Good Programming Practice

Vertical spacing above and below control statements, as well as indentation within control statements, enhances readability.

Let's examine this `for` repetition statement. The `for` statement's first line (including the keyword **for** and everything in parentheses after for)—line 1 of Fig. 10.8—is informally called the **for statement header**, or simply the **for header**. The `for` header specifies all four essential elements for counter-controlled repetition. The first expression in the `for` statement specifies the name and initial value of the control variable `counter`. The second expression specifies the loop-continuation condition (in this case, `counter <= 5`). The last expression specifies the increment (the amount by which `counter` is modified each time the `for` body is executed). The line should be read "*for each value of counter starting at 2 and ending at 5, do the following statements then add one to counter.*"

The initial value of `counter` is 2, so the loop-continuation condition is satisfied and the payment calculations within the `for` body are executed. After executing the `for` body, the right brace is reached (line 13). This marks the end of the `for` statement. When the right brace is reached, control returns to the rightmost portion of the `for` header in line 1, which increments `counter` by 1 and begins the loop again with the loop-continuation condition test. The `for` statement repeats until the loop-continuation condition becomes `false` (that is, when `counter` becomes greater than 5), when repetition terminates.

Error-Prevention Tip

Although the value of the control variable can be changed in the body of a **for** loop, avoid doing so, because this practice can lead to subtle errors.

Figure 10.9 takes a closer look at the `for` statement in Fig. 10.8. Notice that the `for` statement "does it all": It specifies each of the items needed for the counter-controlled repetition with a control variable.]

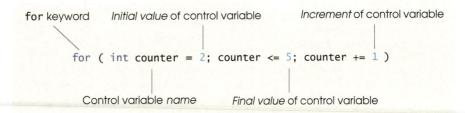

Error-Prevention Tip

Using a `for` loop for counter-controlled repetition helps eliminate off-by-one errors (which occur when a loop is executed for one more or one fewer iteration than is necessary), because the final value of the control variable is clear.

Figure 10.9 `for` header components.

Each `for` statement begins with the keyword `for`. Then the statement names and initializes a control variable (in this case, `counter` is set to 2). [*Note:* You do not need to declare (using the `int` keyword) the counter variable before the `for` statement. It can be done within the header as shown in Fig. 10.9. If the counter variable is declared this way, however, it will only exist within the bounds of the `for` statement. If the counter variable needs to be accessed after the `for` statement, it will need to be declared outside of the `for` statement.] Following the initial value of the control variable is a semicolon, followed by the loop-continuation condition. This is followed by another semicolon, then the increment of the control variable. The following box describes each step as the repetition statement (Fig. 10.9) executes.

Executing the for Repetition Statement	1. The application declares `int` variable `counter` and sets its value to 2.
	2. The loop-continuation condition is checked. The condition evaluates to `true` (`counter` is 2, which is less than or equal to 5), so the application executes the first statement in the body of the `for` statement.
	3. The value of `counter` is increased by 1; `counter` now contains the value 3.
	4. The loop-continuation condition is checked. The condition evaluates to `true` (`counter` is 3, which is less than or equal to 5), so the application executes the first statement in the `for` loop's body.
	5. The value of `counter` is increased by 1; `counter` now contains the value 4.
	6. The loop-continuation condition is checked. The condition evaluates to `true` (`counter` is 4, which is less than or equal to 5), so the application executes the first statement in the `for` loop's body.
	7. The value of `counter` is increased by 1; `counter` now contains the value 5.
	8. The loop-continuation condition is checked. The condition evaluates to `true` (`counter` is 5, which is less than or equal to 5), so the application executes the first statement in the `for` loop's body.
	9. The value of `counter` is increased by 1; `counter` now contains the value 6.
	10. The loop-continuation condition is checked. The condition evaluates to `false` (`counter` is 6, which is not less than or equal to 5), so the application exits the `for` loop.

The starting value, ending value and increment portions of a `for` statement can contain arithmetic expressions. For example, if a = 2 and b = 10, the header

```
for ( int i = a; i <= 4 * a * b; i += ( b / a ) )
```

is equivalent to the header

```
for ( int i = 2; i <= 80; i += 5 )
```

Common Programming Error

Counter-controlled loops should not be controlled with floating-point variables. Floating-point variables are represented only approximately in the computer's memory, possibly resulting in imprecise counter values and inaccurate tests for termination that could lead to logic errors.

Common Programming Error

Using an increment expression that does not modify the control variable's value (such as **counter + 1** when **counter++** or **counter += 1** should be used) normally causes an infinite loop.

If the loop-continuation condition is initially **false** (for example, if the initial value of control variable **i** is 5 and the loop-continuation condition is **i <= 4**), the **for**'s body is not performed. Instead, execution proceeds with the first statement after the **for** statement.

The control variable frequently is displayed or used in calculations within the **for** loop, but it does not have to be. It is common to use the control variable only to control repetition and not use within the loop.

Figure 10.10 contains the UML activity diagram of the **for** statement in Fig. 10.8. This activity diagram is similar to that of the **while** statement. Notice that the UML diagram shows that the initialization occurs only once and that incrementing occurs *after* each execution of the body statement. Also note that, besides small circles and flowlines, the activity diagram contains only rounded rectangle symbols and small diamond symbols. The rounded rectangle symbols are filled with the actions, and the flowlines coming out of the small diamond symbols are labeled with the appropriate guard conditions for this algorithm.

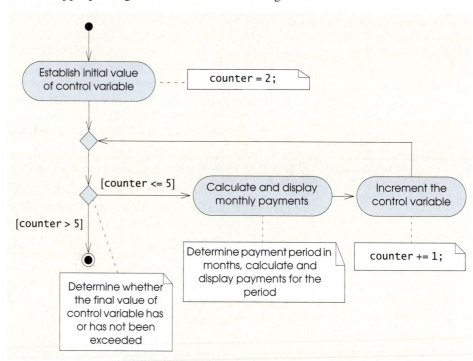

Figure 10.10 **for** repetition statement UML activity diagram.

SELF-REVIEW

1. The value before the first semicolon in a **for** statement specifies the _____.
   a) initial value of the counter variable   b) final value of the counter variable
   c) increment   d) number of times the statement iterates

2. The first line of the **for** repetition statement is informally known as the _____.
   a) **for** body   b) **for** header
   c) **for** counter   d) **for** expression

Answers: 1) a. 2) b.

10.4 Examples Using the for Statement

The following examples demonstrate ways to vary the control variable in a **for** statement. In each case, you are provided with the appropriate **for** header:

■ Vary the control variable from 1 to 100 in increments of 1.

```
for ( int i = 1; i <= 100; i++ )
```

- Vary the control variable from 100 to 1 in increments of −1 (that is, decrements of 1). Notice that when counting downwards, the loop-continuation condition, i >= 1, now uses the relational operator >=.

  ```
  for ( int i = 100; i >= 1; i-- )
  ```

- Vary the control variable from 7 to 77 in increments of 7.

  ```
  for ( int i = 7; i <= 77; i += 7 )
  ```

- Vary the control variable from 20 to 2 in increments of −2 (that is, decrements of 2).

  ```
  for ( int i = 20; i >= 2; i -= 2 )
  ```

- Vary the control variable over the sequence of the following values: 2, 5, 8, 11, 14, 17, 20.

  ```
  for ( int i = 2; i <= 20; i += 3 )
  ```

- Vary the control variable over the sequence of the following values: 99, 88, 77, 66, 55, 44, 33, 22, 11, 0.

  ```
  for ( int i = 99; i >= 0; i -= 11 )
  ```

SELF-REVIEW

1. Which of the following is the appropriate for header to vary the control variable over the following sequence of values: 25, 20, 15, 10, 5?

   a) `for ( int i = 5; i <= 25; i += 5 )`
   b) `for ( int i = 25; i >= 5; i -= 5 )`
   c) `for ( int i = 5; i <= 25; i -= 5 )`
   d) `for ( int i = 25; i >= 5; i += 5 )`

2. Which of the following statements describes what the following for header does?

   ```
   for ( int i = 81; i <= 102; i++ )
   ```

   a) Vary the control variable from 81 to 102 in increments of 1.
   b) Vary the control variable from 81 to 102 in increments of 0.
   c) Vary the control variable from 102 to 81 in increments of −1.
   d) Vary the control variable from 81 to 102 in increments of 2.

Answers: 1) b. 2) a.

10.5 Constructing the Interest Calculator Application

Now you will build your **Interest Calculator** application by using a JSpinner to regulate input, scrollbars to display large output and a for statement to calculate the value of the investment after each year. The following pseudocode describes the basic operation of the **Interest Calculator** application, which executes when the user clicks the **Calculate** JButton:

> When the user clicks the Calculate JButton:
>> Get the values for the principal, interest rate and years entered by the user
>> Display a header in the JTextArea to label the output
>
>> For each year, starting at 1 and ending with the number of years entered,
>>> Calculate and display the year
>>> Calculate and display the current value of the investment

The template application you will use for this tutorial contains the **Calculate** JButton, plus two JLabels and their corresponding JTextFields—the **Principal:** JLabel and JTextField, and the **Interest rate:** JLabel and JTextField. Your application has a **Years:** JLabel, but you will customize the JSpinner component

for this input. You will customize a JTextArea with a scrollbar and add it to your application's GUI. Finally, you will add functionality to your application with a for statement.

Now that you have test-driven the **Interest Calculator** application and studied its pseudocode representation, you will use an ACE table to help you convert the pseudocode to Java. Figure 10.11 lists the actions, components and events that will help you complete your own version of this application.

Action/Component/ Event (ACE) Table for the Interest Calculator Application

Action	Component	Event
Label the application's fields	`interestRateJLabel,` `principalJLabel,` `yearsJLabel,` `yearlyBalanceJLabel`	Application is run
	`calculateJButton`	User clicks **Calculate** JButton
Get the values for the principal, interest rate and years entered by the user	`principalJTextField,` `interestRateJTextField,` `yearsJSpinner`	
Display a header in the JTextArea to label the output	`yearlyBalanceJTextArea`	
For each year, starting at 1 and ending with the number of years entered		
Calculate and display the year	`yearlyBalanceJTextArea`	
Calculate and display the current value of the investment	`yearlyBalanceJTextArea`	

Figure 10.11 ACE table for **Interest Calculator** application.

You will now begin building your **Interest Calculator** application. First, you will customize a JSpinner component to allow the user to select the number of years within a specified range, using the JSpinner's up arrow and down arrow. Next, you learn how to set the limits of the range (minimum and maximum values) for a JSpinner. You will use 1 as the minimum value and 10 as the maximum value for this component.

Customizing a JSpinner Component

1. *Copying the template application to your working directory.* Copy the `C:\Examples\Tutorial10\TemplateApplication\InterestCalcula-tor` directory to your `C:\SimplyJava` directory.

2. *Opening the Interest Calculator application's template file.* Open the template file `InterestCalculator.java` in your text editor.

3. *Setting the JSpinner's range values.* Enter the values highlighted in line 83 of Fig. 10.12 between the two parentheses following `SpinnerNumberModel`. **SpinnerNumberModel** is a class specifying that a JSpinner will contain a range of numerical values, as opposed to other types of data, such as dates. You will learn how to display dates in a JSpinner in Tutorial 25. The statement in lines 82–83 specifies the values that will be included in your JSpinner's range. The first value, 1, specifies the initial value that will be displayed in the JSpinner when your application is run. The next two values, 1 and 10, specify the minimum and maximum values in the range, respectively. The final value (or step size), 1, indicates that each value in the range is one more than the previous value. The **step size** specifies by how much the current number in the JSpinner component changes when the user clicks the component's up arrow (for incrementing) or down arrow (for decrementing).

Good Programming Practice

Suffix JSpinner component names with JSpinner.

(cont.)

Creating a number `JSpinner` and setting its range.

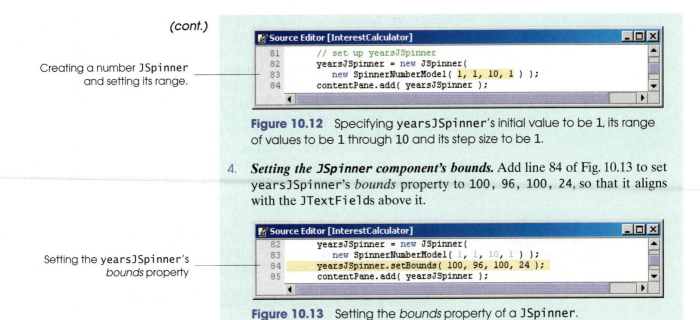

Figure 10.12   Specifying `yearsJSpinner`'s initial value to be 1, its range of values to be 1 through 10 and its step size to be 1.

4. **Setting the JSpinner component's bounds.** Add line 84 of Fig. 10.13 to set `yearsJSpinner`'s *bounds* property to 100, 96, 100, 24, so that it aligns with the `JTextField`s above it.

Setting the `yearsJSpinner`'s *bounds* property

```
Source Editor [InterestCalculator]
82        yearsJSpinner = new JSpinner(
83           new SpinnerNumberModel( 1, 1, 10, 1 ) );
84        yearsJSpinner.setBounds( 100, 96, 100, 24 );
85        contentPane.add( yearsJSpinner );
```

Figure 10.13   Setting the *bounds* property of a `JSpinner`.

5. **Saving the application.** Save your modified source code file.

6. **Opening the Command Prompt window and changing directories.** Open the **Command Prompt** window by selecting **Start > Programs > Accessories > Command Prompt**. Change to your working directory by typing `cd C:\SimplyJava\InterestCalculator`.

7. **Compiling the application.** Compile your application by typing `javac InterestCalculator.java`.

8. **Running the application.** When your application compiles correctly, run it by typing `java InterestCalculator`. Figure 10.14 shows the updated application running. Notice that the `JSpinner` contains the initial value 1. Use the up arrow and down arrow to change the value displayed. Notice also that when you click the **Calculate** `JButton`, no action occurs. You will add this functionality later in the tutorial.

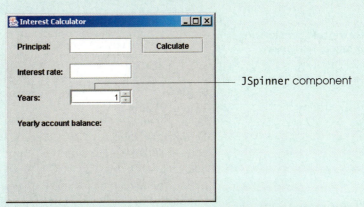

Figure 10.14   `JSpinner` added to **Interest Calculator** application.

9. **Closing the application.** Close your running application by clicking its close button.

10. **Closing the Command Prompt window.** Close the **Command Prompt** window by clicking its close button.

The **Interest Calculator** application displays the results of its calculations in a JTextArea. You will configure the JTextArea to have a scrollbar, so that if the JTextArea is too small to display its contents, the user can scroll up and down to view the entire contents of the box. To do this, Java provides a **JScrollPane** component. A JScrollPane is a **container**, meaning it (like your application's content pane) contains other components. A JScrollPane is not a component that you can view—rather, the JScrollPane causes scrollbars to appear as needed for a component that has been added to the JScrollPane. The JScrollPane is in turn added to the content pane. The component stored in the JScrollPane will appear as it normally would, except that scrollbars will appear as needed, depending on the amount of data being displayed. Next, you will use a JScrollPane to add scrollbars to your JTextArea.

Customizing a JTextArea with Scrollbars

1. **Setting the editable property.** Add line 95 of Fig. 10.15 to your code. This line sets the *editable* property to false so that the user cannot change the output in the **Yearly account balance:** JTextArea.

Setting
yearlyBalanceJTextArea's
editable property

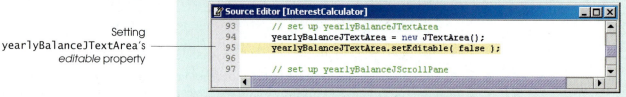

```
93        // set up yearlyBalanceJTextArea
94        yearlyBalanceJTextArea = new JTextArea();
95        yearlyBalanceJTextArea.setEditable( false );
96
97        // set up yearlyBalanceJScrollPane
```

Figure 10.15 Setting the JTextArea's *editable* property to false.

GUI Design Tip

If a JTextArea will display many lines of output, attach the JTextArea to a JScrollPane to allow users to scroll through the lines of output displayed in the JTextArea.

2. **Adding the JTextArea to the JScrollPane.** Enter the text, highlighted in line 99 of Fig. 10.16, between the parentheses following JScrollPane. Notice that we have placed part of this statement on a second line for clarity. This line attaches our JTextArea to the JScrollPane. This enables the JScrollPane to add scrollbars to the JTextArea as needed—that is, a horizontal scrollbar will be added if there is more text than can fit in the width of the JTextArea, and a vertical scrollbar will be added if there is more text than can fit in the height of the JTextArea.

Adding scrollbars to
yearlyBalanceJTextArea

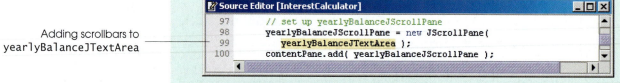

```
97        // set up yearlyBalanceJScrollPane
98        yearlyBalanceJScrollPane = new JScrollPane(
99           yearlyBalanceJTextArea );
100       contentPane.add( yearlyBalanceJScrollPane );
```

Figure 10.16 Adding yearlyBalanceJTextArea to yearlyBalance-JScrollPane.

3. **Setting the bounds of the JScrollPane.** Add line 100 of Fig. 10.17 to your code. This statement sets the JScrollPane's *bounds* property to 16, 160, 300, 92, so that it aligns with the components above it. These bounds also define the size and location of yearlyBalanceJTextArea, which is contained within yearlyBalanceJScrollPane.

Setting
yearlyBalanceJTextArea's
bounds property

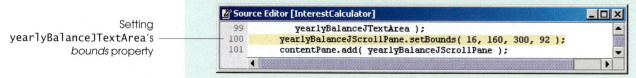

```
99           yearlyBalanceJTextArea );
100       yearlyBalanceJScrollPane.setBounds( 16, 160, 300, 92 );
101       contentPane.add( yearlyBalanceJScrollPane );
```

Figure 10.17 Adding a JScrollPane that will hold a JTextArea.

4. **Saving the application.** Save your modified source code file.

(cont.)

5. ***Opening the Command Prompt window and changing directories.*** Open the **Command Prompt** window by selecting **Start > Programs > Accessories > Command Prompt**. Change to your working directory by typing cd C:\SimplyJava\InterestCalculator.

6. ***Compiling the application.*** Compile your application by typing javac InterestCalculator.java.

7. ***Running the application.*** When your application compiles correctly, run it by typing java InterestCalculator. Figure 10.18 shows the updated application running. Notice that the JTextArea component is now displayed. A scrollbar is visible only when it is needed (that is, when there is more text than will fit in the JTextArea).

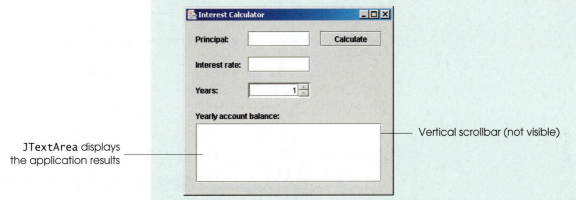

JTextArea displays the application results

Vertical scrollbar (not visible)

Figure 10.18 JTextArea with a JScrollPane added to the application.

8. ***Closing the application.*** Close your running application by clicking its close button.

9. ***Closing the Command Prompt window.*** Close the **Command Prompt** window by clicking its close button.

Now that you have finished designing your GUI, you will add functionality to your application. When the user clicks the **Calculate** JButton, you want your application to retrieve the inputs, then output a table containing the amount on deposit at the end of each year.

Adding Code to the *calculateJButton-ActionPerformed* Event Handler

1. ***Adding code to the `calculateJButtonActionPerformed` event handler.*** Add lines 133–140 of Fig. 10.19 to the calculateJButtonActionPerformed event handler. These lines declare the variables needed to store user inputs and initialize their values. Variable principal stores the principal entered by the user as a double (lines 134–135). Variable rate stores the interest rate, as double (lines 136–137). Variable year stores the number of years the user selected in the JSpinner component (lines 139–140). Line 139 uses the JSpinner component's **getValue** method to obtain the user's selection. This method returns an object that is converted to type **Integer** via the cast (Integer) and assigned to the variable integerObject. An Integer object contains a single piece of int data and has methods that can manipulate ints. Objects cannot be used in the arithmetic calculations, so you must obtain the int value from the Integer object. Line 140 does this by calling the Integer object's **intValue** method. The int returned from intValue is assigned to variable year for use in the interest calculations that you will implement in the next box.

(cont.)

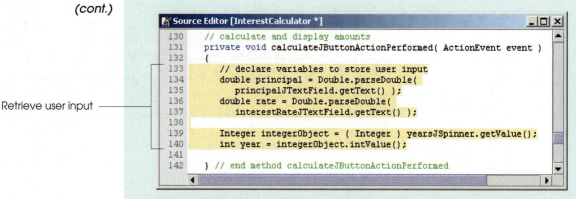

Retrieve user input ⎯

```
 Source Editor [InterestCalculator *]                              _ □ X
130        // calculate and display amounts
131        private void calculateJButtonActionPerformed( ActionEvent event )
132        {
133            // declare variables to store user input
134            double principal = Double.parseDouble(
135                principalJTextField.getText() );
136            double rate = Double.parseDouble(
137                interestRateJTextField.getText() );
138
139            Integer integerObject = ( Integer ) yearsJSpinner.getValue();
140            int year = integerObject.intValue();
141
142        } // end method calculateJButtonActionPerformed
```

Figure 10.19 Application code for retrieving and storing user input.

2. *Adding the header to your JTextArea.* Add lines 142–143 of Fig. 10.20 to the event handler. Line 142 sets the text that will be displayed at the top of the JTextArea. This text provides a header for your application's output. The JTextArea displays the results in two columns. The header labels the two columns as Year and Amount on Deposit, respectively. The "\t" escape sequence inserts a tab character between the word Year and the text Amount on Deposit. Line 143 creates a DecimalFormat object, which you will use shortly to format monetary results.

Placing a header in the
JTextArea and creating
a DecimalFormat to
format dollar amounts

```
 Source Editor [InterestCalculator]                               _ □ X
140            int year = integerObject.intValue();
141
142            yearlyBalanceJTextArea.setText( "Year\tAmount on Deposit" );
143            DecimalFormat dollars = new DecimalFormat( "$0.00" );
144
145        } // end method calculateJButtonActionPerformed
```

Figure 10.20 Application code for displaying a header in a JTextArea.

3. *Saving the application.* Save your modified source code file.

4. *Opening the Command Prompt window and changing directories.* Open the **Command Prompt** window by selecting **Start > Programs > Accessories > Command Prompt**. Change to your working directory by typing cd C:\SimplyJava\InterestCalculator.

5. *Compiling the application.* Compile your application by typing javac InterestCalculator.java.

6. *Running the application.* When your application compiles correctly, run it by typing java InterestCalculator. Figure 10.21 shows the updated application running. Enter a principal value, interest rate and number of years, then press the **Calculate** JButton. The header is displayed in the JTextArea. You will add the functionality to produce the rest of the output in the next box. Notice that the scrollbar has still not appeared because the output does not fill the JTextArea.

(cont.)

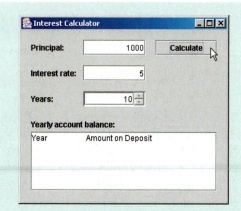

Figure 10.21   Header output in the JTextArea.

7. *Closing the application.* Close your running application by clicking its close button.

8. *Closing the Command Prompt window.* Close the **Command Prompt** window by clicking its close button.

Next, you will write a for statement to perform the interest calculations for the specified number of years. You will also learn to use the Math.pow method to perform exponentiation.

Calculating Cumulative Interest with a for Statement

1. *Creating an empty for statement.* Add lines 145–149 of Fig. 10.22 to the calculateJButtonActionPerformed event handler. The for header in line 146 initializes control variable count to 1. The test after the first semicolon (the loop-continuation condition) causes the loop to continue while the control variable is less than or equal to the number of years specified by the user. The for statement executes its body once for each year up to the value of year, varying control variable count from 1 to year in increments of 1.

```
Source Editor [InterestCalculator]
143          DecimalFormat dollars = new DecimalFormat( "$0.00" );
144
145          // calculate the total value for each year
146          for ( int count = 1; count <= year; count++ )
147          {
148
149          } // end for
150
151      } // end method calculateJButtonActionPerformed
```

Empty for statement

Figure 10.22   Creating the for statement.

2. *Performing the interest calculation.* Add lines 148–149 of Fig. 10.23 to the body of your for statement. Lines 148–149 perform the calculation from the formula

$$a = p\ (1 + r)^n$$

where a is amount, p is principal, r is rate and n is the number of years.

Line 149 calls the **Math.pow** method, which performs exponentiation. Math.pow takes two arguments—the first argument specifies the value that will be raised to a power, and the second argument specifies the power to which the first argument will be raised. For instance, Math.pow(4, 2) is used to represent the expression 4^2, which evaluates to 16.

(cont.)

Using **Math** method **pow** to
calculate the amount on
deposit after the specified
number of years

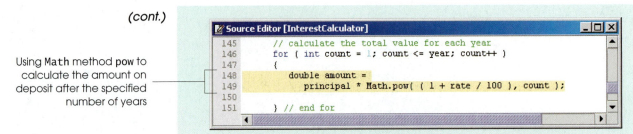

```
Source Editor [InterestCalculator]                          _ □ ×
145        // calculate the total value for each year
146        for ( int count = 1; count <= year; count++ )
147        {
148            double amount =
149                principal * Math.pow( ( 1 + rate / 100 ), count );
150
151        } // end for
```

Figure 10.23   Application code for calculating interest amount.

Line 149 also performs the *(1 + r)^n* portion of the formula. The first
argument to **Math.pow** is (1 + **rate** / 100), representing the *(1 + r)* portion of the formula. The division by 100 converts the input (which is in percentage format) into a decimal value that can be used in the interest
calculation. The second argument to **Math.pow**, **counter**, represents the
power that (1 + **rate** / 100) is raised to (the *n* in the formula above).

3. *Appending the calculation to the JTextArea.* Add lines 150–151 of
Fig. 10.24 to your **for** statement. These lines append additional text to the
end of the output **JTextArea**, using the **append** method. The text includes
a newline character (**"\n"**) to start the next output on the next line, the current **count** value, a tab character (**"\t"**) to position to the second column,
and the result of the method call **dollars.format(amount)**, which
returns the value in **amount** in monetary format.

After the body of the loop is performed, application execution reaches
the right brace, which is now in line 153. The counter (**count**) is incremented by 1, and the loop begins again with the loop-continuation test in
the **for** header. The **for** statement executes until the control variable
exceeds the number of years specified by the user.

Appending one line of text
to the **JTextArea**. (Note the
use of the escape sequence
\n to create a new line of text
and the escape sequence **\t**
to tab to the next column.)

```
Source Editor [InterestCalculator]                          _ □ ×
148            double amount =
149                principal * Math.pow( ( 1 + rate / 100 ), count );
150            yearlyBalanceJTextArea.append( "\n" + count + "\t" +
151                dollars.format( amount ) );
152
153        } // end for
```

Figure 10.24   Appending output to **yearlyBalanceJTextArea**.

4. *Saving the application.* Save your modified source code file.

5. *Opening the Command Prompt window and changing directories.* Open
the **Command Prompt** window by selecting **Start > Programs > Accessories > Command Prompt**. Change to your working directory by typing
cd C:\SimplyJava\InterestCalculator.

6. *Compiling the application.* Compile your application by typing **javac
InterestCalculator.java**.

7. *Running the application.* When your application compiles correctly, run it
by typing **java InterestCalculator**. Figure 10.25 shows the completed
application running. Note that the output is now larger than the **JTextArea**, so that the vertical scrollbar now appears. Use the scrollbar to
examine the full output (Fig. 10.26).

(cont.)

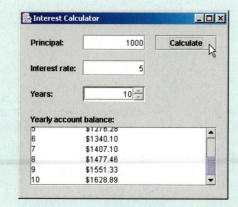

Figure 10.25 Completed application (with initial output).

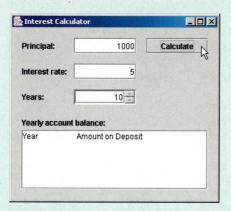

Figure 10.26 Completed application (with remainder of output).

8. ***Closing the application***. Close your running application by clicking its close button.

9. ***Closing the Command Prompt window***. Close the **Command Prompt** window by clicking its close button.

Figure 10.27 presents the source code for your **Interest Calculator** application. The lines of code that you added, viewed or modified are highlighted.

```
1   // Tutorial 10: InterestCalculator.java
2   // Calculate the total value of an investment.
3   import java.awt.*;
4   import java.awt.event.*;
5   import javax.swing.*;
6   import java.text.*;
7
8   public class InterestCalculator extends JFrame
9   {
10      // JLabel and JTextField for principal invested
11      private JLabel principalJLabel;
12      private JTextField principalJTextField;
13
14      // JLabel and JTextField for interest rate
15      private JLabel interestRateJLabel;
16      private JTextField interestRateJTextField;
```

Figure 10.27 **Interest Calculator** application code. (Part 1 of 4.)

```
17
18      // JLabel and JTextField for the number of years
19      private JLabel yearsJLabel;
20      private JSpinner yearsJSpinner;
21
22      // JLabel and JTextArea display amount on deposit at
23      // the end of each year up to number of years entered
24      private JLabel yearlyBalanceJLabel;
25      private JTextArea yearlyBalanceJTextArea;
26
27      // JScrollPane adds scrollbars to JTextArea for lengthy output
28      private JScrollPane yearlyBalanceJScrollPane;
29
30      // JButton calculates amount on deposit at the
31      // end of each year up to number of years entered
32      private JButton calculateJButton;
33
34      // no-argument constructor
35      public InterestCalculator()
36      {
37         createUserInterface();
38      }
39
40      // create and position GUI components; register event handlers
41      private void createUserInterface()
42      {
43         // get content pane for attaching GUI components
44         Container contentPane = getContentPane();
45
46         // enable explicit positioning of GUI components
47         contentPane.setLayout( null );
48
49         // set up principalJLabel
50         principalJLabel = new JLabel();
51         principalJLabel.setBounds( 16, 16, 56, 24 );
52         principalJLabel.setText( "Principal:" );
53         contentPane.add( principalJLabel );
54
55         // set up principalJTextField
56         principalJTextField = new JTextField();
57         principalJTextField.setBounds( 100, 16, 100, 24 );
58         principalJTextField.setHorizontalAlignment(
59            JTextField.RIGHT );
60         contentPane.add( principalJTextField );
61
62         // set up interestRateJLabel
63         interestRateJLabel = new JLabel();
64         interestRateJLabel.setBounds( 16, 56, 80, 24 );
65         interestRateJLabel.setText( "Interest rate:" );
66         contentPane.add( interestRateJLabel );
67
68         // set up interestRateJTextField
69         interestRateJTextField = new JTextField();
70         interestRateJTextField.setBounds( 100, 56, 100, 24 );
71         interestRateJTextField.setHorizontalAlignment(
72            JTextField.RIGHT );
73         contentPane.add( interestRateJTextField );
74
```

Figure 10.27 **Interest Calculator** application code. (Part 2 of 4.)

```
75          // set up yearsJLabel
76          yearsJLabel = new JLabel();
77          yearsJLabel.setBounds( 16, 96, 48, 24 );
78          yearsJLabel.setText( "Years:" );
79          contentPane.add( yearsJLabel );
80
81          // set up yearsJSpinner
82          yearsJSpinner = new JSpinner(
83             new SpinnerNumberModel( 1, 1, 10, 1 ) );
84          yearsJSpinner.setBounds( 100, 96, 100, 24 );
85          contentPane.add( yearsJSpinner );
86
87          // set up yearlyBalanceJLabel
88          yearlyBalanceJLabel = new JLabel();
89          yearlyBalanceJLabel.setBounds( 16, 136, 150, 24 );
90          yearlyBalanceJLabel.setText( "Yearly account balance:" );
91          contentPane.add( yearlyBalanceJLabel );
92
93          // set up yearlyBalanceJTextArea
94          yearlyBalanceJTextArea = new JTextArea();
95          yearlyBalanceJTextArea.setEditable( false );
96
97          // set up yearlyBalanceJScrollPane
98          yearlyBalanceJScrollPane = new JScrollPane(
99             yearlyBalanceJTextArea );
100         yearlyBalanceJScrollPane.setBounds( 16, 160, 300, 92 );
101         contentPane.add( yearlyBalanceJScrollPane );
102
103         // set up calculateJButton
104         calculateJButton = new JButton();
105         calculateJButton.setBounds( 216, 16, 100, 24 );
106         calculateJButton.setText( "Calculate" );
107         contentPane.add( calculateJButton );
108         calculateJButton.addActionListener(
109
110            new ActionListener() // anonymous inner class
111            {
112               // event handler called when calculateJButton is clicked
113               public void actionPerformed( ActionEvent event )
114               {
115                  calculateJButtonActionPerformed( event );
116               }
117
118            } // end anonymous inner class
119
120         ); // end call to addActionListener
121
122
123         // set properties of application's window
124         setTitle( "Interest Calculator" ); // set title bar text
125         setSize( 340, 296 );                // set window size
126         setVisible( true );                 // display window
127
128      } // end method createUserInterface
129
130      // calculate and display amounts
131      private void calculateJButtonActionPerformed( ActionEvent event )
132      {
```

Setting the range of your JSpinner

Customizing the *bounds* property of yearsJSpinner

Setting yearlyBalanceJTextArea's *editable* property to **false**

Adding a JTextArea to a JScrollPane and setting the bounds of the JScrollPane

Figure 10.27   **Interest Calculator** application code. (Part 3 of 4.)

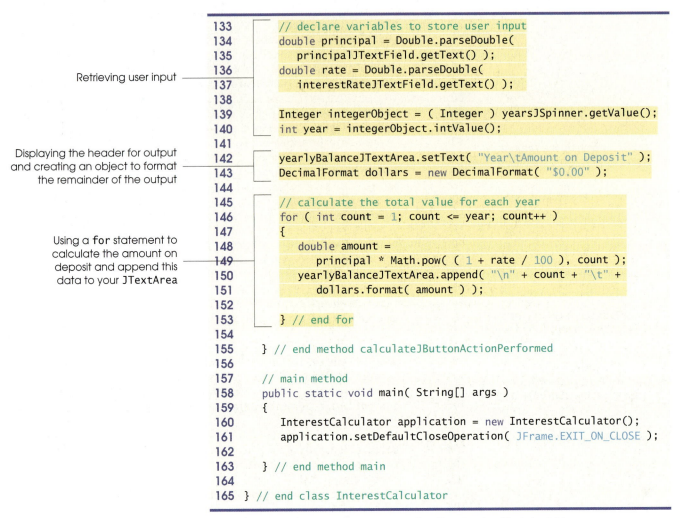

Retrieving user input ⎯⎯

```
133    // declare variables to store user input
134    double principal = Double.parseDouble(
135       principalJTextField.getText() );
136    double rate = Double.parseDouble(
137       interestRateJTextField.getText() );
138
139    Integer integerObject = ( Integer ) yearsJSpinner.getValue();
140    int year = integerObject.intValue();
141
```

Displaying the header for output and creating an object to format the remainder of the output ⎯⎯

```
142    yearlyBalanceJTextArea.setText( "Year\tAmount on Deposit" );
143    DecimalFormat dollars = new DecimalFormat( "$0.00" );
144
```

Using a **for** statement to calculate the amount on deposit and append this data to your **JTextArea** ⎯⎯

```
145    // calculate the total value for each year
146    for ( int count = 1; count <= year; count++ )
147    {
148       double amount =
149          principal * Math.pow( ( 1 + rate / 100 ), count );
150       yearlyBalanceJTextArea.append( "\n" + count + "\t" +
151          dollars.format( amount ) );
152
153    } // end for
154
155    } // end method calculateJButtonActionPerformed
156
157    // main method
158    public static void main( String[] args )
159    {
160       InterestCalculator application = new InterestCalculator();
161       application.setDefaultCloseOperation( JFrame.EXIT_ON_CLOSE );
162
163    } // end method main
164
165    } // end class InterestCalculator
```

Figure 10.27 **Interest Calculator** application code. (Part 4 of 4.)

SELF-REVIEW

1. The _____ determines how much the number in a JSpinner component changes when the user clicks the up arrow or the down arrow.

   a) minimum   b) step size

   c) maximum   d) *value* property

2. The _____ method returns the int data of an Integer object.

   a) intData   b) getValue

   c) getData   d) intValue

Answers: 1) b. 2) d.

10.6 Wrap-Up

In this tutorial, you learned that the essential elements of counter-controlled repetition are the name of a control variable, the initial value of the control variable, the increment (or decrement) by which the control variable is modified each time through the loop and the condition that tests the final value of the control variable. You then explored the **for** repetition statement, which combines these essentials of counter-controlled repetition in its header.

After becoming familiar with the **for** repetition statement, you changed the **Car Payment Calculator** application's **while** statement into a **for** statement. You then built an **Interest Calculator**, after analyzing its pseudocode and ACE table. In

the **Interest Calculator**'s GUI, you used new design elements, including a JSpinner component and a JTextArea inside a JScrollPane.

In the next tutorial, you will learn to use the switch multiple-selection statement. You have learned that the if...else selection statement can be used in code to select between multiple courses of action, depending on the value of a condition. You will see that a switch multiple-selection statement can save development time and improve code readability if the number of conditions is large. You will use a switch multiple-selection statement to build a **Security Panel** application.

SKILLS SUMMARY

Using the for Repetition Statement

- Specify the initial value of the control variable before the first semicolon.
- Specify the loop-continuation condition after the first semicolon.
- Specify the increment (or decrement) after the second semicolon.
- Use curly braces ({ and }) to delineate the body of the for repetition statement.

Performing Exponentiation

- Call the Math.pow method.
- Pass as the first argument to Math.pow the value that is to be raised to a power.
- Pass as the second argument to Math.pow the value of the power.

Retrieving Input from a JSpinner Component

- Call the getValue method.
- Use an (Integer) cast to convert the return value to an Integer object.
- Retrieve the int data from the Integer object by using the intValue method.

KEY TERMS

container—An object that contains components.

control variable—A variable used to control the number of iterations of a counter-controlled loop.

final value of a control variable—The last value a control variable will hold before a counter-controlled loop terminates.

for keyword—The keyword that begins each for statement.

for statement header/for header—The first line in a for statement. The for header specifies all four essential elements for counter-controlled repetition—the name of a control variable, the initial value, the increment or decrement value and the final value.

for repetition statement—A repetition statement that conveniently handles the details of counter-controlled repetition. The for header uses all four elements essential to counter-controlled repetition.

getValue method of class JSpinner—Returns the current value displayed in a JSpinner component.

increment (or decrement) of a control variable—The amount by which the control variable's value changes during each iteration of the loop.

initial value of a control variable—The value a control variable will hold when counter-controlled repetition begins.

Integer object—An object that contains a single piece of int data.

intValue method of class Integer—Returns the primitive int data in an Integer object.

JScrollPane component—Adds scrollbars to another component. When a component is added to a JScrollPane, the component will display scrollbars as necessary (that is, when more information appears in the added component than can be displayed at once).

JSpinner component—Limits user input to a specific range of values. The programmer can specify a maximum and minimum for the range, an increment (or decrement) when the user clicks the up (or down) arrow and an initial value to be displayed.

Math.pow method—Performs exponentiation. The first argument specifies the value that will be raised to a power, and the second argument specifies the power to which the first argument will be raised.

name of a control variable—Identifier used to reference the control variable of a loop.

SpinnerNumberModel object—The object that specifies that a JSpinner will contain numerical values for its range.

step size—Specifies by how much the value of a JSpinner component changes when the user clicks the component's up arrow (for incrementing) or down arrow (for decrementing).

GUI DESIGN GUIDELINES

JTextArea

■ If a JTextArea will display many lines of output, attach the JTextArea to a JScrollPane to allow users to scroll through the lines of output displayed in the JTextArea.

JSpinner

■ Use a JSpinner when you would use a JTextField, but when you want the user to enter input values only within a specified range. The JSpinner prevents invalid input by rejecting values that either are of the wrong type or are out-of-range values. When invalid data is rejected, the previous value in the JSpinner is restored.

■ Use the same GUI design guidelines for JSpinners and JTextFields. (See Appendix C, GUI Design Guidelines.)

JAVA LIBRARY REFERENCE

Integer This class is used to represent and manipulate int data.

■ *Methods*

intValue—Returns the int data of an Integer object.

JScrollPane This component is used to add horizontal and/or vertical scrollbars to other components. When a component, such as a JTextArea, is added to a JScrollPane, the component will display scrollbars as necessary.

■ *In action*

Scrollbar appears as necessary for components contained within a JScrollPane

■ *Methods*

setBounds—Sets the bounds (location and size) of a JScrollPane component.

JSpinner This component allows you to specify input within a specified range. The range can include numeric values, or values of another type. Input can be entered from the keyboard or by clicking up and down arrows provided on the right of the JSpinner. Invalid input is rejected and replaced with the most recent valid input value.

■ *In action*

JSpinner component

■ *Methods*

getValue—Returns the data in the *value* property of a JSpinner component.

setBounds—Sets the bounds (location and size) of a JSpinner component.

Math This class contains several methods used for common mathematical calculations.

■ *Methods*

pow—Performs exponentiation. The first argument specifies the value that will be raised to a power, and the second argument specifies the power to which the first argument will be raised.

MULTIPLE-CHOICE QUESTIONS

10.1 The `JSpinner` component allows you to specify a _____.
a) maximum value the user can select
b) minimum value the user can select
c) step size for the values presented to the user
d) All of the above.

10.2 _____ is used to determine whether a `for` loop continues to iterate.
a) The initial value of the control variable   b) The right brace
c) The left brace   d) The control variable

10.3 In a `for` loop, the control variable is incremented (or decremented) _____.
a) after the body of the loop executes
b) before the body of the loop executes
c) while the loop-continuation condition is `false`
d) while the body of the loop executes

10.4 An _____ object contains `int` data.
a) `IntegerObject`   b) `Int`
c) `IntData`   d) `Integer`

10.5 The `for` header _____ can be used to vary the control variable over the odd numbers between 1 and 10.
a) `for ( int i = 1; i <= 10; i += 1 )`
b) `for ( int i = 1; i <= 10; i += 2 )`
c) `for ( int i = 1; i <= 10; i -= 1 )`
d) `for ( int i = 1; i <= 10; i -= 2 )`

10.6 The body of the `for` loop with the header `for ( int i = 0; i <= 50; i += 5 )` will be executed _____ times.
a) 50   b) 10
c) 11   d) None of the above.

10.7 The _____ method will return the current value in the `JSpinner`.
a) `intValue`   b) `getValue`
c) `getNumber`   d) `getCurrentValue`

10.8 A `JScrollPane` is a _____, which means that other objects can be added to it.
a) container   b) holder
c) shell   d) `JFrame`

10.9 The body of the `for` loop with the header `for ( int i = 1; i <= 10; i -= 1 )` will be executed _____ times.
a) a very large number of   b) 9
c) 10   d) 11

10.10 The `Math.`_____ method returns the value of one number raised to power of another number.
a) `power`   b) `exponent`
c) `pow`   d) `exp`

EXERCISES

10.11 *(Present Value Calculator Application)* A bank wants to show its customers how much they would need to invest to achieve a specified financial goal (future value) in 5, 10, 15, 20, 25 or 30 years. Users must provide their financial goal (the amount of money desired after the specified number of years has elapsed), an interest rate and the length of the investment in years. Create an application that calculates and displays the principal (initial amount to invest) needed to achieve the user's financial goal. Your application should allow the user to invest money for 5, 10, 15, 20, 25 or 30 years. For example, if a customer wants to reach the

financial goal of $15,000 over a period of 5 years when the interest rate is 6.6%, the customer would need to invest $10,896.96 as shown in Fig. 10.28.

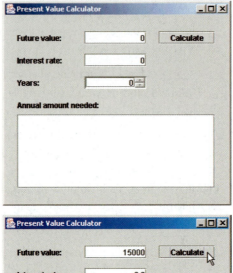

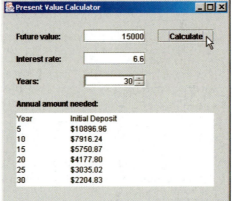

Figure 10.28 Present Value Calculator GUI.

a) *Copying the template to your working directory.* Copy the `C:\Examples\Tutorial10\Exercises\PresentValue` directory to your `C:\SimplyJava` directory.

b) *Opening the template file.* Open the `PresentValue.java` file in your text editor.

c) *Customizing the JSpinner.* You must customize the `JSpinner` to display the number of years. The name of this `JSpinner` is `yearsJSpinner`. This `JSpinner` should display every multiple of 5 from 0 to 30, inclusive. Modify line 83 so that the initial value in the `JSpinner` is 0, the minimum value is 0, the maximum value is 30 and the step size is 5. In line 84, insert code to set the *bounds* property to 130, 95, 100, 20.

d) *Customizing the JTextArea.* You must customize the `JTextArea` that will display the various amounts needed on deposit. The name of this `JTextArea` is `amountNeeded-JTextArea`. Insert a blank line at line 94. On line 95, insert code to set the *bounds* property to 20, 155, 320, 115. On the next line, insert code to set `amountNeeded-JTextArea`'s *editable* property to `false`.

e) *Retrieving input from a JSpinner.* In line 133, access the `JSpinner`'s *value* property and use the (`Integer`) cast to convert the result to an object of type `Integer`. Store the result in `Integer` object `integerObject`. Insert a blank line at line 133. On line 134, retrieve the `int` data in `integerObject`, and store this data in `int` variable `years`.

f) *Completing a for statement header.* In line 140 you will see a `for` statement header with only two semicolons. Before the first semicolon, declare and initialize variable `counter` to 5. Before the second semicolon, enter a loop-continuation condition that will cause the `for` statement to loop until `counter` has reached the number of years specified by the user. After the second semicolon, enter the increment of `counter` so that the `for` statement executes for every fifth year.

g) *Calculating present values.* You will now calculate the amount needed to achieve the future value for each five-year interval. To do this, you will need to implement the following formula within the `for` statement:

$$p = a / (1 + r)^n$$

where

p is the amount needed to achieve the future value

r is the annual interest rate

n is the number of years

a is the future value amount (the amount the user would like to have after n years)

In lines 142–143, use the Math.pow method (as well as the variables defined for you in lines 129 and 131) to calculate the present value needed for the current number of years. Use two lines for clarity. In lines 144–145, use the append method to output the present value calculated in the application's JTextArea. Use the DecimalFormat object (dollars) created for you in line 137. Use two lines for clarity.

h) *Saving the application.* Save your modified source code file.

i) *Opening the Command Prompt window and changing directories.* Open the **Command Prompt** window by selecting **Start > Programs > Accessories > Command Prompt**. Change to your working directory by typing cd C:\SimplyJava\PresentValue.

j) *Compiling the application.* Compile your application by typing javac PresentValue.java.

k) *Running the completed application.* When your application compiles correctly, run it by typing java PresentValue. Input a future value, interest rate and number of years, then click the **Calculate** JButton. View the results to ensure that the correct number of years is displayed, and that the initial deposit results are correct.

l) *Closing the application.* Close your running application by clicking its close button.

m) *Closing the Command Prompt window.* Close the **Command Prompt** window by clicking its close button.

10.12 *(Compound Interest: Comparing Rates Application)* Write an application that calculates the amount of money in an account after 10 years for interest rates of 5–10%, inclusive (Fig. 10.29). For this application, users must provide the initial principal.

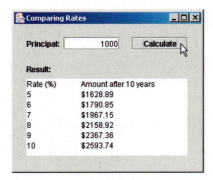

Figure 10.29   Comparing Rates GUI.

a) *Copying the template to your working directory.* Copy the directory C:\Examples\Tutorial10\Exercises\ComparingRates to your C:\SimplyJava directory.

b) *Opening the template file.* Open the ComparingRates.java file in your text editor.

c) *Customizing the JTextArea.* You must customize the JTextArea to display the rate and amount after 10 years. The name of this JTextArea is resultJTextArea. In line 58, insert code to set the *bounds* property to 20, 85, 260, 120. In line 59, insert code to set resultJTextArea's *editable* property to false.

d) *Completing a for statement header.* In line 98, you will see a for statement header with only two semicolons. Before the first semicolon, declare and initialize variable rate (which will be used as our counter) to 5. Before the second semicolon, enter a loop-continuation condition that will cause the for statement to loop until the counter has reached 10. After the second semicolon, enter the increment of the counter so that the for statement executes for every rate percentage from 5 to 10.

e) *Calculating the amount after 10 years.* You will now calculate the amount on deposit after 10 years, for different interest rates. To do this, you will need to implement the following formula within the **for** statement:

$$a = p \, (1 + r)^{\, n}$$

where

p is the original amount invested (the principal)
r is the annual interest rate
n is the number of years
a is the investment's value at the end of the nth year.

In lines 100–101, use the **Math.pow** method (as well as the variable defined for you in lines 94–95) to calculate the amount on deposit in 10 years with the **for** statement's current interest rate. Use the **(double)** cast operator as necessary to ensure that the first argument to **Math.pow** is a **double**. Use two lines for clarity. In lines 102–103, use the **append** method to output the value calculated in the application's JTextArea. Use the **DecimalFormat** object (**dollars**) created for you in line 92. Use two lines for clarity.

f) *Saving the application.* Save your modified source code file.

g) *Opening the Command Prompt window and changing directories.* Open the **Command Prompt** window by selecting **Start > Programs > Accessories > Command Prompt**. Change to your working directory by typing cd C:\SimplyJava\ComparingRates.

h) *Compiling the application.* Compile your application by typing javac ComparingRates.java.

i) *Running the completed application.* When your application compiles correctly, run it by typing java ComparingRates. Input a principal value and click the **Calculate** JButton. View the results to ensure that the correct rate percentages are displayed, and that the future value results are correct.

j) *Closing the application.* Close your running application by clicking its close button.

k) *Closing the Command Prompt window.* Close the **Command Prompt** window by clicking its close button.

10.13 *(Validating Input to the Interest Calculator Application)* Enhance the **Interest Calculator** application you built in this tutorial with error checking. Test whether the user has entered valid values for the principal and interest rate. If the user enters an invalid value, display a message in a message dialog. Figure 10.30 demonstrates the application handling invalid input.

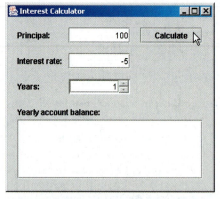

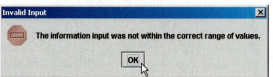

Figure 10.30 **Interest Calculator** application with error checking.

a) *Copying the template to your working directory.* Copy the directory C:\Examples\ Tutorial10\Exercises\InterestCalculatorEnhanced to your C:\SimplyJava directory.

b) *Opening the template file.* Open the InterestCalculator.java file in your text editor.

c) *Customizing the calculateJButtonActionPerformed method to handle invalid input.* In line 143, enter a condition into the if statement that returns true when the principal or rate are negative, or when the rate is over 10.

d) *Displaying the error message.* In lines 145–147, display the message dialog shown in Fig. 10.30. Use three lines for clarity.

e) *Saving the application.* Save your modified source code file.

f) *Opening the Command Prompt window and changing directories.* Open the **Command Prompt** window by selecting **Start > Programs > Accessories > Command Prompt**. Change to your working directory by typing cd C:\SimplyJava\Interest-CalculatorEnhanced.

g) *Compiling the application.* Compile your application by typing javac Interest-Calculator.java.

h) *Running the completed application.* When your application compiles correctly, run it by typing java InterestCalculator. Input a principal value, interest rate and number of years, then click the **Calculate** JButton. Make sure all your input is valid. View the results to ensure that the correct number of years is displayed and that the initial deposit results are correct. Now, modify your input values so that you are entering invalid input and click the **Calculate** JButton. Make sure the message dialog displays, containing the correct text.

i) *Closing the application.* Close your running application by clicking its close button.

j) *Closing the Command Prompt window.* Close the **Command Prompt** window by clicking its close button.

What does this code do? ▶

10.14 What is the output when the following code executes? Assume that power and number are declared as ints.

```
1    power = 5;
2    number = 10;
3    mysteryJTextArea.setText( "" );
4
5    for ( int counter = 1; counter <= power; counter++ )
6    {
7        mysteryJTextArea.append( Math.pow( number, counter ) + "\n" );
8    }
```

What's wrong with this code? ▶

10.15 Identify and correct the error(s) in each of the following:

a) This code should display in a JTextArea all integers from 100 to 1 in decreasing order.

```
1    String output;
2
3    for ( int counter = 100; counter >= 1; counter++ )
4    {
5        output += counter + "\n";
6    }
7
8    displayTextArea.setText( output );
```

b) The following code should set a JSpinner's range to include the even numbers from 2–100. The initial value on the JSpinner should be 2.

```
1  yearsJSpinner = new JSpinner(
2      new SpinnerNumberModel( 100, 2, 100, 1 ) );
3  yearsJSpinner.setBounds( 2, 2, 100, 100 );
4  contentPane.add( yearsJSpinner );
```

Using the Debugger ▶

10.16 (*Savings Calculator Application*) The **Savings Calculator** application calculates the amount that the user will have on deposit after one year. The application gets the initial amount on deposit from the user, and assumes that the user will add $100 to the account every month for the entire year. No interest is added to the account. While testing the application, you noticed that the amount calculated by the application was incorrect. Use the debugger to locate and correct any logic error(s). Figure 10.31 displays the correct output for this application.

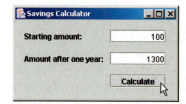

Figure 10.31 Correct output for the **Savings Calculator** application.

a) *Copying the template to your working directory.* Copy the directory C:\Examples\ Tutorial10\Exercises\Debugging\SavingsCalculator to your C:\SimplyJava directory.

b) *Opening the template file.* Open the SavingsCalculator.java file in your text editor.

c) *Running the application.* Run the **Savings Calculator** application by typing java SavingsCalculator. Enter 100 as the starting amount and click the **Calculate** JButton. Notice that the amount after one year is 1200, whereas the correct output would be 1300 (Fig. 10.31).

d) *Compiling with the -g option.* Close your application (but leave the **Command Prompt** open), and compile the application by typing javac -g SavingsCalcula- tor.java.

e) *Starting the debugger.* Start the debugger by typing jdb.

f) *Finding and correcting the error(s).* Use the debugging skills learned in previous tutorials to determine where the application's logic errors exist. Modify the application so that it displays the correct message dialogs.

g) *Saving the application.* Save your modified source code file.

h) *Compiling the application.* Compile your application by typing javac SavingsCal- culator.java.

i) *Running the completed application.* When your application compiles correctly, run it by typing java SavingsCalculator. Test the application using several different inputs, and make sure the resulting savings output is correct.

j) *Closing the application.* Close your running application by clicking its close button.

k) *Closing the Command Prompt window.* Close the **Command Prompt** window by clicking its close button.

Programming Challenge ▶

10.17 (*Pay Raise Calculator Application*) Develop an application that computes the amount of money an employee makes each year over a user-specified number of years. Assume the employee receives a weekly wage of $500 and a pay raise once every year. The user specifies in the application the amount of the raise (in percent per year) and the number

of years for which the amounts earned will be calculated. The application should run as shown in Fig. 10.32.

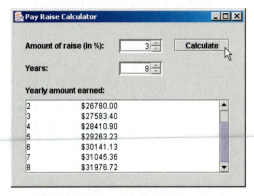

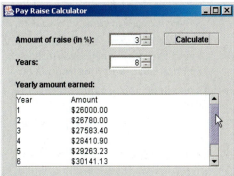

Figure 10.32 **Pay Raise** application.

a) *Copying the template to your working directory.* Copy the directory C:\Examples\ Tutorial10\Exercises\PayRaise to your C:\SimplyJava directory.

b) *Opening the template file.* Open the PayRaise.java file in your text editor.

c) *Customizing the Amount of raise (in%): JSpinner.* You must customize this JSpinner to display the pay raise percentage. The name of this JSpinner is raiseJSpinner. The user should only be able to specify percentages in the range of 3%–8%. Modify line 53 so that raiseJSpinner's initial value is 3, its minimum value is 3, its maximum value is 8 and its step size is 1. In line 54, insert code to set the *bounds* property to 170, 25, 70, 22.

d) *Customizing the Years: JSpinner.* You must customize this JSpinner to display the number of years in the range 1–50. The name of this JSpinner is yearsJSpinner. Modify line 65 so that yearsJSpinner's initial value is 1, its minimum value is 1, its maximum value is 50 and its step size is 1. In line 66, insert code to set the *bounds* property to 170, 60, 70, 22.

e) *Customizing the JTextArea.* You must customize amountEarnedJTextArea, which will display multiple lines of the yearly amount earned. In line 77, insert code to set amountEarnedJTextArea's *editable* property to false.

f) *Customizing the JScrollPane.* You must customize the JScrollPane to contain amountEarnedJTextArea, so that amountEarnedJTextArea will display scrollbars when necessary. Modify line 80 so that amountEarnedJTextArea is added to this application's JScrollPane. Use two line to increase readability. In line 82, insert code to set the *bounds* property to 20, 120, 330, 115.

g) *Retrieving input from the raise JSpinner.* In lines 117–118, access raiseJSpinner's *value* property and use the (Integer) cast to convert the result to an object of type Integer. Store the result in Integer object integerRaiseObject. Use two lines for readability. In line 119, retrieve the int data in integerRaiseObject, and store this data in int variable rate.

h) *Retrieving input from the years JSpinner.* In lines 121–122, access yearsJSpinner's *value* property and use the (Integer) cast to convert the result to an object of type

Integer. Store the result in `Integer` object `integerYearsObject`. In line 123, retrieve the `int` data in `integerYearsObject`, and store this data in `int` variable `years`. Insert a blank line at line after line 123 to separate these lines from the remainder of the code.

i) *Completing a **for** statement header.* In line 129, you will see a `for` statement header with only two semicolons. Before the first semicolon, declare and initialize variable `counter` to 1. Before the second semicolon, enter a loop-continuation condition that will cause the `for` statement to loop until `counter` has reached the number of years entered. After the second semicolon, enter the increment of `counter` so that the `for` statement executes once for each number of years.

j) *Calculating the pay raise.* In line 131, multiply the wage (set to 500 in line 115) by the number of weeks in a year, and store the result in a `double` variable named `amount`. In lines 132–133, display the wage in the `JTextArea`. Use two lines for readability. In line 135, calculate the new wage for the following year, and store the resulting value in variable `wage`. To do this, add 1 to the percentage increase and multiply the result by the current value in `wage`.

k) *Saving the application.* Save your modified source code file.

l) *Opening the Command Prompt window and changing directories.* Open the **Command Prompt** window by selecting **Start > Programs > Accessories > Command Prompt**. Change to your working directory by typing cd C:\SimplyJava\PayRaise.

m) *Compiling the application.* Compile your application by typing javac PayRaise.java.

n) *Running the completed application.* When your application compiles correctly, run it by typing java PayRaise. Input a raise percentage and a number of years for the wage increase, and click the **Calculate** `JButton`. View the results to ensure that the correct years are displayed, and that the future wage results are correct. Also examine the `JSpinner`s to ensure that they are making the correct values available to the user.

o) *Closing the application.* Close your running application by clicking its close button.

p) *Closing the Command Prompt window.* Close the **Command Prompt** window by clicking its close button.

Objectives

In this tutorial, you will learn to:

- Use the `switch` multiple-selection statement.
- Use `case` labels.
- Display a date and time.
- Use a `JPasswordField`.
- Use a `Date` to determine the system's current date and time.
- Use a `DateFormat` to format the date and time.

Outline

11.1 Test-Driving the Security Panel Application

11.2 Introducing the `switch` Multiple-Selection Statement

11.3 Constructing the Security Panel Application

11.4 Wrap-Up

Security Panel Application

Introducing the *switch Multiple-Selection Statement, Date and DateFormat*

In Tutorial 6, you learned that the `if` control statement is used to either choose or ignore a single statement (or sequence of statements), so it is called a single-selection statement. You also learned that the `if...else` control statement is used to choose between alternative statements (or sequences of statements) based on a condition, so `if...else` is called a double-selection statement. In this tutorial, you will learn the `switch` multiple-selection statement, which is used to choose among many possible actions (or sequences of actions).

11.1 Test-Driving the Security Panel Application

In this tutorial, you will use the `switch` multiple-selection statement to construct a **Security Panel** application. This application must meet the following requirements:

> **Application Requirements**
>
> A pharmaceutical company wants to install a security panel outside its laboratory facility. Only authorized personnel may enter the lab, using their security codes. The following are the valid security codes (also called access codes) and the groups of employees they represent:
>
> | Security code | Groups |
> |---|---|
> | 1645 | Technicians |
> | 8345 | Custodians |
> | 9998, 1006–1008 | Scientists |
>
> When a security code is entered, it should not be visible to anyone standing near the security panel. For each security code, access is either granted or denied. All access attempts are displayed in a screen below the keypad. If access is granted, the date, time and group (scientists, custodians, etc.) are displayed on the screen. If access is denied, the date, the time and a message, "Access Denied," are displayed on the screen. Furthermore, an employee can enter the access code 7, 8 or 9 to summon a security guard for assistance. The date, the time and a message, "Restricted Access," are then displayed on the screen to indicate that the request has been received.

You begin by test-driving the application. Then, you will learn the additional Java technologies you will need to create your own version of this application.

GUI Design Tip

If your GUI is modeling a real-world object, your GUI design should mimic the physical appearance of that object.

1. *Locating the completed application.* Open the **Command Prompt** window by selecting **Start > Programs > Accessories > Command Prompt**. Change to your completed **Security Panel** application directory by typing `cd C:\Examples\Tutorial11\CompletedApplication\SecurityPanel`.

2. *Running the Security Panel application.* Type `java SecurityPanel` to run the application (Fig. 11.1). Notice that the GUI keypad looks much like a real-world keypad. (You will mimic real-world conditions when possible.)

Keypad

Output `JTextArea`

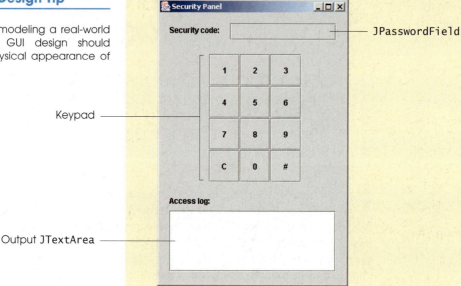

Figure 11.1   **Security Panel** application.

3. *Keying in an invalid security code.* Use the keypad to enter the invalid security code 1212 (Fig. 11.2). To the right of the **Security code:** `JLabel` is a `JPasswordField` that displays an asterisk for each digit in the security code entered using the GUI keypad. A **`JPasswordField`** (which is similar to a `JTextField`) does not display the actual characters that the user types in the application. To keep passwords secure, a `JPasswordField` displays asterisks instead. These characters hide the security code so that no other people will see the access code. This is just like what you experience when you log in to your computer.

4. When you finish entering the security code, click the `#` `JButton` to enable the application to process what you entered. Results are displayed in the `JTextArea` at the bottom of the application. In this case, a message indicating that access is denied appears in the `JTextArea` (Fig. 11.3). Notice that the `JPasswordField` is cleared when the `#` `JButton` is pressed.

5. *Using the C JButton.* Press a few numeric keys, then click the **C** **`JButton`** to clear the **Security code:** `JPasswordField`. All the asterisks displayed in the `JPasswordField` disappear. Users often make mistakes when keystroking or when clicking `JButton`s. The **C** `JButton` enables users to clear the `JPasswordField` and start again if they make a mistake.

(cont.)

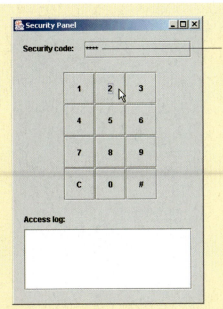

JPasswordField displays one asterisk (*) for each numeric key the user presses (so no one can see the actual security code entered).

 **GUI Design Tip**

Mask passwords or other sensitive pieces of information in JPass-wordFields.

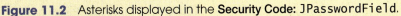

Figure 11.2   Asterisks displayed in the **Security Code:** JPasswordField.

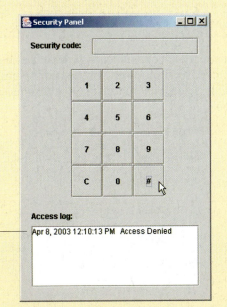

Message indicating that an invalid security code was entered

Figure 11.3   **Security Panel** displaying the **Access Denied** message.

6. ***Entering a valid security code.*** Use the keypad to enter 1006, then click the # JButton. Notice that a second message appears in the JTextArea, as in Fig. 11.4.

7. ***Closing the running application.*** Close your running application by clicking its close button.

8. ***Closing the Command Prompt.*** Close the **Command Prompt** window by clicking its close button.

(cont.)

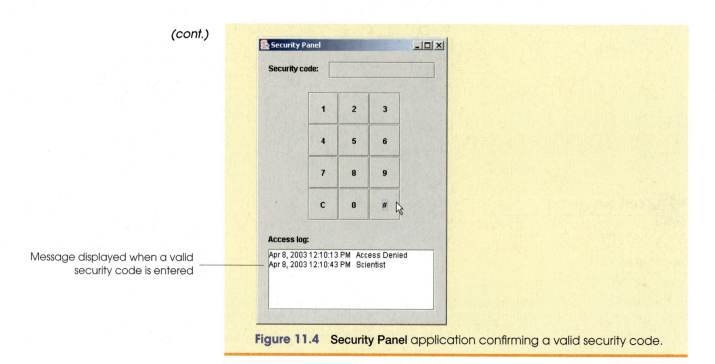

Message displayed when a valid security code is entered

Figure 11.4 **Security Panel** application confirming a valid security code.

11.2 Introducing the `switch` Multiple-Selection Statement

In this section, you will learn how to use the **switch multiple-selection statement**. For comparison purposes, first consider a nested `if...else` statement that performs multiple selections and displays a text message based on a student's grade in a `JLabel`:

```
if ( grade == 'A' )
{
    displayJLabel.setText( "Excellent!" );
}
else if ( grade == 'B' )
{
    displayJLabel.setText( "Very good!" );
}
else if ( grade == 'C' )
{
    displayJLabel.setText( "Good." );
}
else if ( grade == 'D' )
{
    displayJLabel.setText( "Poor." );
}
else if ( grade == 'F' )
{
    displayJLabel.setText( "Failure." );
}
else
{
    displayJLabel.setText( "Invalid grade." );
}
```

This statement is used to produce an appropriate output when selecting among multiple values of `grade`. However, by using the `switch` statement, you can simplify every instance like

```
if ( grade == 'A' )
```

to one like

```
case 'A':
```

In this example, grade is of type **char**, which is one of Java's eight primitive types (see Appendix F for a complete list of Java's primitive types). The value of a variable of the char type is a **character constant** (or **character literal**) which is a single character or escape sequence within single quotes. Character constants include letters (such as 'A'), digits (such as '5'), special characters (such as ','—the comma), whitespace (such as ' '—a space) and escape sequences (such as '\n'—the newline character).

The following switch multiple-selection statement performs the same function as the preceding if...else statement:

```java
switch ( grade )
{
    case 'A':
        displayJLabel.setText( "Excellent!" );
        break;

    case 'B':
        displayJLabel.setText( "Very good!" );
        break;

    case 'C':
        displayJLabel.setText( "Good." );
        break;

    case 'D':
        displayJLabel.setText( "Poor." );
        break;

    case 'F':
        displayJLabel.setText( "Failure." );
        break;

    default:
        displayJLabel.setText( "Invalid grade." );
}
```

The switch statement begins with the keyword switch, followed by a **controlling expression** inside parentheses and a left brace, then terminates with a right brace. The preceding switch contains five **case labels** and the optional **default case**, which will execute if the controlling expression's value does not match any of the other cases. Each case label contains the keyword case followed by a **constant expression** and a colon. The constant expression can be a character literal, such as 'A' (which is a char type) or an integer literal, such as 707, but cannot be a floating-point literal such as 9.9. The constant expression also can be a variable that contains a character or integer constant (that is, a final variable). Only values of types char, byte, short and int can be tested in a switch statement. Although a switch statement can have any number of case labels, it can have at most one default case, and no two cases can specify the same constant expression.

Figure 11.5 shows the UML activity diagram for the preceding switch multiple-selection statement. The first guard condition to be evaluated is grade == 'A'. If this condition is true, the text "Excellent!" is displayed, and the **break** statement at the end of the case transfers program control to the first statement after the switch statement. If the condition is false (that is, the other guard condition, grade != 'A', is true), the statement continues by testing the next condition, grade == 'B'. If this condition is true, the text "Very good!" is displayed, and the break statement at the end of the case transfers program control to the first statement after the switch statement. If the condition is false (that is, the other guard condition, grade != 'B', is true), the statement continues to test the next condition. This process continues until a matching case is found or until the final guard condition, grade != 'F', evaluates to false. If the latter occurs, the default case's body is executed, and the text "Invalid grade." is displayed. The application then continues with the first statement after the switch statement. If the controlling

Good Programming Practice

Placing a blank line before and after each case in a switch statement improves readability.

Good Programming Practice

Indenting the statements in the body of a case improves readability.

Common Programming Error

Specifying two or more cases with the same constant expression is a syntax error.

Common Programming Error

Forgetting the break statement in a case is often a logic error.

Error-Prevention Tip

Always include a `default` case in a `switch` statement to ensure that improper values are handled.

expression's value does not match any of the cases and there is no `default` case, no statements in the `switch` will execute.

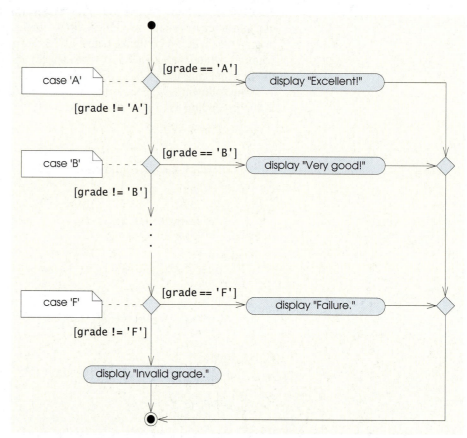

Figure 11.5 `switch` multiple-selection statement UML activity diagram.

When the controlling expression's value matches a `case` and that `case`'s statements do not end with a `break` statement, program control will continue ("fall through") with the statements in the next `case`. This will occur until either a `break` statement is encountered or until the end of the `switch` statement is reached.

SELF-REVIEW

1. `switch` is a _____-selection statement.

   a) single   b) double

   c) multiple   d) None of the above.

2. When does the `default` case execute?

   a) Every time a `switch` statement executes.

   b) When several `cases` match the controlling expression.

   c) When no `cases` match the controlling expression.

   d) None of the above.

Answers: 1) c. 2) c.

11.3 Constructing the Security Panel Application

The **Security Panel** application contains 10 `JButtons` that display digits (the numeric `JButtons`). You will create a method that will execute for each `JButton`. These `JButtons` make up the GUI keypad. The following pseudocode describes the actions for each of these numeric `JButtons`:

When the user clicks a numeric JButton:
    Append the appropriate digit to the text in the JPasswordField

The user will be able to use the numeric JButtons to enter digits and have those digits concatenated to the text in the JPasswordField. Note that each digit appears as the corresponding JButton is clicked; however, the digit is displayed as an asterisk (*) in the JPasswordField.

In addition to the numeric JButtons, this application also contains a **C** JButton and a **#** JButton. The following pseudocode describes the basic operation of the **Security Panel** application when the user presses the **C** JButton:

> When the user presses the C JButton:
>   Set the JPasswordField's text property to the empty string

The following pseudocode describes the basic operation of the **Security Panel** application when the user presses the **#** JButton:

> When the user clicks the # JButton:
>   Get the security code input by the user from the JPasswordField
>   Clear the JPasswordField
>
>   Switch based on the security code
>   If access code is 7, 8 or 9
>   Store "Restricted Access" in a String variable
>   If access code is 1645
>   Store "Technician" in a String variable
>   If access code is 8345
>   Store "Custodian" in a String variable
>   If access code is 9998 or is in the range 1006 to 1008
>   Store "Scientist" in a String variable
>   If access code is invalid
>   Store "Access Denied" in a String variable
>
>   Display a message in the JTextArea with the current time and the String variable's contents

Now that you have test-driven the **Security Panel** application and studied its pseudocode representation, you will use an ACE table to help you convert the pseudocode to Java. Figure 11.6 lists the actions, components and events that will help you complete your own version of this application. The first row specifies that you will be using JLabels to identify the JPasswordField and JTextArea components. The second row introduces the JButtons for the numeric keypad. When one of these JButtons is clicked, the value on the JButton is appended to the text in the JPasswordField's *text* property. The next row indicates that securityCodeJPasswordField will store the security code that is input by the user. The next two rows specify the JButton (clearJButton) that the user can click to clear securityCodeJPasswordField and the method used to clear the JPasswordField. The next row specifies the JButton (enterJButton) that the user can click to submit the security code so the application can determine whether the code is valid. The remaining rows indicate tasks performed when the enterJButton is clicked.

Action/Control/Event (ACE) Table for the Security Panel Application	Action	Component/Object	Event
	Label all the application's components	securityCodeJLabel, accessLogJLabel	Application is run
		zeroJButton, oneJButton, twoJButton, threeJButton, fourJButton, fiveJButton, sixJButton, sevenJButton, eightJButton, nineJButton	User clicks a numeric JButton
	Append the appropriate digit to the text in the JPasswordField	securityCodeJPasswordField	

Figure 11.6   ACE table for **Security Panel** application. (Part 1 of 2.)

Action	Component/Object	Event
	`clearJButton`	User clicks
Set the JPasswordField's text property to the empty string	`securityCodeJPasswordField`	`C JButton`
	`enterJButton`	User clicks
Get the security code input by the user from the JPasswordField	`securityCodeJPasswordField`	`# JButton`
Clear the JPasswordField	`securityCodeJPasswordField`	
Switch based on the security code		
If access code is 7, 8 or 9 Store text "Restricted Access" in a String variable	`message (String)`	
If access code is 1645 Store "Technician" in a String variable	`message (String)`	
If access code is 8345 Store "Custodian" in a String variable	`message (String)`	
If access code is 9998 or is in the range 1006 to 1008 Store "Scientist" in a String variable	`message (String)`	
If access code is invalid Store "Access Denied" in a String variable	`message (String)`	
Display a message in the JTextArea with the current time and the String variable's contents	`accessLogJTextArea, message (String)`	

Figure 11.6   ACE table for **Security Panel** application. (Part 2 of 2.)

Next, you will customize a `JPasswordField` component that will store the user's access code. Later in this tutorial you will use a `switch` statement to build the **Security Panel** application.

Customizing the JPasswordField Component

1. ***Copying the template to your working directory.*** Copy the `C:\Examples\ Tutorial11\TemplateApplication\SecurityPanel` directory to your `C:\SimplyJava` directory. You will begin with an empty content pane.

2. ***Opening the Security Panel application's template file.*** Open the template file `SecurityPanel.java` in your text editor.

3. ***Customizing the JPasswordField.*** Insert lines 57–58 of Fig. 11.7. Line 57 sets the *bounds* property of `securityCodeJPasswordField` to 114, 16, 172, 26. Text displayed in a `JPasswordField` will be hidden, or masked, with the asterisk character (`'*'`). Rather than displaying the actual text that the user types, these **echo characters** (also called **masked characters**) are displayed. The `JPasswordField`'s *password* property contains the text the user typed. For example, if a user enters 5469, the `JPasswordField` displays `****`, yet stores `"5469"` in its *password* property. You can change the character that is displayed by using the `JPasswordField`'s **setEchoChar** method and passing it a character constant.

(cont.)

In this application, the user enters the security code by pressing the numeric keypad buttons, and the JPasswordField simply displays the masked security code. Line 58 prevents users from modifying the text in the JPasswordField, which forces users to interact with the numeric keypad. This is accomplished by setting the JPasswordField's *editable* property to false.

Set the *bounds* and *editable* properties of the JPasswordField

```
55        // set up securityCodeJPasswordField
56        securityCodeJPasswordField = new JPasswordField();
57        securityCodeJPasswordField.setBounds( 114, 16, 172, 26 );
58        securityCodeJPasswordField.setEditable( false );
59        contentPane.add( securityCodeJPasswordField );
```

Figure 11.7 Setting the securityCodeJPasswordField's *bounds* and *editable* properties.

4. ***Saving the application.*** Save your modified source code file.

5. ***Opening the Command Prompt window and changing directories.*** Open the **Command Prompt** window by selecting **Start > Programs > Accessories > Command Prompt**. Change to your working directory by typing cd C:\SimplyJava\SecurityPanel.

6. ***Compiling the application.*** Compile your application by typing javac SecurityPanel.java.

7. ***Running the application.*** When your application compiles correctly, run it by typing java SecurityPanel. Figure 11.8 shows the updated application running. Try pressing the JButtons. Nothing happens because the methods that will execute when these JButtons are clicked have not been written yet.

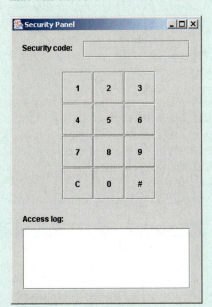

Figure 11.8 **Security Panel** application after customizing the JPassword-Field.

8. ***Closing the application.*** Close your running application by clicking its close button.

9. ***Closing the Command Prompt window.*** Close the **Command Prompt** window by clicking its close button.

Now that you have designed the GUI for your application, you will initialize the variables for your method and code your `switch` statement. This statement will determine the user's access level based on the code input.

Adding a switch Statement to the Application

1. **Declaring and initializing local variables.** Add lines 379–385 of Fig. 11.9 to the `enterJButtonActionPerformed` method. Line 379 declares `String` variable `message`, which will store the message that will be displayed to the user based on the access code entered. Lines 382–383 call `securityCode-JPasswordField`'s **getPassword** method to get the password the user typed. The password is sent to method `String.valueOf` to convert it to a `String`, which is then converted to an `int` with `Integer.parseInt`. The `int` value of the password is then assigned to variable `accessCode`. Line 385 clears the **Security code:** `JPasswordField` so that the user can enter another code.

Declare `message`

Store the access code

Clear the `JPasswordField`

```
376    // gets access code and determines level of clearance
377    private void enterJButtonActionPerformed( ActionEvent event )
378    {
379        String message; // displays access status of users
380
381        // stores access code entered
382        int accessCode = Integer.parseInt( String.valueOf(
383            securityCodeJPasswordField.getPassword() ) );
384
385        securityCodeJPasswordField.setText( "" );
386
```

Figure 11.9 Storing the access code and clearing the **Security code:** `JPasswordField`.

2. **Adding a switch statement to enterJButtonActionPerformed.** Insert lines 387–390 of Fig. 11.10 to the `enterJButtonActionPerformed` method. Line 387 begins the `switch` statement, which contains the controlling expression `accessCode`—the access code entered by the user. Remember that this expression (the value `accessCode`) is compared sequentially with each `case`. If a matching `case` is found, the body of that `case` executes and the `break` statement in that `case`'s body causes program control to shift to the first statement after the right brace. If the `switch` statement contains a `default` case and the controlling expression does not match any other case, the statement(s) in the body of the `default` case will execute. If there are no matches and the `switch` does not contain a `default` case, the body of the `switch` is skipped and the application continues with the next statement after the `switch`. Line 390 is a right brace which terminates the `switch` statement.

Beginning of the `switch` statement

```
385        securityCodeJPasswordField.setText( "" );
386
387        switch ( accessCode ) // check access code input
388        {
389
390        } // end switch statement
391
```

Figure 11.10 Adding a `switch` statement to the method.

3. **Adding a case to the switch statement.** Insert lines 389–394 of Fig. 11.11 in the `switch` statement. Lines 390–392 specify three `case` labels. This means that lines 393–394 will be performed if any of these three `case` labels match the controlling expression. For this example, if the value in `accessCode` is 7, 8 or 9, the code on lines 393–394 will execute, causing the `String` `"Restricted Access"` to be assigned to `message`.

(cont.)

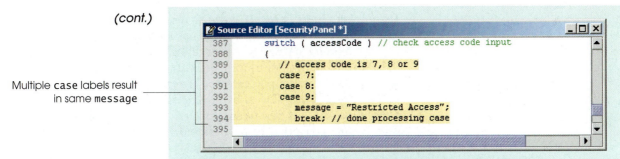

Multiple **case** labels result in same **message**

Figure 11.11 Adding **case** labels to the **switch** statement.

4. *Specifying cases for the remaining access codes.* Add lines 396–412 of Fig. 11.12 to the body of the **switch** statement. The **case** label in line 397 determines whether the value of **accessCode** is equal to 1645. If the user enters this access code, the body of the **case** sets **message** to "Technician". The next **case** label (line 402) checks for the value 8345. If the user enters this access code, the body of the **case** sets **message** to "Custodian". The next set of **case** labels (lines 407–410) determine whether **accessCode** is 9998, 1006, 1007 or 1008. If any of these access codes are entered, the body of the **case** sets **message** to "Scientist".

Access code 1645 for technicians

Access code 8345 for custodians

Access codes 9998, 1006, 1007 and 1008 for scientists

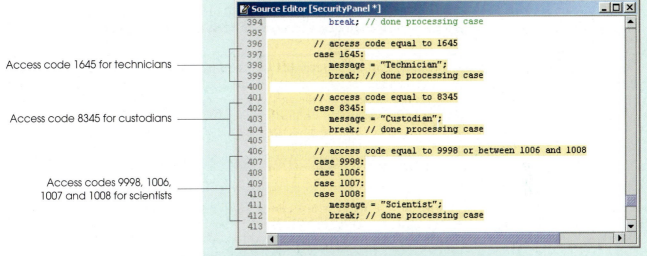

Figure 11.12 Finishing the **switch** statement.

5. *Adding a default case to the switch statement.* Add lines 414–416 of Fig. 11.13 to the **switch** statement. These lines contain the optional **default** case, which is executed if the controlling expression does not match any **cases**. When the **default** case appears at the end of the **switch** statement's body, you do not need to add the **break** statement. The body of the **default** case sets **message** to "Access Denied".

Good Programming Practice

Always place the **default** case at the end of a **switch** statement's body.

default case at the end of the **switch** statement

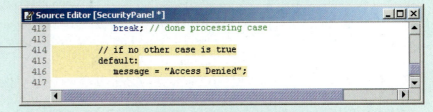

Figure 11.13 Adding a **default** case to the **switch** statement.

(cont.)

6. **Displaying results in the JTextArea.** Insert lines 420–423 of Fig. 11.14 after the `switch` statement. Line 421 obtains a **DateFormat** object (using Date-Format method `getDateTimeInstance`) and stores it in `formatter`. A `DateFormat` allows you to format a date and time as a `String`. Lines 422–423 append a `String` to `accessLogJTextArea` consisting of the current system date and time, followed by three spaces and the value assigned to `message`. Line 422 uses `new Date()`, which returns the current date and time. This is then converted to a formatted `String` with `formatter`'s `format` method and is appended to the `JTextArea` using the `append` method.

```
 Source Editor [SecurityPanel *]                          _ □ ×
418        } // end switch statement
419
420        // display time and message in accessLogJTextArea
421        DateFormat formatter = DateFormat.getDateTimeInstance();
422        accessLogJTextArea.append( formatter.format( new Date() ) +
423          "   " + message + "\n" );
424
```

Format for the date and time → (line 421)

Add the date and time to the message → (lines 422–423)

Figure 11.14 Outputting the current date, the time and the message.

7. **Saving the application.** Save your modified source code file.

Now that you have defined the `enterJButtonActionPerformed` method, you will create methods for each numeric `JButton` and for the **C** `JButton`.

Programming the Remaining Methods

1. **Coding the `oneJButtonActionPerformed` method.** Insert lines 313–314 of Fig. 11.16 in the method. These lines use the + operator to concatenate the `String` value `"1"` to the end of `securityCodeJPasswordField`'s *password* property value. You do this to append the numeric `JButton`'s value to the access code currently in the `JPasswordField`.

```
 Source Editor [SecurityPanel *]                          _ □ ×
310        // append 1 to the security code
311        private void oneJButtonActionPerformed( ActionEvent event )
312        {
313          securityCodeJPasswordField.setText( String.valueOf(
314            securityCodeJPasswordField.getPassword() ) + "1" );
315
316        } // end method oneJButtonActionPerformed
```

Add 1 to the end of the security code → (lines 313–314)

Figure 11.15 Appending a one to the end of the security code.

2. **Code the other numeric JButtons' methods.** Repeat *Step 1* for the remaining numeric JButtons (**2** through **9** and **0**). Be sure to substitute the JButton's number for the value between the quotes (for example, `twoJButtonActionPerformed` appends `"2"` to the access code currently in `securityCodeJPasswordField`). Figure 11.16 shows the methods for the JButtons called `twoJButton` and `threeJButton`.

3. **Coding the `clearJButtonActionPerformed` method.** Add line 393 of Fig. 11.17. This line clears the **Security code:** `JPasswordField`.

4. **Saving the application.** Save your modified source code file.

5. **Opening the Command Prompt window and changing directories.** Open the **Command Prompt** window by selecting **Start > Programs > Accessories > Command Prompt**. Change to your working directory by typing `cd C:\SimplyJava\SecurityPanel`.

(cont.)

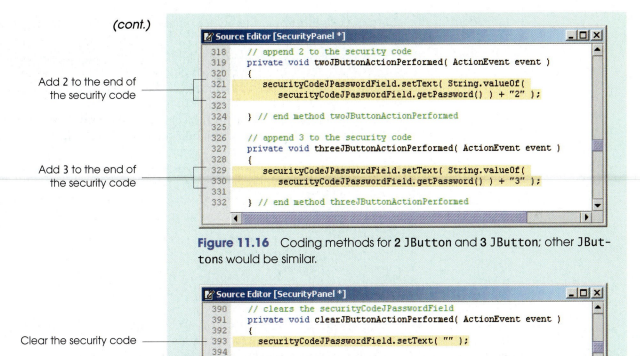

Add 2 to the end of the security code

Add 3 to the end of the security code

Figure 11.16   Coding methods for **2** JButton and **3** JButton; other JButtons would be similar.

Clear the security code

Figure 11.17   Clearing the **Security Code:** JPasswordField.

6. ***Compiling the application.*** Compile your application by typing javac SecurityPanel.java.

7. ***Running the application.*** When your application compiles correctly, run it by typing java SecurityPanel. Figure 11.18 shows the completed application running. Use the keypad to enter each of the following codes: 9998, 8345, 7777, 8, 1006 and 8345. Remember to follow each code by pressing the enter (#) button.

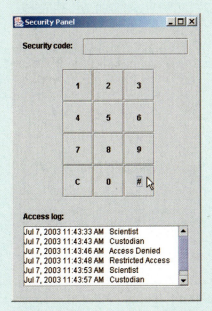

Figure 11.18   Completed **Security Panel** application.

(cont.)

8. ***Closing the application.*** Close your running application by clicking its close button.

9. ***Closing the Command Prompt window.*** Close the **Command Prompt** window by clicking its close button.

Figure 11.19 displays the code for the completed **Security Panel** application. The lines of code you added, viewed or modified in this tutorial are highlighted.

```java
1   // Tutorial 11: SecurityPanel.java
2   // Enable user to enter security codes specifying access privileges.
3   import java.awt.*;
4   import java.awt.event.*;
5   import java.text.DateFormat;
6   import java.util.Date;
7   import javax.swing.*;
8
9   public class SecurityPanel extends JFrame
10  {
11     // JLabel and JPasswordField for user to input security code
12     private JLabel securityCodeJLabel;
13     private JPasswordField securityCodeJPasswordField;
14
15     // JButtons to represent security keypad
16     private JButton oneJButton;
17     private JButton twoJButton;
18     private JButton threeJButton;
19     private JButton fourJButton;
20     private JButton fiveJButton;
21     private JButton sixJButton;
22     private JButton sevenJButton;
23     private JButton eightJButton;
24     private JButton nineJButton;
25     private JButton clearJButton;
26     private JButton zeroJButton;
27     private JButton enterJButton;
28
29     // JLabel, JTextArea and JScrollPane to display access log
30     private JLabel accessLogJLabel;
31     private JTextArea accessLogJTextArea;
32     private JScrollPane accessLogJScrollPane;
33
34     // no-argument constructor
35     public SecurityPanel()
36     {
37        createUserInterface();
38     }
39
40     // create and position GUI components; register event handlers
41     private void createUserInterface()
42     {
43        // get content pane for attaching GUI components
44        Container contentPane = getContentPane();
```

Figure 11.19 Security Panel application code. (Part 1 of 9.)

```
45
46        // enable explicit positioning of GUI components
47        contentPane.setLayout( null );
48
49        // set up securityCodeJLabel
50        securityCodeJLabel = new JLabel();
51        securityCodeJLabel.setBounds( 16, 16, 90, 21 );
52        securityCodeJLabel.setText( "Security code:" );
53        contentPane.add( securityCodeJLabel );
54
55        // set up securityCodeJPasswordField
56        securityCodeJPasswordField = new JPasswordField();
57        securityCodeJPasswordField.setBounds( 114, 16, 172, 26 );
58        securityCodeJPasswordField.setEditable( false );
59        contentPane.add( securityCodeJPasswordField );
60
61        // set up oneJButton
62        oneJButton = new JButton();
63        oneJButton.setBounds( 80, 64, 50, 50 );
64        oneJButton.setText( "1" );
65        contentPane.add( oneJButton );
66        oneJButton.addActionListener(
67
68           new ActionListener() // anonymous inner class
69           {
70              // event handler called when oneJButton is pressed
71              public void actionPerformed( ActionEvent event )
72              {
73                 oneJButtonActionPerformed( event );
74              }
75
76           } // end anonymous inner class
77
78        ); // end call to addActionListener
79
80        // set up twoJButton
81        twoJButton = new JButton();
82        twoJButton.setBounds( 130, 64, 50, 50 );
83        twoJButton.setText( "2" );
84        contentPane.add( twoJButton );
85        twoJButton.addActionListener(
86
87           new ActionListener() // anonymous inner class
88           {
89              // event handler called when twoJButton is pressed
90              public void actionPerformed( ActionEvent event )
91              {
92                 twoJButtonActionPerformed( event );
93              }
94
95           } // end anonymous inner class
96
97        ); // end call to addActionListener
98
99        // set up threeJButton
100       threeJButton = new JButton();
101       threeJButton.setBounds( 180, 64, 50, 50 );
102       threeJButton.setText( "3" );
```

Set the *bounds* and *editable* properties of the JPasswordField

Figure 11.19 **Security Panel** application code. (Part 2 of 9.)

```
103    contentPane.add( threeJButton );
104    threeJButton.addActionListener(
105
106       new ActionListener() // anonymous inner class
107       {
108          // event handler called when threeJButton is pressed
109          public void actionPerformed( ActionEvent event )
110          {
111             threeJButtonActionPerformed( event );
112          }
113
114       } // end anonymous inner class
115
116    ); // end call to addActionListener
117
118    // set up fourJButton
119    fourJButton = new JButton();
120    fourJButton.setBounds( 80, 114, 50, 50 );
121    fourJButton.setText( "4" );
122    contentPane.add( fourJButton );
123    fourJButton.addActionListener(
124
125       new ActionListener() // anonymous inner class
126       {
127          // event handler called when fourJButton is pressed
128          public void actionPerformed( ActionEvent event )
129          {
130             fourJButtonActionPerformed( event );
131          }
132
133       } // end anonymous inner class
134
135    ); // end call to addActionListener
136
137    // set up fiveJButton
138    fiveJButton = new JButton();
139    fiveJButton.setBounds( 130, 114, 50, 50 );
140    fiveJButton.setText( "5" );
141    contentPane.add( fiveJButton );
142    fiveJButton.addActionListener(
143
144       new ActionListener() // anonymous inner class
145       {
146          // event handler called when fiveJButton is pressed
147          public void actionPerformed( ActionEvent event )
148          {
149             fiveJButtonActionPerformed( event );
150          }
151
152       } // end anonymous inner class
153
154    ); // end call to addActionListener
155
156    // set up sixJButton
157    sixJButton = new JButton();
158    sixJButton.setBounds( 180, 114, 50, 50 );
159    sixJButton.setText( "6" );
160    contentPane.add( sixJButton );
```

Figure 11.19 **Security Panel** application code. (Part 3 of 9.)

```
161        sixJButton.addActionListener(
162
163            new ActionListener() // anonymous inner class
164            {
165                // event handler called when sixJButton is pressed
166                public void actionPerformed( ActionEvent event )
167                {
168                    sixJButtonActionPerformed( event );
169                }
170
171            } // end anonymous inner class
172
173        ); // end call to addActionListener
174
175        // set up sevenJButton
176        sevenJButton = new JButton();
177        sevenJButton.setBounds( 80, 164, 50, 50 );
178        sevenJButton.setText( "7" );
179        contentPane.add( sevenJButton );
180        sevenJButton.addActionListener(
181
182            new ActionListener() // anonymous inner class
183            {
184                // event handler called when sevenJButton is pressed
185                public void actionPerformed( ActionEvent event )
186                {
187                    sevenJButtonActionPerformed( event );
188                }
189
190            } // end anonymous inner class
191
192        ); // end call to addActionListener
193
194        // set up eightJButton
195        eightJButton = new JButton();
196        eightJButton.setBounds( 130, 164, 50, 50 );
197        eightJButton.setText( "8" );
198        contentPane.add( eightJButton );
199        eightJButton.addActionListener(
200
201            new ActionListener() // anonymous inner class
202            {
203                // event handler called when eightJButton is pressed
204                public void actionPerformed( ActionEvent event )
205                {
206                    eightJButtonActionPerformed( event );
207                }
208
209            } // end anonymous inner class
210
211        ); // end call to addActionListener
212
213        // set up nineJButton
214        nineJButton = new JButton();
215        nineJButton.setBounds( 180, 164, 50, 50 );
216        nineJButton.setText( "9" );
217        contentPane.add( nineJButton );
218        nineJButton.addActionListener(
```

Figure 11.19 **Security Panel** application code. (Part 4 of 9.)

```
219
220         new ActionListener() // anonymous inner class
221         {
222            // event handler called when nineJButton is pressed
223            public void actionPerformed( ActionEvent event )
224            {
225               nineJButtonActionPerformed( event );
226            }
227
228         } // end anonymous inner class
229
230      ); // end call to addActionListener
231
232      // set up clearJButton
233      clearJButton = new JButton();
234      clearJButton.setBounds( 80, 214, 50, 50 );
235      clearJButton.setText( "C" );
236      contentPane.add( clearJButton );
237      clearJButton.addActionListener(
238
239         new ActionListener() // anonymous inner class
240         {
241            // event handler called when clearJButton is pressed
242            public void actionPerformed( ActionEvent event )
243            {
244               clearJButtonActionPerformed( event );
245            }
246
247         } // end anonymous inner class
248
249      ); // end call to addActionListener
250
251      // set up zeroJButton
252      zeroJButton = new JButton();
253      zeroJButton.setBounds( 130, 214, 50, 50 );
254      zeroJButton.setText( "0" );
255      contentPane.add( zeroJButton );
256      zeroJButton.addActionListener(
257
258         new ActionListener() // anonymous inner class
259         {
260            // event handler called when zeroJButton is pressed
261            public void actionPerformed( ActionEvent event )
262            {
263               zeroJButtonActionPerformed( event );
264            }
265
266         } // end anonymous inner class
267
268      ); // end call to addActionListener
269
270      // set up enterJButton
271      enterJButton = new JButton();
272      enterJButton.setBounds( 180, 214, 50, 50 );
273      enterJButton.setText( "#" );
274      contentPane.add( enterJButton );
275      enterJButton.addActionListener(
276
```

Figure 11.19 Security Panel application code. (Part 5 of 9.)

```
277            new ActionListener() // anonymous inner class
278            {
279                // event handler called when enterJButton is pressed
280                public void actionPerformed( ActionEvent event )
281                {
282                    enterJButtonActionPerformed( event );
283                }
284
285            } // end anonymous inner class
286
287        ); // end call to addActionListener
288
289        // set up accessLogJLabel
290        accessLogJLabel = new JLabel();
291        accessLogJLabel.setBounds( 16, 285, 100, 16 );
292        accessLogJLabel.setText( "Access log:" );
293        contentPane.add( accessLogJLabel );
294
295        // set up accessLogJTextArea
296        accessLogJTextArea = new JTextArea();
297
298        // set up accessLogJScrollPane
299        accessLogJScrollPane = new JScrollPane( accessLogJTextArea );
300        accessLogJScrollPane.setBounds( 16, 309, 270, 95 );
301        contentPane.add( accessLogJScrollPane );
302
303        // set properties of application's window
304        setTitle( "Security Panel" ); // set title bar string
305        setSize( 310, 450 );          // set window's size
306        setVisible( true );           // display window
307
308    } // end method createUserInterface
309
310    // append 1 to the security code
311    private void oneJButtonActionPerformed( ActionEvent event )
312    {
313        securityCodeJPasswordField.setText( String.valueOf(
314            securityCodeJPasswordField.getPassword() ) + "1" );
315
316    } // end method oneJButtonActionPerformed
317
318    // append 2 to the security code
319    private void twoJButtonActionPerformed( ActionEvent event )
320    {
321        securityCodeJPasswordField.setText( String.valueOf(
322            securityCodeJPasswordField.getPassword() ) + "2" );
323
324    } // end method twoJButtonActionPerformed
325
326    // append 3 to the security code
327    private void threeJButtonActionPerformed( ActionEvent event )
328    {
329        securityCodeJPasswordField.setText( String.valueOf(
330            securityCodeJPasswordField.getPassword() ) + "3" );
331
332    } // end method threeJButtonActionPerformed
333
```

Append the numeric JButton value "1" to the password stored in the JPasswordField — (lines 313–314)

Append the numeric JButton value "2" to the password stored in the JPasswordField — (lines 321–322)

Append the numeric JButton value "3" to the password stored in the JPasswordField — (lines 329–330)

Figure 11.19   **Security Panel** application code. (Part 6 of 9.)

Append the numeric `JButton` value "4" to the password stored in the `JPasswordField`

```
334    // append 4 to the security code
335    private void fourJButtonActionPerformed( ActionEvent event )
336    {
337       securityCodeJPasswordField.setText( String.valueOf(
338          securityCodeJPasswordField.getPassword() ) + "4" );
339
340    } // end method fourJButtonActionPerformed
341
342    // append 5 to the security code
343    private void fiveJButtonActionPerformed( ActionEvent event )
344    {
345       securityCodeJPasswordField.setText( String.valueOf(
346          securityCodeJPasswordField.getPassword() ) + "5" );
347
348    } // end method fiveJButtonActionPerformed
349
350    // append 6 to the security code
351    private void sixJButtonActionPerformed( ActionEvent event )
352    {
353       securityCodeJPasswordField.setText( String.valueOf(
354          securityCodeJPasswordField.getPassword() ) + "6" );
355
356    } // end method sixJButtonActionPerformed
357
358    // append 7 to the security code
359    private void sevenJButtonActionPerformed( ActionEvent event )
360    {
361       securityCodeJPasswordField.setText( String.valueOf(
362          securityCodeJPasswordField.getPassword() ) + "7" );
363
364    } // end method sevenJButtonActionPerformed
365
366    // append 8 to the security code
367    private void eightJButtonActionPerformed( ActionEvent event )
368    {
369       securityCodeJPasswordField.setText( String.valueOf(
370          securityCodeJPasswordField.getPassword() ) + "8" );
371
372    } // end method eightJButtonActionPerformed
373
374    // append 9 to the security code
375    private void nineJButtonActionPerformed( ActionEvent event )
376    {
377       securityCodeJPasswordField.setText( String.valueOf(
378          securityCodeJPasswordField.getPassword() ) + "9" );
379
380    } // end method nineJButtonActionPerformed
381
382    // append 0 to the security code
383    private void zeroJButtonActionPerformed( ActionEvent event )
384    {
385       securityCodeJPasswordField.setText( String.valueOf(
386          securityCodeJPasswordField.getPassword() ) + "0" );
387
388    } // end method zeroJButtonActionPerformed
389
```

Append the numeric `JButton` value "5" to the password stored in the `JPasswordField`

Append the numeric `JButton` value "6" to the password stored in the `JPasswordField`

Append the numeric `JButton` value "7" to the password stored in the `JPasswordField`

Append the numeric `JButton` value "8" to the password stored in the `JPasswordField`

Append the numeric `JButton` value "9" to the password stored in the `JPasswordField`

Append the numeric `JButton` value "0" to the password stored in the `JPasswordField`

Figure 11.19 **Security Panel** application code. (Part 7 of 9.)

```
390    // clears the securityCodeJPasswordField
391    private void clearJButtonActionPerformed( ActionEvent event )
392    {
393        securityCodeJPasswordField.setText( "" );
394
395    } // end method clearJButtonActionPerformed
396
397    // gets access code and determines level of clearance
398    private void enterJButtonActionPerformed( ActionEvent event )
399    {
400        String message; // displays access status of users
401
402        // stores access code entered
403        int accessCode = Integer.parseInt( String.valueOf(
404            securityCodeJPasswordField.getPassword() ) );
405
406        securityCodeJPasswordField.setText( "" );
407
408        switch ( accessCode ) // check access code input
409        {
410            // access code is 7, 8 or 9
411            case 7:
412            case 8:
413            case 9:
414                message = "Restricted Access";
415                break; // done processing case
416
417            // access code equal to 1645
418            case 1645:
419                message = "Technician";
420                break; // done processing case
421
422            // access code equal to 8345
423            case 8345:
424                message = "Custodian";
425                break; // done processing case
426
427            // access code equal to 9998 or between 1006 and 1008
428            case 9998:
429            case 1006:
430            case 1007:
431            case 1008:
432                message = "Scientist";
433                break; // done processing case
434
435            // if no other case is true
436            default:
437                message = "Access Denied";
438
439        } // end switch statement
440
441        // display time and message in accessLogJTextArea
442        DateFormat formatter = DateFormat.getDateTimeInstance();
443        accessLogJTextArea.append( formatter.format( new Date() ) +
444            "   " + message + "\n" );
445
446    } // end method enterJButtonActionPerformed
447
```

Labels (left margin):
- Clear the JPasswordField — line 393
- String for message to display — line 400
- Get *password* property — lines 403–404
- Clear the JPasswordField — line 406
- Using a switch statement to determine user access level — line 408
- Three case labels result in the same message — lines 411–413
- Terminate switch statement and continue execution with next statement after switch — line 415
- Access code 1645 for Technicians — line 419
- Access code 8345 for Custodians — line 424
- Access codes 9998, 1006, 1007 and 1008 for Scientists — lines 428–431
- default case executes if no other cases match — line 436
- Right brace ends the switch statement — line 439
- Append the current date and time to the message — lines 442–443

Figure 11.19 **Security Panel** application code. (Part 8 of 9.)

```
448     // main method
449     public static void main( String[] args )
450     {
451        SecurityPanel application = new SecurityPanel();
452        application.setDefaultCloseOperation( JFrame.EXIT_ON_CLOSE );
453
454     } // end method main
455
456  } // end class SecurityPanel
```

Figure 11.19   **Security Panel** application code. (Part 9 of 9.)

SELF-REVIEW

1. By default, when a user types in a `JPasswordField`, _____ is (are) displayed on the screen.
   a) nothing
   b) asterisks
   c) the text typed
   d) only numbers

2. A(n) _____ causes program control to proceed with the first statement after the `switch`.
   a) semicolon
   b) `stop` keyword
   c) `break` statement
   d) end of a `case` statement

Answers: 1) b. 2) c.

11.4 Wrap-Up

In this tutorial, you learned how to use the `switch` multiple-selection statement and discovered its similarities to nested `if...else` statements. You studied a UML activity diagram that illustrates the flow of control in a `switch` statement.

You then applied what you learned to create your **Security Panel** application. You used a `switch` statement to determine whether the user entered a correct security code. You also declared several `cases` and included an optional `default` case, which executes if a valid security code is not provided. You learned that if you don't provide the optional `default` case, invalid codes will cause the `switch` statement to be skipped, so it is indeed important to provide the `default` case. You also learned that `break` statements are used to end `case` statements. If a `break` statement is omitted for a `case` statement, execution will "fall through" to the next `case` statement.

In the next tutorial, you will learn how to construct applications from small, manageable pieces of reusable code called methods. You have actually been working with existing methods all along, but now you will learn how to write your own methods—these are often called programmer-declared methods. You will use methods to enhance the **Wage Calculator** application you created earlier in the book.

SKILLS SUMMARY

Coding a `switch` statement

- Use the keyword `switch` followed by a controlling expression.
- For each `case`, use the keyword `case` followed by an expression to compare with the controlling expression.
- For each `case`, declare the statements that execute if the `case`'s expression matches the controlling expression.
- Use a `break` statement to end each `case` statement. If the `break` statement is omitted execution "falls through" to the next `case` statement.
- Use the `default` label followed by statements to execute if the controlling expression does not match any of the provided `cases`.

Hiding User Input in a `JPasswordField`

- Use a `JPasswordField` to hide user input.
- Retrieve the value typed by the user in the `JPasswordField` with method `getPassword`.
- (Optional) Specify the echo character displayed in the `JPasswordField` with method `setEchoChar`.

Obtaining a Formatted `String` Containing the Current Date and Time

- Use `DateFormat.getDateTimeInstance` to get a `DateFormat` to display a date and time.
- Pass `new Date()` to the `DateFormat`'s `format` method to obtain the formatted `String` containing the date and time.

KEY TERMS

break statement—Typically appears at the end of each `case`. This statement immediately terminates the `switch` statement, and program control continues with the next statement after the `switch`.

case label—Precedes the statements that will execute if the `switch`'s controlling expression matches the expression in the `case` label.

char type—Type used to store character values.

character constant—Another name for a character literal.

character literal—The value of a variable of type `char`, it is represented by a character within single quotes, such as `'A'`, `'d'`, `'*'`, `'.'` and the like.

constant expression—A value that cannot be changed. A `case` label consists of the keyword `case` followed by a constant expression. This constant expression must be a character literal or an integer literal.

controlling expression—The expression in a `switch` statement whose value is compared sequentially with each `case` until either a match occurs, the `default` case is executed or the right brace is reached.

Date class—Stores date and time information.

DateFormat class—Formats date and time information.

default case—The optional case whose statements execute if the `switch`'s controlling expression does not match any of the `cases`' values.

echo character—Replaces each character displayed in a `JPasswordField`. The default echo character is *, but the programmer can specify the echo character by calling the `JPasswordField`'s `setEchoChar` method.

editable **property of a `JPasswordField`**—Determines whether the `JPasswordField` will allow user input.

getPassword method—Returns the text in the `JPasswordField`.

JPasswordField—Displays or inputs a password. The characters displayed in a `JPasswordField` are replaced with asterisks (*). Users can type passwords into an editable `JPasswordField`.

mask character—Another name for an echo character.

multiple-selection statement—A statement, such as a `switch` statement, that selects one of many actions (or sequences of actions), depending on the value of the controlling expression.

password **property of a `JPasswordField`**—Holds the text entered in the `JPasswordField`.

setEchoChar method—Specifies the echo character in a `JPasswordField`.

switch statement—The multiple-selection statement used to make a decision by comparing a controlling expression to a series of case values. The algorithm then takes different actions based on those values.

GUI DESIGN GUIDELINES

Overall Design

- If your GUI is modeling a real-world object, your GUI design should mimic the physical appearance of that object.

`JPasswordField`

- Mask passwords or other sensitive pieces of information in `JPasswordField`s.

JAVA LIBRARY REFERENCE

Date   Represents a date and time. Use the code `new Date()` to get the current system date and time.

DateFormat   Class for formatting `Date` objects.

■ *Methods*

    `format`—Formats a `Date` object and returns a `String`.

    `getDateTimeInstance`—Returns a `DateFormat` object which can be used to format `Date` objects.

JPasswordField   Allows the user to input data from the keyboard and displays each character as an asterisk (*) for security reasons.

■ *In action*

■ *Methods*

    `setBounds`—Sets the *bounds* property which determines the location and size of a `JPasswordField`.

    `setEditable`—Specifies whether users can edit a `JPasswordField`.

    `getPassword`—Returns the password in a `JPasswordField`.

    `setEchoChar`—Specifies the echo character for a `JPasswordField`.

    `setText`—Specifies the text displayed in a `JPasswordField`.

MULTIPLE-CHOICE QUESTIONS

11.1 The _____ signifies the end of a `switch` statement.

  a) `end` keyword   b) `}` character

  c) `break` keyword   d) `default` keyword

11.2 The expression _____ returns the current system time and date.

  a) `DateFormat.getDateTime()`   b) `new Date()`

  c) `DateFormat.getDateTimeInstance()`   d) `new CurrentDate()`

11.3 You can hide information entered by the user with a _____ component; by default, an asterisk (*) will be displayed for every character entered by the user.

  a) `JTextField`   b) `JPassword`

  c) `JMaskedField`   d) `JPasswordField`

11.4 Which of the following is a syntax error?

  a) Having duplicate `case` statements in the same `switch` statement.   b) Beginning and ending a `switch` statement body with braces.

  c) Preceding a `case` label with the `default` label in a `switch` statement.   d) Failing to end a `case` with the `break` statement.

11.5 If the controlling expression in the `switch` statement is not equal to any of the `case` labels and there is no `default` case, _____.

  a) an error occurs   b) an infinite loop occurs

  c) the application continues execution with the next statement after the `switch`   d) the first `case`'s statements are executed

11.6 _____ separates the `case` label from the code that will execute if the `case` label matches the controlling expression.

  a) A colon   b) An underscore

  c) `break` keyword   d) A semicolon

11.7 The _____ primitive type is not compatible with a `switch` statement.

a) `double`
b) `int`
c) `short`
d) `char`

11.8 The correct syntax for a `default` case is _____.

a) `default case`
b) `default`
c) `default case:`
d) `default:`

11.9 The expression in parentheses following the `switch` keyword is called a _____.

a) guard condition
b) controlling expression
c) selection expression
d) case expression

11.10 To prevent a user from modifying text in a `JPasswordField`, set its _____ property to `false`.

a) *masked*
b) *text*
c) *textChange*
d) *editable*

EXERCISES

11.11 *(Sales Commission Calculator Application)* Develop an application that calculates a salesperson's commission from the number of items sold (Fig. 11.20). Assume that all items have a fixed price of 100 dollars per unit. Use a `switch` statement to implement the following sales commission schedule:

> Fewer than 10 items sold = 1% commission
> Between 10 and 39 items sold = 2% commission
> Between 40 and 99 items sold = 3% commission
> More than 99 items sold = 4% commission

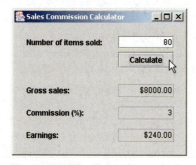

Figure 11.20   Sales Commission Calculator GUI.

a) *Copying the template to your working directory.* Copy the directory `C:\Examples\Tutorial11\Exercises\SalesCommissionCalculator` to your `C:\SimplyJava` directory.

b) *Opening the template file.* Open the `SalesCommissionCalculator.java` file in your text editor. In the template, line 127 in the `calculateJButtonActionPerformed` method obtains the number of items sold that was entered by the user, converts the number to an `int` value and assigns the value to the `int` local variable `items`. Line 129 declares the `double` constant `DOLLARS_PER_UNIT` to represent the cost for each item sold. Line 132 creates the `DecimalFormat` variable `dollars` that will be used to format the gross sales and the salesperson's earnings for display purposes.

c) *Calculate the gross sales.* In `calculateJButtonActionPerformed`, insert a statement in line 130 that multiplies the number of items that the salesperson has sold (`items`) by the cost per item (`DOLLARS_PER_UNIT`), and assigns the result to `double` variable `sales`.

d) *Determine the salesperson's commission percentage.* In line 131 in `calculateJButtonActionPerformed`, declare an `int` local variable `commission` to store the commission percentage. Next, insert a `switch` statement to determine the salesperson's commission percentage from the number of items sold. In this `switch` statement, assign the commission percentage as a whole number to variable `commission`.

For example, if the commission percentage is 2%, assign 2 to `commission`. The controlling expression should be `items / 10`. Because this is integer arithmetic, any number of items in the range 0–9 will result in 0, any number of items in the range 10–19 will result in 1, etc. Inside the `switch` statement, provide `cases` that enable the `switch` to test for values in the ranges specified by the problem statement.

e) *Calculate the decimal value of commission percentage.* After the `switch` statement, insert a statement that divides `commission` by `100.0` and assigns the result to `double` local variable `commissionRate`.

f) *Calculate the salesperson's earnings.* After the statement you inserted in *Step e*, insert a statement that multiplies the salesperson's `sales` (calculated in *Step c*) by `commissionRate`, then assign the result to `double` local variable `earnings`.

g) *Display the gross sales, the commission percentage and the salesperson's earnings.* After the statement in `calculateJButtonActionPerformed` that creates `DecimalFormat dollars`, add three statements that display the values of local variables `sales`, `commission` and `earnings` in the `salesJTextField`, `commissionJTextField` and `earningsJTextField`, respectively. For the sales and earnings values, use `DecimalFormat dollars` to format the values as dollar amounts.

h) *Saving the application.* Save your modified source code file.

i) *Opening the Command Prompt window and changing directories.* Open the **Command Prompt** window by selecting **Start > Programs > Accessories > Command Prompt**. Change to your working directory by typing `cd C:\SimplyJava\SalesCommissionCalculator`.

j) *Compiling the application.* Compile your application by typing `javac SalesCommissionCalculator.java`.

k) *Running the completed application.* Run the application by typing `java SalesCommissionCalculator`. To test your application, enter different numbers in the **Number of items sold:** `JTextField` and click the **Calculate** `JButton` to calculate the sales commission.

l) *Closing the application.* Close your running application by clicking its close button.

m) *Closing the Command Prompt window.* Close the **Command Prompt** window by clicking its close button.

11.12 *(Federal Income Tax Calculator Application)* Create an application that computes the amount of Federal income tax that a person must pay, depending upon that person's salary. [*Note:* The actual U.S. Federal income tax rates vary based on many factors. For more information, see the information in IRS Form 1040-ES, which is located at www.irs.gov/pub/irs-pdf/f1040e03.pdf.] Your application should operate as shown in Fig. 11.21. Assume all salaries are input as integers that are greater than or equal to 0. Use the following income ranges and corresponding tax rates:

Under $25,000 = 2% income tax
$25,000 – 49,999 = 5% income tax
$50,000 – 74,999 = 10% income tax
$75,000 – 99,999 = 15% income tax
$100,000 and over = 20% income tax

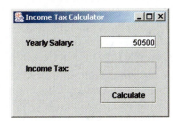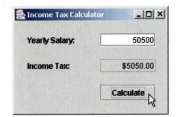

Figure 11.21 Federal Income Tax Calculator GUI.

a) *Copying the template to your working directory.* Copy the directory `C:\Examples\Tutorial11\Exercises\IncomeTaxCalculator` to your `C:\SimplyJava` directory.

b) *Opening the template file.* Open the IncomeTaxCalculator.java file in your text editor.

c) *Inserting a switch statement in the `calculateJButtonActionPerformed` method.* In the calculateJButtonActionPerformed method (lines 110–118 in the template), insert a switch statement at line 114 to determine the tax rate and assign it to the double variable taxRate (declared on line 112). The int variable salary (line 113) contains the salary input by the user. Use the controlling expression salary / 25000 to determine the tax rate. If the salary is less than $25,000, the controlling expression's value will be 0. For salaries in the range $25,000–$49,999, the controlling expression's value will be 1. For salaries in the range $50,000–$74,999, the controlling expression's value will be 2. For salaries in the range $75,000–$99,999, the controlling expression's value will be 3. For all other salaries, use the default case.

d) *Calculating and displaying the income tax in the `calculateJButtonAction-Performed` method.* After the switch statement you inserted in *Step c*, insert a statement that calculates the person's income tax by multiplying the salary and taxRate values, then stores the result in the double variable incomeTax. After the statement that creates the DecimalFormat called dollars, insert a statement that formats the value of incomeTax and displays the formatted value in incomeTaxJTextField.

e) *Saving the application.* Save your modified source code file.

f) *Opening the Command Prompt window and changing directories.* Open the **Command Prompt** window by selecting **Start > Programs > Accessories > Command Prompt**. Change to your working directory by typing cd C:\SimplyJava\ IncomeTaxCalculator.

g) *Compiling the application.* Compile your application by typing javac IncomeTax-Calculator.java.

h) *Running the completed application.* When you application compiles correctly, run it by typing java IncomeTaxCalculator. To test your application, enter different yearly salaries and calculate the income tax.

i) *Closing the application.* Close your running application by clicking its close button.

j) *Closing the Command Prompt window.* Close the **Command Prompt** window by clicking its close button.

What does this code do?   **11.13** What is output by the following code? Discuss the output for grade values of 'A', 'B', 'C', 'D', 'F' and an invalid grade.

```
1  switch ( grade )
2  {
3     case 'A':
4        displayJLabel.setText( "Excellent!" );
5
6     case 'B':
7        displayJLabel.setText( "Very good!" );
8
9     case 'C':
10        displayJLabel.setText( "Good." );
11
12     case 'D':
13        displayJLabel.setText( "Poor." );
14
15     case 'F':
16        displayJLabel.setText( "Failure." );
17
18     default:
19        displayJLabel.setText( "Invalid grade." );
20  }
```

What's wrong with this code? **11.14** This `switch` statement should determine whether an `int` is even or odd. Find the error(s) in the following code:

```
1   switch ( value % 2 )
2   {
3      case 0:
4         outputJTextField.setText( "Even Integer" );
5
6      case 1:
7         outputJTextField.setText( "Odd Integer" );
8         break;
9
10  } // end switch
```

Using the Debugger **11.15** (*Discount Calculator Application*) The **Discount Calculator** application determines the discount the user will receive based on how much money the user spends. A 15% discount is received for purchases of $150 or more, a 10% discount is received for purchases from $100–$149 and a 5% discount is received for purchases from $50–$99. Purchases less than $50 do not receive a discount. While testing your application, you notice that the application is not calculating the discount properly for some values. Use the debugger to find and fix the logic error(s) in the application. Figure 11.22 displays the correct output for values in each range.

Figure 11.22 Correct output for the **Discount Calculator** application.

a) *Copying the template to your working directory.* Copy the `C:\Examples\ Tutorial11\Exercises\Debugger\DiscountCalculator` directory to your `C:\ SimplyJava` directory.

b) *Opening the template file.* Open the `DiscountCalculator.java` file in your text editor.

c) *Opening the Command Prompt window and changing directories.* Open the **Command Prompt** window by selecting **Start > Programs > Accessories > Command Prompt**. Change to your working directory by typing `cd C:\SimplyJava\Discount-Calculator`.

d) *Compiling the application for debugging.* Compile your application by typing `javac -g DiscountCalculator.java`,.

e) *Running the application.* When your application compiles correctly, run it by typing `java DiscountCalculator`. To test your application, enter the amounts shown in Fig. 11.22. When you enter the value 75 (or any other value in the range 50–99), notice that the application incorrectly indicates a discount of 15%.

f) *Starting the debugger.* Close the application (but leave the **Command Prompt** open) and start the debugger by typing `jdb`.

g) *Finding and correcting the error(s).* Use the debugging skills learned in previous tutorials to determine where the application's logic errors exist. In the `discountJButtonActionPerformed` method set breakpoints at the `break` statement in each `case` (lines 81 and 85) and at line 93 (the first statement after the `switch`). Use the debugger's `print` command to inspect the value of the variable `discountRate` each time the application enters break mode. Use the debugger's `cont` command to continue execution after you inspect the `discountRate` at each breakpoint. When you find the logic error, modify the application's `switch` statement so that the proper discount rate is chosen.

h) *Saving the application.* Save your modified source code file.

i) *Compiling the application.* Compile your application by typing `javac DiscountCalculator.java`.

j) *Running the completed application.* When your application compiles correctly, run it by typing `java DiscountCalculator`. Test your application by entering the amounts shown in Fig. 11.22 and make sure the resulting discounts are correct.

k) *Closing the application.* Close your running application by clicking its close button.

l) *Closing the Command Prompt window.* Close the **Command Prompt** window by clicking its close button.

Programming Challenge ▶ **11.16** *(Cash Register Application)* Create a **Cash Register** application (Fig. 11.23) with a numeric keypad similar to that in the **Security Panel** application you built in this tutorial. In addition to numbers, the cash register includes a decimal point `JButton`. Also, there are **Enter**, **Total**, **Delete** and **Clear** `JButton`s. These `JButton`s add an amount to the subtotal, calculate the tax and total, delete the current amount in the **$** `JTextField` (in case the user makes an error during input) and clear the current amounts displayed, respectively. You will implement the methods for the **Enter** and **Total** `JButton`s. Assume the user enters positive, non-zero amounts. Sales tax should be calculated on the amount purchased using a `switch` statement. Add the tax amount to the subtotal to calculate the total. Display the subtotal, tax and total for the user. Use a `switch` statement to determine the tax rate based on the following dollar amounts:

Amounts under $100 = 5% (.05) sales tax
Amounts between $100 and $499 = 7.5% (.075) sales tax
Amounts $500 and over = 10% (.10) sales tax

Figure 11.23 Cash Register GUI.

a) ***Copying the template to your working directory.*** Copy the directory `C:\Examples\Tutorial11\Exercises\CashRegister` to your `C:\SimplyJava` directory.

b) ***Opening the template file.*** Open the `CashRegister.java` file in your text editor.

c) ***Adding code to the enterJButtonActionPerformed method.*** In the enter-JButtonActionPerformed method (lines 496–499 in the template code), insert a statement that converts the value in `amountJTextField` to type `double` and adds the value to instance variable `subtotal`. Using the `DecimalFormat` variable `dollars` (created in line 56), insert a statement that formats the new value of `subtotal` and displays it in `subtotalJTextField`. Insert a statement that clears the `amountJTextField` (so the user can enter the next amount).

d) ***Determining the tax rate.*** In the `totalJButtonActionPerformed` method (which immediately follows `enterJButtonActionPerformed` in the template code), begin by declaring a `double` local variable called `taxRate` to store the tax rate that will be applied to the subtotal. Next, insert a `switch` statement that determines the tax rate and assigns the value to variable `taxRate`. In the `switch` statement, use the controlling expression `(int) subtotal / 100`, which converts the subtotal to an `int`, then divides the subtotal by 100. The value of this expression will be 0 for subtotals less than $100 and 1–4 for subtotals in the range $100–499. All other values should be handled by the `default` case in this exercise.

e) ***Calculating and displaying the tax and total.*** In the `totalJButtonAction-Performed` method (and after the statements you inserted in *Step d*, insert a statement that multiplies `subtotal` by the `taxRate` determined in *Step d* and stores the result in `double` variable `tax`. Next, add `subtotal` and `tax` and store the result in `double` variable `total`. Using the `DecimalFormat` variable `dollars` (created in line 56), insert statements that format the values of `tax` and `total` and displays those formatted values in `taxJTextField` and `totalJTextField`, respectively.

f) ***Clearing amountJTextField and resetting the subtotal.*** In the `totalJButton-ActionPerformed` method (and after the statements you inserted in *Step e*, insert statements that clear `amountJTextField` and reset `subtotal` to `0.0`.

g) ***Saving the application.*** Save your modified source code file.

h) ***Opening the Command Prompt window and changing directories.*** Open the **Command Prompt** window by selecting **Start > Programs > Accessories > Command Prompt**. Change to your working directory by typing cd `C:\SimplyJava\CashRegister`.

i) ***Compiling the application.*** Compile your application by typing `javac CashRegister.java`.

j) ***Running the completed application.*** When your application compiles correctly, run it by typing `java CashRegister`. To test your application, enter different costs using the numeric JButtons and the **Enter** JButton. Determine the tax and total cost by clicking the **Total** JButton. Also be sure to test the **Delete** and **Clear** JButtons by deleting one number from the JTextField and clearing all JTextFields.

k) ***Closing the application.*** Close your running application by clicking its close button.

l) ***Closing the Command Prompt window.*** Close the **Command Prompt** window by clicking its close button.

Objectives

In this tutorial, you will learn to:
- Construct applications modularly from pieces called methods.
- Work with "built-in" methods.
- Create your own methods.

Outline

Enhancing the Wage Calculator Application

Introducing Methods

Most software applications that solve real-world problems are much larger than the applications presented in the first few tutorials of this text. Experience has shown that the best way to develop and maintain a large application is to construct it from smaller, more manageable pieces. This is known as the **divide-and-conquer technique**. These manageable pieces include program blocks, known as **methods**, that simplify the design, implementation and maintenance of large applications. In this tutorial, you will learn how to use predeclared methods from the Java class library and how to create your own methods.

12.1 Test-Driving the Enhanced Wage Calculator Application

You will use methods to enhance the **Wage Calculator** application that you created in Tutorial 6. This enhanced application must meet the following requirements:

Application Requirements

Recall the problem statement from Tutorial 6: A payroll company calculates the gross earnings per week of employees from the number of hours they worked and their hourly wages. Create an application that takes this information and calculates the gross earnings by multiplying the employee's hourly wages by the number of hours worked. The application assumes a standard work week of 40 hours. Any hours worked over 40 hours in a week are considered overtime and earn time-and-a-half (that is, one and one-half times the hourly wage). Salary for time-and-a-half is calculated by multiplying the employee's hourly wage by 1.5 and multiplying the result of that calculation by the number of overtime hours worked. This value is then added to the user's earnings for the regular 40 hours of work to calculate the total earnings for that week. Use a method to calculate and return the user's pay.

The completed application has the same functionality as that application in Tutorial 6, but uses a method to better organize the code. This application calculates wages that are based on an employee's hourly salary and the number of hours worked per week. Normally, an employee who works 40 or fewer hours

earns the hourly wage multiplied by the number of hours worked. The calculation differs if the employee has worked more than the standard 40-hour work week. In this tutorial, you will learn about methods that perform calculations based on values that may differ with each execution of the application. You begin by test-driving the completed application. Then, you will learn the additional Java technologies you will need to create your own version of this application.

Test-Driving the Enhanced Wage Calculator Application

1. *Locating the completed application.* Open the **Command Prompt** by selecting **Start > Programs > Accessories > Command Prompt**. Change to your completed **Wage Calculator** application directory by typing cd `C:\Examples\Tutorial12\CompletedApplication\WageCalculator2`.

2. *Running the Wage Calculator application.* Type java `WageCalculator` in the **Command Prompt** window to run the application (Fig. 12.1). `JText-Fields` are provided for the user to enter an hourly wage and number of hours worked in a week. Once these values are entered, the user clicks the **Calculate** `JButton` and the gross earnings for the week are displayed in the **Gross wages:** `JTextField`.

3. *Entering the employee's hourly wage and weekly hours.* Enter 10 in the **Hourly wage:** `JTextField` and enter 45 in the **Hours worked:** `JTextField`.

4. *Calculating wages earned.* Click the **Calculate** `JButton`. The result ($475.00) is displayed in the **Gross wages:** `JTextField` (Fig. 12.1).

Figure 12.1   **Wage Calculator** executing.

5. *Closing the running application.* Close your running application by clicking its close button.

6. *Closing the Command Prompt window.* Close the **Command Prompt** window by clicking its close button.

12.2 Classes and Methods

The key to creating large applications is to break the applications into smaller pieces. In object-oriented programming, these pieces consist primarily of classes, which can be further broken down into methods.

Programmers typically combine **programmer-declared** classes and methods with pre-existing (also predeclared) code available in the Java class library. Using pre-existing code saves time, effort and money. This concept of **code reuse** increases efficiency for application developers. Figure 12.2 explains and demonstrates several pre-existing Java methods.

Method	Description	Example
`Math.max(x, y)`	Returns the larger value of x and y	`Math.max(2.3, 12.7)` is `12.7`
		`Math.max(-2.3, -12.7)` is `-2.3`

Figure 12.2   Some predeclared Java methods. (Part 1 of 2.)

Method	Description	Example
Math.min(x, y)	Returns the smaller value of x and y	Math.min(2.3, 12.7) is 2.3 Math.min(-2.3, -12.7) is -12.7
Math.sqrt(x)	Returns the square root of x	Math.sqrt(9) is 3.0 Math.sqrt(2) is 1.4142135623731
Integer.parseInt(x)	Converts a String into an int	Integer.parseInt("1") is 1
Double.parseDouble(x)	Converts a String into a double	Double.parseDouble("5.4") is 5.4
String.valueOf(x)	Returns the String value of x	String.valueOf(1.23) is "1.23"

Figure 12.2   Some predeclared Java methods. (Part 2 of 2.)

You have already used several pre-existing classes and methods in the Java class library. For example, all of the GUI components you have used in your applications are declared in the Java class library as classes. You have also used pre-existing Java classes, such as DecimalFormat, to format the output to display properly in your applications. Without class DecimalFormat, you would need to code this functionality yourself—a task that would include many lines of code and programming techniques that have not been introduced yet. These pre-existing classes are also thoroughly tested to eliminate bugs. You will learn to use many more Java class library classes and methods in this book.

The Java class libraries cannot provide every conceivable feature that you might need to build all your applications, so Java allows you to create your own programmer-declared classes and methods to meet the unique requirements of your particular applications. In the next section, you will learn about method declarations; later in this tutorial, you will create your own methods. In Tutorial 18, you will create your own classes.

SELF-REVIEW

1. The _____ provides the programmer with pre-existing classes that perform common tasks.

   a) Java class library   b) preExisting keyword
   c) Java code library   d) library keyword

2. Programmers normally use _____.

   a) programmer-declared methods   b) pre-existing methods
   c) both programmer-declared and pre-existing methods
   d) neither programmer-declared nor pre-existing methods

Answers: 1) a. 2) c.

12.3 Method Declarations

The applications presented earlier in this book have called Java class library methods (such as Integer.parseInt) to help accomplish the applications' tasks. You will now learn how to write your own programmer-declared methods. You will first learn how to create methods in the context of two small applications, before you create the enhanced **Wage Calculator** application. The first application uses the Pythagorean Theorem to calculate the length of the hypotenuse of a right triangle. The second application determines the maximum of three numbers. Let us begin by reviewing the Pythagorean Theorem. A right triangle (which is a triangle with a 90-

degree angle) always satisfies the following relationship—the sum of the squares of the two smaller sides of the triangle equals the square of the largest side of the triangle, which is known as the hypotenuse. In this application, the two smaller sides are called sides A and B and their lengths are used to calculate the length of the hypotenuse.

Creating the Hypotenuse Calculator Application

1. **Copying the template application to your working directory.** Copy the `C:\Examples\Tutorial12\TemplateApplication\HypotenuseCalcu-lator` directory to your `C:\SimplyJava` directory.

2. **Opening the Command Prompt window and changing directories.** Open the **Command Prompt** window by selecting **Start > Programs > Accessories > Command Prompt**. Change to your working directory by typing `cd C:\SimplyJava\HypotenuseCalculator`.

3. **Running the Hypotenuse Calculator template application.** Type `java HypotenuseCalculator` in the **Command Prompt** window to run the application (Fig. 12.3). When this application is running, the user enters the lengths of a triangle's two shorter sides into the **Length of side A:** and **Length of side B:** `JTextFields`, then clicks the **Calculate** `JButton`. The completed application will calculate the length of the hypotenuse and display the result in the **Length of hypotenuse:** output `JTextField`.

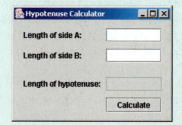

Figure 12.3 Running the **Hypotenuse Calculator** application.

4. **Closing the application.** Close your running application by clicking its close button.

5. **Closing the Command Prompt window.** Close the **Command Prompt** window by clicking its close button.

6. **Opening the Hypotenuse Calculator application's template file.** Open the template file `HypotenuseCalculator.java` in your text editor.

7. **Examining the template code.** Examine the code provided in the template, as shown in Fig. 12.4. We have provided an incomplete method for the **Calculate** `JButton` (lines 107–124). This method declares two local variables (lines 111–114). Variables `sideA` and `sideB` contain the lengths of sides A and B converted to `double` values. Lines 117–122 contain an `if` statement. The `if` statement's body displays a message dialog if a negative value (or zero) is input as the length of side A or side B.

8. **Creating an empty method.** Add lines 126–130 of Fig. 12.5 after the `calculateJButtonActionPerformed` method. Notice the comment on line 130—this comment is used to identify the method being terminated.

Good Programming Practice

Add comments at the end of your methods, indicating which method is being terminated.

(cont.)

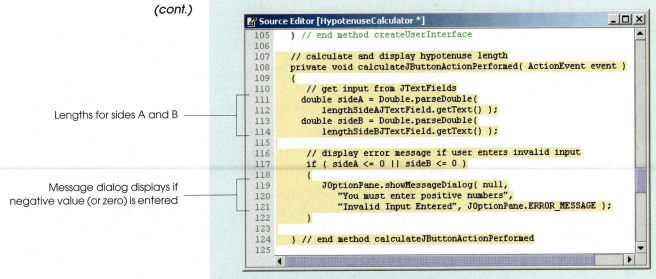

Lengths for sides A and B

Message dialog displays if
negative value (or zero) is entered

Figure 12.4 **Hypotenuse Calculator** template code.

Method header

A right brace marks the end
of a method declaration

Figure 12.5 Declaring method `square`.

9. ***Understanding the method.*** The method begins on line 127 (Fig. 12.5) with keywords `private` and `double`, followed by a **method name** (in this case, `square`). The method name can be any valid identifier. The method name is followed by a set of parentheses containing a variable declaration. The type name between `private` and `square` (in this case `double`) is known as the **return type**. Methods can return either a single piece of information or no information to the caller. If a method returns no information, its return type is declared with the **void** keyword.

The declaration within the parentheses is known as the **parameter list**, where variables (called **parameters**) are declared. Although this applica-tion's parameter list contains only one declaration, a parameter list can contain multiple declarations separated by commas. The parameter list declares each parameter's type and name. Parameter variables are used in the method body. Parameters allow methods to receive data that is required to performed the methods' tasks.

The first line of a method (including the keyword `private` or `public`, the return type, the method name and the parameter list) is called the **method header**. The method header for the `square` method declares one parameter variable, `side`, to be of type `double` and sets the return type of `square` to be `double`.

The declarations and statements that appear between the braces on lines 128 and 130 of Fig. 12.5 form the **method body**. The method body contains code that performs actions, generally by manipulating the parameters from the parameter list. In the next step, you will add statements to the body of the `square` method. The method header, the braces and the body state-ments collectively make up the **method declaration**.

(cont.)

10. ***Adding code to the body of a method.*** You want your method to square the value it receives in the `side` parameter and return that result to the method's caller. Add line 129 of Fig. 12.6 to `square`'s body.

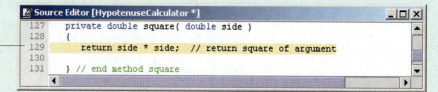

The `return` statement sends a value back to the method's caller

Figure 12.6 Coding the `square` method.

Line 129 uses the `*` operator to calculate the square of `side`—the parameter of this method. Line 129 also uses a **return statement** to return this value. This statement begins with the `return` keyword, followed by an expression. The `return` statement returns the result of the expression following `return` keyword—in this case, `side * side`—and terminates execution of the method. This value is returned to the point at which the method was called so that the returned value may be used by the method's caller. You will write the code to call the `square` method in the next step.

11. ***Saving the application.*** Save your modified source code file.

12. ***Opening the Command Prompt window and changing directories.*** Open the **Command Prompt** window by selecting **Start > Programs > Accessories > Command Prompt**. Change to your working directory by typing `cd C:\SimplyJava\HypotenuseCalculator`.

13. ***Compiling the application.*** Compile your application by typing `javac HypotenuseCalculator.java`.

14. ***Running the application.*** When your application compiles correctly, run it by typing `java HypotenuseCalculator`. Figure 12.7 shows the updated application running. Enter lengths for sides A and B then click the **Calculate** JButton. Notice that the length of the hypotenuse is not displayed. You will add the functionality to calculate and display the length of the hypotenuse in the next box.

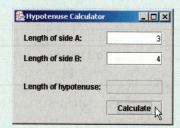

Figure 12.7 **Hypotenuse Calculator** application updated.

15. ***Closing the application.*** Close your running application by clicking its close button.

16. ***Closing the Command Prompt window.*** Close the **Command Prompt** window by clicking its close button.

Now you will insert code into your application to call your new method. You will see the benefits of code reuse by calling the method several times, rather than having to repeat code.

Good Programming Practice

Method names should be verbs and should begin with a lowercase letter. Each subsequent word in the name should begin with an uppercase letter.

Good Programming Practice

Placing a blank line between method declarations enhances application readability.

Calling a Method

1. **Calling the square method.** Now you will call your new method from method `calculateJButtonActionPerformed`. Add lines 123–129 of Fig. 12.8 to your application, to add an `else` block to the `if` statement. Lines 126–127 call `square` using the method name followed by a set of parentheses containing the method's argument. In this case, the arguments are variables `sideA` and `sideB`.

```
  Source Editor [HypotenuseCalculator *]                      _|□|×|
122        }
123        else
124        {
125            // calculate the squares of sides A and B
126            double squaredSideA = square( sideA );
127            double squaredSideB = square( sideB );
128
129        } // end else
130
131    } // end method calculateJButtonActionPerformed
```

Calling method `square` for each side

Figure 12.8 Invoking the `square` method.

A method is **invoked** (that is, made to perform its designated task) by a **method call**. The method call specifies the method name and provides information (**arguments**) that the **callee** (the method being called) receives as parameters and uses to do its job. When the called method completes its task, it returns control to the **caller** (the calling method). For example, you have typically called the `Integer.parseInt` method as follows:

```
result = Integer.parseInt( inputJTextField.getText() );
```

where `Integer.parseInt` is the name of the method and `inputJText-Field`'s *text* property is the argument passed to this function. The method uses this value to perform its defined task (returning the value of `inputJTextField`'s *text* property as an `int`). [*Note:* The method call uses arguments while the method has parameters.]

When program control reaches line 126 of Fig. 12.8, the application calls the `square` method. At this point, the application makes a copy of the value of variable `sideA` (for this example, let's assume the value of `sideA` is 3), program control transfers to the `square` method and the statements of the `square` method are executed.

Argument `sideA`, specified in the `square` method call, indicates that a copy of `sideA`'s value (the length of side A) should be passed to `square`; `square` receives the copy of this value (3) and stores it in the parameter `side`. When the `return` statement in `square` is reached, the calculated value to the right of keyword `return` (3 times 3, or 9) is returned to the point in line 126 (of Fig. 12.8) where the `square` method was called and the called method's execution completes. Program control will also be transferred to this point and the application will continue by assigning the return value of `square` (9) to variable `squaredSideA`. These same actions will occur again when program control reaches the second call to `square` in line 127. With this call, the value passed to `square` is the value of variable `sideB` (for this example, let's assume the value of `sideB` is 4) and the value returned (the square of `sideB`, or 16) is assigned to variable `squaredSideB`.

(cont.)

2. ***Calling a preexisting method of the Java class libraries.*** Add lines 129–143 of Fig. 12.9 to the `else` clause of the `if...else` statement in your application. Line 131 adds the square of side A and the square of side B, resulting in the square of the hypotenuse, which is assigned to variable `squaredHypotenuse`. Line 135 then calls Java library method **`sqrt`** of class `Math` (by qualifying the method name with the class name, using the dot separator). This method will calculate the square root of the square of the hypotenuse to find the length of the hypotenuse. Line 140 uses the built-in `format` method of the `Decimal-Format` class to ensure that only two decimal digits are displayed for the hypotenuse. The formatted output is then displayed in line 143.

```
 Source Editor [HypotenuseCalculator]
127          double squaredSideB = square( sideB );
128
129              // use the Pythagorean theorem to calculate
130              // square of the hypotenuse
131          double squaredHypotenuse = squaredSideA + squaredSideB;
132
133              // use built-in method Math.sqrt to calculate the square
134              // root of the hypotenuse squared (this is the hypotenuse)
135          double hypotenuse = Math.sqrt( squaredHypotenuse );
136
137          DecimalFormat twoDigits = new DecimalFormat( "0.00" );
138
139              // format hypotenuse value
140          String hypotenuseText = twoDigits.format( hypotenuse );
141
142              // display hypotenuse in JTextField
143          lengthHypotenuseJTextField.setText( hypotenuseText );
144
145      } // end else
```

Calling `Math` method `sqrt`

Format and display the length of the hypotenuse

Figure 12.9 Completing method `calculateJButtonActionPerformed`.

3. ***Saving the application.*** Save your modified source code file.

4. ***Opening the Command Prompt window and changing directories.*** Open the **Command Prompt** window by selecting **Start > Programs > Accessories > Command Prompt**. Change to your working directory by typing `cd C:\SimplyJava\HypotenuseCalculator`.

5. ***Running the application.*** When your application compiles correctly, run it by typing `java HypotenuseCalculator`. Figure 12.10 shows the completed application running. Enter lengths for sides A and B, then press the **Calculate JButton**. The length of the hypotenuse will be displayed. Notice that for sides A and B of lengths 3 and 4, the hypotenuse has a length of exactly 5. Test your application using a right triangle where the lengths of sides A and B are 5 and 12 (with a resulting hypotenuse of 13) and a right triangle where the lengths of sides A and B are 8 and 15 (with a resulting hypotenuse of 17).

![Error-Prevention Tip icon]

Error-Prevention Tip

Small methods are easier to test, debug and understand than are large ones.

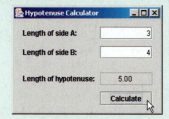

Figure 12.10 Running the completed **Hypotenuse Calculator** application.

6. ***Closing the application.*** Close your running application by clicking its close button.

7. ***Closing the Command Prompt window.*** Close the **Command Prompt** window by clicking its close button.

You have now successfully created your first programmer-declared method. You have also tested this method (by running the application) to confirm that it works correctly. This method can now be used in any Java application where you wish to calculate the square of a `double`. All you need to do is include the method declaration in your application. This is an example of code reuse, which helps programmers create applications faster.

As demonstrated in the **Hypotenuse Calculator** application, the syntax used to call a method follows the format

name(*argument list*)

Where the **argument list** is a comma-separated list of the arguments sent to a method. The number, order and type of arguments must agree with the parameters in the method's parameter list. If a method's parameter list is empty (that is, the method name is followed by an empty set of parentheses), it does not require any arguments.

As you saw in the previous example, the statement

`return` *expression*;

can occur anywhere in a method body and returns the value of *expression* to the caller. Methods return exactly one value. When a `return` statement is executed, control returns immediately to the point at which that method was called, where the value returned can be used. [*Note:* an expression can be any Java expression, even a call to another method.]

SELF-REVIEW

1. A method is invoked by a(n) _____.
   a) callee   b) caller
   c) argument   d) parameter

2. The _____ statement in a method sends a value back to the calling method.
   a) `return`   b) `back`
   c) `end`   d) None of the above.

Answers: 1) b. 2) a.

12.4 Finishing the `Maximum` Application

You will now create another method. This method, which is part of the **Maximum** application, returns the largest of three numbers input by the user.

Creating a Method That Returns the Largest of Three Numbers

1. *Copying the template application to your working directory.* Copy the `C:\Examples\Tutorial12\TemplateApplication\Maximum` directory to your `C:\SimplyJava` directory.

2. *Opening the Command Prompt window and changing directories.* Open the **Command Prompt** window by selecting **Start > Programs > Accessories > Command Prompt**. Change to your working directory by typing `cd C:\SimplyJava\Maximum`.

3. *Running the Maximum template application.* Type `java Maximum` in the **Command Prompt** window to run the application (Fig. 12.11). When this application is running, the user enters three numbers, one into each of the **First value:**, **Second value:** and **Third value:** `JTextField`s, then clicks the **Maximum** `JButton`. The completed application will determine the largest of the three numbers and display the result in the **Maximum:** `JTextField`.

(cont.)

Figure 12.11 **Maximum** application executing.

4. *Closing the application.* Close your running application by clicking its close button.

5. *Closing the Command Prompt window.* Close the **Command Prompt** window by clicking its close button.

6. *Opening the Maximum application's template file.* Open the template file Maximum.java in your text editor.

7. *Coding the maximumJButtonActionPerformed method.* This method, which executes as a result of the user clicking the **Maximum** JButton, is declared in lines 122–137. Add lines 124–135 of Fig. 12.12 to the method. Line 133 calls the determineMaximum method and passes it the three values the user has input into the application's JTextFields. The determineMaximum method has not yet been declared, so this method call will result in a syntax error if you try to compile the code. Misspelling the name of a method in a method call is also a syntax error. You will declare the determineMaximum method in the next step.

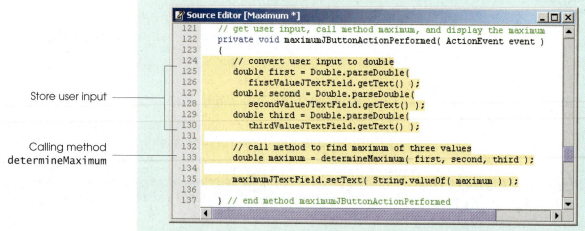

Store user input

Calling method determineMaximum

```
121    // get user input, call method maximum, and display the maximum
122    private void maximumJButtonActionPerformed( ActionEvent event )
123    {
124       // convert user input to double
125       double first = Double.parseDouble(
126          firstValueJTextField.getText() );
127       double second = Double.parseDouble(
128          secondValueJTextField.getText() );
129       double third = Double.parseDouble(
130          thirdValueJTextField.getText() );
131
132       // call method to find maximum of three values
133       double maximum = determineMaximum( first, second, third );
134
135       maximumJTextField.setText( String.valueOf( maximum ) );
136
137    } // end method maximumJButtonActionPerformed
```

Figure 12.12 Invoking the determineMaximum method.

8. *Creating the determineMaximum method.* Add lines 139–144 of Fig. 12.13 after the maximumJButtonActionPerformed method. Line 140 declares the return type of the determineMaximum method to be double. The parameter list (line 141) specifies that the values of the three arguments passed to the determineMaximum method will be stored in parameters one, two and three, all of which are variables of type double.

Common Programming Error

Calling a method that does not yet exist or misspelling the method name in a method call is a syntax error.

(cont.)

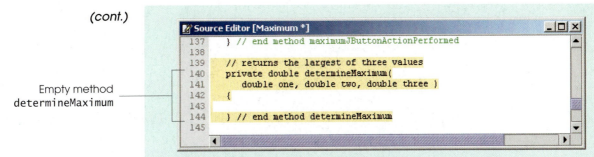

Empty method
`determineMaximum`

Figure 12.13 Declaring the `determineMaximum` method.

9. ***Adding functionality to the determineMaximum method.*** Add lines 143–146 of Fig. 12.14 to the body of `determineMaximum`. Line 143 creates the variable `temporary` to contain the maximum of the first two numbers passed to this method. This maximum is determined by using the **max** method of Java library class `Math`. This method takes two `double`s and returns the larger of the values. The value returned by the `max` method is assigned to the variable `temporary`. Line 144 then compares that value to the `determineMaximum` method's third parameter, `three`. The maximum determined in this line, `maximumValue`, is the maximum of the three values. The `return` statement terminates execution of the method and returns the value of variable `maximumValue` to the calling method. The result is returned to the point (line 133 of Fig. 12.12) where the `determineMaximum` method was called.

Calling `Math.max` twice
to determine the
maximum of three values

Return maximum
of all three values

```
142         {
143             double temporary = Math.max( one, two );
144             double maximumValue = Math.max( temporary, three );
145
146             return maximumValue;
147
```

Figure 12.14 `Math.max` returns the larger of its two arguments.

10. ***Saving the application.*** Save your modified source code file.

11. ***Opening the Command Prompt window and changing directories.*** Open the **Command Prompt** window by selecting **Start > Programs > Accessories > Command Prompt**. Change to your working directory by typing `cd C:\SimplyJava\Maximum`.

12. ***Compiling the application.*** Compile your application by typing `javac Maximum.java`.

13. ***Running the application.*** When your application compiles correctly, run it by typing `java Maximum`. Figure 12.15 shows the completed application running. Test the application by entering the values 2, 34 and 5 in the JTextFields. Notice that the largest value, `34.0`, is displayed in the **Maximum:** JTextField after the **Maximum** JButton is clicked. You should now enter several sets of values, making sure to enter the maximum value in each of the different input JTextFields. Notice that in each case, the application does indeed determine and display the correct maximum value.

(cont.)

Figure 12.15 **Maximum** application executing.

14. *Closing the application*. Close your running application by clicking its close button.

15. *Closing the Command Prompt window*. Close the **Command Prompt** window by clicking its close button.

You have now completed the **Maximum** application. Notice that you can easily modify this application to take and return `int` data. To do this, you will need to store user input in `int` variables (using `Integer.parseInt` instead of `Double.parseDouble`). You will also need to modify the header of the `determineMaximum` method to take three `ints` and return an `int`. In the body of the `determineMaximum` method, store the return values of the calls to the `Math.max` method in `int` variables. Finally, make sure that the returned value of the `determineMaximum` method is stored in an `int` variable.

SELF-REVIEW

1. The _____ method returns the larger of its two arguments.
   a) `max`   b) `maximum`
   c) `larger`   d) `greater`

2. The _____ is sent to a method when it is called.
   a) return value   b) return type
   c) parameter list   d) argument list

Answers: 1) a. 2) d.

12.5 Using Methods in the Wage Calculator Application

The `calculateJButtonActionPerformed` method in the original version of the **Wage Calculator** application (Tutorial 6) calculated the wages and displayed the result in a `JTextField`. Next, you will write the `calculatePay` method to calculate the user's wages. When the user clicks the **Calculate** JButton, the `calculateJButtonActionPerformed` method will call the `calculatePay` method. By taking one piece of the application's functionality and placing it in a method, you will successfully divide the **Wage Calculator** application into smaller, more manageable pieces. Using the divide-and-conquer technique provides several advantages. You can now more easily isolate errors in your application making it easier to debug. For instance, if the final application does not correctly calculate the user's pay, you know that the problem lies within either the `calculatePay` method or the call to the `calculatePay` method. There is no need to look at the other statements in the application, as they are not related to the calculation of the user's pay. Another advantage is reuseability. You will create a method that can be called several times,

if you should wish to modify the application to calculate several sets of wages. All you need to do is call the `calculatePay` method with the correct arguments.

Creating a Method within the Wage Calculator Application

1. ***Copying the template to your working directory.*** Copy the `C:\Examples\Tutorial12\TemplateApplication\WageCalculator2` directory to your `C:\SimplyJava` directory.

2. ***Opening the Wage Calculator application's template file.*** Open the template file `WageCalculator.java` in your text editor.

3. ***Coding the `calculateJButtonActionPerformed` method.*** Add lines 111–126 of Fig. 12.16 to the empty `calculateJButtonActionPerformed` method. Lines 111–117 retrieve the user input from the `JTextField`s and assign the values to the variables `hourlyWage` and `hoursWorked`. Line 120 calls the `calculatePay` method, which you will declare shortly. This method takes two arguments–the hours worked and the hourly wage. Notice that the method's arguments in this example are variables. Arguments also can be constants or expressions.

Store the user input ———

Call to method `calculatePay` ———

Format and display the total wage ———

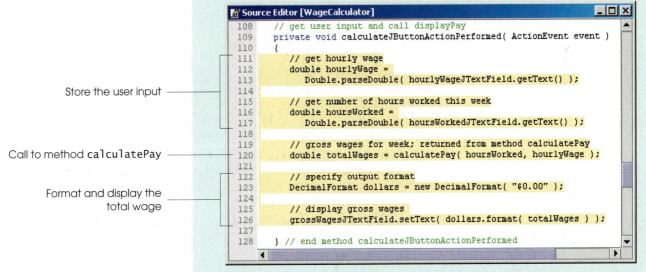

```
108      // get user input and call displayPay
109      private void calculateJButtonActionPerformed( ActionEvent event )
110      {
111          // get hourly wage
112          double hourlyWage =
113              Double.parseDouble( hourlyWageJTextField.getText() );
114
115          // get number of hours worked this week
116          double hoursWorked =
117              Double.parseDouble( hoursWorkedJTextField.getText() );
118
119          // gross wages for week; returned from method calculatePay
120          double totalWages = calculatePay( hoursWorked, hourlyWage );
121
122          // specify output format
123          DecimalFormat dollars = new DecimalFormat( "$0.00" );
124
125          // display gross wages
126          grossWagesJTextField.setText( dollars.format( totalWages ) );
127
128      } // end method calculateJButtonActionPerformed
```

Figure 12.16 `calculateJButtonActionPerformed` calls the `calculatePay` method.

4. ***Creating a method.*** Add the `calculatePay` method to your application (lines 130–155 of Fig. 12.17) after the `calculateJButtonActionPerformed` method.

    The `calculatePay` method receives the argument values and stores them in the parameters `hours` and `wages`. Lines 141–151 declare an `if...else` statement that determines the employee's pay based on the amount of hours worked. The condition for this statement determines whether `hours` is less than or equal to the `HOUR_LIMIT` constant. If it is, then the employee's earnings without overtime are calculated. Otherwise, the employee's earnings including overtime are calculated.

    When the return statement in line 153 is encountered, control is returned to the calling method, `calculateJButtonActionPerformed` (line 120 in Fig. 12.16). The result is stored in variable `totalWages`. In line 126 of Fig. 12.16, the result (formatted as currency) is displayed in the `grossWagesJTextField`.

Software Design Tip

The method header and method call must agree with regard to the number, type and order of parameters.

Common Programming Error

Declaring a variable in the method's body with the same name as a parameter in the method header is a syntax error.

(cont.)

Method header ⎯

Calculate gross wages based on the number of hours worked ⎯

Return the wages for the week ⎯

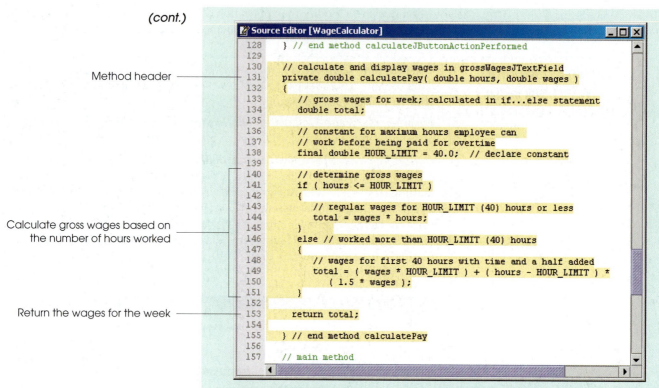

```
128        } // end method calculateJButtonActionPerformed
129
130        // calculate and display wages in grossWagesJTextField
131        private double calculatePay( double hours, double wages )
132        {
133            // gross wages for week; calculated in if...else statement
134            double total;
135
136            // constant for maximum hours employee can
137            // work before being paid for overtime
138            final double HOUR_LIMIT = 40.0;  // declare constant
139
140            // determine gross wages
141            if ( hours <= HOUR_LIMIT )
142            {
143                // regular wages for HOUR_LIMIT (40) hours or less
144                total = wages * hours;
145            }
146            else // worked more than HOUR_LIMIT (40) hours
147            {
148                // wages for first 40 hours with time and a half added
149                total = ( wages * HOUR_LIMIT ) + ( hours - HOUR_LIMIT ) *
150                    ( 1.5 * wages );
151            }
152
153            return total;
154
155        } // end method calculatePay
156
157        // main method
```

Figure 12.17   Declaring the `calculatePay` method.

5. *Saving the application*. Save your modified source code file.

6. *Opening the Command Prompt window and changing directories*. Open the **Command Prompt** window by selecting **Start > Programs > Accessories > Command Prompt**. Change to your working directory by typing `cd C:\SimplyJava\WageCalculator2`.

7. *Compiling the application*. Compile your application by typing `javac WageCalculator.java`.

8. *Running the application.* When your application compiles correctly, run it by typing `java WageCalculator`. Figure 12.18 shows the completed application running. Enter 10 in the **Hourly Wage:** JTextField, enter 45 in the **Hours worked:** JTextField, then press the **Calculate** JButton to test the application. The result (`$475.00`) is displayed in the **Gross wages:** JTextField.

Figure 12.18   **WageCalculator** application executing.

9. *Closing the application*. Close your running application by clicking its close button.

10. *Closing the Command Prompt window*. Close the **Command Prompt** window by clicking its close button.

Figure 12.19 presents the source code for the **Wage Calculator** application. The lines of code that you added, viewed or modified in this tutorial are highlighted.

```java
1   // Tutorial 12: WageCalculator.java
2   // This application inputs the hourly wage and number of hours
3   // worked for an employee, then calculates the employee's gross
4   // wages (with overtime for hours worked over 40 hours).
5   import java.awt.*;
6   import java.awt.event.*;
7   import javax.swing.*;
8   import java.text.*;
9
10  public class WageCalculator extends JFrame
11  {
12     // JLabel and JTextField for wage per hour
13     private JLabel hourlyWageJLabel;
14     private JTextField hourlyWageJTextField;
15
16     // JLabel and JTextField for hours worked in a week
17     private JLabel hoursWorkedJLabel;
18     private JTextField hoursWorkedJTextField;
19
20     // JLabel and JTextField for gross wages
21     private JLabel grossWagesJLabel;
22     private JTextField grossWagesJTextField;
23
24     // JButton to initiate wage calculation
25     private JButton calculateJButton;
26
27     // no-argument constructor
28     public WageCalculator()
29     {
30        createUserInterface();
31     }
32
33     // create and position GUI components; register event handlers
34     public void createUserInterface()
35     {
36        // get content pane for attaching GUI components
37        Container contentPane = getContentPane();
38
39        // enable explicit positioning of GUI components
40        contentPane.setLayout( null );
41
42        // set up hourlyWageJLabel
43        hourlyWageJLabel = new JLabel();
44        hourlyWageJLabel.setBounds( 16, 16, 90, 21 );
45        hourlyWageJLabel.setText( "Hourly wage:" );
46        contentPane.add( hourlyWageJLabel );
47
48        // set up hourlyWageJTextField
49        hourlyWageJTextField = new JTextField();
50        hourlyWageJTextField.setBounds( 120, 16, 90, 21 );
51        hourlyWageJTextField.setHorizontalAlignment(
52           JTextField.RIGHT );
53        contentPane.add( hourlyWageJTextField );
54
```

Figure 12.19 Enhanced **WageCalculator** code. (Part 1 of 3.)

```
55          // set up hoursWorkedJLabel
56          hoursWorkedJLabel = new JLabel();
57          hoursWorkedJLabel.setBounds( 16, 56, 90, 21 );
58          hoursWorkedJLabel.setText( "Hours worked:" );
59          contentPane.add( hoursWorkedJLabel );
60
61          // set up hoursWorkedJTextField
62          hoursWorkedJTextField = new JTextField();
63          hoursWorkedJTextField.setBounds( 120, 56, 90, 21 );
64          hoursWorkedJTextField.setHorizontalAlignment(
65             JTextField.RIGHT );
66          contentPane.add( hoursWorkedJTextField );
67
68          // set up grossWagesJLabel
69          grossWagesJLabel = new JLabel();
70          grossWagesJLabel.setBounds( 16, 96, 90, 21 );
71          grossWagesJLabel.setText( "Gross wages:" );
72          contentPane.add( grossWagesJLabel );
73
74          // set up grossWagesJTextField
75          grossWagesJTextField = new JTextField();
76          grossWagesJTextField.setBounds( 120, 96, 90, 21 );
77          grossWagesJTextField.setHorizontalAlignment(
78             JTextField.RIGHT );
79          grossWagesJTextField.setEditable( false );
80          contentPane.add( grossWagesJTextField );
81
82          // set up calculateJButton
83          calculateJButton = new JButton();
84          calculateJButton.setBounds( 120, 136, 90, 24 );
85          calculateJButton.setText( "Calculate" );
86          contentPane.add( calculateJButton );
87          calculateJButton.addActionListener(
88
89             new ActionListener() // anonymous inner class
90             {
91                // event handler called when calculateJButton clicked
92                public void actionPerformed ( ActionEvent event )
93                {
94                   calculateJButtonActionPerformed( event );
95                }
96
97             } // end anonymous inner class
98
99          ); // end call to addActionListener
100
101         // set properties of application's window
102         setTitle( "Wage Calculator" ); // set title bar string
103         setSize( 230, 200 );           // set window size
104         setVisible( true );            // display window
105
106      } // end method createUserInterface
107
```

Figure 12.19 Enhanced **WageCalculator** code. (Part 2 of 3.)

```
108        // get user input and call calculatePay
109        private void calculateJButtonActionPerformed( ActionEvent event )
110        {
111           // get hourly wage
112           double hourlyWage =
113              Double.parseDouble( hourlyWageJTextField.getText() );
114
115           // get number of hours worked this week
116           double hoursWorked =
117              Double.parseDouble( hoursWorkedJTextField.getText() );
118
119           // gross wages for week; returned from method calculatePay
120           double totalWages = calculatePay( hoursWorked, hourlyWage );
121
122           // specify output format
123           DecimalFormat dollars = new DecimalFormat( "$0.00" );
124
125           // display gross wages
126           grossWagesJTextField.setText( dollars.format( totalWages ) );
127
128        } // end method calculateJButtonActionPerformed
129
130        // calculate and display wages in grossWagesJTextField
131        private double calculatePay( double hours, double wages )
132        {
133           // gross wages for week; calculated in if...else statement
134           double total;
135
136           // constant for maximum hours employee can
137           // work before being paid for overtime
138           final double HOUR_LIMIT = 40.0;   // declare constant
139
140           // determine gross wages
141           if ( hours <= HOUR_LIMIT )
142           {
143              // regular wages for HOUR_LIMIT (40) hours or less
144              total = wages * hours;
145           }
146           else // worked more than HOUR_LIMIT (40) hours
147           {
148              // wages for first 40 hours with time and a half added
149              total = ( wages * HOUR_LIMIT ) + ( hours - HOUR_LIMIT ) *
150                 ( 1.5 * wages );
151           }
152
153           return total;
154
155        } // end method calculatePay
156
157        // main method
158        public static void main( String[] args )
159        {
160           WageCalculator application = new WageCalculator();
161           application.setDefaultCloseOperation( JFrame.EXIT_ON_CLOSE );
162
163        } // end method main
164
165     } // end class WageCalculator
```

Labels (left margin annotations):

- Storing user input → (lines 111–117)
- Calling method `calculatePay` → (line 120)
- Formatting and displaying value returned from the `calculatePay` method → (lines 122–126)
- Method `calculatePay` takes two **double** parameters, returns a **double** → (line 131)
- Variable **total** will contain user's wages for the week → (line 134)
- Overtime for more than 40 hours worked → (line 138)
- Calculating wages based on the number of hours worked → (lines 140–151)
- Returning **total** to calling method → (line 153)
- Closing brace ends method body → (line 155)

Figure 12.19 Enhanced **WageCalculator** code. (Part 3 of 3.)

1. Arguments to a method can be _____.

    a) constants   b) expressions

    c) variables   d) All of the above.

2. The _____ is a comma-separated list of declarations in a method header.

    a) argument list   b) parameter list

    c) value list   d) variable list

Answers: 1) d. 2) b.

12.6 Using the Debugger: Controlling Execution Using the `step`, `step up` and `next` Commands

In earlier tutorials, you learned how to debug your applications by setting breakpoints and either printing or setting values at those breakpoints. You also learned how to use the `cont` command to execute a set of statements. Often, however, you will want to walk through the application line by line to find and fix errors. In this section, you will learn how to use the debugger for this task. Walking through a portion of your application line by line can be useful to verify that a method's code is executing correctly. The statements you will learn in this section allow you to walk through the execution of a method line by line, execute all the statements of a method at once or execute only the remaining statements of a method (if you have already executed some statements within the method).

Using the Debugger: Controlling Execution Using the `step`, `step up` and `next` Commands

1. ***Opening the Command Prompt window and changing directories.*** Open the **Command Prompt** window by selecting **Start > Programs > Accessories > Command Prompt**. Change to your working directory by typing `cd C:\SimplyJava\WageCalculator2`.

2. ***Compiling the application for debugging.*** Compile your application by typing `javac -g WageCalculator.java`.

3. ***Starting the debugger.*** Start the debugger by typing `jdb`.

4. ***Setting a breakpoint.*** Type `stop at WageCalculator:120` to set a breakpoint at line 120 (Fig. 12.20).

Starting the debugger ⟶

Setting a breakpoint ⟶

```
Command Prompt - jdb

C:\>cd C:\SimplyJava\WageCalculator2

C:\SimplyJava\WageCalculator2>javac -g WageCalculator.java

C:\SimplyJava\WageCalculator2>jdb
Initializing jdb ...
> stop at WageCalculator:120
Deferring breakpoint WageCalculator:120.
It will be set after the class is loaded.
>
```

Figure 12.20 Setting a breakpoint in the **Wage Calculator** application.

5. ***Running the application.*** Run the application by typing `run WageCalculator` (Fig. 12.21).

(cont.)

Running the application ⎯⎯⎯

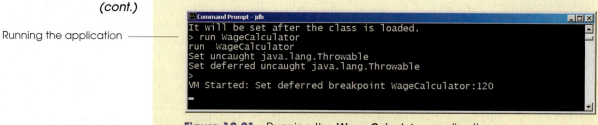

Figure 12.21 Running the **Wage Calculator** application.

6. ***Reaching the breakpoint.*** Enter the value 7.50 in the **Hourly wage:** JTextField and enter the value 35 in the **Hours worked:** JTextField. Click the **Calculate** JButton (Fig. 12.22). The calculateJButtonActionPerformed method executes, reaching the breakpoint at line 120. The debugger indicates that the breakpoint has been reached and displays the line of code for you (Fig. 12.22). The debugger and application then pause and wait for the next command to be entered in the **Command Prompt**.

Reaching a breakpoint ⎯⎯⎯

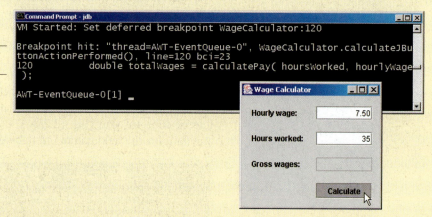

Figure 12.22 Reaching the breakpoint in the **Wage Calculator** application.

7. ***Using the step command.*** The **step** command executes the next statement in the application. If the next statement to execute is a method call and the step command is used, control is transferred to the called method. The step command is for entering a method and studying the individual statements of that method, using jdb commands. For instance, you can use the print and set commands to view and modify the variables within the method. You will now use the step command to enter the calculatePay method by typing step (Fig. 12.23). The debugger indicates that the step has been completed and displays the next executable statement—in this case, line 138. Recall that the first statement of the calculatePay method (double total;) is located in line 134. jdb does not consider declarations that do not include an initialization to be executable statements. Therefore, the step command pauses execution at line 138 rather than line 134.

Stepping through an application ⎯⎯⎯

Application currently paused at line 138 in method calculatePay ⎯⎯⎯

```
Command Prompt - jdb                                          _ □ ×
AWT-EventQueue-0[1] step
>
Step completed: "thread=AWT-EventQueue-0", WageCalculator.calculatePay
(), line=138 bci=0
138              final double HOUR_LIMIT = 40.0;  // declare constant

AWT-EventQueue-0[1] _
```

Figure 12.23 Stepping into the **calculatePay** method.

(cont.)

8. ***Using the step up command.*** After you have stepped into the `calculate-Pay` method, type **step up**. This command executes the statements in the method and returns control to the place where the method was called. Thus, the next action to occur will be assigning the value returned from `calculatePay` to variable `totalWages` (Fig. 12.24). In lengthy methods, you will often want to look at a few key lines of code then continue debugging the caller's code. The `step up` command is useful for such situations, where you do not want to continue stepping through the entire method line by line.

Execute remaining statements in the current method ——————

```
138          final double HOUR_LIMIT = 40.0;  // declare constant

AWT-EventQueue-0[1] step up
>
Step completed: "thread=AWT-EventQueue-0", WageCalculator.calculateJBu
ttonActionPerformed(), line=120 bci=30
120          double totalWages = calculatePay( hoursWorked, hourlyWage
);

AWT-EventQueue-0[1]
```

Figure 12.24   Stepping out of a method.

9. ***Using the cont command and reaching the breakpoint again.*** Enter the cont command by typing `cont` (Fig. 12.25). In the **Wage Calculator** application, click the **Calculate** JButton. The `calculateJButtonActionPerformed` method executes again, reaching the breakpoint at line 120. The debugger indicates that the breakpoint has been reached and displays the line of code for you (Fig. 12.25). The debugger and application then pause and wait for the next command to be entered in the **Command Prompt**.

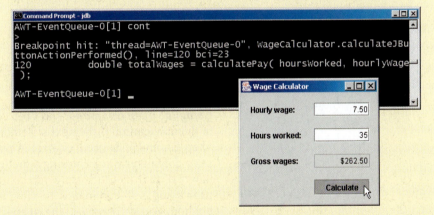

Figure 12.25   Reaching the breakpoint in the **Wage Calculator** application.

10. ***Using the next command.*** Type **next**. This command behaves like the `step` command, except when the next statement to execute contains a method call. Recall from *Step 7* that the `step` command allows you to enter a method when the next statement to execute is a method call. When using the `next` command in such a situation, however, the called method executes in its entirety (without transferring control and entering the method) and the application advances to the next executable line after the method call (Fig. 12.26).

(cont.)

Using the **next** command ————

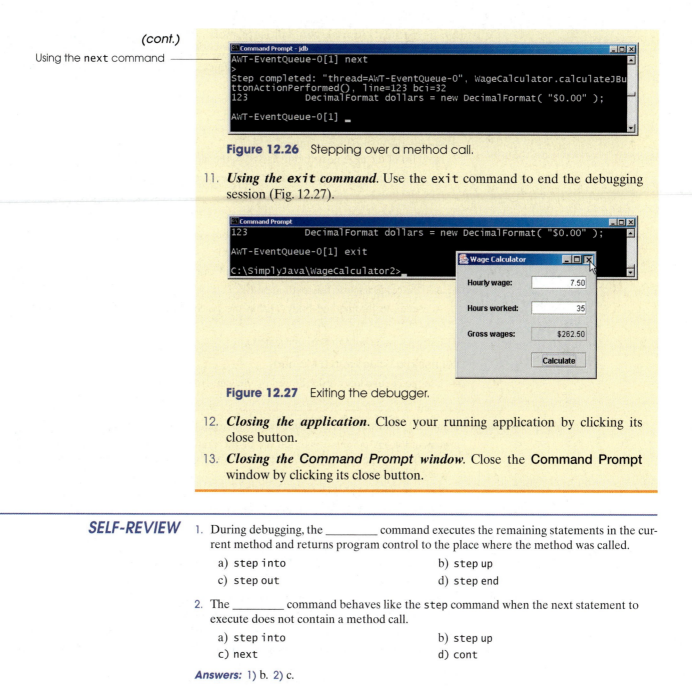

Figure 12.26 Stepping over a method call.

11. ***Using the exit command.*** Use the **exit** command to end the debugging session (Fig. 12.27).

Figure 12.27 Exiting the debugger.

12. ***Closing the application.*** Close your running application by clicking its close button.

13. ***Closing the Command Prompt window.*** Close the **Command Prompt** window by clicking its close button.

SELF-REVIEW

1. During debugging, the _____ command executes the remaining statements in the current method and returns program control to the place where the method was called.

   a) step into   b) step up
   c) step out   d) step end

2. The _____ command behaves like the step command when the next statement to execute does not contain a method call.

   a) step into   b) step up
   c) next   d) cont

Answers: 1) b. 2) c.

12.7 Wrap-Up

In this tutorial, you learned about methods and how they can be used to better organize an application. You learned about the concept of code reuse, where time and effort can be saved by using pre-existing code. You used pre-existing methods provided by the Java class library and learned to create your own methods.

You learned the syntax for declaring and invoking methods. You learned the components of a method, including the method header, the parameter list, the body and the return statement. You learned the order in which execution occurs—from the line where a method is called (invoked) to the method declaration, then back to the point of invocation. You created three programmer-declared methods—square, determineMaximum and calculatePay.

You learned debugger commands (including the step, next and step up commands) that you can use to determine whether a method is executing correctly.

In the next tutorial, you will learn more about event handling in Java, which requires declaring and calling a number of methods. You will also learn that to be able to handle events of a certain type of object, you must register an event handler, which you will do with a method call.

SKILLS SUMMARY

Invoking (Calling) a Method

■ Specify the method name, followed by a pair of parentheses that contain a comma-separated list of the arguments being passed to the method.

■ Ensure that the arguments passed match the method declaration's parameters in number, type and order.

Declaring a Method

■ Give the method a meaningful name, usually a verb that describes what the method does.

■ Place the return type before the method name.

■ Specify a parameter list declaring each parameter's name and type.

■ Add braces to enclose the method body.

■ Add code to the method body (within the braces add previously) to perform a specific task.

■ Return a value with the `return` statement.

Returning a Value From a Method

■ Use the `return` keyword followed by the value to be returned.

KEY TERMS

argument—Information that a method call sends to the called method.

argument list—A comma-separated list of the arguments sent to a method. The number, order and type of arguments must agree with the parameters in the method's parameter list.

callee—The method being called.

caller—The method that calls another method. Also known as the calling method.

code reuse—Using pre-existing code to save time, effort and money.

divide-and-conquer technique—The techniques of constructing large applications from small, manageable pieces to make development and maintenance of those applications easier.

invoke a method—Call a method.

`Math.max`—Returns the maximum of two argument values.

`Math.sqrt`—Returns the square root of the argument value.

method—An application block that performs a task. Methods are used to divide an application into smaller, more manageable pieces that can be called from multiple places within an application.

method body—The declarations and statements that appear between the braces after the method header. The method body contains statements that perform actions, generally by manipulating the parameters from the parameter list.

method call—Invokes a method, by specifying the method name and providing information (arguments) that the callee (the method being called) requires to perform its task.

method declaration—The method header followed by the method body.

method header—The beginning portion of a method (including the keyword `private`, the return type, the method name and the parameter list).

method name—The identifier for a method, which distinguishes one method from another. The method name follows the return type, can be any valid identifier and is used to call the method.

next (debugger command)—The debugger command used to execute the next statement in an application. The `next` command executes method calls in their entirety.

parameter—A variable declared in a method's parameter list. Values passed to a method are stored in that method's parameters and can be used within the method body.

parameter list—A comma-separated list in which a method declares each parameter's type and name.

programmer-declared method—A method created by a programmer to meet the unique needs of a particular application.

return statement—The statement that returns a value from a method. A `return` statement begins with the keyword `return`, followed by an expression.

return type—Type of the result returned from a method to its caller.

step (debugger command)—The debugger command used in the debugger to execute the next statement in an application. The step command steps into method calls, allowing users to execute the called method's statements line by line.

step up (debugger command)—The debugger command used to execute the remaining statements in the current method and move control to the location where the method was called.

void keyword—A return type that specifies that the method does not return any information.

JAVA LIBRARY REFERENCE

`Math` This class provides methods that perform common arithmetic calculations.

■ *Methods*

`min`—Returns the smaller of two numeric arguments.

`max`—Returns the larger of two numeric arguments.

`sqrt`—Returns the square root of a numeric argument.

MULTIPLE-CHOICE QUESTIONS

12.1 A method declaration is made up of _____.

     a) a method header   b) a method body

     c) braces   d) All of the above.

12.2 The technique of developing large applications from small, manageable pieces is known as _____.

     a) divide and conquer   b) counter-controlled repetition

     c) debugging   d) GUI development

12.3 Variables in the parentheses after the method name in a method call are known as _____.

     a) arguments   b) parameters

     c) statements   d) declarations

12.4 What occurs after a method call?

     a) Control is given to the called method. After the method is run, the application continues execution at the point where the method was called.

     b) Control is given to the called method. After the method is run, the application continues execution with the statement after the called method's declaration.

     c) The statement before the method call is executed.

     d) The application terminates.

12.5 How many values can a `return` statement return to a caller?

     a) zero   b) one

     c) any number   d) Both a and b.

12.6 Which of the following must be true when making a method call?

     a) The number of arguments in the method call must match the number of parameters in the method header.

     b) The argument types must be compatible with their corresponding parameter types.

     c) Both a and b.   d) None of the above.

12.7 Which of the following statements correctly returns the `int` variable `value` from a method?

a) `return value();`   b) `return int value;`

c) `value return;`   d) `return value;`

12.8 The _____ debugger command executes the remaining statements in the current method and returns control to the caller.

a) `step up`   b) `step into`

c) `step`   d) `cont`

12.9 The first line of a method (including the method name, the parameter list and the method return type) is known as the method _____.

a) body   b) title

c) caller   d) header

12.10 Method _____ of class `Math` calculates the square root of the value passed as an argument.

a) `squareRoot`   b) `root`

c) `sqrt`   d) `square`

EXERCISES

12.11 (*Temperature Converter Application*) Write an application that performs two types of temperature conversions: degrees Fahrenheit to degrees Celsius and degrees Celsius to degrees Fahrenheit. Your output should look like Fig. 12.28.

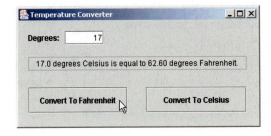

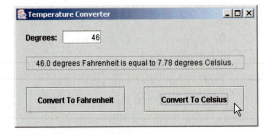

Figure 12.28 Temperature Converter GUI.

a) *Copying the template to your working directory.* Copy the `C:\Examples\Tutorial12\Exercises\TemperatureConverter` directory to your `C:\SimplyJava` directory.

b) *Opening the template file.* Open the `TemperatureConverter.java` file in your text editor.

c) *Adding a method to your application to convert from Celsius to Fahrenheit.* In line 147, add a comment indicating that the method will convert the temperature from Celsius to Fahrenheit. In line 148, add the method header for this method. The method will be called `convertToFahrenheit`. This method returns a value of type `double` and takes an argument of type `double`. Name the `double` parameter `degree`. In line 149, add a left brace to begin the body of the method. In line 150, add a return statement that performs the conversion calculation. To do this, follow the `return` keyword with the following expression:

```
( 9.0 / 5.0 ) * degree + 32.0;
```

In line 152, add the right brace to end the body of the method. Follow the brace with a comment indicating the end of this method. Leave line 151 blank for readability.

d) ***Adding a method to your application to convert the temperature from Fahrenheit to Celsius.*** In line 154, add a comment indicating that the method will convert from Fahrenheit to Celsius and in line 155, add the method header for this method. The method will be called `convertToCelsius`. This method returns a value of type `double` and takes an argument of type `double`. Name the `double` parameter `degree`. In line 156, add a left brace to begin the body of the method. In line 157, add a `return` statement that performs the conversion calculation. To do this, follow the `return` keyword with the following expression:

```
( 5.0 / 9.0 ) * ( degree - 32.0 );
```

In line 159, add the right brace to end the body of the method. Follow the brace with a comment indicating the end of this method. Leave line 158 blank for readability.

e) ***Invoking method `convertToFahrenheit`.*** You will now invoke the `convertToFahrenheit` method and store the result in variable `convertedDegree`, to be displayed in `outputJTextField`. In line 115, replace `0.00` with a call to method `convertToFahrenheit`. Pass variable `degreeCelsius` to the `convertToFahrenheit` method. Variable `degreeCelsius` contains the degrees entered by user, converted to a `double` (lines 111–112).

f) ***Invoking method `convertToCelsius`.*** You will now invoke the `convertToCelsius` method and store the result in variable `convertedDegree`, to be displayed in `outputJTextField`. In line 137, replace `0.00` with a call to the `convertToCelsius` method. Pass variable `degreeFahrenheit` to the `convertToCelsius` method. Variable `degreeFahrenheit` contains the degrees entered by user, converted to `double` (lines 133–134).

g) ***Saving the application.*** Save your modified source code file.

h) ***Opening the Command Prompt window and changing directories.*** Open the **Command Prompt** window by selecting **Start > Programs > Accessories > Command Prompt**. Change to your working directory by typing `cd C:\SimplyJava\TemperatureConverter`.

i) ***Compiling the application.*** Compile your application by typing `javac TemperatureConverter.java`.

j) ***Running the completed application.*** When your application compiles correctly, run it by typing `java TemperatureConverter`. Test the application by entering different degree values and by pressing both the **Convert To Fahrenheit** and **Convert To Celsius** `JButtons`. View the output to ensure that the input is being converted correctly.

k) ***Closing the application.*** Close your running application by clicking its close button.

l) ***Closing the Command Prompt window.*** Close the **Command Prompt** window by clicking its close button.

12.12 *(Display Square Application)* Write an application that displays a solid square composed of a character input by the user (Fig. 12.29). The user also should input the size of the side of the square.

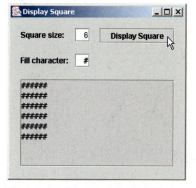

Figure 12.29 Display Square application.

a) *Copying the template to your working directory.* Copy the C:\Examples\ Tutorial12\Exercises\DisplaySquare directory to your C:\SimplyJava directory.

b) *Opening the template file.* Open the DisplaySquare.java file in your text editor.

c) *Adding a method to your application that displays a square of characters.* In line 141, add a comment indicating that the method will display a square in a JTextArea. In line 142, add the method header for this method. The method will be called displaySquare. This method contains two parameters–the first, of type int, should be called size, the second, of type String, should be called character. This method does not return a value, but simply performs a task (displaying a square). For such methods, the return type is specified as void. Specify the return type for display-Square as void. In line 143, add a left brace to begin the body of the method. In line 145, add the right brace to end the body of the method. Follow the brace with a comment indicating the end of this method. You will add functionality to this method in the next step.

d) *Adding functionality to method displaySquare.* Copy (but do not remove) the code from lines 118–130. Paste this code into lines 144–156. This code contains the functionality needed to display the square. Now that this code has been placed within its own method, you will need to replace the variables used with the parameters of this method. In lines 147 and 150, replace squareSize with size. In line 152, replace fillCharacter with character.

e) *Invoking the displaySquare method.* Now that you have placed the logic for displaying a square within the displaySquare method, you can replace the original functionality with a call to method displaySquare. Replace lines 118–130 with a call to the displaySquare method and pass to this method the size of the square and the fill character as entered by the user. The data entered by the user has been stored in variables for you on lines 114–116.

f) *Saving the application.* Save your modified source code file.

g) *Opening the Command Prompt window and changing directories.* Open the **Command Prompt** window by selecting **Start > Programs > Accessories > Command Prompt**. Change to your working directory by typing cd C:\SimplyJava\Display-Square.

h) *Compiling the application.* Compile your application by typing javac Display-Square.java.

i) *Running the completed application.* When your application compiles correctly, run it by typing java DisplaySquare. Test your application by entering various values for the size and fill character of the square. For each set of input, press the **Display Square** JButton and ensure that the square displayed is the correct size and made up of the correct character.

j) *Closing the application.* Close your running application by clicking its close button.

k) *Closing the Command Prompt window.* Close the **Command Prompt** window by clicking its close button.

12.13 (*Miles Per Gallon Application*) Drivers often want to know the miles per gallon their cars get so they can estimate gasoline costs. Develop an application that allows the user to input the number of miles driven and the number of gallons used for a tank of gas (Fig. 12.30).

Figure 12.30 **Miles Per Gallon** application.

a) *Copying the template to your working directory.* Copy the C:\Examples\ Tutorial12\Exercises\MilesPerGallon directory to your C:\SimplyJava directory.

b) *Opening the template file.* Open the MilesPerGallon.java file in your text editor.

c) *Adding a method to calculate miles per gallon.* In line 124, add a comment indicating that the method will calculate the amount of miles per gallon. In lines 125–126, add the method header for this method (use two lines for readability). The method will be called milesPerGallon. This method returns a value of type double and takes two arguments of type double. Name the first double parameter milesDriven and the second parameter gallonsUsed. In line 127, add a left brace to begin the body of the method. In line 128, add a return statement that performs the calculation. To do this, follow the return keyword with the following expression:

```
milesDriven / gallonsUsed;
```

In line 130, add the right brace to end the body of the method. Follow the brace with a comment indicating the end of this method. Leave line 129 blank for readability.

d) *Invoking method milesPerGallon.* Lines 119–120 display the value 0.00 in the milesPerGallonJTextField. You will now call the milesPerGallon method to display the proper miles per gallon, based on the user's input. In line 120, replace 0.00 with a call to the milesPerGallon method. Use the variables created in lines 113–116 to pass this method, the miles driven and gallons used, as specified by the user.

e) *Saving the application.* Save your modified source code file.

f) *Opening the Command Prompt window and changing directories.* Open the **Command Prompt** window by selecting **Start > Programs > Accessories > Command Prompt**. Change to your working directory by typing cd C:\SimplyJava\MilesPerGallon.

g) *Compiling the application.* Compile your application by typing javac MilesPerGallon.java.

h) *Running the completed application.* When your application compiles correctly, run it by typing java MilesPerGallon. Test your application by entering various values for the number of miles driven and gallons used. For each set of input, press the **Calculate MPG** JButton and view the output to ensure that it is correct.

i) *Closing the application.* Close your running application by clicking its close button.

j) *Closing the Command Prompt window.* Close the **Command Prompt** window by clicking its close button.

What does this code do? ▶ **12.14** What does the following code do? Assume this method is invoked by the method call mystery(70, 80). What value is returned from this method call?

```
1    private int mystery( int number1, int number2 )
2    {
3       int x;
4       int y;
5
6       x = number1 + number2;
7       y = x / 2;
8
9       if ( y <= 60 )
10      {
11         return x;
12      }
13      else
14      {
15         return y;
16      }
17
18   } // end method mystery
```

What's wrong with this code? ▶

12.15 Find the error(s) in the following code, which should take an `int` value as an argument and return the value of that argument multiplied by `2.5`. The value returned should be a `double`.

```
1   private int timesTwo( number )
2   {
3      double result;
4
5      result = number * 2.5;
6
7   } // end method timesTwo
```

Using the Debugger ▶

12.16 (*Gas Pump Application*) The **Gas Pump** application (Fig. 12.31) calculates the cost of gas at a local gas station. This gas station charges `$1.61` per gallon for **Regular** grade gas, `$1.67` per gallon for **Special** grade gas and `$1.77` per gallon for **Super+** grade gas. The user enters the number of gallons to purchase and clicks the desired grade. The application calls a method to compute the total cost from the number of gallons entered and the selected grade. The application provided contains a logic error. In this exercise, you will find and fix the error.

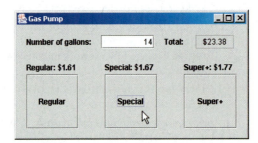

Figure 12.31 **Gas Pump** application running correctly.

a) *Copying the template to your working directory.* Copy the `C:\Examples\Tutorial12\Exercises\Debugging\GasPump` directory to your `C:\SimplyJava` directory.

b) *Opening the template file.* Open the `GasPump.java` file in your text editor.

c) *Compiling the application for debugging.* Compile the application with the `-g` command-line option by typing `javac -g GasPump.java`.

d) *Running the application.* Run the **Gas Pump** application by typing `java GasPump`. Enter 14 as the starting amount and click the **Special** `JButton`. Notice that the output is incorrect (the correct output is displayed in Fig. 12.31).

e) *Starting the debugger.* Close your application (but leave the **Command Prompt** open) and start the debugger by typing `jdb`.

f) *Finding and correcting the error(s).* Add a breakpoint at the beginning of the `specialJButtonActionPerformed` method. Use the `step`, `step up` and `next` commands as necessary to walk through the different statements of this method and any methods called from `specialJButtonActionPerformed`. You specifically want to walk through the `total` method when it is called from `specialJButtonActionPerformed`. Once you have found the error, modify the application so that it displays the correct message dialogs.

g) *Saving the application.* Save your modified source code file.

h) *Compiling the application.* Compile your application by typing `javac -g GasPump.java`.

i) *Running the completed application.* When your application compiles correctly, run it by typing `java GasPump`. Test the application using several different inputs and make sure the resulting output for each `JButton` is correct.

j) *Closing the application.* Close your running application by clicking its close button.

k) *Closing the Command Prompt window.* Close the **Command Prompt** window by clicking its close button.

Programming Challenge ▶

12.17 *(Prime Numbers Application)* An int greater than 1 is said to be prime if it is divisible by only 1 and itself. For example, 2, 3, 5 and 7 are prime numbers, but 4, 6, 8 and 9 are not. Write an application that takes two numbers (representing a lower bound and an upper bound) and determines all of the prime numbers within the specified bounds, inclusive. Your application should appear as in Fig. 12.32.

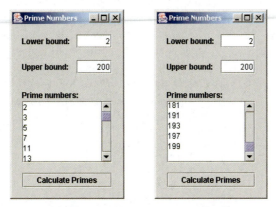

Figure 12.32   Prime Numbers application.

a) *Copying the template to your working directory.* Copy the C:\Examples\ Tutorial12\Exercises\PrimeNumbers directory to your C:\SimplyJava directory.

b) *Opening the template file.* Open the PrimeNumbers.java file in your text editor.

c) *Adding a method to determine if a number is prime.* In line 154, add a comment indicating that the method will determine if a number is a prime number. In line 155, add the method header for this method. The method will be called isPrime. This method returns a value of type boolean and takes an argument of type int. Name the parameter number. In line 156, add a left brace to begin the body of the method. In line 158, add the right brace to end the body of the method. Follow the brace with a comment indicating the end of this method. You will add functionality to this method in the next step.

d) *Dealing with the number 1.* The number 1 is not a prime number. On line 157, add a comment stating that 1 is not a valid prime number. On line 158, add an if statement to test whether the value of the parameter number is equal to 1. On line 159, start the if statement with a left brace. On line 160, return the boolean value false, indicating that 1 is not a prime number. On line 161, end the if statement with a right brace.

e) *Adding functionality to method isPrime.* The algorithm to determine if a number is prime is as follows: Find the square root of the number in question. Loop through the integers from 2 to the square root value. For each iteration of the loop, divide the number in question by the current value of the loop. If any of these divisions result in a remainder of 0, the number is not prime. If the loop finishes all iterations and none of the divisions have resulted in a remainder of 0, the number is prime. To implement this algorithm, in lines 157–158, declare int variable limit and assign to this variable the square root of number. Use line 157 for a comment and line 158 to declare and initialize limit. On lines 160–168, declare a for loop that iterates from the value 2 to limit and increments the counter by 1 with each iteration. In the body of the for loop, declare an if statement that executes when the value of number divided by the counter results in a remainder of 0. In the body of the if statement, use a return statement to return false from the method. Use comments and proper spacing so that the for statement runs from lines 160–168. On line 170, use a return statement to return true from the method.

f) *Invoking method isPrime.* Lines 138–148 loop from the lower bound to the upper bound, displaying every value in primeNumbersJTextArea in line 145. You will now

modify this code so that only the prime numbers are displayed. In line 143, replace `true` with a call to method `isPrime`. Pass to this method the current value in the `for` loop.

g) *Saving the application.* Save your modified source code file.

h) *Opening the Command Prompt window and changing directories.* Open the **Command Prompt** window by selecting **Start > Programs > Accessories > Command Prompt**. Change to your working directory by typing cd C:\SimplyJava\PrimeNumbers.

i) *Compiling the application.* Compile your application by typing javac PrimeNumbers.java.

j) *Running the completed application.* When your application compiles correctly, run it by typing java PrimeNumbers. Test your application by entering various lower and upper bounds. For each set of input, press the **Calculate Primes** JButton and view the output to ensure that it is correct.

k) *Closing the application.* Close your running application by clicking its close button.

l) *Closing the Command Prompt window.* Close the **Command Prompt** window by clicking its close button.

Enhancing the Interest Calculator Application

Introduction to Event Handling

Objectives

In this tutorial, you will learn to:
- Create an event handler.
- Understand how objects are used to represent events.
- Handle the **ChangeEvent** which is generated when the value in a **JSpinner** is changed.

Outline

In the previous tutorial, you learned about methods. In this tutorial, you will learn about event handlers, which are a special type of method. When the user interacts with a GUI-based application (such as by clicking a **JButton**), event objects are generated and sent to event handlers. You will also learn which type of event object is generated when the value in a **JSpinner** component is changed.

13.1 Test-Driving the Enhanced Interest Calculator Application

In this tutorial, you will enhance the **Interest Calculator** application that you created in Tutorial 10. This enhanced application must meet the following requirements:

Application Requirements

Recall the application requirements from Tutorial 10: You are considering investing in a savings account, and you want to determine how your investment will grow. Assuming that you will leave all interest on deposit, calculate and print the amount of money in your account at the end of each year over a period of n years. To compute these amounts, use the following formula:

$$a = p (1 + r/100)^n$$

where

p is the original amount of money invested (the principal)
r is the annual interest rate (for example, 5 is equivalent to 5%)
n is the number of years
a is the amount on deposit at the end of the nth year.

*The range of years is 1 to 10 and should be input with a **JSpinner**. Your application should clear the output when any of the input values change. It should also provide users with a **JButton** that, when clicked, causes the input **JTextFields** to be cleared and resets the value in the **JSpinner** to the initial value.*

The completed application has all the functionality of the application created in Tutorial 10. The updated application clears the output whenever the value in any of the components changes and also provides a **Clear** JButton to clear the components. You begin by test-driving the completed application. Then, you will learn the additional Java technologies you will need to create your own version of this application.

Test-Driving the Enhanced *Interest Calculator* **Application**

1. *Locating the completed application.* Open the **Command Prompt** window by selecting **Start > Programs > Accessories > Command Prompt**. Change to your completed **Interest Calculator** application directory by typing `cd C:\Examples\Tutorial13\CompletedApplication\Interest-Calculator2`.

2. *Running the Interest Calculator application.* Type `java InterestCalculator` in the **Command Prompt** window to run the application (Fig. 13.1).

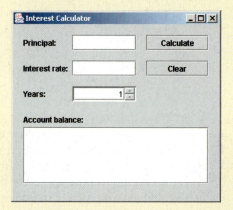

Figure 13.1   Running the **Interest Calculator** application.

3. *Entering values.* Enter the value 1000 in the **Principal:** JTextField and the value 5 in the **Interest rate:** JTextField, then click the **Calculate** JButton (Fig. 13.2).

Enter values in the components →

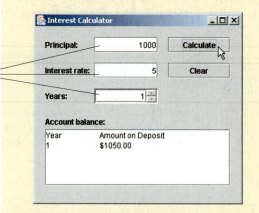

Figure 13.2   Entering values in the running **Interest Calculator** application.

4. *Editing the principal.* Change the value in the **Principal:** JTextField to 2000. The JTextArea is cleared (Fig. 13.3).

(cont.)

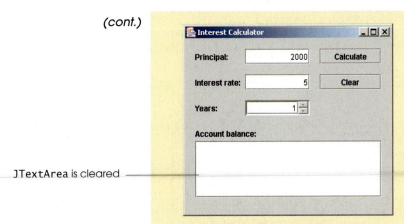

JTextArea is cleared ——————

Figure 13.3   Clearing the output.

5. ***Calculating the account balance.*** Click the **Calculate** JButton to update the JTextArea with the new principal (Fig. 13.4).

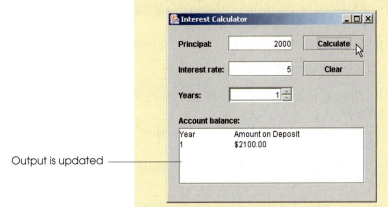

Output is updated ——————

Figure 13.4   Calculating the new account balance.

6. ***Editing the years.*** Press the up arrow in the **Years:** JSpinner. Notice that this also clears the JTextArea (Fig. 13.5).

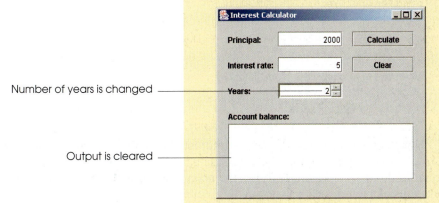

Number of years is changed ——————

Output is cleared ——————

Figure 13.5   Changing the value in a JSpinner.

7. ***Clearing the application.*** Click the **Clear** JButton. The principal and interest rate will be cleared and the year will be set to 1. The JTextArea will also be cleared (Fig. 13.6).

(cont.)

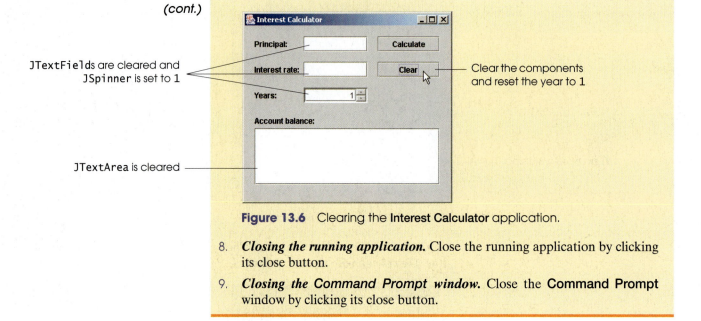

JTextFields are cleared and
JSpinner is set to 1

JTextArea is cleared

Clear the components
and reset the year to 1

Figure 13.6 Clearing the **Interest Calculator** application.

8. *Closing the running application.* Close the running application by clicking its close button.

9. *Closing the Command Prompt window.* Close the **Command Prompt** window by clicking its close button.

13.2 Event Handlers

The following pseudocode describes the basic operation of the **Interest Calculator** application:

> When the user clicks the Calculate JButton:
> >   Get the values for the principal, interest rate and years
> >   Display a header in the JTextArea to label the output
>
> >   For each year, starting at 1 and ending with the number of years entered,
> > >   Calculate the value of the investment
> > >   Display the year and the value of the investment
>
> When the user changes the value in the Years JSpinner
> >   Clear the JTextArea
>
> When the user types in the Principal JTextField:
> >   Clear the JTextArea
>
> When the user types in the Interest rate JTextField:
> >   Clear the JTextArea
>
> When the user clicks the Clear JButton:
> >   Clear the JTextArea
> >   Clear the JTextFields
> >   Reset the JSpinner to the default value

Now that you have test-driven the **Interest Calculator** application and studied its pseudocode representation, you will use an ACE table to help you convert the pseudocode to Java. Figure 13.7 lists the actions, components and events that will help you complete your own version of this application.

	Action	Component	Event
Action/Component/ Event (ACE) Table for the Interest Calculator Application	Label the application's fields	`interestRateJLabel,` `principalJLabel,` `yearsJLabel,` `yearlyBalanceJLabel`	
		`calculateJButton`	User clicks **Calculate** `JButton`
	Get values for principal, interest rate and years	`principalJTextField,` `interestRateJTextField,` `yearsJSpinner`	
	Display a header in the JTextArea to label the output	`yearlyBalanceJTextArea`	
	For each year, starting at 1 and ending with the number of years entered		
	Calculate the value of the investment		
	Display the year and the value of the investment	`yearlyBalanceJTextArea`	
		`yearsJSpinner`	User changes value in **Years:** `JSpinner`
	Clear the JTextArea	`yearlyBalanceJTextArea`	
		`principalJTextField`	User types in **Principal:** `JTextField`
	Clear the JTextArea	`yearlyBalanceJTextArea`	
		`rateJTextField`	User types in **Interest rate:** `JTextField`
	Clear the JTextArea	`yearlyBalanceJTextArea`	
		`clearJButton`	User clicks **Clear** `JButton`
	Clear the JTextArea	`yearlyBalanceJTextArea`	
	Clear the JTextFields	`principalJTextField,` `interestRateJTextField`	
	Reset the JSpinner to the default value	`yearsJSpinner`	

Figure 13.7   ACE table for **Interest Calculator** application.

GUI applications are **event driven**—they wait for certain actions (or **events**) such as the user clicking a JButton or editing a JTextField, that generate **event objects**. The applications then receive the event objects and respond to these actions. When the user is not interacting with the application, the application simply waits for the next action to occur.

In Tutorial 4, you learned that clicking a JButton generates an event object and calls a method named `actionPerformed`. Method `actionPerformed` is known as an **event handler**.

In the previous tutorial, you learned how to declare and call your own methods. Now you will explore Java's event-handling mechanism in more detail. You begin by completing the **Calculate** JButton's event handler.

Coding an `actionPerformed` Event Handler

1. *Copying the template to your working directory.* Copy the `C:\Examples\ Tutorial13\TemplateApplication\InterestCalculator2` directory to your `C:\SimplyJava` directory.

2. *Opening the Interest Calculator application's template file.* Open the template file `InterestCalculator.java` in your text editor.

(cont.)

3. **Viewing an event handler.** Consider lines 133–137 of Fig. 13.8. Line 134 is the method header for an event handler. This line declares an event handler named `actionPerformed`. This declaration uses the keyword void to specify that the method returns no value and takes a single parameter, an `ActionEvent` object which we call `event`. An **ActionEvent** object is the type of event object generated when a user clicks a `JButton`. You can use `ActionEvent` objects to get information about the event, such as the event source. You will learn how to do this in Tutorial 22. In later tutorials, you will learn about other types of event objects, including `KeyEvents` and `MouseEvents`. The keyword **public** in the method header is an access modifier. This modifier allows objects of other classes to access this event handler. You will learn more about classes and access modifiers in Tutorial 18.

Declaration of event handler `actionPerformed`

```
Source Editor [InterestCalculator *]                              _ □ ×
131            new ActionListener() // anonymous inner class
132            {
133                // event handler called when calculateJButton is clicked
134                public void actionPerformed( ActionEvent event )
135                {
136
137                }
138
139            } // end anonymous inner class
```

Figure 13.8 Examining `calculateJButton`'s `actionPerformed` event handler.

4. **Finishing the Calculate JButton event handler.** Finish the `actionPerformed` event handler by inserting line 136 of Fig. 13.9. This line of code calls the `calculateJButtonActionPerformed` method which contains the code that updates the `JTextArea` with the results of the interest calculations.

Call programmer-declared method

```
Source Editor [InterestCalculator *]                              _ □ ×
133                // event handler called when calculateJButton is clicked
134                public void actionPerformed( ActionEvent event )
135                {
136                    calculateJButtonActionPerformed( event );
137                }
```

Figure 13.9 Finishing `calculateJButton`'s `actionPerformed` event handler.

Notice that the code to update the `JTextArea` is placed in the `calculateJButtonActionPerformed` method and not directly in the event handler. Calling `calculateJButtonActionPerformed` to update the `JTextArea` makes the application easier to read by separating the code to handle the event (located in Fig. 13.9) from the code to process the event (located in `calculateJButtonActionPerformed`). The name of the method (`calculateJButtonActionPerformed`) makes it clear which component (`calculateJButton`) and event handler (`actionPerformed`) define the clicking of the **Calculate** `JButton`.

5. **Saving the application.** Save your modified source code file.

6. **Opening the Command Prompt window and changing directories.** Open the **Command Prompt** window by selecting **Start > Programs > Accessories > Command Prompt**. Change to your working directory by typing cd `C:\SimplyJava\InterestCalculator2`.

7. **Compiling the application.** Compile your application by typing javac `InterestCalculator.java`.

(cont.)   8. ***Running the application.*** When your application compiles correctly, run it by typing `java InterestCalculator`. Enter 1000 in the **Principal:** JText-Field and 5 in the **Interest rate:** JTextField. Click the **Calculate** JButton to update the JTextArea (Fig. 13.10). You have not declared event handlers for the **Clear** JButton or **Years:** JSpinner, so interacting with these two components will not have any effect on the application.

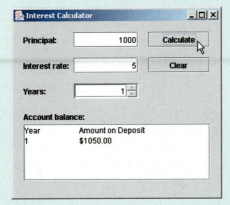

Figure 13.10   Running the updated **Interest Calculator** application.

9. ***Closing the application.*** Close the running application by clicking its close button.

10. ***Closing the Command Prompt window.*** Close the **Command Prompt** window by clicking its close button.

SELF-REVIEW   1. An event object is generated and passed to an _____ when certain user actions, such as clicking a JButton, are performed.

a) event driver   b) action method

c) event handler   d) action driver

2. ActionEvent objects are sent to event handler _____.

a) addChangeListener   b) addActionListener

c) stateChanged   d) actionPerformed

Answers: 1) c. 2) d.

13.3 Event Handler Registration

When an event object is generated (such as in response to a user clicking a JBut-ton), only appropriate event handlers for that event object will be called. The **Interest Calculator** application declares two JButtons and an `actionPerformed` event handler for each. Each event handler must be registered with its corresponding component. **Registering an event handler** with a component tells that component which event handler to call when a particular type of event object is generated. If a component does not have an appropriate event handler registered, then the application will not respond when the user interacts with that component. Next, you will code another event handler and learn how to register each event handler with its corresponding component.

Coding another actionPerformed Event Handler

1. **Finishing the second actionPerformed event handler.** Add line 155 of Fig. 13.11 to event handler actionPerformed. This line of code calls the clearJButtonActionPerformed method, which clears the values in the JTextFields, sets the JSpinner to 1 and clears the JTextArea.

Call programmer-declared method

```
Source Editor [InterestCalculator *]                          _ □ ×
152           // event handler called when clearJButton is clicked
153           public void actionPerformed( ActionEvent event )
154           {
155               clearJButtonActionPerformed( event );
156           }
```

Figure 13.11 Completing the clearJButton event handler.

2. **Registering the event handler.** Consider lines 148 and 160 of Fig. 13.12. Line 148 begins a call to the clearJButton.addActionListener method and line 160 ends the method call with a right parenthesis. The **addAction-Listener** method is used to register an event handler with a component. This method call registers the actionPerformed event handler declared on lines 153–156 with clearJButton. Now, when the user clicks the **Clear JButton**, this actionPerformed event handler is called.

   [*Note:* Part of setting up the event handler for a given GUI component is defining a special class called an anonymous inner class (lines 150–158). You will learn the details of anonymous inner classes in Tutorial 21 when you learn the remaining details of the event-handling mechanism.]

Register event handler for clearJButton

```
Source Editor [InterestCalculator *]                          _ □ ×
147        contentPane.add( clearJButton );
148        clearJButton.addActionListener(
149
150           new ActionListener() // anonymous inner class
151           {
152               // event handler called when clearJButton is clicked
153               public void actionPerformed( ActionEvent event )
154               {
155                   clearJButtonActionPerformed( event );
156               }
157
158           } // end anonymous inner class
159
160        ); // end call to addActionListener
161
```

Figure 13.12 Event handler registration for the clearJButton.

Lines 129 and 141 of Fig. 13.13 have a similar form. These lines begin and end a call to the calculateJButton.addActionListener method to register the actionPerformed event handler declared on lines 134–137 with calculateJButton.

3. **Declaring method clearJButtonActionPerformed.** Add lines 223–227 of Fig. 13.14 after the calculateJButtonActionPerformed method. These lines declare the clearJButtonActionPerformed method, which is called from the actionPerformed event handler when the **Clear** JButton is clicked.

4. **Setting the components to the default values.** Add lines 226–234 of Fig. 13.15 to the clearJButtonActionPerformed method. These lines clear the JTextFields and JTextArea and set the value of the JSpinner to 1. Line 234 invokes method **setValue** to set the *value* property of the JSpinner to an Integer object representing the value 1.

(cont.)

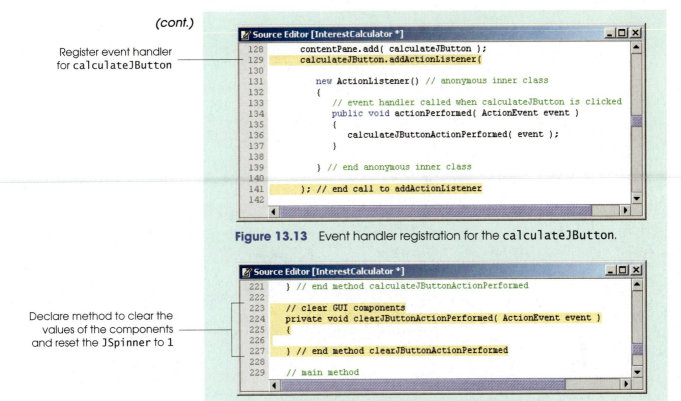

Register event handler for calculateJButton

```
Source Editor [InterestCalculator *]
128         contentPane.add( calculateJButton );
129         calculateJButton.addActionListener(
130
131             new ActionListener() // anonymous inner class
132             {
133                 // event handler called when calculateJButton is clicked
134                 public void actionPerformed( ActionEvent event )
135                 {
136                     calculateJButtonActionPerformed( event );
137                 }
138
139             } // end anonymous inner class
140
141         ); // end call to addActionListener
142
```

Figure 13.13 Event handler registration for the calculateJButton.

Declare method to clear the values of the components and reset the JSpinner to 1

```
Source Editor [InterestCalculator *]
221     } // end method calculateJButtonActionPerformed
222
223     // clear GUI components
224     private void clearJButtonActionPerformed( ActionEvent event )
225     {
226
227     } // end method clearJButtonActionPerformed
228
229     // main method
```

Figure 13.14 Declaring method clearJButtonActionPerformed.

Clear components and reset the JSpinner to 1

```
Source Editor [InterestCalculator *]
223     // clear GUI components
224     private void clearJButtonActionPerformed( ActionEvent event )
225     {
226         // clear the JTextFields
227         principalJTextField.setText( "" );
228         rateJTextField.setText( "" );
229
230         // clear the JTextArea
231         accountJTextArea.setText( "" );
232
233         // reset the value of the JSpinner
234         yearsJSpinner.setValue( new Integer( 1 ) );
235
236     } // end method clearJButtonActionPerformed
```

Figure 13.15 Clearing the values in the components.

5. ***Saving the application.*** Save your modified source code file.

6. ***Opening the Command Prompt window and changing directories.*** Open the **Command Prompt** window by selecting **Start > Programs > Accessories > Command Prompt**. Change to your working directory by typing cd C:\SimplyJava\InterestCalculator2.

7. ***Compiling the application.*** Compile your application by typing javac InterestCalculator.java.

8. ***Running the application.*** When your application compiles correctly, run it by typing java InterestCalculator. Enter 1000 in the **Principal:** JTextField and 5 in the **Interest rate:** JTextField. Click the **Calculate** JButton to update the JTextArea. Now click the **Clear** JButton to clear the components (Fig. 13.16). Changing the value in the JSpinner will still not clear the JTextArea, because you have not declared an event handler for that component. You will do that shortly.

(cont.)

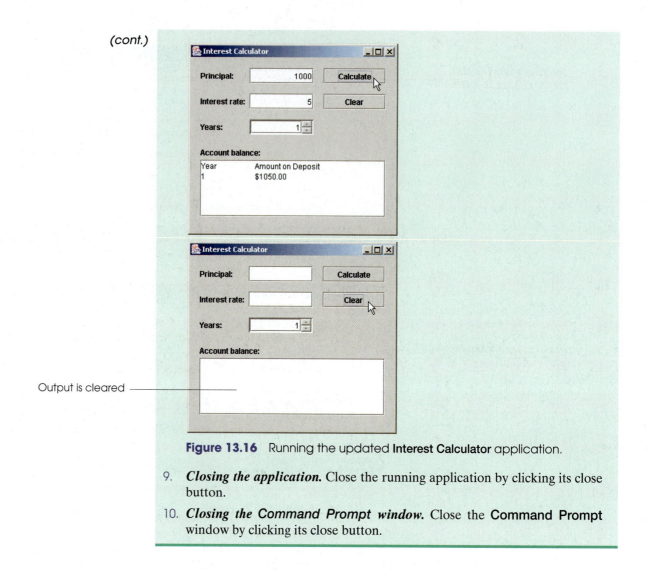

Output is cleared

Figure 13.16 Running the updated **Interest Calculator** application.

9. *Closing the application.* Close the running application by clicking its close button.

10. *Closing the Command Prompt window.* Close the **Command Prompt** window by clicking its close button.

SELF-REVIEW

1. Registering an event handler associates it with a(n) _____.

   a) JButton   b) event object

   c) application   d) component

2. Method _____ is used to register an actionPerformed event handler with a component.

   a) addEventHandler   b) addActionListener

   c) registerEventHandler   d) registerActionListener

Answers: 1) d. 2) b.

13.4 Handling a ChangeEvent

Different components respond to different kinds of actions. Clicking a JButton, for example, generates an ActionEvent object and calls an actionPerformed event handler. Every event handler for a particular type of event object must have a specific name—in the case of an ActionEvent, for example, the event handler must be named actionPerformed. Changing the value in a JSpinner (by clicking on one of its arrows or entering a value) generates a **ChangeEvent**. A ChangeEvent generated on a component results in a call to the **stateChanged** event handler for that component. You can use ChangeEvent objects to get information about the event, such as the event source.

Handling a ChangeEvent

1. ***Viewing the `stateChanged` event handler.*** Lines 115–118 of Fig. 13.17 declare another event handler. When a `JSpinner`'s value changes, a `ChangeEvent` object is generated and sent to the `stateChanged` event handler.

Event handler `stateChanged`

```
Source Editor [InterestCalculator *]
111          new ChangeListener() // anonymous inner class
112          {
113             // event handler called when value in
114             // yearsJSpinner changes
115             public void stateChanged( ChangeEvent event )
116             {
117
118             }
119
120          } // end anonymous inner class
```

Figure 13.17 Event handler `stateChanged` for a `ChangeEvent`.

2. ***Completing the `stateChanged` event handler.*** Add line 117 of Fig. 13.18 to the `stateChanged` event handler. This line calls the `yearsJSpinnerStateChanged` method, which clears the `JTextArea`. While the event handler must be named `stateChanged`, method `yearsJSpinnerStateChanged` follows our naming convention—appending an event handler name (`stateChanged`) to a component name (`yearsJSpinner`).

Call programmer-declared method from event handler

```
Source Editor [InterestCalculator *]
113             // event handler called when value in
114             // yearsJSpinner changes
115             public void stateChanged( ChangeEvent event )
116             {
117                yearsJSpinnerStateChanged( event );
118             }
```

Figure 13.18 Calling the programmer-declared method `yearsJSpinnerStateChanged` from event handler `stateChanged`.

3. ***Registering the `stateChanged` event handler.*** Consider lines 109 and 122 of Fig. 13.19. Line 109 begins a call to the `yearsJSpinner`.**`addChangeListener`** method, which ends on line 122. This method registers the `stateChanged` event handler declared on lines 115–118 of Fig. 13.19 with the `yearsJSpinner` component. As a result, each time the value in `yearsJSpinner` is changed, a `ChangeEvent` object is generated and passed to the `stateChanged` event handler, which calls the `yearsJSpinnerStateChanged` method.

Call method `addChangeListener`

```
Source Editor [InterestCalculator *]
108       contentPane.add( yearsJSpinner );
109       yearsJSpinner.addChangeListener(
110
111          new ChangeListener() // anonymous inner class
112          {
113             // event handler called when value in
114             // yearsJSpinner changes
115             public void stateChanged( ChangeEvent event )
116             {
117                yearsJSpinnerStateChanged( event );
118             }
119
120          } // end anonymous inner class
121
122       ); // end call to addChangeListener
123
```

Figure 13.19 Registering the event handler `stateChanged` to handle `ChangeEvent`s.

(cont.)

4. ***Declaring the yearsJSpinnerStateChanged method.*** Insert lines 238–243 of Fig. 13.20 after the `clearJButtonActionPerformed` method. These lines declare the `yearsJSpinnerStateChanged` method. This method is called from line 117 of Fig. 13.18. Line 241 clears the text in the `JTextArea`.

Clear the `JTextArea` ———

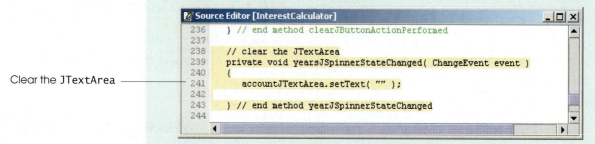

Figure 13.20   Clearing the `accountJTextArea`.

5. ***Saving the application.*** Save your modified source code file.

6. ***Opening the Command Prompt window and changing directories.*** Open the **Command Prompt** window by selecting **Start > Programs > Accessories > Command Prompt**. Change to your working directory by typing `cd C:\SimplyJava\InterestCalculator2`.

7. ***Compiling the application.*** Compile your application by typing `javac InterestCalculator.java`.

8. ***Running the application.*** When your application compiles correctly, run it by typing `java InterestCalculator`. Enter 1000 in the **Principal:** `JTextField` and 5 in the **Interest rate:** `JTextField`. Click the **Calculate** `JButton` to update the `JTextArea`. Change the value in the `JSpinner` to 2. This will clear the `JTextArea` (Fig. 13.21).

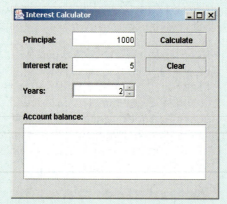

Figure 13.21   Completed **Interest Calculator** application responding to `ChangeEvent` by clearing the `JTextArea`.

9. ***Closing the application.*** Close the running application by clicking its close button.

10. ***Closing the Command Prompt window.*** Close the **Command Prompt** window by clicking its close button.

Figure 13.22 presents the source code of the **Interest Calculator** application. The lines of code that you added, viewed or modified in this tutorial are highlighted.

```
1    // Tutorial 13: InterestCalculator.java
2    // Calculate the total value of an investment.
3    import java.text.*;
4    import java.awt.*;
5    import java.awt.event.*;
6    import javax.swing.*;
7    import javax.swing.event.*;
8
9    public class InterestCalculator extends JFrame
10   {
11      // JLabel and JTextField for principal
12      private JLabel principalJLabel;
13      private JTextField principalJTextField;
14
15      // JLabel and JTextField for interest rate
16      private JLabel rateJLabel;
17      private JTextField rateJTextField;
18
19      // JLabel and JSpinner for years
20      private JLabel yearsJLabel;
21      private JSpinner yearsJSpinner;
22
23      // JLabel, JTextArea and JScrollPane for yearly balances
24      private JLabel accountJLabel;
25      private JTextArea accountJTextArea;
26      private JScrollPane accountJScrollPane;
27
28      // JButton to calculate the yearly balances
29      private JButton calculateJButton;
30
31      // JButton to clear the components
32      private JButton clearJButton;
33
34      // no-argument constructor
35      public InterestCalculator()
36      {
37         createUserInterface();
38      }
39
40      // create and position GUI components; register event handlers
41      private void createUserInterface()
42      {
43         // get content pane and set layout to null
44         Container contentPane = getContentPane();
45         contentPane.setLayout( null );
46
47         // set up principalJLabel
48         principalJLabel = new JLabel();
49         principalJLabel.setText( "Principal:" );
50         principalJLabel.setBounds( 16, 16, 56, 24 );
51         contentPane.add( principalJLabel );
52
53         // set up principalJTextField
54         principalJTextField = new JTextField();
55         principalJTextField.setHorizontalAlignment( JTextField.RIGHT );
56         principalJTextField.setBounds( 96, 16, 104, 24 );
57         contentPane.add( principalJTextField );
58         principalJTextField.addKeyListener(
```

Figure 13.22   Code for the enhanced **Interest Calculator** application. (Part 1 of 5.)

```
59
60        new KeyAdapter() // anonymous inner class
61        {
62           // event handler called when principalJTextField
63           // is edited
64           public void keyPressed( KeyEvent event )
65           {
66              principalJTextFieldKeyPressed( event );
67           }
68
69        } // end anonymous inner class
70
71     ); // end call to addKeyListener
72
73     // set up rateJLabel
74     rateJLabel = new JLabel();
75     rateJLabel.setText( "Interest rate:" );
76     rateJLabel.setBounds( 16, 56, 80, 24 );
77     contentPane.add( rateJLabel );
78
79     // set up rateJTextField
80     rateJTextField = new JTextField();
81     rateJTextField.setHorizontalAlignment( JTextField.RIGHT );
82     rateJTextField.setBounds( 96, 56, 104, 24 );
83     contentPane.add( rateJTextField );
84     rateJTextField.addKeyListener(
85
86        new KeyAdapter() // anonymous inner class
87        {
88           // event handler called when rateJTextField is edited
89           public void keyPressed( KeyEvent event )
90           {
91              rateJTextFieldKeyPressed( event );
92           }
93
94        } // end anonymous inner class
95
96     ); // end call to addKeyListener
97
98     // set up yearsJLabel
99     yearsJLabel = new JLabel();
100    yearsJLabel.setText( "Years:" );
101    yearsJLabel.setBounds( 16, 96, 48, 24 );
102    contentPane.add( yearsJLabel );
103
104    // set up yearsJSpinner
105    yearsJSpinner = new JSpinner(
106       new SpinnerNumberModel( 1, 1, 10, 1 ) );
107    yearsJSpinner.setBounds( 96, 96, 104, 24 );
108    contentPane.add( yearsJSpinner );
109    yearsJSpinner.addChangeListener(
110
111       new ChangeListener() // anonymous inner class
112       {
113          // event handler called when value in
114          // yearsJSpinner changes
115          public void stateChanged( ChangeEvent event )
116          {
```

Calling method addChangeListener — (line 109)

Event handler stateChanged — (line 115)

Figure 13.22 Code for the enhanced **Interest Calculator** application. (Part 2 of 5.)

Calling a programmer-declared method from an event handler

```
117                    yearsJSpinnerStateChanged( event );
118                }
119
120         } // end anonymous inner class
121
122      ); // end call to addChangeListener
123
124      // set up calculateJButton
125      calculateJButton = new JButton();
126      calculateJButton.setText( "Calculate" );
127      calculateJButton.setBounds( 216, 16, 100, 24 );
128      contentPane.add( calculateJButton );
129      calculateJButton.addActionListener(
130
131         new ActionListener() // anonymous inner class
132         {
133            // event handler called when calculateJButton is clicked
134            public void actionPerformed( ActionEvent event )
135            {
136               calculateJButtonActionPerformed( event );
137            }
138
139         } // end anonymous inner class
140
141      ); // end call to addActionListener
142
143      // set up clearJButton
144      clearJButton = new JButton();
145      clearJButton.setBounds( 216, 56, 100, 24 );
146      clearJButton.setText( "Clear" );
147      contentPane.add( clearJButton );
148      clearJButton.addActionListener(
149
150         new ActionListener() // anonymous inner class
151         {
152            // event handler called when clearJButton is clicked
153            public void actionPerformed( ActionEvent event )
154            {
155               clearJButtonActionPerformed( event );
156            }
157
158         } // end anonymous inner class
159
160      ); // end call to addActionListener
161
162      // set up accountJLabel
163      accountJLabel = new JLabel();
164      accountJLabel.setText( "Yearly account balance:" );
165      accountJLabel.setBounds( 16, 136, 150, 24 );
166      contentPane.add( accountJLabel );
167
168      // set up accountJTextArea
169      accountJTextArea = new JTextArea();
170      accountJTextArea.setEditable( false );
171
172      // set up accountJScrollPane
173      accountJScrollPane = new JScrollPane( accountJTextArea );
174      accountJScrollPane.setBounds( 16, 160, 300, 88 );
```

Registering an event handler for `calculateJButton`

Event handler `actionPerformed`

Calling a programmer-declared method from an event handler

Registering an event handler for `clearJButton`

Event handler `actionPerformed`

Calling a programmer-declared method from an event handler

Figure 13.22 Code for the enhanced **Interest Calculator** application. (Part 3 of 5.)

```
175        contentPane.add( accountJScrollPane );
176
177        // set properties of application's window
178        setTitle( "Interest Calculator" ); // set title bar string
179        setSize( 340, 300 );                // set window size
180        setVisible( true );                 // show window
181
182     } // end method createUserInterface
183
184     // clear the accountJTextArea
185     private void rateJTextFieldKeyPressed( KeyEvent event )
186     {
187        accountJTextArea.setText( "" );
188
189     } // end method rateJTextFieldKeyPressed
190
191     // clear the accountJTextArea
192     private void principalJTextFieldKeyPressed( KeyEvent event )
193     {
194        accountJTextArea.setText( "" );
195
196     } // end method principalJTextFieldKeyPressed
197
198     // calculate yearly values of investment
199     private void calculateJButtonActionPerformed( ActionEvent event )
200     {
201        // declare variables to store user input
202        double principal = Double.parseDouble(
203           principalJTextField.getText() );
204        double rate = Double.parseDouble( rateJTextField.getText() );
205        Integer integerObject = ( Integer ) yearsJSpinner.getValue();
206        int year = integerObject.intValue();
207
208        accountJTextArea.setText( "Year\tAmount on Deposit" );
209        DecimalFormat dollars = new DecimalFormat( "$0.00" );
210
211        // calculate the total value for each year
212        for ( int count = 1; count <= year; count++ )
213        {
214           double amount = principal *
215              Math.pow( ( 1 + rate / 100 ), count );
216           accountJTextArea.append( "\n" + count + "\t" +
217              dollars.format( amount ) );
218
219        } // end for
220
221     } // end method calculateJButtonActionPerformed
222
223     // clear GUI components
224     private void clearJButtonActionPerformed( ActionEvent event )
225     {
226        // clear the JTextFields
227        principalJTextField.setText( "" );
228        rateJTextField.setText( "" );
229
230        // clear the JTextArea
231        accountJTextArea.setText( "" );
232
```

Programmer-declared method — line 224

Clearing the JTextFields — lines 227–228

Figure 13.22 Code for the enhanced **Interest Calculator** application. (Part 4 of 5.)

Clearing the JTextArea

Reseting JSpinner to original value

Programmer-declared method

Clearing the JTextArea

```
233        // reset the value of the JSpinner
234        yearsJSpinner.setValue( new Integer( 1 ) );
235
236    } // end method clearJButtonActionPerformed
237
238    // clear the JTextArea
239    private void yearsJSpinnerStateChanged( ChangeEvent event )
240    {
241        accountJTextArea.setText( "" );
242
243    } // end method yearsJSpinnerStateChanged
244
245    // main method
246    public static void main( String args[] )
247    {
248        InterestCalculator application = new InterestCalculator();
249        application.setDefaultCloseOperation( JFrame.EXIT_ON_CLOSE );
250
251    } // end method main
252
253 } // end class InterestCalculator
```

Figure 13.22   Code for the enhanced **Interest Calculator** application. (Part 5 of 5.)

SELF-REVIEW

1. Changing the value in a JSpinner generates a(n)_____.

   a) `ActionEvent`   b) `NextEvent`

   c) `SwitchEvent`   d) `ChangeEvent`

2. Clicking on a JButton generates a(n) _____.

   a) `ActionEvent`   b) `ClickEvent`

   c) `KeyEvent`   d) `PressEvent`

Answers: 1) d. 2) a.

13.5 Wrap-Up

In this tutorial, you learned about event objects and event handlers. You learned that different types of event objects are generated in response to different types of actions. You also learned how to register an event handler with its corresponding component so that the event handler is called when event objects are generated.

    You began by test-driving an application that uses event handlers to calculate the value of an investment. You learned that an `ActionEvent` is generated by clicking a `JButton` and results in a call to an `actionPerformed` event handler. You then learned how to register `actionPerformed` event handlers using the `addAction-Listener` method. Finally, you learned how to handle the `ChangeEvent` for a `JSpinner`—the event object generated when the value of a `JSpinner` changes (by clicking on one of its arrows or entering a value). A `ChangeEvent` results in a call to event handler `stateChanged`.

    In the next tutorial, you will learn about scope rules and conversions of primitive types as you implement a **Fund Raiser** application. Learning these concepts will help you understand how Java keeps track of variables throughout your application.

SKILLS SUMMARY

Handling a JButton click

- Write code inside a registered `actionPerformed` event handler that executes when a `JButton` is clicked.
- Generate an `ActionEvent` by clicking a `JButton`.

Updating a JSpinner

- Change the value of a JSpinner with a setValue call.

Interacting with a JSpinner

- Change the value in a JSpinner by clicking on one of its arrows or entering a value to generate a ChangeEvent.
- Write code inside a registered stateChanged event handler that executes when the value of a JSpinner is changed.

KEY TERMS

ActionEvent—The type of event object generated when a JButton is clicked. This object is sent to event handler actionPerformed (if one is registered for that JButton).

addActionListener method of JButton—Registers an actionPerformed event handler with a component. The actionPerformed event handler will then be called if an ActionEvent is generated by a user's interaction with the component.

addChangeListener method of JSpinner—Registers a stateChanged event handler with a component. The stateChanged event handler will then be called if a ChangeEvent is generated by a user's interaction with the component.

ChangeEvent class—The type of event object generated when a JSpinner's value is changed by clicking on one of its arrows or entering a value. This object is sent to event handler stateChanged.

event—An action that generates an event object and initiates a call to an appropriate registered event handler.

event object—An object generated when the user interacts with a component. The event object contains information about the event that occurred.

event-driven programming—The type of programming in which the application waits for certain events to occur, then responds to those events.

event handler—Handles, or processes, an event object. Event handlers must be registered with a component.

public keyword—The access modifier that allows objects of other classes to call a method.

registering an event handler—Specifying which event handler to call on a component when an event object is generated by the component.

setValue method of JSpinner—Called to change the value in a JSpinner.

stateChanged event handler—Called when a JSpinner's value is changed.

JAVA LIBRARY REFERENCE

ActionEvent This class represents the event object created when a JButton is clicked. Objects of this class contain information about the event that was generated, such as the event source.

ChangeEvent This class represents the event object created when a JSpinner's value is changed. Objects of this class contain information about the event that was generated, such as the event source.

JSpinner This component allows you to collect input within a specified range. The range can include numeric values, or values of another data type. Input can be entered at the keyboard, or by clicking up and down arrows provided on the right of the JSpinner. Invalid input is rejected and replaced with the most recent valid input value.

- *In action*

- *Events*

  stateChanged—Occurs when the value in a JSpinner is changed by clicking on one of its arrows or entering a value.

■ *Methods*

getValue—Returns the data in the *value* property of a JSpinner component.

setBounds—Sets the *bounds* property which determines the location and size of a JSpinner component.

setValue—Sets the *value* property of a JSpinner component.

MULTIPLE-CHOICE QUESTIONS

13.1 Applications that wait for certain actions and inputs and then respond to them are known as _____ applications.

a) object-oriented

b) stepping

c) event-driven

d) movement-oriented

13.2 Method _____ registers a stateChanged event handler with a component.

a) addChangeListener

b) addActionListener

c) addKeyListener

d) addStateListener

13.3 _____ an event handler with a component tells the component which event handler to call for a certain event type.

a) Declaring

b) Defining

c) Storing

d) Registering

13.4 Method _____ sets a JSpinner to a specific value.

a) setJSpinner

b) setText

c) setNumber

d) setValue

13.5 A method called when an action is performed is known as a(n) _____.

a) event listener

b) JButton method

c) event handler

d) action method

13.6 If the user interacts with a component that has no registered event handler, _____.

a) the application executes a default event handler

b) nothing happens

c) the application ends

d) an error occurs

13.7 When a ChangeEvent is generated, the event handler _____ is called.

a) actionPerformed

b) valueChanged

c) stateChanged

d) changeValue

13.8 An example of a component that can generate a ChangeEvent is _____.

a) JTextField

b) JButton

c) JTextArea

d) JSpinner

13.9 The _____ access modifier allows other classes to call a method.

a) public

b) private

c) default

d) None of the above.

13.10 ActionEvent is a type of _____.

a) event handler

b) event object

c) method

d) GUI component

EXERCISES

13.11 (*Enhanced Present Value Calculator Application*) Modify the application you developed in Exercise 10.11 to calculate the present investment value needed to achieve a future financial goal. Recall that to calculate the present investment you should use the formula:

$$p = a / (1 + r/100)^n$$

where

> p is the amount needed to achieve the future value
> r is the annual interest rate (for example, 5 is equivalent to 5%)
> n is the number of years
> a is the future-value amount.

For example, if a customer wants to reach the financial goal of $15,000 over a period of five years when the interest rate is 6.6%, the customer would need to invest $10,896.96 as shown in Fig. 13.23. The years are to be entered with a JSpinner in the range from 0 to 30 in increments of 5. Your application should clear the JTextArea if the values in any of the input components are modified. Your application should also provide the user with a **Clear** JButton, which will clear the JTextFields and JTextArea and reset the value in the JSpinner to the initial value (0).

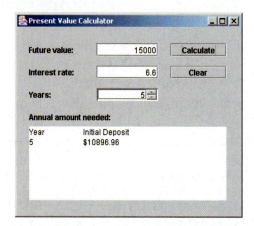

Figure 13.23   Enhanced **Present Value Calculator** GUI.

a) *Copying the template to your working directory.* Copy the directory C:\Examples\ Tutorial13\Exercises\PresentValue2 to your C:\SimplyJava directory.

b) *Opening the template file.* Open the PresentValue.java file in your text editor.

c) *Completing the stateChanged event handler for yearsJSpinner.* On line 123, add code to call the yearsJSpinnerStateChanged method. Send the method the ChangeEvent object event as the argument.

d) *Coding the yearsJSpinnerStateChanged method.* Starting after the interestRateJTextFieldKeyPressed method, on line 226, declare the yearsJSpinnerStateChanged method. This method should clear amountNeededJTextArea.

e) *Completing the actionPerformed event handler for clearJButton.* On line 172, add code to call method clearJButtonActionPerformed. Send the method the ActionEvent object event as the argument.

f) *Coding the clearJButtonActionPerformed method.* Starting after method yearsJSpinnerStateChanged, on line 233, declare method clearJButtonActionPerformed. This method should clear the JTextFields, reset the value of the JSpinner and clear the JTextArea.

g) *Saving the application.* Save your modified source code file.

h) *Opening the Command Prompt window and changing directories.* Open the **Command Prompt** window by selecting **Start > Programs > Accessories > Command Prompt**. Change to your working directory by typing cd C:\SimplyJava\ PresentValue2.

i) *Compiling the application.* Compile your application by typing javac PresentValue.java.

j) *Running the completed application.* When your application compiles correctly, run it by typing java PresentValue. Test the application by calculating initial values for a given future value, interest rate and number of years. Test the JSpinner's event handling by changing the value in the JSpinner. The JTextArea should be cleared. Calculate the new set of values and then test the **Clear** JButton. All of the components should be cleared.

k) *Closing the application.* Close your running application by clicking its close button.

l) *Closing the Command Prompt window.* Close the **Command Prompt** window by clicking its close button.

13.12 (*Temperature Conversion Application*) Write an application that performs various temperature conversions. The application should be capable of performing two types of conversions: degrees Fahrenheit to degrees Celsius and degrees Celsius to degrees Fahrenheit. Your output should look like Fig. 13.24.

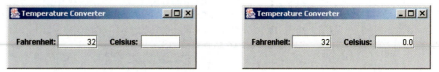

Figure 13.24   **Temperature Conversion** GUI.

The conversion should take place when the user enters a temperature in one of the JTextFields, then presses *Enter*. Pressing *Enter* while the focus is on a JTextField generates an ActionEvent and calls event handler actionPerformed.

a) *Copying the template to your working directory.* Copy the directory C:\Examples\ Tutorial13\Exercises\TemperatureConversion2 to your C:\SimplyJava directory.

b) *Opening the template file.* Open the TemperatureConversion.java file in your text editor.

c) *Completing the actionPerformed event handler for fahrenheitJTextField.* On line 57, add code to call the fahrenheitJTextFieldActionPerformed method. Pass to the method the ActionEvent object event as the argument.

d) *Coding the fahrenheitJTextFieldActionPerformed method.* Starting after the createUserInterface method, on line 97, declare the fahrenheitJTextFieldActionPerformed method. This method should get the value from fahrenheitJTextField, convert it to Celsius and display it in celsiusJTextField. DecimalFormat temperature should be used to format the output. To convert degrees Fahrenheit to degrees Celsius, use this formula:

```
degreesCelsius = ( degreesFahrenheit - 32.0 ) * 5.0 / 9.0;
```

e) *Completing the actionPerformed event handler for celsiusJTextField.* On line 83, add code to call the celsiusJTextFieldActionPerformed method. Pass to the method the ActionEvent object event as the argument.

f) *Coding the celsiusJTextFieldActionPerformed method.* Starting after the fahrenheitJTextFieldActionPerformed method, on line 115, declare the celsiusJTextFieldActionPerformed method. This method should get the value from celsiusJTextField, convert it to Fahrenheit and display it in fahrenheitJTextField. DecimalFormat temperature should be used to format the output. To convert degrees Celsius to degrees Fahrenheit, use this formula:

```
degreesFahrenheit = 9.0 / 5.0 * degreesCelsius + 32.0;
```

g) *Saving the application.* Save your modified source code file.

h) *Opening the Command Prompt window and changing directories.* Open the **Command Prompt** window by selecting **Start > Programs > Accessories > Command Prompt**. Change to your working directory by typing cd C:\SimplyJava\ TemperatureConversion2.

i) *Compiling the application.* Compile your application by typing javac TemperatureConversion.java.

j) *Running the completed application.* When your application compiles correctly, run it by typing java TemperatureConversion. Test the application by entering the value 32 in fahrenheitJTextField and press *Enter*. The value 0.0 should appear in celsiusJTextField. Now enter the value 100 in celsiusJTextField and press *Enter*. The value 212.0 should appear in fahrenheitJTextField.

k) *Closing the application.* Close your running application by clicking its close button.

l) *Closing the Command Prompt window.* Close the **Command Prompt** window by clicking its close button.

13.13 *(Enhanced Sales Commission Calculator Application)* Modify the application you developed in Exercise 11.11 to allow the user to input the price of the items and the sales commission percentage. The user enters the number of items sold and the price of items, and the gross sales is calculated from this. The commission percentage will be in the range from 1 to 10. The user has been provided with a JSpinner to choose the commission percentage (Fig. 13.25). When the value in the JSpinner changes, the calculated earnings should automatically be updated.

Figure 13.25 Enhanced **Sales Commission Calculator** GUI.

a) *Copying the template to your working directory.* Copy the directory C:\Examples\ Tutorial13\Exercises\SalesCommissionCalculator2 to your C:\SimplyJava directory.

b) *Opening the template file.* Open the SalesCommissionCalculator.java file in your text editor.

c) *Completing the stateChanged event handler for commissionJSpinner.* On line 107, add code to call the commissionJSpinnerStateChanged method. Pass to the method the ChangeEvent object event as the argument.

d) *Coding the commissionJSpinnerStateChanged method.* Starting after the calculateEarnings method, on line 174, declare the commissionJSpinnerStateChanged method. This method should call the calculateEarnings method, which has already been declared for you.

e) *Completing the actionPerformed event handler for calculateJButton.* On line 139, add code to call method calculateJButtonActionPerformed. Pass to the method the ActionEvent object event as the argument.

f) *Coding the calculateJButtonActionPerformed method.* Starting after the commissionJSpinnerStateChanged method, on line 181, declare the calculateJButtonActionPerformed method. This method should call method calculateEarnings.

g) *Saving the application.* Save your modified source code file.

h) *Opening the Command Prompt window and changing directories.* Open the **Command Prompt** window by selecting **Start > Programs > Accessories > Command Prompt**. Change to your working directory by typing cd C:\SimplyJava\ SalesCommissionCalculator2.

i) *Compiling the application.* Compile your application by typing javac SalesCommissionCalculator.java.

j) *Running the completed application.* When your application compiles correctly, run it by typing java SalesCommissionCalculator. Test the application by typing an int into the **Number of items sold:** JTextField and a double into the **Price of items:** JTextField and pressing the **Calculate** JButton. Change the value in the **Commission (%):** JSpinner and watch the earnings update automatically.

k) *Closing the application.* Close your running application by clicking its close button.

l) *Closing the Command Prompt window.* Close the **Command Prompt** window by clicking its close button.

What does this code do? ▶

13.14 What does the following code do? Assume that monthsJSpinner has been declared.

```
1  private void createUserInterface()
2  {
3      yearsJSpinner.addChangeListener(
4
5          new ChangeListener() // anonymous inner class
6          {
7              // event handler called when yearsJSpinner is changed
8              public void stateChanged( ChangeEvent event )
9              {
10                 yearsJSpinnerStateChanged( event );
11             }
12
13         } // end anonymous inner class
14
15     ); // end call to addChangeListener
16
17 } // end method createUserInterface
18
19 private void yearsJSpinnerStateChanged( ChangeEvent event )
20 {
21     monthsJSpinner.setValue( new Integer( 1 ) );
22
23 } // end method yearsJSpinnerStateChanged
```

What's wrong with this code? ▶

13.15 Find the error(s) in the following code, which should handle the event that occurs when the value in itemsJSpinner changes.

```
1  itemsJSpinner.addChangeListener(
2
3      new ChangeListener() // anonymous inner class
4      {
5          // event handler called when value in itemsJSpinner is changed
6          public void valueChanged( ChangeEvent event )
7          {
8              itemsJSpinnerValueChanged( event );
9          }
10
11     } // end anonymous inner class
12
13 ); // end call to addChangeListener
```

Programming Challenge ▶

13.16 *(Enhanced Pay Raise Calculator Application)* Modify the application you developed in Exercise 10.17 to calculate the yearly salary every time one of the JSpinner's values is changed. The user specifies the amount of the annual raise (as a percentage) and the numbers of years for which the raise applies in the application. The application should run as shown in Fig. 13.26.

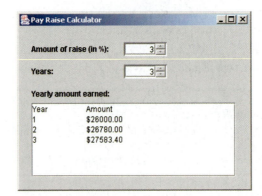

Figure 13.26 Enhanced **Pay Raise Calculator** application's GUI.

a) *Copying the template to your working directory.* Copy the directory C:\Examples\Tutorial13\Exercises\PayRaise2 to your C:\SimplyJava directory.

b) *Opening the template file.* Open the PayRaise.java file in your text editor.

c) *Handling the stateChanged event for raiseJSpinner.* Add code to the state-Changed event handler for raiseJSpinner to call the raiseJSpinnerStateChanged method. This method must then be declared and it should call calculateWages.

d) *Handling the stateChanged event for yearsJSpinner.* Add code to the state-Changed event handler for yearsJSpinner to call the yearsJSpinnerStateChanged method. This method must then be declared and it should call calculateWages.

e) *Saving the application.* Save your modified source code file.

f) *Opening the Command Prompt window and changing directories.* Open the **Command Prompt** window by selecting **Start > Programs > Accessories > Command Prompt**. Change to your working directory by typing cd C:\SimplyJava\PayRaise2.

g) *Compiling the application.* Compile your application by typing javac PayRaise.java.

h) *Running the completed application.* When your application compiles correctly, run it by typing java PayRaise. Test the application by changing the values in the JSpinners. Check that the JTextArea updates the results properly.

i) *Closing the application.* Close your running application by clicking its close button.

j) *Closing the Command Prompt window.* Close the **Command Prompt** window by clicking its close button.

Objectives

In this tutorial, you will learn to:
- Create variables that can be used in all the application's methods.
- Assign a value from a variable of one type to a variable of another type, using implicit conversion.

Outline

Fundraiser Application

Introducing Scope and Conversion of Primitive Types

In this tutorial, you will learn more about instance variables and local variables. You will learn that the difference between a local variable and an instance variable is the scope of the variable—the parts of the application that can access the variable. Also, you will learn how the Java compiler handles conversions between different primitive types.

14.1 Test-Driving the Fundraiser Application

You have been asked to create a fundraiser application that determines how much donated money is available to a charity after operating expenses are taken into consideration. The application must meet the following requirements:

Application Requirements

A fundraising organization collects donations for a charity. A percentage of each donation is used to cover the operating expenses of the fundraising organization, and the rest of the donation goes to the charity. Create an application that allows the organization to keep track of the total amount of money raised. The application should deduct 17% of each donation for operating expenses, while the remaining 83% is given to the charity. The application should display the amount of each donation after the 17% in operating expenses are deducted, and it should display the total amount raised for the charity (that is, the total amount donated minus all operating expenses) for all donations up to that point.

The user inputs the amount of a donation into a `JTextField` and clicks a `JButton` to calculate the net amount the charity receives from that donation after operating expenses have been deducted. In addition, the total amount of money raised for the charity is updated and displayed. You begin by test-driving the completed application. Then, you will learn the additional Java technologies you will need to create your own version of this application.

Test-Driving the Fundraiser Application

1. **Locating the completed application.** Open the **Command Prompt** window by selecting **Start > Programs > Accessories > Command Prompt**. Change to your completed **Fundraiser** application directory by typing cd C:\Examples\Tutorial14\CompletedApplication\Fundraiser.

2. **Running the application.** Type java Fundraiser in the **Command Prompt** window to run the application (Fig. 14.1).

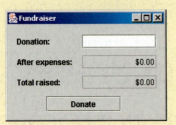

Figure 14.1 Running the completed **Fundraiser** application.

3. **Entering a donation.** Enter 10 in the **Donation:** JTextField. Click the **Donate** JButton. The application calculates the amount of the donation after the operating expenses have been deducted and displays the result (**$8.30**) in the uneditable **After expenses:** JTextField. Because this is the first donation entered, the amount is repeated in the uneditable **Total raised:** JTextField (Fig. 14.2).

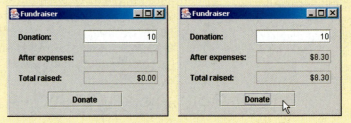

Figure 14.2 **Fundraiser** application with first donation entered.

4. **Entering additional donations.** Enter a **$20** donation and notice that the **After expenses:** JTextField is cleared. Click the **Donate** JButton and notice that the total raised increases (Fig. 14.3).

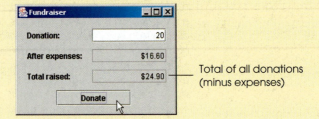

Total of all donations (minus expenses)

Figure 14.3 Making further donations.

5. **Closing the running application.** Close your running application by clicking its close button.

6. **Closing the Command Prompt window.** Close the **Command Prompt** window by clicking its close button.

14.2 Constructing the Fundraiser Application

Now you will create the **Fundraiser** application to enable a user to keep track of the total amount of money raised in a fundraising organization. First you need to analyze the application. The following pseudocode describes the basic operation of the **Fundraiser** application.

> When the user changes the current donation amount in the JTextField
> > Clear the JTextField that displays the current donation after expenses
>
> When the user clicks the Donate JButton
> > Obtain the current donation from the JTextField
> > Calculate and display the current donation after expenses
> > Update and display the total amount raised for the charity

Now that you have test-driven the **Fundraiser** application and studied its pseudocode representation, you will use an ACE table to help you convert the pseudocode to Java. Figure 14.4 lists the actions, components and events required to complete your own version of this application.

Action/Component/ Event Table for the Fundraiser Application

Action	Component	Event
Label all the application's components	`donationJLabel,` `afterExpensesJLabel,` `totalRaisedJLabel`	Application is run
Clear the JTextField that displays the current donation after expenses	`donationJTextField`	User changes value in the **Donation:** JTextField
Obtain the amount of the current donation from the JTextField	`donationJTextField`	User clicks **Donate** JButton
Calculate and display the current donation after expenses	`afterExpensesJTextField`	
Update and display the total amount raised for the charity	`totalRaisedJTextField`	

Figure 14.4 **Fundraiser** application's ACE table.

You're now ready to begin programming your **Fundraiser** application. First, you will declare the variables needed in the application. In this discussion, you will learn a new concept—**scope**. Every variable declaration has a scope, which is the portion of an application in which the variable can be accessed. Some variables can be accessed throughout the lifetime of an application, while others can be referenced only from limited portions of an application (such as within a single method). You will now add code to your application to illustrate these various scopes.

Examining Scope with the Fundraiser Application

1. ***Copying the template to your working directory.*** Copy the C:\Examples\ Tutorial14\TemplateApplication\Fundraiser directory to your C:\SimplyJava directory.

2. ***Opening the Fundraiser application's template file.*** Open the template file Fundraiser.java in your text editor.

3. ***Placing declarations in the code file.*** Add lines 26–27 of Fig. 14.5. In this application, you need a variable that stores the total amount of money (after expenses) raised for the charity.

(cont.)

This variable is created and initialized when the application first executes and retains its value while the application executes (that is, it is not recreated and reinitialized each time a method is invoked). Variable `totalNetDonations` stores the total amount of money raised. This variable is an example of an **instance variable**—it is declared inside a class, but outside any method declarations of that class. The scope of an instance variable is the entire body of the class—all methods in class `Fundraiser` will have access to the variable `totalNetDonations` and will be able to read and modify its value.

Declaring an instance variable —

```
Source Editor [Fundraiser *]                                    _ □ ×
24      private JButton donateJButton;
25
26      // instance variable stores total raised for charity
27      private double totalNetDonations = 0.00;
28
29      // no-argument constructor
```

Figure 14.5   Declaring an instance variable in the application.

4. ***Declaring local variables in the donateJButtonActionPerformed method***
   Add lines 138–143 of Fig. 14.6 to `donateJButtonActionPerformed` method. Variable `grossDonation` (lines 139–140) stores the donation amount, which is an integer. Variable `netDonation` (line 143) stores the donation amount after the operating expenses have been deducted. Line 143 invokes the `calculateDonation` method with the amount of the donation (`grossDonation`). The result of this method—the net amount that goes to charity after the deduction for operation expenses—is assigned to variable `netDonation`.

   Variables, such as `grossDonation` and `netDonation`, that are declared in the body of a method (such as an event handler) are known as **local variables**. The scope of a local variable is from the point at which the declaration appears in the block to the end of that block (denoted with a right brace, }). For example, the scope of `grossDonation` is from the line of its declaration in the method (line 139) to the closing right brace of the method declaration (line 145).

Declaration of a local variable is the beginning of the variable's scope —

Right brace ends the scope of the local variables —

```
Source Editor [Fundraiser *]                                         _ □ ×
136      private void donateJButtonActionPerformed( ActionEvent event )
137      {
138          // get donation amount
139          int grossDonation =
140              Integer.parseInt( donationJTextField.getText() );
141
142          // obtain donation amount after operating expenses deduction
143          double netDonation = calculateDonation( grossDonation );
144
145      } // end method donateJButtonActionPerformed
```

Figure 14.6   Declaring local variables in the **Fundraiser** application.

Local variables cannot be referenced outside the block in which they are declared. If a local variable has the same name as an instance variable, the instance variable is **hidden** in that block. Any expression containing the variable name will use the local variable's value and not the instance variable's value. The instance variable's value is not destroyed, though—it can still be accessed outside that block.

(cont.)

Error-Prevention Tip

Hidden variable names can sometimes lead to subtle logic errors. Use unique names for all variables, regardless of scope, to prevent an instance variable from becoming hidden.

5. ***Examining the `calculateDonation` method.*** The template application provides the `calculateDonation` method (lines 125–133 of Fig. 14.7). The method header (line 126) declares a parameter (`donatedAmount`).

Line 128 declares constant `NET_PERCENTAGE`, which is the net donation percentage (`0.83` for 83%). This constant is a local variable and cannot be accessed elsewhere in the application. The net donation (the amount that goes to the charity) is calculated by multiplying constant `NET_PERCENTAGE` by the donation amount. The result is then returned by the method to the calling point on line 131.

The expression in the `return` statement on line 131 consists of an `int` value (`donatedAmount`) multiplied by a `double` value (`NET_PERCENTAGE`). Java knows how to evaluate only arithmetic expressions in which the operands' types are identical. To ensure that the operands are of the same type, Java performs an operation called **implicit conversion** on selected operands. In this example, Java converts the value of `donatedAmount` (with type `int`) to type `double`, then the application performs the calculation. Variable `donatedAmount` is not actually changed, rather a temporary copy of its value is converted to a `double` in order to perform the calculation. In the next section, you will learn the implicit conversion rules of the standard primitive types.

Value of `donatedAmount` implicitly converted to `double`

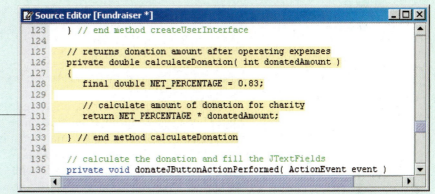

```
123        } // end method createUserInterface
124
125        // returns donation amount after operating expenses
126        private double calculateDonation( int donatedAmount )
127        {
128            final double NET_PERCENTAGE = 0.83;
129
130            // calculate amount of donation for charity
131            return NET_PERCENTAGE * donatedAmount;
132
133        } // end method calculateDonation
134
135        // calculate the donation and fill the JTextFields
136        private void donateJButtonActionPerformed( ActionEvent event )
```

Figure 14.7   Value of `donatedAmount` converted to `double` to perform the calculation.

6. ***Saving the application.*** Save your modified source code file.

SELF-REVIEW

1. The scope of instance variables is the entire _____.

    a) block   b) method

    c) class   d) None of the above.

2. Variables that are defined within a method are called _____.

    a) instance variables   b) local variables

    c) class variables   d) hidden variables

Answers: 1) c. 2) b.

14.3 Conversions

When the computer accesses data, it needs to know the type of the data for the data to make sense. Imagine that you are purchasing a book from an online store that ships internationally. You notice that the price for the book is 20, but no currency is associated with the price—it could be dollars, euros, pesos, yen or some other currency. Without this information, it is impossible to know the true cost of the book.

Therefore, it is important to know what type of currency is being used. If the currency is different from the one you normally use, you will need to perform a conversion to get the correct price of the book.

These types of conversions occur in applications as well. The computer determines the type of a value and converts that value into the type that is needed for a certain operation. Implicit conversions are those performed by Java without requiring any extra code. For example, you are allowed to assign an `int` value to a `double` variable without writing code that tells the application to do the conversion. When an attempted conversion doesn't make sense, such as assigning the `String` value `"hello"` to an `int` variable, a compilation error occurs. Figure 14.8 lists Java's primitive types and their allowed implicit conversions. Primitive types `float`, `long`, `short` and `byte` will not be discussed in this book.

Primitive type	Can be implicitly converted to these (larger) types
double	none
float	double
long	float or double
int	long, float or double
char	int, long, float or double
short	int, long, float or double
byte	short, int, long, float or double
boolean	none

Figure 14.8 Primitive types and their allowed conversions.

Only certain conversions are allowed. The types listed in the right column are "larger" types, in that they can store more data than the types in the left column. For example, `int` values (left column) can be converted to `long` values (right column, which includes two other types). An `int` variable can store values in the approximate range –2.1 billion to +2.1 billion, while a `long` variable can store numbers in the approximate range -9×10^{18} to $+9 \times 10^{18}$ (9 followed by 18 zeros). This means that any `int` value can be assigned to a `long` variable without losing any data. These kinds of conversions are called **widening conversions**, because the value of a "smaller" or "narrower" type (`int`) is being converted to a value of a "larger" or "wider" type (`long`).

Conversions that change a value of a "larger" type to a value of a "smaller" type are known as **narrowing conversions**. Narrowing conversions require you to explicitly specify the conversion. That is why these conversions are called **explicit conversions** (or casting). Explicit conversions require a **cast operator** (or cast) which is a type name contained in parentheses. According to Fig. 14.8, Java does not allow the implicit conversion of `double` values to `int` values (because information could be lost). You can force this conversion to take place using a cast. For example, if `intValue` is of type `int` and `doubleValue` is of type `double`, you can write

```
intValue = ( int ) doubleValue;
```

Error-Prevention Tip

Avoid narrowing conversions where possible because they can result in a loss of information.

without causing a compilation error. Note that the value stored in `doubleValue` may lose some precision when it is cast to an `int`. If there is a fractional part of `doubleValue`, it will be truncated.

You have now learned the Java technology required to create and complete this application. Now you will display the net donation amount and the total donation amount.

Finishing the Fundraiser Application

1. ***Displaying the donation amount after the operating expenses are deducted.*** Add lines 145–150 of Fig. 14.9 to the `donateJButtonActionPerformed` method. The donation amount after expenses is formatted as a dollar amount and displayed in the **After expenses:** `JTextField`.

Display the donation amount after expenses are subtracted →

```
Source Editor [Fundraiser *]                                          _ □ ×

143          double netDonation = calculateDonation( grossDonation );
144
145             // specify display format
146             DecimalFormat dollars = new DecimalFormat( "$0.00" );
147
148             // display amount of donation after expenses
149             afterExpensesJTextField.setText(
150                dollars.format( netDonation ) );
151
152       } // end method donateJButtonActionPerformed
```

Figure 14.9 Displaying the donation amount after operating expenses are deducted.

2. ***Updating and displaying the total donation.*** Add lines 152–157 of Fig. 14.10 to the `donateJButtonActionPerformed` method. Line 153 updates instance variable `totalNetDonations`, which stores the total amount given to the charity after the operating expenses have been deducted. Lines 156–157 display the total amount raised for charity.

   Local variables, such as `grossDonation` (line 139 of Fig. 14.6), are declared in a block and go out of scope at the end of that block. This means that local variables cannot retain their value between method calls. Instance variables however, maintain their value because their scope is the entire class. Variable `totalNetDonations` is an instance variable so it can be used to store the total of the donations over repeated calls to the `donateJButtonActionPerformed` method.

Update instance variable →

Display total amount raised for charity →

```
Source Editor [Fundraiser *]                                          _ □ ×

150             dollars.format( netDonation ) );
151
152             // update total amount of donations received
153             totalNetDonations += netDonation;
154
155             // display total amount collected for charity
156             totalRaisedJTextField.setText(
157                dollars.format( totalNetDonations ) );
158
159       } // end method donateJButtonActionPerformed
```

Figure 14.10 Updating and displaying the total amount raised for charity.

3. ***Clearing the After expenses: JTextField.*** The template application includes the `donationJTextFieldKeyPressed` method (lines 161–167 of Fig. 14.11) for the **Donation:** `JTextField`'s keyPressed event handler. When the user enters data into the **Donation:** `JTextField`, the `donationJTextFieldKeyPressed` method is eventually called, and line 165 clears the net donation from the **After expenses:** `JTextField`.

4. ***Saving the application.*** Save your modified source code file.

5. ***Opening the Command Prompt window and changing directories.*** Open the **Command Prompt** window by selecting **Start > Programs > Accessories > Command Prompt**. Change to your working directory by typing cd `C:\SimplyJava\Fundraiser`.

6. ***Compiling the application.*** Compile your application by typing javac `Fundraiser.java`.

(cont.)

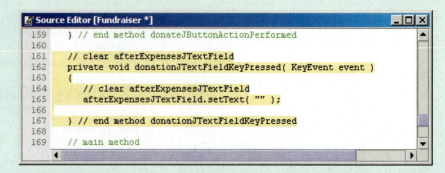

Figure 14.11 Clearing the **After Expenses:** JTextField.

7. **Running the application.** When your application compiles correctly, run it by typing java Fundraiser. Figure 14.12 shows the completed application running.

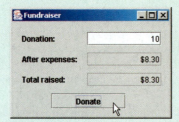

Figure 14.12 Running the completed application.

8. **Closing the application.** Close your running application by clicking its close button.

9. **Closing the Command Prompt window.** Close the **Command Prompt** window by clicking its close button.

Figure 14.13 presents the source code for the **Fundraiser** application. The lines of code that you added, viewed or modified in this tutorial are highlighted.

```
1   // Tutorial 14: Fundraiser.java
2   // Calculates the amount of a donation after expenses and then
3   // totals repeated donations.
4   import java.awt.*;
5   import java.awt.event.*;
6   import java.text.*;
7   import javax.swing.*;
8
9   public class Fundraiser extends JFrame
10  {
11     // JLabel and JTextField to hold donation
12     private JLabel donationJLabel;
13     private JTextField donationJTextField;
14
15     // JLabel and JTextField to display amount after expenses
16     private JLabel afterExpensesJLabel;
17     private JTextField afterExpensesJTextField;
18
19     // JLabel and JTextField to display total amount raised
20     private JLabel totalRaisedJLabel;
21     private JTextField totalRaisedJTextField;
```

Figure 14.13 **Fundraiser** application code. (Part 1 of 4.)

```
22
23       // JButton to allow user to enter donation
24       private JButton donateJButton;
25
26       // instance variable stores total raised for charity
27       private double totalNetDonations = 0.00;
28
29       // no-argument constructor
30       public Fundraiser()
31       {
32          createUserInterface();
33       }
34
35       // create and position GUI components; register event handlers
36       private void createUserInterface()
37       {
38          // get content pane for attaching GUI components
39          Container contentPane = getContentPane();
40
41          // enable explicit positioning of GUI components
42          contentPane.setLayout( null );
43
44          // set up donationJLabel
45          donationJLabel = new JLabel();
46          donationJLabel.setBounds( 16, 16, 80, 20 );
47          donationJLabel.setText( "Donation:" );
48          contentPane.add( donationJLabel );
49
50          // set up donationJTextField
51          donationJTextField = new JTextField();
52          donationJTextField.setBounds( 122, 16, 120, 21 );
53          donationJTextField.setHorizontalAlignment( JTextField.RIGHT );
54          contentPane.add( donationJTextField );
55          donationJTextField.addKeyListener(
56
57             new KeyAdapter() // anonymous inner class
58             {
59                // event handler called when donationJTextField is edited
60                public void keyPressed( KeyEvent event )
61                {
62                   donationJTextFieldKeyPressed( event );
63                }
64
65             } // end anonymous inner class
66
67          ); // end call to addKeyListener
68
69          // set up afterExpensesJLabel
70          afterExpensesJLabel = new JLabel();
71          afterExpensesJLabel.setBounds( 16, 48, 98, 20 );
72          afterExpensesJLabel.setText( "After expenses:" );
73          contentPane.add( afterExpensesJLabel );
74
75          // set up afterExpensesJTextField
76          afterExpensesJTextField = new JTextField();
77          afterExpensesJTextField.setBounds( 122, 48, 120, 20 );
78          afterExpensesJTextField.setText( "$0.00" );
79          afterExpensesJTextField.setEditable( false );
```

Declaring instance variable —

Figure 14.13 **Fundraiser** application code. (Part 2 of 4.)

```
80      afterExpensesJTextField.setHorizontalAlignment(
81         JTextField.RIGHT );
82      contentPane.add( afterExpensesJTextField );
83
84      // set up totalRaisedJLabel
85      totalRaisedJLabel = new JLabel();
86      totalRaisedJLabel.setBounds( 16, 80, 88, 20 );
87      totalRaisedJLabel.setText( "Total raised:" );
88      contentPane.add( totalRaisedJLabel );
89
90      // set up totalRaisedJTextField
91      totalRaisedJTextField = new JTextField();
92      totalRaisedJTextField.setBounds( 122, 80, 120, 20 );
93      totalRaisedJTextField.setText( "$0.00" );
94      totalRaisedJTextField.setEditable( false );
95      totalRaisedJTextField.setHorizontalAlignment(
96         JTextField.RIGHT );
97      contentPane.add( totalRaisedJTextField );
98
99      // set up donateJButton
100     donateJButton = new JButton();
101     donateJButton.setBounds( 63, 112, 122, 24 );
102     donateJButton.setText( "Donate" );
103     contentPane.add( donateJButton );
104     donateJButton.addActionListener(
105
106        new ActionListener() // anonymous inner class
107        {
108           // event handler called when donateJButton is clicked
109           public void actionPerformed( ActionEvent event )
110           {
111              donateJButtonActionPerformed( event );
112           }
113
114        } // end anonymous inner class
115
116     ); // end call to addActionListener
117
118     // set properties of application's window
119     setTitle( "Fundraiser" );  // set title bar string
120     setSize( 263, 174 );       // set window size
121     setVisible( true );        // display window
122
123  } // end method createUserInterface
124
125  // returns donation amount after operating expenses
126  private double calculateDonation( int donatedAmount )
127  {
128     final double NET_PERCENTAGE = 0.83;
129
130     // calculate amount of donation for charity
131     return NET_PERCENTAGE * donatedAmount;
132
133  } // end method calculateDonation
134
135  // calculate the donation and fill the JTextFields
136  private void donateJButtonActionPerformed( ActionEvent event )
137  {
```

Declaring the method
calculateDonation

Figure 14.13 Fundraiser application code. (Part 3 of 4.)

Obtaining the donation amount

Calling the `calculateDonation` method to obtain donation amount after deducting operating expenses

Displaying the donation amount

Updating the total amount of donations received

Displaying the total amount of donations to the charity after expenses

Clearing `afterExpensesJTextField`

```
138        // get donation amount
139        int grossDonation =
140           Integer.parseInt( donationJTextField.getText() );
141
142        // obtain donation amount after operating expenses deduction
143        double netDonation = calculateDonation( grossDonation );
144
145        // specify display format
146        DecimalFormat dollars = new DecimalFormat( "$0.00" );
147
148        // display amount of donation after expenses
149        afterExpensesJTextField.setText(
150           dollars.format( netDonation ) );
151
152        // update total amount of donations received
153        totalNetDonations += netDonation;
154
155        // display total amount collected for charity
156        totalRaisedJTextField.setText(
157           dollars.format( totalNetDonations ) );
158
159     } // end method donateJButtonActionPerformed
160
161     // clear afterExpensesJTextField
162     private void donationJTextFieldKeyPressed( KeyEvent event )
163     {
164        // clear afterExpensesJTextField
165        afterExpensesJTextField.setText( "" );
166
167     } // end method donationJTextFieldKeyPressed
168
169     // main method
170     public static void main( String args[] )
171     {
172        Fundraiser application = new Fundraiser();
173        application.setDefaultCloseOperation( JFrame.EXIT_ON_CLOSE );
174
175     } // end method main
176
177  } // end class Fundraiser
```

Figure 14.13　**Fundraiser** application code. (Part 4 of 4.)

You have learned the rules governing when a variable is in and out of scope. You will now learn what happens when you try to access a local variable that is not in scope.

Accessing a Variable that is Out of Scope

1. *Attempting to access a local variable that is out of scope.* Now you will learn the limits of local variables. In line 131 of Fig. 14.14, temporarily replace `donatedAmount` in the multiplication operation with `grossDona-tion`. Variable `grossDonation` is a local variable declared in line 139 of Fig. 14.13 in the `donateJButtonActionPerformed` method. This variable is only in scope within the `donateJButtonActionPerformed` method. Attempting to access it inside the `calculateDonation` method (line 131 of Fig. 14.14) causes a compilation error.

(cont.)

Try to access local variable `grossDonation`, which is out of scope

```
Source Editor [Fundraiser *]                              _ □ X
125    // returns donation amount after operating expenses
126    private double calculateDonation( int donatedAmount )
127    {
128        final double NET_PERCENTAGE = 0.83;
129
130        // calculate amount of donation for charity
131        return NET_PERCENTAGE * grossDonation;
132
133    } // end method calculateDonation
```

Figure 14.14 Attempting to access `donateJButtonActionPerformed`'s local variable `grossDonation` when it is out of scope.

2. *Saving the application.* Save your modified source code file.

3. *Opening the Command Prompt window and changing directories.* Open the **Command Prompt** window by selecting **Start > Programs > Accessories > Command Prompt**. Change to your working directory by typing cd C:\SimplyJava\Fundraiser.

4. *Compiling the application.* Compile your application by typing javac Fundraiser.java. Note that a compilation error occurs (Fig. 14.15). Because the variable grossDonation is local to donateJButtonAction-Performed, the calculateDonation method cannot access that variable.

```
Command Prompt                                             _ □ X
C:\SimplyJava\Fundraiser>javac Fundraiser.java
Fundraiser.java:131: cannot resolve symbol
symbol  : variable grossDonation
location: class Fundraiser
        return NET_PERCENTAGE * grossDonation;
                                ^
1 error

C:\SimplyJava\Fundraiser>
```

Figure 14.15 Attempting to access `donateJButtonActionPerformed`'s local variable `grossDonation` causes a compilation error.

5. *Returning to the text editor and undoing the change.* Replace variable grossDonation in line 131 of Fig. 14.14 with donatedAmount.

6. *Saving the application.* Save your modified source code file.

SELF-REVIEW

1. An int variable can be implicitly converted to _____.
   a) long
   b) double
   c) float
   d) All of the above.

2. The operation that assigns the value of a "larger" type to a variable of a "smaller" type is known as a _____.
   a) restricted conversion
   b) narrowing conversion
   c) widening conversion
   d) None of the above.

Answers: 1) d. 2) b.

14.4 Wrap-Up

In this tutorial, you learned about types and variables, and you built the **Fundraiser** application to demonstrate these concepts.

You learned that the scope of the instance variables of a class is the entire class, which means that instance variables are accessible to all methods in the class in which they are declared. You declared an instance variable in the Fundraiser class.

In Tutorial 18, you will learn how to create your own classes and how to declare instance variables in them. You learned that the scope of a local variable is from the point at which the declaration appears to the end of the block containing the declaration. Local variables are accessible only within the block (such as the body of an `if` statement or a method) in which they are declared.

You also learned about primitive type conversions. You learned that Java performs implicit conversions on selected operands to ensure that the operands of an expression are of the same type before the expression is evaluated. You learned the casting operator is required for explicit conversions.

In the next tutorial, you will learn about random number generation, and you will create an application that simulates the dice game called Craps.

SKILLS SUMMARY

Understanding Scope

■ Instance variables of a class can be accessed by all methods of that class.

■ Local variables cannot be referenced outside the block in which they are declared.

Understanding Implicit Conversion

■ Values of certain primitive types can be converted to values of other primitive types. A temporary value of the appropriate type is created, but the original value remains unchanged.

■ Values of type `double` cannot be implicitly converted to any other primitive type.

■ Values of type `float` can be implicitly converted to type `double`.

■ Values of type `long` can be implicitly converted to type `float` or `double`.

■ Values of type `int` can be implicitly converted to type `long`, `float` or `double`.

■ Values of type `char` can be implicitly converted to type `int`, `long`, `float` or `double`.

■ Values of type `short` can be implicitly converted to type `int`, `long`, `float` or `double`.

■ Values of type `byte` can be implicitly converted to type `short`, `int`, `long`, `float` or `double`.

■ Values of type `boolean` cannot be implicitly converted to any other primitive type.

KEY TERMS

cast operator—A type name enclosed in parentheses. A cast operator is used to perform explicit conversions. A temporary value of the type in the parentheses will be created and used in the expression.

explicit conversion—An operation converting a value of one type to a value of another type requiring a cast operator. Also called casting.

hidden variable—An instance variable with the same name as a local variable is hidden while the local variable has scope. Hidden variables can lead to logic errors.

implicit conversion—An operation that converts a primitive type to another type without writing code to (explicitly) tell the application to do the conversion.

instance variable—Declared inside a class but outside any methods of that class. The scope of an instance variable is its entire class.

local variable—Declared inside a block. The scope of a local variable is from the point at which the declaration appears in the block to the end of that block.

narrowing conversion—An operation that converts a "larger" type value to a "smaller" type value. These conversions are dangerous because information about the value can be lost.

scope—The portion of an application in which an identifier (such as a variable name) can be referenced. Some identifiers can be referenced throughout an application, while others can be referenced only from limited portions of an application (such as within a single method or block).

widening conversion—An operation that converts a "smaller" type value to a "larger" type value.

MULTIPLE-CHOICE QUESTIONS

14.1 An instance variable with the same name as a local variable is known as a(n) _____ while the local variable has scope.

a) narrowing variable   b) implicit variable

c) hidden variable   d) widening variable

14.2 Explicit conversions are also known as _____.

a) implicit conversions   b) casting

c) widening conversions   d) hiding

14.3 A variable declared inside a class, but outside a method, is called a(n) _____.

a) local variable   b) hidden variable

c) instance variable   d) constant variable

14.4 _____ happens when addition occurs between an int value and a double value.

a) Implicit conversion   b) Casting

c) Assignment   d) None of the above.

14.5 Accessing a local variable outside the block in which the local variable is defined causes a _____.

a) logic error   b) compilation error

c) runtime error   d) None of the above.

14.6 A cast operator must be used for all _____.

a) implicit conversions   b) widening conversions

c) local variables   d) Both (b) and (c).

14.7 A double value can be implicitly converted to a(n) _____.

a) int   b) float

c) long   d) None of the above.

14.8 Instance variables _____.

a) are declared inside a class   b) have scope in the entire class

c) can be accessed by any method in the same class

d) All of the above.

14.9 Assigning a "smaller" type to a "larger" type is a(n) _____ conversion.

a) narrowing   b) shortening

c) widening   d) illegal

14.10 A value of type boolean can be implicitly converted to _____.

a) int   b) double

c) long   d) None of the above.

EXERCISES

14.11 (*Task List Application*) Create an application that allows users to add items to a daily task list. The application's GUI should appear as in Fig. 14.16. The tasks should be placed in a JTextArea, one task per line. The application should also display the number of tasks to be performed. Use method String.valueOf to display the number of tasks in numberJText-Field.

a) *Copying the template to your working directory.* Copy the directory C:\Examples\Tutorial14\Exercises\TaskList to your C:\SimplyJava directory.

b) *Opening the template file.* Open the TaskList.java file in your text editor.

c) *Declaring an instance variable.* At line 24, declare instance variable counter of type int and initialize its value to 0. Add a comment before you declare the instance variable.

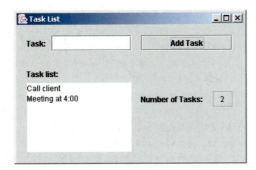

Figure 14.16 Task List application's GUI

d) *Adding code to the Add Task JButton's actionPerformed event handler.* At line 108, add code to the addTaskJButtonActionPerformed method. This method should display the user input in the taskListJTextArea, increment the instance variable created in the previous step, update the numberJTextField that displays the number of tasks and clear the user input from the taskJTextField. Use method String.valueOf to display the number of tasks in the numberJTextField.

e) *Saving the application.* Save your modified source code file.

f) *Opening the Command Prompt window and changing directories.* Open the **Command Prompt** window by selecting **Start > Programs > Accessories > Command Prompt**. Change to your working directory by typing cd C:\SimplyJava\TaskList.

g) *Compiling the application.* Compile your application by typing javac TaskList.java.

h) *Running the completed application.* When your application compiles correctly, run it by typing java TaskList. Test the application by adding tasks to the task list.

i) *Closing the application.* Close your running application by clicking its close button.

j) *Closing the Command Prompt window.* Close the **Command Prompt** window by clicking its close button.

14.12 (*Quiz Average Application*) Develop an application that computes a student's average quiz score for all of the quiz scores entered. The application's GUI should appear as in Fig. 14.17. Use method Integer.parseInt to convert the user input to an int, and assign that value to a double. [*Note:* Implicit conversion occurs when you assign an int value to a double.] Use instance variables to keep track of the sum of all the quiz scores entered and the number of quiz scores entered. Each time a score is submitted, your application should recalculate the average.

Figure 14.17 Quiz Average application's GUI.

a) *Copying the template to your working directory.* Copy the C:\Examples\Tutorial14\Exercises\QuizAverage directory to your C:\SimplyJava directory.

b) *Opening the template file.* Open the QuizAverage.java file in your text editor.

c) *Adding instance variables.* At line 26, add two instance variables. The int instance variable quizzesTaken will keep track of the number of quiz scores entered. The double instance variable totalScore will keep track of the sum of all the quiz scores entered. These two variables will be used to calculate the class average. Add a comment before you declare the instance variables.

d) *Adding code to the submitJButtonActionPerformed method.* Find the submitJButtonActionPerformed method (line 110) located just after method createUserInterface. The code required in *Steps e–j* should be placed in this method.

e) *Obtaining user input.* Use method `Integer.parseInt` to convert the user input from the `quizJTextField` to an `int` which should then be assigned to a variable of type `double`.

f) *Updating the number of quiz scores entered.* Add code to increment the number of quiz scores entered.

g) *Updating the sum of all the quiz scores entered.* Add code that will add the current quiz score to the current total to update the sum of all the quiz scores entered.

h) *Calculating the average score.* Add code to divide the sum of all the quiz scores by the number of quiz scores entered to calculate the average score. Notice that the number of quiz scores is an `int`, but will be implicitly converted to a `double` for the division calculation.

i) *Displaying the number of quizzes taken.* Use method `String.valueOf` to display the number of quiz scores entered in the `numberJTextField`.

j) *Displaying the average score.* Display the average quiz grade in the `averageJText-Field` using `DecimalFormat` with two digits of precision.

k) *Saving the application.* Save your modified source code file.

l) *Opening the Command Prompt window and changing directories.* Open the **Command Prompt** by selecting **Start > Programs > Accessories > Command Prompt**. Change to your working directory by typing `cd C:\SimplyJava\QuizAverage`.

m) *Compiling the application.* Compile your application by typing `javac QuizAverage.java`.

n) *Running the completed application.* When your application compiles correctly, run it by typing `java QuizAverage`. Test the application by submitting a number of quiz scores. Check that the average is calculated correctly.

o) *Closing the application.* Close your running application by clicking its close button.

p) *Closing the Command Prompt window.* Close the **Command Prompt** window by clicking its close button.

14.13 (*Vending Machine Application*) Create an application that mimics the functionality of a vending machine. Your application's GUI has been completed for you (Fig. 14.18). Store the prices of each item for sale in the vending machine in an instance variable. Also, add the code that will display the price of an item when the item's number has been entered and **Enter** `JButton` has been clicked.

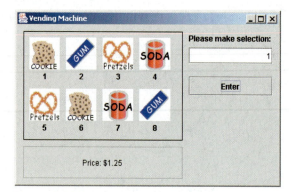

Figure 14.18 **Vending Machine** application displaying a price.

a) *Copying the template to your working directory.* Copy the directory `C:\Examples\Tutorial14\Exercises\VendingMachine2` to your `C:\SimplyJava` directory.

b) *Opening the template file.* Open the `VendingMachine.java` file in your text editor.

c) *Adding instance variables.* After the last GUI component is declared (line 53), declare `private String` instance variables to store the prices of each of the snacks. Each `String` should be in the form `"$0.00"` where the price of the snack is substituted for the zeros. The variables' names and prices should be `snackPrice1` (`"$1.25"`), `snackPrice2` (`"$0.50"`), `snackPrice3` (`"$1.25"`), `snackPrice4` (`"$1.00"`), `snackPrice5` (`"$1.25"`), `snackPrice6` (`"$1.25"`), `snackPrice7` (`"$1.00"`) and `snackPrice8` (`"$0.50"`).

d) *Coding the enterJButtonActionPerformed method.* Locate the enterJButtonActionPerformed method. In this method, store the user input entered in the inputJTextField. Then, use a switch statement to display in displayJTextField the String resulting from concatenation of "Price: " with the price of the item selected. Use a default case for when the user does not enter a numeric value from 1–8.

e) *Saving the application.* Save your modified source code file.

f) *Opening the Command Prompt window and changing directories.* Open the **Command Prompt** window by selecting **Start > Programs > Accessories > Command Prompt**. Change to your working directory by typing cd C:\SimplyJava\ VendingMachine2.

g) *Compiling the application.* Compile your application by typing javac Vending-Machine.java.

h) *Running the completed application.* When your application compiles correctly, run it by typing java VendingMachine. Test your application by entering the number 1 in the inputJTextField and clicking the **Enter** JButton. The displayJTextField should display the first String instance variable (it should appear similar to Fig. 14.18).

i) *Closing the application.* Close your running application by clicking its close button.

j) *Closing the Command Prompt window.* Close the **Command Prompt** window by clicking its close button.

What does this code do?

14.14 What is displayed in the message dialog when the following code is executed? Assume that the following two methods are placed within a class which contains an instance variable, intValue2. This instance variable was initialized to the value 5 when it was declared. The enterJButtonActionPerformed method will execute when one of the class's JButtons, enterJButton, is clicked.

```
1  private void enterJButtonActionPerformed( ActionEvent )
2  {
3     int intValue1 = 10;
4     int intValue2 = 3;
5     int result = mystery( intValue1 );
6
7     // display output
8     JOptionPane.showMessageDialog( this, String.valueOf( result ),
9        "Mystery Message", JOptionPane.INFORMATION_MESSAGE );
10
11 } // end method enterJButtonActionPerformed
12
13 private int mystery( int inputValue )
14 {
15    return inputValue * intValue2;
16
17 } // end method mystery
```

What's wrong with this code?

14.15 Find the error(s) in the following code (the method should assign the value 14 to variable result).

```
1  private void sum()
2  {
3     String number4 = "4";
4     int number10 = 10;
5
6     int result = number4 + number10;
7
8  } // end method sum
```

Programming Challenge

14.16 (*Decryption Application*) Develop an application that allows a user to decrypt a secret message (a string of numbers). The user should enter each number of the message one at a time in a `JTextField`. When the **Decrypt** `JButton` is clicked, the number should be decrypted to a letter. That letter should then be appended to the **Decrypted message:** `JTextField`. When the user enters the numbers 39, 79, 79, 68, 0, 55, 79, 82, 75, 1 in order, your application should appear as in Fig. 14.19.

Figure 14.19 **Decryption** application displays a message.

a) *Copying the template to your working directory.* Copy the directory `C:\Examples\Tutorial14\Exercises\Decryption` to your `C:\SimplyJava` directory.

b) *Opening the template file.* Open the `Decryption.java` file in your text editor.

c) *Adding an instance variable.* After the last GUI component is declared (line 18), add a declaration for a `private String` named `message` which will hold the decrypted message. Initialize `message` to the empty string. Use one line for a comment.

d) *Storing the user input.* Add code in the `decryptJButtonActionPerformed` method that will store the user input in an `int` variable named `encryptedLetter`. The rest of the code you will add in this exercises should be placed in the `decryptJButtonActionPerformed` method.

e) *Testing the user input.* Your application should only accept user input in the range 0 to 94. Add an `if` statement that will test whether the user's input is in the accepted range of values.

f) *Decrypting the input.* Add code to the `if` statement that will decrypt `encryptedLetter` and append it to the `String message`. Letters should be decrypted by first adding 32 to the `int`. This value should then be converted to a `char` type. Note: To convert from an `int` to a `char` requires the cast operator (`char`). This calculation results in the number 1 decrypted to the character `'!'` and the number 33 decrypted to the character `'A'`.

g) *Displaying output and clearing the user input.* Inside the `if` statement, add code to display `String message` in `messageJTextField`. After the `if` statement, add code to clear `encryptedLetterJTextField`.

h) *Saving the application.* Save your modified source code file.

i) *Opening the Command Prompt window and changing directories.* Open the **Command Prompt** by selecting **Start > Programs > Accessories > Command Prompt**. Change to your working directory by typing cd `C:\SimplyJava\Decryption`.

j) *Compiling the application.* Compile your application by typing `javac Decryption.java`.

k) *Running the completed application.* When your application compiles correctly, run it by typing `java Decryption`. Test your application by entering the number 39 and clicking the **Decrypt** `JButton`. The letter `'G'` should now appear in `messageJTextField`. Now, input the following numbers 79, 79, 68, 0, 55, 79, 82, 75, 1. If your application has been programmed correctly, `messageJTextField` should now display the message "Good Work!".

l) *Closing the application.* Close your running application by clicking its close button.

m) *Closing the Command Prompt window.* Close the **Command Prompt** window by clicking its close button.

Objectives

In this tutorial, you will learn to:
- Use simulation techniques that employ random number generation.
- Use methods of class **Random**.
- Generate random numbers.
- Use constants to enhance code readability.
- Use a **JPanel** and a **TitledBorder** to add a border around components.

Outline

15.1 Test-Driving the **Craps Game** Application
15.2 Random Number Generation
15.3 Using Constants in the **Craps Game** Application
15.4 Using Random Numbers in the **Craps Game** Application
15.5 Wrap-Up

Craps Game Application

Introducing Random Number Generation and the JPanel

You will now study a popular type of application involving simulation and game playing. In this tutorial, you will develop a **Craps Game** application. There is something in the air of a gambling casino that invigorates people—from the high rollers at the plush mahogany-and-felt Craps tables to the quarter-poppers at the one-armed bandits. It is the element of chance—the possibility that luck will convert a pocketful of money into a mountain of wealth. Unfortunately, that rarely happens because the odds, of course, favor the casinos.

The element of chance can be introduced into computer applications using random numbers. This tutorial's **Craps Game** application introduces random number generation and the JPanel component. It also uses important concepts that you learned earlier in this book, including constants, instance variables, methods and the switch multiple-selection statement.

15.1 Test-Driving the Craps Game Application

One of the most popular games of chance is a dice game known as "Craps," played in casinos throughout the world. This application must meet the following requirements:

> ### Application Requirements
>
> *Create an application that simulates playing the world-famous dice game "Craps." In this game, a player rolls two dice. Each die has six faces. Each face contains 1, 2, 3, 4, 5 or 6 spots. After the dice have come to rest, the sum of the spots on the two top faces is calculated. If the sum is 7 or 11 on the first roll, the player wins. If the sum is 2, 3 or 12 on the first roll (called "craps"), the player loses (the "house" wins). If the sum is 4, 5, 6, 8, 9 or 10 on the first roll, that sum becomes the player's "point." To win, a player must continue rolling the dice until the player rolls the point value. The player loses by rolling a 7 before rolling the point.*

You begin by test-driving the completed application. Then, you will learn the additional Java technologies you will need to create your own version of this application.

Test-Driving the Craps Game Application

1. ***Locating the completed application.*** Open the **Command Prompt** window by selecting **Start > Programs > Accessories > Command Prompt**. Change to your completed **Craps Game** application directory by typing `cd C:\Examples\Tutorial15\CompletedApplication\CrapsGame`.

2. ***Running the Craps Game application.*** Type `java CrapsGame` in the **Command Prompt** window to run the application (Fig. 15.1).

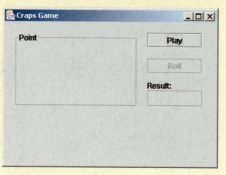

Figure 15.1   Initial appearance of **Craps Game** application.

3. ***Starting the game.*** Click the **Play** `JButton` to make the first roll of the dice. There are three possible outcomes at this point. The player wins by rolling a 7 or an 11 (Fig. 15.2). The player loses by rolling a 2, a 3 or a 12 (Fig. 15.3). Otherwise, the roll becomes the player's point (4, 5, 6, 8, 9 or 10), and the dice are displayed as images in `JLabel`s for the remainder of the game (Fig. 15.4). Note that unlike the real game of Craps, the value of the roll is computed in this application using the forward-facing die faces instead of the top faces.

Figure 15.2   Player winning on first roll by rolling 7.

Figure 15.3   Player losing on first roll by rolling 3.

(cont.)

Figure 15.4   Player's first roll setting the point that the player must match to win.

4. ***Continuing the game.*** If the player does not win or lose on the first roll, the application displays **Roll again!**, as in Fig. 15.4. Click the **Roll** JButton repeatedly until either you win by matching your point value (Fig. 15.5) or you lose by rolling a 7 (Fig. 15.6). When the game ends, you can click the **Play** JButton to start a new game.

Figure 15.5   Player winning the game by matching the point before rolling a 7.

Figure 15.6   Player losing by rolling a 7 before matching the point.

5. ***Closing the running application.*** Close the running application by clicking its close button.

6. ***Closing the Command Prompt window.*** Close the **Command Prompt** window by clicking its close button.

15.2 Random Number Generation

Now you will learn how to use an object of class **Random** to introduce the element of chance into your applications. You will learn more about working with objects of the Java class library over the next few tutorials, then you will learn to create your own classes and objects of those classes in Tutorial 18. Consider the following statements:

```
Random randomGenerator = new Random();
int randomNumber = randomGenerator.nextInt();
```

The first statement declares `randomGenerator` as a variable of type `Random` and assigns it a **reference** to a Random object. A reference is a variable that refers to an object. A reference specifies the location in the computer's memory of an object. The keyword **new** creates an object and assigns it a location in memory.

The second statement declares `int` variable `randomNumber`. The statement then assigns to `randomNumber` the value returned by calling the `nextInt` method on the Random object `randomGenerator`. The **nextInt** method generates a random `int` value selected from all possible `int` values (positive and negative). You can use the `nextInt` method to generate random values of type `int`, or you can use the **nextDouble** method to generate random values of type `double`. The `nextDouble` method returns a positive `double` value between `0.0` and `1.0` (not including `1.0`). Class Random also contains methods to randomly generate values of the primitive types `boolean`, `float` and `long`.

If the `nextInt` method was to produce truly random values, then every `int` value would have an equal chance (or probability) of being chosen when `nextInt` is called. The `nextInt` method comes close to achieving this goal.

The range of values produced by `nextInt` often is different from the range needed in a particular application. For example, an application that simulates coin tossing might require only the random integers 0 for "heads" and 1 for "tails." An application that simulates the rolling of a six-sided die might require only the random integers from 1 to 6. Similarly, an application that randomly predicts the next type of spaceship (out of four possibilities) that flies across the horizon in a video game might require only the random integers from 1 to 4.

By passing an argument to the `nextInt`[1] method as follows

```
value = 1 + randomGenerator.nextInt( 6 );
```

you can produce random integers in the range from 1 to 6. When a single argument is passed to `nextInt`, the values returned by `nextInt` will be in the range from 0 to one less than the value of that argument (5 in the preceding statement). You can change the range of numbers produced by `nextInt` by adding 1 to the previous result, so that the return values are between 1 and 6, rather than 0 and 5. That new range, 1 to 6, corresponds nicely with the roll of a six-sided die, for example.

As with the `nextInt` method, the range of values produced by the `nextDouble` method (that is, values greater than or equal to `0.0` and less than `1.0`) is also usually different from the range needed in a particular application. By multiplying the value returned from the `nextDouble` method as follows

```
doubleValue = 10 * randomGenerator.nextDouble();
```

you can produce `double` values in the range from `0.0` to `10.0` (not including `10.0`). Figure 15.7 shows examples of the ranges of random numbers returned by expressions containing calls to methods `nextInt` and `nextDouble`.

Expression	Resulting range
`randomGenerator.nextInt()`	(-2^{32}) to $(2^{32} - 1)$ [all possible values of `int`]
`randomGenerator.nextInt( 30 )`	0 to 29

Figure 15.7 `nextInt` and `nextDouble` method call expressions with ranges of random numbers produced. (Part 1 of 2.)

---

1. In Tutorial 12, you learned that the number, type and order of arguments to a method must exactly match the method declaration. You may have noticed that the `nextInt` method of class `Random` can be called using zero arguments or one argument. Java has a capability called **method overloading** that allows several methods to have the same name but different numbers or types of arguments.

Expression	Resulting range
10 + randomGenerator.nextInt(10)	10 to 19
randomGenerator.nextDouble()	0.0 to less than 1.0
8 * randomGenerator.nextDouble()	0.0 to less than 8.0

Figure 15.7 nextInt and nextDouble method call expressions with ranges of random numbers produced. (Part 2 of 2.)

SELF-REVIEW

1. The statement _____ returns an integer in the range 8–300.

   a) 7 + randomObject.nextInt(293);   b) 8 + randomObject.nextInt(292);
   c) 8 + randomObject.nextInt(293);   d) None of the above.

2. The statement _____ returns a number in the range 15–35.

   a) 10 + randomObject.nextInt(26);   b) 15 + randomObject.nextInt(21);
   c) 10 + randomObject.nextInt(25);   d) 15 + randomObject.nextInt(35);

Answers: 1) c. 2) b.

15.3 Using Constants in the Craps Game Application

The following pseudocode describes the basic operation of the **Craps Game** application when the **Play** JButton is clicked:

> When the player clicks the Play JButton
>   Roll the two dice using random numbers
>   Calculate the sum of the two dice
>   Display images of the rolled dice
>
>   Switch based on the sum of the two dice:
>
>   Case where the sum is 7 or 11
>   Display the winning message
>
>   Case where the sum is 2, 3 or 12
>   Display the losing message
>
>   Default case
>   Set the value of the point to the sum of the dice and display the
>   value
>   Disable the Play JButton and enable the Roll JButton
>
> When the player clicks the Roll JButton
>   Roll the two dice using random numbers
>   Calculate the sum of the two dice
>   Display images of the rolled dice
>
>   If the player rolls the point
>   Display the winning message
>   Clear the value of the point
>   Enable the Play JButton and disable the Roll JButton
>
>   If the player rolls a 7
>   Display the losing message
>   Clear the value of the point
>   Enable the Play JButton and disable the Roll JButton

Now that you have test-driven the **Craps Game** application and studied its pseudocode representation, you will use an ACE table to help you convert the pseudocode to Java. Figure 15.8 lists the actions, components and events that will help you complete your own version of this application.

Action	Component	Event
Label the application's components	`resultJLabel`	
	`playJButton`	User clicks **Play** `JButton`
Roll the two dice using random numbers	`randomObject` `(Random)`	
Calculate the sum of the two dice		
Display images of the rolled dice	`die1JLabel,` `die2JLabel`	
Switch based on the sum of the two dice:		
Case where the sum is 7 or 11　　Display the winning message	`resultJTextField`	
Case where the sum is 2, 3 or 12　　Display the losing message	`resultJTextField`	
Default case　　Display the value of the point	`pointDie1JLabel,` `pointDie2JLabel`	
Disable the Play JButton and　　enable the Roll JButton	`playJButton,` `rollJButton`	
	`rollJButton`	User clicks **Roll** `JButton`
Roll the two dice using random numbers	`randomObject` `(Random)`	
Calculate the sum of the two dice		
Display images of the rolled dice	`die1JLabel,` `die2JLabel`	
If the player rolls the point　　Display the winning message	`resultJTextField`	
Clear the value of the point	`pointDie1JLabel,` `pointDie2JLabel`	
Enable the Play JButton and　　disable the Roll JButton	`playJButton,` `rollJButton`	
If the player rolls a 7　　Display the losing message	`resultJTextField`	
Clear the value of the point	`pointDie1JLabel,` `pointDie2JLabel`	
Enable the Play JButton and　　disable the Roll JButton	`playJButton,` `rollJButton`	

Figure 15.8　ACE table for the **Craps Game** application.

In the following boxes, you will create an entertaining application that simulates playing the game Craps. As you have learned, Java has access to the Java class library, which is a rich collection of classes that can be used to enhance applications. The Java class library includes classes for enabling your applications to use files, graphics, multimedia, perform arithmetic operations and much more. These predefined classes are grouped into categories of related classes called **packages**. The **java.util package** provides random number processing capabilities with class Random. Importing a class (using the keyword **import**) allows your application to access that class. You will need to use code to generate random numbers for the **Craps Game** application; therefore, you will now import the Random class from the java.util package.

Importing the Random Class from the Java Class Library

1. **Copying the template to your working directory.** Copy the C:\Examples\ Tutorial15\TemplateApplication\CrapsGame directory to your C:\SimplyJava directory.

2. **Opening the Craps Game application's template file.** Open the template file CrapsGame.java in your text editor.

3. **Importing class Random.** Add line 5 of Fig. 15.9 into your code. This line imports class Random from the java.util package. Lines 3, 4, 6 and 7 are also import declarations. These lines use an asterisk (*), which allows the application to access entire packages. These packages allow you to create and manipulate GUIs, and enable event handling for GUI components.

Importing the
java.util.Random class

```
Source Editor [CrapsGame *]                              _ |□| x|
1  // Tutorial 15: CrapsGame.java
2  // This application plays a simple craps game
3  import java.awt.*;
4  import java.awt.event.*;
5  import java.util.Random;
6  import javax.swing.*;
7  import javax.swing.border.*;
```

Figure 15.9   Importing class **Random** of the java.util package.

4. **Saving the application.** Save your modified source code file.

Notice that the numbers 2, 3, 7, 11 and 12 have special meanings during a game of Craps. It would be helpful to create these constants and assign them meaningful names for use in your application. Java allows you to create a constant with the keyword final. You will now create constants whose identifiers describe significant dice combinations in Craps (such as SNAKE_EYES, TREY, CRAPS, LUCKY_SEVEN, YO_LEVEN and BOX_CARS). You will use these to enhance the readability of your code and ensure that numbers are consistent throughout your application.

Declaring Constants and Instance Variables

1. **Declaring constants.** Add lines 31–39 of Fig. 15.10 to your application. Recall that constant declarations contain the keyword final before the type of the variable. Notice that you can assign the same value to multiple constants, as in lines 32 and 39—in this case, because 7 has a different meaning on the first roll than on subsequent rolls.

Declaring constants

```
Source Editor [CrapsGame *]                              _ |□| x|
29      private JTextField resultJTextField;
30
31      // constants representing winning dice rolls
32      private final int LUCKY_SEVEN = 7;
33      private final int YO_LEVEN = 11;
34
35      // constants representing losing dice rolls
36      private final int SNAKE_EYES = 2;
37      private final int TREY = 3;
38      private final int BOX_CARS = 12;
39      private final int CRAPS = 7;
40
41      // no-argument constructor
```

Figure 15.10   Declaring constants in the **Craps Game** application.

(cont.)

2. Add lines 41–43 of Fig. 15.11 to your application. In this application, you will need to access images that display the six faces of a die. For convenience, each file has a name that differs only by one number. For example, the image for the die face displaying 1 is named `die1.png`, and the image for the die face displaying 6 is named `die6.png`. Recall that png is an image file name extension that is short for Portable Network Graphics. These images are stored in the directory named `Images` in your working directory, `C:\SimplyJava\CrapsGame`. As such, the `String Images/die1.png` would correctly indicate the location of the die face image displaying 1 relative to your working directory. To help create a `String` representing the path to the image, `Strings FILE_PREFIX (Images/die)` and `FILE_SUFFIX (.png)` are used (as constants) to store the prefix and suffix of the file name. An image name is thus the combination of FILE_PREFIX, number and FILE_SUFFIX.

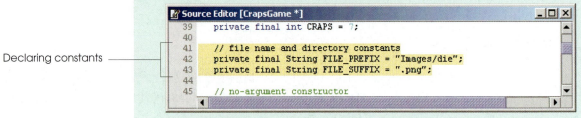

Declaring constants

```
Source Editor [CrapsGame *]
39      private final int CRAPS = 7;
40
41          // file name and directory constants
42          private final String FILE_PREFIX = "Images/die";
43          private final String FILE_SUFFIX = ".png";
44
45          // no-argument constructor
```

Figure 15.11 Declaring constants in the **Craps Game** application.

3. ***Declaring instance variables.*** Add lines 45–47 of Fig. 15.12 below the constant declarations to declare and initialize two instance variables. The game of Craps requires that you store the user's point, once established on the first roll, for the duration of the game. Therefore, variable `myPoint` (line 46) is declared as an `int` to store the sum of the dice on the first roll. You will use the `Random` object referenced by `randomObject` (line 47) to "roll" the dice.

Declaring variable for point value
Using **new** to create
a **Random** object

```
Source Editor [CrapsGame *]
43      private final String FILE_SUFFIX = ".png";
44
45          // instance variables
46          private int myPoint = 0;
47          private Random randomObject = new Random();
48
49          // no-argument constructor
```

Figure 15.12 Adding instance variables to the **Craps Game** application.

4. ***Saving the application.*** Save your modified source code file.

You have now declared constants and instance variables for your application. Before you use these variables, you must first customize a **JPanel**. A JPanel is a container that allows you to group related components. Multiple JPanels can be added to your application's content pane. In this application, you use a JPanel to add a **TitledBorder** around two JLabels. A TitledBorder places a line and a title around a GUI component. Any GUI component attached to the component with the border will appear inside the border. A **border** can be added to any GUI component by setting its *border* property. Some GUI components (such as JButtons and JTextFields) already have default borders.

Adding a
TitledBorder

1. ***Customizing a JPanel.*** Add lines 69–70 of Fig. 15.13. Line 69 sets the *bounds* property of the JPanel. Line 70 sets the JPanel's *layout* property to **null** using the **setLayout** method. The *layout* property controls how components are arranged on a JPanel. Setting the value to **null** allows **absolute positioning** of components. Absolute positioning means that you specify exactly where the component will appear on a container (such as a JPanel). Other layouts usually involve **relative positioning**, which means that components are placed in relation to other components in a container. Line 71 adds the JPanel to the content pane. This JPanel will contain the two JLabels that display the images of the point dice (pointDie1JLabel and pointDie2JLabel).

Customizing the JPanel

```
65        pointDiceTitledBorder = new TitledBorder( "Point" );
66
67        // set up pointDiceJPanel
68        pointDiceJPanel = new JPanel();
69        pointDiceJPanel.setBounds( 16, 16, 200, 116 );
70        pointDiceJPanel.setLayout( null );
71        contentPane.add( pointDiceJPanel );
72
73        // set up pointDie1JLabel
```

Figure 15.13 Customizing pointDiceJPanel.

2. ***Adding components to the JPanel.*** Add lines 75–76 and lines 80–81 of Fig. 15.14. Line 75 sets the *bounds* property of pointDie1JLabel. Line 76 adds pointDie1JLabel to pointDiceJPanel. Recall that the first two values of the *bounds* property are the *x* and *y* values of the component. Because you add pointDie1JLabel to pointDiceJPanel, not to the content pane, *x* and *y* values of 0, 0 refer to the upper left corner of pointDiceJPanel, not of the content pane. In this case, line 69 of Fig. 15.13 specifies that the upper-left corner of the JPanel is located at 16, 16 on the content pane. Lines 80–81 set the *bounds* property of pointDie2JLabel and add it to pointDiceJPanel.

Adding a JLabel to the JPanel

Adding a JLabel to the JPanel

```
71        contentPane.add( pointDiceJPanel );
72
73        // set up pointDie1JLabel
74        pointDie1JLabel = new JLabel();
75        pointDie1JLabel.setBounds( 24, 34, 64, 56 );
76        pointDiceJPanel.add( pointDie1JLabel );
77
78        // set up pointDie2JLabel
79        pointDie2JLabel = new JLabel();
80        pointDie2JLabel.setBounds( 120, 34, 64, 56 );
81        pointDiceJPanel.add( pointDie2JLabel );
82
83        // set up die1JLabel
```

Figure 15.14 Adding components to the JPanel.

3. ***Setting the border of the JPanel.*** Look at line 65 of Fig. 15.15 which creates a TitledBorder with the title "Point". This line uses the keyword **new** to create a TitledBorder object. Add line 71 of Fig. 15.15. This line calls the **setBorder** method to set the *border* property of pointDiceJPanel. The TitledBorder object, pointDiceTitledBorder, is passed to the **setBorder** method to add pointDiceTitledBorder to pointDiceJPanel. This border shows up as a thin line around pointDiceJPanel. The title is displayed in the upper-left part of the border.

(cont.)

Creating a TitledBorder

Setting the *border* property

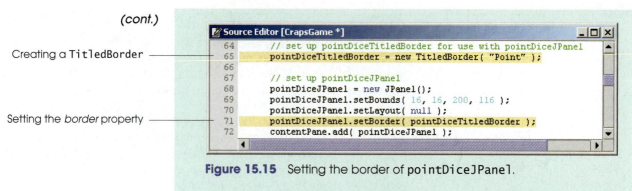

Figure 15.15 Setting the border of pointDiceJPanel.

4. *Saving the application.* Save your modified source code file.

5. *Opening the Command Prompt window and changing directories.* Open the **Command Prompt** window by selecting **Start > Programs > Accessories > Command Prompt.** Change to your working directory by typing cd C:\SimplyJava\CrapsGame.

6. *Compiling the application.* Compile your application by typing javac CrapsGame.java.

7. *Running the application.* When your application compiles correctly, run it by typing java CrapsGame. Figure 15.16 shows the updated application running. You have not coded methods for the **Play** or **Roll** JButtons yet, so your application will not function. You will code these methods shortly.

TitledBorder is displayed with **Point** as the title

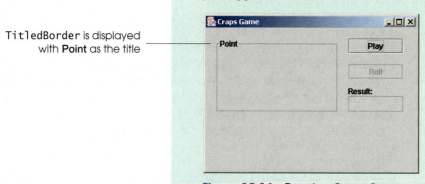

Figure 15.16 Running **Craps Game** application.

8. *Closing the application.* Close your running application by clicking its close button.

9. *Closing the Command Prompt window.* Close the **Command Prompt** window by clicking its close button.

SELF-REVIEW

1. Use the keyword _____ to define constants.

   a) readOnly   b) final

   c) constants   d) constant

2. Package _____ contains class Random.

   a) java.awt   b) java.utility

   c) java.swing   d) java.util

Answers: 1) b. 2) d.

15.4 Using Random Numbers in the Craps Game Application

Now you will add code that executes when the user clicks the **Craps Game** application's JButtons. You begin by inserting the code that will execute when the user clicks the **Play** JButton.

Coding the
playJButton-
ActionPerformed
Method

1. ***Removing Images from a JLabel and rolling dice.*** Begin coding the playJButtonActionPerformed method by adding lines 156–164 of Fig. 15.17. Lines 157–158 remove any images from the JLabels used to display the "point dice." Though there are no images when the application is first run, the images from the previous game must be cleared if the user chooses to play again. Setting the *icon* property to the keyword null indicates that there is no image to display.

```
Source Editor [CrapsGame *]                                      _ □ ×
153    // start new game of craps
154    private void playJButtonActionPerformed( ActionEvent event )
155    {
156        // clear point icons
157        pointDie1JLabel.setIcon( null );
158        pointDie2JLabel.setIcon( null );
159
160        // reset title of border
161        pointDiceTitledBorder.setTitle( "Point" );
162        pointDiceJPanel.repaint();
163
164        int sumOfDice = rollDice(); // roll dice
165
166    } // end method playJButtonActionPerformed
```

Removing images from JLabels —→ (lines 157–158)

Setting the title of the border and updating the JPanel —→ (lines 161–162)

"Rolling" the dice —→ (line 164)

Figure 15.17   Clearing images and rolling the dice.

Line 161 changes the text displayed on pointDiceTitledBorder to "Point", using the **setTitle** method. This method sets the TitledBorder's *title* property, which controls the text that is displayed in the border. The rollJButtonActionPerformed method (declared later) changes the title of the border. This line resets the title of the border. Line 162 redraws the JPanel using the **repaint** method. The repaint method is used when a component needs to be updated, such as when the title of its border is changed. Once the repaint method is called, the JPanel is redrawn as soon as possible so that the title of the border is displayed with the current value (set at line 161).

Line 164 declares an int variable sumOfDice and assigns to it the value returned by rolling the dice. This is accomplished by calling the rollDice method, which you will define later in this tutorial. The rollDice method rolls the two dice, displays the dice images in the lower two JLabels and returns the sum of the dice values.

2. ***Using a switch statement to determine the result of rolling the dice.*** Recall that if the player rolls 7 or 11 on the first roll, the player wins, and if the player rolls 2, 3 or 12 on the first roll, the player loses. To enable your application to handle the cases in which the player wins or loses on the first roll, add lines 166–182 of Fig. 15.18 to the playJButtonActionPerformed method beneath the code you added in the previous step.

(cont.)

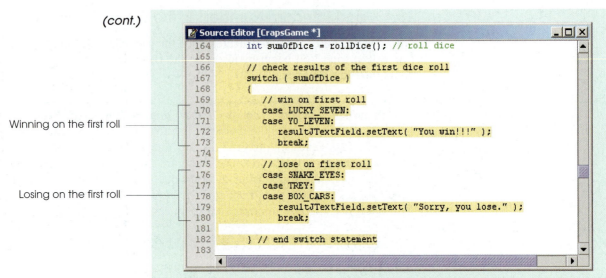

Figure 15.18 `switch` statement in `playJButtonActionPerformed`.

The first `case` (lines 170–173) executes for first-roll values of 7 or 11, using the constant values `LUCKY_SEVEN` and `YO_LEVEN`. Recall that several case labels can be specified to execute the same statements. If the sum of the dice is 7 (`LUCKY_SEVEN`) or 11 (`YO_LEVEN`), the code at line 172 displays `"You win!!!"` in `resultJTextField`. If the sum of the dice is 2 (`SNAKE_EYES`), 3 (`TREY`) or 12 (`BOX_CARS`), the code at line 179 executes and displays `"Sorry, you lose."` in `resultJTextField`. Line 182 ends the `switch` statement.

3. ***Using the default case to continue the game.*** Add lines 182–200 of Fig. 15.19. If the player did not roll a 2, 3, 7, 11 or 12, then the sum of the dice becomes the point and the player must roll again. Line 186 in the `default` case's body sets instance variable `myPoint` to the sum of the die values. Next, line 187 sets the *text* property of `resultJTextField` to notify the user to roll again.

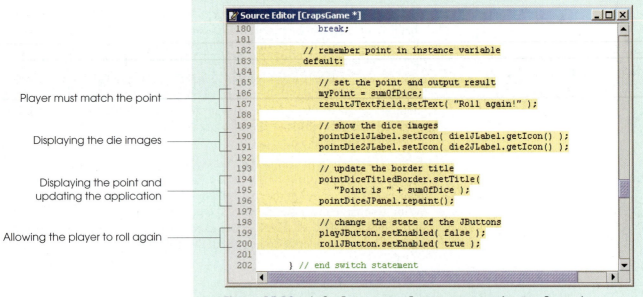

Figure 15.19 `default` case in `playJButtonActionPerformed`.

(cont.)

The user must match the point to win, so you will display the images corresponding to the point roll. This is done by setting the images in the point JLabels to the images currently in the die JLabels. In Tutorial 2, you learned how to display an image in a JLabel by setting its *icon* property. Lines 190–191 display the die faces for the point JLabels by setting the *icon* property of each point JLabel to the value of the *icon* property of its corresponding die JLabel (retrieved using the getIcon method of JLabel). Lines 194–195 change the title on the pointDiceTitledBorder, using its *title* property to display the value of the current point. Finally, the **Play** JButton is disabled (line 199) and the **Roll** JButton is enabled (line 200), limiting users to clicking the **Roll** JButton for all the rolls in the rest of the game.

4. ***Saving the application.*** Save your modified source code file.

The **Roll** JButton is enabled after the user has started the game. The user presses the **Roll** JButton and tries to match the point. Next, you code the event handler method for the **Roll** JButton.

Coding the RollJButton-ActionPerformed Method

1. ***Rolling the dice.*** The user clicks the **Roll** JButton to roll the dice and try to match the point. Begin coding the rollJButtonActionPerformed method by adding line 209 of Fig. 15.20. Line 209 declares an int variable sumOfDice, calls the rollDice method to roll the dice and display the die images, and assigns the sum of the dice to variable sumOfDice.

"Rolling" the dice ⎯

```
Source Editor [CrapsGame *]                               _ □ ×
206        // continue the game
207        private void rollJButtonActionPerformed( ActionEvent event )
208        {
209            int sumOfDice = rollDice(); // roll dice
210
211        } // end method rollJButtonActionPerformed
```

Figure 15.20   Rolling the dice in rollJButtonActionPerformed.

2. ***Determining the output of the roll.*** If the roll matches the point, the user wins and the game ends. However, if the user rolls a 7 (CRAPS), the user loses and the game ends. Add lines 211–224 of Fig. 15.21 in the rollJButton-ActionPerformed method.

Displaying winning message ⎯

Displaying losing message ⎯

```
Source Editor [CrapsGame *]                               _ □ ×
209            int sumOfDice = rollDice(); // roll dice
210
211            // determine outcome of roll, player matches point
212            if ( sumOfDice == myPoint )
213            {
214                resultJTextField.setText( "You win!!!" );
215                rollJButton.setEnabled( false );
216                playJButton.setEnabled( true );
217            }
218            // determine outcome of roll, player loses
219            else if ( sumOfDice == CRAPS )
220            {
221                resultJTextField.setText( "Sorry, you lose." );
222                rollJButton.setEnabled( false );
223                playJButton.setEnabled( true );
224            }
225
226        } // end method rollJButtonActionPerformed
```

Figure 15.21   Determining the outcome of a roll.

(cont.)

The if (line 212) determines whether the sum of the dice in the current roll matches the point. If the sum and point match, the application displays the winning message in resultJTextField. It then allows the user to start a new game, by disabling the **Roll** JButton and enabling the **Play** JButton.

The else (line 219) contains an if (lines 219–224) that determines whether the sum of the dice in the current roll is 7 (CRAPS). If so, the application displays the message that the user has lost (in resultJTextField) and ends the game by disabling the **Roll** JButton and enabling the **Play** JButton. If the player neither matches the point nor rolls a 7, then the player is allowed to roll again. The player can roll the dice again by clicking the **Roll** JButton.

3. **Saving the application.** Save your modified source code file.

Next, you will add code that will simulate rolling the dice and display the dice images in the appropriate JLabels.

Using Random Numbers to Simulate Rolling Dice

1. **Using the Random object to simulate dice rolling.** At several places in this application, it will be necessary to roll and display two dice. Therefore, it is a good idea to create two methods: one to roll the dice (rollDice) and one to display a die image (displayDie) that can be called from different locations in the application. Declare the rollDice method first, by adding lines 228–241 of Fig. 15.22 after the rollJButtonActionPerformed method.

Getting two random numbers

Displaying the die images

Returning the sum of the dice

```
226        } // end method rollJButtonActionPerformed
227
228        // generate random die rolls
229        private int rollDice()
230        {
231            // generate random die values
232            int die1 = 1 + randomObject.nextInt( 6 );
233            int die2 = 1 + randomObject.nextInt( 6 );
234
235            // display the dice images
236            displayDie( die1JLabel, die1 );
237            displayDie( die2JLabel, die2 );
238
239            return die1 + die2; // return sum of dice values
240
241        } // end method rollDice
242
243        // main method
```

Figure 15.22 Declaring the rollDice method.

This code sets the values of die1 and die2 to random integers between 1 to 6, inclusive. Lines 232–233 accomplish this using the expression 1 + randomObject.nextInt(6). Remember that the value returned from nextInt is a non-negative integer between zero and one less than the argument (in this case, the range 0–5).

The method then makes two calls to displayDie (lines 236–237), a method that displays the image of the die corresponding to a face value in the range 1–6. The first parameter in displayDie is the JLabel that will display the image, and the second parameter is the number that appears on the face of the die. You will declare the displayDie method in *Step 2*. Finally, the method returns the sum of the values of the dice (line 239), which the application uses to determine the outcome of the Craps game.

(cont.)

2. ***Displaying the dice images.*** You will now declare the `displayDie` method to display the die images corresponding to the random die values generated in the `rollDice` method. Add lines 243–252 of Fig. 15.23 (after the `roll-Dice` method) to declare the `displayDie` method. This method takes a `JLa-bel` and an `int` as the arguments. The method uses the `int` to get an image, which is then displayed in the `JLabel`.

```
241      } // end method rollDice
242
243      // displays the die image
244      private void displayDie( JLabel picDieJLabel, int face )
245      {
246         ImageIcon image =
247            new ImageIcon( FILE_PREFIX + face + FILE_SUFFIX );
248
249         // display die images in picDieJLabel
250         picDieJLabel.setIcon( image );
251
252      } // end method displayDie
253
254      // main method
```

Creating a new `ImageIcon` → (line 247)

Displaying a die image → (line 250)

Figure 15.23 Declaring the `displayDie` method.

Lines 246–247 create an `ImageIcon`. Recall that `FILE_PREFIX` and `FILE_SUFFIX` were declared earlier as constants. The `String FILE_PREFIX + face + FILE_SUFFIX` specifies the location of the file (line 247). If the value of face is 1, the expression would result in `"Images/die1.png"`. This is the location of the image of a die face showing 1. Line 250 sets the *icon* property for the specified `JLabel` to the `ImageIcon` created in lines 246–247.

3. ***Saving the application.*** Save your modified source code file.

4. ***Opening the Command Prompt window and changing directories.*** Open the **Command Prompt** window by selecting **Start > Programs > Accessories > Command Prompt**. Change to your working directory by typing cd `C:\SimplyJava\CrapsGame`.

5. ***Compiling the application.*** Compile your application by typing javac `CrapsGame.java`.

6. ***Running the application.*** When your application compiles correctly, run it by typing java `CrapsGame`. Figure 15.24 shows the completed application running.

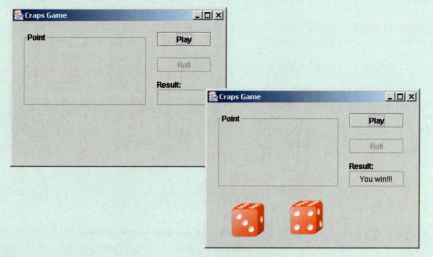

Figure 15.24 Running the completed **Craps Game** application.

(cont.)

Figure 15.25 presents the source code for the **Craps Game** application. The lines of code that you added, viewed or modified in this tutorial are highlighted.

```java
1   // Tutorial 15: CrapsGame.java
2   // This application plays a simple craps game.
3   import java.awt.*;
4   import java.awt.event.*;
5   import java.util.Random;
6   import javax.swing.*;
7   import javax.swing.border.*;
8
9   public class CrapsGame extends JFrame
10  {
11     // JPanel and TitledBorder to contain dice
12     private JPanel pointDiceJPanel;
13     private TitledBorder pointDiceTitledBorder;
14
15     // JLabels to display the die images in pointDiceJPanel
16     private JLabel pointDie1JLabel;
17     private JLabel pointDie2JLabel;
18
19     // JLabels to display the die images from the rolls of the dice
20     private JLabel die1JLabel;
21     private JLabel die2JLabel;
22
23     // JButtons to allow user to interact with game
24     private JButton playJButton;
25     private JButton rollJButton;
26
27     // JLabel and JTextField show results of game
28     private JLabel resultJLabel;
29     private JTextField resultJTextField;
30
31     // constants representing winning dice rolls
32     private final int LUCKY_SEVEN = 7;
33     private final int YO_LEVEN = 11;
34
35     // constants representing losing dice rolls
36     private final int SNAKE_EYES = 2;
37     private final int TREY = 3;
38     private final int BOX_CARS = 12;
39     private final int CRAPS = 7;
40
41     // file name and directory constants
42     private final String FILE_PREFIX = "Images/die";
43     private final String FILE_SUFFIX = ".png";
44
45     // instance variables
46     private int myPoint = 0;
47     private Random randomObject = new Random();
48
```

Importing the class `java.util.Random` → (line 5)

Declaring the constants for the dice rolls → (lines 35–39)

Declaring the constants for the file name → (lines 42–43)

Declaring instance variable `myPoint` → (line 46)

Creating a **Random** object using the **new** keyword → (line 47)

Figure 15.25 **Craps Game** application code listing. (Part 1 of 5.)

```
49    // no-argument constructor
50    public CrapsGame()
51    {
52       createUserInterface();
53    }
54
55    // create and position GUI components; register event handlers
56    private void createUserInterface()
57    {
58       // get content pane for attaching GUI components
59       Container contentPane = getContentPane();
60
61       // enable explicit positioning of GUI components
62       contentPane.setLayout( null );
63
64       // set up pointDiceTitledBorder for use with pointDiceJPanel
65       pointDiceTitledBorder = new TitledBorder( "Point" );
66
67       // set up pointDiceJPanel
68       pointDiceJPanel = new JPanel();
69       pointDiceJPanel.setBounds( 16, 16, 200, 116 );
70       pointDiceJPanel.setLayout( null );
71       pointDiceJPanel.setBorder( pointDiceTitledBorder );
72       contentPane.add( pointDiceJPanel );
73
74       // set up pointDie1JLabel
75       pointDie1JLabel = new JLabel();
76       pointDie1JLabel.setBounds( 24, 34, 64, 56 );
77       pointDiceJPanel.add( pointDie1JLabel );
78
79       // set up pointDie2JLabel
80       pointDie2JLabel = new JLabel();
81       pointDie2JLabel.setBounds( 120, 34, 64, 56 );
82       pointDiceJPanel.add( pointDie2JLabel );
83
84       // set up die1JLabel
85       die1JLabel = new JLabel();
86       die1JLabel.setBounds( 40, 150, 64, 64 );
87       contentPane.add( die1JLabel );
88
89       // set up die2JLabel
90       die2JLabel = new JLabel();
91       die2JLabel.setBounds( 136, 150, 64, 56 );
92       contentPane.add( die2JLabel );
93
94       // set up playJButton
95       playJButton = new JButton();
96       playJButton.setBounds( 232, 16, 88, 23 );
97       playJButton.setText( "Play" );
98       contentPane.add( playJButton );
99       playJButton.addActionListener(
100
101          new ActionListener() // anonymous inner class
102          {
103             // event handler called when playJButton is clicked
104             public void actionPerformed ( ActionEvent event )
105             {
106                playJButtonActionPerformed( event );
```

Creating a TitledBorder object → (line 65)

Adding a border to the JPanel → (line 71)

Adding a JLabel to a JPanel using the **add** method → (line 77)

Adding a JLabel to a JPanel using the **add** method → (line 82)

Figure 15.25　Craps Game application code listing. (Part 2 of 5.)

```
107                    }
108
109              } // end anonymous inner class
110
111          ); // end call to addActionListener
112
113          // set up rollJButton
114          rollJButton = new JButton();
115          rollJButton.setBounds( 232, 56, 88, 23 );
116          rollJButton.setText( "Roll" );
117          rollJButton.setEnabled( false );
118          contentPane.add( rollJButton );
119          rollJButton.addActionListener(
120
121              new ActionListener() // anonymous inner class
122              {
123                  // event handler called when rollJButton is clicked
124                  public void actionPerformed ( ActionEvent event )
125                  {
126                      rollJButtonActionPerformed( event );
127                  }
128
129              } // end anonymous inner class
130
131          ); // end call to addActionListener
132
133          // set up resultJLabel
134          resultJLabel = new JLabel();
135          resultJLabel.setBounds( 232, 90, 48, 16 );
136          resultJLabel.setText( "Result:" );
137          contentPane.add( resultJLabel );
138
139          // set up resultJTextField
140          resultJTextField = new JTextField();
141          resultJTextField.setBounds( 232, 106, 88, 24 );
142          resultJTextField.setHorizontalAlignment( JTextField.CENTER );
143          resultJTextField.setEditable( false );
144          contentPane.add( resultJTextField );
145
146          // set properties of application's window
147          setTitle( "Craps Game" ); // set title bar string
148          setSize( 350, 250 );       // set window size
149          setVisible( true );        // display window
150
151      } // end method createUserInterface
152
153      // start new game of craps
154      private void playJButtonActionPerformed( ActionEvent event )
155      {
156          // clear point icons
157          pointDie1JLabel.setIcon( null );
158          pointDie2JLabel.setIcon( null );
159
160          // reset title of border
161          pointDiceTitledBorder.setTitle( "Point" );
162          pointDiceJPanel.repaint();
163
164          int sumOfDice = rollDice(); // roll dice
```

Removing images from JLabels → (lines 157–158)

Setting the title of the border and updating the JPanel → (lines 161–162)

Figure 15.25   **Craps Game** application code listing. (Part 3 of 5.)

```
165
166        // check results of the first dice roll
167        switch ( sumOfDice )
168        {
169            // win on first roll
170            case LUCKY_SEVEN:
171            case YO_LEVEN:
172                resultJTextField.setText( "You win!!!" );
173                break;
174
175            // lose on first roll
176            case SNAKE_EYES:
177            case TREY:
178            case BOX_CARS:
179                resultJTextField.setText( "Sorry, you lose." );
180                break;
181
182            // remember point in instance variable
183            default:
184
185                // set the point and output result
186                myPoint = sumOfDice;
187                resultJTextField.setText( "Roll again!" );
188
189                // show the dice images
190                pointDie1JLabel.setIcon( die1JLabel.getIcon() );
191                pointDie2JLabel.setIcon( die2JLabel.getIcon() );
192
193                // update the border title
194                pointDiceTitledBorder.setTitle(
195                    "Point is " + sumOfDice );
196                pointDiceJPanel.repaint();
197
198                // change the state of the JButtons
199                playJButton.setEnabled( false );
200                rollJButton.setEnabled( true );
201
202        } // end switch statement
203
204    } // end method playJButtonActionPerformed
205
206    // continue the game
207    private void rollJButtonActionPerformed( ActionEvent event )
208    {
209        int sumOfDice = rollDice();   // roll dice
210
211        // determine outcome of roll, player matches point
212        if ( sumOfDice == myPoint )
213        {
214            resultJTextField.setText( "You win!!!" );
215            rollJButton.setEnabled( false );
216            playJButton.setEnabled( true );
217        }
218        // determine outcome of roll, player loses
219        else if ( sumOfDice == CRAPS )
220        {
221            resultJTextField.setText( "Sorry, you lose" );
222            rollJButton.setEnabled( false );
```

Labels on the left side:
- Winning on the first roll (lines 170–173)
- Losing on the first roll (lines 176–180)
- Player must match the point (lines 186–187)
- Displaying die images (lines 190–191)
- Displaying point and updating the JPanel (lines 194–196)
- Allowing the player to roll again (lines 199–200)

Figure 15.25 **Craps Game** application code listing. (Part 4 of 5.)

```
223              playJButton.setEnabled( true );
224           }
225
226        } // end method rollJButtonActionPerformed
227
228        // generate random die rolls
229        private int rollDice()
230        {
231           // generate random die values
232           int die1 = 1 + randomObject.nextInt( 6 );
233           int die2 = 1 + randomObject.nextInt( 6 );
234
235           // display the dice images
236           displayDie( die1JLabel, die1 );
237           displayDie( die2JLabel, die2 );
238
239           return die1 + die2; // return sum of dice values
240
241        } // end method rollDice
242
243        // displays the die image
244        private void displayDie( JLabel picDieJLabel, int face )
245        {
246           ImageIcon image =
247              new ImageIcon( FILE_PREFIX + face + FILE_SUFFIX );
248
249           // display die images in picDieJLabel
250           picDieJLabel.setIcon( image );
251
252        } // end method displayDie
253
254        // main method
255        public static void main( String args[] )
256        {
257           CrapsGame application = new CrapsGame();
258           application.setDefaultCloseOperation( JFrame.EXIT_ON_CLOSE );
259
260        } // end method main
261
262 } // end class CrapsGame
```

Generating random numbers — lines 232, 233

Displaying the image in the `JLabel` — line 248

Figure 15.25 **Craps Game** application code listing. (Part 5 of 5.)

SELF-REVIEW

1. You request components in a `JPanel` to be redisplayed by calling the _____ method.
   a) paint   b) update
   c) repaint   d) redraw

2. To clear the image in a `JLabel`, set its *icon* property to _____.
   a) "" (double quotes)   b) null
   c) none   d) 0

Answers: 1) c. 2) b.

15.5 Wrap-Up

In this tutorial, you created the **Craps Game** application to simulate playing the popular dice game Craps. You learned about the Random class and how it can be used to generate random numbers by creating a Random object and calling its next-

`Int` method. You then learned how to specify the range of values within which random numbers should be generated by passing an argument to the `nextInt` method. You also learned that the `Random` class can be used to generate random `doubles` using the `nextDouble` method. Later, you learned about borders and how to set the border of a component.

Using your knowledge of random number generation and methods, you wrote code that added functionality to your **Craps Game** application. You used random-number generation to simulate the element of chance, and you learned how to use code to display an image in a `JLabel`.

In the next tutorial, you will learn how to use arrays, which allow you to use one name to store many values. You will apply your knowledge of random numbers and arrays to create a **Flag Quiz** application that tests a user's knowledge of various national flags.

SKILLS SUMMARY

Generating Random Numbers

■ Create an object of class `Random` and call the object's `nextInt` method.

Generating Random Numbers within a Specified Range

■ Call the `Random` class's `nextInt` method. Use an argument to specify a range of random numbers from zero to one less than the argument. Add a number to this value to shift the range.

■ Call the `Random` class's `nextDouble` method. Multiply a number by the return value to change the size of the range. Add a number to this value to shift the range.

Adding a `TitledBorder` to a Component

■ Use the `setBorder` method and pass to it a `TitledBorder` object to add a title and border to a component.

KEY TERMS

absolute positioning—Specifies the exact size and location of a component in a container.

border **property**—Allows a border to be added to some GUI components.

`import` **declaration**—Used to import classes or packages.

`java.util` **package**—Provides, among other capabilities, random number generation capabilities with class `Random`.

`JPanel` **component**—Groups related components.

layout **property**—Controls how components are arranged in a container (such as the content pane or `JPanel`).

method overloading—Allows several methods to have the same name but different numbers of arguments or different types of arguments.

new keyword—Creates an object and assigns it a location in memory.

`nextDouble` **method of** `Random`—Generates a random positive `double` value that is greater than or equal to 0.0 and less than 1.0.

`nextInt` **method of** `Random`—Generates an `int` value selected from all possible `int` values, when called with no arguments. When called with an `int` argument, it generates an int value from 0 to one less than the argument.

`null` **keyword**—Value that clears a reference.

package—A group of related classes. A package can be imported to add functionality to an application.

Random class—Contains methods to generate random numbers. Declared in package `java.util`.

reference—A variable that refers to an object. A reference specifies the location in the computer's memory of an object.

relative positioning—Specifies the size and location of components in relation to other components on a container.

`repaint` **method of** `JPanel`—Redisplays the `JPanel` as soon as possible.

setBorder method of JPanel—Sets the border that is displayed around the `JPanel`.

setLayout method of JPanel—Sets the way components are arranged in the `JPanel`.

setTitle method of TitledBorder—Sets the text displayed in the `TitledBorder`.

title **property of TitledBorder**—Controls the text that is displayed in the border.

TitledBorder class—Allows a component to have a border with a `String` title.

JAVA LIBRARY REFERENCE

Random This class is used to generate random numbers.

■ *Methods*

`nextInt`—Generates an `int` value selected from all possible `int` values, when called with no arguments. When called with an `int` argument, it generates an `int` value from 0 to one less than that argument.

`nextDouble`—Generates a positive `double` value that is greater than or equal to `0.0` and less than `1.0`.

JPanel This component groups other related components. This grouping allows a single border to be placed around multiple components. Components placed in a `JPanel` are positioned with respect to the upper-left corner of the `JPanel`, so changing the location of the `JPanel` moves all of the components contained inside it.

■ *Methods*

`add`—Adds a component to the `JPanel`.

`setBorder`—Sets the border displayed around the `JPanel`.

`setBounds`—Sets the *bounds* property, which specifies the location and size of a `JPanel`.

`setLayout`—Sets the *layout* property, which controls how components are displayed on the `JPanel`.

TitledBorder This class allows the user to add a `String` title and line border to a component.

■ *Methods*

`setTitle`—Sets the title that is displayed in the border.

MULTIPLE-CHOICE QUESTIONS

15.1 A Random object can generate random numbers of type _____.

    a) `int`

    b) `String`

    c) `double`

    d) Both a and c.

15.2 Import declarations allow the application access to _____ from the Java class library.

    a) packages and classes

    b) classes and objects

    c) objects and methods

    d) methods and variables

15.3 The _____ method sets the title of a `TitledBorder`.

    a) `title`

    b) `setText`

    c) `setBorder`

    d) `setTitle`

15.4 The `nextInt` method of class Random can be called using _____.

    a) one argument

    b) no arguments

    c) two arguments

    d) Both a and b.

15.5 The statement _____ assigns to `value` a random number in the range 5 to 20.

    a) `value = 4 + randomObject.nextInt( 16 );`

    b) `value = randomObject.nextInt( 21 );`

    c) `value = 5 + randomObject.nextInt( 15 );`

    d) `value = 5 + randomObject.nextInt( 16 );`

15.6 The _____ method displays an image on a JLabel.

a) setImage

b) setIcon

c) setImageIcon

d) None of the above.

15.7 The java.util package contains class Random to _____.

a) generate positive integers

b) generate positive doubles

c) provide random number generation capabilities

d) All of the above.

15.8 Assume that randomGenerator is an object of class Random. The expression random-Generator.nextDouble() produces random numbers in the range _____.

a) 0.0 to less than 1.0

b) greater than 0.0 to less than 1.0

c) 0.0 to 1.0

d) greater than 0.0 to 1.0

15.9 When creating random numbers, the argument passed to the nextInt method needs to be _____.

a) equal to the maximum value you wish to generate

b) equal to one more than the maximum value you wish to generate

c) equal to one less than the maximum value you wish to generate

d) equal to the minimum value you wish to generate

15.10 When a variable is used throughout the lifetime of the application and its value will not change, it should be declared as a(n)_____.

a) local variable

b) constant

c) instance variable

d) None of the above.

EXERCISES

15.11 (_Guess the Number Application_) Develop an application that generates a random number and prompts the user to guess the number as in Fig. 15.26. When the user clicks the **New Game** JButton, the application chooses a number in the range from 1 to 100 at random. The user enters guesses into the **Guess:** JTextField and clicks the **Enter** JButton. If the guess is correct, the game ends, and the user can start a new game. If the guess is not correct, the application should indicate if the guess is higher or lower than the correct number.

Figure 15.26 **Guess the Number** application.

a) _Copying the template to your working directory._ Copy the directory C:\Examples\ Tutorial15\Exercises\GuessNumber to your C:\SimplyJava directory.

b) _Opening the template file._ Open the GuessNumber.java file in your text editor.

c) _Creating a Random object._ In line 28, create two instance variables. The first variable should store a Random object and the second variable should store a randomly generated number in the range 1 to 100 created using the Random object.

d) _Adding code to the enterJButtonActionPerformed method._ Add code starting in line 133 to the enterJButtonActionPerformed method that retrieves the value entered by the user in guessJTextField and compares that value to the randomly generated number. If the user's guess is lower than the correct answer, display **Too low...** in resultJTextField. If the user's guess is higher than the correct answer, display **Too high...** in resultJTextField. If the guess is correct, display **Correct!** in resultJTextField. Then disable the **Enter** JButton and enable the **New Game** JButton.

e) *Adding code to the newGameJButtonActionPerformed method.* Add code to the newGameJButtonActionPerformed method (after the enterJButtonAction-Performed method) that clears resultJTextField and generates a new random number for the instance variable. The method should then disable the **New Game** JButton and enable the **Enter** JButton.

f) *Saving the application.* Save your modified source code file.

g) *Opening the Command Prompt window and changing directories.* Open the **Command Prompt** by selecting **Start > Programs > Accessories > Command Prompt**. Change to your working directory by typing cd C:\SimplyJava\GuessNumber.

h) *Compiling the application.* Compile your application by typing javac Guess-Number.java

i) *Running the application.* When your application compiles correctly, run it by typing java GuessNumber. Test your application by playing the game until you guess the correct number. Then click **New Game** and play once more.

j) *Closing the application.* Close your running application by clicking its close button.

k) *Closing the Command Prompt window.* Close the **Command Prompt** window by clicking its close button.

15.12 (*Dice Simulator Application*) Develop an application that simulates rolling two six-sided dice. Your application should have a **Roll** JButton that, when clicked, displays two die faces (images) corresponding to random numbers. It should also display the number of times each face has appeared. Your application should appear similar to Fig. 15.27. This application will help you see if rolling dice on your computer is really random. If it is, the number of 1s, 2s, 3s, 4s, 5s and 6s you roll should be about the same, at least for a large number of rolls. The **Total:** JTextField should hold the number of rolls of the dice (each time the **Roll** JButton is clicked, the value in the **Total:** JTextField should be incremented by 2).

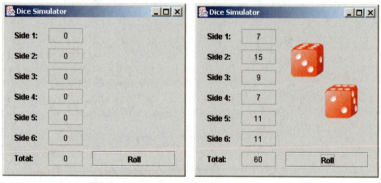

Figure 15.27   **Dice Simulator** application.

a) *Copying the template to your working directory.* Copy the directory C:\Examples\Tutorial15\Exercises\DiceSimulator to your C:\SimplyJava directory.

b) *Opening the template file.* Open the DiceSimulator.java file in your text editor.

c) *Displaying the die image.* After the rollJButtonActionPerformed method, in line 211, create a method named displayDie that takes a JLabel component as its argument. This method should create a new random integer from 1 to 6 using the next-Int method of the Random object generator and assign that value to the variable face. Display the die image in the JLabel component that was passed as an argument. The die image should correspond to the random number that was generated. To set the image, refer to the code presented in Fig. 15.25. Finally, this method should call the displayFrequency method to display the number of times each face has occurred.

d) *Coding the rollJButtonActionPerformed method.* Add code to the roll-JButtonActionPerformed method to call the displayDie method twice to display the images for die1JLabel and die2JLabel. Add code to increment the value displayed in the **Total:** JTextField by 2.

e) *Displaying the frequency.* After the displayDie method, Create a method named displayFrequency that takes an int representing a die roll as its argument. This

method will use a switch statement with the int parameter as the control variable. Each case should update the number of times its corresponding face has appeared.

f) *Saving the application.* Save your modified source code file.

g) *Opening the Command Prompt window and changing directories.* Open the **Command Prompt** by selecting **Start > Programs > Accessories > Command Prompt**. Change to your working directory by typing cd C:\SimplyJava\DiceSimulator.

h) *Compiling the application.* Compile your application by typing javac Dice-Simulator.java.

i) *Running the application.* When your application compiles correctly, run it by typing java DiceSimulator. Test your application by clicking the **Roll** JButton 30 times (to roll 60 dice). Make sure that the total number of rolls adds up to 60.

j) *Closing the application.* Close your running application by clicking its close button.

k) *Closing the Command Prompt window.* Close the **Command Prompt** window by clicking its close button

15.13 (*Lottery Picker Application*) A lottery commission offers four different lottery games to play: Three number, Four number, Five number and Five number + 1 lotteries. Each game has independent numbers. Develop an application that randomly picks numbers for all four games and displays the generated numbers in a GUI (Fig. 15.28). The games are played as follows:

- Three number lotteries require players to choose three numbers in the range from 0–9.
- Four number lotteries require players to choose four numbers, in the range from 0–9.
- Five number lotteries require players to choose five numbers in the range from 1–39.
- Five number + 1 lotteries require players to choose five numbers in the range 1–49 and an additional number in the range from 1–42.

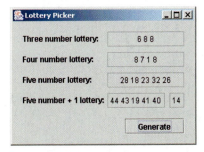

Figure 15.28 Lottery Picker application.

a) *Copying the template to your working directory.* Copy the directory C:\Examples\ Tutorial15\Exercises\LotteryPicker to your C:\SimplyJava directory.

b) *Opening the template file.* Open the LotteryPicker.java file in your text editor.

c) *Generating random numbers.* Create a method in line 142 named generate that will take two ints, representing the low and high end of a range of random numbers, and return a String containing a generated random number.

d) *Drawing numbers for the games.* Add code to the generateJButtonAction-Performed method to call the generate method and display the generated numbers for all four games. Some lotteries allow repetition of numbers. To make this application simple, allow repetition of numbers for all the lotteries.

e) *Saving the application.* Save your modified source code file.

f) *Opening the Command Prompt window and changing directories.* Open the **Command Prompt** by selecting **Start > Programs > Accessories > Command Prompt**. Change to your working directory by typing cd C:\SimplyJava\Lottery-Picker.

g) *Compiling the application.* Compile your application by typing javac Lottery-Picker.java.

h) *Running the application.* When your application compiles correctly, run it by typing java LotteryPicker. Test your application by clicking the **Generate** JButton. Make sure that the resulting lottery numbers are within the bounds given in the rules above.

i) *Closing the application.* Close your running application by clicking its close button.

j) *Closing the Command Prompt window.* Close the **Command Prompt** window by clicking its close button.

What does this code do? ▶

15.14 This code displays text in `integer1JTextField`, `double1JTextField`, and `integer2JTextField`. What is displayed in these JTextFields?

```
1   private void pickRandomNumbers()
2   {
3      Random randomObject = new Random();
4
5      int number1 = randomObject.nextInt();
6      double number = 5 * randomObject.nextDouble();
7      int number2 = 1 + randomObject.nextInt( 11 );
8      integer1JTextField.setText = String.valueOf( number1 );
9      double1JTextField.setText = String.valueOf( number );
10     integer2JTextField.setText = String.valueOf( number2 );
11
12  } // end method pickRandomNumbers
```

What's wrong with this code? ▶

15.15 This `randomDecimal` method should assign a random `double` number (in the range 0.0 to less than 50.0) to `double number` and display it in `displayJLabel`. Find the error(s) in the following code.

```
1   private void randomDecimal()
2   {
3      double number;
4      Random randomObject = new Random();
5
6      number = randomObject.nextDouble();
7      displayJLabel.setText = String.valueOf( number );
8
9   } // end method randomDecimal
```

Programming Challenge ▶

15.16 (*Multiplication Teacher Application*)   Develop an application that helps children learn multiplication as in Fig. 15.29. Use random-number generation to produce two positive one-digit integers that display in a question, such as "How much is 6 times 7?" The student should type the answer into a JTextField. If the answer is correct, then the application randomly displays one of three messages: **Very Good!**, **Excellent!** or **Great Job!** in a JLabel and displays the next question. If the student is wrong, the JLabel displays the message **No. Please try again.**

a) *Copying the template to your working directory.* Copy the directory C:\Examples\ Tutorial15\Exercises\MultiplicationTeacher to your C:\SimplyJava directory.

b) *Opening the template file.* Open the MultiplicationTeacher.java file in your text editor.

c) *Generating the questions.* Declare a method named generateQuestion in your application to generate and display each new question in questionJLabel.

d) *Adding a call to the generateQuestion method.* Add a call to the generate-Question method at the end of the createUserInterface method.

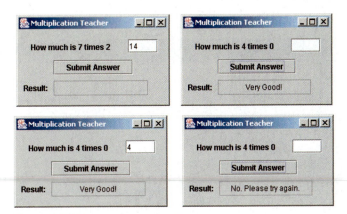

Figure 15.29 Multiplication Teacher application.

e) *Displaying a random message.* Add a method named `generateOutput` that displays a random message congratulating the student if they answer correctly.

f) *Determining whether the right answer was entered.* Add code to the `submit-JButtonActionPerformed` method declared in your application. Determine whether the student answered the question correctly and display an appropriate message. If the student answered the question correctly, call the `generateOutput` method, then call the `generateQuestion` method. Otherwise, display a message indicating the user is wrong. After displaying either result, clear `answerJTextField`.

g) *Saving the application.* Save your modified source code file.

h) *Opening the Command Prompt window and changing directories.* Open the **Command Prompt** window by selecting **Start > Programs > Accessories > Command Prompt**. Change to your working directory by typing cd C:\SimplyJava\MultiplicationTeacher.

i) *Compiling the application.* Compile your application by typing javac MultiplicationTeacher.java.

j) *Running the application.* When your application compiles correctly, run it by typing java MultiplicationTeacher. Test your application by answering the questions and clicking the **Submit Answer** JButton. Make sure that if you continue answering questions, you will see all four possible result messages.

k) *Closing the application.* Close your running application by clicking its close button.

l) *Closing the Command Prompt window.* Close the **Command Prompt** window by clicking its close button.

Objectives

In this tutorial, you will learn to:
- Create and initialize arrays.
- Store information in an array.
- Refer to individual elements of an array.
- Sort arrays.
- Use **JComboBox**es to display options in a drop-down list.

Outline

Flag Quiz Application

Introducing One-Dimensional Arrays and JComboBoxes

This tutorial introduces basic concepts and features of **data structures**. Data structures group together and organize related data. **Arrays** are data structures that consist of data items of the same type (called **elements**). Each element is referenced by its **index** (position number starting from 0) within the array. You will learn how to create arrays and how to access the information that they contain. You also will learn how to sort a `String` array's information alphabetically.

This tutorial's **Flag Quiz** application also includes a **JComboBox** component. A JComboBox presents user options in a drop-down list. This will be the first time that you will add a JComboBox to an application, but you have used them in previous tutorials. For example, in the **Moving Shapes** application of Tutorial 1, you were provided with a JComboBox to select different shapes to draw in the application.

16.1 Test-Driving the Flag Quiz Application

You will now create an application that tests a student's knowledge of the flags of various countries. Your application will use arrays to store information, such as the country names, a numerical value for each flag and `boolean` values to determine if a country name has been previously selected and displayed by your application. Your application must meet the following requirements:

Application Requirements

A geography teacher would like to quiz students on their knowledge of the flags of various countries. The teacher has asked you to write an application that displays a flag and allows the student to select the corresponding country name from a list. The application should inform the user whether the answer is correct and display the next flag. The application should display five flags randomly chosen from the flags of Australia, Brazil, China, Italy, Russia, South Africa, Spain and the United States. When the application is executed, a given flag should be displayed only once.

You begin by test-driving the completed application. Then, you will learn the additional Java technologies you will need to create your own version of this application.

Test-Driving the Flag Quiz Application

1. ***Locating the completed application.*** Open the **Command Prompt** window by selecting **Start > Programs > Accessories > Command Prompt**. Change to your completed **Flag Quiz** application directory by typing cd C:\Examples\Tutorial16\CompletedApplication\FlagQuiz.

2. ***Running the Flag Quiz application.*** Type java FlagQuiz in the **Command Prompt** window to run the application (Fig. 16.1). On the left side of the application, you will see a flag. This flag is chosen at random, so the flag you see will likely be different than the one that appears in Fig. 16.1.

JLabel displays a flag

JComboBox contains answers (country names)

Figure 16.1   Running the completed **Flag Quiz** application.

3. ***Selecting an answer.*** The JComboBox contains eight country names. One country name corresponds to the displayed flag and is the correct answer. The scrollbar allows you to browse through the JComboBox's drop-down list. Select an answer from the JComboBox, as shown in Fig. 16.2.

Answer being selected

Scrollbar in JComboBox's drop-down list

Figure 16.2   Selecting an answer from the JComboBox.

4. ***Submitting a correct answer.*** Click the **Submit** JButton to check your answer. If it is correct, the message "Correct!" is displayed in an output JTextField (Fig. 16.3). Whether or not the correct answer is given, the **Submit** JButton is disabled and the **Next Flag** JButton is enabled. Because this application simulates a quiz, the user has only one chance to answer correctly for each of the five flags that will be displayed.

User can select the next flag

Feedback provided to the user

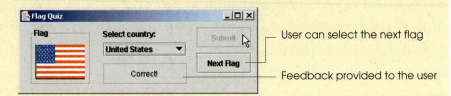

Figure 16.3   Submitting the correct answer.

5. ***Displaying the next flag.*** Click the **Next Flag** JButton to display a different flag (Fig. 16.4). Notice that the **Submit** JButton is now enabled, the **Next Flag** JButton is disabled, the JComboBox displays **Australia** (the first country listed in the JComboBox) and the output JTextField is cleared.

(cont.)

Figure 16.4 Displaying the next flag.

6. *Submitting an incorrect answer.* To demonstrate the application's response, select an incorrect answer and click **Submit** as in Fig. 16.5. The application displays "Sorry, incorrect." in the output JTextField.

Figure 16.5 Submitting an incorrect answer.

7. *Finishing the quiz.* After the application has displayed five flags and the user has submitted five answers, the quiz ends (Fig. 16.6). Notice that the two JButtons and the JComboBox are disabled.

Figure 16.6 Finishing the quiz.

8. *Closing the running application.* Close your running application by clicking its close button.

9. *Closing the Command Prompt window.* Close the **Command Prompt** window by clicking its close button.

16.2 Introducing Arrays

An array is a group of variables (elements) that all have the same type. Array names follow the same conventions that apply to other identifiers. To refer to a particular variable in an array, you specify the name of the array and the index (position number) of the variable, which is an integer that indicates a specific location within an array. Position numbers begin at 0 (zero) and range as high as one less than the number of elements in the array.

Figure 16.7 depicts an int array named units Sold that might be used in a bookstore sales application. This array contains 13 elements. Each element represents the net number of "units sold" of a particular book in a given month at a bookstore. If the bookstore wishes to track sales on a monthly basis it would be convenient to use month numbers to access the array elements. For example, unitsSold[1] is the net sales of that book for January (month 1), unitsSold[2] is the net sales for February (month 2), etc. In this example, you simply ignore the first element of the array (at index 0), because there is no month zero.

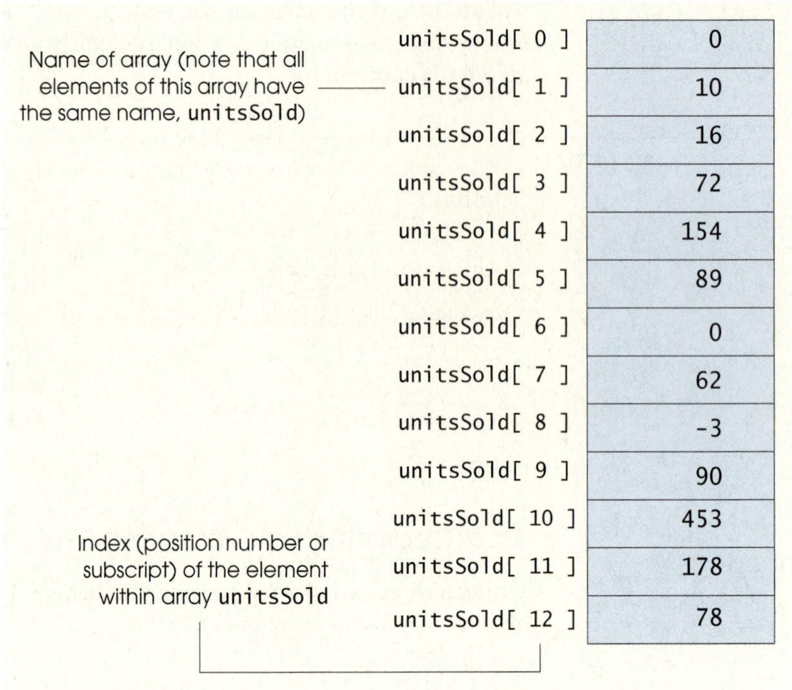

Figure 16.7 Array unitsSold, consisting of 13 elements.

Each array element is referred to by providing the array name followed by the index (**position number** or **subscript**) of the element in brackets—[]. The indices for the elements in an array begin with 0. Thus, the **zeroth element** of array units-Sold is referred to as unitsSold[0], element 1 of array unitsSold is referred to as unitsSold[1], element 6 of array unitsSold is referred to as unitsSold[6] and so on. Element *i* of array unitsSold is referred to as unitsSold[i]. An index must be either zero, a positive integer or an integer expression that yields a positive result. If an application uses an integer expression as an index, the expression is evaluated first to determine the index. For example, if variable value1 is equal to 5, and variable value2 is equal to 6, then the statement

```
unitsSold[ value1 + value2 ] += 2;
```

adds 2 to array element unitsSold[11] to get a value of 180. Note that an **indexed array name** (the array name followed by an index enclosed in brackets) references a variable in the array and can be used on the left side of an assignment statement to place a new value into an array element.

Let's examine the unitsSold array in Fig. 16.7 more closely. The name of the array is unitsSold. The 13 elements of the array are referred to as unitsSold[0] through unitsSold[12]. The value of unitsSold[1] is 10, the value of unitsSold[2] is 16, the value of unitsSold[3] is 72, the value of unitsSold[7] is 62 and the value of unitsSold[11] is 178. A positive value for an element in this array indicates that more books were bought than were returned. A negative value for an element in this array indicates that more books were returned than were bought. A value of zero indicates that the number of books sold was equal to the number of books returned, possibly zero.

Values stored in arrays can be used in various calculations and applications. For example, to determine the units sold in the first three months of the year and store the result in variable firstQuarterUnits, you would write

```
firstQuarterUnits = unitsSold[ 1 ] + unitsSold[ 2 ] + unitsSold[ 3 ];
```

You will deal exclusively with **one-dimensional** arrays, such as unitsSold, in this tutorial. One-dimensional arrays use only one index. In the next tutorial, you

will study two-dimensional arrays, which are like tables consisting of rows and columns; they use two indices—one to identify an element's row and one to identify an element's column.

SELF-REVIEW

1. The number that refers to a particular element of an array is called its _____ (or subscript).
   a) value
   b) size
   c) indexed array name
   d) index

2. The indexed array name of the third element of the one-dimensional array `units` is _____.

   a) `units[ 2 ]`
   b) `units( 2 )`
   c) `units[ 0, 2 ]`
   d) `units{ 2 }`

Answers: 1) d. 2) a.

16.3 Declaring and Creating Arrays

To declare an array, you provide the array's type and name. The following statement declares the array in Fig. 16.7:

```
int[] unitsSold;
```

The brackets that follow the array type indicate that `unitsSold` is an array. Arrays can be declared to contain any type. Every element of the array is a variable of the declared type. For example, every element of an `int` array is an `int` variable.

Before you can use an array, you must specify the size of the array and create the array. Recall from Tutorial 15 that the keyword `new` can be used to create an object. Arrays are objects in Java, so they too are created using the keyword `new`. The value stored in an array variable (such as `unitsSold`) is actually a reference to the array object. To create the array `unitsSold` after it has been declared, use the statement

```
unitsSold = new int[ 13 ];
```

Array bounds determine what indices can be used to access an element in the array. Here, the array bounds are 0 (which is implicit in the preceding statement) and 12 (one less than the number of elements in the array). Notice that because of array element 0, the actual number of elements in the array (13) is one larger than the upper bound of the array (12). When an array is created as in the preceding statement, the elements in the array are initialized to the default value for the array's type. Again, the default values are 0 for numeric primitive-type variables (such as `int`), `false` for `boolean` variables and `null` for reference variables. Recall that the keyword `null` indicates that a reference variable does not refer to an object.

Another way to create an array (`salesPerDay`) is with a statement such as

```
int[] salesPerDay = { 0, 2, 3, 6, 1, 4, 5, 6 };
```

Common Programming Error

Attempting to access elements in the array by using an index outside the array bounds is a runtime error.

where the comma-separated list enclosed in the braces—{ and }—is called an **array initializer** and specifies the initial values of the elements in the array. The preceding statement declares and creates an array containing eight `int`s. Java determines the array's size and bounds from the number of elements in the initializer. The `new` keyword is not required in this case.

Now, you will declare and initialize an array, and access the array's elements as you develop code that will total the values in the array.

Computing the Sum of an Array's Elements

1. ***Copying the template to your working directory.*** Copy the C:\Examples\ Tutorial16\TemplateApplication\SumArray directory to your C:\SimplyJava directory.

2. ***Opening the Command Prompt window and changing directories.*** Open the **Command Prompt** window by selecting **Start > Programs > Accessories > Command Prompt**. Change to your working directory by typing cd C:\SimplyJava\SumArray.

3. ***Running the template application.*** Type java SumArray in the **Command Prompt** window to run the application (Fig. 16.8). Notice that if you click the **Sum Array** JButton, no action occurs. In the next several steps, you will program this application to declare an array containing the integers 1–10, add these values and display the total in the **Total of array elements:** JText-Field.

Figure 16.8 Running the **Sum Array** template application.

4. ***Closing the application.*** Close your running application by clicking its close button. Leave the **Command Prompt** window open because you will use it later.

5. ***Opening the Sum Array application's template file.*** Open the template file SumArray.java in your text editor.

6. ***Combining the declaration and creation of an array.*** Add lines 73–75 of Fig. 16.9 to the sumArrayJButtonActionPerformed method. Line 74 combines the declaration and creation of an array into one statement. Line 75 declares and initializes variable total, which will store the sum of array's elements.

```
Source Editor [SumArray *]
70    // method called to determine sum of array
71    private void sumArrayJButtonActionPerformed( ActionEvent event )
72    {
73       // declare and initialize array
74       int[] array = { 1, 2, 3, 4, 5, 6, 7, 8, 9, 10 };
75       int total = 0;
76
77    } // end method sumArrayJButtonActionPerformed
```

Creating an array of ints ——

Figure 16.9 Declaring an array in the sumArrayJButtonActionPerformed method.

7. ***Calculating the sum.*** Add lines 77–81 of Fig. 16.10 to the method. Every array in Java "knows" its own length. To get the size of an array, you write ***arrayName*.length**, where *arrayName* is the name of the array whose length you are trying to determine. In this example, the expression array.length returns the value 10. The for header (line 78) uses this expression in the loop-continuation condition to iterate through the elements of array. Line 80 retrieves each element's value (one at a time) and adds it to total.

(cont.)

Retrieve the value of each element and add it to the total, one at a time

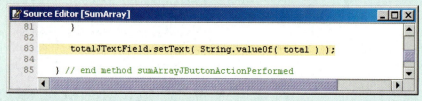

Figure 16.10 Summing of the values of an array's elements.

Let's look more closely at this for statement. The first time this statement iterates, index contains the value 0, so line 80 adds the value of array[0] (which is 1) to total. The value of total was set to 0 in line 75, so the new value of total is 0 + 1, or 1. At the end of the first iteration, the value of index is incremented to 1. Line 80 adds the value of array[1] (which is 2) to total. The value of total contains 1 from the last iteration, so the new value of total is 1 + 2, or 3. The statement continues iterating, adding each value in array to total. The last iteration occurs when index contains the value 9. The value of array[9] (which is 10) will be added to total (total at this point will contain the value 55, as you will see shortly). At the end of this iteration, the value of index is incremented and now contains the value 10. The loop-continuation condition is checked. Because 10 is not less than array.length (which is also 10), the loop finishes iterating and the application continues with the first statement after the loop.

Error-Prevention Tip

Use an expression of the form *arrayName*.length when you need to find the size of an array. Using an actual numerical value for the upper bound instead could lead to errors if you change the number of array elements.

8. ***Displaying the sum.*** Add line 83 of Fig. 16.11 to the method. This line displays the sum of the values of the array's elements.

```
 81        }
 82
 83          totalJTextField.setText( String.valueOf( total ) );
 84
 85      } // end method sumArrayJButtonActionPerformed
```

Figure 16.11 Displaying the sum of the values of an array's elements.

9. ***Saving the application.*** Save your modified source code file.

10. ***Compiling the application.*** Compile your application by typing javac SumArray.java.

11. ***Running the application.*** When your application compiles correctly, run it by typing java SumArray. Figure 16.12 shows the completed application running. Now the total value of the array elements (55) is displayed when you click the **Sum Array** JButton.

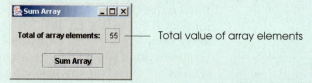
Total value of array elements

Figure 16.12 Running the completed **Sum Array** application.

12. ***Closing the application.*** Close your running application by clicking its close button.

13. ***Closing the Command Prompt window.*** Close the **Command Prompt** window by clicking its close button.

SELF-REVIEW

1. Arrays can be created using keyword _____.

   a) declare
   b) create
   c) new
   d) make

2. An array's length is _____.

   a) one more than the array's last index
   b) one less than the array's last index
   c) the same as the array's last index
   d) None of the above.

   Answers: 1) c. 2) a.

16.4 Constructing the Flag Quiz Application

Now you will build your **Flag Quiz** application by using arrays and a JComboBox. The arrays will be used to store the names of the countries whose flags you are displaying and to keep track of which flags have already been displayed. The JComboBox will display the list of countries from which the user will be able to choose. The following pseudocode describes the basic operation of the **Flag Quiz** application, which executes when the application first begins, and when the **Submit** and **Next Flag** JButtons are clicked.

> When the user runs the application:
>   Sort the country names alphabetically
>   Place country names in the JComboBox
>   Randomly select a flag
>   Display the flag
>
> When the user clicks the Submit JButton:
>   Retrieve the index of the selected country name from the JComboBox
>
>   If the selected country's index matches the index of the current flag
>   Display "Correct!" in the feedback output JTextField
>   Else
>   Display "Sorry, incorrect." in the feedback output JTextField
>
>   If five images have been displayed
>   Append "Done!" to the feedback output JTextField's text
>   Disable the JButtons and JComboBox
>   Else
>   Disable the Submit JButton
>   Enable the Next Flag JButton
>
> When the user clicks the Next Flag JButton:
>   Randomly select a flag that has not been chosen previously
>   Display the new flag
>   Clear the feedback output JTextField
>   Set the JComboBox to display its first item
>   Enable the Submit JButton
>   Disable the Next Flag JButton

Now that you have test-driven the **Flag Quiz** application and studied its pseudocode representation, you will use an ACE table to help you convert the pseudocode to Java. Figure 16.13 lists the actions, components and events that will help you complete your own version of this application.

Action/Component/ Event (ACE) Table for the Flag Quiz Application

Action	Component/Object	Event
Label the application's components	selectCountryJLabel, flagJPanel	
		Application is run
Sort the countries alphabetically	Arrays	
Place countries in the JComboBox	selectCountryJComboBox	
Randomly select a flag	generator (Random)	
Display the flag	flagIconJLabel	
	submitJButton	User clicks **Submit** JButton
Retrieve the selected country	selectCountryJComboBox	
If the selected country matches the current flag Display "Correct!" in the feedback output JTextField	feedbackJTextField	
Else Display "Sorry, incorrect." in the feedback output JTextField	feedbackJTextField	
If five images have been displayed Append "Done!" to the feedback output JTextField's text	feedbackJTextField	
Disable the JButtons and JComboBox	nextFlagJButton, submitJButton, selectCountryJComboBox	
Else Disable the Submit JButton	submitJButton	
Enable the Next Flag JButton	nextFlagJButton	
	nextFlagJButton	User clicks **Next Flag** JButton
Randomly select a flag that has not been chosen previously	generator (Random)	
Display the new flag	flagIconJLabel	
Clear the feedback output JTextField	feedbackJTextField	
Set the JComboBox to display its first item	selectCountryJComboBox	
Enable the Submit JButton	submitJButton	
Disable the Next Flag JButton	nextFlagJButton	

Figure 16.13 **Flag Quiz** application's ACE table.

Next, you will initialize the variables used in the **Flag Quiz** application. In particular, your application requires two one-dimensional arrays.

Declaring and Initializing Arrays

1. *Copying the template to your working directory.* Copy the C:\Examples\Tutorial16\TemplateApplication\FlagQuiz directory to your C:\SimplyJava directory.

2. *Opening the Flag Quiz application's template file.* Open the template file FlagQuiz.java in your text editor.

(cont.)   3. ***Declaring the array of country names.*** Add lines 12–14 of Fig. 16.14 to your application. Lines 13–14 declare and initialize the `countries` array. Each element is a `String` containing the name of a country. These lines assign the values in the initializer to the elements of the array, combining the declaration and initialization of the array into one statement. The compiler determines the size of the array (in this case, eight elements) by counting the number of items in the initializer.

Creating an array of `Strings` to store country names

```
🗾 Source Editor [FlagQuiz *]                                         _ □ ×
    10  public class FlagQuiz extends JFrame
    11  {
    12      // array of country names
    13      private String[] countries = { "Russia", "China", "United States",
    14          "Italy", "Australia", "South Africa", "Brazil", "Spain" };
    15
    16      // JPanel and JLabel for displaying a flag image
```

Figure 16.14   Creating and initializing the `String` array that stores the country names.

4. ***Creating a boolean array.*** Add lines 16–17 of Fig. 16.15. Your application should not display any flag more than once. Because your application uses random number generation to pick a flag, the same flag could be selected more than once—just as when you roll a six-sided die many times, a die face could be repeated. You will use a `boolean` array to track which flags have been displayed (line 17).

Creating an array of `boolean` values

```
🗾 Source Editor [FlagQuiz *]                                         _ □ ×
    14          "Italy", "Australia", "South Africa", "Brazil", "Spain" };
    15
    16      // boolean array tracks displayed flags
    17      private boolean[] flagsUsed = new boolean[ countries.length ];
    18
```

Figure 16.15   Array of type `boolean` that keeps track of displayed flags.

The `flagsUsed` array has the same size as the array `countries`. The elements of `flagsUsed` correspond to the elements of `countries`—for example, `flagsUsed[ 0 ]` specifies whether the flag corresponding to the country name stored in `countries[ 0 ]` has been displayed. Recall that, by default, each element in a `boolean` array is `false`. Your application will set an element of `flagsUsed` to `true` if its corresponding flag has been displayed.

5. ***Declaring instance variables.*** Add lines 19–22 of Fig. 16.16. Line 19 declares instance variable `currentIndex`, which will store the index of the flag currently being displayed. This value will be used to determine whether the user has entered the correct answer. Line 22 declares and initializes instance variable `count`, which is used to ensure that only five flags are displayed.

Declaring instance variables

```
🗾 Source Editor [FlagQuiz]                                           _ □ ×
    17      private boolean[] used = new boolean[ countries.length ];
    18
    19      private int currentIndex; // contains the index of current flag
    20
    21      // tracks the number of flags that have been displayed
    22      private int count = 1;
    23
    24      // JPanel and JLabel for displaying a flag image
```

Figure 16.16   Declaring instance variables.

6. ***Saving the application.*** Save your modified source code file.

Now you will add another component to the **Flag Quiz** application template. The **Flag Quiz** application allows students to select answers from a JComboBox. A JComboBox appears as text with a down arrow at the right edge. The user can click the down arrow to display a list of predefined items. If a user chooses an item from this list, that item is displayed in the JComboBox. If the list contains more items than the drop-down list can display at once, a vertical scrollbar appears. You will now assign an array's elements to a JComboBox before your application is displayed to users.

Customizing a JComboBox Component

1. **Customizing the JComboBox.** On line 76 of Fig. 16.17, add the array name countries within the parentheses following the text new JComboBox. The name to the right of the new keyword (JComboBox) is called a constructor. This line creates a JComboBox and "loads up" the JComboBox with the options that it will display. Using the countries array specifies that the options loaded into the JComboBox will be the elements of the countries array.

Adding data to a JComboBox —

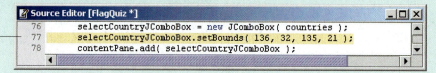

Figure 16.17 Setting selectCountryJComboBox's items.

Good Programming Practice

Suffix JComboBox component names with JComboBox.

2. **Setting the bounds of the JComboBox.** Add line 77 of Fig. 16.18 to set the *bounds* property of selectCountryJComboBox to 136, 32, 135, 21.

Set the bounds of the selectCountryJComboBox —

```
76     selectCountryJComboBox = new JComboBox( countries );
77     selectCountryJComboBox.setBounds( 136, 32, 135, 21 );
78     contentPane.add( selectCountryJComboBox );
```

Figure 16.18 Setting selectCountryJComboBox's bounds.

GUI Design Tip

Each JComboBox should have a descriptive JLabel to describe the JComboBox's contents.

3. **Setting the appearance of selectCountryJComboBox.** Add line 78 of Fig. 16.19. This line uses the **setMaximumRowCount** method of JComboBox to set the number of items displayed at once in selectCountryJComboBox to 3. If the total number of items in selectCountryJComboBox exceeds this number, a vertical scrollbar automatically will be added to the drop-down list to allow the users access to the remaining items. The other rows become visible when the user moves the scrollbar.

Set the number of items displayed in the selectCountryJComboBox —

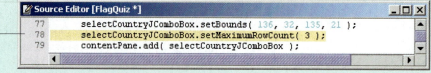

Figure 16.19 Setting the maximum number of items displayed in the selectCountryJComboBox.

4. **Saving the application.** Save your modified source code file.

5. **Opening the Command Prompt window and changing directories.** Open the **Command Prompt** window by selecting **Start > Programs > Accessories > Command Prompt**. Change to your working directory by typing cd C:\SimplyJava\FlagQuiz.

6. **Compiling the application.** Compile your application by typing javac FlagQuiz.java.

(cont.)

7. ***Running the application.*** When your application compiles correctly, run it by typing java FlagQuiz. Figure 16.20 shows the updated application running. The selectCountryJComboBox is now displayed. When you click the down arrow on the right side of the selectCountryJComboBox, the elements of the countries array are displayed. Notice that the country names appear in the same order as the countries array. Later in this tutorial, you will alphabetize the country names before they are displayed.

Figure 16.20   **Flag Quiz** application with selectCountryJComboBox.

8. ***Closing the application.*** Close your running application by clicking its close button.

9. ***Closing the Command Prompt window.*** Close the **Command Prompt** window by clicking its close button.

To ensure that the user is not asked the same question twice, a flag must be displayed no more than once while your application is running. Your application uses boolean array flagsUsed to track which flags have been displayed. Next, you will add code to ensure that your application displays a flag no more than once.

Selecting a Unique Flag to Display

1. ***Generating a random index and ensuring that each flag displays only once.*** Add lines 138–146 of Fig. 16.21 to the empty getUniqueRandomNumber method provided in the template. Line 138 creates generator, an object of type Random, to generate a random number. Line 139 creates variable randomNumber, which will be used to store the random number generated from the generator object. This random number will be used as an index in the flagsUsed array to determine if the flag at this position has been displayed already. If the flag has been displayed, the element of flagsUsed at the generated index is true, and a new random number is generated. The do...while statement (lines 142–146) iterates until it finds a unique index (that is, until flagsUsed[randomNumber] is false).

Determining if a country's flag has been previously displayed ──

```
136     private int getUniqueRandomNumber()
137     {
138         Random generator = new Random();
139         int randomNumber;
140
141         // generate random numbers until unused flag is found
142         do
143         {
144             // generate a number between 0-7
145             randomNumber = generator.nextInt( 8 );
146         }
147         while ( flagsUsed[ randomNumber ] == true );
148
```

Figure 16.21   Generating a unique index.

(cont.)

2. ***Indicating that the index has been used.*** Add lines 149–150 of Fig. 16.22 to the getUniqueRandomNumber method. Line 150 sets the element at the randomNumber index of the flagsUsed array to true. At this point, randomNumber contains an index value for the flag that will be displayed next. Because the flag at this position will be displayed, you want to set this position in the flagsUsed array to true to prevent the flag from being displayed again later in the quiz.

Indicate that a flag is now used

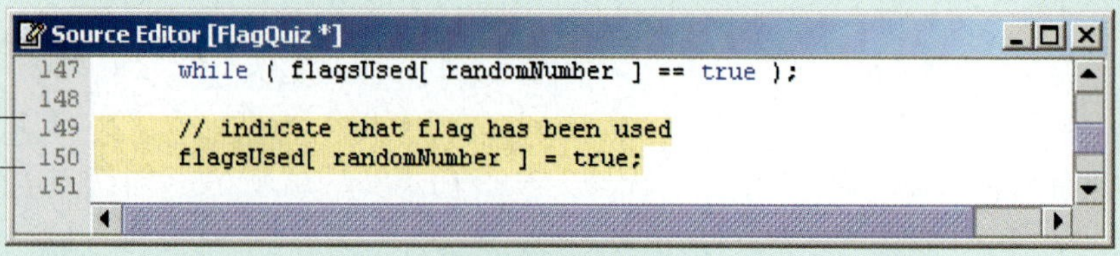

```
Source Editor [FlagQuiz *]                                    _ □ ×
147          while ( flagsUsed[ randomNumber ] == true );
148
149          // indicate that flag has been used
150          flagsUsed[ randomNumber ] = true;
151
```

Figure 16.22 Updating the flagsUsed array for the new flag.

3. ***Returning the unique random number.*** Modify line 152 of Fig. 16.23 to return the unique random index. This line which, originally returned the value 0, was in the template so that your application would compile correctly. You now have a unique random number to return, so you should modify the return statement accordingly.

Returning the value of randomNumber

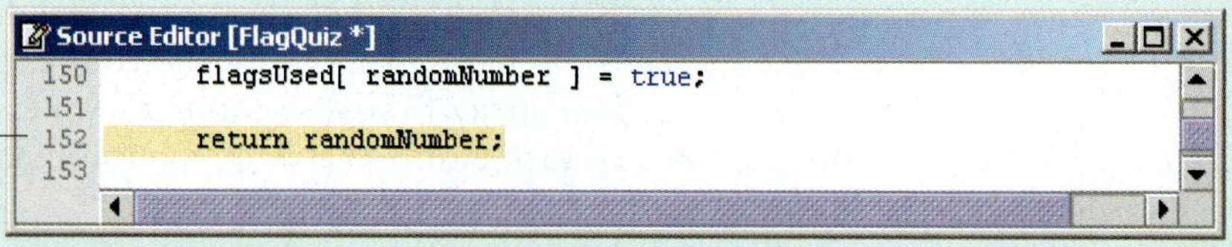

```
Source Editor [FlagQuiz *]                                    _ □ ×
150          flagsUsed[ randomNumber ] = true;
151
152          return randomNumber;
153
```

Figure 16.23 Returning the unique index.

4. ***Saving the application.*** Save your modified source code file.

You have now created a method that will return a unique, randomly selected index each time it is called. You will now use that index to find the location of the flag's image and display that image in flagIconJLabel.

Displaying a Flag

1. ***Using a unique index to retrieve a country name.*** Add lines 159–163 of Fig. 16.24 to the displayFlag method. Line 159 selects a unique index that has not been displayed during your application's execution (by calling the getUniqueRandomNumber method) and assigns it to currentIndex. Lines 162–163 assign to String country the flag's corresponding country name using the **getItemAt** method of JComboBox. This method takes an int argument representing an index and returns the object at that index in the JComboBox which is then converted to a String with the String cast operator. Keep in mind that the index can begin at 0. The values displayed in a JComboBox can be accessed using an index, just as you can use an index to access an array's elements.

(cont.)

Getting the index
of an unused flag

Retrieving the flag's
corresponding country name

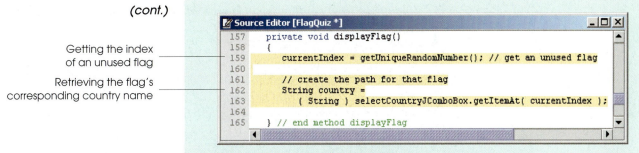

Figure 16.24 Choosing a random country name.

2. ***Building the flag image's path name.*** Add line 164 of Fig. 16.25 to the dis-playFlag method. Line 164 creates the flag image's path name, which begins with the text "images/" (the image files are located in the images directory), followed by the country name, then ends with the ".png" extension (the image files are in PNG format). The result of this expression is assigned to countryPath.

Creating the path name
of the flag's image

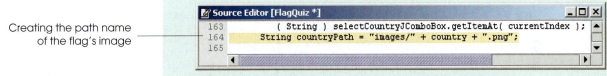

Figure 16.25 Creating the path to the image.

3. ***Displaying the flag image.*** Add lines 166–167 of Fig. 16.26 to the display-Flag method. Line 167 uses the path of the image to create an ImageIcon, which is then assigned to flagIconJLabel's *icon* property.

Use method setIcon
to display the flag image

```
Source Editor [FlagQuiz *]                              _|□|×|
164            String countryPath = "images/" + country + ".png";
165
166            // set the flagIconJLabel to display the flag
167            flagIconJLabel.setIcon( new ImageIcon( countryPath ) );
168
```

Figure 16.26 Displaying a flag image.

4. ***Displaying a flag when your application is running.*** Add line 81 of Fig. 16.27 to your application, after selectCountryJComboBox has been customized. After the selectCountryJComboBox is configured, line 81 calls the displayFlag method, causing the first flag image in the quiz to be displayed.

Displaying a flag when
the application is first run

```
Source Editor [FlagQuiz]                               _|□|×|
79            contentPane.add( selectCountryJComboBox );
80
81            displayFlag(); // display first flag
82
83            // set up feedbackJTextField
```

Figure 16.27 Displaying a flag when your application is run.

5. ***Saving the application.*** Save your modified source code file.

6. ***Opening the Command Prompt window and changing directories.*** Open the **Command Prompt** window by selecting **Start > Programs > Accessories > Command Prompt**. Change to your working directory by typing cd C:\SimplyJava\FlagQuiz.

(cont.)

7. *Compiling the application.* Compile your application by typing javac FlagQuiz.java.

8. *Running the application.* When your application compiles correctly, run it by typing java FlagQuiz. Figure 16.28 shows the updated application running. A randomly selected flag will be displayed. You can select an answer from the selectCountryJComboBox, but clicking the **Submit** JButton will not perform any action yet. You will add this functionality in the next box.

Initial flag is displayed

Figure 16.28 **Flag Quiz** application displaying initial flag.

9. *Closing the application.* Close your running application by clicking its close button.

10. *Closing the Command Prompt window.* Close the **Command Prompt** window by clicking its close button.

The user submits an answer by selecting a country name from the selectCountryJComboBox and clicking the **Submit** JButton. Your application displays whether the user's answer is correct. If your application is finished (that is, five flags have been displayed), your application informs the user that the quiz is done. Otherwise, your application enables the user to view the next flag. Next you will implement this functionality.

Processing a User's Answer

1. *Retrieving the selected selectCountryJComboBox item.* Add lines 176–185 of Fig. 16.29 to the empty submitJButtonActionPerformed method. This if...else statement determines whether the user's response matches the correct answer (currentIndex). Lines 177–178 retrieve the index of the user's answer and compare it to currentIndex. The **getSelectedIndex** method returns the index of the JComboBox's selected item, stored in the *selectedIndex* property. Line 180 displays "Correct!" in the feedbackJTextField if the user's response matches the correct answer. Otherwise, line 184 displays "Sorry, incorrect.".

Retrieving user's answer

Displaying proper feedback

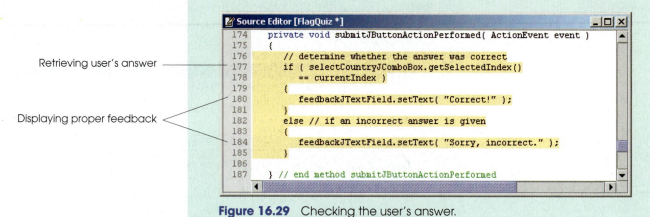

```
174    private void submitJButtonActionPerformed( ActionEvent event )
175    {
176        // determine whether the answer was correct
177        if ( selectCountryJComboBox.getSelectedIndex()
178            == currentIndex )
179        {
180            feedbackJTextField.setText( "Correct!" );
181        }
182        else // if an incorrect answer is given
183        {
184            feedbackJTextField.setText( "Sorry, incorrect." );
185        }
186
187    } // end method submitJButtonActionPerformed
```

Figure 16.29 Checking the user's answer.

(cont.)

2. ***Informing the user that the quiz is over, when five flags have been displayed.*** Add lines 187–195 of Fig. 16.30 to the `submitJButtonAction-Performed` method. If five flags have been displayed (`count` equals 5), the `feedbackJTextField` displays text informing the user that the quiz is over (lines 190–191), and both `JButtons` are disabled (lines 192–193). The `selectCountryJComboBox` is also disabled (line 194).

Actions to perform if quiz is over ⟶

```
Source Editor [FlagQuiz *]                                    _ □ ×
185        }
186
187        // inform user if quiz is over
188        if ( count == 5 )
189        {
190           feedbackJTextField.setText(
191              feedbackJTextField.getText() + "   Done!" );
192           nextFlagJButton.setEnabled( false );
193           submitJButton.setEnabled( false );
194           selectCountryJComboBox.setEnabled( false );
195        }
196
```

Figure 16.30 Testing whether the quiz is finished.

3. ***Continuing the quiz while fewer than five flags have been displayed.*** Add lines 196–200 of Fig. 16.31 to the `submitJButtonActionPerformed` method. If the quiz is not finished (that is, `count` is less than 5), your application disables the **Submit** JButton and enables the **Next Flag** JButton (lines 198–199).

Allow user to continue ⟶

```
Source Editor [FlagQuiz *]                                    _ □ ×
195        }
196        else // if less than 5 flags have been displayed
197        {
198           submitJButton.setEnabled( false );
199           nextFlagJButton.setEnabled( true );
200        }
201
```

Figure 16.31 Enable user to display next flag if quiz is not over.

4. ***Saving the application.*** Save your modified source code file.

5. ***Opening the Command Prompt window and changing directories.*** Open the **Command Prompt** window by selecting **Start > Programs > Accessories > Command Prompt**. Change to your working directory by typing cd `C:\SimplyJava\FlagQuiz`.

6. ***Compiling the application.*** Compile your application by typing javac `FlagQuiz.java`.

7. ***Running the application.*** When your application compiles correctly, run it by typing java `FlagQuiz`. Figure 16.32 shows the updated application running. At this point you can select an answer from the `selectCountryJCom-boBox` and submit it by clicking the **Submit** JButton. You will be informed whether or not you are correct, and the **Next Flag** JButton will be enabled. Clicking this JButton, however, causes no action to occur. You will add this functionality in the next box.

(cont.)

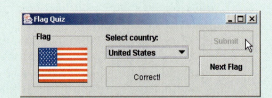

Figure 16.32 **Flag Quiz** application that allows user to submit an answer.

8. *Closing the application.* Close your running application by clicking its close button.

9. *Closing the Command Prompt window.* Close the **Command Prompt** window by clicking its close button.

The user requests the next flag in the quiz by clicking the **Next Flag** JButton. Your application then displays the next flag and increments the number of flags that have been displayed. Next, you will implement this functionality.

Displaying the Next Flag

1. *Displaying the next flag.* Add lines 207–208 of Fig. 16.33 to the next-FlagJButtonActionPerformed method. Line 207 calls the displayFlag method to place the next flag in the JLabel. Line 208 updates count to indicate that one more flag has been displayed.

```
Source Editor [FlagQuiz *]

205     private void nextFlagJButtonActionPerformed( ActionEvent event )
206     {
207         displayFlag(); // display next flag
208         count++;
209
210     } // end method nextFlagJButtonActionPerformed
```

Displaying the next flag for the user to identify

Figure 16.33 Displaying the next flag.

2. *Clearing the previous results and resetting components.* Add lines 210–214 of Fig. 16.34 to nextFlagJButtonActionPerformed. Line 211 clears the feedbackJTextField, deleting the results of the previous question. Line 212 uses the **setSelectedIndex** method to set the *selectedIndex* property of selectCountryJComboBox to 0, which displays the first item in select-CountryJComboBox's drop-down list. Line 213 enables the **Submit** JButton; line 214 disables the **Next Flag** JButton. This forces the user to submit an answer before the next flag can be displayed.

```
Source Editor [FlagQuiz *]

208         count++;
209
210         // reset GUI components to initial states
211         feedbackJTextField.setText( "" );
212         selectCountryJComboBox.setSelectedIndex( 0 );
213         submitJButton.setEnabled( true );
214         nextFlagJButton.setEnabled( false );
215
```

Actions to perform for next question

Figure 16.34 Allowing the user to enter the next answer.

3. *Saving the application.* Save your modified source code file.

4. *Opening the Command Prompt window and changing directories.* Open the **Command Prompt** window by selecting **Start > Programs > Accessories > Command Prompt**. Change to your working directory by typing cd C:\SimplyJava\FlagQuiz.

(cont.)

5. ***Compiling the application.*** Compile your application by typing `javac FlagQuiz.java`.

6. ***Running the application.*** When your application compiles correctly, run it by typing `java FlagQuiz`. Figure 16.35 shows the updated application running. You can now display five flags and submit five answers. The only difference between the application at this point and the completed application is that the country names in the `selectCountryJComboBox` are not alphabetized. You will add this functionality in the next box.

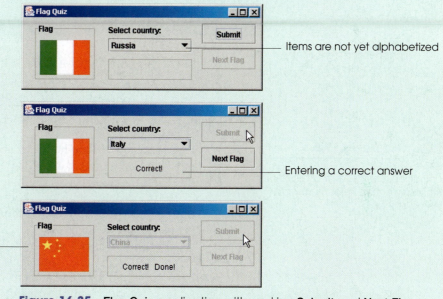

Figure 16.35 **Flag Quiz** application with working **Submit** and **Next Flag** `JButtons`.

7. ***Closing the application.*** Close your running application by clicking its close button.

8. ***Closing the Command Prompt window.*** Close the **Command Prompt** window by clicking its close button.

SELF-REVIEW

1. The _____ method takes an `int` argument representing an index, and returns the value at that index of a `JComboBox`.

   a) `getValueAt`   b) `getSource`
   c) `getIndexValue`   d) `getItemAt`

2. The _____ method of the `JComboBox` class returns the index of the currently selected item in that `JComboBox`.

   a) `getSelectedIndex`   b) `getSelectedValue`
   c) `getSelectedSubscript`   d) `getSelectItem`

Answers: 1) d. 2) a.

16.5 Sorting Arrays

Sorting refers to arranging data in some particular order, such as alphabetical or chronological. For example, a bank sorts checks by account number, so that it can prepare individual bank statements at the end of each month. Telephone companies sort account information alphabetically by last name and, within last name listings, by first name, to make it easy to find phone numbers. Virtually every organization must sort some data—often, massive amounts of it. In this section, you will learn

how to sort the values in an array so that you can alphabetize the list of countries in the **Flag Quiz** application. Users are able to find a country name in the `select-CountryJComboBox` faster if the country names are alphabetized.

Sorting an Array

1. **Sorting the array of country names.** Add line 75 of Fig. 16.36 to your application. Line 75 passes the `countries` array to the **sort** method of class **Arrays**, which sorts the values in the array into ascending alphabetical order. Note that this line is placed prior to setting up the `JComboBox`, so that the items in the `JComboBox` will be displayed in alphabetical order.

Alphabetizing the country names in the array →

```
Source Editor [FlagQuiz]
73          contentPane.add( selectCountryJLabel );
74
75          Arrays.sort( countries ); // sort the array
76
77          // set up selectCountryJComboBox
```

Figure 16.36 Sorting the array of country names.

Notice that the `sort` method does not return a value—the array passed to the `sort` method, `countries`, is sorted "in place." So far, whenever you have passed an argument to a method, a copy of the argument's value has been passed to the method. This is known as **pass-by-value**. Changes made to the copy of the argument in the method do not affect the original variable's value in the calling method.

In contrast, line 75 uses **pass-by-reference**. When an argument is passed by reference, no copy of the argument is made—rather, the called method is given access directly to the argument in the caller. The original data in the caller can be modified by the called method. In Java, objects are always passed by reference, while arguments of primitive types are always passed by value. Arrays are objects, so passing the name of an array to a method causes the array to be passed by reference. This enables the method to access the original array elements in memory.

2. **Saving the application.** Save your modified source code file.

3. **Opening the Command Prompt window and changing directories.** Open the **Command Prompt** window by selecting **Start > Programs > Accessories > Command Prompt**. Change to your working directory by typing `cd C:\SimplyJava\FlagQuiz`.

4. **Compiling the application.** Compile your application by typing `javac FlagQuiz.java`.

5. **Running the application.** When your application compiles correctly, run it by typing `java FlagQuiz`. Figure 16.37 shows the completed application running. Your application now has the same functionality as the completed application shown in the test-drive. Notice that the array was indeed modified by the `Arrays.sort` method, so the elements in the `selectCountryJ-ComboBox` are now in alphabetical order.

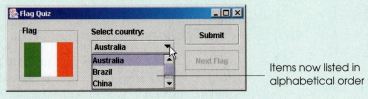

Items now listed in alphabetical order

Figure 16.37 **Flag Quiz** application running.

(cont.)

> 6. ***Closing the application.*** Close your running application by clicking its close button.
>
> 7. ***Closing the Command Prompt window.*** Close the **Command Prompt** window by clicking its close button.

Figure 16.38 presents the source code for the **Flag Quiz** application. The lines of code that you added, viewed or modified in this tutorial are highlighted.

```java
1   // Tutorial 16: FlagQuiz.java
2   // Quiz the user on their knowledge of flags. The user must try to
3   // match five flags to their countries.
4   import java.awt.*;
5   import java.awt.event.*;
6   import java.util.*;
7   import javax.swing.*;
8   import javax.swing.border.*;
9
10  public class FlagQuiz extends JFrame
11  {
12     // array of country names
13     private String[] countries = { "Russia", "China", "United States",
14        "Italy", "Australia", "South Africa", "Brazil", "Spain" };
15
16     // boolean array tracks displayed flags
17     private boolean[] flagsUsed = new boolean[ countries.length ];
18
19     private int currentIndex; // contains the index of current flag
20
21     // tracks the number of flags that have been displayed
22     private int count = 1;
23
24     // JPanel and JLabel for displaying a flag image
25     private JPanel flagJPanel;
26     private JLabel flagIconJLabel;
27
28     // JLabel and JComboBox for choosing a country
29     private JLabel selectCountryJLabel;
30     private JComboBox selectCountryJComboBox;
31
32     // JTextField for giving the user feedback
33     private JTextField feedbackJTextField;
34
35     // JButton to submit an answer
36     private JButton submitJButton;
37
38     // JButton to display the next flag
39     private JButton nextFlagJButton;
40
41     // no-argument constructor
42     public FlagQuiz()
43     {
44        createUserInterface();
45     }
46
```

Creating an array of **Strings** to store country names → (lines 13–14)

Creating a **boolean** array → (lines 16–17)

Variable **currentIndex** stores the index of the flag being displayed → (line 19)

Variable **count** stores the number of flags displayed → (lines 21–22)

Figure 16.38   **Flag Quiz** code. (Part 1 of 5.)

```
47        // create and position GUI components; register event handlers
48        private void createUserInterface()
49        {
50           // get content pane for attaching GUI components
51           Container contentPane = getContentPane();
52
53           // enable explicit positioning of GUI components
54           contentPane.setLayout( null );
55
56           // set up flagJPanel
57           flagJPanel = new JPanel();
58           flagJPanel.setBounds( 16, 8, 100, 90 );
59           flagJPanel.setLayout( null );
60           flagJPanel.setBorder( new TitledBorder( "Flag" ) );
61           contentPane.add( flagJPanel );
62
63           // set up flagIconJLabel
64           flagIconJLabel = new JLabel();
65           flagIconJLabel.setBounds( 10, 14, 80, 80 );
66           flagIconJLabel.setHorizontalAlignment( JLabel.CENTER );
67           flagJPanel.add( flagIconJLabel );
68
69           // set up selectCountryJLabel
70           selectCountryJLabel = new JLabel();
71           selectCountryJLabel.setBounds( 136, 8, 88, 21 );
72           selectCountryJLabel.setText( "Select country:" );
73           contentPane.add( selectCountryJLabel );
74
75           Arrays.sort( countries ); // sort the array
76
77           // set up selectCountryJComboBox
78           selectCountryJComboBox = new JComboBox( countries );
79           selectCountryJComboBox.setBounds( 136, 32, 135, 21 );
80           selectCountryJComboBox.setMaximumRowCount( 3 );
81           contentPane.add( selectCountryJComboBox );
82
83           displayFlag(); // display first flag
84
85           // set up feedbackJTextField
86           feedbackJTextField = new JTextField();
87           feedbackJTextField.setBounds( 136, 64, 135, 32 );
88           feedbackJTextField.setHorizontalAlignment(
89              JTextField.CENTER );
90           feedbackJTextField.setEditable( false );
91           contentPane.add( feedbackJTextField );
92
93           // set up submitJButton
94           submitJButton = new JButton();
95           submitJButton.setBounds( 287, 8, 88, 32 );
96           submitJButton.setText( "Submit" );
97           contentPane.add( submitJButton );
98           submitJButton.addActionListener(
99
100             new ActionListener() // anonymous inner class
101             {
102                // event handler called when submitJButton is pressed
103                public void actionPerformed( ActionEvent event )
104                {
```

Alphabetizing country names in the array — 75

Customizing the selectCountryJComboBox — 78, 79, 80

Displaying the initial flag — 83

Figure 16.38 **Flag Quiz** code. (Part 2 of 5.)

```
105                    submitJButtonActionPerformed( event );
106                 }
107
108              } // end anonymous inner class
109
110           ); // end call to addActionListener
111
112           // set up nextFlagJButton
113           nextFlagJButton = new JButton();
114           nextFlagJButton.setBounds( 287, 48, 88, 32 );
115           nextFlagJButton.setText( "Next Flag" );
116           nextFlagJButton.setEnabled( false );
117           contentPane.add( nextFlagJButton );
118           nextFlagJButton.addActionListener(
119
120              new ActionListener() // anonymous inner class
121              {
122                 // event handler called when nextFlagJButton is pressed
123                 public void actionPerformed( ActionEvent event )
124                 {
125                    nextFlagJButtonActionPerformed( event );
126                 }
127
128              } // end anonymous inner class
129
130           ); // end call to addActionListener
131
132           // set properties of application's window
133           setTitle( "Flag Quiz" ); // set title bar string
134           setSize( 390, 135 );     // set window size
135           setVisible( true );      // display window
136
137        } // end method createUserInterface
138
139        // return an unused random number
140        private int getUniqueRandomNumber()
141        {
142           Random generator = new Random();
143           int randomNumber;
144
145           // generate random numbers until unused flag is found
146           do
147           {
148              // generate a number between 0-7
149              randomNumber = generator.nextInt( 8 );
150           }
151           while ( flagsUsed[ randomNumber ] == true );
152
153           // indicate that flag has been used
154           flagsUsed[ randomNumber ] = true;
155
156           return randomNumber;
157
158        } // end method getUniqueRandomNumber
159
160        // choose a flag and display it in the JLabel
161        private void displayFlag()
162        {
```

Object used to create random values (annotation for line 142)

Determining if a country's flag has been displayed previously (annotation for lines 146–151)

Indicating that an unused flag will be displayed and returning the flag's index for use (annotation for lines 154–156)

Figure 16.38   Flag Quiz code. (Part 3 of 5.)

```
Getting the index of    163    currentIndex = getUniqueRandomNumber(); // get an unused flag
the unused flag         164
                        165        // create the path for that flag
Retrieving the flag's   166        String country =
corresponding country name  167            ( String ) selectCountryJComboBox.getItemAt( currentIndex );
Path name of flag images    168    String countryPath = "images/" + country + ".png";
                        169
                        170        // set the flagIconJLabel to display the flag
Displaying an unused flag   171    flagIconJLabel.setIcon( new ImageIcon( countryPath ) );
                        172
                        173    } // end method displayFlag
                        174
                        175    // check the answer and update the quiz
                        176    private void submitJButtonActionPerformed( ActionEvent event )
                        177    {
                        178        // determine whether the answer was correct
                        179        if ( selectCountryJComboBox.getSelectedIndex()
                        180            == currentIndex )
                        181        {
                        182            feedbackJTextField.setText( "Correct!" );
Retrieving the user's answer  183        }
and displaying feedback     184        else // if an incorrect answer is given
                        185        {
                        186            feedbackJTextField.setText( "Sorry, incorrect." );
                        187        }
                        188
                        189        // inform user if quiz is over
                        190        if ( count == 5 )
                        191        {
                        192            feedbackJTextField.setText(
                        193                feedbackJTextField.getText() + "   Done!" );
                        194            nextFlagJButton.setEnabled( false );
                        195            submitJButton.setEnabled( false );
Determining if the quiz is over  196        selectCountryJComboBox.setEnabled( false );
                        197        }
                        198        else // if less than 5 flags have been displayed
                        199        {
                        200            submitJButton.setEnabled( false );
                        201            nextFlagJButton.setEnabled( true );
                        202        }
                        203
                        204    } // end method submitJButtonActionPerformed
                        205
                        206    // display next flag in the quiz
                        207    private void nextFlagJButtonActionPerformed( ActionEvent event )
                        208    {
Displaying the next flag    209    displayFlag(); // display next flag
for the user to identify    210    count++;
                        211
                        212        // reset GUI components to initial states
                        213        feedbackJTextField.setText( "" );
Setting the JComboBox       214    selectCountryJComboBox.setSelectedIndex( 0 );
to display its first item   215    submitJButton.setEnabled( true );
                        216        nextFlagJButton.setEnabled( false );
                        217
                        218    } // end method nextFlagJButtonActionPerformed
                        219
```

Figure 16.38 **Flag Quiz** code. (Part 4 of 5.)

```
220     // main method
221     public static void main( String[] args )
222     {
223        FlagQuiz application = new FlagQuiz();
224        application.setDefaultCloseOperation( JFrame.EXIT_ON_CLOSE );
225
226     } // end method main
227
228  } // end class FlagQuiz
```

Figure 16.38   **Flag Quiz** code. (Part 5 of 5.)

SELF-REVIEW   1. The process of ordering the elements of an array is called _____ the array.

a) creating   b) sorting
c) declaring   d) initializing

2. Which of the following sorts array `averageRainfall`?

a) `Arrays( averageRainfall ).sort()`   b) `sort.Arrays( averageRainfall )`
c) `sort( averageRainfall )`   d) `Arrays.sort( averageRainfall )`

Answers: 1) b. 2) d.

16.6 Wrap-Up

In this tutorial, you learned about data structures called arrays, which contain elements of the same type. You then learned how to create and initialize one-dimensional arrays. You used an index to access the data of an array and learned that the first index of an array is 0. You used the expression *arrayName*.`length` to retrieve the number of elements in array *arrayName*. You created a simple application called **Sum Array**, which calculated the sum of the `int` values stored in an array. You studied pseudocode and an ACE table to help you begin creating the **Flag Quiz** application.

In building the **Flag Quiz** application, you were introduced to the `JComboBox` component. You learned how to add a `JComboBox` to your application and modify the `JComboBox`'s appearance. You then populated the `JComboBox` with data from an array.

You learned how to sort an array alphabetically by using the `Arrays.sort` method, and you learned the difference between passing data to a method by value and by reference. You learned that arrays are objects and are passed to methods by reference; array arguments in the caller can be modified from the called method.

In the next tutorial, you will learn how to create more sophisticated arrays, consisting of rows and columns of data. These are called two-dimensional arrays. You will use them to create the **Student Grades** application.

SKILLS SUMMARY   **Retrieving an Item at Index *n* of a JComboBox.**

■ Use the `getIndexAt` method.

Creating an Array

■ Declare the array using the format:

arrayType`[]` *arrayName*`;`

where *arrayName* is the reference name of the array and *arrayType* is the type of data that will be stored in the array.

■ Create the array with the expression:

arrayName `= new` *arrayType*`[` *size* `];`

where *size* indicates the number of elements in an array. When an array is created in this way, the elements in the array are initialized to the default value for the array type.

■ Declare an array and create it with the expression:

     arrayType[] *arrayName* = { *arrayInitializerList* };

where *arrayInitializerList* is a comma-separated list of the values that will initialize the elements of the array.

Referring to Element *n* of an Array

■ Use index *n*.

■ Enclose the index in square brackets after the array name.

Obtaining the Length of an Array

■ Use expression *arrayName*.length, where *arrayName* is the name of the array whose length you are trying to obtain.

Providing the User with a Number of Choices

■ Use a JComboBox component.

Setting the Maximum Number of Items a JComboBox Will Display at Once

■ Use the setMaximumRowCount method.

Obtaining a User's Selection in a JComboBox

■ Use the getSelectedIndex method.

Sorting an Array

■ Invoke the Arrays.sort method, passing the array to be sorted as the argument.

KEY TERMS

array—A data structure containing elements of the same type.

array bounds—Integers that determine what indices can be used to access an element in the array. The lower bound is 0; the upper bound is the length of the array minus one.

array initializer—A comma-separated list of expressions enclosed in braces—{ and }—which is used to initialize the elements in an array. When the initializer is empty, the elements in the array are initialized to the default value for the array type.

***arrayName*.length expression**—Contains the number of elements in an array.

Arrays.sort—Sorts the elements in its array argument into ascending or alphabetical order.

data structure—Groups and organizes related data.

element—An item in an array.

getItemAt method of JComboBox—Takes an int argument representing an index and returns the object at that index of a JComboBox.

getSelectedIndex method of JComboBox—Returns the index of the selected item.

index—An array element's position number, also called a subscript. An index must be zero, a positive integer or an integer expression that evaluates to zero or a positive integer. If an application uses an expression as an index, the expression is evaluated first to determine the index.

indexed array name—The array name followed by an index enclosed in square brackets. The indexed array name can be used on the left side of an assignment statement to place a new value into an array element. The indexed array name can be used in the right side of an assignment to retrieve the value of that array element.

JComboBox component—Presents user options in a drop-down list.

one-dimensional array—An array that uses only one index.

pass-by-reference—Arguments in the caller can be accessed and modified by the called method.

pass-by-value—A copy of the caller's argument is passed to the method. Original data cannot be accessed and modified by the called method.

position number—A value that indicates a specific position within an array. Position numbers begin at 0 (zero).

setMaximumRowCount method of JComboBox—Specifies how many items can be displayed in the drop-down list at once.

setSelectedIndex method of JComboBox—Sets the index of the JComboBox's selected item.

sorting—Arranging data into some particular order, such as ascending or descending order.

subscript—Another name for the term index.

zeroth element—The first element in an array.

GUI DESIGN GUIDELINES

JComboBoxes

- Each JComboBox should have a descriptive JLabel to describe the JComboBox's contents.
- Sorting the entries in a JComboBox with many entries helps the user find desired entries.

JAVA LIBRARY REFERENCE

JComboBox—This component allows users to select from a drop-down list of options.

- *In action*

- *Constructor*

    JComboBox—Takes an array as an argument. The items in the array are used to populate the JComboBox.

    ```
    private String[] countries = { "Russia", "China", "United States",
        "Italy", "Australia", "South Africa", "Brazil", "Spain" };
    selectCountryJComboBox = new JComboBox( countries );
    ```

- *Methods*

    setMaximumRowCount—Sets the number of items that can be displayed in the JComboBox's drop-down list.

    setBounds—Specifies the location and size of the JComboBox component on the container component relative to the top-left corner.

    getItemAt—Takes an int argument representing an index and returns the value at that index of a JComboBox.

    getSelectedIndex—Returns the index of the JComboBox's selected item.

    setSelectedIndex—Sets the index of the JComboBox's selected item.

Arrays The class that provides methods to manipulate arrays.

- *Methods*

    sort—Orders an array's elements. An array of numerical values would be organized in ascending order and an array of Strings would be organized in alphabetical order.

MULTIPLE-CHOICE QUESTIONS

16.1 Arrays can be declared to hold values of _____.

   a) type double   b) type int

   c) type String   d) any type

16.2 The elements of an array are related by the fact that they have the same name and _____.

   a) constant value   b) subscript

   c) type   d) value

16.3 The _____ expression returns the largest index in the array.

   a) *arrayName*.getUpperBound   b) *arrayName*.getUpperLimit

   c) *arrayName*.length   d) *arrayName*.length - 1

16.4 The first element in every array is the _____.

    a) subscript   b) zeroth element

    c) length of the array   d) smallest value in the array

16.5 Arrays _____.

    a) are components   b) always have one dimension

    c) keep data in sorted order at all times   d) are objects

16.6 To create an array initializer to specify the initial values of the elements in the array, use symbols _____.

    a) [and]   b) < and >

    c) (and)   d) { and }

16.7 Which method call sorts array words in alphabetical order?

    a) `Arrays.sort( words )`   b) `words.sortArray()`

    c) `Arrays.sort( words, 1 )`   d) `sort( words )`

16.8 The _____ method sets the number of items that can be displayed at once in the JComboBox's drop-down list.

    a) `getUpperBound`   b) `getItemAt`

    c) `setMaximumRowCount`   d) `setBounds`

16.9 When an argument is passed to a method and a copy of the argument's value is passed to the method, this is known as _____.

    a) pass-by-call   b) pass-by-value

    c) pass-by-reference   d) pass-by-method

16.10 The _____ method returns the index of the JComboBox's selected item.

    a) `getUpperBound`   b) `getSelectedIndex`

    c) `setMaximumRowCount`   d) `getItemAt`

EXERCISES

16.11 (*Enhanced Flag Quiz Application*) Enhance the **Flag Quiz** application by counting the number of questions that were answered correctly. After all the questions have been answered, display a message in a JTextField to describe how well the user performed (Fig. 16.39). The JTextField, called commentJTextField, has already been added in the exercise template. The following table (Fig. 16.40) shows which messages to display:

Figure 16.39 Enhanced **Flag Quiz** application's GUI.

Number of correct answers	Message
5	Excellent!
4	Very good!
3	Good.
2	Poor.
1 or 0	Fail.

Figure 16.40 Messages to display to users.

    a) *Copying the template to your working directory.* Copy the directory C:\Examples\ Tutorial16\Exercises\EnhancedFlagQuiz to your C:\SimplyJava directory.

b) *Opening the template file.* Open the `FlagQuiz.java` file in your text editor.

c) *Adding a variable to count the number of correct answers.* In line 24, add a comment indicating that the variable you are about to create will be used to store the number of correct answers from the user. In line 25, declare `int` variable `correct` and initialize it to 0.

d) *Counting the correct answers.* On line 196, increment `correct`. This statement causes `correct` to be incremented each time a correct answer is submitted.

e) *Displaying the message.* Add a `switch` statement on lines 209–227 that displays the proper message in `commentJTextField` depending on the value of `correct`.

f) *Saving the application.* Save your modified source code file.

g) *Opening the Command Prompt window and changing directories.* Open the **Command Prompt** by selecting **Start > Programs > Accessories > Command Prompt**. Change to your working directory by typing `cd C:\SimplyJava\EnhancedFlagQuiz`.

h) *Compiling the application.* Compile your application by typing `javac FlagQuiz.java`

i) *Running the completed application.* When your application compiles correctly, run it by typing `java FlagQuiz`. Run the application several times, each time entering a different number of correct answers. Each time you take the quiz, make sure the proper message is displayed in `commentJTextField` at the end of the application.

j) *Closing the application.* Close your running application by clicking its close button.

k) *Closing the Command Prompt window.* Close the **Command Prompt** window by clicking its close button.

16.12 (*Salary Survey Application*) Use a one-dimensional array to solve the following problem: A company pays its salespeople on a commission basis. The salespeople receive $200 per week, plus 9% of their gross sales for that week. For example, a salesperson who grosses $5000 in sales in a week receives $200 plus 9% of $5000, a total of $650. Write an application (using an array of counters) to determine how many of the salespeople earned salaries in each of the following ranges (assuming that each salesperson's salary is truncated to an integer amount): $200–299, $300–399, $400–499, $500–599, $600–699, $700–799, $800–899, $900–999 and over $999.

Allow the user to enter the sales for each employee in a `JTextField`. The user should click the **Calculate** `JButton` to calculate that salesperson's salary. When the user is done entering this information, clicking the **Show Totals** `JButton` should display how many of the salespeople earned salaries in each of the preceding ranges. The finished application should perform like Figure 16.41. In these screenshots, the user has entered sales of $1230 and $5406. The resulting salaries, $310.70 and $686.54, add 1 each to the ranges $300–$399 and $600–$699 as displayed when the **Show Totals** `JButton` is clicked.

a) *Copying the template to your working directory.* Copy the directory `C:\Examples\Tutorial16\Exercises\SalarySurvey` to your `C:\SimplyJava` directory.

b) *Opening the template file.* Open the `SalarySurvey.java` file in your text editor.

c) *Create an array that represents the number of salaries in each range.* In lines 32–33, create an empty `int` array called `resultArray` to store the number of employees who earn salaries in each range. Use line 32 for a comment and line 33 to create the array. The elements of `resultArray` will represent different ranges in the survey. Specify the size of `resultArray` as 11 the using keyword `new`. There are nine salary ranges in this application. For convenience, we use a slightly larger array, of size 11. You will ignore the first two elements of this array. The elements you will use are at locations 2–10, where each location represents a salary range (location 2 represents the range 200–299, location 3 represents the range 300–399, etc.). The proper location in the array can be calculated by dividing the user's salary (using integer division) by 100. For instance, when a salary of $350 is divided by 100, the result (3) can be used as an index to access the array location for the range $300–$399. The exception to this rule is that salaries over $1000, when divided by 100, will result in values greater than or equal to 10. You will need to handle this range separately in the application. Notice how ignoring the first two elements in `resultArray` allows more convenient, faster programming. If we had used locations 0–8 of `resultArray`, you would need to constantly be subtracting 2 (after you divide by 100) to calculate the proper index!

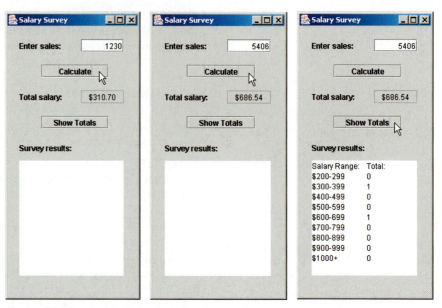

Figure 16.41 **Salary Survey** application's GUI.

d) *Storing the application's results.* Line 136, provided in the template, calculates the user's salary based on the sales input and stores this value in variable `salary`. You now need to increment the element in `resultArray` that represents the proper salary range. Recall that you need to divide the user's salary by 100 to access the proper location in `resultArray`. In line 137, declare `int` variable `index`, and store in it the result when salary is divided by 100. You may need to cast the result to an `int`. In lines 139–146, define an `if...else` statement to increment the proper element of `resultArray`. Use the value stored in `index` as the location in `resultArray` to increment. Keep in mind that for salaries in the final range, the value of `index` may be more than 10.

e) *Displaying the salary ranges.* You will now add the code to display the values in `resultArray`. In line 160, add the header for a `for` statement that will iterate for the values 2–9. This `for` statement will be used to display the results of the first eight ranges, where the value of the `for` statement's counter (`i`) will be used as the index into `resultArray`. The final range is a special case that will be handled after the `for` statement. In line 161, add the left brace to begin the body of the `for` statement. In lines 162–163, initialize variables `lowerBound` and `upperBound` (declared on lines 155–156). Set variable `lowerBound` to contain the lower bound of the current range and `upperBound` to contain the upper bound of the current range. For instance, if the current value of `i` is 4, the lower bound is 400 and the upper bound is 499. In lines 165–166, use the append method to add text to `resultJTextArea`. Use `lowerBound`, `upperBound` and `resultArray` to add a line to the `JTextArea` for that range. Add dollar signs, hyphens, tabs and newline characters to format the output as shown in Fig. 16.41. In line 167, add the right brace to close the `for` statement's body. In line 169, add the final range to `resultJTextArea`, again using the append method.

f) *Saving the application.* Save your modified source code file.

g) *Opening the Command Prompt window and changing directories.* Open the **Command Prompt** by selecting **Start > Programs > Accessories > Command Prompt**. Change to your working directory by typing `cd C:\SimplyJava\SalarySurvey`.

h) *Compiling the application.* Compile your application by typing `javac SalarySurvey.java`.

i) *Running the completed application.* When your application compiles correctly, run it by typing `java SalarySurvey`. Enter several different sales inputs and press the **Calculate** JButton after each. Check that the proper salaries are displayed in the **Total salary:** JTextField. After entering several sales amounts, press the **Show Totals** JButton. Check that the output in the **Survey results:** JTextArea accurately reflects the amount in each range for your calculated salaries.

    j) ***Closing the application.*** Close your running application by clicking its close button.

    k) ***Closing the Command Prompt window.*** Close the **Command Prompt** window by clicking its close button.

16.13 (*Cafeteria Survey Application*) Twenty students were asked to rate, on the scale from 1 to 10, the quality of the food in the student cafeteria, with 1 being "awful" and 10 being "excellent." Allow the user input to be entered using a JComboBox. Place the 20 responses in an int array and determine the frequency of each rating. Display the frequencies as a histogram in a multiline JTextField. A histogram (also known as a bar chart) is a chart where numeric values are displayed as bars. In such a chart, longer bars represent larger numeric values. One simple way to display numeric data graphically is with a histogram that shows each numeric value as a bar of asterisks (*). Figure 16.42 demonstrates the completed application.

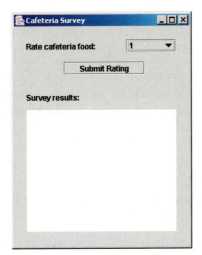 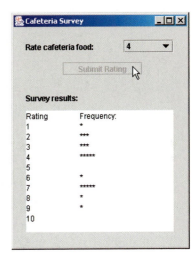

Figure 16.42   **Cafeteria Survey** GUI.

    a) ***Copying the template to your working directory.*** Copy the directory C:\Examples\ Tutorial16\Exercises\CafeteriaSurvey to your C:\SimplyJava directory.

    b) ***Opening the template file.*** Open the CafeteriaSurvey.java file in your text editor.

    c) ***Creating an array of the possible ratings.*** In lines 23–25, create String array choices consisting of 10 consecutive integers in String format (such as "1", "2", etc.) to contain the integers in the range from 1–10, inclusive. Use line 23 for a comment and lines 24–25 to create and initialize the array.

    d) ***Creating an array to store the responses.*** In lines 27–28, create an int array of length 11 named responses. This will be used to store the number of responses in each of the 10 categories (element 0 will not be used). Use line 27 for a comment and line 28 to create the array.

    e) ***Customizing the ratingJComboBox.*** Customize the ratingJComboBox in line 54 so it will display the possible ratings.

    f) ***Storing the responses.*** Let's now look at the submitRatingJButtonActionPerformed method, which executes when the **Submit Rating** JButton is clicked. Line 101 (provided in the template) increments variable responseCounter, which stores the number of responses entered. Line 102 then stores the rating entered by the user into variable input. We have added 1 to the result of ratingJComboBox.getSelectedIndex because the indices of a JComboBox start at 0. The value in variable input now contains the index for that specific rating in array responses. In line 103, use input to increment the proper element of array responses.

    g) ***Displaying the histogram.*** You will now display the results in the form of a histogram. Line 106 begins an if statement that executes when 20 responses have been entered. Within this if statement, a for statement is defined on lines 110–116. This statement loops once for each rating, displaying the rating in line 112 (followed by a tab character) and a newline character in line 114. You will add the number of stars that will be displayed to the right of each rating. Place your cursor at the end of line

112. In line 114, add the header of a for statement that loops from 1 until the number of votes for the current rating (stored in responses). In line 115, add the left brace to begin the for statement's body. In line 116, add an asterisk to the output. Because this for statement will loop the same number of times as there are votes for the current rating, the proper number of asterisks will be displayed. In line 118, add the right brace to end the for statement's body. Follow the brace with a comment indicating the end of the for statement.

h) *Saving the application.* Save your modified source code file.

i) *Opening the Command Prompt window and changing directories.* Open the **Command Prompt** by selecting **Start > Programs > Accessories > Command Prompt**. Change to your working directory by typing cd C:\SimplyJava\CafeteriaSurvey.

j) *Compiling the application.* Compile your application by typing javac Cafeteria-Survey.java.

k) *Running the completed application.* When your application compiles correctly, run it by typing java CafeteriaSurvey. Enter 20 different ratings by selecting values from ratingJComboBox then pressing the **Submit Rating** JButton. After 20 ratings have been entered, check that resultJTextArea contains the proper number of asterisks for each rating.

l) *Closing the application.* Close your running application by clicking its close button.

m) *Closing the Command Prompt window.* Close the **Command Prompt** window by clicking its close button.

What does this code do? ▶

16.14 The mystery method uses the numbers array to modify the elements in the mystery-Array array. What does mysteryArray contain at the end of the method?

```
1   private int mystery()
2   {
3      int[] numbers = { 0, 1, 2, 3, 4 };
4      int[] mysteryArray = new int[ numbers.length ];
5
6      for ( int i = numbers.length; i > 0; i-- )
7      {
8         mysteryArray[ numbers.length - i ] = numbers[ i - 1 ];
9      }
10
11  } // end method mystery
```

What's wrong with this code? ▶

16.15 The following code uses a for loop to sum the elements of an array. Find the error(s) in the following code:

```
1   public void sumArray()
2   {
3      int[] numbers = new int[] { 1, 2, 3, 4, 5, 6, 7, 8 };
4
5      for ( int counter = 0; counter <= numbers.size; counter++ )
6      {
7         int sum += numbers[ counter ];
8      }
9   } // end method sumArray
```

Programming Challenge ▶

16.16 (*Road Sign Test Application*) Write an application that will test the user's knowledge of road signs. Your application should display a random sign image and ask the user to select the sign name from a JComboBox. This application should look like Fig. 16.43. [*Hint*: The application is similar to the **Flag Quiz** application.] You can find the road sign images in C:\Examples\Tutorial16\Exercises\RoadSignTest\images.

Figure 16.43   Road Sign Test GUI.

a) *Copying the template to your working directory.* Copy the directory C:\Examples\ Tutorial16\Exercises\RoadSignTest to your C:\SimplyJava directory.

b) *Opening the template file.* Open the RoadSignTest.java file in your text editor.

c) *Declaring an array to contain the user's options.* In lines 29–33, create String array signs (use line 29 for a comment and lines 30–33 to declare and initialize the array). Have the array contain the values "Do Not Enter", "Narrow Bridge", "No Bicycles", "No Left Turn", "No Pedestrians", "No U-turn", "Road Narrows", "Stop", "Stop Sign Ahead", "Traffic Signals Ahead", "Winding Road Ahead" and "Yield".

d) *Declaring an array to store which signs are used.* On lines 35–36, create a boolean array named signsUsed (use line 35 for a comment and line 36 to create the array). Specify the array to be of size 12.

e) *Sorting array signs.* In line 73, sort array signs alphabetically.

f) *Customizing signJComboBox.* Modify line 76 so that signJComboBox will display the options provided in array signs. On line 78, customize signJComboBox to display at most four items at once.

g) *Modifying the getUniqueRandomNumber method.* The getUniqueRandomNumber method uses the signsUsed array to generate a random sign that has not yet been displayed. Random object generator is created to generate random numbers. You will now add code to generate a random value not used yet in the road sign test. In lines 142–147, define a do...while statement that generates random numbers until one that has not yet been used is found. The body of the do...while statement will generate a random value between 0 and 11. The do...while statement will loop until the random number is not one that has been used before. In line 149, modify the signsUsed array to indicate that the sign specified by the new random number will be used.

h) *Saving the application.* Save your modified source code file.

i) *Opening the Command Prompt window and changing directories.* Open the **Command Prompt** by selecting **Start > Programs > Accessories > Command Prompt**. Change to your working directory by typing cd C:\SimplyJava\RoadSignTest.

j) *Compiling the application.* Compile your application by typing javac RoadSignTest.java.

k) *Running the completed application.* When your application compiles correctly, run it by typing java RoadSignTest. Enter both correct and incorrect answers to make sure that the correct feedback is being given. View the JComboBox to ensure that only four options are available at once.

l) *Closing the application.* Close your running application by clicking its close button.

m) *Closing the* **Command Prompt** *window.* Close the **Command Prompt** window by clicking its close button.

17

Objectives

In this tutorial, you will learn to:
- Differentiate between one-dimensional and two-dimensional arrays.
- Declare and manipulate two-dimensional arrays.
- Understand applications of two-dimensional arrays.
- Use `JRadioButtons` to enable users to select only one option out of many.

Outline

Student Grades Application

Introducing Two-Dimensional Arrays and *JRadioButtons*

In this tutorial, you will learn about two-dimensional arrays, which, like one-dimensional arrays, store multiple values. However, two-dimensional arrays allow you to store multiple rows of values. Also, you will learn about the `JRadioButton` component, which you will employ to enable users to chose only one option out of many.

17.1 Test-Driving the Student Grades Application

In this tutorial, you will implement the **Student Grades** application by using a two-dimensional array. The application must meet the following requirements:

Application Requirements

A teacher issues three tests to a class of ten students. The grades on these tests are integers in the range from 0 to 100. The teacher has asked you to develop an application to keep track of each student's average and the average of the class as a whole. The teacher has also asked that there be a choice to view the grades as either numbers or letters. Letter grades should be calculated according to the grading system:

90-100	*A*
80-89	*B*
70-79	*C*
60-69	*D*
Below 60	*F*

The application should allow a user to input the student's name and three test grades, then compute each student's average and the class average. The application should display number grades by default.

The student's average is equal to the sum of the student's three grades divided by three. The class average is equal to the sum of all of the students' averages divided by the number of students in the class (ten in this case). You begin by test-driving the completed application. Then, you will learn the additional Java technologies you will need to create your own version of this application.

Test-Driving the Student Grades Application

1. *Locating the completed application.* Open the **Command Prompt** window by selecting **Start > Programs > Accessories > Command Prompt**. Change to your completed **Student Grades** application directory by typing cd C:\Examples\Tutorial17\CompletedApplication\StudentGrades.

2. *Running the Student Grades application.* Type java StudentGrades in the **Command Prompt** window to run the application (Fig. 17.1).

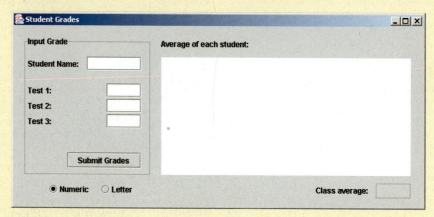

Figure 17.1   Running the completed **Student Grades** application.

3. *Entering data.* Type Gretta Green in the **Student Name:** JTextField. Type 87, 94 and 93 in the **Test 1:**, **Test 2:** and **Test 3:** JTextFields, respectively (Fig. 17.2). Click the **Submit Grades** JButton to display the data in the JTextArea (Fig. 17.3).

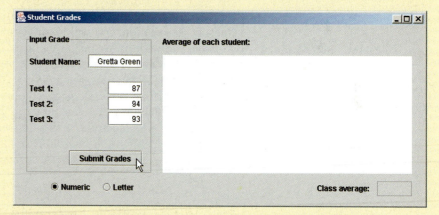

Figure 17.2   Inputting data to the **Student Grades** application.

Numeric JRadioButton selected as the default

Figure 17.3   Displaying the student's numerical grade.

(cont.)

4. ***Changing the JTextArea's appearance.*** Change the JTextArea's appearance by clicking the **Letter** JRadioButton (Fig. 17.4). The JTextArea will display the data using the letter grading system. Click the **Numeric** JRadio-Button to once again display the data in numeric form. (Fig. 17.3).

Select the **Letter** JRadioButton ⎯⎯⎯⎯⎯⎯

Figure 17.4 Displaying the student's resulting letter grade.

5. ***Closing the running application.*** Close your running application by clicking its close button.

6. ***Closing the Command Prompt window.*** Close the **Command Prompt** window by clicking its close button.

17.2 Two-Dimensional Arrays

So far, you have studied one-dimensional arrays, which contain one sequence of values. In this section, you will learn about **two-dimensional arrays**, which require two indices to identify particular elements. Two-dimensional arrays are often used to represent **tables** of values, consisting of information arranged in **rows** and **columns**. Each row is the same size and therefore has the same number of columns. To identify a particular table element, you must specify the two indices—by convention, the first identifies the element's row and the second identifies the element's column. Figure 17.5 illustrates a two-dimensional array, myArray, containing three rows and four columns. A two-dimensional array with *m* rows and *n* columns is called an ***m-by-n* array**; therefore, the array in Fig. 17.5 is a 3-by-4 array.

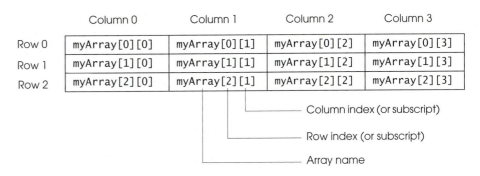

Figure 17.5 Two-dimensional array with three rows and four columns.

Every element in the myArray array is identified in Fig. 17.5 by an element name of the form myArray[i][j], where myArray is the name of the array and i and j are the indices that uniquely identify the row and column of each element in the myArray array. Notice that, because row numbers and column numbers in two-dimensional arrays each begin with zero, the elements in the first row each have a first index of 0, and the elements in the last column each have a second index of 3.

Two-dimensional arrays are initialized in declarations through the same process and notations employed for one-dimensional arrays. For example, a two-dimensional array, `numbers`, with three rows and two columns, can be declared and initialized with

```
int numbers[][] = new int[ 3 ][ 2 ];
numbers[ 0 ][ 0 ] = 1;
numbers[ 0 ][ 1 ] = 2;
numbers[ 1 ][ 0 ] = 3;
numbers[ 1 ][ 1 ] = 4;
numbers[ 2 ][ 0 ] = 5;
numbers[ 2 ][ 1 ] = 6;
```

Notice that the integers used to specify the number of rows and columns when the array is created (in this case, 3 and 2) always indicate *exactly* the number of elements in the row or column. The indices in a row or column vary from zero to one less than the number of elements in that row or column. The preceding declaration and initialization statements can be written in a single statement, using an array initializer, as follows:

```
int numbers[][] = { { 1, 2 }, { 3, 4 }, { 5, 6 } };
```

The values are grouped by row in braces, with 1 and 2 initializing `numbers[ 0 ][ 0 ]` and `numbers[ 0 ][ 1 ]`, respectively, 3 and 4 initializing `numbers[ 1 ][ 0 ]` and `numbers[ 1 ][ 1 ]`, respectively, and 5 and 6 initializing `numbers[ 2 ][ 0 ]` and `numbers[ 2 ][ 1 ]`, respectively.

SELF-REVIEW

1. Arrays that use two indices are referred to as _____ arrays.

   a) single-subscripted   b) two-dimensional

   c) square   d) one-dimensional

2. _____ creates an `int` array of two rows and five columns.

   a) `new integer[ 2 ][ 5 ];`   b) `new integer[ 5 ][ 2 ];`

   c) `new int[ 2 ][ 5 ];`   d) `new int[ 1 ][ 4 ];`

Answers: 1) b. 2) c.

17.3 Using JRadioButtons

A **JRadioButton** is a small circle that is either blank (when it is unselected) or filled with a smaller black dot (when it is selected). A JRadioButton is known as a **state button** because it can be only in the "on" state or in the "off" state. You have also learned about the JCheckBox state button, which was introduced in Tutorial 7.

JRadioButtons are normally grouped in a **ButtonGroup**, which can contail any number of JRadioButtons. A ButtonGroup can contain any number of JRadioButtons. Initially, zero or one JRadioButtons in each ButtonGroup will be selected. Once a JRadioButton has been selected, the ButtonGroup guarantees that only one JRadioButton will be selected at a time. When another JRadioButton in the ButtonGroup is selected, the previously selected JRadioButton is deselected. There is no default group for JRadioButtons; you must explicitly add each JRadioButton to a ButtonGroup. You will want at least one ButtonGroup in your application to accompany your JRadioButtons.

If the JRadioButton is selected (contains a small black dot), the **isSelected** method returns the `boolean` value `true`. If the JRadioButton is not selected (blank), it returns `false`.

A JRadioButton also generates an `ActionEvent` when it is selected. The `actionPerformed` event handler is called when a JRadioButton is selected.

GUI Design Tip

Use JRadioButtons when the user should choose only one option from a group.

GUI Design Tip

Always place each group of JRadioButtons in a separate Button-Group.

The following pseudocode describes the basic operation of the **Student Grades** application:

> When the user clicks the Submit Grades JButton:
>   Retrieve the student's name and grades from the JTextFields
>   Add the student's information to the arrays
>   Display each student's name, test grades and average in the JTextArea
>   Display the class's average in the Class average: JTextField
>   Clear the student's name and grades from the JTextFields
>
>   If 10 students have been entered
>   Disable the Submit Grades JButton
>
> When the user selects the Numeric JRadioButton:
>   Display each student's name, numeric test grades and numeric average in the
>   JTextArea
>   Display the class's numeric average in the Class average: JTextField
>
> When the user selects the Letter JRadioButton:
>   Display each students' name, letter test grades and letter average in the
>   JTextArea
>   Display the class's letter average in the Class average: JTextField

Your **Student Grades** application uses the JRadioButton component's actionPerformed event handler to update the JTextArea when the user selects to display either letter grades or numeric grades. Now that you have test-driven the **Student Grades** application and studied its pseudocode representation, you will use an ACE table to help you convert the pseudocode to Java. Figure 17.6 lists the actions, components and events that will help you complete your own version of this application.

<table>
<tr><td rowspan="8">*Action/Component/ Event (ACE) Table for the Student Grades Application*
</td><td>**Action**</td><td>**Component**</td><td>**Event**</td></tr>
<tr><td>Label the application's components</td><td>studentNameJLabel, test1JLabel, test2JLabel, test3JLabel, displayJLabel, classAverageJLabel, inputGradeJPanel</td><td>Application is run</td></tr>
<tr><td></td><td>submitGradesJButton</td><td rowspan="6">User clicks **Submit Grades** JButton</td></tr>
<tr><td>Retrieve student's name and grades from the JTextFields</td><td>studentNameJTextField, test1JTextField, test2JTextField, test3JTextField</td></tr>
<tr><td>Add the student's information to the arrays</td><td>studentNames, studentGrades</td></tr>
<tr><td>Display each student's name, test grades and average in the JTextArea</td><td>displayJTextArea</td></tr>
<tr><td>Display the class's average in the Class average: JTextField</td><td>classAverageJTextField</td></tr>
<tr><td>Clear the student's name and grades from the JTextFields</td><td>studentNameJTextField, test1JTextField, test2JTextField, test3JTextField</td></tr>
<tr><td>If 10 students have been entered Disable the Submit Grades JButton</td><td>submitGradesJButton</td><td></td></tr>
</table>

Figure 17.6   ACE table for the **Student Grades** application. (Part 1 of 2.)

Action	Component	Event
	`numericJRadioButton`	User selects **Numeric** JRadioButton
Display each student's name, numeric test grades and numeric average in the JTextArea	`displayJTextArea`	
Display the class's numeric average in the Class average: JTextField	`classAverageJTextField`	
	`letterJRadioButton`	User selects **Letter** JRadioButton
Display each students' name, letter test grades and letter average in the JTextArea	`displayJTextArea`	
Display the class's letter average in the Class average: JTextField	`classAverageJTextField`	

Figure 17.6 ACE table for the **Student Grades** application. (Part 2 of 2.)

Now you will build your **Student Grades** application, using JRadioButtons for the first time in this book. The JRadioButtons will allow the user to view the students' grades as letters or numbers.

Using *JRadioButtons* in Your Application

1. *Copying the template to your working directory.* Copy the C:\Examples\ Tutorial17\TemplateApplication\StudentGrades directory to your C:\SimplyJava directory.

2. *Opening the Student Grades application template file.* Open the template file StudentGrades.java in your text editor.

3. *Customizing* ***numericJRadioButton.*** Add lines 166–168 of Fig. 17.7 to your code. Line 166 uses the setBounds method of JRadioButton to set numericJRadioButton's bounds to 55, 244, 75, 23. Line 167 uses numericJRadioButton's setText method to display "Numeric" to the right of numericJRadioButton. Line 168 uses numericJRadioButton's **setSelected** method to indicate that numericJRadioButton should be selected (true). JRadioButtons are unselected by default when they are created.

Error-Prevention Tip

To avoid subtle logic errors, one JRadioButton in a group should be selected as the default by setting its *selected* property to true.

Setting the properties of `numericJRadioButton`

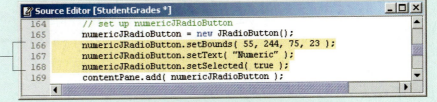

```
164        // set up numericJRadioButton
165        numericJRadioButton = new JRadioButton();
166        numericJRadioButton.setBounds( 55, 244, 75, 23 );
167        numericJRadioButton.setText( "Numeric" );
168        numericJRadioButton.setSelected( true );
169        contentPane.add( numericJRadioButton );
```

Figure 17.7 Customizing `numericJRadioButton`.

4. *Customizing* ***letterJRadioButton.*** Add lines 187–188 of Fig. 17.8 to your code. Line 187 sets the bounds of letterJRadioButton to 140, 244, 75, 23. Line 188 sets the text of letterJRadioButton to "Letter".

Setting the properties of `letterJRadioButton`

```
185        // set up letterJRadioButton
186        letterJRadioButton = new JRadioButton();
187        letterJRadioButton.setBounds( 140, 244, 75, 23 );
188        letterJRadioButton.setText( "Letter" );
189        contentPane.add( letterJRadioButton );
```

Figure 17.8 Customizing `letterJRadioButton`.

(cont.)

GUI Design Tip

Align groups of JRadioButtons either horizontally or vertically.

5. ***Adding numericJRadioButton to the ButtonGroup.*** Add line 169 of Fig. 17.9 to your code. This line adds numericJRadioButton to display-ButtonGroup using the **add** method of ButtonGroup. When another JRadioButton in displayButtonGroup is selected, numericJRadioButton will be deselected.

Calling ButtonGroup method add to add a JRadioButton

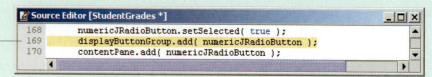

```
168        numericJRadioButton.setSelected( true );
169        displayButtonGroup.add( numericJRadioButton );
170        contentPane.add( numericJRadioButton );
```

Figure 17.9   Adding numericJRadioButton to the ButtonGroup.

6. ***Adding letterJRadioButton to the ButtonGroup.*** Add line 190 of Fig. 17.10 to your code. This line adds letterJRadioButton to display-ButtonGroup.

Calling ButtonGroup method add to add a JRadioButton

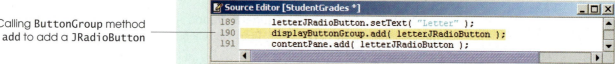

```
189        letterJRadioButton.setText( "Letter" );
190        displayButtonGroup.add( letterJRadioButton );
191        contentPane.add( letterJRadioButton );
```

Figure 17.10   Adding letterJRadioButton to the ButtonGroup.

7. ***Saving the application.*** Save your modified source code file.

8. ***Opening the Command Prompt window and changing directories.*** Open the **Command Prompt** window by selecting **Start > Programs > Accessories > Command Prompt**. Change to your working directory by typing cd C:\SimplyJava\StudentGrades.

9. ***Compiling the application.*** Compile your application by typing javac StudentGrades.java.

10. ***Running the application.*** When your application compiles correctly, run it by typing java StudentGrades. Figure 17.11 shows the updated application running. You are able to enter a student name, enter grades and click the JRadioButtons, but when you click the **Submit** JButton, the average is not computed.

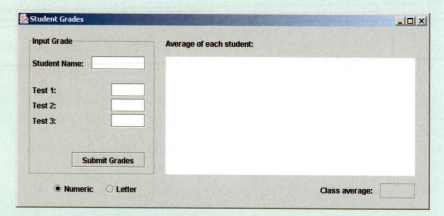

Figure 17.11   Running the application after adding the JRadioButtons.

11. ***Closing the application.*** Close your running application by clicking its close button.

12. ***Closing the Command Prompt window.*** Close the **Command Prompt** window by clicking its close button.

SELF-REVIEW

1. Which method determines the state of a `JRadioButton`?
   a) `isSelected` b) `getSelected`
   c) `isChecked` d) `getChecked`

2. The _________ event handler is called when a `JRadioButton` is selected.
   a) `checkedChanged` b) `actionPerformed`
   c) `selectedChanged` d) None of the above.

Answers: 1) a. 2) b.

17.4 Inserting Code into the Student Grades Application

Now that you have placed the components on the application you are ready to write code to interact with the data given by the user. First you will finish the `submitGradesJButtonActionPerformed` method.

Finishing the `submitGradesJButton` `ActionPerformed` method

1. ***Adding the student to the array.*** Add lines 276–282 of Fig. 17.12 to your code. Line 277 adds the student's name to the one-dimensional array `studentNames`. Lines 278–280 add the student's three test grades to the two-dimensional `StudentGrades` array. Note that the arrays are created in lines 60 and 63. Line 282 increments the number of students in the class.

Store the student name and test grades in the arrays

Increment `studentCount`

Source Editor [StudentGrades *]

```
274       int test3 = Integer.parseInt( test3JTextField.getText() );
275
276       // add user input to arrays
277       studentNames[ studentCount ] = nameOfStudent;
278       studentGrades[ studentCount ][ FIRST_TEST ] = test1;
279       studentGrades[ studentCount ][ SECOND_TEST ] = test2;
280       studentGrades[ studentCount ][ THIRD_TEST ] = test3;
281
282       studentCount++; // increment studentCount
283
```

Figure 17.12 Storing the input.

2. ***Displaying the output.*** Insert lines 284–291 of Fig. 17.13 into your code. Line 284 uses the `isSelected` method of `JRadioButton` to determine how the user would like the student's grades displayed. Line 286 calls the `displayNumericGrades` method and line 290 calls the `displayLetterGrades` method. These methods will be declared later in this tutorial.

Calling method `displayNumericGrades`

Calling method `displayLetterGrades`

Source Editor [StudentGrades *]

```
282       studentCount++; // increment studentCount
283
284       if ( numericJRadioButton.isSelected() )
285       {
286          displayNumericGrades();
287       }
288       else
289       {
290          displayLetterGrades();
291       }
292
```

Figure 17.13 Displaying the output.

3. ***Disabling the* Submit Grades *`JButton`.*** Insert lines 299–304 of Fig. 17.14 into your code. If 10 students have already been entered into the array, line 303 will disable the **Submit Grades** `JButton` so that no more grades can be entered.

(cont.)

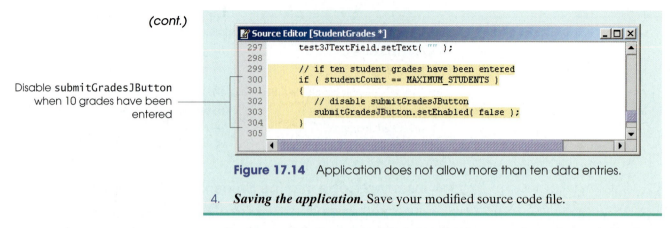

Figure 17.14 Application does not allow more than ten data entries.

Disable submitGradesJButton when 10 grades have been entered

4. **Saving the application.** Save your modified source code file.

In the previous box, you called the displayNumericGrades and display-LetterGrades methods, which are not yet declared to display the appropriate data. Next, you will declare the displayNumericGrades method.

Declaring a Method to Display Numeric Grades

1. **Declaring the displayNumericGrades method.** Add lines 308–318 of Fig. 17.15 after the submitGradesJButtonActionPerformed method. These lines declare the displayNumericGrades method, which will be used to display the grades as numbers. Lines 312–313 add a header to displayJ-TextArea. Lines 315–316 declare and initialize variables to store the student's and class's total grades.

```
306    } // end method submitGradesJButtonActionPerformed
307
308    // display student grades and averages as numbers
309    private void displayNumericGrades()
310    {
311       // add a header to displayJTextArea
312       displayJTextArea.setText(
313          "Name\tTest 1\tTest 2\tTest 3\tAverage\n" );
314
315       int studentTotal = 0; // store the student's total grades
316       int classTotal = 0;   // store the class's total grades
317
318    } // end method displayNumericGrades
319
```

Displaying a header

Figure 17.15 Adding a header to displayJTextArea.

2. **Outputting the student's name.** Add lines 318–325 of Fig. 17.16 to your code. This for statement iterates over each student that has been added to the class. Line 321 appends the name of the student to the displayJTextArea. Line 323 initializes the variable to store the student's total grades. This variable will be initialized to 0 for each student in the class.

```
316       int classTotal = 0;    // store the class's total grades
317
318       for ( int student = 0; student < studentCount; student++ )
319       {
320          // display student names
321          displayJTextArea.append( studentNames[ student ] + "\t" );
322
323          studentTotal = 0; // initialize the student's total grades
324
325       } // end outer for
326
```

Outputting the student's name

Figure 17.16 Appending the student's name to displayJTextArea.

(cont.)   3. ***Outputting the student's grades.*** Add lines 325–334 of Fig. 17.17 inside the
for statement from the previous step. This for statement is called a **nested
loop** because it is enclosed (nested) inside another control statement (the for
statement from the previous step). Nested loops are often useful for processing two-dimensional arrays. This for statement steps through each test in the
studentGrades array. Lines 328–329 append each test grade to display-
JTextArea. Line 332 adds the test grade to the studentTotal variable.

Output each test grade

Add the test grade to
the student's total

```
🗐 Source Editor [StudentGrades *]                                    _ □ ×
323          studentTotal = 0; // initialize the student's total grades  ▲
324
325          for ( int test = 0; test < NUMBER_OF_TESTS; test++ )
326          {
327              // append each test grade to displayJTextArea
328              displayJTextArea.append(
329                  studentGrades[ student ][ test ] + "\t" );
330
331              // add the test grade to the student's total
332              studentTotal += studentGrades[ student ][ test ];
333
334          } // end inner for
335                                                                        ▼
```

Figure 17.17   Outputting each test grade and calculating the student's
total grade.

4. ***Outputting the student's average.*** Add lines 336–343 of Fig. 17.18 to your
code. Line 337 adds the student's total grade to the class's total. Lines 340–
341 calculate the student's average grade, and lines 342–343 append the student's average to displayJTextArea. The instance variable twoDigits,
declared in line 67, is used to format the value.

Add the student's total
to the class's total

Calculate and display
the student's average

```
🗐 Source Editor [StudentGrades *]                                    _ □ ×
334          } // end inner for                                           ▲
335
336          // add the student's total grade to the class's total
337          classTotal += studentTotal;
338
339          // calculate the student average and display it
340          double studentAverage =
341              ( double ) studentTotal / NUMBER_OF_TESTS;
342          displayJTextArea.append(
343              twoDigits.format( studentAverage ) + "\n" );
344                                                                        ▼
```

Figure 17.18   Calculating and displaying the student's average grade.

5. ***Outputting the class's average.*** Add lines 347–351 of Fig. 17.19 to your code.
Lines 348–349 calculate the class's average test grade. Lines 350–351 output
the class's average in classAverageJTextField.

Calculate and display
the class's average

```
🗐 Source Editor [StudentGrades *]                                    _ □ ×
345          } // end outer for                                           ▲
346
347          // calculate the class average and display it
348          double classAverage =
349              ( double ) classTotal / studentCount / NUMBER_OF_TESTS;
350          classAverageJTextField.setText(
351              twoDigits.format( classAverage ) );
352                                                                        ▼
```

Figure 17.19   Calculating and displaying the class's average grade.

6. ***Saving the application.*** Save your modified source code file.

You have now declared the displayNumericGrades method to output the students' grades, the students' averages and the class's averages in displayJTextArea as numbers. Now you will declare the displayLetterGrades method to output the same information as letter grades.

Declaring a Method to Display Letter Grades

1. **Declaring the displayLetterGrades method.** Add lines 355–365 of Fig. 17.20 to your code. These lines declare the displayLetterGrades method, which will be used to display grades as letters. Lines 359–360 add a header to the displayJTextArea. Lines 362–363 declare and initialize variables to store the student's total grade and the class's total grade.

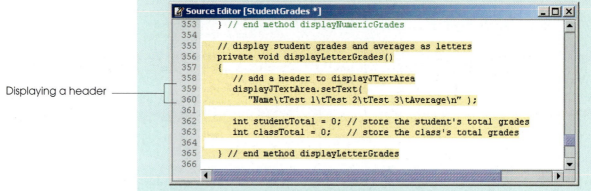

Displaying a header

```
353        } // end method displayNumericGrades
354
355        // display student grades and averages as letters
356        private void displayLetterGrades()
357        {
358           // add a header to displayJTextArea
359           displayJTextArea.setText(
360              "Name\tTest 1\tTest 2\tTest 3\tAverage\n" );
361
362           int studentTotal = 0; // store the student's total grades
363           int classTotal = 0;   // store the class's total grades
364
365        } // end method displayLetterGrades
366
```

Figure 17.20 Outputting a header.

2. **Outputting the student's name and initializing studentTotal.** Add lines 365–372 of Fig. 17.21 to your code. Line 365 starts a for statement that iterates over each student that has been added to the class. Line 368 appends each student's name to displayJTextArea. Line 370 initializes the variable to store the student's total grade.

Outputting the student's name

```
363           int classTotal = 0;   // store the class's total grades
364
365           for ( int student = 0; student < studentCount; student++ )
366           {
367              // display student names
368              displayJTextArea.append( studentNames[ student ] + "\t" );
369
370              studentTotal = 0; // initialize the student's total grades
371
372           } // end outer for
373
```

Figure 17.21 Outputting each student's name.

3. **Outputting the student's grades.** Add lines 372–381 of Fig. 17.22 inside the for statement from the previous step to declare a nested loop. These lines iterate over each student's test grades. Lines 375–376 append the current test grade to displayJTextArea. Line 379 adds each grade to the student's total. Notice that line 375 calls the convertToLetterGrade method. This method (which has been provided for you) converts a student's number grade (in the range 0–100) to a letter grade (in the range A–F).

(cont.)

Convert the test grade to a letter

Add the test grade to
the student's total

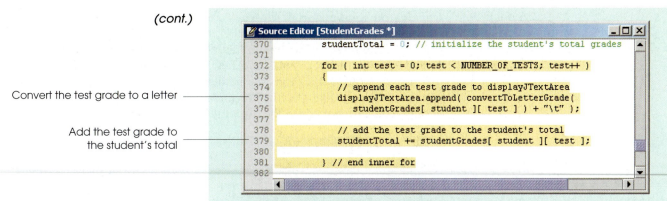

```
370        studentTotal = 0; // initialize the student's total grades
371
372        for ( int test = 0; test < NUMBER_OF_TESTS; test++ )
373        {
374           // append each test grade to displayJTextArea
375           displayJTextArea.append( convertToLetterGrade(
376              studentGrades[ student ][ test ] ) + "\t" );
377
378           // add the test grade to the student's total
379           studentTotal += studentGrades[ student ][ test ];
380
381        } // end inner for
382
```

Figure 17.22   Outputting the student's letter grades and calculating the student's total grade.

4. ***Outputting the student's average.*** Add lines 383–390 of Fig. 17.23 to your code. Lines 387–388 calculate the student's average. Lines 389–390 append the student's average to displayJTextArea. Notice that line 390 calls the convertToLetterGrade method again.

Add the student's total
to the class's total

Convert student's average
to a letter grade

```
381        } // end inner for
382
383        // add the student's total grade to the class's total
384        classTotal += studentTotal;
385
386        // calculate the student average and display it
387        double studentAverage =
388           ( double ) studentTotal / NUMBER_OF_TESTS;
389        displayJTextArea.append(
390           convertToLetterGrade( studentAverage ) + "\n" );
391
```

Figure 17.23   Calculating and displaying the student's average letter grade.

5. ***Outputting the class's average.*** Add lines 394–398 of Fig. 17.24 to your code. Lines 395–396 calculate the class's average. Lines 397–398 output the class's average to classAverageJTextField. Line 398 calls the convertToLetterGrade method again.

Convert class's average
to a letter grade

```
392        } // end outer for
393
394        // calculate the class average and display it
395        double classAverage =
396           ( double ) classTotal / studentCount / NUMBER_OF_TESTS;
397        classAverageJTextField.setText(
398           convertToLetterGrade( classAverage ) );
399
```

Figure 17.24   Calculating and displaying the class's average letter grade.

6. ***Saving the application.*** Save your modified source code file.

7. ***Opening the Command Prompt window and changing directories.*** Open the **Command Prompt** window by selecting **Start > Programs > Accessories > Command Prompt**. Change to your working directory by typing cd C:\SimplyJava\StudentGrades.

8. ***Compiling the application.*** Compile your application by typing javac StudentGrades.java.

(cont.)

9. ***Running the application.*** When your application compiles correctly, run it by typing java StudentGrades. Figure 17.25 shows the updated application running. Enter Gretta Green in the **Student Name:** JTextField. Enter 87, 94 and 93 in the **Test 1:**, **Test 2:** and **Test 3:** JTextFields respectively. Click the **Submit Grades** JButton. The numeric grades will be displayed in the JTextArea. Notice that selecting the **Letter** JRadioButton does nothing yet because you have not added the functionality.

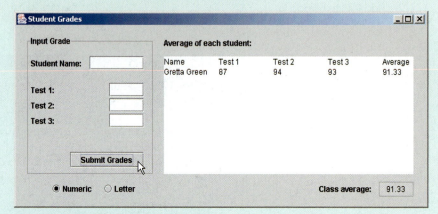

Figure 17.25 Running the application after declaring new methods.

10. ***Closing the application.*** Close your running application by clicking its close button.

11. ***Closing the Command Prompt window.*** Close the **Command Prompt** window by clicking its close button.

You will now code an event handler to enhance the application's functionality by allowing the user to select whether the results will be presented as letter grades or numeric grades.

Coding Event Handlers for the *JRadioButtons*

1. ***Finishing the*** `actionPerformed` ***event handler for*** `numericJRadioButton`***.*** Add line 179 of Fig. 17.26 to your code. The numericJRadioButton-ActionPerformed method will now be called when the **Numeric** JRadioButton is selected.

Coding an event handler for the numericJRadioButton

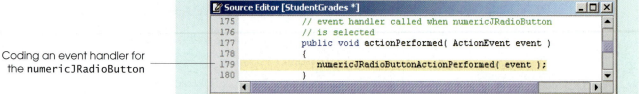

Figure 17.26 numericJRadioButton's actionPerformed event handler.

2. ***Finishing the*** `actionPerformed` ***event handler for*** `letterJRadioButton`***.*** Add line 200 of Fig. 17.27 to your code. The letterJRadioButtonAction-Performed method will now be called when the **Letter** JRadioButton is selected.

(cont.)

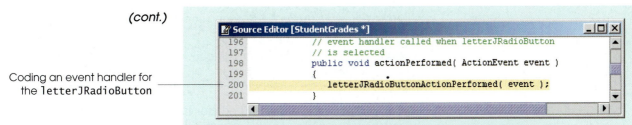

```
Source Editor [StudentGrades *]                          _ □ ×
196          // event handler called when letterJRadioButton
197          // is selected
198          public void actionPerformed( ActionEvent event )
199          {
200              letterJRadioButtonActionPerformed( event );
201          }
```

Figure 17.27 letterJRadioButton's actionPerformed event handler.

3. ***Declaring method numericJRadioButtonActionPerformed.*** Add lines 402–408 of Fig. 17.28 to your code to declare method numericJRadioButtonActionPerformed. Line 406 calls method displayNumericGrades. This method displays data in the displayJTextArea as numeric grades.

```
Source Editor [StudentGrades *]                          _ □ ×
400      } // end method displayLetterGrades
401
402      // user selected numeric display
403      private void numericJRadioButtonActionPerformed(
404          ActionEvent event )
405      {
406          displayNumericGrades();
407
408      } // end method numericJRadioButtonActionPerformed
409
```

Calling method
displayNumericGrades

Figure 17.28 Method numericJRadioButtonActionPerformed.

4. ***Declaring the letterJRadioButtonActionPerformed method.*** Add lines 410–416 of Fig. 17.29 to your code to call the displayLetterGrades method. This method displays the data in displayJTextArea as letter grades.

```
Source Editor [StudentGrades *]                          _ □ ×
408      } // end method numericJRadioButtonActionPerformed
409
410      // user selected letter display
411      private void letterJRadioButtonActionPerformed(
412          ActionEvent event )
413      {
414          displayLetterGrades();
415
416      } // end method letterJRadioButtonActionPerformed
417
```

Calling method
displayLetterGrades

Figure 17.29 Method letterJRadioButtonActionPerformed.

5. ***Saving the application.*** Save your modified source code file.

6. ***Opening the Command Prompt window and changing directories.*** Open the **Command Prompt** window by selecting **Start > Programs > Accessories > Command Prompt**. Change to your working directory by typing cd C:\SimplyJava\StudentGrades.

7. ***Compiling the application.*** Compile your application by typing javac StudentGrades.java.

8. ***Running the application.*** When your application compiles correctly, run it by typing java StudentGrades. You can now select to view the grades as letters or numbers.

(cont.)

9. ***Closing the application.*** Close your running application by clicking its close button.

10. ***Closing the Command Prompt window.*** Close the **Command Prompt** window by clicking its close button.

Figure 17.30 presents the source code for the **Student Grades** application. The lines of code that you added, viewed or modified in this tutorial are highlighted.

```java
1   // Tutorial 17: StudentGrades.java
2   // This application computes each student's grade average and
3   // the class average for ten students.
4   import java.awt.*;
5   import java.awt.event.*;
6   import java.text.*;
7   import javax.swing.*;
8   import javax.swing.border.*;
9
10  public class StudentGrades extends JFrame
11  {
12     // JPanel for user inputs
13     private JPanel inputGradeJPanel;
14
15     // JLabel and JTextField for student name
16     private JLabel studentNameJLabel;
17     private JTextField studentNameJTextField;
18
19     // JLabel and JTextField for test 1 score
20     private JLabel test1JLabel;
21     private JTextField test1JTextField;
22
23     // JLabel and JTextField for test 2 score
24     private JLabel test2JLabel;
25     private JTextField test2JTextField;
26
27     // JLabel and JTextField for test 3 score
28     private JLabel test3JLabel;
29     private JTextField test3JTextField;
30
31     // JButton to calculate student and class average
32     private JButton submitGradesJButton;
33
34     // ButtonGroup to control numeric and letter JRadioButtons
35     private ButtonGroup displayButtonGroup;
36
37     // JRadioButtons to choose to display numerically or as letters
38     private JRadioButton numericJRadioButton;
39     private JRadioButton letterJRadioButton;
40
41     // JLabel, JTextArea and JScrollPane to display students averages
42     private JLabel displayJLabel;
43     private JTextArea displayJTextArea;
44
45     // JLabel and JTextField to display the class average
46     private JLabel classAverageJLabel;
47     private JTextField classAverageJTextField;
48
```

Figure 17.30 Student Grades code. (Part 1 of 8.)

Creating array for student names ——

Creating array for student grades ——

```
49      // initialize number of students to zero
50      private int studentCount = 0;
51
52      // constants
53      private final int NUMBER_OF_TESTS = 3;
54      private final int MAXIMUM_STUDENTS = 10;
55      private final int FIRST_TEST = 0;
56      private final int SECOND_TEST = 1;
57      private final int THIRD_TEST = 2;
58
59      // one-dimensional array to store student names
60      private String studentNames[] = new String[ MAXIMUM_STUDENTS ];
61
62      // two-dimensional array to store student grades
63      private int studentGrades[][] =
64         new int[ MAXIMUM_STUDENTS ][ NUMBER_OF_TESTS ];
65
66      // DecimalFormat for two digits of precision
67      private DecimalFormat twoDigits = new DecimalFormat( "0.00" );
68
69      // no-argument constructor
70      public StudentGrades()
71      {
72         createUserInterface();
73      }
74
75      // create and position GUI components; register event handlers
76      private void createUserInterface()
77      {
78         // get content pane for attaching GUI components
79         Container contentPane = getContentPane();
80
81         // enable explicit positioning of GUI components
82         contentPane.setLayout( null );
83
84         // set up inputGradeJPanel
85         inputGradeJPanel = new JPanel();
86         inputGradeJPanel.setBounds( 16, 16, 208, 218 );
87         inputGradeJPanel.setBorder(
88            new TitledBorder( "Input Grade" ) );
89         inputGradeJPanel.setLayout( null );
90         contentPane.add( inputGradeJPanel );
91
92         // set up studentNameJLabel
93         studentNameJLabel = new JLabel();
94         studentNameJLabel.setBounds( 8, 32, 90, 23 );
95         studentNameJLabel.setText( "Student Name:" );
96         inputGradeJPanel.add( studentNameJLabel );
97
98         // set up studentNameJTextField
99         studentNameJTextField = new JTextField();
100        studentNameJTextField.setBounds( 104, 32, 88, 21 );
101        studentNameJTextField.setHorizontalAlignment(
102           JTextField.RIGHT );
103        inputGradeJPanel.add( studentNameJTextField );
104
105        // set up test1JLabel
106        test1JLabel = new JLabel();
```

Figure 17.30 Student Grades code. (Part 2 of 8.)

```
107        test1JLabel.setBounds( 8, 74, 60, 23 );
108        test1JLabel.setText( "Test 1:" );
109        inputGradeJPanel.add( test1JLabel );
110
111        // set up test1JTextField
112        test1JTextField = new JTextField();
113        test1JTextField.setBounds( 136, 74, 56, 21 );
114        test1JTextField.setHorizontalAlignment( JTextField.RIGHT );
115        inputGradeJPanel.add( test1JTextField );
116
117        // set up test2JLabel
118        test2JLabel = new JLabel();
119        test2JLabel.setBounds( 8, 98, 60, 23 );
120        test2JLabel.setText( "Test 2:" );
121        inputGradeJPanel.add( test2JLabel );
122
123        // set up test2JTextField
124        test2JTextField = new JTextField();
125        test2JTextField.setBounds( 136, 98, 56, 21 );
126        test2JTextField.setHorizontalAlignment( JTextField.RIGHT );
127        inputGradeJPanel.add( test2JTextField );
128
129        // set up test3JLabel
130        test3JLabel = new JLabel();
131        test3JLabel.setBounds( 8, 122, 60, 23 );
132        test3JLabel.setText( "Test 3:" );
133        inputGradeJPanel.add( test3JLabel );
134
135        // set up test3JTextField
136        test3JTextField = new JTextField();
137        test3JTextField.setBounds( 136, 122, 56, 21 );
138        test3JTextField.setHorizontalAlignment( JTextField.RIGHT );
139        inputGradeJPanel.add( test3JTextField );
140
141        // set up submitGradesJButton
142        submitGradesJButton = new JButton();
143        submitGradesJButton.setBounds( 72, 182, 120, 24 );
144        submitGradesJButton.setText( "Submit Grades" );
145        inputGradeJPanel.add( submitGradesJButton );
146        submitGradesJButton.addActionListener(
147
148           new ActionListener() // anonymous inner class
149           {
150              // event handler called when submitGradesJButton
151              // is clicked
152              public void actionPerformed( ActionEvent event )
153              {
154                 submitGradesJButtonActionPerformed( event );
155              }
156
157           } // end anonymous inner class
158
159        ); // end call to addActionListener
160
161        // set up displayButtonGroup
162        displayButtonGroup = new ButtonGroup();
163
```

Figure 17.30 **Student Grades** code. (Part 3 of 8.)

```
164        // set up numericJRadioButton
165        numericJRadioButton = new JRadioButton();
166        numericJRadioButton.setBounds( 55, 244, 75, 23 );
167        numericJRadioButton.setText( "Numeric" );
168        numericJRadioButton.setSelected( true );
169        displayButtonGroup.add( numericJRadioButton );
170        contentPane.add( numericJRadioButton );
171        numericJRadioButton.addActionListener(
172
173           new ActionListener()  // anonymous inner class
174           {
175              // event handler called when numericJRadioButton
176              // is selected
177              public void actionPerformed( ActionEvent event )
178              {
179                 numericJRadioButtonActionPerformed( event );
180              }
181
182           } // end anonymous inner class
183
184        ); // end call to addActionListener
185
186        // set up letterJRadioButton
187        letterJRadioButton = new JRadioButton();
188        letterJRadioButton.setBounds( 140, 244, 75, 23 );
189        letterJRadioButton.setText( "Letter" );
190        displayButtonGroup.add( letterJRadioButton );
191        contentPane.add( letterJRadioButton );
192        letterJRadioButton.addActionListener(
193
194           new ActionListener()  // anonymous inner class
195           {
196              // event handler called when letterJRadioButton
197              // is selected
198              public void actionPerformed( ActionEvent event )
199              {
200                 letterJRadioButtonActionPerformed( event );
201              }
202
203           } // end anonymous inner class
204
205        ); // end call to addActionListener
206
207        // set up displayJLabel
208        displayJLabel = new JLabel();
209        displayJLabel.setBounds( 240, 16, 150, 23 );
210        displayJLabel.setText( "Average of each student:" );
211        contentPane.add( displayJLabel );
212
213        // set up displayJTextArea
214        displayJTextArea = new JTextArea();
215        displayJTextArea.setBounds( 240, 48, 402, 184 );
216        displayJTextArea.setEditable( false );
217        contentPane.add( displayJTextArea );
218
219        // set up classAverageJLabel
220        classAverageJLabel = new JLabel();
221        classAverageJLabel.setBounds( 490, 244, 96, 23 );
```

Setting the properties of `numericJRadioButton`

Adding `numericJRadioButton` to the `displayButtonGroup`

Coding an event handler for the `numericJRadioButton`

Setting the properties of the `letterJRadioButton`

Adding the `letterJRadioButton` to the `displayButtonGroup`

Coding an event handler for the `letterJRadioButton`

Figure 17.30   **Student Grades** code. (Part 4 of 8.)

```
222         classAverageJLabel.setText( "Class average:" );
223         contentPane.add( classAverageJLabel );
224
225         // set up classAverageJTextField
226         classAverageJTextField = new JTextField();
227         classAverageJTextField.setBounds( 586, 244, 56, 23 );
228         classAverageJTextField.setHorizontalAlignment(
229            JTextField.CENTER );
230         classAverageJTextField.setEditable( false );
231         contentPane.add( classAverageJTextField );
232
233         // set properties of application's window
234         setTitle( "Student Grades" ); // set title bar string
235         setSize( 670, 308 );          // set window size
236         setVisible( true );           // display window
237
238      } // end method createUserInterface
239
240      // convert a number to a letter grade
241      private String convertToLetterGrade( double grade )
242      {
243         if ( grade >= 90 )
244         {
245            return "A";
246         }
247         else if ( grade >= 80 )
248         {
249            return "B";
250         }
251         else if ( grade >= 70 )
252         {
253            return "C";
254         }
255         else if ( grade >= 60 )
256         {
257            return "D";
258         }
259         else
260         {
261            return "F";
262         }
263
264      } // end method convertToLetterGrade
265
266      // calculate and display the student and class average
267      private void submitGradesJButtonActionPerformed(
268         ActionEvent event )
269      {
270         // get user input
271         String nameOfStudent = studentNameJTextField.getText();
272         int test1 = Integer.parseInt( test1JTextField.getText() );
273         int test2 = Integer.parseInt( test2JTextField.getText() );
274         int test3 = Integer.parseInt( test3JTextField.getText() );
275
```

Figure 17.30 Student Grades code. (Part 5 of 8.)

```
276        // add user input to arrays
277        studentNames[ studentCount ] = nameOfStudent;
278        studentGrades[ studentCount ][ FIRST_TEST ] = test1;
279        studentGrades[ studentCount ][ SECOND_TEST ] = test2;
280        studentGrades[ studentCount ][ THIRD_TEST ] = test3;
281
282        studentCount++; // increment studentCount
283
284        if ( numericJRadioButton.isSelected() )
285        {
286           displayNumericGrades();
287        }
288        else
289        {
290           displayLetterGrades();
291        }
292
293        // clear other JTextFields for new data
294        studentNameJTextField.setText( "" );
295        test1JTextField.setText( "" );
296        test2JTextField.setText( "" );
297        test3JTextField.setText( "" );
298
299        // if ten student grades have been entered
300        if ( studentCount == MAXIMUM_STUDENTS )
301        {
302           // disable submitGradesJButton
303           submitGradesJButton.setEnabled( false );
304        }
305
306     } // end method submitGradesJButtonActionPerformed
307
308     // display student grades and averages as numbers
309     private void displayNumericGrades()
310     {
311        // add a header to displayJTextArea
312        displayJTextArea.setText(
313           "Name\tTest 1\tTest 2\tTest 3\tAverage\n" );
314
315        int studentTotal = 0; // store the student's total grades
316        int classTotal = 0;   // store the class's total grades
317
318        for ( int student = 0; student < studentCount; student++ )
319        {
320           // display student names
321           displayJTextArea.append( studentNames[ student ] + "\t" );
322
323           studentTotal = 0; // initialize the student's total grades
324
325           for ( int test = 0; test < NUMBER_OF_TESTS; test++ )
326           {
327              // append each test grade to displayJTextArea
328              displayJTextArea.append(
329                 studentGrades[ student ][ test ] + "\t" );
```

Labels (left margin):
- Storing the student name and test grades in the arrays — lines 277–280
- Increment studentCount — line 282
- Calling method displayNumericGrades — line 286
- Calling method displayLetterGrades — line 290
- Disabling submitGradesJButton if 10 students have been entered — line 302
- Displaying a header — lines 312–313
- Outputting the student's name — line 321
- Outputting each test grade — lines 328–329

Figure 17.30   **Student Grades** code. (Part 6 of 8.)

```
330
331                     // add the test grade to the student's total
332                     studentTotal += studentGrades[ student ][ test ];
333
334              } // end inner for
335
336              // add the student's total grade to the class's total
337              classTotal += studentTotal;
338
339              // calculate the student average and display it
340              double studentAverage =
341                 ( double ) studentTotal / NUMBER_OF_TESTS;
342              displayJTextArea.append(
343                 twoDigits.format( studentAverage ) + "\n" );
344
345           } // end outer for
346
347           // calculate the class average and display it
348           double classAverage =
349              ( double ) classTotal / studentCount / NUMBER_OF_TESTS;
350           classAverageJTextField.setText(
351              twoDigits.format( classAverage ) );
352
353        } // end method displayNumericGrades
354
355        // display student grades and averages as letters
356        private void displayLetterGrades()
357        {
358           // add a header to displayJTextArea
359           displayJTextArea.setText(
360              "Name\tTest 1\tTest 2\tTest 3\tAverage\n" );
361
362           int studentTotal = 0; // store the student's total grades
363           int classTotal = 0;   // store the class's total grades
364
365           for ( int student = 0; student < studentCount; student++ )
366           {
367              // display student names
368              displayJTextArea.append( studentNames[ student ] + "\t" );
369
370              studentTotal = 0; // initialize the student's total grades
371
372              for ( int test = 0; test < NUMBER_OF_TESTS; test++ )
373              {
374                 // append each test grade to displayJTextArea
375                 displayJTextArea.append( convertToLetterGrade(
376                    studentGrades[ student ][ test ] ) + "\t" );
377
378                 // add the test grade to the student's total
379                 studentTotal += studentGrades[ student ][ test ];
380
381              } // end inner for
382
383              // add the student's total grade to the class's total
384              classTotal += studentTotal;
385
```

Labels (left margin):
- Adding the test grade to the student's total — (line 332)
- Adding the student's total to the class's total — (line 337)
- Calculating and displaying the student's average — (lines 340–343)
- Calculating and displaying the class's average — (lines 348–351)
- Displaying a header — (lines 359–360)
- Outputting the student's name — (line 368)
- Converting the test grade to a letter — (lines 375–376)
- Adding the test grade to the student's total — (line 379)
- Adding the student's total to the class's total — (line 384)

Figure 17.30 **Student Grades** code. (Part 7 of 8.)

Converting student's average to a letter grade

```
386        // calculate the student average and display it
387        double studentAverage =
388           ( double ) studentTotal / NUMBER_OF_TESTS;
389        displayJTextArea.append(
390           convertToLetterGrade( studentAverage ) + "\n" );
391
392     } // end outer for
393
394        // calculate the class average and display it
395        double classAverage =
396           ( double ) classTotal / studentCount / NUMBER_OF_TESTS;
397        classAverageJTextField.setText(
398           convertToLetterGrade( classAverage ) );
399
400  } // end method displayLetterGrades
401
402  // user selected numeric display
403  private void numericJRadioButtonActionPerformed(
404     ActionEvent event )
405  {
406     displayNumericGrades();
407
408  } // end method numericJRadioButtonActionPerformed
409
410  // user selected letter display
411  private void letterJRadioButtonActionPerformed(
412     ActionEvent event )
413  {
414     displayLetterGrades();
415
416  } // end method letterJRadioButtonActionPerformed
417
418  // main method
419  public static void main( String[] args )
420  {
421     StudentGrades application = new StudentGrades();
422     application.setDefaultCloseOperation( JFrame.EXIT_ON_CLOSE );
423
424  } // end method main
425
426  } // end class StudentGrades
```

Converting class's average to a letter grade

Calling method displayNumericGrades

Calling method displayLetterGrades

Figure 17.30   **Student Grades** code. (Part 8 of 8.)

SELF-REVIEW

1. A ButtonGroup can contain _____ JRadioButton(s).
   a) exactly two   b) no more than one
   c) no more than three   d) any number of

2. When one JRadioButton in a ButtonGroup is selected, _____ .
   a) others can be selected at the same time   b) up to two can be selected together
   c) all others are deselected   d) Both a and c.

Answers: 1.) d. 2.) c.

17.5 Wrap-Up

In this tutorial, you learned how to use two-dimensional arrays to store data and how to declare and assign values to a two-dimensional array. You also used nested loops to process data stored in a two-dimensional array.

To help you complete the **Student Grades** application, you used JRadioButtons. You learned that you must group related JRadioButtons by placing them in a ButtonGroup. Initially, zero or one JRadioButton in each ButtonGroup will be selected. Once a JRadioButton has been selected, the ButtonGroup guarantees that only one JRadioButton will be selected at a time. When another JRadioButton in a ButtonGroup is selected, the previously selected JRadioButton in the ButtonGroup is deselected.

After learning about JRadioButtons, you used code to store user input in a two-dimensional array. You also learned that selecting a JRadioButton calls an actionPerformed event handler.

You have been using classes all along, from the JFrame class that represents the application's GUI to the Random class that you used to generate random numbers. In the next tutorial, you will learn how to create your own classes for use in your applications.

SKILLS SUMMARY

Using Two-Dimensional Arrays

- Declare a two-dimensional array to create a table of values (each row will contain the same number of columns). For example, use the code

```
int numbers[][] = new int[ 3 ][ 2 ];
```

to declare an array with three rows and two columns.

Using a JRadioButton

- Use JRadioButtons in an application to allow the user to select one of a group of options.

Selecting a JRadioButton at Runtime

- Click the hollow circle of the JRadioButton. A small black dot will appear inside the circle.

Determining Whether a JRadioButton Is Selected

- Determine the JRadioButton's state with the isSelected method. This method returns true if the JRadioButton is selected and false otherwise.

Executing Code When a JRadioButton Has Been Selected

- Use the actionPerformed event handler, which executes when a JRadioButton is selected.

KEY TERMS

add method of ButtonGroup—Adds a JRadioButton to the ButtonGroup.

ButtonGroup—A group of any number of JRadioButtons. Only one JRadioButton in the ButtonGroup can be selected at a time. When one JRadioButton is selected, the previously selected JRadioButton is deselected.

column—In referring to an element of a two-dimensional array, the second index specifies the column.

isSelected method of JRadioButton—Returns true if the JRadioButton is selected and false otherwise.

JRadioButton component—A component that appears as a small circle that is either blank (unselected) or contains a smaller black dot (selected). Usually these components appear in groups of two or more.

m-by-n array—A two-dimensional array with *m* rows and *n* columns.

nested loop—A loop (such as a for statement) which is enclosed inside another control statement.

row—In referring to an element of a two-dimensional array, the first index specifies the row.

setSelected method of JRadioButton—Sets the state of the JRadioButton to selected (true) or unselected (false).

state button—A button that can only be in an "on" or "off" state (for example, a JRadioButton or JCheckBox).

table—A two-dimensional array used to contain information arranged in rows and columns.

two-dimensional array—An array requiring two indices to specify a value. These arrays are often used to represent tables of information with values arranged in rows and columns.

GUI DESIGN GUIDELINES

JRadioButton

- Use JRadioButtons when the user should choose only one option from a group.
- Always place each group of JRadioButtons in a separate ButtonGroup.
- Align groups of JRadioButtons either horizontally or vertically.

JAVA LIBRARY REFERENCE

JRadioButton This component is used to enable users to select only one of several options.

- *In action*

- *Event handlers*

  actionPerformed—Called when the component is selected.

- *Methods*

  isSelected—Returns true if the JRadioButton is selected and false otherwise.

  setBounds—Specifies the location of the JRadioButton component on the container control relative to the top-left corner, as well as the height and width (in pixels) of the component.

  setSelected—Sets the state of the JRadioButton to selected or unselected. When true, the JRadioButton displays a small black dot inside a circle. When false, the JRadioButton displays an empty circle.

  setText—Specifies the text displayed in the JRadioButton.

ButtonGroup This class is used to group JRadioButton components. Initially, zero or one JRadioButtons will be selected. Once a JRadioButton has been selected, only one JRadioButton in the ButtonGroup can be selected at any time.

- *Methods*

  add—Adds a JRadioButton to the ButtonGroup.

MULTIPLE-CHOICE QUESTIONS

17.1 Use the _____ method to select or deselect a JRadioButton component.

    a) setSelected   b) setChecked

    c) setDefault   d) setEnabled

17.2 A _____ component is considered a state button.

    a) JRadioButton   b) JCheckBox

    c) JButton   d) Both a and b.

17.3 In an *m*-by-*n* array, the *m* stands for _____.

    a) the number of columns in the array   b) the total number of array elements

    c) the number of rows in the array   d) the number of elements in each row

17.4 The statement _____ assigns an array of three columns and five rows to the two-dimensional int array variable myArray.

    a) myArray = new int[5][3];   b) myArray = new int[4][2];

    c) myArray = new int[3][5];   d) myArray = new int[2][4];

17.5 A JRadioButton is a type of _____ button.

    a) check   b) change

    c) state   d) action

17.6 Use a _____ to group JRadioButtons on the JFrame.

  a) GroupBox   b) ButtonBox

  c) ButtonGroup   d) None of the above.

17.7 Use the _____ method to add a JRadioButton to a ButtonGroup.

  a) add   b) addJButton

  c) addJRadioButton   d) newJRadioButton

17.8 Two-dimensional arrays are often used to represent _____.

  a) a pie chart   b) distances

  c) lines   d) tables

17.9 When a JRadioButton is created it _____.

  a) is selected   b) is not selected

  c) is added to the content pane   d) is added to a default ButtonGroup

17.10 _____ is the correct way to create a new two-dimensional integer array myArray with 5 rows and 5 columns.

  a) int myArray[][] = new int[5][5]

  b) int myArray[2] = new int(5, 5)

  c) int myArray[,] = new int[5, 5]

  d) int myArray[] = new int[5, 5]

EXERCISES

17.11 *(Food Survey Application)* A school cafeteria is giving an electronic survey to its students to improve their lunch menu. Create an application that will use a two-dimensional array to hold counters for the survey (Fig. 17.31). You will also provide JRadioButtons for the students to indicate whether they like or dislike a particular food.

Figure 17.31   **Food Survey** application.

a) *Copying the template to your working directory.* Copy the directory C:\Examples\ Tutorial17\Exercises\FoodSurvey to your C:\SimplyJava directory.

b) *Opening the template file.* Open the FoodSurvey.java file in your text editor.

c) *Declaring a two-dimensional int array.* In lines 29–30, insert code to declare a two-dimensional int array named display, with 4 rows and 2 columns.

d) *Declaring local variables.* In line 105, in method addJButtonActionPerformed, set the text of displayJTextArea to "Food\tLike\tDislike" for the header. Create a local int variable index. This variable should contain the index of the selected item in foodJComboBox.

e) *Using a for loop to display the data.* Insert a for statement that will loop through each row in the foodChoices array (0–3). In the body of the loop, append the appropriate food to displayJTextArea. The counter variable of the for statement will be used as the index of the foodChoices array. Add the "\n" escape sequence to displayJTextArea before the food and the "\t" escape sequence after the food.

f) *Determining which counter to increment.* Insert an if statement inside the for statement you created in *Step e.* It should check if the likeJRadioButton is selected and if the variable index is equal to the counter of your for statement. If both conditions are true, increment the counter in column 0 in the display array. Insert an else containing a nested if that determines whether the dislikeJRadioButton is selected

and whether the variable `index` is equal to the counter of your `for` statement. If both conditions are `true`, increment the counter in column 1 of the `display` array.

g) ***Adding contents of the `display` array to output.*** Use a nested `for` statement to append the contents of your `display` array to `displayJTextArea`. Use the counter of your first `for` statement as the first index (row) of `display` and the counter of your nested `for` statement as the second index (column) of `display`. Add the `"\t"` escape sequence to `output` after adding each cell of the array.

h) ***Saving the application.*** Save your modified source code file.

i) ***Opening the Command Prompt window and changing directories.*** Open the **Command Prompt** by selecting **Start > Programs > Accessories > Command Prompt**. Change to your working directory by typing cd C:\SimplyJava\FoodSurvey.

j) ***Compiling the application.*** Compile your application by typing javac FoodSurvey.java.

k) ***Running the completed application.*** When your application compiles correctly, run it by typing java FoodSurvey. Chose either the **Like** or **Dislike** `JRadioButton`. Click the **Add** `JButton` and check to make sure all `Strings` and numbers in the `JTextArea` are correct. Add several other selections to the **Food Survey** and make sure that the numbers are correct.

l) ***Closing the application.*** Close your running application by clicking its close button.

m) ***Closing the Command Prompt window.*** Close the **Command Prompt** window by clicking its close button.

17.12 *(Sales Report Application)* A clothing manufacturer has asked you to create an application that will calculate the total sales of that manufacturer in a week. Sales values should be input separately for each clothing item, but the amount of sales for all five weekdays should be input at once. The application should calculate the total amount of sales for each item in the week and also calculate the total sales for the manufacturer for all the items in the week. Because the manufacturer is a small company, it will produce at most ten items in any week. The application is shown in Fig. 17.32.

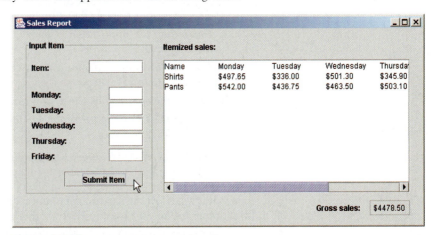

Figure 17.32 **Sales Report** application.

a) ***Copying the template to your working directory.*** Copy the directory C:\Examples\Tutorial17\Exercises\SalesReport to your C:\SimplyJava directory.

b) ***Opening the template file.*** Open the SalesReport.java file in your text editor.

c) ***Inputting data from the user.*** Add code starting in line 231 to input the data from the user. Variable `nameOfItem` stores the name of the item. This must be assigned to the `itemNames` array, indexed with `itemCount` (which stores the number of items added). Variables `monday`, `tuesday`, `wednesday`, `thursday` and `friday` store the sales data for each of the five weekdays. These variables must be assigned to the two-dimensional `dailyItems` array. The first index to this array should be `itemCount`, and the second will range from 0 to 4. Finally, increment variable `itemCount` to record that another item's sales data has been added.

d) *Iterating over all the items added.* Inside the `displaySales` method, after variable `salesTotal` has been declared (line 270), add code to begin a `for` statement. This `for` statement should iterate from 0 to `itemCount`. Declare the variable `item` as the `for` statement's counter.

e) *Displaying the item's name.* Insert code in this `for` statement to append the item's name to `displayJTextArea`. Remember that the items' names are stored in `String` array `itemNames`. Append the escape sequence "\t" to format the output properly.

f) *Iterating over the days in the week.* Add code to initialize variable `weekTotal` to 0. This variable keeps track of the total sales for each item over the course of the week. Add code to start a `for` statement. This `for` statement will iterate from 0 to the number of days in a week (stored in the `NUMBER_OF_DAYS` constant, which is declared in the template).

g) *Appending daily sales and summing sales for the week.* Add code in this `for` statement to append the daily sales to `displayJTextArea`. These sales are stored in the `dailyItems` array. This array must be accessed with the current item and the day of the week. The output is money, so use `DecimalFormat` variable `dollars` to format the value. Also append the escape sequence "\t" to format the output properly.

h) *Calculating weekly sales.* Insert code to add the amount of the daily sales to variable `weekTotal`. This variable stores the weekly sales for each item. Add a right brace to end the `for` statement started in *Step f*.

i) *Calculating total sales and outputting weekly sales.* Insert code to add the weekly sales to variable `salesTotal`. This variable keeps track of the total sales for all the items for the week. Add code to append the weekly sales to `displayJTextArea`. The weekly sales are also stored as money, so use `DecimalFormat` dollars again. Also append the escape sequence "\n" to move to the next line in the `JTextArea`. Insert a right brace to end the `for` statement started in *Step d*.

j) *Saving the application.* Save your modified source code file.

k) *Opening the Command Prompt window and changing directories.* Open the **Command Prompt** by selecting **Start > Programs > Accessories > Command Prompt**. Change to your working directory by typing `cd C:\SimplyJava\SalesReport`.

l) *Compiling the application.* Compile your application by typing `javac SalesReport.java`.

m) *Running the completed application.* When your application compiles correctly, run it by typing `java SalesReport`.

n) *Closing the application.* Close your running application by clicking its close button.

o) *Closing the Command Prompt window.* Close the **Command Prompt** window by clicking its close button.

17.13 *(Profit Report Application)* The clothing manufacturer was so impressed with the **Sales Report** application you created for them (Exercise 17.12) they want you to create a **Profit Report** application as well. This application will be similar to the **Sales Report** application, but it will allow the user to input information as gains or losses. It should provide `JRadioButtons` to allow the user to select whether a certain item is a gain or a loss (Fig. 17.33).

a) *Copying the template to your working directory.* Copy the directory `C:\Examples\Tutorial17\Exercises\ProfitReport` to your `C:\SimplyJava` directory.

b) *Opening the template file.* Open the `ProfitReport.java` file in your text editor.

c) *Modifying the template application.* Modify the template as you did in Exercise 17.12.

d) *Customizing the Gain JRadioButton.* Add code to the `createUserInterface` method to customize `gainJRadioButton`. Set the bounds and text so that the component appears as in Fig. 17.33. Set the `JRadioButton` to be selected when the application starts (the default). Add the `JRadioButton` to `profitButtonGroup`.

e) *Customizing the Loss JRadioButton.* Add code to the `createUserInterface` method to customize `lossJRadioButton`. Set the bounds and text so that the component appears as in Fig. 17.33. Add the `JRadioButton` to `profitButtonGroup`.

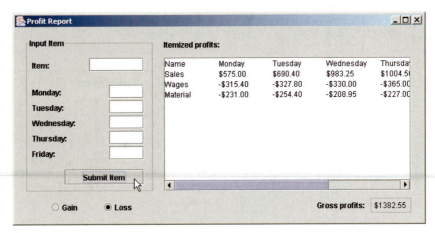

Figure 17.33 **Profit Report** application.

f) *Testing which JRadioButton was selected.* Add code to the submitItem-JButtonActionPerformed method to test which JRadioButton was selected. If the **Gain** JRadioButton was selected, add the input values to the array normally. If the **Loss** JRadioButton was selected, add the input value to the array as negative values.

g) *Saving the application.* Save your modified source code file.

h) *Opening the Command Prompt window and changing directories.* Open the **Command Prompt** by selecting **Start > Programs > Accessories > Command Prompt.** Change to your working directory by typing cd C:\SimplyJava\ProfitReport.

i) *Compiling the application.* Compile your application by typing javac Profit-Report.java.

j) *Running the completed application.* When your application compiles correctly, run it by typing java ProfitReport.

k) *Closing the application.* Close your running application by clicking its close button.

l) *Closing the Command Prompt window.* Close the **Command Prompt** window by clicking its close button.

What does this code do? ▶

17.14 What is returned by the following code? Assume that getStockPrices is a method that returns a 2-by-31 array, with the first row containing the stock price at the beginning of the day and the last row containing the stock price at the end of the day, for each day of the month.

```
1   private int[] mystery()
2   {
3      int[][] prices = new int[ 2 ][ 31 ];
4
5      prices = getStockPrices();
6
7      int[] result = new int[ 31 ];
8
9      for ( int i = 0; i<= 30; i++ )
10     {
11        result[ i ] = prices[ 0 ][ i ] - prices[ 1 ][ i ];
12
13     } // end for
14
15     return result;
16
17  } // end method mystery
```

What's wrong with this code? ▶

17.15 Find the error(s) in the following code. The `twoDArrays` method should create a two-dimensional array and initialize all its values to 1.

```
1   private void twoDArrays()
2   {
3      int[][] intArray;
4
5      intArray = new int[ 4 ][ 4 ];
6
7      // assign 1 to all cell values
8      for ( int i = 0; i < 4; i++ )
9      {
10        intArray[ i ][ i ] = 1;
11
12     } // end for
13
14  } // end method twoDArrays
```

Programming Challenge ▶

17.16 *(Enhanced Lottery Picker Application)* In Tutorial 15, your **Lottery Picker** application selected numbers for four different types of lotteries. In this exercise, you enhance the **Lottery Picker** to select four different sets of number for the five-number lottery and to prevent duplicate numbers from being selected (Fig. 17.34). Recall that the lottery is played as follows: Five number lotteries require players to choose five unique numbers in the range from 0–39.

Figure 17.34 Enhanced **Lottery Picker** application.

a) *Copying the template to your working directory.* Copy the directory C:\Examples\ Tutorial17\Exercises\EnhancedLotteryPicker to your C:\SimplyJava directory.

b) *Opening the template file.* Open the LotteryPicker.java file in your text editor.

c) *Iterating over the four lotteries.* Add code in line 138 to begin a `for` statement in your application that will execute four times—once for each lottery. Use variable `lottery` as the `for` statement's counter.

d) *Initialize the boolean array.* To generate unique numbers in each lottery, you will use a two-dimensional `boolean` array, `uniqueNumber` (declared for you in the template). When a number has been selected for a lottery, the value of that variable in the array (indexed by the lottery and the number selected) will be `true`. First, you must initialize the value for the lottery's numbers to `false`. Add a nested `for` statement to set the 40 values in the array for this lottery to `false`. You will need to use `lottery` and the counter in this `for` statement to index the array. Add a right brace to end this inner `for` statement.

e) *Initialize a String to hold the selections.* The output array has been provided for you in the template. It is a `String` array with four values—one for each lottery. This array will hold the output as each lottery number is generated. Add code to initialize the lottery's `String` to the empty string (""). You will need to use `lottery` to index the array.

f) *Iterating over the five numbers selected.* Five unique numbers will need to be selected for each lottery. Add code to begin another for statement that will iterate five times. Each time this for statement executes, a single unique lottery number will be generated.

g) *Generating a unique lottery number.* Add a do...while statement inside this for statement. The body of this do...while statement should use method generate (declared for you in the template) and pass it the arguments 0 and 39 to return a random number between 0 and 39, inclusive. This value should be assigned to variable selection (also declared for you in the template). The loop continuation condition should test whether the number stored in selection has been used for this lottery. This is done using array uniqueNumber indexed with lottery and selection.

h) *Updating the value in uniqueNumber.* Add code to set the value in uniqueNumber represented by the selected number (indexed with lottery and selection) to true. This number will not be selected again for this lottery.

i) *Adding the number to the output.* Insert code to add a space and the selected number to the output String for this lottery. This String is stored in the output array indexed with lottery. Add a right brace to end the inner for statement (*Step f*) and another right brace to end the outer for statement (*Step c*).

j) *Displaying the generated numbers.* The output array will now hold the generated sequences in its four indices. Add code to set the text of each JTextField—oneJTextField, twoJTextField, threeJTextField and fourJTextField—to one of the Strings in array output.

k) *Saving the application.* Save your modified source code file.

l) *Opening the Command Prompt window and changing directories.* Open the **Command Prompt** window by selecting **Start > Programs > Accessories > Command Prompt**. Change to your working directory by typing cd C:\SimplyJava\Enhanced-LotteryPicker.

m) *Compiling the application.* Compile your application by typing javac Lottery-Picker.java.

n) *Running the completed application.* When your application compiles correctly, run it by typing java LotteryPicker. Click the **Generate** JButton and check to make sure all numbers in each of the four five number lotteries are unique. Do this several more times to make sure.

o) *Closing the application.* Close your running application by clicking its close button.

p) *Closing the Command Prompt window.* Close the **Command Prompt** window by clicking its close button.

TUTORIAL

Microwave Oven Application

Building Your Own Classes and Objects

In earlier tutorials, you used the following application-development methodology: You analyzed many typical problems that required an application to be built and determined what classes from the Java class library were needed to implement each application. You then selected appropriate methods from these classes and created any additional methods to complete each application.

You have now seen many Java class library classes. Each GUI component is declared as a class. When you add a component to your application, an object (also known as an **instance**) of that class is created and added to your application. You can have many instances of one class; for example, many of the applications you have worked with in this book have included two or more `JButtons`. You have also seen Java class library classes that are not GUI components. Class `DecimalFormat`, for example, has been used to create `DecimalFormat` objects (for textual data). When you create and use an object of a class in an application, your application is known as a **client** of that class.

In this tutorial, you will learn to create and use your own classes (sometimes known as **programmer-declared classes**). Creating your own classes is a key part of object-oriented programming (OOP) because classes can be reused by many applications. In the world of Java programming, applications are created by using a combination of Java class library classes and methods and programmer-declared classes and methods. You have already created several methods in this book. Now you will learn to create the classes that contain these methods.

You will create a microwave-oven simulator where the user will enter the cooking time. To handle the time data, you will create a class called `CookingTime`. This class will store a number of minutes and a number of seconds (which your **Microwave Oven** application will use to keep track of the remaining cooking time). The class will also provide *get* and *set* methods, which clients of this class can use to access and change, respectively, the number of minutes and seconds.

18.1 Test-Driving the Microwave Oven Application

In this tutorial you will build your own class as you construct your **Microwave Oven** application. This application must meet the following requirements:

Application Requirements

*An electronics company is considering building microwave ovens. The company has asked you to develop an application that simulates a microwave oven. The oven will contain a keypad that allows the user to specify the microwave cooking time, which is displayed for the user. Once a time is entered, the user clicks the **Start JButton** to begin the cooking process. The microwave's glass window changes color (from gray to yellow) to simulate the oven's light that remains on while the food cooks, and a timer counts down one second at a time. Once the time expires, the color of the microwave's glass window returns to gray (indicating that the microwave's light is now off) and the microwave displays the text **Done!**. The user can click the **Clear JButton** at any time to stop the microwave and enter a new time. The user should be able to enter a number of minutes no greater than 59 and a number of seconds no greater than 59; otherwise, the invalid cooking time will be set to zero.*

You begin by test-driving the completed application. Then, you will learn the additional Java technologies you will need to create your own version of this application.

Test-Driving the Microwave Oven Application

1. **Locating the completed application.** Open the **Command Prompt** window by selecting **Start > Programs > Accessories > Command Prompt**. Change to the completed **Microwave Oven** application directory by typing cd C:\Examples\Tutorial18\CompletedApplication\MicrowaveOven.

2. **Running the Microwave Oven application.** Type java MicrowaveOven in the **Command Prompt** window to run the application (Fig. 18.1). Your application contains a large rectangle on the left (representing the microwave oven's glass window) and a keypad on the right, including a JTextField with the text **Microwave Oven**. The numeric JButtons are used to enter the cooking time, which will be displayed in the JTextField on the top right.

Microwave's glass window ⎯⎯⎯⎯⎯⎯⎯

Numeric keypad

Figure 18.1 **Microwave Oven** application GUI displayed when your application is executed.

3. **Entering a time.** Click the numeric JButtons: **1**, **2**, **3**, **4** and **5** in order. Notice that you can enter no more than four digits (the first two for the minutes and the second two for the seconds)—any extra digits will not appear (Fig. 18.2). The number of minutes and the number of seconds must each be 59 or less. If the user enters an invalid number of minutes or seconds (such as 89), the invalid amount will be set to zero.

(cont.)

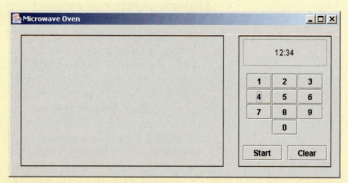

Figure 18.2 **Microwave Oven** application accepts only four digits.

4. ***Entering invalid data.*** Click the **Clear** JButton to clear your input. Click the numeric JButtons: **7**, **2**, **3** and **5** in order (Fig. 18.3). This input is invalid because the number of minutes, 72, is larger than the maximum allowed value, 59, so the number of minutes is set to zero when the **Start** JButton is clicked. Click the **Start** JButton. Notice that the number of minutes has been reset to **00**, though the number of seconds has been left unchanged (Fig. 18.4). Also, notice that the microwave oven's window has changed to yellow, to simulate the light that goes on inside the oven so that the user can watch the food cooking.

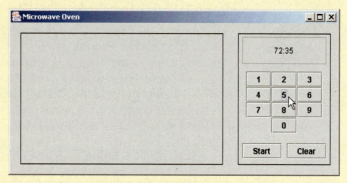

Figure 18.3 **Microwave Oven** application with invalid input.

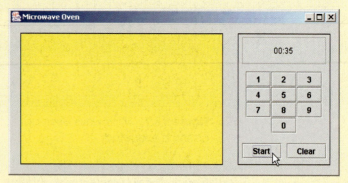

Figure 18.4 **Microwave Oven** application after invalid input has been entered and the **Start** JButton clicked.

5. ***Entering valid data.*** Click the **Clear** JButton to enter a new cooking time. Click the **5** JButton (to indicate 5 seconds); then, click the **Start** JButton (Fig. 18.5).

(cont.)

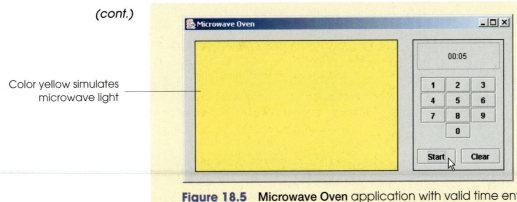

Figure 18.5 **Microwave Oven** application with valid time entered and inside light turned on (it's now cooking).

6. *Viewing your application after the cooking time has expired.* Wait five seconds. Notice that the display `JTextField` shows the time counting down by `1` each second. When the time has reached zero, the display `JTextField` changes to contain the text **Done!** and the microwave oven's window changes back to the same color as the `JFrame`, indicating that the oven light has been turned off (Fig. 18.6).

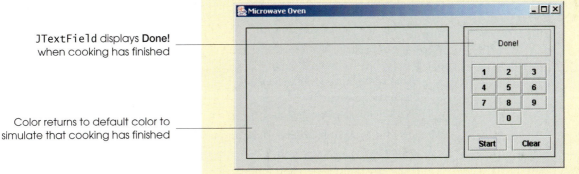

Figure 18.6 **Microwave Oven** application after the cooking time has elapsed.

7. *Closing the running application.* Close the running application by clicking its close button.

8. *Closing the Command Prompt window.* Close the **Command Prompt** window by clicking its close button.

18.2 Designing the Microwave Oven Application

The **Microwave Oven** application groups components using a `JPanel` component. The application requires two `JPanel`s—one to contain your application's `JButton`s and `JTextField`s, and the other to represent the microwave oven's glass window. The template application provided for you contains one of these `JPanel`s. You will soon add the other.

The **Microwave Oven** application contains a class (called `CookingTime`) whose objects store the cooking time in minutes and seconds. All of the components you have used (including the `JFrame` itself) are declared in the Java class library as classes. You will create the `CookingTime` class before you create the class for the **Microwave Oven**. The following pseudocode describes the basic operation of class `CookingTime`:

> When the time object is created:
>   Set the number of minutes and number of seconds to 0

When setting the number of minutes:
>   If the number of minutes is greater than 0 and less than 60
>   set the number of minutes to specified value
>   else
>   set the number of minutes to 0

When setting the number of seconds:
>   If the number of seconds is greater than 0 and less than 60
>   set the number of seconds to specified value
>   else
>   set the number of seconds to 0

When the time object is decremented:
>   If the number of seconds is greater than 0
>   reduce the number of seconds by 1
>   else if the number of minutes is greater than 0
>   reduce the number of minutes by 1
>   set the number of seconds to 59

When an object of class `CookingTime` is created, the number of minutes and number of seconds will both be initialized to 0. Invalid data for the number of minutes or the number of seconds will cause the value to be set to 0. The following pseudocode describes the basic operation of your **Microwave Oven** application:

When the user clicks a numeric JButton:
>   Display the formatted time

When the user clicks the Start JButton:
>   Display the formatted time
>   Store the minutes and seconds
>   Begin the countdown
>   Turn the microwave light on

When the timer interval expires (once per second):
>   Decrease the time by one second
>
>   If the new time is not zero
>   Display the new time
>   Else
>   Stop the countdown
>   Display the text "Done!"
>   Turn the microwave light off

When the user clicks the Clear JButton:
>   Stop the countdown
>   Display the text "Microwave Oven"
>   Turn the microwave light off

The user enters input by clicking the numeric `JButtons`. Each time a numeric `JButton` is clicked, the number on that `JButton` is appended to the end of the cooking time that is displayed in the GUI's `JTextField`. After entering the cooking time, the user can click the **Start** `JButton` to begin the cooking process or click the **Clear** `JButton` and enter a new time. If the **Start** `JButton` is clicked, a countdown using a `Timer` component begins, and the microwave oven's window changes to yellow, indicating that the microwave oven's light is on (so that the user can watch the food cook). Each second, the display is updated to show the remaining cooking time. When the countdown finishes, the `displayJTextField` displays the text **Done!** and the microwave oven's "light" is turned off, by changing the window's color back to its default gray.

Before you begin to build your application, it is helpful to create an ACE table for the application. Figure 18.7 lists the actions, components and events required to complete the **Microwave Oven** application.

Action/Component/Event (ACE) Table for the Microwave Oven Application

Action	Component/Object	Event
	oneJButton, twoJButton, threeJButton, fourJButton, fiveJButton, sixJButton, sevenJButton, eightJButton, nineJButton	User clicks a numeric JButton
Display the formatted time	displayJTextField	
	startJButton	User clicks **Start** JButton
Display the formatted time	displayJTextField	
Store the minutes and seconds	microwaveTime (CookingTime)	
Begin the countdown	clockTimer (Timer)	
Turn the microwave light on	windowJPanel	
	clockTimer (Timer)	Timer interval expires (once per second)
Decrease the time by one second	microwaveTime (CookingTime)	
If the new time is not zero 　Display the new time	microwaveTime, displayJTextField	
Else 　Stop the countdown	clockTimer (Timer)	
Display the text "Done!"	displayJTextField	
Turn the microwave light off	windowJPanel	
	clearJButton	User clicks **Clear** JButton
Stop the countdown	clockTimer (Timer)	
Display the text "Microwave Oven"	displayJTextField	
Turn the microwave light off	windowJPanel	

Figure 18.7　ACE table for the **Microwave Oven** application.

　　Input is sent to your application when the user clicks one of the numeric JButtons. Values are displayed in displayJTextField as they are entered. Once all input has been entered, the user clicks the **Start** JButton to begin the countdown. The windowJPanel's background color is set to yellow to simulate the microwave oven's light being turned on, and Timer clockTimer will update displayJTextField each second during the countdown. To clear the input and start over, the user can click the **Clear** JButton.

　　Next, you will learn how to add a class to your application. This class will be used to create objects that contain the time in minutes and seconds.

Creating a Class

1. ***Copying the template to your working directory.*** Copy the C:\Examples\Tutorial18\TemplateApplication\MicrowaveOven directory to your C:\SimplyJava directory.

2. ***Opening the CookingTime class template file.*** Open the template file CookingTime.java in your text editor. Remember that in Java, every source code file must have the same name as the public class that it contains followed by the file name extension, .java. The files, MicrowaveOven.java and CookingTime.java contain the classes MicrowaveOven and CookingTime, respectively. Both of these classes are necessary in building the **Microwave Oven** application.

(cont.)

Good Programming Practice

By convention, always begin a class name with a capital letter and start each subsequent word in the class name with a capital letter.

Good Programming Practice

Add comments at the beginning of programmer-declared classes to increase readability. The comments should indicate the name of the file that contains the class and the purpose of the class being declared.

3. **Viewing the template code.** Look at lines 1–7 of Fig. 18.8. Lines 1–2 are comments that indicate the name and purpose of your class file. Line 4, which begins the CookingTime class declaration, contains the keywords public and class, followed by the name of the class (in this case, CookingTime). Keyword **class** indicates that what follows is a class declaration. All classes in this book are declared public. This is the first step in creating classes that can be used by many applications. A class is reusable only if it is declared public and placed in a package that other applications can import. Creating packages is beyond the scope of this book. The left and right brace (lines 5 and 7) indicate the beginning and end of the **class's body**, respectively. Methods or variables declared in the body of a class are said to be **members** of that class.

Empty class declaration ——

```
Source Editor [CookingTime]                                    _ □ X
1  // Tutorial 18: CookingTime.java
2  // Represents time data and contains get and set methods.
3
4  public class CookingTime
5  {
6
7  } // end class CookingTime
8
```

Figure 18.8 Empty class declaration.

4. **Adding instance variables to your application.** Add lines 6–8 of Fig. 18.9 to the CookingTime class declaration. Lines 7–8 declare two int instance variables—minute and second. The CookingTime class will store a time value containing minutes and seconds—the value for minutes is stored in minute and the value for seconds is stored in second. Recall from Tutorial 14 that the scope of an instance variable is its entire class. All methods declared in class CookingTime will be able to access instance variables minute and second.

Instance variables store minute and second information ——

```
Source Editor [CookingTime *]                                  _ □ X
4  public class CookingTime
5  {
6      // integers for storing minutes and seconds
7      private int minute;
8      private int second;
9
```

Figure 18.9 CookingTime's instance variables.

5. **Saving the application.** Save your modified source code file.

SELF-REVIEW
1. Keyword _____ begins a class declaration.
   a) declare   b) new
   c) class   d) None of the above.

2. A class declaration must include a pair of _____.
   a) square brackets b) braces
   c) commas   d) parentheses

Answers: 1) c. 2) b.

18.3 Initializing Objects: Constructors

A class can contain methods and instance variables. You have already used methods such as the format method of class DecimalFormat and the nextInt method of class Random. A **constructor** is used to initialize instance variables. The constructor

has the same name as the name of the class that contains it. The declaration of a constructor is similar to a method, but unlike a method, a constructor cannot specify a return type (not even `void`). In Tutorial 15, you learned how to use constructors to create objects. Next, you will declare a constructor for your `CookingTime` class, allowing clients to create `CookingTime` objects and initialize those objects' instance variables.

Declaring a Constructor

1. **Adding a constructor to a class.** Add lines 10–14 of Fig. 18.10 to the body of class `CookingTime`. These lines declare a constructor for class `CookingTime`. Notice that the constructor's name (`CookingTime`) is the same as the class's name. The constructor is invoked each time an object of that class is **instantiated** (created). You will add the body statements of this constructor in the following steps. Statements within a constructor usually initialize instance variables.

```
Source Editor [CookingTime *]
 8      public int second;
 9
10      // CookingTime constructor, minute and second supplied
11      public CookingTime( int minuteValue, int secondValue )
12      {
13
14      } // end constructor
15
16  } // end class CookingTime
```

Constructor ──── (lines 10–14)

Figure 18.10   Declaring an empty constructor.

The constructor in Fig. 18.10 expects two arguments. You'll see how to provide arguments to constructors momentarily. Constructors return an object of its class (for example, the `CookingTime` constructor returns an instance of the `CookingTime` class). Constructors cannot specify a different return type. This is an important difference between constructors and methods. A class's instance variables can be initialized in the constructor, or when those variables are declared in the class declaration. Variable `second`, for example, can be initialized where it is declared (line 8) or it can be initialized in `CookingTime`'s constructor.

2. **Initializing variables in a constructor.** Add lines 13–14 of Fig. 18.11 to the constructor. These lines initialize `CookingTime`'s instance variables to the values of the constructor's parameters (line 11). When an object is created in a client of a class, values are often specified for that object. For example, a `CookingTime` object (such as `microwaveTime`) can now be created with the statement

```
microwaveTime = new CookingTime( 0, 0 );
```

This `CookingTime` object will be created and the constructor will execute. The values 0 and 0 will be assigned to the constructor's parameters, which the constructor will use to initialize `minute` and `second`.

 **Error-Prevention Tip**

Providing a constructor to ensure that every object is initialized with meaningful values can help eliminate logic errors.

Constructor arguments assigned to instance variables ────

```
Source Editor [CookingTime *]
11      public CookingTime( int minuteValue, int secondValue )
12      {
13          minute = minuteValue;
14          second = secondValue;
15
16      } // end constructor
```

Figure 18.11   Constructor initializing instance variables.

(cont.)

3. **Saving the application.** Save your modified source code file.

4. **Opening the Microwave Oven application's template file.** Open the template file `MicrowaveOven.java` in your text editor.

5. **Creating a CookingTime object.** After declaring your new CookingTime class, you can declare your own objects of type CookingTime. Add lines 42–43 of Fig. 18.12 to your application.

Declaring an instance of
class CookingTime

```
40      private String timeToDisplay = "";
41
42      // Time instance for storing the current time
43      private CookingTime microwaveTime = new CookingTime( 0, 0 );
44
```

Figure 18.12   Declaring an object of type CookingTime.

Notice the use of the class name, CookingTime, as a type. Just as you can create many variables from a primitive type, such as int, you can create many objects from a class (a reference type). You can also create your own classes as needed. Java is known as an **extensible language** because the language can be "extended" with new classes.

The instance variable microwaveTime is initialized on the same line that it is declared (line 43). After keyword **new**, the CookingTime constructor is called to initialize the instance variables of the CookingTime object. The constructor of class CookingTime is passed two 0's as arguments, which initialize CookingTime's instance variables minute and second to 0. The expression results in a reference to the newly created object; this reference is assigned to microwaveTime.

6. **Saving the application.** Save your modified source code file.

SELF-REVIEW

1. A(n) _____ language is one that can be "extended" with new classes.
   a) data
   b) extensible
   c) typeable
   d) extended

2. Instance variables can be initialized _____.
   a) when they are declared
   b) to their default values
   c) in a constructor
   d) All of the above.

Answers: 1) b.   2) d.

18.4 *Get* and *Set* Methods

Clients of a class usually want to manipulate that class's instance variables. For example, assume a class (Person) that stores information about a person, including age information (stored in int instance variable age). Clients who create an object of class Person could want to modify age—perhaps incorrectly, by assigning a negative value to age. Classes often provide *get* and *set* **methods** (sometimes called **accessors** and **mutators**, respectively) to allow clients to access and modify instance variables in a regular and safe way. *Get* methods (accessors) typically retrieve a value from an object. *Set* methods (mutators) typically modify data in an object. You have already seen and used several of these methods in previous tutorials. For example, JLabels have setText and getText methods to retrieve or modify the text displayed.

The *get* method allows clients to get (that is, obtain the value of) an instance variable. When the code

```
minuteValue = timeObject.getMinute();
```

executes, the getMinute method executes and returns the value of timeObject's minute instance variable, which is then assigned to minuteValue.

The *set* method allows clients to set (that is, assign a value to) an instance variable. For example, when the code

```
timeObject.setMinute( 35 );
```

executes, the setMinute method assigns a new value to the instance variable minute. A *set* method could—and should—carefully scrutinize attempts to modify the variable's value. This ensures that the new value is appropriate for that data item. Maintaining an object's data in this manner is known as keeping the data in a **consistent state**. The setMinute method keeps variable minute in a consistent state by assigning a valid value to minute even if invalid data is passed to the *set* method. Users can specify an amount of minutes only in the range of 0 to 59. Values not in this range will be discarded by the *set* method, and minute will be assigned the value 0.

In this tutorial, you will learn how to create your own *get* and *set* methods to help clients of a class read and modify the class's instance variables. You will create four methods, getMinute, setMinute, getSecond and setSecond, for your CookingTime class.

Good Programming Practice

While it is not required, it is a good idea to include the words get and set in the names of *get* and *set* methods.

Declaring the Methods of Class CookingTime

1. ***Declaring a*** **get** ***method for minute.*** Add lines 18–23 of Fig. 18.13 to class CookingTime. Line 19 begins with the keyword public. The public keyword is an access modifier that allows clients of instances of MicrowaveOven to call the method it modifies (getMinute). After the keyword public, the return type (int) indicates that the method should return an int, then the method name (getMinute) is followed by its parameter list which is normally empty for a *get* method. When the getMinute method is called, it should return the value of minute, so it uses the keyword return followed by the identifier minute (line 21).

```
Source Editor [CookingTime *]                                    _□×
16        } // end constructor
17
18        // return minute value
19        public int getMinute()
20        {
21            return minute;
22
23        } // end method getMinute
24
```

Returning a value from a *get* method →

Figure 18.13 getMinute declaration.

2. ***Declaring a*** **set** ***method for minute.*** Add lines 25–37 of Fig. 18.14 to class CookingTime. This method should set the value of minute to the int argument it receives but first, it should test the argument to make sure that it is valid. The setMinute method should accept a value less than 60 and greater than 0, a condition that is tested on line 28. If the argument (value) is valid, it will be assigned to minute on line 30. Otherwise, the value 0 will be assigned to minute on line 34. This keeps the value of minute in a consistent state.

(cont.)

Code used to validate data ⟶

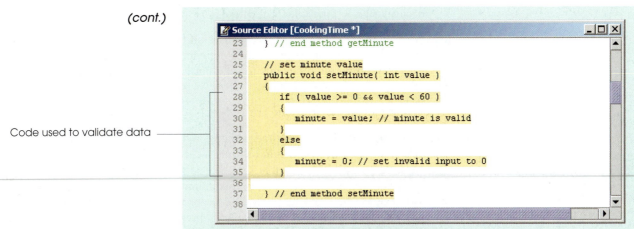

```
23        } // end method getMinute
24
25        // set minute value
26        public void setMinute( int value )
27        {
28            if ( value >= 0 && value < 60 )
29            {
30                minute = value; // minute is valid
31            }
32            else
33            {
34                minute = 0; // set invalid input to 0
35            }
36
37        } // end method setMinute
38
```

Figure 18.14   setMinute declaration.

3. *Declaring a* **get** *method for second.* Add lines 39–44 of Fig. 18.15 to your application. The getSecond method should return the value of second just as the getMinute method returned the value of minute in *Step 3*.

Code to return the **second** value ⟶

```
37        } // end method setMinute
38
39        // return second value
40        public int getSecond()
41        {
42            return second;
43
44        } // end method getSecond
45
```

Figure 18.15   getSecond declaration.

4. *Declaring a* **set** *method for second.* Add lines 46–58 of Fig. 18.16 to the CookingTime class declaration. Notice that the *set* and *get* methods for second are similar to the *set* and *get* methods for minute, except that variable second is being accessed, as opposed to the variable minute.

Method setSecond is similar to setMinute ⟶

```
44        } // end method getSecond
45
46        // set second value
47        public void setSecond( int value )
48        {
49            if ( value >= 0 && value < 60 )
50            {
51                second = value; // second is valid
52            }
53            else
54            {
55                second = 0; // set invalid input to 0
56            }
57
58        } // end method setSecond
59
```

Figure 18.16   setSecond declaration.

(cont.)

5. ***Adding the `isDone` method.*** Add lines 60–65 of Fig. 18.17 to the Cooking-Time class declaration. The `isDone` method returns a `boolean` value. It will return `true` when the time has reached zero and `false` otherwise. Line 63 tests whether `minute` and `second` are both equal to 0. If they are equal to 0, `true` is returned, otherwise `false` is returned.

Testing whether both `minute` and `second` are equal to 0

```
Source Editor [CookingTime *]                                        _ □ ×
58      } // end method setSecond
59
60      // return whether or not the time has reached zero
61      public boolean isDone()
62      {
63          return ( minute == 0 && second == 0 );
64
65      } // end method isDone
66
```

Figure 18.17   `isDone` declaration.

6. ***Using `set` methods.*** Modify lines 13–14 of Fig. 18.11 (as shown in Fig. 18.18) to call the correct *set* methods instead of storing values in `minute` and `second` directly. Now that you have declared *set* methods, you should use these *set* methods to initialize instance variables in the class constructor to ensure that only valid data will be assigned to `minute` and `second`.

Assign data by calling methods `setMinute` and `setSecond`

```
Source Editor [CookingTime *]                                        _ □ ×
11      public CookingTime( int minuteValue, int secondValue )
12      {
13          setMinute( minuteValue );
14          setSecond( secondValue );
15
16      } // end constructor
```

Figure 18.18   Constructor using *set* methods to initialize variables.

Most method calls you have written required you to precede the method call with a class name and a dot (as in `Integer.parseInt`) or a variable name and a dot (as in `calculateJButton.setBounds`). You may have noticed that some method calls do not require a class name or an object name, such as the call to `setMinute` on line 13 of Fig. 18.18. The method call on line 13 implicitly invokes `setMinute` on the object that is being constructed. Inside a method, you can explicitly refer to the object of that class on which the method was called with the keyword **this**, also called the **this reference**. For example, line 13 can be written as

```
this.setMinute( minuteValue );
```

When the compiler encounters method calls like the one in line 13, it automatically adds "`this.`" to the beginning of the method call.

7. ***Declaring the `tick` method.*** Add lines 67–82 of Fig. 18.19 to the Cooking-Time class declaration. The `tick` method will decrement the CookingTime object by one second. The class MicrowaveOven will call the `tick` method once per second to mimic an actual microwave oven timer. If the number of seconds is greater than zero (line 71), the number of seconds is decremented by one (line 73). If the value of seconds is zero but the value of minutes is greater than zero (line 76), the number of minutes is decremented by one (line 78) and the number of seconds is set to 59 (line 79).

(cont.)

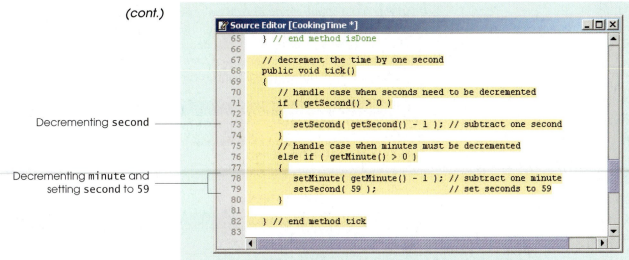

Decrementing **second**

Decrementing **minute** and setting **second** to 59

```
65        } // end method isDone
66
67        // decrement the time by one second
68        public void tick()
69        {
70            // handle case when seconds need to be decremented
71            if ( getSecond() > 0 )
72            {
73                setSecond( getSecond() - 1 ); // subtract one second
74            }
75            // handle case when minutes must be decremented
76            else if ( getMinute() > 0 )
77            {
78                setMinute( getMinute() - 1 ); // subtract one minute
79                setSecond( 59 );              // set seconds to 59
80            }
81
82        } // end method tick
83
```

Figure 18.19 Decrementing the time in the **tick** method.

8. *Saving the application.* Save your modified source code file.

9. *Opening the Command Prompt window and changing directories.* Open the **Command Prompt** window by selecting **Start > Programs > Accessories > Command Prompt**. Change to your working directory by typing cd C:\SimplyJava\MicrowaveOven.

10. *Compiling the class.* Compile the class by typing javac CookingTime.java. If your application does not compile correctly, fix the errors in your code before proceeding to the next section.

11. *Closing the Command Prompt window.* Close the **Command Prompt** window by clicking its close button.

SELF-REVIEW

1. A(n) _____ is used to ensure that data is kept in a consistent state.
   a) *get* method
   b) *return* statement
   c) boolean value
   d) *set* method

2. A *get* method is also known as a(n) _____ .
   a) constructor
   b) access modifier
   c) accessor
   d) mutator

Answers: 1) d. 2) c.

18.5 Completing the Microwave Oven Application

Now that you have completed your CookingTime class, you will use an object of this class to maintain the cooking time in your application.

Completing the Microwave Oven Application

1. *Setting the Timer's delay.* Modify line 326 as shown in Figure 18.20 in MicrowaveOven.java file. An object of class **Timer** generates an ActionEvent as each specified interval of time passes. This is similar to the ticking of a clock. The amount of time that passes during an interval between ticks is specified as the first argument in the Timer constructor and is measured in milliseconds (1/1000 second). In this application, the Timer will generate an event every 1000 milliseconds (1 second). The second argument (timerActionListener) has been declared for you in the template to handle the events generated by clockTimer.

(cont.)

Setting `clockTimer`'s delay

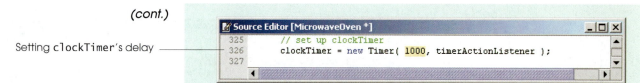

```
Source Editor [MicrowaveOven *]                              _ | □ | x |
325         // set up clockTimer
326         clockTimer = new Timer( 1000, timerActionListener );
327
```

Figure 18.20 Creating `clockTimer` with a delay of 1000 milliseconds.

2. *Formatting `currentTime`.* Remove the `return` statement that returns an empty `String` on line 408 and add lines 408–424 of Fig. 18.21 to `format-Time`. Line 409 declares `String currentTime` to hold the formatted value of `timeToDisplay` (declared in the template on line 40). The `for` loop in lines 412–415 adds `"0"` to the left of `currentTime` until its length is at least 4. Lines 418–422 shorten `currentTime` to 4 characters if it is longer. Line 424 returns `currentTime` to the calling method. To shorten `currentTime` to four characters, the `String` method **substring** is used. This method returns a `String` that is a specified portion of the original `String`, but does not modify the original `String`. Line 421 selects the first four characters of `currentTime` and assigns this value to `currentTime` by calling `substring` and passing it two arguments. The first argument, 0, indicates that the `String` returned from this method starts with the first character (at position 0) of `currentTime`. The second argument, 4, indicates that the returned `String` should end just before the character at position 4. After this line, `currentTime` will be exactly four characters long.

Copy `timeToDisplay`
into `currentTime`

```
Source Editor [MicrowaveOven *]                                      _ | □ | x |
406      private String formatTime()
407      {
408          // declare String currentTime to manipulate output
409          String currentTime = timeToDisplay;
410
411          // add zeros until currentTime is at least 4 characters long
412          for ( int i = currentTime.length(); i < 4; i++ )
413          {
414              currentTime = "0" + currentTime;
415          }
416
417          // if the length of currentTime is greater than four
418          if ( currentTime.length() > 4 )
419          {
420              // shorten currentTime to the first four characters
421              currentTime = currentTime.substring( 0, 4 );
422          }
423
424          return currentTime;
425
426      } // end method formatTime
```

Figure 18.21 Declaring `currentTime` to hold `timeToDisplay` value.

3. *Finishing the `startJButtonActionPerformed` method.* Add lines 431–445 of Fig. 18.22 to method `startJButtonActionPerformed`. Line 432 calls method `formatTime` and stores the returned `String` in `fourDigit-Time`. Lines 435–436 declare variables `minute` and `second` and assign to those variables the minute and second values entered by the user. Lines 439–440 use the `setMinute` and `setSecond` methods of your `CookingTime` object (`microwaveTime`) to set your application's initial cooking time. Lines 443–445 display the formatted, initial cooking time as a `String` containing two digits (for minutes), a colon (`:`) and another two digits (for seconds). If the time entered was 3 minutes and 20 seconds, lines 443–445 will display `"03:20"`. Each number is formatted properly by using `micro-waveTime`'s *get* methods and `timeFormat`'s format method. The `timeFormat` object is an instance of the `DecimalFormat` class created to convert a number to a `String` with at least two digits.

(cont.)

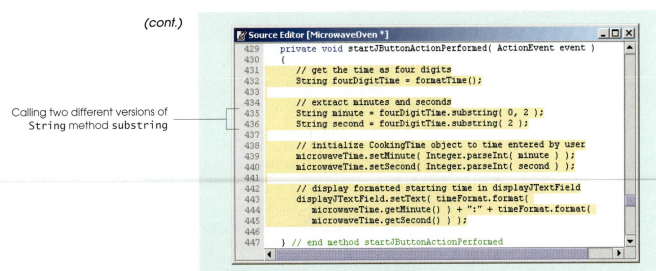

Calling two different versions of `String` method `substring`

```
Source Editor [MicrowaveOven *]                                    _ □ X

429    private void startJButtonActionPerformed( ActionEvent event )
430    {
431        // get the time as four digits
432        String fourDigitTime = formatTime();
433
434        // extract minutes and seconds
435        String minute = fourDigitTime.substring( 0, 2 );
436        String second = fourDigitTime.substring( 2 );
437
438        // initialize CookingTime object to time entered by user
439        microwaveTime.setMinute( Integer.parseInt( minute ) );
440        microwaveTime.setSecond( Integer.parseInt( second ) );
441
442        // display formatted starting time in displayJTextField
443        displayJTextField.setText( timeFormat.format(
444            microwaveTime.getMinute() ) + ":" + timeFormat.format(
445            microwaveTime.getSecond() ) );
446
447    } // end method startJButtonActionPerformed
```

Figure 18.22 Extracting minutes and seconds from `currentTime`.

Lines 435 and 436 use two different versions of the `substring` method. Line 435 uses the method that you saw previously, in *Step 3*. This method returns a substring of `fourDigits` starting at position 0 (the first argument to the method) and ending at position 2 (the second argument to the method).

Line 436 uses a second version of the `substring` method. This version takes a single argument which specifies the beginning index of the substring. This method call returns a substring of `fourDigits` beginning at index 2 and continuing to the end of the `String`.

Recall from Tutorial 14 that a class can contain two methods with the same name, but with different sets of parameters—this is called method overloading. The `substring` method is an example of an overloaded method.

4. *Starting the cooking process.* Add lines 447–450 of Fig. 18.23 to your application. Line 447 clears the user's input (`timeToDisplay`), so that the user can enter a new cooking time (after the current cook cycle). The **start** method of class `Timer` will start generating an `ActionEvent` as each interval of time (line 326 of Figure 18.20) passes. Line 449 starts `clockTimer` by calling its `start` method. The `clockTimerActionPerformed` method (which you will be implementing shortly) will now be called every second. Line 450 sets `windowJPanel`'s *background* property to yellow to simulate turning on the light inside the microwave oven.

Start timer and turn "light" on to indicate microwave oven is cooking

```
Source Editor [MicrowaveOven *]                                    _ □ X

445            microwaveTime.getSecond() ) );
446
447        timeToDisplay = ""; // clear timeToDisplay for future input
448
449        clockTimer.start();                          // start timer
450        windowJPanel.setBackground( Color.YELLOW ); // turn "light" on
451
```

Figure 18.23 Starting the **Microwave Oven** application's countdown.

(cont.)

5. ***Clearing the cooking time.*** Add lines 457–461 of Fig. 18.24 to the clear-JButtonActionPerformed method. The **stop** method of class Timer will stop clockTimer, preventing further ActionEvents from being generated. Line 458 calls clockTimer's stop method, which stops the countdown. Line 459 sets displayJTextField's text to "Microwave Oven". Line 459 clears the String timeToDisplay. Line 461 sets the JPanel's *background* property to the JPanel's original gray color to simulate turning off the light inside the microwave oven.

Code that turns off microwave and resets variables

```
Source Editor [MicrowaveOven *]                           _ □ ×
455    private void clearJButtonActionPerformed( ActionEvent event )
456    {
457        // stop Timer and reset variables to their initial settings
458        clockTimer.stop();
459        displayJTextField.setText( "Microwave Oven" );
460        timeToDisplay = "";
461        windowJPanel.setBackground( new Color( 204, 204, 204 ) );
462
```

Figure 18.24 Clearing the **Microwave Oven** input.

6. ***Displaying data as it is being input.*** Add lines 468–479 of Fig. 18.25 to the displayTime method. This method is called with a String argument, digit, each time the user enters another digit for the cooking time. On line 469, digit is appended to String timeToDisplay, which is the String that holds user input. On line 472, the formatTime method is called to turn the timeToDisplay String into four digits. Lines 475–476 declare variables minute and second and assign to those variables their respective pieces of the fourDigitTime String. Line 479 uses the setText method to display the application's initial cooking time.

Appending digit to instance variable timeToDisplay

```
Source Editor [MicrowaveOven *]                           _ □ ×
466    public void displayTime( String digit )
467    {
468        // append digit to timeToDisplay
469        timeToDisplay += digit;
470
471        // get the time as four digits
472        String fourDigitTime = formatTime();
473
474        // extract minutes and seconds
475        String minute = fourDigitTime.substring( 0, 2 );
476        String second = fourDigitTime.substring( 2 );
477
478        // display number of minutes, ":", then number of seconds
479        displayJTextField.setText( minute + ":" + second );
480
481    } // end method displayTime
```

Figure 18.25 Appending digit and formatting timeToDisplay.

7. ***Performing the countdown.*** Add lines 486–497 of Fig. 18.26 to the clockTimerActionPerformed method. Remember that this method executes once per second while the Timer is running. Line 487 calls the tick method that you declared earlier in the CookingTime class. The tick method will decrement object microwaveTime by one second. The if statement on line 490 calls the isDone method that you also declared earlier in the CookingTime class. This method will determine if the number of minutes and seconds is zero. Because of the logical negation operator (!), the if statement evaluates to true if the isDone method is false, or, in other words, if the time has not reached zero. The code in lines 493–495 displays in the displayJTextField the cooking time remaining. These lines use CookingTime's *get* methods and Decimal-Format's format method to display the cooking time properly.

(cont.)

Decrements `time` during countdown

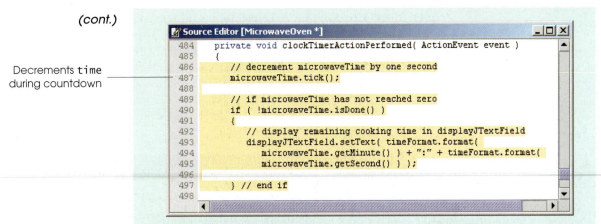

```
Source Editor [MicrowaveOven *]                              _ □ ×
484    private void clockTimerActionPerformed( ActionEvent event )
485    {
486        // decrement microwaveTime by one second
487        microwaveTime.tick();
488
489        // if microwaveTime has not reached zero
490        if ( !microwaveTime.isDone() )
491        {
492            // display remaining cooking time in displayJTextField
493            displayJTextField.setText( timeFormat.format(
494                microwaveTime.getMinute() ) + ":" + timeFormat.format(
495                microwaveTime.getSecond() ) );
496
497        } // end if
498
```

Figure 18.26 Modifying the display during countdown.

8. ***Completing the `clockTimerActionPerformed` method.*** Add lines 498–506 of Fig. 18.27 to the `clockTimerActionPerformed` method. If the `isDone` method returns `true` in the `if` statement of the previous step, then the time has reached zero and the code within the `else` statement (lines 500–504) will execute. The cooking process is stopped by calling Timer's `stop` method (line 500), the `displayJTextField` is set to `"Done!"` (line 503) and `windowJPanel`'s background color is set to its default gray color (line 504).

Stopping `clockTimer`

```
Source Editor [MicrowaveOven *]                              _ □ ×
497        } // end if
498        else // microwaveTime has reached zero
499        {
500            clockTimer.stop(); // stop timer
501
502            // inform user timer is finished
503            displayJTextField.setText( "Done!" );
504            windowJPanel.setBackground( new Color( 204, 204, 204 ) );
505
506        } // end else
507
```

Figure 18.27 Turning off the microwave when the timer runs out.

9. ***Saving the application.*** Save your modified source code file.

10. ***Opening the Command Prompt window and changing directories.*** Open the **Command Prompt** window by selecting **Start > Programs > Accessories > Command Prompt**. Change to your working directory by typing `cd C:\SimplyJava\MicrowaveOven`.

11. ***Compiling the application.*** Compile your application by typing `javac MicrowaveOven.java`.

12. ***Running the application.*** When your application compiles correctly, run it by typing `java MicrowaveOven`. Figure 18.28 shows the completed application running. Notice that your application performs as it did in the test-drive.

13. ***Closing the application.*** Close the running application by clicking its close button.

14. ***Closing the Command Prompt window.*** Close the **Command Prompt** window by clicking its close button.

(cont.)

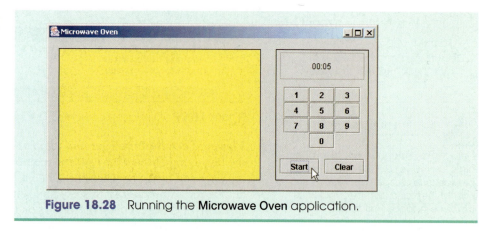

Figure 18.28   Running the **Microwave Oven** application.

SELF-REVIEW

1. Use an instance of class _____ to generate events each time an interval of time expires.

   a) Timer   b) Interval
   c) Generator   d) Clock

2. The expression example.substring(3, 4) returns the character(s) _____.

   a) that begin at position three and continues for four characters
   b) that begin at position three and ends before position four
   c) at position three and position four   d) at position 3, repeated 4 times

   Answers: 1) a. 2) b.

18.6 Controlling Access to Members

Common Programming Error

Attempting to access a private class member from outside that class is a syntax error.

Keywords **public** and **private** are called **access modifiers**. You declared instance variables with access modifier private and methods with access modifiers private and public earlier in this tutorial. Class members that are declared public are available outside of their class's declaration. The classes of the Java class library provide public methods that enable you to interact with objects of those classes (for example, calling a JTextField's setText method to display text in the JText-Field). The declaration of instance variables or methods with access modifier private makes them available only to methods of the same class. Attempting to access a class's private members from outside the class declaration is a compilation error. The classes of the Java class library also include many private variables and methods that they use to provide functionality for you, but that you cannot use directly in your own applications. Normally, instance variables are declared private, whereas methods are declared public. Now you will review the access modifiers of some of your classes' members.

Controlling Access to Members

1. ***Opening the application.*** If CookingTime.java is closed, open it in your text editor.

2. ***Viewing CookingTime's instance variables.*** View lines 7–8 of Fig. 18.29. These lines declare two private instance variables minute and second, which means that they are accessible only to members of class CookingTime. A class's private instance variables may be accessed only by methods of that class. This provides you with complete control over how the instance variables are accessed and modified by users of your class.

(cont.)

Declaring instance variables of class CookingTime, private

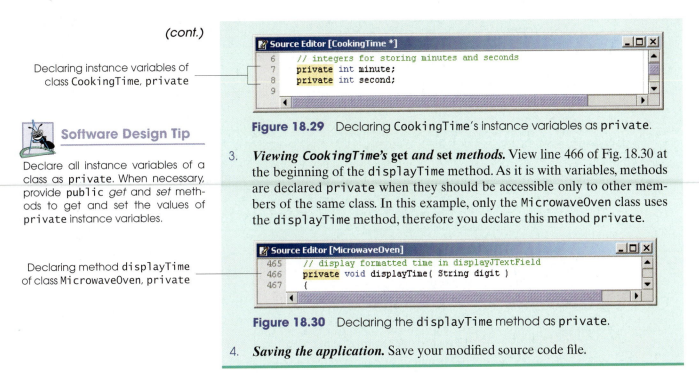

Figure 18.29 Declaring CookingTime's instance variables as private.

3. *Viewing CookingTime's get and set methods.* View line 466 of Fig. 18.30 at the beginning of the displayTime method. As it is with variables, methods are declared private when they should be accessible only to other members of the same class. In this example, only the MicrowaveOven class uses the displayTime method, therefore you declare this method private.

Declaring method displayTime of class MicrowaveOven, private

Figure 18.30 Declaring the displayTime method as private.

4. *Saving the application.* Save your modified source code file.

Software Design Tip

Declare all instance variables of a class as private. When necessary, provide public *get* and *set* methods to get and set the values of private instance variables.

Figure 18.31 and Figure 18.32 present the source code for the **Microwave Oven** application. The lines of code that you added, viewed or modified in this tutorial are highlighted.

```
1   // Tutorial 18: MicrowaveOven.java
2   // Mimics the behavior of a microwave oven.
3   import java.awt.*;
4   import java.awt.event.*;
5   import java.text.DecimalFormat;
6   import javax.swing.*;
7   import javax.swing.border.*;
8
9   public class MicrowaveOven extends JFrame
10  {
11     // JPanel for microwave window
12     private JPanel windowJPanel;
13
14     // JPanel for microwave controls
15     private JPanel controlJPanel;
16
17     // JTextField for cooking time
18     private JTextField displayJTextField;
19
20     // JButtons to set cooking time
21     private JButton oneJButton;
22     private JButton twoJButton;
23     private JButton threeJButton;
24     private JButton fourJButton;
25     private JButton fiveJButton;
26     private JButton sixJButton;
27     private JButton sevenJButton;
28     private JButton eightJButton;
29     private JButton nineJButton;
30     private JButton zeroJButton;
```

Figure 18.31 Completed **Microwave Oven** source code. (Part 1 of 10.)

```
31
32        // JButtons to start and clear timer
33        private JButton startJButton;
34        private JButton clearJButton;
35
36        // Timer to count down seconds
37        private Timer clockTimer;
38
39        // String for storing digits entered by user
40        private String timeToDisplay = "";
41
42        // CookingTime instance for storing the current time
43        private CookingTime microwaveTime = new CookingTime( 0, 0 );
44
45        // DecimalFormat to format time output
46        private DecimalFormat timeFormat = new DecimalFormat( "00" );
47
48        // no-argument constructor
49        public MicrowaveOven()
50        {
51           createUserInterface();
52        }
53
54        // create and position GUI components; register event handlers
55        private void createUserInterface()
56        {
57           // get content pane for attaching GUI components
58           Container contentPane = getContentPane();
59
60           // enable explicit positioning of GUI components
61           contentPane.setLayout( null );
62
63           // set up windowJPanel
64           windowJPanel = new JPanel();
65           windowJPanel.setBounds( 16, 16, 328, 205 );
66           windowJPanel.setBorder( new LineBorder( Color.BLACK ) );
67           contentPane.add( windowJPanel );
68
69           // set up controlJPanel
70           controlJPanel = new JPanel();
71           controlJPanel.setBounds( 368, 16, 149, 205 );
72           controlJPanel.setBorder( new LineBorder( Color.BLACK ) );
73           controlJPanel.setLayout( null );
74           contentPane.add( controlJPanel );
75
76           // set up displayJTextField
77           displayJTextField = new JTextField();
78           displayJTextField.setBounds( 7, 5, 135, 42 );
79           displayJTextField.setText( "Microwave Oven" );
80           displayJTextField.setHorizontalAlignment( JTextField.CENTER );
81           displayJTextField.setEditable( false );
82           controlJPanel.add( displayJTextField );
83
84           // set up oneJButton
85           oneJButton = new JButton();
86           oneJButton.setBounds( 13, 59, 41, 24 );
87           oneJButton.setText( "1" );
88           controlJPanel.add( oneJButton );
```

Declaring private instance
variable timeToDisplay

Declaring private instance
variable cookingTime

Figure 18.31 Completed **Microwave Oven** source code. (Part 2 of 10.)

```
89          oneJButton.addActionListener(
90
91             new ActionListener() // anonymous inner class
92             {
93                // event handler called when oneJButton is pressed
94                public void actionPerformed( ActionEvent event )
95                {
96                   oneJButtonActionPerformed( event );
97                }
98
99             } // end anonymous inner class
100
101         ); // end call to addActionListener
102
103         // set up twoJButton
104         twoJButton = new JButton();
105         twoJButton.setBounds( 54, 59, 41, 24 );
106         twoJButton.setText( "2" );
107         controlJPanel.add( twoJButton );
108         twoJButton.addActionListener(
109
110            new ActionListener() // anonymous inner class
111            {
112               // event handler called when twoJButton is pressed
113               public void actionPerformed( ActionEvent event )
114               {
115                  twoJButtonActionPerformed( event );
116               }
117
118            } // end anonymous inner class
119
120         ); // end call to addActionListener
121
122         // set up threeJButton
123         threeJButton = new JButton();
124         threeJButton.setBounds( 95, 59, 41, 24 );
125         threeJButton.setText( "3" );
126         controlJPanel.add( threeJButton );
127         threeJButton.addActionListener(
128
129            new ActionListener() // anonymous inner class
130            {
131               // event handler called when threeJButton is pressed
132               public void actionPerformed( ActionEvent event )
133               {
134                  threeJButtonActionPerformed( event );
135               }
136
137            } // end anonymous inner class
138
139         ); // end call to addActionListener
140
141         // set up fourJButton
142         fourJButton = new JButton();
143         fourJButton.setBounds( 13, 83, 41, 24 );
144         fourJButton.setText( "4" );
145         controlJPanel.add( fourJButton );
146         fourJButton.addActionListener(
```

Figure 18.31 Completed **Microwave Oven** source code. (Part 3 of 10.)

```
147
148          new ActionListener() // anonymous inner class
149          {
150             // event handler called when fourJButton is pressed
151             public void actionPerformed( ActionEvent event )
152             {
153                fourJButtonActionPerformed( event );
154             }
155
156          } // end anonymous inner class
157
158       ); // end call to addActionListener
159
160       // set up fiveJButton
161       fiveJButton = new JButton();
162       fiveJButton.setBounds( 54, 83, 41, 24 );
163       fiveJButton.setText( "5" );
164       controlJPanel.add( fiveJButton );
165       fiveJButton.addActionListener(
166
167          new ActionListener() // anonymous inner class
168          {
169             // event handler called when fiveJButton is pressed
170             public void actionPerformed( ActionEvent event )
171             {
172                fiveJButtonActionPerformed( event );
173             }
174
175          } // end anonymous inner class
176
177       ); // end call to addActionListener
178
179       // set up sixJButton
180       sixJButton = new JButton();
181       sixJButton.setBounds( 95, 83, 41, 24 );
182       sixJButton.setText( "6" );
183       controlJPanel.add( sixJButton );
184       sixJButton.addActionListener(
185
186          new ActionListener() // anonymous inner class
187          {
188             // event handler called when sixJButton is pressed
189             public void actionPerformed( ActionEvent event )
190             {
191                sixJButtonActionPerformed( event );
192             }
193
194          } // end anonymous inner class
195
196       ); // end call to addActionListener
197
198       // set up sevenJButton
199       sevenJButton = new JButton();
200       sevenJButton.setBounds( 13, 107, 41, 24 );
201       sevenJButton.setText( "7" );
202       controlJPanel.add( sevenJButton );
203       sevenJButton.addActionListener(
204
```

Figure 18.31 Completed **Microwave Oven** source code. (Part 4 of 10.)

```
205          new ActionListener() // anonymous inner class
206          {
207             // event handler called when sevenJButton is pressed
208             public void actionPerformed( ActionEvent event )
209             {
210                sevenJButtonActionPerformed( event );
211             }
212
213          } // end anonymous inner class
214
215       ); // end call to addActionListener
216
217       // set up eightJButton
218       eightJButton = new JButton();
219       eightJButton.setBounds( 54, 107, 41, 24 );
220       eightJButton.setText( "8" );
221       controlJPanel.add( eightJButton );
222       eightJButton.addActionListener(
223
224          new ActionListener() // anonymous inner class
225          {
226             // event handler called when eightJButton is pressed
227             public void actionPerformed( ActionEvent event )
228             {
229                eightJButtonActionPerformed( event );
230             }
231
232          } // end anonymous inner class
233
234       ); // end call to addActionListener
235
236       // set up nineJButton
237       nineJButton = new JButton();
238       nineJButton.setBounds( 95, 107, 41, 24 );
239       nineJButton.setText( "9" );
240       controlJPanel.add( nineJButton );
241       nineJButton.addActionListener(
242
243          new ActionListener() // anonymous inner class
244          {
245             // event handler called when nineJButton is pressed
246             public void actionPerformed( ActionEvent event )
247             {
248                nineJButtonActionPerformed( event );
249             }
250
251          } // end anonymous inner class
252
253       ); // end call to addActionListener
254
255       // set up zeroJButton
256       zeroJButton = new JButton();
257       zeroJButton.setBounds( 54, 131, 41, 24 );
258       zeroJButton.setText( "0" );
259       controlJPanel.add( zeroJButton );
260       zeroJButton.addActionListener(
261
```

Figure 18.31 Completed **Microwave Oven** source code. (Part 5 of 10.)

```
262              new ActionListener() // anonymous inner class
263              {
264                 // event handler called when zeroJButton is pressed
265                 public void actionPerformed( ActionEvent event )
266                 {
267                    zeroJButtonActionPerformed( event );
268                 }
269
270              } // end anonymous inner class
271
272           ); // end call to addActionListener
273
274           // set up startJButton
275           startJButton = new JButton();
276           startJButton.setBounds( 7, 171, 64, 24 );
277           startJButton.setText( "Start" );
278           controlJPanel.add( startJButton );
279           startJButton.addActionListener(
280
281              new ActionListener() // anonymous inner class
282              {
283                 // event handler called when startJButton is pressed
284                 public void actionPerformed( ActionEvent event )
285                 {
286                    startJButtonActionPerformed( event );
287                 }
288
289              } // end anonymous inner class
290
291           ); // end call to addActionListener
292
293           // set up clearJButton
294           clearJButton = new JButton();
295           clearJButton.setBounds( 79, 171, 64, 24 );
296           clearJButton.setText( "Clear" );
297           controlJPanel.add( clearJButton );
298           clearJButton.addActionListener(
299
300              new ActionListener() // anonymous inner class
301              {
302                 // event handler called when clearJButton is pressed
303                 public void actionPerformed( ActionEvent event )
304                 {
305                    clearJButtonActionPerformed( event );
306                 }
307
308              } // end anonymous inner class
309
310           ); // end call to addActionListener
311
312           // set up timerActionListener
313           ActionListener timerActionListener =
314
315              new ActionListener() // anonymous inner class
316              {
317                 // event handler called every 1000 milliseconds
318                 public void actionPerformed( ActionEvent event )
319                 {
```

Figure 18.31   Completed **Microwave Oven** source code. (Part 6 of 10.)

```
320                    clockTimerActionPerformed( event );
321              }
322
323          }; // end anonymous inner class
324
325       // set up clockTimer
326       clockTimer = new Timer( 1000, timerActionListener );
327
328       // set properties of application's window
329       setTitle( "Microwave Oven" ); // set title bar string
330       setSize( 536, 261 );          // set window size
331       setVisible( true );           // display window
332
333    } // end method createUserInterface
334
335    // add digit 1 to timeToDisplay
336    private void oneJButtonActionPerformed( ActionEvent event )
337    {
338       displayTime( "1" ); // display time input properly
339
340    } // end method oneJButtonActionPerformed
341
342    // add digit 2 to timeToDisplay
343    private void twoJButtonActionPerformed( ActionEvent event )
344    {
345       displayTime( "2" ); // display time input properly
346
347    } // end method twoJButtonActionPerformed
348
349    // add digit 3 to timeToDisplay
350    private void threeJButtonActionPerformed( ActionEvent event )
351    {
352       displayTime( "3" ); // display time input properly
353
354    } // end method threeJButtonActionPerformed
355
356    // add digit 4 to timeToDisplay
357    private void fourJButtonActionPerformed( ActionEvent event )
358    {
359       displayTime( "4" ); // display time input properly
360
361    } // end method fourJButtonActionPerformed
362
363    // add digit 5 to timeToDisplay
364    private void fiveJButtonActionPerformed( ActionEvent event )
365    {
366       displayTime( "5" ); // display time input properly
367
368    } // end method fiveJButtonActionPerformed
369
370    // add digit 6 to timeToDisplay
371    private void sixJButtonActionPerformed( ActionEvent event )
372    {
373       displayTime( "6" ); // display time input properly
374
375    } // end method sixJButtonActionPerformed
376
```

Figure 18.31　Completed **Microwave Oven** source code. (Part 7 of 10.)

```
377    // add digit 7 to timeToDisplay
378    private void sevenJButtonActionPerformed( ActionEvent event )
379    {
380       displayTime( "7" ); // display time input properly
381
382    } // end method sevenJButtonActionPerformed
383
384    // add digit 8 to timeToDisplay
385    private void eightJButtonActionPerformed( ActionEvent event )
386    {
387       displayTime( "8" ); // display time input properly
388
389    } // end method eightJButtonActionPerformed
390
391    // add digit 9 to timeToDisplay
392    private void nineJButtonActionPerformed( ActionEvent event )
393    {
394       displayTime( "9" ); // display time input properly
395
396    } // end method nineJButtonActionPerformed
397
398    // add digit 0 to timeToDisplay
399    private void zeroJButtonActionPerformed( ActionEvent event )
400    {
401       displayTime( "0" ); // display time input properly
402
403    } // end method zeroJButtonActionPerformed
404
405    // format the time so that it has exactly four digits
406    private String formatTime()
407    {
408       // declare String currentTime to manipulate output
409       String currentTime = timeToDisplay;
410
411       // add zeros to currentTime until it is 4 characters long
412       for ( int i = currentTime.length(); i < 4; i++ )
413       {
414          currentTime = "0" + currentTime;
415       }
416
417       // if the length of currentTime is greater than four
418       if ( currentTime.length() > 4 )
419       {
420          // shorten currentTime to the first four characters
421          currentTime = currentTime.substring( 0, 4 );
422       }
423
424       return currentTime;
425
426    } // end method formatTime
427
428    // start the microwave oven
429    private void startJButtonActionPerformed( ActionEvent event )
430    {
431       // get the time as four digits
432       String fourDigitTime = formatTime();
433
```

Lengthening the time, if necessary —— (line 414)

Shortening the time, if necessary —— (line 421)

Storing the time as exactly four digitis —— (line 432)

Figure 18.31   Completed **Microwave Oven** source code. (Part 8 of 10.)

```
434          // extract minutes and seconds
435          String minute = fourDigitTime.substring( 0, 2 );
436          String second = fourDigitTime.substring( 2 );
437
438          // initialize CookingTime object to time entered by user
439          microwaveTime.setMinute( Integer.parseInt( minute ) );
440          microwaveTime.setSecond( Integer.parseInt( second ) );
441
442          // display formatted starting time in displayJTextField
443          displayJTextField.setText( timeFormat.format(
444             microwaveTime.getMinute() ) + ":" + timeFormat.format(
445             microwaveTime.getSecond() ) );
446
447          timeToDisplay = ""; // clear timeToDisplay for future input
448
449          clockTimer.start();                          // start timer
450          windowJPanel.setBackground( Color.YELLOW ); // turn "light" on
451
452       } // end method startJButtonActionPerformed
453
454       // clear the microwave oven
455       private void clearJButtonActionPerformed( ActionEvent event )
456       {
457          // stop Timer and reset variables to their initial settings
458          clockTimer.stop();
459          displayJTextField.setText( "Microwave Oven" );
460          timeToDisplay = "";
461          windowJPanel.setBackground( new Color( 204, 204, 204 ) );
462
463       } // end method clearJButtonActionPerformed
464
465       // display formatted time in displayJTextField
466       private void displayTime( String digit )
467       {
468          // append digit to timeToDisplay
469          timeToDisplay += digit;
470
471          // get the time as four digits
472          String fourDigitTime = formatTime();
473
474          // extract minutes and seconds
475          String minute = fourDigitTime.substring( 0, 2 );
476          String second = fourDigitTime.substring( 2 );
477
478          // display number of minutes, ":", and then number of seconds
479          displayJTextField.setText( minute + ":" + second );
480
481       } // end method displayTime
482
483       // decrement displayJTextField by one second
484       private void clockTimerActionPerformed( ActionEvent event )
485       {
486          // decrement microwaveTime by one second
487          microwaveTime.tick();
488
489          // if microwaveTime has not reached zero
490          if ( !microwaveTime.isDone() )
491          {
```

Labels (left margin, top to bottom):
- Obtaining the minutes and seconds → lines 435–436
- Setting the minutes and seconds for the cooking time → lines 439–440
- Displaying the initial cooking time → lines 443–445
- Starting the microwave → line 449
- Stopping the microwave and clearing the cooking time → lines 458–461
- Adding a digit to the time → line 469
- Storing the time as exactly four digitis → line 472
- Obtaining the minutes and seconds → lines 475–476
- Outputting the formatted time → line 479
- Decrementing the cooking time → line 487

Figure 18.31 Completed **Microwave Oven** source code. (Part 9 of 10.)

Displaying the remaining cooking time

```
492          // display remaining cooking time in displayJTextField
493          displayJTextField.setText( timeFormat.format(
494             microwaveTime.getMinute() ) + ":" + timeFormat.format(
495             microwaveTime.getSecond() ) );
496
497       } // end if
498       else // microwaveTime has reached zero
499       {
500          clockTimer.stop(); // stop timer
501
502          // inform user timer is finished
503          displayJTextField.setText( "Done!" );
504          windowJPanel.setBackground( new Color( 204, 204, 204 ) );
505
506       } // end else
507
508    } // end method clockTimerActionPerformed
509
510    // main method
511    public static void main( String args[] )
512    {
513       MicrowaveOven application = new MicrowaveOven();
514       application.setDefaultCloseOperation( JFrame.EXIT_ON_CLOSE );
515
516    } // end method main
517
518 } // end class MicrowaveOven
```

Stopping the microwave — line 500

Notifying the user that the microwave has stopped — lines 503–504

Figure 18.31   Completed **Microwave Oven** source code. (Part 10 of 10.)

```
1  // Tutorial 18: CookingTime.java
2  // Represents time data and contains get and set methods.
3
4  public class CookingTime
5  {
6     // integers for storing minutes and seconds
7     private int minute;
8     private int second;
9
10    // CookingTime constructor, minute and second supplied
11    public CookingTime( int minuteValue, int secondValue )
12    {
13       setMinute( minuteValue );
14       setSecond( secondValue );
15
16    } // end constructor
17
18    // return minute value
19    public int getMinute()
20    {
21       return minute;
22
23    } // end method getMinute
24
25    // set minute value
26    public void setMinute( int value )
27    {
```

Declaring private instance variables of class CookingTime — lines 7–8

Constructor of class CookingTime — lines 11–16

Returning value of instance variable minute — line 21

Figure 18.32   Completed class **CookingTime** source code (Part 1 of 2.)

```
28          if ( value >= 0 && value < 60 )
29          {
30              minute = value; // minute is valid
31          }
32          else
33          {
34              minute = 0; // set invalid input to 0
35          }
36
37       } // end method setMinute
38
39       // return second value
40       public int getSecond()
41       {
42          return second;
43
44       } // end method getSecond
45
46       // set second value
47       public void setSecond( int value )
48       {
49          if ( value >= 0 && value < 60 )
50          {
51              second = value; // second is valid
52          }
53          else
54          {
55              second = 0; // set invalid input to 0
56          }
57
58       } // end method setSecond
59
60       // return whether or not the time has reached zero
61       public boolean isDone()
62       {
63          return ( minute == 0 && second == 0 );
64
65       } // end method isDone
66
67       // decrement the time by one second
68       public void tick()
69       {
70          // handle case when seconds need to be decremented
71          if ( getSecond() > 0 )
72          {
73              setSecond( getSecond() - 1 ); // subtract one second
74          }
75          // handle case when minutes must be decremented
76          else if ( getMinute() > 0 )
77          {
78              setMinute( getMinute() - 1 ); // subtract one minute
79              setSecond( 59 );              // set seconds to 59
80          }
81
82       } // end method tick
83
84    } // end class CookingTime
```

Annotations:
- Validating user input for instance variable **minute** (lines 28–35)
- Returning value of instance variable **second** (line 42)
- Validating user input for instance variable **second** (lines 49–56)
- Testing whether both **minute** and **second** are equal to 0 (line 63)
- Decrementing **second** (line 73)
- Decrementing **minute** and setting **second** to 59 (lines 78–79)

Figure 18.32   Completed class CookingTime source code (Part 2 of 2.)

1. All instance variable declarations should begin with which of the following keywords?

   a) `int`   b) `private`
   c) `public`   d) any of the above.

2. The access modifier _____ specifies that members can only be accessed from within the member's class.

   a) `private`   b) `public`
   c) `dimensional`   d) none of the above.

Answers: 1) b. 2) a.

18.7 `main` Method

You have learned that methods declared `public` are accessible outside of the class in which they are declared. You will now learn about a special `public` method in Java, the **`main`** method. The `main` method is the **entry point** of the application—when the application starts, `main` is the first method that executes. The job of the `main` method is to start the application's execution.

Viewing the main Method

1. *Opening the application.* If `MicrowaveOven.java` is closed, open it in your text editor.

2. *Viewing the `main` Method.* Consider line 511 of Fig. 18.33. This line is the method header for the `main` method. This method is declared `public`, which allows it to be called from outside the class. It returns `void` and takes a `String` array named `args` as its argument. This array allows the user to pass **command-line arguments** to the application when it starts. (You will use this functionality in Tutorial 26.) The `main` method is also declared **`static`**. A method that is `static` can be called without first creating an instance (object) of the class. You have already seen examples of `static` methods—for example, method `parseInt` is a `static` method of class `Integer` and method `showMessageDialog` is a `static` method of class `JOptionPane`.

   Declaring the `main` method `static` allows Java to invoke `main` without creating an instance of the class. In many applications `main`'s task is to create an instance of the class, which creates the GUI and displays the application window. Line 513 in the `main` method creates a new instance of type `Micro-waveOven`. This line calls `MicrowaveOven`'s constructor.

   main is declared `static`
   Calling `MicrowaveOven`'s constructor

```
510        // main method
511        public static void main( String args[] )
512        {
513            MicrowaveOven application = new MicrowaveOven();
514            application.setDefaultCloseOperation( JFrame.EXIT_ON_CLOSE );
```

Figure 18.33 Method header for the `main` method.

3. *Viewing `MicrowaveOven`'s constructor.* Consider lines 49–52 of Fig. 18.34. Line 49 begins the declaration of class `MicrowaveOven`'s constructor. Line 51 calls method `createUserInterface` (declared in lines 54–332), which then creates and sets up all the GUI components, registers the event handlers and displays the GUI.

(cont.)

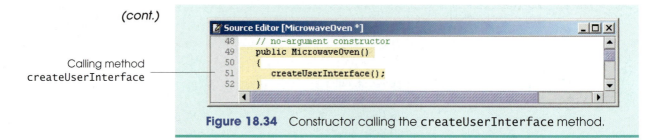

Figure 18.34 Constructor calling the `createUserInterface` method.

Calling method
`createUserInterface`

18.8 Using the Debugger: The watch Command

Now you will enhance your knowledge of the debugger by studying the **watch** command. The **watch** command tells the debugger to watch an instance variable. When that instance variable changes, the debugger will notify you. In this section, you will learn how to use the **watch** command to see how the `CookingTime` object's instance variable `second` is modified during the execution of the application.

Using the Debugger: Using the watch command

1. **Opening the Command Prompt and changing directories.** Open the **Command Prompt** window by selecting **Start > Programs > Accessories > Command Prompt.** Change to your working directory by typing cd `C:\SimplyJava\MicrowaveOven`.

2. **Compiling the application for debugging.** Compile your application by typing `javac -g MicrowaveOven.java CookingTime.java`. This command compiles both `MicrowaveOven.java` and `CookingTime.java`. Recall that the `-g` option compiles the application for use with the debugger.

3. **Starting the debugger.** Start the debugger by typing `jdb`.

4. **Watching a class's instance variable.** Set a watch on `CookingTime`'s `second` field by typing **watch** `CookingTime.second` (Fig. 18.35). You can set a watch on any instance variable during execution of the debugger. Whenever the value in an instance variable is changed, the debugger enters break mode and notifies you that the value will change. Watches can be placed only on instance variables.

Setting a watch

```
C:\SimplyJava\MicrowaveOven>jdb
Initializing jdb ...
> watch CookingTime.second
Deferring watch modification of CookingTime.second.
It will be set after the class is loaded.
>
```

Figure 18.35 Setting a watch on `CookingTime`'s instance variable `second`.

5. **Running the application.** Run the application with the command run `MicrowaveOven`. The debugger will now notify you that instance variable `second` will change (Fig. 18.36). When the application begins, an instance of `CookingTime` is created and a reference to it is assigned to the `microwaveTime` instance variable. When the constructor for this object runs, it sets both `minute` and `second` of the `CookingTime` object to 0. The debugger notifies you that the value of `second` will be set to 0. Type `cont` to continue.

(cont.)

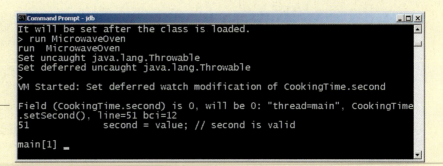

Debugger notifying you when the value changes

Figure 18.36 **Microwave Oven** application stops when `microwaveTime` is created.

6. *Adding time to the microwave oven.* Press the JButtons **1, 3** and **0** in that order (Fig. 18.37). Press the **Start** JButton—the code on line 439 of Fig. 18.31 sets the `second` variable. The debugger notifies you that instance variable `second` will change. Note that while line 439 of Microwave-Oven.java calls method `setSecond`, it is line 51 of CookingTime's method `setSecond` which actually changes the value of `second`.

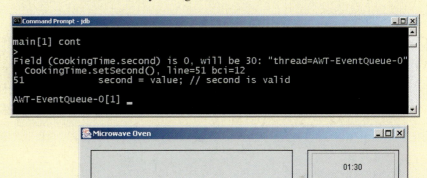

Figure 18.37 Changing the value of **second** by starting the microwave.

7. *Continuing execution.* Type `cont`—the application will continue executing (Fig. 18.38). After about a second, the timer will generate an event and the application will enter break mode again. When the timer generates an event, the `cookingTime` is decremented. This causes a change in instance variable `second`. The debugger again notifie\s you that `second` will change.

8. *Removing the watch on the variable.* Remove the debugger's watch on the variable by typing **unwatch** `CookingTime.second` (Fig. 18.39). Type `cont`—the application will continue executing without re-entering break mode.

9. *Closing the running application.* Close your running application by clicking its close button. The debugger will stop when the application closes.

10. *Closing the Command Prompt window.* Close the **Command Prompt** window by clicking its close button.

(cont.)

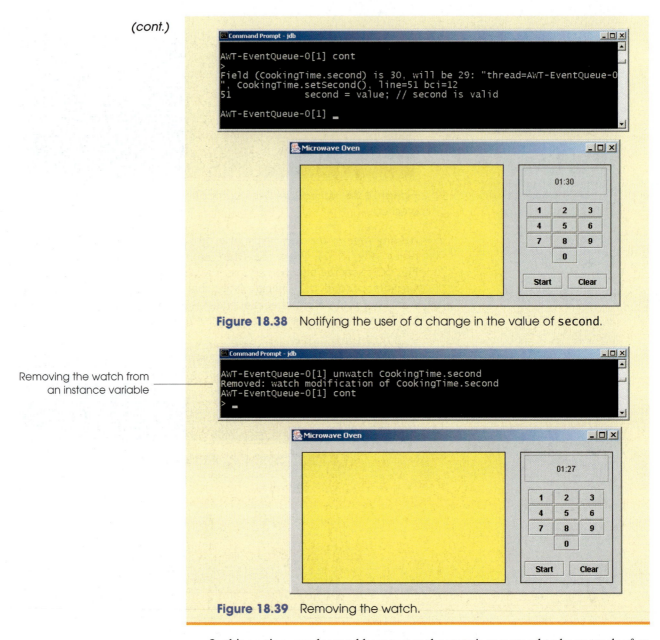

Figure 18.38   Notifying the user of a change in the value of **second**.

Removing the watch from
an instance variable

Figure 18.39   Removing the watch.

In this section, you learned how to use the `watch` command to keep track of an instance variable throughout the life of an application.

SELF-REVIEW   1. The `watch` command allows you to view all changes to a(n) _____.

    a) object   b) `int` variable

    c) local variable   d) instance variable

2. Watches can be removed using the _____ command.

    a) `unwatch`   b) `remove`

    c) `ignore`   d) `clear`

Answers: 1) d. 2) a.

18.9 Wrap-Up

In this tutorial, you learned how to create your own classes—also known as programmer-declared classes—to provide functionality not available in the Java class

library. In the world of Java programming, applications are created by using a combination of Java class library classes and methods and programmer-declared classes and methods.

You created a microwave oven simulator using a programmer-declared class called CookingTime. You added a constructor, instance variables and two pairs of *get* and *set* methods to the CookingTime class. You declared your constructor to initialize the class's instance variables. For each instance variable, you declared *get* and *set* methods that allow the class's instance variables to be safely accessed and modified. You then applied what you have already learned about using classes and methods to create a CookingTime object. You used the methods of class CookingTime to access and display the number of minutes and number of seconds that the user has specified as the microwave oven's cooking time and used a JPanel to simulate the microwave oven's glass door. You concluded the tutorial by learning how to follow the value of a variable as it changes in the debugger using the watch command.

In the next tutorial, you will learn about collections. The Java class library provides several collection classes, which enable you to store collections of data in an organized way. A collection can be thought of as a group of items. You will use collections to create a shipping hub application that stores information about several parcels that are being shipped to various destinations. Each parcel will be declared by using a Parcel programmer-declared class. Several Parcel objects will be maintained by using collections.

SKILLS SUMMARY

Declaring a Class

- Use keyword class, followed by the name of the class.
- Add instance variables and methods to the class's body.

Declaring *Get* and *Set* Methods

- Declare *get* and *set* methods to access and modify instance variables, respectively.
- In the *get* method, provide code to return the value of an instance variable.
- In the *set* method, provide code to modify and perform validity checking on the value of an instance variable.

Declaring a Constructor

- Use keyword public, followed by the name of the class, followed by a set of parentheses enclosing any parameters for the constructor.
- Add code to the constructor to initialize the object's data.

Getting a Substring

- Call String method substring with two arguments. The first argument is the beginning position of the substring and the second argument is one past the end position.
- Call String method substring with one argument. The argument is the beginning position of the substring and it continues to the end of the original String.

Controlling access to members

- Declare a member public if you want to allow clients of the class access to that member.
- Declare a member private if you do not want to allow clients of the class access to that member.

KEY TERMS

access modifier—Keywords public and private are called access modifier.

accessor—A *get* method.

class keyword—Indicates that what follows is a class declaration.

class's body—Code that is included in the { and } of a class declaration.

client—When you create and use an object of a class in an application, your application is known as a client of that class.

command-line arguments—Information passed to an application during startup.

consistent state—A way to maintain the values of an object's instance variables such that those values are always valid.

constructor—Initializes a class's variables and has the same name as the class that contains it. They are similar to methods, but do not have a return type.

entry point—The location in an application's source code where execution begins. In Java, the entry point for an application is the `main` method.

extensible language—A language that can be "extended" with new classes.

get **method**—Used to retrieve a value of an instance variable.

instance—Also known as an object.

instantiate an object—Create an object of a class.

`main` **method**—When an application is run, this is the first method of the application class that is called by Java.

members of a class—Methods and variables declared within the body of a class.

mutator—A *set* method.

new keyword—Creates a new instance of the object that follows this keyword.

`private` **keyword**—Access modifier that makes instance variables or methods accessible only to methods of that class.

programmer-declared class—Class that a programmer declares, as opposed to a class predeclared in the Java class library.

`public` **keyword**—Access modifier that makes instance variables or methods accessible wherever your application has a reference to that object.

set **method**—Sets the value of an instance variable. Validates the value to ensure that it is appropriate for the variable that is being set.

`start` **method of class** `Timer`—Starts generating an `ActionEvent` as each interval of time (specified in `Timer`'s constructor) passes.

`static`—Modifier which allows access to a method without requiring an instance of that method's class.

`stop` **method of class** `Timer`—Stops the `Timer` and prevents further `ActionEvents` from being generated.

`substring` **method of class** `String`—Returns a `String` that is a specified portion of the original `String`.

`this` `keyword`—Provides a reference to the current object.

`Timer` **class**—An object of class `Timer` can generate an `ActionEvent` as each specified interval of time passes. This is similar to the ticking of a clock in the real world.

unwatch command (in the debugger)—Removes the watch from a variable.

watch command (in the debugger)—Puts a watch on an instance variable. The debugger then notifies you every time the variable is modified.

JAVA LIBRARY REFERENCE

`Timer`   The `Timer` class provides methods to schedule tasks to be performed at future times.

■ *Constructor*

`Timer`—Takes an `int` and an object that handles `ActionEvents` as arguments. The first argument is the interval (in milliseconds) for the `Timer`. Each time the interval expires, an `ActionEvent` will be generated.

```
private Timer clockTimer = new Timer( 1000, timerActionListener )
```

■ *Methods*

`start`—Starts the timer.
`stop`—Stops the timer.

`String`   The `String` class represents a series of characters treated as a single unit.

■ *Methods*

`substring`—Returns a `String` that is a specified portion of the original `String`.

MULTIPLE-CHOICE QUESTIONS

18.1 A good name for a method that would set the value of instance variable `number` while ensuring its validity is _____.

   a) `number`   b) `set`

   c) `setNumber`   d) `setValid`

18.2 Keyword(s) _____ begin(s) a class declaration.

   a) `new class`   b) `declare class`

   c) `declare`   d) `class`

18.3 Keyword _____ is used to create an object.

   a) `object`   b) `instantiate`

   c) `create`   d) `new`

18.4 The code segment, `sample`_____ returns the length of `String sample`.

   a) `.getLength`   b) `.getLength()`

   c) `.length`   d) `.length()`

18.5 A _____ is used to retrieve the value of an instance variable.

   a) *get* method   b) `return` statement

   c) value method   d) *set* method

18.6 A `private` instance variable can not be initialized _____.

   a) when declared   b) outside of its declaring class

   c) in a constructor   d) to its default values

18.7 An important difference between constructors and methods is that _____.

   a) constructors cannot specify a return type

   b) constructors cannot specify any parameters

   c) constructors appear before methods in the same file

   d) constructors can assign values to instance variables

18.8 A class can yield many _____, just as a primitive type can yield many variables.

   a) names   b) objects

   c) values   d) types

18.9 *Set* methods enable you to _____.

   a) provide range checking   b) modify data

   c) provide data validation   d) All of the above.

18.10 Instance variables declared `private` are not directly accessible _____.

   a) outside the class   b) by other methods of the same class

   c) by the constructor of the class d) inside the same class

EXERCISES

18.11 (*Triangle Creator Application*) Create an application that allows the user to enter the lengths for the three sides of a triangle as integers. Your application should then determine whether the triangle is a right triangle (two sides of the triangle form a 90-degree angle), an equilateral triangle (all sides of equal length) or neither. Your application's GUI is completed for you (Fig. 18.40). You must create a class to represent a triangle object and declare the `createJButtonActionPerformed` method.

   a) *Copying the template to your working directory.* Copy the directory `C:\Examples\ Tutorial18\Exercises\TriangleCreator` to your `C:\SimplyJava` directory.

   b) *Opening the template files.* Open the `TriangleCreator.java` and `Triangle.java` files in your text editor.

   c) *Declaring variables.* View the `Triangle.java` file and declare three `int` variables (`side1`, `side2`, `side3`) starting on line 6 to hold the length of each side. They should all be declared `private` so that only the methods of this class can access them.

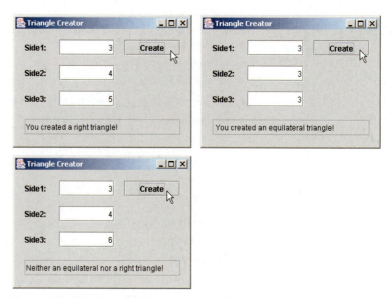

Figure 18.40 **Triangle Creator** application with all possible outputs.

d) *Declaring the necessary* **get** *and* **set** *methods.* After the instance variable declarations declare a constructor that will take the lengths of the three sides of a triangle as arguments. Your constructor should always set instance variables by using corresponding *set* methods. Following the constructor, create three pairs of *get* and *set* methods that enable clients to access and modify the lengths of the three sides. If the user enters a negative value, that side should be assigned the value zero. Use this tutorial's CookingTime class as your guide in creating the *get* and *set* methods.

e) *Adding additional features.* Following the *get* and *set* methods, create a method named isRightTriangle and a method named isEquilateral in the Triangle class. These methods are similar to *get* methods except that they return boolean values. The isRightTriangle method returns whether or not the sides form a right triangle using the Pythagorean theorem. This theorem states that in a right triangle the sum of the squares of the two shorter sides of the triangle equal the square of the longest side of the triangle. Make sure that your method's return value is not affected by the order of sides, as any of the three sides could be the largest. The isEquilateral method returns whether or not the sides form an equilateral triangle, which is true only if all the sides are equal.

f) *Adding code to the* **createJButtonActionPerformed** *method.* Now that you have created your Triangle class, you can use it to create objects in your application. Switch to the TriangleCreator.java file. In the createJButtonActionPerformed method declare three new ints starting on line 114 to store the three lengths from the JTextFields; then, use those values to create a new Triangle object.

g) *Displaying the result.* Use an if...else statement to determine if the triangle is a right triangle, an equilateral triangle or neither. Display the result in the messageJTextField.

h) *Saving the application.* Save your modified source code files.

i) *Opening the Command Prompt window and changing directories.* Open the **Command Prompt** by selecting **Start > Programs > Accessories > Command Prompt**. Change to your working directory by typing cd C:\SimplyJava\TriangleCreator.

j) *Compiling the application.* Compile your application by typing javac TriangleCreator.java Triangle.java.

k) *Running the application.* When your application compiles correctly, run it by typing java TriangleCreator. Test your application by entering sides all of length 3 and make sure that the displayed message indicates your triangle is equilateral. Then, make sure that inputs of 3, 4 and 5 indicate a right triangle and inputs of 3, 4 and 6 indicate neither. Finally, try inputting sides of 4, 5 and 3 and the message should indicate that your triangle is a right triangle.

l) *Closing the application.* Close the running application by clicking its close button.

m) *Closing the Command Prompt window.* Close the **Command Prompt** window by clicking its close button.

18.12 (*Modified Microwave Oven Application*) Modify the tutorial's **Microwave Oven** application to include an additional digit, which would represent the hour. Allow the user to enter up to 9 hours, 59 minutes and 59 seconds (Fig. 18.41).

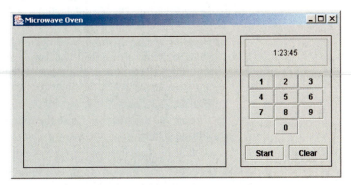

Figure 18.41   **Microwave Oven** application's GUI.

a) *Copying the template to your working directory.* Copy the directory C:\Examples\ Tutorial18\Exercises\MicrowaveOven2 to your C:\SimplyJava directory.

b) *Opening the template files.* Open the MicrowaveOven.java and CookingTime.java files in your text editor.

c) *Adding the hour variable.* To allow users to enter a cooking time that includes the hour digit, you will need to modify the CookingTime.java template file. Declare a new private instance variable hour (line 7). Change the CookingTime constructor starting on line 11, to take a third int named hourValue as its first parameter. The constructor header should be split into two lines for readability. Call method setHour from inside the constructor to set the hour instance variable.

d) *Adding the getHour and setHour methods.* Use the *get* and *set* methods already declared in class CookingTime as your template to create the *get* and *set* methods beginning on line 21 for the instance variable hour, in the CookingTime class. Allow only a single digit to represent the hour (hour < 10).

e) *Modifying the isDone method.* Change the return statement of the isDone method to include a check whether instance variable hour is equal to 0.

f) *Modifying the tick method.* At the end of the tick method, add an else statement that will handle the case when hour must be decremented. Both the minutes and the seconds values must be changed as well.

g) *Modifying the declaration of microwaveTime.* Switch to the MicrowaveOven.java file. Change the code on line 43 to call the CookingTime constructor with three arguments.

h) *Modifying the startJButtonActionPerformed method.* Change the name of the startJButtonActionPerformed method's local variable, fourDigitTime (on line 409), to fiveDigitTime. Declare a variable of type String named hour on line 412. Initialize hour to fiveDigitTime.substring(0, 1), then modify the substring arguments that follow it accordingly. On line 417, add a setHour call similar to the setMinute and setSecond calls below it. In this method, modifications will also need to be made to the setText method on line 422.

i) *Modifying the formatTime method.* Change any occurrence of the number 4 in the formatTime method to the number 5.

j) *Modifying the displayTime method.* Change the name of the displayTime method's local variable, fourDigitTime (on line 474), to fiveDigitTime. Declare a variable of type String named hour on line 477. Initialize hour to fiveDigit-Time.substring(0, 1) then modify the substring arguments that follow it accordingly. Again, the setText method on line 482 will have to be modified as well. Split this line into two lines for readability.

k) *Modifying the* **clockTimerActionPerformed** *method.* On line 497 of the clockTimerActionPerformed method, modify the setText method one last time.

l) *Saving the application.* Save your modified source code files.

m) *Opening the Command Prompt window and changing directories.* Open the **Command Prompt** by selecting **Start > Programs > Accessories > Command Prompt**. Change to your working directory by typing cd C:\SimplyJava\ MicrowaveOven2.

n) *Compiling the application.* Compile your application by typing javac MicrowaveOven.java CookingTime.java.

o) *Running the application.* When your application compiles correctly, run it by typing java MicrowaveOven. Test your application by starting the timer several times after entering different times. Make sure the microwave handles invalid data correctly, that it ends correctly when the timer reaches zero, and that the **Clear** JButton works correctly.

p) *Closing the application.* Close the running application by clicking its close button.

q) *Closing the Command Prompt window.* Close the **Command Prompt** window by clicking its close button.

18.13 (*Account Information Application*) A bank wants you to create an application that will allow them to view their clients' information. The interface is created for you (Fig. 18.42); you need to implement the Client class which stores the data. Once your application is completed, the bank manager should be able to click the **Next** or **Previous** JButtons to run through each client's information. The GUI is implemented such that clicking the **Next** JButton at the last account returns the user to the first account and clicking the **Previous** JButton at the first account returns the user to the last account. The information is stored in four arrays containing first names, last names, account numbers and account balances.

Figure 18.42   **Account Information** application GUI.

a) *Copying the template to your working directory.* Copy the directory C:\Examples\ Tutorial18\Exercises\AccountInformation2 to your C:\SimplyJava directory.

b) *Opening the template files.* Open the AccountInformation.java and Client.java files in your text editor.

c) *Determining variables for the class.* Examine the code from AccountInformation.java, including all the *get* method calls that the Client object uses to retrieve information. These method calls can be found in the displayInformation method, beginning on line 197.

d) *Creating the* **Client** *class.* Switch to your Client.java file. Declare four private instance variables beginning on line 6 to represent an account number, a balance amount, a first name and a last name. Use *get* and *set* methods (which you will declare in the next step) for those variables to declare a constructor on lines 16–26.

e) *Declaring the* **get** *and* **set** *methods.* Each instance variable should have a corresponding *get* and *set* method. Use this tutorial's CookingTime class as your guide in creating the *get* and *set* methods.

f) *Adding more information.* Now switch to your AccountInformation.java file. In the AccountInformation constructor (beginning on line 36), add one more account. Include name, account number and balance. To add an account, insert an additional

comma and a number or `String` value into each of the four array declarations starting on line 41.

g) *Saving the application.* Save your modified source code files.

h) *Opening the Command Prompt window and changing directories.* Open the **Command Prompt** window by selecting **Start > Programs > Accessories > Command Prompt**. Change to your working directory by typing cd C:\SimplyJava\ AccountInformation2.

i) *Compiling the application.* Compile your application by typing javac Account-Information.java Client.java.

j) *Running the application.* When your application compiles correctly, run it by typing java AccountInformation. Test your application by clicking the **Next** and **Previous** JButtons. Make sure that each account indexed in the accountRecords array can be displayed. The information stored in accountRecords can be found in four array declarations starting on line 41.

k) *Closing the application.* Close the running application by clicking its close button.

l) *Closing the Command Prompt window.* Close the **Command Prompt** window by clicking its close button.

What does this code do? ▶

18.14 What does the following code do? The first code listing contains the declaration of class Shape. Each Shape object represents a closed shape with a number of sides (a closed shape must have three or more sides). The second code listing contains a method (mystery) declared by a client of class Shape. What does this method do?

```
1   public class Shape
2   {
3      // integer for storing number of sides.
4      private int sides;
5
6      // Shape constructor, number of sides supplied
7      public Shape( int numSides )
8      {
9         setSides( numSides );
10
11     } // end constructor
12
13     // return sides value
14     public int getSides()
15     {
16        return sides;
17
18     } // end method getSides
19
20     // set sides value
21     public void setSides( int numSides )
22     {
23        if ( numSides > 2 )
24        {
25           sides = numSides;
26        }
27        else // set invalid input to 0
28        {
29           sides = 0;
30        }
31
32     } // end method setSides
33
34  } // end class Shape
```

```
1   public String mystery( Shape shape )
2   {
3      String shapeText;
4
5      // determine case with shape.getSides()
6      switch ( shape.getSides() )
7      {
8         case 3:
9            shapeText = "Triangle";
10           break;
11
12        case 4:
13           shapeText = "Quadrilateral";
14           break;
15
16        default:
17           shapeText = "Other polygon";
18
19     } // end switch
20
21     return shapeText;
22
23  } // end method mystery
```

What's wrong with this code? ▶ **18.15** Find the error(s) in the following code. The following method should create a new Shape object with numberSides sides. Assume the Shape class is from Exercise 18.14.

```
1   private void manipulateShape( int numberSides )
2   {
3      Shape shape = new Shape( 3 );
4
5      shape.sides = numberSides;
6   }
```

Using the Debugger ▶ **18.16** (*View Name Application*) The **View Name** application allows the user to enter the user's first and last name. When the user clicks the **View Name** JButton, a JOptionPane that displays the user's first and last name appears. Your application creates an instance of Class Name. This class uses *set* methods to set the first-name and last-name instance variables. While testing your application, you noticed that the JOptionPane did not display the correct output. The last name is displayed, but the first name is not. The GUI is shown in Fig. 18.43.

Figure 18.43 **View Name** application with correct output.

a) *Copying the template to your working directory.* Copy the directory C:\Examples\ Tutorial18\Exercises\Debugger\ViewName to your C:\SimplyJava directory.

b) *Opening the Command Prompt window and changing directories.* Open the **Command Prompt** window by selecting **Start > Programs > Accessories > Command Prompt**. Change to your working directory by typing cd C:\SimplyJava\ViewName.

c) *Using the debugger.* Use the debugger to find the logic error(s) in your application. Use the `watch` command to see all the changes to the instance variables of class `Name`. When you have found the logic error, change the code appropriately. The application with the correct output is displayed in Fig. 18.43.

d) *Saving the application.* Save your modified source code files.

e) *Compiling the application.* Compile the application by typing `javac ViewName.java Name.java`.

f) *Running the application.* When your application compiles correctly, run it by typing `java ViewName`. Test your application by entering various names into the input `JTextFields` and clicking the **View Name** `JButton`. A message should appear which displays the exact name that you entered.

g) *Closing the application.* Close the running application by clicking its close button.

h) *Closing the Command Prompt window.* Close the **Command Prompt** window by clicking its close button.

Programming Challenge ▶

18.17 (*DVD Inventory Application*) Create an application that allows the user to inventory DVDs. Users input the title of the DVD and bonus materials and that information is stored in an object. The GUI is provided for you (Fig. 18.44). You will create a class (`DVDInfo`) to represent the DVD object and another class (`BonusInfo`) to represent bonus materials for a DVD object such as the movie's trailer.

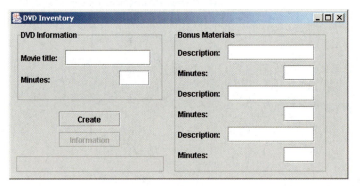

Figure 18.44 **DVD Inventory** application.

a) *Copying the template to your working directory.* Copy the directory `C:\Examples\ Tutorial18\Exercises\DVDInventory` to your `C:\SimplyJava` directory.

b) *Opening the Command Prompt window and changing directories.* Open the **Command Prompt** by selecting **Start > Programs > Accessories > Command Prompt**. Change to your working directory by typing `cd C:\SimplyJava\DVDInventory`.

c) *Opening the template files.* Open the `DVDInventory.java`, `DVDInfo.java` and `BonusInfo.java` files in your text editor.

d) *Creating the BonusInfo class.* View the `BonusInfo` class. Add code to this class so that its objects will each represent one bonus material item on the DVD. Each `BonusInfo` object should have a name (`name`) and a length (`itemLength`). Use this tutorial's `CookingTime` class as your guide in creating the *get* and *set* methods for the name and length of each bonus material. Have your *set* methods truncate a name longer than twenty characters and set the minutes of an item to zero if it is a negative value. You will also need to declare a constructor to create an instance of this class.

e) *Creating the DVDInfo class.* Now, view the `DVDInfo` class. Add the code so that this class contains the movie title (`movieTitle`) and the length of the movie (`movieLength`). It should also include an array of `BonusInfo` items (`bonusMaterial`). Again, use this tutorial's `CookingTime` class as your guide in creating the *get* and *set* methods for the name, length and bonus materials. The *get* method of `bonusMaterial` should return a `String`. You will also need to declare a constructor to create an instance of this class.

f) *Creating the necessary variables.* View the `DVDInventory` class. First, create a `DVDInfo` instance variable. Once that is done, in the `createJButtonAction-`

Performed method, store the information from the JTextFields in variables. You will need to create local variables to store this information.

g) ***Adding bonus material information.*** Create an array of BonusInfo objects to store bonus materials. Use the variables you declared in *Step f* to create BonusInfo objects to go in this array.

h) ***Creating an instance of DVDInfo.*** Use the movie title, length and the array of bonus materials to make your DVDInfo object.

i) ***Displaying the output.*** Locate the informationJButtonActionPerformed method. It is already partially declared for you. Initialize String information to contain the complete information on the DVD object that you created earlier. Use the *get* methods you declared in *Steps d–e*. The String information will be displayed in a JOptionPane.

j) ***Saving the application.*** Save your modified source code files.

k) ***Compiling the application.*** Compile your source code files by typing javac DVDInventory.java DVDInfo.java BonusInfo.java.

l) ***Running the application.*** When your application compiles correctly, run it by typing java DVDInventory. Test your application by entering various values into the input JTextFields and clicking the **Create** JButton. A message in the lower JTextField will let you know that you have created a DVD successfully. Click the **Information** JButton and verify that all information in the JOptionPane is correct.

m) ***Closing the application.*** Close the running application by clicking its close button.

n) ***Closing the Command Prompt window.*** Close the **Command Prompt** window by clicking its close button.

19

Objectives

In this tutorial, you will learn to:
- Create and manipulate an `ArrayList` object.
- Create a mnemonic for a component.
- Use an iterator to iterate through an `ArrayList`.
- Display items in a `JList`.

Outline

Shipping Hub Application

Introducing Collections, ArrayList and Iterators

In this tutorial, you will develop an application that simulates parcel processing at a shipping hub. Your application will use **collections**, which provide you with a quick and easy way to organize and manipulate data. Collections can contain several data items, or elements. This tutorial focuses on the `ArrayList` collection, which includes the data storage and manipulation capabilities of an array, but with much greater flexibility. You will also learn to use **iterators**, which allow you to loop through each element in a collection.

19.1 Test-Driving the Shipping Hub Application

In this section, you will test-drive the **Shipping Hub** application. This application must meet the following requirements:

Application Requirements

A shipping company receives parcels at its shipping hub. Parcels will be represented as Parcel objects, where class Parcel is provided for you. The company then ships these Parcels to a distribution center in one of the following states: Alabama, Florida, Georgia, Kentucky, Mississippi, North Carolina, South Carolina, Tennessee, Virginia or West Virginia. The company needs an application to track the Parcels that pass through its shipping hub. When the user clicks the application's Scan New JButton, the application generates an ID and arrival time for the new Parcel. Once a Parcel has been scanned, the user should be able to enter the recipient's name and shipping address for the Parcel. JButtons should be provided for the user to remove or modify the information of Parcels that have already been scanned. The user should be able to navigate through the list of scanned Parcels by using the < Back or Next > JButtons. Finally, users should be able to view a list of all Parcels destined for a particular state.

You begin by test-driving the completed application. Then, you will learn the additional Java technologies you will need to create your own version of this application.

1. *Locating the completed application.* Open the **Command Prompt** window by selecting **Start > Programs > Accessories > Command Prompt.** Change to your completed **Shipping Hub** application directory by typing cd C:\Examples\Tutorial19\CompletedApplication\ShippingHub.

2. *Running the Shipping Hub application.* Type java ShippingHub in the **Command Prompt** window to run the application (Fig. 19.1). At the top of the application, you will see the **Arrived at:** JTextField that will display the date and time that the Parcel arrived. Below this is the **Parcel Information** JPanel which contains fields for the user to view or edit the Parcel's identification number, and the recipient's name and shipping address. Notice that a JComboBox is provided to limit the states from which the user may choose. To the right of the **Parcel Information** JPanel is the **Parcels by State** JPanel. This JPanel also contains a JComboBox that allows the user to select a state. Once a state is selected, all packages destined for that state will be displayed in the **JList** below the JComboBox. A JList is a component that, like a JTextArea, displays multiple lines of text. Unlike a JTextArea, a JList displays a series of items from which the user may make selections. Finally, seven JButtons are displayed below the application's JPanels. The **Scan New** JButton allows you to scan a new Parcel and enter information for that Parcel. The **Add** JButton adds the new Parcel to the application's list of Parcels, while the **Remove** JButton removes the current Parcel displayed from the application's list of Parcels. The **Edit** JButton makes the application's name and address fields editable, so that you can modify an existing Parcel. The **Update** JButton allows the modifications to be stored. The **< Back** and **Next >** JButtons allow you to navigate from one Parcel to another, where each Parcel's information is displayed in the **Parcel Information** JPanel.

JPanel contains fields for user to view or edit the Parcel

JComboBoxes list available states

Figure 19.1   Running the completed **Shipping Hub** application.

3. *Scanning a new Parcel.* Click the **Scan New** JButton. The application displays the time and date the Parcel arrived and a Parcel ID number (Fig. 19.2). The JTextFields are made editable and the **State:** JComboBox is enabled, allowing the user to enter the Parcel's information. Notice that the **Parcel ID:** JTextField remains uneditable. You do not want the user to be able to modify the Parcel ID or the arrival time.

Keep in mind that this application is a simulation. When Parcels arrive at an actual shipping hub, a scanner is used to read the Parcel's ID, which is preprinted on a slip that is attached to the Parcel. The **Shipping Hub** application generates the Parcel's ID to simulate this action of scanning a Parcel.

(cont.)

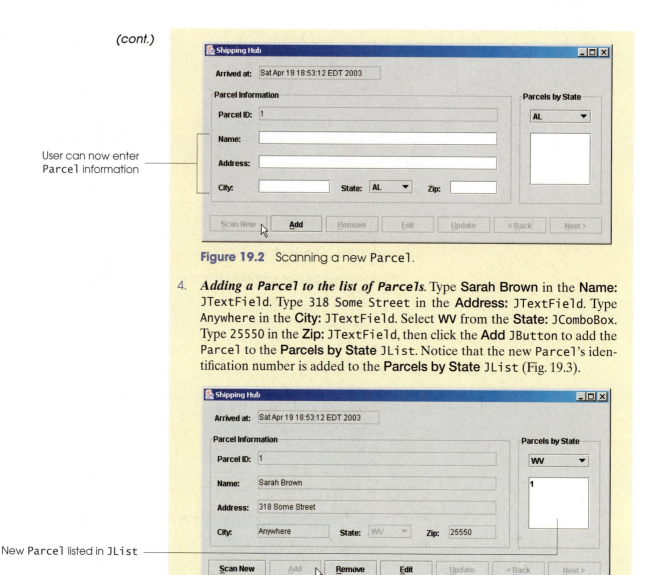

User can now enter
`Parcel` information

Figure 19.2   Scanning a new `Parcel`.

4. ***Adding a Parcel to the list of Parcels.*** Type **Sarah Brown** in the **Name:** JTextField. Type 318 Some Street in the **Address:** JTextField. Type Anywhere in the **City:** JTextField. Select **WV** from the **State:** JComboBox. Type 25550 in the **Zip:** JTextField, then click the **Add** JButton to add the `Parcel` to the **Parcels by State** JList. Notice that the new `Parcel`'s identification number is added to the **Parcels by State** JList (Fig. 19.3).

New `Parcel` listed in `JList`

Figure 19.3   Entering a new `Parcel`'s information.

5. ***Using mnemonics.*** Notice that one letter of each JButton is underlined. Such underlines are used to indicate a keyboard shortcut, or **mnemonic** that is available to the user. Mnemonics allow the user to perform an action on a component using the keyboard. Press and hold the *Alt* key, then press the *S* key ('S' being the underlined character). This action causes the **Scan New** JButton to be "clicked." Notice that the user can still use the mouse to click the JButton; mnemonics are provided as another option to the user. Enter a `Parcel` with the following information

   ■ Derek Blue, 9 Some Road, Townsville, SC, 29445

   then "click" the **Add** JButton by holding down the *Alt* key and pressing the *A* key.

6. ***Adding more Parcels.*** Use the **Scan New** and **Add** JButtons to enter three more `Parcel`s with the following information:

   ■ John Green, 234 Some Place, Townsville, SC, 29486

   ■ Alicia Purple, 46 Main Street, Anytown, KY, 42259

   ■ Lisa Orange, 3 Some Avenue, Some City, MS, 39194

(cont.)

7. ***Browsing Parcels.*** The application's **Next >** and **< Back** JButtons allow the user to navigate the list of Parcels. Press each JButton several times to move through the list of Parcels. Notice that the JTextFields are kept uneditable so that the user can view, but not modify the Parcels' information.

8. ***Editing Parcels.*** Use the **Next >** JButton or **< Back** JButton to navigate to the first Parcel entered. Click the **Edit** JButton using the mouse or using the 'E' mnemonic. The JTextFields that display the Parcel's address information are made editable, and the **State:** JComboBox is enabled (Fig. 19.4). The **Update** JButton is enabled while the **Edit** JButton is disabled. Modify the number in the **Address:** JTextField from 318 to 313 and modify the zip code in the **Zip:** JTextField from 25550 to 25551. Click the **Update** JButton to save your changes (Fig. 19.5). The **Edit** JButton is enabled while the **Update** JButton is disabled.

Fields are made editable —

Update JButton is enabled —

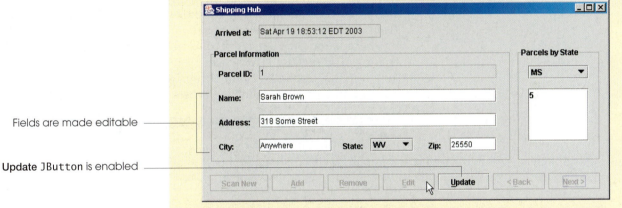

Figure 19.4 Parcel information is editable when **Edit** JButton is clicked.

Updated zip code —

Figure 19.5 New information is stored when **Update** JButton is clicked.

9. ***Removing Parcels.*** The **Remove** JButton allows the user to delete a Parcel. Use the **Next >** JButton or **< Back** JButton to navigate to the fourth Parcel entered, whose ID is 4. Click the **Remove** JButton using the mouse or using the 'R' mnemonic. The current Parcel's information is replaced with the information of the next Parcel that was entered (Fig. 19.6).

(cont.)

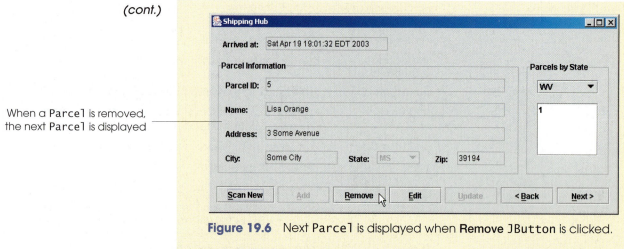

When a `Parcel` is removed, the next `Parcel` is displayed

Figure 19.6 Next `Parcel` is displayed when **Remove** `JButton` is clicked.

10. ***Viewing all Parcels going to the same state.*** The **Parcels by State** `JComboBox` on the right side of the application's GUI allows the user to select a two-letter state code. When a state code is selected, all of the `Parcel` ID numbers of `Parcel`s destined for that state are displayed in a `JList` (Fig. 19.7). [*Note*: You will add the `JList` to a `JScrollPane` so that scrollbars will be added if necessary.]

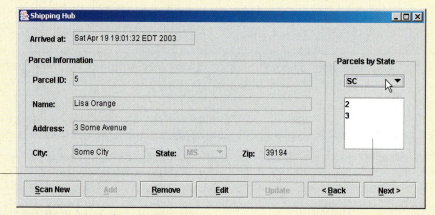

All `Parcel`s being sent to South Carolina

Figure 19.7 Viewing all `Parcel`s going to South Carolina.

11. ***Closing the running application.*** Close your running application by clicking its close button.

12. ***Closing the Command Prompt window.*** Close the **Command Prompt** window by clicking its close button.

19.2 Parcel Class

Your application must store each `Parcel`'s shipping information, including recipient's name, address, city, state and zip code. However, multiple `Parcel`s can be shipped to the same person at the same location, therefore, each `Parcel` will be identified by a unique identification number. The `Parcel` class, included with the template application, provides the necessary methods and instance variables to keep track of a `Parcel`'s information. The instance variables are made `private`, and therefore must be accessed using the class's `public` methods. The table in Fig. 19.8 describes the `public` methods for class `Parcel`. Notice that there is no `setParcelID` or `setArrivalTime` method—this is because the user of class `Parcel` should not be able to modify the `Parcel`'s identification number or arrival time after the `Parcel` object has been created. The code for the completed `Parcel` class is displayed in Fig. 19.54 at the end of this tutorial.

Method	Description
getName/setName	Provide access to instance variable name (a String).
getAddress/ setAddress	Provide access to instance variable address (a String).
getCity/setCity	Provide access to instance variable city (a String).
getState/ setState	Provide access to instance variable state (a String). States are represented as two-letter abbreviations.
getZip/setZip	Provide access to instance variable zip (an int).
getParcelID	Provides access to instance variable parcelID (an int).
getArrivalTime	Provides access to instance variable arrivalTime (a String).
Parcel	Constructor that is used to create a new Parcel object with two arguments parcelID (an int) and arrivalTime (a String).

Figure 19.8 `public` Methods listing for class `Parcel`.

19.3 JList Component

Recall that a `JList` displays a series of items from which the user may select one or more items. The **setListData** method is called to set the items displayed in the `JList`. This method takes as an argument a one-dimensional array containing the items to be displayed. Next, you will create a `JList` and attached it to a `JScrollPane`. Then, you will populate the `JList` using the `setListData` method.

Adding the `JList`

1. *Copying the template to your working directory.* Copy the C:\Examples\Tutorial19\TemplateApplication\ShippingHub directory to your C:\SimplyJava directory.

2. *Opening the Shipping Hub application's template file.* Open the template file ShippingHub.java in your text editor.

3. *Declaring references to a JList and JScrollPane.* Add lines 46–47 of Fig. 19.9 to your code to declare references to the JList and JScrollPane components.

Good Programming Practice

Suffix JList component names with JList.

```
44      // JComboBox, JList and JScrollPane for Parcel number
45      private JComboBox parcelStateJComboBox;
46      private JList parcelStateJList;
47      private JScrollPane parcelStateJScrollPane;
48
49      // JButtons to manipulate Parcels
```

Figure 19.9 Declaring new references to a JList and JScrollPane.

4. *Creating a new JList.* Add lines 205–206 of Fig. 19.10 to your code. Line 206 initializes parcelStateJList with a new JList.

Initializing parcelStateJList with a new JList

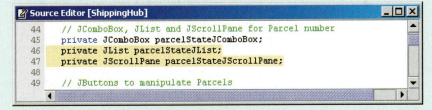

```
203        ); // end call to addActionListener
204
205        // set up parcelStateJList
206        parcelStateJList = new JList();
207
208        // set up parcelStateJScrollPane
```

Figure 19.10 Creating a new JList object.

(cont.)

GUI Design Tip

Attaching a `JList` to a `JScroll-Pane` allows users to scroll items in a `JList`.

Adding the `parcelStateJList` to the `parcelStateJScrollPane`

5. ***Adding the `JList` to a `JScrollPane`.*** Unlike a `JComboBox`, a `JList` does not provide a scrollbar if there are more items in the list than the number of visible rows. In this case, you must add the `JList` to a `JScrollPane` to allow the other items in the `JList` to be displayed and selected. Add line 209 of Fig. 19.11 to your code to add the `JList` to `parcelStateJScrollPane`.

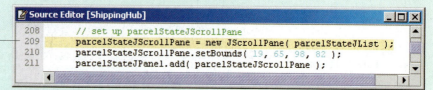

Figure 19.11 Declaring a new `JScrollPane` containing the `JList`.

6. ***Saving the application.*** Save your modified source code file. You have not yet created some of the application's instance variables, so your code will not yet compile. You will add these variables shortly.

SELF-REVIEW

1. The _____ method is used to set the data displayed in a `JList`.
   a) `add`   b) `setText`
   c) `setListData`   d) `append`

2. Items can be assigned to a `JList` from a(n) _____.
   a) one-dimensional array   b) two-dimensional array
   c) `ArrayList`   d) All of the above.

Answers: 1) c. 2) a.

19.4 Using Mnemonics (Keyboard Shortcuts)

Mnemonics (or keyboard shortcuts) allow the user to perform an action on a component using the keyboard. You have already seen examples of mnemonics in the application's test-drive.

GUI Design Tip

Use mnemonics to allow users to "click" a component using the keyboard. This provides an added convenience for the user, especially for applications that require the user to enter a great deal of text data.

To specify a mnemonic key for a component, set the component's ***mnemonic*** property (using the **`setMnemonic`** method) to the character you wish to use as a mnemonic. If you wish to use **S** as the mnemonic on the **Scan New** `JButton`, set its *mnemonic* property to the constant **`KeyEvent.VK_S`**. This constant is known as a **virtual key code**. Java uses virtual key codes to represent the keys on the keyboard. Each key has a unique code. These constants are declared in class **`KeyEvent`**, which contains information about keyboard events (such as the pressing of a key on the keyboard). You will learn more about keyboard events in Tutorial 22. For example, the `KeyEvent.VK_S` constant is an `int` that represents the *S* key. You can specify many mnemonics in an application, but each character used as a mnemonic in any particular container (such as a particular `JPanel` or `JScrollPane`) must be unique. Recall from the test-drive that to use the mnemonic, you must hold down the *Alt* key while pressing the mnemonic character on the keyboard (release both keys after pressing the mnemonic character). In the case of the **Scan New** `JButton`, you would hold down the *Alt* key while pressing the *S* key (also written as *Alt+S*). You would then release both keys.

Mnemonics are often used on `JButton` components and on the `JMenuItem` component, which will be introduced in Tutorial 22. Normally, the mnemonic is chosen as the first letter of the text displayed on the component. In the case of a "tie," where you want to create mnemonics for two components in a container whose text start with the same letter, use the next most prominent letter (usually the second letter in the component's text). You will now add mnemonics to your **Shipping Hub** application.

Creating Mnemonics

1. *Creating a mnemonic for the Scan New **JButton.*** Add line 217 of Fig. 19.12 to set the *mnemonic* property of the **Scan New** `JButton`. When you run your application, the letter S will be underlined on the `JButton` (Fig. 19.13). If the user presses *Alt+S* during execution, this will have the same effect as if the user "clicks" the **Scan New** `JButton`.

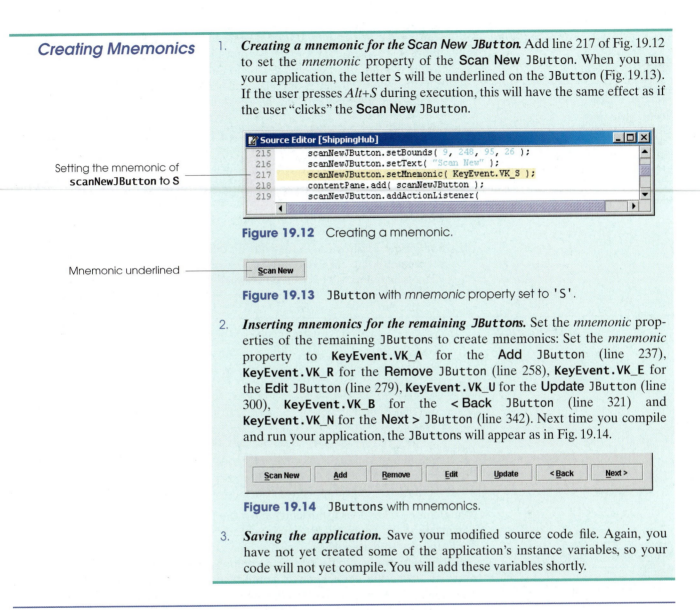

Setting the mnemonic of **scanNewJButton** to **S**

```
215     scanNewJButton.setBounds( 9, 248, 95, 26 );
216     scanNewJButton.setText( "Scan New" );
217     scanNewJButton.setMnemonic( KeyEvent.VK_S );
218     contentPane.add( scanNewJButton );
219     scanNewJButton.addActionListener(
```

Figure 19.12 Creating a mnemonic.

Mnemonic underlined — [Scan New]

Figure 19.13 `JButton` with *mnemonic* property set to `'S'`.

2. *Inserting mnemonics for the remaining **JButtons.*** Set the *mnemonic* properties of the remaining `JButtons` to create mnemonics: Set the *mnemonic* property to **KeyEvent.VK_A** for the **Add** `JButton` (line 237), **KeyEvent.VK_R** for the **Remove** `JButton` (line 258), **KeyEvent.VK_E** for the **Edit** `JButton` (line 279), **KeyEvent.VK_U** for the **Update** `JButton` (line 300), **KeyEvent.VK_B** for the **< Back** `JButton` (line 321) and **KeyEvent.VK_N** for the **Next >** `JButton` (line 342). Next time you compile and run your application, the `JButtons` will appear as in Fig. 19.14.

| Scan New | Add | Remove | Edit | Update | < Back | Next > |

Figure 19.14 `JButtons` with mnemonics.

3. *Saving the application.* Save your modified source code file. Again, you have not yet created some of the application's instance variables, so your code will not yet compile. You will add these variables shortly.

SELF-REVIEW

1. Set a `JButton`'s *mnemonic* property using the _____ method.

   a) `setKeyboardShortcut`
   b) `setMnemonic`
   c) `isKeyboardShortcut`
   d) `isMnemonic`

2. Hold down the _____ key then press the underlined character on a `JButton` to use that `JButton`'s mnemonic.

   a) *Control*
   b) *Shift*
   c) *Alt*
   d) *Tab*

Answers: 1) b. 2) c.

19.5 Collections

Java provides several predefined classes, called collections, where objects can store groups of related objects. These classes provide methods that make it easier for you to store, organize and retrieve your data. This capability reduces application development time because you do not have to write code to organize your data; also, the methods in the collection classes are reliable and efficient.

In Tutorials 16 and 17, you learned how to declare and use arrays in your applications. Once an array is declared, its size is fixed over the life of your application.

Software Design Tip

Use an ArrayList (instead of an array) to store a group of values when the number of elements in the group varies during the execution of an application.

This poses a problem if the number of items that your application needs to store will vary over time.

Class ArrayList (in the java.util package) provides a convenient solution to this problem. The **ArrayList** collection provides all of the capabilities of an array, as well as dynamic resizing capabilities. **Dynamic resizing** enables an ArrayList object to change its size to meet the varying storage demands of your application. Also, ArrayLists (and other collections) can store objects of any type. In fact, one ArrayList may contain objects of several different types.

SELF-REVIEW

1. Collections _____.
   a) force you to focus on how your data is stored
   b) speed up application development
   c) are predefined classes provided by Java
   d) Both b and c.

2. One limitation of arrays is that _____.
   a) the size of an array cannot change dynamically
   b) they can only store primitive types
   c) Strings cannot be placed in them
   d) All of the above.

Answers: 1) d. 2) a.

19.6 Constructing the Shipping Hub Application

Now you will build your **Shipping Hub** application by using ArrayLists to maintain several Parcel objects. This tutorial's template file provides much of the **Shipping Hub** application's functionality so that you may concentrate on the code that manipulates your ArrayLists. The following pseudocode describes the basic operation of your **Shipping Hub** application:

When the user runs the application:
     Create a list to contain all parcels being sent
     Create a list to contain the parcels being sent to a specific state

When the user clicks the Scan New JButton:
     Generate a unique parcel ID number
     Display the arrival time and the ID number of the new parcel
     Create a Parcel object for the new entry

When the user clicks the Add JButton:
     Store the name, address, city, state and zip code values in the new parcel
     Add the new parcel to the list of all parcels
     Add the parcel ID to the Parcels by State JList

When the user clicks the Remove JButton:
     Remove the parcel ID from the list of parcels sent to a specific state
     Remove the parcel from the list of all parcels

     If the removed parcel was last in the list of parcels
          Display the first parcel
     Else
          Display the next Parcel

When the user clicks the Edit JButton:
     Enable the input components

When the Update JButton is clicked:
     Store the new name, address, city, state and zip code values in the parcel
     Update the Parcels by State JList based on the user's changes

When the < Back JButton is clicked:
    If the parcel was first in the list of parcels
        Display the last parcel
    Else
        Display the previous Parcel

When the Next > JButton is clicked:
    If the parcel was last in the list of parcels
        Display the first parcel
    Else
        Display the next Parcel

When the user chooses a different state in the Parcels by State JComboBox:
    Iterate through each parcel in the list of all parcels
    Add IDs of parcels destined for the selected state to the list of parcels being
        sent to a specific state
    Display the parcel IDs from the list of parcels being sent to a specific state in
        the Parcels by State JList

The **Shipping Hub** application must store a list of `Parcels` through which the user can navigate using the **Next >** and **< Back** JButtons. Each time your application executes, it must allow for any number of `Parcels` to be added (one at a time). Using arrays (which are not resizable), you would be limited by the number of values that you could store in the array. The `ArrayList` collection solves this problem by combining the functionality of an array with dynamic resizing capabilities. Now that you have test-driven the **Shipping Hub** application and studied its pseudocode representation, you will use an ACE table to help you convert the pseudocode to Java. Figure 19.15 lists the actions, components and events that will help you to complete your own version of this application.

Action/Component/
Event (ACE) Table for the
Shipping Hub
Application

Action	Component	Event
Label the application's components	`arrivedAtJLabel,` `parcelIDJLabel, nameJLabel,` `addressJLabel, cityJLabel,` `stateJLabel, zipJLabel,` `parcelInformationJPanel,` `parcelStateJPanel`	Application is run
Create a list to contain all parcels being sent	`parcelsArrayList`	
Create a list to contain the parcels being sent to a specific state	`parcelStateArrayList`	
	`scanNewJButton`	User clicks **Scan New** JButton
Generate a unique parcel ID number		
Display the arrival time and the ID number of the new Parcel	`arrivedAtJTextField,` `parcelIDJTextField`	
Create a Parcel object for the new entry	`newParcel`	
	`addJButton`	User clicks **Add** JButton
Store the name, address, city, state and zip code values in the new parcel	`newParcel`	
Add the new parcel to the list of all parcels	`parcelsArrayList`	
Add the parcel ID to the Parcels by State JList	`parcelStateJList`	

Figure 19.15 ACE table for the **Shipping Hub** application. (Part 1 of 3.)

Action	Component	Event
	removeJButton	User clicks **Remove** JButton
Remove the parcel ID from the list of parcels sent to a specific state	parcelStateJList	
Remove the parcel from the list of all parcels	parcelsArrayList	
If the removed parcel was last in the list of parcels	parcelsArrayList	
Display the first parcel	nameJTextField, addressJTextField, cityJTextField, zipJTextField, stateJComboBox	
Else Display the next Parcel	nameJTextField, addressJTextField, cityJTextField, zipJTextField, stateJComboBox	
	editJButton	User clicks **Edit** JButton
Enable the input components	nameJTextField, addressJTextField, cityJTextField, zipJTextField, stateJComboBox	
	updateJButton	User clicks **Update** JButton
Store the new name, address, city, state and zip code values in the parcel	nameJTextField, addressJTextField, cityJTextField, zipJTextField, stateJComboBox, newParcel	
Update the Parcels by State JList based on the user's changes	parcelStateJList	
	backJButton	User clicks **< Back** JButton
If the parcel was first in the list of parcels Display the last parcel	nameJTextField, addressJTextField, cityJTextField, zipJTextField, stateJComboBox	
Else Display the previous Parcel	nameJTextField, addressJTextField, cityJTextField, zipJTextField, stateJComboBox	
	nextJButton	User clicks **Next >** JButton
If the parcel was last in the list of parcels Display the first parcel	nameJTextField, addressJTextField, cityJTextField, zipJTextField, stateJComboBox	
Else Display the next Parcel	nameJTextField, addressJTextField, cityJTextField, zipJTextField, stateJComboBox	

Figure 19.15   ACE table for the **Shipping Hub** application. (Part 2 of 3.)

Action	Component	Event
	`parcelStateJComboBox`	User selects a state in JComboBox
Iterate through each parcel in the list of all parcels	`parcelsArrayList`	
Add IDs of parcels destined for the selected state to the list of parcels being sent to a specific state	`parcelStateArrayList`	
Display the parcel IDs from the list of parcels being sent to a specific state in the Parcels by State JList	`parcelStateJList`	

Figure 19.15 ACE table for the **Shipping Hub** application. (Part 3 of 3.)

In this tutorial, you will use an `ArrayList` in the **Shipping Hub** application to keep track of all `Parcel`s. You will now create this `ArrayList` and another to keep track of the `Parcel`s going to a specific state.

Creating ArrayLists

1. ***Importing the java.util package.*** Insert line 5 of Fig. 19.16 in your application to import the `java.util` package. This `import` declaration allows access to all predefined classes contained in the `java.util` package, including class `ArrayList`.

Importing the `java.util` package

```
Source Editor [ShippingHub]
3  import java.awt.*;
4  import java.awt.event.*;
5  import java.util.*;
6  import javax.swing.*;
7  import javax.swing.border.TitledBorder;
```

Figure 19.16 Importing package `java.util`.

2. ***Initializing the ArrayList.*** To use an `ArrayList`, you must first create a new `ArrayList` object. Insert lines 66–71 (Fig. 19.17) to your application. Lines 67 and 71 use the `new` keyword to create two empty `ArrayList` objects when your application is run. The `parcelsArrayList` will contain the `Parcel`s entered by the user. The `parcelStateArrayList` will contain the `Parcel`s destined for a particular state.

Creating the `ArrayLists`

```
Source Editor [ShippingHub]
63      // Parcel object contains data for newly entered parcels
64      private Parcel newParcel;
65
66      // ArrayList contains Parcels entered by user
67      private ArrayList parcelsArrayList = new ArrayList();
68
69      // ArrayList used to modify and display the Parcel objects
70      // for a specific state
71      private ArrayList parcelStateArrayList = new ArrayList();
72
73      private int parcelID = 0; // ID for new parcels
```

Figure 19.17 Creating the `ArrayLists`.

3. ***Saving the application.*** Save your modified source code file.

4. ***Opening the Command Prompt window and changing directories.*** Open the **Command Prompt** window by selecting **Start > Programs > Accessories > Command Prompt**. Change to your working directory by typing `cd C:\SimplyJava\ShippingHub`.

(cont.)

5. ***Compiling the application.*** Compile your application by typing `javac ShippingHub.java`.

6. ***Running the application.*** When your application compiles correctly, run it by typing `java ShippingHub`. Figure 19.18 shows the updated application running. Click the **Scan New** `JButton`. The `Parcel` information fields are made editable, but neither the `Parcel` ID nor the arrival time are displayed. You will add this functionality later. Enter the name and address information, then click the **Add** `JButton`. A new `Parcel` object is not yet created—this functionality, too, will be added later.

Parcel's arrival time and ID not yet displayed

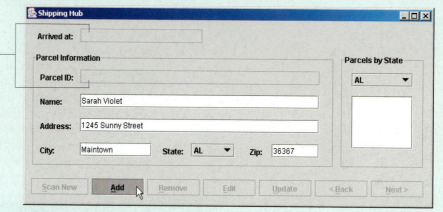

Figure 19.18 Entering information for a new `Parcel`.

7. ***Closing the application.*** Close your running application by clicking its close button.

8. ***Closing the Command Prompt window.*** Close the **Command Prompt** window by clicking its close button.

Now that you have created the `parcelsArrayList`, you will need to insert code that allows the user to add `Parcel`s to this `ArrayList`. To accomplish this, you will create a reference to an object of class `Parcel` and use the `ArrayList`'s **add** method to store the reference in the `ArrayList`—more specifically, the add method appends its argument at the end of an `ArrayList`.

Creating and Adding Parcels

1. ***Displaying the Parcel number and arrival time.*** The user presses the **Scan New** `JButton` when a new `Parcel` arrives at the shipping hub. When this `JButton` is clicked, your application should generate an identification number and arrival time, then allow the user to enter the shipping address. Recall that the ID is generated because this application is a simulation; you don't actually have access to a bar-code scanner, for example. Insert lines 380–386 of Fig. 19.19 into the `scanNewJButtonActionPerformed` method. Line 381 creates a `Date` object to access the current date and time, which is displayed on line 382. Class `Date`'s **toString** method (line 382) returns the current date as a `String`, in the format `Tue Feb 13 16:50:00 EST 2003`. Line 385 increments `parcelID` to ensure that all `Parcel`s have a unique identification number. The new `Parcel`'s ID is displayed in `parcelIDJTextField` on line 386.

(cont.)

Displaying the arrival time and `Parcel`'s ID number in the `JTextFields`

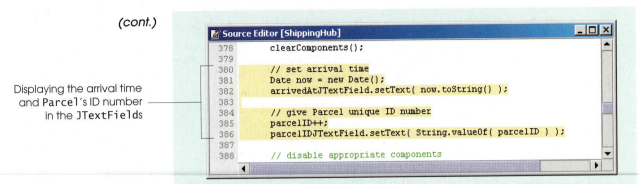

```
Source Editor [ShippingHub]
378          clearComponents();
379
380          // set arrival time
381          Date now = new Date();
382          arrivedAtJTextField.setText( now.toString() );
383
384          // give Parcel unique ID number
385          parcelID++;
386          parcelIDJTextField.setText( String.valueOf( parcelID ) );
387
388          // disable appropriate components
```

Figure 19.19 Displaying the `Parcel`'s number and arrival time.

2. **Creating a Parcel.** After the `Parcel` has been "scanned," your application should create the new `Parcel` object. Insert lines 388–390 of Fig. 19.20 into your application. Lines 389–390 pass the identification number and arrival time as arguments to the constructor for class `Parcel`. The values that you pass to the `Parcel` constructor can then be accessed using class `Parcel`'s `getParcelID` and `getArrivalTime` methods. Note that line 389 uses the same reference, `newParcel`, every time the **Scan New** JButton is pressed. This object temporarily stores the `Parcel`'s data before the `Parcel` is added to `parcelsArrayList`.

Create a new `Parcel` object with an ID and arrival time

```
Source Editor [ShippingHub]
386          parcelIDJTextField.setText( String.valueOf( parcelID ) );
387
388          // create new Parcel object
389          newParcel = new Parcel( parcelID,
390             arrivedAtJTextField.getText() );
391
392          // disable appropriate components
```

Figure 19.20 Creating a `Parcel` object.

3. **Adding a Parcel to the ArrayList.** To add the `Parcel` to `parcelsArray-List` after entering the `Parcel`'s information, the user presses the **Add** JButton. Insert lines 410–412 of Fig. 19.21 to the `addJButtonActionPer-formed` method. Line 411 adds the new `Parcel` to `parcelsArrayList` using the `ArrayList`'s add method.

Adding a `Parcel` object to the `ArrayList`

```
Source Editor [ShippingHub]
407          // set information for new Parcel
408          setParcelData();
409
410          // add new Parcel to parcelsArrayList
411          parcelsArrayList.add( newParcel );
412          position = parcelsArrayList.size() - 1;
413
414          // disable or make uneditable appropriate components
```

Figure 19.21 Adding a `Parcel` to the `ArrayList`.

(cont.)

Line 412 updates the value of variable `position`. This variable, declared in the template as an instance variable, is used to store the location of the current `Parcel` in `parcelsArrayList`. As with arrays, you refer to an object's location in an `ArrayList` as the object's **index**. Much like an array, the index of an object at the beginning of the `ArrayList` is zero and the index of an object at the end of the `ArrayList` is one less than the number of objects in the `ArrayList`. Each time you add an object to the `ArrayList` by calling the add method, the object is appended at the end of the `ArrayList`. The **size** method of class `ArrayList` returns the number of elements in the `ArrayList` object on which that method is called. Line 412 subtracts 1 from the number of elements in `parcelsArrayList` to determine the index of the last element and stores this index in variable `position`. This variable will be used as an index to display the current `Parcel`'s information. The current `Parcel` is already displayed, so you do not need to use this variable yet.

4. ***Saving the application.*** Save your modified source code file.

5. ***Opening the Command Prompt window and changing directories.*** Open the **Command Prompt** window by selecting **Start > Programs > Accessories > Command Prompt**. Change to your working directory by typing `cd C:\SimplyJava\ShippingHub`.

6. ***Compiling the application.*** Compile your application by typing `javac ShippingHub.java`.

7. ***Running the application.*** When your application compiles correctly, run it by typing `java ShippingHub`. Figure 19.22 shows the updated application running. Click the **Scan New** JButton. The arrival date and time, and the `Parcel` ID will be displayed. Enter a name and address for the new `Parcel`, then press the **Add** JButton (Fig. 19.23). The `Parcel` is added to `parcelsArrayList`, but it is not yet listed in the **Parcels by State** JList—you will add this functionality later. The input fields are made uneditable, but the new `Parcel`'s information is still displayed. Functionality is not yet provided for the **Remove**, **Edit**, **Update**, **< Back** and **Next >** JButtons.

Arrival time and ID now displayed ————

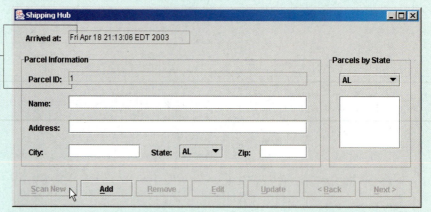

Figure 19.22 Newly scanned items have the `Parcel`'s arrival time and ID displayed.

8. ***Closing the application.*** Close your running application by clicking its close button.

9. ***Closing the Command Prompt window.*** Close the **Command Prompt** window by clicking its close button.

(cont.)

New **Parcel** not yet added to **JList**

Panel information is made uneditable

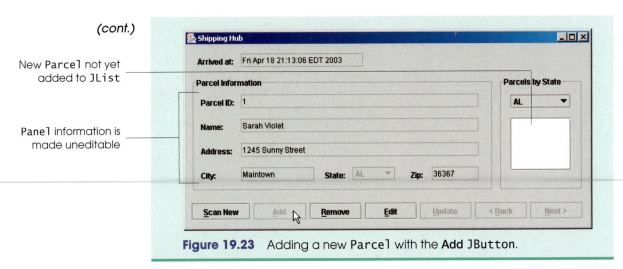

Figure 19.23 Adding a new **Parcel** with the **Add** JButton.

Now you will learn how to remove a Parcel from an ArrayList with the ArrayList method **remove**.

Removing Parcels

1. ***Removing a Parcel from parcelsArrayList.*** When the user selects a Parcel and presses the **Remove** JButton, your application should remove the Parcel from parcelsArrayList. The ArrayList class provides a simple way to remove objects. Insert lines 429–430 of Fig. 19.24 into the remove-JButtonActionPerformed method. This line uses the remove method to remove a Parcel from parcelsArrayList. The argument passed to the remove method is the index of the current Parcel in parcelsArrayList, contained in variable position.

Removing the current **Parcel** from the **ArrayList**

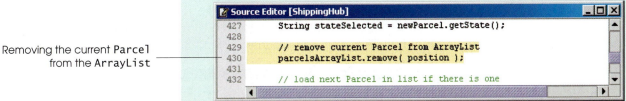

Figure 19.24 Removing a **Parcel** from **parcelsArrayList**.

Whenever an object is removed from an ArrayList, the ArrayList automatically updates the indices accordingly. For example, if a Parcel at index 3 is removed from the ArrayList, the Parcel that was previously at index 4 will then be located at index 3.

2. ***Saving the application.*** Save your modified source code file.

3. ***Opening the Command Prompt window and changing directories.*** Open the **Command Prompt** window by selecting **Start > Programs > Accessories > Command Prompt**. Change to your working directory by typing cd C:\SimplyJava\ShippingHub.

4. ***Compiling the application.*** Compile your application by typing javac ShippingHub.java.

(cont.)

5. ***Running the application.*** When your application compiles correctly, run it by typing `java ShippingHub`. Figure 19.25 shows the updated application running. Click the **Scan New** JButton. The arrival time and `Parcel`'s ID will be displayed. Enter a name and address for the new `Parcel`, then press the **Add** JButton (Fig. 19.25). Click the **Remove** JButton to remove the new `Parcel` (Fig. 19.26). [*Note:* You may notice that if several `Parcel`s are added and you then click the **Remove** JButton, the current `Parcel` will be removed but will still be displayed in the **Parcel Information** JPanel. Later in the tutorial, you will add the functionality to modify which `Parcel` is displayed after a removal.]

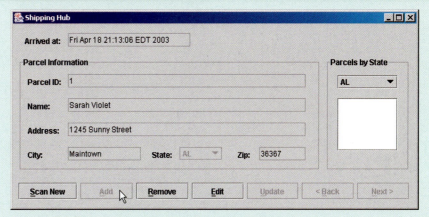

Figure 19.25 Adding a `Parcel` to `parcelsArrayList`.

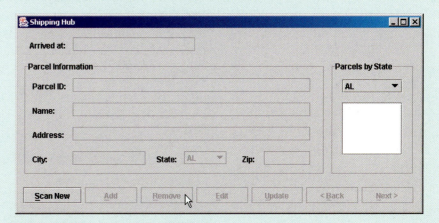

Figure 19.26 Removing a `Parcel` from `parcelsArrayList`.

6. ***Closing the application.*** Close your running application by clicking its close button.

7. ***Closing the Command Prompt window.*** Close the **Command Prompt** window by clicking its close button.

Once a `Parcel` has been added to the `parcelsArrayList`, the **Shipping Hub** application disables the JTextFields so that the user can not accidentally modify the `Parcel` information. To allow users to modify any of the `Parcel`'s information (except for the arrival time and identification number), an **Edit** JButton is provided. When the user clicks the **Edit** JButton, its event handler enable's the components that allow the user to modify the `Parcel`'s data, but not the `Parcel`'s identification number or arrival time. The **Edit** JButton's functionality is provided in the template. Once the user has clicked the **Edit** JButton and made changes to the `Parcel`, the user clicks the **Update** JButton, which will store the new data in the `Parcel` object. You will now add the functionality of the **Update** JButton to your application.

Updating Parcel Information

1. **Updating the Parcel's data.** When users want to modify a `Parcel`'s data, they will click the **Edit** `JButton`. This event causes the `Parcel`'s information to become editable, and enable **Update** `JButton` (the code for these actions has already been provided in the template). The user then modifies the `Parcel`'s information and clicks the **Update** `JButton`. Insert line 468 of Fig. 19.27 into the `updateJButtonActionPerformed` method. This line calls the `setParcelData` method, which retrieves the information entered by the user and stores this data in the current `Parcel` object, using reference `newParcel`.

Updating the `ArrayList` with new `Parcel` information

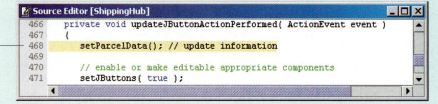

```
466    private void updateJButtonActionPerformed( ActionEvent event )
467    {
468        setParcelData(); // update information
469
470        // enable or make editable appropriate components
471        setJButtons( true );
```

Figure 19.27   Removing and inserting a `Parcel` to update data.

2. **Saving the application.** Save your modified source code file.

3. **Opening the Command Prompt window and changing directories.** Open the **Command Prompt** window by selecting **Start > Programs > Accessories > Command Prompt**. Change to your working directory by typing `cd C:\SimplyJava\ShippingHub`.

4. **Compiling the application.** Compile your application by typing `javac ShippingHub.java`.

5. **Running the application.** When your application compiles correctly, run it by typing `java ShippingHub`. Figure 19.28 shows the updated application running. Use the **Scan New** and **Add** `JButtons` to add a `Parcel` to `parcelsArrayList` (Fig. 19.28). Click the **Edit** `JButton`—notice that the **Update** `JButton` is enabled. Modify the `Parcel`'s information (Fig. 19.29), then click the **Update** `JButton`. The `Parcel` has now been modified (Fig. 19.30).

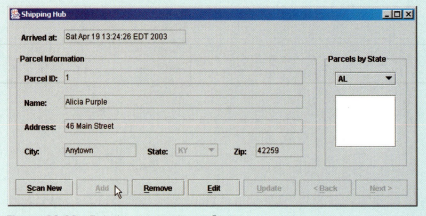

Figure 19.28   Entering a new `Parcel`.

(cont.)

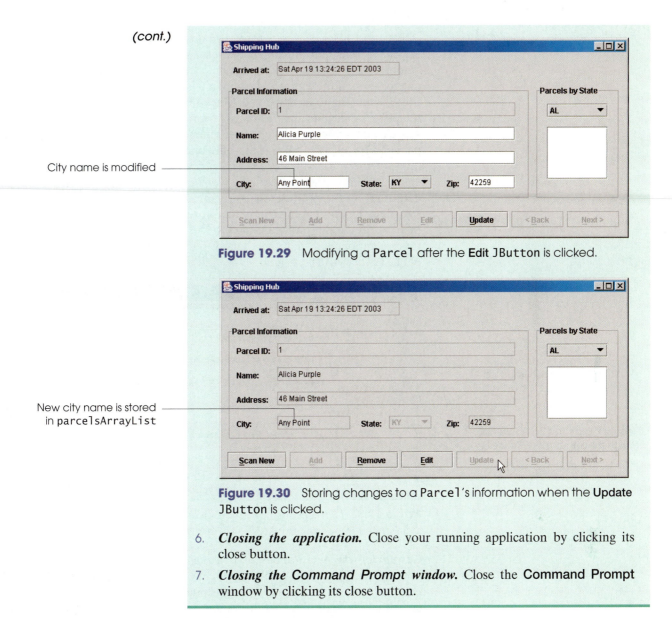

Figure 19.29   Modifying a `Parcel` after the **Edit** `JButton` is clicked.

Figure 19.30   Storing changes to a `Parcel`'s information when the **Update** `JButton` is clicked.

6. ***Closing the application.*** Close your running application by clicking its close button.

7. ***Closing the Command Prompt window.*** Close the **Command Prompt** window by clicking its close button.

The user navigates `parcelsArrayList` by clicking the **Next >** and **< Back** `JButtons`. When the **Remove** `JButton` is clicked, the next `Parcel` in `parcels-ArrayList` is displayed. When any of these `JButtons` are clicked, the `Parcel`'s information displayed in your application's components must be updated. You will define this functionality in the `loadParcel` method. This method will use variable `position` to retrieve the appropriate `Parcel`'s information from the `parcels-ArrayList`. You will first update `position` in the **Next >**, **< Back** and **Remove** `JButtons` and call the `loadParcel` method. Then you will define the `loadParcel` method.

Displaying a `Parcel`

1. ***Determining which `Parcel` to display after a removal.*** When a `Parcel` is removed, the next `Parcel` is displayed. There are two exceptions to this rule: When the last `Parcel` in `parcelsArrayList` is removed, the "next" `Parcel` should be the first `Parcel` in `parcelsArrayList`. The other exception occurs when the removed `Parcel` was the only element in `parcelsArray-List`. When this occurs, your application's components should be cleared. To display the appropriate information, variable `position` must contain the index of the "next" `Parcel`.

(cont.)

For most cases, variable `position` does not need to be updated when a `Parcel` is removed. Recall that when a removal occurs, the `ArrayList` is automatically updated—each element after the one removed is moved back one location. If the `Parcel` at position 6 is removed, the new `Parcel` at position 6 is the one to be displayed. Lines 432–444 of Fig. 19.31, provided in the template, determine the "next" appropriate `Parcel` to display. Lines 433–439 set `position` to 0 when the element removed was the last one in the `parcelsArrayList`, but not the only one. The condition on line 433 determines if there are still `Parcel`s in `parcelsArrayList` (and therefore, the element removed wasn't the only element), while the condition on line 435 determines if the position of the removed element is larger or equal to the size of `parcelsArrayList` (and therefore, the element removed was the element at the end of `parcelsArrayList`). Lines 440–444 clear your application's components when the element removed was the only element in the `parcelsArrayList`.

Set `position` to display first `Parcel` when last `Parcel` is removed ────

Clear application's components when there are no more `Parcel`s ────

```
430        parcelsArrayList.remove( position );
431
432        // load next Parcel in list if there is one
433        if ( parcelsArrayList.size() > 0 )
434        {
435           if ( position >= parcelsArrayList.size() )
436           {
437              position = 0; // go to beginning
438           }
439        }
440        else
441        {
442           // if no other Parcels remain
443           clearComponents();
444        }
445
446        setJButtons( true ); // enabled appropriate JButtons
```

Figure 19.31 Setting `position` to 0 (to display the first `Parcel`) when the last `Parcel` in `parcelsArrayList` is removed.

2. ***Displaying the next Parcel after a removal***. Add line 440 of Fig. 19.32 to your application. After the `if` statement on lines 435–438 of Fig. 19.31 is executed, `position` contains the proper index of the next element (if there are still elements to display). At this point, you will call the `loadParcel` method (which will be defined shortly) to display the next `Parcel`'s information.

Call method `loadParcel` to display next `Parcel` ────

```
437              position = 0; // go to beginning
438           }
439
440        loadParcel();
441        }
442        else
```

Figure 19.32 Display appropriate `Parcel` after a `Parcel` is removed.

3. ***Determining which Parcel to display when the < Back JButton is clicked***. When the **< Back** JButton is clicked, the previous `Parcel` in `parcelsArrayList` is displayed. If the current `Parcel` is the first element in `parcelsArrayList`, clicking the **< Back** JButton should display the last element in the `parcelsArrayList`. Lines 484–491 of Fig. 19.33, provided in the template, update variable `position` accordingly. If the current `Parcel` is not the first element, decrement `position` (line 486). Otherwise, set `position` to contain the location of the last element (line 490).

(cont.)

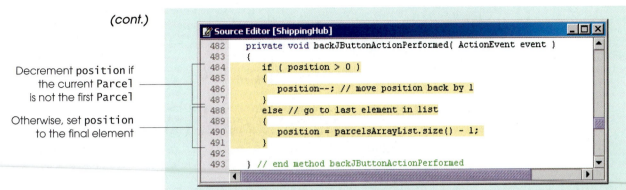

Decrement `position` if
the current `Parcel`
is not the first `Parcel`

Otherwise, set `position`
to the final element

Figure 19.33 Set `position` to the index of the previous `Parcel` when **< Back** JButton is clicked.

4. ***Displaying the previous Parcel.*** Add lines 493–494 of Fig. 19.34 to your application. Variable `position` has already been updated, causing `loadParcel` to display the proper element of the `parcelsArrayList`.

```
Source Editor [ShippingHub *]
490            position = parcelsArrayList.size() - 1;
491        }
492
493        // set and load Parcel
494        loadParcel();
495
496    } // end method backJButtonActionPerformed
```

Figure 19.34 Calling the `loadParcel` method to display the previous `Parcel`'s information.

5. ***Determining which Parcel to display when the Next > JButton is clicked.*** When the **Next >** JButton is clicked, the next `Parcel` in the `parcelsArrayList` is displayed. If the current `Parcel` is the last element in the `parcelsArrayList`, clicking the **Next >** JButton should display the first element in the `parcelsArrayList`. Lines 501–508 of Fig. 19.35, provided in the template, update variable `position`. If the current `Parcel` is not the last element, `position` is incremented (line 503). Otherwise, `position` is set to contain the location of the first element (line 507).

```
Source Editor [ShippingHub]
498    // move to next Parcel
499    private void nextJButtonActionPerformed( ActionEvent event )
500    {
501        if ( position < parcelsArrayList.size() - 1 )
502        {
503            position++; // move position forward by 1
504        }
505        else
506        {
507            position = 0; // go to first element in list
508        }
509
510    } // end method nextJButtonActionPerformed
```

Increment `position` if
the current `Parcel`
is not the last `Parcel`

Otherwise, set `position`
to the first element

Figure 19.35 Set `position` to next `Parcel` when **Next >** JButton is clicked.

6. ***Displaying the next Parcel.*** Add lines 510–511 of Fig. 19.36 to your application. Variable `position` has already been updated, causing `loadParcel` to display the proper element of `parcelsArrayList`.

(cont.)

```
Source Editor [ShippingHub *]                                    _ □ X
507        position = 0; // go to first element in list
508      }
509
510      // load information of Parcel
511      loadParcel();
512
513    } // end method nextJButtonActionPerformed
```

Figure 19.36 Calling the `loadParcel` method to display the next `Parcel`'s information.

7. ***Displaying the Parcel's information.*** Insert lines 538–549 of Fig. 19.37 into your application. Line 539 uses `ArrayList` method **get**, which returns the element in the `parcelsArrayList` at the index specified by the argument, `position`. `ArrayLists` store objects of type `Object`, which need to be cast to the expected type—in this case with the cast (`Parcel`)—when they are retrieved. The resulting `Parcel` is assigned to `newParcel`. Lines 542–549 retrieve the `Parcel` information from `newParcel` and display the data in the corresponding components in your application.

```
Source Editor [ShippingHub]                                      _ □ X
535      // display all information about the Parcel
536      private void loadParcel()
537      {
538          // retrieve package from list
539          newParcel = ( Parcel ) parcelsArrayList.get( position );
540
541          // display package data
542          arrivedAtJTextField.setText( newParcel.getArrivalTime() );
543          parcelIDJTextField.setText(
544              String.valueOf( newParcel.getParcelID() ) );
545          nameJTextField.setText( newParcel.getName() );
546          addressJTextField.setText( newParcel.getAddress() );
547          cityJTextField.setText( newParcel.getCity() );
548          stateJComboBox.setSelectedItem( newParcel.getState() );
549          zipJTextField.setText( String.valueOf( newParcel.getZip() ) );
550
551      } // end method loadParcel
```

Retrieving `Parcel` at index `position` in `parcelsArrayList`

Displaying the data stored in the `Parcel` object

Figure 19.37 Displaying the `Parcel`'s data in your application's components.

8. ***Saving the application.*** Save your modified source code file.

9. ***Opening the Command Prompt window and changing directories.*** Open the **Command Prompt** window by selecting **Start > Programs > Accessories > Command Prompt**. Change to your working directory, `Shipping-Hub`, by typing `cd C:\SimplyJava\ShippingHub`.

10. ***Compiling the application.*** Compile your application by typing `javac ShippingHub.java`.

11. ***Running the application.*** When your application compiles correctly, run it by typing `java ShippingHub`. Figure 19.38 shows the updated application running. Use the **Scan New** and **Add** `JButtons` to add at least two `Parcels` to `parcelsArrayList`. Click the **< Back** and **Next >** `JButtons` to ensure that the previous and next `Parcels` are displayed, respectively (Fig. 19.38 and Fig. 19.39). Use the **Remove** `JButton` to remove each of the `Parcels`, and notice that the next appropriate `Parcel` is displayed, unless there are no more `Parcels` left (in which case your application's components should be cleared).

(cont.)

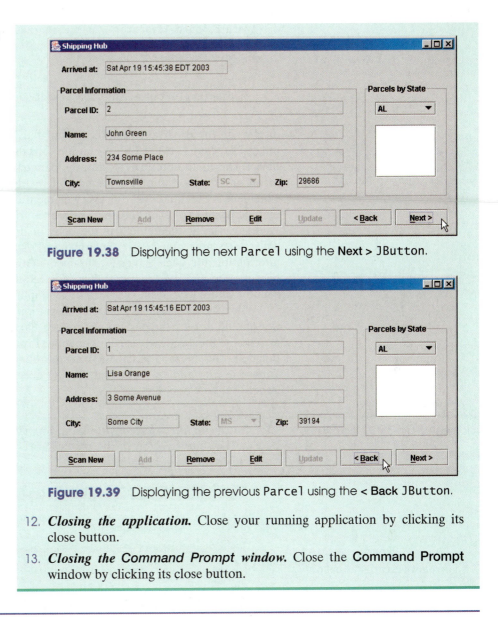

Figure 19.38   Displaying the next `Parcel` using the **Next >** `JButton`.

Figure 19.39   Displaying the previous `Parcel` using the **< Back** `JButton`.

12. ***Closing the application.*** Close your running application by clicking its close button.

13. ***Closing the Command Prompt window.*** Close the **Command Prompt** window by clicking its close button.

SELF-REVIEW

1. The _____ method of class `ArrayList` can be used to retrieve an element of an `ArrayList` at a specified location.

   a) `get`   b) `insert`

   c) `getAt`   d) `retrieve`

2. The **Shipping Hub** application uses an `ArrayList` because class `ArrayList` _____.

   a) can store a variable number of objects   b) allows the addition of `Parcel`s

   c) allows the removal of `Parcel`s   d) All of the above.

Answers: 1) a. 2) d.

19.7 Using Iterators

Software Design Tip

Use an `Iterator` to iterate through the values in a collection without using a counter variable.

An **Iterator** can be used to traverse the elements of a collection. Instead of setting initial and final values for a counter variable, `Iterator` objects provide the **next** method that can access each object of a collection in order. The **iterator** method of the `ArrayList` class returns an `Iterator` object used for traversing through the `ArrayList`. Assuming that you have created the `ArrayList` `parcelsArrayList` that contains only `Parcel` objects, the code

```
Iterator parcelIterator = parcelsArrayList.iterator();

while ( parcelIterator.hasNext() )
{
    Parcel currentParcel = ( Parcel ) parcelIterator.next();
    displayJTextArea.append( currentParcel.getParcelID() + "\n" );
}
```

displays in the `displayJTextArea` all of the ID numbers for the `Parcel`s in the `parcelsArrayList`. The loop condition calls the **hasNext** method of the `Iterator` object. This method returns `true` if the `parcelsArrayList` contains any more elements and `false` if there are no more elements. This means the body of the `while` statement is executed once for every element in the `parcelsArrayList`. The `next` method of an `Iterator` returns a reference to the next object in the `parcelsArrayList`. The first statement in the body of the preceding `while` loop assigns the collection's next object to `currentParcel`. You use this reference to manipulate information for each `Parcel` contained in the `parcelsArrayList`. Notice that because the `while` statement does not require you to specify initial and final counter values when using an iterator, it simplifies accessing groups of values.

When the user selects a state abbreviation from the `JComboBox`, your application should display the `parcelID` for each `Parcel` destined for that state. You will now define the `parcelStateJComboBoxActionPerformed` method to perform this function. This method is called from the `parcelStateJComboBox`'s **actionPerformed** event handler. This event handler executes when an item is selected in the `parcelStateJComboBox`.

Inserting an *Iterator*

1. ***Retrieving the selected state.*** First, you will need a variable to hold the name of the state selected in the `parcelStateJComboBox`. Add lines 519–521 of Fig. 19.40 to your application.

Obtaining the state selected in `parcelStateJComboBox`

```
Source Editor [ShippingHub]
515     // change the list of Parcels in the parcelStateJList
516     private void parcelStateJComboBoxActionPerformed(
517         ActionEvent event )
518     {
519         // create string to compare states
520         String state =
521             ( String ) parcelStateJComboBox.getSelectedItem();
522
523     } // end method parcelStateJComboBoxActionPerformed
```

Figure 19.40   Declaring a variable for the state selected.

2. ***Declaring an Iterator.*** Insert lines 523–524 of Fig. 19.41 to your `parcelStateJComboBoxActionPerformed` method. Line 524 declares variable `parcelIterator` of type `Iterator`. The variable will be used to access each `Parcel` object (one at a time) as you iterate through the `parcelsArrayList`.

Declaring the `Iterator` for the `while` repetition statement

```
Source Editor [ShippingHub]
521             ( String ) parcelStateJComboBox.getSelectedItem();
522
523         // create iterator
524         Iterator parcelIterator = parcelsArrayList.iterator();
525
526     } // end method parcelStateJComboBoxActionPerformed
```

Figure 19.41   Declaring an `Iterator`.

(cont.)

3. ***Clearing the ArrayList.*** Insert lines 526–527 of Fig. 19.42 to your application. Line 527 removes all previous Parcels from the parcelStateArrayList using ArrayList method **clear**. Now parcelStateArrayList contains zero elements, and therefore has a length of zero.

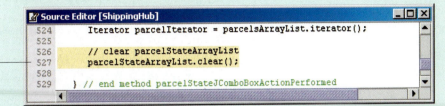

Removing all elements from
the parcelStateArrayList

```
524        Iterator parcelIterator = parcelsArrayList.iterator();
525
526        // clear parcelStateArrayList
527        parcelStateArrayList.clear();
528
529    } // end method parcelStateJComboBoxActionPerformed
```

Figure 19.42   Clearing parcelStateArrayList.

4. ***Inserting a while statement.*** Insert lines 529–534 of Fig. 19.43 to your application. This while statement will iterate through the parcelsArrayList using the parcelIterator. The while loop executes each time the hasNext method returns true.

Using an Iterator in
the while condition

```
527        parcelStateArrayList.clear();
528
529        // create parcelStateArrayList with ID numbers of Parcels
530        // to be displayed
531        while ( parcelIterator.hasNext() )
532        {
533
534        } // end while
535
536    } // end method parcelStateJComboBoxActionPerformed
```

Figure 19.43   Iterator used in a while condition.

5. ***Getting the next Parcel.*** Insert lines 533–534 of Fig. 19.44 to the body of the while loop. Line 534 calls the next method of the Iterator to obtain a reference to the next object in parcelsArrayList. You then cast it to a Parcel type. Recall that ArrayLists and other collections can store objects of several types at the same time. For this reason, it is necessary to use a cast to indicate the type of the object you are retrieving.

Retrieving the next Parcel
in the parcelIterator

```
531        while ( parcelIterator.hasNext() )
532        {
533            // create temporary reference to Parcel object
534            Parcel currentParcel = ( Parcel ) parcelIterator.next();
535
536        } // end while
```

Figure 19.44   Creating a reference using the next method of Iterator.

6. ***Determining a Parcel's destination state.*** Insert lines 536–541 of Fig. 19.45 into your application. These lines contain an if statement that tests each Parcel's destination state code against the state code displayed in the **Parcels By State** JComboBox. If the two state codes match, lines 539–540 add the parcelID to parcelStateArrayList.

The call to the getState method (line 537) will generate a compilation error if the reference returned by the parcelIterator.next() method is not cast to a Parcel type. This occurs because the next method of an Iterator returns a reference to an Object, which has no getState or getParcelID method. You must cast this to a Parcel type so that you will have access to these methods of class Parcel.

Common Programming Error

The **next** method of class Iterator returns a reference of type Object. If this reference is not converted to the expected type, attempting to accesses members of the expected type will cause compilation errors to occur.

(cont.)

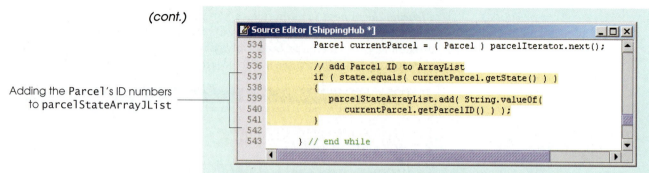

Adding the Parcel's ID numbers to parcelStateArrayJList

Figure 19.45 Adding all shipments going to selected state.

7. *Displaying results in a* **JList**. Insert lines 545–547 of Fig. 19.46 into your application. These lines use the setListData method to set the text displayed in the JList. This method takes an array as an argument, and displays the array's elements in a JList, with each item on its own line.

The class ArrayList contains the method **toArray**, which converts the information stored in the ArrayList directly to an array of Objects. The method call in line 547 converts the parcelStateArrayList to a one-dimensional array. Using this method, you can set the JList to display in the parcelStateJList the parcelID of each Parcel object.

![Common Programming Error icon] **Common Programming Error**

Method setListData expects an array as an argument. It is an error to pass this method an object of type ArrayList. Instead, convert the ArrayList to an array with method toArray.

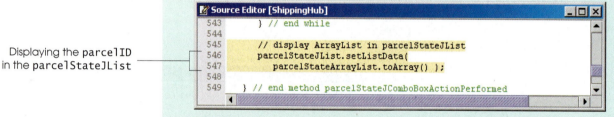

Displaying the parcelID in the parcelStateJList

Figure 19.46 Displaying all Parcels going to the selected state.

8. *Saving the application.* Save your modified source code file.

9. *Opening the Command Prompt window and changing directories.* Open the **Command Prompt** window by selecting **Start > Programs > Accessories > Command Prompt**. Change to your working directory by typing cd C:\SimplyJava\ShippingHub.

10. *Compiling the application.* Compile your application by typing javac ShippingHub.java.

11. *Running the application.* When your application compiles correctly, run it by typing java ShippingHub. Figure 19.47 shows the updated application running. Use the **Scan New** and **Add** JButtons to add several Parcels. Make sure that multiple Parcels have the same state entered in the **State:** JComboBox. Once you have entered the Parcels, select different states using the **Parcels by State** JComboBox to see all Parcels being sent to a specific state. In Fig. 19.47, four of the added Parcels are bound for Florida. Selecting **FL** in the **Parcels by State** JComboBox displays the IDs of these Parcels. Keep in mind that the application does not yet automatically update the **Parcels by State** JList—you need to explicitly select a state to see a list of Parcels.

(cont.)

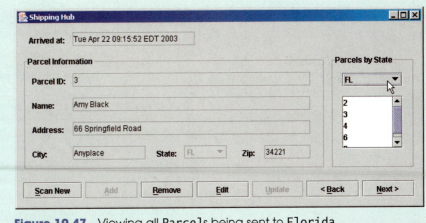

Figure 19.47 Viewing all `Parcels` being sent to `Florida`.

12. ***Closing the application.*** Close your running application by clicking its close button.

13. ***Closing the Command Prompt window.*** Close the **Command Prompt** window by clicking its close button.

You have now completed the `parcelStateJComboBoxActionPerformed` method. This method executes when a state is selected from the `parcelStateJComboBox`, updating the `parcelStateJList`. However, the `parcelStateJList` is still not automatically updated when a `Parcel` is added, updated or removed. You will now add this functionality.

Selecting a State   1. ***Selecting an item in a JComboBox to execute the JComboBox's actionPerformed event handler.*** Add lines 421–423 of Fig. 19.48 to the `addJButtonActionPerformed` method. Lines 422–423 select the state in `parcelStateJComboBox` that was selected by the user in `stateJComboBox`. This selection causes `parcelStateJComboBox`'s `actionPerformed` event handler to execute, which calls the `parcelStateJComboBoxActionPerformed` method. This method determines and displays the `Parcels` bound for the selected state. Add lines 483–485 of Fig. 19.49 to the `updateJButtonActionPerformed` method. These lines again cause the `parcelStateJComboBoxActionPerformed` method to execute. You want this method to execute at this time, because the user may have modified the `Parcel`'s state code after clicking the **Edit** `JButton`. If this information has been modified, `parcelStateJList` will need to be modified as well.

Selecting the state in
`parcelStateJComboBox`
that was selected by the
user in `stateJComboBox`

```
     Source Editor [ShippingHub]
419        setJButtons( true );
420
421        // change selected item in parcelStateJComboBox
422        parcelStateJComboBox.setSelectedIndex(
423          stateJComboBox.getSelectedIndex() );
424
425    } // end method addJButtonActionPerformed
```

Figure 19.48 Adding an element to `parcelStateJList`.

(cont.)

Selecting the state in `parcelStateJComboBox` that was selected by the user in `stateJComboBox`

```
Source Editor [ShippingHub]
481        parcelInformationJPanelEditable( false );
482
483        // change selected item in parcelStateJComboBox
484        parcelStateJComboBox.setSelectedIndex(
485           stateJComboBox.getSelectedIndex() );
486
487     } // end method updateJButtonActionPerformed
```

Figure 19.49   Updating elements in `parcelStateJList`.

2. ***Updating parcelStateJList when a Parcel is removed.*** Add lines 433–439 of Fig. 19.50 to the removeJButtonActionPerformed method. This if statement's condition determines whether the state selected in parcel-StateJComboBox is also the state of the Parcel being removed. When this occurs, the Parcel being removed from parcelsArrayList must also be removed from parcelStateJList. Add lines 438–445 of Fig. 19.51 to your application. Lines 439–440 access the index of the Parcel to be removed in parcelStateArrayList. Method **indexOf** of class ArrayList takes an object, and returns the index in the ArrayList where that object is stored. If the object does not exist in the ArrayList, method indexOf returns -1. Line 441 removes this element, and lines 444–445 assign the remaining Parcel IDs to parcelStateJList using the setListData method of JList.

Determine if the state selected in `parcelStateJComboBox` is also the state of the `Parcel` being removed

```
Source Editor [ShippingHub]
431        String stateSelected = newParcel.getState();
432
433        // if same state is selected, remove ID number from
434        // parcelStateJList
435        if ( stateSelected.equals(
436           parcelStateJComboBox.getSelectedItem() ) )
437        {
438
439        } // end if
440
441        // remove current parcel from ArrayList
```

Figure 19.50   Determining if an element needs to be removed from `parcelStateJList`.

Removing the `Parcel` ID from the `parcelStateArrayList`

Assigning the remaining `Parcel` IDs to `parcelStateJList`

```
Source Editor [ShippingHub]
435        if ( stateSelected.equals(
436           parcelStateJComboBox.getSelectedItem() ) )
437        {
438           // index of current Parcel
439           int index = parcelStateArrayList.indexOf(
440              String.valueOf( newParcel.getParcelID() ) );
441           parcelStateArrayList.remove( index );
442
443           // reset JList data
444           parcelStateJList.setListData(
445              parcelStateArrayList.toArray() );
446
447        } // end if
```

Figure 19.51   Removing an element from `parcelStateJList`.

3. ***Saving the application.*** Save your modified source code file.

4. ***Opening the Command Prompt window and changing directories.*** Open the **Command Prompt** window by selecting **Start > Programs > Accessories > Command Prompt**. Change to your working directory by typing cd C:\SimplyJava\ShippingHub.

(cont.)

5. ***Compiling the application.*** Compile your application by typing `javac ShippingHub.java`.

6. ***Running the application.*** When your application compiles correctly, run it by typing `java ShippingHub`. Figure 19.52 shows the completed application running. Use the **Scan New** and **Add** `JButton`s to add several `Parcel`s. Notice that as you add each `Parcel`, the proper state and items are displayed in the **Parcels by State** `JPanel`. In Fig. 19.52, five of the added `Parcel`s are bound for Florida (the fifth `Parcel` to Florida, `Parcel 9`, can be seen using the scrollbar). Selecting **FL** in the **Parcels by State** `JComboBox` displays the IDs of these `Parcel`s. You then remove the third `Parcel` in Fig. 19.53. Notice that the **Parcels by State** `JList` is updated to remove this item. Use the **Edit** and **Update** `JButton`s to modify one of your entries, and notice that the **Parcels by State** `JPanel` will update accordingly.

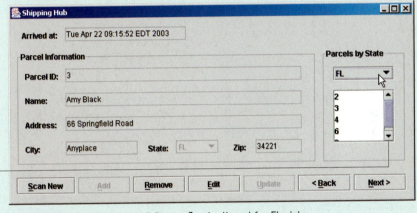

Scrollbar appears for more than four `Parcel` IDs

Figure 19.52 Viewing all `Parcel`s destined for Florida.

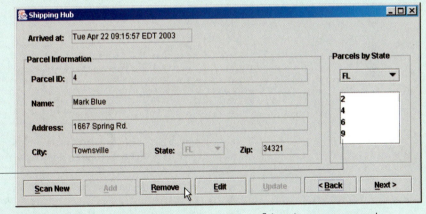

`Parcel 3` is removed

Figure 19.53 Resulting `JList` after a `Parcel` has been removed.

7. ***Closing the application.*** Close your running application by clicking its close button.

8. ***Closing the Command Prompt window.*** Close the **Command Prompt** window by clicking its close button.

Figure 19.54 and Fig. 19.55 present the source code for the **Shipping Hub** application. The lines of code that you added, viewed or modified in this tutorial are highlighted.

```
1    // Tutorial 19: Parcel.java
2    // This class defines the Parcel object.
3    public class Parcel
4    {
5       // member data
6       private String name;
7       private String address;
8       private String city;
9       private String state;
10      private String arrivalTime;
11      private int zip;
12      private int parcelID;
13
14      // constructor
15      public Parcel( int number, String time )
16      {
17         setParcel( "", "", "", "", 99999, "" );
18         parcelID = number;
19         arrivalTime = time;
20      }
21
22      // set the parcel properties
23      private void setParcel( String nameValue, String addressValue,
24         String cityValue, String stateValue, int zipValue,
25         String timeValue )
26      {
27         name = nameValue;
28         address = addressValue;
29         city = cityValue;
30         state = stateValue;
31         zip = zipValue;
32         arrivalTime = timeValue;
33      }
34
35      // get the name
36      public String getName()
37      {
38         return name;
39      }
40
41      // set the name
42      public void setName( String nameValue )
43      {
44         name = nameValue;
45      }
46
47      // get the address
48      public String getAddress()
49      {
50         return address;
51      }
52
53      // set the address
54      public void setAddress( String addressValue )
55      {
56         address = addressValue;
57      }
58
```

Figure 19.54   Parcel code. (Part 1 of 2.)

```
59      // get the city
60      public String getCity()
61      {
62         return city;
63      }
64
65      // set the city
66      public void setCity( String cityValue )
67      {
68         city = cityValue;
69      }
70
71      // get the state
72      public String getState()
73      {
74         return state;
75      }
76
77      // set the state
78      public void setState( String stateValue )
79      {
80         state = stateValue;
81      }
82
83      // get the zip code
84      public int getZip()
85      {
86         return zip;
87      }
88
89      // set the zip code
90      public void setZip( int zipValue )
91      {
92         zip = zipValue;
93      }
94
95      // get the parcel number
96      public int getParcelID()
97      {
98         return parcelID;
99      }
100
101      // get the arrival time
102      public String getArrivalTime()
103      {
104         return arrivalTime;
105      }
106
107  } // end class Parcel
```

Figure 19.54 `Parcel` code. (Part 2 of 2.)

```
1   // Tutorial 19: ShippingHub.java
2   // This application tracks Parcels that pass through a shipping hub.
3   import java.awt.*;
4   import java.awt.event.*;
5   import java.util.*;
```

Import the package containing
class `ArrayList`

Figure 19.55 **Shipping Hub** code. (Part 1 of 13.)

```java
 6   import javax.swing.*;
 7   import javax.swing.border.TitledBorder;
 8
 9   public class ShippingHub extends JFrame
10   {
11      // JLabel and JTextField to display time of arrival
12      private JLabel arrivedAtJLabel;
13      private JTextField arrivedAtJTextField;
14
15      // JPanel to contain Parcel information
16      private JPanel parcelInformationJPanel;
17
18      // JLabel and JTextField to display Parcel identification number
19      private JLabel parcelIDJLabel;
20      private JTextField parcelIDJTextField;
21
22      // JLabel and JTextField for name
23      private JLabel nameJLabel;
24      private JTextField nameJTextField;
25
26      // JLabel and JTextField for address
27      private JLabel addressJLabel;
28      private JTextField addressJTextField;
29
30      // JLabel and JTextField for city
31      private JLabel cityJLabel;
32      private JTextField cityJTextField;
33
34      // JLabel and JTextField for state
35      private JLabel stateJLabel;
36      private JComboBox stateJComboBox;
37
38      // JLabel and JTextField for zip code
39      private JLabel zipJLabel;
40      private JTextField zipJTextField;
41
42      // JPanel for Parcel number by state
43      private JPanel parcelStateJPanel;
44
45      // JComboBox, JList and JScrollPane for Parcel number
46      private JComboBox parcelStateJComboBox;
47      private JList parcelStateJList;
48      private JScrollPane parcelStateJScrollPane;
49
50      // JButtons to manipulate Parcels
51      private JButton scanNewJButton;
52      private JButton addJButton;
53      private JButton removeJButton;
54      private JButton editJButton;
55      private JButton updateJButton;
56      private JButton backJButton;
57      private JButton nextJButton;
58
59      // array contains options for ParcelStateJComboBox
60      private String[] states = { "AL", "FL", "GA", "KY", "MS", "NC",
61         "SC", "TN", "VA", "WV" };
62
```

parcelStateJList and parcelStateJScrollPane used to display a scrollable list of Parcels bound for the same state

Figure 19.55   **Shipping Hub** code. (Part 2 of 13.)

ArrayList contains the
Parcels entered by user

ArrayList contains the Parcel
IDs destined for a specific state

```
63      // Parcel object contains data for newly entered Parcels
64      private Parcel newParcel;
65
66      // ArrayList contains Parcel objects entered by user
67      private ArrayList parcelsArrayList = new ArrayList();
68
69      // ArrayList used to modify and display the Parcel objects
70      // for a specific state
71      private ArrayList parcelStateArrayList = new ArrayList();
72
73      private int parcelID = 0; // ID for new Parcels
74
75      // position used to track location when the user is
76      // browsing through the list of Parcels
77      private int position = 0;
78
79      // no-argument constructor
80      public ShippingHub()
81      {
82         createUserInterface();
83      }
84
85      // create and position GUI components; register event handlers
86      private void createUserInterface()
87      {
88         // get content pane for attaching GUI components
89         Container contentPane = getContentPane();
90
91         // enable explicit positioning of GUI components
92         contentPane.setLayout( null );
93
94         // set up arrivedAtJLabel
95         arrivedAtJLabel = new JLabel();
96         arrivedAtJLabel.setBounds( 19, 14, 74, 24 );
97         arrivedAtJLabel.setText( "Arrived at:" );
98         contentPane.add( arrivedAtJLabel );
99
100        // set up arrivedAtJTextField
101        arrivedAtJTextField = new JTextField();
102        arrivedAtJTextField.setBounds( 89, 14, 207, 21 );
103        arrivedAtJTextField.setEditable( false );
104        contentPane.add( arrivedAtJTextField );
105
106        // set up parcelInformationJPanel
107        parcelInformationJPanel = new JPanel();
108        parcelInformationJPanel.setBounds( 9, 51, 490, 178 );
109        parcelInformationJPanel.setBorder(
110           new TitledBorder( "Parcel Information" ) );
111        parcelInformationJPanel.setLayout( null );
112        contentPane.add( parcelInformationJPanel );
113
114        // set up parcelIDJLabel
115        parcelIDJLabel = new JLabel();
116        parcelIDJLabel.setBounds( 15, 27, 84, 24 );
117        parcelIDJLabel.setText( "Parcel ID:" );
118        parcelInformationJPanel.add( parcelIDJLabel );
119
```

Figure 19.55 Shipping Hub code. (Part 3 of 13.)

```
120      // set up parcelIDJTextField
121      parcelIDJTextField = new JTextField();
122      parcelIDJTextField.setBounds( 80, 27, 386, 21 );
123      parcelIDJTextField.setEditable( false );
124      parcelInformationJPanel.add( parcelIDJTextField );
125
126      // set up nameJLabel
127      nameJLabel = new JLabel();
128      nameJLabel.setBounds( 15, 65, 66, 25 );
129      nameJLabel.setText( "Name:" );
130      parcelInformationJPanel.add( nameJLabel );
131
132      // set up nameJTextField
133      nameJTextField = new JTextField();
134      nameJTextField.setBounds( 80, 65, 386, 21 );
135      nameJTextField.setEditable( false );
136      parcelInformationJPanel.add( nameJTextField );
137
138      // set up addressJLabel
139      addressJLabel = new JLabel();
140      addressJLabel.setBounds( 15, 103, 66, 25 );
141      addressJLabel.setText( "Address:" );
142      parcelInformationJPanel.add( addressJLabel );
143
144      // set up addressJTextField
145      addressJTextField = new JTextField();
146      addressJTextField.setBounds( 80, 103, 386, 21 );
147      addressJTextField.setEditable( false );
148      parcelInformationJPanel.add( addressJTextField );
149
150      // set up cityJLabel
151      cityJLabel = new JLabel();
152      cityJLabel.setBounds( 15, 141, 37, 24 );
153      cityJLabel.setText( "City:" );
154      parcelInformationJPanel.add( cityJLabel );
155
156      // set up cityJTextField
157      cityJTextField = new JTextField();
158      cityJTextField.setBounds( 80, 141, 117, 21 );
159      cityJTextField.setEditable( false );
160      parcelInformationJPanel.add( cityJTextField );
161
162      // set up stateJLabel
163      stateJLabel = new JLabel();
164      stateJLabel.setBounds( 215, 141, 47, 24 );
165      stateJLabel.setText( "State:" );
166      parcelInformationJPanel.add( stateJLabel );
167
168      // set up stateJComboBox
169      stateJComboBox = new JComboBox( states );
170      stateJComboBox.setBounds( 260, 141, 70, 21 );
171      stateJComboBox.setEnabled( false );
172      parcelInformationJPanel.add( stateJComboBox );
173
174      // set up zipJLabel
175      zipJLabel = new JLabel();
176      zipJLabel.setBounds( 355, 141, 28, 24 );
177      zipJLabel.setText( "Zip:" );
```

Figure 19.55 **Shipping Hub** code. (Part 4 of 13.)

```
178          parcelInformationJPanel.add( zipJLabel );
179
180          // set up zipJTextField
181          zipJTextField = new JTextField();
182          zipJTextField.setBounds( 390, 141, 76, 21 );
183          zipJTextField.setEditable( false );
184          parcelInformationJPanel.add( zipJTextField );
185
186          // set up parcelStateJPanel
187          parcelStateJPanel = new JPanel();
188          parcelStateJPanel.setBounds( 508, 51, 136, 178 );
189          parcelStateJPanel.setBorder(
190             new TitledBorder( "Parcels by State" ) );
191          parcelStateJPanel.setLayout( null );
192          contentPane.add( parcelStateJPanel );
193
194          // set up parcelStateJComboBox
195          parcelStateJComboBox = new JComboBox( states );
196          parcelStateJComboBox.setBounds( 19, 29, 98, 21 );
197          parcelStateJPanel.add( parcelStateJComboBox );
198          parcelStateJComboBox.addActionListener(
199
200             new ActionListener() // anonymous inner class
201             {
202                // event handler called when parcelStateJComboBox
203                // is selected
204                public void actionPerformed( ActionEvent event )
205                {
206                   parcelStateJComboBoxActionPerformed( event );
207                }
208
209             } // end anonymous inner class
210
211          ); // end call to addActionListener
212
213          // set up parcelStateJList
214          parcelStateJList = new JList();
215
216          // set up parcelStateJScrollPane
217          parcelStateJScrollPane = new JScrollPane( parcelStateJList );
218          parcelStateJScrollPane.setBounds( 19, 65, 98, 82 );
219          parcelStateJPanel.add( parcelStateJScrollPane );
220
221          // set up scanNewJButton
222          scanNewJButton = new JButton();
223          scanNewJButton.setBounds( 9, 248, 95, 26 );
224          scanNewJButton.setText( "Scan New" );
225          scanNewJButton.setMnemonic( KeyEvent.VK_S );
226          contentPane.add( scanNewJButton );
227          scanNewJButton.addActionListener(
228
229             new ActionListener() // anonymous inner class
230             {
231                // event handler called when scanNewJButton is pressed
232                public void actionPerformed( ActionEvent event )
233                {
234                   scanNewJButtonActionPerformed( event );
235                }
```

Define the `parcelStateJList` as an empty `JList`

Add the `parcelStateJList` to a `JScrollPane` so that scrollbars will be added as necessary

Set the mnemonic of `scanNewJButton` to 'S'

Figure 19.55 Shipping Hub code. (Part 5 of 13.)

```
236
237              } // end anonymous inner class
238
239          ); // end call to addActionListener
240
241          // set up addJButton
242          addJButton = new JButton();
243          addJButton.setBounds( 109, 248, 85, 26 );
244          addJButton.setText( "Add" );
245          addJButton.setMnemonic( KeyEvent.VK_A );
246          addJButton.setEnabled( false );
247          contentPane.add( addJButton );
248          addJButton.addActionListener(
249
250              new ActionListener() // anonymous inner class
251              {
252                  // event handler called when addJButton is pressed
253                  public void actionPerformed( ActionEvent event )
254                  {
255                      addJButtonActionPerformed( event );
256                  }
257
258              } // end anonymous inner class
259
260          ); // end call to addActionListener
261
262          // set up removeJButton
263          removeJButton = new JButton();
264          removeJButton.setBounds( 199, 248, 85, 26 );
265          removeJButton.setText( "Remove" );
266          removeJButton.setMnemonic( KeyEvent.VK_R );
267          removeJButton.setEnabled( false );
268          contentPane.add( removeJButton );
269          removeJButton.addActionListener(
270
271              new ActionListener() // anonymous inner class
272              {
273                  // event handler called when removeJButton is pressed
274                  public void actionPerformed( ActionEvent event )
275                  {
276                      removeJButtonActionPerformed( event );
277                  }
278
279              } // end anonymous inner class
280
281          ); // end call to addActionListener
282
283          // set up editJButton
284          editJButton = new JButton();
285          editJButton.setBounds( 289, 248, 85, 26 );
286          editJButton.setText( "Edit" );
287          editJButton.setMnemonic( KeyEvent.VK_E );
288          editJButton.setEnabled( false );
289          contentPane.add( editJButton );
290          editJButton.addActionListener(
291
292              new ActionListener() // anonymous inner class
293              {
```

Set the mnemonic of addJButton to 'A' *(annotation pointing to line 245)*

Set the mnemonic of removeJButton to 'R' *(annotation pointing to line 266)*

Set the mnemonic of editJButton to 'E' *(annotation pointing to line 287)*

Figure 19.55 Shipping Hub code. (Part 6 of 13.)

```
294        // event handler called when editJButton is pressed
295        public void actionPerformed( ActionEvent event )
296        {
297            editJButtonActionPerformed( event );
298        }
299
300     } // end anonymous inner class
301
302  ); // end call to addActionListener
303
304  // set up updateJButton
305  updateJButton = new JButton();
306  updateJButton.setBounds( 379, 248, 85, 26 );
307  updateJButton.setText( "Update" );
308  updateJButton.setMnemonic( KeyEvent.VK_U );
309  updateJButton.setEnabled( false );
310  contentPane.add( updateJButton );
311  updateJButton.addActionListener(
312
313     new ActionListener() // anonymous inner class
314     {
315        // event handler called when updateJButton is pressed
316        public void actionPerformed( ActionEvent event )
317        {
318            updateJButtonActionPerformed( event );
319        }
320
321     } // end anonymous inner class
322
323  ); // end call to addActionListener
324
325  // set up backJButton
326  backJButton = new JButton();
327  backJButton.setBounds( 469, 248, 85, 26 );
328  backJButton.setText( "< Back" );
329  backJButton.setMnemonic( KeyEvent.VK_B );
330  backJButton.setEnabled( false );
331  contentPane.add( backJButton );
332  backJButton.addActionListener(
333
334     new ActionListener() // anonymous inner class
335     {
336        // event handler called when backJButton is pressed
337        public void actionPerformed( ActionEvent event )
338        {
339            backJButtonActionPerformed( event );
340        }
341
342     } // end anonymous inner class
343
344  ); // end call to addActionListener
345
346  // set up nextJButton
347  nextJButton = new JButton();
348  nextJButton.setBounds( 559, 248, 85, 26 );
349  nextJButton.setText( "Next >" );
350  nextJButton.setMnemonic( KeyEvent.VK_N );
351  nextJButton.setEnabled( false );
```

Set the mnemonic of updateJButton to 'U'

Set the mnemonic of backJButton to 'B'

Set the mnemonic of nextJButton to 'N'

Figure 19.55 **Shipping Hub** code. (Part 7 of 13.)

```
352          contentPane.add( nextJButton );
353          nextJButton.addActionListener(
354
355             new ActionListener() // anonymous inner class
356             {
357                // event handler called when nextJButton is pressed
358                public void actionPerformed( ActionEvent event )
359                {
360                   nextJButtonActionPerformed( event );
361                }
362
363             } // end anonymous inner class
364
365          ); // end call to addActionListener
366
367          // set properties of application's window
368          setTitle( "Shipping Hub" ); // set title bar string
369          setSize( 663, 313 );        // set window size
370          setVisible( true );         // display window
371
372       } // end method createUserInterface
373
374       // prepare to scan a new Parcel
375       private void scanNewJButtonActionPerformed( ActionEvent event )
376       {
377          // clear JTextFields
378          clearComponents();
379
380          // set arrival time
381          Date now = new Date();
382          arrivedAtJTextField.setText( now.toString() );
383
384          // give Parcel unique ID number
385          parcelID++;
386          parcelIDJTextField.setText( String.valueOf( parcelID ) );
387
388          // create new Parcel object
389          newParcel = new Parcel( parcelID,
390             arrivedAtJTextField.getText() );
391
392          // disable appropriate components
393          setJButtons( false );
394
395          // enable or make editable appropriate components
396          addJButton.setEnabled( true );
397          parcelInformationJPanelEditable( true );
398
399          // grab focus
400          nameJTextField.requestFocusInWindow();
401
402       } // end method scanNewJButtonActionPerformed
403
404       // add a new Parcel
405       private void addJButtonActionPerformed( ActionEvent event )
406       {
407          // set information for new Parcel
408          setParcelData();
409
```

Create a new **Date** object to set the arrival time of the **Parcel** → (lines 381–382)

Create a unique ID number for the new **Parcel** → (line 385)

Create a **Parcel** object to contain the user's data → (lines 389–390)

Figure 19.55 **Shipping Hub** code. (Part 8 of 13.)

Add the `Parcel` to the `ArrayList` and set position to the last element in the `ArrayList`

```
410        // add new Parcel to parcelsArrayList
411        parcelsArrayList.add( newParcel );
412        position = parcelsArrayList.size() - 1;
413
414        // disable or make uneditable appropriate components
415        addJButton.setEnabled( false );
416        parcelInformationJPanelEditable( false );
417
418        // enable appropriate components
419        setJButtons( true );
420
```

Change the selected item, causing the `parcelStateJComboBox`'s `actionPerformed` event handler to execute

```
421        // change selected item in parcelStateJComboBox
422        parcelStateJComboBox.setSelectedIndex(
423           stateJComboBox.getSelectedIndex() );
424
425     } // end method addJButtonActionPerformed
426
427     // remove a Parcel
428     private void removeJButtonActionPerformed( ActionEvent event )
429     {
430        // retrieve the state of the current Parcel
431        String stateSelected = newParcel.getState();
432
433        // if same state is selected, remove ID number from
434        // parcelStateJList
435        if ( stateSelected.equals(
436           parcelStateJComboBox.getSelectedItem() ) )
437        {
438           // index of current Parcel
439           int index = parcelStateArrayList.indexOf(
440              String.valueOf( newParcel.getParcelID() ) );
441           parcelStateArrayList.remove( index );
442
443           // reset JList data
444           parcelStateJList.setListData(
445              parcelStateArrayList.toArray() );
446
447        } // end if
448
449        // remove current Parcel from ArrayList
450        parcelsArrayList.remove( position );
451
452        // load next Parcel in list if there is one
453        if ( parcelsArrayList.size() > 0 )
454        {
455           if ( position >= parcelsArrayList.size() )
456           {
457              position = 0; // go to beginning
458           }
459
460           loadParcel();
461        }
462        else
463        {
464           // if no other Parcels remain
465           clearComponents();
466        }
467
```

If the state in the `parcelStateJComboBox` is the same as the state of the `Parcel` to be removed, remove the `Parcel` ID from the `parcelStateArrayList`

The `setListData` method displays an array's elements in a `JList`

Remove the current `Parcel` from the `parcelsArrayList`

Determine the position of the next `Parcel` to be displayed, and call `loadParcel` to display it

If the removed `Parcel` was the only `Parcel`, clear the application's components

Figure 19.55   **Shipping Hub** code. (Part 9 of 13.)

```
468        setJButtons( true ); // enabled appropriate JButtons
469
470        // set focus to scanNewJButton
471        scanNewJButton.requestFocusInWindow();
472
473     } // end method removeJButtonActionPerformed
474
475     // allow user to edit Parcel information
476     private void editJButtonActionPerformed( ActionEvent event )
477     {
478        // disable appropriate components
479        setJButtons( false );
480
481        // make user able to update Parcel information
482        updateJButton.setEnabled( true );
483        parcelInformationJPanelEditable( true );
484
485     } // end method editJButtonActionPerformed
486
487     // move to next Parcel
488     private void updateJButtonActionPerformed( ActionEvent event )
489     {
490        setParcelData(); // update information
491
492        // enable or make editable appropriate components
493        setJButtons( true );
494
495        // disable or make uneditable appropriate components
496        updateJButton.setEnabled( false );
497        parcelInformationJPanelEditable( false );
498
499        // change selected item in parcelStateJComboBox
500        parcelStateJComboBox.setSelectedIndex(
501           stateJComboBox.getSelectedIndex() );
502
503     } // end method updateJButtonActionPerformed
504
505     // move to previous Parcel
506     private void backJButtonActionPerformed( ActionEvent event )
507     {
508        if ( position > 0 )
509        {
510           position--; // move position back by 1
511        }
512        else // go to last element in list
513        {
514           position = parcelsArrayList.size() - 1;
515        }
516
517        // set and load Parcel
518        loadParcel();
519
520     } // end method backJButtonActionPerformed
521
522     // move to next Parcel
523     private void nextJButtonActionPerformed( ActionEvent event )
524     {
```

The `setParcelData` method sets the `Parcel`'s properties to the values entered by the user

Change the selected item, causing the `parcelStateJComboBox`'s `actionPerformed` event handler to execute

When the user clicks the **< Back** `JButton`, decrement `position`. If `position` was zero, set `position` to the last object in the `ArrayList`

Display the previous `Parcel`

Figure 19.55   **Shipping Hub** code. (Part 10 of 13.)

When the user clicks the **Next >** JButton, increment `position`. If `position` was the index of the last object in the ArrayList, set `position` to zero

```
525     if ( position < parcelsArrayList.size() - 1 )
526     {
527         position++; // move position forward by 1
528     }
529     else
530     {
531         position = 0; // go to first element in list
532     }
533
534     // load information of Parcel
```

Display the next Parcel

```
535     loadParcel();
536
537 } // end method nextJButtonActionPerformed
538
539 // change the list of Parcels in the parcelStateJList
540 private void parcelStateJComboBoxActionPerformed(
541     ActionEvent event )
542 {
543     // create string to compare states
```

Retrieve the state code selected in parcelStateJComboBox

```
544     String state =
545         ( String ) parcelStateJComboBox.getSelectedItem();
546
547     // create iterator
```

Create a new Iterator object

```
548     Iterator parcelIterator = parcelsArrayList.iterator();
549
550     // clear parcelStateArrayList
```

Remove all elements from the parcelStateArrayList

```
551     parcelStateArrayList.clear();
552
553     // create parcelStateArrayList with ID numbers of Parcels
554     // to be displayed
```

Iterate through every element in the ArrayList

```
555     while ( parcelIterator.hasNext() )
556     {
557         // create temporary reference to Parcel object
```

Retrieve the next Parcel in the parcelsArrayList

```
558         Parcel currentParcel = ( Parcel ) parcelIterator.next();
559
560         // add parcel ID to ArrayList
561         if ( state.equals( currentParcel.getState() ) )
562         {
```

Add the Parcel ID to the parcelStateArrayList

```
563             parcelStateArrayList.add( String.valueOf(
564                 currentParcel.getParcelID() ) );
565         }
566
567     } // end while
568
569     // display ArrayList in parcelStateJList
```

Display the parcel IDs in the parcelStateArrayJList

```
570     parcelStateJList.setListData(
571         parcelStateArrayList.toArray() );
572
573 } // end method parcelStateJComboBoxActionPerformed
574
575 // set all information about the Parcel
576 private void setParcelData()
577 {
578     newParcel.setName( nameJTextField.getText() );
579     newParcel.setAddress( addressJTextField.getText() );
580     newParcel.setCity( cityJTextField.getText() );
581     newParcel.setState( states[
582         stateJComboBox.getSelectedIndex() ] );
```

Figure 19.55   Shipping Hub code. (Part 11 of 13.)

```
583         newParcel.setZip( Integer.parseInt(
584            zipJTextField.getText() ) );
585
586      } // end method setParcelData
587
588      // display all information about the Parcel
589      private void loadParcel()
590      {
591         // retrieve package from list
592         newParcel = ( Parcel ) parcelsArrayList.get( position );
593
594         // display package data
595         arrivedAtJTextField.setText( newParcel.getArrivalTime() );
596         parcelIDJTextField.setText(
597            String.valueOf( newParcel.getParcelID() ) );
598         nameJTextField.setText( newParcel.getName() );
599         addressJTextField.setText( newParcel.getAddress() );
600         cityJTextField.setText( newParcel.getCity() );
601         stateJComboBox.setSelectedItem( newParcel.getState() );
602         zipJTextField.setText( String.valueOf( newParcel.getZip() ) );
603
604      } // end method loadParcel
605
606      // clear all information about the Parcel
607      private void clearComponents()
608      {
609         nameJTextField.setText( "" );
610         addressJTextField.setText( "" );
611         cityJTextField.setText( "" );
612         zipJTextField.setText( "" );
613         arrivedAtJTextField.setText( "" );
614         parcelIDJTextField.setText( "" );
615
616      } // end method clearComponents
617
618      // enabled/disable JButtons
619      private void setJButtons( boolean state )
620      {
621         backJButton.setEnabled( state );
622         scanNewJButton.setEnabled( state );
623         removeJButton.setEnabled( state );
624         editJButton.setEnabled( state );
625         nextJButton.setEnabled( state );
626
627         // disable navigation if not multiple packages
628         if ( parcelsArrayList.size() < 2 )
629         {
630            nextJButton.setEnabled( false );
631            backJButton.setEnabled( false );
632         }
633
634         // if no items, disable Remove, Edit and Update JButtons
635         if ( parcelsArrayList.size() == 0 )
636         {
637            editJButton.setEnabled( false );
638            updateJButton.setEnabled( false );
639            removeJButton.setEnabled( false );
640         }
```

Retrieve `Parcel` at index position in `parcelsArrayList`

Display all `Parcel` information in the applicaton's components

Figure 19.55 **Shipping Hub** code. (Part 12 of 13.)

```
641
642     } // end method setJButtons
643
644     // make editable or uneditable components
645     // in parcelInformationJPanel
646     private void parcelInformationJPanelEditable( boolean editable )
647     {
648        nameJTextField.setEditable( editable );
649        addressJTextField.setEditable( editable );
650        cityJTextField.setEditable( editable );
651        stateJComboBox.setEnabled( editable );
652        zipJTextField.setEditable( editable );
653
654     } // end method parcelInformationJPanelEditable
655
656     // main method
657     public static void main( String[] args )
658     {
659        ShippingHub application = new ShippingHub();
660        application.setDefaultCloseOperation( JFrame.EXIT_ON_CLOSE );
661
662     } // end method main
663
664  } // end class ShippingHub
```

Figure 19.55   Shipping Hub code. (Part 13 of 13.)

SELF-REVIEW

1. The _____ method of an `Iterator` returns true if there are more elements in the collection.

   a) `next`   b) `isNext`

   c) `hasNext`   d) `iterator.next`

2. Iterators provide a(n) _____ to access each element in a collection.

   a) counter   b) element

   c) reference   d) instance variable

Answers: 1) c. 2) c.

19.8 Wrap-Up

In this tutorial, you created mnemonics to allow the user to "press" `JButtons` in the **Shipping Hub** application by pressing the *Alt* key, then the mnemonic key for the particular `JButton`.

You learned about the `JList` component. You added a `JList` to a `JScroll-Pane` so that scrollbars will be displayed as necessary. You also set the elements to be displayed in the `JList` using the `setListData` method.

You learned about the `ArrayList` collection. You used `ArrayList` methods to add a `Parcel` object to the `parcelsArrayList` and remove the `Parcel` from a specific index in the `parcelsArrayList`. These methods helped you store, edit and navigate the `parcelsArrayList` in the **Shipping Hub** application. You also created the `parcelStateArrayList`, which contained the IDs of the `Parcels` bound for a specific state.

Finally, you learned about `Iterators`. You used the `hasNext` method in a `while` loop and used the `next` method to iterate through each element in a collection. Then you used the `while` statement to iterate through `Parcel` objects in the `ArrayList` in your **Shipping Hub** application.

In the next tutorial, you will learn about inheritance, a technique for creating classes that build upon existing classes. You will use inheritance and the Graphics object to draw rectangles on a JPanel, to create a screen saver application.

SKILLS SUMMARY

Using a JList

- Create an object of type JList using keyword new.
- Add this JList to a JScrollPane so that scrollbars will be displayed as necessary.
- Call the JList's setListData method, and pass it an array containing the items you want to display in the JList.

Adding a Mnemonic to a JButton

- Use the JButton's setMnemonic method, and pass it the KeyEvent constant for the character you wish to use as the mnemonic (keyboard shortcut).

Using a Mnemonic to a JButton

- Press the mnemonic character (which will be underlined on the JButton) while holding down the *Alt* key, then release both keys.

Creating an ArrayList

- Create an object of type ArrayList using keyword new.

Adding an Element to an ArrayList

- Call the add method on an ArrayList object and pass the method the object that will be added at the end of the ArrayList.

Removing Elements From an ArrayList

- To remove a specific element, call the remove method on an ArrayList object and pass the method the index of the element in the ArrayList that should be removed.
- To remove all elements in an ArrayList, call the clear method.
- An ArrayList's indices will be updated automatically after removals.

Finding the Index of an Element in an ArrayList

- Call the indexOf method on an ArrayList object and pass the method the element that you wish to find.

Retrieving Elements From an ArrayList

- Call the get method on an ArrayList object and pass the method the index of the element in the ArrayList that you wish to access.
- Cast the reference returned from method get to the appropriate type.

Converting an ArrayList to a One-Dimensional Array

- Call the toArray method on an ArrayList object.

Determining the Size of an ArrayList

- Call the size method on an ArrayList object.

Using an Iterator

- Use the iterator method of ArrayList to obtain a reference to an Iterator.
- Code a while statement that executes as long as there are still elements in the Iterator, using the hasNext method.
- In the body of the while statement, use the next method to retrieve the next element, and cast the reference that is returned to the appropriate type. In the rest of the while loop, perform any functionality needed on the current element. When there are no more elements to retrieve, the while statement will finish looping.

KEY TERMS

`actionPerformed` event handler for the `JComboBox` component—The event handler that is called when a new value is selected in a `JComboBox`.

`add` method of class `ArrayList`—Adds a specified object at the end of an `ArrayList`.

`ArrayList` collection/class—Used to store a group of objects. Unlike arrays, `ArrayList`s can be dynamically resized and have access to several methods that allow programmers to easily manipulate the contents of the `ArrayList`.

`clear` method of class `ArrayList`—Removes all elements in an `ArrayList`.

collection—An object that stores groups of related objects.

dynamic resizing—Enables an `ArrayList` object to vary its size to meet the storage demands of your application.

`get` method of class `ArrayList`—Returns a reference to the element in the `ArrayList` at the specified index.

`hasNext` method of class `Iterator`—Tests if there are any remaining elements in the `ArrayList` accessed by this `Iterator` object.

`indexOf` method of class `ArrayList`—Returns the index in the `ArrayList` where a specified object is stored. If the object does not exist in the `ArrayList`, `indexOf` returns `-1`.

index of an `ArrayList`—The value with which you can refer to a specific element in an `ArrayList`, based on the element's location in that `ArrayList`.

iterator—An object that allows you to loop through each element in a collection.

`Iterator` interface—Implemented by iterator objects, which allow you to loop through each element in a collection.

`iterator` method of class `ArrayList`—Creates a new object of type `Iterator` used for iterating through each element contained in the `ArrayList`.

`JList` component—Displays a series of items from which the user may select one or more.

`KeyEvent` class—Contains information about keyboard events (such as the pressing of a key on the keyboard).

`KeyEvent.VK_A` constant—Represents the A key on the keyboard.

`KeyEvent.VK_B` constant—Represents the B key on the keyboard.

`KeyEvent.VK_E` constant—Represents the E key on the keyboard.

`KeyEvent.VK_N` constant—Represents the N key on the keyboard.

`KeyEvent.VK_R` constant—Represents the R key on the keyboard.

`KeyEvent.VK_S` constant—Represents the S key on the keyboard.

`KeyEvent.VK_U` constant—Represents the U key on the keyboard.

mnemonic—Allows the user to perform an action on a component using the keyboard.

***mnemonic* property of class `JButton`**—The mnemonic used to perform an action on a `JButton`.

`next` method of interface `Iterator`—Returns a reference to the next element in the `ArrayList`.

`remove` method of class `ArrayList`—Removes the object located at a specified location of an `ArrayList`.

`setListData` method of class `JList`—Sets the text to be displayed in the `JList`.

`setMnemonic` method of class `JButton`—Sets the mnemonic to be used to "press" the `JButton`.

`size` method of class `ArrayList`—Returns the number of objects contained in the `ArrayList`.

`toArray` method of class `ArrayList`—Converts the `ArrayList` to a one-dimensional array. This is convenient for cases when the elements of an `ArrayList` need to be passed to a method that is expecting a one-dimensional array.

`toString` method of class `Date`—Returns the current date as a `String`, in the format `Tue Feb 13 16:50:00 EST 2003`.

virtual key code—A constant that represents a key on the keyboard.

GUI DESIGN GUIDELINES

Overall Design

- Use mnemonics to allow users to "click" a component using the keyboard. This provides an added convenience for the user, especially for applications that require the user to enter a great deal of text data.

- Attaching a `JList` to a `JScrollPane` allows users to scroll items in a `JList`.

JAVA LIBRARY REFERENCE

ArrayList This class is used to store a set of objects. Unlike arrays, `ArrayList`s can be dynamically resized and have access to several methods that allows programmers to easily manipulate the contents of the `ArrayList`.

- *Methods*

  add—Adds an element to the `ArrayList` object.

  clear—Removes all elements in an `ArrayList`.

  get—Returns a reference to the element in the `ArrayList` at the specified index.

  indexOf—Returns the index in the `ArrayList` where a specified object is stored. If the object does not exist in the `ArrayList`, indexOf returns -1.

  iterator—Creates a new object of type `Iterator` used for iterating through each element contained in the `ArrayList`.

  remove—Removes an element from the `ArrayList` object at the specified index.

  size—Returns the number of elements in the `ArrayList`.

  toArray—Converts the `ArrayList` to a one-dimensional array. This is convenient for cases when the elements of an `ArrayList` need to be passed to a method that is expecting a one-dimensional array.

Date This class is used to store date and time information.

- *Methods*

  toString—Returns the current date as a `String`, in the format Tue Feb 13 16:50:00 EST 2003.

Iterator This interface is used for iterating, or traversing, through a collection.

- *Methods*

  hasNext—Tests if there are any remaining elements in the `ArrayList` accessed by this `Iterator` object.

  next—Returns a reference to the next element in the `ArrayList`.

JButton This component allows the user to generate an action.

- *In action*

- *Event Handlers*

  actionPerformed—This is called when the `JButton` is clicked.

- *Methods*

  requestFocusInWindow—Sets the `JButton` to have the focus.

  setBounds—Sets the *bounds* property of the `JButton`, which determines the location and size.

  setEnabled—Sets the *enabled* property of the `JButton` to `true` or `false`.

  setMnemonic—Sets the *mnemonic* property of the `JButton`. The argument passed to this method is the KeyEvent constant for the character that will be used as a mnemonic, or keyboard shortcut that allows the user to "click" the `JButton` using the keyboard.

  setText—Sets the *text* property of a `JButton`.

JComboBox   This component allows users to select from a drop-down list of options.

- ***In action***

- ***Event Handlers***

  `actionPerformed`—This is called when a new value is selected in the `JComboBox`.

- ***Methods***

  `getItemAt`—Takes an `int` argument representing an index and returns the value at that index of a `JComboBox`.

  `getSelectedIndex`—Returns the index of the `JComboBox`'s selected item, stored in the *selectedIndex* property.

  `setBounds`—Specifies the location and size of the `JComboBox` component on the container component relative to the top-left corner.

  `setEnabled`—Controls whether the user can select items from the `JComboBox`.

  `setMaximumRowCount`—Sets the number of items that can be displayed in the `JComboBox`'s drop-down list.

  `setSelectedIndex`—Sets the index of the `JComboBox`'s selected item, stored in the *selectedIndex* property.

JList   This component allows users to view and select items in a list.

- ***In action***

- ***Methods***

  `setBounds`—Specifies the location and size of the `JList`.

  `setListData`—Sets the text displayed in the `JList`.

KeyEvent   This class contains information about keyboard events (such as the pressing of a key on the keyboard).

- ***Constants***

  `KeyEvent.VK_A`—Represents the *A* key on the keyboard.

  `KeyEvent.VK_B`—Represents the *B* key on the keyboard.

  `KeyEvent.VK_E`—Represents the *E* key on the keyboard.

  `KeyEvent.VK_N`—Represents the *N* key on the keyboard.

  `KeyEvent.VK_R`—Represents the *R* key on the keyboard.

  `KeyEvent.VK_S`—Represents the *S* key on the keyboard.

  `KeyEvent.VK_U`—Represents the *U* key on the keyboard.

MULTIPLE-CHOICE QUESTIONS

19.1 _____ are specifically designed to store groups of values.

    a) Collections   b) Properties

    c) Accessors   d) None of the above.

19.2 The `ArrayList` class is located in the _____ package.

    a) `java.util`   b) `java.awt`

    c) `javax.swing`   d) `java.awt.event`

19.3 The _____ method converts an `ArrayList` to a one-dimensional array.

a) `to1DArray`
b) `toOneDimensionalArray`
c) `fromArrayList`
d) `toArray`

19.4 The reference returned by the next method of `Iterator` _____.

a) must be of type `int`
b) is of type `Object`
c) must be of type `ArrayList`
d) None of the above.

19.5 The _____ method returns the number of elements in an `ArrayList`.

a) `length`
b) `lengthOf`
c) `numberElements`
d) `size`

19.6 The `setListData` method of the `JList` component takes a(n) _____ as an argument.

a) `int`
b) `String`
c) one-dimensional array
d) `ArrayList`

19.7 Use the _____ method of `Iterator` to return a reference to the next element in the collection.

a) `next`
b) `getNext`
c) `hasNext`
d) `isNext`

19.8 To add an element at the end of an `ArrayList`, call the _____ method.

a) `add`
b) `addToEnd`
c) `append`
d) `insertAt`

19.9 To remove an element at a specific index in the `ArrayList`, use method _____.

a) `remove`
b) `removeAt`
c) `delete`
d) `deleteAt`

19.10 Use the _____ method of the `ArrayList` class to generate an `Iterator`.

a) `getIterator`
b) `makeIterator`
c) `iterator`
d) `iterate`

EXERCISES

19.11 (*Modified Salary Survey Application*) In this exercise, you will create a **Salary Survey** application that is similar to the one you created in Exercise 16.12. This application includes an `ArrayList` that has already been added for you, to contain the salary ranges for use by an `Iterator`. Note that the salary ranges are for whole dollar amounts—the amount of cents in the user's salary is truncated before the salary is placed in a specific range. You will use the `Iterator` with a `while` statement to replace the `for` statement that is used in Tutorial 16 (Fig. 19.56).

a) *Copying the template to your working directory.* Copy the directory `C:\Examples\Tutorial19\Exercises\ModifiedSalarySurvey` to your `C:\SimplyJava` directory.

b) *Opening the template file.* Open the `SalarySurvey.java` file in your text editor.

c) *Clearing the JTextArea from previous output.* Find the `showTotalsJButtonActionPerformed` method, which begins at line 174. Inside the `showTotalsJButtonActionPerformed` method, clear the **Survey results:** `JTextArea`'s text.

d) *Adding a header to the output.* The first portion of your application's output is the header. Use method `append` to add the header as a `String` to the **Survey results:** `JTextArea` (`surveyResultsJTextArea`).

e) *Creating a counter variable.* `ArrayList rangesArrayList` contains each range as a `String`. In the next step, you will create an `Iterator` to cycle through each element in this `ArrayList`. However, you will still need to use a counter to access the number of results for the current range. Declare counter variable `i` and initialize it to 2. Recall that in this exercise, the first two elements of `resultArray` are not used.

f) *Creating the `Iterator`.* Create an `Iterator` (`rangeIterator`) for `rangesArrayList`.

g) *Creating the `while` statement.* Add a `while` statement that loops while there are still elements to be referenced by `rangeIterator`.

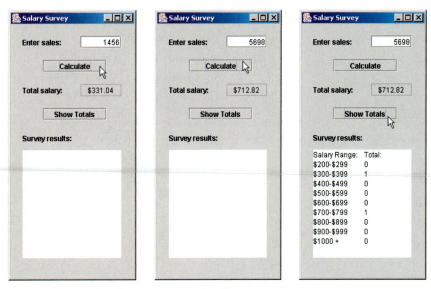

Figure 19.56 Modified **Salary Survey** GUI.

h) *Creating the reference variable.* Inside the `while` loop, create a `String` variable for the next element in `rangesArrayList`.

i) *Adding text to surveyResultsJTextArea.* After creating the `String` variable, add to `surveyResultsJTextArea` the current salary range along with the survey results for that range (stored in `resultArray`). Then, increment `i` for the next iteration of the `while` statement.

j) *Saving the application.* Save your modified source code file.

k) *Opening the Command Prompt window and changing directories.* Open the **Command Prompt** window by selecting **Start > Programs > Accessories > Command Prompt**. Change to your working directory by typing `cd C:\SimplyJava\Modified-SalarySurvey`.

l) *Compiling the application.* Compile your application by typing `javac SalarySurvey.java`.

m) *Running the completed application.* When your application compiles correctly, run it by typing `java SalarySurvey`. Enter various sales totals and click the **Show Totals** `JButton` to make sure that the proper output is displayed.

n) *Closing the application.* Close your running application by clicking its close button.

o) *Closing the Command Prompt window.* Close the **Command Prompt** window by clicking its close button.

19.12 (*Modified Shipping Hub Application*) Modify the **Shipping Hub** application created in this tutorial so that when the user double clicks a `Parcel`'s ID in `parcelStateJList`, that `Parcel`'s information will be displayed in a `JOptionPane` (Fig. 19.57). An empty method called `parcelStateJListMouseDoubleClicked` is provided for you. This method will execute when an item in `parcelStateJList` is double clicked. You will add this exercise's functionality to this method. At this point, you do not need to understand how to handle events related to the mouse—this will be covered in Tutorial 21.

a) *Copying the template to your working directory.* Copy the directory `C:\Examples\Tutorial19\Exercises\ModifiedShippingHub` to your `C:\SimplyJava` directory.

b) *Opening the template file.* Open the `ShippingHub.java` file in your text editor.

c) *Retrieving the selected Parcel's ID.* Find the `parcelStateJListMouseDoubleClicked` method, which begins at line 593. Inside the `parcelStateJListMouseDoubleClicked` method, declare variable `int number` to hold the number of the `Parcel` the user has selected to display. To do this, you need to call the `getSelectedValue` method of class `JList`. This method returns the item currently selected in the `JList` as an `Object`. You will need to convert this `Object` to a `String`, then to an `Integer`, before finally storing the value in `number`.

Figure 19.57 Modified **Shipping Hub** application's GUI and J0ptionPane.

d) *Creating the Iterator.* To cycle through the Parcels in parcelsArrayList, you need to create an Iterator. Create an Iterator (parcelIterator) to iterate through parcelsArrayList.

e) *Creating the while statement.* Add a while statement that loops while there are still elements to be referenced by parcelIterator.

f) *Creating the reference variable.* Inside the while loop, create a reference variable for the next element in parcelsArrayList.

g) *Determining whether the current selected Parcel is correct.* Inside the while loop, add an if statement to determine whether the ID of the current Parcel matches the selected item from the JList. Once the correct Parcel is matched, display that Parcel's information in the J0ptionPane.

h) *Saving the application.* Save your modified source code file.

i) *Opening the Command Prompt window and changing directories.* Open the **Command Prompt** window by selecting **Start > Programs > Accessories > Command Prompt**. Change to your working directory by typing cd C:\SimplyJava\Modified-ShippingHub.

j) *Compiling the application.* Compile your application by typing javac Shipping-Hub.java.

k) *Running the completed application.* When your application compiles correctly, run it by typing java ShippingHub. Scan a new Parcel, and after adding it, double click on its number in the parcelIDJList. View the resulting J0ptionPane to determine if the correct information is displayed.

l) *Closing the application.* Close your running application by clicking its close button.

m) *Closing the Command Prompt window.* Close the **Command Prompt** window by clicking its close button.

19.13 (*Components Collection Application*) Java provides methods to access your application's components, as well as property values for those components. In this exercise, componentsArrayList is provided and contains a reference to each component in the application. You will use a while statement to iterate through each component. As each component is encountered, add the component's identifier (that is, the component's name) to another ArrayList, called outputArrayList. Finally, you will display the component names in a JList and change the component's background color to magenta (Fig. 19.58). [*Note:* We will explain how to change background colors in the exercise steps.]

Figure 19.58 Components Collection GUI.

a) *Copying the template to your working directory.* Copy the directory C:\Examples\ Tutorial19\Exercises\ComponentsCollection to your C:\SimplyJava directory.

b) *Opening the template file.* Open the ComponentsCollection.java file in your text editor.

c) *Clearing outputArrayList.* ArrayList outputArrayList will be used to specify the output that will be displayed in **List of components:** JList. Find the submitJButtonActionPerformed method, which begins at line 146. Inside the submitJButtonActionPerformed method, add code to remove all previous elements that were stored in outputArrayList.

d) *Creating the Iterator.* After clearing the outputArrayList, declare an Iterator (componentIterator) for componentsArrayList. ArrayList componentsArrayList already contains references to each component in the application. These references are of type **Component**, which can be used to access information about any component, such as the name of the component.

e) *Creating the while statement.* Add a while statement that loops while there are still elements to be referenced by componentIterator.

f) *Creating the reference variable.* In the while loop, create a variable for the next element in componentsArrayList. Be sure to cast the element to type Component.

g) *Changing the component's background color.* Inside the while loop, use class Component's **setBackground** method to change its background color. You will learn more about using colors later in the text. For now, simply pass the constant **Color.MAGENTA** to method setBackground. Note that you do not see the background color of bookPictureJLabel change because its image fills the entire JLabel.

h) *Adding text to outputArrayList.* Inside the while loop, add to outputArrayList the name of the current Component object. You can do this by calling the **getName** method of class Component. This method does not require any arguments.

i) *Displaying the output in the JList.* After the while loop, convert outputArrayList to a one-dimensional array and set the list data for listComponentsJList to that array.

j) *Saving the application.* Save your modified source code file.

k) *Opening the Command Prompt window and changing directories.* Open the **Command Prompt** window by selecting **Start > Programs > Accessories > Command Prompt**. Change to your working directory by typing cd C:\SimplyJava\ComponentsCollection.

l) *Compiling the application.* Compile your application by typing javac ComponentsCollection.java.

m) *Running the completed application.* When your application compiles correctly, run it by typing java ComponentsCollection. Click the **Submit** JButton to ensure the application functions correctly.

n) *Closing the application.* Close your running application by clicking its close button.

o) *Closing the Command Prompt window.* Close the **Command Prompt** window by clicking its close button.

What does this code do? ▶   **19.14** What is the result of the following code?

```
1   ArrayList mysteryArrayList = new ArrayList();
2   String output = "";
3
4   mysteryArrayList.add( "1" );
5   mysteryArrayList.add( "2" );
6   mysteryArrayList.add( "3" );
7   mysteryArrayList.add( "4" );
8   mysteryArrayList.add( "5" );
9   mysteryArrayList.remove( 1 );
10  mysteryArrayList.remove( 2 );
11
12  Iterator mysteryIterator = mysteryArrayList.iterator();
13
14  while ( mysteryIterator.hasNext() )
15  {
16     String currentElement = ( String ) mysteryIterator.next();
17
18     output += ( currentElement + " " );
19  }
20
21  JOptionPane.showMessageDialog( null, output, "Mystery",
22     JOptionPane.INFORMATION_MESSAGE );
```

What's wrong with this code? ▶   **19.15** This code should iterate through an array of `Parcel`s in `ArrayList valueArrayList` and print each `Parcel`'s number in `displayJTextArea`. Find the error(s) in the following code.

```
1   Iterator valueIterator = valueArrayList.iterator();
2
3   while ( valueIterator.hasNext() )
4   {
5      displayJTextArea.setText( String.valueOf(
6         valueIterator.getParcelID() ) );
7
8   } // end while loop
```

Programming Challenge ▶   **19.16** (***Enhanced Shipping Hub Application***) Enhance the **Shipping Hub** application created in Exercise 19.12 to allow the user to move a maximum of five parcels from the warehouse to a truck for shipping. When the user selects an item in the `parcelStateJList` and clicks the **Ship** `JButton`, the item will be removed from this `JList` and added to the **Parcels to Ship** `JList` (`parcelShipJList`, shown in Fig. 19.59). After five `Parcel` IDs have been added to this `JList`, no more may be added. The five `Parcel` limit has already been coded for you. You will only be adding the functionality to modify the `JList`s.

a) ***Copying the template to your working directory.*** Copy the directory `C:\Examples\Tutorial19\Exercises\EnhancedShippingHub` to your `C:\SimplyJava` directory.

b) ***Opening the template file.*** Open the `ShippingHub.java` file in your text editor.

c) ***Retrieving the selected Parcel's ID.*** Find the `shipJButtonActionPerformed` method, which begins at 440. The first statement inside the `shipJButtonActionPerformed` is an `if` statement. This `if` statement will execute when the user has clicked `shipJButton` and there are still less than five items in `toBeShippedArrayList`. This `ArrayList` will be used to contain the `Parcel` IDs that will be added to the **Parcels to Ship** `JList`. At line 445, declare variable `int currentNumber` to hold the ID of the `Parcel` the user has selected in `parcelStateJList`. Remember to use the `getSelectedValue` method and convert the return value to the proper type.

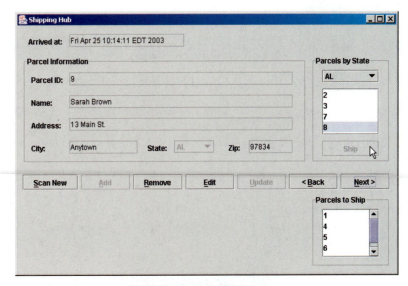

Figure 19.59   Enhanced **Shipping Hub** GUI.

d) *Adding the selected ID to toBeShippedArrayList.* Add the String version of the ID selected to toBeShippedArrayList. Then, set the elements of toBeShippedArrayList to be displayed in parcelShipJList.

e) *Creating the Iterator.* You now need to remove the selected ID from parcelStateJList. To do this, you will cycle through the Parcels in parcelsArrayList using an Iterator. Create an Iterator (parcelIterator) to iterate through parcelsArrayList.

f) *Creating the while statement.* Add a while statement that loops while there are still elements to be referenced by parcelIterator.

g) *Creating the reference variable.* Inside the while loop, create a reference variable for the next element in parcelsArrayList.

h) *Removing the selected Parcel.* Inside the while loop, define an if statement that will execute when the ID of the current Parcel matches the ID of the Parcel selected in parcelStateJList. Within the if statement, use method indexOf to retrieve the location of the current Parcel's ID in parcelStateArrayList. Use this index to remove the ID from parcelStateArrayList. Finally, use parcelStateArrayList to update the contents of parcelStateJList.

i) *Saving the application.* Save your modified source code file.

j) *Opening the Command Prompt window and changing directories.* Open the **Command Prompt** window by selecting **Start > Programs > Accessories > Command Prompt**. Change to your working directory by typing cd C:\SimplyJava\EnhancedShippingHub.

k) *Compiling the application.* Compile your application by typing javac ShippingHub.java.

l) *Running the completed application.* When your application compiles correctly, run it by typing java ShippingHub. Scan a new Parcel, and after adding it, click on its number in the parcelIDJList. Then, click the **Ship** JButton to add it to the truck. To view the parcel information, double click the parcel number in the parcelIDJList.

m) *Closing the application.* Close your running application by clicking its close button.

n) *Closing the Command Prompt window.* Close the **Command Prompt** window by clicking its close button.

Objectives

In this tutorial, you will learn to:
- Understand inheritance.
- Form new classes quickly from existing classes using inheritance.
- Use the `Graphics` object to draw rectangles on a `JPanel`.

Outline

Screen Saver Application

Introducing Inheritance and Graphics

Inheritance is one of the most useful and important features of object-oriented programming. **Inheritance** is a form of software reuse in which a new class is created by absorbing an existing class's fields (attributes) and methods (behaviors) and embellishing them with new or modified capabilities. Software reusability saves time during application development. It also encourages the reuse of proven and debugged high-quality software, which increases the likelihood that a system will be implemented effectively. In this tutorial, you will learn how to create a class by reusing an existing class through inheritance.

This tutorial also introduces basic concepts and features of graphics. Part of Java's initial appeal was that it supported graphics, enabling Java programmers to visually enhance their applications. You will learn several of Java's capabilities for drawing two-dimensional shapes and controlling colors.

20.1 Test-Driving the Screen Saver Application

In this tutorial, you will create a **Screen Saver** application. This application must meet the following requirements:

Application Requirements

*A local retail chain continuously displays a single screen on its customer service monitors. To prevent this image from being burned into the monitor, the owner of the chain has asked you to create an application that will display rectangles of random size, position, and color every .25 seconds when no customers need help. This program should also contain a **Clear `JButton`** to clear the previously drawn rectangles.*

You begin by test-driving the completed application. Next, you learn the additional Java technologies you will need to create your own version of this application.

Test-Driving the Screen Saver Application

1. **Locating the completed application.** Open a **Command Prompt** window by selecting **Start > Programs > Accessories > Command Prompt**. Change to your completed **Screen Saver** application directory by typing cd C:\Examples\Tutorial20\CompletedApplication\ScreenSaver.

2. **Running the Screen Saver application.** Type java ScreenSaver in the **Command Prompt** window and press *Enter* to run the application (Fig. 20.1). Notice that this application begins to draw rectangles immediately.

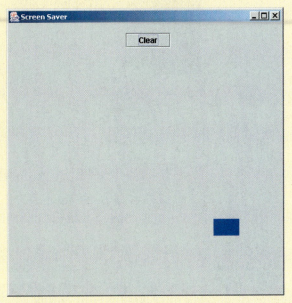

Figure 20.1   Running the completed **Screen Saver** application.

3. **Allowing the application to run.** Allow the application to run for a few seconds (Fig. 20.2) and notice what happens. Each new rectangle has a random size, location and color, and is added to the JPanel on top of the existing rectangles.

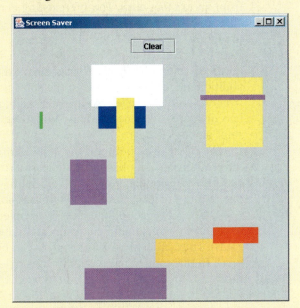

Figure 20.2   **Screen Saver** application after running for a few seconds.

(cont.)

4. ***Clearing the JPanel.*** Click the **Clear** JButton (Fig. 20.3). Notice that the application clears all previously drawn rectangles from the JPanel, then continues to draw rectangles.

Figure 20.3 **Screen Saver** application after clicking the **Clear** JButton.

5. ***Closing the running application.*** Close your running application by clicking its close button.

6. ***Closing the Command Prompt window.*** Close the **Command Prompt** window by clicking its close button.

20.2 Inheritance Overview

When creating a class, rather than declaring completely new members (instance variables and methods), you can designate the new class to inherit the members from an existing class. The pre-existing class is called the **superclass**, and the new class is called the **subclass**. Once created, each subclass can become the superclass for future subclasses. A subclass normally adds its own fields and methods. Therefore, a subclass is more specialized than its superclass and represents a smaller group of objects. Typically, the subclass exhibits the behaviors of its superclass and additional behaviors specific to the subclass. The **direct superclass** is the superclass from which the subclass explicitly inherits. An **indirect superclass** is inherited from two or more levels up the **class hierarchy**, which defines the inheritance relationships among classes.

We distinguish between the *is a* **relationship** and the *has a* **relationship**. In an *is a* relationship, an object of a subclass also can be treated as an object of its superclasses. For example, a car is a vehicle. In a *has a* relationship, an object contains one or more object references. For example, a car has a steering wheel.

Often, an object of one class *is an* object of another class as well. For example, in geometry, a rectangle is a quadrilateral (as are squares, parallelograms and trapezoids). Thus, in Java, class Rectangle can be said to inherit from class Quadrilateral. In this context, class Quadrilateral is a superclass, and class Rectangle is a subclass. A rectangle is a specific type of quadrilateral, but it is incorrect to claim that every quadrilateral is a rectangle—the quadrilateral could be a parallelogram or some other shape. Figure 20.4 lists several simple examples of superclasses and subclasses.

Superclass	Subclasses
Student	GraduateStudent, UndergraduateStudent
Shape	Circle, Triangle, Rectangle
Loan	CarLoan, HomeImprovementLoan, MortgageLoan
Employee	Faculty, Staff
BankAccount	CheckingAccount, SavingsAccount

Figure 20.4 Inheritance examples.

Because every subclass object *is an* object of its superclass, and because one superclass can have many subclasses, the set of objects represented by a superclass typically is larger than the set of objects represented by any of its subclasses. For example, the superclass Vehicle represents all vehicles, including cars, trucks, boats, bicycles and so on. By contrast, subclass Car represents a smaller, more specific subset of all vehicles.

Inheritance relationships form tree-like hierarchical structures (Fig. 20.5). A superclass exists in a hierarchical relationship with its subclasses. Although classes can exist independently, when they participate in inheritance relationships, they become affiliated with other classes. A class becomes either a superclass, supplying fields and methods to other classes, or a subclass, inheriting fields and methods from other classes.

Let's develop a simple class hierarchy (also called an **inheritance hierarchy**). A university community has thousands of community members (first line of Fig. 20.5), consisting of employees, students and alumni (second line of Fig. 20.5). Employees are either faculty members or staff members (third line of Fig. 20.5). Faculty members are either administrators (such as deans and department chairpersons) or teachers (fourth line of Fig. 20.5). Note that this inheritance hierarchy could contain many other classes. For example, students can be graduate or undergraduate students. Undergraduate students can be freshmen, sophomores, juniors or seniors. Each upward pointing arrow in the hierarchy represents an *is a* relationship. For instance, as you follow the arrows in this class hierarchy, you can state, "an Employee is a CommunityMember" and "a Teacher is a Faculty member." CommunityMember is the direct superclass of Employee, Student and Alumnus, and is an indirect superclass of all the other classes in the diagram. Starting from the bottom of the hierarchy, the reader can follow the arrows and apply the *is a* relationship to the topmost superclass. For example, an Administrator is a Faculty member, is an Employee and is a CommunityMember.

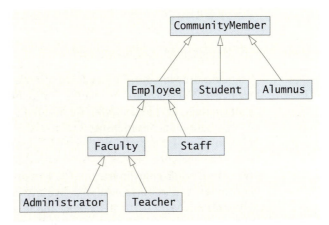

Figure 20.5 Inheritance hierarchy for university CommunityMembers.

Another example of an inheritance hierarchy is the Shape hierarchy of Fig. 20.6. To specify that class TwoDimensionalShape extends (or inherits from) class Shape, class TwoDimensionalShape could be declared in Java as follows:

```
public class TwoDimensionalShape extends Shape
```

The **extends** keyword indicates that the subclass TwoDimensionalShape inherits existing members (fields and methods) from the superclass Shape.

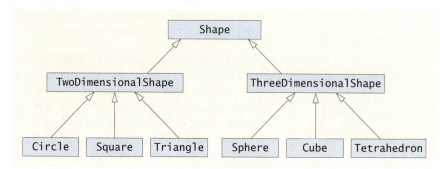

Figure 20.6   Inheritance hierarchy for **Shapes**.

One problem with inheritance is that a subclass can inherit methods it does not need or should not have. Even when a superclass method is appropriate for a subclass, that subclass often requires the method to perform its task in a manner specific to the subclass. In such cases, the subclass can **override** the superclass method with an appropriate implementation, which means the new method declared in the subclass supersedes the old method declared in the superclass. Do not confuse this concept with overloading, which refers to methods with the same name but different parameter lists. You will override a superclass method in *Step 5* of the box *Drawing the Rectangles* later in this tutorial.

SELF-REVIEW

1. A(n) _____ defines the inheritance relationships among a set of related classes.
   a) method override   b) class hierarchy
   c) *has a* relationship   d) None of the above.

2. When an _____ occurs, the new method declared in the subclass supersedes the old method declared in the superclass.
   a) override   b) indirect superclass
   c) overload   d) None of the above.

Answers: 1) b. 2) a.

20.3 Graphics Overview

To begin drawing graphics in Java, you must first understand Java's **coordinate system** (Fig. 20.7), which is a scheme for identifying every possible point on the computer screen. Text and shapes are displayed on the screen by specifying coordinates. Coordinate units are measured in pixels. A **pixel** is a display monitor's smallest unit of resolution. By default, the upper-left corner of a GUI component (such as a window) has the coordinates (0, 0). A **coordinate pair** is composed of an *x*-**coordinate** (the **horizontal coordinate**) and a *y*-**coordinate** (the **vertical coordinate**). The *x*-coordinate is the horizontal distance moving right from the upper-left corner. The *y*-coordinate is the vertical distance moving down from the upper-left corner. The *x*-**axis** describes every horizontal coordinate, and the *y*-**axis** describes every vertical coordinate.

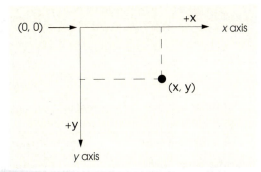

Figure 20.7   Java coordinate system. Units are measured in pixels.

A **Graphics** object allows you to draw pixels on the screen to represent text and other graphical objects (such as lines, ellipses, rectangles and other polygons). **Graphics** objects contain methods for drawing, font manipulation, color manipulation and more. You will soon work with **Graphics** objects.

SELF-REVIEW   1. The upper-left corner of a GUI component has the coordinates _____.

    a) $(500, 500)$ b) (x, y)

    c) $(0, 0)$ d) None of the above.

2. A(n) _____ object manages a graphics context and draws pixels on the screen that represent text and other graphical objects.

    a) `Image`   b) `Coordinates`

    c) `Graphics`   d) None of the above.

Answers: 1) c. 2) c.

20.4 Creating the Screen Saver Application

Now that you have been introduced to inheritance, you can begin to develop the **Screen Saver** application. First, you will use pseudocode to list the actions to be executed and to specify the order of execution. The following pseudocode describes the basic operation of the **Screen Saver** application:

> When the user runs the application:
>   Start the timer
>
> When the timer interval expires (every quarter second):
>   Get random values for x, y, width and height
>   Pick a random color
>   Create a rectangle
>   Place the rectangle in the ArrayList
>   Repaint the DrawJPanel
>
> When paintComponent is called:
>   Create an Iterator for the ArrayList
>   Use the Iterator to reference each Rectangle in the ArrayList and draw each
>   rectangle
>
> When the user clicks the Clear JButton:
>   Clear the ArrayList
>   Repaint the DrawJPanel

Before you begin to build your application, it is helpful to create an ACE table. Figure 20.8 lists the actions, components and events required to complete the application.

Action	Component/Object	Event/Method
		Application is run
Start the timer	drawTimer	
	drawTimer	Timer interval expires
Get random values for x, y, width and height	randomNumber	
Pick a random color	randomNumber	
Create a rectangle	rectangle	
Place the rectangle in the ArrayList	rectangleArrayList	
Repaint the DrawJPanel	drawingJPanel	
	drawingJPanel	paintComponent is called
Create an Iterator for the ArrayList	rectangleArrayList	
Reference each Rectangle in the ArrayList	rectangleIterator	
Draw each rectangle	currentRectangle	
	clearJButton	User clicks **Clear** JButton
Clear the ArrayList	rectangleArrayList	
Repaint the DrawJPanel	drawingJPanel	

Figure 20.8   **Screen Saver** application's ACE table.

To complete the **Screen Saver** application, you will need to create two new classes. The MyRectangle class will be a subclass of the existing **Rectangle** class from the java.awt package. (The **java.awt** package contains classes for graphics and images.) The Rectangle class specifies a rectangle that is defined by the *x*- and *y*-coordinates of its upper-left point, its width and its height. MyRectangle creates a Rectangle object and adds a Color instance variable. The DrawJPanel class will be a subclass of the JPanel class. DrawJPanel creates the JPanel on which the MyRectangles will be drawn and also draws the colored MyRectangle object.

20.5 Using Inheritance to Create the MyRectangle Class

You will create the MyRectangle class to store the information you will need to draw a rectangle.

1. ***Copying the template to your working directory.*** Copy the C:\Examples\Tutorial20\TemplateApplication\ScreenSaver directory to your C:\SimplyJava directory.

2. ***Opening the MyRectangle template file.*** Open the template file MyRectangle.java in your text editor.

3. ***Adding the MyRectangle class declaration.*** Insert lines 5–8 of Fig. 20.9 into the MyRectangle.java file. Line 5 uses the **extends** keyword to indicate that the MyRectangle class will inherit from the existing Rectangle class. This Rectangle class, which is predefined in the java.awt package, provides most of the data (such as the *x*- and *y*-coordinates of the upper-left point, the width and the height of the rectangle) you will need.

(cont.)

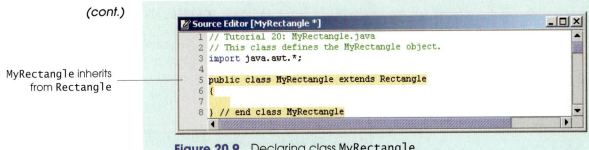

Figure 20.9 Declaring class `MyRectangle`.

*MyRectangle inherits
from Rectangle*

4. *Adding an instance variable to the MyRectangle class.* Insert lines 7–8 of Fig. 20.10 into the MyRectangle class. The Rectangle class you are extending has no instance variable for color. Line 8 adds a Color instance variable, fillColor, to your new MyRectangle class.

*Creating an instance
variable for color*

```
5  public class MyRectangle extends Rectangle
6  {
7      // instance variable to hold fillColor of MyRectangle
8      private Color fillColor;
9
10 } // end class MyRectangle
```

Figure 20.10 Instance variable to hold the fill color.

5. *Creating the constructor for MyRectangle.* Insert lines 10–17 of Fig. 20.11 into the MyRectangle class to add the MyRectangle constructor. You need add a constructor to MyRectangle because subclass does not inherit superclass's constructor, The MyRectangle constructor accepts five arguments. The first four arguments are passed to the Rectangle constructor. The fifth argument specifies the color of the rectangle. The MyRectangle constructor invokes the Rectangle constructor by using the **superclass constructor call syntax**—the **super** keyword, followed by a set of parentheses containing the superclass constructor arguments. The superclass (Rectangle) constructor takes four arguments—xValue, yValue, widthValue and heightValue. xValue and yValue determine the *x*- and *y*-coordinates of the upper-left corner of the rectangle. heightValue specifies the height of the rectangle. widthValue specifies the width of the rectangle. The first statement in a subclass constructor must be a call to one of the superclass's constructors—this initializes the part of the subclass that was inherited from the superclass.

*Declaring class
MyRectangle's constructor*

```
8      private Color fillColor;
9
10     // constructor
11     public MyRectangle( int xValue, int yValue, int widthValue,
12         int heightValue, Color colorValue )
13     {
14         // call constructor of superclass
15         super( xValue, yValue, widthValue, heightValue );
16
17     } // end constructor
18
```

Figure 20.11 Calling the superclass's constructor.

(cont.)

6. ***Setting the color for MyRectangle.*** The superclass's constructor sets the upper-left corner's *x*- and *y*-coordinates and the width and height of the rectangle, but not the color. You must set the color within the MyRectangle constructor. Insert lines 17–18 of Fig. 20.12 into the MyRectangle constructor to call the setFillColor method (which you will declare in *Step 7*), which will assign the argument colorValue to the instance variable fillColor.

Setting the rectangle's color ——————

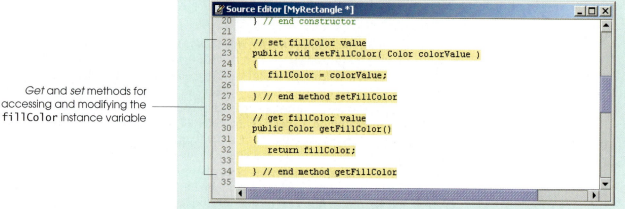

```
15        super( xValue, yValue, widthValue, heightValue );
16
17        // set fillColor of MyRectangle
18        setFillColor( colorValue );
19
```

Figure 20.12 Calling method setFillColor to set the color of MyRectangle.

7. ***Adding the*** **set** ***and*** **get** ***methods.*** Now you will create methods to access the fillColor instance variable. Insert lines 22–34 of Fig. 20.13 into the MyRectangle class to declare methods that *set* and *get* the instance variable fillColor.

Get and *set* methods for accessing and modifying the fillColor instance variable ——————

```
20        } // end constructor
21
22        // set fillColor value
23        public void setFillColor( Color colorValue )
24        {
25            fillColor = colorValue;
26
27        } // end method setFillColor
28
29        // get fillColor value
30        public Color getFillColor()
31        {
32            return fillColor;
33
34        } // end method getFillColor
35
```

Figure 20.13 *Set* and *get* methods for the instance variable fillColor.

8. ***Declaring the draw method.*** Insert lines 36–42 of Fig. 20.14 into the MyRectangle class to draw a rectangle. Line 39 invokes the **setColor** method of the Graphics class, which takes a Color object as an argument and sets the color that will be drawn. Line 40 invokes the **fillRect** method of the Graphics class, which takes four int arguments and draws a filled rectangle with the upper-left corner at the x and y values and with the specified width and height values. Notice that you did not declare the four fields in your MyRectangle class—x, y, width and height—that are passed to the fillRect method because these fields were declared as public instance variables in the superclass Rectangle, so they were inherited into the MyRectangle class as public members.

9. ***Saving the application.*** Save your modified source code file.

(cont.)

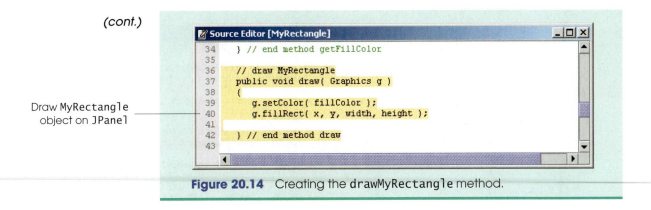

Draw MyRectangle object on JPanel

Figure 20.14 Creating the drawMyRectangle method.

SELF-REVIEW 1. In the class declaration, use the _____ keyword to create a subclass of an existing class.

    a) extends   b) implements

    c) inherits   d) modifies

2. To call the superclass constructor, use the _____ keyword followed by a set of parentheses containing the superclass constructor arguments.

    a) superclass   b) superconstructor

    c) super   d) None of the above.

Answers: 1) a. 2) c.

20.6 Graphics in Java

This section continues our discussion of graphics in Java. A Graphics object controls how information is drawn in an application. In addition to providing methods for drawing various shapes, Graphics objects contain methods for font manipulation, color manipulation and other graphics-related actions.

You will now create the DrawJPanel class, which extends the JPanel class. This class uses a Timer object to draw a rectangle every 250 milliseconds.

Creating the DrawJPanel Class

1. ***Opening the DrawJPanel template file.*** Open the template file DrawJPanel.java in your text editor.

2. ***Declaring class DrawJPanel.*** Insert the highlighted code at the end of line 10 (Fig. 20.15) into the DrawJPanel class. Line 10 declares that class DrawJPanel extends the JPanel class.

DrawJPanel inherits from JPanel

Figure 20.15 Declaring class DrawJPanel.

3. ***Adding instance variables.*** Insert lines 12–24 of Fig. 20.16 into the DrawJPanel class. Line 13 creates a Random object you will use to generate random dimensions for your rectangles. Line 16 creates a Timer object you will use to draw a rectangle every 250 milliseconds. Line 19 creates an ArrayList you will use to hold all the rectangle objects to be drawn. Lines 22–24 create an array of Color constants. All rectangles will be drawn with one of these constants.

(cont.)

Creating a `Random` object

Creating a `Timer` object

Creating an `ArrayList`

Declaring an array to hold `MyRectangle` colors

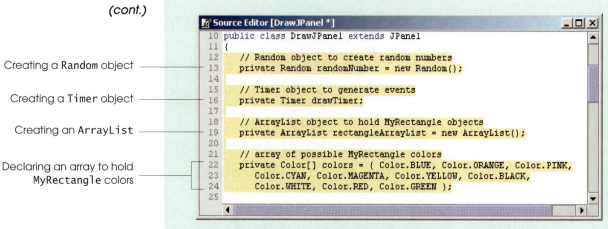

```
10  public class DrawJPanel extends JPanel
11  {
12        // Random object to create random numbers
13        private Random randomNumber = new Random();
14
15        // Timer object to generate events
16        private Timer drawTimer;
17
18        // ArrayList object to hold MyRectangle objects
19        private ArrayList rectangleArrayList = new ArrayList();
20
21        // array of possible MyRectangle colors
22        private Color[] colors = { Color.BLUE, Color.ORANGE, Color.PINK,
23           Color.CYAN, Color.MAGENTA, Color.YELLOW, Color.BLACK,
24           Color.WHITE, Color.RED, Color.GREEN };
25
```

Figure 20.16   Declaring instance variables.

4. **Calling the superclass constructor.** Insert line 29 of Fig. 20.17 into the `DrawJPanel` constructor. Line 29 explicitly calls the superclass's (`JPanel`'s) no-argument constructor. Recall that the first statement in a constructor must be a call to the superclass's constructor. If line 29 is omitted, Java will implicitly call the superclass's no-argument constructor. You explicitly call the superclass constructor so that you can pass arguments to it. Line 31 of Fig. 20.17 specifies that `drawTimer` will call the `actionPerformed` event handler every 250 milliseconds.

Call the superclass constructor

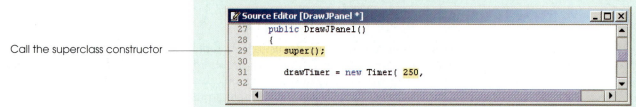

```
27     public DrawJPanel()
28     {
29        super();
30
31        drawTimer = new Timer( 250,
32
```

Figure 20.17   Calling the superclass's no-argument constructor.

5. **Starting the Timer object.** Insert line 45 of Fig. 20.18 into the `DrawJPanel` constructor. Line 45 invokes the `start` method of `Timer` to start `drawTimer`.

Start the timer

```
43        ); // end call to new Timer
44
45        drawTimer.start(); // start timer
46
```

Figure 20.18   Starting the `drawTimer` object.

6. **Saving the application.** Save your modified source code file.

Now that you have completed your `MyRectangle` class and the constructor of the `DrawJPanel` class, you can add methods to the `DrawJPanel` class to draw the rectangles defined by the `MyRectangle` objects in your application.

Drawing the Rectangles

1. **Creating random dimensions of a rectangle.** Insert lines 49–59 of Fig. 20.19 into your `DrawJPanel` class. These lines declare the `drawTimerActionPer-formed` method, which is called from the `actionPerformed` event handler for `drawTimer`. Lines 53–56 create a random *x*-coordinate, random *y*-coordinate, random width and random height for the rectangle. Line 57 creates a random index for the `colors` array.

(cont.)

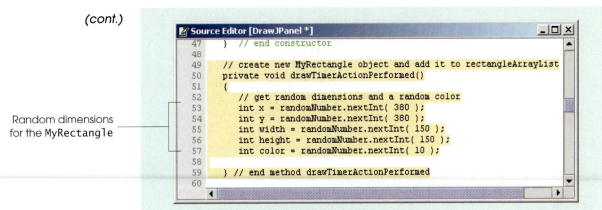

```
47     }  // end constructor
48
49     // create new MyRectangle object and add it to rectangleArrayList
50     private void drawTimerActionPerformed()
51     {
52         // get random dimensions and a random color
53         int x = randomNumber.nextInt( 380 );
54         int y = randomNumber.nextInt( 380 );
55         int width = randomNumber.nextInt( 150 );
56         int height = randomNumber.nextInt( 150 );
57         int color = randomNumber.nextInt( 10 );
58
59     } // end method drawTimerActionPerformed
60
```

Random dimensions for the MyRectangle

Figure 20.19   Creating random color and dimensions for the rectangle.

2. *Creating a new MyRectangle object.* Insert lines 59–61 of Fig. 20.20 into the drawTimerActionPerformed method to create a new MyRectangle object with random dimensions and color.

```
57         int color = randomNumber.nextInt( 10 );
58
59         // create MyRectangle object and add it to rectangleArrayList
60         MyRectangle rectangle = new MyRectangle( x, y, width, height,
61             colors[ color ] );
62
```

Figure 20.20   Creating a new MyRectangle object.

3. *Adding MyRectangle to the ArrayList.* Insert line 62 of Fig. 20.21 into the drawTimerActionPerformed method to add rectangle to rectangleArrayList. When the DrawJPanel is painted, it will iterate through rectangleArrayList and draw each MyRectangle object.

```
61             colors[ color ] );
62         rectangleArrayList.add( rectangle );
63
```

Add MyRectangle object to rectangleArrayList

Figure 20.21   Adding rectangle to rectangleArrayList.

4. *Calling the repaint method to update the DrawJPanel.* Insert line 64 of Fig. 20.22 into the drawTimerActionPerformed method. This line calls the **repaint** method, which clears the background of the DrawJPanel and eventually results in a call to the **paintComponent** method. Next, you will declare the paintComponent method to draw the rectangles. Note that the paintComponent method is called automatically by the repaint method, so you do not need to provide code to call the paintComponent method.

```
62         rectangleArrayList.add( rectangle );
63
64         repaint();
65
```

Call repaint method to update the JPanel

Figure 20.22   Calling the repaint method.

(cont.)

5. *Overriding the paintComponent method.* Insert lines 68–73 of Fig. 20.23 into the DrawJPanel class after the drawTimerActionPerformed method. The paintComponent method is originally declared in DrawJPanel's indirect superclass JComponent (which is the direct superclass of the JPanel class). These lines override the declaration of paintComponent in the superclass so that this class's version of the method is called. Overriding paint-Component enables you to define how to draw on an object of your DrawJPanel class. Line 71 calls the superclass's paintComponent method using the super keyword. Preceding a method call with the super keyword and a dot (.) calls the direct superclass's version of that method. Calling the superclass's paintComponent method clears the DrawJPanel and ensures that the JPanel portion of DrawJPanel is displayed properly. You will now add functionality to this method.

Call paintComponent method of superclass

```
66        } // end method drawTimerActionPerformed
67
68        // draw all rectangles
69        public void paintComponent( Graphics g )
70        {
71            super.paintComponent( g );
72
73        } // end method paintComponent
74
```

Figure 20.23 Overriding the superclass's paintComponent method.

6. *Creating an Iterator.* Insert lines 73–85 of Fig. 20.24 into the paintComponent method. Line 74 creates an Iterator object to iterate through rectangleArrayList. Lines 79–85 will loop while there are more MyRectangle objects in rectangleArrayList. Lines 81–82 get a MyRectangle reference from rectangleArrayList, and line 84 calls the draw method (declared in the MyRectangle class) to draw each rectangle. Recall that the next method of Iterator returns an Object type, therefore requiring an explicit cast to a MyRectangle type (line 82).

Iterate through rectangleArrayList

Draw MyRectangle object

```
71            super.paintComponent( g );
72
73        // create iterator
74        Iterator rectangleIterator = rectangleArrayList.iterator();
75
76        MyRectangle currentRectangle; // create MyRectangle
77
78        // iterate through ArrayList and draw all MyRectangles
79        while ( rectangleIterator.hasNext() )
80        {
81            currentRectangle =
82                ( MyRectangle ) rectangleIterator.next();
83
84            currentRectangle.draw( g ); // draw rectangle
85        }
86
87    } // end method paintComponent
```

Figure 20.24 Iterating through rectangleArrayList.

7. *Declaring the clear method.* Insert lines 89-96 of Fig. 20.25 into the DrawJPanel class. Line 92 invokes the clear method of rectangleArrayList to remove all MyRectangle objects from it. Line 94 invokes the repaint method. When paintComponent is called, the superclass's paintComponent method will clear the previously drawn rectangles. Variable rectangleArrayList is empty, so the previous rectangles will not be drawn.

(cont.)

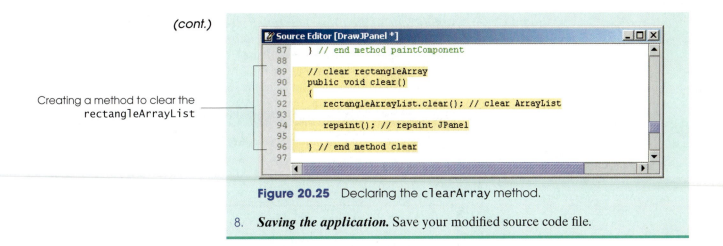

Figure 20.25   Declaring the `clearArray` method.

8. *Saving the application.* Save your modified source code file.

SELF-REVIEW

1. Use the _____ statement to call the superclass's no-argument constructor.

    a) `super();`
           b) `superclass();`

    c) `superClass();`
           d) None of the above.

2. The `repaint` method calls the _____ method to paint all current objects on the `JPanel`.

    a) `repaint`
           b) `paint`

    c) `paintComponent`
       d) `update`

Answers: 1) a. 2) c.

20.7 Completing the Screen Saver Application

Now that you have created the `DrawJPanel` class, you can create an instance of it in your **Screen Saver** application. You must also define the event handler for the **Clear** `JButton`. When clicked, this `JButton` will clear all previous rectangles from the `JPanel`. The `Timer` object that is part of the `DrawJPanel` class will continue to create a new rectangle every 250 milliseconds.

Adding a DrawJPanel

1. *Opening the Screen Saver template file.* Open the template file Screen-Saver.java in your text editor.

2. *Adding a DrawJPanel to the application.* Insert lines 49–52 of Fig. 20.26 into `ScreenSaver.java`. Line 50 calls the constructor—which you declared previously—to create a new instance of the `DrawJPanel` class and assign it to `drawingJPanel`. Line 51 calls the `setBounds` method, which is inherited from the `DrawJPanel` class's `JPanel` superclass. Line 52 adds `drawingJ-Panel` to `contentPane`.

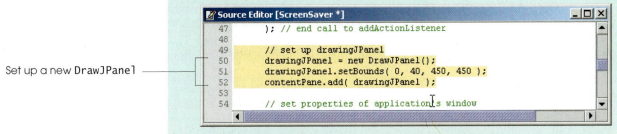

Figure 20.26   Creating a new `DrawJPanel` object.

(cont.)

3. ***Adding code to the `clearJButtonActionPerformed` method.*** Insert line 64 of Fig. 20.27 into the `clearJButtonActionPerformed` method. This line calls the `clear` method of `DrawJPanel` object `drawingJPanel`. The `clear` method clears the background of the `DrawJPanel`; new rectangles will continue to be drawn.

Calling the `clear` method of
`DrawJPanel` `drawingJPanel`

```
Source Editor [ScreenSaver *]                                      _ □ X
    61      // reset drawingJPanel
    62      private void clearJButtonActionPerformed( ActionEvent event )
    63      {
    64          drawingJPanel.clear();
    65
    66      } // end method clearJButtonActionPerformed
```

Figure 20.27 Calling the `clear` method to clear `drawingJPanel`.

4. ***Saving the application.*** Save your modified source code file.

5. ***Opening the Command Prompt window and changing directories.*** Open the **Command Prompt** window by selecting **Start > Programs > Accessories > Command Prompt**. Change to your working directory, **ScreenSaver**, by typing `cd C:\SimplyJava\ScreenSaver`.

6. ***Compiling the application.*** Compile your three source code files. Type `javac ScreenSaver.java MyRectangle.java DrawJPanel.java`.

7. ***Running the application.*** When your application compiles correctly, run it by typing `java ScreenSaver`. Figure 20.28 shows the completed **Screen Saver** application running.

Figure 20.28 Completed **Screen Saver** application.

8. ***Closing the application.*** Close your running application by clicking its close button.

9. ***Closing the Command Prompt window.*** Close the **Command Prompt** window by clicking its close button.

Figure 20.29 presents the source code for the **Screen Saver** application. Figure 20.30 presents the source code for the `MyRectangle` class. Figure 20.31 pre-

sents the source code for the `DrawJPanel` class. The lines of code that you added, viewed or modified in this tutorial are highlighted.

```
1   // Tutorial 20: ScreenSaver.java
2   // Application simulates screen saver by drawing random shapes.
3   import java.awt.*;
4   import java.awt.event.*;
5   import javax.swing.*;
6
7   public class ScreenSaver extends JFrame
8   {
9      // JButton to clear drawingJPanel
10     private JButton clearJButton;
11
12     // DrawJPanel for displaying rectangles
13     private DrawJPanel drawingJPanel;
14
15     // no-argument constructor
16     public ScreenSaver()
17     {
18        createUserInterface();
19     }
20
21     // create and position GUI components; register event handlers
22     private void createUserInterface()
23     {
24        // get content pane for attaching GUI components
25        Container contentPane = getContentPane();
26
27        // enable explicit positioning of GUI components
28        contentPane.setLayout( null );
29
30        // set up clearJButton
31        clearJButton = new JButton();
32        clearJButton.setBounds( 189, 16, 72, 23 );
33        clearJButton.setText( "Clear" );
34        contentPane.add( clearJButton );
35        clearJButton.addActionListener(
36
37           new ActionListener() // anonymous inner class
38           {
39              // event handler called when clearJButton is pressed
40              public void actionPerformed( ActionEvent event )
41              {
42                 clearJButtonActionPerformed( event );
43              }
44
45           } // end anonymous inner class
46
47        ); // end call to addActionListener
48
49        // set up drawingJPanel
50        drawingJPanel = new DrawJPanel();
51        drawingJPanel.setBounds( 0, 40, 450, 450 );
52        contentPane.add( drawingJPanel );
53
54        // set properties of application's window
55        setTitle( "Screen Saver" ); // set title bar text
```

Creating and customizing the DrawJPanel

Figure 20.29   Screen Saver code. (Part 1 of 2.)

```
56        setSize( 500, 500 );        // set window size
57        setVisible( true );          // display window
58
59     } // end method createUserInterface
60
61     // clear drawingJPanel
62     private void clearJButtonActionPerformed( ActionEvent event )
63     {
64        drawingJPanel.clear();
65
66     } // end method clearJButtonActionPerformed
67
68     // main method
69     public static void main( String[] args )
70     {
71        ScreenSaver application = new ScreenSaver();
72        application.setDefaultCloseOperation( JFrame.EXIT_ON_CLOSE );
73
74     } // end method main
75
76  } // end class ScreenSaver
```

Clearing the DrawJPanel — 64

Figure 20.29 **Screen Saver** code. (Part 2 of 2.)

```
1   // Tutorial 20: MyRectangle.java
2   // This class defines the MyRectangle object
3   import java.awt.*;
4
5   public class MyRectangle extends Rectangle
6   {
7      // instance variable to hold fillColor of MyRectangle
8      private Color fillColor;
9
10     // constructor
11     public MyRectangle( int xValue, int yValue, int widthValue,
12        int heightValue, Color colorValue )
13     {
14        // call constructor of superclass
15        super( xValue, yValue, widthValue, heightValue );
16
17        // set fillColor of MyRectangle
18        setFillColor( colorValue );
19
20     } // end constructor
21
22     // set fillColor value
23     public void setFillColor( Color colorValue )
24     {
25        fillColor = colorValue;
26
27     } // end method setFillColor
28
29     // get fillColor value
30     public Color getFillColor()
31     {
32        return fillColor;
33
34     } // end method getFillColor
```

MyRectangle inherits from Rectangle — 5

Creating an instance variable for color — 8

Declaring class MyRectangle's constructor — 16

Get and set methods for Color instance variable — 28

Figure 20.30 **MyRectangle** class code. (Part 1 of 2.)

```
35
36        // draw MyRectangle
37        public void draw( Graphics g )
38        {
39           g.setColor( color );
40           g.fillRect( x, y, width, height );
41
42        } // end method draw
43
44     } // end class MyRectangle
```

Drawing MyRectangle object on JPanel → (lines 39–40)

Figure 20.30 MyRectangle class code. (Part 2 of 2.)

```
1     // Tutorial 20: DrawJPanel.java
2     // This class draws a random rectangle every .25 seconds.
3     import java.awt.*;
4     import java.awt.event.*;
5     import java.util.ArrayList;
6     import java.util.Iterator;
7     import java.util.Random;
8     import javax.swing.*;
9
10    public class DrawJPanel extends JPanel
11    {
12       // Random object to create random numbers
13       private Random randomNumber = new Random():
14
15       // Timer object to generate events
16       private Timer drawTimer;
17
18       // ArrayList object to hold MyRectangle objects
19       private ArrayList rectangleArrayList = new ArrayList();
20
21       // array of possible MyRectangle colors
22       private Color[] colors = { Color.BLUE, Color.ORANGE, Color.PINK,
23          Color.CYAN, Color.MAGENTA, Color.YELLOW, Color.BLACK,
24          Color.WHITE, Color.RED, Color.GREEN };
25
26       // no-argument constructor
27       public DrawJPanel()
28       {
29          super();
30
31          drawTimer = new Timer( 250,
32
33             new ActionListener() // anonymous inner class
34             {
35                // event handler called every 250 microseconds
36                public void actionPerformed( ActionEvent event )
37                {
38                   drawTimerActionPerformed();
39                }
40
41             } // end anonymous inner class
42
43          ); // end call to new Timer
44
45          drawTimer.start(); // start timer
```

DrawJPanel inherits from JPanel → (line 10)
Creating a Timer object → (line 16)
Creating an ArrayList → (line 19)
Array to hold MyRectangle Colors → (lines 22–24)
Calling superclass constructor → (line 29)
Calling Timer method start → (line 45)

Figure 20.31 DrawJPanel class code. (Part 1 of 2.)

```
46
47        } // end constructor
48
49           // create MyRectangle object and add it to rectangleArrayList
50           private void drawTimerActionPerformed()
51           {
52              // get random color and dimensions
53              int x = randomNumber.nextInt( 380 );
54              int y = randomNumber.nextInt( 380 );
55              int width = randomNumber.nextInt( 150 );
56              int height = randomNumber.nextInt( 150 );
57              int color = randomNumber.nextInt( 10 );
58
59              // create MyRectangle object and add it to rectangleArrayList
60              MyRectangle rectangle = new MyRectangle( x, y, width, height,
61                 colors[ color ] );
62              rectangleArrayList.add( rectangle );
63
64              repaint();
65
66           } // end method drawTimerActionPerformed
67
68           // draw all rectangles
69           public void paintComponent( Graphics g )
70           {
71              super.paintComponent( g );
72
73              // create iterator
74              Iterator rectangleIterator = rectangleArrayList.iterator();
75
76              MyRectangle currentRectangle; // create MyRectangle
77
78              // iterate through ArrayList and draw all MyRectangles
79              while ( rectangleIterator.hasNext() )
80              {
81                 currentRectangle =
82                    ( MyRectangle ) rectangleIterator.next();
83
84                 currentRectangle.draw( g ); // draw rectangle
85              }
86
87           } // end method paintComponent
88
89           // clear rectangleArrayList
90           public void clear()
91           {
92              rectangleArrayList.clear(); // clear ArrayList
93
94              repaint(); // repaint JPanel
95
96           } // end method clear
97
98        } // end class DrawJPanel
```

Random dimensions for the MyRectangle

Adding rectangle object to rectangleArrayList
Call ingrepaint method to update JPanel

Calling paintComponent method of superclass

Iterate through rectangleArrayList

Draw MyRectangle object

Call repaint method to update JPanel

Figure 20.31 DrawJPanel class code. (Part 2 of 2.)

1.   When a subclass method overrides a superclass method, the superclass method can be accessed from the subclass by preceding the superclass method name with the _____ keyword and a _____.

   a) super, colon(:)   b) super, comma (,)

   c) super, dot (.)   d) None of the above.

2.   The _____ method of the ArrayList object returns an Iterator over the elements in the ArrayList.

   a) iterator   b) getIterator

   c) returnIterator   d) None of the above.

   Answers: 1) c. 2) a.

20.8 Wrap-Up

In this tutorial, you learned about inheritance. You learned about the relationships among superclasses and subclasses within a class hierarchy. You also learned method overriding. You defined two new classes that extended other classes and added additional methods to the subclasses.

You used inheritance and a Graphics object in the **Screen Saver** application. You created the MyRectangle class by extending the Rectangle class and adding color functionality to the new subclass. You created the DrawJPanel class by extending the JPanel class and added a DrawJPanel to the **Screen Saver** application. You called the repaint method to draw the rectangles.

You learned how to use a Graphics object to draw shapes on a JPanel. You used method overriding to modify the superclass's paintComponent method and used an Iterator to paint each rectangle contained in the ArrayList. You created the drawMyRectangle method to take a Graphics object, set the color and dimensions, and then draw that object on the JPanel.

The **Screen Saver** application draws a rectangle with random dimensions and color every 250 milliseconds. The application also contains a **Clear** JButton that, when clicked, clears all previously drawn rectangles from the JPanel. You used the ArrayList's clear method along with the repaint method to handle this.

In the next tutorial, you will learn how to use event handlers that are called in response to user interactions with the mouse. You will then build an application that allows the user to draw complex shapes using the mouse.

SKILLS SUMMARY

Accessing Superclass Methods

■ Use the super keyword to access methods of the superclass you are extending.

Calling Superclass Constructor

■ Use the super keyword followed by a set of parentheses containing the superclass constructor arguments to call the superclass constructor.

Creating a Subclass of an Existing Class

■ Use keyword extends in the class declaration to create a subclass. In this tutorial, class MyRectangle extended class Rectangle.

Drawing on a JPanel

■ Use Graphics methods, such as fillRect, to draw shapes on a JPanel.

■ Use the repaint method to clear the JPanel's background and call method paintComponent.

■ Use the paintComponent method to draw with the Graphics object on the JPanel.

Drawing a Rectangle

■ Use the Graphics method fillRect to fill the rectangle specified by its *x*- and *y*-coordinates, height and width.

Overriding a Superclass Method

■ Use the same method header in the subclass to override the superclass method.

Setting Graphics Color

■ Use the `Graphics` method `setColor` to set the color of drawn objects.

KEY TERMS

class hierarchy—Also known as inheritance hierarchy, this defines the inheritance relationships among classes.

coordinate pair—Composed of an *x*-coordinate (the horizontal coordinate) and a *y*-coordinate (the vertical coordinate). A coordinate pair can be used to reference a single pixel on a GUI component.

coordinate system—A scheme for identifying every possible point on the computer screen.

direct superclass—The superclass from which the subclass inherits.

extends keyword—The keyword indicating that a subclass inherits members (fields and methods) from the superclass.

fillRect method of class Graphics—A method that draws a filled rectangle defined by the arguments: *x*- and *y*- coordinates of the upper-left corner, the width and the height of the rectangle.

Graphics object—An object that draws pixels on the screen to represent text and other graphical objects (such as lines, ellipses, rectangles and other polygons).

***has a* relationship**—A relationship, in which an object contains one or more references to other objects.

horizontal coordinate—The horizontal distance moving right from the upper-left corner of a GUI component. Also known as the *x*-coordinate.

indirect superclass—A superclass that is two or more levels up the class hierarchy.

inheritance—A form of software reuse in which classes are based on an existing class's fields (attributes) and methods (behaviors) and extend them with new or modified capabilities.

inheritance hierarchy—The inheritance relationships among classes. Also known as the class hierarchy.

***is a* relationship**—A relationship, in which an object of a subclass also can be treated as an object of its superclass.

java.awt—The package containing classes for graphics and images.

override—Supersedes a superclass method with a new implementation declared in the subclass.

paintComponent method of class JPanel—Draws graphics on the `JPanel`.

pixel—A display monitor's smallest unit of resolution.

Rectangle class—Specifies a rectangle defined by the *x*- and the *y*-coordinates of the upper-left corner, the width and the height of a rectangle.

repaint method of class JPanel—Clears all previous drawings and updates any current drawings in the `JPanel`.

setColor method of class Graphics—Sets the color of an object to be drawn.

subclass—A class that extends (inherits from) another class (called a superclass).

super keyword—The keyword used for accessing the superclass's constructor and members.

superclass—A class that is extended by another class to form a subclass. The subclass inherits from the superclass.

superclass constructor call syntax—Uses the `super` keyword, followed by a set of parentheses containing the superclass constructor arguments.

vertical coordinate—The vertical distance moving down from the upper-left corner of a GUI component. Also known as the *y*-coordinate.

***x*-axis**—Describes every horizontal coordinate.

***x*-coordinate**—The horizontal distance moving right from the upper-left corner of a GUI component.

***y*-axis**—Describes every vertical coordinate.

***y*-coordinate**—Vertical distance moving down from the upper-left corner of a GUI component.

JAVA LIBRARY REFERENCE

Graphics The class that contains methods used to draw text, lines and shapes.

■ *Methods*

fillRect—Draws a filled rectangle of a specified size at a specified location.

setColor—Sets the color of the object to be drawn.

JPanel This component groups other related components. This allows a single border to be placed around multiple components. Components placed in a JPanel are positioned with respect to the upper-left corner of the JPanel, so changing the location of the JPanel moves all of the components contained inside it.

■ *Method*

add—Adds a component to the JPanel.

paintComponent—Paints components in the Graphics object that is the passed to this method.

repaint—Clears all previous drawings and updates any current drawings in the JPanel.

setBorder—Sets the border displayed around the JPanel.

setBounds—Sets the *bounds* property, which specifies the location and size of a JPanel.

setLayout—Sets the *layout* property, which controls how components are displayed on the JPanel.

MULTIPLE-CHOICE QUESTIONS

20.1 The _____ corner of a GUI component has the coordinate pair $(0, 0)$.

     a) upper-left   b) upper-right

     c) bottom-left   d) bottom-right

20.2 The _____ method of the Graphics class draws a filled rectangle.

     a) filledRect   b) rectangle

     c) solidRect   d) fillRect

20.3 If the Truck class extends the Vehicle class, and you want to call the Vehicle class's no-argument constructor from the Truck class, you would write _____.

     a) Truck()   b) superClass()

     c) super()   d) noArgument()

20.4 If the Truck class extends the Vehicle class, the Truck class is called the _____, and the Vehicle class is called the _____.

     a) superclass, subclass   b) subclass, superclass

     c) superclass, direct superclass   d) direct superclass, superclass

20.5 When a subclass overrides its superclass's method, _____.

     a) the superclass's method has the same header as the subclass's method

     b) the superclass's method is superseded by the subclass's method in the subclass

     c) you can use the keyword super followed by a dot (.) to access the superclass's method from the subclass

     d) All of the above.

20.6 The Rectangle class takes four arguments, which define _____.

     a) the coordinate pair of the four corners of the rectangle

     b) the *x*- and *y*-coordinates of the upper-left corner and the bottom-right corner

     c) the *x*- and *y*-coordinates of the upper-right corner and the bottom-left corner

     d) the *x*- and *y*-coordinates of the upper-left corner, the width and the height

20.7 The _____ class declares methods and constants for manipulating colors in a Java application.

     a) Color   b) GraphicsColor

     c) Colors   d) GraphicsColors

20.8 The _____ class contains methods for drawing text, lines, rectangles and other shapes.

a) Pictures

b) Drawings

c) Graphics

d) Illustrations

20.9 In a(n) _____ relationship, an object of a subclass also can be treated as an object of its superclass.

a) *is a*

b) *like a*

c) *has a*

d) None of the above.

20.10 In a(n) _____ relationship, a class contains references to objects of other classes.

a) *is a*

b) *like a*

c) *has a*

d) None of the above.

EXERCISES

20.11 (*Brick Wall Application*) A software company that writes applications used to landscape property wants to add a feature to its application that helps users design brick walls around their property. Write an application that will display a brick wall that is 10 bricks high and 9 bricks wide. You must leave some room between each brick, and every other row must be offset horizontally by half a brick from the bricks in the adjacent row. The completed application should appear as in Fig. 20.32.

Figure 20.32 Brick Wall application's GUI.

a) *Copying the template to your working directory.* Copy the directory C:\Examples\ Tutorial20\Exercises\BrickWall to your C:\SimplyJava directory.

b) *Opening the DrawJPanel template file.* Open the template file DrawJPanel.java in your text editor.

c) *Cycling through each row and column of bricks.* Inside the drawBricks method (starts at line 45), start an outer for loop to cycle through each row of bricks before the repaint method call (line 58). The counter should start at 0 and iterate through 9 (inclusive), because there are a total of 10 rows. Inside the outer for loop, declare a new int variable y. Initialize this variable to 25 times the row variable. Then begin an inner for loop to iterate through each column of bricks. This for loop should also start at 0 and iterate through 9 (inclusive). Since some rows only have 9 columns of bricks, some bricks will be printed outside of the drawingJPanel. However, these bricks will be invisible to the application user, so you will not remove them to keep the code more readable. Inside the inner for loop, declare a new int variable x and initialize it to 50 times the column variable.

d) *Drawing the bricks.* After the declaration of the int variable x that you added in *Step c*, add an if...else statement in which you will initialize your MyRectangle object brick to represent each brick in the wall. The if statement should determine if your row number is odd by using the remainder operator (%). If row % 2 equals 1, then row is odd. Otherwise, row is even. If your row number is odd, display a row of nine bricks. When calling the MyRectangle constructor, the x and y variables you defined in the previous step should be the first two parameters. The height, width and color variables that have been declared for you should be your third, fourth and

fifth parameters, respectively. After you create this new MyRectangle object, add it to brickArrayList, which is an instance variable declared in the template. Since each row of a brick wall is offset by half a brick, if the row variable is even, you should display a row of bricks in which each MyRectangle object is offset to the left by 25 pixels.

e) *Saving the application.* Save your modified source code file.

f) *Compiling the application.* Compile the three source code files. Type javac MyRectangle.java DrawJPanel.java BrickWall.java.

g) *Running the completed application.* When all your files compile correctly, run your application by typing java BrickWall. When the application starts, the bricks should appear in the JPanel as shown in Fig. 20.32.

h) *Closing the running application.* Close your running application by clicking its close button.

i) *Closing the Command Prompt window.* Close the **Command Prompt** window by clicking its close button.

20.12 (*Enhanced Brick Wall Application*) The electronic landscaping company would like users to be able to customize their brick walls. Modify the **Brick Wall** application so that the user can enter the number of rows and columns of their brick wall.

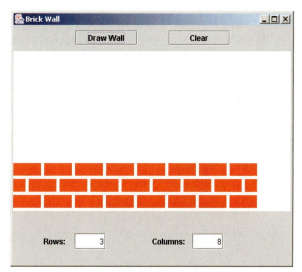

Figure 20.33 Enhanced **Brick Wall** application's GUI.

a) *Copying the template to your working directory.* Copy the directory C:\Examples\Tutorial20\Exercises\EnhancedBrickWall to your C:\SimplyJava directory.

b) *Opening the Brick Wall template file.* Open the template file BrickWall.java in your text editor.

c) *Declaring and initializing local variables.* Inside the drawJButtonActionPerformed method (starts at line 125), declare an int variable named numberOfRows. Initialize this variable by using the parseInt method to get the value the user enters in the rowsJTextField. Then declare the second int variable named numberOfColumns, which is initialized to the value in the columnsJTextField.

d) *Calling the drawBricks method.* After the variable declarations that you added in *Step c*, call the drawBricks method, which takes the two integers you just declared as arguments. Remember, since the drawBricks method is in a separate class, you will need to utilize drawingJPanel (declared as an instance variable in line 16), followed by the dot separator to access the method.

e) *Saving the application.* Save your modified source code file.

f) *Opening the DrawJPanel template file.* Open the template file DrawJPanel.java in your text editor.

g) *Modifying the drawBricks method.* Modify the drawBricks method header (line 43) so that it will now take two integers (wallRows and wallColumns) as arguments.

h) *Clearing the JPanel.* Inside the drawBricks method, at line 45, call the clearArray method, which has already been defined for you.

i) *Modifying the nested for statements.* Inside the drawBricks method, modify the outer for loop (starts at line 58) so that it iterates up to wallRows (exclusive). Modify the variable y (line 60) so that it equals (9 - row) * 25. Then, modify the inner for loop (starts at line 63) so that it iterates up to wallColumns (exclusive). Finally, in line 88, modify the first argument passed to the MyRectangle constructor to wallColumns * 50 - 25.

j) *Saving the application.* Save your modified source code file.

k) *Compiling the application.* Compile the three source code files. Type javac MyRectangle.java DrawJPanel.java BrickWall.java.

l) *Running the completed application.* When your application compiles correctly, run it by typing java BrickWall. To build a new wall, enter integer values in the JTextFields and press the **Draw Wall** JButton. The wall will appear on the JPanel with the desired number of rows and columns. If you wish to clear the JPanel, click the **Clear** JButton.

m) *Closing the application.* Close your running application by clicking its close button.

n) *Closing the Command Prompt window.* Close the **Command Prompt** window by clicking its close button.

20.13 (*Elevator Application*) A hotel is expanding and wants to install an elevator system in its building. You have been asked to create a simulation of this new elevator system. Create an application simulating the buttons in the elevator and displaying a simple picture of the elevator (a black rectangle) moving to the correct floor when a JButton is pressed (Fig. 20.34).

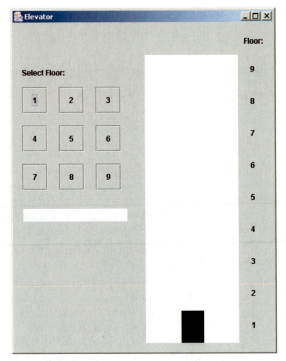

Figure 20.34 **Elevator** application's GUI.

a) *Copying the template to your working directory.* Copy the directory C:\Examples\ Tutorial20\Exercises\Elevator to your C:\SimplyJava directory.

b) *Opening the DrawJPanel template file.* Open the template file DrawJPanel.java in your text editor.

c) *Creating a new MyRectangle object.* Inside the DrawJPanel no-argument constructor, create your new MyRectangle object buildingElevator (at line 47) after the creation of delayTimer. The template already declares buildingElevator as an

instance variable. When calling the `MyRectangle` constructor, the `x` and `y` variables should be the first two parameters and be set to 57 and 400 respectively. The `height`, `width` and `color` variables should be set to 36, 50 and `Color.BLACK` and are the third, fourth and fifth parameters, respectively.

d) *Adding code to the `moveEelevator` method.* Find the `moveElevator` method, which immediately follows `moveElevatorToFloor`. Inside the `moveElevator` method, add an `if...else` statement that tests if `currentPosition` is less than `moveToPosition`. If this is the case, increment `currentPosition` by 1. Otherwise, decrement `currentPosition` by 1. Then, use the `setLocation` method to move the `buildingEle-vator` to its new position. Finally, call the `repaint` method.

e) *Saving the application.* Save your modified source code file.

f) *Compiling the application.* Compile the three source code files. Type `javac MyRect-angle.java DrawJPanel.java Elevator.java`.

g) *Running the completed application.* When your application compiles correctly, run it by typing `java Elevator`.

h) *Closing the application.* Close your running application by clicking its close button.

i) *Closing the Command Prompt window.* Close the **Command Prompt** window by clicking its close button.

What does this code do? ▶   **20.14** What does the `drawImages` method draw?

```
1   private void drawImages( Graphics g )
2   {
3       g.setColor( Color.GREEN );
4       g.fillRect( 50, 50, 50, 50 );
5   }
```

What's wrong with this code? ▶   **20.15** Find the error(s) in the following code. The `rectangleArray` is an instance variable of type `ArrayList`, which contains `MyRectangle` objects.

```
1    private void paintComponent( Graphics g )
2    {
3        superclass.paintComponent( g );
4        Iterator traverse = rectangleArray.iterator();
5
6        while ( traverse.hasMoreElements() )
7        {
8            MyRectangle currentRectangle = ( MyRectangle ) traverse.next();
9            currentRectangle.drawMyRectangle( g );
10
11       } // end while
12
13   } // end method paintComponent
```

Programming Challenge ▶   **20.16** *(Enhanced Cafeteria Survey Application)* Enhance the **Cafeteria Survey** application from Tutorial 16 so that it draws a bar, instead of asterisks, for each rating. The user should still be able to choose ratings from a `JComboBox` and press a `JButton` to enter the selected rating. As ratings are input by the user, a horizontal bar graph appears in the `JPanel` as seen in Fig. 20.35. When 20 ratings have been entered, disable the **Submit Rating** `JButton`.

a) *Copying the template to your working directory.* Copy the directory `C:\Examples\Tutorial20\Exercises\EnhancedCafeteriaSurvey` to your `C:\SimplyJava` directory.

b) *Opening the DrawJPanel template file.* Open the template file `DrawJPanel.java` in your text editor.

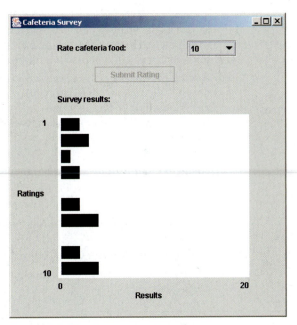

Figure 20.35 Enhanced **Cafeteria Survey** application's GUI.

c) *Initializing variables.* Inside the drawGraph method, before the repaint method call, declare two new int variables x and y, and initialize them to the value 5. Then, declare a new int variable width, but do not initialize it. The value of width will depend on the number of responses for each number. Declare a fourth int variable, height, which will be initialized to 20.

d) *Creating a new MyRectangle object.* After the declaration of the four int variables that you added in *Step c*, create a new MyRectangle object and assign it to variable bar.

e) *Looping through the responses.* After the declaration you added in *Step d*, begin a for statement that loops from 1 to 10, incrementing by one each time through the loop. Inside the for loop, set the width to 15 times the index of the answers array equal to the counter variable. The answers array is the parameter of the drawGraph method.

f) *Drawing the bar graph.* After setting the width as you did in *Step e*, initialize your bar object to the variables you declared in *Step d*. Set the color to the constant Color.BLACK. Then add the newly created MyRectangle to your barArray.

g) *Updating the y position.* After adding the newly created MyRectangle to barArray as you did in *Step f*, add 25 to variable y. This will ensure the graph is evenly spaced. This is the last statement inside the for statement.

h) *Saving the application.* Save your modified source code file.

i) *Opening the Command Prompt window and changing directories.* Open the **Command Prompt** window by selecting **Start > Programs > Accessories > Command Prompt**. Change to your working directory by typing cd C:\SimplyJava\Enhanced-CafeteriaSurvey.

j) *Compiling the application.* Compile all three of your source code files. Type javac CafeteriaSurvey.java DrawJPanel.java MyRectangle.java.

k) *Running the completed application.* When your application compiles correctly, run it by typing java CafeteriaSurvey. Choose a rating from the JComboBox and press the selectRatingJButton to select the desired rating. Make sure the bar graph correctly displays the results.

l) *Closing the application.* Close your running application by clicking the window's close button.

m) *Closing the Command Prompt window.* Close the **Command Prompt** window by clicking its close button.

Objectives

In this tutorial, you will learn to:

- Use mouse events to allow user interaction with an application.
- Use the mousePressed, mouseReleased and mouseDragged event handlers.
- Use the Graphics object to draw circles on a JPanel.
- Determine which mouse button was pressed.

Outline

"Cat and Mouse" Painter Application

Introducing Interfaces, Mouse Input; the Event-Handling Mechanism

The mouse is one of the computer's most important input devices. It is essential to GUI applications. With the mouse, the user can point to, press and drag items in applications. There are events associated with pressing, releasing and moving the mouse.

In this tutorial, you create a **Painter** application that handles **mouse events**—events that occur when the user interacts with the application by using the mouse. The **Painter** application contains a single component of programmer-declared type DrawJPanel, which is a subclass of the JPanel class. By moving the mouse cursor over the DrawJPanel with the left mouse button held down, the user can create line drawings composed of small, filled circles. By moving the mouse cursor over the DrawJPanel with the right mouse button held down (also called dragging the mouse), the user can erase those small, filled circles. (This application uses a method that draws ovals. Ovals whose width and height are the same are circles.)

21.1 Test-Driving the Painter Application

In this tutorial, you will create a **Painter** application. This application must meet the following requirements:

Application Requirements

The principal of an elementary school wants to introduce children to computers by appealing to their creative side. Many elementary-level applications test skills in mathematics, but the principal wishes to use an application that allows children to express their artistic skills. Develop an application that allows the student to "paint" on a JPanel, using the mouse. The application should draw when the user moves the mouse with the left mouse button held down and stop drawing when the left mouse button is released. The application should draw small, filled, blue circles side by side to trace out lines, curves and shapes. An important part of any drawing application is the ability to erase mistakes. The user can erase a portion of the drawing by moving the mouse over that portion of the drawing with the right mouse button held down.

You begin by test-driving the completed application. Next, you will learn the additional Java technologies you will need to create your own version of this application.

Test-Driving the Painter Application

1. **Locating the completed application.** Open the **Command Prompt** window by selecting **Start > Programs > Accessories > Command Prompt**. Change to your completed **Painter** application directory by typing `cd C:\Examples\Tutorial21\CompletedApplication\Painter`.

2. **Running the Painter application.** Type `java Painter` in the **Command Prompt** window to run the application (Fig. 21.1).

Figure 21.1 **Painter** application before drawing.

3. **Drawing with the mouse.** To draw on the `DrawJPanel`, press and hold down the left mouse button while the mouse cursor is anywhere over the `DrawJPanel` and drag the mouse (Fig. 21.2). To stop drawing, release the mouse button. Note that the application draws little blue circles as you move the mouse while holding down the left mouse button.

Drawing lines composed of small, colored circles

Figure 21.2 Drawing on the **Painter** application's `DrawJPanel`.

4. **Being creative.** Draw a cat and a computer mouse, as shown in Fig. 21.3. Be creative and have fun—your drawing need not look like the image shown.

5. **Using the eraser.** Hold down the right mouse button and drag the mouse cursor over part of your drawing. This "erases" the drawing wherever the mouse cursor comes into contact with the colored line (Fig. 21.4). The eraser stops when you release the right mouse button. You will see that when you add code to the application to erase, you are actually drawing little circles in the application's background color.

(cont.)

Figure 21.3   Drawing a cat and a computer mouse on the DrawJPanel.

Erasing by drawing circles that are the same color as the DrawJPanel's background

Figure 21.4   Erasing part of the drawing.

6. ***Closing the running application.*** Close your running application by clicking its close button.

7. ***Closing the Command Prompt window.*** Close the **Command Prompt** window by clicking its close button.

21.2 Constructing the Painter Application

Before you begin building the **Painter** application, you should review its functionality. The following pseudocode describes the basic operation of the **Painter** application when the user moves the mouse cursor over the application's DrawJPanel:

> When the mouse is pressed:
>   Get the mouse's location
>   Store the mouse's location
>
>   If the left mouse button is pressed
>   Set the color to blue
>   Set the diameter for drawing
>   Else
>   Set the color to the DrawJPanel's background color
>   Set the diameter for erasing
>
>   Repaint the DrawJPanel
>
> When the mouse is dragged:
>   Store the mouse's location
>   Repaint the DrawJPanel

When the paintComponent method is called:
Set the drawing color
Draw a circle with the appropriate diameter at the mouse's location

You begin by learning about interfaces, then you learn how to implement three mouse event handlers—the event handler that is called when you press a mouse button, the event handler that is called when you release that mouse button and the event handler that is called when you press a mouse button and drag the mouse. At first, your **Painter** application will draw a circle when the user presses any mouse button. Then, you will enhance your application to draw another circle when the user releases that mouse button. The circles drawn by pressing a mouse button will be larger and colored blue, while the circles drawn by releasing the mouse button will be smaller and colored green. Next, you will modify the application so that it draws when the user moves the mouse while the left button is pressed and erases when the user moves the mouse while the right button is pressed. If the user moves the mouse without pressing a mouse button, nothing will be drawn or erased.

Now that you have test-driven the **Painter** application and studied its pseudocode representation, you will use an ACE table to help you convert the pseudocode to Java. Figure 21.5 lists the actions, components and events required to complete your own version of this application.

Action/Component/ Event (ACE) Table for the Painter Application

Action	Component/Object	Event/Method
	myDrawJPanel	User presses a mouse button
Get the mouse's location	event (MouseEvent)	
Store the mouse's location	currentPoint (Point)	
If left mouse button is pressed	event (MouseEvent)	
Set the color to blue	drawColor (Color)	
Set the diameter for drawing	drawDiameter (int)	

Else
   Set color to DrawJPanel's
   background color
	drawColor (Color)	

Set the diameter for erasing	drawDiameter (int)	
Repaint the DrawJPanel	myDrawJPanel	
	myDrawJPanel	User drags the mouse
Store the mouse's location	event (MouseEvent)	
Repaint the DrawJPanel	myDrawJPanel	
	myDrawJPanel	paintComponent method is called
Set the drawing color	g (Graphics object)	
Draw a circle with appropriate diameter at mouse's location	g (Graphics object)	

Figure 21.5 **Painter** application's ACE table.

To complete the **Painter** application, you will need to add the erasing capability, which requires you to determine which mouse button the user presses. The last section of this tutorial will show you how to assign the drawing capability to the left mouse button and the erasing capability to the right mouse button.

21.3 Interfaces

There are three parts to the event-handling mechanism—the **event source**, the event object and the **event listener**. The event source is the GUI component with which the user interacts. The event object you learned about in Tutorial 13; it is generated by Java and contains information about the event that occurred. The event listener is the object that is notified by the event source when an event occurs; in effect, it "listens" for an event and executes in response to the event. This occurs only if you register the listener with the event source by calling an appropriate add listener method, such as addMouseListener (introduced shortly). Event listeners are created by implementing an interface.

An **interface** is a description of *what* a class does, but not *how* it is done. Interfaces declare method headers but do not declare the methods' bodies. A class **implements an interface** by implementing all the methods in the interface. For example, ActionListener is the interface that declares the actionPerformed event handler (called when the user clicks a JButton). Any class that implements the ActionListener interface must provide the actionPerformed event handler.

You will now learn about the **MouseListener** interface which declares event handler headers for mouse events. The MouseListener interface declares five event handler headers. The **mouseClicked** event handler is called when the mouse is clicked (pressed and released without moving the mouse) on a component. The **mouseEntered** event handler is called when the mouse cursor enters the bounds of a component. The **mouseExited** event handler is called when the mouse cursor exits the bounds of a component. The **mousePressed** event handler is called when the mouse button is pressed on a component. The **mouseReleased** event handler is called when the mouse button is released on a component.

Adding a MouseListener

1. *Copying the template to your working directory.* Copy the C:\Examples\Tutorial21\TemplateApplication\Painter directory to your C:\SimplyJava directory.

2. *Opening the Painter application's template file.* Open the template file DrawJPanel.java in your text editor.

3. *Registering a MouseListener.* Add lines 23–25 of Fig. 21.6 to your code. Line 23 calls the **addMouseListener** method. This method call registers an event listener (which you will create next) with an event source (the DrawJPanel). Recall that the compiler includes an implicit this reference before the addMouseListener method call on line 23. The this reference refers to the current object, which is the DrawJPanel.

Adding a MouseListener object ——
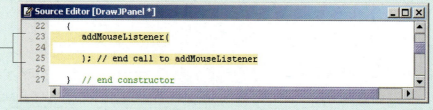

Figure 21.6 Calling the addMouseListener method.

4. *Creating an anonymous inner class.* Add lines 25–28 of Fig. 21.7 to your code. These lines create an object that is the event listener. This object is known as an anonymous inner class. An **inner class** is a class that is declared inside another class. In this example, the class that implements MouseListener is declared inside the DrawJPanel class. An **anonymous inner class** is an inner class that has no name.

(cont.)

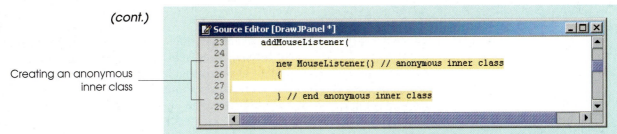

Figure 21.7 Creating an instance of the `MouseListener` interface.

Anonymous inner classes can be referenced only at the point where they are declared. An anonymous inner class, however, can only be instantiated where it is declared.

Line 25 creates an instance of this class (using the `new` keyword) and begins the class declaration. The class must now declare the five event handlers in the `MouseListener` interface. The braces on lines 26 and 28 will enclose these event handler declarations.

5. ***Declaring the event handlers.*** Add lines 27–50 of Fig. 21.8 to your code. Lines 28–30 declare the `mouseClicked` event handler. Lines 33–35 declare the `mouseEntered` event handler. Lines 38–40 declare the `mouseExited` event handler. Lines 43–45 declare the `mousePressed` event handler. Lines 48–50 declare the `mouseReleased` event handler. In this tutorial, you will use only the `mousePressed` and `mouseReleased` event handlers. Even though you will leave the other three event handlers empty, you must still implement them. *Every* method in an interface *must* be implemented.

Common Programming Error

Implementing an interface and forgetting to implement one of the interface's methods is a compile-time error.

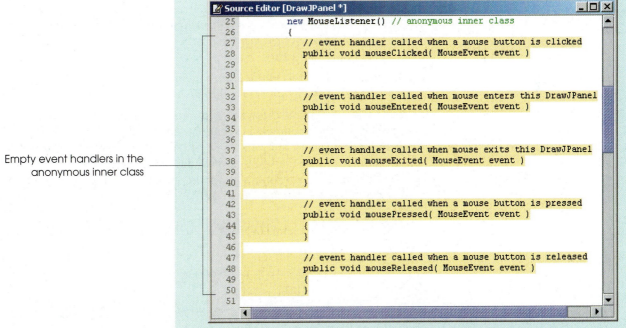

Figure 21.8 Implementing event handlers for the `MouseListener` interface.

(cont.)

In this example, the event source is the `DrawJPanel` object. Recall that the compiler includes an implicit `this` reference, referring to the `Draw-JPanel`, before the `addMouseListener` method call in line 23 of Fig. 21.6. The event object is the **MouseEvent** object that is generated (lines 28, 33, 38, 43 and 48). Later in this tutorial, you will use the event object to determine the position of the mouse on the `DrawJPanel`. The event listener is the object (the anonymous inner class declared in lines 25–52 of Fig. 21.8) that implements the `MouseListener` interface. The `addMouseListener` method of class `DrawJPanel` registers the event listener with the event source.

6. **Saving the application.** Save your modified source code file.

SELF-REVIEW

1. When a class implements an interface, it must _____.

   a) declare an extra instance variable   b) implement all methods in the interface

   c) declare that it `extends` the interface   d) None of the above.

2. An anonymous inner class _____.

   a) has no name

   b) is declared inside of another class

   c) has an instance created at the same point it is declared

   d) All of the above.

Answers: 1) b. 2) d.

21.4 The mousePressed Event Handler

A `mousePressed` event handler is called when a mouse button is pressed while the mouse cursor is over a component. Pressing any mouse button will call the `mouse-Pressed` event handler. Later in this tutorial, you will learn how to determine which mouse button was pressed.

Implementing the mousePressed Event Handler

1. **Coding the mousePressed event handler.** Insert line 45 of Fig. 21.9 in your `mousePressed` event handler. When the mouse is pressed while inside the `DrawJPanel`'s bounds, the `mousePressed` event handler is called and passed a `MouseEvent` as an argument. This event handler then calls method `draw-JPanelMousePressed`. This method uses our standard naming scheme—following the component name (`drawJPanel`) with the event handler name (`mousePressed`).

Adding code to the
mousePressed event handler

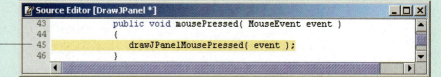

Figure 21.9   Coding the `mousePressed` event handler.

2. **Getting the location of the mouse cursor.** Add lines 59–65 of Fig. 21.10 to your code to create the `drawJPanelMousePressed` method. Line 63 calls the **getPoint** method on `event` (an instance of `MouseEvent`). This method returns a **Point** object, which has *x* and *y* values corresponding to the location of the mouse cursor in relation to the event source—in this example, the values 0, 0 represent the upper-left corner of the `DrawJPanel`. Note that variable `currentPoint` is an instance variable of the `Point` type declared in the `DrawJPanel` class (line 10).

(cont.)

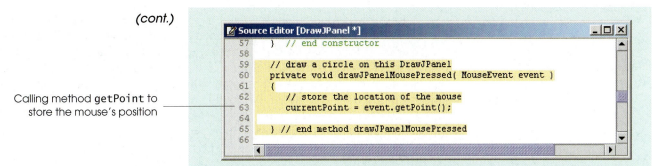

Figure 21.10 Storing the position of the mouse cursor.

Calling method getPoint to store the mouse's position

3. **Setting the circle diameter and color.** Insert lines 65–69 of Fig. 21.11 in the drawJPanelMousePressed method. Line 66 sets instance variable draw-Color to the constant DRAW_COLOR (which is assigned the Color constant BLUE in the template). This variable is used to set the color of the circle to be drawn. Line 67 sets instance variable drawDiameter to the constant DRAW_DIAMETER (which is set equal to 8 in the template). This variable is used to set the diameter of the circle. Line 69 calls the repaint method, which calls the DrawJPanel's paintComponent method. The paintComponent method will draw a little blue filled circle on the DrawJPanel.

```
Source Editor [DrawJPanel *]
63          currentPoint = event.getPoint();
64
65          // set the instance variables to the drawing values
66          drawColor = DRAW_COLOR;
67          drawDiameter = DRAW_DIAMETER;
68
69          repaint(); // repaint this DrawJPanel
70
```

Figure 21.11 Setting the color and diameter of the circle.

4. **Setting the drawing color.** Insert lines 73–78 of Fig. 21.12 in your code. Line 76 calls the setColor method on Graphics object g with the instance variable drawColor (which was set to the constant DRAW_COLOR in line 66 of Fig. 21.11). This method sets the color of the shapes drawn with Graphics object g.

```
Source Editor [DrawJPanel *]
71          } // end method drawJPanelMousePressed
72
73          // draw a small circle at the mouse's location
74          public void paintComponent( Graphics g )
75          {
76              g.setColor( drawColor ); // set the color
77
78          } // end method paintComponent
79
```

Figure 21.12 Setting the color using method setColor.

5. **Drawing on the DrawJPanel.** Insert lines 78–83 of Fig. 21.13 in your paintComponent method. Line 78 tests whether currentPoint is null. When the application starts, the paintComponent method is called, but you do not want a circle to be drawn. So instance variable currentPoint is initialized to null. This if statement ensures that a circle will not be drawn when the application starts. The Graphics class does not provide a method for drawing circles, but an oval whose width and height are the same is a circle. Lines 81–82 use the **fillOval** method of the Graphics class to draw a circle (an oval whose width and height are equal) on the DrawJPanel.

(cont.)

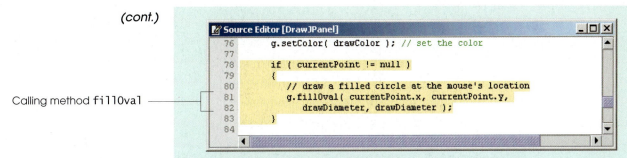

Calling method `fillOval`

Figure 21.13   Drawing the circle using method `fillOval`.

Figure 21.14 shows a diagram of a general oval. The dotted rectangle is known as the oval's **bounding box**. The bounding box specifies the oval's location, width and height. The `fillOval` method takes four arguments. The first two arguments specify the upper-left corner's *x* and *y* coordinates of the bounding box. The last two arguments specify the oval's width and height, respectively. The first two arguments are specified using `current-Point`'s **x** and **y** instance variables, which indicate the location of the mouse cursor when it was pressed. The next two arguments (the height and width) are specified by `drawDiameter`.

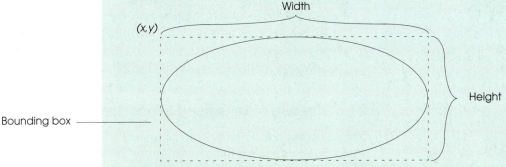

Figure 21.14   General oval.

6. ***Saving the application.*** Save your modified source code file.

7. ***Opening the Command Prompt window and changing directories.*** Open the **Command Prompt** window by selecting **Start > Programs > Accessories > Command Prompt**. Change to your working directory, `Painter`, by typing cd `C:\SimplyJava\Painter`.

8. ***Compiling the application.*** Compile your application by typing `javac DrawJPanel.java`.

9. ***Running the application.*** When your application compiles correctly, run it by typing `java Painter`. Figure 21.15 shows the updated application running. Notice that your **Painter** application will draw a circle when you presse any mouse button.

10. ***Closing the application.*** Close your running application by clicking its close button.

11. ***Closing the Command Prompt window.*** Close the **Command Prompt** window by clicking its close button.

(cont.)

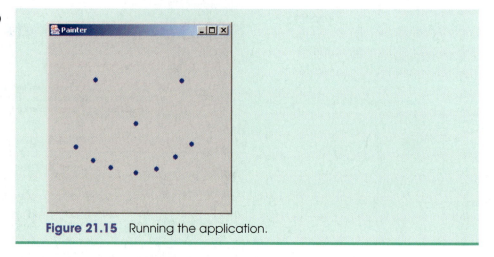

Figure 21.15 Running the application.

---

1. To draw a filled oval, call the _____ method.

   a) `fillEllipse`   b) `drawOval`

   c) `drawEllipse`   d) `fillOval`

2. The `getPoint` method of _____ returns a `Point` object, which has x and y values corresponding to the location of the mouse cursor in relation to the event source.

   a) `Point`   b) `JPanel`

   c) `MouseEvent`   d) `Graphics`

Answers: 1) d. 2) c.

21.5 The `mouseReleased` Event Handler

You can now press anywhere on the `DrawJPanel` and draw a little blue filled circle. You will now enhance the application to draw a green circle on the `DrawJPanel` when the user releases the mouse button. The `mouseReleased` event handler is called when a mouse button is released while the cursor is over a component. You will now add functionality to examine the `mouseReleased` event handler. This functionality is not in the application requirements, and you will remove it from the application later.

Implementing the
`mouseReleased` Event
Handler

1. ***Adding constants for releasing the mouse.*** Insert lines 16–18 of Fig. 21.16 into your code. Line 17 declares a constant that stores the color of the circles drawn when a mouse button is released (`Color.GREEN`). Line 18 declares a constant to store the diameter of these circles in pixels (4).

```
Source Editor [DrawJPanel *]
14      private final int DRAW_DIAMETER = 8;
15
16      // constants for the release circle
17      private final Color RELEASE_COLOR = Color.GREEN;
18      private final int RELEASE_DIAMETER = 4;
19
```

Figure 21.16 Declaring constants for the released circle's color and size.

2. ***Adding code to the `mouseReleased` event handler.*** Add line 55 of Fig. 21.17 to your code. The `mouseReleased` event handler calls the `drawJPanel-MouseReleased` method when a mouse button is released.

(cont.)

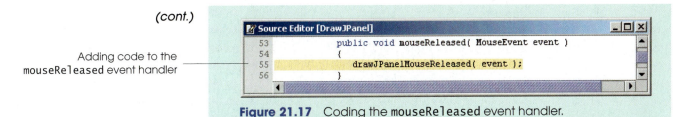

Adding code to the
`mouseReleased` event handler

Figure 21.17 Coding the `mouseReleased` event handler.

3. ***Storing the mouse cursor's location.*** Insert lines 92–98 of Fig. 21.18 in your
   code. These lines declare the `drawJPanelMouseReleased` method. Line 96
   stores the mouse's location in `currentPoint` using the `getPoint` method
   of the `MouseEvent` class.

Coding the
`drawJPanelMouseReleased`
method

Figure 21.18 Storing the location of the mouse's cursor.

4. ***Setting the diameter and color.*** Add lines 98–102 of Fig. 21.19 to the `draw-
   JPanelMouseReleased` method. Line 99 sets the color of the circle to the
   constant `RELEASE_COLOR`, and line 100 sets the diameter of the circle to the
   constant `RELEASE_DIAMETER`. These two constants were declared and initialized in lines 17–18 of Fig. 21.16. Line 102 calls the `repaint` method,
   which will call the `paintComponent` method you declared earlier.

Figure 21.19 Setting the color and size of the circle to be drawn.

5. ***Saving the application.*** Save your modified source code file.

6. ***Opening the Command Prompt window and changing directories.*** Open
   the **Command Prompt** window by selecting **Start > Programs > Accessories > Command Prompt**. Change to your working directory, `Painter`, by
   typing `cd C:\SimplyJava\Painter`.

7. ***Compiling the application.*** Compile your application by typing `javac
   DrawJPanel.java`.

8. ***Running the application.*** When your application compiles correctly, run it
   by typing `java Painter`. Figure 21.20 shows the updated application running.

9. ***Closing the application.*** Close your running application by clicking its
   close button.

10. ***Closing the Command Prompt window.*** Close the **Command Prompt**
    window by clicking its close button.

(cont.)

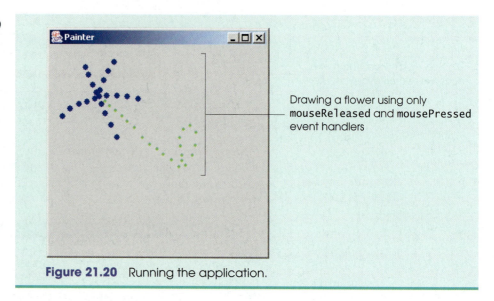

Figure 21.20   Running the application.

Drawing a flower using only `mouseReleased` and `mousePressed` event handlers

SELF-REVIEW

1. The _____ event handler is called when a mouse button is released.
   a) `mouseReleased`   b) `mouseUp`
   c) `mouseOff`   d) `mouseLetGo`

2. The first and second arguments of the `fillOval` method specify the *x*- and *y*-coordinates of the _____.
   a) oval's center   b) bounding box's center
   c) bounding box's upper-right corner   d) bounding box's upper-left corner

Answers: 1) a. 2) d.

21.6 mouseDragged Event Handler

Currently, your application allows you to draw only isolated circles when a mouse button is pressed or released. It does not yet allow you to continuously draw circles while the mouse is dragged (to create lines, arcs or shapes, for example). Next, you will enhance the application to provide more drawing capabilities. The application should continuously draw little blue filled circles while the mouse is being dragged over the `DrawJPanel` with the left mouse button held down. If the mouse is dragged with the right mouse button held down, the application should continuously erase by drawing little filled circles of the same color as the `DrawJPanel`'s background. If no mouse button is pressed, moving the mouse across the `DrawJPanel` should not draw or erase anything.

Determining Which Mouse Button Was Pressed

1. ***Modifying constants.*** Modify lines 16–18 of your code as shown in Fig. 21.21. Line 17 declares constant ERASE_COLOR to be the color of this DrawJPanel's background. This line calls the **getBackground** method. This method returns a Color object representing the color of the DrawJPanel's background. Line 18 declares the constant ERASE_DIAMETER which is equal to 8.

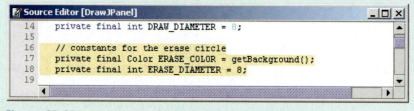

```
14    private final int DRAW_DIAMETER = 8;
15
16       // constants for the erase circle
17       private final Color ERASE_COLOR = getBackground();
18       private final int ERASE_DIAMETER = 8;
19
```

Figure 21.21   Adding constants for the erasing circle.

(cont.)

2. ***Removing code from the `mouseReleased` event handler.*** Remove line 55 from your application. This line calls the `drawJPanelMouseReleased` method. In the final application, you will not need this functionality. The `mouseReleased` event handler should now look like Fig. 21.22.

```
 52            // event handler called when a mouse button is released
 53            public void mouseReleased( MouseEvent event )
 54            {
 55            }
```

Figure 21.22 Removing the method call to `drawJPanelMouseReleased`.

3. ***Removing methods.*** Remove lines 92–104 of code from your application. These lines declared the `drawJPanelMouseReleased` method, which is not used in the final application. Leave the `paintComponent` and `drawJPanelMousePressed` methods declared.

4. ***Determining which mouse button was pressed.*** Add lines 69–78 of Fig. 21.23 to the `drawJPanelMousePressed` method (lines 76–77 should already be included). Line 69 uses the **`isMetaDown`** method of `MouseEvent` object event. This method returns `true` when the user presses the right mouse button on a mouse with two or three buttons. (If your mouse has only one button, pressing the right mouse button can be simulated by holding down the *Meta* key on the keyboard and pressing the mouse button. For example, on a Macintosh computer, hold down the *Option* key and press the mouse button.) If the right mouse button was pressed while the mouse was dragged, you want to erase points on the `DrawJPanel`. Line 71 sets the color of the circle that will be drawn to `ERASE_COLOR`, and line 72 sets the diameter of the circle that will be drawn to `ERASE_DIAMETER`. These constants are declared on lines 17–18 of Fig. 21.21.

Determining which mouse button is pressed

```
 67            currentPoint = event.getPoint();
 68
 69            if ( event.isMetaDown() ) // right mouse button is pressed
 70            {
 71                drawColor = ERASE_COLOR;
 72                drawDiameter = ERASE_DIAMETER;
 73            }
 74            else // left mouse button is pressed
 75            {
 76                drawColor = DRAW_COLOR;
 77                drawDiameter = DRAW_DIAMETER;
 78            }
 79
```

Figure 21.23 Using the `isMetaDown` method to determine which mouse button is pressed.

5. ***Saving the application.*** Save your modified source code file.

Next, you will add a **`MouseMotionListener`** interface. This interface, like the `MouseListener`, declares event handlers for mouse events. The `MouseMotionListener` interface declares two event handlers. The **`mouseDragged`** event handler is called when a mouse button is pressed and the mouse is moved. The **`mouseMoved`** event handler is called when the mouse is moved without any buttons pressed.

Unlike most events you have studied so far, moving the mouse and dragging the mouse (moving the mouse with a button pressed) each call the associated event handler continuously. When the mouse is moved, the `mouseMoved` event handler is called each time the mouse cursor's location on the screen changes. When the

mouse is dragged, the `mouseDragged` event handler is called each time the mouse cursor's location on the screen changes. Moving the mouse even a small distance can call these event handlers multiple times. Your application may draw multiple circles when the mouse is moved only once.

Adding the mouseDragged Event Handler

1. ***Registering a MouseMotionListener.*** Add lines 61–63 of Fig. 21.24 to your code. Line 61 calls the **addMouseMotionListener** method of the Draw-JPanel class, which registers an event listener (which you will create next) with an event source (which is the DrawJPanel).

Adding a `MouseMotionListener` to the `DrawJPanel`

```
 59         ); // end call to addMouseMotionListener
 60
 61         addMouseMotionListener(
 62
 63         ); // end call to addMouseMotionListener
 64
```

Figure 21.24   Calling method `addMouseMotionListener`.

2. ***Creating an anonymous inner class.*** Add lines 63–75 of Fig. 21.25 to your code. Line 63 uses the new keyword to create an object of the MouseMotion-Listener type. Before creating the object, the two event handlers in the MouseMotionListener interface must be implemented. Lines 66–68 implement the mouseDragged event handler. Lines 71–73 implement the mouse-Moved event handler.

Creating an anonymous inner class that implements the `MouseMotionListener` interface

```
 61         addMouseMotionListener(
 62
 63           new MouseMotionListener() // anonymous inner class
 64           {
 65              // event handler called when the mouse is dragged
 66              public void mouseDragged( MouseEvent event )
 67              {
 68              }
 69
 70              // event handler called when the mouse is moved
 71              public void mouseMoved( MouseEvent event )
 72              {
 73              }
 74
 75           } // end anonymous inner class
 76
```

Figure 21.25   Creating an anonymous inner class.

3. ***Coding the mouseDragged event handler.*** Add line 68 of Fig. 21.26 to the mouseDragged event handler. This line calls the drawJPanelMouseDragged method, which you will declare next. Note that this method will likely be called multiple times when the mouse moves.

```
 66         public void mouseDragged( MouseEvent event )
 67         {
 68            drawJPanelMouseDragged( event );
 69         }
```

Figure 21.26   Coding the `mouseDragged` event handler.

(cont.)

4. ***Storing the mouse's location.*** Add lines 117–125 of Fig. 21.27 to your code after the `paintComponent` method. These lines declare the `drawJPanel-MouseDragged` method. Line 121 stores the mouse's location in `current-Point` using the `getPoint` method. The `drawJPanelMouseDragged` method is called each time the mouse's location changes. The location returned from `getPoint` reflects the location of the mouse when this method is called. Line 123 calls the `repaint` method, which causes the `paintComponent` method to be called to update the `DrawJPanel`. When it is called, `paintComponent` draws a circle on the `DrawJPanel` with the color specified in `drawColor` and the diameter specified in `drawDiameter`.

```
Source Editor [DrawJPanel *]                              _ □ X
115      } // end method paintComponent
116
117      // draw a circle on this DrawJPanel
118      private void drawJPanelMouseDragged( MouseEvent event )
119      {
120         // store the location of the mouse
121         currentPoint = event.getPoint();
122
123         repaint(); // repaint this DrawJPanel
124
125      } // end method drawJPanelMouseDragged
126
```

Figure 21.27 Storing the location of the mouse's cursor.

5. ***Saving the application.*** Save your modified source code file.

6. ***Opening the Command Prompt window and changing directories.*** Open the **Command Prompt** window by selecting **Start > Programs > Accessories > Command Prompt**. Change to your working directory, `Painter`, by typing `cd C:\SimplyJava\Painter`.

7. ***Compiling the application.*** Compile your application by typing `javac DrawJPanel.java`.

8. ***Running the application.*** When your application compiles correctly, run it by typing `java Painter`. Figure 21.28 shows the completed application running.

Figure 21.28 Running the completed **Painter** application.

9. ***Closing the application.*** Close your running application by clicking the window's close button.

10. ***Closing the Command Prompt window.*** Close the **Command Prompt** window by clicking its close button.

Figure 21.29 presents the source code for the DrawJPanel class. Figure 21.30 presents the source code for the **Painter** application. The lines of code that you added, viewed and modified in this tutorial are highlighted.

```java
1   // Tutorial 21: DrawJPanel.java
2   // This class allows the user to draw and erase on the application.
3   import java.awt.*;
4   import java.awt.event.*;
5   import javax.swing.*;
6
7   public class DrawJPanel extends JPanel
8   {
9      // Point to hold the mouse cursor's location
10     private Point currentPoint;
11
12     // constants for the drawn circle
13     private final Color DRAW_COLOR = Color.BLUE;
14     private final int DRAW_DIAMETER = 8;
15
16     // constants for the erase circle
17     private final Color ERASE_COLOR = getBackground();
18     private final int ERASE_DIAMETER = 8;
19
20     // instance variables for the circle
21     private Color drawColor;
22     private int drawDiameter;
23
24     // constructor
25     public DrawJPanel()
26     {
27        addMouseListener(
28
29           new MouseListener() // anonymous inner class
30           {
31              // event handler called when a mouse button is clicked
32              public void mouseClicked( MouseEvent event )
33              {
34              }
35
36              // event handler called when mouse enters this DrawJPanel
37              public void mouseEntered( MouseEvent event )
38              {
39              }
40
41              // event handler called when mouse exits this DrawJPanel
42              public void mouseExited( MouseEvent event )
43              {
44              }
45
46              // event handler called when a mouse button is pressed
47              public void mousePressed( MouseEvent event )
48              {
49                 drawJPanelMousePressed( event );
50              }
51
```

Adding a MouseListener — *line 27*

Creating an anonymous inner class — *line 29*

Empty event handlers in the anonymous inner class. To implement the MouseListener, these methods must be implemented — *lines 31–44*

Calling the drawJPanelMousePressed method when mouse is pressed — *line 49*

Figure 21.29 DrawJPanel source code. (Part 1 of 3.)

Empty event handlers in
the anonymous inner class

```
52                        // event handler called when a mouse button is released
53                        public void mouseReleased( MouseEvent event )
54                        {
55                        }
56
57                   } // end anonymous inner class
58
59                ); // end call to addMouseListener
60
61         addMouseMotionListener(
62
63                new MouseMotionListener() // anonymous inner class
64                {
65                        // event handler called when the mouse is dragged
66                        public void mouseDragged( MouseEvent event )
67                        {
68                            drawJPanelMouseDragged( event );
69                        }
70
71                        // event handler called when the mouse is moved
72                        public void mouseMoved( MouseEvent event )
73                        {
74                        }
75
76                   } // end anonymous inner class
77
78                ); // end call to addMouseMotionListener
79
80      } // end constructor
81
82      // draw a circle on this DrawJPanel
83      private void drawJPanelMousePressed( MouseEvent event )
84      {
85          // store the location of the mouse
86          currentPoint = event.getPoint();
87
88          if ( event.isMetaDown() ) // right mouse button is pressed
89          {
90              drawColor = ERASE_COLOR;
91              drawDiameter = ERASE_DIAMETER;
92          }
93          else // left mouse button is pressed
94          {
95              drawColor = DRAW_COLOR;
96              drawDiameter = DRAW_DIAMETER;
97          }
98
99          repaint(); // repaint this DrawJPanel
100
101     } // end method drawJPanelMousePressed
102
103     // draw a small circle at the mouse's location
104     public void paintComponent( Graphics g )
105     {
106         g.setColor( drawColor ); // set the color
107
108         if ( currentPoint != null )
109         {
```

Adding a MouseMotionListener
to the DrawJPanel

Creating an anonymous inner
class that implements the
MouseMotionListener interface

Calling the
drawJPanelMouseDragged
method when mouse is dragged

Calling method getPoint to
store the mouse's position

Determining which mouse
button was pressed

Figure 21.29 DrawJPanel source code. (Part 2 of 3.)

Using the Graphics
object to draw a circle

```
110          // draw a filled circle at the mouse's location
111          g.fillOval( currentPoint.x, currentPoint.y,
112             drawDiameter, drawDiameter );
113       }
114
115    } // end method paintComponent
116
117    // draw a circle on this DrawJPanel
118    private void drawJPanelMouseDragged( MouseEvent event )
119    {
120       // store the location of the mouse in currentPoint
121       currentPoint = event.getPoint();
122
123       repaint(); // repaint this DrawJPanel
124
125    } // end method drawJPanelMouseDragged
126
127 } // end class DrawJPanel
```

Figure 21.29 DrawJPanel source code. (Part 3 of 3.)

```
1  // Tutorial 21: Painter.java
2  // Application enables user to draw on a subclass of JPanel.
3  import java.awt.*;
4  import java.awt.event.*;
5  import javax.swing.*;
6  import java.util.*;
7
8  public class Painter extends JFrame
9  {
10    // DrawJPanel for circles drawn by user
11    private DrawJPanel myDrawJPanel;
12
13    // no-argument constructor
14    public Painter()
15    {
16       createUserInterface();
17    }
18
19    // set up the GUI components
20    public void createUserInterface()
21    {
22       // get content pane for attaching GUI components
23       Container contentPane = getContentPane();
24
25       // enable explicit positioning of GUI components
26       contentPane.setLayout( null );
27
28       // set up myDrawJPanel
29       myDrawJPanel = new DrawJPanel();
30       myDrawJPanel.setBounds( 0, 0, 300, 300 );
31       contentPane.add( myDrawJPanel );
32
33       // set properties of application's window
34       setTitle( "Painter" ); // set title bar text
35       setSize( 300, 300 );   // set window size
36       setVisible( true );    // display window
```

Figure 21.30 **Painter** application source code. (Part 1 of 2.)

```
37
38       } // end method createUserInterface
39
40       // main method
41       public static void main( String[] args )
42       {
43          Painter application = new Painter();
44          application.setDefaultCloseOperation( JFrame.EXIT_ON_CLOSE );
45
46       } // end method main
47
48    } // end class Painter
```

Figure 21.30 **Painter** application source code. (Part 2 of 2.)

SELF-REVIEW

1. Moving the mouse with its button pressed invokes the _____ event handler.
   a) mouseDragged   b) mousePositionChanged
   c) mouseMoved   d) mouseChanged

2. Call the _____ method to register the listen for the mouse being dragged.
   a) addMouseListener   b) addMouseDraggedListener
   c) addMouseMotionListener   d) addMouseMovementListener

Answers: 1) a. 2) c.

21.7 Wrap-Up

In this tutorial, you learned the essential elements of mouse event handling. You learned what an interface is and how to implement an interface. You added a MouseListener and a MouseMotionListener to the DrawJPanel. You implemented three common mouse event handlers—mousePressed, mouseReleased and mouseDragged. You then used these event handlers and the fillOval method of the Graphics class to draw filled circles for the **Painter** application.

You used the MouseEvent class, which provides information about mouse events, such as the *x*- and *y*-coordinates where the mouse event occurred. The MouseEvent class also provides the isMetaDown method, which you used to distinguish which mouse button was pressed to provide the **Painter** application with an eraser.

In the next tutorial, you will learn how to use event handlers that respond to user interactions with the keyboard. You will then build an application that uses keyboard events. You will also learn how to create menus and dialogs.

SKILLS SUMMARY

Handling Mouse Events

■ Clicking a mouse button (pressing and releasing) invokes the mouseClicked event handler.

■ Moving the mouse into the bounds of a component invokes the mouseEntered event handler.

■ Moving the mouse out of the bounds of a component invokes the mouseExited event handler.

■ Pressing a mouse button invokes the mousePressed event handler.

■ Releasing a mouse button invokes the mouseReleased event handler.

Handling Mouse Motion Events

■ Moving the mouse with a button pressed invokes the mouseDragged event handler.

■ Moving the mouse without a button pressed invokes the mouseMoved event handler.

Distinguishing Between Mouse Buttons

■ Method `isMetaDown` returns `true` if the right mouse button was pressed, `false` otherwise.

Drawing a Filled Oval

■ Use the `Graphics` method `setColor` to specify the oval's color.

■ Use the `Graphics` method `fillOval` to draw a filled oval.

■ Specify the height and width of the bounding box and the coordinates of the bounding box's upper-left corner. When the height and width of the bounding box are equal, a circle is drawn.

KEY TERMS

addMouseListener method—Registers with a GUI component an event listener object that implements the `MouseListener` interface. The component can now react to mouse events.

addMouseMotionListener method—Registers with a GUI component an event listener object that implements the `MouseMotionListener` interface. The component can now react to mouse motion events.

anonymous inner class—An unnamed inner class that must be used to instantiate one object at the same time the class is declared. Anonymous inner classes are often used for event handling.

bounding box—A box encompassing an oval or other graphic, that specifies height, width, and location.

event listener—The object notified by an event source when an event is generated.

event source—The GUI component the user acts on to generate an event.

fillOval method of Graphics—Draws an oval. This method takes as arguments the coordinates of the upper-left corner of the oval's bounding box and the width and height of the bounding box.

getBackground method of JPanel—Returns a `Color` object that is the color of the background.

getPoint method of class MouseEvent—Returns a `Point` object containing the coordinates of the mouse cursor.

implement an interface—Implementing a method body for each method declared in an interface.

inner class—A class that is declared completely inside another class. A type of inner class, the anonymous inner class, is often used for event handling.

interface—A way to declare *what* a class does without declaring *how* it does it.

isMetaDown method—Returns `true` if the right mouse button is pressed, `false` otherwise.

mouse event—An event that is generated when a user interacts with an application using the computer's mouse.

mouseClicked event handler—Invoked when a mouse button is clicked (pressed and released).

mouseDragged event handler—Invoked when a mouse cursor is moved while one of the mouse buttons is pressed.

mouseEntered event handler—Invoked when a mouse cursor enters the bounds of the component.

MouseEvent—The type of event object generated when the mouse is used to interact with an application.

mouseExited event handler—Invoked when a mouse cursor leaves the bounds of the component.

MouseListener interface—Declares five event handlers for mouse events. These event handlers are: `mouseClicked`, `mouseEntered`, `mouseExited`, `mousePressed` and `mouseReleased`.

MouseMotionListener interface—Declares two event handlers for mouse motion events. These event handlers: `mouseDragged` and `mouseMoved`.

mouseMoved event handler—Invoked when the mouse is moved.

mousePressed event handler—Invoked when a mouse button is pressed.

mouseReleased event handler—Invoked when a mouse button is released.

Point—This class represents a location in the component.

x instance variable of class Point—The instance variable of the Point class that specifies the *x*-coordinate.

y instance variable of class Point—The instance variable of the Point class that specifies the *y*-coordinate.

JAVA LIBRARY REFERENCE

JPanel This component groups other related components, allowing a single border to be placed around multiple components. Components placed in a JPanel are positioned with respect to the upper-left corner of the JPanel, so changing the location of the JPanel moves all of the components contained inside it.

■ *Event handlers*

mousePressed—Invoked when a mouse button is pressed.

mouseDragged—Invoked when the mouse is moved while a mouse button is pressed.

mouseReleased—Invoked when a mouse button is released.

mouseEntered—Invoked when the mouse cursor enters the bounds of the component.

mouseExited—Invoked when the mouse cursor leaves the bounds of the component.

mouseClicked—Invoked when a mouse button is clicked (pressed and released).

■ *Methods*

add—Adds a component to the JPanel.

addMouseListener—Adds a MouseListener to the JPanel.

addMouseMotionListener—Adds a MouseMotionListener to the JPanel.

getBackground—Returns a Color object that is the color of the JPanel's background.

paintComponent—Paints components in the Graphics object, which is the argument passed to this method.

repaint—Clears all previous drawings and updates any current drawings in the JPanel.

setBorder—Sets the border displayed around the JPanel.

setBounds—Sets the *bounds* property, which specifies the location and size of the JPanel.

setLayout—Sets the *layout* property, which controls how components are displayed on the JPanel.

Graphics This class contains methods used to draw text, lines and shapes.

■ *Method*

fillOval—Draws a solid oval of a specified size at the specified location.

fillRect—Draws a solid rectangle of a specified size at the specified location.

setColor—Sets the color with which to fill the oval.

MouseEvent This class contains information about mouse events.

■ *Methods*

getPoint—Returns a Point object representing where the mouse cursor is.

isMetaDown—Returns true if the right mouse button was pressed, and false otherwise.

MouseListener This interface declares five event handlers for mouse events.

■ *Event Handlers*

mouseClicked—Invoked when a mouse button is clicked (pressed and released).

mouseEntered—Invoked when a mouse cursor enters the bounds of the component.

mouseExited—Invoked when a mouse cursor leaves the bounds of the component.

mousePressed—Invoked when a mouse button is pressed.

mouseReleased—Invoked when a mouse button is released.

MouseMotionListener This interface declares two event handlers for mouse motion events.

■ *Event Handlers*

mouseDragged—Invoked when a mouse cursor is moved while one of the mouse buttons is pressed.

mouseMoved—Invoked when the mouse is moved.

Point This class represents a single point on the screen.

■ *Instance variables*

x—The *x*-coordinate of the Point.

y—The *y*-coordinate of the Point.

MULTIPLE-CHOICE QUESTIONS

21.1 The *x*- and *y*-coordinates of the MouseEvent object are relative to _____.

a) the screen

b) the application

c) the GUI component that raises the event

d) None of the above.

21.2 A(n) _____ describes a set of methods that can be called on an object.

a) interface
b) constructor
c) template file
d) anonymous inner class

21.3 The _____ object passed to a mouse event handler contains information about the mouse event that was raised.

a) EventHandler
b) MouseEventHandler
c) MouseEvent
d) EventArgs

21.4 The _____ event handler is invoked when a mouse button is pressed.

a) mouseDown
b) mouseClick
c) mousePressed
d) mouseButtonDown

21.5 The mouseDragged event handler is declared in the _____ interface.

a) MouseMotionListener
b) MouseListener
c) MouseDraggedListener
d) ActionListener

21.6 Use the _____ method to get the location of the mouse cursor.

a) getPoint
b) getLocation
c) getMouse
d) getCursor

21.7 The _____ method of MouseEvent can be used to determine which mouse button was pressed.

a) isPressed
b) rightButton
c) leftButton
d) isMetaDown

21.8 The _____ event handler is not declared in the MouseListener interface.

a) mouseEntered
b) mouseExited
c) mouseMoved
d) mouseClicked

21.9 An oval whose _____ is a circle.

a) height is twice the length of its width
b) width is set to zero
c) height is half the length of its width
d) height is equal to its width

21.10 A bounding box will not tell you an object's _____.

   a) height   b) color

   c) width   d) position

EXERCISES

21.11 *(Line Length Application)* The **Line Length** application should draw a straight black line on a JFrame and calculate the length of the line. The line should begin at the coordinates where the mouse button is pressed and should stop at the point where the mouse button is released. The application should display the line's length (that is, the distance between the two endpoints) in the **Length=** JTextField. Use the following formula to calculate the line's length, where (x_1, y_1) is the first endpoint (the coordinates where the mouse button is pressed) and (x_2, y_2) is the second endpoint (the coordinates where the mouse button is released). To calculate the distance (or length) between the two points, use the following equation:

$$d = \sqrt{(x_1 - x_2)^2 + (y_1 - y_2)^2}$$

To draw a straight line, you need to use the **drawLine** method on a Graphics object. Use the following method call to draw a black line between the two points using a Graphics object reference g:

g.drawLine(x_1 , y_1 , x_2 , y_2)

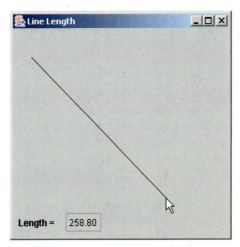

Figure 21.31   **Line Length** application's GUI.

  a) *Copying the template to your working directory.* Copy the directory C:\Examples\ Tutorial21\Exercises\LineLength to your C:\SimplyJava directory.

  b) *Opening the template file.* Open the LineLength.java file in your text editor.

  c) *Coding the lineLengthMousePressed method.* Find the lineLengthMousePressed method, which starts at line 97. Inside the lineLengthMousePressed method, add code to clear lengthJTextField, store the *x*-coordinate in instance variable point1x (declared for you in the template) using the statement event.getX()and store the *y*-coordinate in instance variable point1y (declared for you in the template) using the statement event.getY().

  d) *Coding the lineLengthMouseReleased method.* Find the lineLengthMouseReleased method, which immediately follows lineLengthMousePressed. Add code to the lineLengthMouseReleased method to store the *x*- coordinate in instance variable point2x (declared for you in the template) and store the *y*- coordinate in instance variable point2y (declared for you in the template). Then declare a variable named distance of type double and assign to it the value returned by a call to the lineLength method. Display the value of distance in lengthJTextField using DecimalFormat value, which is declared for you in the template. Finally, call the repaint method.

e) *Coding the `lineLength` method.* Find the `lineLength` method, which immediately follows `lineLengthMouseReleased`. Inside the `lineLength` method, before the `return` statement, declare a variable named `xDistance` of type `double` and assign to it the value of `point2x` subtracted from `point1x`. Declare a variable named `yDistance` of type `double` and assign to it the value of `point2y` subtracted from `point1y`. Modify the `return` statement that performs the length calculation. To do this, follow the `return` keyword with the following expression:

```
Math.Sqrt( ( xDistance * xDistance ) + ( yDistance * yDistance ) )
```

f) *Coding the `paint` method.* Find the `paint` method, which immediately follows `lineLength`. Inside the paint method, after the call to the superclass's `paint` method, draw the line by calling the `Graphics` object's `drawLine` method. The arguments to the `drawLine` method will be the *x*-coordinate of the first endpoint, the *y*-coordinate of the first endpoint, the *x*-coordinate of the second endpoint and the *y*-coordinate of the second endpoint.

g) *Saving the application.* Save your modified source code file.

h) *Opening the Command Prompt window and changing directories.* Open the **Command Prompt** by selecting **Start > Programs > Accessories > Command Prompt**. Change to your working directory, `LineLength`, by typing `cd C:\SimplyJava\ LineLength`.

i) *Compiling the application.* Compile your application by typing `javac Line-Length.java`.

j) *Running the completed application.* When your application compiles correctly, run it by typing `java LineLength`.

k) *Closing the application.* Close your running application by clicking its close button.

l) *Closing the Command Prompt window.* Close the **Command Prompt** window by clicking its close button.

21.12 *(Circle Painter Application)* The **Circle Painter** application should draw a blue circle of a randomly chosen size when the user presses a mouse button anywhere over the `JPanel` (Fig. 21.32). The application should randomly select a circle diameter in the range from 5 to 199, inclusive. To draw a blue circle with a given diameter (`diameter`), use the following statement:

```
g.drawOval( x, y, diameter, diameter );
```

The `drawOval` method draws the outline of an oval. Recall that an oval is a circle if the height and width arguments are the same (in this case, the randomly selected `width` and `height`). Use the *x*- and *y*-coordinates of the `mousePressed` event as the *x*- and *y*-coordinates of the circle's bounding box (that is, the first and second arguments to the `drawOval` method).

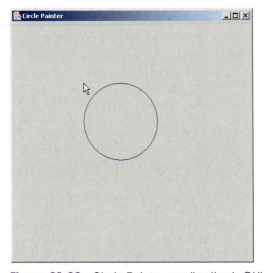

Figure 21.32   Circle Painter application's GUI.

a) *Copying the template to your working directory.* Copy the directory C:\Examples\ Tutorial21\Exercises\CirclePainter to your C:\SimplyJava directory.

b) *Opening the template file.* Open the DrawJPanel.java file in your text editor.

c) *Coding the drawJPanelMousePressed method.* Find the drawJPanelMousePressed method, which starts at line 58. Add code to the drawJPanelMousePressed method to store the *x*-coordinate in instance variable x (declared for you in the template) and store the *y*-coordinate in instance variable y (declared for you in the template), Then, store a random int in the range 5 to 199 into the instance variable diameter (declared for you in the template). Call the repaint method to update the drawing.

d) *Coding the paintComponent method.* Find the paintComponent method, which immediately follows the drawJPanelMousePressed method. After the call to the superclass's paintComponent method, set the color of g to Color.BLUE and call the drawOval method to draw a blue circle on the JPanel with the diameter generated by the Random object.

e) *Saving the application.* Save your modified source code file.

f) *Opening the Command Prompt window and changing directories.* Open the **Command Prompt** by selecting **Start > Programs > Accessories > Command Prompt**. Change to your working directory, CirclePainter, by typing cd C:\SimplyJava\ CirclePainter.

g) *Compiling the application.* Compile your application by typing javac Draw-JPanel.java.

h) *Running the completed application.* When your application compiles correctly, run it by typing java CirclePainter.

i) *Closing the application.* Close your running application by clicking its close button.

j) *Closing the Command Prompt window.* Close the **Command Prompt** window by clicking its close button.

21.13 *(Advanced Circle Painter Application)* In this exercise, you will enhance the application you created in Exercise 21.12. The advanced **Circle Painter** application should draw blue circles with a randomly generated diameter when the user presses the left mouse button. When the user presses the right mouse button, the application should draw a red circle with a randomly generated diameter (Fig. 21.33).

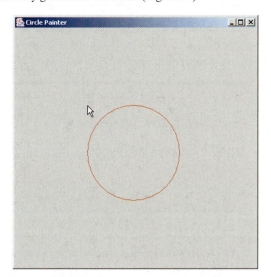

Figure 21.33 Advanced **Circle Painter** application's GUI.

a) *Copying the template to your working directory.* Copy the directory C:\Examples\ Tutorial21\Exercises\AdvancedCirclePainter to your C:\SimplyJava directory.

b) *Opening the template file.* Open the DrawJPanel.java file in your text editor.

c) *Adding a Color instance variable.* In line 17, add instance variable circleColor of type Color to hold the color of the circle to be painted.

d) *Determining which button was pressed.* Find the drawJPanelMousePressed method, which starts at line 60. In line 68 (before the method call repaint), add an if...else statement that sets circleColor to Color.RED if right mouse button is pressed and sets circleColor to Color.BLUE if left mouse button is pressed.

e) *Drawing the appropriate color.* Find the paintComponent method, which immediately follows drawJPanelMousePressed. Replace the parameter passed to the set-Color method (Color.BLUE) with circleColor since the color of the drawn circle will change depending on the mouse button that was pressed.

f) *Saving the application.* Save your modified source code file.

g) *Opening the Command Prompt window and changing directories.* Open the **Command Prompt** window by selecting **Start > Programs > Accessories > Command Prompt**. Change to your working directory, AdvancedCirclePainter, by typing cd C:\SimplyJava\AdvancedCirclePainter.

h) *Compiling the application.* Compile your application by typing javac Draw-JPanel.java.

i) *Running the completed application.* When your application compiles correctly, run it by typing java CirclePainter.

j) *Closing the application.* Close your running application by clicking its close button.

k) *Closing the Command Prompt window.* Close the **Command Prompt** window by clicking its close button.

What does this code do? ▶   **21.14** Consider the code in Fig. 21.29 (lines 118–125). Suppose we change the drawJPanel-MouseDragged method to the code below. What happens when the user drags the mouse? Assume that displayJTextField has been added to the application.

```
1   private void drawJPanelMouseDragged( MouseEvent event )
2   {
3       displayJTextField.setText = "I'm at " + event.getX()
4           + ", " + event.getY() + ".";
5
6   } // end method drawJPanelMouseDragged
```

What's wrong with this code? ▶   **21.15** The following code should draw a blue, filled, circle of diameter 4 that corresponds to the movement of the mouse. Find the error(s) in the following code:

```
1   public void paintComponent( Graphics g )
2   {
3      if ( currentPoint != null )
4      {
5          g.fillOval( Color.BLUE, currentPoint.y, currentPoint.x, 4, 5 );
6      }
7
8   } // end method paintComponent
```

Programming Challenge ▶   **21.16** *(Advanced Painter Application)* Extend the Painter application to enable a user to change the size and color of the circles drawn (Fig. 21.34). This application will use an Array-List to keep track of the data for all previously drawn circles (as in the **Screen Saver** application). Each time the paintComponent method is called, draw all previously drawn circles.

a) *Copying the template to your working directory.* Copy the directory C:\Examples\Tutorial21\Exercises\AdvancedPainter to your C:\SimplyJava directory.

b) *Opening the template file.* Open the PainterJPanel.java file in your text editor.

c) *Coding the mouseDragged event handler.* Inside the mouseDragged event handler (lines 30–32), add code to call the painterJPanelMouseDragged method with the argument event. You will declare this method in the next step.

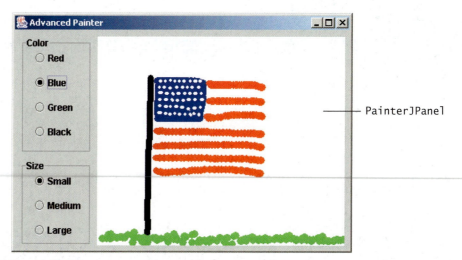

Figure 21.34　Advanced Painter application's GUI.

d) **Declaring the *painterJPanelMouseDragged* method.** After the paintComponent method, add the method header for painterJPanelMouseDragged. This method should be declared private, return void and take a MouseEvent object as its parameter. Inside the painterJPanelMouseDragged method, add an if…else statement to test if the right mouse button was pressed. If the right mouse button was pressed, create a new Circle object and assign it to instance variable newCircle. The Circle constructor should take the diameter of the circle (stored in instance variable circleDiameter), the location of the mouse's cursor (as a Point object) and the color of this PainterJPanel's background. If the left mouse button was pressed, create a new Circle object and assign it to instance variable newCircle. The constructor for this Circle object should take as arguments the diameter of the circle, the location of the mouse's cursor and the color of the circle (stored in instance variable circleColor). After the if…else statement, add code to add the newCircle object to circleArrayList. At the end of the method, call repaint to draw the new circle.

e) **Opening the template file.** Open the Circle.java file in your text editor.

f) **Coding the draw method of class *Circle*.** Find the draw method in the Circle.java class, which starts at line 62. Add code to set the color of the Graphics object to the color of this Circle object. Use the getDrawnColor method declared in the template to get the Circle's color. Use the fillOval method of the Graphics class to draw the circle. Remember that the fillOval method takes the *x* and *y* coordinates of the upper-left corner of the bounding box along with the width and height (which will be equal for a circle). Use the getLocation and getDiameter methods declared for you in the template. The getLocation method returns a Point object, and the getDiameter method returns an int.

g) **Saving the application.** Save your modified source code files.

h) **Opening the Command Prompt window and changing directories.** Open the **Command Prompt** by selecting **Start > Programs > Accessories > Command Prompt**. Change to your working directory, AdvancedPainter, by typing cd C:\SimplyJava\ AdvancedPainter.

i) **Compiling the application.** Compile your application by typing javac Painter-JPanel.java Circle.java.

j) **Running the completed application.** When your application compiles correctly, run it by typing java AdvancedPainter.

k) **Closing the application.** Close your running application by clicking its close button.

l) **Closing the Command Prompt window.** Close the **Command Prompt** window by clicking its close button.

TUTORIAL

Objectives

In this tutorial, you will learn to:
- Handle keyboard events.
- Create menus for your Java applications.
- Display a color dialog to enable users to choose colors.

Outline

Typing Skills Developer Application

Introducing Keyboard Events and JMenus

Text editor applications enable you to perform a wide variety of tasks, from writing e-mail to creating business proposals. These applications often use **menus** and dialogs to help you customize the appearance of your documents. In this tutorial, you will learn how to handle **keyboard events**, which occur when keys on the keyboard are pressed, released or typed. Handling keyboard events allows you to specify the actions the application should take when the user interacts with the keyboard. You will also learn to create **JMenus**, which group related commands, allowing the user to select various actions the application should take. Finally, you will learn about the **JColorChooser**, which is a color dialog that allows a user to select colors.

22.1 Test-Driving the Typing Skills Developer Application

In this tutorial, you will create a **Typing Skills Developer** application to help students learn how to type. The application must meet the following requirements:

> **Application Requirements**
>
> *A high-school course teaches students how to "touch type." The instructor would like to use an application that allows the student to watch what he or she is typing on the screen without looking at the keyboard. Your application should display a virtual keyboard that highlights any key the student presses on the real keyboard. This application should also contain menu commands for selecting the font style, size and color of the text, and for clearing the displayed text.*

This application allows the user to type text. As the user presses each key, the application highlights the corresponding key on the GUI and adds the character to a JTextArea that shows what the user has typed so far. The user can select the color and style of the characters typed and can clear the JTextArea. You begin by test-driving the completed application. Then, you will learn the additional Java technologies you will need to create your own version of this application.

Test-Driving the Typing Skills Developer Application

1. ***Locating the completed application.*** Open the **Command Prompt** by selecting **Start > Programs > Accessories > Command Prompt**. Change to your completed **Typing Skills Developer** directory by typing cd C:\Examples\ Tutorial22\CompletedApplication\TypingSkillsDeveloper.

2. ***Running the Typing Skills Developer application.*** Type java TypingApplication in the **Command Prompt** window to run the application (Fig. 22.1). Once the application has loaded, type the sentence "Programming in Java is simple." Notice that as you type, the corresponding keys light up on the application's virtual keyboard, and the text is displayed in the JTextArea.

Virtual keyboard ——————

Highlighted key ——————

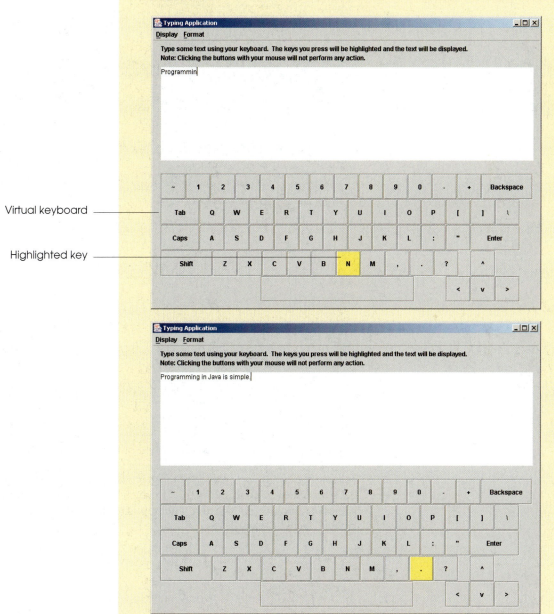

Figure 22.1   **Typing Skills Developer** application with a key pressed.

3. ***Changing the font.*** Select **Format > Style > Bold**, then select **Format > Size > 20** (Fig. 22.2). Notice that the text you typed in *Step 2* is now larger and bold.

(cont.)

Style submenu

JCheckBoxMenuItem

Size submenu

JRadioButtonMenuItem

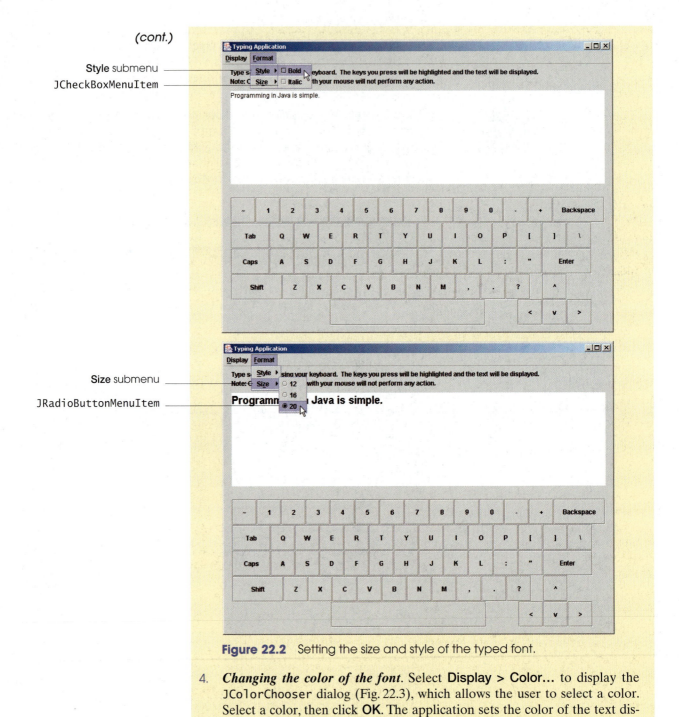

Figure 22.2 Setting the size and style of the typed font.

4. *Changing the color of the font*. Select **Display > Color...** to display the **JColorChooser** dialog (Fig. 22.3), which allows the user to select a color. Select a color, then click **OK**. The application sets the color of the text displayed to the selected color.

(cont.)

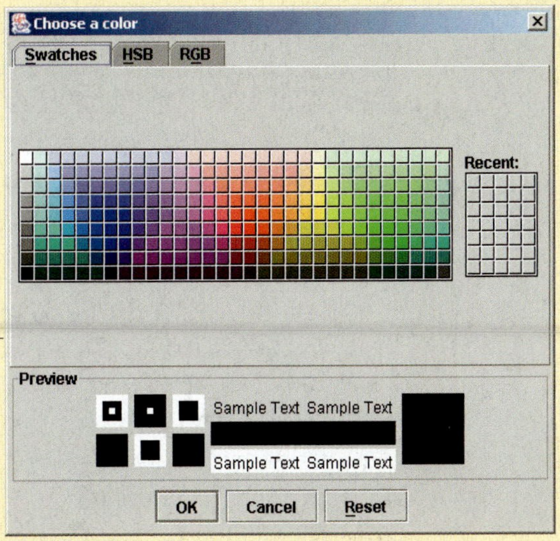

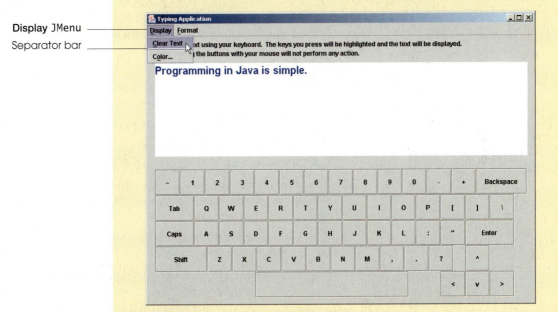

Figure 22.3   JColorChooser dialog displayed when **Display > Color...** is selected.

5. ***Clearing the JTextArea.*** Select **Display > Clear Text** (Fig. 22.4) to clear the text from the JTextArea (Fig. 22.5). The horizontal rule in the menu is called a **separator bar** and is used to group related menu items.

Figure 22.4   Selecting the **Clear Text** JMenuItem.

6. ***Closing the running application.*** Close your running application by clicking its close button.

7. ***Closing the Command Prompt.*** Close the **Command Prompt** window by clicking its close button.

(cont.)

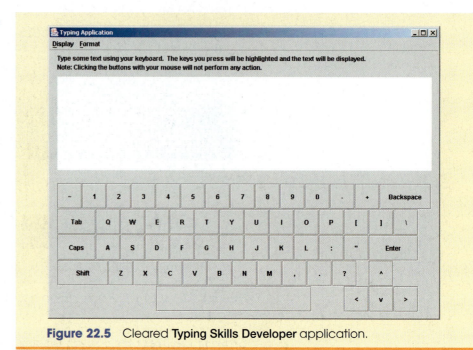

Figure 22.5 Cleared **Typing Skills Developer** application.

22.2 Keyboard Events

Before you begin building your **Typing Skills Developer** application, you should review its functionality. The following pseudocode describes the basic operation of the **Typing Skills Developer** application:

> When the user presses a key
> > Highlight in yellow the corresponding JButton on the virtual keyboard
>
> When the user releases a key
> > Reset the corresponding JButton to its default color
>
> When the user selects the Clear Text JMenuItem
> > Clear the JTextArea
>
> When the user selects the Color... JMenuItem
> > Display the JColorChooser dialog so the user can choose a color
> > Update the JTextArea text's color
>
> When the user selects a Style JCheckBoxMenuItem
> > Update the JTextArea font's style
>
> When the user selects a Size JRadioButtonMenuItem
> > Update the JTextArea font's size

Now that you have test-driven the **Typing Skills Developer** application and studied its pseudocode representation, you will use an ACE table to help you convert the pseudocode to Java. Figure 22.6 lists the actions, components and events that will help you complete your own version of this application.

*Action/Component/
Event (ACE) Table for the
Typing Skills Developer
Application*

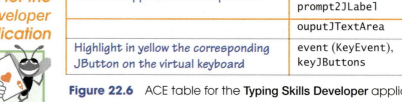

Action	Component/Class/Object	Event
Label the application's components	`prompt1JLabel` `prompt2JLabel`	Application is run
	`ouputJTextArea`	key is pressed
Highlight in yellow the corresponding JButton on the virtual keyboard	`event (KeyEvent)`, `keyJButtons`	

Figure 22.6 ACE table for the **Typing Skills Developer** application. (Part 1 of 2.)

Action	Component/Class/Object	Event
	ouputJTextArea	key is released
Reset the corresponding JButton to its default color	lastJButton	
Clear the JTextArea	clearJMenuItem	User selects **Clear Text** JMenuItem
	outputJTextArea	
Display the JColorChooser dialog so the user can choose a color	colorJMenuItem	User selects **Color...** JMenuItem
	JColorChooser class	
Update the JTextArea text's color	outputJTextArea	
Update the JTextArea font's style	styleMenuItems	User selects a **Style** JCheck-BoxMenuItem
	outputJTextArea, outputFont (Font)	
Update the JTextArea font's size	sizeMenuItems	User selects a **Size** JRadioButton MenuItem
	outputJTextArea, outputFont (Font)	

Figure 22.6   ACE table for the **Typing Skills Developer** application. (Part 2 of 2.)

You will now learn how to handle keyboard events, which are generated when keys on the keyboard are pressed and when they are released. The **KeyListener** interface declares three event handlers for keyboard events. The **keyPressed** event handler is called when a key is pressed. The **keyReleased** event handler is called when a key is released. The **keyTyped** event handler is called when a character key (such as 'a') is pressed. When you press a non-character key, such as the **Shift** key or the **Backspace** key, the keyPressed event handler is called and the keyTyped event handler is not called. You will not use the keyTyped event handler in this book, but you must implement it (with an empty body) to implement the interface because you must implement all methods declared in an interface.

You will now insert code for the keyPressed and keyReleased event handlers. When the user presses a key, your application will highlight in yellow the JButton associated with that key. When the key is released, your application will remove the highlight color from the JButton.

<table>
<tr>
<td valign="top">

Coding the outputJTextArea KeyPressed method

</td>
<td>

1. ***Copying the template to your working directory.*** Copy the C:\Examples\ Tutorial22\TemplateApplication\TypingSkillsDeveloper directory to your C:\SimplyJava directory.

2. ***Opening the Typing Skills Developer application's template file.*** Open the template file TypingApplication.java in your text editor.

3. ***Registering a KeyListener.*** Add lines 191–212 of Fig. 22.7 to your code. Line 191 calls the **addKeyListener** method. This method call registers an event listener with an event source (outputJTextArea). Line 193 creates an object of an anonymous inner class to implement the KeyListener inter-face. Recall from Tutorial 21 that to create an object of an interface type, you must declare every event handler in that interface. Lines 196–198 declare the keyPressed event handler, lines 201–203 declare the keyReleased event handler and lines 206–208 declare the keyTyped event handler. Each of these event handlers takes a **KeyEvent** object, which is the event object gen-erated when keyboard event occurs.

</td>
</tr>
</table>

(cont.)

Adding a KeyListener

Creating an anonymous inner class

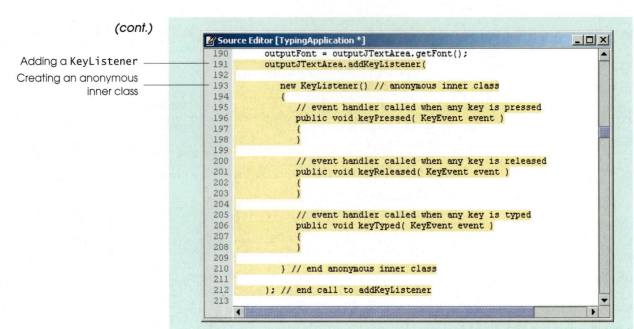

```
Source Editor [TypingApplication *]                              _ □ ×
190        outputFont = outputJTextArea.getFont();
191        outputJTextArea.addKeyListener(
192
193           new KeyListener() // anonymous inner class
194           {
195              // event handler called when any key is pressed
196              public void keyPressed( KeyEvent event )
197              {
198              }
199
200              // event handler called when any key is released
201              public void keyReleased( KeyEvent event )
202              {
203              }
204
205              // event handler called when any key is typed
206              public void keyTyped( KeyEvent event )
207              {
208              }
209
210           } // end anonymous inner class
211
212        ); // end call to addKeyListener
213
```

Figure 22.7   Adding a KeyListener to outputJTextArea.

4. *Coding the event handlers.* Add line 198 of Fig. 22.8 to the keyPressed event handler. This line calls the outputJTextAreaKeyPressed method. Add line 204 to the keyReleased event handler. This line calls the outputJTextAreaKeyReleased method. Leave the keyTyped event handler blank. Although you will not code any functionality for this event handler, you must still implement it (here, with no statements in its body), because it is in the KeyListener interface.

```
Source Editor [TypingApplication *]                              _ □ ×
196           public void keyPressed( KeyEvent event )
197           {
198              outputJTextAreaKeyPressed( event );
199           }
200
201           // event handler called when any key is released
202           public void keyReleased( KeyEvent event )
203           {
204              outputJTextAreaKeyReleased( event );
205           }
```

Figure 22.8   Coding the keyPressed and keyReleased event handlers.

5. *Viewing the array of JButtons.* View lines 66–67 of Fig. 22.9. These lines create an array of JButtons to hold all of the keyboard JButtons for this application. You will use the value associated with the key that was pressed to index the array and return the JButton associated with that key. The size of this array is equal to **KeyEvent.KEY_LAST** + 1. The KeyEvent (in package **java.awt.event**) class declares a number of constants for use with keyboard events. Most of these constants are unique; each one is associated with a single key on the keyboard. The KEY_LAST constant is the maximum value of these constants. Using the value KeyEvent.KEY_LAST + 1 guarantees that you can index this array with any of the key constants. The java.awt.event package provides interfaces and classes for handling all kinds of events, such as keyboard events and mouse events.

Tutorial 22   Typing Skills Developer Application   **609**

(cont.)

Using KeyEvent constant
KEY_LAST

```
Source Editor [TypingApplication *]                              _ |□| x|
65      // array of JButtons
66      private JButton[] keyJButtons =
67         new JButton[ KeyEvent.KEY_LAST + 1 ];
68
```

Figure 22.9   Creating an array of JButtons.

6. ***Adding JButtons to the array.*** Add lines 324 and 330 of Fig. 22.10 to your code. These lines add JButtons to your array. Recall from Tutorial 19 that Java uses virtual key codes to represent the keys on the keyboard. Each key has a unique code. For example, the **KeyEvent.VK_Q** (line 324) constant is an int that represents the *Q* key qJButton. Line 324 uses the KeyEvent constant VK_Q to index the array. Line 330 uses the KeyEvent constant **VK_W** to index the array. This constant is associated with the *W* key (wJButton). The rest of the JButtons have been added to the array in the template code.

Adding qJButton to the array

Adding wJButton to the array

```
Source Editor [TypingApplication *]                              _ |□| x|
321         qJButton = new JButton( "Q" );
322         qJButton.setBounds( 90, 298, 48, 48 );
323         contentPane.add( qJButton );
324         keyJButtons[ KeyEvent.VK_Q ] = qJButton;
325
326         // set up wJButton
327         wJButton = new JButton( "W" );
328         wJButton.setBounds( 138, 298, 48, 48 );
329         contentPane.add( wJButton );
330         keyJButtons[ KeyEvent.VK_W ] = wJButton;
331
```

Figure 22.10   Adding JButtons to the array.

7. ***Declaring the outputJTextAreaKeyPressed method.*** Add lines 633–642 of Fig. 22.11 to your code after the sizeMenuItemsActionPerformed method. These lines declare the outputJTextAreaKeyPressed method. Line 637 uses KeyEvent method **getKeyCode**. This method returns an int, which is the virtual key code associated with the key that was pressed. Line 640 uses this int to index the keyJButtons array and obtain the JButton associated with that key. This JButton is then passed to the changeColor method (provided for you in the template in lines 593–603), which changes the JButton's background color to yellow. The complete list of key codes can be found at java.sun.com/j2se/1.4.1/docs/api/java/awt/event/KeyEvent.html.

Calling the getKeyCode method

Using the virtual key code
to index the array

```
Source Editor [TypingApplication *]                              _ |□| x|
631   } // end method sizeMenuItemsActionPerformed
632
633      // highlight corresponding JButton when a key is pressed
634      private void outputJTextAreaKeyPressed( KeyEvent event )
635      {
636         // get the key code for this event
637         int buttonIndex = event.getKeyCode();
638
639         // change the color of the associated JButton
640         changeColor( keyJButtons[ buttonIndex ] );
641
642      } // end method outputJTextAreaKeyPressed
643
```

Figure 22.11   Highlighting the JButton associated with the pressed key.

(cont.)

8. ***Declaring the outputJTextAreaKeyReleased method.*** Add lines 644–649 of Fig. 22.12 to your code after the outputJTextAreaKeyPressed method. These lines declare the outputJTextAreaKeyReleased method. Line 647 calls the resetColor method (provided for you in the template on lines 605–613), which resets the color of the JButton associated with the key pressed to its default gray color.

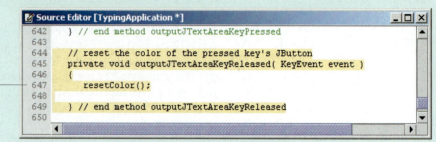

Resetting the color of the JButton ——

```
642        } // end method outputJTextAreaKeyPressed
643
644        // reset the color of the pressed key's JButton
645        private void outputJTextAreaKeyReleased( KeyEvent event )
646        {
647            resetColor();
648
649        } // end method outputJTextAreaKeyReleased
650
```

Figure 22.12 Removing the highlight from the JButton.

9. ***Saving the application.*** Save your modified source code file.

Now that you have added code to enable the user to see what they are typing by highlighting the corresponding JButtons and displaying output in a JTextArea, you will allow the user to alter the appearance of the display. You will do this by adding JMenus to your application; these will allow the user to perform tasks such as changing the color of the text, the size of the text and the style of the text.

SELF-REVIEW

1. A _____ event is raised when a key on the keyboard is pressed or released.
   a) keyboard   b) KeyPressedEvent
   c) KeyChar   d) KeyReleasedEvent

2. The _____ event handler is called when a key is released.
   a) KeyEventReleased   b) KeyUp
   c) KeyReleased   d) None of the above.

Answers: 1) a. 2) c.

22.3 JMenus

Menus allow you to group related commands for your applications. Although most menus and commands vary among applications, some—such as **Open** and **Save**—are common to many applications. Menus are an important part of GUIs because they organize commands without "cluttering" the GUI. Instead of being placed alongside other components, menus are often added to a **menu bar**, which usually runs along the top of the application's interface. In this section, you will learn how to enhance your **Typing Skills Developer** application by adding JMenus to allow the user to control the color, size and style of the text in the JTextArea. You begin by creating a JMenuBar, then adding JMenus and JMenuItems.

Creating the Display JMenu

1. ***Adding a menu bar to your application.*** Add lines 93–95 of Fig. 22.13 to your code to create a JMenuBar. The **JMenuBar** component is a container for the menus in your application. Line 94 creates the JMenuBar (named typingJMenuBar), and line 95 calls the **setJMenuBar** method inherited from JFrame to set the JMenuBar for this application.

(cont.)

Creating a JMenuBar ——

```
91          contentPane.setLayout( null );
92
93          // set up typingJMenuBar
94          typingJMenuBar = new JMenuBar();
95          setJMenuBar( typingJMenuBar );
96
```

Figure 22.13   Creating a JMenuBar.

2. ***Adding a menu to your menu bar.*** Add lines 97–100 of Fig. 22.14 to your code. Line 98 creates a new JMenu component named displayJMenu. You pass the constructor on this line the String "Display" to set the name of the JMenu. Previously, you have set the text displayed in a component using a call to its setText method. In this application, you will set the text by passing a String to the JMenu constructor. This will reduce the number of lines of code in the application. Line 99 calls the **setMnemonic** method and passes it the KeyEvent constant VK_D to set the mnemonic for this component to D. You learned in Tutorial 19 that mnemonics allow the user to select a component using the keyboard. Now, when the user presses the *Alt* and *D* keys, the **Display** JMenu will be selected. Line 100 uses the **add** method of JMenuBar to add displayJMenu to typingJMenuBar. JMenus are displayed left to right in the JMenuBar in the order that they are added. The **Display** JMenu will be the leftmost JMenu in your application's JMenuBar. A JMenu component that is added directly to a JMenuBar is called a **top-level menu**.

Creating a JMenu ——
Adding a JMenu to a JMenuBar ——

```
95          setJMenuBar( typingJMenuBar );
96
97          // set up displayJMenu
98          displayJMenu = new JMenu( "Display" );
99          displayJMenu.setMnemonic( KeyEvent.VK_D );
100         typingJMenuBar.add( displayJMenu );
101
```

Figure 22.14   Creating displayJMenu.

GUI Design Tip

Use book-title capitalization in menu item text.

GUI Design Tip

Use separator bars in a JMenu to group related JMenuItems.

3. ***Creating a menu item.*** Add lines 104–106 of Fig. 22.15 to your code. Line 103 creates a new **JMenuItem** component, which is a single menu item. A **menu item** performs some action when it is selected by the user. Line 104 sets the mnemonic for this JMenuItem. Line 105 uses the add method of JMenu to add clearJMenuItem to displayJMenu. Line 106 uses the **addSeparator** method of the JMenu class to create a recessed, horizontal rule after the **Clear Text** menu item.

Creating a JMenuItem ——
Adding a JMenuItem to a JMenu ——
Adding a separator bar ——

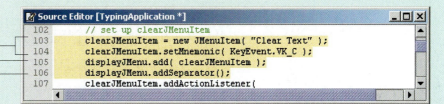

```
102         // set up clearJMenuItem
103         clearJMenuItem = new JMenuItem( "Clear Text" );
104         clearJMenuItem.setMnemonic( KeyEvent.VK_C );
105         displayJMenu.add( clearJMenuItem );
106         displayJMenu.addSeparator();
107         clearJMenuItem.addActionListener(
```

Figure 22.15   Adding a JMenuItem to your application.

GUI Design Tip

If clicking a menu item opens a dialog, an ellipsis (...) should follow the the menu item's text.

4. ***Adding the Color... JMenuItem.*** Add lines 123–124 of Fig. 22.16 to your code. Line 122 creates a new JMenuItem named colorJMenuItem. Line 123 sets the mnemonic for colorJMenuItem. Line 124 adds colorJMenuItem to displayJMenu. The **Color...** JMenuItem will appear at the bottom of the **Display** JMenu, after the separator bar.

(cont.)

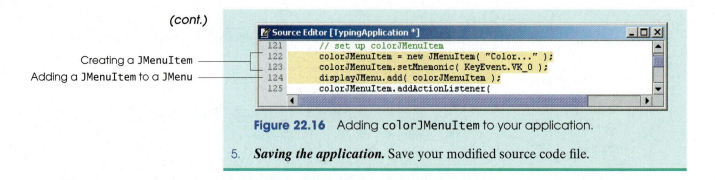

Creating a JMenuItem ———
Adding a JMenuItem to a JMenu ———

```
Source Editor [TypingApplication *]                    _ |□| x|
121        // set up colorJMenuItem
122        colorJMenuItem = new JMenuItem( "Color..." );
123        colorJMenuItem.setMnemonic( KeyEvent.VK_O );
124        displayJMenu.add( colorJMenuItem );
125        colorJMenuItem.addActionListener(
```

Figure 22.16 Adding `colorJMenuItem` to your application.

5. ***Saving the application.*** Save your modified source code file.

You just learned how to create menus and menu items. Next, you will learn how to add another menu to your application and create other kinds of menu items.

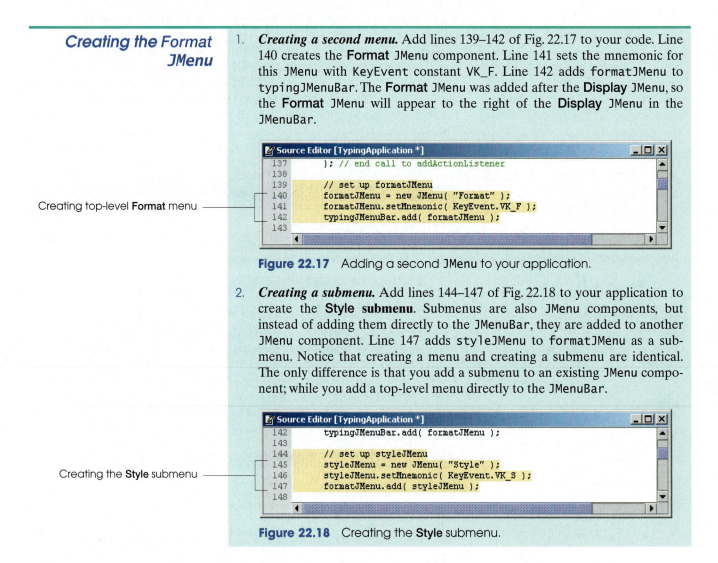

Creating the Format JMenu

1. ***Creating a second menu.*** Add lines 139–142 of Fig. 22.17 to your code. Line 140 creates the **Format** JMenu component. Line 141 sets the mnemonic for this JMenu with KeyEvent constant VK_F. Line 142 adds `formatJMenu` to `typingJMenuBar`. The **Format** JMenu was added after the **Display** JMenu, so the **Format** JMenu will appear to the right of the **Display** JMenu in the JMenuBar.

Creating top-level **Format** menu ———

```
Source Editor [TypingApplication *]                    _ |□| x|
137        ); // end call to addActionListener
138
139        // set up formatJMenu
140        formatJMenu = new JMenu( "Format" );
141        formatJMenu.setMnemonic( KeyEvent.VK_F );
142        typingJMenuBar.add( formatJMenu );
143
```

Figure 22.17 Adding a second JMenu to your application.

2. ***Creating a submenu.*** Add lines 144–147 of Fig. 22.18 to your application to create the **Style** submenu. Submenus are also JMenu components, but instead of adding them directly to the JMenuBar, they are added to another JMenu component. Line 147 adds `styleJMenu` to `formatJMenu` as a submenu. Notice that creating a menu and creating a submenu are identical. The only difference is that you add a submenu to an existing JMenu component; while you add a top-level menu directly to the JMenuBar.

Creating the **Style** submenu ———

```
Source Editor [TypingApplication *]                    _ |□| x|
142        typingJMenuBar.add( formatJMenu );
143
144        // set up styleJMenu
145        styleJMenu = new JMenu( "Style" );
146        styleJMenu.setMnemonic( KeyEvent.VK_S );
147        formatJMenu.add( styleJMenu );
148
```

Figure 22.18 Creating the **Style** submenu.

(cont.)

GUI Design Tip

A JCheckBoxMenuItem's text should be descriptive, be as short as possible and use book-title capitalization.

GUI Design Tip

Use JCheckBoxMenuItem when the user should be able to choose multiple options from a menu containing a group of JCheckBoxMenuItems.

Adding a JCheckBoxMenuItem to a JMenu ————

3. **Creating JCheckBoxMenuItems.** Add line 156 of Fig. 22.19 to your code. Lines 154–155 create a new **JCheckBoxMenuItem** component. A JCheck-BoxMenuItem has a check box to its left, allowing the user to see if the item is currently selected. Line 156 adds this JCheckBoxMenuItem to styleJMenu. Both styleMenuItems and styleNames are arrays that are already declared as instance variables in the template. The variable styleMenuItems is an array of JCheckBoxMenuItems. The variable styleNames is an array of Strings that stores font style names, such as Bold and Italic. The for statement that begins at line 152 creates and adds each JCheckBoxMenuItem stored in the styleMenuItems array to styleJMenu, then registers each menu item's event listener. All JCheckBoxMenuItems in the styleMenu-Items array use the same event handler, which is called when you select any JCheckBoxMenuItem.

```
152          for ( int count = 0; count < styleMenuItems.length; count++ )
153          {
154             styleMenuItems[ count ] = new JCheckBoxMenuItem(
155                styleNames[ count ] );
156             styleJMenu.add( styleMenuItems[ count ] );
157             styleMenuItems[ count ].addItemListener(
```

Figure 22.19   Creating JCheckBoxMenuItems.

4. **Creating the Size submenu.** Add lines 173–176 of Fig. 22.20 to your application to create the **Size** submenu. This code is identical to the code used to create the **Style** submenu.

Creating the **Size** submenu ————

```
171          } // end for
172
173          // set up sizeJMenu
174          sizeJMenu = new JMenu( "Size" );
175          sizeJMenu.setMnemonic( KeyEvent.VK_Z );
176          formatJMenu.add( sizeJMenu );
177
```

Figure 22.20   Creating the **Size** submenu.

GUI Design Tip

Use JRadioButtonMenuItem when the user should choose only one option from a menu containing a group of JRadioButtonMenuItems.

5. **Creating JRadioButtonMenuItems.** Add lines 186–187 of Fig. 22.21 to your code. Lines 184–185 create a new **JRadioButtonMenuItem** component. A JRadioButtonMenuItem has a JRadioButton to its left, allowing the user to see if the item is currently selected. Line 186 adds each JRadioButtonMenu-Item to sizeJMenu. Line 187 adds each JRadioButtonMenuItem to size-ButtonGroup to ensure that only one JRadioButtonMenuItem will be selected at a time. Both sizeMenuItems and sizeNames are arrays that are already declared as instance variables in the template. The variable size-MenuItems is an array of JRadioButtonMenuItems. The variable size-Names is an array of Strings that stores font sizes, such as 12, 16 and 20. The for statement that begins at line 182 creates and adds each JRadioButton-MenuItem stored in the sizeMenuItems array to sizeJMenu, then registers each menu item's event listener. All JRadioButtonMenuItems in the size-MenuItems array use the same event handler, which is called when you select any JRadioButtonMenuItem.

6. **Saving the application.** Save your modified source code file.

(cont.)

Adding `JRadioButtonMenuItems` to the menu

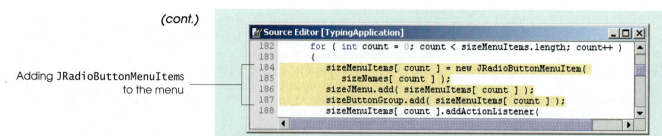

Figure 22.21 Creating the **Size** `JRadioButtonMenuItems`.

7. *Opening the Command Prompt window and changing directories.* Open the **Command Prompt** window by selecting **Start > Programs > Accessories > Command Prompt**. Change to your working directory by typing `cd C:\SimplyJava\TypingApplication`.

8. *Compiling the application.* Compile your application by typing `javac TypingApplication.java`.

9. *Running the application.* When your application compiles correctly, run it by typing `java TypingApplication`. The **Display** and **Format** JMenus will now appear in the JMenuBar (Fig. 22.22).

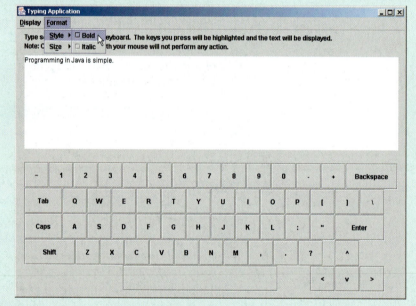

Figure 22.22 **Typing Skills Developer** application with JMenus added.

10. *Closing the application.* Close your running application by clicking its close button.

11. *Closing the Command Prompt window.* Close the **Command Prompt** window by clicking its close button.

SELF-REVIEW

1. JMenus can contain _____.

   a) commands that the user can select   b) submenus

   c) separator bars   d) All of the above.

2. A submenu is a JMenu component added to a _____ component.

   a) JMenu   b) JMenuBar

   c) JMenuItem   d) JSeparator

Answers: 1) d. 2) a.

22.4 JColorChooser

For a menu item to perform some action when it is selected, an event handler must be added for that item. The **Typing Skills Developer** application provides menus to allow the user to specify the color of the text that is output in the JTextArea. You will now learn how to allow the user to select a color using JColorChooser. JColorChooser allows the user interactively select a Color from a color dialog.

Coding the colorJMenuItem ActionPerformed Method

1. **Opening the JColorChooser.** Add lines 650–651 of Fig. 22.23 to the color-JMenuItemActionPerformed method. These lines call the **showDialog** method of class JColorChooser to open a color dialog that allows the user to choose a color and assign the return value to foregroundColor. The first argument passed to this method is the parent of the component. When a dialog is displayed, it is centered over its parent. Using the this reference centers the JColorChooser dialog over the application. The second argument is the text that will appear in the JColorChooser's title bar. The third argument specifies the initial color selected when the JColorChooser opens. If the user clicks the **OK** JButton, the showDialog method returns a Color object that represents the color selected. If the user clicks the **Cancel** JButton, the showDialog method returns null.

Displaying the JColorChooser

```
Source Editor [TypingApplication *]                          _□×
647      // change text color when user selects Colors... JMenuItem
648      private void colorJMenuItemActionPerformed( ActionEvent event )
649      {
650          Color foregroundColor = JColorChooser.showDialog(
651              this, "Choose a color", Color.BLACK );
652
653      } // end method colorMenuItemActionPerformed
```

Figure 22.23 Displaying the JColorChooser dialog.

2. **Setting the text's color.** Add lines 653–658 of Fig. 22.24 to your application. The if statement on line 654 tests whether foregroundColor is not equal to null (which will occur if the user clicks the **Cancel** JButton). Line 657 uses the **setForeground** method to set the text's color to the color selected by the user in the JColorChooser.

Changing the text to the color selected by the user

```
Source Editor [TypingApplication *]                          _□×
651              this, "Choose a color", Color.BLACK );
652
653          // if the user selected a color
654          if ( foregroundColor != null )
655          {
656              // set foreground color of outputJTextArea
657              outputJTextArea.setForeground( foregroundColor );
658          }
659
```

Figure 22.24 Setting the JTextArea's text color.

3. **Saving the application.** Save your modified source code file.

You will now allow the user to change the style of the font of the text in out-putJTextArea. To specify a font in Java, you must specify the font name, size and style. In this application, you will allow the user to change the size and style of the font.

Changing the Style of the Font

1. **Declaring a variable to store the style.** Add line 665 of Fig. 22.25 to your code. This line initializes variable `style` to the constant **Font.PLAIN**. The **Font** class allows you to create and manipulate objects that represent fonts. It also provides constants for the style of a font. The constant `Font.PLAIN` specifies a plain style (or normal style), that is neither italic nor bold.

```
Source Editor [TypingApplication *]                        _ |□| X|
662      // change font when user selects an item from Style submenu
663      private void styleMenuItemsStateChanged( ItemEvent event )
664      {
665          int style = Font.PLAIN;
666
667      } // end method styleMenuItemsStateChanged
```

Initializing a variable to hold the font style

Figure 22.25 Declaring a variable for the Font's style.

2. **Modifying the style.** Add lines 667–677 of Fig. 22.26 to your code. Line 668 checks if the **Bold** JCheckBoxMenuItem is selected. The **Bold** JCheckBox-MenuItem was placed in the first element (index 0) of the `styleMenuItems` array. If the bold style was selected, line 670 adds the constant **Font.BOLD** to the variable `style`. The constant `Font.BOLD` specifies bold style. Line 674 checks if the **Italic** JCheckBoxMenuItem is selected. The **Italic** JCheckBox-MenuItem was placed in the second element (index 1) of the `styleMenuItems` array. If the italic style was selected, line 676 adds the constant **Font.ITALIC** to the variable `style`. The constant `Font.ITALIC` specifies italic style.

```
Source Editor [TypingApplication *]                        _ |□| X|
665          int style = Font.PLAIN;
666
667          // check for bold selection
668          if ( styleMenuItems[ 0 ].isSelected() )
669          {
670              style += Font.BOLD;
671          }
672
673          // check for italic selection
674          if ( styleMenuItems[ 1 ].isSelected() )
675          {
676              style += Font.ITALIC;
677          }
678
```

Testing whether the **Bold** menu item was selected

Testing whether the **Italic** menu item was selected

Figure 22.26 Determining the style of the Font.

3. **Creating a new Font object.** Add lines 679–681 of Fig. 22.27 to create a new object of the Font class. The three parameters for the Font constructor are the name, style and size of the font, respectively. This method should change only the style, so you will want to preserve the name and size of the font. To preserve the name, pass the constructor the name of outputJTextArea's Font. This Font is stored in the instance variable outputFont (declared in the template in line 70). You can determine the name of the Font by calling the **getName** method of the Font class. The return value from this method is passed to the constructor as the first argument (line 680). The second argument should be `style` so that the user's modification to the style will be reflected in your new Font. You also want to preserve the size of the Font. The **getSize** method of the Font class returns the size of the Font, which is passed to the constructor as the third argument (line 681).

4. **Setting the font of outputJTextArea.** Add line 683 of Fig. 22.28 to your code. This line sets the font of outputJTextArea using the **setFont** method, passing the Font object you created in the previous step.

(cont.)

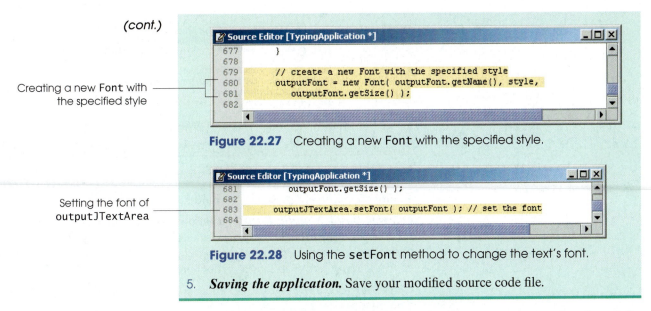

Creating a new **Font** with
the specified style

Figure 22.27   Creating a new **Font** with the specified style.

Setting the font of
`outputJTextArea`

Figure 22.28   Using the `setFont` method to change the text's font.

5. ***Saving the application.*** Save your modified source code file.

You will now add functionality to allow the user to change the size of the
JTextArea's font.

Changing the Size of the Font

1. ***Finding the event source.*** Add lines 690–691 of Fig. 22.29 to your code. In the
test-drive of the completed application, the **Format > Size** menu has three
JRadioButtonMenuItems with values 12, 16 and 20. When you click any of
these JRadioButtonMenuItems, the sizeMenuItemActionPerformed
method is called. You can decide which JRadioButtonMenuItem was chosen
by calling the getSource method of the ActionEvent class. Line 691 calls
the **getSource** method, which returns a reference (the source for this event)
of the Object type, which is then cast to the JRadioButtonMenuItem type.
This reference to the JRadioButtonMenuItem selected by the user is then
assigned to sizeMenuItem.

Storing a reference to the
`JRadioButtonMenuItem`

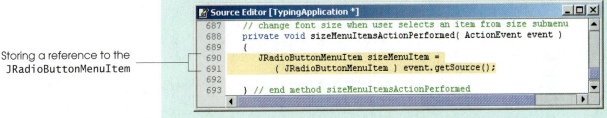

Figure 22.29   Obtaining a reference to the event source.

2. ***Creating a new Font object.*** Add lines 693–698 of Fig. 22.30 to create a new
Font. This method should change only the size, so you will want to preserve
the name and style of the font. Use the getName method again to pass the
constructor the name of the font (line 694). To preserve the style of the Font,
use the **getStyle** method of the Font class and pass its return value to the
constructor as the second argument (line 695). To determine the size of the
Font, line 696 uses the reference (sizeMenuItem) you created in the previous step. This line calls the getText method, which returns the text displayed in the JRadioButtonMenuItem as a String. That String is then
converted to an int using the Integer.parseInt method. This int is then
passed to the Font constructor as the third argument. Line 698 sets the font
of outputJTextArea.

(cont.)

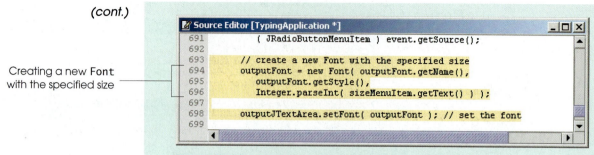

Creating a new Font with the specified size

Figure 22.30 Setting the Font for the new size.

3. **Saving the application.** Save your modified source code file.

4. **Opening the Command Prompt window and changing directories.** Open the **Command Prompt** window by selecting **Start > Programs > Accessories > Command Prompt**. Change to your working directory by typing cd C:\SimplyJava\TypingApplication.

5. **Compiling the application.** Compile your application by typing javac TypingApplication.java.

6. **Running the application.** When your application compiles correctly, run it by typing java TypingApplication.

7. **Closing the application.** Close your running application by clicking its close button.

8. **Closing the Command Prompt window.** Close the **Command Prompt** window by clicking its close button.

Figure 22.31 presents the source code for the **Typing Skills Developer** application. The lines of code that you added, viewed or modified in this tutorial are highlighted.

```
1   // Tutorial 22: TypingApplication.java
2   // Application enables users to practice typing
3   import java.awt.*;
4   import java.awt.event.*;
5   import javax.swing.*;
6   import java.text.*;
7
8   public class TypingApplication extends JFrame
9   {
10     // JMenuBar for display and format options
11     private JMenuBar typingJMenuBar;
12
13     // JMenu to show display options clear, invert colors and color
14     private JMenu displayJMenu;
15
16     // JMenuItems to clear the JTextArea and choose color
17     private JMenuItem clearJMenuItem;
18     private JMenuItem colorJMenuItem;
19
20     // JMenu to display format options style and size
21     private JMenu formatJMenu;
22
23     // JMenu and array of JCheckBoxMenuItems to display style options
24     private JMenu styleJMenu;
25     private JCheckBoxMenuItem styleMenuItems[];
```

Figure 22.31 **Typing Skills Developer** application source code. (Part 1 of 14.)

```
26
27        // JMenu, array of JRadioButtonMenuItems and ButtonGroup to
28        // display size options
29        private JMenu sizeJMenu;
30        private JRadioButtonMenuItem sizeMenuItems[];
31        private ButtonGroup sizeButtonGroup;
32
33        // JLabel and JTextArea to display text output
34        private JLabel prompt1JLabel, prompt2JLabel;
35        private JTextArea outputJTextArea;
36
37        // JButtons to represent first row of keys
38        private JButton tildeJButton, oneJButton, twoJButton,
39           threeJButton, fourJButton, fiveJButton, sixJButton,
40           sevenJButton, eightJButton, nineJButton, zeroJButton,
41           hyphenJButton, plusJButton, backspaceJButton;
42
43        // JButtons to represent second row of keys
44        private JButton tabJButton, qJButton, wJButton, eJButton,
45           rJButton, tJButton, yJButton, uJButton, iJButton, oJButton,
46           pJButton, leftBraceJButton, rightBraceJButton, slashJButton;
47
48        // JButtons to represent third row of keys
49        private JButton capsJButton, aJButton, sJButton, dJButton,
50           fJButton, gJButton, hJButton, jJButton, kJButton, lJButton,
51           colonJButton, quoteJButton, enterJButton;
52
53        // JButtons to represent fourth row of keys
54        private JButton shiftLeftJButton, zJButton, xJButton, cJButton,
55           vJButton, bJButton, nJButton, mJButton, commaJButton,
56           periodJButton, questionJButton, upJButton;
57
58        // JButtons to represent fifth row of keys
59        private JButton spaceJButton, leftJButton, downJButton,
60           rightJButton;
61
62        // JButton to store the last JButton typed
63        private JButton lastJButton;
64
65        // array of JButtons
66        private JButton[] keyJButtons =
67           new JButton[ KeyEvent.KEY_LAST + 1 ];
68
69        // Font of outputJTextArea
70        private Font outputFont;
71
72        // String array of font sizes
73        String sizeNames[] = { "12", "16", "20" };
74
75        // String array of font styles
76        String styleNames[] = { "Bold", "Italic" };
77
78        // no-argument constructor
79        public TypingApplication()
80        {
81           createUserInterface();
82        }
83
```

Array of `JButton` references
indexed by virtual key constant

Figure 22.31 **Typing Skills Developer** application source code. (Part 2 of 14.)

```
84      // set and position GUI components; register event handlers
85      private void createUserInterface()
86      {
87          // get content pane for attaching GUI components
88          Container contentPane = getContentPane();
89
90          // enable explicit positioning of GUI components
91          contentPane.setLayout( null );
92
93          // set up typingJMenuBar
94          typingJMenuBar = new JMenuBar();
95          setJMenuBar( typingJMenuBar );
96
97          // set up displayJMenu
98          displayJMenu = new JMenu( "Display" );
99          displayJMenu.setMnemonic( KeyEvent.VK_D );
100         typingJMenuBar.add( displayJMenu );
101
102         // set up clearJMenuItem
103         clearJMenuItem = new JMenuItem( "Clear Text" );
104         clearJMenuItem.setMnemonic( KeyEvent.VK_C );
105         displayJMenu.add( clearJMenuItem );
106         displayJMenu.addSeparator();
107         clearJMenuItem.addActionListener(
108
109             new ActionListener() // anonymous inner class
110             {
111                 // event handler called when clearJMenuItem is selected
112                 public void actionPerformed( ActionEvent event )
113                 {
114                     clearJMenuItemActionPerformed( event );
115                 }
116
117             } // end anonymous inner class
118
119         ); // end call to addActionListener
120
121         // set up colorJMenuItem
122         colorJMenuItem = new JMenuItem( "Color..." );
123         colorJMenuItem.setMnemonic( KeyEvent.VK_O );
124         displayJMenu.add( colorJMenuItem );
125         colorJMenuItem.addActionListener(
126
127             new ActionListener() // anonymous inner class
128             {
129                 // event handler called when colorJMenuItem is selected
130                 public void actionPerformed( ActionEvent event )
131                 {
132                     colorJMenuItemActionPerformed( event );
133                 }
134
135             } // end anonymous inner class
136
137         ); // end call to addActionListener
138
139         // set up formatJMenu
140         formatJMenu = new JMenu( "Format" );
141         formatJMenu.setMnemonic( KeyEvent.VK_F );
142         typingJMenuBar.add( formatJMenu );
```

Labels (left margin annotations):
- Creating a JMenuBar — lines 94–95
- Creating a JMenu — lines 98–99
- Adding a JMenu to a JMenuBar — line 100
- Creating a JMenuItem — lines 103–104
- Adding a JMenuItem to a JMenu — line 105
- Adding a separator bar to a JMenu — line 106
- Creating a JMenuItem — lines 122–123
- Adding a JMenuItem to a JMenu — line 124
- Creating top-level **Format** menu — lines 140–142

Figure 22.31   Typing Skills Developer application source code. (Part 3 of 14.)

```
143
144      // set up styleJMenu
145      styleJMenu = new JMenu( "Style" );
146      styleJMenu.setMnemonic( KeyEvent.VK_S );
147      formatJMenu.add( styleJMenu );
148
149      styleMenuItems = new JCheckBoxMenuItem[ styleNames.length ];
150
151      // set up styleMenuItems
152      for ( int count = 0; count < styleMenuItems.length; count++ )
153      {
154         styleMenuItems[ count ] = new JCheckBoxMenuItem(
155            styleNames[ count ] );
156         styleJMenu.add( styleMenuItems[ count ] );
157         styleMenuItems[ count ].addItemListener(
158
159            new ItemListener() // anonymous inner class
160            {
161               // event handler called when styleMenuItems selected
162               public void itemStateChanged( ItemEvent event )
163               {
164                  styleMenuItemsStateChanged( event );
165               }
166
167            } // end anonymous inner class
168
169         ); // end call to addItemListener
170
171      } // end for
172
173      // set up sizeJMenu
174      sizeJMenu = new JMenu( "Size" );
175      sizeJMenu.setMnemonic( KeyEvent.VK_Z );
176      formatJMenu.add( sizeJMenu );
177
178      sizeMenuItems = new JRadioButtonMenuItem[ sizeNames.length ];
179      sizeButtonGroup = new ButtonGroup();
180
181      // set up sizeMenuItems
182      for ( int count = 0; count < sizeMenuItems.length; count++ )
183      {
184         sizeMenuItems[ count ] = new JRadioButtonMenuItem(
185            sizeNames[ count ] );
186         sizeJMenu.add( sizeMenuItems[ count ] );
187         sizeButtonGroup.add( sizeMenuItems[ count ] );
188         sizeMenuItems[ count ].addActionListener(
189
190            new ActionListener()  // anonymous inner class
191            {
192               // event handler called when sizeMenuItems is selected
193               public void actionPerformed( ActionEvent event )
194               {
195                  sizeMenuItemsActionPerformed( event );
196               }
197
198            } // end anonymous inner class
199
200         ); // end call to addActionListener
```

Creating the **Style** submenu — (lines 144–147)

Adding JCheckBoxMenuItems to a JMenu — (lines 154–156)

Creating the **Size** submenu — (lines 173–176)

Creating the JRadioButtonMenuItem — (lines 184–185)

Adding JRadioButtonMenuItems to the menu — (lines 186–187)

Figure 22.31   **Typing Skills Developer** application source code. (Part 4 of 14.)

```
201
202         } // end for
203
204         // set up prompt1JLabel
205         prompt1JLabel = new JLabel( "Type some text using your " +
206            "keyboard.  The keys you press will be highlighted and " +
207            "the text will be displayed." );
208         prompt1JLabel.setBounds( 15, 5, 725, 20 );
209         contentPane.add( prompt1JLabel );
210
211         // set up prompt2JLabel
212         prompt2JLabel = new JLabel( "Note: Clicking the buttons " +
213            "with your mouse will not perform any action."  );
214         prompt2JLabel.setBounds( 15, 20, 725, 25 );
215         contentPane.add( prompt2JLabel );
216
217         // set up outputJTextArea
218         outputJTextArea = new JTextArea();
219         outputJTextArea.setBounds( 15, 50, 725, 175 );
220         outputJTextArea.setLineWrap( true );
221         contentPane.add( outputJTextArea );
222         outputFont = outputJTextArea.getFont();
223         outputJTextArea.addKeyListener(
224
225            new KeyListener() // anonymous inner class
226            {
227               // event handler called when any key is pressed
228               public void keyPressed( KeyEvent event )
229               {
230                  outputJTextAreaKeyPressed( event );
231               }
232
233               // event handler called when any key is released
234               public void keyReleased( KeyEvent event )
235               {
236                  outputJTextAreaKeyReleased( event );
237               }
238
239               // event handler called when any key is typed
240               public void keyTyped( KeyEvent event )
241               {
242               }
243
244            } // end anonymous inner class
245
246         ); // end call to addKeyListener
247
248         outputJTextArea.addFocusListener(
249
250            new FocusAdapter() // anonymous inner class
251            {
252               // event handler called when outputJTextArea loses focus
253               public void focusLost( FocusEvent event )
254               {
255                  outputJTextAreaFocusLost( event );
256               }
257
258            } // end anonymous inner class
```

Calling the **addKeyListener** method to register a **KeyListener** object *(line 223)*

Declaring the **keyPressed** event handler *(line 228)*

Declaring the **keyReleased** event handler *(line 234)*

Declaring the empty **keyTyped** event handler *(line 240)*

Figure 22.31 **Typing Skills Developer** application source code. (Part 5 of 14.)

```
259
260        ); // end call to addFocusListener
261
262        // set up tildeJButton
263        tildeJButton = new JButton( "~" );
264        tildeJButton.setBounds( 15, 250, 48, 48 );
265        contentPane.add( tildeJButton );
266        keyJButtons[ KeyEvent.VK_BACK_QUOTE ] = tildeJButton;
267
268        // set up oneJButton
269        oneJButton = new JButton( "1" );
270        oneJButton.setBounds( 63, 250, 48, 48 );
271        contentPane.add( oneJButton );
272        keyJButtons[ KeyEvent.VK_1 ] = oneJButton;
273
274        // set up twoJButton
275        twoJButton = new JButton( "2" );
276        twoJButton.setBounds( 111, 250, 48, 48 );
277        contentPane.add( twoJButton );
278        keyJButtons[ KeyEvent.VK_2 ] = twoJButton;
279
280        // set up threeJButton
281        threeJButton = new JButton( "3" );
282        threeJButton.setBounds( 159, 250, 48, 48 );
283        contentPane.add( threeJButton );
284        keyJButtons[ KeyEvent.VK_3 ] = threeJButton;
285
286        // set up fourJButton
287        fourJButton = new JButton( "4" );
288        fourJButton.setBounds( 207, 250, 48, 48 );
289        contentPane.add( fourJButton );
290        keyJButtons[ KeyEvent.VK_4 ] = fourJButton;
291
292        // set up fiveJButton
293        fiveJButton = new JButton( "5" );
294        fiveJButton.setBounds( 255, 250, 48, 48 );
295        contentPane.add( fiveJButton );
296        keyJButtons[ KeyEvent.VK_5 ] = fiveJButton;
297
298        // set up sixJButton
299        sixJButton = new JButton( "6" );
300        sixJButton.setBounds( 303, 250, 48, 48 );
301        contentPane.add( sixJButton );
302        keyJButtons[ KeyEvent.VK_6 ] = sixJButton;
303
304        // set up sevenJButton
305        sevenJButton = new JButton( "7" );
306        sevenJButton.setBounds( 351, 250, 48, 48 );
307        contentPane.add( sevenJButton );
308        keyJButtons[ KeyEvent.VK_7 ] = sevenJButton;
309
310        // set up eightJButton
311        eightJButton = new JButton( "8" );
312        eightJButton.setBounds( 399, 250, 48, 48 );
313        contentPane.add( eightJButton );
314        keyJButtons[ KeyEvent.VK_8 ] = eightJButton;
315
```

Figure 22.31 **Typing Skills Developer** application source code. (Part 6 of 14.)

```
316    // set up nineJButton
317    nineJButton = new JButton( "9" );
318    nineJButton.setBounds( 447, 250, 48, 48 );
319    contentPane.add( nineJButton );
320    keyJButtons[ KeyEvent.VK_9 ] = nineJButton;
321
322    // set up zeroJButton
323    zeroJButton = new JButton( "0" );
324    zeroJButton.setBounds( 495, 250, 48, 48 );
325    contentPane.add( zeroJButton );
326    keyJButtons[ KeyEvent.VK_0 ] = zeroJButton;
327
328    // set up hyphenJButton
329    hyphenJButton = new JButton( "-" );
330    hyphenJButton.setBounds( 543, 250, 48, 48 );
331    contentPane.add( hyphenJButton );
332    keyJButtons[ KeyEvent.VK_MINUS ] = hyphenJButton;
333
334    // set up plusJButton
335    plusJButton = new JButton( "+" );
336    plusJButton.setBounds( 591, 250, 48, 48 );
337    contentPane.add( plusJButton );
338    keyJButtons[ KeyEvent.VK_EQUALS ] = plusJButton;
339
340    // set up backspaceJButton
341    backspaceJButton = new JButton( "Backspace" );
342    backspaceJButton.setBounds( 639, 250, 100, 48 );
343    contentPane.add( backspaceJButton );
344    keyJButtons[ KeyEvent.VK_BACK_SPACE ] = backspaceJButton;
345
346    // set up tabJButton
347    tabJButton = new JButton( "Tab" );
348    tabJButton.setBounds( 15, 298, 75, 48 );
349    contentPane.add( tabJButton );
350    keyJButtons[ KeyEvent.VK_TAB ] = tabJButton;
351
352    // set up qJButton
353    qJButton = new JButton( "Q" );
354    qJButton.setBounds( 90, 298, 48, 48 );
355    contentPane.add( qJButton );
356    keyJButtons[ KeyEvent.VK_Q ] = qJButton;
357
358    // set up wJButton
359    wJButton = new JButton( "W" );
360    wJButton.setBounds( 138, 298, 48, 48);
361    contentPane.add( wJButton );
362    keyJButtons[ KeyEvent.VK_W ] = wJButton;
363
364    // set up eJButton
365    eJButton = new JButton( "E" );
366    eJButton.setBounds( 186, 298, 48, 48 );
367    contentPane.add( eJButton );
368    keyJButtons[ KeyEvent.VK_E ] = eJButton;
369
370    // set up rJButton
371    rJButton = new JButton( "R" );
372    rJButton.setBounds( 234, 298, 48, 48 );
373    contentPane.add( rJButton );
```

Figure 22.31 **Typing Skills Developer** application source code. (Part 7 of 14.)

```
374         keyJButtons[ KeyEvent.VK_R ] = rJButton;
375
376         // set up tJButton
377         tJButton = new JButton( "T" );
378         tJButton.setBounds( 282, 298, 48, 48 );
379         contentPane.add( tJButton );
380         keyJButtons[ KeyEvent.VK_T ] = tJButton;
381
382         // set up yJButton
383         yJButton = new JButton( "Y" );
384         yJButton.setBounds( 330, 298, 48, 48 );
385         contentPane.add( yJButton );
386         keyJButtons[ KeyEvent.VK_Y ] = yJButton;
387
388         // set up uJButton
389         uJButton = new JButton( "U" );
390         uJButton.setBounds( 378, 298, 48, 48 );
391         contentPane.add( uJButton );
392         keyJButtons[ KeyEvent.VK_U ] = uJButton;
393
394         // set up iJButton
395         iJButton = new JButton( "I" );
396         iJButton.setBounds( 426, 298, 48, 48 );
397         contentPane.add( iJButton );
398         keyJButtons[ KeyEvent.VK_I ] = iJButton;
399
400         // set up oJButton
401         oJButton = new JButton( "O" );
402         oJButton.setBounds( 474, 298, 48, 48 );
403         contentPane.add( oJButton );
404         keyJButtons[ KeyEvent.VK_O ] = oJButton;
405
406         // set up pJButton
407         pJButton = new JButton( "P" );
408         pJButton.setBounds( 522, 298, 48, 48 );
409         contentPane.add( pJButton );
410         keyJButtons[ KeyEvent.VK_P ] = pJButton;
411
412         // set up leftBraceJButton
413         leftBraceJButton = new JButton( "[" );
414         leftBraceJButton.setBounds( 570, 298, 48, 48 );
415         contentPane.add( leftBraceJButton );
416         keyJButtons[ KeyEvent.VK_OPEN_BRACKET ] = leftBraceJButton;
417
418         // set up rightBraceJButton
419         rightBraceJButton = new JButton( "]" );
420         rightBraceJButton.setBounds( 618, 298, 48, 48 );
421         contentPane.add( rightBraceJButton );
422         keyJButtons[ KeyEvent.VK_CLOSE_BRACKET ] = rightBraceJButton;
423
424         // set up slashJButton
425         slashJButton = new JButton( "\\" );
426         slashJButton.setBounds( 666, 298, 48, v );
427         contentPane.add( slashJButton );
428         keyJButtons[ KeyEvent.VK_BACK_SLASH ] = slashJButton;
429
430         // set up capsJButton
431         capsJButton = new JButton( "Caps" );
```

Figure 22.31 **Typing Skills Developer** application source code. (Part 8 of 14.)

```
432     capsJButton.setBounds( 15, 346, 75, 48 );
433     contentPane.add( capsJButton );
434     keyJButtons[ KeyEvent.VK_CAPS_LOCK ] = capsJButton;
435
436     // set up aJButton
437     aJButton = new JButton( "A" );
438     aJButton.setBounds( 90, 346, 48, 48 );
439     contentPane.add( aJButton );
440     keyJButtons[ KeyEvent.VK_A ] = aJButton;
441
442     // set up sJButton
443     sJButton = new JButton( "S" );
444     sJButton.setBounds( 138, 346, 48, 48 );
445     contentPane.add( sJButton );
446     keyJButtons[ KeyEvent.VK_S ] = sJButton;
447
448     // set up dJButton
449     dJButton = new JButton( "D" );
450     dJButton.setBounds( 186, 346, 48, 48 );
451     contentPane.add( dJButton );
452     keyJButtons[ KeyEvent.VK_D ] = dJButton;
453
454     // set up fJButton
455     fJButton = new JButton( "F" );
456     fJButton.setBounds( 234, 346, 48, 48 );
457     contentPane.add( fJButton );
458     keyJButtons[ KeyEvent.VK_F ] = fJButton;
459
460     // set up gJButton
461     gJButton = new JButton( "G" );
462     gJButton.setBounds( 282, 346, 48, 48 );
463     contentPane.add( gJButton );
464     keyJButtons[ KeyEvent.VK_G ] = gJButton;
465
466     // set up hJButton
467     hJButton = new JButton( "H" );
468     hJButton.setBounds( 330, 346, 48, 48 );
469     contentPane.add( hJButton );
470     keyJButtons[ KeyEvent.VK_H ] = hJButton;
471
472     // set up jJButton
473     jJButton = new JButton( "J" );
474     jJButton.setBounds( 378, 346, 48, 48 );
475     contentPane.add( jJButton );
476     keyJButtons[ KeyEvent.VK_J ] = jJButton;
477
478     // set up kJButton
479     kJButton = new JButton( "K" );
480     kJButton.setBounds( 426, 346, 48, 48 );
481     contentPane.add( kJButton );
482     keyJButtons[ KeyEvent.VK_K ] = kJButton;
483
484     // set up lJButton
485     lJButton = new JButton( "L" );
486     lJButton.setBounds( 474, 346, 48, 48 );
487     contentPane.add( lJButton );
488     keyJButtons[ KeyEvent.VK_L ] = lJButton;
489
```

Figure 22.31 **Typing Skills Developer** application source code. (Part 9 of 14.)

```
490            // set up colonJButton
491            colonJButton = new JButton( ":" );
492            colonJButton.setBounds( 522, 346, 48, 48 );
493            contentPane.add( colonJButton );
494            keyJButtons[ KeyEvent.VK_SEMICOLON ] = colonJButton;
495
496            // set up quoteJButton
497            quoteJButton = new JButton( "\"" );
498            quoteJButton.setBounds( 570, 346, 48, 48 );
499            contentPane.add( quoteJButton );
500            keyJButtons[ KeyEvent.VK_QUOTE ] = quoteJButton;
501
502            // set up enterJButton
503            enterJButton = new JButton( "Enter" );
504            enterJButton.setBounds( 618, 346, 96, 48 );
505            contentPane.add( enterJButton );
506            keyJButtons[ KeyEvent.VK_ENTER ] = enterJButton;
507
508            // set up shiftLeftJButton
509            shiftLeftJButton = new JButton( "Shift" );
510            shiftLeftJButton.setBounds( 15, 394, 100, 48 );
511            contentPane.add( shiftLeftJButton );
512            keyJButtons[ KeyEvent.VK_SHIFT ] = shiftLeftJButton;
513
514            // set up zJButton
515            zJButton = new JButton( "Z" );
516            zJButton.setBounds( 115, 394, 48, 48 );
517            contentPane.add( zJButton );
518            keyJButtons[ KeyEvent.VK_Z ] = zJButton;
519
520            // set up xJButton
521            xJButton = new JButton( "X" );
522            xJButton.setBounds( 163, 394, 48, 48 );
523            contentPane.add( xJButton );
524            keyJButtons[ KeyEvent.VK_X ] = xJButton;
525
526            // set up cJButton
527            cJButton = new JButton( "C" );
528            cJButton.setBounds( 211, 394, 48, 48 );
529            contentPane.add( cJButton );
530            keyJButtons[ KeyEvent.VK_C ] = cJButton;
531
532            // set up vJButton
533            vJButton = new JButton( "V" );
534            vJButton.setBounds( 259, 394, 48, 48 );
535            contentPane.add( vJButton );
536            keyJButtons[ KeyEvent.VK_V ] = vJButton;
537
538            // set up bJButton
539            bJButton = new JButton( "B" );
540            bJButton.setBounds( 307, 394, 48, 48 );
541            contentPane.add( bJButton );
542            keyJButtons[ KeyEvent.VK_B ] = bJButton;
543
544            // set up nJButton
545            nJButton = new JButton( "N" );
546            nJButton.setBounds( 355, 394, 48, 48 );
547            contentPane.add( nJButton );
```

Figure 22.31 **Typing Skills Developer** application source code. (Part 10 of 14.)

```
548        keyJButtons[ KeyEvent.VK_N ] = nJButton;
549
550        // set up mJButton
551        mJButton = new JButton( "M" );
552        mJButton.setBounds( 403, 394, 48, 48 );
553        contentPane.add( mJButton );
554        keyJButtons[ KeyEvent.VK_M ] = mJButton;
555
556        // set up commaJButton
557        commaJButton = new JButton( "," );
558        commaJButton.setBounds( 451, 394, 48, 48 );
559        contentPane.add( commaJButton );
560        keyJButtons[ KeyEvent.VK_COMMA ] = commaJButton;
561
562        // set up periodJButton
563        periodJButton = new JButton( "." );
564        periodJButton.setBounds( 499, 394, 48, 48 );
565        contentPane.add( periodJButton );
566        keyJButtons[ KeyEvent.VK_PERIOD ] = periodJButton;
567
568        // set up questionJButton
569        questionJButton = new JButton( "?" );
570        questionJButton.setBounds( 547, 394, 48, 48 );
571        contentPane.add( questionJButton );
572        keyJButtons[ KeyEvent.VK_SLASH ] = questionJButton;
573
574        // set up upJButton
575        upJButton = new JButton( "^" );
576        upJButton.setBounds( 618, 394, 48, 48 );
577        contentPane.add( upJButton );
578        keyJButtons[ KeyEvent.VK_UP ] = upJButton;
579
580        // set up spaceJButton
581        spaceJButton = new JButton( "" );
582        spaceJButton.setBounds( 208, 442, 300, 48 );
583        contentPane.add( spaceJButton );
584        keyJButtons[ KeyEvent.VK_SPACE ] = spaceJButton;
585
586        // set up leftJButton
587        leftJButton = new JButton( "<" );
588        leftJButton.setBounds( 570, 442, 48, 48 );
589        contentPane.add( leftJButton );
590        keyJButtons[ KeyEvent.VK_LEFT ] = leftJButton;
591
592        // set up downJButton
593        downJButton = new JButton( "v" );
594        downJButton.setBounds( 618, 442, 48, 48 );
595        contentPane.add( downJButton );
596        keyJButtons[ KeyEvent.VK_DOWN ] = downJButton;
597
598        // set up rightJButton
599        rightJButton = new JButton( ">" );
600        rightJButton.setBounds( 666, 442, 48, 48 );
601        contentPane.add( rightJButton );
602        keyJButtons[ KeyEvent.VK_RIGHT ] = rightJButton;
603
604        // set properties of application's window
605        setTitle( "Typing Skills Developer" ); // set title bar string
```

Figure 22.31 **Typing Skills Developer** application source code. (Part 11 of 14.)

```
606       setSize( 760, 550 );                    // set window size
607       setVisible( true );                     // display window
608
609    } // end method createUserInterface
610
611    // reset the color of the lastJButton
612    private void outputJTextAreaFocusLost( FocusEvent event )
613    {
614       resetColor();
615
616    } // end method outputJTextAreaFocusLost
617
618    // clear text
619    private void clearJMenuItemActionPerformed( ActionEvent event )
620    {
621       outputJTextArea.setText( "" );
622
623    } // end method clearJMenuItemActionPerformed
624
625    // highlight JButton passed as argument
626    private void changeColor( JButton changeJButton )
627    {
628       if ( changeJButton != null )
629       {
630          resetColor();
631          changeJButton.setBackground( Color.YELLOW );
632          lastJButton = changeJButton;
633       }
634
635    } // end method changeColor
636
637    // changes lastJButton's color back to default
638    private void resetColor()
639    {
640       if ( lastJButton != null )
641       {
642          lastJButton.setBackground( this.getBackground() );
643       }
644
645    } // end method resetColor
646
647    // change text color when user selects Colors... JMenuItem
648    private void colorJMenuItemActionPerformed( ActionEvent event )
649    {
650       Color foregroundColor = JColorChooser.showDialog(
651          this, "Choose a color", Color.BLACK );
652
653       // if the user selected a color
654       if ( foregroundColor != null )
655       {
656          // set foreground color of outputJTextArea
657          outputJTextArea.setForeground( foregroundColor );
658       }
659
660    } // end method colorMenuItemActionPerformed
661
```

Displaying JColorChooser — (line 650)

Changing the text to the color selected by the user — (line 657)

Figure 22.31 **Typing Skills Developer** application source code. (Part 12 of 14.)

Initializing a variable
to hold the style

Testing whether the **Bold**
menu item was selected

Testing whether the **Italic**
menu item was selected

Creating a new **Font**
with the specified style

Setting the font of
outputJTextArea

Storing a reference to the
JRadioButtonMenuItem

Creating a new **Font**
with the specified size

Using the getKeyCode method to
determine which key was pressed

Changing the background
color for the lastJButton
to the default color

```
662    // change font when user selects an item from Style submenu
663    private void styleMenuItemsStateChanged( ItemEvent event )
664    {
665       int style = Font.PLAIN;
666
667       // check for bold selection
668       if ( styleMenuItems[ 0 ].isSelected() )
669       {
670          style += Font.BOLD;
671       }
672
673       // check for italic selection
674       if ( styleMenuItems[ 1 ].isSelected() )
675       {
676          style += Font.ITALIC;
677       }
678
679       // create a new Font with the specified style
680       outputFont = new Font( outputFont.getName(), style,
681          outputFont.getSize() );
682
683       outputJTextArea.setFont( outputFont ); // set the font
684
685    } // end method styleMenuItemsStateChanged
686
687    // change font size when user selects an item from size submenu
688    private void sizeMenuItemsActionPerformed( ActionEvent event )
689    {
690       JRadioButtonMenuItem sizeMenuItem =
691          ( JRadioButtonMenuItem ) event.getSource();
692
693       // create a new Font with the specified size
694       outputFont = new Font( outputFont.getName(),
695          outputFont.getStyle(),
696          Integer.parseInt( sizeMenuItem.getText() ) );
697
698       outputJTextArea.setFont( outputFont ); // set the font
699
700    } // end method sizeMenuItemsActionPerformed
701
702    // highlight corresponding JButton when a key is pressed
703    private void outputJTextAreaKeyPressed( KeyEvent event )
704    {
705       // get the key code for this event
706       int buttonIndex = event.getKeyCode();
707
708       // change the color of the associated JButton
709       changeColor( keyJButtons[ buttonIndex ] );
710
711    } // end method outputJTextAreaKeyPressed
712
713    // reset the color of the pressed key's JButton
714    private void outputJTextAreaKeyReleased( KeyEvent event )
715    {
716       resetColor();
717
718    } // end method outputJTextAreaKeyReleased
719
```

Figure 22.31 **Typing Skills Developer** application source code. (Part 13 of 14.)

```
720        // main method
721        public static void main( String[] args )
722        {
723           TypingApplication application = new TypingApplication();
724           application.setDefaultCloseOperation( JFrame.EXIT_ON_CLOSE );
725
726        } // end method main
727
728   } // end class TypingApplication
```

Figure 22.31   Typing Skills Developer application source code. (Part 14 of 14.)

SELF-REVIEW

1. The _____ dialog allows the user to select a color.

    a) `ColorChooser`   b) `JColorChooser`

    c) `ChooseColor`   d) `JChooseColor`

2. Use the _____ method to get the event source.

    a) `getSource`   b) `getEventSource`

    c) `eventSource`   d) `source`

    Answers: 1) b. 2) a.

22.5 Wrap-Up

In this tutorial, you learned about keyboard events. You learned how to handle (with the `keyPressed` event handler) the event raised when the user presses a key on the keyboard. You then learned how to use the `keyReleased` event handler to handle the event raised when the user releases a key.

You added `JMenus` to your **Typing Skills Developer** application. You learned that `JMenus` allow you to add functionality to your application without cluttering the GUI with added components. You added `JMenus` to a `JMenuBar`. You then added separator bar and `JMenuItems` to a `JMenu` to organize menus. You also learned how to display the `JColorChooser` dialog, allowing the user to specify the color of the text in the `JTextArea`.

In the next tutorial, you will learn about the methods in the `String` class that allow you to manipulate `Strings`. These methods will help you build a screen scraper application that can search the text on a Web page for specific information.

SKILLS SUMMARY

Executing Code When the User Presses a Key on the Keyboard

■ Use the `keyPressed` event handler.

■ Use the `getKeyCode` method of `KeyEvent` to determine which key was pressed.

■ Compare the pressed key to a virtual key code value in each `case`.

Executing Code When the User Releases a Key

■ Use the `keyReleased` event handler.

Adding JMenus to Your Application

■ Create a `JMenuBar` to hold all menus.

■ Create `JMenus` and add them to the `JMenuBar` using the add method of the `JMenuBar` class.

■ Create `JMenuItems` and add them to `JMenus` using the add method of the `JMenu` class.

■ Use the `setMnemonic` method to give `JMenus` and `JMenuItems` mnemonics for easier access.

Adding a Color Dialog to Your Application

■ Use the `showDialog` method of the `JColorChooser` class to display a dialog to allow the user to choose a color.

Adding JCheckBoxMenuItems to JMenus

■ Create a JCheckBoxMenuItem.

■ Add the JCheckBoxMenuItem to a JMenu using the add method of the JMenu class.

Adding JRadioButtonMenuItems to JMenus

■ Create a JRadioButtonMenuItem.

■ Add the JRadioButtonMenuItem to a JMenu using the add method of the JMenu class.

Adding JMenuItems to JMenus

■ Create a JMenuItem.

■ Add the JMenuItem to a JMenu using the add method of the JMenu class.

KEY TERMS

addkeyListener method—Registers an event listener with an event source, such as a JTextArea.

add method of JMenu—Adds a JMenu, JMenuItem, JCheckBoxMenuItem or JRadioButton-MenuItem to the JMenu.

add method of JMenuBar—Adds a JMenu to the JMenuBar.

addSeparator method of JMenu—Adds a separator bar to the JMenu.

Font class—Creates and manipulates fonts.

Font.BOLD constant—Represents the bold font style.

Font.ITALIC constant—Represents the italic font style.

Font.PLAIN constant—Represents the plain font style.

getKeyCode method of KeyEvent—Returns the virtual key code associated with the key that the user interacted with.

getName method of Font—Returns the name of the Font.

getSize method of Font—Returns the size of the Font.

getSource method of ActionEvent—Returns the GUI component that raised the event (also called the source of the event).

getStyle method of Font—Returns the style of the Font.

java.awt.event package—Provides interfaces and classes for handling all kinds of events, such as keyboard events and mouse events.

JCheckBoxMenuItem component—A specific type of menu item that has a check box to its left, allowing the user to see if the item is currently selected.

JColorChooser component—Displays a dialog containing color options to a user.

JMenu component—A menu that can be added to a JMenuBar and can contain other JMenus and JMenuItems.

JMenuBar component—The bar at the top of an application that hold JMenus.

JMenuItem component—An item within a menu.

JRadioButtonMenuItem component—A specific type of menu item that has a JRadioButton to its left, allowing the user to see if an item is currently selected.

keyboard event—An event raised when a key on the keyboard is pressed or released.

KeyEvent—The event object generated when the user presses, releases or types a key.

KeyEvent.KEY_LAST—The constant equal to the maximum value of the virtual key constants.

KeyListener interface—Declares event handler headers for keyboard events.

keyPressed event handler—Invoked when a key is pressed.

keyReleased event handler—Invoked when a key is released.

keyTyped event handler—Declared in the KeyListener interface. Invoked when a key is typed.

menu—A component that groups related commands for GUI applications. Menus are an integral part of GUIs, because they organize commands without cluttering the GUI. In Java, a menu is created with a JMenu component.

menu bar—A bar at the top of an application that contains the menus. In Java, a menu is created with a `JMenuBar` component.

menu item—An item located in a menu that, when selected, causes the application to perform a specific action. In Java, a menu item is created with a `JMenuItem` component.

separator bar—A bar placed in a menu to separate related menu items.

setFont method of JTextArea—Sets the `Font` of the `JTextArea`.

setForeground method of JTextArea—Sets the foreground `Color` of the `JTextArea`.

setJMenuBar method of JFrame—Sets the `JMenuBar` of the `JFrame`.

setMnemonic method of JMenu—Sets the keyboard shortcut of the `JMenu`.

setMnemonic method of JMenuItem—Sets the keyboard shortcut of the `JMenuItem`.

showDialog method of JColorChooser—Displays the `JColorChooser` color dialog.

submenu—A menu within another menu.

top-level menu—A menu that is added directly to the menu bar.

GUI DESIGN GUIDELINES

Menus

- Use book-title capitalization in menu item text.
- If clicking a menu item opens a dialog, an ellipsis (…) should follow the menu item's text.
- Use separator bars in a menu to group related menu items.

JCheckBoxMenuItem

- A `JCheckBoxMenuItem`'s text should be description, be as short as possible and use book-title capitalization.
- Use `JCheckBoxMenuItem` when the user should be able to choose multiple options from a menu containing a group of `JCheckBoxMenuItems`.

JRadioButtonMenuItem

- Use `JRadioButtonMenuItem` when the user should choose only one option from a menu containing a group of `JRadioButtonMenuItems`.

JAVA LIBRARY REFERENCE

ActionEvent   This class represents arguments passed to the `actionPerformed` event handler.

- *Methods*

  `getSource`—Returns the event source.

Font   This class represents a unique font specified by its name, size and style.

- *Constructor*

  `Font`—Takes three arguments—the name, style and size of the font.

  ```
  outputFont = new Font( outputFont.getName(), Font.BOLD, 16 );
  ```

- *Constants*

  `Font.BOLD`—Represents the bold style.

  `Font.ITALIC`—Represents the italic style.

  `Font.PLAIN`—Represents the plain style.

- *Methods*

  `getName`—Returns the name of the `Font` as a `String`.

  `getSize`—Returns the size of the `Font` as an `int`.

  `getStyle`—Returns the style of the `Font` as an `int`.

JCheckBoxMenuItem This component represents a menu object that has a `JCheckBox` to its left so the user can tell if the object is selected.

- ■ *In action*

- ■ *Method*

getText—Returns the text of the `JCheckBoxMenuItem`.

isSelected—Returns whether this component is selected or not selected.

JColorChooser This component allows the user to select a color.

- ■ *Method*

showDialog—Displays the `JColorChooser` dialog.

JMenu This component allows you to group related menu items for your application.

- ■ *Constructor*

JMenu—Takes one argument that specifies the name of the `JMenu`.

```
displayJMenu = new JMenu( "Display" );
```

- ■ *In action*

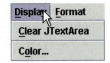

- ■ *Methods*

add—Adds a menu or a menu item to the menu.

addSeparator—Adds a separator bar to the menu.

setMnemonic—Sets the keyboard shortcut of the menu.

JMenuBar This component allows you to add menus to your application.

- ■ *In action*

- ■ *Methods*

add—Adds a menu to the menu bar.

JMenuItem This component represents a menu item that can be added to a `JMenu`.

- ■ *In action*

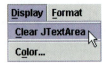

- ■ *Methods*

setMnemonic—Returns the keyboard shortcut of the `JMenuItem`.

JRadioButtonMenuItem   This component represents a menu object that has a radio button to its left so that the user can tell if the object is selected.

■ *In action*

■ *Method*

getText—Returns the text of the JRadioButtonMenuItem.

JTextArea   This component allows the user to input data from the keyboard.

■ *In action*

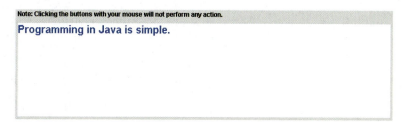

■ *Methods*

addKeyListener—Adds a KeyListener object to the JTextArea.

append—Adds text to a JTextArea.

grabFocus—Transfers the focus of the application to the JTextArea.

setBounds—Sets the position and size of the JTextArea.

setEditable—Sets whether the text in the JTextArea can be edited (true) or not (false).

setEnabled—Sets the *enabled* property which determines whether the JTextArea will respond to user actions (true) or not (false).

setFont—Sets the font of the JTextArea.

setForeground—Sets the foreground Color of the JTextArea.

setHorizontalAlignment—Specifies how the text is aligned within the JTextArea (JTextArea.LEFT, JTextArea.CENTER, JTextArea.RIGHT).

setText—Sets the text displayed in the JTextArea.

KeyEvent   This class represents an event object generated when a key is pressed, typed or released.

■ *Constants*

KeyEvent.KEY_LAST—The largest virtual key code declared in the KeyEvent class.

KeyEvent.VK_A—Represents the A key on the keyboard.

KeyEvent.VK_B—Represents the B key on the keyboard.

■ *Method*

getKeyCode—Returns the virtual key code for the key that the user interacted with.

KeyListener   This interface declares three event handlers for keyboard events.

■ *Event Handlers*

keyPressed—Invoked when a key is pressed.

keyReleased—Invoked when a key is released.

keyTyped—Invoked when a character key is pressed.

MULTIPLE-CHOICE QUESTIONS

22.1 The _____ KeyEvent constant is equal to the greatest virtual key code.

   a) MAXIMUM

   b) KEY_FINAL

   c) VK_MAX

   d) KEY_LAST

22.2 A _____ is a container for menus.

   a) keyboard event

   b) menu bar

   c) separator bar

   d) menu item

22.3 The GUI component you would add to a JMenu to create a submenu is a _____.

   a) JSubmenu

   b) JMenuItem

   c) JMenu

   d) JMenuBar

22.4 The addSeparator method adds a separator _____ to a menu.

   a) bar

   b) mnemonic

   c) submenu

   d) menu item

22.5 A _____ provides a group of related commands for your applications.

   a) separator bar

   b) hot key

   c) menu

   d) margin indicator bar

22.6 The _____ method of KeyEvent returns the key pressed by the user.

   a) keys

   b) KeyCode

   c) add

   d) getKeyCode

22.7 The _____ event handler is invoked when a key is pressed by the user.

   a) keyDown

   b) keyReleased

   c) keyPressed

   d) none of the above

22.8 Use JTextArea method _____ to set the text color in the JTextArea.

   a) setForeground

   b) setTextColor

   c) setBackground

   d) setColor

22.9 Which of the following methods sets the mnemonic of a menu item?

   a) setFont

   b) setMnemonic

   c) setMenuMnemonic

   d) setText

22.10 Create _____ when a user should be able to select only a single menu item at a time.

   a) submenus

   b) JRadioButtonMenuItems

   c) a JColorChooser

   d) JCheckBoxMenuItems

EXERCISES

22.11 (*Enhanced Inventory Application*) Enhance the **Inventory** application that you developed in Tutorial 4 to prevent the user from entering input that is not a number. Use keyboard events to allow the user to press the number keys (*0* to *9*), the left and right arrow keys, the *Backspace* key and the *Enter* key. If any other key is pressed, display a JOptionPane instructing the user to enter a number (Fig. 22.32).

Figure 22.32 Enhanced **Inventory** application.

   a) *Copying the template to your working directory.* Copy the directory C:\Examples\Tutorial22\Exercises\InventoryEnhanced to your C:\SimplyJava directory.

   b) *Opening the template file.* Open the Inventory.java file in your text editor.

   c) *Adding a switch statement.* In line 132 (in the cartonsJTextFieldKeyPressed method), begin a switch statement that determines whether a number key, a left or

right arrow key or the *Backspace* key was pressed. Use KeyEvent constants VK_0, VK_1, VK_2, VK_3, VK_4, VK_5, VK_6, VK_7, VK_8, VK_9, VK_LEFT, VK_RIGHT, VK_BACK_SPACE and VK_ENTER. If one of these keys was pressed, use the break statement to continue execution.

d) *Adding the default statement.* At the end of the switch statement, add a default case to determine whether a key other than a valid one for this application was pressed. If an invalid key was pressed, display a JOptionPane that instructs the user to enter a number. Also, reset the text of cartonsJTextField to "0".

e) *Adding a second switch statement.* In the itemsJTextFieldKeyPressed method, begin a switch statement to determine whether a number key, a left or right arrow key or the *Backspace* key was pressed. Use the same KeyEvent constants from *Step c*. If one of these keys was pressed, use the break statement to continue execution.

f) *Adding the default statement.* At the end of the switch statement, add a default case to determine whether a key that is invalid for this application was pressed. If an invalid key was pressed, display a JOptionPane that instructs the user to enter a number. Also, reset the text of itemsJTextField to "0".

g) *Saving the application.* Save your modified source code file.

h) *Opening the Command Prompt window and changing directories.* Open the **Command Prompt** by selecting **Start > Programs > Accessories > Command Prompt**. Change to your working directory by typing cd C:\SimplyJava\InventoryEnhanced.

i) *Compiling the application.* Compile your application by typing javac Inventory.java.

j) *Running the completed application.* When your application compiles correctly, run it by typing java Inventory. To test your application, press both valid and invalid keys in each JTextArea. A JOptionPane should appear when you press an invalid key.

k) *Closing the application.* Close your running application by clicking its close button.

l) *Closing the Command Prompt window.* Close the **Command Prompt** window by clicking its close button.

22.12 (*Bouncing Ball Application*) Write an application that allows the user to play a game, the goal of which is to prevent a bouncing ball from falling off the bottom of the application. When the user presses the *S* key, the game starts and a blue ball bounces off the top, left and right sides (the "walls") of the application. There should be a horizontal bar on the bottom of the application, which serves as a paddle, and prevents the ball from hitting the bottom of the application (the ball can bounce off the paddle, but not off the bottom of the application.) The user can move the paddle using the left and right arrow keys. If the ball hits the paddle, the ball should bounce up, and the game should continue. If the ball hits the bottom of the application, the game should end. Most of the geometric processing, along with the GUI (Fig. 22.33), is provided for you in the template.

Figure 22.33   **Bouncing Ball** application.

a) *Copying the template to your working directory.* Copy the directory C:\Examples\ Tutorial22\Exercises\BouncingBall to your C:\SimplyJava directory.

b) *Opening the template file.* Open the BouncingBall.java file in your text editor.

c) *Writing code to start the game.* In line 131 (in the bouncingBallKeyPressed method), begin an if statement to determine if the *S* key has been pressed. You will need to use the KeyEvent constant VK_S. Inside the if statement, start ballTimer by calling the start method of ballTimer, which is a Timer declared as an instance variable in the template.

d) *Inserting code to move the paddle left.* Following the if statement you added in *Step c*, add an else if statement that tests if the user pressed the left arrow key and if the paddle's horizontal position, stored in rectX, is greater than ten. You will need to use KeyEvent constant VK_LEFT. If the paddle's horizontal position equals ten, the left edge of the paddle is touching the left wall and the paddle should not be allowed to move farther to the left. Inside the else if statement, decrease the paddle's horizontal position by 10 pixels.

e) *Inserting code to move the paddle right.* Following the else if statement you added in *Step d*, begin another else if statement that tests if the user pressed the right arrow key and if the paddle's horizontal position, stored in rectX, is less than 400 minus the size of the paddle, stored in rectWidth. Inside the else if statement, increase the paddle's horizontal position by 10 pixels.

f) *Saving the application.* Save your modified source code file.

g) *Opening the Command Prompt window and changing directories.* Open the **Command Prompt** by selecting **Start > Programs > Accessories > Command Prompt**. Change to your working directory by typing cd C:\SimplyJava\BouncingBall.

h) *Compiling the application.* Compile your application by typing javac Bouncing-Ball.java.

i) *Running the completed application.* When your application compiles correctly, run it by typing java BouncingBall. To test your application, be sure that the ball begins to move when the *S* key is pressed and continues to move when it hits the paddle. The ball should stop when it gets below the paddle.

j) *Closing the application.* Close your running application by clicking its close button.

k) *Closing the Command Prompt window.* Close the **Command Prompt** window by clicking its close button.

22.13 (*Enhanced Painter Application*) Enhance the **Painter** application that you developed in Tutorial 21 to include menus to allow the user to select the size and color of the painted ellipses and the color of the JFrame (Fig. 22.34). (The menus replace the JRadioButtons.) Also, add a multiline JTextArea that allows the user to type text to accompany the painting. The user should be able to use menus to select the font style and color of the text and the background color of the JTextArea.

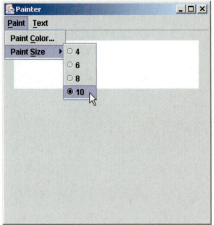

Figure 22.34 Enhanced **Painter** GUI.

a) *Copying the template to your working directory.* Copy the directory C:\Examples\ Tutorial22\Exercises\PainterEnhanced to your C:\SimplyJava directory.

b) *Opening the template file.* Open the Painter.java file in your text editor.

c) *Creating paintJMenu.* In line 75, add the code that will set up paintJMenu. To do this, create a new JMenu and assign it to paintJMenu. Next, set the text of paintJ-Menu to "Paint". Set the mnemonic for paintJMenu to the *P* key. You will need to use KeyEvent constant VK_P. The, add paintJMenu to painterJMenuBar.

d) *Creating textJMenu.* Before the code that sets up textColorJMenuItem, add the code that will set up textJMenu. To do this, create a new JMenu and assign it to text-JMenu. Next, set the text of textJMenu to "Text". Set the mnemonic for textJMenu to the *T* key. You will need to use KeyEvent constant VK_T. Then, add textJMenu to painterJMenuBar.

e) *Allowing the user to select the paint color.* In the paintColorJMenuItemAction-Performed method, declare local Color variable paintColor and assign to it the return value from the showDialog method of the JColorChooser class. Then, add an if statement to test if paintColor is not equal to null. Inside the if statement, set the color of myPainterJPanel using the setColor method. Pass paintColor to this method.

f) *Allowing the user to select the font size.* In the fontSizeItemsActionPerformed method, call the getSource method of the event ActionEvent object. Cast this return value to a JRadioButtonMenuItem and assign it to a new local variable named sizeMenuItem. The variable sizeMenuItem must also be of the JRadioButtonMenu-Item type. Then, create a new font and assign it to instance variable displayFont. The first two arguments passed to the Font class's constructor should be the name of displayFont and the style of displayFont. The last argument should be the text of sizeMenuItem as an int. You will need to call the getText method on sizeMenu-Item, then pass the returned value to the Integer.parseInt method. Finally, set the font of displayJTextArea to displayFont.

g) *Saving the application.* Save your modified source code file.

h) *Opening the Command Prompt window and changing directories.* Open the **Command Prompt** window by selecting **Start > Programs > Accessories > Command Prompt**. Change to your working directory by typing cd C:\SimplyJava\Painter-Enhanced.

i) *Compiling the application.* Compile your application by typing javac Painter.java.

j) *Running the completed application.* When your application compiles correctly, run it by typing java Painter. Test your application by creating a picture using different colors, and by adding a description in the JTextArea. Make sure you can change the color and style of the typed text using the menus that you added to your application.

k) *Closing the application.* Close your running application by clicking its close button.

l) *Closing the Command Prompt window.* Close the **Command Prompt** window by clicking its close button.

What does this code do? ▶   **22.14** What is the result of the following code, assuming that outputJTextArea is a JText-Area?

```
1   private void colorJMenuItemActionPerformed( ActionPerformed event )
2   {
3      Color backgroundColor = JColorChooser.showDialog(
4         null, "Choose a color", Color.BLACK );
5
6      if ( backgroundColor != null )
7      {
8         outputJTextArea.setBackground( backgroundColor );
9      }
10
11  } // end method colorJMenuItemActionPerformed
```

What's wrong with this code? ▶ **22.15** This code should increment the variable bCount every time the *B* key is pressed. Find the error(s) in the following code, assuming that bCount and outputJTextArea are declared as an int and a JTextArea, respectively.

```
1  private void outputJTextAreaKeyPressed( KeyEvent event)
2  {
3     // receive code for key pressed by user
4     switch ( event.KeyCode() )
5     {
6        case VK_B: // B key
7           bCount++;
8           break;
9     }
10 } // end event handler outputJTextAreaKeyPressed
```

Programming Challenge ▶ **22.16** (*Dvorak Keyboard Application*) Create an application that simulates the letters on the Dvorak keyboard (see http://www.mwbrooks.com/dvorak/, http://www.mit.edu/people/jcb/Dvorak/ and http://www.cse.ogi.edu/~dylan/dvorak/dvorak.html). A Dvorak keyboard allows faster typing than the widely used "QWERTY" keyboard by placing the most commonly used keys in the most accessible locations. Use keyboard events to create an application similar to the **Typing Skills Developer** application, except simulating the Dvorak keyboard instead of the standard keyboard (Fig. 22.35). The correct Dvorak key should be highlighted on the virtual keyboard and the correct character should be displayed in the JTextArea. The keys and characters map as follows:

- On the top row, the *P* key of the Dvorak keyboard corresponds to the *R* key on a standard keyboard, and the *L* key of the Dvorak keyboard corresponds to the *P* key on a standard keyboard.

- On the middle row, the *A* key remains in the same position, and the *S* key on the Dvorak keyboard corresponds to the semicolon key on the standard keyboard.

- On the bottom row, the *Q* key on the Dvorak keyboard corresponds to the *X* key on the standard keyboard, and the *Z* key corresponds to the question mark key.

- All of the other keys on the Dvorak keyboard correspond to the locations shown in Fig. 22.35.

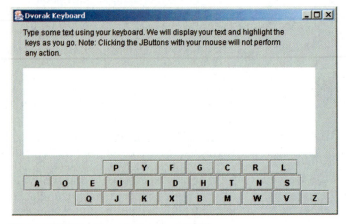

Figure 22.35 Dvorak Keyboard GUI.

a) *Copying the template to your working directory.* Copy the directory C:\Examples\Tutorial22\Exercises\DvorakKeyboard to your C:\SimplyJava directory.

b) *Opening the template file.* Open the DvorakKeyboard.java file in your text editor.

c) *Adding a KeyListener.* Starting in line 72, call the addKeyListener method on displayJTextArea. Pass to this method an anonymous inner class which implements the KeyListener interface. In the anonymous inner class, declare the three event handlers—keyPressed, keyReleased and keyTyped. In the keyPressed event handler, call the displayJTextAreaKeyPressed method and pass to it the KeyEvent that is generated. In the keyReleased event handler, call the displayJTextAreaKeyReleased method and pass to it the KeyEvent which is generated. Leave the keyTyped event handler blank.

d) *Declaring the displayJTextAreaKeyPressed method.* After the createUser-Interface method, your application declares the changeColor and resetColor to manipulate the JButtons. After the resetColor method, declare the displayJTextAreaKeyPressed method. In this method, get a reference to the JButton corresponding to the pressed key. Use the getKeyCode method of the KeyEvent class to get the virtual key code. Use this to index the keyJButtons array (declared for you in the template). Use an if statement to determine whether the returned JButton reference is null. If the reference is not null, add the JButton's text to String instance variable display (declared for you in the template). This String is used to store the typed text. Set the text of displayJTextArea to display. Finally, call the changeColor method and pass to it the JButton.

e) *Declaring the displayJTextAreaKeyReleased method.* After the displayJTextAreaKeyPressed method, declare the displayJTextAreaKeyReleased method. This method should call the resetColor method.

f) *Saving the application.* Save your modified source code file.

g) *Opening the Command Prompt window and changing directories.* Open the **Command Prompt** window by selecting **Start > Programs > Accessories > Command Prompt**. Change to your working directory by typing cd C:\SimplyJava\ DvorakKeyboard.

h) *Compiling the application.* Compile your application by typing javac DvorakKeyboard.java.

i) *Running the completed application.* When your application compiles correctly, run it by typing java DvorakKeyboard. To test your application, attempt to type using the Dvorak keyboard. As you are typing, make sure the correct JButton is highlighted and the correct output appears in the JTextArea.

j) *Closing the application.* Close your running application by clicking the window's close button.

k) *Closing the Command Prompt window.* Close the **Command Prompt** window by clicking its close button.

23

Objectives

In this tutorial, you will learn to:
- Create and manipulate `String` objects.
- Use properties and methods of class `String`.
- Search for substrings within `Strings`.
- Extract substrings from `Strings`.
- Replace substrings within `Strings`.

Outline

Screen Scraping Application

Introducing `String` Processing

This tutorial introduces Java's `String` processing capabilities. The techniques presented in this tutorial can be used to create applications that process text. Earlier tutorials introduced the `String` class and several of its methods. In this tutorial, you will learn how to search `Strings`, retrieve substrings from `Strings` and replace substrings in `Strings`. You will create an application that uses these `String` processing capabilities to manipulate a `String` containing **HTML (Hyper-Text Markup Language)**. HTML is a technology used for describing Web content. Extracting desired information from the HTML that composes a Web page is called **screen scraping**. A screen-scraper is a tool used to extract data from Web sites. Applications that perform screen scraping can be used to extract specific information, such as weather conditions or stock prices, from Web pages so that the information can be formatted and manipulated more easily by computer applications. In this tutorial, you will create a simple **Screen Scraping** application.

23.1 Test-Driving the Screen Scraping Application

This application must meet the following requirements:

Application Requirements

An online European auction house wants to expand its business to include bidders from the United States. However, all of the auction house's Web pages currently display their prices in euros, not dollars. The auction house wants to generate separate Web pages for American bidders that will display the prices of auction items in dollars. These new Web pages will be generated by using screen-scraping techniques on the already existing Web pages. You have been asked to build a prototype application that will test the screen-scraping functionality. The application should search a sample string of HTML and extract information about the price of a specified auction item. For testing purposes, a `JComboBox` should be provided that contains auction items listed in the HTML. The selected item's amount must then be converted to dollars, so a `JTextField` is provided where the user can enter the current conversion rate. The application will search and extract the price in euros of the item selected, convert this value to dollars and display the resulting price.

The **Screen Scraping** application searches for the name of a specified auction item in a string of HTML. Users select the item from a JComboBox whose price they want to find. The application then extracts, converts and displays the price of this item in dollars. You begin by test-driving the completed application. Then, you will learn the additional Java technologies you will need to create your own version of this application.

Test-Driving the Screen Scraping Application

1. *Locating the completed application.* Open the **Command Prompt** window by selecting **Start > Programs > Accessories > Command Prompt**. Change to your completed **Screen Scraping** application directory by typing cd C:\Examples\Tutorial23\CompletedApplication\ScreenScraping.

2. *Running the Screen Scraping application.* Type java ScreenScraping in the **Command Prompt** window to run the application (Fig. 23.1). Notice that the HTML string is displayed in a JTextArea at the bottom of the application. You will learn about this text shortly. Above the JTextArea, the **Item:** JComboBox provides the user with a list of items from which to select. The **Rate:** JTextField is provided for the user to enter the conversion rate. For instance, if the current conversion rate is 1.5 (meaning that 1 euros is equal to 1.5 dollars), the user would enter 1.5 into the **Rate:** JTextField. Once the user selects an item, enters a conversion rate and clicks the **Search** JButton, the price in euros for that item will be found in the HTML, converted to dollars and displayed in the **Price:** JTextField. Figure 23.2 displays the HTML page in Internet Explorer.

JTextArea containing HTML ———

Figure 23.1   Running the completed **Screen Scraping** application.

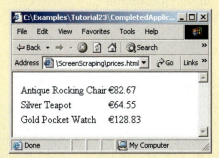

Figure 23.2   Displaying the HTML page in Internet Explorer.

3. *Selecting an item name.* The JComboBox contains three item names. Select **Silver Teapot** from the JComboBox as shown in Fig. 23.3.

(cont.)

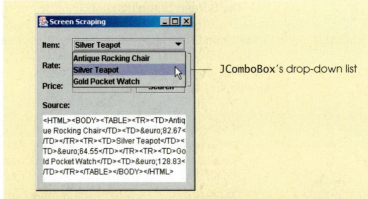

Figure 23.3 Selecting an item name from the `JComboBox`.

4. **Searching for an item's price.** Enter a conversion rate of `1.14284` into the **Rate:** `JTextField`. Conversion rates change almost constantly, which is why we have provided an input `JTextField` rather than defining a constant conversion rate. Current conversion rates are provided by various Web sites. One such site, known as the The Universal Currency Converter[®], can be found at `www.xe.com/ucc`. Click the **Search** `JButton` to display the price for the selected item. The extracted price in dollars is displayed in an uneditable `JTextField` (Fig. 23.4).

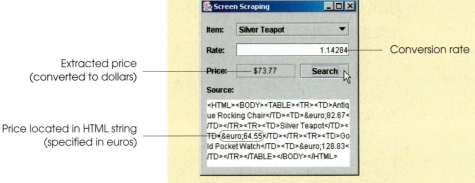

Figure 23.4 Searching for the item's price.

5. **Closing the running application.** Close your running application by clicking its close button.

6. **Closing the Command Prompt window.** Close the **Command Prompt** window by clicking its close button.

23.2 Fundamentals of `Strings`

A **string** is a sequence of characters treated as a single unit. These characters can be uppercase letters, lowercase letters, digits and various **special characters**, such as +, -, *, /, $, white space (that is, blank lines, spaces and tabs) and others. A string is an object of class `String` in the `java.lang` package. You write **string literals**, or **string constants** (often called **literal `String` objects**), as sequences of characters in double quotation marks:

```
"This is a String!"
```

You've created and used `Strings` in previous tutorials. You know that a declaration can assign a string literal to a `String` variable. For example, the declaration

```
String color = "blue";
```

initializes `String color` with a reference to the `String` object referenced by string literal `"blue"`.

Like arrays, `Strings` always "know" their own size. But unlike arrays, `Strings` use a method to get their size. `String` method **length** returns the length of the `String` (that is, the number of characters in the `String`). For example, the method call `color.length()` returns 4 for the `String "blue"`.

Another useful method of class `String` is **charAt**, which returns the character located at a specific index in a `String`. Method `charAt` takes an `int` argument specifying the index and returns the character at that index. An index ranges from 0 to the length of the `String` minus 1. As with arrays, the first element of a `String` is at index 0. For example, the following code

```
if ( string1.charAt( 0 ) == string2.charAt( 0 ) )
{
   messageJLabel.setText(
      "The first characters of string1 and string2 are the same." );
}
```

compares the character at index 0 (that is, the first character) of `string1` with the character (also at index 0) of `string2` and prints a message when they are equal.

In earlier tutorials, you used methods `valueOf` (Section 4.3) and `equals` (Section 7.4) of class `String` to manipulate `String` objects. You will learn new `String` methods later in this tutorial.

Any `String` method that may appear to modify a `String` actually returns a new `String` that contains the results. This occurs because `Strings` are **immutable** objects—that is, characters in `Strings` cannot be changed after the `Strings` are created.

SELF-REVIEW

1. The _____ method of the `String` class returns the number of characters in the `String`.

   a) `maxChars`   b) `length`

   c) `characterCount`   d) `size`

2. A `String` can be composed of _____.

   a) digits   b) lowercase letters

   c) special characters   d) All of the above.

Answers: 1) b. 2) d.

23.3 Constructing the Screen Scraping Application

Now you will build your **Screen Scraping** application by using `String` processing to locate and manipulate `String` data. The following pseudocode describes the basic operation of the **Screen Scraping** application, which executes when the user clicks the **Search** `JButton`.

> When the user runs the application:
>   Display the HTML that contains the items' prices in a JTextArea
>
> When the user clicks the Search JButton:
>   Retrieve the item selected from the JComboBox
>   Search the HTML for the item the user selected
>   Extract the item's price
>   Convert the item's price from euros to dollars
>   Display the item's price in a JTextField

Now that you have test-driven the **Screen Scraping** application and studied its pseudocode representation, you will use an ACE table to help you convert the pseudocode to Java. Figure 23.5 lists the actions, components and events that will help you complete your own version of this application.

**Action/Component/
Event (ACE) Table for the
Screen Scraping
Application**

Action	Component/Object	Event

Label the application's components	`itemJLabel`
	`rateJLabel`
	`priceJLabel`
	`sourceJLabel`
		Application is run

Display the HTML that contains the items' prices in a JTextArea	`sourceJTextArea`	
	`searchJButton`	User clicks **Search** `JButton`
Retrieve the item selected from the JComboBox	`itemJComboBox`	
Search the HTML for the item the user selected	`htmlText (String)`	
Extract the item's price	`htmlText (String)`	
Convert the item's price from euros to dollars	`price (String)`	
Display the item's price in a JTextField	`priceJTextField`	

Figure 23.5   ACE table for **Screen Scraping** application.

Now that you've analyzed the **Screen Scraping** application's components, you will learn about the `String` methods that you will use to construct the application.

23.4 Locating Substrings in `Strings`

In many applications, it is necessary to search for a character or a group of characters in a `String`. For example, a word processing application might provide capabilities that allow users to search their documents. Class `String` provides methods that search for specified **substrings** in a `String`. A substring is a sequence of characters that make up part or all of a `String`. For instance, `"lo"` is a substring of the `String "hello"`, as is `"ll"`, `"he"`, `"e"` and many others, including `"hello"` itself. Next, you will use the `indexOf` method to search for substrings in `Strings`.

**Locating the Selected
Item's Price**

1. ***Copying the template to your working directory.*** Copy the directory `C:\Examples\Tutorial23\TemplateApplication\ScreenScraping` to your `C:\SimplyJava` directory.

2. ***Opening the Screen Scraping application's template file.*** Open the template file `ScreenScraping.java` in your text editor.

3. ***Viewing the application's HTML.*** The HTML displayed in the **Source:** JTextArea is included in a `String` on lines 34–42 of Fig. 23.6. You are not expected at this point to understand HTML—in this tutorial, we will briefly describe only the HTML of Fig. 23.6. You will learn more HTML in Tutorial 30, where you will see it used in the operation of a Web-based **Bookstore** application. In addition, we include two chapters on the book's CD that provide you with a thorough introduction to HTML. The following HTML contains the names and prices of three auction items. Lines 36–37 display the portion of HTML that contains the name and price of the first item. The name of the item is specified on line 36 as `"Antique Rocking Chair"`, and the price of this item is specified on line 37 as `"&euro;82.67"`. The `String "&euro;"` is the HTML representation of the euro symbol (€), which appears before every price value in the HTML string in this application. You do not need to worry about the text surrounding the name and price values—most of this text is used only to specify how the name and price of the item should be displayed on a Web page. In this application, you will be concerned only with the name and price in euros of each item. Lines 38–39 display the portion of HTML that contains the name and price of the second item, and lines 40–41 display the portion of HTML that contains the name and price of the third item.

(cont.)

```
Source Editor [ScreenScraping]                                    _ |□| X|
32          "Silver Teapot", "Gold Pocket Watch" };
33
34       // small piece of HTML code containing items and prices
35       private String htmlText = "<HTML><BODY><TABLE>"
36          + "<TR><TD>Antique Rocking Chair</TD>"
37          + "<TD>&euro;82.67</TD></TR>"
38          + "<TR><TD>Silver Teapot</TD>"
39          + "<TD>&euro;64.55</TD></TR>"
40          + "<TR><TD>Gold Pocket Watch</TD>"
41          + "<TD>&euro;128.83</TD></TR>"
42          + "</TABLE></BODY></HTML>";
43
44       // no-argument constructor
```

Figure 23.6   HTML containing price of auction items.

4. *Locating the specified item name*. Add lines 150–153 of Fig. 23.7 to the
searchJButtonActionPerformed method. Lines 151–152 obtain the user
selected item and store it in the String selectedItem. Line 153 calls the
String method **indexOf** to locate the first occurrence of the specified item
name in the HTML string htmlText. You will use two versions of indexOf
in this application. Line 153 uses the version that takes a single argument—
the substring for which to search. The indexOf method locates the first
occurrence of the specified substring (in this case, the name of the selected
item) within the htmlText. The index at which the substring begins in htmlText is returned. If the specified substring doesn't exist within htmlText,
indexOf returns –1. Line 153 stores the result in itemLocation.

```
Source Editor [ScreenScraping *]                                 _ |□| X|
147          return; // exit method
148       }
149
150       // search for location of item and price
151       String selectedItem =
152          ( String ) itemJComboBox.getSelectedItem();
153       int itemLocation = htmlText.indexOf( selectedItem );
154
155    } // end method searchJButtonActionPerformed
```

Search for the selectedItem in
the String htmlText

Figure 23.7   Locating the desired item's name.

5. *Locating the start of the price*. Add line 154 of Fig. 23.8 to the
searchJButtonActionPerformed method. Line 154 locates the index at
which the item's price begins. This line of code uses the version of the
indexOf method that takes two arguments—the substring for which to
search ("€") and the starting index in the String at which the search
should begin. The method does not examine any characters that occur prior
to the starting index (specified by itemLocation), because you are concerned only with the portion of htmlText that includes the price of the
selected item. Remember that the first price that follows the specified item
name will be the desired price, which will begin with the "€" substring. The index returned from the indexOf method is stored in variable
priceBegin.

```
Source Editor [ScreenScraping *]                                 _ |□| X|
153          int itemLocation = htmlText.indexOf( selectedItem );
154          int priceBegin = htmlText.indexOf( "&euro;", itemLocation );
155
156    } // end method searchJButtonActionPerformed
```

Locate the beginning of
the price in htmlText

Figure 23.8   Locating the desired item's price.

(cont.)

6. ***Locating the end of the price.*** Add line 155 of Fig. 23.9 to the `searchJBut-tonActionPerformed` method. Line 155 finds the index at which the desired price ends by passing the `String` "`</TD>`" and the starting index `priceBegin` to the `indexOf` method. A `</TD>` tag directly follows every price (excluding any spaces) in the HTML string, so the index of the first `</TD>` tag after `priceBegin` marks the end of the current price. The tags `<TD>` and `</TD>` are used to display data in a table. Again, you do not need to understand HTML tables at this time. In this tutorial, all that is important is that each price is followed by `</TD>`, which marks the end of table data. The index returned from method `indexOf` is stored in variable `priceEnd`.

Locate the end of the price in `htmlText`

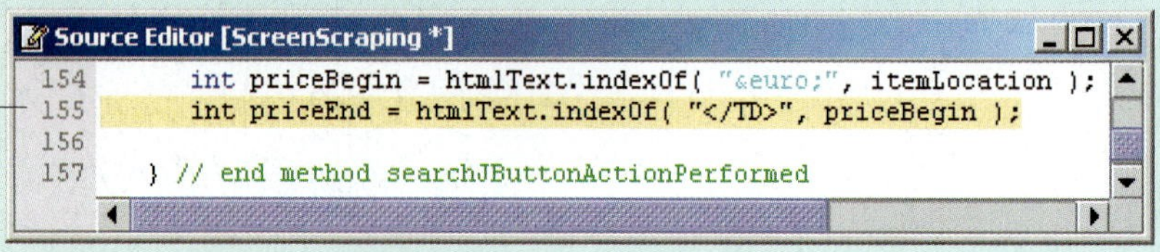

```
Source Editor [ScreenScraping *]
154        int priceBegin = htmlText.indexOf( "&euro;", itemLocation );
155        int priceEnd = htmlText.indexOf( "</TD>", priceBegin );
156
157    } // end method searchJButtonActionPerformed
```

Figure 23.9 Locating the end of the item's price.

7. ***Saving the application.*** Save your modified source code file. You have now stored the index where the price of the selected item begins (`priceBegin`) and the index directly after the location where the price of the selected item ends (`priceEnd`). No output is yet displayed, so if you compile and run your application then click the **Search** JButton, no price will be displayed in the **Price:** JTextField. You will add this functionality later in the tutorial.

Another `String` class method that is similar to the `indexOf` method is the **`lastIndexOf`** method. This method locates the last occurrence of a substring in a `String`; it performs the search backwards, starting from the end of the `String`. The `lastIndexOf` method returns the starting index of the specified substring in the `String`. If the specified substring does not exist in the `String` on which `lastIndexOf` was called, –1 is returned.

There are two versions of method `lastIndexOf` that search for substrings in a `String`. The first takes a single argument—the substring for which to search. The second takes two arguments—the substring for which to search and the index from which to begin searching backward for the substring. Figure 23.10 demonstrates searching for substrings using the `indexOf` and `lastIndexOf` methods.

Method	Example Expression (assume text = "My String is a long String")	Returns
`indexOf`(*String*)	`text.indexOf( "ring" )`	5
`indexOf`(*String, int*)	`text.indexOf( "ring", 10 )`	22
`lastIndexOf`(*String*)	`text.lastIndexOf( "ring" )`	22
`lastIndexOf`(*String, int*)	`text.lastIndexOf( "ring", 3 )`	–1

Figure 23.10 Demonstration of `indexOf` and `lastIndexOf` methods.

SELF-REVIEW

1. The _____ method locates the first occurrence of a substring within the `String` on which the method was called.

    a) `indexOf`   b) `firstIndexOf`

    c) `findFirst`   d) `locate`

2. In the version of the lastIndexOf method that takes a String followed by an int as arguments, the second argument passed to the lastIndexOf method is _____.

   a) the number of characters to search

   b) the starting index from which to start searching forward

   c) the length of the substring to locate

   d) the starting index from which to start searching backward

Answers: 1) a. 2) d.

23.5 Extracting Substrings from Strings

You will now learn how to use the **substring** method to retrieve the price of the selected item from the HTML string. The substring method returns a new String object that contains a copy of a specified part of an existing String object.

Retrieving the Desired Item's Price	1. **Extracting the price.** Add lines 157–160 of Fig. 23.11 to the searchJButtonActionPerformed method. Lines 158–159 extract the price from htmlText using the substring method. The first argument (priceBegin + 6), specifies the starting index from which the method copies characters from the original String. Remember that priceBegin contains the index where the price of the current item begins (including the String "€"). Because you will be displaying the monetary values as dollars, you do not need the euro symbol; by adding 6 to priceBegin, you are excluding the first 6 characters, namely "€". The second argument (priceEnd) specifies the index one beyond the last character to be copied (that is, copy up to, but not including, that index in the String). Variable priceEnd contains the index where the text "</TD>" begins, which is found directly after the price of the current item. The substring returned on line 158 (priceText) contains a copy of the specified characters from the original String. In this case, the substring returned is the item's price (without the euro symbol). For example, if the item selected were the **Antique Rocking Chair**, the String stored in price would be "82.67", as you can see from the data in Fig. 23.1. (This value is found in the HTML's second line of text.)

```
Source Editor [ScreenScraping *]                              _ □ ×
155         int priceEnd = htmlText.indexOf( "</TD>", priceBegin );
156
157         // store price found in double price
158         String priceText = htmlText.substring(
159            priceBegin + 6, priceEnd );
160         double price = Double.parseDouble( priceText );
161
162      } // end method searchJButtonActionPerformed
```

Set priceText to htmlText substring, convert priceText to double and store in price

Figure 23.11 Retrieving the desired price.

Class String provides two versions of the substring method. The other version takes only one int argument. The argument specifies the starting index from which the method copies characters in the original String. The substring returned contains a copy of the characters from the starting index to the end of the String. You will not use this version of the substring method in the **Screen Scraping** application. Line 160 converts priceText into a double (stored in variable price), so that this price may be multiplied by the conversion rate.

(cont.)

2. *Converting from euros to dollars.* You must now multiply the price extracted from the HTML by the conversion rate entered by the user. Add lines 162–165 of Fig. 23.12 to the `searchJButtonActionPerformed` method. Lines 163–164 retrieve the conversion rate and store this value as a `double` in variable `conversionRate`. Line 165 multiplies this value by `price` and stores the result in `price`. Recall that the `*=` operator multiplies its left and right operands, and stores the result in the left operand.

Convert the price from euros to dollars using the conversion rate entered by the user

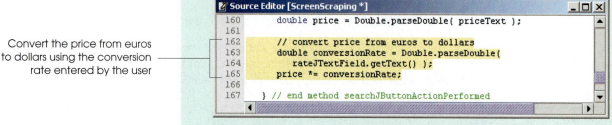

```
160        double price = Double.parseDouble( priceText );
161
162        // convert price from euros to dollars
163        double conversionRate = Double.parseDouble(
164           rateJTextField.getText() );
165        price *= conversionRate;
166
167     } // end method searchJButtonActionPerformed
```

Figure 23.12 Converting prices from euros to dollars.

3. *Displaying the price.* Add lines 167–169 of Fig. 23.13 to the `searchJButtonActionPerformed` method. Line 169 formats and displays the price in dollars, using the `DecimalFormat` object `dollars` that is created on line 168.

Display price in dollars

```
165        price *= conversionRate;
166
167        // display price of item in priceJTextField
168        DecimalFormat dollars = new DecimalFormat( "$0.00" );
169        priceJTextField.setText( dollars.format( price ) );
170
171     } // end method searchJButtonActionPerformed
```

Figure 23.13 Displaying the price in the `priceJTextField`.

4. *Saving the application.* Save your modified source code file.

5. *Opening the Command Prompt window and changing directories.* Open the **Command Prompt** window by selecting **Start > Programs > Accessories > Command Prompt**. Change to your working directory by typing `cd C:\SimplyJava\ScreenScraping`.

6. *Compiling the application.* Compile your application by typing `javac ScreenScraping.java`.

7. *Running the application.* When your application compiles correctly, run it by typing `java ScreenScraping`. Figure 23.14 shows the completed application running. Select an item from the **Item:** JComboBox, enter a conversion rate and click the **Search** JButton to display the price of that item in dollars.

Figure 23.14 Running the completed **Screen Scraping** application.

(cont.)   8.   ***Closing the application.*** Close your running application by clicking its close
          button.

     9.   ***Closing the Command Prompt window.*** Close the **Command Prompt** win-
          dow by clicking its close button.

---

1. The substring method _____.

   a) accepts either one or two arguments

   b) returns a new String object

   c) creates a String object by copying part of an existing String object

   d) All of the above

2. When a call is made to the two-argument version of the substring method, the second
   argument specifies _____.

   a) the index from which to begin copying backwards

   b) the length of the substring to copy

   c) the index one beyond the last character to be copied

   d) the last index to be copied

Answers: 1) d. 2) c.

23.6 Other String Methods

Class String provides several additional methods that allow you to manipulate
Strings. Figure 23.15 lists some of these methods.

Method	Description	Sample Expression (assume text = " My String")
startsWith(*String*)	Returns true if a String starts with the argument *String*; otherwise, returns false.	text.startsWith("Your"); Returns: false
endsWith(*String*)	Returns true if a String ends with the argument *String*; otherwise, returns false.	text.endsWith("ing"); Returns: true
trim()	Removes any whitespace from the beginning and end of a String.	text.trim(); Returns: "My String"

Figure 23.15   Description of other String methods.

Figure 23.16 presents the source code for the **Screen Scraping** application. The
lines of code that you added, viewed or modified in this tutorial are highlighted.

```
1   // Tutorial 23: ScreenScraping.java
2   // Search an HTML code String for an item and display its price
3   // converted from euros to American dollars.
4   import java.awt.*;
5   import java.awt.event.*;
6   import java.text.*;
7   import javax.swing.*;
8
```

Figure 23.16   **Screen Scraping** code. (Part 1 of 4.)

```
9  public class ScreenScraping extends JFrame
10 {
11     // JLabel and JComboBox for item names
12     private JLabel itemJLabel;
13     private JComboBox itemJComboBox;
14
15     // JLabel and JTextField for conversion rate
16     private JLabel rateJLabel;
17     private JTextField rateJTextField;
18
19     // JLabel and JTextField for item price
20     private JLabel priceJLabel;
21     private JTextField priceJTextField;
22
23     // JButton to search HTML code for item price
24     private JButton searchJButton;
25
26     // JLabel and JTextArea for HTML code
27     private JLabel sourceJLabel;
28     private JTextArea sourceJTextArea;
29
30     // items that can be found in HTML code
31     private String[] items = { "Antique Rocking Chair",
32        "Silver Teapot", "Gold Pocket Watch" };
33
34     // small piece of HTML code containing items and prices
35     private String htmlText = "<HTML><BODY><TABLE>"
36        + "<TR><TD>Antique Rocking Chair</TD>"
37        + "<TD>&euro;82.67</TD></TR>"
38        + "<TR><TD>Silver Teapot</TD>"
39        + "<TD>&euro;64.55</TD></TR>"
40        + "<TR><TD>Gold Pocket Watch</TD>"
41        + "<TD>&euro;128.83</TD></TR>"
42        + "</TABLE></BODY></HTML>";
43
44     // no-argument constructor
45     public ScreenScraping()
46     {
47        createUserInterface();
48     }
49
50     // create and position GUI components; register event handlers
51     private void createUserInterface()
52     {
53        // get content pane for attaching GUI components
54        Container contentPane = getContentPane();
55
56        // enable explicit positioning of GUI components
57        contentPane.setLayout( null );
58
59        // set up itemJLabel
60        itemJLabel = new JLabel();
61        itemJLabel.setBounds( 8, 16, 40, 21 );
62        itemJLabel.setText( "Item:" );
63        contentPane.add( itemJLabel );
64
65        // set up itemJComboBox
66        itemJComboBox = new JComboBox( items );
```

HTML provided in template describes three auction items and their prices in euros — (lines 35–42)

Figure 23.16 Screen Scraping code. (Part 2 of 4.)

```
67          itemJComboBox.setBounds( 56, 16, 184, 21 );
68          contentPane.add( itemJComboBox );
69
70          // set up rateJLabel
71          rateJLabel = new JLabel();
72          rateJLabel.setBounds( 8, 48, 40, 21 );
73          rateJLabel.setText( "Rate:" );
74          contentPane.add( rateJLabel );
75
76          // set up rateJTextField
77          rateJTextField = new JTextField();
78          rateJTextField.setBounds( 56, 48, 184, 21 );
79          rateJTextField.setHorizontalAlignment( JTextField.RIGHT );
80          contentPane.add( rateJTextField );
81
82          // set up priceJLabel
83          priceJLabel = new JLabel();
84          priceJLabel.setBounds( 8, 80, 40, 21 );
85          priceJLabel.setText( "Price:" );
86          contentPane.add( priceJLabel );
87
88          // set up priceJTextField
89          priceJTextField = new JTextField();
90          priceJTextField.setBounds( 56, 80, 96, 21 );
91          priceJTextField.setHorizontalAlignment( JTextField.CENTER );
92          priceJTextField.setEditable( false );
93          contentPane.add( priceJTextField );
94
95          // set up searchJButton
96          searchJButton = new JButton();
97          searchJButton.setBounds( 160, 80, 80, 23 );
98          searchJButton.setText( "Search" );
99          contentPane.add( searchJButton );
100         searchJButton.addActionListener(
101
102            new ActionListener() // anonymous inner class
103            {
104               // event handler called when searchJButton is pressed
105               public void actionPerformed( ActionEvent event )
106               {
107                  searchJButtonActionPerformed( event );
108               }
109
110            } // end anonymous inner class
111
112         ); // end call to addActionListener
113
114         // set up sourceJLabel
115         sourceJLabel = new JLabel();
116         sourceJLabel.setBounds( 8, 112, 48, 16 );
117         sourceJLabel.setText( "Source:" );
118         contentPane.add( sourceJLabel );
119
120         // set up sourceJTextArea
121         sourceJTextArea = new JTextArea();
122         sourceJTextArea.setBounds( 8, 136, 232, 105 );
123         sourceJTextArea.setText( htmlText );
124         sourceJTextArea.setLineWrap( true );
```

Figure 23.16   Screen Scraping code. (Part 3 of 4.)

```
125          contentPane.add( sourceJTextArea );
126
127          // set properties of application's window
128          setTitle( "Screen Scraping" ); // set title bar string
129          setSize( 259, 278 );            // set window size
130          setVisible( true );             // display window
131
132       } // end method createUserInterface
133
134       // find and display price substring
135       private void searchJButtonActionPerformed( ActionEvent event )
136       {
137          // get rate
138          String rate = rateJTextField.getText();
139
140          // rate is an empty string
141          if ( rate.equals( "" ) )
142          {
143             JOptionPane.showMessageDialog( null,
144                "Please enter conversion rate first.",
145                "Missing Rate", JOptionPane.WARNING_MESSAGE );
146
147             return; // exit method
148          }
149
150          // search for location of item and price
151          String selectedItem =
152             ( String ) itemJComboBox.getSelectedItem();
153          int itemLocation = htmlText.indexOf( selectedItem );
154          int priceBegin = htmlText.indexOf( "&euro;", itemLocation );
155          int priceEnd = htmlText.indexOf( "</TD>", priceBegin );
156
157          // store price found in double price
158          String priceText = htmlText.substring(
159             priceBegin + 6, priceEnd );
160          double price = Double.parseDouble( priceText );
161
162          // convert price from euros to dollars
163          double conversionRate = Double.parseDouble(
164             rateJTextField.getText() );
165          price *= conversionRate;
166
167          // display price of item in priceJTextField
168          DecimalFormat dollars = new DecimalFormat( "$0.00" );
169          priceJTextField.setText( dollars.format( price ) );
170
171       } // end method searchJButtonActionPerformed
172
173       // main method
174       public static void main( String args[] )
175       {
176          ScreenScraping application = new ScreenScraping();
177          application.setDefaultCloseOperation( JFrame.EXIT_ON_CLOSE );
178
179       } // end method main
180
181    } // end class ScreenScraping
```

Retrieve the selected item and locate the indices where the price in euros begins and ends

Set priceText to htmlText substring, convert priceText to double and store in price

Convert the price from euros to dollars using the conversion rate entered by the user

Display the price in dollars

Figure 23.16 **Screen Scraping** code. (Part 4 of 4.)

1. The _____ method removes all white space that appears at the beginning and end of a `String`.

   a) `removeSpaces`   b) `squeeze`

   c) `trim`   d) `truncate`

2. The `startsWith` method returns _____ if the `String` on which the method is called begins with the `String` passed as an argument.

   a) `true`   b) `false`

   c) `1`   d) the index of the substring

   Answers: 1) c. 2) a.

23.7 Wrap-Up

In this tutorial, you were introduced to `String` processing using the methods of class `String`. You learned how to create and manipulate `String` objects. You learned how to locate, retrieve and replace substrings in `Strings` using `String` methods `indexOf` and `substring`. You applied your knowledge of `Strings` in Java to create a simple **Screen Scraping** application. You learned that screen scraping is the process of extracting desired information from HTML in a Web page. You also learned about the `String` methods `length`, `charAt`, `endsWith`, `startsWith` and `trim`, which enable you to further access and manipulate `String` data.

In the next tutorial, you will learn how to use exception handling in your applications; exception handling is a technique for resolving problems within an application. Using exception handling enables your applications to detect and handle problems without having to end execution. You will enhance your **Car Payment Calculator** application so that it will use exception handling to recognize and react properly to invalid input from the user.

SKILLS SUMMARY

Determining the Size of a `String`

- Use `String` method `length`.

Locating Substrings in `Strings`

- Use `String` method `indexOf` to locate the first occurrence of a substring in a `String`. The return value is the index where the first occurrence of the substring begins. If the substring is not found in the `String`, `-1` is returned.

- Use `String` method `lastIndexOf` to locate the last occurrence of a substring in a `String`. The return value is the index where the last occurrence of the substring begins. If the substring is not found in the `String`, `-1` is returned.

Retrieving Substrings from `Strings`

- Use `String` method `substring` with one argument to obtain a substring that begins at the specified starting index and contains the remainder of the original `String`.

- Use `String` method `substring` with two arguments to obtain a substring that begins at the specified starting index (the first argument) and ends one location before the ending index (the second argument).

Comparing Substrings to the Beginning or End of a `String`

- Use `String` method `startsWith` to determine whether a `String` starts with a particular substring.

- Use `String` method `endsWith` to determine whether a `String` ends with a particular substring.

Removing Whitespace from a `String`

- Use `String` method `trim` to remove all white space that appear at the beginning and end of a `String`.

KEY TERMS

charAt method of class String—Returns the character located at a specific index in a `String`.

endsWith method of class String—Returns `true` if a `String` ends with a particular substring and `false` otherwise.

HTML (HyperText Markup Language)—A technology used for describing Web content and how that content should be formatted.

immutable—`Strings` in Java are immutable, meaning that the contents of a `String` cannot be changed after it is created.

indexOf method of class String—Returns the index of the first occurrence of a substring in a `String`; returns −1 if the substring is not found.

lastIndexOf method of class String—Returns the index of the last occurrence of a substring in a `String`; returns −1 if the substring is not found.

length method of class String—Returns the number of characters in a `String`.

literal String objects—A `String` constant written as a sequence of characters in double quotation marks (also called a string constant or string literal).

screen scraping—The process of extracting desired information from the HTML that composes a Web page.

special character—Characters such as +, -, *, /, $, white space and others. Does not include letters or digits.

startsWith method of class String—Returns `true` if a `String` starts with a particular substring and `false` otherwise.

String—A class that represents a series of characters treated as a single unit.

string constant—Another term for string literal or literal `String` object.

string literal—Another term for string constant or literal `String` object.

substring—A sequence of characters that makes up part or all of a `String`.

substring method of class String—Returns a new `String` object by copying a specified part of an existing `String` object.

trim method of class String—Returns a new `String` object with all white space removed from the beginning and end of a `String`.

JAVA LIBRARY REFERENCE

String The `String` class represents a sequence of characters treated as a single unit.

- *Methods*

  `charAt`—Returns the character located at a specific index in a `String`.

  `endsWith`—Returns `true` if a `String` ends with a particular substring and `false` otherwise.

  `equals`—Compares the contents of two `Strings`, returning `true` if the two `Strings` contain the same characters in the same order and `false` otherwise.

  `indexOf`—Returns the index of the first occurrence of a substring in a `String`, or −1 if the substring is not found.

  `lastIndexOf`—Returns the index of the last occurrence of a substring in a `String`. It returns −1 if the substring is not found.

  `length`—Returns the number of characters in a `String`.

  `startsWith`—Returns `true` if a `String` starts with a particular substring and `false` otherwise.

  `substring`—Creates a new `String` object by copying part of an existing `String` object.

  `trim`—Removes all white space from the beginning and end of a `String`.

  `valueOf`—Converts numeric values to a `String`.

MULTIPLE-CHOICE QUESTIONS

23.1 Extracting desired information from Web pages is called _____.

a) Web crawling	b) screen scraping
c) querying	d) redirection

23.2 If the indexOf method does not find the specified substring, it returns _____.

  a) false
                               b) 0

  c) -1
                                 d) None of the above.

23.3 The String class allows you to _____ Strings.

  a) search
                                b) retrieve characters from

  c) determine the number of characters in   d) All of the above.

23.4 _____ is a technology for describing Web content.

  a) Class String
                               b) A String literal

  c) HTML
                                d) A screen scraper

23.5 The _____ method returns the character located at a specific index in a String.

  a) get
                                b) char

  c) getAt
                              d) charAt

23.6 The _____ method creates a new String object by copying part of an existing String object.

  a) stringCopy
                           b) substring

  c) copyString
                         d) copySubString

23.7 All String objects are _____.

  a) the same size

  b) always equal to each other

  c) preceded by at least one white space

  d) immutable

23.8 The version of the indexOf method that takes two arguments does not examine any characters that occur prior to the _____.

  a) second argument
                         b) first match

  c) last character of the String
           d) None of the above.

23.9 The _____ method determines whether a String ends with a particular substring.

  a) checkEnd
                           b) stringEnd

  c) endsWith
                            d) endIs

23.10 The trim method removes all white space that appear _____ a String.

  a) in
                                b) at the beginning of

  c) at the end of
                            d) Both (b) and (c).

EXERCISES

23.11 (*Supply Cost Calculator Application*) Write an application that calculates the cost of all the supplies added to the user's shopping list (Fig. 23.17). The application should contain two JLists. The first JList contains all the supplies offered and their respective prices. Users should be able to select the desired supplies from the first JList and add them to the second JList. The user may select an item in the first JList multiple times. Provide a **Calculate** JButton that displays the total price for the user's shopping list (the contents of the second JList).

  a) *Copying the template to your working directory.* Copy the directory C:\Examples\ Tutorial23\Exercises\SupplyCalculator to your C:\SimplyJava directory.

  b) *Opening the template file.* Open the SupplyCalculator.java file in your text editor.

  c) *Adding code to the calculcateJButtonActionPerformed method.* In the calculateJButtonActionPerformed method (lines 242–245), declare two variables—the first should be a double (called total), which will keep track of the total price. The second will be a String (called price) used as a temporary variable for the price. Then, add a for statement to loop through all the items in the ArrayList userArrayList. You will use this for statement to iterate through each item in the **Items in Your List:** JList. These items have already been added to the userArrayList for you.

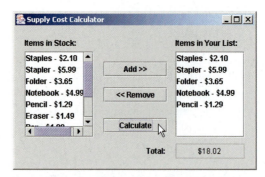

Figure 23.17 Supply Cost Calculator application's GUI.

d) *Extracting the prices and calculating the total.* Inside the `for` statement you added in *Step c*, convert the current item from the `userArrayList` into a `String`. Store this `String` in variable `price`. Extract the price from the `String` variable `price`. To do this, you need to first find the location where the price begins (directly after `"$"`), and use this index to extract all the characters after the `"$"`. Store the resulting substring in `price`. Then, convert `price` to a `double` and add its value to `total`.

e) *Displaying the total.* Immediately following the `for` statement you completed in *Step e*, create a new `DecimalFormat` object named `dollars` that will be used to display a `String` in currency format. Use the `format` method of `dollars` to display the `total` in `totalJTextField`.

f) *Saving the application.* Save your modified source code file.

g) *Opening the Command Prompt window and changing directories.* Open the **Command Prompt** by selecting **Start > Programs > Accessories > Command Prompt**. Change to your working directory by typing `cd C:\SimplyJava\SupplyCalculator`.

h) *Compiling the application.* Compile your application by typing `javac SupplyCalculator.java`.

i) *Running the completed application.* When your application compiles correctly, run it by typing `java SupplyCalculator`. To test your application, add and remove items from your list and check that the total calculates correctly.

j) *Closing the application.* Close your running application by clicking its close button.

k) *Closing the Command Prompt window.* Close the **Command Prompt** window by clicking its close button.

23.12 (*Encryption Application*) Write an application that encrypts a message from the user (Fig. 23.18). The application should be able to encrypt the message in two different ways: substitution cipher and transposition cipher (both described below). The user should be able to enter the message in a `JTextField` and select the desired method of encryption. The encrypted message is then displayed in an uneditable `JTextField`.

In a substitution cipher, every character in the English alphabet is represented by a different character in a substitution `String`, which we will refer to as the substitution alphabet. Every time a letter occurs in the English sentence, it is replaced by the letter in the corresponding index of the substitution `String`. As an example of a substitution cipher, let's encrypt the `String` `"code"`. If the corresponding characters for `"c"`, `"o"`, `"d"` and `"e"` in the substitution alphabet are `"e"`, `" "`, `"f"` and `"g"` (respectively), the encrypted `String` is `"e fg"`.

In a transposition cipher, two `Strings` are created. The first new `String` contains all the characters at the even indices of the input `String`. The second new `String` contains all of the characters at the odd indices. The second `String` is then appended to the first `String` with a space between them. For example a transposition cipher for the word `"code"` would be: `"cd oe."`

a) *Copying the template to your working directory.* Copy the directory `C:\Examples\Tutorial23\Exercises\CipherEncryption` to your `C:\SimplyJava` directory.

b) *Opening the template file.* Open the `Encryption.java` file in your text editor.

Figure 23.18 Encryption application's GUI.

c) *Adding code to the **substitutionCipher** method.* In the substitutionCipher method (lines 126–140), English and substitution alphabet Strings have been declared for you as normalAlphabet and cipherAlphabet, respectively. Other Strings that you will be using have already been defined for you—cipher is an empty String you will use to store the encrypted text and plain contains the text entered by the user. After the declaration of the Strings, add an empty for statement that loops for each character in plain.

d) *Performing the substitution encryption.* Inside the for statement you added in *Step c*, create an int variable index and assign to it the index in normalAlphabet where the current character in plain appears. If index is not equal to -1, retrieve the character in cipherAlphabet at the location stored in index and append this character to the end of cipher. Now the original String has been substituted with all the corresponding cipher characters. After the for statement, add code to display cipher in cipherJTextField.

e) *Adding code to the **transpositionCipher** method.* Find the transpositionCipher method, which immediately follows substitutionCipher. Strings firstWord and lastWord have been declared for you in this method as well as plainText, which contains the text entered by the user. After the declaration of the Strings, add an empty for statement that loops for each character in plainText. This for statement will be used to add each proper character to the two words.

f) *Performing the transposition encryption.* Inside the for statement you added in *Step e*, add an if...else statement whose if statement executes when counter is an even number. [*Hint:* Recall that when an even number is divided by 2, the remainder is 0.] Within the if statement, extract the current character in plainText and append it to firstWord. Within the else statement, extract the current character in plainText and append it to lastWord. After the for statement, add code to display in cipherJTextField the firstWord followed by the lastWord, separated by a space.

g) *Saving the application.* Save your modified source code file.

h) *Opening the Command Prompt window and changing directories.* Open the **Command Prompt** by selecting **Start > Programs > Accessories > Command Prompt**. Change to your working directory by typing cd C:\SimplyJava\Encryption.

i) *Compiling the application.* Compile your application by typing javac Encryption.java.

j) *Running the completed application.* When your application compiles correctly, run it by typing java Encryption. To test your application, use both ciphers on different texts. Check that you can get the same results as the **Encryption** application shown in Figure 23.18.

k) *Closing the application.* Close your running application by clicking its close button.

l) *Closing the Command Prompt window.* Close the **Command Prompt** window by clicking its close button.

23.13 (*Anagram Game Application*) Write an **Anagram Game** application that contains an array of pre-set words. The game should randomly select a word and scramble its letters (Fig. 23.19). The first letter is extracted and placed back in the String at a random location. This process is repeated 20 times to ensure that the String is sufficiently scrambled. A JLabel displays the scrambled word for the user to guess. If the user guesses correctly, display a message and repeat the process with a different word. If the guess is incorrect, display a message and let the user try again.

Figure 23.19 **Anagram Game** application's GUI.

a) *Copying the template to your working directory.* Copy the directory `C:\Examples\Tutorial23\Exercises\Anagram` to your `C:\SimplyJava` directory.

b) *Opening the template file.* Open the `Anagram.java` file in your text editor.

c) *Adding a for statement to the generateAnagram method.* The generateAnagram method (lines 133–145) selects a `String` from a predefined array and scrambles this `String` for the user. The `String` to be scrambled is stored in variable `scrambled` for you. A random index in this `String` has also been generated for you and stored in variable `randomIndex`. In this exercise, you will be completing only the generate-Anagram method—the rest of the application has been provided for you. After the variable declarations inside the generateAnagram method, add an empty for statement that will loop 20 times.

d) *Generating the scrambled word.* Inside the for statement you added in *Step c*, declare char `firstCharacter` and assign to it the first character in `scrambled`. Use the substring method to remove the first character from `scrambled`. Then, create `String` variables `temporary1` and `temporary2`. In `temporary1`, store the characters in `scrambled` from the beginning of the `String` until `randomIndex`. In `temporary2`, store the remaining characters from `scrambled`. Append the `firstCharacter` to `temporary1`, then concatenate `temporary1` and `temporary2` and store the result in `scrambled`. You have moved the first character of `scrambled` to a random location. This process is repeated 20 times to further scramble the `String` before it is displayed for the user.

e) *Generating a random index.* You now need to generate a new `randomIndex` for the next iteration of the for statement. After concatenating `temporary1` and `temporary2` in *Step d*, use randomGenerator (a Random object created for you in the template) to generate a random integer between the values 0 and the last index of `scrambled`, inclusive. Store the random integer in `randomIndex`.

f) *Displaying the anagram.* After the for statement you completed in *Steps c–e*, display `scrambled` in anagramJTextField.

g) *Saving the application.* Save your modified source code file.

h) *Opening the Command Prompt window and changing directories.* Open the **Command Prompt** window by selecting **Start > Programs > Accessories > Command Prompt**. Change to your working directory by typing cd `C:\SimplyJava\Anagram`.

i) *Compiling the application.* Compile your application by typing javac `Anagram.java`.

j) *Running the completed application.* When your application compiles correctly, run it by typing java Anagram. To test your application, enter both correct and incorrect answers for multiple words.

k) *Closing the application.* Close your running application by clicking its close button.

l) *Closing the Command Prompt window.* Close the **Command Prompt** window by clicking its close button.

What does this code do? ▶   **23.14** What Strings are stored in array words after the following code executes?

```
1  String words[] = { "dance", "walk", "talking", "eat" };
2
3  for ( int counter = 0; counter <= words.length - 1; counter++ )
4  {
5     if ( words[ counter ].endsWith( "e" ) )
6     {
7        words[ counter ] = words[ counter ].substring(
8           0, words[ counter ].length() - 1 );
9     }
10
11    if ( !( words[ counter ].endsWith( "ing" ) ) )
12    {
13       words[ counter ] += "ing";
14    }
15
16 } // end for loop
```

What's wrong with this code? ▶   **23.15** This code should remove each space from test. Find the error(s) in the following code.

```
1  String test = "s p a c e s";
2  int index;
3
4  while( test.indexOf( " " ) == -1 )
5  {
6     index = test.indexOf( " " );
7     test = test.substring( 0, index - 1 ) + test.substring( index );
8  }
```

Programming Challenge ▶   **23.16** (*Pig Latin Application*) Write an application that encodes English language phrases into Pig Latin (Fig. 23.20). Pig Latin is a form of coded language often used for amusement. Use the following algorithm to form the Pig Latin words:

> *To form a Pig Latin word from an English-language phrase, the translation proceeds one word at a time. To translate an English word into a Pig Latin word, place the first letter of the English word (if it is not a vowel) at the end of the English word and add the letters "ay." If the first letter of the English word is a vowel, place it at the end of the word and add "y." Using this method, the word "jump" becomes "umpjay," the word "the" becomes "hetay" and the word "ace" becomes "ceay." Blanks between words remain blanks.*

Assume the following: The English phrase entered by the user consists of words separated by blanks, there are no punctuation marks and all words have two or more letters. The translateToPigLatin method should translate the sentence into Pig Latin, word by word.

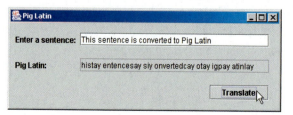

Figure 23.20 Pig Latin application.

a) **Copying the template to your working directory.** Copy the directory C:\Examples\ Tutorial23\Exercises\PigLatin to your C:\SimplyJava directory.

b) **Opening the template file.** Open the PigLatin.java file in your text editor.

c) **Adding a for statement to the translateToPigLatin method.** In the translateToPigLatin method (lines 97–109), four variables have been provided for you—Strings prefix and suffix (which you will use shortly to convert each word), String array words, which contains each word in the text entered by the user and String translatedText, which will be used to store the translated sentence. After the variable declaration, add an empty for statement that will loop through each String in words.

d) **Retrieving the word's first letter.** Inside the for statement you added in *Step c*, retrieve the first letter of the current word and store its lowercase equivalent in prefix. [*Hint*: Use the substring method to retrieve the first letter and assign it to prefix. Then use prefix to call String method **toLowerCase**. This method will return the letter's lowercase equivalent.]

e) **Determining the suffix.** After retrieving the first letter, add an if...else statement whose if statement executes when the letter in prefix is a vowel (that is, when the letter in prefix is equal to one of the following letters: a, e, i, o or u). In the body of the if statement, assign the String "y" to suffix. In the else statement, assign "ay" to suffix.

f) **Translating the current word to Pig Latin.** After the if...else statement, translate the current word to its Pig Latin equivalent as follows: Have the first portion contain all the letters in the original word except for the first letter. Append to this text the value in prefix then the value in suffix. Assign the new word to the current location in array words. Then, append the current element in words to translatedText, followed by a space. This line concatenates all the converted Pig Latin words back into a sentence.

g) **Returning the new sentence.** After the for statements, modify the return statement to return translatedText.

h) **Saving the application.** Save your modified source code file.

i) **Opening the Command Prompt window and changing directories.** Open the **Command Prompt** window by selecting **Start > Programs > Accessories > Command Prompt**. Change to your working directory by typing cd C:\SimplyJava\PigLatin.

j) **Compiling the application.** Compile your application by typing javac PigLatin.java.

k) **Running the completed application.** When your application compiles correctly, run it by typing java PigLatin. To test your application, translate multiple sentences into Pig Latin and check that each translates correctly.

l) **Closing the application.** Close your running application by clicking its close button.

m) **Closing the Command Prompt window.** Close the **Command Prompt** window by clicking its close button.

Objectives

In this tutorial, you will learn to:
- Understand exception handling.
- Use the `try` block, the `catch` block, the `finally` block and the `throws` block to handle exceptions.
- Understand the exception inheritance hierarchy.
- Distinguish checked and unchecked exceptions.

Outline

Enhanced Car Payment Calculator Application

Introducing Exception Handling

I n this tutorial, you will learn about **exception handling**. An **exception** is an indication of a problem that occurs during an application's execution. The name "exception" comes from the fact that, although a problem can occur, the problem occurs infrequently—if the "rule" is that a statement normally executes correctly, then the "exception to the rule" is that a problem occurs. Exception handling enables you to create applications that can resolve (or handle) exceptions as the applications execute. In many cases, handling an exception allows an application to continue executing as if no problem had been encountered.

This tutorial begins with a test-drive of the **Enhanced Car Payment Calculator** application, then overviews exception handling concepts and demonstrates basic exception handling techniques. You will learn the specifics of exception handling with the `try`, `catch` and `finally` blocks and the `throws` block and the inheritance hierarchy of exception classes.

24.1 Test-Driving the Enhanced Car Payment Calculator Application

In this tutorial, you will enhance the **Car Payment Calculator** application from Tutorial 8 by adding exception handling statements. Your application must meet the following requirements:

Application Requirements

*A bank wishes to prevent users from entering incorrect data on their car loans. Although the application you developed in Tutorial 8 continues running when incorrect data is entered, it will not calculate the result. Alter the **Car Payment Calculator** application to allow users to enter only integers in the **Price:** `JTextField` and **Down payment:** `JTextField`. If the user enters anything besides an integer (such as a `double` or any non-numeric data), a message should be displayed instructing the user to enter an integer. Similarly, users should be allowed to enter only `double` values in the **Annual interest rate:** `JTextField`. If the user enters anything besides a `double`, a message should be displayed instructing the user to enter a `double` value between 0.0 and 100.0. The interest rate should be entered such that an input of 5 is equal to 5%.*

The **Enhanced Car Payment Calculator** application calculates monthly payments for a car when financed for 24, 36, 48 and 60 months if the user provides valid input. Users input the car price, the down payment and the annual interest rate. You begin by test-driving the completed application. Next, you will learn the additional Java technologies you will need to create your own version of this application.

<table>
<tr>
<td>

*Test-Driving the
Completed Enhanced
Car Payment Calculator
Application*

</td>
<td>

1. ***Locating the completed application.*** Open the **Command Prompt** window by selecting **Start > Programs > Accessories > Command Prompt**. Change to your completed **Enhanced Car Payment Calculator** application directory by typing cd C:\Examples\Tutorial24\CompletedApplication\ EnhancedCarPayment.

2. ***Running the Enhanced Car Payment Calculator application.*** Type java CarPayment in the **Command Prompt** window to run your application (Fig. 24.1).

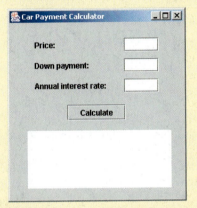

Figure 24.1 Running the completed **Enhanced Car Payment Calculator** application.

3. ***Entering a double in the Down payment: JTextField.*** Enter 16900 in the **Price:** JTextField. Enter 6000.50 in the **Down payment:** JTextField. The application window appears as in Fig. 24.2.

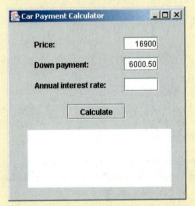

Figure 24.2 Entering a double in the **Down payment:** JTextField.

4. ***Calculating the monthly payment amounts.*** Click the **Calculate** JButton to attempt to display the monthly payment in the JTextArea. Notice that an error message dialog (Fig. 24.3) appears.

</td>
</tr>
</table>

(cont.)

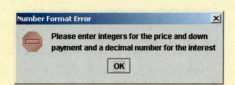

Figure 24.3   Message dialog displayed for incorrect down payment input.

5. ***Entering non-numeric data in the Down payment: JTextField.*** Change the value 6000.50 in the **Down payment:** JTextField to 600p. The application window appears as in Fig. 24.4. Click the **Calculate** JButton to attempt to display the monthly payment in the JTextArea. The error message dialog shown in Fig. 24.3 appears again (a non-numeric character like p cannot be entered when an integer is expected).

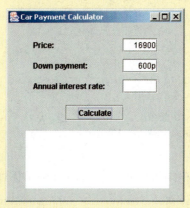

Figure 24.4   Entering a non-numeric character in the **Down payment:** JTextField.

6. ***Entering non-numeric data in the Annual interest rate: JTextField.*** Change the value 600p in the **Down payment:** JTextField to 6000. Enter 7.5% in the **Annual interest rate:** JTextField. The application window appears as in Fig. 24.5. Click the **Calculate** JButton to attempt to display the monthly payment in the JTextArea. The error message dialog shown in Fig. 24.3 appears again (7.5 is the correct input; entering the % special character is incorrect).

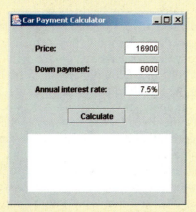

Figure 24.5   Entering a non-numeric character in the **Annual interest rate:** JTextField.

(cont.)   7. *Correcting the input*. Change the value 7.5% in the **Annual interest rate:** JTextField to 7.5, and click the **Calculate** JButton to display the monthly payments (Fig. 24.6).

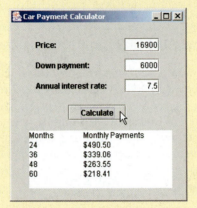

Figure 24.6 Displaying monthly payments after input is corrected.

8. *Closing the application.* Close your running application by clicking the window's close button.

9. *Closing the Command Prompt*. Close the **Command Prompt** window by clicking its close button.

24.2 Introduction to Exception Handling

Application logic frequently tests conditions that determine how application execution should proceed. Consider the following pseudocode:

Perform a task

If the preceding task did not execute correctly
    Perform error processing

Perform next task

If the preceding task did not execute correctly
    Perform error processing

...

In this pseudocode, you begin by performing a task. Then, you test whether the task executed correctly. If not, you perform error processing. Otherwise, you continue with the next task. Although this form of error checking works, intermixing application logic with error-handling logic can make the application difficult to read, modify, maintain and debug—especially in large applications. In fact, if potential problems occur infrequently, intermixing application and error-handling logic can degrade an application's performance, because the application must explicitly test for errors after each task to determine whether the next task can be performed.

Exception handling enables you to remove error-handling code from the code that implements your application's logic, which improves application clarity and enhances modifiability. You can decide to handle only the exceptions you choose—all exceptions, all exceptions of a certain type or all exceptions of a group of related types (such as exception types that belong to an inheritance hierarchy). Such flexibility reduces the likelihood that errors will be overlooked, thereby making an application more robust.

A method **throws an exception** if a problem occurs during the method execution but the method is unable to correct the problem. There is no guarantee that there will be an **exception handler**—code that executes when the application detects an exception—to process that kind of exception. If there is, the exception handler

catches and handles the exception. An **uncaught exception**—an exception that does not have an exception handler—might cause the application to terminate execution.

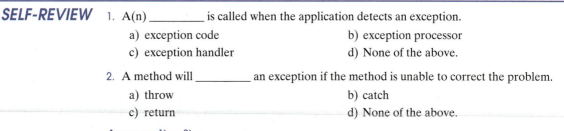

24.3 Exception Handling in Java

Java provides **try statements** to enable exception handling. A `try` statement consists of the keyword `try`, followed by braces (`{}`) that delimit a **try block**, followed by one or more **catch blocks**, optionally followed by a single **finally block**.

The purpose of the `try` block is to contain statements that might cause exceptions and statements that should not execute if an exception occurs. At least one `catch` block (also called an **exception handler**) or a `finally` block must immediately follow the `try` block. Each `catch` block specifies in parentheses a parameter (known as the **exception parameter**) that identifies the exception type the exception handler can process. The parameter enables the `catch` block to interact with the caught exception object. After the last `catch` block, an optional `finally` block provides code that always executes, whether or not an exception occurs. In Tutorial 25, you will see that the `finally` block is an ideal location for code to release resources to prevent "resource leaks."

If an exception occurs in a `try` block, the `try` block terminates immediately. As with any other block of code, when a `try` block terminates, local variables declared in the block go out of scope. Next, the application searches for the first `catch` block (immediately following the `try` block) that can process the type of exception that occurred. The application locates the matching `catch` by comparing the thrown exception's type with each `catch`'s exception-parameter type. A match occurs if the types are identical or if the thrown exception's type is a subclass of the exception parameter's type. When a match occurs, the block associated with the matching `catch` block executes. When a `catch` block finishes processing, local variables declared within the `catch` block (as well as the exception parameter) go out of scope. Any remaining `catch` blocks that correspond to the `try` block are ignored, and execution resumes at the first line of code after the `try` statement if there is no `finally` block. Otherwise, execution resumes at the `finally` block.

If there is no `catch` block that matches the exception thrown in the corresponding `try` block, the execution resumes at the first line of code after the `try` statement if no `finally` block is presented. Otherwise, execution resumes at the `finally` block.

If no exceptions occur in a `try` block, the application ignores the `catch` block(s) for that block. Application execution resumes with the next statement after the `try` statement if there is no `finally` block. Otherwise, execution resumes at the `finally` blockblock. A `finally` block (if one is present) will execute whether or not an exception is thrown in the corresponding `try` block or any of its corresponding `catch` blocks.

In a method declaration, a **throws block** specifies the exceptions the method throws. The `throws` block appears after the parameter list and before the method body. The block contains a comma-separated list of exceptions the method will throw if a problem occurs when the method executes. Such exceptions may be thrown by statements in the method's body, or they may be thrown by methods

called in the body. A method can throw exceptions of the indicated classes, or it can throw exceptions of their subclasses. The usage of the `throws` block is beyond the scope of this book.

Most readers of this text will be concerned with exceptions thrown by methods of library classes. Java allows programmers to create their own exception types, which throw all kinds of exceptions. To handle the programmer-defined exceptions, you would include a `throws` block in your code to indicate that those exceptions have occurred, and include `catch` blocks to handle those kinds of errors.

It is possible that a `catch` block might decide that either it cannot process that exception or it can only partially process the exception. In such cases, the exception handler can defer the handling (or perhaps a portion of it) to another `catch` block. In either case, the handler achieves this by **rethrowing the exception** using the **throw** keyword via the statement

`throw` *exceptionReference*;

where *exceptionReference* is the parameter for the exception in the `catch` block. When a rethrow occurs, the next enclosing `try` block (if any) detects the rethrown exception and one of its `catch` blocks attempts to handle the exception.

SELF-REVIEW
1. The _____ (if there is one) is always executed regardless of whether an exception occurs.
   a) catch block
   b) finally block
   c) both catch and finally blocks
   d) None of the above.

2. If no exceptions occur in a `try` block, the application ignores the _____ for that block.
   a) finally block
   b) return statement
   c) catch block(s)
   d) None of the above.

Answers: 1) b. 2) c.

24.4 Java Exception Hierarchy

This section examines Java's inheritance hierarchy of exceptions. Exceptions are objects. Thus, programmers can create exception-class hierarchies. Figure 24.7 shows a small portion of the inheritance hierarchy for the **Throwable** class, which is the superclass of all exceptions. Only Throwable objects can be used with the exception-handling mechanism. The Throwable class has two subclasses: **Exception** and **Error**. The Exception class and its subclasses represent exceptional situations that occur in a Java application that should be caught by the application. The Error class and its subclasses represent exceptional situations that happen in the Java runtime system, but typically should not be caught by applications.

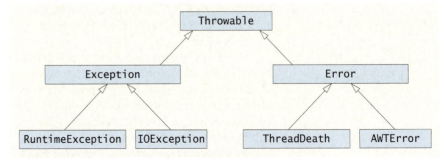

Figure 24.7   Inheritance hierarchy for class `Throwable`.

Java distinguishes between two categories of exceptions: **checked exceptions** and **unchecked exceptions**. The **RuntimeException** class (package `java.lang`) is

the superclass of all exceptions that can be thrown during application execution. All exception types that are not subclasses of RuntimeException are checked exceptions. All exception types that are subclasses of RuntimeException are unchecked exceptions.

The distinction between a checked exception and an unchecked exception is important, because the Java compiler enforces a **catch-or-declare requirement** for checked exceptions. The compiler checks each method call and method declaration to determine whether the method throws checked exceptions. If so, the compiler ensures that the checked exception is caught in a catch block or declared in a throws block. To satisfy the catch part of the catch-or-declare requirement, the code that generates the exception must be wrapped in a try block, and a catch block must be provided for the checked exception type (or one of its superclass types). To satisfy the declare part of the catch-or-declare requirement, the method containing the code that generates the exception must provide a throws clause containing the checked exception type after the parameter list and before the method body. If the catch-or-declare requirement is not satisfied, the compiler will issue an error message indicating that the exception must be caught or declared.

Although the Java compiler does not force you to provide exception handlers to deal with unchecked exceptions, it is a good practice for you to provide appropriate exception handling code when it is known that such exceptions might occur. For example, an application should process NumberFormatExceptions from Integer method parseInt, even though NumberFormatExceptions are unchecked exceptions (The NumberFormatException class is a subclass of RuntimeException). You will learn about NumberFormatExceptions and how to catch them shortly.

Various exception classes can be derived from a common superclass. If an exception handler is written to catch exception objects of a superclass type, it can also catch all objects of that class's subclasses. For example, an exception handler that catches exceptions of type RuntimeException will also catch exceptions of type NumberFormatException. This enables a catch block to handle related errors with a concise notation.

You could also catch each subclass exception object individually if those exceptions require different processing. Catching related exceptions in one catch block makes sense only if the handling behavior would be the same for all the subclasses. Otherwise, you should handle each subclass exception individually by declaring separate catch blocks for each. In such cases, you must handle exceptions of a subclass before handling those of a superclass.

Common Programming Error

If an uncaught exception is a checked exception, then an error occurs when you attempt to compile the application.

Common Programming Error

If an uncaught exception is an unchecked exception, then an error occurs when you attempt to run the application.

SELF-REVIEW

1. All exception types that are subclasses of _____ are unchecked exceptions.

   a) RuntimeException   b) Exception

   c) Error   d) None of the above.

2. The Java compiler enforces a catch-or-declare requirement for _____.

   a) exceptions   b) errors

   c) unchecked exceptions   d) checked exceptions

Answers: 1) a. 2) d.

24.5 Constructing the Enhanced Car Payment Calculator Application

Now that you have been introduced to exception handling, you will construct your **Enhanced Car Payment Calculator** application. The following pseudocode describes the basic operation of the **Enhanced Car Payment Calculator** application:

When the user clicks the Calculate JButton:
  Clear the JTextArea of any previous text

  Try
      Get the car price from the Price: JTextField
      Get the down payment from the Down Payment: JTextField
      Get the annual interest rate from the Annual Interest Rate: JTextField
      Calculate monthly payments for 2, 3, 4 and 5 years
      Display the results

  Catch NumberFormatException
      Display the error message dialog

When the user calls method calculateMonthlyPayment:
      Calculate the monthly payment based on loan amount, monthly interest rate
      and loan length in months

Now that you have test-driven the **Enhanced Car Payment Calculator** application and studied its pseudocode representation, you will use an ACE table to help you convert the pseudocode to Java. Figure 24.8 lists the actions, components and events required to complete your own version of this application.

Action/Control/Event (ACE) Table for the Enhanced Car Payment Calculator Application	Action	Component/Class	Event/Method
	Label all the application's components	`priceJLabel`, `downPaymentJLabel`, `interestRateJLabel`	Application is run
		`calculateJButton`	User clicks **Calculate JButton**
	Clear the JTextArea of any previous text	`monthlyPaymentsJTextArea`	
	Try Get the car price from the Price: JTextField	`priceJTextField`	
	Get the down payment from the Down Payment: JTextField	`downPaymentJTextField`	
	Get the annual interest rate from the Annual Interest Rate: JTextField	`interestRateJTextField`	
	Calculate monthly payments for 2, 3, 4 and 5 years		
	Display the results	`monthlyPaymentsJTextArea`	
	Catch NumberFormatException Display the error message dialog	`JOptionPane`	
			Method `calculate Monthly-Payment` is called
	Calculate the monthly payment based on loan amount, monthly interest rate and loan length in months		

Figure 24.8 Enhanced **Car Payment Calculator** application ACE table.

Now that you've analyzed the **Enhanced Car Payment Calculator** application's components, you will learn how to place exception handling in your application's code.

Handling the
NumberFormat
Exception

1. ***Copying the template to your working directory.*** Copy the C:\Examples\ Tutorial24\TemplateApplication\EnhancedCarPayment directory to your C:\SimplyJava directory.

2. ***Opening the template application.*** Open the template file CarPayment.java in your text editor.

3. ***Studying the code.*** In Fig. 24.9, the statements that read the integers from the JTextFields (lines 120–124) each use the Integer.parseInt method to convert a String to an int value. The statement that reads the double from the JTextField (lines 127–128) uses the Double.parseDouble method to convert a String to a double value.

   Methods parseInt and parseDouble throw a NumberFormatException if their arguments do not represent a valid integer or double, respectively. The **NumberFormatException** class, a subclass of RuntimeException, is thrown when the application cannot convert a string to a desired numeric type, such as int or double. The parseInt method throws a NumberFormatException when the application attempts to convert a string that does not represent an integer (such as "6000.50" or "600p") to an int. The parseDouble method throws a NumberFormatException when the application attempts to convert a string that does not represent a decimal number (such as "7.5%") to a double. However, the parseDouble method does not throw a NumberFormatException if the argument passed to it is a string that represents an integer (such as "7"), because an integer is also a valid double value. Once the data has been read and the contents of the JTextFields have been converted to ints and a double, the processData method is called to determine the monthly payments (line 131).

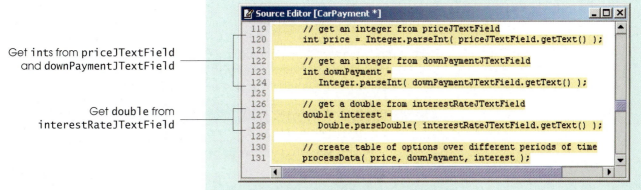

Get ints from priceJTextField and downPaymentJTextField

Get double from interestRateJTextField

Figure 24.9   Obtaining the user input.

4. ***Adding a try statement.*** Add lines 122–123 and line 138 of Fig. 24.10 to your code. The try statement will attempt to get int values from the **Price:** and **Down payment:** JTextFields, and a double value from the **Annual interest rate:** JTextField. You need to indent lines 125–137 after adding the highlighted code in Fig. 24.10. Lines 125–134 are included in the try block since they might throw an exception. Line 137 is included even though it will not throw an exception. Instead, it is included because you do not want it to execute if an exception occurs. If an exception occurs in one of the previous lines, line 137 will be skipped.

(cont.)

```
Source Editor [CarPayment *]                                      _ □ ×
122        // try to retrieve price and down payment
123        try
124        {
125            // get an integer from priceJTextField
126            int price = Integer.parseInt( priceJTextField.getText() );
127
128            // get an integer from downPaymentJTextField
129            int downPayment =
130                Integer.parseInt( downPaymentJTextField.getText() );
131
132            // get a double from interestRateJTextField
133            double interest =
134                Double.parseDouble( interestRateJTextField.getText() );
135
136            // create table of options over different periods of time
137            processData( price, downPayment, interest );
138        }
```

Adding a `try` statement

Figure 24.10 Creating a `try` statement in the `calculateJButton` event handler.

5. ***Adding a catch block.*** Only one `catch` block is needed following the `try` block in this example because only one type of exception—a Number-FormatException will be thrown. Add lines 139–142 of Fig. 24.11 to your code. Line 139 specifies the type of exception that this block catches. In this case, you are trying to stop users from entering numbers with decimal points in a `JTextField` in which an integer is expected and entering non-numeric data, like 600p instead of 6000, in a `JTextField` in which numeric data is expected. If the user does not enter an `int` in priceJTextField, line 126 throws an exception of type NumberFormatException. Likewise, if the user does not enter an `int` in downPaymentJTextField, line 130 throws a NumberFormatException. If the user does not enter a `double` (or an `int`) into interestJTextField, line 134 (Fig. 24.10) also throws a NumberFormatException. The type of exception that you are handling is always declared in a `catch` block of the `try` statement. If you are attempting to catch multiple errors, you may use several `catch` block after the `try` block.

```
Source Editor [CarPayment *]                                      _ □ ×
137            processData( price, downPayment, interest );
138        }
139        catch ( NumberFormatException exception )
140        {
141
142        }
143
144    } // end method calculateJButtonActionPerformed
```

Adding a `catch` block

Figure 24.11 Adding a `catch` block.

6. ***Displaying an error message dialog.*** Add lines 138–142 of Fig. 24.12 to your code. If a NumberFormatException does occur, you want to inform the user of the error and ask the user to enter correct data. To do this, you will display a message dialog in a `JOptionPane` (Fig. 24.3). Since you are dealing with exceptions, you use the `JOptionPane`'s ERROR_MESSAGE constant. Recall that you use the `this` keyword to refer to the current object. In this example, the first argument passed to the showMessageDialog is the `this` keyword, which causes the error message dialog to appear in the center of the running application window. The second argument passed to the showMessageDialog is the message displayed in the dialog, the third argument sets the text displayed in the title bar of the message dialog and the last argument specifies the message type.

(cont.)

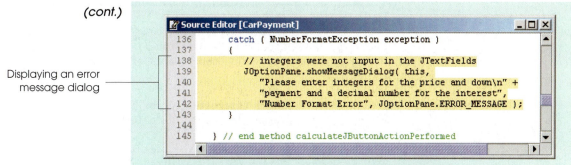

Displaying an error
message dialog

Figure 24.12 Displaying an error message dialog.

7. **Saving the application.** Save your modified source code file.

8. **Opening the Command Prompt window and changing directories.** Open the **Command Prompt** window by selecting **Start > Programs > Accessories > Command Prompt**. Change to your working directory, Enhanced-CarPayment, by typing cd C:\SimplyJava\EnhancedCarPayment.

9. **Compiling the application.** Compile your application by typing javac CarPayment.java.

10. **Running the application.** When your application compiles correctly, run it by typing java CarPayment. Figure 24.13 shows the result when the user attempts to enter invalid input. Redo the test drive using your new version of the application to see that it works properly. Click the **OK** JButton to close the message dialog.

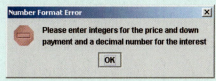

Figure 24.13 Error message dialog displayed when NumberFormatException occurs.

11. **Closing the application.** Close your running application by clicking the window's close button.

12. **Closing the Command Prompt window.** Close the **Command Prompt** window by clicking its close button.

Figure 24.14 presents the source code for the **Enhanced Car Payment Calculator** application. The lines of code you added, viewed or modified in this tutorial are highlighted with a yellow background.

```
1   // Tutorial 24: CarPayment.java
2   // This application uses exception-handling to handle invalid input.
3   import java.awt.*;
4   import java.text.DecimalFormat;
5   import java.awt.event.*;
6   import javax.swing.*;
7
8   public class CarPayment extends JFrame
9   {
10      // JLabel and JTextField for price
11      private JLabel priceJLabel;
12      private JTextField priceJTextField;
```

Figure 24.14 **Enhanced Car Payment Calculator** application's code. (Part 1 of 5.)

```
13
14      // JLabel and JTextField for down payment
15      private JLabel downPaymentJLabel;
16      private JTextField downPaymentJTextField;
17
18      // JLabel and JTextField for interest rate
19      private JLabel interestRateJLabel;
20      private JTextField interestRateJTextField;
21
22      // JButton to calculate the monthly payments
23      private JButton calculateJButton;
24
25      // JTextArea to display the monthly payments
26      private JTextArea monthlyPaymentsJTextArea;
27
28      // no-argument constructor
29      public CarPayment()
30      {
31         createUserInterface();
32      }
33
34      // create and position GUI components; register event handlers
35      private void createUserInterface()
36      {
37         // get content pane and set layout to null
38         Container contentPane = getContentPane();
39
40         // enable explicit positioning of GUI components
41         contentPane.setLayout( null );
42
43         // set up priceJLabel
44         priceJLabel = new JLabel();
45         priceJLabel.setBounds( 40, 24, 80, 21 );
46         priceJLabel.setText( "Price:" );
47         contentPane.add( priceJLabel );
48
49         // set up priceJTextField
50         priceJTextField = new JTextField();
51         priceJTextField.setBounds( 184, 24, 56, 21 );
52         priceJTextField.setHorizontalAlignment( JTextField.RIGHT );
53         contentPane.add( priceJTextField );
54
55         // set up downPaymentJLabel
56         downPaymentJLabel = new JLabel();
57         downPaymentJLabel.setBounds( 40, 56, 96, 21 );
58         downPaymentJLabel.setText( "Down payment:" );
59         contentPane.add( downPaymentJLabel );
60
61         // set up downPaymentJTextField
62         downPaymentJTextField = new JTextField();
63         downPaymentJTextField.setBounds( 184, 56, 56, 21 );
64         downPaymentJTextField.setHorizontalAlignment(
65            JTextField.RIGHT );
66         contentPane.add( downPaymentJTextField );
67
68         // set up interestRateJLabel
69         interestRateJLabel = new JLabel();
70         interestRateJLabel.setBounds( 40, 88, 120, 21 );
```

Figure 24.14 **Enhanced Car Payment Calculator** application's code. (Part 2 of 5.)

```
71      interestRateJLabel.setText( "Annual interest rate:" );
72      contentPane.add( interestRateJLabel );
73
74      // set up interestRateJTextField
75      interestRateJTextField = new JTextField();
76      interestRateJTextField.setBounds( 184, 88, 56, 21 );
77      interestRateJTextField.setHorizontalAlignment(
78         JTextField.RIGHT );
79      contentPane.add( interestRateJTextField );
80
81      // set up calculateJButton
82      calculateJButton = new JButton();
83      calculateJButton.setBounds( 92, 128, 94, 24 );
84      calculateJButton.setText( "Calculate" );
85      contentPane.add( calculateJButton );
86      calculateJButton.addActionListener(
87
88         new ActionListener() // anonymous inner class
89         {
90            // event handler called when calculateJButton is clicked
91            public void actionPerformed( ActionEvent event )
92            {
93               calculateJButtonActionPerformed( event );
94            }
95
96         } // end anonymous inner class
97
98      ); // end call to addActionListener
99
100     // set up monthlyPaymentsJTextArea
101     monthlyPaymentsJTextArea = new JTextArea();
102     monthlyPaymentsJTextArea.setEditable( false );
103     monthlyPaymentsJTextArea.setBounds( 28, 168, 232, 90 );
104     contentPane.add( monthlyPaymentsJTextArea );
105
106     // set properties of application's window
107     setTitle( "Car Payment Calculator" ); // set title-bar string
108     setSize( 288, 302 );                  // set window size
109     setVisible( true );                   // display window
110
111  } // end method createUserInterface
112
113  // calculate the monthly car payments
114  private void calculateJButtonActionPerformed( ActionEvent event )
115  {
116     // clear JTextArea
117     monthlyPaymentsJTextArea.setText( "" );
118
119     // try to retrieve price and down payment
120     try
121     {
122        // get an integer from priceJTextField
123        int price = Integer.parseInt( priceJTextField.getText() );
124
125        // get an integer from downPaymentJTextField
126        int downPayment =
127           Integer.parseInt( downPaymentJTextField.getText() );
128
```

Enclosing the code that may cause exceptions in a **try** block

Figure 24.14 Enhanced Car Payment Calculator application's code. (Part 3 of 5.)

```
129              // get a double from interestRateJTextField
130              double interest =
131                 Double.parseDouble( interestRateJTextField.getText() );
132
133              // create table of options over different periods of time
134              processData( price, downPayment, interest );
135           }
136           catch ( NumberFormatException exception )
137           {
138              // integers were not input in the JTextFields
139              JOptionPane.showMessageDialog( this,
140                 "Please enter integers for the price and down\n" +
141                 "payment and a decimal number for the interest",
142                 "Number Format Error", JOptionPane.ERROR_MESSAGE );
143           }
144
145        } // end method calculateJButtonActionPerformed
146
147        // process entered data and calculate payments over
148        // each time interval
149        private void processData( int price, int downPayment,
150           double interest )
151        {
152           // calculate loan amount and monthly interest
153           int loanAmount = price - downPayment;
154           double monthlyInterest = interest / 1200;
155
156           // format to display monthlyPayment in currency format
157           DecimalFormat dollars = new DecimalFormat( "$0.00" );
158
159           int years = 2; // repetition counter
160
161           // add header JTextArea
162           monthlyPaymentsJTextArea.append( "Months\tMonthly Payments" );
163
164           // while years is less than or equal to five years
165           while ( years <= 5 )
166           {
167              // calculate payment period
168              int months = 12 * years;
169
170              // get monthlyPayment
171              double monthlyPayment = calculateMonthlyPayment(
172                 monthlyInterest, months, loanAmount );
173
174              // insert result into JTextArea
175              monthlyPaymentsJTextArea.append( "\n" + months + "\t" +
176                 dollars.format( monthlyPayment ) );
177
178              years++; // increment counter
179
180           } // end while
181
182        } // end method processData
183
```

End of **try** block → line 135

Add a catch block to handle **NumberFormatException** → lines 136–143

Figure 24.14 Enhanced Car Payment Calculator application's code. (Part 4 of 5.)

```
184    // calculate monthlyPayment
185    private double calculateMonthlyPayment( double monthlyInterest,
186       int months, int loanAmount )
187    {
188       double base = Math.pow( 1 + monthlyInterest, months );
189       return loanAmount * monthlyInterest / ( 1 - ( 1 / base ) );
190
191    } // end method calculateMonthlyPayment
192
193    // main method
194    public static void main( String[] args )
195    {
196       CarPayment application = new CarPayment();
197       application.setDefaultCloseOperation( JFrame.EXIT_ON_CLOSE );
198
199    } // end method main
200
201 } // end class CarPayment
```

Figure 24.14   Enhanced Car Payment Calculator application's code. (Part 5 of 5.)

SELF-REVIEW   1. If you are attempting to catch multiple errors, you may use several _____ blocks after the _____ block.

    a) `try, catch`   b) `catch, try`

    c) `finally, try`   d) None of the above.

2. The exception you wish to handle should be declared as a parameter of the _____ block.

    a) `try`   b) `catch`

    c) `finally`   d) None of the above.

Answers: 1) b. 2) b.

24.6 Wrap-Up

In this tutorial, you learned exception handling concepts and how exception handling is used in Java. You learned how to use the `try` statement and the `catch` block to handle exceptions in your applications, and how to use the `throws` block to throw exceptions in your methods. You also learned how to use the `throw` keyword to rethrow an exception than cannot be handled in the `catch` block. Next, you learned the inheritance hierarchy of exception classes. You applied your knowledge of exception handling in Java to enhance your **Car Payment Calculator** application to calculate the price of a car while checking for input errors. You used the `try` block to enclose the statements that may throw a `NumberFormatException` and the `catch` block to handle the `NumberFormatException`.

In the next tutorial, you will learn how data is represented in a computer. You will be introduced to the concepts of files and streams, and you will learn how to store data in sequential-access files. You also will learn how to use the `finally` block to close the streams for reading from and writing to files.

SKILLS SUMMARY   **Handling an exception**

- Enclose in a `try` block code that may generate an exception and any code that should not execute if an exception occurs.

- Follow the `try` block with one or more `catch` blocks. Each `catch` block is an exception handler that specifies the type of exception it can handle.

KEY TERMS

catch block—Also called an exception handler, this block executes when the corresponding `try` block in the application detects an exceptional situation and throws an exception of the type the `catch` block declares.

catch-or-declare requirement—The code that generates a checked exception should be wrapped in a `try` block and provide a `catch` block for that checked exception. The method that contains the code that generates a checked exception must provide a `throws` block containing the checked exception unless it provides a handler for it.

checked exception—An exception type that is not a subclass of `RuntimeException`, which must satisfy the catch-or-declare requirement.

Error class—The class that represents exceptional situations happening in the Java runtime system that typically should not be caught by an application.

exception—An indication of a problem that occurs during an application's execution.

Exception class—The class that represents exceptional situations occuring in a Java application that should be caught and handled by the application.

exception handler—A block that executes (in a `catch` block) when the application detects an exceptional situation and throws an exception.

exception handling—Creating applications that can resolve (or handle) problems during application execution.

exception parameter—Identifies the exception type the exception handler can process.

finally block—A block that is guaranteed to execute if its corresponding try block executes. Typically, the `finally` block is used to release resources.

NumberFormatException class—A subclass of `RuntimeException` that is thrown when the application cannot convert a string to a desired numeric type, such as `int` or `double`.

rethrow the exception—The `catch` block can defer the exception handling (or perhaps a portion of it) to another `catch` block using the `throw` keyword.

RuntimeException class—The superclass of all unchecked exceptions that can be thrown during application execution.

Throwable class—The superclass of all exceptions and errors.

throw keyword—The keyword used to rethrow an exception in a `catch` block.

throws an exception—A method throws an exception if a problem occurs during method execution that the method is unable to handle.

throws clause—The `throws` clause appears after the parameter list and before the method body. It specifies the exceptions the method throws, but does not handle. The clause contains a comma-separated list of exceptions the method will throw if a problem occurs when the method executes.

try block—A block that contains statements that might cause exceptions and statements that should not execute if an exception occurs.

try statement—A statement that consists of keyword `try`, followed by braces ({}) that delimit a `try` block, followed by one or more `catch` blocks, optionally followed by a `finally` block.

uncaught exception—An exception that does not have an exception handler. Uncaught exceptions might terminate application execution.

unchecked exception—An exception type that is a subclass of `RuntimeException`. Such exceptions are thrown during application execution.

JAVA LIBRARY REFERENCE

Error A class that represents exceptional situations happening in the Java runtime system that typically should not be caught by an application.

Exception A class that represents exceptional situations occuring in a Java application that should be caught by the application.

NumberFormatException A subclass of `RuntimeException` that is thrown when the application cannot convert a string to a desired numeric type, such as `int` or `double`.

RunTimeException The superclass of all unchecked exceptions that can be thrown during application execution.

Throwable The superclass of all exceptions and errors.

MULTIPLE-CHOICE QUESTIONS

24.1 Dealing with exceptional situations as a program executes is called exception _____.
- a) detection
- b) handling
- c) resolution
- d) debugging

24.2 A(n) _____ is always followed by at least one catch block or at least one finally block.
- a) if statement
- b) throws block
- c) try block
- d) None of the above.

24.3 The method call Integer.parseInt("123.45"); will throw a(n) _____.
- a) NumberFormatException
- b) ParsingException
- c) ArithmeticException
- d) None of the above.

24.4 If no exceptions are thrown in a try block, _____.
- a) the catch block(s) are skipped
- b) all catch blocks are executed
- c) an error occurs
- d) the default exception is thrown

24.5 Each catch block specifies a(n) _____ that identifies the exception type the handler can process.
- a) try block
- b) parameter
- c) error handler
- d) thrower

24.6 A try block can have _____ associated with it.
- a) only one catch block
- b) several finally blocks
- c) one or more catch blocks
- d) None of the above.

24.7 All exception types that are subclasses of RuntimeException are _____.
- a) fatal errors
- b) logic errors
- c) checked exceptions
- d) unchecked exceptions

24.8 _____ is the superclass of all Exceptions and Errors.
- a) Throwable
- b) CheckedException
- c) Catchable
- d) RuntimeException

24.9 The _____ class and its subclasses typically should not be caught by an application you will develop.
- a) NumberFormatException
- b) Exception
- c) RuntimeException
- d) Error

24.10 A _____ is executed if an exception is thrown from a try block or if no exception is thrown.
- a) catch block
- b) finally block
- c) exception handler
- d) All of the above.

EXERCISES

24.11 (*Enhanced Miles Per Gallon Application*) Modify the **Miles Per Gallon** application (Exercise 12.13) to include exception handling to handle the NumberFormatException when converting the strings in the JTextFields to doubles (Fig. 24.15). The original application allowed the user to input the number of miles driven and the number of gallons used for a tank of gas, in order to determine the number of miles the user was able to drive on one gallon of gas.

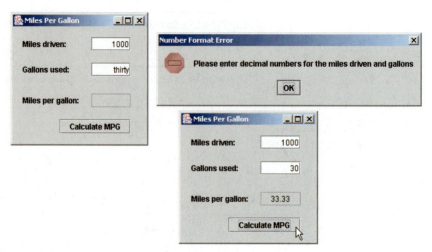

Figure 24.15 Enhanced **Miles Per Gallon** application's GUI.

a) *Copying the template to your working directory*. Copy the directory C:\Examples\ Tutorial24\Exercises\EnhancedMilesPerGallon to your C:\SimplyJava direc- tory.

b) *Opening the template file*. Open the MilesPerGallon.java file in your text editor.

c) *Adding a try block*. Find the calculateMPGJButtonActionPerformed method, which immediately follows createUserInterface. Enclose lines 113–120 in a try block.

d) *Adding a catch block*. Immediately following the try block you added in *Step c*, add a catch block to catch a NumberFormatException. Inside the catch block, add code to display an error message dialog at the center of the running application.

e) *Saving the application*. Save your modified source code file.

f) *Opening the Command Prompt window and changing directories*. Open the **Com- mand Prompt** window by selecting **Start > Programs > Accessories > Command Prompt**. Change to your working directory, EnhancedMilesPerGallon, by typing cd C:\SimplyJava\EnhancedMilesPerGallon.

g) *Compiling the application*. Compile the application by typing javac MilesPerGal- lon.java.

h) *Running the completed application*. When your application compiles correctly, run it by typing java MilesPerGallon. The error message dialog displayed when your completed **Miles Per Gallon** application throws an exception should look similar to the dialog shown in Fig. 24.15.

i) *Closing the application*. Close your running application by clicking the window's close button.

j) *Closing the Command Prompt window*. Close the **Command Prompt** window by clicking its close button.

24.12 (*Enhanced Prime Numbers Application*) Modify the **Prime Numbers** application (Exercise 12.17) to include exception handling to handle the NumberFormatException when converting the strings in the JTextFields to ints (Fig. 24.16). The original application took two numbers (representing a lower bound and an upper bound) and determined all of the prime numbers within the specified bounds, inclusive. An int greater than 1 is said to be prime if it is divisible by only 1 and itself. For example, 2, 3, 5 and 7 are prime numbers, but 4, 6, 8 and 9 are not.

a) *Copying the template to your working directory*. Copy the directory C:\Examples\ Tutorial24\Exercises\EnhancedPrimeNumbers to your C:\SimplyJava directory.

b) *Opening the template file*. Open the PrimeNumbers.java file in your text editor.

c) *Adding a try block*. Find the calculatePrimesJButtonActionPerformed method, which immediately follows createUserInterface. Enclose lines 116–123 in a try block.

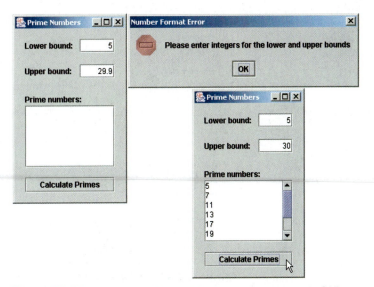

Figure 24.16 Enhanced **Prime Numbers** application's GUI.

d) *Adding a catch block*. Immediately following the try block you added in *Step c*, add a catch block to catch a NumberFormatException. Inside the catch block, add code to display an error message dialog at the center of the running application.

e) *Saving the application*. Save your modified source code file.

f) *Opening the Command Prompt window and changing directories*. Open the **Command Prompt** window by selecting **Start > Programs > Accessories > Command Prompt**. Change to your working directory, EnhancedPrimeNumbers, by typing cd C:\SimplyJava\EnhancedPrimeNumbers.

g) *Compiling the application*. Compile your application by typing javac PrimeNumbers.java.

h) *Running the completed application*. When your application compiles correctly, run it by typing java PrimeNumbers. The error message dialog displayed when your completed **Prime Numbers** application throws an exception should look similar to the dialog shown in Fig. 24.16.

i) *Closing the application*. Close your running application by clicking the window's close button.

j) *Closing the Command Prompt window*. Close the **Command Prompt** window by clicking its close button.

24.13 (*Enhanced Simple Calculator Application*) Modify the **Simple Calculator** application (Exercise 5.13) to include exception handling to handle the NumberFormatException when converting the strings in the JTextFields to ints and the ArithmeticException when performing the division (Fig. 24.17). The application should still perform simple addition, subtraction, multiplication and division.

a) *Copying the template to your working directory*. Copy the directory C:\Examples\Tutorial24\Exercises\EnhancedSimpleCalculator to your C:\SimplyJava directory.

b) *Opening the template file*. Open the SimpleCalculator.java file in your text editor.

c) *Adding a try block to the addJButtonActionPerformed method*. Find the addJButtonActionPerformed method, which immediately follows secondNumberJ-TextFieldKeyPressed. Enclose the body of the addJButtonActionPerformed method (lines 220–229) in a try block.

d) *Adding a catch block to the addJButtonActionPerformed method*. Immediately following the try block inside the addJButtonActionPerformed method, add a catch block to catch a NumberFormatException. Inside the catch block, add code to display an error message dialog at the center of the running application.

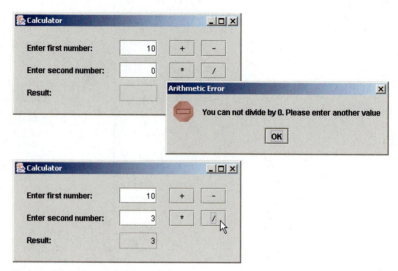

Figure 24.17 Enhanced **Simple Calculator** application.

e) *Adding a try block to the subtractJButtonActionPerformed method.* Find the subtractJButtonActionPerformed method, which immediately follows addJButtonActionPerformed. Enclose the body of the subtractJButtonActionPerformed in a try block.

f) *Adding a catch block to the subtractJButtonActionPerformed method.* Immediately following the try block inside the subtractJButtonActionPerformed method, add a catch block to catch a NumberFormatException. Inside the catch block, add code to display an error message dialog at the center of the running application.

g) *Adding a try block to the multiplyJButtonActionPerformed method.* Find the multiplyJButtonActionPerformed method, which immediately follows subtractJButtonActionPerformed. Enclose the body of the multiplayJButtonActionPerformed in a try block.

h) *Adding a catch block to the multiplyJButtonActionPerformed method.* Immediately following the try block inside the multiplyJButtonActionPerformed method, add a catch block to catch a NumberFormatException. Inside the catch block, add code to display an error message dialog at the center of the running application.

i) *Adding a try block to the divideJButtonActionPerformed method.* Find the divideJButtonActionPerformed method, which immediately follows multiplyJButtonActionPerformed. Enclose the body of the divideJButtonActionPerformed in a try block.

j) *Adding a catch block to the divideJButtonActionPerformed method.* Immediately following the try block inside the divideJButtonActionPerformed method, add a catch block to catch a NumberFormatException. Inside the catch block, add code to display an error message dialog at the center of the running application.

k) *Adding a second catch block to the divideJButtonActionPerformed method.* Immediately following the first catch block inside the divideJButtonActionPerformed method, add a catch block to catch an ArithmeticException. An ArithmeticException is thrown when division by zero in integer arithmetic occurs. Inside the catch block, add code to display an error message dialog at the center of the running application.

l) *Saving the application.* Save your modified source code file.

m) *Opening the Command Prompt window and changing directories.* Open the **Command Prompt** window by selecting **Start > Programs > Accessories > Command Prompt**. Change to your working directory, EnhancedSimpleCalculator, by typing cd C:\SimplyJava\EnhancedSimpleCalculator.

n) *Compiling the application.* Compile your application by typing javac SimpleCalculator.java.

o) *Running the completed application.* When your application compiles correctly, run it by typing java SimpleCalculator. The error message dialog displayed when your

completed **Simple Calculator** application throws a `NumberFormatException` should look similar to the two previous exercises. When a user attempts to divide a number by zero, the error message dialog in Fig. 24.17 should appear.

p) *Closing the application*. Close your running application by clicking the window's close button.

q) *Closing the Command Prompt window*. Close the **Command Prompt** window by clicking its close button.

What does this code do? ▶ | **24.14** What does the following code do?

```
1   try
2   {
3      double myDouble1 =
4         Double.parseDouble( double1JTextField.getText() );
5      double myDouble2 =
6         Double.parseDouble( double2JTextField.getText() );
7      double result = myDouble1 * myDouble2;
8      resultJTextField.setText( String.valueOf( result ) );
9   }
10  catch( NumberFormatException exception )
11  {
12     JOptionPane.showMessageDialog( this,
13        "Please enter decimal numbers",
14        "NumberFormatException occurs", JOptionPane.ERROR_MESSAGE );
15  }
```

What's wrong with this code? ▶ | **24.15** The following code should add integers from two `JTextFields` and display the result in `resultJTextField`. Find the error(s) in the following code:

```
1   try
2   {
3      int first = Integer.parseInt( firstJTextField.getText() );
4      int second = Integer.parseInt( secondJTextField.getText() );
5      int result = first + second;
6   }
7
8   resultJTextField.setText( String.valueOf( result ) );
9
10  catch()
11  {
12     JOptionPane.showMessageDialog( this,
13        "Please enter valid integers", "Number Format Error",
14        OptionPane.ERROR_MESSAGE );
15  }
```

Programming Challenge ▶ | **24.16** (*Enhanced Vending Machine Application*) The **Vending Machine** application from Tutorial 2 has been modified to add exception handling to handle the `ArrayIndexOutOf-BoundsException` exception when selecting items out of the range 0 through 7 (Fig. 24.18). To get a snack, the user must type the number of the desired snack in the `inputJTextField` then press the **Dispense Snack:** `JButton`. The name of the snack is displayed in the `dis-playJTextField`.

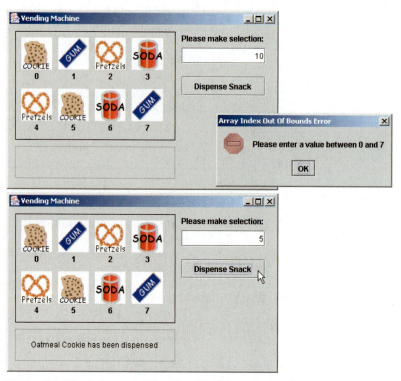

Figure 24.18 Enhanced **Vending Machine** application.

a) *Copying the template to your working directory*. Copy the directory C:\Examples\ Tutorial24\Exercises\EnhancedVendingMachine to your C:\SimplyJava direc- tory.

b) *Opening the template file*. Open the VendingMachine.java file in your text editor.

c) *Adding a try block*. Find the dispenseJButtonActionPerformed method, which immediately follows createUserInterface. Enclose lines 236–240 in a try block.

d) *Adding a catch block*. Immediately following the try block you added in *Step c*, add a catch block to catch a NumberFormatException. Inside the catch block, add code to display an error message dialog at the center of the running application.

e) *Adding a second catch block*. Immediately following the catch block you added in *Step d*, add a second catch block to catch an ArrayIndexOutOfBoundsException. An ArrayIndexOutOfBoundsException occurs when the application attempts to access an array with an invalid index. Inside the catch block, add code to display an error message dialog at the center of the running application.

f) *Saving the application*. Save your modified source code file.

g) *Opening the Command Prompt window and changing directories*. Open the **Com- mand Prompt** by selecting **Start > Programs > Accessories > Command Prompt**. Change to your working directory, VendingMachine, by typing cd C:\SimplyJava\ VendingMachine.

h) *Compiling the application*. Compile the application by typing javac VendingMa- chine.java.

i) *Running the completed application*. When your application compiles correctly, run it by typing java VendingMachine. The JOptionPane displayed when your completed **Vending Machine** application throws a NumberFormatException should look simi- lar to the previous exercises. When a user attempts to access an element out of the range 0 through 7, the JOptionPane in Fig. 24.18 should appear.

j) *Closing the application*. Close your running application by clicking the window's close button.

k) *Closing the Command Prompt window*. Close the **Command Prompt** window by clicking its close button.

Objectives

In this tutorial, you will learn to:
- Create, read from, write to and update files.
- Understand a computer's data hierarchy.
- Become familiar with sequential-access file processing.
- Use the FileReader with BufferedReader capabilities to read a line of text from sequential-access files.
- Use the FileWriter with PrintWriter capabilities to write text to sequential-access files.
- Use the finally block with exception handling to ensure that certain actions are always performed.

Outline

Ticket Information Application

Introducing Sequential-Access Files

You have used variables and arrays to store data temporarily—the data are lost when a method or application terminates. When you want to store data for a longer period of time, you use **files**. A file is a collection of data that is given a name such as data.txt or Welcome.java. Data in files exist even after the application that created the data terminates. This type of data often is called **persistent data**. Computers store files on **secondary storage media**, including magnetic disks (for example, the hard drive of your computer), optical disks (such as CD-ROMs or DVDs) and magnetic tapes (which are similar to music cassette tapes).

File processing, which includes creating, reading from and writing to files, is an important capability of Java. It enables Java to support commercial applications that typically process massive amounts of persistent data. In this tutorial, you will learn about **sequential-access files**, which contain information that is read from a file in the same order that it was originally written to the file. You will learn how to create, open and write to a sequential-access file by building a **Write Event** application. This application allows the user to create or open a **text file** (a file containing human-readable characters) and to input the dates, times and descriptions of community events (such as concerts or sporting matches).

You will then learn how to read data from a file by building the **Ticket Information** application. This application displays data from a file created by the **Write Event** application. Along the way, you will get more practice using two-dimensional arrays, which are used in this application to store data read from a file.

25.1 Test-Driving the Write Event and Ticket Information Applications

Many communities and businesses use computer applications to allow their members and customers to view information about upcoming events, such as movies, concerts, and sporting events. The **Write Event** application that you will build in this tutorial writes the community event information to a sequential-access file. The **Write Event** application must meet the following requirements:

Application Requirements

To create an application that reads event information from a file, you will need first to create another application that writes event information to a file. The user should be provided with input fields for the day, time, price, name and description of each event. The user should be able to specify the file's location and name.

The **Ticket Information** application that you will build displays the data stored in the file generated by the **Write Event** application. The **Ticket Information** application must meet the following requirements:

Application Requirements

A local town has asked you to write an application that allows its residents to view community events for the current month, such as concerts, sporting events, movies and other forms of entertainment. The events have already been written to the file `calendar.txt` *using the **Write Event** application. When the user selects a day, the application should indicate whether there are events scheduled for that day. The application should list the scheduled events and allow the user to select a particular event. The application should then display the time, price and a brief description of the event. The application should inform the user when there are no events scheduled for a selected day.*

Your application will allow a user to select a date from a `JSpinner` GUI component. For simplicity, the day will be an integer value between 1 and 31 (inclusive). It is assumed that the events are for the current month of the current year, so the user should only be interested in the day of the month. We also assume that the month contains 31 days. The application will open a text file and read its contents to display information about events scheduled for the selected date. You begin by test-driving the completed application. Next, you will learn the additional Java technologies you will need to create your own version of this application.

Test-Driving the Ticket Information and Write Event Applications

1. *Locating the completed application.* Open the **Command Prompt** window by selecting **Start > Programs > Accessories > Command Prompt**. Change to your completed **Ticket Information** application directory by typing `cd C:\Examples\Tutorial25\CompletedApplication\TicketInformation`.

2. *Running the Ticket Information application.* Type `java TicketInformation` in the **Command Prompt** window to run the application (Fig. 25.1). At the top of the application, a `JSpinner` is provided for you to select a day. The `JSpinner` currently displays the value 1, indicating the first day of the current month. You are also provided with a `JComboBox` listing any events for the day specified in the `JSpinner`. The text **- No Events -** in the `JComboBox` indicates that there are no events for the specified day.

3. *Getting event information.* Select the 19th day of the month. Notice that the `JComboBox` now displays an event's information (Fig. 25.2). The time, price and description of the event appear in the **Description:** `JTextArea`. Click the down arrow on the **Pick an event:** `JComboBox`. There is only one event, **Film Festival**, for this day. If there were multiple events in one day, they would all be listed in the `JComboBox`. The **Description:** `JTextArea` would display information about the first event in the list. To view a description of another event, you need to select that event in the **Pick an event:** `JComboBox`. You will see an example of this shortly.

(cont.)

JSpinner

JComboBox lists any events

JTextArea displays
event details

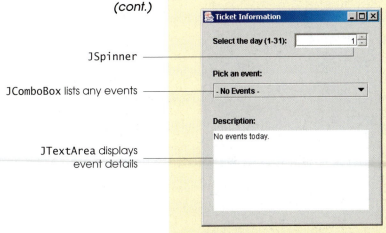

Figure 25.1 **Ticket Information** application's GUI.

Event information displayed

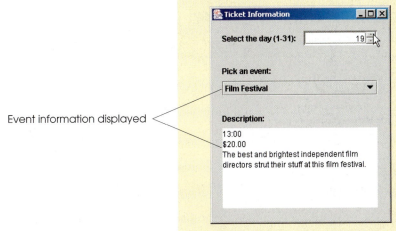

Figure 25.2 **Ticket Information** application displaying event information.

4. *Viewing other events.* Select other dates (such as the 4th, the 5th and the 28th) and view the results. The 4th should display no events, the 5th should display information about a talent show, and the 28th should display information about a city tour.

5. *Closing the running application.* Close your running application by clicking the window's close button. Leave the **Command Prompt** window open.

6. *Adding events using the Write Event application.* In the **Command Prompt** window, change to your completed **Write Event** application directory by typing cd C:\Examples\Tutorial25\CompletedApplication\ WriteEvent. Type java WriteEvent in the **Command Prompt** window to run the application (Fig. 25.3). Input fields are provided for the user to enter the day, time, price, name and description of an event. The **Time:** JSpinner initially displays the current time (you will learn how to read the system clock in this tutorial). There are three JButtons, but only the **Open File...** JButton is enabled. A file must be opened before event data can be written to it.

7. *Opening a file.* The file used by your **Ticket Information** application is cal- endar.txt, located in the TicketInformation directory. To add events to this file, you need to open it. Click the **Open File...** JButton to open the **Open File for Write Event** dialog (Fig. 25.4). Browse to the C:\Examples\ Tutorial25\CompletedApplication\TicketInformation directory and select calendar.txt. Click the **Open** JButton.

(cont.)

JSpinner for the day of the event —

JTextField for the price of the event

JTextArea displays the event description

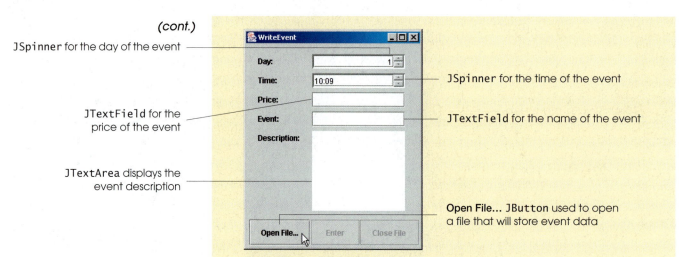

JSpinner for the time of the event

JTextField for the name of the event

Open File... JButton used to open a file that will store event data

Figure 25.3 **Write Event** application enables user to store event data.

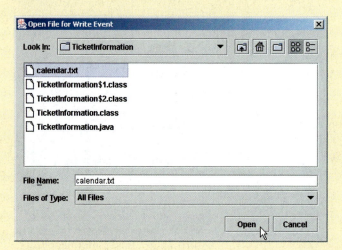

Figure 25.4 Dialog enables users to specify a file that will store event data.

8. ***Entering an event.*** You will now be returned to the application's window. Notice that the **Open File...** JButton is disabled (because the file has been opened) and that the **Enter** and **Close File** JButtons are enabled. Enter information for an event as shown in the left image of Fig. 25.5, then click the **Enter** JButton. Do not press *Enter* while writing into the **Description:** JTextArea, because doing so adds extra lines of text to the calendar.txt. The data entered is written to the file specified in the previous step (calendar.txt), and the fields for the event's price, name and description are cleared (right image of Fig. 25.5). Also notice that highlighting the hours portion of the JSpinner enables you to click the up/down arrows and go forwards or backwords with hours using a 24 hour clock. You can do the same with the minutes portion of the JSpinner.

9. ***Closing the file.*** Enter another event as shown in the left image of Fig. 25.6, then click the **Enter** JButton. Next, click the **Close File** JButton (right image of Fig. 25.6). The file calendar.txt has now been closed. Notice that the price, name and description fields are again cleared and that the **Open File...** JButton is enabled, so that you can open another file or reopen calendar.txt. Because there is no file currently open, the **Enter** and **Close File** JButtons are disabled.

10. ***Closing the running application.*** Close your running application by clicking the window's close button.

(cont.)

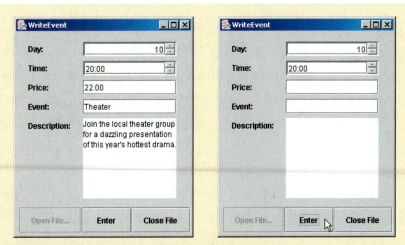

Figure 25.5   Adding an event to `calendar.txt`.

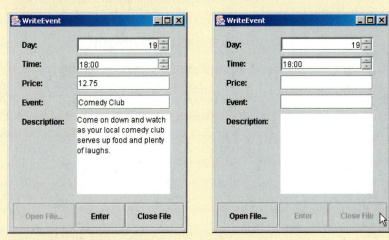

Figure 25.6   Entering another event and closing the file.

11. ***Viewing the new events.*** Change to your completed **Ticket Information** application directory by typing `cd C:\Examples\Tutorial25\Com-pletedApplication\TicketInformation`. Type the command `java TicketInformation` in the **Command Prompt** window to run the application. You have now added events on the 10th and 19th. Select these days and notice that the events are now displayed. Recall from Fig. 25.2 that the 19th had only one event. With **19** selected in the `JSpinner`, click the down arrow on the **Pick an event:** `JComboBox` and notice that there are now two events, including the event added in *Step 9* (Fig. 25.7). "Toggle" back and forth between these to confirm that the correct event is displayed each time in the **Description:** `JTextArea`.

12. ***Closing the running application.*** Close your running application by clicking the window's close button.

13. ***Closing the Command Prompt window.*** Close the **Command Prompt** window by clicking its close button.

(cont.)

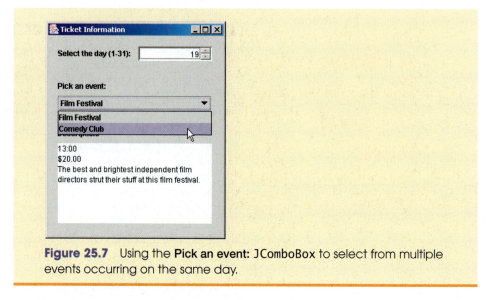

Figure 25.7 Using the **Pick an event: JComboBox** to select from multiple events occurring on the same day.

25.2 Data Hierarchy

Data items processed by computers form a **data hierarchy** (Fig. 25.8), in which data items become larger and more complex in structure as they progress from bits, to characters to fields and, finally, to larger data structures.

Throughout this book, you have been manipulating data in your applications. The data has been in several forms: **decimal digits** (0, 1, 2, 3, 4, 5, 6, 7, 8 and 9), **letters** (A–Z and a–z) and **special symbols** ($, @, %, &, *, (,), -, +, ", :, ?, / and many others). Digits, letters and special symbols are referred to as **characters**. The set of all characters used to write applications and represent data items on a particular computer is called that computer's **character set**.

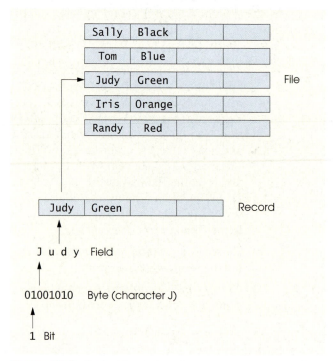

Figure 25.8 Data hierarchy.

Ultimately, all data items processed by a computer are reduced to combinations of zeros and ones. The smallest data item that computers support is called a **bit**.

"Bit" is short for "**binary digit**"—a digit that can be one of two values. Each bit can be set only to the value 0 or the value 1. Computer circuitry performs various simple bit manipulations, such as examining the value of a bit, setting the value of a bit and reversing the value of a bit (from 1 to 0 or from 0 to 1). This approach has been adopted because it is simple and economical to build electronic devices that can assume two stable states—one state representing 0 and the other representing 1. It is remarkable that the extensive functions performed by computers involve only the most fundamental manipulations of 0s and 1s.

Every character in a computer's character set is represented as a pattern of 0s and 1s. **Bytes** are composed of 8 bits. Characters in Java are **Unicode® characters**, which are composed of 2 bytes (16 bits). Programming with data in the low-level form of bits is difficult, so programmers create applications and data items with characters, and computers manipulate and process these characters as patterns of bits.

Just as characters are composed of bits, **fields** are composed of characters (Fig. 25.8). A field is a group of characters that conveys some meaning. For example, a field consisting of uppercase and lowercase letters can represent a person's name.

Typically, a **record** (which usually is represented as a class in Java) is a collection of several related fields (called instance variables in Java). In a payroll system, for example, a record for a particular employee might include the following fields:

1. Employee identification number

2. Name

3. Address

4. Hourly pay rate

5. Number of exemptions claimed

6. Year-to-date earnings

7. Amount of taxes withheld

Thus, a record is a group of related fields. In the preceding example, each field is associated with the same employee. A file is a group of related records. A company's payroll file normally contains one record for each employee. Hence, a payroll file for a small company might contain only 22 records, whereas a payroll file for a large company might contain 100,000 or more records. It is not unusual for a company to have many files, some containing millions, billions or even trillions of characters of information.

To facilitate the retrieval of specific records from a file, at least one field in each record is chosen as a **record key**. A record key identifies a record as belonging to a particular person or entity and distinguishes that record from all other records. Therefore, the record key must be unique. In the payroll record just described, the employee identification number normally would be chosen as the record key because each employee's identification number is different.

There are many ways to organize records in a file. The most common type of organization is called a sequential file, in which records typically are stored in order by a record key field. In a payroll file, records usually are placed in order by employee identification number. The first employee record in the file contains the lowest employee identification number, and subsequent records contain increasingly higher employee identification numbers.

Most businesses use many different files to store data. For example, a company might have payroll files, accounts receivable files (listing money due from clients), accounts payable files (listing money due to suppliers), inventory files (listing facts about all the items handled by the business) and many other types of files. Sometimes, a group of related files is called a **database**. A collection of programs designed to create and manage databases is called a **database management system** (DBMS). You will learn more about databases in Tutorial 26 and Tutorial 31.

1. The smallest data item a computer can process is called a _____.

    a) database   b) byte

    c) file   d) bit

2. A _____ is a group of related records.

    a) file   b) field

    c) bit   d) byte

Answers: 1) d. 2) a.

25.3 Files and Streams

Java views files as sequences of bytes or characters called **streams** (Fig. 25.9). In this tutorial, you will learn how to manipulate files that contain characters. File processing is performed in Java applications by using objects of classes from the **java.io** package. This package contains many classes, including those you will use to write characters into a file and to read characters from a file. You will be briefly introduced to some of these classes in this section.

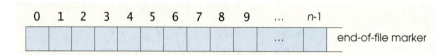

Figure 25.9 Java's conceptual view of an *n*-byte file.

You will use objects of the **FileWriter** and **FileReader** classes to open files for output and input of characters, respectively. These classes allow you to write characters to and read characters from files.

In the test-drive of the **Write Events** application, you saw the application process information such as strings and numbers. However, a FileWriter object can write only characters to a file. Java enables you to output strings and numbers (and any other types) as text (that is, characters) with a **PrintWriter** object, but a PrintWriter does not know how to write to a file. In this tutorial, you will learn how to combine the FileWriter and PrintWriter capabilities so that your application can output strings and numbers to a text file.

In a similar manner, the **Ticket Information** application reads one line of text at a time from the file created by the **Write Events** application. However, a FileReader object can read only characters from a file. Java enables you to read lines of text with an object of the **BufferedReader** class, but a BufferedReader does not know how to read from a file. You will learn how to combine the FileReader and BufferedReader capabilities so that your application can read lines of text from a file.

1. When used together with FileWriter, the _____ can write strings and numbers to a text file.

    a) OutputFile   b) StreamWriter

    c) PrintWriter   d) BufferedReader

2. Java views a file as a sequential _____ of bytes.

    a) stream   b) loop

    c) string   d) record

Answers: 1) c. 2) a.

25.4 Creating the Write Event Application: Writing to a File

Now you will create the **Write Event** application to enable a user to write community-event information to a sequential-access text file. First you need to analyze the application. The following pseudocode describes the basic operation of the **Write Event** application.

> When the user clicks the Open File... JButton:
>   Display a JFileChooser dialog
>   Retrieve the file selected by the user
>   Open the selected file for writing
>   Disable the Open File... JButton
>   Enable the Enter JButton
>   Enable the Close File JButton
>   Reset input fields
>
> When the user clicks the Enter JButton:
>   Add the day of the event and a newline to the file
>   Add the time of the event and a newline to the file
>   Add the price of the event and a newline to the file
>   Add the name of the event and a newline to the file
>   Add a description of the event and a newline to the file
>   Reset input fields
>
> When the user clicks the Close File JButton:
>   Close the file
>   Disable the Enter JButton
>   Enable the Open File... JButton
>   Disable the Close File JButton
>   Reset input fields

Now that you have test-driven the **Write Event** application and studied its pseudocode representation, you will use an ACE table to help you convert the pseudocode to Java. Figure 25.10 lists the actions, components and events required to complete your own version of this application.

Action/Component/ Event (ACE) Table for the Write Event Application

Action	Component/Object	Event
Label the application's components	`dayJLabel,` `timeJLabel,` `priceJLabel,` `eventJLabel,` `descriptionJLabel`	Application is run
	`openFileJButton`	User clicks **Open File...** JButton
Display a JFileChooser dialog	`fileChooser` `(JFileChooser)`	
Retrieve the file selected by the user	`fileChooser,` `selectedFile (File)`	
Open the selected file for writing	`outputFile (FileWriter),` `output (PrintWriter)`	
Disable the Open File... JButton	`openFileJButton`	
Enable the Enter JButton	`enterJButton`	
Enable the Close File JButton	`closeFileJButton`	
Reset input fields	`priceJTextField,` `eventJTextField,` `descriptionJTextArea`	

Figure 25.10 ACE table for the **Write Event** application. (Part 1 of 2.)

Action	Component/Object	Event
	enterJButton	User clicks **Enter** JButton
Add the day of the event and a newline to the file	dayJSpinner, output (PrintWriter)	
Add the time of the event and a newline to the file	timeJSpinner, output (PrintWriter)	
Add the price of the event and a newline to the file	priceJTextField, output (PrintWriter)	
Add the name of the event and a newline to the file	eventJTextField, output (PrintWriter)	
Add a description of the event and a newline to the file	descriptionJTextArea, output (PrintWriter)	
Reset input fields	priceJTextField, eventJTextField, descriptionJTextArea	
	closeFileJButton	User clicks **Close File** JButton
Close the file	output (PrintWriter)	
Disable the Enter JButton	enterJButton	
Enable the Open File... JButton	openFileJButton	
Disable the Close File JButton	closeFileJButton	
Reset input fields	priceJTextField, eventJTextField, descriptionJTextArea	

Figure 25.10   ACE table for the **Write Event** application. (Part 2 of 2.)

An important aspect of the **Ticket Information** application is its ability to read data sequentially from a file. You will need to create the file from which the **Ticket Information** application will read its data. Therefore, before you create the **Ticket Information** application, you must learn how to write data to a file sequentially.

The **Write Event** application stores in a text file the information input by a user. Input fields are provided for the user to enter the day, time, price, name and description of an event. JButtons are provided to allow the user to open a file, enter data into the file and close the file. Data is entered into the input fields and written to a file specified by the user. To open and write to this text file, your application will create a FileWriter object and a PrintWriter object. The **Write Event** application should enable the user to create a new file or open an existing file—if an existing file is opened, the new events will be added to the end of the file.

Creating a *PrintWriter* Object

1. ***Copying the template to your working directory.*** Copy the directory C:\Examples\Tutorial25\TemplateApplication\WriteEvent to your C:\SimplyJava directory.

2. ***Opening the Write Event application's template file.*** Open the template file WriteEvent.java in your text editor.

3. ***Importing the package java.io to enable file processing.*** Add line 6 of Fig. 25.11 to your code to import the java.io package. This package will allow you to access the classes and methods needed to perform file processing with sequential-access files.

(cont.)

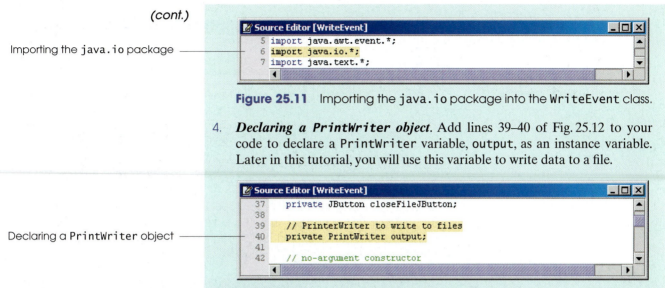

Importing the `java.io` package ——

Figure 25.11   Importing the `java.io` package into the `WriteEvent` class.

4. ***Declaring a PrintWriter object***. Add lines 39–40 of Fig. 25.12 to your code to declare a `PrintWriter` variable, `output`, as an instance variable. Later in this tutorial, you will use this variable to write data to a file.

Declaring a `PrintWriter` object ——

```
37        private JButton closeFileJButton;
38
39        // PrinterWriter to write to files
40        private PrintWriter output;
41
42        // no-argument constructor
```

Figure 25.12   Declaring a `PrintWriter` object.

5. ***Displaying the JFileChooser dialog***. Add lines 186–189 of Fig. 25.13 to the `openFileJButtonActionPerformed` method. Line 187 creates a **JFileChooser** object to allow the user to open a file. A `JFileChooser` object is used to display a dialog enabling users to select a file from a disk drive. In this application, if the user specifies a file that does not exist, a new file will be created with the specified name. Line 188 invokes the `JFileChooser`'s **setDialogTitle** method to set the title bar string of the `JFileChooser` dialog. Line 189 invokes the **showOpenDialog** method to display the `JFileChooser` dialog. The `showOpenDialog` method takes as an argument a reference to the parent GUI component (`this`), indicating that the dialog will appear centered over the application window. This method returns an `int` that indicates whether the user clicked the **OK** or **Cancel** JButton in the dialog. For instance, the `showOpenDialog` method returns the `int` constant **JFileChooser.CANCEL_OPTION** if the user clicks the **Cancel** JButton or the `int` constant **JFileChooser.APPROVE_OPTION** if the user clicks the **OK** JButton. The `int` constant **JFile-Chooser.ERROR_OPTION** is returned if an error occurs.

Displaying the
`JFileChooser` dialog ——

```
184      private void openFileJButtonActionPerformed( ActionEvent event )
185      {
186          // display file dialog so user can select file to open
187          JFileChooser fileChooser = new JFileChooser();
188          fileChooser.setDialogTitle( "Open File for Write Event" );
189          int result = fileChooser.showOpenDialog( this );
190
191      } // end method openFileJButtonActionPerformed
```

Figure 25.13   Displaying the `JFileChooser` dialog and retrieving the result.

6. ***Exiting the method if the user clicks the Cancel JButton***. Add lines 191–195 of Fig. 25.14 to your code. If the user clicks the **Cancel** JButton (line 192), the `return` statement in line 194 causes the method to exit, which allows the user to click the **Open File...** JButton again and restart the process of selecting a file to open.

(cont.)

If the user clicks the **Cancel** JButton, the method returns

```
189        int result = fileChooser.showOpenDialog( this );
190
191        // if user clicked Cancel JButton on dialog, return
192        if ( result == JFileChooser.CANCEL_OPTION )
193        {
194            return; // exit method openFileJButtonActionPerformed
195        }
196
197     } // end method openFileJButtonActionPerformed
```

Figure 25.14   Exiting the method if the user clicks the **Cancel** JButton.

7. *Retrieving the file.* Add lines 197–198 of Fig. 25.15 to your code. Line 198 invokes the **getSelectedFile** method of JFileChooser to retrieve the file that the user selected—this file is returned as an object of the **File** class. The File class, as you will see in the next step, is used to retrieve information about a file or directory.

Getting the selected file

```
195        }
196
197        // get selected file
198        File selectedFile = fileChooser.getSelectedFile();
199
200     } // end method openFileJButtonActionPerformed
```

Figure 25.15   Retrieving the file selected by the user.

8. *Getting the selected file name.* Add lines 200–201 of Fig. 25.16 to your code. The **getName** method of the File class returns the name of the selected file (line 201) as a String.

Retrieving the name of the selected file

```
198        File selectedFile = fileChooser.getSelectedFile();
199
200        // get selected file name
201        String fileName = selectedFile.getName();
202
203     } // end method openFileJButtonActionPerformed
```

Figure 25.16   Retrieving the name of the file using the getName method.

9. *Checking for a missing file name.* Add lines 203–208 of Fig. 25.17 to your code. Line 204 determines if the file name is missing. If it is, lines 206–207 display a dialog with an error message.

Checking for a missing file name

```
201        String fileName = selectedFile.getName();
202
203        // display error if file name missing
204        if ( fileName.equals( "" ) )
205        {
206            JOptionPane.showMessageDialog( this, "File name missing.",
207                "File Name Missing", JOptionPane.ERROR_MESSAGE );
208        }
209
210     } // end method openFileJButtonActionPerformed
```

Figure 25.17   Validating the file name.

(cont.)

10. *Initializing a PrintWriter object.* Add lines 209–220 of Fig. 25.18 to your code. Lines 215–216 create a `FileWriter` object to write characters to the file specified by `selectedFile` (the first argument to the `FileWriter` constructor). Recall that `selectedFile` represents the file selected by the user in the `JFileChooser` dialog. The second argument indicates where new characters will be added to the file. If this argument is `true` (as it is in line 216), any new data written to the file will be appended to the end of the file. If this argument is `false`, data will be written at the beginning of the file, overwriting previously stored data. Once the `FileWriter` has been created in lines 215–216, this file can be writen to. Line 217 passes this `FileWriter` as an argument to the `PrintWriter` constructor to initialize the `Print-Writer` called `output`, which you will use to write text to the file specified by `fileName`.

Notice that this code is placed within a `try` block because the `File-Writer`'s constructor might throw an **IOException** (indicating an input/output error) if a problem occurs while opening the file (such as when a file is opened on a drive with insufficient space). You will handle the exception in a `catch` block shortly.

Software Design Tip

When you open an existing file by invoking the `FileWriter` constructor with a second argument of `false`, data previously contained in the file will be lost.

Common Programming Error

Attempting to process a file without first opening it causes an `IOException`, which indicates that an input/output error occurred.

Create a `FileWriter` and pass it to `PrintWriter` constructor

```
208            }
209        else
210        {
211            // open file
212            try
213            {
214                // open file for writing
215                FileWriter outputFile =
216                    new FileWriter( selectedFile, true );
217                output = new PrintWriter( outputFile );
218            }
219
220        } // end else
221
222    } // end method openFileJButtonActionPerformed
```

Figure 25.18 Opening the file to which the information will be written.

11. *Changing the state of the JButtons.* Add lines 219–222 of Fig. 25.19 to your code to change the state of the `JButtons`. Line 220 prevents the user from attempting to open another file before the current file is closed. Lines 221–222 enable the user to add data to the file or close the file.

```
217                output = new PrintWriter( outputFile, true );
218
219                // change state of JButtons
220                openFileJButton.setEnabled( false );
221                enterJButton.setEnabled( true );
222                closeFileJButton.setEnabled( true );
223            }
224
225        } // end else
```

Figure 25.19 Changing the state of the `JButtons`.

12. *Catching an IOException.* Add lines 224–229 of Fig. 25.20 to your code. These lines catch the `IOException` that might occur in the `try` block of lines 212–223.

(cont.)

Catching any IOException thrown from the **try** block

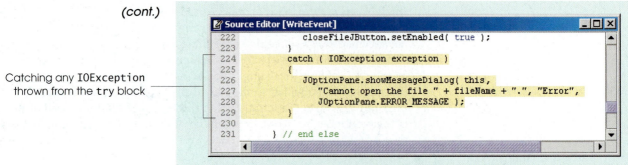

```
222              closeFileJButton.setEnabled( true );
223          }
224          catch ( IOException exception )
225          {
226              JOptionPane.showMessageDialog( this,
227                  "Cannot open the file " + fileName + ".", "Error",
228                  JOptionPane.ERROR_MESSAGE );
229          }
230
231      } // end else
```

Figure 25.20   Displaying a JOptionPane if an IOException is caught.

13. **Resetting the input fields.** Add lines 233–234 of Fig. 25.21 to your code. Line 234 calls the resetUserInput method. This method, provided in the template, clears the priceJTextField, eventJTextField and descriptionJTextArea.

Clearing the user input components

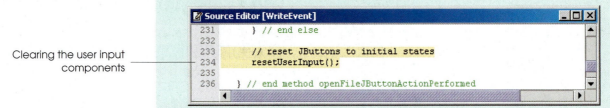

```
231      } // end else
232
233      // reset JButtons to initial states
234      resetUserInput();
235
236  } // end method openFileJButtonActionPerformed
```

Figure 25.21   Calling method resetUserInput.

14. **Saving the application.** Save your modified source code file.

15. **Compiling the application.** Compile your application by typing javac WriteEvent.java.

16. **Running the application.** When your application compiles correctly, run it by typing java WriteEvent. Fig. 25.22 shows the updated application running. The time shown in the **Time:** JSpinner is the current time (8 PM).

Figure 25.22   WriteEvent application with opening files capability.

17. **Creating a file.** Click the **Open File...** JButton. The **Open File for Write Event** dialog will appear. Browse to the C:\SimplyJava\WriteEvent directory and type test.txt in the **File Name:** field. Click the **Open** JButton. This will create the file test.txt and store it in your WriteEvent directory.

(cont.)

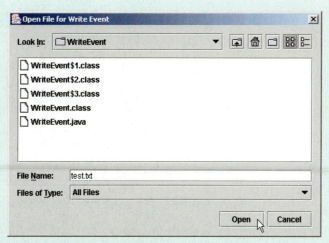

Figure 25.23   Creating a file.

You will be returned to the application window. Although the **Enter** and **Close File** JButtons are now enabled, you have not yet added the functionality for these JButtons, so no action will occur when they are clicked. Once you have closed the application, browse to your WriteEvent directory. Notice that test.txt has been created but does not yet contain any data. You can also open an existing file with the current application, but you will not be able to add data to the file until the next box, where you will learn to write data to a file.

18. **Closing the application.** Close your running application by clicking the window's close button.

19. **Closing the Command Prompt window.** Close the **Command Prompt** window by clicking its close button.

Good Programming Practice

Closing the file as soon as the application no longer needs the file. This minimizes the chance of corrupting the file and allows other application to access that file.

Now that the application can open a file, you will learn how to enable the user to input information that will be written to that file. Next, you will add code to the enterJButtonActionPerformed method, which executes when the **Enter** JButton is clicked. This method will write data entered by the user into a text file. You will also add code to close the file when the **Close File** JButton is clicked. A file should be closed as soon as the application no longer needs the file. This minimizes the chance of corrupting the file and allows other applications to access that file.

Writing Information to a Sequential-Access File

1. **Writing the date and time of the event to a file.** Add lines 241–249 of Fig. 25.24 to the enterJButtonActionPerformed method. Lines 242–249 write the user input line-by-line to the file by using the PrintWriter's **println** method. This method takes as an argument a value of any primitive type or Object and writes the String version of that value to the file, followed by a newline. In line 242, the println method writes the day entered by the user to the file, followed by a newline to start a new line in the file. You will add each piece of information on a separate line in the file. Line 245 retrieves the time entered by the user. The data returned from timeJSpinner.getValue actually returns more data than needed, such as the current month. All we are interested in from this component is the time of the event in hours and minutes. Line 246 uses the substring method to extract this information. Line 249 writes this time information to the file, followed by a newline.

(cont.)

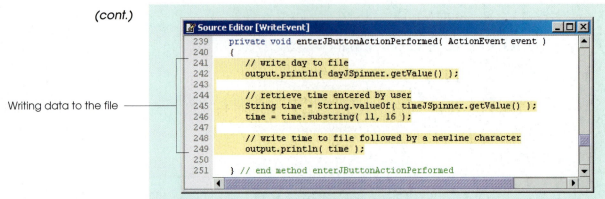

Writing data to the file

Figure 25.24 PrintWriter writing to a file.

2. ***Adding the price, name and description of the event to the file.*** Add lines 251–261 of Fig. 25.25 to your code. Line 252 adds to the file a line containing a dollar sign and the price entered in the priceJTextField. Line 255 adds the name of the event to the file. Line 258 adds a description of the event to the file. Line 261 invokes the resetUserInput method to clear the input JTextFields.

```
249          output.println( time );
250
251          // write price to file followed by a newline character
252          output.println( "$" + priceJTextField.getText() );
253
254          // write event name to file followed by a newline character
255          output.println( eventJTextField.getText() );
256
257          // write event description to file
258          output.println( descriptionJTextArea.getText() );
259
260          // clear JTextFields
261          resetUserInput();
262
263       } // end method enterJButtonActionPerformed
```

Figure 25.25 Adding the price, event name and event description to the file.

3. ***Closing the file.*** Add lines 268–269 of Fig. 25.26 to the closeFileJButtonActionPerformed method. Line 269 uses the PrintWriter's **close** method to close the stream that writes to the file.

Closing the PrintWriter

```
266       private void closeFileJButtonActionPerformed( ActionEvent event )
267       {
268          // close file
269          output.close();
270
271          // reset state of JButtons
```

Figure 25.26 Closing the PrintWriter.

4. ***Saving the application.*** Save your modified source code file.

5. ***Compiling the application.*** Compile your application by typing javac WriteEvent.java.

6. ***Running the application.*** When your application compiles correctly, run it by typing java WriteEvent. Fig. 25.27 shows the completed application running.

(cont.)

Figure 25.27   **Write Event** application executing.

7. **Creating or opening a file.** Click the **Open File...** JButton to create or open the file to which you will write. The **Open** dialog appears (Fig. 25.28). Browse to the C:\SimplyJava\WriteEvent directory and open the test.txt file.

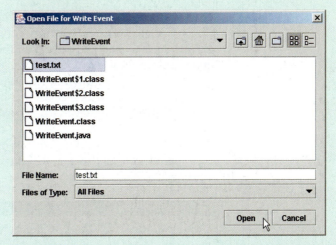

Figure 25.28   **Open File for Write Event** dialog displaying contents of the template **Write Event** application's directory.

8. **Inputting event information.** In the **Day:** JSpinner, select 4 to indicate that the event is scheduled for the 4th day of the month. Enter 14:30 in the **Time:** JSpinner. Type 12.50 in the **Price:** JTextField. Enter Arts and Crafts Fair in the **Event:** JTextField. In the **Description:** JTextArea, enter the information Take part in creating various types of arts and crafts at this fair. Click the **Enter** JButton to add this event's information to the test.txt file.

9. **Closing the file.** When you have entered all the events you wish, click the **Close File** JButton. This closes the test.txt file and prevents any more events from being written until another file is opened (or test.txt is reopened). Be sure to click the **Close File** JButton before closing the application.

(cont.)

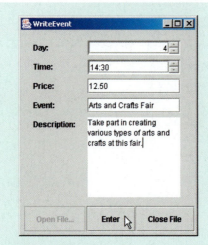

Figure 25.29 Adding the **Arts and Crafts Fair** event to `test.txt`.

10. *Closing the application.* Close your running application by clicking the window's close button.

11. *Closing the Command Prompt window.* Close the **Command Prompt** window by clicking its close button.

12. *Opening and closing the sequential-access file.* Open `test.txt` with a text editor. Scroll down towards the bottom of the file. The information you entered in *Step 8* should appear in the file, similar to Fig. 25.30. Normally, information is not stored in this way, with each piece of data on a separate line. Rather, the information for an event would be all on one line, with each piece of information separated by a special character, such as a space or a tab. We have chosen to organize the file as shown in Fig. 25.30 for simplicity—now we can read each piece of information by reading a line from the file, rather than reading all the information at once and splitting the data based on the special characters that separate them. Close the `test.txt` file.

Data written to file ————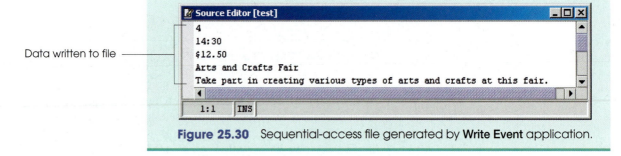

Figure 25.30 Sequential-access file generated by **Write Event** application.

Figure 25.31 presents the source code for the **Write Event** application. The lines of code that you added, viewed or modified in this tutorial are highlighted.

```
1   // Tutorial 25: WriteEvent.java
2   // This application writes information about an event on a given
3   // date to a file.
4   import java.awt.*;
5   import java.awt.event.*;
6   import java.io.*;
7   import java.text.*;
```
Importing the package `java.io` ———— 6

Figure 25.31 **Write Event** code. (Part 1 of 6.)

```
 8   import java.util.Date;
 9   import javax.swing.*;
10   import javax.swing.event.*;
11
12   public class WriteEvent extends JFrame
13   {
14      // JLabel and JSpinner to display day of month
15      private JLabel dayJLabel;
16      private JSpinner dayJSpinner;
17
18      // JLabel and JSpinner to display time
19      private JLabel timeJLabel;
20      private JSpinner timeJSpinner;
21
22      // JLabel and JTextField to display price
23      private JLabel priceJLabel;
24      private JTextField priceJTextField;
25
26      // JLabel and JTextField to display event name
27      private JLabel eventJLabel;
28      private JTextField eventJTextField;
29
30      // JLabel and JTextArea to display event description
31      private JLabel descriptionJLabel;
32      private JTextArea descriptionJTextArea;
33
34      // JButtons to allow user to write to files
35      private JButton openFileJButton;
36      private JButton enterJButton;
37      private JButton closeFileJButton;
38
39      // PrinterWriter to write to files
40      private PrintWriter output;
41
42      // no-argument constructor
43      public WriteEvent()
44      {
45         createUserInterface();
46      }
47
48      // create and position GUI components; register event handlers
49      private void createUserInterface()
50      {
51         // get content pane for attaching GUI components
52         Container contentPane = getContentPane();
53
54         // enable explicit positioning of GUI components
55         contentPane.setLayout( null );
56
57         // set up dayJLabel
58         dayJLabel = new JLabel();
59         dayJLabel.setBounds( 20, 16, 75, 23 );
60         dayJLabel.setText( "Day:" );
61         contentPane.add( dayJLabel );
62
63         // set up dayJSpinner
64         dayJSpinner = new JSpinner(
65            new SpinnerNumberModel( 1, 1, 31, 1 ) );
```

Declaring a new
PrintWriter variable

Figure 25.31   **Write Event** code. (Part 2 of 6.)

```
66          dayJSpinner.setBounds( 108, 16, 150, 23 );
67          contentPane.add( dayJSpinner );
68
69          // set up timeJLabel
70          timeJLabel = new JLabel();
71          timeJLabel.setBounds( 20, 46, 75, 23 );
72          timeJLabel.setText( "Time:" );
73          contentPane.add( timeJLabel );
74
75          // set up timeJSpinner
76          timeJSpinner = new JSpinner( new SpinnerDateModel() );
77          timeJSpinner.setBounds( 108, 46, 150, 23 );
78          timeJSpinner.setEditor(
79             new JSpinner.DateEditor( timeJSpinner, "HH:mm" ) );
80          contentPane.add( timeJSpinner );
81
82          // set up priceJLabel
83          priceJLabel = new JLabel();
84          priceJLabel.setBounds( 20, 76, 75, 23 );
85          priceJLabel.setText( "Price:" );
86          contentPane.add( priceJLabel );
87
88          // set up priceJTextField
89          priceJTextField = new JTextField();
90          priceJTextField.setBounds( 108, 76, 150, 23 );
91          contentPane.add( priceJTextField );
92
93          // set up eventJLabel
94          eventJLabel = new JLabel();
95          eventJLabel.setBounds( 20, 106, 75, 23 );
96          eventJLabel.setText( "Event:" );
97          contentPane.add( eventJLabel );
98
99          // set up eventJTextField
100         eventJTextField = new JTextField();
101         eventJTextField.setBounds( 108, 106, 150, 23 );
102         contentPane.add( eventJTextField );
103
104         // set up descriptionJLabel
105         descriptionJLabel = new JLabel();
106         descriptionJLabel.setBounds( 20, 136, 75, 23 );
107         descriptionJLabel.setText( "Description:" );
108         contentPane.add( descriptionJLabel );
109
110         // set up descriptionJTextArea
111         descriptionJTextArea = new JTextArea();
112         descriptionJTextArea.setBounds( 108, 136, 150, 125 );
113         descriptionJTextArea.setLineWrap( true );
114         descriptionJTextArea.setWrapStyleWord( true );
115         contentPane.add( descriptionJTextArea );
116
117         // set up openFileJButton
118         openFileJButton = new JButton();
119         openFileJButton.setBounds( 5, 275, 100, 40 );
120         openFileJButton.setText( "Open File..." );
121         contentPane.add( openFileJButton );
122         openFileJButton.addActionListener(
123
```

Figure 25.31   **Write Event** code. (Part 3 of 6.)

```
124              new ActionListener() // anonymous inner class
125              {
126                 // event handler called when openFileJButton is clicked
127                 public void actionPerformed( ActionEvent event )
128                 {
129                    openFileJButtonActionPerformed( event );
130                 }
131
132              } // end anonymous inner class
133
134           ); // end call to addActionListener
135
136           // set up enterJButton
137           enterJButton = new JButton();
138           enterJButton.setBounds( 106, 275, 80, 40 );
139           enterJButton.setText( "Enter" );
140           enterJButton.setEnabled( false );
141           contentPane.add( enterJButton );
142           enterJButton.addActionListener(
143
144              new ActionListener() // anonymous inner class
145              {
146                 // event handler called when enterJButton is clicked
147                 public void actionPerformed( ActionEvent event )
148                 {
149                    enterJButtonActionPerformed( event );
150                 }
151
152              } // end anonymous inner class
153
154           ); // end call to addActionListener
155
156           // set up closeFileJButton
157           closeFileJButton = new JButton();
158           closeFileJButton.setBounds( 186, 275, 95, 40 );
159           closeFileJButton.setText( "Close File" );
160           closeFileJButton.setEnabled( false );
161           contentPane.add( closeFileJButton );
162           closeFileJButton.addActionListener(
163
164              new ActionListener() // anonymous inner class
165              {
166                 // event handler called when closeFileJButton is clicked
167                 public void actionPerformed( ActionEvent event )
168                 {
169                    closeFileJButtonActionPerformed( event );
170                 }
171
172              } // end anonymous inner class
173
174           ); // end call to addActionListener
175
176           // set properties of application's window
177           setTitle( "WriteEvent" ); // set title bar string
178           setSize( 290, 345 );       // set window size
179           setVisible( true );        // display window
180
181        } // end method createUserInterface
```

Figure 25.31   **Write Event** code. (Part 4 of 6.)

```
182
183         // open a file for writing
184         private void openFileJButtonActionPerformed( ActionEvent event )
185         {
186             // display file dialog so user can select file to open
187             JFileChooser fileChooser = new JFileChooser();
188             fileChooser.setDialogTitle( "Open File for Write Event" );
189             int result = fileChooser.showOpenDialog( this );
190
191             // if user clicked Cancel JButton on dialog, return
192             if ( result == JFileChooser.CANCEL_OPTION )
193             {
194                 return; // exit method openFileJButtonActionPerformed
195             }
196
197             // get selected file
198             File selectedFile = fileChooser.getSelectedFile();
199
200             // get selected file name
201             String fileName = selectedFile.getName();
202
203             // display error if file name missing
204             if ( fileName.equals( "" ) )
205             {
206                 JOptionPane.showMessageDialog( this, "File name missing.",
207                     "File Name Missing", JOptionPane.ERROR_MESSAGE );
208             }
209             else
210             {
211                 // open file
212                 try
213                 {
214                     // open file for writing
215                     FileWriter outputFile =
216                         new FileWriter( selectedFile, true );
217                     output = new PrintWriter( outputFile );
218
219                     // change state of JButtons
220                     openFileJButton.setEnabled( false );
221                     enterJButton.setEnabled( true );
222                     closeFileJButton.setEnabled( true );
223                 }
224                 catch ( IOException exception )
225                 {
226                     JOptionPane.showMessageDialog( this,
227                         "Cannot open the file " + fileName + ".", "Error",
228                         JOptionPane.ERROR_MESSAGE );
229                 }
230
231             } // end else
232
233             // reset JButtons to initial states
234             resetUserInput();
235
236         } // end method openFileJButtonActionPerformed
237
238         // save data entered to specified file
239         private void enterJButtonActionPerformed( ActionEvent event )
240         {
```

Labels (left margin):
- Displaying the JFileChooser dialog — (lines 187–189)
- User clicks **Cancel** JButton — (line 192)
- Exit the method — (line 194)
- Get the selected file — (line 198)
- Get the selected file name — (line 201)
- Checking for a missing file name — (line 204)
- Create a FileWriter and pass it to the PrintWriter constructor — (lines 215–217)
- Catch any IOException thrown from the try block — (lines 226–227)
- Clearing the user input components — (line 234)

Figure 25.31 **Write Event** code. (Part 5 of 6.)

```
241              // write day to file
242              output.println( dayJSpinner.getValue() );
243
244              // retrieve time entered by user
245              String time = String.valueOf( timeJSpinner.getValue() );
246              time = time.substring( 11, 16 );
247
248              // write time to file followed by a newline character
249              output.println( time );
250
251              // write price to file followed by a newline character
252              output.println( "$" + priceJTextField.getText() );
253
254              // write event name to file followed by a newline character
255              output.println( eventJTextField.getText() );
256
257              // write event description to file
258              output.println( descriptionJTextArea.getText() );
259
260              // clear JTextFields
261              resetUserInput();
262
263          } // end method enterJButtonActionPerformed
264
265          // file is closed after user is finished with it
266          private void closeFileJButtonActionPerformed( ActionEvent event )
267          {
268              // close file
269              output.close();
270
271              // reset state of JButtons
272              enterJButton.setEnabled( false );
273              openFileJButton.setEnabled( true );
274              closeFileJButton.setEnabled( false );
275
276              // clear JTextFields
277              resetUserInput();
278
279          } // end method closeFileJButtonActionPerformed
280
281          // clear JTextFields
282          private void resetUserInput()
283          {
284              priceJTextField.setText( "" );
285              eventJTextField.setText( "" );
286              descriptionJTextArea.setText( "" );
287
288          } // end method resetUserInput
289
290          // main method
291          public static void main( String[] args )
292          {
293              WriteEvent application = new WriteEvent();
294              application.setDefaultCloseOperation( JFrame.EXIT_ON_CLOSE );
295
296          } // end method main
297
298      } // end class WriteEvent
```

Write data to the file — (lines 241–258)

Clearing the user input components — (line 261)

Close the file — (line 269)

Figure 25.31 Write Event code. (Part 6 of 6.)

SELF-REVIEW

1. A _____ object displays a dialog enabling a user to select a file from a disk drive.
   a) JFileDialog
   b) JFileChooser
   c) JFileOption
   d) JOptionPane

2. The _____ class is used to retrieve information about a file or directory.
   a) File
   b) FileDirectory
   c) FileInformation
   d) DirectoryInformation

Answers: 1) b. 2) a.

25.5 Creating the Ticket Information Application

Now that you have created the **Write Event** application to enable a user to write community event information to a sequential-access text file, you will create the **Ticket Information** application from the test-drive section at the beginning of the tutorial. First you need to analyze the application. The following pseudocode describes the basic operation of the **Ticket Information** application.

> When the user selects a day from the Date JSpinner:
>   Retrieve the day selected in the Date JSpinner
>   Open calendar.txt file to read from
>
>   While there are events left in the file
>
>   If the current event is for the day selected by the user
>   Store the event information
>   Increment the number of events for the selected day
>
>   Read the next event's information
>
>   Close the file
>
>   If events are scheduled for that day
>   Add each event to the Event JComboBox
>   Else
>   DIsplay "- No Events -" in the Event JComboBox
>   Display "No events today." in the Description: JTextArea
>
> When the user selects an event from the Event JComboBox:
>   Retrieve index of selected item in the Event JComboBox
>   Display event information in the Description: JTextArea

Now that you have test-driven the **Ticket Information** application and studied its pseudocode representation, you will use an ACE table to help you convert the pseudocode to Java. Figure 25.32 lists the actions, components and events required to complete your own version of this application.

*Action/Component/
Event (ACE) Table for the
Ticket Information
Application*

Action	Component/Object	Event
Label the application's components	`dateJLabel`, `eventJLabel`, `descriptionJLabel`	Application is run
	`dateJSpinner`	User selects a date from the **Date** JSpinner
Retrieve the day selected in the Date JSpinner	`dateJSpinner`	
Open calendar.txt file to read from	`currentFile (FileReader)`, `input (BufferedReader)`	
While there are events left in the file If the current event is for the day selected by the user Store the event information	`daysEvents (String array)`, `input (BufferedReader)`	
Increment the number of events for the selected day		
Read the next event's information	`input (BufferedReader)`	
Close the file	`input (BufferedReader)`	
If events are scheduled for that day Add each event to the Event JComboBox	`daysEvents (String array)`, `eventJComboBox`	
Else Display "- No Events -" in the Event JComboBox	`eventJComboBox`	
Display "No events today." in the Description: JTextArea	`descriptionJTextArea`	
	`eventJComboBox`	User selects an event from the **Event** JComboBox
Retrieve index of selected item in the Event JComboBox	`eventJComboBox`	
Display event information in the Description: JTextArea	`daysEvents (String array)`, `descriptionJTextArea`	

Figure 25.32 ACE table for the **Ticket Information** application.

For this application, you will create the `createEventList` and `extractData` methods. The method headers for these methods are in the template application. Method `createEventList` retrieves the events for the day selected by the user and displays them in the `eventJComboBox`. This method calls `extractData` to retrieve the events from `calendar.txt`.

*Beginning to Build the
Ticket Information
Application*

1. ***Copying the template to your working directory.*** Copy the `C:\Examples\Tutorial25\TemplateApplication\TicketInformation` directory to your `C:\SimplyJava` directory.

2. ***Opening the Ticket Information application's template file.*** Open the template file `TicketInformation.java` in your text editor.

3. ***Adding an instance variable.*** Add lines 26–27 of Fig. 25.33 to your code. Line 27 declares instance variable `input`, which is of `BufferedReader` type. You will use `input` to read data from a file.

(cont.)

Declare a
BufferedReader variable

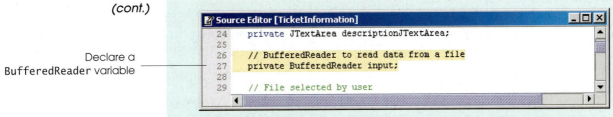

Figure 25.33 Declaring an instance variable in the **Ticket Information** application.

4. *Invoking the `createEventList` method.* Add line 128 of Fig. 25.34 to the dateJSpinnerStateChanged method, which is called when you change the date in the dateJSpinner. This line invokes the createEventList method; you will add code to this method in the following box.

Calling the
createEventList method

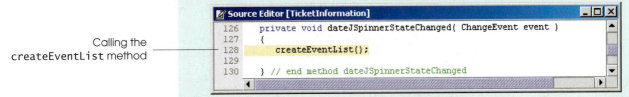

Figure 25.34 Invoking the `createEventList` method.

5. *Saving the application.* Save your modified source code file. You may run the application at this time, but no events will be displayed for any day, as createEventList has not yet been defined.

The application invokes the createEventList method from the constructor and the dateJSpinnerStateChanged method. The createEventList method will populate the JComboBox with event names if there are events scheduled for the date the user chooses, or it will indicate that the event list is empty if there are no events for that day.

Adding Code to the `createEventList` Method

1. *Setting variables and clearing the JComboBox.* Add lines 141–146 of Fig. 25.35 to the createEventList method. Line 142 invokes the extractData method, to which you will add code later in this tutorial. Line 145 calls the **removeAllItems** method of JComboBox to remove all items (events currently displayed) from the eventJComboBox. The createEventList method is called when a new day is selected, so we first need to remove the events displayed for the previously selected day. Line 146 clears the text displayed in the descriptionJTextArea.

The extractData method will
read events from calendar.txt

```
Source Editor [TicketInformation]
139      private void createEventList()
140      {
141          // get data from file
142          extractData();
143
144          // remove all information from last date
145          eventJComboBox.removeAllItems();
146          descriptionJTextArea.setText( "" );
147
148      } // end method createEventList
```

Figure 25.35 Calling the **extractData** method and clearing the **eventJ-ComboBox**.

(cont.)

2. ***Setting events displayed in the JComboBox.*** Add lines 148–161 of Fig. 25.36 to the createEventList method. Instance variable eventNumber, declared in the template, keeps track of how many events are scheduled for the selected day. If there are events scheduled, the expression in line 149 will evaluate to true, and the for statement (lines 152–155) will iterate through the two-dimensional array daysEvents and add the name of each event to the eventJComboBox (line 154). The daysEvents array is created in the template with ten rows and five columns. The ten rows represent a maximum of 10 events per day. The five columns represent the date, time, price, name and description of the event, respectively. In line 154, x represents the current event in the for statement. The expression daysEvents[x] returns an array containing that event's information. The value at index 3 of this event contains the name of the event. Therefore, daysEvents[x][3] returns the name of the current event. This name is then added to eventJComboBox using the addItem method. If there are no events for the chosen day, the eventJComboBox displays **- No events -** and the descriptionJTextArea displays **No events today.** (lines 159–160).

Indicating that events are scheduled for the day

Extracting the event name from the array and displaying it in the eventJComboBox

Indicating that no events are scheduled for the day

Figure 25.36 Displaying the events scheduled for the specified day.

3. ***Saving the application.*** Save your modified source code file. If you run the application at this time, no events will be displayed for any day, as extractData does not yet read the events from calendar.txt.

The extractData method reads information from the file, assigns to the daysEvents array the information about any events scheduled for that day and assigns to the eventNumber variable the number of events for that day.

Reading a Sequential-Access File

1. ***Adding variables to the extractData method.*** Add lines 168–175 of Fig. 25.37 to the extractData method. The extractData method will assign the number of events scheduled for the specified date to the variable eventNumber, which is initialized to 0 in line 168. Lines 170–172 get the selected day from the dateJSpinner and store it as a String (currentDate), which will later be compared to the String date stored in the file. Line 175 calls the initialize method to initialize te daysEvents array.

(cont.)

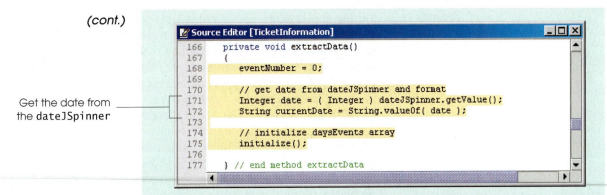

Get the date from
the dateJSpinner

```
Source Editor [TicketInformation]                        _ □ X
166        private void extractData()
167        {
168            eventNumber = 0;
169
170            // get date from dateJSpinner and format
171            Integer date = ( Integer ) dateJSpinner.getValue();
172            String currentDate = String.valueOf( date );
173
174            // initialize daysEvents array
175            initialize();
176
177        } // end method extractData
```

Figure 25.37 Declaring variables in the extractData method.

2. *Using a BufferedReader to read from the file.* Add lines 177–189 of Fig. 25.38 to your code. Line 181 creates a File object calendarFile for the file calendar.txt, which contains the events to be displayed in your application. Line 184 creates a FileReader object currentFile for reading characters from a selected file. The FileReader constructor takes one argument, which specifies the file (represented by the File object calendarFile) from which you will read characters. When a FileReader is created as in line 184, the file can be read from. Line 185 passes a FileReader as an argument to the BufferedReader constructor to initialize the BufferedReader input, which provides methods to read from the file specified by the user.

The **readLine** method (line 188) of the BufferedReader object reads a line of characters up to and including a newline character from the specified stream (input) and returns the characters as a String. Line 188 assigns the first line of the file to contents. This first line contains the day of the first event in the file. If the first event in the file is a talent show on the 12th, the value returned by the first line of the file is 12.

Notice that the code added in this step forms a try block, because the readLine method (called on line 188) may generate an IOException. You will create the corresponding catch block for this exception in *Step 6*.

Create a FileReader and pass it
to the BufferedReader
constructor

Read a line from the file

```
Source Editor [TicketInformation]                        _ □ X
175            initialize();
176
177            // find and display events for current date
178            try
179            {
180                // get file
181                calendarFile = new File( "calendar.txt" );
182
183                // open file
184                FileReader currentFile = new FileReader( calendarFile );
185                input = new BufferedReader( currentFile );
186
187                // read a line from the file
188                String contents = input.readLine();
189            }
190
191        } // end method extractData
```

Figure 25.38 Using a BufferedReader object to read data from a sequential-access file.

(cont.)

3. ***Extracting the day from an event in the file.*** Add lines 190–196 of Fig. 25.39 to the extractData method. The while statement (line 191) begins by determining whether there is more data to read in the file. If there is, line 194 calls the readLine method to read the next line of text in the file. If the end of the file is reached (that is, there is no more data to read from the file), null is returned and the while loop ends. If the end of the file has not been reached, the current line will be stored in variable contents.

Check to see if end of file has been reached

```
Source Editor [TicketInformation]                                    _ |□| X
188           String contents = input.readLine();
189
190           // while more lines are in the file
191           while ( contents != null )
192           {
193               // read a line from the file
194               contents = input.readLine();
195
196           } // end while
197       }
```

Figure 25.39   Reading through each line in a file.

4. ***Reading event information from the sequential-access file.*** Add lines 193–203 of Fig. 25.40 to the while statement to read each event's information sequentially from the file. If the day of the event read from the file (contents) and the specified day (currentDate) are equal (line 194), then the event information (day, time, ticket price, name and description) is read from the file and is stored in the daysEvents array (lines 197–201).

Store event information in a row of the array

```
Source Editor [TicketInformation]                                    _ |□| X
191           while ( contents != null )
192           {
193               // if day selected is equal to the day read from the file
194               if ( contents.equals( currentDate ) )
195               {
196                   // read event information
197                   daysEvents[ eventNumber ][ 0 ] = contents;
198                   daysEvents[ eventNumber ][ 1 ] = input.readLine();
199                   daysEvents[ eventNumber ][ 2 ] = input.readLine();
200                   daysEvents[ eventNumber ][ 3 ] = input.readLine();
201                   daysEvents[ eventNumber ][ 4 ] = input.readLine();
202                   eventNumber++;
203               }
204
205               // read a line from the file
```

Figure 25.40   Sequentially reading event entries from the file.

Recall that the **Write Event** application writes each piece of data (day, time, price, event and description) to calendar.txt on a separate line, so the event data can be retrieved using the readLine method. Each event for the chosen day is placed in its own row of the array (indicated by eventNumber), and each piece of event information is placed (within that row) in its own column of the array. Line 202 increments eventNumber, which indicates the number of events scheduled for that date.

5. ***Finding the next date in the sequential-access file.*** Add lines 204–211 of Fig. 25.41 to your code. If contents and the selected day do not match, then the BufferedReader skips to the next event, using a for statement (lines 207–210) that reads, but does not store any information from, the next four lines of text. After the for statement, the next line is read from the file. This line contains the next event's date. This entire process is repeated until the end of the file is reached.

(cont.)

```
 Source Editor [TicketInformation]                                    _ □ ×
202                    eventNumber++;
203                }
204                else // if date was not equal
205                {
206                    // move to next date in file
207                    for ( int x = 0; x < 4; x++ )
208                    {
209                        input.readLine();
210                    }
211                }
212
213                // read a line from the file
```

Figure 25.41   Finding the next date in the file.

6. **Catching the IOException.** Add lines 218–228 of Fig. 25.42 to your code. Lines 220–223 display an error message. Lines 226–227 disable eventJ-ComboBox and dateJSpinner. If the file cannot be opened, the user should not be able to look for events using these components.

```
 Source Editor [TicketInformation]                                    _ □ ×
216                } // end while
217            }
218            catch ( IOException exception )
219            {
220                JOptionPane.showMessageDialog( this,
221                    "Please make sure the file exists and is of the " +
222                    "right format.", "I/O Error",
223                    JOptionPane.ERROR_MESSAGE );
224
225                // disable components
226                eventJComboBox.setEnabled( false );
227                dateJSpinner.setEnabled( false );
228            }
229
230        } // end method extractData
```

Figure 25.42   Displaying an error message if there is an error reading from the file.

7. **Saving the application.** Save your modified source code file.

SELF-REVIEW

1. To open a file for reading, you would use a _____ object.
   a) InputFile   b) StreamReader
   c) BufferedReader   d) FileReader

2. The _____ method of the JComboBox class removes all items from a JComboBox.
   a) clear   b) removeAll
   c) clearAll   d) removeAllItems

Answers: 1) d. 2) d.

25.6 Using the `finally` block

In Tutorial 24, you learned that a `finally` block will execute whether or not an exception is thrown in the corresponding `try` block or any of its corresponding `catch` blocks. The `finally` block, if it exists, is placed directly after the `catch` block and is used to perform any functionality whether or not an exception is thrown within the `try` block. The closing of a file typically is placed in a `finally` block to guarantee that the file will be closed regardless of whether or not an exception is thrown while the file is being processed. You will now add a `finally` block that closes the file represented by the `BufferedReader` input.

Closing the File

1. ***Adding a finally block.*** Add lines 229–232 of Fig. 25.43 to your code. This finally block is located after the try and catch blocks that opened calendar.txt for reading. Whether or not an exception occurs while reading data from the file, the code in the finally block will execute (either after the last statement in the try block if there was no exception thrown, or after the last statement of the catch block if there was an exception thrown). You will use this finally block to close calendar.txt.

Code in the finally block always executes

```
Source Editor [TicketInformation]                                   _ □ X
227            dateJSpinner.setEnabled( false );
228        }
229        finally // close the file
230        {
231
232        }
233
234    } // end method extractData
```

Figure 25.43 Adding a finally block to your code.

2. ***Closing the file.*** Add lines 231–242 of Fig. 25.44 to your code. The **close** method of the BufferedReader class closes the file (line 234) so that other methods or applications can view and modify it. The next time the file is opened, the first line read will be the first line of text in the file. Because the close method could potentially cause an I/O error, it is contained within another try block (lines 232–235) and is followed by another catch block (lines 236–242). The method then returns to the point in createEventList where it was called, and the events read from the file are displayed for the user. The user can then select another day from the dateJSpinner or an event from the eventJComboBox.

Close the input file

```
Source Editor [TicketInformation]                                   _ □ X
229        finally // close the file
230        {
231            // close the file
232            try
233            {
234                input.close();
235            }
236            catch( IOException exception )
237            {
238                JOptionPane.showMessageDialog( this,
239                    "Please make sure the file exists and is of the " +
240                    "right format.", "I/O Error",
241                    JOptionPane.ERROR_MESSAGE );
242            }
243        }
```

Figure 25.44 Closing the BufferedReader file.

3. ***Saving the application.*** Save your modified source code file.

4. ***Opening the Command Prompt window and changing directories.*** Open the **Command Prompt** window by selecting **Start > Programs > Accessories > Command Prompt**. Change to your working directory by typing cd C:\SimplyJava\TicketInformation.

5. ***Compiling the application.*** Compile your updated application by typing javac TicketInformation.java.

(cont.)

6. **Running the application.** When your application compiles correctly, run it by typing `java TicketInformation`. Figure 25.45 shows the updated application running. Scroll through the different days. Notice that the event names are displayed but not the event descriptions. You will add this functionality shortly.

Figure 25.45 **Write Event** application with event names.

7. **Closing the application.** Close your running application by clicking the window's close button.

8. **Closing the Command Prompt window.** Close the **Command Prompt** window by clicking its close button.

The `eventJComboBox` displays the names of any events scheduled for the date specified in the `dateJSpinner`. When the user selects the event from `eventJComboBox`, the event description should be displayed in `descriptionJTextArea`.

Displaying Event Information

1. **Displaying event information in the `descriptionJTextArea`.** Add lines 135–139 of Fig. 25.46 to the `eventJComboBoxActionPerformed` method. The event number is determined by the event selected in `eventJComboBox`. The `descriptionJTextArea` displays the time, price and a description of the event.

Display the event information in `descriptionJTextArea`

```
Source Editor [TicketInformation]
132    // display event information
133    private void eventJComboBoxActionPerformed( ActionEvent event )
134    {
135        int selectedEvent = eventJComboBox.getSelectedIndex();
136        descriptionJTextArea.setText(
137            daysEvents[ selectedEvent ][ 1 ] + "\n" +   // time
138            daysEvents[ selectedEvent ][ 2 ] + "\n" +   // price
139            daysEvents[ selectedEvent ][ 4 ] );          // description
140
141    } // end method eventJComboBoxActionPerformed
```

Figure 25.46 Displaying event information in `descriptionJTextArea`.

2. **Saving the application.** Save your modified source code file.

3. **Opening the Command Prompt window and changing directories.** Open the **Command Prompt** window by selecting **Start > Programs > Accessories > Command Prompt**. Change to your working directory by typing `cd C:\SimplyJava\TicketInformation`.

(cont.)

4. ***Compiling the application.*** Compile your completed application by typing `javac TicketInformation.java`.

5. ***Running the application.*** When your application compiles correctly, run it by typing `java TicketInformation`. Figure 25.47 shows the completed application running. Notice that now event names and descriptions are displayed.

Figure 25.47 Completed **Ticket Information** application.

6. ***Closing the application.*** Close your running application by clicking the window's close button.

7. ***Closing the Command Prompt window.*** Close the **Command Prompt** window by clicking its close button.

Figure 25.48 presents the source code for the **Ticket Information** application. The lines of code that you added, viewed or modified in this tutorial are highlighted.

```
1   // Tutorial 25: TicketInformation.java
2   // This application reads information about events on different dates
3   // from a file created by class WriteEvent.
4   import java.awt.*;
5   import java.awt.event.*;
6   import java.io.*;
7   import java.text.*;
8   import java.util.Date;
9   import javax.swing.*;
10  import javax.swing.event.*;
11
12  public class TicketInformation extends JFrame
13  {
14     // JLabel and JSpinner to display date
15     private JLabel dateJLabel;
16     private JSpinner dateJSpinner;
17
18     // JLabel and JComboBox to display day's events
19     private JLabel eventJLabel;
20     private JComboBox eventJComboBox;
21
22     // JLabel and JTextArea to display details of events
23     private JLabel descriptionJLabel;
24     private JTextArea descriptionJTextArea;
```

Figure 25.48 **Ticket Information** code. (Part 1 of 6.)

Declare a `BufferedReader` variable ——

```java
25
26      // BufferedReader to read data from a file
27      private BufferedReader input;
28
29      // File selected by user
30      private File calendarFile;
31
32      // instance variables to store event information and number
33      private String[][] daysEvents = new String[ 10 ][ 5 ];
34      private int eventNumber;
35
36      // no-argument constructor
37      public TicketInformation()
38      {
39         createUserInterface();
40
41         createEventList(); // read file and display events on given day
42      }
43
44      // create and position GUI components; register event handlers
45      private void createUserInterface()
46      {
47         // get content pane for attaching GUI components
48         Container contentPane = getContentPane();
49
50         // enable explicit positioning of GUI components
51         contentPane.setLayout( null );
52
53         // set up dateJLabel
54         dateJLabel = new JLabel();
55         dateJLabel.setBounds( 16, 16, 121, 23 );
56         dateJLabel.setText( "Select the day (1-31):" );
57         contentPane.add( dateJLabel );
58
59         // set up dateJSpinner
60         dateJSpinner = new JSpinner(
61            new SpinnerNumberModel( 1, 1, 31, 1 ) );
62         dateJSpinner.setBounds( 147, 16, 119, 23 );
63         contentPane.add( dateJSpinner );
64         dateJSpinner.addChangeListener(
65
66            new ChangeListener() // anonymous inner class
67            {
68               // event handler called when dateJSpinner is changed
69               public void stateChanged( ChangeEvent event )
70               {
71                  dateJSpinnerStateChanged( event );
72               }
73
74            } // end anonymous inner class
75
76         ); // end call to addActionListener
77
78         // set up eventJLabel
79         eventJLabel = new JLabel();
80         eventJLabel.setBounds( 16, 67, 100, 23 );
81         eventJLabel.setText( "Pick an event: " );
82         contentPane.add( eventJLabel );
```

Figure 25.48 **Ticket Information** code. (Part 2 of 6.)

```
83
84          // set up eventJComboBox
85          eventJComboBox = new JComboBox();
86          eventJComboBox.setBounds( 16, 94, 250, 23 );
87          eventJComboBox.addItem( "- No Events -" );
88          contentPane.add( eventJComboBox );
89          eventJComboBox.addActionListener(
90
91             new ActionListener() // anonymous inner class
92             {
93                // event handler called when eventJComboBox is changed
94                public void actionPerformed( ActionEvent event )
95                {
96                   eventJComboBoxActionPerformed( event );
97                }
98
99             } // end anonymous inner class
100
101         ); // end call to addActionListener
102
103         // set up descriptionJLabel
104         descriptionJLabel = new JLabel();
105         descriptionJLabel.setBounds( 16, 141, 100, 23 );
106         descriptionJLabel.setText( "Description: " );
107         contentPane.add( descriptionJLabel );
108
109         // set up descriptionJTextArea
110         descriptionJTextArea = new JTextArea();
111         descriptionJTextArea.setBounds( 16, 168, 250, 125 );
112         descriptionJTextArea.setText( "No events today." );
113         descriptionJTextArea.setLineWrap( true );
114         descriptionJTextArea.setWrapStyleWord( true );
115         descriptionJTextArea.setEditable( false );
116         contentPane.add( descriptionJTextArea );
117
118         // set properties of application's window
119         setTitle( "Ticket Information" ); // set title bar string
120         setSize( 292, 340 );               // set window size
121         setVisible( true );                // display window
122
123      } // end method createUserInterface
124
125      // read event information from a file for a given date
126      private void dateJSpinnerStateChanged( ChangeEvent event )
127      {
128         createEventList();
129
130      } // end method dateJSpinnerStateChanged
131
132      // display event information
133      private void eventJComboBoxActionPerformed( ActionEvent event )
134      {
135         int selectedEvent = eventJComboBox.getSelectedIndex();
136         descriptionJTextArea.setText(
137            daysEvents[ selectedEvent ][ 1 ] + "\n" +  // time
138            daysEvents[ selectedEvent ][ 2 ] + "\n" +  // price
139            daysEvents[ selectedEvent ][ 4 ] );        // description
140
141      } // end method eventJComboBoxActionPerformed
```

Create a list of events when dateJSpinner is changed → (line 128)

Display the event information in descriptionJTextArea → (lines 136–139)

Figure 25.48   **Ticket Information** code. (Part 3 of 6.)

The extractData method will read events from calendar.txt

Indicating that events are scheduled for the day

Add the events for the day to eventJComboBox

Indicating that no events are scheduled for the day

Get the date from dateJSpinner

Create a FileReader and pass it to the BufferedReader constructor

Read a line from the file

Check to see if end of file has been reached

```
142
143        // read events for current day and display events in application
144        private void createEventList()
145        {
146            // get data from file
147            extractData();
148
149            // remove all information from last date
150            eventJComboBox.removeAllItems();
151            descriptionJTextArea.setText( "" );
152
153            // if there are events scheduled for the current day
154            if ( eventNumber > 0 )
155            {
156                // add events to the eventJComboBox
157                for ( int x = 0; x < eventNumber; x++ )
158                {
159                    eventJComboBox.addItem( daysEvents[ x ][ 3 ] );
160                }
161            }
162            else // no events for the day
163            {
164                eventJComboBox.addItem( "- No Events -" );
165                descriptionJTextArea.setText( "No events today." );
166            }
167
168        } // end method createEventList
169
170        // read data from file
171        private void extractData()
172        {
173            eventNumber = 0;
174
175            // get date from dateJSpinner and format
176            Integer date = ( Integer ) dateJSpinner.getValue();
177            String currentDate = String.valueOf( date );
178
179            // initialize daysEvents array
180            initialize();
181
182            // find and display events for current date
183            try
184            {
185                // get file
186                calendarFile = new File( "calendar.txt" );
187
188                // open file
189                FileReader currentFile = new FileReader( calendarFile );
190                input = new BufferedReader( currentFile );
191
192                // read a line from the file
193                String contents = input.readLine();
194
195                // while more lines are in the file
196                while ( contents != null )
197                {
198                    // if day selected is equal to the day read from the file
199                    if ( contents.equals( currentDate ) )
200                    {
```

Figure 25.48 Ticket Information code. (Part 4 of 6.)

```
201                        // read event information
202                        daysEvents[ eventNumber ][ 0 ] = contents;
203                        daysEvents[ eventNumber ][ 1 ] = input.readLine();
204                        daysEvents[ eventNumber ][ 2 ] = input.readLine();
205                        daysEvents[ eventNumber ][ 3 ] = input.readLine();
206                        daysEvents[ eventNumber ][ 4 ] = input.readLine();
207                        eventNumber++;
208                     }
209                  else // if date was not equal
210                  {
211                     // move to next date in file
212                     for ( int x = 0; x < 4; x++ )
213                     {
214                        input.readLine();
215                     }
216                  }
217
218                  // read a line from the file
219                  contents = input.readLine();
220
221               } // end while
222            }
223            catch ( IOException exception )
224            {
225               JOptionPane.showMessageDialog( this,
226                  "Please make sure the file exists and is of the " +
227                  "right format.", "I/O Error",
228                  JOptionPane.ERROR_MESSAGE );
229
230               // disable components
231               eventJComboBox.setEnabled( false );
232               dateJSpinner.setEnabled( false );
233            }
234            finally // close the file
235            {
236               // close the file
237               try
238               {
239                  input.close();
240               }
241               catch( IOException exception )
242               {
243                  JOptionPane.showMessageDialog( this,
244                     "Please make sure the file exists and is of the " +
245                     "right format.", "I/O Error",
246                     JOptionPane.ERROR_MESSAGE );
247               }
248            }
249
250         } // end method extractData
251
252         // initialize daysEvents array
253         private void initialize()
254         {
255            // for each of ten possible events per day
256            for ( int i = 0; i <= 9; i++ )
257            {
```

Store the event information in a two-dimensional array — (lines 202–206)

Search the entire file — (line 219)

Closing the file — (line 239)

Figure 25.48 **Ticket Information** code. (Part 5 of 6.)

```
258              // for each of five fields per event
259              for ( int j = 0; j <= 4; j++ )
260              {
261                 daysEvents[ i ][ j ] = "";
262              }
263           }
264
265           daysEvents[ 0 ][ 3 ] = "- No Events -";
266           daysEvents[ 0 ][ 4 ] = "No events today.";
267
268        } // end method initialize
269
270        // main method
271        public static void main( String[] args )
272        {
273           TicketInformation application = new TicketInformation();
274           application.setDefaultCloseOperation( JFrame.EXIT_ON_CLOSE );
275
276        } // end method main
277
278 } // end class TicketInformation
```

Figure 25.48   Ticket Information code. (Part 6 of 6.)

SELF-REVIEW

1. A(n) _____ will execute whether or not an exception occurs.
   a) try block   b) catch block
   c) finally block   d) return statement

2. The readLine method _____ when there is no more data to be read from the file.
   a) returns 0   b) throws an EndOfFileException
   c) returns null   d) All of the above.

Answers: 1) c. 2) c.

25.7 Wrap-Up

In this tutorial, you learned how to store and retrieve data in sequential-access files. This type of data is called persistent because it is maintained after the application that generates the data terminates. Computers store files on secondary storage devices.

Sequential-access files store data items in the order that they are written to the files. These files can be composed of records, which are collections of related fields. Fields are made up of characters, which in Java are composed of two bytes. (Remember that Java uses the Unicode character set, where each character is represented using two bytes.) Bytes are composed of bits—the smallest data items that computers can support.

You learned that Java views each file as a sequential stream of bytes. You created a sequential-access file in the **Write Event** application by associating a Print-Writer object with a specified file name. You used the PrintWriter object to add information to that file. After creating a file of community events with the **Write Event** application, you developed the **Ticket Information** application, which uses a BufferedReader object to read information from that file sequentially. The user selects a date in the **Ticket Information** application's JSpinner component and extracts event information from a sequential-access file about any events scheduled for that date. You learned how to close a file within a finally block and how the finally block interacts with the catch block.

In the next tutorial, you will be introduced to databases, which were mentioned briefly in this tutorial. Databases provide another common mechanism for maintaining persistent data. You will learn how databases are organized, and how to access and modify a database using SQL (the Structured Query Language). Using databases and SQL, you will create an **ATM** (automated teller machine) application that accesses account information from a database. The user will enter an account number, and the **ATM** application will use this data to retrieve the user's account information.

SKILLS SUMMARY

Displaying a Dialog to Open a File

- Add a dialog to open a file in your application by creating a new `JFileChooser`.
- Invoke the `JFileChooser`'s `showOpenDialog` method.
- To retrieve the file selected, use the `getSelectedFile` method of the `JFileChooser` object, which returns a `File` object representing the selected file.

Retrieve the Name of a File

- Use the `getName` method of the `File` class.

Writing to a Sequential-Access File

- Import the `java.io` package.
- Create a `FileWriter` object that takes two arguments—the name of the file to write to and a `boolean` value that determines whether information will be appended to the file (`true` means information will be appended to the file; `false` means information will be written at the beginning of the file, overwriting any old data).
- Create a `PrintWriter` object by passing the `FileWriter` object as an argument to the `PrintWriter`'s constructor.
- Use the `println` method of `PrintWriter` to write information to the file, followed by a newline character.

Reading from a Sequential-Access File

- Import the `java.io` package.
- Create a `FileReader` object that takes as its argument the name of the file to read from.
- Create a `BufferedReader` object by passing the `FileReader` object to the constructor.
- Use the `readLine` method of `BufferedReader` to read information from the file.

KEY TERMS

binary digit—A digit that can assume one of two values (0 or 1).

bit—Short for "binary digit."

BufferedReader class—Provides the functionality of reading lines of text from a file.

byte—A piece of data typically composed of eight bits.

character—A digit, letter or special symbol (characters in Java are Unicode characters, which are composed of 2 bytes).

character set—The set of all characters used to write applications and represent data items on a particular computer. Java uses the Unicode character set.

close method of BufferedReader—Closes the file being read.

close method of PrintWriter—Closes the file to which information is being written.

data hierarchy—The collection of data items processed by computers, which become larger and more complex in structure as you progress from bits to characters to fields to files, and so on.

database—A group of related files.

database management system (DBMS)—A collection of programs designed to create and manage databases.

decimal digits—The digits 0, 1, 2, 3, 4, 5, 6, 7, 8 and 9.

field—A group of characters that conveys some meaning. For example, a field consisting of uppercase and lowercase letters can represent a person's name.

file—A group of related records that is assigned a name. Files are used for long-term persistence of data, even after the application that created the data terminates.

File class—Represents a file and can be used to retrieve information about a file, such as the name of the file.

file processing—A capability of Java that includes creating, reading from and writing to files.

FileReader class—Used to read characters from a file.

FileWriter class—Used to write characters from a file.

getName method of File—Returns the name of the selected file.

getSelectedFile method of JFileChooser—Returns File object containing the selected file from the JFileChooser.

IOException—An error that indicates that a problem occurred while opening, reading or writing a file.

java.io package—Includes classes that enable you to access and manipulate files.

JFileChooser component—Allows a user to select a file.

JFileChooser.APPROVE_OPTION constant—A value representing the **OK** JButton being clicked in the JFileChooser.

JFileChooser.CANCEL_OPTION constant—A value representing the **Cancel** JButton being clicked in the JFileChooser.

JFileChooser.ERROR_OPTION constant—A value specifying that an error occurred in a JFileChooser dialog.

letter—An uppercase letter A–Z or a lowercase letter a–z.

persistent data—Data that exists even after the application that created the data terminates.

println method of PrintWriter—Takes as an argument a value of any primitive type or Object and writes the String version of that value to the file, followed by a newline.

PrintWriter class—Provides the functionality of writing lines of text, but does not know how to open a file for output.

readLine method of the BufferedReader class—Reads a line of text from a stream and returns it as a String.

record—A collection of related fields. A record is usually represented as a class in Java.

record key—A unique field used to identify a record and distinguish that record from all other records.

removeAllItems method of JComboBox—Removes all items in the JComboBox.

secondary storage media—Devices such as magnetic disks, optical disks and magnetic tapes on which computers store files.

special symbols—$, @, %, &, *, (,), -, +, ", :, ?, / and the like.

sequential-access file—A file that contains data that is read in the order that it was written.

setDialogTitle method of JFileChooser—Changes the text displayed in the title bar of the JFileChooser.

showOpenDialog method of JFileChooser—Displays a dialog allowing a user to select a file or directory.

stream—Object that has access to a sequence of characters.

text file—A file containing human-readable characters.

Unicode character—Composed of 2 bytes. Characters are represented in Java using the Unicode character set.

JAVA LIBRARY REFERENCE

BufferedReader This class is used to read data from a file.

- *Constructor*

  BufferedReader—Takes a FileReader object as an argument. The resulting BufferedReader object can read data from the file opened by the FileReader. The following code demonstrates the use of this constructor.

  ```
  File currentFile = new File( "current.txt" );
  FileReader currentReader = new FileReader( currentFile );
  BufferedReader input = new BufferedReader( currentReader );
  ```

■ *Methods*

close—Closes the file.

readLine—Reads a line of data from a particular file.

File This class represents a file.

■ *Method*

getName—Returns the name of the File.

FileReader A class whose objects read characters from a file.

■ *Constructor*

FileReader—Takes a File object as an argument and opens the corresponding file for reading. The following lines of text demonstrate use of this constructor.

```
File currentFile = new File( "current.txt" );
FileReader currentReader = new FileReader( currentFile );
```

FileWriter A class whose objects write characters to a file.

■ *Constructor*

FileWriter—Takes a File object as the first argument and a boolean as the second argument. The first argument indicates the file that should be opened for writing. The second argument indicates whether new data should be appended (true) to the end of the file. The following lines of text demonstrate use of this constructor.

```
File currentFile = new File( "current.txt" );
FileWriter currentWriter = new FileWriter( currentFile, true );
```

JComboBox This component allows users to select from a drop-down list of options.

■ *In action*

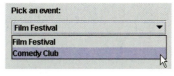   

■ *Event handler*

actionPerformed—Event handler called when a new value is selected in the JComboBox.

■ *Methods*

getItemAt—Takes an int argument representing an index and returns the value at that index of a JComboBox.

getSelectedIndex—Returns the index of the JComboBox's selected item, stored in the *selectedIndex* property.

removeAllItems—Removes all items in the JComboBox.

setBounds—Specifies the location and size of the JComboBox component on the container component relative to the top-left corner.

setEnabled—Controls whether the user can select items from a JComboBox.

setMaximumRowCount—Sets the number of items that can be displayed in the JComboBox's drop-down list.

setSelectedIndex—Sets the index of the JComboBox's selected item, stored in the *selectedIndex* property.

JFileChooser This class defines a dialog which enables the user to open a file.

■ *Constants*

JFileChooser.APPROVE_OPTION—A value representing the **OK** JButton being clicked in the JFileChooser.

JFileChooser.CANCEL_OPTION—A value representing the **Cancel** JButton being clicked in the JFileChooser.

JFileChooser.ERROR_OPTION—A value specifying that an error occurred in a JFileChooser dialog.

■ *Methods*

getSelectedFile—Returns the file selected by the user.

setDialogTitle—Sets the title of the dialog.

showOpenDialog—Displays the **Open** dialog and returns the result of the user interaction with the dialog.

PrintWriter This class is used to write data to a file.

■ *Constructor*

PrintWriter—Takes a FileWriter as an argument. The FileWriter specifies the file to which data will be written. The following lines of text demonstrate use of this constructor.

```
File currentFile = new File( "current.txt" );
FileWriter currentWriter = new FileWriter( currentFile, true );
PrintWriter output = new PrintWriter( currentWriter );
```

■ *Methods*

close—Closes the file.

println—Outputs the data specified in its argument, followed by a newline character.

MULTIPLE-CHOICE QUESTIONS

25.1 Data maintained in a file are called _____.

a) persistent data
b) bits
c) secondary data
d) databases

25.2 The _____ package provides the classes and methods that you need to use to perform file processing.

a) java.io
b) java.files
c) java.stream
d) none of the above

25.3 A _____ is a group of related files.

a) field
b) database
c) collection
d) byte

25.4 Digits, letters and special symbols are referred to as _____.

a) constants
b) ints
c) Strings
d) characters

25.5 The _____ method of the BufferedReader class reads a line from a file.

a) readLine
b) read
c) line
d) lineRead

25.6 Bytes are typically composed of _____ bits.

a) 4
b) 8
c) 1
d) 2

25.7 The _____ method of the BufferedReader class is used to close a file that has been opened for reading.

a) flush
b) closeBufferedReader
c) closeFile
d) close

25.8 The _____ method of the JFileChooser class returns the file selected in a dialog used to open files.

a) getFile

b) get

c) getSelectedFile

d) getFileSelected

25.9 The type of exception that occurs when there is an error opening a file is known as a(n) _____.

a) IOException

b) OpenException

c) FileException

d) InputOutputException

25.10 The _____ method of class JFileChooser is used to display a dialog used to open a file.

a) showOpenFileDialog

b) showOpenDialog

c) showFileDialog

d) showMessageDialog

EXERCISES

25.11 (*Birthday Saver Application*) Create an application that stores people's names and birthdays in a file (Fig. 25.49). The user creates a file and inputs each person's first name, last name and birthday in the application. The information is then written to the file as shown in the right image of Fig. 25.49. Note that only the month and day are written to the file.

Figure 25.49   **Birthday Saver** application's GUI.

a) *Copying the template to your working directory.* Copy the directory C:\Examples\ Tutorial25\Exercises\BirthdaySaver to your C:\SimplyJava directory.

b) *Opening the template file.* Open the BirthdaySaver.java file in your text editor.

c) *Viewing the PrintWriter instance variable.* In lines 29–30, view the PrintWriter instance variable named output that will be used to write output to a file.

d) *Opening a JFileChooser dialog.* For this exercise, you will define only the open-FileJButtonActionPerformed method (lines 160–163 in the template). Functionality for writing data to a file and closing a file is provided in the template. Starting on line 163, add and display a new JFileChooser to allow the user to select the file to which to write. Then, define an if statement that causes the method to be exited if the user clicks the **Cancel** JButton.

e) *Validating the file name.* Retrieve the file selected by the user (as a File object) and the name of the file. Create a File object, selectedFile, to contain the file selected by the user and create String fileName to contain the name of the selected file. Next, define an if statement that displays a message dialog when an invalid file name has been entered (that is, when fileName is the empty String).

f) *Opening the file to write to.* Begin an else statement to correspond to the if statement you created in the previous step. Inside the else statement, add a try block that opens the selected file. In this try block, define a FileWriter that opens the selectedFile. Use this FileWriter to initialize the PrintWriter declared on line 31. Also in this try block, disable the openFileJButton and enable the enterJButton and closeFileJButton. Then, add a catch block that will display a message dialog in the event of an IOException.

g) *Saving the application.* Save your modified source code file.

h) *Opening the Command Prompt window and changing directories.* Open the **Command Prompt** by selecting **Start > Programs > Accessories > Command Prompt**. Change to your working directory by typing cd C:\SimplyJava\BirthdaySaver.

i) *Compiling the application.* Compile your application by typing javac Birthday-Saver.java.

j) *Running the completed application.* When your application compiles correctly, run it by typing `java BirthdaySaver`. To test your application, enter several names and birthdays into a text file. Then, open the text file in your text editor to make sure it was written properly.

k) *Closing the application.* Close your running application by clicking the window's close button.

l) *Closing the Command Prompt window.* Close the **Command Prompt** window by clicking its close button.

25.12 (*Image Album Application*) Create an application that displays images for the user, as shown in Fig. 25.50. This application will display images of book covers, but you can easily modify the application to display your own images. You learned in Tutorial 2 that images can be displayed using the *icon* property of a JLabel. This application should display the current image on a large JLabel and display the previous and next images in smaller JLabels. The images are specified in the file `books.txt`. To display the next image as the large image, the user clicks the **Next Image** JButton. To display the previous image as the large image, the user clicks the **Previous Image** JButton. When either of these JButtons are pressed, the previous and next images are updated based on the next and previous images specified in a text file. When the last image in the file is displayed as the large image, no image will be displayed above the **Next Image** JButton. When the first image in the file is displayed as the large image, no image will be displayed above the **Previous Image** JButton. A description of the book represented by the large image should be displayed in a JTextArea. Figure 25.50 displays the cover of *C++ How to Program, 4/e* as the large image. Figure 25.51 shows the corresponding entry in `books.txt` that contains the name used for this book's image as well as a description of the book. You will examine the organization of this file more closely in the following steps. [*Note*: For presentation proposes, Fig. 25.51 does not show the entire description of the current text.]

Figure 25.50 **Image Album** application GUI.

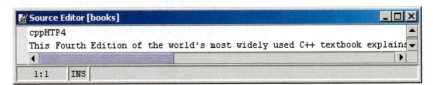

Figure 25.51 Contents of `books.txt`.

a) *Copying the template to your working directory.* Copy the directory `C:\Examples\Tutorial25\Exercises\ImageAlbum` to your `C:\SimplyJava` directory.

b) *Opening the template file.* Open the `ImageAlbum.java` file in your text editor.

c) *Declaring the BufferedReader.* In lines 26–27, declare BufferedReader input, which will be used to read information from a file.

d) *Calling the retrieveData method.* In this application, you will be defining the retrieveData method, which reads information from books.txt. This method is called at the start of the application and stores the image information in various instance variables (as you will see shortly). At line 122, call the retrieveData method. This method does not take any arguments.

e) *Opening a file to read from.* Inside the retrieveData method, add a try block. Inside the try block, open books.txt (located in the same directory as the application) for reading. To do so, create a File object for this file and create a FileReader. Then, initialize BufferedReader input using the FileReader created previously.

f) *Reading information from the file.* Each book has two lines of data in books.txt. The first line contains a prefix used to access the large and small images of this book's cover. Each book cover has two corresponding files—a small image file and a large image file. The large images are located in the images\large directory, and the small images are located in the images\small directory. The small image's file name ends with _thumb.jpg (that is, *filename*_thumb.jpg) while the large image's file name ends with _large.jpg (that is, *filename*_large.jpg). These files have similar names, beginning with the prefix *filename*. This prefix is the text that is stored as the first line of each entry in books.txt. For example, the entry in Fig. 25.51 has a first line of cppHTP4. This prefix is used to form the file names cppHTP4_thumb.jpg and cppHTP4_large.jpg and thus access these image files. The second line of each entry contains a description of the book whose cover is being displayed. You will now read information from this file. Inside the try block, add the code to read the first line from the file and store this line in String imageName. This String now contains the prefix for the first image. Declare int variable counter and initialize it to 0. This counter will be used shortly in a while statement.

g) *Storing information from the file.* Three arrays have already been declared for you. The largeImage array was created to contain the file names for the large image files. The smallImage array was created to contain the file names for the small image files. Finally, array descriptions was created to contain descriptions for each image. You will now fill these arrays with data from the file. After the declaration of int variable counter, define a while statement that loops while String imageName is not null (imageName will contain the value null when there is no more data to be read from the file). Whinin the while loop, use the prefix to form the name of the larger image file, and store this file name as the current element (using index counter) of the largeImage array. Use the prefix to form the name of the small image file and store this file name as the current element of the smallImage array. Next, read the next line from the file (the description for the current image) and store this information in the current element of array descriptions. Then, read the next line from the file (for the next iteration of the loop), increment the counter and close the while statement. These arrays can now be used later in the application to display the proper images and their descriptions.

h) *Closing the file.* After the try block, define a catch block that displays a message dialog if an IOException occurs. Then, add a finally block that close the BufferedReader input.

i) *Saving the application.* Save your modified source code file.

j) *Opening the Command Prompt window and changing directories.* Open the **Command Prompt** by selecting **Start > Programs > Accessories > Command Prompt**. Change to your working directory by typing cd C:\SimplyJava\ImageAlbum.

k) *Compiling the application.* Compile your application by typing javac Image-Album.java.

l) *Running the completed application.* When your application compiles correctly, run it by typing java ImageAlbum. To test your application, click the **Next Image** JButton until you have cycled through all the pictures.

m) *Closing the application.* Close your running application by clicking the window's close button.

n) *Closing the Command Prompt window.* Close the **Command Prompt** window by clicking its close button.

What does this code do? ▶   **25.13** What is the result of the following code?

```
1    String file1 = "oldFile.txt";
2    String file2 = "newFile.txt";
3    String line;
4
5    PrintWriter output;
6    BufferedReader input;
7
8    try
9    {
10      File oldFile = new File( file1 );
11      File newFile = new File( file2 );
12
13      FileWriter outputFile = new FileWriter( file2, false );
14      output = new PrintWriter( outputFile );
15
16      FileReader inputFile = new FileReader( file1 );
17      input = new BufferedReader( inputFile );
18
19      line = input.readLine();
20
21      while ( line != null )
22      {
23         output.println( line );
24         line = input.readLine();
25      }
26
27   }
28   catch( IOException exception )
29   {
30      JOptionPane.showMessageDialog( this, "IOException occurred." );
31   }
32   finally
33   {
34      try
35      {
36         output.close();
37         input.close();
38      }
39      catch( IOExcetpion exception )
40      {
41         JOptionPane.showMessageDialog( this, "IOException occurred." );
42      }
43   }
```

What's wrong with this code? ▶   **25.14** Find the error(s) in the following code, which is supposed to read a line from some-file.txt, convert the line to uppercase and append it to somefile.txt.

```
 1   String file = "someFile.txt";
 2   String contents;
 3
 4   File someFile = new File( file );
 5   FileReader inputFile = new FileReader( someFile );
 6   BufferedReader input = new BufferedReader( inputFile );
 7
 8   contents = input.readLine();
 9
10   contents = contents.toUpperCase();
11
12   input.close();
13
14   FileWriter outputFile = new FileWriter( someFile, false );
15   PrintWriter output = new PrintWriter( outputFile );
16
17   output.println( contents );
18   output.close();
```

Programming Challenge ▶   **25.15** (*Car Reservation Application*) Create an application that allows a user to reserve a car for a specified day (Fig. 25.52). The car reservation company can rent out only four cars per day. Let the application allow the user to specify a certain day. If four cars have already been reserved for that day, then indicate to the user that no vehicles are available. Reservations are stored in reservations.txt.

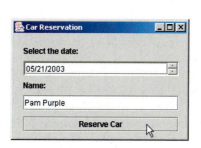

Figure 25.52   Car Reservation application GUI.

a) *Copying the template to your working directory.* Copy the directory C:\Examples\Tutorial25\Exercises\CarReservation to your C:\SimplyJava directory.

b) *Opening the template file.* Open the CarReservation.java file in your text editor.

c) *Declaring a BufferedReader and a PrintWriter instance variable.* At lines 24, declare two instance variables—a BufferedReader object named input, which will be used to read from a file, and a PrintWriter object named output, which will be used to write to a file.

d) *Opening a file to read from.* In the reserveCarJButtonActionPerformed method (which immediately follows createUserInterface), create a new File object reserveFile for the file reservations.txt. Then, add a try block. Inside the try block, create a FileReader by passing the reserveFile to its constructor . Use this FileReader to initialize BufferedReader input.

e) *Retrieving the selected date.* For this application, you should store in reservations.txt the date selected, including the day, month and year. To access this information, you will need to extract text from the selected Date in dateJSpinner.

Continue adding code to the try block. Your code should retrieve the selected value in dateJSpinner, use a cast to convert it to a Date object and store this object in Date fullDate. Convert the Date object to a String and store it in String currentDate. Use the substring method to extract the first 10 characters from currentDate, and store this substring in String monthDay. This substring contains the day of the week, the day of the month and the month. Use the substring method to extract the characters at indices 24–27 (inclusive) from currentDate and store this substring in String year. This substring contains the current year. Append monthDay and year, separated by a space, and store the resulting String in currentDate.

f) *Reading text from the file.* Still inside the try block, declare an int variable date-Count and assign to it the value 1. This variable is used to store the number of people who reserve a car for a specific day. Also, read a line from the file and store the line in String contents. Next, add a while statement that will read data from the file. Have the while statement loop while the value of contents is not null. Inside the while loop, add an if statement that executes when the value of contents equals the value of currentDate. Within this if statement, define an if...else statement where the if part increments dateCount if there are still less than four people reserving a car on that day. The else part should display a message dialog informing the user that there are no more cars available for this day, disable the reserveCar-JButton and exit the method. After the outer if statement, read the next line of the file for the next iteration of the while loop. After the while loop, close the file.

g) *Writing to the text file.* If the remainder of the method is reached, there is still room for a reservation on the current day. After the code that close the file (still inside the try block), open the reservations.txt for writing. Create a FileWriter with variable reserveFile, and then use the created FileWriter to initialize PrintWriter output. Next, write the value of currentDate to the file (in its own line), followed by the name entered into nameJTextField (also on its own line). Display a message dialog informing the user that the car has been reserved. Then, close the file, which is the last statement in the try block. Add a catch block to catch IOExceptions. The catch block should display a message dialog to indicate that an error occurs and disable the dateJSpinner and reserveCarJButton. After the catch block, add code to clear the nameJTextField.

h) *Saving the application.* Save your modified source code file.

i) *Opening the Command Prompt window and changing directories.* Open the **Command Prompt** by selecting **Start > Programs > Accessories > Command Prompt**. Change to your working directory by typing cd C:\SimplyJava\CarReservation.

j) *Compiling the application.* Compile your application by typing javac CarReservation.java.

k) *Running the completed application.* When your application compiles correctly, run it by typing java CarReservation. To test your application, reserve cars on different dates. Also, be sure that you receive an error message when trying to reserve too many cars for one day.

l) *Closing the application.* Close your running application by clicking the window's close button.

m) *Closing the Command Prompt window.* Close the **Command Prompt** window by clicking its close button.

ATM Application

Introducing Database Programming and Using Command-Line Arguments

Objectives

In this tutorial, you will learn to:
- Install the Cloudscape database.
- Connect to databases.
- Create SQL queries.
- Retrieve and update information in databases.
- Use command-line arguments to pass options to an application as it begins executing.

Outline

In the last tutorial, you learned how to create sequential-access files and how to search through such files to locate information. Sequential-access files are inappropriate for so-called **instant-access applications**, in which information must be located immediately. Popular instant-access applications include airline-reservation systems, banking systems, point-of-sale systems, automated teller machines (ATMs) and other transaction-processing systems that require rapid access to specific data. The bank where you have your account might have hundreds of thousands, or even millions, of other customers, but when you use an ATM, the bank's computers retrieve your account information in as little as a fraction of a second. This type of instant access is made possible by databases. Individual database records can be accessed directly (and quickly) without sequentially searching through large numbers of other records, as is required with sequential-access files. In this tutorial, you will be introduced to databases and the part of Java—the **JDBC™ API**—used to interact with databases. You will learn about databases and the JDBC API as you create the **ATM** application.

When the application executes with the java interpreter, you can supply arguments to the application (called **command-line arguments**) that specify options (such as database name) to run the application. You will learn how to pass command-line arguments to your application and how to use command-line arguments in your application.

26.1 IBM Cloudscape Database

The CD that accompanies this book includes a 60-day trial of Cloudscape 5.1.3—a pure-Java embedded database management system from IBM. Complete information about Cloudscape is available at

www-3.ibm.com/software/data/cloudscape/

Before you can test-drive the completed application you must install Cloudscape. [*Note*: If you want to use Microsoft Access instead of Cloudscape, we provide the Access version of the database used in this tutorial and the instructions on how to run the example with the Access database at www.deitel.com/books/simplyJava1/index.html.] Follow the steps in the box, *Installing Cloudscape,*

to install this software on your computer. [*Note*: If Cloudscape is already installed on your computer, you can skip this step.] Cloudscape executes on many platforms, including Windows, Solaris, Linux, Macintosh and others. For a complete list of these platforms, visit

www-3.ibm.com/software/data/cloudscape/requirements.html

Installing Cloudscape	1. ***Opening the Command Prompt window.*** Open the **Command Prompt** by selecting **Start > Programs > Accessories > Command Prompt**.

2. ***Installing Cloudscape.*** In the **Command Prompt** window, type `java -jar D:\software\Cloudscape513\cloudscape_eval_513.jar` to start the installer. [*Note*: If your CD drive is not drive `D:`, replace `D:` with the correct drive letter for your CD drive.] Click the **Next** button as shown in Fig. 26.1 to continue the installation. |

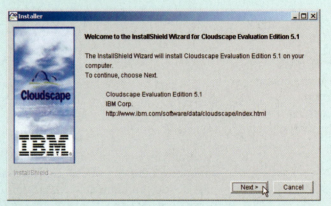

Figure 26.1 Welcome page of Cloudscape installer. (Courtesy of IBM Corporation.)

3. ***Reading release notes.*** The installer allows you to choose whether you want to read the release notes before installing Cloudscape. The release notes contain information about Cloudscape, such as the various platforms on which Cloudscape can run. Click the **Next** button (Fig. 26.2) to view the release notes (Fig. 26.3). If you do not want to read the release notes at this time, uncheck the check box in Fig. 26.2 and click the **Next** button to continue on to *Step 4*.

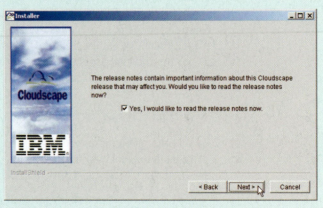

Figure 26.2 Option to view the release notes. (Courtesy of IBM Corporation.)

(cont.)

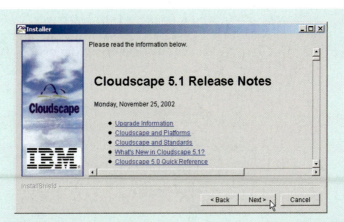

Figure 26.3 Cloudscape 5.1 release notes. (Courtesy of IBM Corporation.)

4. *Accepting the license agreement.* To install Cloudscape, you must accept the license agreement. Read the license agreement, then click the **I accept the terms in the license agreement** radio button and click the **Next** button to continue (Fig. 26.4).

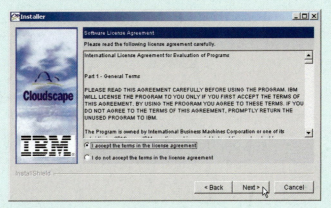

Figure 26.4 Accepting the Cloudscape license agreement. (Courtesy of IBM Corporation.)

5. *Specifying the installation directory.* When prompted to select an installation directory (Fig. 26.5), click **Next** to use the default directory (`C:\Cloudscape_5.1`). Cloudscape will be installed in the directory you specify here. If you choose a directory that does not exist, Cloudscape will create a directory of that name and proceed with the installation.

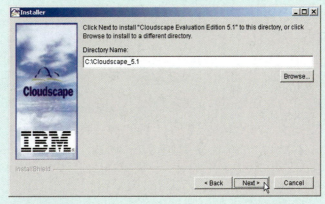

Figure 26.5 Choosing the Cloudscape installation directory. (Courtesy of IBM Corporation.)

(cont.)

6. ***Choosing the default setup type.*** When prompted to choose the setup type, click **Next** to accept the default setup type **Typical** (Fig. 26.6). This will install Cloudscape's standard components. If you wish to customize your installation by adding or removing Cloudscape components, select the **Custom** radio button, then click **Next**.

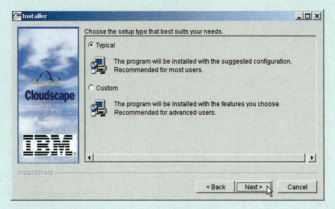

Figure 26.6   Choosing the default setup type. (Courtesy of IBM Corporation.)

7. ***Confirming the installation location.*** In Fig. 26.7, click **Next** to confirm the installation directory of Cloudscape and continue the install process.

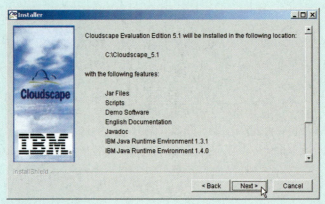

Figure 26.7   Confirming the location of the Cloudscape installation. (Courtesy of IBM Corporation.)

8. ***Monitoring the installation process.*** The installer program will begin to install Cloudscape on your computer (Fig. 26.8). This process may take a few minutes.

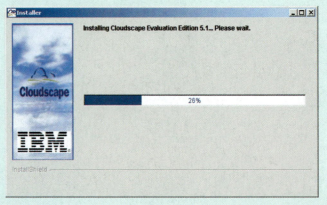

Figure 26.8   Cloudscape installation progress dialog. (Courtesy of IBM Corporation.)

(cont.) 9. **Completing the Cloudscape installation.** Once the Cloudscape installation completes, click **Next** to finish the installation (Fig. 26.9).

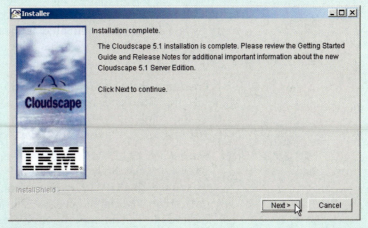

Figure 26.9 Completing the Cloudscape installation. (Courtesy of IBM Corporation.)

10. **Exiting the wizard.** Click the **Finish** button (Fig. 26.10) to exit the wizard.

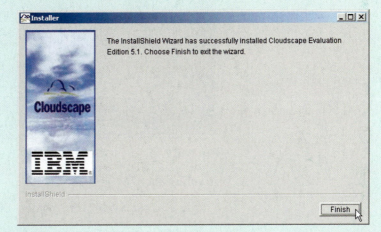

Figure 26.10 Exiting the installer wizard. (Courtesy of IBM Corporation.)

26.2 Test-Driving the ATM Application

Many banks offer ATMs to provide their customers with quick and easy access to their bank accounts. When customers use these machines, their account information is updated immediately to reflect the transactions they perform, such as deposits, withdrawals and fund transfers between accounts. This application must meet the following requirements:

> **Application Requirements**
>
> *A local bank has asked you to create a prototype automated teller machine (ATM) application to access a database that contains sample customer records. Each record consists of an account number, a Personal Identification Number (PIN), a first name and a balance amount. For testing purposes, valid account numbers will be provided in a JComboBox. The ATM application should allow the user to log in to an account by providing a valid PIN. Once logged in, the user should be able to view the account balance and withdraw money from the account (if the account contains sufficient funds). If money is withdrawn, the application should update the database.*

Your **ATM** application will allow the user to enter a PIN. If the user provides a correct PIN, then the ATM will retrieve information about the requested account, such as the account holder's name and balance, from the database. If the PIN entered is invalid, a message is displayed asking the user to re-enter the PIN. You begin by test-driving the completed application. Next, you learn the additional Java technologies you will need to create your own version of this application.

<table>
<tr>
<td>

Test-Driving the ATM Application

</td>
<td>

1. ***Locating the completed application.*** Open the **Command Prompt** by selecting **Start > Programs > Accessories > Command Prompt**. Change to the completed **ATM** application directory by typing `cd C:\Examples\Tutorial26\CompletedApplication\ATM`.

2. ***Setting the CLASSPATH environment variable.*** Type `C:\Cloudscape_5.1\frameworks\embedded\bin\setCP.bat` in the **Command Prompt** window (Fig. 26.11) to set the **CLASSPATH environment variable** (Fig. 26.11). The CLASSPATH environment variable specifies the location of the class libraries that are required to run an application. By default, Java knows where the classes of the Java class library are located. Performing this step will enable the application to interact with Cloudscape by using the Java classes supplied with Cloudscape.

</td>
</tr>
</table>

Result of running `setCP.bat` —

```
Command Prompt

C:\Examples\Tutorial26\CompletedApplication\ATM>C:\Cloudscape_5.1\frameworks\embedded\bin\setCP.bat

C:\Examples\Tutorial26\CompletedApplication\ATM>set DB2J_INSTALL=C:\Cloudscape_5.1

C:\Examples\Tutorial26\CompletedApplication\ATM>set CLASSPATH=C:\Cloudscape_5.1\lib\db2j.jar;C:\Cloudscape_5.1\lib\db2jtools.jar;C:\Cloudscape_5.1\lib\db2jcview.jar;C:\Cloudscape_5.1\lib\jh.jar;C:\Cloudscape_5.1\lib\license.jar;

C:\Examples\Tutorial26\CompletedApplication\ATM>
```

Figure 26.11 Setting the CLASSPATH environment variable.

3. ***Running the ATM application.*** Type

```
java ATM com.ibm.db2j.jdbc.DB2jDriver jdbc:db2j:ATM
```

in the **Command Prompt** window (Fig. 26.12) to run the application (Fig. 26.13). Notice the two command-line arguments passed to the **ATM** application—`com.ibm.db2j.jdbc.DB2jDriver` and `jdbc:db2j:ATM`. Command-line arguments allow you to provide information to an application as it begins execution. In this case, the command-line arguments represent the JDBC driver class and the database URL. The application shown in Fig. 26.13 will appear with the keypad **JButtons** and the **Enter**, **Balance**, **Withdraw** and **Done JButtons** initially disabled. The **JTextArea** at the top of the ATM displays a message informing you to select an account number.

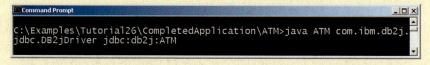

Figure 26.12 Passing command-line arguments to the **ATM** application.

(cont.)

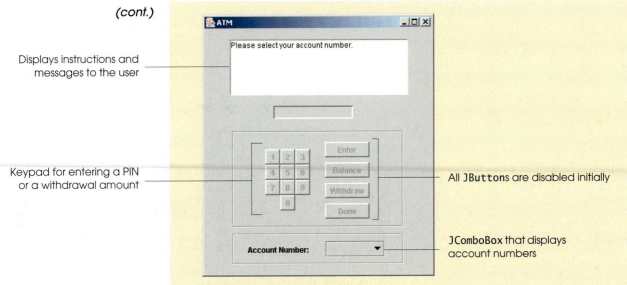

Displays instructions and messages to the user

Keypad for entering a PIN or a withdrawal amount

All JButtons are disabled initially

JComboBox that displays account numbers

Figure 26.13   ATM application.

4. *Selecting an account number.* Use the **Account Number:** JComboBox at the bottom of the application to select your account number (assume that it is 12548693). Notice that the JTextArea now prompts the user to provide a PIN (Fig. 26.14). The JComboBox has been disabled, preventing the user from selecting another account until the current transaction is complete. The **Done** JButton has been enabled, allowing you to indicate that the current transaction is complete, so the next user can begin a transaction. The keypad JButtons have also been enabled allowing the user to enter the PIN.

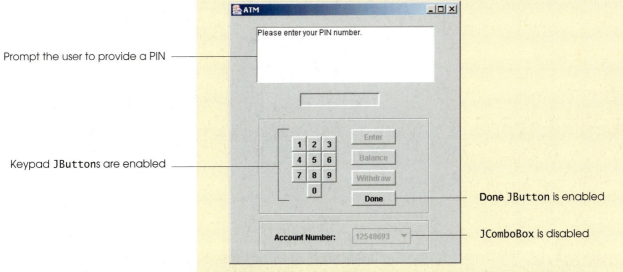

Prompt the user to provide a PIN

Keypad JButtons are enabled

Done JButton is enabled

JComboBox is disabled

Figure 26.14   Selecting an account number from the JComboBox.

5. *Entering a PIN.* Use the keypad to input 1234 the PIN. Notice that each time you click a digit on the numeric keypad, an asterisk (*) is displayed to conceal your input. The **Enter** JButton should be enabled now (Fig. 26.15).

(cont.)

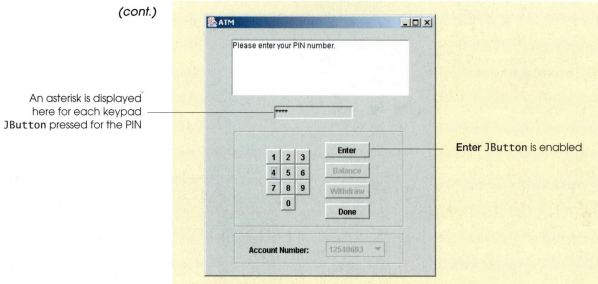

An asterisk is displayed here for each keypad JButton pressed for the PIN

Enter JButton is enabled

Figure 26.15 Entering the PIN for the selected account.

6. *Clicking the Enter JButton.* Click **Enter** to submit your PIN. The JTextArea at the top of the ATM will display a welcome message telling you to select a transaction (Fig. 26.16). Notice that the **Balance** and **Withdraw** JButtons have been enabled, allowing you to perform these types of transactions. The **Enter** JButton and the keypad JButtons are disabled to prevent you from entering numbers without selecting the transaction type.

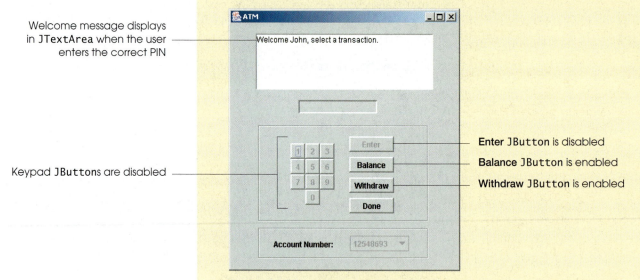

Welcome message displays in JTextArea when the user enters the correct PIN

Keypad JButtons are disabled

Enter JButton is disabled

Balance JButton is enabled

Withdraw JButton is enabled

Figure 26.16 ATM displaying welcome message.

7. *Viewing the account balance.* Click the **Balance** JButton to view the account balance. The amount displays in the JTextArea at the top of the application (Fig. 26.17).

8. *Withdrawing money from the account.* Click the **Withdraw** JButton to initiate a withdrawal. The JTextArea at the top of the application asks you to input the amount you want to withdraw (Fig. 26.18). The keypad JButtons are enabled, allowing you to enter the withdrawal amount. The **Balance** and **Withdraw** JButtons are disabled, preventing you from performing another transaction without first completing the withdrawal.

(cont.)

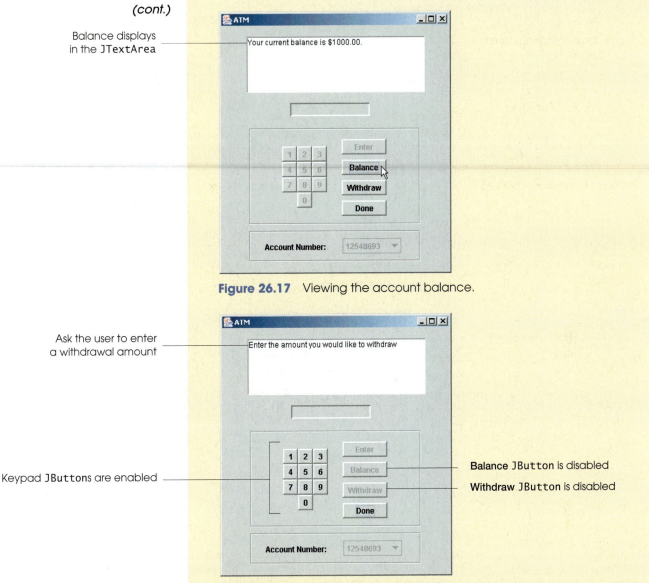

Balance displays
in the JTextArea

Figure 26.17   Viewing the account balance.

Ask the user to enter
a withdrawal amount

Keypad JButtons are enabled

Balance JButton is disabled

Withdraw JButton is disabled

Figure 26.18   Withdrawing money from the account.

9. ***Entering the withdrawal amount.*** Use the keypad to input 20 for the withdrawal amount. Notice that once you click the **2** JButton, the **Enter** JButton is enabled. After inputting 20, click **Enter**. The JTextArea displays the withdrawal amount, which is $20.00 (Fig. 26.19). Both the **Balance** and **Withdraw** JButtons are enabled for the next transaction, and the **Enter** JButton and the keypad JButtons are disabled.

10. ***Confirm that the account information has been updated.*** Click the **Balance** JButton to check the balance of the account (Fig. 26.20). Notice that the balance amount reflects the withdrawal you performed in *Step* 9.

11. ***Ending the transaction.*** Click the **Done** JButton to complete the transaction. The transaction ends and the instructions for the next customer are displayed in the JTextArea (Fig. 26.21). The **Enter**, **Balance**, **Withdraw**, **Done** and keypad JButtons are disabled. The JComboBox is enabled, allowing the new customer to select an account number.

(cont.)

Display the withdrawal amount

Keypad JButtons are disabled

Balance JButton is enabled

Withdraw JButton is enabled

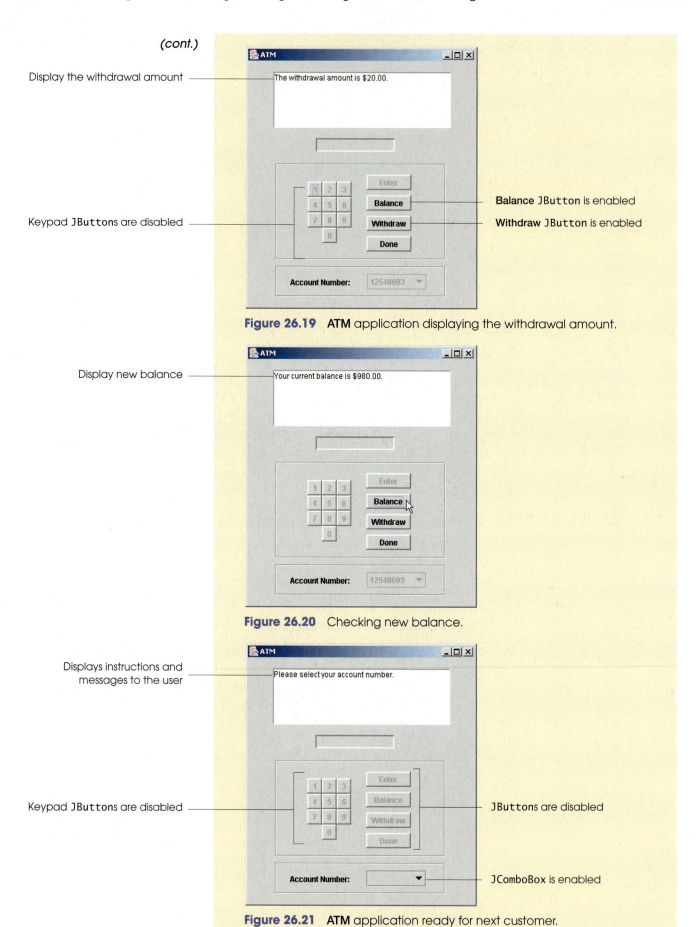

Figure 26.19 **ATM** application displaying the withdrawal amount.

Display new balance

Figure 26.20 Checking new balance.

Displays instructions and messages to the user

Keypad JButtons are disabled

JButtons are disabled

JComboBox is enabled

Figure 26.21 **ATM** application ready for next customer.

(cont.)   12. ***Closing the running application***. Close the running application by clicking its close button.

13. ***Closing the Command Prompt window***. Close the **Command Prompt** window by clicking its close button.

26.3 Planning the ATM Application

Now that you have test-driven the **ATM** application, you will begin by analyzing the application. The following pseudocode describes the basic operation of the **ATM** application.

```
When the user selects an account number from the JComboBox:
    Disable the JComboBox
    Clear the JTextField for the PIN
    Prompt the user to enter a PIN
    Enable the keypad JButtons
    Enable the Done JButton

When the user enters the PIN:
    Enable the Enter JButton
    Append the number to the PIN

When the user clicks the Enter JButton to submit the PIN:
    Search the database for the account number's corresponding account
    information

    If the user provided a correct PIN
        Clear the JTextField
        Disable the Enter JButton
        Disable the keypad JButtons
        Enable the Balance and Withdraw JButtons
        Display the status to the user
    Else
        Clear the JTextField
        Prompt the user to enter a valid PIN

When the user clicks the Balance JButton:
    Display the balance

When the user clicks the Withdraw JButton:
    Disable the Balance and Withdraw JButtons
    Enable the keypad JButtons
    Prompt the user to enter the withdrawal amount

When the user clicks the Enter JButton to submit the withdrawal amount:
    Disable the Enter JButton
    Disable the keypad JButtons
    Process the withdrawal and display the withdrawal amount
    Clear the withdrawal amount in the JTextField
    Enable the Balance and Withdraw JButtons

When the user clicks the Done JButton:
    Disable the keypad JButtons
    Disable the Enter, Balance, Withdraw and Done JButtons
    Enable the JComboBox
    Display instructions for the next customer in the JTextArea
```

Now that you have test-driven the **ATM** application and studied its pseudocode representation, you will use an ACE table to help you convert the pseudocode to Java. Fig. 26.22 lists the actions, components and events required to complete your own version of this application.

Action/Component/ Event (ACE) Table for the ATM Application	Action	Component	Event
		accountNumberJComboBox	User selects an account number from JComboBox
	Disable the JComboBox	accountNumberJComboBox	
	Clear the JTextField for the PIN	numberJTextField	
	Prompt user to enter a PIN	messageJTextArea	
	Enable the keypad JButtons	zeroJButton, oneJButton, twoJButton, threeJButton, fourJButton, fiveJButton, sixJButton, sevenJButton, eightJButton, nineJButton	
	Enable the Done JButton	doneJButton	
		zeroJButton, oneJButton, twoJButton, threeJButton, fourJButton, fiveJButton, sixJButton, sevenJButton, eightJButton, nineJButton	User clicks keypad JButton
	Enable the Enter JButton	enterJButton	
	Append the number to the PIN	numberJTextField	
		enterJButton	User clicks **Enter** JButton
	Search the database for the account number's corresponding account information	myStatement myResultSet	
	If the user provided a correct PIN Clear the JTextField	numberJTextField	
	Disable the Enter JButton	enterJButton	
	Disable the keypad JButtons	zeroJButton, oneJButton, twoJButton, threeJButton, fourJButton, fiveJButton, sixJButton, sevenJButton, eightJButton, nineJButton	
	Enable the Balance and Withdraw JButtons	balanceJButton, withdrawJButton	
	Display status to the user	messageJTextArea	
	Else Clear the JTextField	numberJTextField	
	Prompt the user to enter a valid PIN	messageJTextArea	
		balanceJButton	User clicks **Balance** JButton
	Display the balance	messageJTextArea	

Figure 26.22 ACE table for the **ATM** application. (Part 1 of 2.)

Action	Component	Event
	`withdrawJButton`	User clicks **Withdraw** JButton
Disable the Balance and Withdraw JButtons	`balanceJButton` `withdrawJButton`	
Enable the keypad JButtons	`zeroJButton, oneJButton, twoJButton, threeJButton, fourJButton, fiveJButton, sixJButton, sevenJButton, eightJButton, nineJButton`	
Prompt the user to enter the withdrawal amount	`messageJTextArea`	
	`enterJButton`	User clicks **Enter** JButton
Disable the Enter JButton	`enterJButton`	
Disable the keypad JButtons	`zeroJButton, oneJButton, twoJButton, threeJButton, fourJButton, fiveJButton, sixJButton, sevenJButton, eightJButton, nineJButton`	
Process the withdrawal and display the withdrawal amount	`myStatement` `messageJTextArea`	
Clear withdrawal amount in the JTextField	`numberJTextField`	
Enable the Balance and Withdraw JButtons	`balanceJButton` `withdrawJButton`	
	`doneJButton`	User clicks **Done** JButton
Disable the keypad JButtons	`zeroJButton, oneJButton, twoJButton, threeJButton, fourJButton, fiveJButton, sixJButton, sevenJButton, eightJButton, nineJButton`	
Disable the Enter, Balance, Withdraw and Done JButtons	`enterJButton, balanceJButton, withdrawJButton, doneJButton`	
Enable the JComboBox	`accountNumberJComboBox`	
Display instructions for the next customer in the JTextArea	`messageJTextArea`	

Figure 26.22 ACE table for the **ATM** application. (Part 2 of 2.)

26.4 Relational Database Overview: The ATM Database

In this section, you will become familiar with the **ATM** database used in this application. A **database** is an organized collection of data. Many different strategies exist for organizing databases to allow easy access to and manipulation of the data within them. A **database management system (DBMS)** enables applications to access and store data without worrying about how the data is organized.

Today's most popular database systems are relational databases. A **relational database** consists of data items stored in simple tables from which the data can be accessed. A **table** is used to store information in rows and columns. A **row** uniquely represents a set of values in a relational database. A **column** represents an individual data attribute. Some popular **relational database management systems (RDBMSs)** are Microsoft SQL Server, Oracle, Sybase, IBM DB2, Informix and MySQL. In this tutorial, we present examples using Cloudscape 5.1—a Java-based

RDBMS from IBM. Figure 26.23 displays the simple database used in the **ATM** application. This database consists of a single table.

accountNumber	pin	firstName	balanceAmount
12548693	1234	John	980.0
24578648	8568	Susan	125.0
35682458	5689	Joseph	3400.99
45632598	8790	Michael	1254.76
52489635	2940	Donna	9200.02
55698632	3457	Elizabeth	788.9
69857425	6765	Jennifer	677.87
71869534	5678	Al	7799.24
88965723	1245	Ben	736.78
98657425	2456	Bob	946.09

Figure 26.23 accountInformation table of the ATM database.

The name of the table is accountInformation, and the table's primary purpose is to store the attributes of multiple accounts. This table contains ten rows and four columns. For example, in this table, the row containing 12548693, 1234, John and 980.0 represents a single account. The accountNumber, pin, firstName and balanceAmount columns represent the data in each row. The values stored in the accountNumber, pin and firstName columns are Strings. The values stored in the balanceAmount column are doubles.

In addition to rows and columns, a table should contain a **primary key**, which is a column (or combination of columns) that contains unique values. Primary keys are used to distinguish rows from one another. In this table, the accountNumber column is the primary key for referencing the data. Because no two account number values are the same, the accountNumber column can act as the primary key.

Different users of a database often are interested in different data and different relationships among those data. Users often require only subsets of the rows and columns. To obtain these subsets, we use **Structured Query Language (SQL)** to specify which data to select from a table. SQL—pronounced "sequel"—is the international standard language, used almost universally with relational databases to perform **queries**—requests for information that satisfy a given criteria—and to manipulate data. In the next section, you will learn how to write basic SQL statements.

SELF-REVIEW

1. Relational databases are composed of one or more _____.
   a) charts
   b) relatives
   c) tables
   d) None of the above.

2. The _____ contains unique values that are used to distinguish rows from one another.
   a) primary key
   b) SQL
   c) query
   d) None of the above.

Answers: 1) c. 2) a.

26.5 SQL

In this section, you will learn to use basic SQL queries in the context of our ATM sample database. You will write your own SQL queries as you answer the exercises at the end of the tutorial.

26.5.1 Basic SELECT Query

You begin by considering several SQL queries that extract information from the ATM database. A SQL query "selects" rows and columns from one or more tables in a database. Such selections are performed by **SELECT** queries. The basic form of a query is

    SELECT * FROM tableName

In the preceding query, the **FROM** keyword indicates the table from which the query is taken and the asterisk (*) indicates that all columns from the *tableName* table should be retrieved. For example, to retrieve all the data in the accountInformation table, you would use the query

    SELECT * FROM accountInformation

To retrieve only specific columns from a table, replace the asterisk (*) with a comma-separated list of the column names. For example, to retrieve only the columns accountNumber and firstName for all rows in the accountInformation table, use the query

    SELECT accountNumber, firstName FROM accountInformation

This query returns the data listed in Fig. 26.24.

accountNumber	firstName
12548693	John
24578648	Susan
35682458	Joseph
45632598	Michael
52489635	Donna
55698632	Elizabeth
69857425	Jennifer
71869534	Al
88965723	Ben
98657425	Bob

Figure 26.24   Selecting the accountNumber and firstName columns of the accountInformation table.

26.5.2 WHERE Clause

In most cases, it is necessary to locate rows in a database that satisfy certain **selection criteria**. Only rows that satisfy the selection criteria are selected. SQL uses the optional **WHERE** clause to specify the selection criteria for a query. The basic form of a SELECT query with selection criteria is

    SELECT columnName1, columnName2, ... FROM tableName WHERE criteria

For example, to select from table accountInformation the pin, firstName and balanceAmount columns for which the accountNumber equals "12548693", use the query

    SELECT pin, firstName, balanceAmount
        FROM accountInformation
        WHERE accountNumber = '12548693'

Figure 26.25 shows the single row that is the result of the preceding query. Notice that SQL uses the single quote (') character as a delimiter for strings. The accountNumber 12548693 appears in quotes, because the values stored in the accountNumber column are represented as Strings in this database. Quotes are not used with numeric values, such as ints and doubles.

Common Programming Error

If a programmer assumes that the columns in a result are always returned in the same order from a SQL statement that uses the asterisk (*), the application may process the result incorrectly. If the column order in the table(s) changes, the order of the columns in the result would change accordingly.

Good Programming Practice

Specifying the column names to select guarantees that the columns are always returned in the specified order and also avoids returning unneeded columns, even if the actual order of the columns in the table(s) changes.

pin	firstName	balanceAmount
1234	John	980.0

Figure 26.25 Selecting the `pin`, `firstName` and `balanceAccount` for the person with `accountNumber` 12548693.

26.5.3 UPDATE Statement

An **UPDATE** statement modifies data in a table. The basic form of the UPDATE statement is

```
UPDATE tableName
    SET columnName1 = value1, columnName2 = value2, ..., columnNameN = valueN
    WHERE criteria
```

where *tableName* is the table to update. The *tableName* is followed by the **SET** keyword and a comma-separated list of column name/value pairs in the format *columnName = value*. The WHERE clause provides criteria to determine which rows to update. The UPDATE statement

```
UPDATE accountInformation
    SET balanceAmount = 1000
    WHERE accountNumber = '12548693'
```

updates a row in the `accountInformation` table. The statement indicates that `balanceAmount` will be assigned the value 1000 for the row in which `accountNumber` is equal to 12548693. The `balanceAmount` 1000 does not appear in quotes, because the values stored in the `accountNumber` column are represented as `doubles` in this database. Figure 26.26 shows the `accountInformation` table after the UPDATE operation completes.

accountNumber	pin	firstName	balanceAmount
12548693	1234	John	1000.0
24578648	8568	Susan	125.0
35682458	5689	Joseph	3400.99
45632598	8790	Michael	1254.76
52489635	2940	Donna	9200.02
55698632	3457	Elizabeth	788.9
69857425	6765	Jennifer	677.87
71869534	5678	Al	7799.24
88965723	1245	Ben	736.78
98657425	2456	Bob	946.09

Figure 26.26 `accountInformation` table after executing an UPDATE statement.

SELF-REVIEW

1. SQL keyword _____ is followed by the selection criteria that specify the rows to select in a query.

    a) SELECT   b) WHERE

    c) UPDATE   d) None of the above.

2. Use a SQL _____ statement to modify data in a table.

    a) SELECT   b) WHERE

    c) UPDATE   d) None of the above.

Answers: 1) b. 2) c.

26.6 Using Command-Line Arguments

In the test-drive, you supplied two command-line arguments (Fig. 26.12) to the **ATM** application. Now, you will learn how to access the command-line arguments that were passed to your application.

Passing the Command-Line Arguments to the Application

1. ***Copying the template to your working directory.*** Copy the C:\Examples\ Tutorial26\TemplateApplication\ATM directory to your C:\Simply-Java directory.

2. ***Opening the template application.*** Open the template file ATM.java in your text editor.

3. ***Viewing the main method.*** When the **ATM** application executes, it calls the main method first (lines 798–816 of Fig. 26.27). Java passes the command-line arguments to main as an array of Strings called args (line 798). When you ran the **ATM** application in the test-drive, the first argument (com.ibm.db2j.jdbc.DB2jDriver) after the application class name was the first String in the args array and the second argument (jdbc:db2j:ATM) was the second String in args. The length of the array is the total number of command-line arguments that appear after the application's class name.

Start the main method declaration
Check the number of command-line arguments
Get the command-line arguments
Pass the command-line arguments to the constructor
Display a line of text that indicates the syntax to run the application

```
797     // method main
798     public static void main( String[] args )
799     {
800         // check command-line arguments
801         if ( args.length == 2 )
802         {
803             // get command-line arguments
804             String databaseDriver = args[ 0 ];
805             String databaseURL = args[ 1 ];
806
807             // create new ATM
808             ATM atm = new ATM( databaseDriver, databaseURL );
809         }
810         else // invalid command-line arguments
811         {
812             System.out.println(
813                 "Usage: java ATM databaseDriver databaseURL" );
814         }
815
816     } // end method main
```

Figure 26.27 Viewing the main method.

If the length of the args array is 2 (line 801), lines 804–805 retrieve the command-line arguments from the array, and line 808 passes the arguments to the **ATM** constructor. If the number of command-line arguments is incorrect, lines 812–813 call the **System.out.println** method to display a line of text in the **Command Prompt** window. This text indicates the proper syntax required to run the application from the **Command Prompt** window. **System.out** is known as the **standard output object**. It allows Java applications to display text in the **Command Prompt** window.

SELF-REVIEW

1. The length of the array args (the parameter of the main method) is the total number of _____.

a) commands to run the application b) methods in the application
c) command-line arguments d) None of the above.

2. The `println` method of the _____ object displays a line of text in the **Command Prompt** window.

    a) `System`
                            b) `System.out`

    c) `System.output`
                  d) None of the above.

Answers: 1) c. 2) b.

26.7 Creating Database Connections

Java applications communicate with databases and manipulate their data using the JDBC™ API. In this tutorial, you will be introduced to JDBC and use it to manipulate a Cloudscape database. The techniques demonstrated here also can be used to manipulate other databases that have JDBC drivers. A **JDBC driver** is a class provided by a DBMS vendor that enables Java applications to access a particular database, such as `com.ibm.db2j.jdbc.DB2jDriver` for the Cloudscape database. To access a database with JDBC, you first must connect to the database. [*Note*: If you want to use the Microsoft Access database instead of Cloudscape, we provide the Access version of the database used in this tutorial and the instructions on how to run the example with the Access database on our Web site—www.deitel.com/books/simplyJava1/index.html.]

Adding a Database Connection to the ATM Application	1. ***Importing the `java.sql` package.*** Add line 6 of Fig. 26.28 to import the `java.sql` package. Importing this package will allow you to perform database processing and omit typing `java.sql` when referring to the JDBC classes and interfaces in this package.

Importing the `java.sql` package ⎯

```
Source Editor [ATM]
4  import java.awt.*;
5  import java.awt.event.*;
6  import java.sql.*;
7  import java.text.*;
8  import javax.swing.*;
```

Figure 26.28   Importing the `java.sql` package.

2. ***Declaring instance variables for database processing.*** Add lines 71–74 of Fig. 26.29 to declare the instance variables used to manipulate the database. Line 72 declares the `Connection` variable `myConnection`. This **Connection** object manages the connection between the Java application and the database. `Connection` objects enable applications to create SQL statements that manipulate databases. As long as the connection remains open, SQL statements may be executed. Line 73 declares the `Statement` variable `myStatement`. This **Statement** object enables applications to execute SQL. If the SQL executed is a query, a **ResultSet** containing the rows and columns selected from the database is returned. The rows of the table are returned in sequence. Line 74 declares the `ResultSet` variable `myResultSet`. Only one `ResultSet` can be open per `Statement` at any time.

Declaring instance variables for managing the database connection ⎯

```
Source Editor [ATM]
69      private double balance;
70
71      // instance variables used to manipulate database
72      private Connection myConnection;
73      private Statement myStatement;
74      private ResultSet myResultSet;
75
76      // no-argument constructor
```

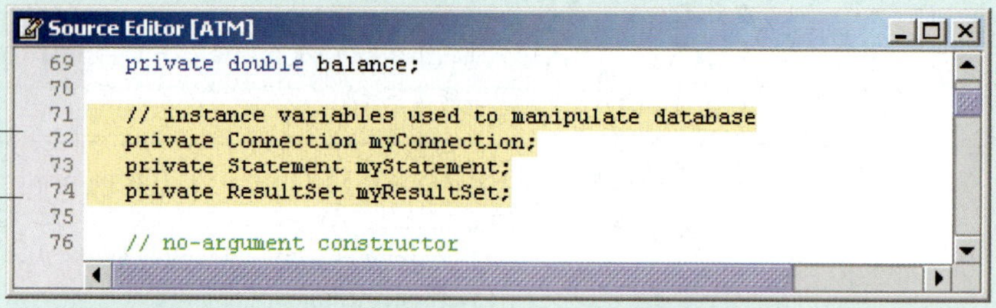

Figure 26.29   Declaring instance variables for database processing.

(cont.)   3.   ***Connecting to the database.*** To access and manipulate data in a database, you must first establish a connection to the database. Add lines 79–99 of Fig. 26.30 to the ATM constructor to connect to the database. The `try` block (lines 80–91) will establish the database connection and create a `Statement` object.

The application must load the database driver before attempting to connect to the database. Line 83 calls the **forName** method of class **Class** to load the class for the database driver. The `Class` object represents a class in a running Java application. The class name of the database driver (`databaseDriver`), which is received from `main`, is specified as the first command-line argument (`com.ibm.db2j.jdbc.DB2jDriver`). Line 83 throws a **ClassNotFoundException** if the class loader cannot locate the driver class, which means the path to the database driver class is not specified in the CLASSPATH environment variable. Lines 86–87 assign to `myConnection` the result of a call to the **getConnection** method of the `DriverManager` class. The **DriverManager** class manages JDBC drivers and uses them to establish database connections.

The `getConnection` method attempts to connect to the database specified by its argument, `databaseURL` (received from `main`). Recall that when you test-drove the **ATM** application, you passed `jdbc:db2j:ATM` (the JDBC URL) as the second command-line argument to the application. A **JDBC URL** can be thought of as an address that directs a JDBC driver to a database location. The argument to the `getConnection` method—a JDBC URL—has the form *protocol:subprotocol:subname*. The JDBC URL specifies the protocol for communication (`jdbc`), the subprotocol for communication (such as `db2j`) and the name of the database (such as ATM). **Protocols** and **subprotocols** are sets of rules that defines how data is transferred between the Java application and the database. The database is located in your `C:\SimplyJava\ATM` directory. The subprotocol `db2j` indicates that the application uses IBM-specific rules to connect to the Cloudscape database. If the `DriverManager` cannot connect to the database, the `getConnection` method throws a `SQLException`. A **SQLException** indicates database connection or processing errors.

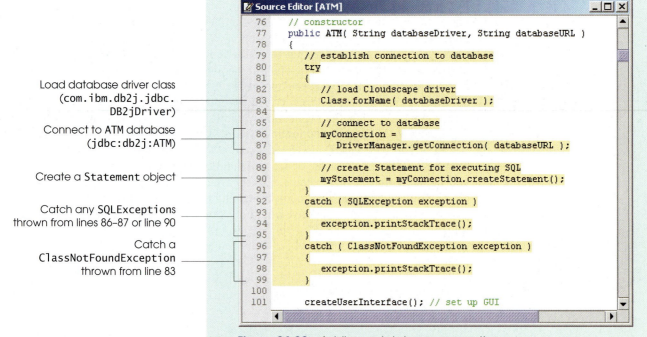

Load database driver class (`com.ibm.db2j.jdbc.DB2jDriver`)

Connect to ATM database (`jdbc:db2j:ATM`)

Create a `Statement` object

Catch any SQLExceptions thrown from lines 86–87 or line 90

Catch a ClassNotFoundException thrown from line 83

```
76    // constructor
77    public ATM( String databaseDriver, String databaseURL )
78    {
79        // establish connection to database
80        try
81        {
82            // load Cloudscape driver
83            Class.forName( databaseDriver );
84
85            // connect to database
86            myConnection =
87                DriverManager.getConnection( databaseURL );
88
89            // create Statement for executing SQL
90            myStatement = myConnection.createStatement();
91        }
92        catch ( SQLException exception )
93        {
94            exception.printStackTrace();
95        }
96        catch ( ClassNotFoundException exception )
97        {
98            exception.printStackTrace();
99        }
100
101       createUserInterface(); // set up GUI
```

Figure 26.30   Adding a database connection.

(cont.)

Line 90 invokes Connection method **createStatement** to obtain a Statement object. The application uses the Statement object to submit SQL to the database. The createStatement method throws a SQLException. Lines 92–95 catch the SQLException that may be thrown by lines 86–87 or line 90, and lines 96–99 catch the ClassNotFoundException that may be thrown by line 83.

4. *Saving the application.* Save your modified source code file.

5. *Opening the Command Prompt window and changing directories.* Open the **Command Prompt** window by selecting **Start > Programs > Accessories > Command Prompt**. Change to your ATM working directory by typing cd C:\SimplyJava\ATM.

6. *Compiling the application.* Compile your application by typing javac ATM.java. If your application does not compile correctly, fix the errors in your code before proceeding to the next section.

7. *Closing the Command Prompt window.* Close the **Command Prompt** window by clicking its close button.

SELF-REVIEW

1. Importing the _____ package will allow you to use the classes and interfaces for database processing.

   a) java.text
   b) java.db
   c) java.sql
   d) None of the above.

2. The getConnection method throws a _____ if the DriverManager cannot connect to the database.

   a) SQLException
   b) ClassNotFoundException
   c) DatabaseNotFoundException
   d) None of the above.

Answers: 1) c. 2) a.

26.8 Programming the ATM Application

Now that you have established a connection to the ATM Cloudscape database and have obtained a Statement object to manipulate the database, you will write the necessary code to complete the application. When you view the template code file (ATM.java), you will notice that the basic functionality of the **ATM** application is already provided. However, you will be declaring the loadAccountNumbers, retrieveAccountInformation and updateBalance methods that will access the database. You also will declare the frameWindowClosing method to close the database connection when the application window is closed. The empty method headers for these have been provided for you. Your task will be to code their functionality.

Now you will declare the loadAccountNumbers method to fill the account-NumberJComboBox with a list of account numbers from the database. This will allow you to select an existing account number when the **ATM** application is executed. [*Note:* You provide the JComboBox containing the account numbers for demonstration purposes only. A real ATM would not provide a list of account numbers like this.]

Displaying Existing Account Numbers in the JComboBox

1. ***Filling the JComboBox with account numbers.*** Insert lines 804–824 of Fig. 26.31 into the `loadAccountNumbers` method. Lines 807–808 use the `Statement` object's **`executeQuery`** method to submit a SQL query to the database. The specified query selects all the account numbers from the `accountInformation` table. The `executeQuery` method takes a `String` argument that specifies the query and returns an object that implements `ResultSet` interface. The `ResultSet` object enables the application to manipulate the query results. The `executeQuery` method throws a `SQLException` if an error occurs while accessing the database.

```
Source Editor [ATM]                                                  _ | □ | ✕
801        // load account numbers to accountNumberJComboBox
802        private void loadAccountNumbers()
803        {
804            // get all account numbers from database
805            try
806            {
807                myResultSet = myStatement.executeQuery(
808                    "SELECT accountNumber FROM accountInformation" );
809
810                // add account numbers to accountNumberJComboBox
811                while ( myResultSet.next() )
812                {
813                    accountNumberJComboBox.addItem(
814                        myResultSet.getString( "accountNumber" ) );
815                }
816
817                myResultSet.close(); // close myResultSet
818
819            } // end try
820
821            catch ( SQLException exception )
822            {
823                exception.printStackTrace();
824            }
825
826        } // end method loadAccountNumbers
```

Submit a query that selects the account numbers from table `accountInformation` — *(line 807–808)*

Process the `ResultSet` and fill the `accountNumberJComboBox` with account numbers — *(lines 811–815)*

Close `myResultSet` to release database resources — *(line 817)*

Catch any `SQLExceptions` thrown from the `try` block — *(lines 821–824)*

Figure 26.31 Filling the `accountNumberJComboBox` with account numbers.

The loop in lines 811–815 processes the `ResultSet` and fills the `accountNumberJComboBox` with account numbers. Before processing the data in a `ResultSet`, you must position the `ResultSet` **cursor** (a pointer which points to a row in a `ResultSet`) to the first row in the `ResultSet`. Initially, the `ResultSet` cursor is positioned before the first row. As a result, the first time you call the `next` method, it will move the cursor to the first row. Line 811 calls the **`next`** method to move the cursor down one row from its current position. The cursor points to the current row in the `ResultSet`. The `next` method returns the `boolean` value `true` if it can be positioned in the next row; otherwise, the method returns `false` to indicate that there are no more rows to process in the `ResultSet`.

If there are rows in the `ResultSet`, lines 813–814 extract the account number of the current row (line 814) and adds it to the `accountNumberJComboBox` using the `JComboBox` method `addItem` (line 813), which adds an item to the end of the list of items in the `JComboBox`. When processing a `ResultSet`, you extract each column of the `ResultSet` as a specific Java type. For example, `ResultSet` method **`getString`** returns the column value as a `String`, method **`getInt`** returns the column value as an `int` and method **`getDouble`** returns the column value as a `double`. In this example, `ResultSet` method `getString` is used (line 814) to get the column value as a `String`. The `getString` method accepts as an argument a column name (as a `String`, such as `"accountNumber"`), indicating which column's value to obtain.

(cont.)

Line 817 uses the `ResultSet` object's **close** method to close the Result-Set. Closing the `ResultSet` releases its resources and prevents it from being used to continue processing results of a prior query. The `close` method throws a `SQLException` if an error occurs while accessing the database. Lines 821–824 catch any `SQLException`s thrown from the `try` block.

2. *Saving the application.* Save your modified source code file.

3. *Opening the Command Prompt window and changing directories.* Open the **Command Prompt** window by selecting **Start > Programs > Accessories > Command Prompt**. Change to your ATM working directory by typing `cd C:\SimplyJava\ATM`.

4. *Compiling the application.* Compile your application by typing `javac ATM.java`. If your application does not compile correctly, fix the errors in your code before proceeding to the steps in the next box.

5. *Closing the Command Prompt window.* Close the **Command Prompt** window by clicking its close button.

Now you are ready to define the `retrieveAccountInformation` method, which will determine whether the PIN number provided by the user is valid.

Retrieving Account Information from the Database

1. *Retrieving account information.* Insert lines 831–853 of Fig. 26.32 into the `retrieveAccountInformation` method. Lines 834–836 use the `Statement` object's `executeQuery` method to submit a query that selects from the `accountInformation` table the `pin`, `firstName` and `balanceAmount` values for the specified account number (`userAccountNumber`). The variable `userAccountNumber` (an instance variable provided at line 66 of the template) contains the account number selected by the user from `accountNumberJComboBox`. At line 836, note the use of single quotes and dynamically created selection criteria of the WHERE clause.

Submit a query that selects the `pin`, `firstName` and `balanceAmount` values for the specified account number

Get the `pin`, `firstName` and `balanceAmount` values from the `ResultSet`

Close `myResultSet` to release database resources

Catch any `SQLException`s thrown from the `try` block

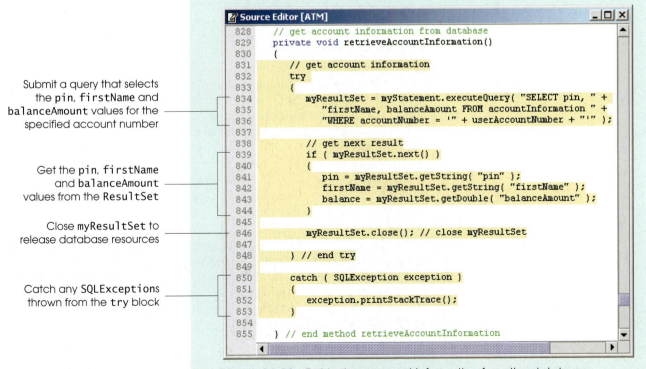

```
828     // get account information from database
829     private void retrieveAccountInformation()
830     {
831         // get account information
832         try
833         {
834             myResultSet = myStatement.executeQuery( "SELECT pin, " +
835                 "firstName, balanceAmount FROM accountInformation " +
836                 "WHERE accountNumber = '" + userAccountNumber + "'" );
837
838             // get next result
839             if ( myResultSet.next() )
840             {
841                 pin = myResultSet.getString( "pin" );
842                 firstName = myResultSet.getString( "firstName" );
843                 balance = myResultSet.getDouble( "balanceAmount" );
844             }
845
846             myResultSet.close(); // close myResultSet
847
848         } // end try
849
850         catch ( SQLException exception )
851         {
852             exception.printStackTrace();
853         }
854
855     } // end method retrieveAccountInformation
```

Figure 26.32 Retrieving account information from the database.

(cont.) The `if` statement in lines 839–844 accesses the information that is returned from the database. Recall that the `next` method must be called to position the cursor to the `ResultSet`'s first row. Lines 841–843 set the instance variables `pin`, `firstName` and `balance` to the PIN, first name and balance amount stored in the database for the requested account number. Each account number is unique, so there can be only one row in the `ResultSet` if the specified `accountNumber` is found in the database. Recall that the `getString` method returns the column value as a `String`, so lines 841–842 get the `String` representation of the PIN number and first name, respectively. The column `balanceAmount` contains floating-point numbers, so line 843 calls `ResultSet` method `getDouble` to get the `double` value of the account balance. The `getDouble` method accepts as an argument a column name (as a `String`, such as `"balanceAmount"`) indicating which column's value to obtain.

2. *Saving the application.* Save your modified source code file.

3. *Opening the Command Prompt window and changing directories.* Open the **Command Prompt** window by selecting **Start > Programs > Accessories > Command Prompt**. Change to your ATM working directory by typing `cd C:\SimplyJava\ATM`.

4. *Compiling the application.* Compile your application by typing `javac ATM.java`. If your application does not compile correctly, fix the errors in your code before continuing.

5. *Closing the Command Prompt window.* Close the **Command Prompt** window by clicking its close button.

Next, you will implement the `updateBalance` method, which will be invoked if the user-requested withdrawal amount can be deducted from the account balance. The `updateBalance` method updates the account balance in the database.

Updating the Balance Amount in the Database

1. *Updating the balance amount.* Insert lines 860–870 of Fig. 26.33 into the `updateBalance` method. Lines 863–865 use the `Statement` object's **executeUpdate** method to submit a SQL statement that updates the `balanceAmount` column in the `accountInformation` table for the row with the specified `accountNumber`. The `balanceAmount` for that row will be set to the value of `balance`, which is an instance variable that contains the new balance amount after a withdrawal. The `executeUpdate` method takes a `String` argument that specifies the SQL to execute and returns an `int` that indicates how many rows were updated. You should use the `executeUpdate` method for SQL statements that modify database data, such as UPDATE statements. The `executeUpdate` method throws a `SQLException` if an error occurs while accessing the database. Lines 867–870 catch any `SQLExceptions` thrown from the `try` block.

2. *Saving the application.* Save your modified source code file.

3. *Opening the Command Prompt window and changing directories.* Open the **Command Prompt** window by selecting **Start > Programs > Accessories > Command Prompt**. Change to your ATM working directory by typing `cd C:\SimplyJava\ATM`.

4. *Compiling the application.* Compile your application by typing `javac ATM.java`. If your application does not compile correctly, fix the errors in your code before continuing.

5. *Closing the Command Prompt window.* Close the **Command Prompt** window by clicking its close button.

(cont.)

Submit a SQL statement that updates the balanceAmount in the accountInformation table for the row with the specified accountNumber

Catch any SQLExceptions thrown from the try block

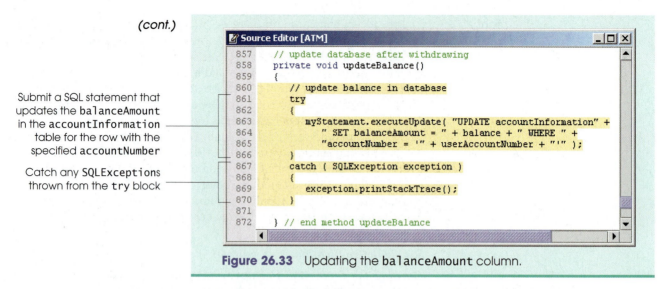

```
857        // update database after withdrawing
858        private void updateBalance()
859        {
860            // update balance in database
861            try
862            {
863                myStatement.executeUpdate( "UPDATE accountInformation" +
864                    " SET balanceAmount = " + balance + " WHERE " +
865                    "accountNumber = '" + userAccountNumber + "'" );
866            }
867            catch ( SQLException exception )
868            {
869                exception.printStackTrace();
870            }
871
872        } // end method updateBalance
```

Figure 26.33 Updating the balanceAmount column.

Next, you will implement the frameWindowClosing method, which will close the database connection when the user terminates the application by closing the window.

Closing the Database Connection

1. ***Closing the database connection.*** In the frameWindowClosing method, you will release the database resources and close the database connection. Add lines 877–890 of Fig. 26.34 to the frameWindowClosing method. Lines 880–881 use the **close** methods of the Statement and Connection objects to close the myStatement and myConnection, respectively. Closing the Statement releases its resources and prevents it from being used to execute any more SQL statements. Closing the Connection terminates the connection between the application and the database management system. The close method throws a SQLException if an error occurs while accessing the database. Lines 883–886 catch any SQLExceptions that are thrown from the try block. Line 889 invokes System method exit to terminate the application.

Close Statement and Connection to release database resources

Catch any SQLExceptions thrown from the try block

Terminate the application

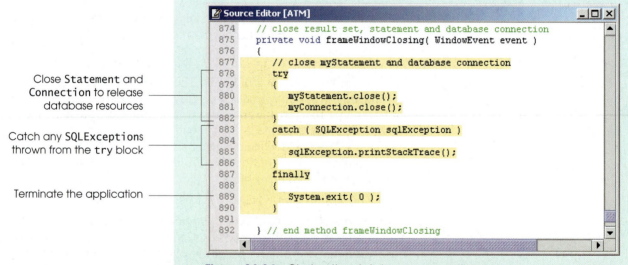

```
874        // close result set, statement and database connection
875        private void frameWindowClosing( WindowEvent event )
876        {
877            // close myStatement and database connection
878            try
879            {
880                myStatement.close();
881                myConnection.close();
882            }
883            catch ( SQLException sqlException )
884            {
885                sqlException.printStackTrace();
886            }
887            finally
888            {
889                System.exit( 0 );
890            }
891
892        } // end method frameWindowClosing
```

Figure 26.34 Closing the database connection.

2. ***Saving the application.*** Save your modified source code file.

3. ***Opening the Command Prompt window and changing directories.*** Open the **Command Prompt** window by selecting **Start > Programs > Accessories > Command Prompt**. Change to your ATM working directory by typing cd C:\SimplyJava\ATM.

(cont.)

4. ***Setting the CLASSPATH environment variable.*** Type `C:\Cloudscape_5.1\` `frameworks\embedded\bin\setCP.bat` in the **Command Prompt** window to set the CLASSPATH environment variable.

5. ***Compiling the application.*** Compile the application by typing `javac ATM.java`. If your application does not compile correctly, fix the errors in your code before continuing.

6. ***Running the application.*** Type `java ATM com.ibm.db2j.jdbc.DB2jDriver jdbc:db2j:ATM` in the **Command Prompt** window to run the application. Figure 26.35 shows the completed application running.

7. ***Closing the running application.*** Close the running application by clicking its close button.

8. ***Closing the Command Prompt window.*** Close the **Command Prompt** window by clicking its close button.

Figure 26.35   Running the completed **ATM** application.

Figure 26.36 presents the source code for the **ATM** application. The lines of code that you added, modified or viewed in this tutorial are highlighted.

```
1   // Tutorial 26: ATM.java
2   // ATM application allows users to access an account,
3   // view the balance and withdraw money from the account.
4   import java.awt.*;
5   import java.awt.event.*;
6   import java.sql.*;
7   import java.text.*;
8   import javax.swing.*;
9   import javax.swing.event.*;
10
11  public class ATM extends JFrame
12  {
13     // JTextArea to display message
14     private JTextArea messageJTextArea;
15
16     // JTextField to enter PIN or withdrawal amount
17     private JTextField numberJTextField;
18
```

Importing the `java.sql` package ——— (line 6)

Figure 26.36   **ATM** application code. (Part 1 of 17.)

```
19        // JPanel for number JButtons
20        private JPanel buttonsJPanel;
21
22        // JButtons for input of PIN or withdrawal amount
23        private JButton oneJButton;
24        private JButton twoJButton;
25        private JButton threeJButton;
26        private JButton fourJButton;
27        private JButton fiveJButton;
28        private JButton sixJButton;
29        private JButton sevenJButton;
30        private JButton eightJButton;
31        private JButton nineJButton;
32        private JButton zeroJButton;
33
34        // JButton to submit PIN or withdrawal amount
35        private JButton enterJButton;
36
37        // JButton to view balance
38        private JButton balanceJButton;
39
40        // JButton to withdraw from account
41        private JButton withdrawJButton;
42
43        // JButton to close the transaction
44        private JButton doneJButton;
45
46        // JPanel to get account numbers
47        private JPanel accountNumberJPanel;
48
49        // JLabel and JComboBox for account numbers
50        private JLabel accountNumberJLabel;
51        private JComboBox accountNumberJComboBox;
52
53        // constants for user action
54        private final static int ENTER_PIN = 1;
55        private final static int WITHDRAWAL = 2;
56
57        // instance variables used to store PIN and
58        // firstName from database
59        private String pin, firstName;
60
61        // instance variable used to distinguish user action
62        private int action;
63
64        // instance variables used to store user selected account number
65        // and PIN
66        private String userAccountNumber, userPIN;
67
68        // instance variable used to store account balance
69        private double balance;
70
71        // instance variables used to manipulate database
72        private Connection myConnection;
73        private Statement myStatement;
74        private ResultSet myResultSet;
75
```

Declaring instance variables to manage the database connection —

Figure 26.36   **ATM** application code. (Part 2 of 17.)

```
76    // constructor
77    public ATM( String databaseDriver, String databaseURL )
78    {
79        // establish connection to database
80        try
81        {
82            // load Cloudscape driver
83            Class.forName( databaseDriver );
84
85            // connect to database
86            myConnection =
87                DriverManager.getConnection( databaseURL );
88
89            // create Statement for executing SQL
90            myStatement = myConnection.createStatement();
91        }
92        catch ( SQLException exception )
93        {
94            exception.printStackTrace();
95        }
96        catch ( ClassNotFoundException exception )
97        {
98            exception.printStackTrace();
99        }
100
101       createUserInterface(); // set up GUI
102
103   } // end constructor
104
105   // create and position GUI components; register event handler
106   private void createUserInterface()
107   {
108       // get content pane for attaching GUI components
109       Container contentPane = getContentPane();
110
111       // enable explicit positioning of GUI components
112       contentPane.setLayout( null );
113
114       // set up messageJTextArea
115       messageJTextArea = new JTextArea();
116       messageJTextArea.setBounds( 40, 16, 288, 88 );
117       messageJTextArea.setText(
118           "Please select your account number." );
119       messageJTextArea.setBorder(
120           BorderFactory.createLoweredBevelBorder() );
121       messageJTextArea.setEditable( false );
122       contentPane.add( messageJTextArea );
123
124       // set up numberJTextField
125       numberJTextField = new JTextField();
126       numberJTextField.setBounds( 110, 120, 128, 21 );
127       numberJTextField.setBorder(
128           BorderFactory.createLoweredBevelBorder() );
129       numberJTextField.setEditable( false );
130       contentPane.add( numberJTextField );
131
132       // set up buttonsJPanel
133       buttonsJPanel = new JPanel();
```

Loading database driver class (`com.ibm.db2j.jdbc.DB2jDriver`) — line 83

Connecting to **ATM** database (`jdbc:db2j:ATM`) — lines 86–87

Creating a `Statement` object — line 90

Catching `ClassNotFoundException` thrown from line 83 — lines 96–99

Figure 26.36　**ATM** application code. (Part 3 of 17.)

```
134        buttonsJPanel.setBounds( 44, 160, 276, 150 );
135        buttonsJPanel.setBorder( BorderFactory.createEtchedBorder() );
136        buttonsJPanel.setLayout( null );
137        contentPane.add( buttonsJPanel );
138
139        // set up oneJButton
140        oneJButton = new JButton();
141        oneJButton.setBounds( 53, 28, 24, 24 );
142        oneJButton.setText( "1" );
143        oneJButton.setBorder(
144           BorderFactory.createRaisedBevelBorder() );
145        buttonsJPanel.add( oneJButton );
146        oneJButton.addActionListener(
147
148           new ActionListener() // anonymous inner class
149           {
150              // event handler called when oneJButton is clicked
151              public void actionPerformed( ActionEvent event )
152              {
153                 oneJButtonActionPerformed( event );
154              }
155
156           } // end anonymous inner class
157
158        ); // end call to addActionListener
159
160        // set up twoJButton
161        twoJButton = new JButton();
162        twoJButton.setBounds( 77, 28, 24, 24 );
163        twoJButton.setText( "2" );
164        twoJButton.setBorder(
165           BorderFactory.createRaisedBevelBorder() );
166        buttonsJPanel.add( twoJButton );
167        twoJButton.addActionListener(
168
169           new ActionListener() // anonymous inner class
170           {
171              // event handler called when twoJButton is clicked
172              public void actionPerformed( ActionEvent event )
173              {
174                 twoJButtonActionPerformed( event );
175              }
176
177           } // end anonymous inner class
178
179        ); // end call to addActionListener
180
181        // set up threeJButton
182        threeJButton = new JButton();
183        threeJButton.setBounds( 101, 28, 24, 24 );
184        threeJButton.setText( "3" );
185        threeJButton.setBorder(
186           BorderFactory.createRaisedBevelBorder() );
187        buttonsJPanel.add( threeJButton );
188        threeJButton.addActionListener(
189
190           new ActionListener() // anonymous inner class
191           {
```

Figure 26.36 ATM application code. (Part 4 of 17.)

```
192                    // event handler called when threeJButton is clicked
193                    public void actionPerformed( ActionEvent event )
194                    {
195                        threeJButtonActionPerformed( event );
196                    }
197
198                } // end anonymous inner class
199
200            ); // end call to addActionListener
201
202            // set up fourJButton
203            fourJButton = new JButton();
204            fourJButton.setBounds( 53, 52, 24, 24 );
205            fourJButton.setText( "4" );
206            fourJButton.setBorder(
207                BorderFactory.createRaisedBevelBorder() );
208            buttonsJPanel.add( fourJButton );
209            fourJButton.addActionListener(
210
211                new ActionListener() // anonymous inner class
212                {
213                    // event handler called when fourJButton is clicked
214                    public void actionPerformed( ActionEvent event )
215                    {
216                        fourJButtonActionPerformed( event );
217                    }
218
219                } // end anonymous inner class
220
221            ); // end call to addActionListener
222
223            // set up fiveJButton
224            fiveJButton = new JButton();
225            fiveJButton.setBounds( 77, 52, 24, 24 );
226            fiveJButton.setText( "5" );
227            fiveJButton.setBorder(
228                BorderFactory.createRaisedBevelBorder() );
229            buttonsJPanel.add( fiveJButton );
230            fiveJButton.addActionListener(
231
232                new ActionListener() // anonymous inner class
233                {
234                    // event handler called when fiveJButton is clicked
235                    public void actionPerformed( ActionEvent event )
236                    {
237                        fiveJButtonActionPerformed( event );
238                    }
239
240                } // end anonymous inner class
241
242            ); // end call to addActionListener
243
244            // set up sixJButton
245            sixJButton = new JButton();
246            sixJButton.setBounds( 101, 52, 24, 24 );
247            sixJButton.setText( "6" );
248            sixJButton.setBorder(
249                BorderFactory.createRaisedBevelBorder() );
```

Figure 26.36   **ATM** application code. (Part 5 of 17.)

```
250        buttonsJPanel.add( sixJButton );
251        sixJButton.addActionListener(
252
253           new ActionListener() // anonymous inner class
254           {
255              // event handler called when sixJButton is clicked
256              public void actionPerformed( ActionEvent event )
257              {
258                 sixJButtonActionPerformed( event );
259              }
260
261           } // end anonymous inner class
262
263        ); // end call to addActionListener
264
265        // set up sevenJButton
266        sevenJButton = new JButton();
267        sevenJButton.setBounds( 53, 76, 24, 24 );
268        sevenJButton.setText( "7" );
269        sevenJButton.setBorder(
270           BorderFactory.createRaisedBevelBorder() );
271        buttonsJPanel.add( sevenJButton );
272        sevenJButton.addActionListener(
273
274           new ActionListener() // anonymous inner class
275           {
276              // event handler called when sevenJButton is clicked
277              public void actionPerformed( ActionEvent event )
278              {
279                 sevenJButtonActionPerformed( event );
280              }
281
282           } // end anonymous inner class
283
284        ); // end call to addActionListener
285
286        // set up eightJButton
287        eightJButton = new JButton();
288        eightJButton.setBounds( 77, 76, 24, 24 );
289        eightJButton.setText( "8" );
290        eightJButton.setBorder(
291           BorderFactory.createRaisedBevelBorder() );
292        buttonsJPanel.add( eightJButton );
293        eightJButton.addActionListener(
294
295           new ActionListener() // anonymous inner class
296           {
297              // event handler called when eightJButton is clicked
298              public void actionPerformed( ActionEvent event )
299              {
300                 eightJButtonActionPerformed( event );
301              }
302
303           } // end anonymous inner class
304
305        ); // end call to addActionListener
306
```

Figure 26.36 ATM application code. (Part 6 of 17.)

```
307        // set up nineJButton
308        nineJButton = new JButton();
309        nineJButton.setBounds( 101, 76, 24, 24 );
310        nineJButton.setText( "9" );
311        nineJButton.setBorder(
312           BorderFactory.createRaisedBevelBorder() );
313        buttonsJPanel.add( nineJButton );
314        nineJButton.addActionListener(
315
316           new ActionListener() // anonymous inner class
317           {
318              // event handler called when nineJButton is clicked
319              public void actionPerformed( ActionEvent event )
320              {
321                 nineJButtonActionPerformed( event );
322              }
323
324           } // end anonymous inner class
325
326        ); // end call to addActionListener
327
328        // set up zeroJButton
329        zeroJButton = new JButton();
330        zeroJButton.setBounds( 77, 100, 24, 24 );
331        zeroJButton.setText( "0" );
332        zeroJButton.setBorder(
333           BorderFactory.createRaisedBevelBorder() );
334        buttonsJPanel.add( zeroJButton );
335        zeroJButton.addActionListener(
336
337           new ActionListener() // anonymous inner class
338           {
339              // event handler called when zeroJButton is clicked
340              public void actionPerformed( ActionEvent event )
341              {
342                 zeroJButtonActionPerformed( event );
343              }
344
345           } // end anonymous inner class
346
347        ); // end call to addActionListener
348
349        disableKeyPad(); // disable numeric JButtons
350
351        // set up enterJButton
352        enterJButton = new JButton();
353        enterJButton.setBounds( 149, 17, 72, 24 );
354        enterJButton.setText( "Enter" );
355        enterJButton.setBorder(
356           BorderFactory.createRaisedBevelBorder() );
357        buttonsJPanel.add( enterJButton );
358        enterJButton.setEnabled( false );
359        enterJButton.addActionListener(
360
361           new ActionListener() // anonymous inner class
362           {
```

Figure 26.36 **ATM** application code. (Part 7 of 17.)

```
363                // event handler called when enterJButton is clicked
364                public void actionPerformed( ActionEvent event )
365                {
366                    enterJButtonActionPerformed( event );
367                }
368
369            } // end anonymous inner class
370
371        ); // end call to addActionListener
372
373        // set up balanceJButton
374        balanceJButton = new JButton();
375        balanceJButton.setBounds( 149, 49, 72, 24 );
376        balanceJButton.setText( "Balance" );
377        balanceJButton.setBorder(
378            BorderFactory.createRaisedBevelBorder() );
379        buttonsJPanel.add( balanceJButton );
380        balanceJButton.setEnabled( false );
381        balanceJButton.addActionListener(
382
383            new ActionListener() // anonymous inner class
384            {
385                // event handler called when balanceJButton is clicked
386                public void actionPerformed( ActionEvent event )
387                {
388                    balanceJButtonActionPerformed( event );
389                }
390
391            } // end anonymous inner class
392
393        ); // end call to addActionListener
394
395        // set up withdrawJButton
396        withdrawJButton = new JButton();
397        withdrawJButton.setBounds( 149, 81, 72, 24 );
398        withdrawJButton.setText( "Withdraw" );
399        withdrawJButton.setBorder(
400            BorderFactory.createRaisedBevelBorder() );
401        withdrawJButton.setEnabled( false );
402        buttonsJPanel.add( withdrawJButton );
403        withdrawJButton.addActionListener(
404
405            new ActionListener() // anonymous inner class
406            {
407                // event handler called when withdrawJButton is clicked
408                public void actionPerformed( ActionEvent event )
409                {
410                    withdrawJButtonActionPerformed( event );
411                }
412
413            } // end anonymous inner class
414
415        ); // end call to addActionListener
416
417        // set up doneJButton
418        doneJButton = new JButton();
419        doneJButton.setBounds( 149, 113, 72, 24 );
420        doneJButton.setText( "Done" );
```

Figure 26.36 **ATM** application code. (Part 8 of 17.)

```
421          doneJButton.setBorder(
422             BorderFactory.createRaisedBevelBorder() );
423          doneJButton.setEnabled( false );
424          buttonsJPanel.add( doneJButton );
425          doneJButton.addActionListener(
426
427             new ActionListener() // anonymous inner class
428             {
429                // event handler called when doneJButton is clicked
430                public void actionPerformed( ActionEvent event )
431                {
432                   doneJButtonActionPerformed( event );
433                }
434
435             } // end anonymous inner class
436
437          ); // end call to addActionListener
438
439          // set up accountNumberJPanel
440          accountNumberJPanel = new JPanel();
441          accountNumberJPanel.setBounds( 44, 320, 276, 48 );
442          accountNumberJPanel.setBorder(
443             BorderFactory.createEtchedBorder() );
444          accountNumberJPanel.setLayout( null );
445          contentPane.add( accountNumberJPanel );
446
447          // set up accountNumberJLabel
448          accountNumberJLabel = new JLabel();
449          accountNumberJLabel.setBounds( 25, 15, 100, 20 );
450          accountNumberJLabel.setText( "Account Number:" );
451          accountNumberJPanel.add( accountNumberJLabel );
452
453          // set up accountNumberJComboBox
454          accountNumberJComboBox = new JComboBox();
455          accountNumberJComboBox.setBounds( 150, 12, 96, 25 );
456          accountNumberJComboBox.addItem( "" );
457          accountNumberJComboBox.setSelectedIndex( 0 );
458          accountNumberJPanel.add( accountNumberJComboBox );
459          accountNumberJComboBox.addItemListener(
460
461             new ItemListener() // anonymous inner class
462             {
463                // event handler called when account number is chosen
464                public void itemStateChanged( ItemEvent event )
465                {
466                   accountNumberJComboBoxItemStateChanged( event );
467                }
468
469             } // end anonymous inner class
470
471          ); // end call to addItemListener
472
473          // read account numbers from database and
474          // place them in accountNumberJComboBox
475          loadAccountNumbers();
476
477          // set properties of application's window
478          setTitle( "ATM" );   // set title bar string
```

Figure 26.36 ATM application code. (Part 9 of 17.)

```
479            setSize( 375, 410 ); // set window size
480            setVisible( true );   // display window
481
482            // ensure database connection is closed
483            // when user closes application window
484            addWindowListener(
485
486               new WindowAdapter() // anonymous inner class
487               {
488                  public void windowClosing( WindowEvent event )
489                  {
490                     frameWindowClosing( event );
491                  }
492
493               } // end anonymous inner class
494
495            ); // end addWindowListener
496
497      } // end method createUserInterface
498
499      // process oneJButton click
500      private void oneJButtonActionPerformed( ActionEvent event )
501      {
502         zeroToNineJButtonActionPerformed( "1" );
503
504      } // end method oneJButtonActionPerformed
505
506      // process twoJButton click
507      private void twoJButtonActionPerformed( ActionEvent event )
508      {
509         zeroToNineJButtonActionPerformed( "2" );
510
511      } // end method twoJButtonActionPerformed
512
513      // process threeJButton click
514      private void threeJButtonActionPerformed( ActionEvent event )
515      {
516         zeroToNineJButtonActionPerformed( "3" );
517
518      } // end method threeJButtonActionPerformed
519
520      // process fourJButton click
521      private void fourJButtonActionPerformed( ActionEvent event )
522      {
523         zeroToNineJButtonActionPerformed( "4" );
524
525      } // end method fourJButtonActionPerformed
526
527      // process fiveJButton click
528      private void fiveJButtonActionPerformed( ActionEvent event )
529      {
530         zeroToNineJButtonActionPerformed( "5" );
531
532      } // end method fiveJButtonActionPerformed
533
534      // process sixJButton click
535      private void sixJButtonActionPerformed( ActionEvent event )
536      {
```

Figure 26.36   **ATM** application code. (Part 10 of 17.)

```
537            zeroToNineJButtonActionPerformed( "6" );
538
539     } // end method sixJButtonActionPerformed
540
541     // process sevenJButton click
542     private void sevenJButtonActionPerformed( ActionEvent event )
543     {
544            zeroToNineJButtonActionPerformed( "7" );
545
546     } // end method sevenJButtonActionPerformed
547
548     // process eightJButton click
549     private void eightJButtonActionPerformed( ActionEvent event )
550     {
551            zeroToNineJButtonActionPerformed( "8" );
552
553     } // end method eightJButtonActionPerformed
554
555     // process nineJButton click
556     private void nineJButtonActionPerformed( ActionEvent event )
557     {
558            zeroToNineJButtonActionPerformed( "9" );
559
560     } // end method nineJButtonActionPerformed
561
562     // process zeroJButton click
563     private void zeroJButtonActionPerformed( ActionEvent event )
564     {
565            zeroToNineJButtonActionPerformed( "0" );
566
567     } // end method zeroJButtonActionPerformed
568
569     // process clicks of a numeric JButton
570     private void zeroToNineJButtonActionPerformed( String number )
571     {
572        // enable enterJButton if it is disabled
573        if ( !enterJButton.isEnabled() )
574        {
575           enterJButton.setEnabled( true );
576        }
577
578        // if user is entering PIN number display * to conceal PIN
579        if ( action == ENTER_PIN )
580        {
581           userPIN += number; // append number to current PIN
582           numberJTextField.setText(
583              numberJTextField.getText() + "*" );
584        }
585
586        else // otherwise display number of JButton user clicked
587        {
588           numberJTextField.setText(
589              numberJTextField.getText() + number );
590        }
591
592     } // end method zeroToNineJButtonsActionPerformed
593
```

Figure 26.36   ATM application code. (Part 11 of 17.)

```
594    // verify PIN or withdraw from account
595    private void enterJButtonActionPerformed( ActionEvent event )
596    {
597       if ( action == ENTER_PIN ) // checking PIN
598       {
599          // get pin, first name and balance for account number
600          // selected in accountNumberJComboBox
601          retrieveAccountInformation();
602
603          numberJTextField.setText( "" ); // clear numberJTextField
604
605          // correct PIN number
606          if ( userPIN.equals( pin ) )
607          {
608             // disable enterJButton
609             enterJButton.setEnabled( false );
610
611             disableKeyPad(); // disable numeric JButtons
612
613             // enable balanceJButton and withdrawJButton
614             balanceJButton.setEnabled( true );
615             withdrawJButton.setEnabled( true );
616
617             // display status to user
618             messageJTextArea.setText(
619                "Welcome " + firstName + ", select a transaction." );
620
621          } // end if part of if...else
622
623          else // wrong PIN number
624          {
625             // indicate that incorrect PIN was provided
626             messageJTextArea.setText(
627                "Sorry, PIN number is incorrect." +
628                "\nPlease re-enter the PIN number." );
629
630             userPIN = ""; // clear user's previous PIN entry
631
632          } // end else part of if...else
633
634       } // end if that processes PIN
635
636       else if ( action == WITHDRAWAL ) // process withdrawal
637       {
638          enterJButton.setEnabled( false ); // disable enterJButton
639
640          disableKeyPad(); // disable numeric JButtons
641
642          // process withdrawal
643          withdraw(
644             Double.parseDouble( numberJTextField.getText() ) );
645
646          numberJTextField.setText( "" ); // clear numberJTextField
647
648          // enable balanceJButton and withdrawJButton
649          balanceJButton.setEnabled( true );
650          withdrawJButton.setEnabled( true );
```

Figure 26.36   **ATM** application code. (Part 12 of 17.)

```
651
652          } // end if that processes withdrawal
653
654      } // end method enterJButtonActionPerformed
655
656      // display account balance
657      private void balanceJButtonActionPerformed( ActionEvent event )
658      {
659         // define display format
660         DecimalFormat dollars = new DecimalFormat( "0.00" );
661
662         // display user's balance
663         messageJTextArea.setText( "Your current balance is $" +
664            dollars.format( balance ) + "." );
665
666      } // end method balanceJButtonActionPerformed
667
668      // display withdraw action
669      private void withdrawJButtonActionPerformed( ActionEvent event )
670      {
671         // disable Balance and Withdraw JButtons
672         balanceJButton.setEnabled( false );
673         withdrawJButton.setEnabled( false );
674
675         enableKeyPad(); // enable numeric JButtons
676
677         // display message to user
678         messageJTextArea.setText(
679            "Enter the amount you would like to withdraw" );
680
681         // change action to indicate user will provide
682         // withdrawal amount
683         action = WITHDRAWAL;
684
685      } // end method withdrawJButtonActionPerformed
686
687      // reset GUI
688      private void doneJButtonActionPerformed( ActionEvent event )
689      {
690         userPIN = ""; // clear userPIN
691
692         disableKeyPad(); // disable numeric JButtons
693
694         // disable OK, Balance, Withdraw and Done JButtons
695         enterJButton.setEnabled( false );
696         balanceJButton.setEnabled( false );
697         withdrawJButton.setEnabled( false );
698         doneJButton.setEnabled( false );
699
700         // enable and reset accountNumberJComboBox
701         accountNumberJComboBox.setEnabled( true );
702         accountNumberJComboBox.setSelectedIndex( 0 );
703
704         // reset messageJTextArea
705         messageJTextArea.setText(
706            "Please select your account number." );
707
708      } // end method doneJButtonActionPerformed
```

Figure 26.36 **ATM** application code. (Part 13 of 17.)

```
709
710    // get account number and enable OK and Done JButtons
711    private void accountNumberJComboBoxItemStateChanged(
712       ItemEvent event )
713    {
714       // get user selected account number if no transaction is
715       // in process
716       if ( ( event.getStateChange() == ItemEvent.SELECTED ) &&
717          ( accountNumberJComboBox.getSelectedIndex() != 0 ) )
718       {
719          // disable accountNumberJComboBox
720          accountNumberJComboBox.setEnabled( false );
721
722          // get selected account number
723          userAccountNumber =
724             ( String ) accountNumberJComboBox.getSelectedItem();
725
726          // change action to indicate that user will provide
727          // PIN number
728          action = ENTER_PIN;
729          userPIN = "";
730
731          // prompt user to enter PIN number
732          messageJTextArea.setText(
733             "Please enter your PIN number." );
734
735          numberJTextField.setText( "" ); // clear numberJTextField
736          enableKeyPad();                 // enable numeric JButtons
737          doneJButton.setEnabled( true ); // enable doneJButton
738
739       } // end if
740
741    } // end method accountNumberJComboBoxItemStateChanged
742
743    // enable numeric JButtons
744    private void enableKeyPad()
745    {
746       oneJButton.setEnabled( true );   // enable oneJButton
747       twoJButton.setEnabled( true );   // enable twoJButton
748       threeJButton.setEnabled( true ); // enable threeJButton
749       fourJButton.setEnabled( true );  // enable fourJButton
750       fiveJButton.setEnabled( true );  // enable fiveJButton
751       sixJButton.setEnabled( true );   // enable sixJButton
752       sevenJButton.setEnabled( true ); // enable sevenJButton
753       eightJButton.setEnabled( true ); // enable eightJButton
754       nineJButton.setEnabled( true );  // enable nineJButton
755       zeroJButton.setEnabled( true );  // enable zeroJButton
756
757    } // end method enableKeyPad
758
759    // disable numeric JButtons
760    private void disableKeyPad()
761    {
762       oneJButton.setEnabled( false );   // disable oneJButton
763       twoJButton.setEnabled( false );   // disable twoJButton
764       threeJButton.setEnabled( false ); // disable threeJButton
765       fourJButton.setEnabled( false );  // disable fourJButton
766       fiveJButton.setEnabled( false );  // disable fiveJButton
```

Figure 26.36 ATM application code. (Part 14 of 17.)

```
767        sixJButton.setEnabled( false );    // disable sixJButton
768        sevenJButton.setEnabled( false ); // disable sevenJButton
769        eightJButton.setEnabled( false ); // disable eightJButton
770        nineJButton.setEnabled( false );  // disable nineJButton
771        zeroJButton.setEnabled( false );  // disable zeroJButton
772
773     } // end method disableKeyPad
774
775     // withdraw amount from account
776     private void withdraw( double withdrawAmount )
777     {
778        // determine if amount can be withdrawn
779        if ( withdrawAmount <= balance )
780        {
781           balance -= withdrawAmount; // calculate new balance
782
783           updateBalance(); // update row in database
784
785           // define display format
786           DecimalFormat dollars = new DecimalFormat( "0.00" );
787
788           // display balance information to user
789           messageJTextArea.setText( "The withdrawal amount is $" +
790              dollars.format( withdrawAmount ) + "." );
791        }
792        else // amount cannot be withdrawn
793        {
794           messageJTextArea.setText(
795              "The withdrawal amount is too large." +
796              "\nSelect Withdraw and enter a different amount." );
797        }
798
799     } // end method withdraw
800
801     // load account numbers to accountNumberJComboBox
802     private void loadAccountNumbers()
803     {
804        // get all account numbers from database
805        try
806        {
807           myResultSet = myStatement.executeQuery(
808              "SELECT accountNumber FROM accountInformation" );
809
810           // add account numbers to accountNumberJComboBox
811           while ( myResultSet.next() )
812           {
813              accountNumberJComboBox.addItem(
814                 myResultSet.getString( "accountNumber" ) );
815           }
816
817           myResultSet.close(); // close myResultSet
818
819        } // end try
820
821        catch ( SQLException exception )
822        {
823           exception.printStackTrace();
824        }
```

Submit a query that selects the account numbers from the `accountInformation` table

Process the `ResultSet` and fill `accountNumberJComboBox` with account numbers

Close `myResultSet` to release database resources

Catch any `SQLExceptions` thrown from the try block

Figure 26.36 ATM application code. (Part 15 of 17.)

```
825
826     } // end method loadAccountNumbers
827
828     // get account information from database
829     private void retrieveAccountInformation()
830     {
831        // get account information
832        try
833        {
834           myResultSet = myStatement.executeQuery( "SELECT pin, " +
835              "firstName, balanceAmount FROM accountInformation " +
836              "WHERE accountNumber = '" + userAccountNumber + "'" );
837
838           // get next result
839           if ( myResultSet.next() )
840           {
841              pin = myResultSet.getString( "pin" );
842              firstName = myResultSet.getString( "firstName" );
843              balance = myResultSet.getDouble( "balanceAmount" );
844           }
845
846           myResultSet.close(); // close myResultSet
847
848        } // end try
849
850        catch ( SQLException exception )
851        {
852           exception.printStackTrace();
853        }
854
855     } // end method retrieveAccountInformation
856
857     // update database after withdrawing
858     private void updateBalance()
859     {
860        // update balance in database
861        try
862        {
863           myStatement.executeUpdate( "UPDATE accountInformation" +
864              " SET balanceAmount = " + balance + " WHERE " +
865              "accountNumber = '" + userAccountNumber + "'" );
866        }
867        catch ( SQLException exception )
868        {
869           exception.printStackTrace();
870        }
871
872     } // end method updateBalance
873
874     // close statement and database connection
875     private void frameWindowClosing( WindowEvent event )
876     {
877        // close myStatement and database connection
878        try
879        {
880           myStatement.close();
881           myConnection.close();
882        }
```

Descriptions in left margin:

- Submit a query that selects the pin, firstName and balanceAmount values for the specified account number
- Get the pin, firstName and balanceAmount values from the ResultSet
- Close myResultSet to release database resources
- Catch any SQLExceptions thrown from the try block
- Submit a SQL statement that updates the balanceAmount in the accountInformation table for the row with the specified accountNumber
- Catch any SQLExceptions thrown from the try block
- Close myStatement and myConnection to release database resources

Figure 26.36 **ATM** application code. (Part 16 of 17.)

```
883     catch ( SQLException sqlException )
884     {
885         sqlException.printStackTrace();
886     }
887     finally
888     {
889         System.exit( 0 );
890     }
891
892   } // end method frameWindowClosing
893
894   // method main
895   public static void main( String[] args )
896   {
897       // check command-line arguments
898       if ( args.length == 2 )
899       {
900           // get command-line arguments
901           String databaseDriver = args[ 0 ];
902           String databaseURL = args[ 1 ];
903
904           // create new ATM
905           ATM atm = new ATM( databaseDriver, databaseURL );
906       }
907       else // invalid command-line arguments
908       {
909           System.out.println(
910               "Usage: java ATM databaseDriver databaseURL" );
911       }
912
913   } // end method main
914
915 } // end class ATM
```

Catch any SQLExceptions thrown from the try block → (lines 883–886)

Terminate the application → (line 889)

Check the command-line arguments → (line 898)

Get the command-line arguments → (lines 901–902)

Create new **ATM** instance → (line 905)

Display a line of text that indicates the syntax to run the application → (lines 909–910)

Figure 26.36   ATM application code. (Part 17 of 17.)

SELF-REVIEW

1. The method _____ of interface Statement selects data from a database table.
   a) executeQuery   b) select
   c) executeUpdate   d) None of the above.

2. The Statement method _____ modifies data in a database table.
   a) executeQuery   b) modifyTable
   c) executeUpdate   d) None of the above.

Answers: 1) a. 2) c.

26.9 Wrap-Up

In this tutorial, you learned that a database is an organized collection of data and that database management systems provide mechanisms for storing and organizing data in a format consistent with that of a database. You then examined the contents of the Cloudscape database, which was used in the **ATM** application. While examining the ATM database, you learned that relational databases represent data as tables containing rows composed of columns. You also learned that each table should have a primary key, which is used to distinguish one row from another.

After learning about the Cloudscape database, you learned basic SQL to retrieve data from and update data in a database. You then learned how to connect to a database with the DriverManager method getConnection. You used the Con-

nection object returned by getConnection to manage the connection to the database and to create a Statement object to access and manipulate the database. You also used a ResultSet to process query results returned from the database.

In the next tutorial, you will learn additional graphics capabilities and you will learn polymorphism—a fundamental concept that is important for a complete understanding of object-oriented programming. Polymorphism enables you to "program in the general" rather than "program in the specific." You can write programs that process related objects as if they are all objects of their common superclass type. You will use polymorphic programming techniques to implement a drawing application in which the user can select a type of shape to draw, then can drag the mouse to draw that shape. Your application will maintain a collection of all the shapes the user draws. As you will see, the logic for drawing all the shapes will be quite simple with polymorphism. In addition, you will learn how polymorphism makes your drawing application extensible—that is, enables you to add new shape types to your application quickly and easily.

SKILLS SUMMARY

Using command-line arguments

- Supply command-line arguments to the java interpreter.
- Retrieve command-line arguments from the args array, which is the main method's parameter.
- Pass the command-line arguments to the constructor of the application.

Opening a Database Connection

- Load the database driver class by invoking the Class method forName.
- Connect to the database by invoking the DriverManager method getConnection.
- Catch the possible ClassNotFoundException thrown by the forName method.
- Catch the possible SQLException thrown by the getConnection method.

Creating a Statement object

- Invoke the Connection method createStatement to create a Statement object.
- Catch the possible SQLException thrown by the createStatement method.

Retrieving Information from the Database

- Invoke the Statement method executeQuery with a String argument that specifies a query.
- Process the ResultSet returned by the executeQuery method and extract the necessary information.
- Catch the possible SQLExceptions thrown by the Statement method executeQuery and the ResultSet methods.

Updating the Database

- Invoke the Statement method executeUpdate with a String argument that specifies an UPDATE statement.
- Catch the possible SQLException thrown by the executeUpdate method.

Closing the ResultSet Object

- Invoke the close method on the ResultSet object.
- Catch the possible SQLException thrown by the close method.

Closing the Statement Object

- Invoke the close method on the Statement object.
- Catch the possible SQLException thrown by the close method.

Closing the Database Connection

- Invoke the close method on the Connection object.
- Catch the possible SQLException thrown by the close method.

KEY TERMS

Class class—Represents a class in a running Java application.

ClassNotFoundException class—An exception thrown by the `Class` method `forName` if the class the application is attempting to load cannot be found.

CLASSPATH environment variable—Specifies the location of the class libraries that are required to run an application.

close method of Connection—Closes a connection to a database.

close method of Statement—Closes a `Statement` and release its database resources.

close method of ResultSet—Closes a `ResultSet` and release its database resources.

column—Represents an individual data attribute.

command-line arguments—Arguments that are supplied to the `java` interpreter that specify the options to run an application.

Connection object—Manages a connection to a database.

createStatement method of Connection—Creates a `Statement` object for submitting SQL to a DBMS.

cursor—A pointer to a row in a `ResultSet`.

database—An organized collection of data.

database management system (DBMS)—Provides mechanisms for storing and organizing data in a manner consistent with a database's format.

DriverManager class—Provides services for managing JDBC drivers. This class also is used to establish a connection to a database.

executeQuery method of Statement—Used to execute a SQL query. This method returns a `ResultSet` object containing the results of the query.

executeUpdate method of Statement—Used to execute a SQL statement that modifies database data, such as UPDATE. This method returns an `int` value that indicates the number of rows that were updated.

forName method of Class—The method used to load the class for the database driver.

FROM SQL keyword—The keyword used with SELECT to specify the table from which to get data.

getConnection method of DriverManager—A method that attempts to connect to a database.

getDouble method of ResultSet—The method used to get a column value as a `double`.

getInt method of ResultSet—The method used to get a column value as an `int`.

getString method of ResultSet—The method used to get a column value as a `String`.

instant-access application—An application for which particular information must be located immediately.

JDBC API—The part of the Java API that is used to interact with databases.

JDBC driver—A class that enables Java applications to access a particular DBMS.

JDBC URL—An address that directs a JDBC driver to a database location.

next method of ResultSet—Moves the `ResultSet` cursor to the next row in a `ResultSet`.

primary key—A column (or combination of columns) in a database table that contains unique values used to distinguish one row from another.

println method of System.out—The method that displays a line of text in the **Command Prompt** window.

protocol—A set of rules to define how data is transported between the Java application and the database.

query—A request for information from a database that satisfies given criteria.

relational database—A database that maintains data in a set of related tables.

relational database management system (RDBMS)—A database management system for relational databases.

ResultSet object—A table of data that is generated by executing a query statement.

row—Uniquely represents a set of values in a relational database.

SELECT SQL keyword—The keyword used to specify queries that request information from a database.

selection criteria—Specifies what rows to select.

SQLException—An exception that is thrown when an error occurs while accessing a database.

standard output object—A `System.out` object that allows Java applications to display sets of characters in the **Command Prompt** window from which the Java application executes.

Statement object—The object used to execute SQL.

Structured Query Language (SQL)—A language used by relational databases to perform queries and manipulate data.

subprotocol—A set of rules to define how data is transported between the Java application and the database. Typically, the subprotocol contains rules that are specific to a particular DBMS.

System.out object—The object that allows Java applications to display sets of characters in the **Command Prompt** window from which the Java application executes. Also known as the standard output object.

table—This is used to store information in rows and columns.

UPDATE SQL keyword—The keyword used in SQL statements that modify data in a database table.

WHERE SQL keyword—The keyword that specifies criteria that determine the rows to retrieve or update.

JAVA LIBRARY REFERENCE

Class   This object represents a class in a running Java application.

■ *Methods*

forName—Used to load the class for the database driver.

Connection   This object represents a connection to a specific database.

■ *Methods*

close—Closes the connection to the database.

createStatement—Creates a `Statement` object to submit SQL to the database.

DriverManager   This object provides a service for managing JDBC drivers. This object also is used to establish a connection to a database.

■ *Methods*

getConnection—Attempts to connect to a database.

Statement   This object is used to submit SQL to a database.

■ *Methods*

close—Closes a `Statement` and release its database resources.

executeQuery—Executes SQL queries.

executeUpdate—Executes SQL statements that modify a database, such as UPDATEs.

ResultSet   This object is used to manipulate the results of a query.

■ *Methods*

close—Close a `ResultSet` and release its database resources.

getDouble—Gets a column value as a `double`.

getInt—Gets a column value as an `int`.

getString—Gets a column value as a `String`.

next—Moves the `ResultSet` cursor down to the next row in a `ResultSet`.

System.out This object allows a Java application to display sets of characters in the **Command Prompt** window from which the Java application executes.

■ *Methods*

println—Displays a line of text in the **Command Prompt** window.

MULTIPLE-CHOICE QUESTIONS	

26.1 Use the Class method _____ to load a database driver.

a) getClass   b) getName

c) forClass   d) forName

26.2 A _____ uniquely represents a set of values in a relational database.

a) record   b) field

c) row   d) primary key

26.3 A primary key is used to _____.

a) create rows in a database   b) identify columns in a database

c) distinguish between rows in a table   d) None of the above.

26.4 A Statement object allows you to _____.

a) connect to a database   b) load a database driver

c) execute SQL to retrieve   d) None of the above.
   or modify data in a database

26.5 The executeQuery method _____.

a) retrieves information from a database   b) modifies information in a database

c) establishes a connection to a database d) closes a connection to a database

26.6 In a SELECT statement, what immediately follows the SELECT keyword?

a) the name of a table   b) the name of a column or *

c) the name of a database   d) the criteria that the row must meet

26.7 What does the following SELECT statement do?

```
SELECT age FROM people WHERE lastName = 'Purple'
```

a) It selects the age of the person (or people) with the last name Purple from the people table of a database.

b) It selects the value Purple from the age table of the people database.

c) It selects the age of the person with the last name Purple from the people database.

d) It selects the people column from the age table with the lastName value Purple.

26.8 The SQL _____ statement modifies information in a database.

a) SELECT   b) MODIFY

c) CHANGE   d) UPDATE

26.9 Assuming the account number is 2, which of the following modifies the pin column in the accounts table?

a) SELECT pin FROM accounts WHERE accountNumber = 2

b) SELECT accounts FROM accountNumber = 2 WHERE pin

c) UPDATE accounts SET pin = 1243 WHERE accountNumber = 2

d) UPDATE pin = 1243 SET accountNumber = 2 WHERE accounts

26.10 A _____ is an organized collection of data.

a) row   b) database

c) primary key   d) None of the above.

EXERCISES

26.11 *(Stock Portfolio Application)* A stockbroker wants an application that will display a client's stock portfolio (Fig. 26.37). All the companies that the user holds stock in should be displayed in a JComboBox when the application is loaded. When the user selects a company from the JComboBox and clicks the **Stock Information** JButton, the stock information for that company should be displayed in output JTextFields. The provided stocks database contains one table, stockInformation (Fig. 26.38), which has four columns—stockName, stockSymbol, shares and price. The values stored in the stockName and stockSymbol columns are Strings. The values stored in the shares column are ints. The values stored in the price column are doubles.

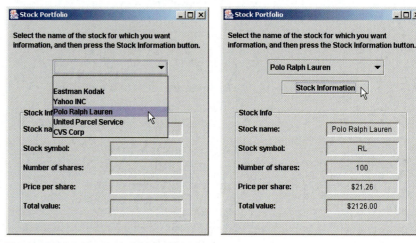

Figure 26.37 **Stock Portfolio** application.

stockName	stockSymbol	shares	price
Eastman Kodak	EK	50	34.95
Yahoo INC	YHOO	25	17.31
Polo Ralph Lauren	RL	100	21.26
United Parcel Service	UPS	65	62.96
CVS Corp	CVS	35	27.62

Figure 26.38 stockInformation table contents.

a) *Copying the template to your working directory.* Copy the directory C:\Examples\ Tutorial26\Exercises\StockPortfolio to your C:\SimplyJava directory.

b) *Copying the database to your working directory.* Copy the stocks database directory from C:\Examples\Tutorial26\Exercises\Databases to your C:\SimplyJava\ StockPortfolio directory.

c) *Opening the template file.* Open the StockPortfolio.java file in your text editor.

d) *Declaring instance variables for database processing.* In line 45, declare three instance variables—myConnection, myStatement and myResultSet—of types Connection, Statement and ResultSet, respectively.

e) *Adding a database connection and creating a Statement object.* In line 52 in the StockPortfolio constructor, insert statements that load the database driver, connect to the stocks database and create a Statement for submitting SQL statements to the database. Assume that the driver class name and JDBC URL are passed to the constructor from main.

f) *Adding code to the loadStockNames database.* Find the loadStockNames method, which immediately follows createUserInterface. In the loadStockNames method, add a statement that queries the database and retrieves the stockName column from the stockInformation table. Insert a loop that processes the ResultSet and adds each stock name to stockNamesJComboBox. Close the ResultSet after the loop.

g) *Adding code to stockInfoJButtonActionPerformed.* Find the stockInfoJButtonActionPerformed method (which immediately follows loadStockNames) and add code to this method that passes the selected stock name in stockNamesJComboBox to the stockData method as a String.

h) *Declaring the stockData method.* Immediately following stockInfoJButtonActionPerformed, create a stockData method that takes a String representing the name of the stock as an argument and does not return anything. In this method, execute a query that retrieves the information for the stock name that was received as an argument. Process the ResultSet and display the stock information in the corresponding output JTextFields (stockNameJTextField, stockSymbolJTextField, sharesJTextField and priceJTextField). Add a DecimalFormat object to format the price before displaying. Close the ResultSet after processing is done. Call the computeTotalValue method, which you declare in the next step, with an int that specifies the number of shares and a double that specifies the price per share to calculate the total value. This method will return a String containing the formatted total which you should display in totalJTextField.

i) *Declaring the computeTotalValue method.* Immediately following stockData, create the computeTotalValue method to compute the total value by multiplying the number of shares by the price per share. The method should return a String containing the value formatted as a dollar amount.

j) *Closing the database connection.* Find the frameWindowClosing method (which is located just before main at the end of the file) and add code to this method that closes myStatement and myConnection.

k) *Saving the application.* Save your modified source code file.

l) *Opening the Command Prompt window and changing directories.* Open the **Command Prompt** by selecting **Start > Programs > Accessories > Command Prompt**. Change to your working directory by typing cd C:\SimplyJava\StockPortfolio.

m) *Setting the CLASSPATH.* Type C:\Cloudscape_5.1\frameworks\embedded\bin\ setCP.bat in the **Command Prompt** window to set the CLASSPATH environment variable.

n) *Compiling the application.* Compile your application by typing javac StockPortfolio.java.

o) *Running the completed application.* When your application compiles correctly, run it by typing

```
java StockPortfolio com.ibm.db2j.jdbc.DB2jDriver jdbc:db2j:stocks
```

p) *Closing the application.* Close your running application by clicking its close button.

q) *Closing the Command Prompt window.* Close the **Command Prompt** window by clicking its close button.

26.12 *(Restaurant Bill Calculator Application)* A restaurant wants you to develop an application that calculates a table's bill (Fig. 26.39). The application should display all the menu items from the restaurant's database in four JComboBoxes. Each JComboBox should contain a category of food offered by the restaurant (**Beverage, Appetizer, Main Course** and **Dessert**). The user can choose one item from each of these JComboBoxes to add items to a table's bill. When the table is finished ordering, the user can click the **Calculate Bill** JButton to display the **Subtotal:, Tax:** and **Total:** for the table. The provided restaurant1 database contains one table, menu (Fig. 26.40), which has four columns—itemID, name, category and price. The values stored in the itemID column are ints. The values stored in the name and category columns are Strings. The values stored in the price column are doubles.

a) *Copying the template to your working directory.* Copy the directory C:\Examples\ Tutorial26\Exercises\RestaurantBillCalculator to your C:\SimplyJava directory.

b) *Copying the database to your working directory.* Copy the restaurant1 database directory from C:\Examples\Tutorial26\Exercises\Databases to the C:\SimplyJava\RestaurantBillCalculator directory.

c) *Opening the template file.* Open the RestaurantBillCalculator.java file in your text editor.

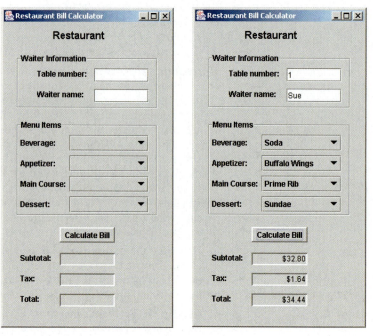

Figure 26.39 **Restaurant Bill Calculator** application.

itemID	name	category	price
1	Soda	Beverage	1.95
2	Tea	Beverage	1.50
3	Coffee	Beverage	1.25
4	Mineral Water	Beverage	2.95
5	Juice	Beverage	2.50
6	Milk	Beverage	1.50
7	Buffalo Wings	Appetizer	5.95
8	Buffalo Fingers	Appetizer	6.95
9	Potato Skins	Appetizer	8.95
10	Nachos	Appetizer	8.95
11	Mushroom Caps	Appetizer	10.95
12	Shrimp Cocktail	Appetizer	12.95
13	Chips And Salsa	Appetizer	6.95
14	Seafood Alfredo	Main Course	15.95
15	Chicken Alfredo	Main Course	13.95
16	Chicken Picatta	Main Course	13.95
17	Turkey Club	Main Course	11.95
18	Lobster Pie	Main Course	19.95
19	Prime Rib	Main Course	20.95
20	Shrimp Scampi	Main Course	18.95
21	Turkey Dinner	Main Course	13.95
22	Stuffed Chicken	Main Course	14.95
23	Apple Pie	Dessert	5.95
24	Sundae	Dessert	3.95

Figure 26.40 **menu** table content. (Part 1 of 2.)

itemID	name	category	price
25	Carrot Cake	Dessert	5.95
26	Mud Pie	Dessert	4.95
27	Apple Crisp	Dessert	5.95

Figure 26.40 menu table content. (Part 2 of 2.)

d) *Adding a database connection and creating a Statement object*. In line 75 in the RestaurantBillCalculator constructor, insert statements that load the database driver, connect to the restaurant1 database and create a Statement to submit SQL to the database. Assume that the driver class name and JDBC URL are passed to the constructor from main. Note that three instance variables—myConnection, myStatement and myResultSet—have already been declared in the template at lines 64–66.

e) *Adding code to the loadCategory method*. Find the loadCategory method, which immediately follows createMenuItemsJPanel. The loadCategory method takes a String, representing the category to load, and the name of the JComboBox to add items to as arguments. Add a statement that queries the database and retrieves the name column from the menu table for the specified category. Insert a loop that processes the ResultSet and adds each name to the categoryJComboBox. Close the ResultSet after the loop.

f) *Adding code to the beverageJComboBoxItemStateChanged method*. Find the beverageJComboBoxItemStateChanged method (which immediately follows loadCategory) and insert code that adds the String representation of the selected item to the ArrayList billItems. [*Hint*: Use the ItemEvent.SELECTED constant to determine whether an item is selected.]

g) *Adding code to the appetizerJComboBoxItemStateChanged method*. Find the appetizerJComboBoxItemStateChanged method (which immediately follows beverageJComboBoxItemStateChanged) and insert code that adds the String representation of the selected item to the ArrayList billItems. [*Hint*: Use the ItemEvent.SELECTED constant to determine whether an item is selected.]

h) *Adding code to the mainCourseJComboBoxItemStateChanged method*. Find the mainCourseJComboBoxItemStateChanged method (which immediately follows appetizerJComboBoxItemStateChanged) and insert code that adds the String representation of the selected item to the ArrayList billItems. [*Hint*: Use the ItemEvent.SELECTED constant to determine whether an item is selected.]

i) *Adding code to the dessertJComboBoxItemStateChanged method*. Find the dessertJComboBoxItemStateChanged method (which immediately follows mainCourseJComboBoxItemStateChanged) and insert code that adds the String representation of the selected item to the ArrayList billItems. [*Hint*: Use the ItemEvent.SELECTED constant to determine whether an item is selected.]

j) *Adding code to the calculateBillJButtonActionPerformed method*. Find the calculateBillJButtonActionPerformed method (which immediately follows dessertJComboBoxItemStateChanged) and add code to ensure that a table number (tableNumberJTextField) and waiter name (waiterNameJTextField) have been entered. If one of these fields is empty, display a JOptionPane informing the user that both fields must contain information. Otherwise, call the calculateSubtotal method, which you implement in the next step, to calculate the subtotal of the bill. The calculateSubtotal method takes no arguments and returns a double containing the subtotal, which you should display in subtotalJTextField. Calculate and display the tax and the total of the bill in JTextFields taxJTextField and totalJTextField, respectively. The tax rate is specified in a constant TAX_RATE.

k) *Adding code to the calculateSubtotal method*. Find the calculateSubtotal method (which immediately follows calculateBillJButtonActionPerformed) and add code that queries the database and retrieves the price column for all the menu items in the billItems ArrayList. This method should then calculate the total price of all the items in the ArrayList and return this value as a double.

l) *Closing the database connection.* Find the frameWindowClosing method (which is located just before main at the end of the class) and add code that closes myStatement and myConnection.

m) *Saving the application.* Save your modified source code file.

n) *Opening the Command Prompt window and changing directories.* Open the **Command Prompt** window by selecting **Start > Programs > Accessories > Command Prompt**. Change to your working directory by typing cd C:\SimplyJava\RestaurantBillCalculator.

o) *Setting the CLASSPATH.* Type C:\Cloudscape_5.1\frameworks\embedded\bin\ setCP.bat in the **Command Prompt** window to set the CLASSPATH environment variable.

p) *Compiling the application.* Compile your application by typing javac RestaurantBillCalculator.java.

q) *Running the completed application.* When your application compiles correctly, run it by typing java RestaurantBillCalculator com.ibm.db2j.jdbc.DB2jDriver jdbc:db2j:restaurant1.

r) *Closing the application.* Close your running application by clicking its close button.

s) *Closing the Command Prompt window.* Close the **Command Prompt** window by clicking its close button.

26.13 *(Airline Reservation Application)* An airline company wants you to develop an application that displays flight information (Fig. 26.41). The database contains two tables, one containing information about the flights and the other containing passenger information. The user should be able to choose a flight number from a JComboBox. When the **View Flight Information** JButton is clicked, the application should display the date of the flight, the flight's departure and arrival cities and the names of the passengers scheduled to take the flight. The provided airline database contains two tables—reservations and flights. The reservations table (Fig. 26.42) has three columns—firstName, lastName and flightNumber. The values in the firstName and lastName column are Strings. The values in the flightNumber column are ints. The flights table (Fig. 26.43) has four columns— flightNumber, departureCity, arrivalCity and flightDate. The values in the flightNumber column are ints. The values in the departureCity, arrivalCity and flightDate columns are Strings.

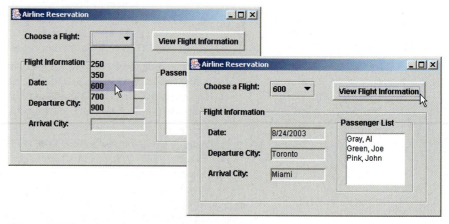

Figure 26.41 **Airline Reservation** application.

a) *Copying the template to your working directory.* Copy the directory C:\Examples\ Tutorial26\Exercises\AirlineReservation to your C:\SimplyJava directory.

b) *Copying the database to your working directory.* Copy the airline database directory from C:\Examples\Tutorial26\Exercises\Databases to your C:\SimplyJava\ AirlineReservation directory.

c) *Opening the template file.* Open the AirlineReservation.java file in your text editor.

lastName	firstName	flightNumber
Black	Bob	350
Blue	Bob	250
Brown	John	250
Cobalt	Alan	700
Gray	Al	600
Green	Joe	600
Indigo	Alan	700
Mix	Bob	350
Orange	Bob	900
Pink	John	600
Purple	John	700
Red	Joe	350
Smith	John	900
White	Joe	900
Yellow	Joe	250

Figure 26.42   reservations table contents.

flightNumber	departureCity	arrivalCity	flightDate
250	Los Angeles	Chicago	7/23/2003
350	Dallas	Las Vegas	7/11/2003
600	Toronto	Miami	8/24/2003
700	San Diego	Providence	6/12/2003
900	Boston	Orlando	6/9/2003

Figure 26.43   flights table contents.

d) *Adding a database connection and creating a Statement object*. In line 45 in the AirlineReservation constructor, insert statements that load the database driver, connect to the airline database and create a Statement to submit SQL to the database. Assume that the driver class name and JDBC URL are passed to the constructor from main. Note that three instance variables—myConnection, myStatement and myResultSet—have already been declared in the template at lines 37–39.

e) *Adding code to the loadFlightNumbers method*. Find the loadFlightNumbers method, which immediately follows createPassengerListJPanel. In loadFlightNumbers, add a statement that queries the database and retrieves the flightNumber column from the flights table in the airline database. Insert a loop that processes the ResultSet and adds each flight number to chooseFlightJComboBox.

f) *Adding code to the flightInfoJButtonActionPerformed method.* Find the flightInfoJButtonActionPerformed method (which immediately follows loadFlightNumbers) and add code that passes the selected flight number (as a String) to the displayFlightInformation method.

g) *Adding code to the displayFlightInformation method.* Find the displayFlightInformation method, which immediately follows flightInfoJButtonActionPerformed. The displayFlightInformation method takes as an argument a String representing the selected flight number. You will need to execute two SQL queries in this method to retrieve information from the two tables in the database. The first SQL query should obtain the flight information for the specified flight number from the flights table. Process the ResultSet from this query and display the flight information in the correct JTextFields (dateJTextField, departureCityJTextField and arrivalCityJTextField). The second SQL query should obtain the pas-

senger information for the specified flight number from the `reservations` table. Clear `displayJTextArea`, process the `ResultSet` and display the passenger names in `displayJTextArea`.

h) *Closing the database connection.* Find the `frameWindowClosing` method (which is located just before `main` at the end of the class) and add code to this method that closes `myStatement` and `myConnection`.

i) *Saving the application.* Save your modified source code file.

j) *Opening the Command Prompt window and changing directories.* Open the **Command Prompt** window by selecting **Start > Programs > Accessories > Command Prompt**. Change to your working directory by typing `cd C:\SimplyJava\Airline-Reservation`.

k) *Setting the CLASSPATH.* Type `C:\Cloudscape_5.1\frameworks\embedded\bin\setCP.bat` in the **Command Prompt** window to set the CLASSPATH environment variable.

l) *Compiling the application.* Compile your application by typing `javac AirlineReservation.java`.

m) *Running the completed application.* When your application compiles correctly, run it by typing `java AirlineReservation com.ibm.db2j.jdbc.DB2jDriver jdbc:db2j:airline`.

n) *Closing the application.* Close your running application by clicking its close button.

o) *Closing the Command Prompt window.* Close the **Command Prompt** window by clicking the window's close button.

What does this code do? ▶   **26.14** What is the result of executing the following code?

```
1  myResultSet = myStatement.executeQuery(
2     "SELECT age FROM people WHERE name = 'Bob'" );
3
4  while ( myResultSet.next() )
5  {
6     displayJTextArea.append( myResultSet.getInt( "age" ) + "\n");
7  }
```

What's wrong with this code? ▶   **26.15** Find the error(s) in the following code. This code should modify the `age` column of table `people`.

```
1  myResultSet = myStatement.executeQuery(
2     "UPDATE people SET age = 30 WHERE name = 'Bob'" );
```

Programming Challenge ▶   **26.16** *(Enhanced Restaurant Bill Calculator Application)* Modify the application you developed in Exercise 26.12 to keep track of multiple table bills at the same time. Sample outputs are shown in Fig. 26.44. The user should be able to calculate a bill for a table and save that table's subtotal and waiter's name. The user should also be able to retrieve that information at a later time. [*Hint:* The `restaurant2` database contains two tables, one for the menu items, as before, and another (`restaurantTables`) for all the tables in the restaurant. The `restaurantTables` table (Fig. 26.45) has three columns—`tableNumber`, `subtotal` and `waiterName`. The values in the `tableNumber` column are `int`s. The values in the `subtotal` column are `double`s. The values in the `waiterName` column are `String`s.]

a) *Copying the template to your working directory.* Copy the directory `C:\Examples\Tutorial26\Exercises\RestaurantBillCalculatorEnhanced` to your `C:\SimplyJava` directory.

b) *Copying the database to your working directory.* Copy the `restaurant2` database directory from `C:\Examples\Tutorial26\Exercises\Databases` to your `C:\SimplyJava\RestaurantBillCalculatorEnhanced` directory.

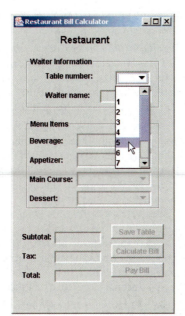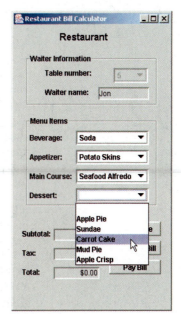

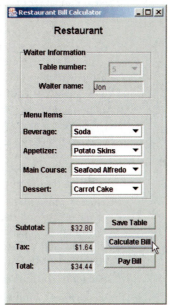

Figure 26.44   Enhanced **Restaurant Bill Calculator** application's GUI.

tableNumber	subtotal	waiterName
1	0.00	Jon
2	0.00	Jon
3	0.00	Jon
4	0.00	Jon
5	0.00	Jon
6	0.00	Sue
7	0.00	Sue
8	0.00	Sue
9	0.00	Sue
10	0.00	Sue

Figure 26.45   Table `restaurantTables` contents.

c) ***Opening the template file.*** Open the `RestaurantBillCalculator.java` file in your text editor.

d) ***Adding code to the `loadTableNumbers` method.*** Find the `loadTableNumbers` method, which immediately follows `createMenuItemsJPanel`. In the `loadTable-Numbers` method, add a statement that queries the database and retrieves the `table-Number` column from the `restaurantTables` table. Insert a loop that processes the `ResultSet` and adds each table number to the `tableNumberJComboBox`.

e) ***Adding code to the `tableNumberJComboBoxItemStateChanged` method.*** Find the `tableNumberJComboBoxItemStateChanged` method, which immediately follows `loadCategory`. In `tableNumberJComboBoxItemStateChanged`, add a statement that queries the database and retrieves all the columns from the `restaurantTables` table for the table that is selected from the `JComboBox`. Process the `ResultSet` and display the waiter's name in `waiterNameJTextField`. Call the `displayTotal` method with the subtotal retrieved from the database, which is provided in the template, to display the subtotal, tax and total in the `subtotalJTextField`, `taxJTextField` and `totalJTextField`, respectively. At the end of the `tableNumberJComboBoxItem-StateChanged` method, enable the `menuItemsJPanel` and all `JComboBoxes` in it and disable the `waiterJPanel` and the `tableNumberJCombox` in it. Finally, enable the `saveTableJButton`, `calculateBillJButton` and `payBillJButton`.

f) ***Adding code to the `saveTableJButtonActionPerformed` method.*** Find the `save-TableJButtonActionPerformed` method, which immediately follows `dessertJCom-boBoxItemStateChanged`. In `saveTableJButtonActionPerformed`, assign the double value returned by the `calculateSubtotal` method (which is already declared in the template) to instance variable `subtotal`. The method should then call the `updateTable` method (which will be created in *Step h*) to update the database. Lastly the method should call the `resetJFrame` method (which is already declared in the template) to reset the components in the `JFrame` to their initial setting.

g) ***Adding code to the `payBillJButtonActionPerformed` method.*** Find the `payBill-JButtonActionPerformed` method, which immediately follows `saveTableJButton-ActionPerformed`. The `payBillJButtonActionPerformed` method should reset `subtotal` to zero, call the `updateTable` method (which is created in the next step) to update the database and call the `resetJFrame` method (which is already declared in the template) to reset the components in the `JFrame` to their initial setting.

h) ***Creating the `updateTable` method.*** Immediately following the `payBillJButton-ActionPerformed` method, create the `updateTable` method, which does not take any arguments and does not return anything. In the `updateTable` method, add a statement that updates the `subtotal` column with the value stored in the instance variable `subtotal` for the selected table number.

i) ***Saving the application.*** Save your modified source code file.

j) ***Opening the Command Prompt window and changing directories.*** Open the **Command Prompt** window by selecting **Start > Programs > Accessories > Command Prompt**. Change to your working directory by typing cd `C:\SimplyJava\Restau-rantBillCalculatorEnhanced`.

k) ***Setting the CLASSPATH.*** Type `C:\Cloudscape_5.1\frameworks\embedded\bin\ setCP.bat` in the **Command Prompt** window to set the CLASSPATH environment variable.

l) ***Compiling the application.*** Compile your application by typing javac `Restaurant-BillCalculator.java`.

m) ***Running the completed application.*** When your application compiles correctly, run it by typing java `RestaurantBillCalculator com.ibm.db2j.jdbc.DB2jDriver jdbc:db2j:restaurant2`.

n) ***Closing the application.*** Close your running application by clicking its close button.

o) ***Closing the Command Prompt window.*** Close the **Command Prompt** window by clicking its close button.

Objectives

In this tutorial, you will learn to:
- Use polymorphism to create an application that process related objects as though they are the same.
- Use additional `Graphics` methods such as `drawLine`.
- Create an application that allows users to draw shapes.

Outline

Drawing Shapes Application

Introduction to Polymorphism; an Expanded Discussion of Graphics

Polymorphism is an object-oriented programming concept that enables you to "program in the general" rather than having to "program in the specific."

In particular, polymorphism makes it easy to write code to process a variety of related objects. The same method call is made on these objects and each of the objects will "do the right thing." If, for example, you ask an object to "talk" it will respond appropriately. If you tell a pig object to talk, it will respond with an "oink." If you tell a dog object to talk, it will respond with a "bark."

Polymorphic applications handle, in a simple and convenient manner, objects of many classes that belong to the same inheritance hierarchy. These applications focus on the similarities between these classes rather than the differences.

With polymorphism, it is also possible to design and implement systems that are easily extended with new capabilities. New classes can be added with little or no modification to the rest of the application, as long as those classes share the similarities of the classes that the application already processes. These new classes simply "plug right in."

In this tutorial, you will add polymorphic processing to the **Drawing Shapes** application. You will also learn additional methods of the `Graphics` class to outline and fill in different types of shapes.

27.1 Test-Driving the Drawing Shapes Application

In this tutorial, you will create a **Drawing Shapes** application that will allow students to draw lines, rectangles and ovals. The application must meet the following requirements:

Application Requirements

*The principal of the elementary school from Tutorial 21 has asked you to modify your **Painter** application. The user should now be able to choose a color from a `JColorChooser` dialog and a type of shape to be drawn from a `JComboBox`. The possible shapes include lines, rectangles and ovals. The user should be able to click a mouse button to create a shape and drag the mouse anywhere on the drawing area to resize that shape. Multiple shapes can be drawn on the drawing area, allowing the user to draw a picture by combining shapes.*

This application allows a user to draw three different kinds of shapes in a variety of colors. The user chooses the shape and color, then presses a mouse button and drags the mouse to create the shape. The user can draw as many shapes as desired. You begin by test-driving the completed application. Then, you will learn the additional Java technologies you will need to create your own version of this application.

Test-Driving the Drawing Shapes Application

1. *Locating the completed application.* Open the **Command Prompt** window by selecting **Start > Programs > Accessories > Command Prompt**. Change to your completed **Drawing Shapes** application directory by typing cd C:\Examples\Tutorial27\CompletedApplication\DrawingShapes.

2. *Running the Drawing Shapes application.* Type java DrawingShapes in the **Command Prompt** window to run the application (Fig. 27.1).

JComboBox for selecting shapes ——

JButton for selecting the drawing color

Drawing area ——

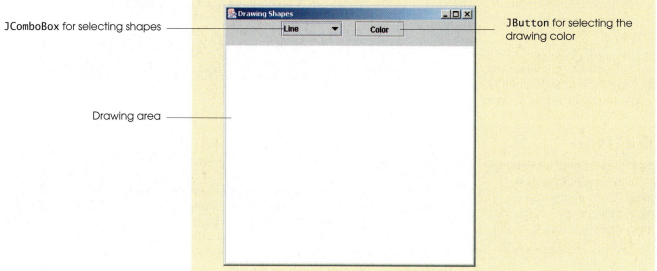

Figure 27.1 Running the completed **Drawing Shapes** application.

3. *Changing the type of shape to draw.* Click the JComboBox at the top of the application and select **Oval** (Fig. 27.2).

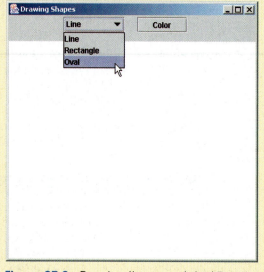

Figure 27.2 Running the completed **Drawing Shapes** application.

(cont.)

4. ***Changing the color of the shape to be drawn.*** Click the **Color** JButton at the top of the application. This will open the JColorChooser dialog which allows you to select a color for the shapes you will draw. The JColor-Chooser dialog will look identical to Fig. 22.3. Select a color and click the **OK** JButton in the JColorChooser dialog. Notice that when you select a new color, the color of the **Color** JButton changes to the newly selected color.

5. ***Drawing an oval.*** Once you have chosen a shape to draw and a color for your shape, move your mouse pointer to the drawing area (the white rectangle). Click and hold the left mouse button to create a new shape. One end of the shape will be positioned at the mouse cursor. Drag the mouse around to position the opposite end of the shape at the location you desire, then release the mouse.

Figure 27.3 Drawing a shape on the application.

6. ***Closing the running application.*** Close your running application by clicking its close button.

7. ***Closing the Command Prompt window.*** Close the **Command Prompt** window by clicking its close button.

27.2 Polymorphism

You will now continue your study of object-oriented programming by learning about polymorphism with inheritance hierarchies. With polymorphism, the same method signature can be used to cause different actions to occur, depending on the type of the object on which the method is invoked.

As an example, suppose you design a video game that manipulates objects of many different types, including objects of classes Bird, Fish and Snake. Also, imagine that each of these classes inherits from a common superclass called Animal, which contains method move. Each subclass implements this method. Your video game application would maintain a collection (such as an ArrayList) of references to objects of the various classes. To move the animals, the application would periodically send each object the same message—namely move. Each object responds to this message in a unique way. For example, a Bird flies across the screen. A Fish swims through a lake. A Snake slithers through the grass. The same message (in this case, move) sent to a variety of objects would have "many forms" of results—hence the term polymorphism which means literally "many forms."

Consider another example—developing a simple payroll system for an Employee inheritance hierarchy. Every Employee has an earnings method that calculates the employee's weekly pay. These earnings methods vary by employee type—a SalariedEmployee is paid a fixed weekly salary regardless of the number of hours worked. An HourlyEmployee is paid by the hour and receives overtime pay. A CommissionEmployee receives a percentage of sales. The same message (in this case, earnings) sent to a variety of objects would have "many forms" of results—again, polymorphism.

For the **Drawing Shapes** application, you will develop a simple inheritance hierarchy. The MyShape class will declare the basic properties of a shape such as its color and location. Three other classes will extend MyShape and each of these classes will declare more specific shape information. These classes are MyLine, MyRectangle and MyOval. The UML class diagram of Fig. 27.4 demonstrates the inheritance hierarchy for your **Drawing Shapes** application.

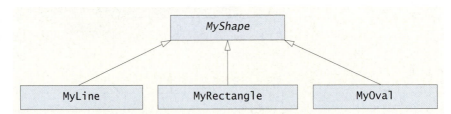

Figure 27.4 UML class diagram for the inheritance hierarchy in the **Drawing Shapes** application.

Calling the draw method on a MyLine object draws a line. Calling the draw method on a MyRectangle object draws a rectangle. [*Note:* The MyOval class is not included in the template application. You will declare it later in this tutorial.] The same message (in this case, draw) sent to a variety of objects would have "many forms" of results—again, polymorphism.

27.3 More Graphics Methods

Before you begin building your **Drawing Shapes** application, you should review its functionality. The following pseudocode describes the basic operation of the **Drawing Shapes** application:

When the user presses the mouse button:

    If Line is selected in the JComboBox
        Create a line

    If Rectangle is selected in the JComboBox
        Create a rectangle

    If Oval is selected in the JComboBox
        Create an oval

When the user clicks the Color JButton:
    Display a JColorChooser dialog
    Update the JButton's color with the selected color
    Set the current shape color to the selected color

When the user selects an item in the JComboBox:
    Get the shape type selected
    Set the current shape type to the selected item

When the user drags the mouse:
    Resize the shape
    Repaint the application

Now that you have test-driven the **Drawing Shapes** application and studied its pseudocode representation, you will use an ACE table to help you convert the pseudocode to Java. Figure 27.5 lists the actions, components and events that will help you complete your own version of the application.

Action/Component/ Event (ACE) Table for the Drawing Shapes Application	Action	Component/Object	Event
		`painterJPanel`	User presses a mouse button
	If Line is selected in JComboBox	`shapeJComboBox`	
	Create a line	`currentShape (MyShape)`	
	If Rectangle is selected in JComboBox	`shapeJComboBox`	
	Create a rectangle	`currentShape (MyShape)`	
	If Oval is selected in JComboBox	`shapeJComboBox`	
	Create an oval	`currentShape (MyShape)`	
		`colorJButton`	User clicks **Color** JButton
	Display a JColorChooser dialog	`JColorChooser`	
	Update the JButton's color	`colorJButton`	
	Set the current shape color to the selected color	`paintJPanel`	
		`shapeJComboBox`	User selects an item in the JComboBox
	Get the shape type selected	`shapeJComboBox`	
	Set the current shape type to the selected item	`paintJPanel`	
		`painterJPanel`	User drags the mouse
	Resize the shape	`currentShape (MyShape)`	
	Repaint the application	`painterPaintJPanel`	

Figure 27.5   **Drawing Shapes** application ACE table.

When you think of a class type, you assume that applications will create objects of that type. However, there are cases in which it is useful to declare classes for which the programmer never intends to instantiate objects. Such classes are called **abstract classes**. Because abstract classes are used only as superclasses in inheritance hierarchies, those classes are often called **abstract superclasses**. These classes cannot be used to instantiate objects, because, as you will see, abstract classes are incomplete. Subclasses must declare the "missing pieces." Abstract superclasses are often used in polymorphic applications which is why polymorphism is sometimes called programming "in the abstract."

The purpose of an abstract class is to provide an appropriate superclass from which other classes can inherit. Classes that can be used to instantiate objects are called **concrete classes**. Abstract superclasses are too generic to create real objects—they specify only what is common among their subclasses. You need to be more specific before you can create objects. Concrete classes provide the specifics that make it possible to instantiate objects.

In the MyShape inheritance hierarchy described previously, MyShape is an abstract superclass. It declares a draw method, but does not provide an implementation of that method. If someone tells you to "draw the shape," your response would likely be "what shape should I draw?" This draw method is the missing piece that makes it impossible to instantiate a MyShape object. If instead you were told to "draw a line" or "draw a rectangle," you could do so. The MyLine class is a concrete subclass of MyShape because the MyLine class includes an implementation of the draw method which specifically draws a line. The MyRectangle class is a concrete subclass of MyShape because the MyRectangle class includes an implementation of the draw method which specifically draws a rectangle.

You will finish the MyShape inheritance hierarchy by declaring the MyShape class abstract and adding a draw method. You will then provide an implementation of the draw method in classes MyLine and MyRectangle.

Declaring an abstract Method

1. ***Copying the template to your working directory.*** Copy the C:\Examples\ Tutorial27\TemplateApplication\DrawingShapes directory to your C:\SimplyJava directory.

2. ***Opening the MyShape template file.*** Open the template file MyShape.java in your text editor.

3. ***Declaring the MyShape class abstract.*** Modify line 5 as shown in Fig. 27.6. This line declares the MyShape class **abstract**. By declaring this class abstract, instances of this class cannot be created. In this application, you will create instances of MyShape's subclasses—MyLine, MyRectangle and MyOval.

Declaring MyShape abstract ⎯⎯⎯⎯⎯⎯

```
4
5 public abstract class MyShape extends Object
6 {
```

Figure 27.6 Declaring the MyShape class abstract.

4. ***Declaring an abstract method.*** Insert lines 95–96 of Fig. 27.7 after method getColor. These lines declare abstract method draw, but provide no implementation for it. Abstract methods are declared by writing a method header followed by a semicolon—no method body is provided. This draw method is the missing piece of the MyShape class that makes it impossible to instantiate. If any method in a class is declared abstract, then the whole class must be declared abstract (as you did in the previous step). The concrete subclasses of MyShape must provide an implementation of the draw method.

(cont.)

Declaring abstract
method draw

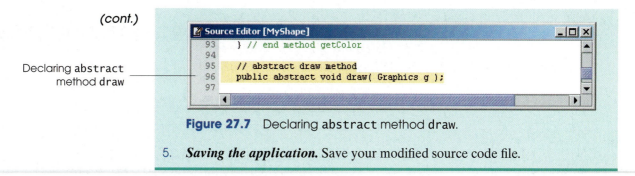

Figure 27.7 Declaring abstract method draw.

5. ***Saving the application.*** Save your modified source code file.

In Tutorial 20, you learned to set the color of drawn shapes using the setColor method and to draw a filled rectangle using the fillRect method. In Tutorial 21, you learned to draw a filled oval using the fillOval method. Each of these methods belongs to class Graphics. Now, you will learn about Graphics methods for drawing lines, rectangles and ovals. Figure 27.8 summarizes the Graphics methods you have learned and introduces several new ones.

Graphics Method	Description
drawLine(x1, y1, x2, y2)	Draws a line from the point (x1, y1) to the point (x2, y2).
drawRect(x, y, width, height)	Draws a rectangle of the specified width and height. The top-left corner of the rectangle is at the point (x, y).
fillRect(x, y, width, height)	Draws a solid rectangle of the specified width and height. The top-left corner of the rectangle is at the point (x, y).
drawOval(x, y, width, height)	Draws an oval inside a rectangular area of the specified width and height. The top-left corner of the rectangular area is at the point (x, y).
fillOval(x, y, width, height)	Draws a filled oval inside a rectangular area of the specified width and height. The top-left corner of the rectangular area is at the point (x, y).
setColor(color)	Sets the drawing color to the specified color.

Figure 27.8 Graphics methods that draw lines, rectangles and ovals.

The MyLine class extends the abstract class MyShape which contains abstract method draw. To declare MyLine as a concrete subclass, you must provide an implementation for the draw method. If you extend an abstract superclass, you must provide an implementation for each of its abstract methods or else the subclass must be declared abstract as well.

You will now provide an implementation of the draw method in the MyLine class. This method should draw a line starting at one of the endpoints specified in the MyLine object and ending at the other one.

Implementing the draw Method in Class MyLine

1. ***Opening the MyLine template file.*** Open the template file MyLine.java in your text editor.

2. ***Implementing the draw method in the MyLine class.*** Insert lines 18–19 of Fig. 27.9 into the draw method. Line 18 calls method getColor to get the color of the MyShape. The return value is passed to method setColor to set the color of the Graphics object (g) for drawing. Line 19 calls the **drawLine** method on the Graphics object. This method takes four int values; the first two are the *x*- and *y*-coordinates of the first endpoint of the line and the second two are the *x*- and *y*-coordinates of the second endpoint of the line.

(cont.)

Implementing the **draw** method to draw a line

```
Source Editor [MyLine *]                                    _ | □ | ×
16    public void draw( Graphics g )
17    {
18        g.setColor( getColor() );
19        g.drawLine( getX1(), getY1(), getX2(), getY2() );
20
```

Figure 27.9 Implementing the **draw** method in class **MyLine**.

3. *Saving the application.* Save your modified source code file.

Your application receives input from the user in the form of two points on the screen—the location at which the user originally clicks the mouse button and the location to which the user drags the mouse cursor. Drawing a line between these two points is simple; the **drawLine** method of class **Graphics** takes the location of two points as arguments. Drawing a rectangle based on these two points is more complicated. The drawn rectangle will have one corner located at one of the points and the diagonally opposite, corner located on the other point. In the **MyRectangle** class's **draw** method, you will need to use these two points to calculate the *x*- and *y*-coordinates of the upper-left corner of the rectangle along with the rectangle's width and height.

You will now implement the **draw** method in the **MyRectangle** class to make **MyRectangle** a concrete subclass of **MyShape**. This method should draw a rectangle on the screen with one corner at one point of the **MyRectangle** object and the opposite corner at the other point.

Implementing the draw Method in Class MyRectangle

1. *Opening the **MyRectangle** template file.* Open the template file MyRectangle.java in your text editor.

2. *Calculating the coordinates of the upper-left corner.* Insert lines 18–19 of Fig. 27.10 into the **draw** method. As you learned in Tutorial 20, the **fillRect** method takes as arguments the *x*- and *y*-coordinates of the upper-left point of the rectangle along with the width and the height. The **MyRectangle** class stores its data in instance variables x1, x2, y1 and y2. Your **draw** method will need to convert the information stored in the **MyRectangle** class to the correct information to pass to the **fillRect** method.

   Line 18 uses the **Math** class's **min** method to determine the smaller of the two *x*-coordinates, which is the one farther left. This method call returns the left edge of the rectangle. Line 19 calls the **min** method to determine the smaller of the two *y*-coordinates, which is the one higher than the other. This method call returns the top of the rectangle.

Determining the *x*- and *y*-coordinates of the upper left corner

```
Source Editor [MyRectangle *]                              _ | □ | ×
16    public void draw( Graphics g )
17    {
18        int upperLeftX = Math.min( getX1(), getX2() );
19        int upperLeftY = Math.min( getY1(), getY2() );
20
```

Figure 27.10 Calculating the coordinates of the upper-left corner.

(cont.)

3. ***Calculating the width and height.*** Insert lines 20–24 of Fig. 27.11 into your code. The **abs** method of class Math returns the **absolute value** (the value of the number without the sign of the number) of the expression it receives. Line 20 uses the abs method to determine the difference between the two *x*-coordinates, which is the width of the rectangle. Line 21 uses the Math class's abs method to determine the difference between the two *y*-coordinates, which is the height of the rectangle. Line 23 sets the color of the rectangle. Line 24 calls method fillRect using the *x*- and *y*-coordinates that you calculated in the previous step, along with the width and height that you calculated in this step.

Calculating the width and
height of the rectangle

```
Source Editor [MyRectangle *]                                    _ | □ | ×
19        int upperLeftY = Math.min( getY1(), getY2() );
20        int width = Math.abs( getX1() - getX2() );
21        int height = Math.abs( getY1() - getY2() );
22
23        g.setColor( getColor() );
24        g.fillRect( upperLeftX, upperLeftY, width, height );
25
```

Figure 27.11 Calculating the width and height and drawing the rectangle.

4. ***Saving the application.*** Save your modified source code file.

You will now finish the PaintJPanel class to allow the user to create and resize shapes.

Finishing the PaintJPanel Class

1. ***Opening the template file.*** Open the template file PaintJPanel.java in your text editor.

2. ***Declaring a MyShape instance variable.*** Add lines 13–14 of Fig. 27.12 into your code. These lines declare a MyShape instance variable to hold the current shape. The MyShape class is an abstract class and cannot be instantiated, but references of the MyShape class can be created. This is one of the keys to polymorphism. This reference is used to resize a shape after it has been created. With polymorphism, you do not need to know what type of shape is stored in the MyShape reference.

Declaring a myShape
instance variable

```
Source Editor [PaintJPanel *]                                    _ | □ | ×
11        private ArrayList shapesArrayList = new ArrayList();
12
13        // current shape that is being drawn
14        private MyShape currentShape;
15
```

Figure 27.12 Declaring a new MyShape object.

3. ***Creating a new MyLine object.*** Insert lines 72–77 of Fig. 27.13 into method paintJPanelMousePressed. Line 73 tests whether the user selected **Line** in the JComboBox. If this is the case, lines 75–76 create a new MyLine object. These lines use methods getX and getY of MouseEvent to determine where the mouse is positioned. This MyLine object is created with the first endpoint the same as the second endpoint. This makes the length of the line 0 and it appears as a single colored pixel. When the user drags the mouse, the second endpoint will be repositioned, changing the size of the line.

(cont.)

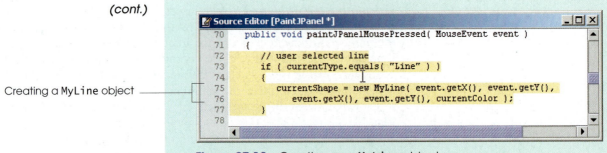

Creating a `MyLine` object

Figure 27.13 Creating new `MyLine` object.

4. ***Creating a new MyRectangle object.*** Insert lines 78–83 of Fig. 27.14 into method `paintJPanelMousePressed`. Line 79 tests whether the user selected **Rectangle** in the `JComboBox`. If this is the case, lines 81–82 create a new `MyRectangle` object. These lines use methods `getX` and `getY` of `MouseEvent` to determine where the mouse is positioned. This `MyRectangle` object is created with the first endpoint the same as the second endpoint. This makes the rectangle appear as a single colored pixel. When the user drags the mouse, the second endpoint will be repositioned, changing the size and shape of the rectangle.

```
 Source Editor [PaintJPanel *]                              _ □ ×
 77          }
 78          // user selected rectangle
 79          else if ( currentType.equals( "Rectangle" ) )
 80          {
 81             currentShape = new MyRectangle( event.getX(), event.getY(),
 82                event.getX(), event.getY(), currentColor );
 83          }
 84
```

Creating a `MyRectangle` object

Figure 27.14 Creating new `MyRectangle` object.

Line 75 of Fig. 27.13 assigns a `MyLine` object to `MyShape` variable `currentShape` and line 81 of Fig. 27.14 assigns a `MyRectangle` object to `currentShape`. Java allows both of these assignments because the `MyLine` and `MyRectangle` classes have an *is a* relationship with the `MyShape` class.

5. ***Adding the MyShape reference to the ArrayList.*** Add line 85 of Fig. 27.15 to method `paintJPanelMousePressed`. This line adds the new `MyShape` object to `shapesArrayList`.

```
 Source Editor [PaintJPanel *]                              _ □ ×
 83          }
 84
 85          shapesArrayList.add( currentShape );
 86
```

Adding `currentShape` to the shapes `ArrayList`

Figure 27.15 Adding the new `MyShape` to `shapesArrayList`.

6. ***Resizing the shape.*** Add lines 92–94 of Fig. 27.16 to method `paintJPanel-MouseDragged`. When the user drags the mouse, `currentShape` must be resized. Lines 92–93 resize the shape by changing the *x*- and *y*-coordinates of the shape's second point. Recall that when the shape is constructed, the first and second points are at the same location. Changing the location of the second point resizes the shape, while keeping the first point in place. These lines use `MouseEvent` methods `getX` and `getY` to get the location of the mouse cursor.

(cont.)

Lines 92–93 use the MyShape variable currentShape without knowing exactly what type of shape is being affected. This is an example of polymorphic processing. The calls to methods setX2 and setY2 are allowed because these methods are declared in the MyShape class. All classes that extend MyShape contain these methods. Line 94 calls the repaint method, which will call the paintComponent method which you will declare next.

```
Source Editor [PaintJPanel *]                                    _ |□| x|
90      public void paintJPanelMouseDragged( MouseEvent event )
91      {
92          currentShape.setX2( event.getX() );
93          currentShape.setY2( event.getY() );
94          repaint();
95
```

Setting the currentShape's *x*-
and *y*-coordinates

Figure 27.16   Resizing the MyShape object.

7. *Paint all the shapes.* Add lines 103–112 of Fig. 27.17 to method paintComponent. Line 104 creates an Iterator to traverse through each element of shapesArrayList. Lines 107–112 iterate through the items in shapesArrayList. Line 110 calls method next to get a reference to the next object in shapesArrayList. This method returns an instance of type Object which is then cast to a MyShape reference and assigned to nextShape. Line 111 calls method draw on nextShape.

At this point, you do not know which draw method will be called—the one in MyLine or the one in MyRectangle. The method call will be resolved only when the application is executed. Each shape in shapesArrayList knows how to draw itself. If nextShape is a MyLine object, the draw method from the MyLine class will be called. If nextShape is instead a MyRectangle object, the draw method from the MyRectangle class will be called.

```
Source Editor [PaintJPanel *]                                    _ |□| x|
101         super.paintComponent( g );
102
103         MyShape nextShape;
104         Iterator shapesIterator = shapesArrayList.iterator();
105
106         // iterate through all the shapes
107         while ( shapesIterator.hasNext() )
108         {
109             // draw each shape
110             nextShape = ( MyShape ) shapesIterator.next();
111             nextShape.draw( g );
112         }
113
```

Using a while statement
to draw each shape

Figure 27.17   Drawing the shapes in shapesArrayList polymorphically.

8. *Saving the application.* Save your modified source code file.

You have now finished coding the PaintJPanel class. Next, you will instantiate an object of PaintJPanel and use it in your **Drawing Shapes** application to allow the user to draw shapes.

**Adding a PaintJPanel
to Your Application**

1. *Opening the template file.* Open the template file DrawingShapes.java in your text editor.

2. *Declaring a PaintJPanel instance variable.* Add lines 19–20 of Fig. 27.18 to your code to declare a PaintJPanel instance variable. This PaintJPanel component listens for mouse events and uses them to draw shapes.

(cont.)

Declaring a `PaintJPanel` instance variable

```
Source Editor [DrawingShapes *]                          _ |□| x|
17      private JButton colorJButton;
18
19      // PaintJPanel for drawing shapes
20      private PaintJPanel painterPaintJPanel;
21
```

Figure 27.18   Declaring a `PaintJPanel` instance variable.

3. ***Creating and customizing the `PaintJPanel`.*** Add lines 46–50 of Fig. 27.19 to your application. Line 47 instantiates a `PaintJPanel` object named `painterPaintJPanel`. Lines 48–49 set the *bounds* and *background* properties for the `painterPaintJPanel`, respectively. Line 50 adds `painterPaintJPanel` to the content pane to display the component and allow the user to interact with it.

```
Source Editor [DrawingShapes *]                          _ |□| x|
44          contentPane.add( controlsJPanel );
45
46          // set up painterPaintJPanel
47          painterPaintJPanel = new PaintJPanel();
48          painterPaintJPanel.setBounds( 0, 40, 400, 340 );
49          painterPaintJPanel.setBackground( Color.WHITE );
50          contentPane.add( painterPaintJPanel );
51
```

Figure 27.19   Creating a new `PaintJPanel` object.

4. ***Setting the color for the next drawn `MyShape`.*** Add line 105 of Fig. 27.20 to method `colorJButtonActionPerformed`. This line sets the color of the shape to be drawn to the color the user selected in the `JColorChooser` dialog. Now, when the user selects a color, that color will be set as the current color of `painterPaintJPanel`.

Setting the `PaintJPanel`'s color

```
Source Editor [DrawingShapes *]                          _ |□| x|
104         colorJButton.setBackground( selection );
105         painterPaintJPanel.setCurrentColor( selection );
106     }
```

Figure 27.20   Setting the color for the next MyShape.

5. ***Setting the type of the drawn `MyShape`.*** Add lines 113–114 of Fig. 27.21 to method `shapeJComboBoxActionPerformed`. These lines take the name of the shape that the user selected from `shapeJComboBox` and pass it to `painterPaintJPanel`. The `getSelectedItem` method returns the `Object` that is currently selected in `shapeJComboBox`, which is then cast to `String` and passed to method `setCurrentShapeType` of `PaintJPanel`. When the user drags the mouse on `painterPaintJPanel`, a shape of the user's selected type and color will appear.

Determining which shape to draw

```
Source Editor [DrawingShapes *]                          _ |□| x|
111     private void shapeJComboBoxActionPerformed( ActionEvent event )
112     {
113         painterPaintJPanel.setCurrentShapeType(
114             ( String )shapeJComboBox.getSelectedItem() );
115
```

Figure 27.21   Changing the type of shape drawn.

6. ***Saving the application.*** Save your modified source code file.

(cont.)

7. ***Opening the Command Prompt window and changing directories.*** Open the **Command Prompt** window by selecting **Start > Programs > Accessories > Command Prompt**. Change to your working directory by typing cd C:\SimplyJava\DrawingShapes.

8. ***Compiling the application.*** Compile your application by typing javac DrawingShapes.java PaintJPanel.java MyShape.java MyLine.java MyRectangle.java.

9. ***Running the application.*** When your application compiles correctly, run it by typing java DrawingShapes. Figure 27.28 shows the completed application running. Users can now select and draw a line or a rectangle, but cannot select or draw an oval.

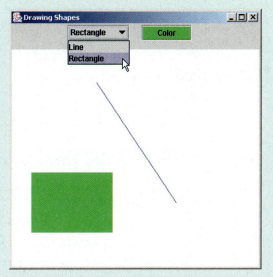

Figure 27.22 Completed **Drawing Shapes** application.

10. ***Closing the application.*** Close your running application by clicking its close button.

11. ***Closing the Command Prompt window.*** Close the **Command Prompt** window by clicking its close button.

SELF-REVIEW

1. The statement, _____, will draw a horizontal line.
   a) drawLine(0, 5, 5, 0)
   b) drawLine(0, 5, 5, 5)
   c) drawLine(5, 5, 5, 0)
   d) drawLine(5, 5, 5, 5)

2. The _____ method of class Graphics can draw the outline of a circle.
   a) fillOval
   b) fillCircle
   c) drawOval
   d) drawCircle

Answers: 1) b. 2) c.

27.4 Adding to the MyShape Inheritance Hierarchy

One of the benefits of polymorphism is that it makes it easy to add new types of objects to an existing application. In your **Drawing Shapes** application, the user can draw a line or a rectangle. Both the MyLine and the MyRectangle class extend the MyShape class and implement the draw method. You will now add to your application by declaring a MyOval class and adding it to the inheritance hierarchy. The MyOval class will also extend the MyShape class and declare a draw method. The application code will require only a few changes.

Adding Class MyOval to the Inheritance Hierarchy

1. **Create the MyOval file.** Create a new source code file. Name this new file MyOval.java. After you have created the file, open it in your text editor.

2. **Declare the MyOval class.** Add lines 1–8 of Fig. 27.23 to MyOval.java. Line 5 declares that class MyOval extends class MyShape. The class declaration ends with the right brace on line 8.

Class MyOval extends class MyShape

```
Source Editor [MyOval *]                                    _ □ ×
1  // Tutorial 27: MyOval.java
2  // Class that declares an oval object.
3  import java.awt.*;
4
5  public class MyOval extends MyShape
6  {
7
8  } // end class MyOval
```

Figure 27.23   Declaring class MyOval to extend MyShape.

3. **Adding a constructor.** Add lines 7–13 of Fig. 27.24 to the class declaration. These lines declare a constructor for MyOval which takes four integer arguments and a Color argument. This constructor calls the superclass's constructor which also takes four int arguments and a Color argument.

MyOval's constructor, which takes five arguments

```
Source Editor [MyOval *]                                    _ □ ×
6  {
7      // constructor
8      public MyOval( int firstX, int firstY, int secondX, int secondY,
9          Color shapeColor )
10     {
11         super( firstX, firstY, secondX, secondY, shapeColor );
12
13     } // end constructor
14
```

Figure 27.24   Declaring a constructor in class MyOval.

4. **Implementing the draw method.** Add lines 15–26 of Fig. 27.25 after the constructor. These lines implement the draw method declared in class MyShape to draw an oval. Lines 18–21 calculate the dimensions of the oval to be drawn. These calculations are the same as those that were required for the MyRectangle class. Recall that the min method returns the smallest of the two values it receives and the abs method returns the absolute value of the expression it receives. Line 24 calls Graphics method fillOval to draw an oval in the application.

Implementing the draw method

```
Source Editor [MyOval *]                                    _ □ ×
13     } // end constructor
14
15     // draw an oval
16     public void draw( Graphics g )
17     {
18         int upperLeftX = Math.min( getX1(), getX2() );
19         int upperLeftY = Math.min( getY1(), getY2() );
20         int width = Math.abs( getX1() - getX2() );
21         int height = Math.abs( getY1() - getY2() );
22
23         g.setColor( getColor() );
24         g.fillOval( upperLeftX, upperLeftY, width, height );
25
26     } // end method draw
27
```

Figure 27.25   Implementing method draw to draw a MyOval object.

5. **Saving the application.** Save your modified source code file.

Now that you have created class `MyOval`, you must modify some of the code in the application. First, you must add an option to the `JComboBox` allowing the user to select an oval to draw.

Allowing the User to Draw an Oval

1. ***Opening the template file.*** Open the template file `DrawingShapes.java` in your text editor.
2. ***Adding an oval option to the `JComboBox`.*** Modify line 23 of your source code file so it looks like line 23 of Fig. 27.26. This adds an "Oval" option to the `JComboBox` which allows the user to select an oval as the shape to draw.

Allow users to select "Oval" from `shapeTypes`

Source Editor [DrawingShapes *]

```
22    // array of shape types
23    private String[] shapeTypes = { "Line", "Rectangle", "Oval" };
24
```

Figure 27.26 Adding the oval option to the `String` array `shapeTypes`.

3. ***Saving the application.*** Save the modified source code file.

The user can now select an oval, but the application must also create a `MyOval` object.

Creating a `MyOval` Object

1. ***Opening the template file.*** Open the template file `PaintJPanel.java` in your text editor.
2. ***Creating a `MyOval` object.*** Add lines 84–89 of Fig. 27.27 to method `paintJPanelMousePressed`. Line 85 tests whether the current shape type is equal to `"Oval"`. If it is, lines 87–88 create a new `MyOval` object.

Drawing an oval if the user has selected this option

Source Editor [PaintJPanel *]

```
83          }
84          // user selected oval
85          else if ( currentType.equals( "Oval" ) )
86          {
87             currentShape = new MyOval( event.getX(), event.getY(),
88                event.getX(), event.getY(), currentColor );
89          }
90
```

Figure 27.27 Creating a `MyOval` object.

Notice that you do not need to make any changes to the method that resizes the shape (`paintJPanelMouseDragged`) or the method that draws the shape (`paintComponent`) because they handle the shapes polymorphically. Line 111 of Fig. 27.17 calls the `draw` method on `MyShape` reference `currentShape`. If `currentShape` actually refers to a `MyOval` object, the `draw` method declared in the `MyOval` class is called. The `MyOval` object knows how to draw itself.

3. ***Saving the application.*** Save your modified source code file.
4. ***Opening the* Command Prompt *window and changing directories.*** Open the **Command Prompt** window by selecting **Start > Programs > Accessories > Command Prompt**. Change to your working directory by typing `cd C:\SimplyJava\DrawingShapes`.
5. ***Compiling the application.*** Compile your application by typing `javac DrawingShapes.java PaintJPanel.java MyOval.java`.

(cont.)

6. ***Running the application.*** When your application compiles correctly, run it by typing `java DrawingShapes`. Figure 27.28 shows the completed application running. Users can now select and draw an oval.

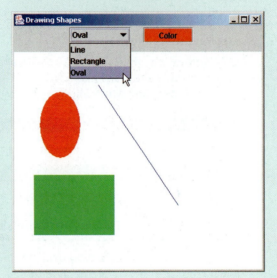

Figure 27.28 Completed **Drawing Shapes** application.

7. ***Closing the application.*** Close your running application by clicking its close button.

8. ***Closing the Command Prompt window.*** Close the **Command Prompt** window by clicking its close button.

Figure 27.29–Fig. 27.30 present the source code for the **Drawing Shapes** application. The lines of code that you added, viewed or modified in this tutorial are highlighted.

```
1   // Tutorial 27: DrawingShapes.java
2   // Application allows user to draw lines, rectangles and ovals and
3   // choose the color of the drawn shape.
4   import java.awt.*;
5   import java.awt.event.*;
6   import javax.swing.*;
7
8   public class DrawingShapes extends JFrame
9   {
10     // JPanel for the shape and color controls
11     private JPanel controlsJPanel;
12
13     // JComboBox to allow selection of a shape
14     private JComboBox shapeJComboBox;
15
16     // JButton to select the color
17     private JButton colorJButton;
18
19     // PaintJPanel for drawing shapes
20     private PaintJPanel painterPaintJPanel;
21
22     // array of shape types
23     private String[] shapeTypes = { "Line", "Rectangle", "Oval" };
24
```

PaintJPanel instance variable ——— 20

Array of shape names ——— 23

Figure 27.29 **Drawing Shapes** code. (Part 1 of 3.)

```
25    // no-argument constructor
26    public DrawingShapes()
27    {
28       createUserInterface();
29    }
30
31    // create and position GUI components; register event handlers
32    private void createUserInterface()
33    {
34       // get content pane for attaching GUI components
35       Container contentPane = getContentPane();
36
37       // enable explicit positioning of GUI components
38       contentPane.setLayout( null );
39
40       // set up controlsJPanel
41       controlsJPanel = new JPanel();
42       controlsJPanel.setBounds( 0, 0, 400, 40 );
43       controlsJPanel.setLayout( null );
44       contentPane.add( controlsJPanel );
45
46       // set up painterPaintJPanel
47       painterPaintJPanel = new PaintJPanel();
48       painterPaintJPanel.setBounds( 0, 40, 400, 340 );
49       painterPaintJPanel.setBackground( Color.WHITE );
50       contentPane.add( painterPaintJPanel );
51
52       // set up shapeJComboBox
53       shapeJComboBox = new JComboBox( shapeTypes );
54       shapeJComboBox.setBounds( 90, 2, 100, 24 );
55       controlsJPanel.add( shapeJComboBox );
56       shapeJComboBox.addActionListener(
57
58          new ActionListener() // anonymous inner class
59          {
60             // event method called when shapeJComboBox is selected
61             public void actionPerformed( ActionEvent event )
62             {
63                shapeJComboBoxActionPerformed( event );
64             }
65
66          } // end anonymous inner class
67
68       ); // end call to addActionListener
69
70       // set up colorJButton
71       colorJButton = new JButton();
72       colorJButton.setBounds( 210, 2, 80, 24 );
73       colorJButton.setText( "Color" );
74       controlsJPanel.add( colorJButton );
75       colorJButton.addActionListener(
76
77          new ActionListener() // anonymous inner class
78          {
79             // event handler called when colorJButton is pressed
80             public void actionPerformed( ActionEvent event )
81             {
82                colorJButtonActionPerformed( event );
```

Figure 27.29 **Drawing Shapes** code. (Part 2 of 3.)

```
83                 }
84
85             } // end anonymous inner class
86
87         ); // end call to addActionListener
88
89         // set properties of application's window
90         setTitle( "Drawing Shapes" ); // set title bar string
91         setSize( 408, 407 );          // set window size
92         setVisible( true );           // display window
93
94     } // end method createUserInterface
95
96     // select a new color for the shape
97     private void colorJButtonActionPerformed( ActionEvent event )
98     {
99         Color selection = JColorChooser.showDialog( null,
100             "Select a Color", Color.BLACK );
101
102         if ( selection != null )
103         {
104             colorJButton.setBackground( selection );
105             painterPaintJPanel.setCurrentColor( selection );
106         }
107
108     } // end method colorJButtonActionPerformed
109
110     // set the selected shape in the painting panel
111     private void shapeJComboBoxActionPerformed( ActionEvent event )
112     {
113         painterPaintJPanel.setCurrentShapeType(
114             ( String )shapeJComboBox.getSelectedItem() );
115
116     } // end method shapeJComboBoxActionPerformed
117
118     // main method
119     public static void main( String args[] )
120     {
121         DrawingShapes application = new DrawingShapes();
122         application.setDefaultCloseOperation( JFrame.EXIT_ON_CLOSE );
123
124     } // end method main
125
126 } // end class DrawingShapes
```

Setting the color of the PaintJPanel — *(annotation pointing to line 105)*

Setting the shape to draw — *(annotation pointing to lines 113–114)*

Figure 27.29 **Drawing Shapes** code. (Part 3 of 3.)

```
1   // Tutorial 27: PaintJPanel.java
2   // Panel allows user to create a shape.
3   import java.awt.*;
4   import java.awt.event.*;
5   import java.util.*;
6   import javax.swing.*;
7
8   public class PaintJPanel extends JPanel {
9
10      // ArrayList to hold the shapes
11      private ArrayList shapesArrayList = new ArrayList();
```

Figure 27.30 **PaintJPanel** code. (Part 1 of 3.)

```
12
13      // current shape that is being drawn
14      private MyShape currentShape;
15
16      // currently selected shape type
17      private String currentType = "Line";
18
19      // currently selected color
20      private Color currentColor = new Color( 204, 204, 204 );
21
22      // no-argument constructor
23      public PaintJPanel()
24      {
25         addMouseListener(
26
27            new MouseAdapter() // anonymous inner class
28            {
29               // event handler called when mouse button is pressed
30               public void mousePressed( MouseEvent event )
31               {
32                  paintJPanelMousePressed( event );
33               }
34
35            } // end anonymous inner class
36
37         ); // end call to addMouseListener
38
39         addMouseMotionListener(
40
41            new MouseMotionAdapter() // anonymous inner class
42            {
43               // event handler called when the mouse is dragged
44               public void mouseDragged( MouseEvent event )
45               {
46                  paintJPanelMouseDragged( event );
47               }
48
49            } // end anonymous inner class
50
51         ); // end call to addMouseMotionListener
52
53      } // end constructor
54
55      // change the current shape type
56      public void setCurrentShapeType( String shape )
57      {
58         currentType = shape;
59
60      } // end method setCurrentShapeType
61
62      // change the current color
63      public void setCurrentColor( Color shapeColor )
64      {
65         currentColor = shapeColor;
66
67      } // end method setCurrentColor
68
```

Figure 27.30   PaintJPanel code. (Part 2 of 3.)

Creating a `MyLine` object and assigning it to a `MyShape` variable

Creating a `MyRectangle` object and assigning it to a `MyShape` variable

Creating a `MyOval` object and assigning it to a `MyShape` variable

Adding `currentShape` to `shapesArrayList`

Setting the `currentShape`'s x- and y- coordinates

Using a `while` statement to draw each shape

```java
69      // create a new shape
70      public void paintJPanelMousePressed( MouseEvent event )
71      {
72         // user selected line
73         if ( currentType.equals( "Line" ) )
74         {
75            currentShape = new MyLine( event.getX(), event.getY(),
76               event.getX(), event.getY(), currentColor );
77         }
78         // user selected rectangle
79         else if ( currentType.equals( "Rectangle" ) )
80         {
81            currentShape = new MyRectangle( event.getX(), event.getY(),
82               event.getX(), event.getY(), currentColor );
83         }
84         // user selected oval
85         else if ( currentType.equals( "Oval" ) )
86         {
87            currentShape = new MyOval( event.getX(), event.getY(),
88               event.getX(), event.getY(), currentColor );
89         }
90
91         shapesArrayList.add( currentShape );
92
93      } // end method paintJPanelMousePressed
94
95      // reset the second point for the shape
96      public void paintJPanelMouseDragged( MouseEvent event )
97      {
98         currentShape.setX2( event.getX() );
99         currentShape.setY2( event.getY() );
100        repaint();
101
102     } // end method paintJPanelMouseDragged
103
104     // paint all the shapes
105     public void paintComponent( Graphics g )
106     {
107        super.paintComponent( g );
108
109        MyShape nextShape;
110        Iterator shapesIterator = shapesArrayList.iterator();
111
112        // iterate through all the shapes
113        while ( shapesIterator.hasNext() )
114        {
115           // draw each shape
116           nextShape = ( MyShape ) shapesIterator.next();
117           nextShape.draw( g );
118        }
119
120     } // end method paintComponent
121
122  } // end class PaintJPanel
```

Figure 27.30 PaintJPanel code. (Part 3 of 3.)

Declaring MyShape abstract ———

```
1   // Tutorial 27: MyShape.java
2   // Superclass for all shape objects.
3   import java.awt.*;
4
5   public abstract class MyShape extends Object
6   {
7      private int x1;
8      private int y1;
9      private int x2;
10     private int y2;
11     private Color color;
12
13     // constructor
14     public MyShape( int firstX, int firstY, int secondX, int secondY,
15        Color shapeColor )
16     {
17        setX1( firstX );
18        setY1( firstY );
19        setX2( secondX );
20        setY2( secondY );
21        setColor( shapeColor );
22
23     } // end constructor
24
25     // set x1 value
26     public void setX1( int x )
27     {
28        x1 = x;
29
30     } // end method setX1
31
32     // get x1 value
33     public int getX1()
34     {
35        return x1;
36
37     } // end method getX1
38
39     // set Y1 value
40     public void setY1( int y )
41     {
42        y1 = y;
43
44     } // end method setY1
45
46     // get Y1 value
47     public int getY1()
48     {
49        return y1;
50
51     } // end method getY1
52
53     // set x2 value
54     public void setX2( int x )
55     {
56        x2 = x;
57
58     } // end method setX2
```

Figure 27.31 My Shape code. (Part 1 of 2.)

```
59
60      // get x2 value
61      public int getX2()
62      {
63         return x2;
64
65      } // end method getX2
66
67      // set y2 value
68      public void setY2( int y )
69      {
70         y2 = y;
71
72      } // end method setY2
73
74      // get y2 value
75      public int getY2()
76      {
77         return y2;
78
79      } // end method getY2
80
81      // set color value
82      public void setColor( Color c )
83      {
84         color = c;
85
86      } // end method setColor
87
88      // get color value
89      public Color getColor()
90      {
91         return color;
92
93      } // end method getColor
94
95      // abstract draw method
96      public abstract void draw( Graphics g );
97
98   } // end class MyShape
```

Declaring **abstract**
method draw ⟶ (line 96)

Figure 27.31   My Shape code. (Part 2 of 2.)

```
1   // Tutorial 27: MyLine.java
2   // Class that declares a line object.
3   import java.awt.*;
4
5   public class MyLine extends MyShape
6   {
7      // constructor
8      public MyLine( int firstX, int firstY, int secondX, int secondY,
9         Color shapeColor )
10     {
11        super( firstX, firstY, secondX, secondY, shapeColor );
12
13     } // end constructor
14
```

Figure 27.32   My Line code. (Part 1 of 2.)

```
15      // draw a line
16      public void draw( Graphics g )
17      {
18          g.setColor( getColor() );
19          g.drawLine( getX1(), getY1(), getX2(), getY2() );
20
21      } // end method draw
22
23   } // end class MyLine
```

Implementing the abstract draw method from MyShape *(annotation pointing to lines 18–19)*

Figure 27.32 **My Line** code. (Part 2 of 2.)

```
1    // Tutorial 27: MyRectangle.java
2    // Class that declares a rectangle object.
3    import java.awt.*;
4
5    public class MyRectangle extends MyShape
6    {
7       // constructor
8       public MyRectangle( int firstX, int firstY, int secondX,
9          int secondY, Color shapeColor )
10      {
11         super( firstX, firstY, secondX, secondY, shapeColor );
12
13      } // end constructor
14
15      // draw a rectangle
16      public void draw( Graphics g )
17      {
18          int upperLeftX = Math.min( getX1(), getX2() );
19          int upperLeftY = Math.min( getY1(), getY2() );
20          int width = Math.abs( getX1() - getX2() );
21          int height = Math.abs( getY1() - getY2() );
22
23          g.setColor( getColor() );
24          g.fillRect( upperLeftX, upperLeftY, width, height );
25
26      } // end method draw
27
28   } // end class MyRectangle
```

Implementing the abstract draw method from MyShape *(annotation pointing to line 16)*

Calculating the *x*- and *y*-coordinates, width and height of the rectangle *(annotation pointing to lines 18–21)*

Drawing a rectangle *(annotation pointing to line 24)*

Figure 27.33 **My Rectangle** code.

```
1    // Tutorial 27: MyOval.java
2    // Class that declares an oval object.
3    import java.awt.*;
4
5    public class MyOval extends MyShape
6    {
7       // constructor
8       public MyOval( int firstX, int firstY, int secondX, int secondY,
9          Color shapeColor )
10      {
11         super( firstX, firstY, secondX, secondY, shapeColor );
12
13      } // end constructor
14
```

Extending class MyShape *(annotation pointing to line 5)*

MyOval's constructor takes five arguments *(annotation pointing to lines 8–11)*

Figure 27.34 **My Oval** code. (Part 1 of 2.)

Implementing the abstract
draw method from MyShape

Calculating the *x*- and *y*-
coordinates, width and height
of the rectangle

```
15      // draw an oval
16      public void draw( Graphics g )
17      {
18          int upperLeftX = Math.min( getX1(), getX2() );
19          int upperLeftY = Math.min( getY1(), getY2() );
20          int width = Math.abs( getX1() - getX2() );
21          int height = Math.abs( getY1() - getY2() );
22
23          g.setColor( getColor() );
24          g.fillOval( upperLeftX, upperLeftY, width, height );
25
26      } // end method draw
27
28  } // end class MyOval
```

Figure 27.34   **My Oval** code. (Part 2 of 2.)

SELF-REVIEW

1. The min and abs methods belong to the _____ class.

   a) Calc
   b) Math
   c) Calculation
   d) Number

2. The drawLine, fillOval and setColor methods belong to the _____ class.

   a) Draw
   b) Graphics
   c) Drawing
   d) Graphic

Answers: 1) b. 2) b.

27.5 Wrap-Up

In this tutorial, you learned about polymorphism. You created a **Drawing Shapes** application, which allows you to draw a picture by combining different colored shapes. You learned how to use additional Graphics methods to draw a line, a filled rectangle and a filled oval.

While building the **Drawing Shapes** application, you used an inheritance hierarchy consisting of the MyShape superclass and the MyLine, MyRectangle and MyOval subclasses. You also handled objects of the three subclasses polymorphically—by treating them as objects of the MyShape superclass.

In the next tutorial, you will learn about the Java Speech API which produces synthetic speech from text input. You will use this technology to create a phone book application that will speak a selected person's phone number.

SKILLS SUMMARY

Drawing a Rectangle

- Use the Graphics method drawRect to draw the rectangle specified by its *x*- and *y*-coordinates, width and height.

Drawing an Oval

- Use the Graphics method drawOval to draw the oval specified by its bounding box's *x*- and *y*-coordinates, width and height.

Drawing a Line

- Use the Graphics method drawLine to draw the line specified by its beginning and ending *x*- and *y*-coordinates.

KEY TERMS

abs method of the Math class—Returns the absolute value of a given value.

absolute value—The value of a number without the sign of the number.

abstract class—A class that cannot be instantiated. Often called an abstract superclass because it is usable only as the superclass in an inheritance hierarchy. These classes are incomplete; they are missing pieces necessary for instantiation which concrete subclasses must implement.

abstract keyword—Used to declare that a class or method is abstract.

abstract method—Declares a method header but no method body. Any class with an abstract method must be an abstract class.

concrete class—A class that can be instantiated.

drawLine method of the Graphics class—Draws a line using the given *x*- and *y*-coordinates.

drawOval method of the Graphics class—Draws an oval using the bounding box's upper-left *x*- and *y*-coordinates and the width and height.

drawRect method of the Graphics class—Draws a rectangle using the given *x*- and *y*-coordinates and the rectangle's width and height.

min method of the Math class—Returns the minimum of two values.

polymorphism—Concept that allows you to write applications that handle, in a more general manner, a wide variety of classes related by inheritance.

JAVA LIBRARY REFERENCE

Graphics   The Graphics class provides methods to draw shapes of varying colors.

■ *Methods*

drawLine—Takes four arguments and draws a line at the specified beginning and ending *x*- and *y*-coordinates.

drawOval—Takes four arguments and draws an unfilled oval inside a bounding rectangular area. The first two arguments are the *x*- and *y*-coordinates of the top-left corner of the rectangular area and the second two are the width and height.

drawRect—Takes four arguments and draws an unfilled rectangle at the specified upper-left *x*- and *y*-coordinates and of the specified width and height.

fillRect—Takes four arguments and draws a solid rectangle at the specified upper-left *x*- and *y*-coordinates and of the specified width and height.

fillOval—Takes four arguments and draws a solid oval inside a bounding rectangular area. The first two arguments are the *x*- and *y*-coordinates of the top-left corner of the rectangular area and the second two are the width and height.

setColor—Sets the color of the Graphics object.

Math   The Math class provides methods to perform different mathematical functions.

■ *Methods*

abs—Returns the absolute value of its argument.

max—Returns the greater of its two arguments.

min—Returns the lesser of its two arguments.

MULTIPLE-CHOICE QUESTIONS

27.1 The code _____ will draw a solid circle.

   a) drawCircle(50, 50, 25);   b) fillOval(50, 25, 50, 25);

   c) fillOval(50, 50, 25, 25);   d) drawOval(50, 50, 50, 50);

27.2 Because of polymorphism, using the same _____ can cause different actions to occur depending on the type of the object on which a method is invoked.

   a) method return type   b) instance variable

   c) local variable   d) method signature

27.3 The _____ method returns the absolute value of a number.

   a) abs   b) absolute

   c) positive   d) positiveValue

27.4 If MyTruck extends MyCar, _____.

a) an object of MyTruck can be assigned to a variable of type MyCar

b) an object of MyCar can be assigned to a variable of type MyTruck

c) objects of either class cannot be assigned to the opposite class

d) both a and b.

27.5 Polymorphism allows you to program _____ .

a) "in the abstract"   b) "in the general"

c) "in the specific"   d) Both a and b.

27.6 The first and third arguments taken by the drawLine method specify the line's _____ coordinates.

a) upper-left   b) x-

c) y-   d) none of the above

27.7 Methods such as drawOval and drawRect are declared in the _____ class.

a) Drawing   b) Paint

c) Graphics   d) Images

27.8 In applications that use polymorphism, the exact type of an object _____.

a) is known only during execution

b) is decided when the application is compiled

c) is known while you are coding

d) is never known

27.9 The code _____ will draw a straight, vertical line.

a) drawLine(50, 50, 25, 25);   b) drawLine(25, 25, 50, 25);

c) drawLine(50, 25, 50, 25);   d) drawLine(50, 25, 50, 50);

27.10 Polymorphism involves using a variable of a _____ type to invoke methods on superclass and subclass objects.

a) primitive   b) superclass

c) subclass   d) none of the above

EXERCISES

27.11 (*Advanced Screen Saver Application*) Write an application that mimics the behavior of a screen saver. It should draw random shapes onto a black background and the shapes should build up on top of each other until the screen saver resets (every 30 seconds). You have been provided with a **Screen Saver** application that does not yet display outlined shapes. It uses the MyRectangle and MyOval classes that you created in this tutorial. Add the code that will display random outlined shapes in your output. Your output should look like Fig. 27.35.

a) *Copying the template to your working directory.* Copy the directory C:\Examples\Tutorial27\Exercises\AdvancedScreenSaver to your C:\SimplyJava directory.

b) *Opening the template file.* Open the MyRectangle.java file in your text editor.

c) *Adding an instance variable to the MyRectangle class.* At line 7, add a comment indicating that the instance variable is a boolean and will indicate whether or not the rectangle is filled. At line 8, add a private instance variable named filled of type boolean.

d) *Modifying the MyRectangle constructor.* You will now modify the MyRectangle constructor so that it can accept an additional boolean argument. At line 12, add a boolean argument named fill to the end of the parameter list. At line 16, set the instance variable filled equal to the value of parameter fill and on the same line, add a comment indicating that filled will specify if the shape will be filled.

e) *Modifying the draw method.* At line 31, add comment indicating that an if statement will execute if the rectangle is filled. At line 32, add an if statement that checks if filled is true. If it is, then the application should call the fillRect method (which is on line 30 of the template).

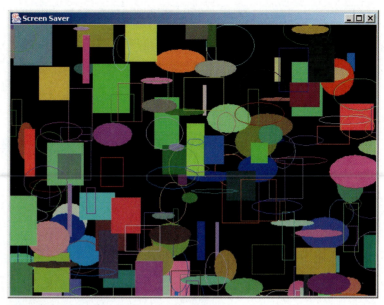

Figure 27.35 Advanced **Screen Saver** application.

f) *Finishing the draw method.* At line 37, add an `else` to the `if` statement from the previous step. If `filled` is `false`, the application should call the `drawRect` method.

g) *Saving the application.* Save your modified source code file.

h) *Opening the template file.* Open the `MyOval.java` file in your text editor.

i) *Modifying the MyOval class.* Apply *Steps c–f* to the `MyOval` class. The line numbers for `MyOval` will be the same as `MyRectangle`. Use the `fillOval` and `drawOval` methods in place of the `fillRect` and `drawRect` methods respectively.

j) *Saving the application.* Save your modified source code file.

k) *Opening the template file.* Open the `DrawJPanel.java` file in your text editor.

l) *Modifying the shape constructor calls.* You will now add a `boolean` argument to the statements that invoke the shape constructors. On line 117, add an additional argument to the end of the list of arguments. The statement being modified is creating an outlined oval, which means it should not be filled. So, the additional argument should be the keyword `false`. This will result in instance variable `filled`, of the `MyOval` class, being set to `false`. On line 123, add the additional argument, `true`, to the end of the list of arguments. Now, when this line of code is executed, a `MyOval` object with instance variable `filled` set to `true` will be created. On line 130, add the additional argument, `false`, to the end of the list of arguments. When this line of code is executed, a `MyRectangle` object with instance variable `filled` set to `false` will be created. Finally, on line 136, add the additional argument, `true`, to the end of the list of arguments. When this line of code is executed, a `MyRectangle` object with instance variable `filled` set to `true` will be created.

m) *Saving the application.* Save your modified source code file.

n) *Opening the Command Prompt window and changing directories.* Open the **Command Prompt** by selecting **Start > Programs > Accessories > Command Prompt**. Change to your working directory by typing `cd C:\SimplyJava\AdvancedScreenSaver`.

o) *Compiling the application.* Compile your application by typing the command `javac ScreenSaver.java DrawJPanel.java MyRectangle.java MyOval.java`.

p) *Running the completed application.* When your application compiles correctly, run it by typing `java ScreenSaver`. Test your application by ensuring that shapes appear and that the screen clears itself every thirty seconds.

q) *Closing the application.* Close your running application by clicking its close button.

r) *Closing the Command Prompt window.* Close the **Command Prompt** window by clicking its close button.

27.12 (*Logo Designer Application*) Write an application that allows users to design a company logo. It should be able to draw lines as well as both filled and empty rectangles and ovals with a simple coordinate input interface. Your GUI should look like Fig. 27.36.

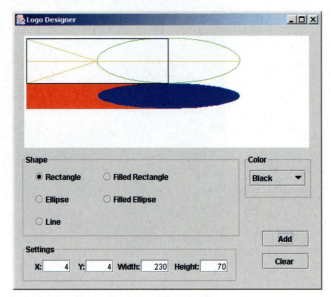

Figure 27.36 **Logo Designer** application.

a) *Copying the template to your working directory.* Copy the directory C:\Examples\Tutorial27\Exercises\LogoDesigner to your C:\SimplyJava directory.

b) *Opening the template file.* Open the MyRectangle.java and MyOval.java files in your text editor.

c) *Modifying the MyRectangle and MyOval classes.* Apply *Steps c–j* of the previous exercise (Exercise 27.11) to your MyRectangle and MyOval classes. This will add the ability to draw both filled and outlined shapes to your shape hierarchy.

d) *Opening the template file.* Open the DrawJPanel.java file in your text editor.

e) *Adding the addShape method.* At line 31, add a comment indicating that the method will add the shape to shapeArray and then repaint. On line 32, add the method header for the addShape method. This method does not return a value and takes an argument of type MyShape named shape. Add shape to shapeArrayList by calling the add method on shapeArrayList and passing it shape. Then, call the repaint method so that the newly added shape will be displayed. Be sure to end the method with a right brace on line 37.

f) *Saving the application.* Save your modified source code file.

g) *Opening the template file.* Open the LogoDesigner.java file in your text editor.

h) *Invoking method addShape to draw a line.* You will now invoke method addShape in order to display a new line on the JPanel. At lines 279–280, call method addShape on variable drawingJPanel. Pass it a new MyLine object created with the arguments x, y, width, height and drawColor.

i) *Invoking method addShape to draw an oval.* You will now invoke method addShape in order to display a new, outlined oval on the JPanel. On lines 284–285, call method addShape on variable drawingJPanel. Pass it a new MyOval object created with the arguments x, y, x + width, y + height, drawColor and false. On lines 289–290, call addShape again, but this time draw a filled oval instead of an outlined one by changing the boolean value at the end of the argument list to true.

j) *Invoking method addShape to draw a rectangle.* You will now invoke method addShape in order to display a new, outlined rectangle on the JPanel. On lines 294–295, call method addShape on variable drawingJPanel. Pass it a new MyRectangle object created with the arguments x, y, x + width, y + height, drawColor and false. On lines 299–300, call addShape again, but this time draw a filled rectangle instead of an outlined one by changing the boolean value at the end of the argument list to true.

k) *Saving the application.* Save your modified source code file.

l) *Opening the Command Prompt window and changing directories.* Open the **Command Prompt** by selecting **Start > Programs > Accessories > Command Prompt**. Change to your working directory by typing cd C:\SimplyJava\LogoDesigner.

m) *Compiling the application.* Compile your application by typing the command javac LogoDesigner.java DrawJPanel.java MyRectangle.java MyOval.java.

n) *Running the completed application.* When your application compiles correctly, run it by typing java LogoDesigner. Test your application by drawing different shapes using different *x*- and *y*- coordinates, heights and widths.

o) *Closing the application.* Close your running application by clicking its close button.

p) *Closing the Command Prompt window.* Close the **Command Prompt** window by clicking its close button.

27.13 (*Whack A Mole Application*) Create a **Whack A Mole**[1] game application that emulates its popular arcade counterpart. Allow players to start a new game by clicking a button. Then, a mole should appear randomly within a single cell of an outlined grid. Clicking on the mole before it moves will add 50 points to the score. Playing the game should result in output similar to Fig. 27.37.

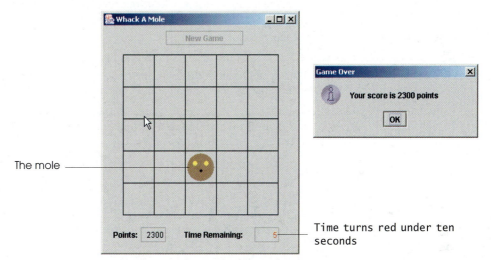

The mole

Time turns red under ten seconds

Figure 27.37   **Whack A Mole** application.

a) *Copying the template to your working directory.* Copy the C:\Examples\ Tutorial27\Exercises\WhackAMole directory to your C:\SimplyJava directory.

b) *Opening the template file.* Open the Mole.java file in your text editor.

c) *Declaring local variables in the drawMole method.* At line 23, add a comment indicating that the cell dimensions will be calculated. At line 24, declare and initialize a local variable of type int named x. Set x equal to moleColumn * 50. Next, declare and initialize another local variable of type int named y. Set y equal to moleRow * 50. Variables x and y represent the *x*- and *y*-coordinates in pixels of each cell. These variables will be used in later calculations.

d) *Drawing the mole's head in the drawMole method.* At line 27, add a comment indicating that the mole's head color will be set. Now, notice that the parameter list of the drawMole method indicates that it will be passed an instance of Graphics named g. On line 28, call the setColor method on g. Pass a new Color to method setColor. Pass the integer values, 155, 126, and 87 to the new Color constructor. Next, add a comment indicating that the mole's head will be drawn, then call the fillOval method on g. Pass the following arguments to method fillOval: x + 38, y + 72, 44 and 44.

e) *Drawing the mole's eyes in the drawMole method.* At line 33, call the setColor method on g to set the mole's eye color. Pass constant Color.YELLOW to the set-

---

1. Be careful before you download any **Whack A Mole** games from the Internet. There has been a virus-infected version that would read your hard drive while you were playing.

Color method. On line 35, add a comment indicating that the mole's eyes will be drawn, then, on line 36, call the fillOval method on g. Pass the following arguments to method fillOval: x + 47, y + 84, 8 and 8. On line 37, call the fillOval method on g. Pass the following arguments to method fillOval: x + 65, y + 84, 8 and 8.

f) *Drawing the mole's nose in the drawMole method.* At line 39, call the setColor method on g. Pass constant Color.BLACK to the setColor method. On line 40, call the fillOval method on g. Pass the following arguments to method fillOval: x + 58, y + 97, 5 and 5.

g) *Saving the application.* Save your modified source code file.

h) *Opening the Command Prompt window and changing directories.* Open the **Command Prompt** by selecting **Start > Programs > Accessories > Command Prompt**. Change to your working directory by typing cd C:\SimplyJava\WhackAMole.

i) *Compiling the application.* Compile your application by typing the command javac WhackAMole.java Mole.java.

j) *Running the completed application.* When your application compiles correctly, run it by typing java WhackAMole. Test your application by playing the game a few times. Make sure that the mole looks as shown in Fig. 27.37.

k) *Closing the application.* Close your running application by clicking its close button.

l) *Closing the Command Prompt window.* Close the **Command Prompt** window by clicking its close button.

What does this code do? ▶ **27.14** What is the result of the following code? Assume that the classes used are those from the **Drawing Shapes** application and that this method is in the PainterJPanel class.

```
1   private void drawJButtonActionPerformed( ActionEvent event )
2   {
3      MyOval oval;
4
5      for ( int i = 0; i <= 50; i += 10 )
6      {
7         oval = new MyOval( i, 20, 10, 10, Color.GREEN );
8         shapes.add( oval );
9
10     } // end for
11
12     repaint();
13
14  } // end method drawJButtonActionPerformed
```

What's wrong with this code? ▶ **27.15** Find the error(s) in the following code. This is the definition for an actionPerformed event handler for a JButton. This event handler should draw a rectangle on a JPanel. Assume that the classes used are those from the **Drawing Shapes** application.

```
1   private void drawImageJButtonActionPerformed( ActionEvent event )
2   {
3      // set shape
4      MyShape rectangle = new MyRectangle( 2, 3, 40, 30 );
5
6      // set color
7      rectangle.setColor( Color.ORANGE );
8
9      // add rectangle to shapesArrayList
10     shapesArrayList.add( rectangle );
11
12  } // end method drawImageJButtonActionPerformed
```

Programming Challenge ▶

27.16 (*Moving Shapes Application*) Enhance the **Drawing Shapes** application that you created in this tutorial. Improve the application so that once you finish drawing a shape, the shape will be given a random velocity and begin to move, bouncing off the walls of the PaintJPanel. Your output should be capable of looking look like Fig. 27.38.

Figure 27.38   **Moving Shapes** application.

a) *Copying the template to your working directory.* Copy the directory C:\Examples\ Tutorial27\Exercises\MovingShapes to your C:\SimplyJava directory.

b) *Opening the template file.* Open the MyMovingShape.java file in your text editor.

c) *Adding a method to your MyMovingShape class to change the position of the shape.* The abstract superclass for this inheritance hierarchy has been renamed MyMoving-Shape. Add a public method named moveShape to the class. It should take no arguments and have no return type. Two new instance variables, dx and dy, have been added to the MyMovingShape class for you. Variable dx holds the distance along the *x*-axis that the shape must travel in one move. Variable dy holds the distance along the *y*-axis that the shape must travel in one move. Add dx to the x1 and x2 values and add dy to the y1 and y2 values. Follow good programming practice by using the corresponding get and set methods instead of modifying the variables directly.

d) *Finishing the moveShape method.* Add two if statements to the moveShape method to reverse the direction of the shape if it has hit a wall. The first if statement should check if either *x*-coordinate (x1 or x2) is less than 0 or greater than 400. If this is true then set the value of dx equal to the negative of itself. Make sure that you use the correct get or set methods to do this. The second if statement should check if either *y*-coordinate (y1 or y2) is less than 0 or greater than 340. If this is true then set the value of dy equal to the negative of itself. Again, make sure that you use the correct get or set methods to do this.

e) *Saving the application.* Save your modified source code file.

f) *Opening the template file.* Open the PaintJPanel.java file in your text editor.

g) *Modifying the moveTimerActionPerformed method.* The moveTimerAction-Performed method will iterate through every shape in shapeArrayList to call the moveShape method of each shape. To do this, first declare a local variable of type MyMovingShape named nextShape. Declare another local variable of type Iterator named, shapesIterator and initialize it to the value returned by calling the iterator method on shapeArrayList. Then, create a while loop whose condition is the boolean returned by calling the hasNext method of shapesIterator. Within the while loop, set nextShape equal to the reference returned by the next method of shapesIterator. The next method will return the next indexed object in shapeArrayList, which may be of type MyLine, MyRectangle, or MyOval. This means that you will have to cast the returned object to a MyMovingShape object before storing it

in a variable of type MyMovingShape. Before ending the while loop, call the move-Shape method on nextShape. The while loop you have created will now iterate through every shape in shapeArrayList to call the moveShape method of each shape.

h) *Saving the application.* Save your modified source code file.

i) *Opening the Command Prompt window and changing directories.* Open the **Command Prompt** by selecting **Start > Programs > Accessories > Command Prompt**. Change to your working directory by typing cd C:\SimplyJava\MovingShapes.

j) *Compiling the application.* Compile your application by typing the command javac MovingShapes.java PaintJPanel.java MyMovingShape.java.

k) *Running the completed application.* When your application compiles correctly, run it by typing java MovingShapes. Test your application by drawing each of the three shapes and pick a different color for each of them. Make sure that the shapes move around and bounce off all of the walls.

l) *Closing the application.* Close your running application by clicking its close button.

m) *Closing the Command Prompt window.* Close the **Command Prompt** window by clicking its close button.

Objectives

In this tutorial, you will learn to:
- Download and install FreeTTS to run the Java Speech application.
- Enhance Java applications using multimedia.
- Use the Java Speech API in a Java application.

Outline

28.1 Java Speech API
28.2 Downloading and Installing FreeTTS
28.3 Test-Driving the **Phone Book** Application
28.4 Constructing the **Phone Book** Application
28.5 Wrap-Up

Phone Book Application

Introducing the Java Speech API

When computers were first introduced, they were large, expensive machines, used primarily to perform arithmetic calculations. **Multimedia** applications, which use a variety of media—including graphics, animation, video and sound—were impractical due to the high cost and slow speed of computers. However, today's affordable, ultrafast processors are making multimedia-based applications commonplace. As the market for multimedia explodes, users are purchasing computers with the faster processors, larger amounts of memory and wider communications bandwidths needed to support multimedia applications.

Users are seeing exciting new three-dimensional multimedia applications that interact with the user by means of animation, audio and video. Multimedia programming is an entertaining and innovative field, but one that presents many challenges. Java enables you to include such multimedia capabilities in your applications.

In this tutorial, you will explore the **Java Speech API**, which produces synthetic speech from text inputs. You will create a phone book application in which the user selects a name from the JComboBox and the application actually speaks the corresponding phone number.

28.1 Java Speech API

Your **Phone Book** application must meet the following requirements:

Application Requirements

A software company's customer service representatives are responsible for calling clients. The representatives need a convenient way to access their clients' phone numbers and have asked you to develop an application that stores and retrieves the names and phone numbers of their clients. The service representatives want an application that employs speech synthesis (using the Java Speech API) to allow them to retrieve the phone numbers by selecting clients' names with the mouse.

The Java Speech API is a technology used to add speech capabilities to applications or Web pages to support convenient human interaction with computers. The Java Speech API supports two core speech technologies: **speech synthesis** and **speech recognition**. Speech synthesis, also known as **text-to-speech technology**, produces synthetic speech from text. Speech recognition produces text from audio input that contains speech.

Sun provides basic information on the Java Speech API at

`java.sun.com/products/java-media/speech/`

The Java Speech API enables users to interact with applications and Web pages by speaking. When the user speaks into a microphone, the control uses a **speech-recognition engine**, an application that translates voice input from a microphone into a language that the computer understands. The Java Speech API also uses a text-to-speech engine, which allows the application to speak lines of text. A **text-to-speech engine** is an application that translates typed words into sound that users can hear through headphones or speakers connected to a computer.

Sun does not provide an implementation of the Java Speech API. Several third-party implementations are available, such as FreeTTS from the Speech Integration Group of Sun Microsystems Laboratories and Speech for Java from IBM. Speech for Java works together with the IBM's speech technology to incorporate speech synthesis and speech recognition into the user interface. In this tutorial, you will use the FreeTTS implementation, which is an **open source** speech synthesis software written entirely in Java. Open source software is freely available for download, both as completed applications for use and source code for reproduction and modification. Your computer needs to have speakers and a sound card to generate speech.

SELF-REVIEW
1. A _____ translates typed words into sound.
   a) speech-recognition engine   b) text-to-speech engine
   c) character-animation set   d) All of the above.

2. An application that translates voice input from a microphone to a language understood by the computer is called a _____.
   a) speech-recognition engine   b) text-to-speech engine
   c) character-animation set   d) All of the above.

Answers: 1) b. 2) a.

28.2 Downloading and Installing FreeTTS

FreeTTS is the Speech Integration Group of Sun Microsystems Laboratories's implementation of the Java Speech API. This tutorial demonstrates how to use FreeTTS to build the **Phone Book** application. To run this tutorial's application, you must download and install FreeTTS from the FreeTTS Web site. FreeTTS can be downloaded from

`prdownloads.sourceforge.net/freetts/freetts-1_1_2.tar.gz?`
`download`

Select the location nearest to you and click the symbol in the rightmost column to download (Fig. 28.1). Save the file `freetts-1_1_2.tar.gz` to your computer. The `freetts-1_1_2.tar.gz` file is a compressed archive that contains the files required to install FreeTTS.

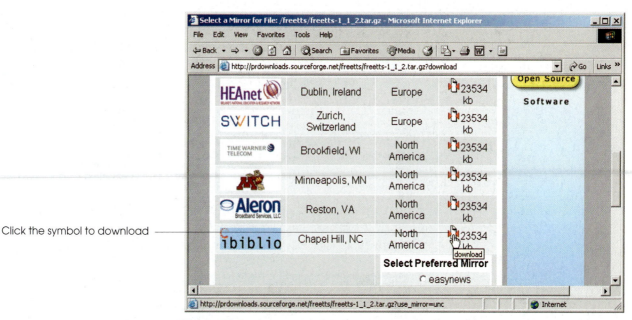

Click the symbol to download

Figure 28.1   Locations for downloading FreeTTS.

Installing FreeTTS

1. ***Unzipping the `freetts-1_1_2.tar.gz`.*** Open the `freetts-1_1_2.tar.gz` `file` with software that can extract files from an archive file, such as WinZip (`www.winzip.com`).

2. ***Decompressing `freetts-1_1_2.tar`.*** When the **WinZip** screen of Fig. 28.2 appears, click the **Yes** button to decompress the `freetts-1_1_2.tar` file to a temporary directory.

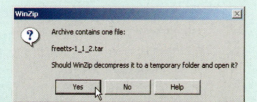

Figure 28.2   Decompressing `freetts-1_1_2.tar`.

3. ***Extracting the content in `freetts-1_1_2.tar`.*** Click the **Extract** button of Fig. 28.3 to extract the contents in `freetts-1_1_2.tar`. Choose the `C:\` directory in Fig. 28.4 as the extract destination—this will create a `FreeTTS` directory in the `C:\` directory.

4. ***Opening the Command Prompt and changing directories.*** Open the **Command Prompt** window by selecting **Start > Programs > Accessories > Command Prompt**. Change to the `FreeTTS\lib` directory by typing `cd C:\FreeTTS\lib`.

5. ***Installing the Java Speech API implementation.*** Type `jsapi.exe` to install the Java Speech API implementation. You must accept the license agreement first (Fig. 28.5). Figure 28.6 appears when the installation completes. Click the **Close** button to dismiss the installation window.

(cont.)

Click the **Extract** button
to extract the content in —
`freetts-1_1_2.tar`

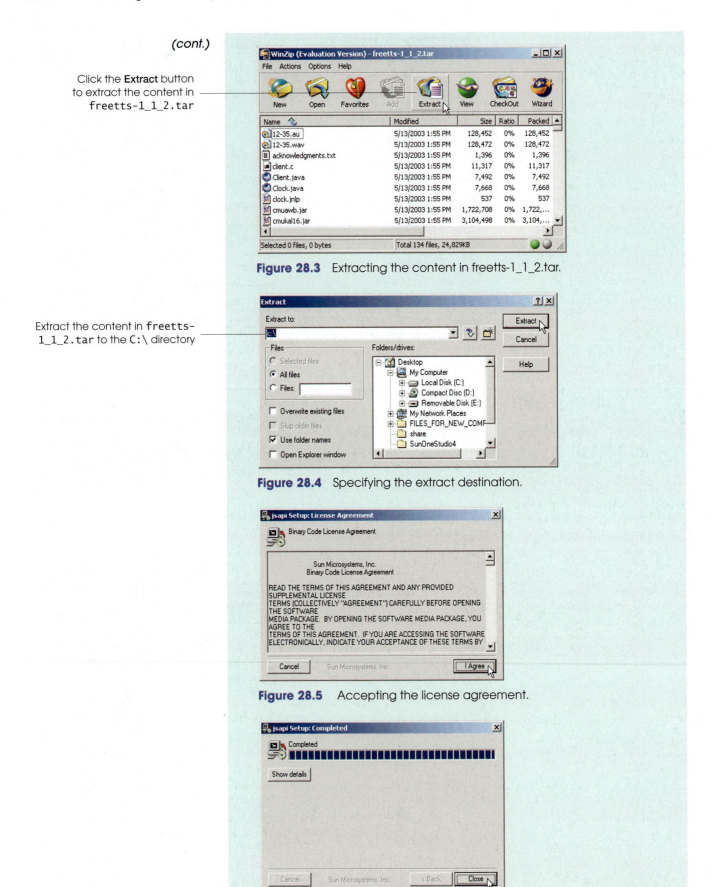

Figure 28.3   Extracting the content in freetts-1_1_2.tar.

Extract the content in `freetts-`
`1_1_2.tar` to the `C:\` directory

Figure 28.4   Specifying the extract destination.

Figure 28.5   Accepting the license agreement.

Figure 28.6   Completing the Java Speech API implementation installation.

(cont.)

6. *Installing the speech.properties file.* Copy the C:\FreeTTS\ speech.properties file to the C:\j2sdk1.4.1_02\jre\lib directory. If you installed J2SE 1.4 (in the *Before You Begin* section at the beginning of this book) in a directory other than C:\j2sdk1.4.1_02, then copy the speech.properties file to the subdirectories jre\lib of your J2SE installation.

28.3 Test-Driving the Phone Book Application

Recall that you will be creating the **Phone Book** application to allow users to search for a phone number using speech synthesis using the Java Speech API. You begin by test-driving the application. Then, you will learn the additional Java technologies you will need to create your own version of this application.

Test-Driving the Phone Book Application

1. *Locating the completed application.* Open the **Command Prompt** window by selecting **Start > Programs > Accessories > Command Prompt**. Change to your completed **Phone Book** application directory by typing cd C:\Examples\Tutorial28\CompletedApplication\PhoneBook.

2. *Setting the CLASSPATH environment variable.* Recall that the CLASSPATH environment variable specifies the location of the class libraries that are required to run an application. Type SetClasspath.bat in the **Command Prompt** window to set the CLASSPATH environment variable. [*Note:* If your FreeTTS is installed in a directory other than C:\FreeTTS, then replace C:\FreeTTS with your FreeTTS installation directory in the SetClasspath.bat file.] The provided SetClasspath.bat file is a batch file that contains the command to set the CLASSPATH environment. You can simply enter the name of the batch file instead of entering the command.

3. *Running the application.* Type java PhoneBook in the **Command Prompt** window to run the application (Fig. 28.7). Select a name from the JComboBox, then click the **Get Phone Number** JButton to listen to the phone number.

When the **Get Phone Number** JButton is clicked, the computer speaks the name John and John's phone number.

Figure 28.7   **Phone Book** application.

4. *Closing the running application.* Close the running application by clicking its close button.

5. *Closing the Command Prompt window.* Close the **Command Prompt** window by clicking its close button.

28.4 Constructing the Phone Book Application

Now you will build the **Phone Book** application using speech synthesis using the Java Speech API. The user can click the JComboBox to select a name and listen for the specified telephone number. The following pseudocode describes the basic operation of the **Phone Book** application that occurs when the user clicks the **Get Phone Number** JButton.

> When the Get Phone Number JButton is clicked:
>   Get the selected name
>   Speak the phone number of the selected person

Now that you have test-driven the **Phone Book** application and studied its pseudocode representation, you will use an ACE table to help you convert the pseudocode to Java. Figure 28.8 lists the actions, components and events that will help you to complete your own version of this application.

Action/Component/ Event (ACE) Table for the Phone Book Application

Action	Component/Object	Event
Display instructions to the user	`instruction1JLabel` `instruction2JLabel`	Application is run
	`getPhoneNumberJButton`	User clicks **Get Phone Number** `JButton`
Get the selected name	`nameJComboBox`	
Speak the phone number	`Synthesizer`	

Figure 28.8 ACE table for the **Phone Book** application.

Now that you understand the purpose of the **Phone Book** application, you will begin to create it. You begin by adding a synthesizer to the application.

Adding the Speech Synthesizer to the Application

1. *Copying the template to your working directory.* Copy the `C:\Examples\ Tutorial28\TemplateApplication\PhoneBook` directory to your `C:\SimplyJava` directory.

2. *Opening the template application.* Open the template file `PhoneBook.java` in your text editor.

3. *Importing Java Speech API packages.* Add lines 7–8 of Fig. 28.9 to your code to import the Java Speech API packages **javax.speech** and **javax.speech.synthesis**. The classes and interfaces in the `javax.speech` package support audio connectivity. The classes and interfaces in the `javax.speech.synthesis` package support speech synthesis. Importing these packages will allow you to perform speech synthesis and omit typing `javax.speech` and `javax.speech.synthesis` when referring to the classes in these packages.

Importing the Java Speech API packages

```
   Source Editor [PhoneBook *]                              _ □ ×
    5  import java.util.*;
    6  import javax.swing.*;
    7  import javax.speech.*;
    8  import javax.speech.synthesis.*;
    9
   10  public class PhoneBook extends JFrame
```

Figure 28.9 Importing the Java Speech API packages.

4. *Declaring an instance variable for the speech synthesizer.* Add lines 22–23 of Fig. 28.10 to your code to declare instance variable `speechSynthesizer`, which will be used to speak phone numbers. You will learn more about the `Synthesizer` object in more detail later in this tutorial.

(cont.)

Declaring an instance variable for the speech synthesizer

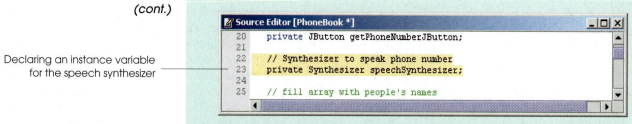

```
20      private JButton getPhoneNumberJButton;
21
22      // Synthesizer to speak phone number
23      private Synthesizer speechSynthesizer;
24
25      // fill array with people's names
```

Figure 28.10 Declaring an instance variable for the speech synthesizer.

5. ***Initializing the speech synthesizer.*** Add lines 35–51 of Fig. 28.11 to your code to initialize the speech synthesizer. Lines 39–41 create a **SynthesizerModeDesc** object, which is a descriptor that specifies the properties of the speech synthesizer, such as the name of the speech engine, the mode of operation of the speech engine, the language supported by the speech engine, the running state of the speech engine and the voice of the speech engine.

Create SynthesizerModeDesc for FreeTTS synthesizer

Create a Synthesizer object

```
33      public PhoneBook()
34      {
35          // initialize Synthesizer
36          try
37          {
38              // create SynthesizerModeDesc for FreeTTS synthesizer.
39              SynthesizerModeDesc descriptor = new SynthesizerModeDesc(
40                  "Unlimited domain FreeTTS Speech Synthesizer " +
41                  "from Sun Labs", null, Locale.US, Boolean.FALSE, null );
42
43              // create a Synthesizer
44              speechSynthesizer = Central.createSynthesizer( descriptor );
45
46          } // end try
47
48          catch ( Exception myException )
49          {
50              myException.printStackTrace();
51          }
52
53          createUserInterface(); // set up GUI
```

Figure 28.11 Initializing the speech synthesizer.

The SynthesizerModeDesc constructor (lines 39–41) takes five arguments, each representing a basic property of the speech engine. The first argument (a String) specifies the name of the text-to-speech engine. You use the text-to-speech engine that comes with the FreeTTS installation, which has the name "Unlimited domain FreeTTS Speech Synthesizer from Sun Labs". The second argument (a String) identifies the mode of operation of the speech engine—setting the second argument to null means that there is no specific requirement for the operation mode of the speech engine. The third argument (a Locale) specifies the language supported by the speech engine. A **Locale** object represents a specific region of the world. The constant **Locale.US** represents a Locale object for the United States, therefore the language associated with this Locale object is English. The fourth argument (a Boolean) indicates whether a speech engine is already running. You pass the constant **Boolean.FALSE** to indicate not to select the engine that is already running. The fifth argument (an array of **Voice** objects, which allows you to specify the output voice of a speech synthesizer) specifies the voice of the speech engine. Setting the fifth argument to null means that there is no specific requirement for the voice of the speech engine.

(cont.)

Line 44 creates the speech synthesizer by invoking the **createSynthesizer** method of the **Central** object. The createSynthesizer method of Central takes a SynthesizerModeDesc (the descriptor) and returns a **Synthesizer** object that matches the properties specified by the descriptor. A Synthesizer object provides speech synthesis capabilities, such as speaking text. The Central class provides access to all speech input and output capabilities, such as the speech synthesis. The Central class is also capable of locating the speech engines, selecting a matching engine based on the set of properties defined by the descriptor and creating speech recognizers and speech synthesizers. The createSynthesizer method of Central throws exceptions if the Central object cannot create the engine or the synthesizer properties specified by SynthesizerModeDesc are unknown. Lines 48–50 use the Exception object to catch all the exceptions that may be thrown by the createSynthesizer method.

6. ***Preparing the Synthesizer object to speak.*** Add lines 46–59 of Fig. 28.12 to the try block (lines 36–61). If the Central object creates the speech synthesizer successfully, lines 47–53 invoke the **allocate** method and the **resume** method of the Synthesizer object to allocate the resources required by the speech engine and get the speech synthesizer ready to speak. If the Central object failed to create the speech synthesizer, lines 55–59 display the error message and terminate the application by calling the exit method of System.

```
Source Editor [PhoneBook *]
44        speechSynthesizer = Central.createSynthesizer( descriptor );
45
46           // Synthesizer created successfully
47           if ( speechSynthesizer != null )
48           {
49              // prepare synthesizer to speak
50              speechSynthesizer.allocate();
51              speechSynthesizer.resume();
52
53           } // end if
54
55           else
56           {
57              System.err.println( "Synthesizer creation failed." );
58              System.exit( 1 );
59           }
60
61        } // end try
```

Get speech synthesizer
ready to speak

Figure 28.12 Getting the Synthesizer object ready to speak.

7. ***Setting the properties of the Synthesizer object.*** Add lines 53–58 of Fig. 28.13 to the if statement from the previous step (lines 47–53). Lines 54–55 invoke the **getSynthesizerProperties** method of the Synthesizer object to obtain the **SynthesizerProperties** object associated with the speech synthesizer. A SynthesizerProperties object contains various properties of a speech synthesizer. Each property can be changed by calling the setProperty method. For example, you can call the **setSpeakingRate** method of SynthesizerProperties to set the *speakingRate* property of the speech synthesizer. The *speakingRate* property specifies the speaking rate in words per minute.

Line 58 invokes the setSpeakingRate method of SynthesizerProperties to set the *speakingRate* property of the speech synthesizer. The setSpeakingRate method takes one argument—a float that specifies the speaking rate of the speech synthesizer. Line 58 passes the float number 100.0f to the setSpeakingRate method.

(cont.)

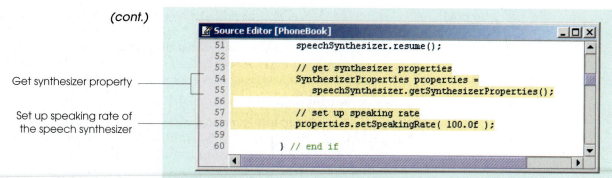

Get synthesizer property

Set up speaking rate of the speech synthesizer

```
51              speechSynthesizer.resume();
52
53              // get synthesizer properties
54              SynthesizerProperties properties =
55                  speechSynthesizer.getSynthesizerProperties();
56
57              // set up speaking rate
58              properties.setSpeakingRate( 100.0f );
59
60          } // end if
```

Figure 28.13   Setting the properties of the `Synthesizer` object.

8. ***Saving the application.*** Save your modified source code file.

9. ***Opening the Command Prompt window and changing directories.*** Open the **Command Prompt** window by selecting **Start > Programs > Accessories > Command Prompt**. Change to your working directory by typing cd C:\SimplyJava\PhoneBook.

10. ***Setting the CLASSPATH.*** Type `SetClasspath.bat` in the **Command Prompt** window to set the CLASSPATH environment variable.

11. ***Compiling the application.*** Compile your application by typing javac PhoneBook.java.

12. ***Closing the Command Prompt window.*** Close the **Command Prompt** window by clicking its close button.

Now that you have added a speech synthesizer to the **Phone Book** application, you will add code to execute when the user clicks the **Get Phone Number** JButton.

Coding the Event Handler for the Get Phone Number *JButton*

1. ***Coding the event handler for getPhoneNumberJButton.*** Add lines 158–166 of Fig. 28.14 to the `getPhoneNumberJButtonActionPerformed` method. Line 159 invokes the `getSelectedIndex` method of the `JComboBox` to get the index of the user-selected person's name. This index corresponds to the index of the person's name in the `namesArray` and the index of the person's phone number in the `numbersArray`. Both `namesArray` and `numbersArray` are instance variables initialized in the template. Lines 162–163 obtain the selected person's name from `namesArray` and the selected person's phone number from `numbersArray`.

Get index of the selected person

Declare the text to speak

Speak the person's name and phone number

```
154     // speak a person's phone number
155     private void getPhoneNumberJButtonActionPerformed(
156        ActionEvent event )
157     {
158        // get index of the selected person
159        int selectedName = nameJComboBox.getSelectedIndex();
160
161        // declare text to speak
162        String textToSpeak = namesArray[ selectedName ] +
163           "'s phone number is " + numbersArray[ selectedName ];
164
165        // speak the person's name and phone number
166        speechSynthesizer.speakPlainText( textToSpeak, null );
167
168     } // end method getPhoneNumberJButtonActionPerformed
```

Figure 28.14   Coding the event handler for getPhoneNumberJButton.

(cont.)

Line 166 invokes the **speakPlainText** method of Synthesizer to speak the text constructed at lines 162–163. The speakPlainText method takes two arguments—a String that specifies the text to speak and a null indicating that no notification of speech events (such as reaching the end of the text to speak) is received as the synthesizer speaks.

2. *Saving the application.* Save your modified source code file.

3. *Opening the Command Prompt window and changing directories.* Open the **Command Prompt** window by selecting **Start > Programs > Accessories > Command Prompt**. Change to your working directory by typing cd C:\SimplyJava\PhoneBook.

4. *Setting the CLASSPATH.* Type SetClasspath.bat in the **Command Prompt** window to set the CLASSPATH environment variable.

5. *Compiling the application.* Compile your application by typing javac PhoneBook.java.

6. *Closing the Command Prompt window.* Close the **Command Prompt** window by clicking its close button.

Now that you have added the event handler to the **Get Phone Number** JButton, you will add code to clean up the speech synthesizer when the user clicks the application's close button.

Cleaning up the Synthesizer object

1. *Cleaning up the Synthesizer object.* Add lines 168–180 of Fig. 28.15 to the frameWindowClosing method. Line 171 invokes the **deallocate** method of Synthesizer to free the resources (such as the speech synthesizer) that are allocated (using the allocate method call) to the speech engine. Line 175 uses the Exception object to catch any exceptions thrown by the deallocate method. Line 179 invokes the exit method of System to terminate the application.

Deallocate the speech synthesizer →

```
 Source Editor [PhoneBook]
165     // clean up synthesizer
166     private void frameWindowClosing( WindowEvent event )
167     {
168         // deallocate synthesizer
169         try
170         {
171             speechSynthesizer.deallocate();
172         }
173         catch ( Exception myException )
174         {
175             myException.printStackTrace();
176         }
177         finally
178         {
179             System.exit( 0 );
180         }
181
182     } // end method frameWindowClosing
```

Figure 28.15 Cleaning up the synthesizer.

2. *Saving the application.* Save your modified source code file.

3. *Opening the Command Prompt window and changing directories.* Open the **Command Prompt** window by selecting **Start > Programs > Accessories > Command Prompt**. Change to your working directory by typing cd C:\SimplyJava\PhoneBook.

(cont.)

4. **Setting the CLASSPATH environment variable.** Type `SetClasspath.bat` in the **Command Prompt** window to set the CLASSPATH environment variable. [*Note*: If your FreeTTS is installed in a directory other than `C:\FreeTTS`, then replace `C:\FreeTTS` with your FreeTTS installation directory in the `SetClasspath.bat` file.]

5. **Compiling the application.** Compile your application by typing `javac PhoneBook.java`.

6. **Running the application.** When your application compiles correctly, run it by typing `java PhoneBook`. Figure 28.16 shows the completed application running.

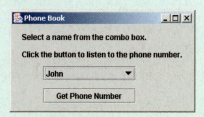

Figure 28.16 Running the completed application.

7. **Closing the application.** Close your running application by clicking its close button.

8. **Closing the Command Prompt window.** Close the **Command Prompt** window by clicking its close button.

Figure 28.17 presents the source code for the **Phone Book** application. The lines of code you added, viewed or modified in this tutorial are highlighted.

```
1   // Tutorial 28: PhoneBook.java
2   // An application announces phone number with FreeTTS.
3   import java.awt.*;
4   import java.awt.event.*;
5   import java.util.*;
6   import javax.swing.*;
7   import javax.speech.*;
8   import javax.speech.synthesis.*;
9
10  public class PhoneBook extends JFrame
11  {
12     // JLabels to display instructions
13     private JLabel instruction1JLabel;
14     private JLabel instruction2JLabel;
15
16     // JComboBox for names
17     private JComboBox nameJComboBox;
18
19     // JButton to get phone number
20     private JButton getPhoneNumberJButton;
21
22     // Synthesizer to speak phone number
23     private Synthesizer speechSynthesizer;
24
25     // fill array with people's names
26     private String[] namesArray = { "John", "Jennifer", "Howard" };
27
```

Import the Java Speech API packages — lines 7–8

Declare the instance variable speechSynthesizer — line 23

Figure 28.17 **Phone Book** application. (Part 1 of 4.)

```
28        // fill array with people's phone numbers
29        private String[] numbersArray =
30           { "(555) 555-9876", "(555) 555-1234", "(555) 555-4567" };
31
32        // no-argument constructor
33        public PhoneBook()
34        {
35           // initialize Synthesizer
36           try
37           {
38              // create SynthesizerModeDesc for FreeTTS synthesizer
39              SynthesizerModeDesc descriptor = new SynthesizerModeDesc(
40                 "Unlimited domain FreeTTS Speech Synthesizer " +
41                 "from Sun Labs", null, Locale.US, Boolean.FALSE, null );
42
43              // create a Synthesizer
44              speechSynthesizer = Central.createSynthesizer( descriptor );
45
46              // Synthesizer created successfully
47              if ( speechSynthesizer != null )
48              {
49                 // prepare synthesizer to speak
50                 speechSynthesizer.allocate();
51                 speechSynthesizer.resume();
52
53                 // get synthesizer properties
54                 SynthesizerProperties properties =
55                    speechSynthesizer.getSynthesizerProperties();
56
57                 // set up speaking rate
58                 properties.setSpeakingRate( 100.0f );
59
60              } // end if
61
62              else
63              {
64                 System.err.println( "Synthesizer creation failed." );
65                 System.exit( 1 );
66              }
67
68           } // end try
69
70           catch ( Exception myException )
71           {
72              myException.printStackTrace();
73           }
74
75           createUserInterface(); // set up GUI
76
77        } // end constructor
78
79        // create and position GUI components; register event handler
80        private void createUserInterface()
81        {
82           // get content pane for attaching GUI components
83           Container contentPane = getContentPane();
84
```

Labels (left margin):
- Create a SynthesizerModeDesc for FreeTTS synthesizer
- Create a Synthesizer object
- Prepare the synthesizer to speak
- Get synthesizer properties
- Set up speaking rate of speech synthesizer
- If synthesizer is not created successfully, print error message and terminate the application
- Catch exceptions

Figure 28.17 **Phone Book** application. (Part 2 of 4.)

```
 85        // enable explicit positioning of GUI components
 86        contentPane.setLayout( null );
 87
 88        // set up instruction1JLabel
 89        instruction1JLabel = new JLabel();
 90        instruction1JLabel.setBounds( 16, 8, 264, 23 );
 91        instruction1JLabel.setText(
 92           "Select a name from the combo box." );
 93        contentPane.add( instruction1JLabel );
 94
 95        // set up instruction2JLabel
 96        instruction2JLabel = new JLabel();
 97        instruction2JLabel.setBounds( 16, 35, 264, 23 );
 98        instruction2JLabel.setText(
 99           "Click the button to listen to the phone number." );
100        contentPane.add( instruction2JLabel );
101
102        // set up nameJComboBox
103        nameJComboBox = new JComboBox( namesArray );
104        nameJComboBox.setBounds( 50, 65, 150, 23 );
105        contentPane.add( nameJComboBox );
106
107        // set up getPhoneNumberJButton
108        getPhoneNumberJButton = new JButton();
109        getPhoneNumberJButton.setBounds( 50, 100, 150, 23 );
110        getPhoneNumberJButton.setText( "Get Phone Number" );
111        contentPane.add( getPhoneNumberJButton );
112        getPhoneNumberJButton.addActionListener(
113
114           new ActionListener()  // anonymous inner class
115           {
116              // event handler called when getPhoneNumberJButton
117              // is clicked
118              public void actionPerformed( ActionEvent event )
119              {
120                 getPhoneNumberJButtonActionPerformed( event );
121              }
122
123           } // end anonymous inner class
124
125        ); // end call to addActionListener
126
127        // set properties of application's window
128        setTitle( "Phone Book" );  // set title bar string
129        setSize( 300, 160 );       // set window size
130        setVisible( true );        // display window
131
132        // ensure synthesizer is cleaned up
133        // when user closes application
134        addWindowListener(
135
136           new WindowAdapter()  // anonymous inner class
137           {
138              public void windowClosing( WindowEvent event )
139              {
140                 frameWindowClosing( event );
141              }
142
```

Figure 28.17   **Phone Book** application. (Part 3 of 4.)

```
143               } // end anonymous inner class
144
145         ); // end addWindowListener
146
147      } // end method createUserInterface
148
149      // speak a person's phone number
150      private void getPhoneNumberJButtonActionPerformed(
151         ActionEvent event )
152      {
153         // get index of the selected person
154         int selectedName = nameJComboBox.getSelectedIndex();
155
156         // declare text to speak
157         String phoneNumberString = namesArray[ selectedName ] +
158            "'s phone number is " + numbersArray[ selectedName ];
159
160         // speak the person's name and phone number
161         speechSynthesizer.speakPlainText( phoneNumberString, null );
162
163      } // end method getPhoneNumberJButtonActionPerformed
164
165      // cleanup synthesizer
166      private void frameWindowClosing( WindowEvent event )
167      {
168         // deallocate synthesizer
169         try
170         {
171            speechSynthesizer.deallocate();
172         }
173         catch ( Exception myException )
174         {
175            myException.printStackTrace();
176         }
177         finally
178         {
179            System.exit( 0 );
180         }
181
182      } // end method frameWindowClosing
183
184      // main method
185      public static void main( String[] args )
186      {
187         PhoneBook application = new PhoneBook();
188
189      } // end method main
190
191 } // end class PhoneBook
```

Labels (left margin):
- Get index of the selected person → line 154
- Declare text to speak → lines 157–158
- Speak the person's name and phone number → line 161
- Deallocate synthesizer → line 171

Figure 28.17 Phone Book application. (Part 4 of 4.)

SELF-REVIEW

1. When the speech engine speaks too fast, you can call the _____ method to ask the speech engine to speak slowly.

   a) `setSpeakingRate`   b) `changeSpeakingRate`

   c) `speakSlowly`   d) None of the above.

2. The _____ method of Synthesizer is used to speak text.
   a) `speakString`   b) `speakText`
   c) `speakPlainText`   d) None of the above.

Answers: 1) a. 2) c.

28.5 Wrap-Up

In this tutorial, you were introduced to the Java Speech API and you learned how it can be used to enhance software applications. You learned what FreeTTS is and how to install it. You then wrote code to use the Java Speech API.

Using the Java Speech API, you created an application that interacts with the user by speaking using speech synthesis. You used the `createSynthesizer` method to create a `Synthesizer` object. You also used the `setSpeakingRate` methods to change the properties of the speech synthesizer. You then used the `Synthesizer` object's `speakPlainText` method to speak phone numbers to the user.

Tutorials 29–32 present a Web-based bookstore application case study. You will learn how to build an application that can be accessed by using a Web browser. You will be introduced to the concept of a three-tier application, in which an application is divided into three major separate pieces that can reside on the same computer or can be distributed among separate computers across a network, such as the Internet.

SKILLS SUMMARY

Installing the FreeTTS

- Unzip the `freetts-1_1_2.tar.gz` file.
- Decompress the `freetts-1_1_2.tar` file.
- Extract the content of the `freetts-1_1_2.tar` file.
- Install the Java Speech API implementation.
- Install the `speech.properties` file.

Creating a Synthesizer object

- Create a `SynthesizerModeDesc` object, which is a descriptor that specifies the basic properties of the speech synthesizer.
- Invoke the `createSynthesizer` method of the `Central` object with a `SynthesizerModeDesc` object.

Preparing the Synthesizer Object to Speak

- Invoke the `allocate` method of the `Synthesizer` object.
- Invoke the `resume` method of the `Synthesizer` object.

Getting the Properties of the Synthesizer Object

- Invoke the `getSynthesizerProperties` method of the `Synthesizer` object to get the `SynthesizerProperties` object which contains various properties of a speech synthesizer.

Setting the *speakingRate* Property of the Speech Synthesizer

- Invoke the `setSpeakingRate` method of the `SynthesizerProperties` object with a `float` value that specifies the speaking rate in words per minute to set the *speakingRate* property of the speech synthesizer.

Causing the Speech Synthesizer to Speak

- Invoke the `speakPlainText` method of the `Synthesizer` object to speak the plain text.

Releasing the Resources Allocated to the Synthesizer Object

- Invoke the `deallocate` method of the `Synthesizer` object to release the resources (such as the speech synthesizer) allocated to the speech engine.

KEY TERMS

allocate method of Synthesizer—Used to allocate the resources required by the speech engine.

Boolean.FALSE—A constant in class `Boolean` that represents a false value as a `Boolean` object. Class `Boolean` also contains a TRUE constant.

Central class—Used to provide access to all speech input and output capabilities, such as speech synthesis. Also used to locate the speech engines, select a matching engine based on the set of properties defined by the descriptor and create speech recognizers and speech synthesizers.

createSynthesizer method of Central—Used to create a speech synthesizer.

deallocate method of Synthesizer—Used to free the resources (such as speech synthesizers) that are allocated to the speech engine.

getSynthesizerProperties method of Synthesizer—Used to obtain the `Synthesizer-Properties` object associated with the speech synthesizer.

javax.speech package—The classes and interfaces in the `javax.speech` package support audio connectivity.

javax.speech.synthesis package—Package of classes and interfaces that support speech synthesis.

Java Speech API—A technology used to add speech capabilities to applications or Web pages to support new means of human interaction with computers.

Java Speech technology—The use of speech synthesis to produce synthetic speech from text.

Locale object—Represents a specific region of the world.

Locale.US constant—Represents a `Locale` object for the United States.

multimedia—The use of various media, such as sound, video and animation, to create content in an application.

open source software—Software that is freely available for download, both as completed applications for use and source code for reproduction and modification.

resume method of Synthesizer—Used to get the speech synthesizer ready to speak.

setSpeakingRate method of SynthesizerProperties—Used to set the *speakingRate* property of the speech synthesizer.

***speakingRate* property of the speech synthesizer**—Specifies the speaking rate in words per minute.

speakPlainText method of Synthesizer—Used to speak text to the user.

speech recognition—A technique that produces text from audio input that contains speech.

speech-recognition engine—An application that translates vocal sound input from a microphone into a language that the computer understands.

speech synthesis—Also known as text-to-speech technology, this produces synthetic speech from text.

Synthesizer object—Provides speech synthesis capabilities, such as speaking text.

SynthesizerModeDesc object—A descriptor that specifies the basic properties of the speech synthesizer.

SynthesizerProperties object—Contains various properties of a speech synthesizer.

text-to-speech engine—An application that translates typed words into spoken sound that users hear through headphones or speakers connected to a computer.

text-to-speech technology—Produces synthetic speech from text.

Voice class—Specifies the output voice of a speech synthesizer.

JAVA LIBRARY REFERENCE

Central This class (in the `javax.speech` package) provides access to all speech input and output capabilities, such as the speech synthesizer.

■ *Methods*

    `createSynthesizer`—Creates a `Synthesizer` object, which is used to speak text to the users.

Locale   This class represents a specific region of the world.

- *Constants*

  Locale.US—Represents a Locale object for the United States.

Synthesizer   This class provides speech synthesis capabilities, such as speaking text.

- *Methods*

  allocate—Allocates the resources such as the speech synthesizer, required by the speech engine.

  deallocate—Frees the resources, such as the speech synthesizer, that are allocated to the speech engine.

  getSynthesizerProperties—Used to obtain the SynthesizerProperties object associated with the speech synthesizer.

  resume—Used to get the speech synthesizer ready to speak.

  speakPlainText—Used to speak text to the user.

SynthesizerModeDesc   This class specifies the basic properties of the speech synthesizer.

- *Constructor*

  SynthesizerModeDesc—Takes five arguments, each representing a basic property of the speech engine. The first argument (a String) specifies the name of the text-to-speech engine. The second argument (a String) identifies the mode of operation of the speech engine. The third argument (a Locale) specifies the language supported by the speech engine. The fourth argument (a Boolean) indicates whether a speech engine is already running. The fifth argument (an array of Voice objects).

  ```
  SynthesizerModeDesc descriptor = new SynthesizerModeDesc(
     "Unlimited domain FreeTTS Speech Synthesizer " +
     "from Sun Labs", null, Locale.US, Boolean.FALSE, null );
  ```

SynthesizerProperties   This class contains various properties of a speech synthesizer.

- *Properties*

  speakingRate—Specifies the speaking rate in words per minute.

- *Methods*

  setSpeakingRate—Sets the *speakingRate* property of the speech synthesizer.

Voice   This class specifies the output voice of a speech synthesizer.

MULTIPLE-CHOICE QUESTIONS

28.1 The _____ method is used to specify what the speech synthesizer will speak.

    a) speakPlainText   b) say

    c) voice   d) None of the above.

28.2 The _____ method is used to get the resources required by a speech engine.

    a) getResource   b) obtainResource

    c) allocate   d) None of the above.

28.3 Method createSynthesizer takes one argument that represents the _____.

    a) location of the speech synthesizer.   b) name of the speech synthesizer.

    c) voice of the speech synthesizer.   d) descriptor that specifies the properties of the speech synthesizer.

28.4 The _____ method of Synthesizer returns an object that presents the properties of a speech synthesizer?

    a) getSynthesizerProperty   b) getSynthesizerProperties

    c) getProperty   d) getProperties

28.5 Use the _____ method to free the resources allocated to a speech engine.

a) `deallocate`

b) `freeResource`

c) `releaseResource`

d) None of the above.

28.6 The *speakingRate* property specifies the speaking rate in _____.

a) characters per second

b) characters per minute

c) words per second

d) words per minute

28.7 The _____ object represents the properties of a speech synthesizer.

e) `SynthesizerProperties`

f) `Central`

g) `SynthesizerModeDesc`

h) None of the above.

28.8 The _____ object represents a specific region of the world..

a) `Locale.WORLD`

b) `Locale`

c) `Region`

d) None of the above.

28.9 The classes and interfaces in the _____ package support speech synthesis.

a) `javax.speech`

b) `javax.speech.synthesis`

c) `java.speech`

d) `java.speech.synthesis`

28.10 Method _____ returns the index of the user-selected item in a JComboBox.

a) `getSelectedItem`

b) `getSelected`

c) `getSelectedIndex`

d) None of the above.

EXERCISES

28.11 (*Appointment Book Application Using the Java Speech API*) Write an application that allows users to add appointments to an appointment book that uses the Java Speech API (Fig. 28.18). When the user clicks the **Add** JButton, the application adds the name, time and date of the appointment to three ArrayLists, respectively. When the user clicks the **Get Appointments** JButton, the application speaks the time and date of the appointment that the user has with the person whose name is shown in the **Appointment With:** JTextField.

Figure 28.18 Appointment Book GUI.

a) *Copying the template to your working directory.* Copy the directory C:\Examples\Tutorial28\Exercises\AppointmentBook to your C:\SimplyJava directory.

b) *Opening the template file.* Open the AppointmentBook.java file in your text editor.

c) *Importing the Java Speech API packages.* Import the javax.speech and the javax.speech.synthesis packages.

d) *Declaring instance variables.* At line 48, declare three instance variables of type ArrayList to store the date, time and person with which the user has an appointment. Declare an instance variable of type Synthesizer, which will be used to speak text.

e) *Creating a Synthesizer object.* Inside the AppointmentBook constructor, create a Synthesizer object, allocate the resource and get the synthesizer ready to speak.

f) *Adding code to the addJButtonActionPerformed method.* Find the addJButtonActionPerformed method, which immediately follows createUserInterface. Add code to the addJButtonActionPerformed method so that the information provided by the user is added to its corresponding ArrayList. The **Appointment With:** JTextField input should be added to the ArrayList containing the names of each person with whom the user has an appointment. The input for the appointment date and

time should also be added to their respective ArrayLists. Display an error message if the user leaves the **Appointment With:** or the **Appointment Time:** JTextField empty.

g) *Adding code to the getAppointmentJButtonActionPerformed method.* Find the getAppointmentJButtonActionPerformed method, which immediately follows addJButtonActionPerformed. Add code to the getAppointmentJButtonActionPerformed method so that the application should state the time and date at which the user has an appointment with the person whose name is specified in the appointmentWithJTextField. Display an error message if the user leaves the **Appointment With:** JTextField empty. If the user did not schedule any appointments, then the application should inform the user that no appointments were scheduled. [*Note:* The date stored in dateJSpinner has the same format as in "Fri Apr 04 16:22:09 EST 2003". It is difficult for the FreeTTS to speak such text, so you need to call the predefined method parseDate in the template to parse the date to a FreeTTS speakable text. For example, method parseDate converts the String "Fri Apr 04 16:22:09 EST 2003" to "Friday April 04 2003".]

h) *Releasing the resources allocated to the speech synthesizer.* Find the frameWindowClosing method, which immediately follows parseMonth. Inside the frameWindowClosing method, add code to release the resources allocated to the speech synthesizer.

i) *Saving the application.* Save your modified source code file.

j) *Opening the Command Prompt window and changing directories.* Open the **Command Prompt** by selecting **Start > Programs > Accessories > Command Prompt**. Change to your working directory by typing cd C:\SimplyJava\AppointmentBook.

k) *Setting the CLASSPATH environment variable.* Type SetClasspath.bat in the **Command Prompt** window to set the CLASSPATH environment variable. [*Note:* if your FreeTTS is installed in a directory other than C:\FreeTTS then replace C:\FreeTTS with your FreeTTS installation directory in the SetClasspath.bat file.]

l) *Compiling the application.* Compile your application by typing the command javac AppointmentBook.java.

m) *Running the completed application.* When your application compiles correctly, run it by typing java AppointmentBook. Add an appointment to the book, then use the **Get Appointment** JButton to have the application repeat the information back to you.

n) *Closing the application.* Close your running application by clicking its close button.

o) *Closing the Command Prompt window.* Close the **Command Prompt** window by clicking its close button.

28.12 *Closing the Command Prompt window.* Close the **Command Prompt** window by clicking its close button(*Craps Game Application Using the Java Speech API*) Modify the **Craps Game** application from Tutorial 15 to use the Java Speech API. The completed application is shown in Fig. 28.19.

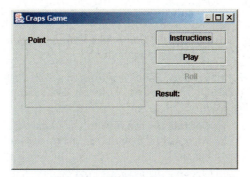

Figure 28.19　Modified **Craps Game** GUI.

a) *Copying the template to your working directory.* Copy the directory C:\Examples\Tutorial28\Exercises\CrapsGameEnhancement to your C:\SimplyJava directory.

b) *Opening the template file.* Open the CrapsGame.java file in your text editor.

c) *Importing Java Speech API packages.* Import the javax.speech and the javax.speech.synthesis packages.

d) *Declaring instance variables.* Above the CrapsGame constructor, declare an instance variable of type Synthesizer, which is used to speak text.

e) *Creating a Synthesizer object.* Inside the CrapsGame constructor, create a Synthesizer object, allocate the resource and prepare the synthesizer to speak.

f) *Adding code to the instructionsJButtonActionPerformed method.* Find the instructionsJButtonActionPerformed method, which immediately follows createUserInterface. Add code to the instructionsJButtonActionPerformed method so that the speech synthesizer speaks the instructions of the game.

g) *Adding code to the playJButtonActionPerformed method.* Find the playJButtonActionPerformed method, which immediately follows instructionsJButtonActionPerformed. Add code to the playJButtonActionPerformed method. When the user wins the game, the application should say aloud "Congratulations, you won!". If the user loses, the application should say aloud "Sorry, you lost!". If the user neither wins nor loses, the application should say aloud "Please roll again.".

h) *Adding code to the rollJButtonActionPerformed method.* Find the rollJButtonActionPerformed method, which immediately follows playJButtonActionPerformed. Add code to the rollJButtonActionPerformed method. If users "make their point," the application should say "Congratulations, you won!". If the user rolls a 7, the application should say "Sorry, you lost!". Otherwise, the application should say "Please roll again.".

i) *Releasing the resources allocated to the speech synthesizer.* Find the frameWindowClosing method, which immediately follows displayDie. Inside the frameWindowClosing method, add code to release the resources allocated to the speech synthesizer.

j) *Saving the application.* Save your modified source code file.

k) *Opening the Command Prompt window and changing directories.* Open the **Command Prompt** window by selecting **Start > Programs > Accessories > Command Prompt**. Change to your working directory by typing cd C:\SimplyJava\CrapsGameEnhancement.

l) *Setting the CLASSPATH environment variable.* Type SetClasspath.bat in the **Command Prompt** window to set the CLASSPATH environment variable. [*Note:* if your FreeTTS is installed in a directory other than C:\FreeTTS then replace C:\FreeTTS with your FreeTTS installation directory in the SetClasspath.bat file.]

m) *Compiling the application.* Compile your application by typing the command javac CrapsGame.java.

n) *Running the completed application.* When your application compiles correctly, run it by typing java CrapsGame. Click the **Play** JButton to start a game of Craps. Roll the dice a few times and check to make sure that the application is speaking the correct messages.

o) *Closing the application.* Close your running application by clicking its close button.

p) *Closing the Command Prompt window.* Close the **Command Prompt** window by clicking its close button.

28.13 (*Security Panel Application Using Java Speech API*) Modify the **Security Panel** application from Tutorial 11 to use Java Speech API. The completed application is shown in Fig. 28.20.

a) *Copying the template to your working directory.* Copy the directory C:\Examples\Tutorial28\Exercises\SecurityPanelEnhancement to your C:\SimplyJava directory.

b) *Opening the template file.* Open the SecurityPanel.java file in your text editor.

c) *Importing Java Speech API packages.* Import the javax.speech and the javax.speech.synthesis packages.

d) *Declaring instance variables.* Above the SecurityPanel constructor, Declare an instance variable of type Synthesizer, which is used to speak text.

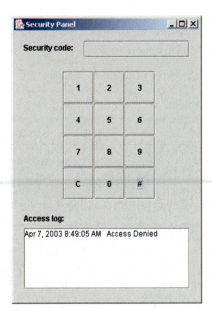

Figure 28.20 Modified **Security Panel** application.

e) *Creating a Synthesizer object*. Inside the SecurityPanel constructor, create a Synthesizer object, allocate the resource and get the synthesizer ready to speak.

f) *Adding code to the enterJButtonActionPerformed method*. Find the enterJButtonActionPerformed method, which immediately follows nineJButtonActionPerformed. Add code to the enterJButtonActionPerformed method to use the speech synthesizer. If the user enters a valid access code, the application should welcome the user and state the type of employee that the access code represents. If the access code is invalid, then the application should state that an invalid code was provided and that access is denied.

g) *Releasing the resources allocated to the speech synthesizer*. Find the frameWindowClosing method, which immediately follows enterJButtonActionPerformed. Inside the frameWindowClosing method, add code to release the resources allocated to the speech synthesizer.

h) *Saving the application*. Save your modified source code file.

i) *Opening the Command Prompt window and changing directories*. Open the **Command Prompt** window by selecting **Start > Programs > Accessories > Command Prompt**. Change to your working directory by typing cd C:\SimplyJava\SecurityPanelEnhancement.

j) *Setting the CLASSPATH environment variable*. Type SetClasspath.bat in the **Command Prompt** window to set the CLASSPATH environment variable. [*Note*: if your FreeTTS is installed in a directory other than C:\FreeTTS then replace C:\FreeTTS with your FreeTTS installation directory in the SetClasspath.bat file.]

k) *Compiling the application*. Compile your application by typing the command javac SecurityPanel.java.

l) *Running the completed application*. When your application compiles correctly, run it by typing java SecurityPanel. Enter a correct access code, then click the # JButton to verify that the application speaks the correct message. Try entering an incorrect access code. You should hear the application speak an error message notifying you that you did not enter a correct code.

m) *Closing the application*. Close your running application by clicking its close button.

n) *Closing the Command Prompt window*. Close the **Command Prompt** window by clicking its close button.

What does this code do? ▶   **28.14** After the user clicks the **Speak** JButton, what does the following method do? The speechSynthesizer variable references a Synthesizer object, which is declared as an instance variable.

```
1   private void speakJButtonActionPerformed( ActionEvent event )
2   {
3      speechSynthesizer.allocate();
4      speechSynthesizer.resume();
5
6   } // end method speakJButtonActionPerformed
```

What's wrong with this code? ▶

28.15 Find the error(s) in the following code. The method should have a Synthesizer object say, "Hello, here are the instructions to run the application." This should happen when the user clicks the **Instructions** JButton. The speechSynthesizer variable references a Synthesizer object, which is declared as an instance variable.

```
1   private void instructionsJButtonActionPerformed( ActionEvent event )
2   {
3      speechSynthesizer.setSpeakingRate( 100.0f );
4      speechSynthesizer.speakPlainText(
5         "Hello, here are the instructions to run the application" );
6
7   } // end method instructionsJButtonActionPerformed
```

Programming Challenge ▶

28.16 (*Car Payment Application Using Java Speech API*) Enhance the **Car Payment Calculator** application from Tutorial 8 to use the Java Speech API (Fig. 28.21). When the user clicks the **Instructions** JButton, the application should explain the purpose of the application. After the user enters information into each field of the **Car Payment Calculator** and clicks the **Calculate** JButton, the application should speak the calculated payment amounts and the period (number of months) over which they were calculated.

Figure 28.21 Enhanced **Car Payment** application.

a) *Copying the template to your working directory*. Copy the directory C:\Examples\Tutorial28\Exercises\CarPaymentCalculatorEnhancement to your C:\SimplyJava directory.

b) *Opening the template file*. Open the CarPayment.java file in your text editor.

c) *Importing Java Speech API packages*. Import the javax.speech and the javax.speech.synthesis packages.

d) *Declaring instance variables*. At line 34, declare an instance variable of type Synthesizer, which is used to speak text.

e) *Creating a Synthesizer object*. Inside the CarPayment constructor, create a Synthesizer object, allocate the resource and get the synthesizer ready to speak.

f) *Adding code to the instructionsJButtonActionPerformed method*. Find the instructionsJButtonActionPerformed method, which immediately follows createUserInterface. Add code to the instructionsJButtonActionPerformed

29.1 Multi-Tier Architecture

Web applications are **multi-tier applications**, sometimes refer
cations. Multi-tier applications divide their functionality acro
is, logical groupings of functionality). The tiers of an applicat
the same computer or on separate computers distributed ac
commonly, the Internet. In this case study, you will implement
computer. Figure 29.1 illustrates the basic structure of a mul
explanation of each tier follows the figure.

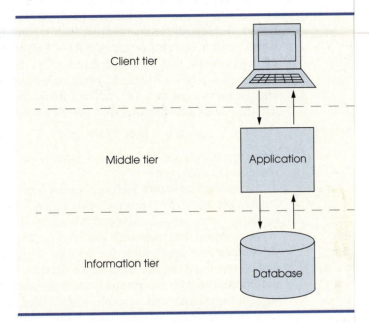

Figure 29.1 Three-tier application model.

The **information tier** (also called the **data tier** or the **bott**
data for the application. For example, the information tier fc
application is implemented as a database that contains produ
book titles, author names, publication dates, edition numbers
descriptions and prices.

The **middle tier** controls the interactions between appli
Web browsers) and application data in the information tier.
application, the middle-tier code determines which book wa
and retrieves the information for that book from the databas
determines the format in which the selected book's data will
middle tier represents the functionality of the Web applicat
the **business logic tier**.

The **client tier**, or **top tier**, is the application's user interfa
Web browser. The user will interact directly with your applica
tier (browser) by entering text, selecting from lists, click
browser reports the user's actions and data entered to the r
cesses the information. The middle tier can also make reques
from, the information tier. The client Web browser then d
data retrieved by the middle tier from the information tier.

SELF-REVIEW   1. The information tier is also called the _____ tier in a typica

a) top   b) middle

c) bottom   d) client

---

method to use the speech synthesizer. Have the synthesizer tell the user to enter the
price of a car, the down payment and the annual interest rate of the loan, then
describe the output of the application so that the user understands what the program
will do.

g) *Modifying the `calculateJButtonActionPerformed` method.* Find the `calculate-
JButtonActionPerformed` method, which immediately follows `instructionsJBut-
tonActionPerformed`. Add code to the `calculateJButtonActionPerformed`
method to declare a `String` named `textToSpeak` that will be used to display the output. Set the `String` to `"You Will Have to Pay:"`, which will be the first line in the
ouput. Add the code that will append the payment values for the loan onto
`textToSpeak`. Finally, have the application speak the result text to the user.

h) *Releasing the resources allocated to the speech synthesizer.* Find the `frameWindow-
Closing` method, which immediately follows `calculateMonthlyPayment`. Inside the
`frameWindowClosing` method, add code to release the resources allocated to the
speech synthesizer.

i) *Saving the application.* Save your modified source code file.

j) *Opening the Command Prompt window and changing directories.* Open the **Command Prompt** window by selecting **Start > Programs > Accessories > Command
Prompt**. Change to your working directory by typing `cd C:\SimplyJava\CarPay-
mentCalculatorEnhancement`.

k) *Setting the CLASSPATH environment variable.* Type `SetClasspath.bat` in the **Command Prompt** window to set the CLASSPATH environment variable. [*Note*: if your
FreeTTS is installed in a directory other than `C:\FreeTTS` then replace `C:\FreeTTS`
with your FreeTTS installation directory in the `SetClasspath.bat` file.]

l) *Compiling the application.* Compile your application by typing the command `javac
CarPayment.java`.

m) *Running the completed application.* When your application compiles correctly, run it
by typing `java CarPayment`.

n) *Closing the application.* Close your running application by clicking its close button.

o) *Closing the Command Prompt window.* Close the **Command Prompt** window by
clicking its close button.

Objectives

In this tutorial, you will learn to:
- Use the Apache Tomcat Web server to serve Web content to Web browser clients.
- Request documents from a Web server.
- Execute a Web application that uses Java Server Pages technology.

Outline

29.1 Multi-Tier Architecture
29.2 Web Servers
29.3 Apache Tomcat Web Server
29.4 Test-Driving the **Bookstore** Web Application
29.5 Wrap-Up

Bookstore W Applicatio

Introducing Web Applicati Apache Tomcat Web

I n previous tutorials, you used Java to develop de application contained a GUI with which the user int Java to create **Web applications**. These applications, applications, can use **JavaServer Pages (JSP)** technolog data that can be viewed in a Web browser, such as Microsoft) or Netscape (from Netscape Communica Web content includes **HTML (HyperText Markup L** images. JSP uses Java and HTML to develop dynamic W guage that is understood by virtually all Web browsers documents with GUI elements, text and images. With Web pages that can access other online documents usin can design forms (containing components similar to and **JButton**) to obtain user input. You will learn the your **Bookstore** Web application in Tutorial 30.

In Tutorial 29, you will learn the multi-tier architec Web applications. You will learn about Web servers an cat Web server, which you will need to run your **Books** will learn important Web development concepts in the Web application. This application consists of two Web plays a list of books. After selecting a book, the user c the browser to a second Web page. Information about retrieved from a database and displayed on the second tains a link that, when clicked, directs the Web brow page, allowing the user to select a different book. Be application, you will learn fundamental Web develo required to understand the **Bookstore** Web applicatio drive. In Tutorial 30–Tutorial 32, you will analyze the ps for the **Bookstore** Web application and you will imp Java using the most advanced techniques you have lea

---

2. In a typical three-tier application, the role of the middle tier is to _____.
   a) control the interaction between the client and information tiers
   b) control the interaction between the client and the user interface
   c) display the application's user interface
   d) provide a database for the application

Answers: 1) c. 2) a.

29.2 Web Servers

A **Web server** is specialized software that responds to client (Web browser) requests by providing requested resources (such as HTML documents and access to databases). To request documents from Web servers, users must know the addresses at which those documents reside. A **URL** (**Uniform Resource Locator**) can be thought of as an address that is used to direct a Web browser to a resource on the Web. A URL contains the protocol of the resource (such as http), the machine name or IP address for the resource (we will discuss machine names and IP addresses shortly) and the name (including the path) of the resource. For example, in the URL

```
http://www.deitel.com/index.html
```

the protocol is http, the machine name is www.deitel.com and the name of the resource is index.html.

Once the **Bookstore** Web application is properly set up, users can run it by typing its URL into a Web browser. This action is translated into a request to the Web server (such as Apache Tomcat) where the **Bookstore** Web application resides. When the user interacts with the Web browser to request information from the **Bookstore** Web application, the Web server retrieves information from the information tier (contains the Cloudscape database) and sends Web content created by the **Bookstore** Web application back to the client Web browser, which displays that content for the user. For example, when a user sends a request to view all the book titles by selecting a title and clicking the button, the Web content created by the **Bookstore** Web application will include a list of book titles and a button. When a user sends a request for viewing book information for a specific book, the Web content created by the **Bookstore** Web application will include information (such as author, price, ISBN number, edition number, copyright year and description) about the book the user selected. You will install the Apache Tomcat Web server and the **Bookstore** Web application in the next section.

To understand how a Web browser is able to locate documents on a Web server, it is helpful for you to know the following terms:

1. Host: A **host** is a computer that stores and maintains resources, such as Web pages, databases and multimedia files. In the case of the **Bookstore** Web application, the host is your computer, because all the application-related resources, including JSPs and databases, are stored in your computer.

2. Domain: A **domain** represents a group of hosts on the Internet. Each domain has a **domain name**, also known as a **Web address**, which uniquely identifies the location of a business or organization on the Internet.

3. Fully qualified domain name: A **fully qualified domain name** (**FQDN**), also known as the machine name, contains a host (for example, www for World Wide Web) and a domain name, including a **top-level domain** (**TLD**). The top-level domain is the last and most significant component of a fully qualified domain name.

To request documents from the Web server, users must know the fully qualified domain names (machine names) on which the Web server software resides. For example, to access the documents from Deitel's Web server, you must know the FQDN www.deitel.com. The FQDN www.deitel.com indicates that the host is

www and the top-level domain is com. In a FQDN, the TLD often describes the type of organization that owns the domain. For example, the com TLD usually refers to a commercial business, the org TLD usually refers to a nonprofit organization and the edu TLD usually refers to an educational institution. In addition, each country has its own TLD, such as cn for China, et for Ethiopia, om for Oman and us for the United States.

Each FQDN corresponds to a numeric address called an **IP (Internet Protocol) address**, which is much like the street address of a house. Just as people use street addresses to locate houses or businesses in a city, computers use IP addresses to locate other computers on the Internet. Each internet host computer has a unique IP address. Each address is comprised of four sets of numbers separated by periods, such as 63.110.43.82. A **Domain Name System (DNS) server** is a computer that maintains a database of FQDNs and their corresponding IP addresses. The process of translating FQDNs to IP addresses is called a **DNS lookup**. For example, to access the Deitel Web site, type the FQDN www.deitel.com into a Web browser. The DNS lookup translates www.deitel.com into the IP address of the Deitel Web server (63.110.43.82). In the next section, you will install the Apache Tomcat Web server and the completed **Bookstore** Web application.

SELF-REVIEW

1. A(n) _____ is a computer that stores and maintains resources.
   a) host   b) IP address
   c) domain name   d) Domain Name System

2. A DNS lookup is a _____.
   a) translation of an IP address to a domain   b) translation of a fully qualified domain
   name   name to an IP address
   c) translation of a fully qualified domain   d) search for a domain name
   name to a host name

Answers: 1) a. 2) b.

29.3 Apache Tomcat Web Server

The **Apache Group's Tomcat** is the Web server you will use to create and deliver Web pages to clients in response to client requests. Before you can test-drive the completed application, you must install Tomcat and the **Bookstore** Web application. You must have the Java 2 Software Development Kit (J2SDK) v1.4 installed before you install Tomcat. [*Note*: You already have J2SDK v1.4 installed if you have been running and building the applications in this book. If you already have the Tomcat installed, you can skip this step.]

Installing Tomcat and the Bookstore Web Application

1. ***Installing Tomcat.*** Locate the jakarta-tomcat-4.1.24-LE-jdk14.exe file on the CD (in the software\windows\tomcat directory) and double click it to run the installer program, which will install Tomcat step-by-step.

2. ***Confirming the location of your Java Development Kit installation.*** The Tomcat installer will locate your J2SDK installation directory automatically. In the first dialog box (Fig. 29.2), click **OK** to confirm the installation directory of J2SDK version 1.4.

Figure 29.2 Locating the Java Development Kit. Copyright © 2000–2003 The Apache Software Foundation (http://www.apache.org). All rights reserved.

(cont.)

3. ***Accepting the license agreement.*** To install Apache Tomcat, you must accept the license agreement. When prompted with the license agreement, read it carefully and, if the terms are acceptable to you, click **I Agree** (Fig. 29.3).

Figure 29.3 Accepting the Tomcat license agreement. Copyright © 2000–2003 The Apache Software Foundation (`http://www.apache.org`). All rights reserved.

4. ***Accepting the default installation options.*** When prompted to choose the type of installation to perform, click **Next** to accept the default options (Fig. 29.4).

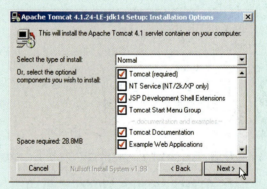

Figure 29.4 Accepting Tomcat default installation options. Copyright © 2000–2003 The Apache Software Foundation (`http://www.apache.org`). All rights reserved.

5. ***Specifying the installation directory.*** When prompted to select an installation directory (Fig. 29.5), click **Install** to use the default directory (`C:\Program Files\Apache Group\Tomcat 4.1`).

Tomcat default installation directory

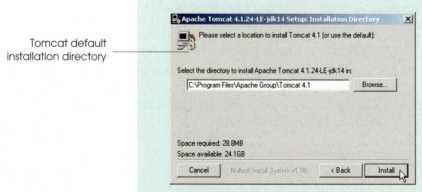

Figure 29.5 Choosing the default Tomcat installation directory. Copyright © 2000–2003 The Apache Software Foundation (`http://www.apache.org`). All rights reserved.

(cont.)   6. ***Monitoring the installation process.*** The installer program will begin copying files to your computer (Fig. 29.6).

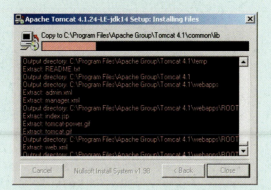

7. ***Selecting an administrator password.*** Tomcat has a password-protected administration program built in. When prompted, type `admin` into the **Password** field for the **User Name** `admin` (Fig. 29.7). [*Note:* You can actually choose any password you like. Be sure to keep track of the password you use.] For security reasons, it is a good idea to choose your own password. This user name and password is used only when you try to access Tomcat's administration tool. You will not use the administration tool in this book. Click the **Next** button to continue.

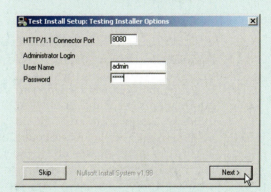

8. ***Completing the Tomcat installation.*** Once the Tomcat installation completes, click **Close** to finish the installation (Fig. 29.8).

9. ***Copying the Bookstore Web application to the Tomcat webapps directory.*** To install the completed **Bookstore** Web application, copy the `C:\Examples\Tutorial29\CompletedApplication\bookstore` directory to Tomcat's `webapps` directory. The default location of the `webapps` directory is `C:\Program Files\Apache Group\Tomcat 4.1\webapps` (Fig. 29.9). [*Note 1:* If you chose a different directory in *Step 6*, then copy the `bookstore` folder to the `webapps` subdirectory of your Tomcat installation.] [*Note 2*: Since the completed **Bookstore** Web application is expecting to find the database information specifically in the `C:\Examples\Tutorial29\Databases` directory, verify that you have copied the `Tutorial29` directory on the CD to the `C:\Examples` directory.] [*Note 3*: At our Web site, we also provide a version for running this Web application on Linux.]

(cont.)

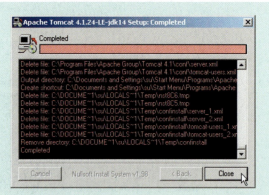

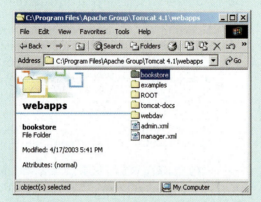

Figure 29.9 Copying the `bookstore` folder to `webapps`.

10. ***Copying the database JAR files to the Bookstore Web application***. The information tier for the **Bookstore** Web application uses the Cloudscape database. You need to copy the `db2j.jar` and `license.jar` files to the `C:\Program Files\Apache Group\Tomcat 4.1\webapps\bookstore\WEB-INF\lib` directory. The `db2j.jar` and `license.jar` files are located in the `C:\Cloudscape_5.1\lib` directory (Fig. 29.10). In Tutorial 26, if you installed Cloudscape in a directory other than `C:\Cloudscape_5.1`, replace `C:\Cloudscape_5.1` with your Cloudscape installation.

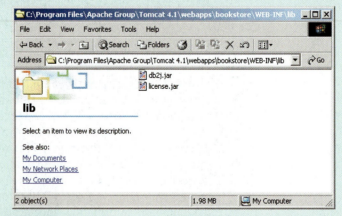

Figure 29.10 Copying the database JAR files to the **Bookstore** Web application.

method to use the speech synthesizer. Have the synthesizer tell the user to enter the price of a car, the down payment and the annual interest rate of the loan, then describe the output of the application so that the user understands what the program will do.

g) *Modifying the* **calculateJButtonActionPerformed** *method*. Find the calculate-JButtonActionPerformed method, which immediately follows instructionsJButtonActionPerformed. Add code to the calculateJButtonActionPerformed method to declare a String named textToSpeak that will be used to display the output. Set the String to "You Will Have to Pay:", which will be the first line in the ouput. Add the code that will append the payment values for the loan onto textToSpeak. Finally, have the application speak the result text to the user.

h) *Releasing the resources allocated to the speech synthesizer.* Find the frameWindow-Closing method, which immediately follows calculateMonthlyPayment. Inside the frameWindowClosing method, add code to release the resources allocated to the speech synthesizer.

i) *Saving the application.* Save your modified source code file.

j) *Opening the Command Prompt window and changing directories.* Open the **Command Prompt** window by selecting **Start > Programs > Accessories > Command Prompt**. Change to your working directory by typing cd C:\SimplyJava\CarPaymentCalculatorEnhancement.

k) *Setting the CLASSPATH environment variable.* Type SetClasspath.bat in the **Command Prompt** window to set the CLASSPATH environment variable. [*Note:* if your FreeTTS is installed in a directory other than C:\FreeTTS then replace C:\FreeTTS with your FreeTTS installation directory in the SetClasspath.bat file.]

l) *Compiling the application.* Compile your application by typing the command javac CarPayment.java.

m) *Running the completed application.* When your application compiles correctly, run it by typing java CarPayment.

n) *Closing the application.* Close your running application by clicking its close button.

o) *Closing the Command Prompt window.* Close the **Command Prompt** window by clicking its close button.

29

TUTORIAL

Bookstore Web Application

Introducing Web Applications and the Apache Tomcat Web Server

In previous tutorials, you used Java to develop desktop applications. Each application contained a GUI with which the user interacted. You can also use Java to create **Web applications**. These applications, also known as Web-based applications, can use **JavaServer Pages (JSP)** technology to create **Web content**—data that can be viewed in a Web browser, such as Internet Explorer (from Microsoft) or Netscape (from Netscape Communications Corporation). This Web content includes **HTML** (**HyperText Markup Language**) documents and images. JSP uses Java and HTML to develop dynamic Web pages. HTML is a language that is understood by virtually all Web browsers and used to publish online documents with GUI elements, text and images. With HTML, you can create Web pages that can access other online documents using hypertext links, and you can design forms (containing components similar to JComboBox, JTextField and JButton) to obtain user input. You will learn the HTML you need to build your **Bookstore** Web application in Tutorial 30.

In Tutorial 29, you will learn the multi-tier architecture that is used to create Web applications. You will learn about Web servers and install the Apache Tomcat Web server, which you will need to run your **Bookstore** Web application. You will learn important Web development concepts in the context of the **Bookstore** Web application. This application consists of two Web pages. The first page displays a list of books. After selecting a book, the user clicks a button that directs the browser to a second Web page. Information about the selected book is then retrieved from a database and displayed on the second Web page. This page contains a link that, when clicked, directs the Web browser back to the first Web page, allowing the user to select a different book. Before you create this Web application, you will learn fundamental Web development concepts that are required to understand the **Bookstore** Web application, which you will then test-drive. In Tutorial 30–Tutorial 32, you will analyze the pseudocode and ACE table for the **Bookstore** Web application and you will implement the application in Java using the most advanced techniques you have learned in this book.

```
1   private void speakJButtonActionPerformed( ActionEvent event )
2   {
3      speechSynthesizer.allocate();
4      speechSynthesizer.resume();
5
6   } // end method speakJButtonActionPerformed
```

What's wrong with this code? ▶

28.15 Find the error(s) in the following code. The method should have a Synthesizer object say, "Hello, here are the instructions to run the application." This should happen when the user clicks the **Instructions** JButton. The speechSynthesizer variable references a Synthesizer object, which is declared as an instance variable.

```
1   private void instructionsJButtonActionPerformed( ActionEvent event )
2   {
3      speechSynthesizer.setSpeakingRate( 100.0f );
4      speechSynthesizer.speakPlainText(
5         "Hello, here are the instructions to run the application" );
6
7   } // end method instructionsJButtonActionPerformed
```

Programming Challenge ▶

28.16 (*Car Payment Application Using Java Speech API*) Enhance the **Car Payment Calculator** application from Tutorial 8 to use the Java Speech API (Fig. 28.21). When the user clicks the **Instructions** JButton, the application should explain the purpose of the application. After the user enters information into each field of the **Car Payment Calculator** and clicks the **Calculate** JButton, the application should speak the calculated payment amounts and the period (number of months) over which they were calculated.

Figure 28.21 Enhanced **Car Payment** application.

a) *Copying the template to your working directory.* Copy the directory C:\Examples\ Tutorial28\Exercises\CarPaymentCalculatorEnhancement to your C:\SimplyJava directory.

b) *Opening the template file.* Open the CarPayment.java file in your text editor.

c) *Importing Java Speech API packages.* Import the javax.speech and the javax.speech.synthesis packages.

d) *Declaring instance variables.* At line 34, declare an instance variable of type Synthesizer, which is used to speak text.

e) *Creating a Synthesizer object.* Inside the CarPayment constructor, create a Synthesizer object, allocate the resource and get the synthesizer ready to speak.

f) *Adding code to the instructionsJButtonActionPerformed method.* Find the instructionsJButtonActionPerformed method, which immediately follows createUserInterface. Add code to the instructionsJButtonActionPerformed

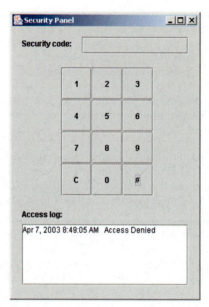

Figure 28.20 Modified **Security Panel** application.

e) *Creating a Synthesizer object.* Inside the SecurityPanel constructor, create a Synthesizer object, allocate the resource and get the synthesizer ready to speak.

f) *Adding code to the enterJButtonActionPerformed method.* Find the enterJButtonActionPerformed method, which immediately follows nineJButtonActionPerformed. Add code to the enterJButtonActionPerformed method to use the speech synthesizer. If the user enters a valid access code, the application should welcome the user and state the type of employee that the access code represents. If the access code is invalid, then the application should state that an invalid code was provided and that access is denied.

g) *Releasing the resources allocated to the speech synthesizer.* Find the frameWindowClosing method, which immediately follows enterJButtonActionPerformed. Inside the frameWindowClosing method, add code to release the resources allocated to the speech synthesizer.

h) *Saving the application.* Save your modified source code file.

i) *Opening the Command Prompt window and changing directories.* Open the **Command Prompt** window by selecting **Start > Programs > Accessories > Command Prompt**. Change to your working directory by typing cd C:\SimplyJava\SecurityPanelEnhancement.

j) *Setting the CLASSPATH environment variable.* Type SetClasspath.bat in the **Command Prompt** window to set the CLASSPATH environment variable. [*Note:* if your FreeTTS is installed in a directory other than C:\FreeTTS then replace C:\FreeTTS with your FreeTTS installation directory in the SetClasspath.bat file.]

k) *Compiling the application.* Compile your application by typing the command javac SecurityPanel.java.

l) *Running the completed application.* When your application compiles correctly, run it by typing java SecurityPanel. Enter a correct access code, then click the # JButton to verify that the application speaks the correct message. Try entering an incorrect access code. You should hear the application speak an error message notifying you that you did not enter a correct code.

m) *Closing the application.* Close your running application by clicking its close button.

n) *Closing the Command Prompt window.* Close the **Command Prompt** window by clicking its close button.

What does this code do? ▶   **28.14** After the user clicks the **Speak** JButton, what does the following method do? The speechSynthesizer variable references a Synthesizer object, which is declared as an instance variable.

2. In a typical three-tier application, the role of the middle tier is to _____.

    a) control the interaction between the client and information tiers

    b) control the interaction between the client and the user interface

    c) display the application's user interface

    d) provide a database for the application

Answers: 1) c. 2) a.

29.2 Web Servers

A **Web server** is specialized software that responds to client (Web browser) requests by providing requested resources (such as HTML documents and access to data-bases). To request documents from Web servers, users must know the addresses at which those documents reside. A **URL** (**Uniform Resource Locator**) can be thought of as an address that is used to direct a Web browser to a resource on the Web. A URL contains the protocol of the resource (such as http), the machine name or IP address for the resource (we will discuss machine names and IP addresses shortly) and the name (including the path) of the resource. For example, in the URL

    http://www.deitel.com/index.html

the protocol is http, the machine name is www.deitel.com and the name of the resource is index.html.

Once the **Bookstore** Web application is properly set up, users can run it by typing its URL into a Web browser. This action is translated into a request to the Web server (such as Apache Tomcat) where the **Bookstore** Web application resides. When the user interacts with the Web browser to request information from the **Bookstore** Web application, the Web server retrieves information from the information tier (contains the Cloudscape database) and sends Web content created by the **Bookstore** Web application back to the client Web browser, which displays that content for the user. For example, when a user sends a request to view all the book titles by selecting a title and clicking the button, the Web content created by the **Bookstore** Web application will include a list of book titles and a button. When a user sends a request for viewing book information for a specific book, the Web content created by the **Bookstore** Web application will include information (such as author, price, ISBN number, edition number, copyright year and description) about the book the user selected. You will install the Apache Tomcat Web server and the **Bookstore** Web application in the next section.

To understand how a Web browser is able to locate documents on a Web server, it is helpful for you to know the following terms:

1. Host: A **host** is a computer that stores and maintains resources, such as Web pages, databases and multimedia files. In the case of the **Bookstore** Web application, the host is your computer, because all the application-related resources, including JSPs and databases, are stored in your computer.

2. Domain: A **domain** represents a group of hosts on the Internet. Each domain has a **domain name**, also known as a **Web address**, which uniquely identifies the location of a business or organization on the Internet.

3. Fully qualified domain name: A **fully qualified domain name** (**FQDN**), also known as the machine name, contains a host (for example, www for World Wide Web) and a domain name, including a **top-level domain** (**TLD**). The top-level domain is the last and most significant component of a fully qualified domain name.

To request documents from the Web server, users must know the fully qualified domain names (machine names) on which the Web server software resides. For example, to access the documents from Deitel's Web server, you must know the FQDN www.deitel.com. The FQDN www.deitel.com indicates that the host is

29.1 Multi-Tier Architecture

Web applications are **multi-tier applications**, sometimes referred to as *n*-**tier applications**. Multi-tier applications divide their functionality across separate **tiers** (that is, logical groupings of functionality). The tiers of an application can be located on the same computer or on separate computers distributed across a network—most commonly, the Internet. In this case study, you will implement all three tiers on one computer. Figure 29.1 illustrates the basic structure of a multi-tier application. An explanation of each tier follows the figure.

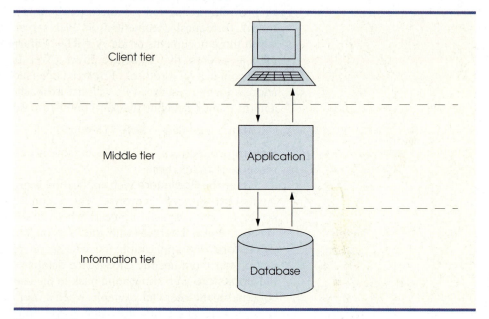

Figure 29.1   Three-tier application model.

The **information tier** (also called the **data tier** or the **bottom tier**) maintains the data for the application. For example, the information tier for the **Bookstore** Web application is implemented as a database that contains product information, such as book titles, author names, publication dates, edition numbers, ISBN numbers, book descriptions and prices.

The **middle tier** controls the interactions between application clients (such as Web browsers) and application data in the information tier. In the **Bookstore** Web application, the middle-tier code determines which book was selected by the user and retrieves the information for that book from the database. The middle tier also determines the format in which the selected book's data will be displayed. Thus, the middle tier represents the functionality of the Web application and is often called the **business logic tier**.

The **client tier**, or **top tier**, is the application's user interface, which is typically a Web browser. The user will interact directly with your application through the client tier (browser) by entering text, selecting from lists, clicking buttons, etc. The browser reports the user's actions and data entered to the middle tier, which processes the information. The middle tier can also make requests to, and retrieve data from, the information tier. The client Web browser then displays to the user the data retrieved by the middle tier from the information tier.

SELF-REVIEW   1. The information tier is also called the _____ tier in a typical three-tier application.

    a) top   b) middle

    c) bottom   d) client

(cont.)

3. ***Accepting the license agreement.*** To install Apache Tomcat, you must accept the license agreement. When prompted with the license agreement, read it carefully and, if the terms are acceptable to you, click **I Agree** (Fig. 29.3).

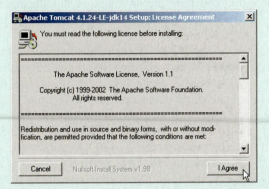

Figure 29.3 Accepting the Tomcat license agreement. Copyright © 2000–2003 The Apache Software Foundation (`http://www.apache.org`). All rights reserved.

4. ***Accepting the default installation options.*** When prompted to choose the type of installation to perform, click **Next** to accept the default options (Fig. 29.4).

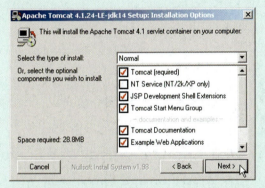

Figure 29.4 Accepting Tomcat default installation options. Copyright © 2000–2003 The Apache Software Foundation (`http://www.apache.org`). All rights reserved.

5. ***Specifying the installation directory.*** When prompted to select an installation directory (Fig. 29.5), click **Install** to use the default directory (`C:\Program Files\Apache Group\Tomcat 4.1`).

Tomcat default installation directory

Figure 29.5 Choosing the default Tomcat installation directory. Copyright © 2000–2003 The Apache Software Foundation (`http://www.apache.org`). All rights reserved.

www and the top-level domain is com. In a FQDN, the TLD often describes the type of organization that owns the domain. For example, the com TLD usually refers to a commercial business, the org TLD usually refers to a nonprofit organization and the edu TLD usually refers to an educational institution. In addition, each country has its own TLD, such as cn for China, et for Ethiopia, om for Oman and us for the United States.

Each FQDN corresponds to a numeric address called an **IP (Internet Protocol) address**, which is much like the street address of a house. Just as people use street addresses to locate houses or businesses in a city, computers use IP addresses to locate other computers on the Internet. Each internet host computer has a unique IP address. Each address is comprised of four sets of numbers separated by periods, such as 63.110.43.82. A **Domain Name System (DNS) server** is a computer that maintains a database of FQDNs and their corresponding IP addresses. The process of translating FQDNs to IP addresses is called a **DNS lookup**. For example, to access the Deitel Web site, type the FQDN www.deitel.com into a Web browser. The DNS lookup translates www.deitel.com into the IP address of the Deitel Web server (63.110.43.82). In the next section, you will install the Apache Tomcat Web server and the completed **Bookstore** Web application.

SELF-REVIEW
1. A(n) _____ is a computer that stores and maintains resources.

    a) host   b) IP address

    c) domain name   d) Domain Name System

2. A DNS lookup is a _____.

    a) translation of an IP address to a domain name   b) translation of a fully qualified domain name to an IP address

    c) translation of a fully qualified domain name to a host name   d) search for a domain name

Answers: 1) a. 2) b.

29.3 Apache Tomcat Web Server

The **Apache Group's Tomcat** is the Web server you will use to create and deliver Web pages to clients in response to client requests. Before you can test-drive the completed application, you must install Tomcat and the **Bookstore** Web application. You must have the Java 2 Software Development Kit (J2SDK) v1.4 installed before you install Tomcat. [*Note:* You already have J2SDK v1.4 installed if you have been running and building the applications in this book. If you already have the Tomcat installed, you can skip this step.]

Installing Tomcat and the Bookstore Web Application

1. ***Installing Tomcat.*** Locate the jakarta-tomcat-4.1.24-LE-jdk14.exe file on the CD (in the software\windows\tomcat directory) and double click it to run the installer program, which will install Tomcat step-by-step.

2. ***Confirming the location of your Java Development Kit installation.*** The Tomcat installer will locate your J2SDK installation directory automatically. In the first dialog box (Fig. 29.2), click **OK** to confirm the installation directory of J2SDK version 1.4.

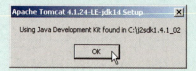

Figure 29.2 Locating the Java Development Kit. Copyright © 2000–2003 The Apache Software Foundation (http://www.apache.org). All rights reserved.

(cont.)

6. ***Monitoring the installation process.*** The installer program will begin copying files to your computer (Fig. 29.6).

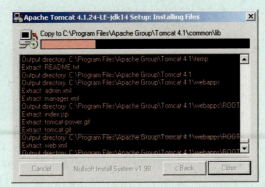

Figure 29.6   Tomcat installation progress dialog. Copyright © 2000-2003 The Apache Software Foundation (`http://www.apache.org`). All rights reserved.

7. ***Selecting an administrator password.*** Tomcat has a password-protected administration program built in. When prompted, type `admin` into the **Password** field for the **User Name** `admin` (Fig. 29.7). [*Note:* You can actually choose any password you like. Be sure to keep track of the password you use.] For security reasons, it is a good idea to choose your own password. This user name and password is used only when you try to access Tomcat's administration tool. You will not use the administration tool in this book. Click the **Next** button to continue.

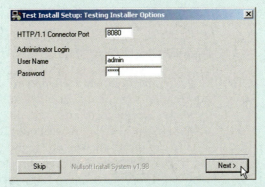

Figure 29.7   Selecting a Tomcat administrator password. Copyright © 2000–2003 The Apache Software Foundation (`http://www.apache.org`). All rights reserved.

8. ***Completing the Tomcat installation.*** Once the Tomcat installation completes, click **Close** to finish the installation (Fig. 29.8).

9. ***Copying the Bookstore Web application to the Tomcat webapps directory.*** To install the completed **Bookstore** Web application, copy the `C:\Examples\Tutorial29\CompletedApplication\bookstore` directory to Tomcat's `webapps` directory. The default location of the `webapps` directory is `C:\Program Files\Apache Group\Tomcat 4.1\webapps` (Fig. 29.9). [*Note 1:* If you chose a different directory in *Step 6,* then copy the `bookstore` folder to the `webapps` subdirectory of your Tomcat installation.] [*Note 2:* Since the completed **Bookstore** Web application is expecting to find the database information specifically in the `C:\Examples\Tutorial29\Databases` directory, verify that you have copied the `Tutorial29` directory on the CD to the `C:\Examples` directory.] [*Note 3:* At our Web site, we also provide a version for running this Web application on Linux.]

(cont.)

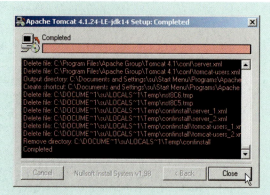

Figure 29.8 Completing the Tomcat installation. Copyright © 2000–2003 The Apache Software Foundation (`http://www.apache.org`). All rights reserved.

Figure 29.9 Copying the `bookstore` folder to `webapps`.

10. ***Copying the database JAR files to the Bookstore Web application***. The information tier for the **Bookstore** Web application uses the Cloudscape database. You need to copy the `db2j.jar` and `license.jar` files to the `C:\Program Files\Apache Group\Tomcat 4.1\webapps\bookstore\WEB-INF\lib` directory. The `db2j.jar` and `license.jar` files are located in the `C:\Cloudscape_5.1\lib` directory (Fig. 29.10). In Tutorial 26, if you installed Cloudscape in a directory other than `C:\Cloudscape_5.1`, replace `C:\Cloudscape_5.1` with your Cloudscape installation.

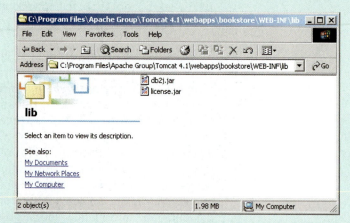

Figure 29.10 Copying the database JAR files to the **Bookstore** Web application.

SELF-REVIEW   1. You must have _____ installed before you install Tomcat.

    a) the Cloudscape database   b) the Java 2 Software Development Kit
                                                        (J2SDK) v1.4

    c) a Web server   d) None of the above.

2. To install the **Bookstore** Web application, you must copy it to the Tomcat _____ directory.

    a) `server`   b) `work`

    c) `webapps`   d) None of the above.

Answers: 1) b. 2) c.

29.4 Test-Driving the Bookstore Web Application

In the next three tutorials, you will build a Web application that displays book information to a user upon request. Your **Bookstore** Web application must meet the following requirements:

> **Application Requirements**
>
> *A bookstore employee receives e-mails from customers asking for information pertaining to the books the store sells online. The employee has asked you to create a Web application that allows users to view online information about various books. This information includes the author, cover image, price, ISBN number, edition number, copyright year and a brief description of the book. The **Bookstore** Web application you create will use JavaServer Pages to implement the middle tier. The client tier will create the application's GUI, which will be implemented using HTML. The application's GUI should allow users to select a book title and view the information about the selected book. The middle tier will retrieve the book information from the information tier and display it in the client tier. The information tier will maintain the database, which has been created using Cloudscape. You will use the JDBC API to access the database, which will be provided for you.*

You begin by test-driving the completed Web application. You will test the **Bookstore** Web application on your local computer. Most computers specify a special host name—`localhost` (which normally corresponds to the IP address 127.0.0.1)—for testing Web-based applications (and other networking applications) on the local computer. As you will see in the test-drive, the URLs you will use to access the **Bookstore** Web application will contain `localhost` as the host name. In most cases, you can also specify your computer's name instead of `localhost` as the host name. [*Note*: If you are running Microsoft Windows on your computer, your computer's name can be determined by selecting **Start > Settings > Control Panel** and double-clicking **System** from the list to display the **System Properties** dialog. In Windows 2000, click the **Network Identification** tab. On this tab, the **Full computer name:** field displays your computer's name. In Windows XP, select the **Computer Name** tab. On this tab, the **Full computer name:** field displays the computer name. For other platforms, see your instructor for details on determining your computer's name.]

1. ***Starting Tomcat.*** Tomcat must be running to respond to client requests. To start Tomcat, select **Start > Programs > Apache Tomcat 4.1 > Start Tomcat**. A window similar to the one shown in Fig. 29.11 will appear.

```
Start Tomcat
Mar 26, 2003 11:16:04 AM org.apache.commons.modeler.Registry loadRegistry
INFO: Loading registry information
Mar 26, 2003 11:16:04 AM org.apache.commons.modeler.Registry getRegistry
INFO: Creating new Registry instance
Mar 26, 2003 11:16:05 AM org.apache.commons.modeler.Registry getServer
INFO: Creating MBeanServer
Mar 26, 2003 11:16:07 AM org.apache.coyote.http11.Http11Protocol init
INFO: Initializing Coyote HTTP/1.1 on port 8080
Starting service Tomcat-Standalone
Apache Tomcat/4.1.24-LE-jdk14
Mar 26, 2003 11:16:15 AM org.apache.coyote.http11.Http11Protocol start
INFO: Starting Coyote HTTP/1.1 on port 8080
Mar 26, 2003 11:16:15 AM org.apache.jk.common.ChannelSocket init
INFO: JK2: ajp13 listening on /0.0.0.0:8009
Mar 26, 2003 11:16:15 AM org.apache.jk.server.JkMain start
INFO: Jk running ID=0 time=0/40  config=C:\Program Files\Apache Group\Tomcat 4.1
\conf\jk2.properties
```

Figure 29.11 Tomcat server output window.

2. ***Running the application.*** Open your Web browser and enter the URL `http://localhost:8080/bookstore/books.jsp`. This will request the Tomcat Web server the page, `books.jsp`, of the **Bookstore** Web application. The `books.jsp` page displays a list of the available books (Fig. 29.12). Although this list GUI component looks similar to the `JComboBox` component you have used in desktop applications, the list is actually an **HTML menu control**, which is defined by the **HTML `select` element**. You will learn how to use the HTML menu control in Tutorial 30. Programmers customize Web pages by adding various HTML elements. As you will learn, some HTML elements look similar to common Java GUI components. The callouts in Fig. 29.12 identify various HTML elements that will be explained throughout this case study (Tutorial 30–Tutorial 32).

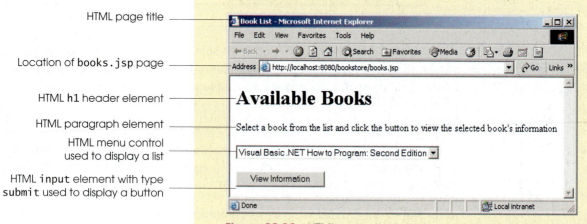

HTML page title

Location of `books.jsp` page

HTML `h1` header element

HTML paragraph element

HTML menu control used to display a list

HTML `input` element with type `submit` used to display a button

Figure 29.12 HTML page that display, a form with a list and a button.

The book titles displayed in the menu control are retrieved from a database. The database is the information tier of this three-tier application. Although only the book titles are displayed on this page, the database includes other information, such as the authors, cover images, prices, ISBN numbers, edition numbers, copyright years and descriptions of the books. In Tutorial 31, you will examine the application's information tier and learn how to connect to the database to access the data.

(cont.)

3. ***Selecting a book.*** Select **C++ How To Program: Fourth Edition** from the book list, then click the **View Information** button. The `bookInformation.jsp` page appears (Fig. 29.13). This page displays the title, author and an image of the book cover of the book you selected. This page also displays the book's price, ISBN number, edition number and copyright year, as well as a description of the book.

Address of
`bookInformation.jsp` page

When clicked, this link
returns the user to `books.jsp`

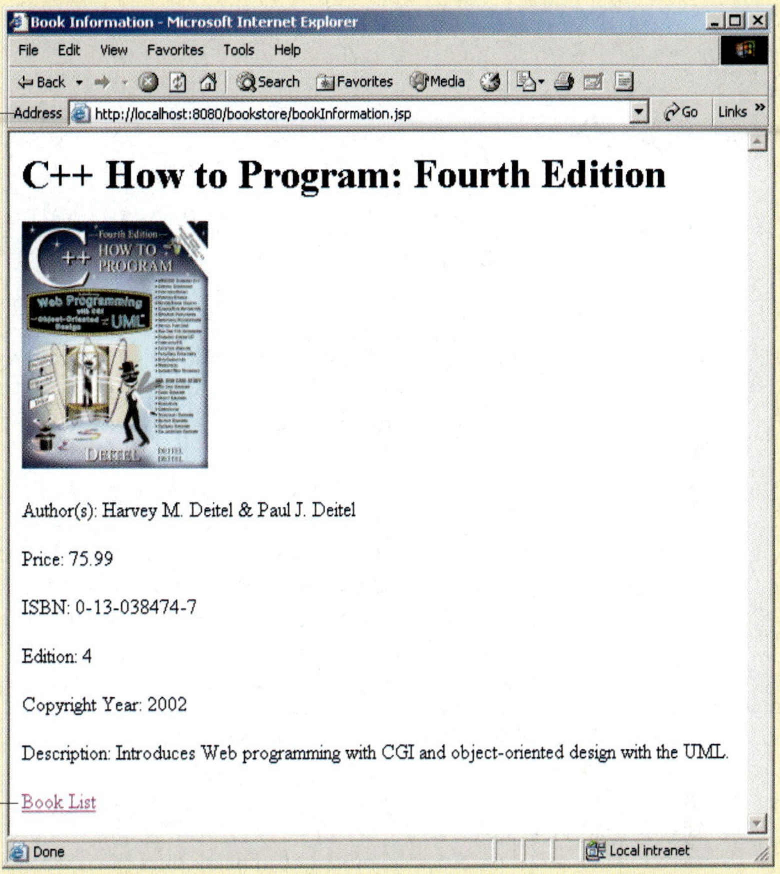

Figure 29.13   Page that displays the selected book's information.

4. ***Returning to `books.jsp`.*** After viewing a book's information, users can decide whether they wish to view information about other books. The bottom of this page contains a **Book List** link that, when clicked, redirects the browser back to the `books.jsp` page to redisplay the form that contains a list of book titles.

5. ***Closing the browser.*** Close the browser window by clicking its close button.

6. ***Removing the completed application from Tomcat's webapps directory.*** You cannot have two applications with the same name in the webapps directory. Therefore, you must delete the completed application before you begin developing your **Bookstore** Web application over the next three tutorials. Stop Tomcat by clicking **Start > Programs > Apache Tomcat 4.1 > Stop Tomcat**. Then, open **Windows Explorer** (by double clicking **My Computer** on your desktop), navigate to Tomcat's webapps folder and delete the **bookstore** folder from the webapps folder (Fig. 29.14) by right-clicking the bookstore folder and selecting **Delete** from the shortcut menu.

(cont.)

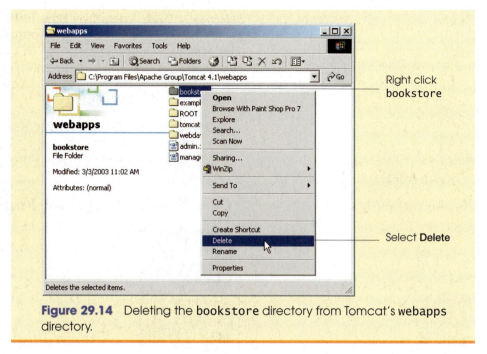

Figure 29.14 Deleting the `bookstore` directory from Tomcat's `webapps` directory.

Notice that this example uses all three tiers of a three-tier application. To review: the information tier contains the database from which the Web application retrieves information; the client tier is represented by the Web pages in which the user views and selects books; and the middle tier is the code that controls what occurs when users interact with the Web pages requesting information from the database.

SELF-REVIEW
1. A button in an HTML document is represented by _____.
   a) an HTML `input` element   b) an HTML `button` element
   c) an HTML `select` element   d) None of the above.

2. A list of items can be displayed in a Web page with _____.
   a) an HTML `input` element   b) an HTML `button` element
   c) an HTML `select` element   d) None of the above.

Answers: 1) a. 2) c.

29.5 Wrap-Up

In this tutorial, you learned about the components of a three-tier, Web-based application. You were introduced to the information tier (also called the bottom tier), which maintains the data for the application, typically as a database. You then learned about the client tier (also called the top tier), which displays the application's user interface, and the business-logic tier (also called the middle tier), which coordinates between the information and client tiers. Next, you were introduced to the Web servers. Then, you installed the Apache Tomcat Web server, which serves Web content, such as JavaServer Pages. You then test-drove the three-tier **Bookstore** Web application, learning how to start and stop Tomcat and how to run JavaServer-Pages-based applications. You also learned that HTML elements are used to create Web pages.

In Tutorial 30, **Bookstore** Web Application: Client Tier, you will create the user interface for this application. You will design the Web pages that display the list of books and the detailed book information. You will then proceed to Tutorial 31, **Bookstore** Web Application: Information Tier, where you will learn about the data-

base used in the application and how the application connects to that database. You will complete the **Bookstore** Web application in Tutorial 32, **Bookstore** Web Application: Business Logic Tier. In that tutorial, you will write the functionality for the entire **Bookstore** Web application.

SKILLS SUMMARY

Installing Tomcat

- Locate `jakarta-tomcat-4.1.24-LE-jdk14.exe` on the CD and double click it to run the installer program.
- Follow the prompted instructions to complete the installation.

Starting Tomcat

- Select **Start > Programs > Apache Tomcat 4.1 > Start Tomcat**.

Stopping Tomcat

- Select **Start > Programs > Apache Tomcat 4.1 > Stop Tomcat**.

Setting up a Web Application on Your Computer

- Place the Web application's folder in your Tomcat webapps directory (if you installed Tomcat in the default directory, this directory is `C:\Program Files\Apache Group\ Tomcat 4.1\webapps`).

Testing the Web Application Using a Web Browser

- Open a Web browser.
- Type the URL `http://localhost:8080/`*nameOfApplication*`/`*nameOfFirstPage*, where *nameOfApplication* is the name of the Web application's directory and *nameOfFirstPage* is the name of the first Web page (such as a JSP page) that loads when the application is run.
- Press *Enter* to run the application.

KEY TERMS

Apache Tomcat—A Web server from the Apache Group that is free and available for many platforms.

bottom tier—The tier (also known as the information tier, or the data tier) containing the application data of a multi-tier application—typically implemented as a database.

client tier—The user interface of a multi-tier application (also called the top tier).

data tier—The tier (also known as the information tier, or the bottom tier) containing the application data of a multi-tier application—typically implemented as a database.

DNS lookup—The process that translates fully qualified domain names into IP addresses.

domain—Represents a group of hosts on the Internet.

domain name—Also known as a Web address, which uniquely identifies the location of a business or organization on the Internet.

Domain Name System (DNS) server—A computer that maintains a database of host names and their corresponding IP addresses.

fully qualified domain name (FQDN)—A host name combined with a domain and top-level domain that provides a user-friendly way to identify a site on the Internet.

host—A computer that stores and maintains resources, such as Web pages, databases and multimedia files.

HTML element—A part of the HTML language, such as `h1`, `select` or `input`, that determines the format of a Web page and the GUI components that appear on a Web page.

HyperText Markup Language (HTML)—A language, understood by virtually all Web browsers, used to publish online documents with forms and images.

information tier—The tier containing the application data of a multi-tier application—typically implemented as a database (also called the bottom tier or database tier).

IP (Internet Protocol) address—A unique address used to locate a computer on the Internet.

JavaServer Pages—A technology to develop dynamic Web pages through the use of Java and HTML.

`localhost`—The host name that identifies the computer you are using.

middle tier—The tier that controls interaction between the client and information tiers of a multi-tier application. This is sometimes known as the business logic tier.

multi-tier application—Application (sometimes referred to as an *n*-tier application) whose functionality is divided into separate tiers, which can be on the same machine or can be distributed to separate machines across a network. One popular form of multi-tier application has three tiers—the client tier, which contains the application's user interface, the information tier, which maintains the data for the application and the business logic tier, which controls interactions between application clients (such as Web browsers) and application data in the information tier. Sometimes referred to as n-tier application.

tier—Logical groupings of functionality.

top-level domain (TLD)—The portion of a Web address that usually describes the type of organization that owns the domain name. For example, the `com` TLD usually refers to a commercial business, the `org` TLD usually refers to a nonprofit organization and the `edu` TLD usually refers to an educational institution.

top tier—The tier containing the application's user interface in a multi-tier application— typically implemented as a GUI.

URL (Uniform Resource Locator)—An address that can be used to direct a browser to a resource on the Web.

Web address—Also known as a domain name, which uniquely identifies the location of a business or organization on the Internet.

Web application—Also known as Web-based application, can use JavaServer Pages (JSP) technology to create Web content.

Web content—Data that can be viewed in a Web browser, such as Internet Explorer or Netscape.

Web server—Specialized software that responds to Web client requests by sending Web pages and other resources back to the client.

MULTIPLE-CHOICE QUESTIONS

29.1 JavaServer pages have the _____ extension.

a) `.html`

b) `.jsp`

c) `.javasp`

d) None of the above.

29.2 _____ applications divide functionality into separate tiers.

a) *n*-tier

b) Multi-tier

c) Both a and b.

d) None of the above.

29.3 All tiers of a multi-tier application _____.

a) must be located on the same computer

b) must be located on different computers

c) can be located on the same computer or on different computers

d) must be arranged so that the client and middle tier are on the same computer and the information tier is on a different computer

29.4 The client tier interacts with the _____ tier to access information from the _____ tier.

a) middle, information

b) information, middle

c) information, bottom

d) bottom, information

29.5 A _____ is specialized software that responds to client requests from Web browsers by providing resources.

a) host

b) host name

c) DNS server

d) Web server

29.6 A(n) _____ can be thought of as an address used to direct a browser to a resource on the Web.

a) middle tier

b) ASPX page

c) URL

d) query string

29.7 A _____ represents a group of _____ on the Internet.

    a) domain, hosts   b) host, domain names

    c) host name, hosts   d) None of the above.

29.8 _____ is a Web server.

    a) Apache Tomcat   b) `localhost`

    c) Java   d) None of the above.

29.9 A _____ is a special host name that identifies the local computer.

    a) `localhost`   b) local Web server

    c) remote Web server   d) None of the above.

29.10 The _____ tier is the application's user interface.

    a) middle   b) client

    c) bottom   d) information

EXERCISES

29.11 (*Phone Book Web Application*) Over the next three tutorials, you will create a **Phone Book** Web application. This phone book should be a Web-based version of the **Phone Book** application created in Tutorial 28. [*Note*: This Web application will not use the Java Speech API as in Tutorial 28.] The **Phone Book** Web application should consist of two JSP pages, which will be named phoneBook and phoneNumber. The phoneBook page displays a list containing the names of several people. The names are retrieved from the phonebook database. When a name is selected and the **Get Number** button is clicked, the client browser is redirected to the phoneNumber JSP page. The telephone number of the selected name should be retrieved from a database and displayed in the phoneNumber JSP page. For this exercise, you need only organize the components (phoneBook and phoneNumber JSP pages, phonebook database and the code that performs the specified functionality) of this Web application into separate tiers. Decide which component belongs in which tier. You will begin building the application in the next tutorial.

29.12 (*US State Facts Web Application*) Over the next three tutorials, you will create a **US State Facts** Web application. This application is designed to allow users to review their knowledge about various U.S. states. This application should consist of two JSP pages. The first page (named `states`) should display a list containing 10 different state names. These state names are stored in the `StateFacts` database. The user should be allowed to select a state name from the list and click a button to retrieve information about the selected state from the database. The information should be displayed on a different JSP page (named `stateFacts`). The `stateFacts` page should display an image of the state flag and list the state capital, state flower, state tree and state bird (retrieved from the database). You will be provided with images of the state flags. For this exercise, you need only organize the components (`states` and `stateFacts` JSP pages, `StateFacts` database and the code that performs the specified functionality) of this Web application into separate tiers. Decide which component belongs in which tier. You will begin building the application in the next tutorial.

29.13 (*Road Sign Review* Web *Application*) Over the next three tutorials, you will create a **Road Sign Review** Web application. The **Road Sign Review** Web application should consist of two JSP pages. This application displays road signs for the user to review and allows the user to schedule a driving test. The first page (named `roadSigns`) should display 15 road sign images that will be provided for you. The page should display the images by retrieving their information from the `RoadSigns` database. This page also will contain two input fields (which look like `JTextField`s) and a button that allow the user to enter information to register for a driving test. When the user clicks the **Register** button, the second page (`roadTestRegistered`) displays information confirming that the user has registered for a driving test. For this exercise, you need only organize the components (`roadSigns` and `roadTestRegistered` JSP pages, `RoadSigns` database and the code that performs the specified functionality) of this Web application into separate tiers. Decide which component belongs in which tier. You will begin building the application in the next tutorial.

30

Objectives

In this tutorial, you will learn to:
- Create a JSP Web Application.
- Create and design JSP pages.
- Use HTML form controls and other HTML elements.
- Use these technologies to implement the client tier of a three-tier web-based application.

Outline

Bookstore Web Application: Client Tier

Introducing HTML

In this tutorial, you will use **HyperText Markup Language** (**HTML**) to create the client tier (also called the top tier)—the user interface of your three-tier **Bookstore** Web application. HTML is a markup language that specifies the format of text that is displayed in a Web browser, such as Internet Explorer (from Microsoft) or Netscape (from Netscape Communications Corporation). You will begin by creating the JavaServer Pages (JSP) Web-based application. You then will use HTML to create the application's GUI.

30.1 Analyzing the Bookstore Web Application

In Tutorial 29, you test-drove the completed three-tier **Bookstore** Web application. Now you will analyze the application's components. The following pseudocode describes the basic operation of the **Bookstore** Web application:

> When the books.jsp page is requested:
>   Retrieve the book titles from the database
>   Display the book titles in an HTML menu
>
> When the user selects a book title from the menu and clicks the View Information (submit) button:
>   Request the bookInformation.jsp page for the selected title
>
> When the bookInformation.jsp page is requested from books.jsp:
>   Retrieve the selected book's information from a database
>   for the selected title
>   Format the retrieved information in the bookInformation.jsp page
>   Return the result to the client browser
>
> When the user clicks the Book List link on the bookInformation.jsp page:
>   Request the books.jsp page

Now that you have test-driven the **Bookstore** Web application and studied its pseudocode representation, you will use an ACE table to help you convert the pseudocode to JSP. Figure 30.1 lists the actions, components and events required to complete your own version of this application.

Action/Component/
Event (ACE) Table for the
Web-Based Bookstore
Application

Action	Component/Class/ HTML element	Event/Method
	`books.jsp`	User requests `books.jsp` page
Retrieve the book titles from the database	`Statement`	
Display the book titles in an HTML menu	`ResultSet`, `select` HTML element, `option` HTML element	
		User clicks the "submit" button
Request the bookInformation.jsp page for the selected title	`input` HTML element with type `submit`	
	`bookInformation.jsp`	User requests `bookInformation.jsp` page
Retrieve the selected book's information from a database for the selected title	`Statement`	
Format the retrieved information in the bookInformation.jsp page	`ResultSet`, `p` (paragraph) HTML elements, `img` HTML element	
Return the result to the client browser		
	`a` (anchor) HTML element	User clicks the hyper-link
Request the books.jsp page	`books.jsp`	

Figure 30.1   ACE table for the Web-based **Bookstore** application.

30.2 Creating JavaServer Pages

In Tutorial 29, you were introduced to the Apache Tomcat Web server and three-tier, Web-based application concepts. Now you will begin creating the **Bookstore** Web application that you test-drove in the last tutorial. This Web-based application allows the user to view information about a selected book. After viewing a book's information, the user can return to the page containing the list of books and select another book. You will create the JavaServer Pages Web application for the **Bookstore** in the boxes, *Creating the* `books.jsp` *Page* and *Creating the* `bookInformation.jsp` *Page*.

In some ways, JavaServer Pages look like standard HTML documents. In fact, JSPs normally include both HTML markup and JSP code. Initially, the `books.jsp` and `bookInformation.jsp` pages you will build in this tutorial contain only HTML. You will add JSP code to these two JSPs in Tutorial 31. [*Note*: On the CD that accompanies this book, we provide two tutorials on HTML from our book *Internet and World Wide Web How to Program*, *Second Edition*. To access these PDF documents, open the file `additional-references.htm` (on the CD in the directory `html\additional-references`) in your Web browser.]

30.3 Creating the `books.jsp` Page

This **Bookstore** Web application consists of two JavaServer Pages. You begin by creating the `books.jsp` page that displays the list of available books.

Creating the books.jsp Page

1. *Copying the template to your working directory.* Copy the `C:\Examples\Tutorial30\TemplateApplication\bookstore` directory to your `C:\SimplyJava` directory.

2. *Opening the books.jsp template file.* Open the `books.jsp` template file in your text editor.

3. *Setting the JSP's title.* Add lines 10–11 of Fig. 30.2 to the JSP. Line 10 is an **HTML comment** that specifies that the next line is the title of the JSP. HTML comments always start with `<!--` and end with `-->`. HTML comments supporting multi-line text. Comments do not cause the Web server to perform any action when the user requests the JSP document for viewing in the Web browser. **HTML markup** contains text that represents the content of a document and **elements** that specify a document's structure and how it will be displayed. HTML delimits each element with start and end tags. A **start tag** consists of the element name in angle brackets (such as `<title>`). An **end tag** consists of the element name preceded by a `/` in angle brackets (such as `</title>`). Line 11 sets the JSP's title to Book List by specifying a **title element**. The `title` element sets the title displayed in the title bar at the top of the browser window. Figure 30.8 shows the `title` element as rendered by the browser. The `title` element always appears inside the **head element** (delimited by the tags on lines 8 and 12 of Fig. 30.2). The head element specifies various settings for the document, such as its title.

Setting the JSP's title ———

```
 8    <head>
 9
10        <!-- specify page title -->
11        <title>Book List</title>
12    </head>
13
14        <!-- begin body of document -->
```

Figure 30.2 Adding the title to the JSP.

4. *Adding a header element to the body of the JSP.* The **body element** (delimited by the tags on lines 15 and 18 of Fig. 30.3) contains the HTML elements that will be displayed in the Web browser window when the JSP is loaded into the browser. The body element contains the document's content, such as text, images and buttons. HTML provides various levels of **header elements** to specify the relative importance of information. Add line 16 of Fig. 30.3 to insert a header element in the JSP that displays text Available Books. Header element **h1** (line 16) is the highest-level header and typically is rendered in a large font by the Web browser. Figure 30.8 shows the `h1` element as rendered by the browser.

Adding an h1 header element ———

```
14        <!-- begin body of document -->
15    <body>
16        <h1>Available Books</h1>
17
18    </body>
19  </html>
```

Figure 30.3 Adding a header to the JSP.

(cont.)   5. ***Creating a form.*** The JSP `books.jsp` should allow the user to select a book title from a menu then click a button to view the book information. HTML provides a mechanism called a **form** for collecting user input. Add lines 18–21 of Fig. 30.4 to insert a form in the JSP.

Creating an HTML form

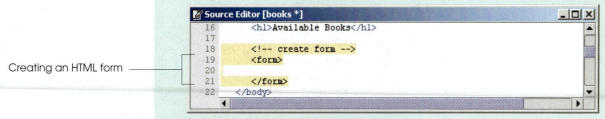

Figure 30.4 Creating a form in the JSP.

6. ***Creating a paragraph of text.*** Add lines 21–22 of Fig. 30.5 inside the form element of the JSP. The **paragraph tag**s (`<p>` and `</p>`) in lines 21–22 delimit text that will be displayed in a **p** (**paragraph**) **element**. All text placed between the `<p>` and `</p>` tags forms one paragraph. Browsers normally place a blank line before and after each paragraph. Figure 30.8 shows the paragraph element as rendered by the browser.

Creating a paragraph of text

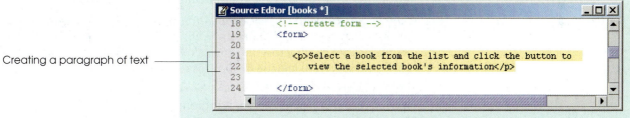

Figure 30.5 Creating a paragraph of text in the JSP.

7. ***Creating a menu.*** Add lines 24–27 of Fig. 30.6 inside the form element of the JSP. The **select element** (lines 25–27) provides a drop-down list, also known as an **HTML menu control**, of items from which the user can select an item. [*Note:* We normally refer to GUI elements as "components" in Java. In HTML, GUI elements are called "controls."] Figure 30.8 shows the select element as rendered by the browser. Notice that the size (width) of the drop-down list is small because you have not added items yet. The **name attribute** identifies the drop-down list and is similar to a variable name in Java code. For the moment, the select element will not display any book titles. In the next two tutorials, you will retrieve information from the database and populate the select element with the titles of the books listed in the database.

Creating an HTML menu control

```
22          view the selected book's information.</p>
23
24          <!-- create list that contains book titles -->
25          <select name = "bookTitle">
26
27          </select>
28
29      </form>
```

Figure 30.6 Creating an empty `select` element in the JSP.

(cont.)

8. ***Adding a button.*** Add lines 29–30 of Fig. 30.7 to insert a button control in the JSP. Line 30 defines an **input** element with the **type** attribute set to **"submit"**, which indicates that this input element is a **"submit" button**. The input element can be used to add various input controls (such as a text input control and a button control) to the JSP. In this JSP, the input element in line 30 defines a button control. In Exercise 30.13, you will use the input element to add a text input control to the JSP. Figure 30.8 shows the **"submit"** button as rendered by the browser. When the user clicks a **"submit"** button, the browser sends the data in the form to the Web server for processing. The **value** attribute sets the text displayed on the button. If the value attribute is not specified, the default value is **Submit**.

Adding a "submit" button ——

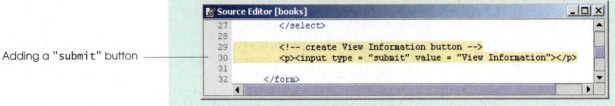

Figure 30.7 Adding the "submit" button to the JSP.

9. ***Saving the application.*** Save your modified source code file.

10. ***Copying the Bookstore Web application to the Tomcat webapps directory.*** To install the updated **Bookstore** Web application, copy the C:\Simply-Java\bookstore directory to Tomcat's webapps directory. This directory is C:\Program Files\Apache Group\Tomcat 4.1\webapps if you installed Tomcat in the default directory.

11. ***Starting Tomcat.*** Click **Start > Programs > Apache Tomcat 4.1 > Start Tomcat**.

12. ***Running the application.*** Open a Web browser and enter the URL http://localhost:8080/bookstore/books.jsp. Figure 30.8 displays the updated JSP. Notice that the HTML menu control does not contain any book titles. This is because you have not yet set up the database connections to retrieve the information. You will add this functionality to your application in the next two tutorials. Click the **View Information** button. Notice that nothing happens. Currently, you have specified only the visual aspects of the page. Thus, when you click the **View Information** button, you are not forwarded to bookInformation.jsp. You will add this functionality to your application in Tutorial 32.

HTML title element ——
Header (h1) element ——
Paragraph (p) element ——
HTML menu control (select element) ——
"submit" button (input element of type "submit") ——

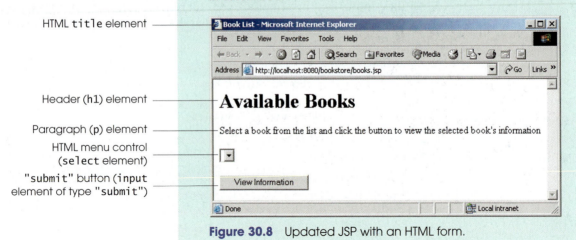

Figure 30.8 Updated JSP with an HTML form.

(cont.)

13. ***Closing the browser.*** Click the browser's close button to close the browser window.

14. ***Stopping Tomcat.*** Select **Start > Programs > Apache Tomcat 4.1 > Stop Tomcat** to stop the Tomcat Web server.

SELF-REVIEW

1. Use the _____ attribute to change the text displayed on the "submit" button.
   a) `text`   b) `name`
   c) `value`   d) None of the above.

2. The _____ element defines an HTML menu control (a drop-down list).
   a) `input`   b) `select`
   c) `h1`   d) `title`

Answers: 1) c. 2) b.

30.4 Creating the `bookInformation.jsp` Page

Now you will create the `bookInformation.jsp` page, which will display the information about the book that was chosen in the selection list.

Creating the
`bookInformation.jsp`
Page

1. ***Opening the `bookInformation.jsp` template file.*** Open the template file `bookInformation.jsp` (located in your working directory, `C:\Simply-Java\bookstore`) in your text editor.

2. ***Setting the JSP's title.*** Add lines 10–11 of Fig. 30.9 to the JSP. Line 11 sets the JSP's title to `Book Information`, which will be displayed in the Web browser's title bar. Figure 30.19 shows the `title` element as rendered by the browser.

Setting the JSP's title ──────

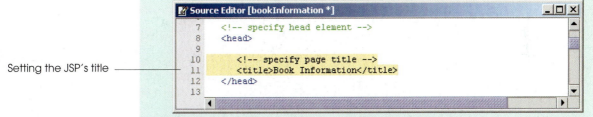

Figure 30.9 Adding a title to `bookInformation.jsp`.

3. ***Adding a header element to the JSP.*** Add lines 17–18 of Fig. 30.10 to the JSP. Line 18 creates an empty `h1` header element that will be used to display the title of the selected book. You will specify the text of this `h1` header in Tutorial 32.

Adding an `h1` header element ──────

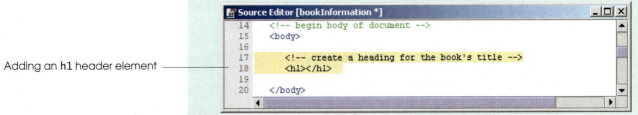

Figure 30.10 Adding the header that will specify the book title.

(cont.)

4. ***Adding an image to the JSP.*** Add lines 20–21 of Fig. 30.11 to the JSP. Line 21 uses an **img** element to insert an image into the JSP. This img element will display the cover image of the selected book. The image file's location (that is, its "source") is specified with the img element's **src** attribute. This is empty now, but you will specify it in Tutorial 32. Every img element has an **alt** attribute—if a browser cannot render an image (this might happen if the Web server cannot find the image file), the browser then displays the alt attribute's value (a string that specifies the text to display). In this case, the values of the src attribute and alt attribute are empty strings. We will change these values in Tutorial 32. Figure 30.19 shows the img element as rendered by the browser. Just like the input element, the img element is an **empty element**, that is, no text is placed between its tags.

Adding an image to the JSP ——

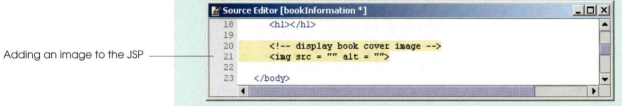

Figure 30.11   Adding the img element that will specify the book's cover.

5. ***Creating the authors paragraph.*** Add lines 23–24 of Fig. 30.12 to the JSP. Line 24 creates the paragraph that displays the label Author(s):. In Tutorial 32, you will retrieve information from the database and populate this p (paragraph) element with the authors of the selected book. Figure 30.19 shows the paragraph element as rendered by the browser.

Adding the authors paragraph ——

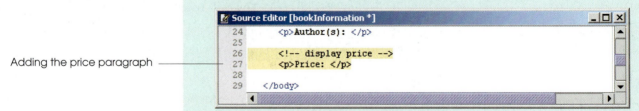

Figure 30.12   Adding the authors paragraph.

6. ***Creating the price paragraph.*** Add lines 26–27 of Fig. 30.13 to the JSP. Line 27 creates the paragraph that displays the label Price:. In Tutorial 32, you will retrieve information from the database and populate this p (paragraph) element with the price of the selected book. Figure 30.19 shows the paragraph element as rendered by the browser.

Adding the price paragraph ——

```
┌─ Source Editor [bookInformation *] ─────────────── _ □ X ┐
│ 24        <p>Author(s): </p>                              ▲ │
│ 25                                                          │
│ 26        <!-- display price -->                           │
│ 27        <p>Price: </p>                                    │
│ 28                                                          │
│ 29     </body>                                            ▼ │
│ ◄                                                        ► │
└──────────────────────────────────────────────────────────┘
```

Figure 30.13   Adding the price paragraph.

7. ***Creating the ISBN paragraph.*** Add lines 29–30 of Fig. 30.14 to the JSP. Line 30 creates the paragraph that displays the label ISBN:. In Tutorial 32, you will retrieve information from the database and populate this p (paragraph) element with the ISBN number of the selected book. Figure 30.19 shows the paragraph element as rendered by the browser.

(cont.)

Adding the ISBN paragraph

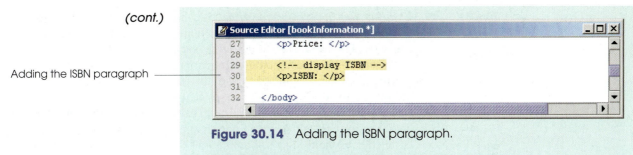

Figure 30.14   Adding the ISBN paragraph.

8. ***Creating the edition paragraph.*** Add lines 32–33 of Fig. 30.15 to the JSP. Line 33 creates the paragraph that displays the label `Edition:`. In Tutorial 32, you will retrieve information from the database and populate this p (`paragraph`) element with the edition number of the selected book. Figure 30.19 shows the paragraph element as rendered by the browser.

Adding the edition paragraph

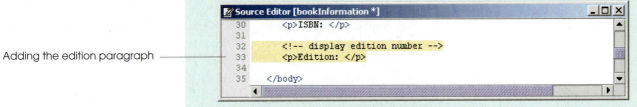

Figure 30.15   Adding the edition paragraph.

9. ***Creating the copyright year paragraph.*** Add lines 35–36 of Fig. 30.16 to the JSP. Line 36 creates the paragraph that displays the label `Copyright Year:`. In Tutorial 32, you will retrieve information from the database and populate this p (`paragraph`) element with the copyright year of the selected book. Figure 30.19 shows the paragraph element as rendered by the browser.

Adding the copyright year paragraph

```
Source Editor [bookInformation *]
33        <p>Edition: </p>
34
35        <!-- display copyright year -->
36        <p>Copyright Year: </p>
37
38   </body>
```

Figure 30.16   Adding the copyright year paragraph.

10. ***Creating the description paragraph.*** Add lines 38–39 of Fig. 30.17 to the JSP. Line 39 creates the paragraph that displays the label `Description:`. In Tutorial 32, you will retrieve information from the database and populate this p (`paragraph`) element with the description of the selected book. Figure 30.19 shows the paragraph element as rendered by the browser.

Adding the description paragraph

```
Source Editor [bookInformation *]
36        <p>Copyright Year: </p>
37
38        <!-- display description -->
39        <p>Description: </p>
40
41   </body>
```

Figure 30.17   Adding the description paragraph.

(cont.)

11. ***Creating the Book List hyperlink.*** Add lines 41–42 of Fig. 30.18 to the JSP. One of the most important HTML features is the **hyperlink**, which references (or links to) another resource, such as an HTML document or JSP. Links are created using the **a** (anchor) element. Figure 30.19 shows the anchor element as rendered by the browser. Line 42 defines a hyperlink that links the text Book List to the URL assigned to attribute **href** (which stands for **hyperlink reference**). The href attribute specifies the location of a linked resource, such as a Web page, a file or an e-mail address. This particular anchor element links to books.jsp. Notice that we used a relative URL to specify the location of the linked resource in line 42. A **relative URL** does not contain the protocol of the resource (such as http), the domain name of the resource or IP address of the resource. The relative URL contains only the path to the resource. In line 42, the relative URL is "books.jsp", which refers to the books.jsp page that is located in the same directory as the current JSP page (bookInformation.jsp). A relative URL should only be used when you specify a link to the Web resource that belongs to the same Web application (such as books.jsp in the **Bookstore** Web application). If you specify a link to the Web resource that does not belong to the same Web application (such as www.deitel.com), then the href attribute value should be the entire URL (such as www.deitel.com). The default operation of a hyperlink is to retrieve the Web resource specified by the href attribute. So when the user clicks the Book List hyperlink in Fig. 30.19, the JSP page books.jsp is retrieved and displayed in the client Web browser.

Adding a hyperlink ——————

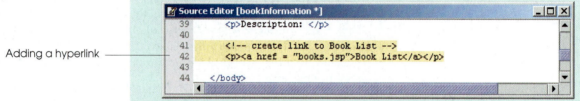

Figure 30.18   Adding the **Book List** hyperlink.

12. ***Saving the application.*** Save your modified source code file.

13. ***Copying bookInformation.jsp to the Tomcat webapps directory.*** Copy your completed bookInformation.jsp file from C:\SimplyJava\bookstore and paste it into the C:\Program Files\Apache Group\Tomcat 4.1\webapps\bookstore directory.

14. ***Starting Tomcat.*** Select **Start > Programs > Apache Tomcat 4.1 > Start Tomcat** to start the Tomcat server.

15. ***Testing the application.*** Open a Web browser and enter the URL http://localhost:8080/bookstore/bookInformation.jsp. Figure 30.19 displays the updated JSP. Notice that the paragraphs do not contain any book information. This is because you have not yet set up the database connections to retrieve the information. You will do this in the next two tutorials. Click the Book List hyperlink to cause the browser to load books.jsp.

16. ***Closing the browser.*** Click the browser's close button to close the browser window.

17. ***Stopping Tomcat.*** Select **Start > Programs > Apache Tomcat 4.1 > Stop Tomcat** to stop the Tomcat server.

(cont.)

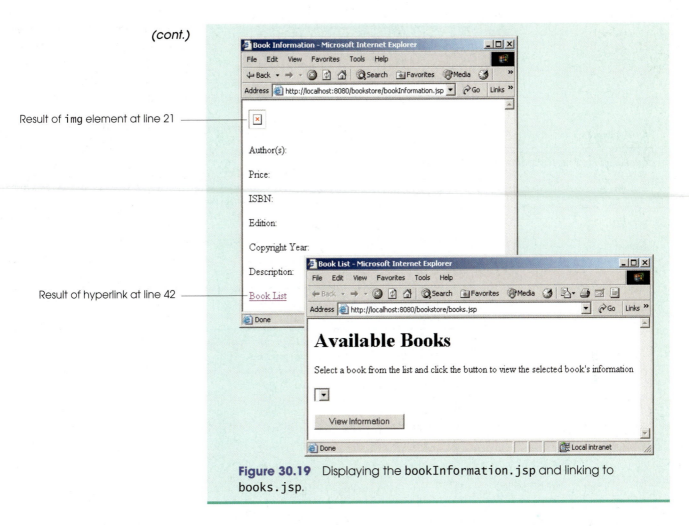

Result of `img` element at line 21

Result of hyperlink at line 42

Figure 30.19 Displaying the `bookInformation.jsp` and linking to `books.jsp`.

Figure 30.20 presents the source code of `books.jsp`. Figure 30.21 presents the source code of `bookInformation.jsp`. The lines of code that you added, viewed or modified in this tutorial are highlighted.

```
1    <!-- Tutorial 30: books.jsp -->
2    <!-- Displays a form.          -->
3
4    <!-- begin HTML document -->
5    <html>
6
7       <!-- specify HTML head element -->
8       <head>
9
10          <!-- specify page title -->
11          <title>Book List</title>
12       </head>
13
14       <!-- begin body of document -->
15       <body>
16          <h1>Available Books</h1>
17
```

Setting the JSP's title

Adding an **h1** header element

Figure 30.20 `books.jsp` code. (Part 1 of 2.)

Adding an HTML form that contains a paragraph, a drop-down list and a "submit" button

```
18      <!-- create form -->
19      <form>
20
21         <p>Select a book from the list and click the button to
22            view the selected book's information</p>
23
24         <!-- create list that contains book titles -->
25         <select name = "bookTitle">
26
27         </select>
28
29         <!-- create View Information button -->
30         <p><input type = "submit" value = "View Information"></p>
31
32      </form>
33   </body>
34 </html>
```

Figure 30.20   `books.jsp` code. (Part 2 of 2.)

```
1  <!-- Tutorial 30: bookInformation.jsp -->
2  <!-- Displays book information.         -->
3
4  <!-- begin HTML document -->
5  <html>
6
7     <!-- specify head element -->
8     <head>
9
10       <!-- specify page title -->
11       <title>Book Information</title>
12    </head>
13
14    <!-- begin body of document -->
15    <body>
16
17       <!-- create a heading for the book's title -->
18       <h1></h1>
19
20       <!-- display book cover image -->
21       <img src = "" alt = "">
22
23       <!-- display authors -->
24       <p>Author(s): </p>
25
26       <!-- display price -->
27       <p>Price: </p>
28
29       <!-- display ISBN -->
30       <p>ISBN: </p>
31
32       <!-- display edition number -->
33       <p>Edition: </p>
34
35       <!-- display copyright year -->
36       <p>Copyright Year: </p>
37
```

Setting the JSP's title — 11

Adding an empty **h1** header element — 18

Adding image — 21

Adding authors paragraph — 24

Adding price paragraph — 27

Adding ISBN paragraph — 30

Adding edition paragraph — 33

Adding copyright year paragraph — 36

Figure 30.21   `bookInformation.jsp` code. (Part 1 of 2.)

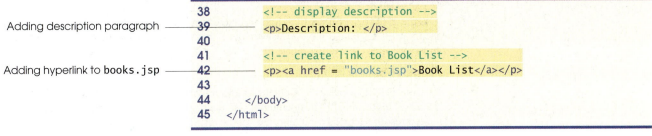

```
38              <!-- display description -->
39              <p>Description: </p>
40
41              <!-- create link to Book List -->
42              <p><a href = "books.jsp">Book List</a></p>
43
44          </body>
45      </html>
```

Adding description paragraph — lines 38–39

Adding hyperlink to `books.jsp` — line 42

Figure 30.21   `bookInformation.jsp` code. (Part 2 of 2.)

SELF-REVIEW   1. The `img` element's _____ attribute is used to set the location of the image file.

    a) `location`   b) `source`

    c) `src`   d) None of the above.

2. The `a` (anchor) element's _____ attribute specifies the location of a linked resource.

    a) `href`   b) `location`

    c) `reference`   d) `link`

Answers: 1) c. 2) a.

30.5 Wrap-Up

In this tutorial, you began creating the JavaServer Pages (JSPs) for your three-tier **Bookstore** Web application. You learned how to add HTML controls and elements to JSPs. The HTML controls you used in this tutorial include the menu control, which is specified by the `select` element, and the `"submit"` button, which is specified by the `input` element with the `type` attribute set to `"submit"`. You used other HTML elements in this tutorial including head, body, `form`, header (`h1`), paragraph (`p`), image (`img`) and hyperlink (`a`). You also learned attributes of various elements, including the `alt` and `src` attributes of the `img` element, the `name` attribute of the `select` element, the `type` and `value` attributes of the `input` element, and the `href` attribute of the `a` (anchor) element.

In the next tutorial, you will access the database, or information tier, of the application, which contains information about the books in the bookstore. You will use SQL to create the statements necessary to retrieve book information from the database. You also will create database `Connection` and `Statement` objects, which are used to perform database connection and processing. After you have created these database components, in Tutorial 32 you will create the middle tier of the bookstore, which provides functionality to the JSPs.

SKILLS SUMMARY

Setting a JSP title

■ Use the HTML `title` element to set the title displayed in the title bar at the top of the browser window.

Adding a header element to a JSP

■ Use the HTML `h1` element to add a header.

Creating an HTML form

■ Use the HTML `form` element to collect user input.

Adding an HTML menu control to a form

■ Use the HTML `select` element to add a drop-down list to an HTML form.

Adding a "submit" button to a form

■ Use the HTML `input` element with the `type` attribute set to `"submit"` to create a `"submit"` button. Use its `value` attribute to specify the text displayed on the button.

Displaying an image in a JSP

■ Use the HTML `img` element to add an image to a JSP. Use the `src` attribute to specify the location of the image file and use the `alt` attribute to specify the text to display if the browser cannot locate the image file.

Adding a hyperlink to a JSP

■ Use the HTML `a` (anchor) element to add a hyperlink, which links to another resource, such as a JSP or an HTML document. Use the `href` attribute to specify the location of the linked resource. Specify the text that will be displayed for the hyperlink in the JSP.

KEY TERMS

a (anchor) element in HTML—Used to create a hyperlink.

alt attribute of HTML img element—Specifies the text to display if the browser cannot locate an image.

body element in HTML—Contains the HTML elements that will be displayed in the Web browser window.

comment in HTML—Starting with `<!--` and ending with `-->`, an HTML comment is used to describe portions of an HTML document or JSP. HTML comments support multi-line text. Browsers ignore comments when they render HTML documents.

element in HTML—Markup used to specify a document's structure.

empty element—An element that does not place text between the start and end tags.

end tag in HTML—Consists of the element name preceded by a / in angle brackets, which ends an HTML element.

form element in HTML—Used to collect user inputs.

h1 element in HTML—The highest-level header element. Typically, an `h1` element is rendered by browsers in a large font.

head element in HTML—Specifies various settings of the document, such as its title.

header element in HTML—Used to specify the relative importance of information.

href (hyperlink reference) attribute of the a (anchor) element in HTML—Specifies a linked resource's location.

HTML markup—Contains text that represents the content of a document and elements that specify a document's structure.

HTML menu control—A drop-down list that is created by an HTML `select` element.

hyperlink in HTML—Used to reference other resources, such as HTML documents and JSPs.

HyperText Markup Language (HTML)—A markup language that specifies the format of text and images displayed in a Web browser, such as Internet Explorer or Netscape.

img element in HTML—Inserts an image in an HTML document.

input element in HTML—Creates a "submit" button.

name attribute of HTML select element—Identifies the drop-down list menu control. The identifier specified is similar to a variable name in Java.

p (paragraph) element in HTML—Adds a paragraph to a JSP or an HTML document.

relative URL—A relative URL does not contain the protocol of the resource (such as `http`), the domain name of the resource or IP address of the resource. The relative URL contains only the path to the resource.

select element in HTML—Creates an HTML menu control (also called a drop-down list).

src attribute of HTML img element—Specifies the location of the image file.

start tag in HTML—Consists of the element name in angle brackets, which starts an HTML element.

"submit" button—A button created by setting the `type` attribute of the input HTML element to `"submit"`.

title element in HTML—Sets the title displayed in the title bar at the top of the browser.

type attribute of HTML input element—Specifies the type of an `input` element. Setting the `type` to `"submit"` indicates that the `input` element is a `"submit"` button.

value attribute of HTML input element—Sets the text displayed on the `"submit"` button.

HTML REFERENCE

a (anchor) This element is used to add a hyperlink in an HTML document.
- *Attributes*

  href—Specifies the location of a linked resource.

---

body This element contains the HTML elements that will be displayed in the Web browser window.

---

form This element is used to insert a form in an HTML document to collect user inputs.

---

h1 This is the highest-level header element. Typically, an h1 element is rendered by browsers in a large font.

---

head This element specifies the settings of the document, such as its title.

---

img This element is used to insert an image in an HTML document.
- *Attributes*

  alt—Specifies the text to display if the browser cannot locate the image.

  src—Specifies the location of the image file.

---

input This element is used to create a "submit" button.
- *Attributes*

  type—Specifies the type of an input element. Setting the type to "submit" indicates that the input element is a "submit" button.

  value—Sets the text displayed on the "submit" button.

---

p (paragraph) This element adds a paragraph to a JSP or an HTML document.

---

select This element is used to create an HTML menu control.
- *Attributes*

  name—This attribute identifies the drop-down list menu control. The identifier used is similar to a variable name in Java.

---

title This element sets the title displayed in the title bar at the top of the browser window.

MULTIPLE-CHOICE QUESTIONS

30.1 You change the _____ attribute of the HTML input element to specify the text to be displayed on a "submit" button.

a) text

b) name

c) value

d) button

30.2 An HTML menu control can be added to a JSP using the _____ element.

a) select

b) menu

c) input

d) None of the above.

30.3 The _____ HTML element can be used to add a hyperlink to the JSP.

a) p

b) link

c) h1

d) a

30.4 The title element sets the _____.

a) text displayed on a button

b) first line displayed in the JSP page

c) title displayed in the title bar at the top of the browser window

d) None of the above.

30.5 The src attribute of the HTML img element _____.

a) specifies the type of the image

b) specifies the location of the image file

c) specifies the text displayed if the browser cannot render the image

d) specifies the size of the image

30.6 The HTML _____ element contains the HTML elements that will be displayed in the Web browser window.

a) input

b) head

c) body

d) title

30.7 The _____ element is used to create an HTML form.

a) form

b) htmlForm

c) h1

d) None of the above.

30.8 An HTML comment starts with _____ and ends with _____.

a) /*, */

b) <!--, -->

c) <--, -->

d) <!--, --!>

30.9 An HTML _____ provides a mechanism to collect user input from a Web page.

a) tag

b) form

c) element

d) comment

30.10 A _____ links to other resources.

a) hyperlink

b) button control

c) menu control

d) None of the above.

EXERCISES

30.11 (*Phone Book Application: GUI*) Create the user interface for the **Phone Book** application. The detailed description of this application can be found in Exercise 29.11. The design for the two pages for this application is displayed in Fig. 30.22. You will develop this application over this and the next two tutorials, so you do not yet have the names and numbers from the database. To help you to better understand what you are setting out to do, Figure 30.23 shows a test-drive-like full final screen output.

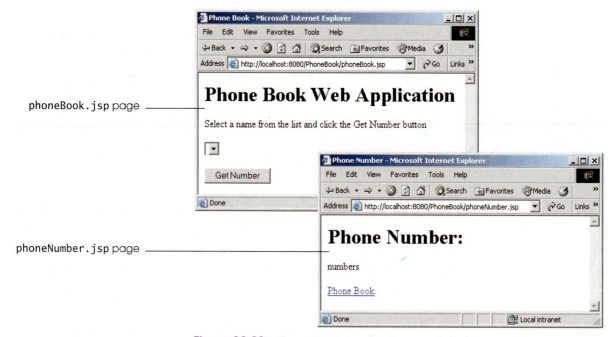

phoneBook.jsp page ——————

phoneNumber.jsp page ——————

Figure 30.22 **Phone Book** application user interface.

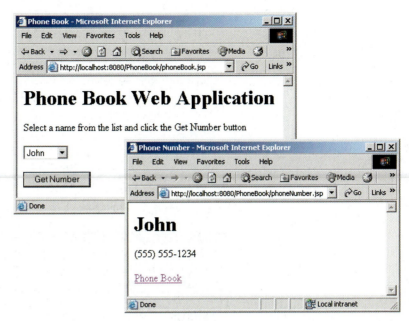

Figure 30.23 Completed **Phone Book** application.

a) *Copying the template to your working directory.* Copy the directory C:\Examples\ Tutorial30\Exercises\PhoneBook to the C:\SimplyJava directory.

b) *Opening the phoneBook.jsp template file.* Open the phoneBook.jsp file in your text editor.

c) *Setting the title of phoneBook.jsp.* Add a title element to set the JSP's title to "Phone Book."

d) *Adding an h1 header element to phoneBook.jsp.* Add an h1 header element that displays "Phone Book Web Application."

e) *Adding a form to phoneBook.jsp.* Add an HTML form element.

f) *Adding a paragraph to phoneBook.jsp.* Within the form element, add a paragraph that displays the instructions "Select a name from the list and click the Get Number button."

g) *Adding a menu control to phoneBook.jsp.* Within the form element, add a select HTML element. The name attribute for this select element is "personName"."

h) *Adding a submit button to phoneBook.jsp.* Within the form element, add a "submit" button. The text displayed on the button should be "Get Number." The "submit" button should be displayed inside a paragraph after the menu control.

i) *Saving the file.* Save your modified phoneBook.jsp.

j) *Opening the phoneNumber.jsp template file.* Open the phoneNumber.jsp file in your text editor.

k) *Setting the title of phoneNumber.jsp.* Add a title element to set the JSP's title to "Phone Number".

l) *Adding an h1 header element to phoneNumber.jsp.* Add an h1 header element that displays "Phone Number:."

m) *Adding a paragraph to phoneNumber.jsp.* Add a paragraph that displays "numbers."

n) *Adding a hyperlink to phoneNumber.jsp.* Add a hyperlink (with the text "Phone Book") that links to "phoneBook.jsp." The hyperlink should be displayed inside a paragraph after the paragraph that displays "numbers."

o) *Saving the file.* Save your modified phoneNumber.jsp.

p) *Copying the Phone Book application to the Tomcat webapps directory.* To install the **Phone Book** application, copy the C:\SimplyJava\PhoneBook directory to Tomcat's webapps directory. This directory is C:\Program Files\ Apache Group\Tomcat 4.1\webapps if you installed Tomcat in the default directory.

q) *Starting Tomcat*. Select **Start > Programs > Apache Tomcat 4.1 > Start Tomcat** to start the Tomcat server.

r) *Testing the application*. Open a Web browser and enter the URLs `http://localhost:8080/PhoneBook/phoneBook.jsp` and `http://localhost:8080/PhoneBook/phoneNumber.jsp` to test the application.

s) *Stopping Tomcat*. Select **Start > Programs > Apache Tomcat 4.1 > Stop Tomcat** to stop the Tomcat server.

30.12 (*US State Facts Application: GUI*) Create the user interface for the **US State Facts** application. The detailed description of this application can be found in Exercise 29.12. The design for the two pages for this application is displayed in Fig. 30.24. You will develop this application over this and the next two tutorials, so you do not yet have the state names, images and information from the database. To help you to better understand what you are setting out to do, Figure 30.25 shows a test-drive-like full final screen output.

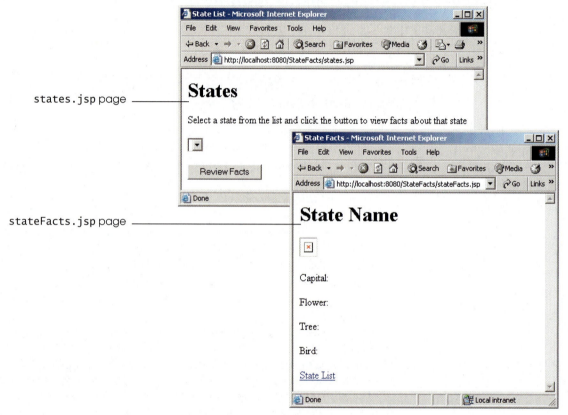

states.jsp page ————

stateFacts.jsp page ————

Figure 30.24 **US State Facts** application user interface.

a) *Copying the template to your working directory*. Copy the directory `C:\Examples\Tutorial30\Exercises\StateFacts` to the `C:\SimplyJava` directory.

b) *Opening the `states.jsp` template file*. Open the `states.jsp` file in your text editor.

c) *Setting the title of `states.jsp`*. Add a `title` element to set the JSP's title to "State List."

d) *Adding an `h1` header element to `states.jsp`*. Add an h1 header element that displays "States."

e) *Adding a `form` to `states.jsp`*. Add an HTML form element.

f) *Adding a paragraph to `states.jsp`*. Within the form element, add a paragraph that displays the instruction "Select a state from the list and click the button to view facts about that state."

g) *Adding a menu control to `states.jsp`*. Within the form element, add a select element. The name attribute for the select element is "stateName".

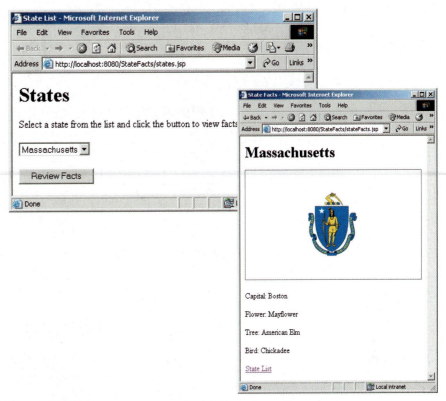

Figure 30.25 Completed **US State Facts** application.

h) *Adding a **submit** button to **states.jsp***. Within the form element, add a "submit" button. The text displayed on the button should be "Review Facts."

i) *Saving the file*. Save your modified states.jsp.

j) *Opening the **stateFacts.jsp** template file*. Open the stateFacts.jsp file in your text editor.

k) *Setting the title of **stateFacts.jsp***. Add a title element to set the JSP's title to "State Facts".

l) *Adding an **h1** header element to **stateFacts.jsp***. Add an h1 header element that displays "State Name".

m) *Adding an image to **stateFacts.jsp***. Add an img element to add an image to the JSP. The values of the src and the alt attributes should set to "" for now. You will modify the values of these attributes in the next two tutorials.

n) *Adding four paragraphs to **stateFacts.jsp***. Add four paragraphs that display "Capital:", "Flower:", "Tree:" and "Bird:" respectively.

o) *Adding a hyperlink to **stateFacts.jsp***. Add a hyperlink (with the text "State List") that links to the "states.jsp."

p) *Saving the file*. Save your modified stateFacts.jsp.

q) *Copying the State Facts application to the Tomcat webapps directory*. To install the **State Facts** application, copy the C:\SimplyJava\StateFacts directory to Tomcat's webapps directory. This directory is C:\Program Files\Apache Group\ Tomcat 4.1\webapps if you installed Tomcat in the default directory.

r) *Starting Tomcat*. Select **Start > Programs > Apache Tomcat 4.1 > Start Tomcat** to start the Tomcat server.

s) *Testing the application*. Open a Web browser and enter the URLs http:// localhost:8080/StateFacts/states.jsp and http://localhost:8080/State- Facts/stateFacts.jsp to test the application.

t) *Stopping Tomcat*. Select **Start > Programs > Apache Tomcat 4.1 > Stop Tomcat** to stop the Tomcat server.

30.13 (*Road Sign Review Application: GUI*) Create the user interface for the **Road Sign Review** application. The detailed description of this application can be found in Exercise 29.13. The design for the two pages for this application is displayed in Fig. 30.26. You will develop this application over this and the next two tutorials, so you do not yet have the images from the database. To help you to better understand what you are setting out to do, Figure 30.27 shows a test-drive-like full final screen output.

roadSigns.jsp page ────

input element with type "text" ────

roadTestRegistered.jsp page ────

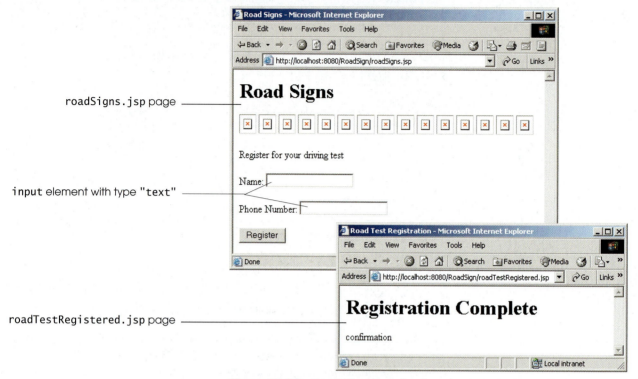

Figure 30.26   **Road Signs** application user interface.

Figure 30.27   Completed **Road Signs** application.

a) ***Copying the template to your working directory.*** Copy the directory `C:\Examples\Tutorial30\Exercises\RoadSign` to the `C:\SimplyJava` directory.

b) ***Opening the roadSigns.jsp template file.*** Open the `roadSigns.jsp` file in your text editor.

c) ***Setting the title of roadSigns.jsp.*** Add a `title` element to set the JSP's title to "Road Signs."

d) ***Adding an h1 header element to roadSigns.jsp.*** Add an h1 header element that displays "Road Signs."

e) ***Adding road sign images to roadSigns.jsp.*** Add 15 img elements to add the road sign images to the JSP. Set the `src` and the `alt` attributes of each element to `""` for now.

f) ***Adding a form to roadSigns.jsp.*** Add an HTML form element.

g) ***Adding a paragraph to roadSigns.jsp.*** Within the form element, add a paragraph that displays "Register for your driving test."

h) ***Adding a paragraph and an input element to roadSigns.jsp.*** Within the form element, add the code `<p>Name: <input type = "text" name = "name"></p>` to add an input element with type `"text"` that will display a text field for a user name.

i) ***Adding another paragraph and an input element to roadSigns.jsp.*** Within the form element, add the code `<p>Phone Number: <input type = "text" name = "phoneNumber"></p>` to add an input element with type `"text"` that will display a text field for the user's phone number.

j) ***Adding a submit button to roadSigns.jsp.*** Within the form element, add a "submit" button. The text displayed on the button should be "Register."

k) ***Saving the file.*** Save your modified roadSigns.jsp.

l) ***Opening the roadTestRegistered.jsp template file.*** Open the `roadTestRegistered.jsp` file in your text editor.

m) ***Setting the title of roadTestRegistered.jsp.*** Add a `title` element to set the JSP's title to "Road Test Registration."

n) ***Adding an h1 header element to roadTestRegistered.jsp.*** Add an h1 header element that displays "Registration Complete."

o) ***Adding a paragraph to roadTestRegistered.jsp.*** Add a paragraph that displays "confirmation."

p) ***Saving the file.*** Save your modified roadTestRegistered.jsp.

q) ***Copying the Road Sign application to the Tomcat webapps directory.*** To install the **Road Sign** application, copy the `C:\SimplyJava\RoadSign` directory to Tomcat's webapps directory—`C:\Program Files\Apache Group\Tomcat 4.1\webapps` if you installed Tomcat in the default directory.

r) ***Starting Tomcat.*** Select **Start > Programs > Apache Tomcat 4.1 > Start Tomcat** to start the Tomcat server.

s) ***Testing the application.*** Test roadSigns.jsp by entering `http://localhost:8080/RoadSign/roadSigns.jsp` in your browser, then test `roadTestRegistered.jsp` by entering `http://localhost:8080/RoadSign/roadTestRegistered.jsp` in your browser.

t) ***Stopping Tomcat.*** Select **Start > Programs > Apache Tomcat 4.1 > Stop Tomcat** to stop the Tomcat server.

Objectives

In this tutorial, you will learn to:
- Connect to a database.
- Create SQL statements that retrieve information from a database.

Outline

Bookstore Web Application: Information Tier

Examining the Database and Creating Database Components

This tutorial focuses on the **Bookstore** Web application's information tier, where the application's data resides. In your **Bookstore** Web application, the information tier is represented by a Cloudscape database, bookstore, that stores each book's information. Before you begin this tutorial, you should be familiar with the database concepts presented in Tutorial 26.

In this tutorial, you will create the Connection and Statement objects that your application will need to connect to the database and execute SQL statements. You also will define the SQL statements that will retrieve data from that database. Actually, the information tier consists solely of the bookstore database. The Connection objects and Statement objects created in this tutorial are actually part of the middle tier, as they perform the task of retrieving data from the database. You create these objects here because they are necessary to interact with the information tier. You will complete the **Bookstore** Web application by creating the middle tier in the next tutorial.

31.1 Reviewing the Bookstore Web Application

You took the three-tier **Bookstore** Web application for a test-drive (Tutorial 29) and have designed the GUI by using HTML elements (Tutorial 30). Now you are ready to create the database components for the application. In this tutorial, you will be creating the objects that are used to retrieve information from the database, including the objects that connect to the database and the objects that execute the SQL statements. Before you begin these tasks, review the ACE table and pseudocode of Tutorial 30, which lists the actions, components and events required to complete the application.

31.2 Information Tier: Database

The information tier maintains the data needed for an application. The database that stores this data might contain product data, such as description, price and quantity in stock, and customer data, such as user name and shipping information.

Databases are an integral part of real-world applications. As soon as a piece of data is entered into the database, it is accessible to users and applications with the proper authorization. Because data is stored electronically, it can be accessed

and manipulated much faster than paper copies. Most databases are relational databases—databases where the data is organized in tables and where those tables relate to one another. A variety of database products (used to build and modify databases) exist, ranging from "personal" products like Microsoft Access to industrial-strength enterprise products such as Oracle, Sybase, IBM's DB2 and Microsoft SQL Server. Database products also can be used to generate reports from information in databases.

The **Bookstore** Web application stores the data for the books in a Cloudscape database called `bookstore`. The data is retrieved from the database by using Java code and the JDBC API—a set of Java classes for working with databases. The database contains one table, named `products`, that stores each book's information.

The `products` table contains nine columns: `productID`, `title`, `authors`, `copyrightYear`, `edition`, `isbn`, `cover`, `description` and `price`. These columns contain the ID number, book title, authors, copyright year, edition number, ISBN (a unique number used to reference a book), cover image file name, description and price of each book, respectively. The contents of the `products` table are shown in Fig. 31.1 and Fig. 31.2. Figure 31.1 shows the data in the first three columns of the `products` table. Figure 31.2 shows the data in the remaining six columns of the `products` table.

productID	title	authors
1	Visual Basic .NET How to Program: Second Edition	Harvey M. Deitel, Paul J. Deitel & Tem R. Nieto
2	C++ How to Program: Fourth Edition	Harvey M. Deitel & Paul J. Deitel
3	C# How to Program: First Edition	Harvey M. Deitel, Paul J. Deitel, Jeff Listfield, Tem R. Nieto, Cheryl Yaeger & Marina Zlatkina

Figure 31.1   `products` table of the `bookstore` database.

copyright-Year	edition	isbn	cover	description	price
2002	2	0-13-029363-6	vbnethtp2.png	Microsoft Visual Basic .NET	75.99
2002	4	0-13-038474-7	cpphtp4.png	Introduces Web programming with CGI and object-oriented design with the UML.	75.99
2002	1	0-13-062221-4	csharphtp1.png	Introduces .NET and Web services	75.99

Figure 31.2   `products` table of the `bookstore` database (continued).

SELF-REVIEW

1. Once data is entered into a database, _____.

   a) the data is immediately accessible to users and applications with the proper authorization

   b) users must wait until the system reboots in order to access the data

   c) all applications using the database must manually be updated

   d) None of the above.

2. In relational databases, data is organized in _____.

   a) classes

   b) tables

   c) result sets

   d) None of the above.

Answers: 1) a. 2) b.

31.3 Using the Cloudscape Database in JSP Pages

Before you begin programming the middle tier of your **Bookstore** Web application in Tutorial 32, you must set up the database connections that will enable your application to retrieve data from the database. Using JDBC, you can create a `Connection` object to connect to a database and `Statement` objects to execute SQL statements. You then process the results of your SQL statements using `ResultSet` objects.

Adding Database Components to the books.jsp Page

1. **Copying the template to your working directory.** Copy the `C:\Examples\Tutorial31\TemplateApplication\bookstore_informationTier` directory to the `C:\SimplyJava` directory.

2. **Opening the books.jsp template file.** Open the `books.jsp` template file in your text editor.

3. **Adding a JSP scriptlet.** Add lines 30–44 of Fig. 31.3 to the JSP. This code adds a JSP **scriptlet** that will perform database connection and processing. A scriptlet enables programmers to insert blocks of Java code into a JSP.

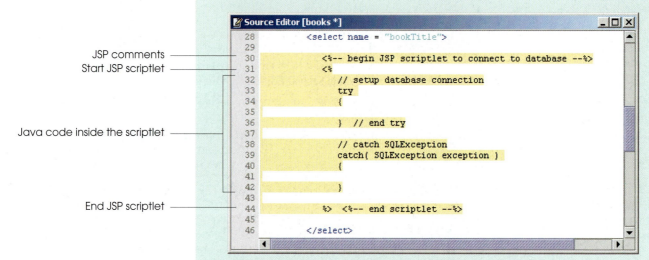

Figure 31.3 Adding the template for the JSP scriptlet.

Line 30 is a JSP comment. **JSP comments** are delimited by **<%--** and **--%>**. JSP comments and HTML comments can be placed throughout a JSP, but not inside scriptlets. Scriptlets are blocks of Java code delimited by **<%** and **%>**. [*Note*: When we show the `books.jsp` source code in Fig. 31.21, we color the symbols **<%** and **%>** in red, which makes it easy to see JSP scriptlets in the code.] Lines 31–44 create a JSP scriptlet. Scriptlets can contain `//` comments and comments delimited by `/*` and `*/`. Lines 33–36 declare a `try` block in which you will soon create `Connection`, `Statement` and `Resultset` objects. The `catch` block in lines 39–42 will catch any `SQLExceptions` that are thrown in the `try` block.

To use the `SQLException` and other classes for database connection and processing you need to import the `java.sql` package. We provide the code to import the `java.sql` package in the template. It is at line 5 of Fig. 31.21.

(cont.)   4. ***Specifying the database location.*** Add lines 35–37 of Fig. 31.4 to the JSP. The Cloudscape JDBC driver determines the locations of database files using system property db2j.system.home. Lines 36–37 calls the **setProperty** method of System to set this property to the location of the bookstore database. Method setProperty takes two String arguments—the first String specifies the system property name and the second String specifies the value to set for the property. In this case, the database should be located in C:\Examples\Tutorial29\Databases. In line 37, note the use of the \\ escape sequence to insert \ characters in the string that represents the database's location. [*Note*: If you copied and pasted the Tutorial29 directory on the CD to a directory other than C:\Examples, then replace C:\\Examples (line 37 of Fig. 31.4) with the directory where you pasted Tutorial29.]

```
Source Editor [books *]
33              try
34              {
35                    // specify database location
36                    System.setProperty( "db2j.system.home",
37                       "C:\\Examples\\Tutorial29\\Databases" );
38
39              } // end try
```

Specifying database location

Figure 31.4   Setting the location of the database.

5. ***Loading the Cloudscape database driver.*** Add lines 39–40 of Fig. 31.5 to the JSP. Line 40 loads the class for the Cloudscape JDBC driver using forName method of Class.

```
Source Editor [books *]
37                       "C:\\Examples\\Tutorial29\\Databases" );
38
39                    // load Cloudscape driver
40                    Class.forName( "com.ibm.db2j.jdbc.DB2jDriver" );
41
42              } // end try
```

Loading database driver class

Figure 31.5   Loading the database driver.

6. ***Creating the Connection object.*** You must set up a connection to the database before accessing its data. You will use a JDBC Connection object to accomplish this task. This Connection will allow you to create Statement objects to read book information from the database. Add lines 42–45 of Fig. 31.6 to the JSP to create the Connection object that connects to the bookstore database. Recall that the parameter passed to the getConnection method is a JDBC URL that specifies the database name and the protocols to access the database.

```
Source Editor [books *]
40                    Class.forName( "com.ibm.db2j.jdbc.DB2jDriver" );
41
42                    // connect to bookstore database
43                    Connection connection =
44                       DriverManager.getConnection(
45                          "jdbc:db2j:bookstore" );
46
47              } //end try
```

Connecting to
bookstore database

Figure 31.6   Connecting to the database.

(cont.)

7. ***Creating the Statement object.*** Add lines 47–53 of Fig. 31.7 to the JSP. Line 48 checks that the connection was created successfully in the previous step. Lines 50–51 create a `Statement` object that will use the database connection to execute SQL statements.

Creating `Statement` object to execute SQL statement

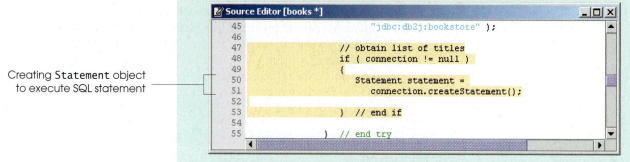

Figure 31.7 Creating a `Statement` object.

8. ***Executing the query.*** You must use the `Statement` object's `executeQuery` method to execute a query that obtains information from the database. The `executeQuery` method returns a `ResultSet` object, which contains the results of the query. Add lines 53–54 of Fig. 31.8 to retrieve the book titles from the `products` table. In Tutorial 32, you will add code to process this `ResultSet` to populate the menu control in the `books.jsp` page.

Executing query to get book titles

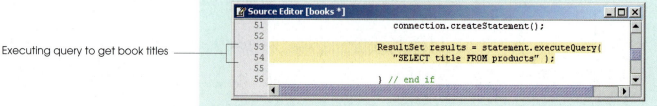

Figure 31.8 Getting information from the database

9. ***Closing the database connection.*** Recall that you need to close the database connection to release the database resource after the data processing is done. Add line 58 of Fig. 31.9 to the JSP. This code will close the database connection by calling the `close` method of class `Connection`.

Closing database connection

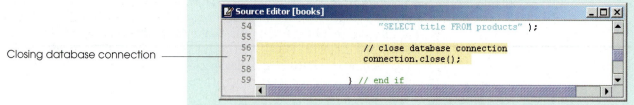

Figure 31.9 Closing the connection to the database.

10. ***Catching exceptions thrown by accessing the database.*** Add lines 66–67 of Fig. 31.10 to the JSP. If an exception is thrown in the `try` block, lines 66–67 will display an appropriate error message. The **out** object in line 66 is an implicit object in JSP. **Implicit objects** are a set of Java objects that provide programmers with access to the request from the client and the response to the client in the context of a JavaServer Page. The programmer does not have to explicitly create the implicit object to use it. This **out** object uses the `println` method to write string content as part of the response to a request.

(cont.)

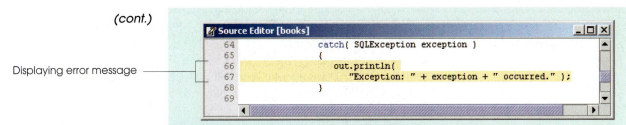

Displaying error message

```
64            catch( SQLException exception )
65            {
66                out.println(
67                    "Exception: " + exception + " occurred." );
68            }
69
```

Figure 31.10 Ending the JSP scriptlet and catching exceptions.

11. *Saving the application.* Save your modified source code file.

12. *Copying books.jsp to the bookstore directory.* Copy your modified books.jsp file and paste it into the C:\Program Files\Apache Group\ Tomcat 4.1\webapps\bookstore directory.

13. *Copying the database JAR files to the Bookstore Web application.* The information tier for the **Bookstore** Web application uses the Cloudscape database. You need to copy the db2j.jar and license.jar files to the C:\Program Files\Apache Group\Tomcat 4.1\webapps\bookstore\ WEB-INF\lib directory. The db2j.jar and license.jar files are located in the C:\Cloudscape_5.1\lib directory. In Tutorial 26, if you installed Cloudscape in a directory other than C:\Cloudscape_5.1, replace C:\Cloudscape_5.1 with your Cloudscape installation.

14. *Starting Tomcat.* Select **Start > Programs > Apache Tomcat 4.1 > Start Tomcat** to start the Tomcat server.

15. *Testing the application.* Open a Web browser and enter the URL http:// localhost:8080/bookstore/books.jsp. Figure 31.11 shows the updated books.jsp page running. Notice that the client GUI is the same as before. This is because you have not yet added the book titles to the menu control. You will add this code in the next tutorial.

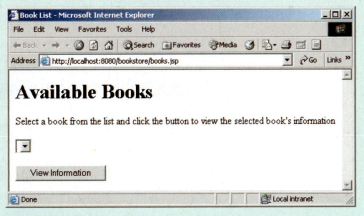

Figure 31.11 Running the updated books.jsp page.

16. *Closing the browser.* Click the browser's close button to close the browser window.

17. *Stopping Tomcat.* Select **Start > Programs > Apache Tomcat 4.1 > Stop Tomcat** to stop the Tomcat server.

Now that you have added database Connection and Statement objects to the books.jsp page, you will do the same for the bookInformation.jsp page.

<table>
<tr><td>

***Adding Database
Components to the
bookInformation.jsp
Page***

</td><td>

1. ***Opening the bookInformation.jsp template file***. Open the bookInforma-tion.jsp template file (located in directory C:\SimplyJava\ bookstore_informationTier) in your text editor.

2. ***Starting a JSP scriptlet.*** Add lines 23–27 of Fig. 31.12 to the JSP. This code starts the JSP scriptlet that will be used to connect to the database.

</td></tr>
</table>

Figure 31.12   Adding the template for the JSP scriptlet.

3. ***Specifying the database location***. Add lines 28–30 of Fig. 31.13 to the JSP. Lines 29–30 specify the location of the database. [*Note*: If you copied and pasted the Tutorial29 directory on the CD to a directory other than C:\Examples, then replace C:\\Examples (line 37 of Fig. 31.4) with the directory where you pasted Tutorial29.]

Figure 31.13   Setting the location of the database.

4. ***Loading the Cloudscape driver.*** Add lines 32–33 of Fig. 31.14 to the JSP. Line 33 loads the Cloudscape JDBC driver.

Figure 31.14   Loading the database driver.

5. ***Creating the Connection object.*** Add lines 35–37 of Fig. 31.15 to the JSP. You must set up a connection to the database before accessing its data. You will use a Connection object to accomplish this task. This Connection will allow you to read book information from the database. Lines 35–37 calls the getConnection method of DriverManager to connect to the bookstore database.

(cont.)

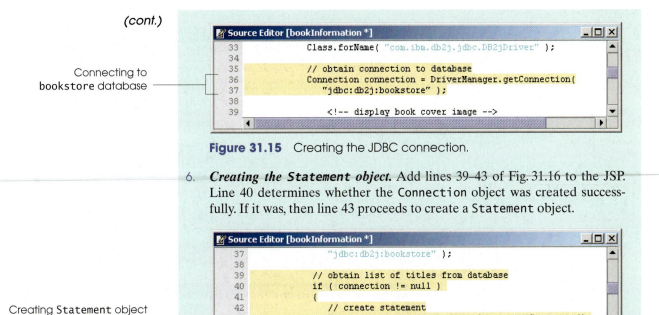

```
Source Editor [bookInformation *]                        _ □ ×
 33              Class.forName( "com.ibm.db2j.jdbc.DB2jDriver" );
 34
 35          // obtain connection to database
 36          Connection connection = DriverManager.getConnection(
 37              "jdbc:db2j:bookstore" );
 38
 39              <!-- display book cover image -->
```

Figure 31.15   Creating the JDBC connection.

6. ***Creating the Statement object.*** Add lines 39–43 of Fig. 31.16 to the JSP. Line 40 determines whether the `Connection` object was created successfully. If it was, then line 43 proceeds to create a `Statement` object.

```
Source Editor [bookInformation *]                        _ □ ×
 37              "jdbc:db2j:bookstore" );
 38
 39          // obtain list of titles from database
 40          if ( connection != null )
 41          {
 42              // create statement
 43              Statement statement = connection.createStatement();
 44
 45              <!-- display book cover image -->
```

Figure 31.16   Creating the `Statement` object.

7. ***Executing the query.*** Next, you must execute a query to obtain information about the selected book from the database. Add lines 45–50 of Fig. 31.17 to the JSP. This statement will retrieve the `cover`, `title`, `authors`, `price`, `isbn`, `edition`, `copyrightYear` and `description` columns from the `products` table for the book title the user selected in the `books.jsp` page. When specifying the SQL statement, line 50 uses the **`getParameter`** method of the JSP implicit object **`request`** to obtain the value for parameter `bookTitle`. Method `getParameter` accepts one `String` argument that specifies the parameter name and returns a `String` which is the value of the specified parameter name. The implicit object `request` represents the request from the Web browser client and is used to access user input and other data in the client Web page. Recall that in Fig. 30.6 of Tutorial 30, we created an empty menu control using the HTML `select` element and specified `bookTitle` as the `name` attribute of the HTML `select` element. When the user clicks the `"submit"` button in `books.jsp`, the browser associates the user-selected title with the name `bookTitle` and passes this information to `bookInformation.jsp` as part of the request. Calling the `request.getParameter` method with the argument `"bookTitle"` will return the book title that the user selected in `books.jsp`. Recall that SQL uses the single-quote (`'`) character as a delimiter for strings. So lines 49–50 use the single-quote character to delimit the `String` returned by the `get-Parameter` method.

Connecting to `bookstore` database

Creating `Statement` object to execute an SQL statement

(cont.)

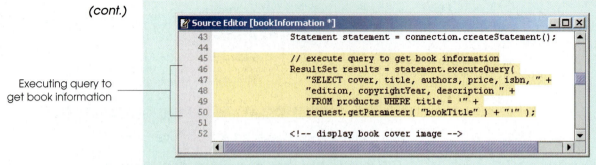

Executing query to get book information

Figure 31.17   Executing the query.

8. ***Ending the scriptlet.*** Add line 52 of Fig. 31.18 to the JSP to end the scriptlet. You need to end the scriptlet here because literal HTML markup cannot be placed in a JSP scriptlet. JSP scriptlet can contain only Java code. You will continue the scriptlet to close the database connection in the next step.

Ending scriptlet

Figure 31.18   Ending the scriptlet so that literal HTML markup can be inserted in the response to the client.

9. ***Closing the connection.*** Recall that you need to close the database connection to release the resource. Add lines 78–92 of Fig. 31.19 to the JSP. Lines 78–92 continue the scriptlet (line 78), close the database connection (line 80) and provide the exception handler (lines 87–90). Line 80 closes the Connection object by calling its close method. Line 82 ends the if statement started in line 40 (Fig. 31.16). Line 84 ends the try statement started at line 26 (Fig. 31.12). Lines 87–90 catch exceptions thrown by the try statement.

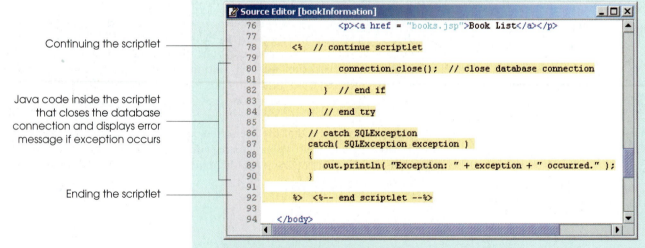

Continuing the scriptlet

Java code inside the scriptlet that closes the database connection and displays error message if exception occurs

Ending the scriptlet

Figure 31.19   Closing the database connection.

10. ***Saving the application.*** Save your modified source code file.

11. ***Copying bookInformation.jsp to the bookstore directory.*** Copy your modified bookInformation.jsp file and paste it into the C:\Program Files\Apache Group\Tomcat 4.1\webapps\bookstore directory.

(cont.)

12. ***Copying the database JAR files to the Bookstore Web application.*** The information tier for the **Bookstore** Web application uses the Cloudscape database. You need to copy the db2j.jar and license.jar files to the C:\Program Files\Apache Group\Tomcat 4.1\webapps\bookstore\WEB-INF\lib directory. The db2j.jar and license.jar files are located in the C:\Cloudscape_5.1\lib directory. In Tutorial 26, if you installed Cloudscape in a directory other than C:\Cloudscape_5.1, replace C:\Cloudscape_5.1 with your Cloudscape installation.

13. ***Starting Tomcat.*** Select **Start > Programs > Apache Tomcat 4.1 > Start Tomcat** to start the Tomcat server.

14. ***Testing the application.*** Open a Web browser and enter the URL http://localhost:8080/bookstore/bookInformation.jsp. Figure 31.20 shows the updated the bookInformation.jsp page running. Notice that the output is the same as in Tutorial 30, because you have not yet inserted the book information in the response to the client.

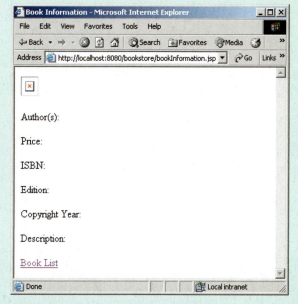

Figure 31.20   Running the updated bookInformation.jsp page.

15. ***Closing the browser.*** Click the browser's close button to close the browser window.

16. ***Stopping Tomcat.*** Select **Start > Programs > Apache Tomcat 4.1 > Stop Tomcat** to stop the Tomcat server.

Figures 31.21 and 31.22 present the source code files of books.jsp and the bookInformation.jsp, respectively. The lines of code that you added, viewed or modified in this tutorial are highlighted.

Import classes from package java.sql ———

```
1   <!-- Tutorial 31: books.jsp -->
2   <!-- Displays a form.          -->
3
4   <%-- import java.sql.* for database classes --%>
5   <%@ page import = "java.sql.*" %>
6
7   <!-- begin HTML document -->
8   <html>
```

Figure 31.21   books.jsp code. (Part 1 of 3.)

```
 9
10      <!-- specify HTML head element -->
11      <head>
12
13         <!-- specify page title -->
14         <title>Book List</title>
15      </head>
16
17      <!-- begin body of document -->
18      <body>
19         <h1>Available Books</h1>
20
21         <!-- create form -->
22         <form>
23
24            <p>Select a book from the list and click the button to view
25               the selected book's information</p>
26
27            <!-- create list that contains book titles -->
28            <select name = "bookTitle">
29
30            <%-- begin JSP scriptlet to connect to database --%>
31            <%
32               // setup database connection
33               try
34               {
35                  // specify database location
36                  System.setProperty( "db2j.system.home",
37                     "C:\\Examples\\Tutorial29\\Databases" );
38
39                  // load Cloudscape driver
40                  Class.forName( "com.ibm.db2j.jdbc.DB2jDriver" );
41
42                  // connect to bookstore database
43                  Connection connection =
44                     DriverManager.getConnection(
45                        "jdbc:db2j:bookstore" );
46
47                  // obtain list of titles
48                  if ( connection != null )
49                  {
50                     Statement statement =
51                        connection.createStatement();
52
53                     ResultSet results = statement.executeQuery(
54                        "SELECT title FROM products" );
55
56                     // close database connection
57                     connection.close();
58
59                  }  // end if
60
61               }  // end try
62
63               // catch SQLException
64               catch( SQLException exception )
65               {
```

Marginal labels (left column, top to bottom):

- JSP comment → line 30
- Start JSP scriptlet → line 31
- Specifying database location → lines 36–37
- Loading database driver class → line 40
- Connecting to the **bookstore** database → lines 43–45
- Creating **Statement** to execute SQL query → lines 50–51
- Executing query to get book titles → lines 53–54
- Closing database connection → line 57

Figure 31.21   books.jsp code. (Part 2 of 3.)

```
66                         out.println(
67                             "Exception: " + exception + " occurred." );
68                     }
69
70              %>   <%-- end scriptlet --%>
71
72          </select>
73
74          <!-- create View Information button -->
75          <p><input type = "submit" value = "View Information"></p>
76          </form>
77
78      </body>
79  </html>
```

Displaying error message — lines 66–67
End the scriptlet — line 70

Figure 31.21   `books.jsp` code. (Part 3 of 3.)

```
1   <!-- Tutorial 31: bookInformation.jsp -->
2   <!-- Displays book information.       -->
3
4   <%-- import java.sql.* for database classes --%>
5   <%@ page import = "java.sql.*" %>
6
7   <!-- begin HTML document -->
8   <html>
9
10    <!-- specify head element -->
11    <head>
12
13      <!-- specify page title -->
14      <title>Book Information</title>
15    </head>
16
17    <!-- begin body of document -->
18    <body>
19
20      <!-- create a heading for the book's title -->
21      <h1></h1>
22
23      <%-- begin JSP scriptlet to connect to a database --%>
24      <%
25          // setup database connection
26          try
27          {
28              // specify database location
29              System.setProperty( "db2j.system.home",
30                  "C:\\Examples\\Tutorial29\\Databases" );
31
32              // load Cloudscape driver
33              Class.forName( "com.ibm.db2j.jdbc.DB2jDriver" );
34
35              // obtain connection to database
36              Connection connection = DriverManager.getConnection(
37                  "jdbc:db2j:bookstore" );
38
39              // obtain list of titles from database
40              if ( connection != null )
41              {
```

Import classes from package `java.sql` — line 5
JSP comment — line 23
Start scriptlet — line 24
Specifying database location — lines 29–30
Loading database driver class — line 33
Connecting to the bookstore database — lines 36–37

Figure 31.22   `bookInformation.jsp` code. (Part 1 of 2.)

Creating `Statement` to execute SQL query

Executing query to get book information

End scriptlet to begin inserting literal HTML markup

Continue scriptlet

Java code inside the scriptlet that closes the database connection and displays error message if exception occurs

End scriptlet

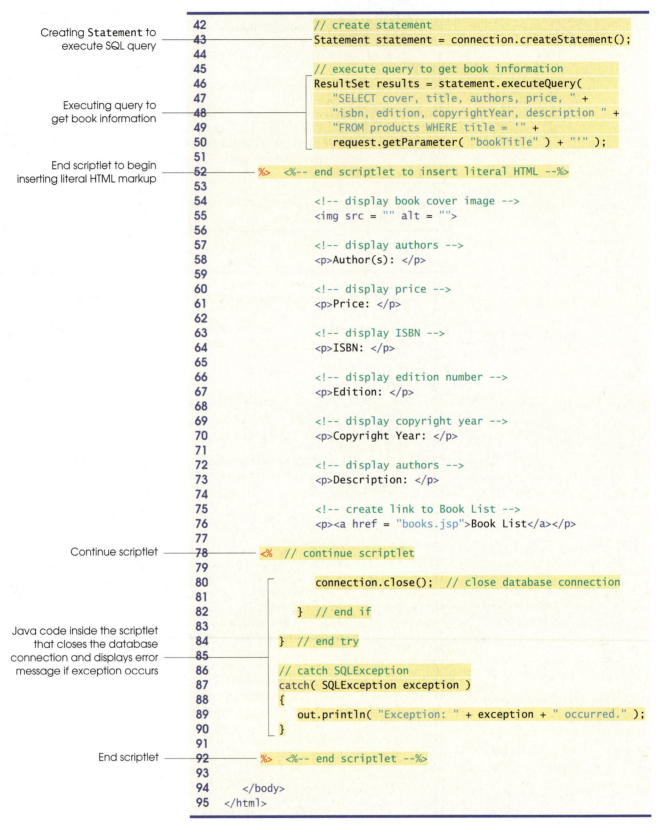

```jsp
42        // create statement
43        Statement statement = connection.createStatement();
44
45        // execute query to get book information
46        ResultSet results = statement.executeQuery(
47           "SELECT cover, title, authors, price, " +
48           "isbn, edition, copyrightYear, description " +
49           "FROM products WHERE title = '" +
50           request.getParameter( "bookTitle" ) + "'" );
51
52     %>  <%-- end scriptlet to insert literal HTML --%>
53
54        <!-- display book cover image -->
55        <img src = "" alt = "">
56
57        <!-- display authors -->
58        <p>Author(s): </p>
59
60        <!-- display price -->
61        <p>Price: </p>
62
63        <!-- display ISBN -->
64        <p>ISBN: </p>
65
66        <!-- display edition number -->
67        <p>Edition: </p>
68
69        <!-- display copyright year -->
70        <p>Copyright Year: </p>
71
72        <!-- display authors -->
73        <p>Description: </p>
74
75        <!-- create link to Book List -->
76        <p><a href = "books.jsp">Book List</a></p>
77
78     <%  // continue scriptlet
79
80              connection.close();  // close database connection
81
82           }  // end if
83
84        }  // end try
85
86        // catch SQLException
87        catch( SQLException exception )
88        {
89           out.println( "Exception: " + exception + " occurred." );
90        }
91
92     %>  <%-- end scriptlet --%>
93
94  </body>
95  </html>
```

Figure 31.22 bookInformation.jsp code. (Part 2 of 2.)

SELF-REVIEW

1. _____ comments can not be used inside scriptlets.

   a) HTML   b) Java

   c) JSP   d) Both a and c.

2. JSP scriptlets are delimited by _____.

   a) <%-- and --%>   b) <% and %>

   c) <!-- and -->   d) None of the above.

Answers: 1) d. 2) b.

31.4 Wrap-Up

In this tutorial, you were introduced to the information tier of the three-tier, Web-based **Bookstore** application. You examined the contents of the bookstore database. You accessed the information tier of the **Bookstore** Web application by creating JDBC Connection and Statement objects.

In the next tutorial, you will complete the middle tier of your **Bookstore** Web application. You will add code to your application to decide what data from the database will be displayed on the JavaServer Pages.

SKILLS SUMMARY

Adding a JSP comment

■ Delimited comment text with <%-- and --%>.

Adding a JSP scriptlet

■ Delimited scriptlet code with <% and %>.

■ Inside the scriptlet, add Java code to perform tasks such as connecting to a database.

Displaying error messages

■ Use the println method of the implicit object out to display error messages in JSP.

Retrieving user input in JSP

■ Use the JSP implicit object request's getParameter method to get the user input in a JSP.

KEY TERMS

getParameter method of the implicit JSP object request—Used to obtain the value of a request parameter.

implicit object—Provides the programmer with access to the request from the client and the response to the client in the context of a JavaServer Page. The programmer does not have to explicitly create the implicit object to use it.

JSP comment—Delimited by <%-- and --%>.

out implicit JSP object—Used to write text as a part of the response to a user request.

println method of the implicit JSP object out—Writes text as part of the response to a user request.

request implicit JSP object—Represents the client request. This object can be used to get data that is submitted to a JSP as part of the client request.

scriptlet—Block of code delimited by <% abd %> that enables programmers to insert Java code in a JSP.

setProperty method of System—Sets the system property, such as db2j.system.home.

JSP REFERENCE

JSP comment   A comment delimited by <%-- and --%>.

out   This implicit JSP object is used to write text as a part of the response to a client request.

■ *Methods*

   println—Writes text as part of the response to a client request.

request   This implicit JSP object represents the client request. This object can be used to get data that is submitted to a JSP as part of the client request.

- ■ *Methods*

   getParameter—Obtains the value of a request parameter.

scriptlet   A JSP scriptlet enables programmers to insert a block of Java code in a JSP. Scriptlets are delimited by <% and %>.

MULTIPLE-CHOICE QUESTIONS

31.1 _____ is an example of a database product.

a) Cloudscape	b) Microsoft SQL Server
c) Oracle	d) All of the above.

31.2 JSP _____ objects provide programmers with access to the request from the client and the response to the client in the context of a JavaServer Page.

a) Scriptlet	b) Explicit
c) Implicit	d) None of the above.

31.3 When a comment appears inside a JSP scriptlet, it must be a(n) _____.

a) // comment or a comment delimited by /* and */
b) HTML comment
c) JSP comment
d) All of the above.

31.4 The system property _____ specifies the database location.

a) db2j.system.home	b) db2j.system.database.home
c) db2j.system.location	d) db2j.system.database.location

31.5 The method getConnection of _____ can be used to create a Connection to a database.

a) DatabaseDriver	b) CloudscapeManager
c) DriverManager	d) None of the above.

31.6 You use a _____ object to execute SQL statements that retrieve data from a database.

a) Connection	b) Statement
c) DriverManager	d) None of the above.

31.7 _____ are used to add Java code to JSP pages.

a) JSP comments	b) JSP scriptlets
c) Both a and b.	d) None of the above.

31.8 You use the _____ object returned by the Statement method executeQuery to retrieve data from a database.

a) Connection	b) Statement
c) ResultSet	d) None of the above.

31.9 You use the _____ method of the implicit object request to get data that is submitted to the JSP as part of the client request.

a) getParameter	b) getValue
c) getField	d) getName

31.10 Another name for the database tier is _____.

a) the information tier	b) the bottom tier
c) Both a and b.	d) None of the above.

EXERCISES   **31.11** (*Phone Book Application: Database*) Use JSP scriptlets to create the database Connection and Statement objects for the **Phone Book** application. The phonebook database has the table phoneNumbers, which contains three columns—id, name and phoneNumber. The id field is a unique number to identify a person. The name field is a string that specifies the person's name. The phoneNumber field is a string that indicates the person's phone number.

a) *Opening **phoneBook.jsp***. Open the phoneBook.jsp file that you created in Exercise 30.11.

b) *Importing classes from **java.sql** for use in the JSP.* Copy lines 4–5 of Fig. 31.21 and insert them in line 4 of phoneBook.jsp.

c) *Adding a JSP scriptlet*. Inside the select HTML element in the phoneBook.jsp source code add a JSP scriptlet that contains a try block and a catch block that catches SQLExceptions thrown from the try block.

d) *Adding a **Connection** to the database*. In the try block declared in the previous step, specify the database location with value "C:\\Examples\\Tutorial31\\Exercises\\Databases", load the database driver class and connect to the phonebook database (jdbc:db2j:phonebook). [*Note:* If you copied and pasted the Tutorial31 directory on the CD to a directory other than C:\Examples, then replace C:\\Examples with the directory where you pasted Tutorial31.]

e) *Creating a **Statement** and executing a query that retrieves names from the database.* In the try block, after the database connection is created successfully, create a Statement object that will be used to execute an SQL query. Execute a query that gets all the names from the database.

f) *Closing the database connection*. After executing the query, invoke the close method of the Connection object to disconnect from the database.

g) *Displaying the **SQLException** error message*. Inside the catch block of the phoneBook.jsp, display the SQLException error message using the println method of the implicit JSP object out.

h) *Saving the file*. Save your modified file phoneBook.jsp file.

i) *Opening **phoneNumber.jsp***. Open the phoneNumber.jsp file that you created in Exercise 30.11.

j) *Importing classes from **java.sql** for use in the JSP.* Copy lines 4–5 of Fig. 31.21 and insert them in line 4 of phoneNumber.jsp.

k) *Starting a JSP scriptlet*. In the phoneNumber.jsp source code, after the h1 HTML element, start a JSP scriptlet. Inside the scriptlet, start a try block.

l) *Adding a **Connection** to the database*. In the try block, specify the database location with value "C:\\Examples\\Tutorial31\\Exercises\\Databases", load the database driver class and connect to the phonebook database. [*Note:* If you copied and pasted the Tutorial31 directory on the CD to a directory other than C:\Examples, then replace C:\\Examples with the directory where you pasted Tutorial31.]

m) *Creating a **Statement** object and executing a query that retrieves information from the database.* After the database connection is created successfully, create a Statement object that will be used to execute an SQL query. Execute a query that gets the information of the person whose name the user selected.

n) *Ending the scriptlet*. Before the p (paragraph) HTML element containing "numbers," end the scriptlet you started in *Step k* so that literal HTML markup can be placed in the response to the client.

o) *Adding a second JSP scriptlet*. In the phoneNumber.jsp source code, after the paragraph HTML element containing the hyperlink to phoneBook.jsp, add a second JSP scriptlet that will close the database connection, end the try block and display an error message if an exception occurs.

p) *Saving the file*. Save your modified phoneNumber.jsp file.

q) *Copying the **phoneBook.jsp** and **phoneNumber.jsp** files to the Tomcat webapps directory*. Copy your updated phoneBook.jsp and phoneNumber.jsp files and paste them into the C:\Program Files\Apache Group\Tomcat 4.1\webapps\PhoneBook directory.

r) *Copying the database JAR files to the Phone Book Web application.* The information tier for the **Phone Book** Web application uses the Cloudscape database. You need to copy the db2j.jar and license.jar files to the C:\Program Files\Apache Group\Tomcat 4.1\webapps\PhoneBook\WEB-INF\lib directory. The db2j.jar and license.jar files are located in the C:\Cloudscape_5.1\lib directory. In Tutorial 26, if you installed Cloudscape in a directory other than C:\Cloudscape_5.1, replace C:\Cloudscape_5.1 with your Cloudscape installation.

s) *Starting Tomcat.* Select **Start > Programs > Apache Tomcat 4.1 > Start Tomcat** to start the Tomcat server.

t) *Testing the application.* Open a Web browser and enter the URLs http://localhost:8080/PhoneBook/phoneBook.jsp and http://localhost:8080/PhoneBook/phoneNumber.jsp to test the application.

u) *Stopping Tomcat.* Select **Start > Programs > Apache Tomcat 4.1 > Stop Tomcat** to stop the Tomcat server.

31.12 (*US State Facts Application: Database*) Use JSP scriptlets to create the database Connection and Statement objects for the **US State Facts** application. The statefacts database has the table states, which contains seven columns—id, name, flag, capital, flower, tree and bird. The id field is a unique number to identify a state. The name field is a string that specifies the state name. The flag field is a string that specifies a file name for an image of the state's flag, such as "flag1.png". The capital field is a string that indicates the state capital. The flower field is a string that indicates the state flower. The tree field is a string that indicates the state tree. The bird field is a string that indicates the state bird.

a) *Opening states.jsp.* Open the states.jsp file that you created in Exercise 30.12.

b) *Importing classes from java.sql for use in the JSP.* Copy lines 4–5 of Fig. 31.21 and insert them in line 4 of states.jsp.

c) *Adding a JSP scriptlet.* Inside the select HTML element of the states.jsp source file, add a JSP scriptlet that contains a try block and a catch block that catches a SQLException.

d) *Adding a Connection to the database.* In the try block declared in the previous step, specify the database location with value "C:\\Examples\\Tutorial31\\Exercises\\Databases", load the database driver class and connect to the statefacts database (jdbc:db2j:statefacts). [*Note:* If you copied and pasted the Tutorial31 directory on the CD to a directory other than C:\Examples, then replace C:\\Examples with the directory where you pasted Tutorial31.]

e) *Creating a Statement object and executing the query to retrieve state names in the database.* After the database connection is created successfully, create a Statement object that will be used to execute an SQL query. Execute a query that gets all the state names from the database.

f) *Closing the database connection.* After executing the query, invoke the close method of the Connection object to disconnect from the database.

g) *Displaying the SQLException error message.* Inside the catch block, display the SQLException error message using the println method of the implicit JSP object out.

h) *Saving the file.* Save your modified states.jsp file.

i) *Opening stateFacts.jsp.* Open the stateFacts.jsp that you created in Exercise 30.12.

j) *Importing classes from java.sql for use in the JSP.* Copy lines 4–5 of Fig. 31.21 and insert them in line 4 of stateFacts.jsp.

k) *Starting a JSP scriptlet.* In the stateFacts.jsp source code, after the h1 HTML element, start a JSP scriptlet. In the scriptlet, start a try block.

l) *Adding a Connection to the database.* In the scriptlet of the stateFacts.jsp, specify the database location with value "C:\\Examples\\Tutorial31\\Exercises\\Databases", load the database driver class and connect to the statefacts database. [*Note:* If you copied and pasted the Tutorial31 directory on the CD to a directory other than C:\Examples, then replace C:\\Examples with the directory where you pasted Tutorial31.]

m) *Creating a Statement and executing the query to retrieve state information in the database.* After the database connection is created successfully, create a `Statement` object that will be used to execute an SQL query. Execute a query that gets the information for the state name selected by the user.

n) *Ending the scriptlet.* End the scriptlet started in *Step k*, so that literal HTML markup can be placed in the response to the client.

o) *Adding a second JSP scriptlet.* In the `stateFacts.jsp` source code, after the paragraph HTML element that will display the bird name retrieved from the database, add a second JSP scriptlet that will close the database connection, end the `try` block and display the `SQLException` error message if an exception occurs.

p) *Saving the file.* Save your modified file `stateFacts.jsp`.

q) *Copying the `states.jsp` and `stateFacts.jsp` files to the Tomcat webapps directory.* Copy your updated `states.jsp` and `stateFacts.jsp` files and paste them into the `C:\Program Files\Apache Group\Tomcat 4.1\webapps\StateFacts` directory.

r) *Copying the database JAR files to the State Facts Web application.* The information tier for the **State Facts** Web application uses the Cloudscape database. You need to copy the `db2j.jar` and `license.jar` files to the `C:\Program Files\Apache Group\Tomcat 4.1\webapps\StateFacts\WEB-INF\lib` directory. The `db2j.jar` and `license.jar` files are located in the `C:\Cloudscape_5.1\lib` directory. In Tutorial 26, if you installed Cloudscape in a directory other than `C:\Cloudscape_5.1`, replace `C:\Cloudscape_5.1` with your Cloudscape installation.

s) *Starting Tomcat.* Select **Start > Programs > Apache Tomcat 4.1 > Start Tomcat** to start the Tomcat server.

t) *Testing the application.* Open a Web browser and enter the URLs `http://localhost:8080/StateFacts/states.jsp` and `http://localhost:8080/StateFacts/stateFacts.jsp` to test your application.

u) *Stopping Tomcat.* Select **Start > Programs > Apache Tomcat 4.1 > Stop Tomcat** to stop the Tomcat server.

31.13 (*Road Sign Review Application: Database*) Use JSP scriptlets to create the database `Connection` and `Statement` objects for the **Road Sign Review** application that you started developing in Tutorial 30. The `roadsigns` database has the table `signs`, which contains three columns—`id`, `name` and `sign`. The `id` field is a unique number to identify a road sign. The `name` field is a string that specifies the name of the road sign. The `sign` field is a string that specifies a file name for an image of the road sign, such as `"sign01.png"`.

a) *Opening `roadSigns.jsp`.* Open the `roadSigns.jsp` file that you created in Exercise 30.13.

b) *Importing classes from `java.sql` for use in the JSP.* Copy lines 4–5 of Fig. 31.21 and insert them in line 4 of `roadSigns.jsp`.

c) *Starting a JSP scriptlet.* In the `roadSigns.jsp` source code, after the h1 HTML element, start a JSP scriptlet. In the scriptlet, start a `try` block.

d) *Adding a Connection to the database.* In the `try` block, specify the database location with value `"C:\\Examples\\Tutorial31\\Exercises\\Databases"`, load the database driver class and connect to the `roadsigns` database (`jdbc:db2j:roadsigns`). [*Note:* If you copied and pasted the `Tutorial31` directory on the CD to a directory other than `C:\Examples`, then replace `C:\\Examples` with the directory where you pasted `Tutorial31`.]

e) *Creating a Statement and executing a query that retrieves road sign information from the database.* After the database connection is created successfully, create a `Statement` object that will be used to execute an SQL query. Execute a query that gets all the road signs from the database.

f) *Ending the scriptlet.* In the `roadSigns.jsp` source code, end the scriptlet started in *Step c* so that literal HTML markup can be placed in the response to the client.

g) *Adding a second JSP scriptlet.* In the `roadSigns.jsp` source code, after the `img` HTML element that will display the last road sign image retrieved from the database, add a second JSP scriptlet that will close the database connection, end the `try` block and display the `SQLException` error message if an exception occurs.

h) *Saving the file.* Save your modified file roadsigns.jsp.

i) *Copying the **roadSigns.jsp** file to the Tomcat **webapps** directory.* Copy your updated roadSigns.jsp file and paste it into the C:\Program Files\ Apache Group\Tomcat 4.1\webapps\RoadSign directory.

j) *Copying the database JAR files to the **Road Signs** Web application.* The information tier for the **Road Signs** Web application uses the Cloudscape database. You need to copy the db2j.jar and license.jar files to the C:\Program Files\Apache Group\Tomcat 4.1\webapps\RoadSign\WEB-INF\lib directory. The db2j.jar and license.jar files are located in the C:\Cloudscape_5.1\lib directory. In Tutorial 26, if you installed Cloudscape in a directory other than C:\Cloudscape_5.1, replace C:\Cloudscape_5.1 with your Cloudscape installation.

k) *Starting Tomcat.* Select **Start > Programs > Apache Tomcat 4.1 > Start Tomcat** to start the Tomcat server.

l) *Testing the application.* Open a Web browser and enter the URLs http:// localhost:8080/RoadSign/roadSigns.jsp to test the application.

m) *Stopping Tomcat.* Select **Start > Programs > Apache Tomcat 4.1 > Stop Tomcat** to stop the Tomcat server.

Objectives

In this tutorial, you will learn to:

- Write the functionality for the middle tier, using JSP.
- Process a **ResultSet** inside a JSP scriptlet.
- Use JSP expressions to insert content in a JSP.

Outline

Bookstore Web Application: Middle Tier

form Attributes method/action and Inserting Query Results in a JSP

I n Tutorial 30 and Tutorial 31, you built the client tier and created connections to the information tier of the **Bookstore** Web application. Using HTML elements, you were able to design the user interface of this Web-based application. In this tutorial, you will learn about the middle tier, then complete the **Bookstore** Web application by programming the middle tier's functionality. Recall that the middle tier is responsible for interacting with the client tier and the information tier. The middle tier accepts user requests for data from the client tier, retrieves the data from the information tier (that is, the database) and responds to the client's requests with Web content.

32.1 Reviewing the Bookstore Web Application

You have taken the three-tier **Bookstore** Web application for a test-drive (Tutorial 29) and have created the HTML elements (Tutorial 30) and database objects (Tutorial 31) for the application. Now you will write code to specify the functionality of the **Bookstore** Web application. In this tutorial, you will implement the interaction between the client tier and the database tier of the **Bookstore** Web application. This means that you will write the code that determines which book image will be displayed in the page and which information will be retrieved from the database and displayed. You also will write the code that redirects the client browser to another page when the **View Information** button is clicked. Before you begin these tasks, review the ACE table and pseudocode of Tutorial 30, which lists the actions, components and events required to complete the application.

32.2 Adding Functionality to the books.jsp Page

Although you have designed your **Bookstore** Web application's GUI and have added database connections, the **Bookstore** currently lacks necessary functionality, such as listing all available book titles, redirecting the client browser to another page when the View Information button is clicked or displaying book information for the user-selected book. You will now begin programming this functionality.

Displaying Book Titles in the `books.jsp` Page

1. ***Copying the template to your working directory.*** Copy the `C:\Examples\Tutorial32\TemplateApplication\bookstore_middleTier` directory to your `C:\SimplyJava` directory.

2. ***Opening the `books.jsp` template file.*** Open the `books.jsp` template file in your text editor.

3. ***Obtaining book titles.*** Add lines 56–62 of Fig. 32.1 to the JSP. This `while` statement will, after we complete it in the next step, display the titles of every book in the database. Lines 59–60 assign the book title retrieved from the `ResultSet` `results` to the `String` variable `currentTitle`.

`while` statement that iterates through the `ResultSet` and gets each book title

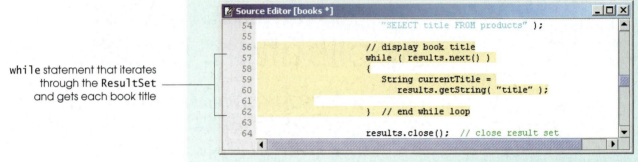

Figure 32.1   `while` statement that gets book titles from the `ResultSet`.

4. ***Displaying the book titles.*** Add lines 62–67 of Fig. 32.2 to the `while` loop begun in line 56. Line 62 ends the scriptlet in order to allow you to insert literal HTML markup as part of the `while` statement. Line 65 uses the HTML **option** element inside the HTML **select** element to add the book title to the HTML menu control. Figure 32.4 displays the output that has the book titles added to the menu control. The `option` element adds items to the menu control defined by the `select` element. You insert a book title in an `option` element by using a **JSP expression**. Each JSP expression is delimited by **<%=** and **%>**. JSP expressions are used to add dynamic content (such as information from a database) to Web pages. In line 65, the expression `<%= currentTitle %>` inserts the value of `currentTitle` (declared in lines 59–60 of Fig. 32.1) in the response to the client. Line 67 resumes the scriptlet, so you can continue inserting Java code in the JSP.

Adding book titles to HTML menu control

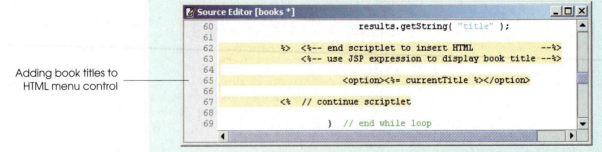

Figure 32.2   Displaying the current book title.

5. ***Closing the ResultSet.*** Add line 71 of Fig. 32.3 to the JSP. Line 71 calls `ResultSet` method `close` to release the resources held by `results`, such as the rows in the `ResultSet`.

(cont.)

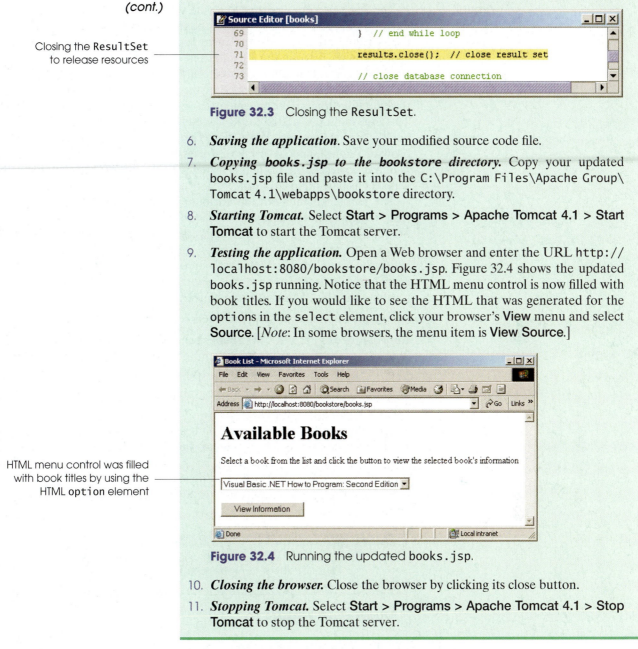

Closing the `ResultSet` to release resources

Figure 32.3   Closing the `ResultSet`.

6. *Saving the application.* Save your modified source code file.

7. *Copying books.jsp to the bookstore directory.* Copy your updated books.jsp file and paste it into the C:\Program Files\Apache Group\ Tomcat 4.1\webapps\bookstore directory.

8. *Starting Tomcat.* Select **Start > Programs > Apache Tomcat 4.1 > Start Tomcat** to start the Tomcat server.

9. *Testing the application.* Open a Web browser and enter the URL http:// localhost:8080/bookstore/books.jsp. Figure 32.4 shows the updated books.jsp running. Notice that the HTML menu control is now filled with book titles. If you would like to see the HTML that was generated for the options in the select element, click your browser's **View** menu and select **Source**. [*Note*: In some browsers, the menu item is **View Source**.]

HTML menu control was filled with book titles by using the HTML `option` element

Figure 32.4   Running the updated books.jsp.

10. *Closing the browser.* Close the browser by clicking its close button.

11. *Stopping Tomcat.* Select **Start > Programs > Apache Tomcat 4.1 > Stop Tomcat** to stop the Tomcat server.

Next, you will define the action for the HTML form in the books.jsp page. When the user clicks the **View Information** button (Fig. 32.4), the HTML form redirects the client browser to bookInformation.jsp.

Defining the action for the form in the books.jsp Page

1. *Specifying the action for a form element.* Modify line 22 as shown in Fig. 32.5 to specify the form elements's method and action attributes.

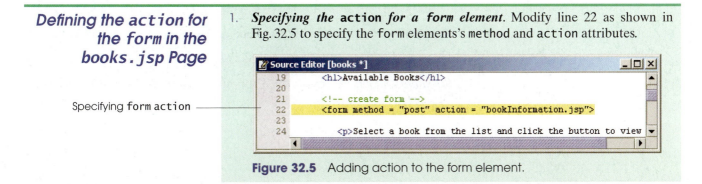

Specifying form action

Figure 32.5   Adding action to the form element.

(cont.)

The `form` element's **method** attribute specifies how the form's data is sent to the Web server. Using `method = "post"` appends user input (such as the user-selected book title) to the client browser request. Upon receiving the client browser request, the JSPs located on the Web server's computer can access the form data that are sent as part of the request. For example, when the user selects a book, the value of the `bookTitle` parameter (a variable that identifies the `select` element) is set to the title of the selected book. This information is added to the `request` object, so that it may be used in `bookInformation.jsp`. When `bookInformation.jsp` receives the client browser request, line 20 of Fig. 32.7 uses the method `getParameter` of the `request` to access the value associated with the `bookTitle` parameter that was sent as part of the request.

The `form` element's **action** attribute specifies where to send form data (user input) when the user submits the form (by clicking the **View Information** button in this application). In this case (line 22), it specifies a JSP named `bookInformation.jsp` that displays information for the selected book. When the user clicks the **View Information** button, the HTML form submits client input to `bookInformation.jsp`, which is the value of the `action` attribute (line 22). This causes the `bookInformation.jsp` to be requested.

2. ***Saving the application.*** Save your modified source code file.

3. ***Copying books.jsp to the bookstore directory.*** Copy your updated `books.jsp` file and paste it into the `C:\Program Files\Apache Group\Tomcat 4.1\webapps\bookstore` directory.

4. ***Starting Tomcat.*** Select **Start > Programs > Apache Tomcat 4.1 > Start Tomcat** to start the Tomcat server.

5. ***Testing the application.*** Open a Web browser and enter the URL `http://localhost:8080/bookstore/books.jsp`. Figure 32.6 shows the updated `books.jsp` running. Notice that the `bookInformation.jsp` page now loads if you click the **View Information** button. However, the actual book information is not displayed because you have not added this capability to `bookInformation.jsp` yet.

Clicking this button forwards the user's request to `bookInformation.jsp`

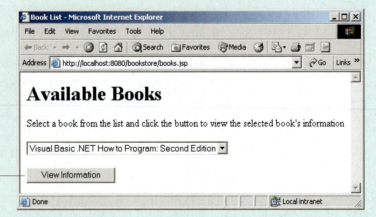

Figure 32.6 Running the updated `books.jsp` page.

6. ***Closing the browser.*** Close the browser by clicking its close button.

7. ***Stopping Tomcat.*** Select **Start > Programs > Apache Tomcat 4.1 > Stop Tomcat** to stop the Tomcat server.

SELF-REVIEW   1. The _____ element adds items to an HTML menu control.

a) `select`   b) `item`

c) `option`   d) None of the above.

2. The _____ attribute of the `form` element specifies the task to perform when the user submits the form.

a) `action`   b) `data`

c) `url`   d) None of the above.

Answers: 1) c. 2) a.

32.3 Adding Functionality to the bookInformation.jsp Page

Now, you will add to the `bookInformation.jsp` page the code that retrieves the requested book's information from the database.

Displaying Book Information in the bookInformation.jsp Page

1. ***Opening the bookInformation.jsp template file.*** Open the template file `bookInformation.jsp` in your text editor.

2. ***Displaying the book title in an h1 header element.*** Modify line 21 as shown in Fig. 32.7. Line 21 uses a JSP expression to get the value of the `bookTitle` parameter from the implicit JSP object `request` and place the value in an `h1` header element. Note that the `bookTitle` parameter corresponds to the name of the menu control (line 25 of Fig. 30.6).

Displaying book title in an **h1** header ─────

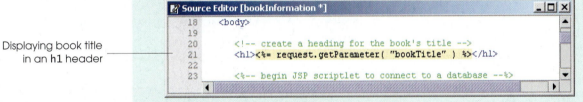

Figure 32.7   Displaying the book title.

3. ***Accessing the ResultSet results.*** Add line 52 of Fig. 32.8 to the JSP. Line 52 moves the cursor to the first row of the `ResultSet` results.

Calling method **next** for the first time positions the **ResultSet** cursor in the first row of the **ResultSet** ─────

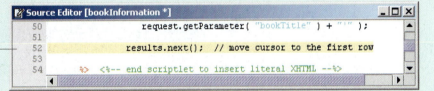

Figure 32.8   Accessing the ResultSet results.

4. ***Displaying the book cover image.*** Replace line 57 of the template file with lines 57–59 of Fig. 32.9. Lines 57–59 use two JSP expressions `<%= results.getString( "cover" ) %>` and `<%= results.getString( "title" ) %>` to retrieve the image file name of the book cover image and the book title from the database. The image file name is appended to `"images/"` then assigned to the attribute `src` of the `img` element. The image files are located in the `C:\Program Files\Apache Group\Tomcat 4.1\webapps\bookstore\images` directory. The book title is appended to `"Book cover for "`, which is then assigned to the attribute `alt` of the `img` element.

(cont.)

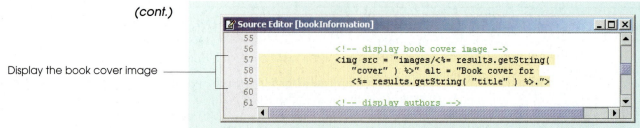

Display the book cover image

Figure 32.9 Displaying book cover image.

5. ***Displaying the authors.*** Replace line 62 of the template file with lines 62–63 of Fig. 32.10. Lines 62–63 use a JSP expression to obtain the `authors` from the `ResultSet results` and displays them in a paragraph element.

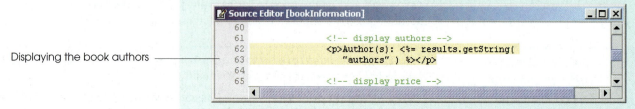

Displaying the book authors

Figure 32.10 Displaying the authors.

6. ***Displaying the price.*** Replace line 66 of the template file with line 66 of Fig. 32.11. Line 66 uses a JSP expression to obtain the `price` from the `ResultSet results` and displays it in a paragraph element.

Displaying the book price

Figure 32.11 Displaying the price.

7. ***Displaying the ISBN.*** Replace line 69 of the template file with line 69 of Fig. 32.12. Line 69 uses a JSP expression to obtain the `isbn` from the `ResultSet results` and displays it in a paragraph element.

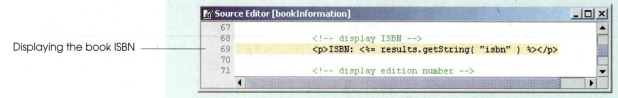

Displaying the book ISBN

Figure 32.12 Displaying the ISBN.

8. ***Displaying the edition.*** Replace line 72 of the template file with line 72 of Fig. 32.13. Line 72 uses a JSP expression to obtain the `edition` from the `ResultSet results` and displays it in a paragraph element. Recall that method `getInt` returns an `int` representation of the value in the `edition` column.

(cont.)

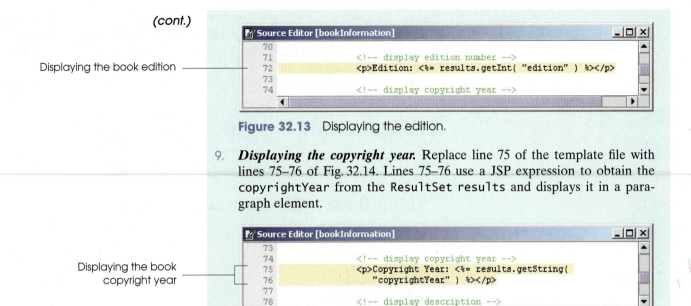

Figure 32.13   Displaying the edition.

Displaying the book edition

9. ***Displaying the copyright year.*** Replace line 75 of the template file with lines 75–76 of Fig. 32.14. Lines 75–76 use a JSP expression to obtain the copyrightYear from the ResultSet results and displays it in a paragraph element.

Displaying the book copyright year

Figure 32.14   Displaying the copyright year.

10. ***Displaying the description.*** Replace line 79 of the template file with lines 79–80 of Fig. 32.15. Lines 79–80 use a JSP expression to obtain the description from the ResultSet results and display it in a paragraph element.

Displaying the book description

Figure 32.15   Displaying the description.

11. ***Closing ResultSet results.*** Add line 87 of Fig. 32.16 to JSP. Line 87 closes the ResultSet results using the close method.

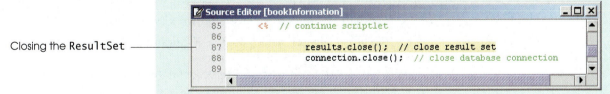

Closing the ResultSet

Figure 32.16   Closing the ResultSet.

12. ***Saving the application.*** Save your modified source code file.

13. ***Copying bookInformation.jsp to the bookstore directory.*** Copy your updated bookInformation.jsp file and paste it into the C:\Program Files\Apache Group\Tomcat 4.1\webapps\bookstore directory.

14. ***Starting Tomcat.*** Select **Start > Programs > Apache Tomcat 4.1 > Start Tomcat** to start the Tomcat server.

(cont.)

15. ***Testing the application.*** Open a Web browser and enter the URL `http://localhost:8080/bookstore/books.jsp`. Select "Visual Basic .NET How to Program: Second Edition" from the HTML menu control. Figure 32.17 shows the completed `bookInformation.jsp` running. Notice that the `bookInformation.jsp` page now displays the book information of the selected book title.

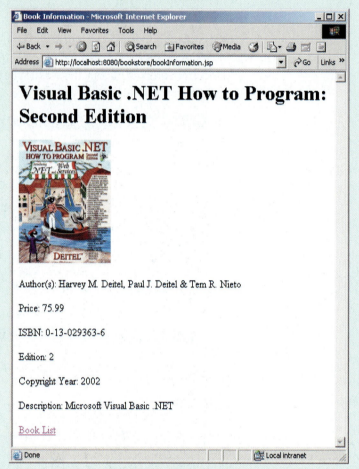

Figure 32.17 `bookInformation.jsp` page displaying book information. (Book image courtesy of Prentice Hall.)

16. ***Closing the browser.*** Close the browser by clicking its close button.

17. ***Stopping Tomcat.*** Select **Start > Programs > Apache Tomcat 4.1 > Stop Tomcat** to stop the Tomcat server.

Figure 32.18 and Fig. 32.19 display the complete code for the `books.jsp` and `bookInformation.jsp` pages of the **Bookstore** Web application, respectively. With the implementation of these JSPs, your three-tier **Bookstore** Web application is now complete.

```
1   <!-- Tutorial 32: books.jsp -->
2   <!-- Displays a form.        -->
3
4   <%-- import java.sql.* for database classes --%>
5   <%@ page import = "java.sql.*" %>
6
```

Figure 32.18 `books.jsp` code. (Part 1 of 3.)

```
 7    <!-- begin HTML document -->
 8    <html>
 9
10       <!-- specify HTML head element -->
11       <head>
12
13          <!-- specify page title -->
14          <title>Book List</title>
15       </head>
16
17       <!-- begin body of document -->
18       <body>
19          <h1>Available Books</h1>
20
21          <!-- create form -->
22          <form method = "post" action = "bookInformation.jsp">
23
24             <p>Select a book from the list and click the button to view
25                the selected book's information</p>
26
27             <!-- create list that contains book titles -->
28             <select name = "bookTitle">
29
30                <%-- begin JSP scriptlet to connect to database --%>
31                <%
32                   // setup database connection
33                   try
34                   {
35                      // specify database location
36                      System.setProperty( "db2j.system.home",
37                         "C:\\Examples\\Tutorial29\\Databases" );
38
39                      // load Cloudscape driver
40                      Class.forName( "com.ibm.db2j.jdbc.DB2jDriver" );
41
42                      // connect to database
43                      Connection connection =
44                         DriverManager.getConnection(
45                            "jdbc:db2j:bookstore" );
46
47                      // obtain list of titles
48                      if ( connection != null )
49                      {
50                         Statement statement =
51                            connection.createStatement();
52
53                         ResultSet results = statement.executeQuery(
54                            "SELECT title FROM products" );
55
56                         // display book title
57                         while ( results.next() )
58                         {
59                            String currentTitle =
60                               results.getString( "title" );
61
62                %>   <%-- end scriptlet to insert HTML        --%>
63                     <%-- JSP expressions output from this loop --%>
```

Specifying the form's action — line 22

Retrieving the book title from the ResultSet — lines 59–60

Figure 32.18   books.jsp code. (Part 2 of 3.)

Adding the book title to the HTML menu `control`

Closing the `ResultSet results`

```
64
65                                          <option><%= currentTitle %></option>
66
67              <%  // continue scriptlet
68
69                 }  // end while loop
70
71              results.close();  // close result set
72
73              // close database connection
74              connection.close();
75
76           }  // end if
77
78        }  // end try
79
80        // catch SQLException
81        catch( SQLException exception )
82        {
83           out.println(
84              "Exception: " + exception + " occurred." );
85        }
86
87        %>  <%-- end scriptlet --%>
88
89     </select>
90
91     <!-- create View Information button -->
92     <p><input type = "submit" value = "View Information"></p>
93  </form>
94
95  </body>
96 </html>
```

Figure 32.18 `books.jsp` code. (Part 3 of 3.)

```
1  <!-- Tutorial 32: bookInformation.jsp -->
2  <!-- Displays book information.         -->
3
4  <%-- import java.sql.* for database classes --%>
5  <%@ page import = "java.sql.*" %>
6
7  <!-- begin HTML document -->
8  <html>
9
10    <!-- specify head element -->
11    <head>
12
13       <!-- specify page title -->
14       <title>Book Information</title>
15    </head>
16
17    <!-- begin body of document -->
18    <body>
19
20       <!-- create a heading for the book's title -->
21       <h1><%= request.getParameter( "bookTitle" ) %></h1>
22
```

Displaying the book title specified in `books.jsp` in an `h1` header

Figure 32.19 `bookInformation.jsp` code. (Part 1 of 3.)

```
23        <%-- begin JSP scriptlet to connect to a database --%>
24        <%
25           // setup database connection
26           try
27           {
28              // specify database location
29              System.setProperty( "db2j.system.home",
30                 "C:\\Examples\\Tutorial29\\Databases" );
31
32              // load Cloudscape driver
33              Class.forName( "com.ibm.db2j.jdbc.DB2jDriver" );
34
35              // obtain connection to database
36              Connection connection = DriverManager.getConnection(
37                 "jdbc:db2j:bookstore" );
38
39              // obtain list of titles from database
40              if ( connection != null )
41              {
42                 // create statement
43                 Statement statement = connection.createStatement();
44
45                 // execute query to get book information
46                 ResultSet results = statement.executeQuery(
47                    "SELECT cover, title, authors, price, isbn, " +
48                    "edition, copyrightYear, description " +
49                    "FROM products WHERE title = '" +
50                    request.getParameter( "bookTitle" ) + "'" );
51
52                 results.next();  // move cursor to the first row
53
54        %>  <%-- end scriptlet to insert literal HTML --%>
55
56           <!-- display book cover image -->
57           <img src = "images/<%= results.getString(
58              "cover" ) %>" alt = "Book cover for
59              <%= results.getString( "title" ) %>.">
60
61           <!-- display authors -->
62           <p>Author(s): <%= results.getString(
63              "authors" ) %></p>
64
65           <!-- display price -->
66           <p>Price: <%= results.getDouble( "price" ) %></p>
67
68           <!-- display ISBN -->
69           <p>ISBN: <%= results.getString( "isbn" ) %></p>
70
71           <!-- display edition number -->
72           <p>Edition: <%= results.getInt( "edition" ) %></p>
73
74           <!-- display copyright year -->
75           <p>Copyright Year: <%= results.getString(
76              "copyrightYear" ) %></p>
77
78           <!-- display description -->
79           <p>Description: <%= results.getString(
80              "description" ) %></p>
```

Moving to the first row of the ResultSet — line 52

Displaying the book cover image — lines 57-59

Displaying the author(s) — lines 62-63

Displaying the price — line 66

Displaying the ISBN — line 69

Displaying the edition number — line 72

Displaying the copyright year — lines 75-76

Displaying the description — lines 79-80

Figure 32.19 bookInformation.jsp code. (Part 2 of 3.)

```
81
82                    <!-- create link to Book List -->
83                    <p><a href = "books.jsp">Book List</a></p>
84
85           <%  // continue scriptlet
86
87                    results.close();  // close result set
88                    connection.close();  // close database connection
89
90              }  // end if
91
92           }  // end try
93
94           // catch SQLException
95           catch( SQLException exception )
96           {
97              out.println( "Exception: " + exception + " occurred." );
98           }
99
100          %>  <%-- end scriptlet --%>
101
102    </body>
103 </html>
```

Closing the `ResultSet` → (line 87)

Figure 32.19   `bookInformation.jsp` code. (Part 3 of 3.)

SELF-REVIEW

1. The _____, which is returned by executing a SQL query, can be used to retrieve information from the database.

   a) `ResultSet`   b) `Connection`
   c) `Statement`   d) None of the above.

2. To get the `String` representation of field `"title"` from the `ResultSet` `results`, you should use statement _____.

   a) `ResultSet.getString( "title" );`   b) `results.getString( "title" );`
   c) `ResultSet.getValue( "title" );`   d) `results.getValue( "title" );`

Answers: 1) a. 2) b.

32.4 Internet and Web Resources

Please take a moment to visit each of these sites. To save typing time, use the hot links on the enclosed CD or at `www.deitel.com`.

`java.sun.com/products/jsp/`
This site overviews JSP and provides JSP tutorials. It also includes links to JSP-related news and highlights.

`java.sun.com/products/jsp/docs.html`
This site includes tutorials, articles, code examples and links to JSP resources.

`www.jspin.com/home/tutorials`
This resource site provides users with JSP tutorials and code samples.

`www.jsp-servlet.net/tomcat_examples.html`
This site provides free JSP demos and source code.

32.5 Wrap-Up

In this tutorial, you programmed the middle tier of your three-tier **Bookstore** Web application. By adding the HTML form element's `method` and `action` attributes, JSP scriptlets and expressions, you specified the actions that execute when the user

interacts with JSP pages. You learned about JSP expressions and how they are used to display content in JSP pages. You then learned about the `method` attribute of the `form` element, which specifies how form's data is sent to the Web server. You also learned about the `action` attribute of the `form` element, which allows you to forward the client browser to other JSP pages.

After learning about JSP expressions and the HTML `form` element's `method` and `action` attributes, you used them in the **Bookstore** Web application. You began with the first JSP page of the application, `books.jsp`. This page retrieves the book titles from the database and displays them in an HTML menu control when the JSP page is loaded. You did this by adding JSP expressions to the `option` HTML element. You then defined the actions that occur when the user clicks the **View Information** button. In the `form` element, you set the `method` attribute to `post` which appends user input to the client browser request and set the `action` attribute to direct users from the `books.jsp` page to the `bookInformation.jsp` page.

You then defined the `bookInformation.jsp` page. You added JSP expressions to display information about the selected book. Recall that you used the value stored in the implicit object `request` to determine the book title selected by the user. You then retrieved the selected book's information and displayed it in HTML `p` (paragraph) elements. Through programming, you were able to control the flow of data from the information tier to the client tier, completing the three-tier **Bookstore** Web application.

SKILLS SUMMARY

Adding JSP Expressions to the JSP

- Delimit the expression with <%= and %>.

Retrieving the Client Request

- Use the method `getParameter` of the implicit object `request` to retrieve data from the client request.

Redirecting the Client Browser to Another Web Page

- Use the `action` attribute of the `form` element to forward the client request to another Web page when the user submits the form.

Creating a Three-Tier Web Application with JSP and JDBC

- Create the client tier of the Web application by placing HTML elements and controls in JSPs.
- Implement the information tier of the Web application by using a database, such as the Cloudscape.
- Add business-logic-tier functionality to the Web application by using JSP technology, such as scriptlets and expressions.

KEY TERMS

action attribute of the form HTML element—The attribute specifying where to send form data when the user submits the `form` by clicking the `"submit"` button.

JSP expression—An expression delimited by <%= and %>. JSP expressions are used to insert dynamic content (such as information from a database) in the response to a client.

method attribute of the form HTML element—The attribute that describes how the HTML form's data is sent to the Web server.

option HTML element—The element that adds items to the HTML menu control, which is defined by the `select` HTML element.

HTML REFERENCE

option   This HTML element is used inside the `select` HTML element to add items to the HTML menu control.

form   This HTML element is used to insert a form in an HTML document that will collect user inputs.

■ *Attributes*

`action`—Specifies where to send form data when the user submits the form by clicking the `"submit"` button.

`method`—Describes how the HTML form's data is sent to the Web server.

JSP REFERENCE

JSP expression   An expression used to insert dynamic content (such as information from a database) in the response to a client. JSP expressions are delimited by <%= and %>.

MULTIPLE-CHOICE QUESTIONS

32.1 A JSP expression _____.

a) redirects the client browser to different Web pages

b) defines the functionality when a `Button` is clicked

c) adds dynamic content to a Web page

d) defines the functionality when a Web control is selected

32.2 The action attribute of the `form` HTML element _____.

a) refreshes the current Web page

b) responds to user input

c) specifies the task to perform when the user submits a form

d) responds to the selection of the HTML menu control

32.3 The JSP implicit object _____ is used in the **Bookstore** Web application to retrieve data from the client request.

a) `out`

b) `request`

c) `clientRequest`

d) None of the above.

32.4 `ResultSet` objects are used for _____.

a) tracking user-specific data

b) retrieving information from a database

c) connection to a database

d) None of the above.

32.5 JSP expressions are delimited by _____.

a) <%-- and --%>

b) <% and %>

c) <%= and %>

d) <%= and =%>

32.6 The method attribute of the `form` element _____.

a) specifies the method to call when the client clicks the `"submit"` button

b) describes how the form's data is sent to the Web server

c) redirects the client to another Web page

d) None of the above.

32.7 The `request.getParameter` method takes a(n) _____ as an argument.

a) URL

b) `int`

c) `boolean`

d) `String`

32.8 The _____ attribute specifies the location of the image that an `img` element displays.

a) `src`

b) `imageURL`

c) `image`

d) `display`

32.9 The _____ element is used to add items to an HTML menu control.

a) `item`

b) `option`

c) `value`

d) None of the above.

32.10 The JSP expression _____ displays the `name` that was passed to the JSP as part of a client request.

a) `<%= request.getName() %>`

b) `<%= request.getPara( "name" ) %>`

c) `<%= request.getParameter( "name" ) %>`

d) None of the above.

EXERCISES

32.11 (*Phone Book Application: Functionality*) Define the middle tier for the **Phone Book** application.

a) *Opening phoneBook.jsp*. Open the phoneBook.jsp file that you modified in Exercise 31.11.

b) *Defining the form's method and action attributes in the phoneBook.jsp page*. In the phoneBook.jsp source code, specify "post" as the form element's method and use the action attribute to forward the client request to phoneNumber.jsp.

c) *Populating the HTML menu control with names*. In the phoneBook.jsp source code, add a while statement to the scriptlet in phoneBook.jsp. The loop should add each person's name (retrieved from the ResultSet) to the HTML menu control. This step requires literal HTML markup, as well as a JSP expression.

d) *Closing the ResultSet*. In the scriptlet that ends the while statement, add code to close the ResultSet by invoking its close method.

e) *Saving the file*. Save your modified source code file.

f) *Opening phoneNumber.jsp*. Open the phoneNumber.jsp file that you modified in Exercise 31.11.

g) *Displaying the selected name*. In the phoneNumber.jsp source code, modify the h1 header element to display the selected name that is received as part of the client request.

h) *Displaying the phone number*. In the phoneNumber.jsp source code, modify the HTML paragraph element that contains "numbers" to display the phone number that corresponds to the selected name. Note that you need to move the cursor to the first row of the ResultSet to retrieve the phone number.

i) *Closing the ResultSet*. In the scriptlet that appears after the code you added in *Step h*, add code to close the ResultSet by invoking its close method.

j) *Saving the file*. Save your modified source code file.

k) *Copying phoneBook.jsp and phoneNumber.jsp to the PhoneBook directory*. Copy your updated phoneBook.jsp and phoneNumber.jsp files and paste them into the C:\Program Files\Apache Group\Tomcat 4.1\webapps\PhoneBook directory.

l) *Starting Tomcat*. Select **Start > Programs > Apache Tomcat 4.1 > Start Tomcat** to start the Tomcat server.

m) *Testing the application*. Open a Web browser and enter the URL http://localhost:8080/PhoneBook/phoneBook.jsp, select a name from the list and click the **Get Number** button to test the application.

n) *Stopping Tomcat*. Select **Start > Programs > Apache Tomcat 4.1 > Stop Tomcat** to stop the Tomcat server.

32.12 (*US State Facts Application: Functionality*) Define the middle tier for the **US State Facts** application.

a) *Opening states.jsp*. Open the states.jsp file that you modified Exercise 31.12.

b) *Defining the form's method and action attributes in the states.jsp page*. In the states.jsp source code, specify "post" as the form element's method and use the action attribute to forward the client request to the stateFacts.jsp.

c) *Populating the HTML menu control with state names*. Aadd a while statement to the scriptlet in states.jsp. The loop should add each state's name (retrieved from the ResultSet) to the HTML menu control. This step requires you to use literal HTML markup, as well as a JSP expression.

d) *Closing the ResultSet*. In the scriptlet, add code to close the ResultSet by invoking its close method.

e) *Saving the file*. Save your modified source code file.

f) *Opening stateFacts.jsp*. Open the stateFacts.jsp that you modified in Exercise 31.12.

g) *Displaying the selected state name*. In the stateFacts.jsp source code, modify the h1 header element that contains "State Name" to display the selected state name.

h) ***Moving to the first row in the ResultSet***. In the scriptlet that obtains the Result-Set, move the `ResultSet` cursor to the first row of the `ResultSet` by calling its `next` method.

i) ***Displaying the state's flag***. In the `stateFacts.jsp` source code, modify the `img` element to display the selected state's flag.

j) ***Displaying the state's capital***. In the `stateFacts.jsp` source code, modify the paragraph element that contains "`Capital:`" to display the selected state's capital.

k) ***Displaying the state's flower***. In the `stateFacts.jsp` source code, modify the paragraph element that contains "`Flower:`" to display the selected state's flower.

l) ***Displaying the state's tree***. In the `stateFacts.jsp` source code, modify the paragraph element that contains "`Tree:`" to display the selected state's tree.

m) ***Displaying the state's bird***. In the `stateFacts.jsp` source code, modify the paragraph element that contains "`Bird:`" to display the selected state's bird.

n) ***Closing the ResultSet.*** In the scriptlet that appears after the code you added in *Steps i–m*, add code to close the `ResultSet` by invoking its `close` method.

o) ***Saving the file.*** Save your modified source code file.

p) ***Copying states.jsp and stateFacts.jsp to the StateFacts directory***. Copy your updated `states.jsp` and `stateFacts.jsp` files and paste them into the `C:\Program Files\Apache Group\Tomcat 4.1\webapps\StateFacts` directory.

q) ***Starting Tomcat***. Select **Start > Programs > Apache Tomcat 4.1 > Start Tomcat** to start the Tomcat server.

r) ***Testing the application***. Open a Web browser and enter the URL `http://localhost:8080/StateFacts/states.jsp`, select a state name from the list and click the **Review Facts** button to test the application.

s) ***Stopping Tomcat***. Select **Start > Programs > Apache Tomcat 4.1 > Stop Tomcat** to stop the Tomcat server.

32.13 (*Road Sign Review Application: Functionality*) Define the middle tier for the **Road Sign Review** application.

a) ***Opening roadSigns.jsp***. Open the `roadSigns.jsp` file that you modified in Exercise 31.13.

b) ***Displaying road sign images***. In the `roadSigns.jsp` source code, add a `while` statement to `roadSigns.jsp`. The loop should obtain the image file name and image name from each row in the `ResultSet` and use them to insert an `img` element in the page. Note that the loop replaces the long list of `img` elements that you added to this JSP in Exercise 30.13. The remaining `img` element will appear as literal HTML markup between the two scriptlets that start and end the `while` statement. Two JSP expressions should be used to obtain the image file name and image name from the `ResultSet`.

c) ***Closing the ResultSet.*** In the second scriptlet and after the `while` statement, add code to close the `ResultSet` invoking its `close` method.

d) ***Defining the form's method and action attributes in the roadSigns.jsp page***. In the `roadSigns.jsp` source code, specify `"post"` as the form element's `method` and use the `action` attribute to forward the client request to `roadTestRegistered.jsp`.

e) ***Saving the file.*** Save your modified source code file.

f) ***Opening roadTestRegistered.jsp***. Open the `roadTestRegistered.jsp` file that you created in Exercise 30.13.

g) ***Displaying the client's name***. In the `roadTestRegistered.jsp` source code, modify the paragraph element that contains "`confirmation`" to use a JSP expression to obtain the client's name from the JSP implicit object `request` and display it in the paragraph.

h) ***Displaying the client's phone number***. Modify the paragraph element from the previous step to use a JSP expression to obtain the client's phone number from the JSP implicit object `request` and display it in the paragraph.

i) ***Saving the file.*** Save your modified source code file.

j) *Copying roadSigns.jsp and roadTestRegistered.jsp to the RoadSign directory.* Copy your updated roadSigns.jsp and roadTestRegistered.jsp files and paste them into the C:\Program Files\Apache Group\Tomcat 4.1\webapps\RoadSign directory.

k) *Starting Tomcat.* Select **Start > Programs > Apache Tomcat 4.1 > Start Tomcat** to start the Tomcat server.

l) *Testing the application.* Open a Web browser and enter the URL http://localhost:8080/RoadSign/roadSigns.jsp, enter your name and phone number, then click the **Register** button to test the application.

m) *Stopping Tomcat.* Select **Start > Programs > Apache Tomcat 4.1 > Stop Tomcat** to stop the Tomcat server.

Operator Precedence Chart

O perators are shown in decreasing order of precedence from top to bottom, with each level of precedence separated by a horizontal line. Java operators associate from left to right.

Operator	Type
++	unary postincrement
--	unary postdecrement
++	unary preincrement
--	unary predecrement
+	unary plus
-	unary minus
!	unary logical negation
~	unary bitwise complement
(*type*)	unary cast
*	multiplication
/	division
%	remainder
+	addition or string concatenation
-	subtraction
<<	left shift
>>	signed right shift
>>>	unsigned right shift
<	less than
<=	less than or equal to
>	greater than
>=	greater than or equal to
instanceof	type comparison
==	is equal to
!=	is not equal to
&	bitwise AND
	boolean logical AND
^	bitwise exclusive OR
	boolean logical exclusive OR

Figure A.1   Operator list (in order of operator precedence). (Part 1 of 2.)

Operator	Type
|	bitwise inclusive OR
	boolean logical inclusive OR
&&	conditional AND
||	conditional OR
?:	conditional
=	assignment
+=	addition assignment
-=	subtraction assignment
*=	multiplication assignment
/=	division assignment
&=	remainder assignment
^=	bitwise AND assignment
|=	bitwise exclusive OR assignment
<<=	bitwise inclusive OR assignment
>>=	bitwise left shift assignment
>>>=	bitwise signed-right-shift assignment
	bitwise unsigned-right-shift assignment

Figure A.1   Operator list (in order of operator precedence). (Part 2 of 2.)

APPENDIX

ASCII Character Set

The digits in the left column of Fig. B.1 are the left digits of the decimal equivalent (0–127) of the character code, and the digits in the top row of Fig. B.1 are the right digits of the character code. For example, the character code for "F" is 70, and the character code for "&" is 38.

Most users of this book are interested in the ASCII character set used to represent English characters on many computers. The ASCII character set is a subset of the Unicode® character set used by Java to represent characters from most of the world's languages.

	0	1	2	3	4	5	6	7	8	9
0	nul	soh	stx	etx	eot	enq	ack	bel	bs	ht
1	lf	vt	ff	cr	so	si	dle	dc1	dc2	dc3
2	dc4	nak	syn	etb	can	em	sub	esc	fs	gs
3	rs	us	sp	!	"	#	$	%	&	'
4	(	)	*	+	,	-	.	/	0	1
5	2	3	4	5	6	7	8	9	:	;
6	<	=	>	?	@	A	B	C	D	E
7	F	G	H	I	J	K	L	M	N	O
8	P	Q	R	S	T	U	V	W	X	Y
9	Z	[	\	]	^	_	'	a	b	c
10	d	e	f	g	h	i	j	k	l	m
11	n	o	p	q	r	s	t	u	v	w
12	x	y	z	{			}	~	del		

Figure B.1 ASCII character set.

APPENDIX

GUI Design Guidelines

This appendix contains a complete list of the GUI design guidelines presented at the end of each tutorial. The guidelines are organized by tutorial; within each tutorial section, they are organized by component.

Tutorial 2: Welcome Application (Introduction to Graphical User Interface Programming)

Overall Design

- Use colors in your applications, but not to the point of distracting the user.

JFrames

- Choose short, descriptive JFrame titles.
- JFrame titles should use book-title capitalization, in which the first letter of each significant word is capitalized and the title does not end with any punctuation.

JLabels

- Use JLabels to display text that users cannot change.
- Ensure that all JLabel components are large enough to display their text.
- Use JLabels with images to enhance GUIs with graphics that users cannot change.
- Ensure that all JLabel components are large enough to display their images.

Tutorial 3: Designing the Inventory Application (Introducing JTextFields and JButtons)

JButton

- JButtons are labeled by using their *text* property. JButton text should use book-title capitalization and be as short as possible while still being meaningful to the user.
- JButtons should be stacked vertically downward from the top right of the JFrame or arranged horizontally on the same line starting from the bottom right of the JFrame.

JFrame

- Place an application's output components below and/or to the right of the application's input components.

JLabel

- Use JLabels to identify other GUI components.
- Descriptive JLabels should use sentence-style capitalization and end with a colon.
- Place each descriptive JLabel either above or to the left of the component (for example, a JTextField) that it identifies.
- Align the left sides of a group of descriptive JLabels if the JLabels are arranged vertically.
- A descriptive JLabel should have the same height as the component it describes if the components are arranged horizontally.
- A descriptive JLabel and the component it identifies should be top aligned if they are arranged horizontally.
- A descriptive JLabel and the component it identifies should be left aligned if they are arranged vertically.

JTextField

- Use editable JTextFields to input data from the keyboard. JTextFields are editable by default
- Each JTextField should have a descriptive JLabel indicating the JTextField's purpose.
- Make JTextFields wide enough for their expected inputs, if possible. Otherwise, the text will scroll as the user types and only part of the text will be visible.
- Align the left sides of JTextFields that are arranged vertically.
- In general, numeric values in JTextFields should be right aligned.
- Output JTextFields should be distinguishable from those used for input. Setting the *editable* property of an output JTextField to false prevents the user from typing in the JTextField and causes the JTextField to appear with a gray background in the user interface.

Tutorial 7: Dental Payment Application (Introducing JCheckBoxes, Message Dialogs and Logical Operators)

JCheckBoxes

- A JCheckBox's text should be descriptive and as short as possible. When a JCheckBox's text contains more than one word, use book-title capitalization.
- Align groups of JCheckBoxes either horizontally or vertically.

Message Dialogs

- Text displayed in a message dialog should be descriptive and as short as possible.

Tutorial 8: Car Payment Calculator Application (Introducing the while Repetition Statement and JTextAreas)

JTextArea

- Use headers in a JTextArea to improve readability when you are displaying tabular data.

Tutorial 9: Class Average Application (Introducing the do...while Repetition Statement)

JButton

- Disable a JButton when its function should not be available to the user.
- Enable a JButton when its function should be available to the user.

JTextArea

- Most JTextAreas should have a descriptive JLabel, indicating what output is expected to be displayed. Use sentence-style capitalization for such a JLabel.

Tutorial 10: Interest Calculator Application (Introducing the for Repetition Statement)

JTextArea

- If a JTextArea will display many lines of output, attach the JTextArea to a JScrollPane to allow users to scroll through the lines of output displayed in the JTextArea.

JSpinner

- Use a JSpinner when you would use a JTextField, but want the user to only enter input values within a specified range. The JSpinner prevents invalid input by rejecting values that either are of the wrong type or are out-of-range values. When invalid data is rejected, the previous value in the JSpinner is restored.
- Use the same GUI design guidelines for JSpinners and JTextFields.

Tutorial 11: Security Panel Application (Introducing the switch Multiple-Selection Statement, Date and DateFormat)

Overall Design

- If your GUI is modeling a real-world object, your GUI design should mimic the physical appearance of that object.

JPasswordField

- Mask passwords or other sensitive pieces of information in JPasswordFields.

Tutorial 16: Flag Quiz Application (Introducing One-Dimensional Arrays and JComboBoxes)

JComboBoxes

- Each JComboBox should have a descriptive JLabel to describe the JComboBox's contents.
- Sorting the entries in a JComboBox with many entries helps the user find desired entries.

Tutorial 17: Student Grades Application (Introducing Two-Dimensional Arrays and JRadioButtons)

JRadioButton

- Use JRadioButtons when the user should choose only one option from a group.
- Always place each group of JRadioButtons in a separate ButtonGroup.
- Align groups of JRadioButtons either horizontally or vertically.

Tutorial 19: Shipping Hub Application (Introducing Collections, ArrayList and Iterators)

Overall Design

- Use mnemonics to allow users to "click" a component using the keyboard. This provides an added convenience for the user, especially for applications that require the user to enter a great deal of text data.
- Attaching a JList to a JScrollPane allows users to scroll items in a JList.

Tutorial 22: Typing Skills Developer Application (Introducing Keyboard Events and JMenus)

Menus

- Use book-title capitalization in menu item text.
- If clicking a menu item opens a dialog, an ellipsis (…) should follow the menu item's text.
- Use separator bars in a menu to group related menu items.

JCheckBoxMenuItem

■ A JCheckBoxMenuItem's text should be description, be as short as possible and use book-title capitalization.

■ Use JCheckBoxMenuItem when the user should be able to choose multiple options from a group of JCheckBoxMenuItems.

JRadioButtonMenuItem

■ Use JRadioButtonMenuItem when the user should choose only one option from a group of JRadioButtonMenuItems.

Java Library Reference

This appendix contains a listing of components and predefined classes used in the text. Each component or class includes a description of its purpose, as well as explanations of events, properties and methods related to that component or class, as covered in the text.

Tutorial 1: Moving Shapes Application (Introducing Computers, the Internet and Java Programming)

No new elements.

Tutorial 2: Welcome Application (Introduction to Graphical User Interface Programming)

JFrame   This component enables a Java application to appear in its own window. All other components in an application are displayed within the application's window.

■ *In action*

■ *Methods*

setBackground—Sets the background color of the JFrame's content pane (or of other components). For example, if the content pane of the JFrame is called content-Pane, then the statement contentPane.setBackground(Color.YELLOW); sets the background color of the content pane to yellow.

setSize—Sets the size (in pixels) of the JFrame.

setTitle—Sets the text displayed in the title bar of the JFrame.

919

JLabel   This component displays text or an image that the user cannot modify.

■ *In action*

Welcome to Java Programming!

■ *Methods*

setBounds—Specifies the size and location in the JLabel.

setFont—Specifies the font name, style and size of the text displayed in the JLabel.

setHorizontalAlignment—Determines how the text is aligned in the JLabel.

setIcon—Specifies the file name and path of the image in the JLabel.

setSize—Specifies the height and width (in pixels) in the JLabel.

setText—Specifies the text displayed in the JLabel.

Tutorial 3: Designing the Inventory Application (Introducing *JTextFields* and *JButtons*)

JButton   This component allows the user to command the application to perform an action.

■ *In action*

Calculate Total

■ *Methods*

setBounds—Sets the *bounds* property, which specifies the location and size of the JButton.

setText—Sets the *text* property of the JButton.

JLabel   This component displays text that the user cannot modify.

■ *In action*

Descriptive JLabel ⎯⎯⎯⎯⎯

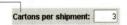

Cartons per shipment: 3

■ *Methods*

setBounds—Sets the *bounds* property, which specifies the location and size of the JLabel.

setFont—Sets the font name, font size and font style of the text displayed in the JLabel. For example, to set the font for textJLabel, use textJLabel.setFont(new Font(*fontName*, *fontStyle*, *fontSize*));. Sample values for *fontName* include "Sans-Serif", "Serif" and "Monospaced". The *fontStyle* can be Font.PLAIN, Font.BOLD, Font.ITALIC or Font.Bold + Font.ITALIC. The *fontSize* can be any positive integer (whole number) value.

setHorizontalAlignment—Specifies how the text is aligned within the JLabel (JLabel.LEFT, JLabel.CENTER, JLabel.RIGHT).

setIcon—Sets the image for the JLabel to display.

setLocation—Sets the position of the JLabel.

setSize—Sets the width and height (in pixels) of the JLabel.

setText—Sets the text displayed in the JLabel.

JTextField   This component obtains input from the keyboard or displays information to the user.

■ *In action*

Editable JTextField ——————

Cartons per shipment: [3]

Uneditable JTextField ——————

Total: [45]

■ *Methods*

setBounds—Sets the *bounds* property, which specifies the location and size of the JText-Field.

setEditable—Specifies whether users can edit the JTextField.

setHorizontalAlignment—Specifies how the text is aligned within the JTextField.

setText—Specifies the text displayed in the JTextField.

Tutorial 4: Completing the Inventory Application (Introducing Programming)

Integer   The Integer class contains methods that process integer values.

■ *Method*

parseInt—Returns the integer equivalent of its String argument.

JButton   This component allows the user to cause an event by pressing a button in an application's graphical user interface.

■ *In action*

[Calculate Total]

■ *Event*

actionPerformed—Occurs when the user clicks the JButton.

■ *Methods*

setBounds—Sets the location and size of the JButton.

setText—Sets the *text* property of the JButton.

JTextField   This component allows the user to input information and can be used to display results to the user.

■ *In action*

Editable JTextField ——————

Cartons per shipment: [3|]

Uneditable JTextField ——————

Total: [45]

■ *Methods*

getText—Returns the text displayed in the JTextField.

setBounds—Sets the location and size of the JTextField.

setEditable—Specifies whether users can edit the JTextField. A true value (the default) means the JTextField is an editable input JTextField and a false value means the JTextField is an uneditable output JTextField.

setHorizontalAlignment—Specifies how the text is aligned within the JTextField (JTextField.LEFT, JTextField.CENTER or JTextField.RIGHT).

setText—Specifies the text displayed in the JTextField.

String   The String class stores and manipulates text data.

- *Method*

  valueOf—Returns the String equivalent of its argument.

Tutorial 5: Enhancing the Inventory Application (Introducing Variables, Memory Concepts, Arithmetic and Keyboard Events)

JTextField   This component allows the user to input information and can be used to display results to the user.

- *In action*

editable JTextField
uneditable JTextField

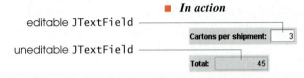

- *Events*

  keyPressed—Raised when any key is pressed in the JTextField.

- *Methods*

  getText—Returns the text displayed in the JTextField.

  setBounds—Sets the location and size of the JTextField.

  setEditable—Specifies whether users can edit the JTextField. A true value (the default) means the JTextField is an editable input JTextField and a false value means the JTextField is an uneditable output JTextField.

  setHorizontalAlignment—Specifies how the text is aligned within the JTextField.

  setText—Specifies the text displayed in the JTextField.

Tutorial 6: Wage Calculator Application (Introducing Algorithms, Pseudocode and Program Control)

DecimalFormat   Class DecimalFormat is used to format floating-point numbers (that is, numbers with decimal points).

- *Methods*

  format—Converts a double value into a specified format.

Tutorial 7: Dental Payment Application (Introducing JCheckBoxes Message Dialogs and Logical Operators)

JCheckBox   This component allows the user to select an option. If an application contains several JCheckBoxes, any number of them (including zero or all) can be selected at once).

- *In action*

- *Methods*

  isSelected—Returns true if a JCheckBox is selected.

  setBounds—Sets the location and size of a JCheckBox component.

  setText—Sets the text displayed alongside a JCheckBox.

JOptionPane   This class allows the user to display dialogs.

■ *Methods*

showMessageDialog—Displays a message dialog, taking four arguments. The first argument (null in the examples so far) specifies the position of the message dialog on the screen. The second and third arguments indicate the text of the dialog's message and the text of the dialog's title bar, respectively. The fourth argument (one of the constants defined in class JOptionPane) specifies the icon that will be displayed in the dialog.

■ *Constants*

ERROR_MESSAGE ()—Icon containing a stop sign. Typically used to alert the user of errors or critical situations.

INFORMATION_MESSAGE ( )—Icon containing the letter "i." Typically used to display information about the state of the application.

PLAIN_MESSAGE—Displays a dialog that simply contains a message, with no icon.

QUESTION_MESSAGE ( )—Icon containing a question mark. Typically used to ask the user a question.

WARNING_MESSAGE ( )—Icon containing an exclamation point. Typically used to caution the user against potential problems.

String   This class is used to manipulate textual data.

■ *Methods*

equals—Returns true when String contains the same text as the String argument to method equals.

Tutorial 8: Car Payment Calculator Application (Introducing the while Repetition Statement and JTextAreas)

JTextArea   This component allows the user to view multiline text in a JTextArea.

■ *In action*

Months	Monthly Payments
24	$490.50
36	$339.06
48	$263.55
60	$218.41

■ *Methods*

append—Adds text to a JTextArea.

setBounds—Sets the *x*-coordinate, *y*-coordinate, width and height of a JTextArea.

setEditable—Specifies whether a JTextArea is editable. If the setEditable is false, then the JTextArea is not able to receive input from the keyboard.

setText—Sets the *text* property of a JTextArea.

Tutorial 9: Class Average Application (Introducing the do...while Repetition Statement)

JButton   This class is used to display message and input dialogs.

■ *In action*

Average —— Enabled JButton

Average —— Enabled JButton with focus

Average —— Disabled JButton

- *Methods*

  requestFocusInWindow—Sets the JButton to have the focus.

  setBounds—Sets the bounds of the JButton, which determines its location and size.

  setEnabled—Sets the *enabled* property of the JButton to true or false.

  setText—Sets the *text* property of a JButton.

JOptionPane   This class is used to display message and input dialogs.

- *Methods*

  showInputDialog—Displays an input dialog.

  showMessageDialog—Displays a message dialog.

Tutorial 10: Interest Calculator Application (Introducing the *for* Repetition Statement)

Integer   This class is used to represent and manipulate int data.

- *Methods*

  intValue—Returns the int data of an Integer object.

JScrollPane   This component is used to add horizontal and/or vertical scrollbars to other components. When a component, such as a JTextArea, is added to a JScrollPane, the component will display scrollbars as necessary.

- *In action*

Scrollbar appears as necessary for components contained within a JScrollPane

- *Methods*

  setBounds—Sets the bounds (location and size) of a JScrollPane component.

JSpinner   This component allows you to specify input within a specified range. The range can include numeric values, or values of another type. Input can be entered from the keyboard or by clicking up and down arrows provided on the right of the JSpinner. Invalid input is rejected and replaced with the most recent valid input value.

- *In action*

JSpinner component

- *Methods*

  getValue—Returns the data in the *value* property of a JSpinner component.

  setBounds—Sets the bounds (location and size) of a JSpinner component.

Math   This class contains several methods used for common mathematical calculations.

- *Methods*

  pow—Performs exponentiation. The first argument specifies the value that will be raised to a power, and the second argument specifies the power to which the first argument will be raised.

Tutorial 11: Security Panel Application (Introducing the switch Multiple-Selection Statement, Date and DateFormat)

Date   Represents a date and time. Use the code new Date() to get the current system date and time.

DateFormat   Class for formatting Date objects.

■ *Methods*

format—Formats a Date object and returns a String.
getDateTimeInstance—Returns a DateFormat object which can be used to format Date objects.

JPasswordField   Allows the user to input data from the keyboard and displays each character as an asterisk (*) for security reasons.

■ *In action*

■ *Methods*

setBounds—Sets the *bounds* property which determines the location and size of a JPasswordField.
setEditable—Specifies whether users can edit a JPasswordField.
getPassword—Returns the password in a JPasswordField.
setEchoChar—Specifies the echo character for a JPasswordField.
setText—Specifies the text displayed in a JPasswordField.

Tutorial 12: Enhancing the Wage Calculator Application (Introducing Methods)

Math   This class provides methods that perform common arithmetic calculations.

■ *Methods*

min—Returns the smaller of two numeric arguments.
max—Returns the larger of two numeric arguments.
sqrt—Returns the square root of a numeric argument.

Tutorial 13: Enhancing the Interest Calculator Application (Introduction to Event Handling)

ActionEvent   This class represents the event object created when a JButton is clicked. Objects of this class contain information about the event that was generated, such as the event source.

ChangeEvent   This class represents the event object created when a JSpinner's value is changed. Objects of this class contain information about the event that was generated, such as the event source.

JSpinner   This component allows you to collect input within a specified range. The range can include numeric values, or values of another data type. Input can be entered at the keyboard, or by clicking up and down arrows provided on the right of the JSpinner. Invalid input is rejected and replaced with the most recent valid input value.

■ *In action*

■ *Events*

stateChanged—Occurs when the value in a JSpinner is changed by clicking on one of its arrows or entering a value.

■ *Methods*

getValue—Returns the data in the *value* property of a JSpinner component.

setBounds—Sets the *bounds* property which determines the location and size of a JSpinner component.

setValue—Sets the *value* property of a JSpinner component.

Tutorial 14: *Fundraiser Application (Introducing Scope and Conversion of Primitive Types)*

No new elements.

Tutorial 15: *Craps Game Application (Introducing Random Number Generation and the JPanel)*

Random   This class is used to generate random numbers.

■ *Methods*

nextInt—Generates an int value selected from all possible int values, when called with no arguments. When called with an int argument, it generates an int value from 0 to one less than that argument.

nextDouble—Generates a positive double value that is greater than or equal to 0.0 and less than 1.0.

JPanel   This component groups other related components. This grouping allows a single border to be placed around multiple components. Components placed in a JPanel are positioned with respect to the upper-left corner of the JPanel, so changing the location of the JPanel moves all of the components contained inside it.

■ *Methods*

add—Adds a component to the JPanel.

setBorder—Sets the border displayed around the JPanel.

setBounds—Sets the *bounds* property, which specifies the location and size of a JPanel.

setLayout—Sets the *layout* property, which controls how components are displayed on the JPanel.

TitledBorder   This class allows the user to add a String title and line border to a component.

■ *Methods*

setTitle—Sets the title that is displayed in the border.

Tutorial 16: *Flag Quiz Application (Introducing One-Dimensional Arrays and JComboBoxes)*

JComboBox   This component allows users to select from a drop-down list of options.

■ *In action*

■ *Constructor*

JComboBox—Takes an array as an argument. The items in the array are used to populate the JComboBox.

```
private String[] countries = { "Russia", "China", "United States",
    "Italy", "Australia", "South Africa", "Brazil", "Spain" };
selectCountryJComboBox = new JComboBox( countries );
```

■ *Methods*

setMaximumRowCount—Sets the number of items that can be displayed in the JComboBox's drop-down list.

setBounds—Specifies the location and size of the JComboBox component on the container component relative to the top-left corner.

getItemAt—Takes an int argument representing an index and returns the value at that index of a JComboBox.

getSelectedIndex—Returns the index of the JComboBox's selected item.

setSelectedIndex—Sets the index of the JComboBox's selected item.

Arrays　　The class that provides methods to manipulate arrays.

■ *Methods*

sort—Orders an array's elements. An array of numerical values would be organized in ascending order and an array of Strings would be organized in alphabetical order.

Tutorial 17: Student Grades Application (Introducing Two-Dimensional Arrays and JRadioButtons)

JRadioButton　　Enable users to select only one of several options.

■ *In action*

■ *Event handlers*

actionPerformed—Called when the component is selected.

■ *Methods*

isSelected—Returns true if the JRadioButton is selected and false otherwise.

setBounds—Specifies the location of the JRadioButton component on the container control relative to the top-left corner, as well as the height and width (in pixels) of the component.

setSelected—Sets the state of the JRadioButton to selected or unselected. When true, the JRadioButton displays a small black dot inside a circle. When false, the JRadioButton displays an empty circle.

setText—Specifies the text displayed in the JRadioButton.

ButtonGroup　　This class is used to group JRadioButton components. Initially, zero or one JRadioButtons will be selected. Once a JRadioButton has been selected, only one JRadioButton in the ButtonGroup can be selected at any time.

■ *Methods*

add—Adds a JRadioButton to the ButtonGroup.

Tutorial 18: Microwave Oven Application (Building Your Own Classes and Objects)

Timer   The Timer class provides methods to schedule tasks to be performed at future times.

■ *Constructor*

Timer—Takes an int and an object that handles ActionEvents as arguments. The first argument is the interval (in milliseconds) for the Timer. Each time the interval expires, an ActionEvent will be generated.

```
private Timer clockTimer = new Timer( 1000, timerActionListener )
```

■ *Methods*

start—This method starts the timer.

stop—This method stops the timer.

String   The String class represents a series of characters treated as a single unit.

■ *Methods*

substring—This method returns a String that is a specified portion of the original String.

Tutorial 19: Shipping Hub Application (Introducing Collections, ArrayList and Iterators)

ArrayList   This class is used to store a set of objects. Unlike arrays, ArrayLists can be dynamically resized and have access to several methods that allows programmers to easily manipulate the contents of the ArrayList.

■ *Methods*

add—This method adds an element to the ArrayList object.

clear—This method removes all elements in an ArrayList.

get—This method returns a reference to the element in the ArrayList at the specified index.

indexOf—This method returns the index in the ArrayList where a specified object is stored. If the object does not exist in the ArrayList, indexOf returns -1.

iterator—This method creates a new object of type Iterator used for iterating through each element contained in the ArrayList.

remove—This method removes an element from the ArrayList object at the specified index.

size—This method returns the number of elements in the ArrayList.

toArray—This method converts the ArrayList to a one-dimensional array. This is convenient for cases when the elements of an ArrayList need to be passed to a method that is expecting a one-dimensional array.

Date   This class is used to store date and time information.

■ *Methods*

toString—This method returns the current date as a String, in the format Tue Feb 13 16:50:00 EST 2003.

Iterator   This interface is used for iterating, or traversing, through a collection.

■ *Methods*

hasNext—This method tests if there are any remaining elements in the ArrayList accessed by this Iterator object.

next—This method returns a reference to the next element in the ArrayList.

JButton   This component allows the user to generate an action.

- ■ *In action*

- ■ *Event Handlers*

    actionPerformed—This event handler is called when the JButton is clicked.

- ■ *Methods*

    requestFocusInWindow—The method sets the JButton to have the focus.

    setBounds—The method sets the *bounds* property, of the JButton, which determines the location and size.

    setEnabled—The method sets the *enabled* property of the JButton to true or false.

    setMnemonic—The method sets the *mnemonic* property of the JButton. The argument passed to this method is the KeyEvent constant for the character that will be used as a mnemonic, or keyboard shortcut that allows the user to "click" the JButton using the keyboard.

    setText—The method sets the *text* property of a JButton.

JComboBox   This component allows users to select from a drop-down list of options.

- ■ *In action*

- ■ *Event Handlers*

    actionPerformed—This event handler is called when a new value is selected in the JComboBox.

- ■ *Methods*

    getItemAt—This method takes an int argument representing an index and returns the value at that index of a JComboBox.

    getSelectedIndex—This method returns the index of the JComboBox's selected item, stored in the *selectedIndex* property.

    setBounds—This method specifies the location and size of the JComboBox component on the container component relative to the top-left corner.

    setEnabled—Controls whether the user can select items from the JComboBox.

    setMaximumRowCount—This method sets the number of items that can be displayed in the JComboBox's drop-down list.

    setSelectedIndex—This method sets the index of the JComboBox's selected item, stored in the *selectedIndex* property.

JList   This component allows users to view and select items in a list.

- ■ *In action*

- ■ *Methods*

    setBounds—This method specifies the location and size of the JList.

    setListData—This method sets the text displayed in the JList.

KeyEvent   This class contains information about keyboard events (such as the pressing of a key on the keyboard).

- *Constants*

  KeyEvent.VK_A—This constant represents the A key on the keyboard.

  KeyEvent.VK_B—This constant represents the B key on the keyboard.

  KeyEvent.VK_E—This constant represents the E key on the keyboard.

  KeyEvent.VK_N—This constant represents the N key on the keyboard.

  KeyEvent.VK_R—This constant represents the R key on the keyboard.

  KeyEvent.VK_S—This constant represents the S key on the keyboard.

  KeyEvent.VK_U—This constant represents the U key on the keyboard.

Tutorial 20: Screen Saver Application (Introducing Inheritance and Graphics)

Graphics   The class that contains methods used to draw text, lines and shapes.

- *Methods*

  fillRect—Draws a filled rectangle of a specified size at a specified location.

  setColor—Sets the color of the object to be drawn.

JPanel   This component groups other related components. This allows a single border to be placed around multiple components. Components placed in a JPanel are positioned with respect to the upper-left corner of the JPanel, so changing the location of the JPanel moves all of the components contained inside it.

- *Methods*

  add—Adds a component to the JPanel.

  paintComponent—Paints components in the Graphics object that is the passed to this method.

  repaint—Clears all previous drawings and updates any current drawings in the JPanel.

  setBorder—Sets the border displayed around the JPanel.

  setBounds—Sets the *bounds* property, which specifies the location and size of a JPanel.

  setLayout—Sets the *layout* property, which controls how components are displayed on the JPanel.

Tutorial 21: "Cat and Mouse" Painter Application (Introducing Interfaces, Mouse Input; the Event-Handling Mechanism)

JPanel   This component groups other related components, allowing a single border to be placed around multiple components. Components placed in a JPanel are positioned with respect to the upper-left corner of the JPanel, so changing the location of the JPanel moves all of the components contained inside it.

- *Event handlers*

  mousePressed—Invoked when a mouse button is pressed.

  mouseDragged—Invoked when the mouse is moved while a mouse button is pressed.

  mouseReleased—Invoked when a mouse button is released.

  mouseEntered—Invoked when the mouse cursor enters the bounds of the component.

  mouseExited—Invoked when the mouse cursor leaves the bounds of the component.

  mouseClicked—Invoked when a mouse button is clicked (pressed and released).

- *Methods*

  add—Adds a component to the JPanel.

  addMouseListener—Adds a MouseListener to the JPanel.

addMouseMotionListener—Adds a MouseMotionListener to the JPanel.

getBackground—Returns a Color object that is the color of the JPanel's background.

paintComponent—Paints components in the Graphics object, which is the argument passed to this method.

repaint—Clears all previous drawings and updates any current drawings in the JPanel.

setBorder—Sets the border displayed around the JPanel.

setBounds—Sets the *bounds* property, which specifies the location and size of the JPanel.

setLayout—Sets the *layout* property, which controls how components are displayed on the JPanel.

Graphics   This class contains methods used to draw text, lines and shapes.

■ *Methods*

fillOval—Draws a solid oval of a specified size at the specified location.

fillRect—Draws a solid rectangle of a specified size at the specified location.

setColor—Sets the color with which to fill the oval.

MouseEvent   This class contains information about mouse events.

■ *Methods*

getPoint—Returns a Point object representing where the mouse cursor is.

isMetaDown—Returns true if the right mouse button was pressed, and false otherwise.

MouseListener   This interface declares five event handlers for mouse events.

■ *Event Handlers*

mouseClicked—Invoked when a mouse button is clicked (pressed and released).

mouseEntered—Invoked when a mouse cursor enters the bounds of the component.

mouseExited—Invoked when a mouse cursor leaves the bounds of the component.

mousePressed—Invoked when a mouse button is pressed.

mouseReleased—Invoked when a mouse button is released.

MouseMotionListener   This interface declares two event handlers for mouse motion events.

■ *Event Handlers*

mouseDragged—Invoked when a mouse cursor is moved while one of the mouse buttons is pressed.

mouseMoved—Invoked when the mouse is moved.

Point   This class represents a single point on the screen.

■ *Instance variables*

x—The *x*-coordinate of the Point.

y—The *y*-coordinate of the Point.

Tutorial 22: Typing Skills Developer Application (Introducing Keyboard Events and JMenus)

ActionEvent   This class represents arguments passed to the actionPerformed event handler.

■ *Methods*

getSource—Returns the event source.

Font   This class represents a unique font specified by its name, size and style.

■ *Constructor*

Font—Takes three arguments—the name, style and size of the font.

```
outputFont = new Font( outputFont.getName(), Font.BOLD, 16 );
```

■ *Constants*

Font.BOLD—Represents the bold style.
Font.ITALIC—Represents the italic style.
Font.PLAIN—Represents the plain style.

■ *Methods*

getName—Returns the name of the Font as a String.
getSize—Returns the size of the Font as an int.
getStyle—Returns the style of the Font as an int.

JCheckBoxMenuItem   This component represents a menu object that has a JCheckBox to its left so the user can tell if the object is selected.

■ *In action*

■ *Methods*

getText—Returns the text of the JCheckBoxMenuItem.
isSelected—Returns whether this component is selected or not selected.

JColorChooser   This component allows the user to select a color.

■ *Method*

showDialog—Displays the JColorChooser dialog.

JMenu   This component allows you to group related menu items for your application.

■ *Constructor*

JMenu—Takes one argument that specifies the name of the JMenu.

```
displayJMenu = new JMenu( "Display" );
```

■ *In action*

■ *Methods*

add—Adds a menu or a menu item to the menu.
addSeparator—Adds a separator bar to the menu.
setMnemonic—Sets the keyboard shortcut of the menu.

JMenuBar   This component allows you to add menus to your application.

■ *In action*

■ *Methods*

add—Adds a menu to the menu bar.

JMenuItem   This component represents a menu item that can be added to a JMenu.

- *In action*

- *Methods*

  setMnemonic—Returns the keyboard shortcut of the JMenuItem.

JRadioButtonMenuItem   This component represents a menu object that has a radio button to its left so that the user can tell if the object is selected.

- *In action*

- *Method*

  getText—Returns the text of the JRadioButtonMenuItem.

JTextArea   This component allows the user to input data from the keyboard.

- *In action*

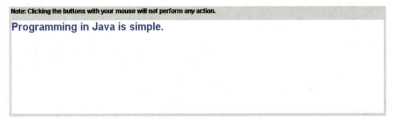

- *Methods*

  addKeyListener—Adds a KeyListener object to the JTextArea.

  append—Adds text to a JTextArea.

  grabFocus—Transfers the focus of the application to the JTextArea.

  setBounds—Sets the position and size of the JTextArea.

  setEditable—Sets whether the text in the JTextArea can be edited (true) or not (false).

  setEnabled—Sets the *enabled* property which determines whether the JTextArea will respond to user actions (true) or not (false).

  setFont—Sets the font of the JTextArea.

  setForeground—Sets the foreground Color of the JTextArea.

  setHorizontalAlignment—Specifies how the text is aligned within the JTextArea (JTextArea.LEFT, JTextArea.CENTER, JTextArea.RIGHT).

  setText—Sets the text displayed in the JTextArea.

KeyEvent   This class represents an event object generated when a key is pressed, typed or released.

- *Constants*

  KeyEvent.KEY_LAST—The largest virtual key code declared in the KeyEvent class.

  KeyEvent.VK_A—Represents the A key on the keyboard.

  KeyEvent.VK_B—Represents the B key on the keyboard.

■ *Method*

getKeyCode—Returns the virtual key code for the key that the user interacted with.

KeyListener   This interface declares three event handlers for keyboard events.

■ *Event Handlers*

keyPressed—Invoked when a key is pressed.

keyReleased—Invoked when a key is released.

keyTyped—Invoked when a character key is pressed.

Tutorial 23: Screen Scraping Application (Introducing String Processing)

String   The String class represents a sequence of characters treated as a single unit.

■ *Methods*

charAt—Returns the character located at a specific index in a String.

endsWith—Returns true if a String ends with a particular substring and false otherwise.

equals—Compares the contents of two Strings, returning true if the two Strings contain the same characters in the same order and false otherwise.

indexOf—Returns the index of the first occurrence of a substring in a String. Returns -1 if the substring is not found.

lastIndexOf—Returns the index of the last occurrence of a substring in a String. It returns -1 if the substring is not found.

length—Returns the number of characters in a String.

startsWith—Returns true if a String starts with a particular substring and false otherwise.

substring—Creates a new String object by copying part of an existing String object.

trim—Removes all white space from the beginning and end of a String.

valueOf—Converts numeric values to a String.

Tutorial 24: Enhanced Car Payment Calculator Application (Introducing Exception Handling)

Error   A class that represents exceptional situations happening in the Java runtime system that typically should not be caught by an application.

Exception   A class that represents exceptional situations occuring in a Java application that should be caught by the application.

NumberFormatException   A subclass of RuntimeException that is thrown when the application cannot convert a string to a desired numeric type, such as int or double.

RunTimeException   The superclass of all unchecked exceptions that can be thrown during application execution.

Throwable   The superclass of all exceptions and errors.

Tutorial 25: Ticket Information Application (Introducing Sequential-Access Files)

BufferedReader   This class is used to read data from a file.

■ *Constructor*

BufferedReader—Takes a FileReader object as an argument. The resulting Buffered-Reader object can read data from the file opened by the FileReader. The following lines of text demonstrate use of this constructor.

```
File currentFile = new File( "current.txt" );
FileReader currentReader = new FileReader( currentFile );
BufferedReader input = new BufferedReader( currentReader );
```

■ *Methods*

close—This method closes the file.

readLine—This method reads a line of data from a particular file.

File   This class represents a file.

■ *Method*

getName—This method returns the name of the File.

FileReader   A class whose objects read characters from a file.

■ *Constructor*

FileReader—This constructor takes a File object as an argument and opens the corresponding file for reading. The following lines of text demonstrate use of this constructor.

```
File currentFile = new File( "current.txt" );
FileReader currentReader = new FileReader( currentFile );
```

FileWriter   A class whose objects write characters to a file.

■ *Constructor*

FileWriter—This constructor takes a File object as the first argument and a boolean as the second argument. The first argument indicates the file that should be opened for writing. The second argument indicates whether new data should be appended (true) to the end of the file. The following lines of text demonstrate use of this constructor.

```
File currentFile = new File( "current.txt" );
FileWriter currentWriter = new FileWriter( currentFile, true );
```

JComboBox   This component allows users to select from a drop-down list of options.

■ *In action*

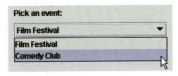 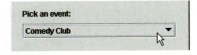

■ *Event handler*

actionPerformed—This event handler is called when a new value is selected in the JComboBox.

■ *Methods*

getItemAt—This method takes an int argument representing an index and returns the value at that index of a JComboBox.

getSelectedIndex—This method returns the index of the JComboBox's selected item, stored in the *selectedIndex* property.

removeAllItems—This method removes all items in the JComboBox.

setBounds—This method specifies the location and size of the JComboBox component on the container component relative to the top-left corner.

setEnabled—This method controls whether the user can select items from a JComboBox.

setMaximumRowCount—This method sets the number of items that can be displayed in the JComboBox's drop-down list.

setSelectedIndex—This method sets the index of the JComboBox's selected item, stored in the *selectedIndex* property.

JFileChooser   This class defines a dialog which enables the user to open a file.

■ *Constants*

JFileChooser.APPROVE_OPTION—A value representing the **OK** JButton being clicked in the JFileChooser.

JFileChooser.CANCEL_OPTION—A value representing the **Cancel** JButton being clicked in the JFileChooser.

JFileChooser.ERROR_OPTION—A value specifying that an error occurred in a JFile-Chooser dialog.

■ *Methods*

getSelectedFile—This method returns the file selected by the user.

setDialogTitle—This method sets the title of the dialog.

showOpenDialog—This method displays the **Open** dialog and returns the result of the user interaction with the dialog.

PrintWriter   This class is used to write data to a file.

■ *Constructor*

PrintWriter—Takes a FileWriter as an argument. The FileWriter specifies the file to which data will be written. The following lines of text demonstrate use of this constructor.

```
File currentFile = new File( "current.txt" );
FileWriter currentWriter = new FileWriter( currentFile, true );
PrintWriter output = new PrintWriter( currentWriter );
```

■ *Methods*

close—This method closes the file.

println—This method writes the data specified in its argument to a file, followed by a newline character.

Tutorial 26: ATM Application (Introducing Database Programming and Using Command-Line Arguments)

Class   This object represents a class in a running Java application.

■ *Methods*

forName—Used to load the class for the database driver.

Connection   This object represents a connection to a specific database.

■ *Methods*

close—Closes the connection to the database.

createStatement—Creates a Statement object to submit SQL to the database.

DriverManager   This object provides a service for managing JDBC drivers. This object also is used to establish a connection to a database.

- **Methods**

  getConnection—Attempts to connect to a database.

Statement   This object is used to submit SQL to a database.

- **Methods**

  close—Closes a Statement and release its database resources.

  executeQuery—Executes SQL queries.

  executeUpdate—Executes SQL statements that modify a database, such as UPDATEs.

ResultSet This object is used to manipulate the results of a query.

- **Methods**

  close—Close a ResultSet and release its database resources.

  getDouble—Gets a column value as a double.

  getInt—Gets a column value as an int.

  getString—Gets a column value as a String.

  next—Moves the ResultSet cursor down to the next row in a ResultSet.

System.out This object allows a Java application to display sets of characters in the **Command Prompt** window from which the Java application executes.

- **Methods**

  println—Displays a line of text in the **Command Prompt** window.

Tutorial 27: Drawing Shapes Application (Introduction to Polymorphism; an Expanded Discussion of Graphics)

Graphics   The Graphics class provides methods to draw shapes of varying colors.

- **Methods**

  drawLine—Takes four arguments and draws a line at the specified beginning and ending x- and y-coordinates.

  drawOval—Takes four arguments and draws an unfilled oval inside a bounding rectangular area. The first two arguments are the x- and y-coordinates of the top-left corner of the rectangular area and the second two are the width and height.

  drawRect—Takes four arguments and draws an unfilled rectangle at the specified upper-left x- and y-coordinates and of the specified width and height.

  fillRect—Takes four arguments and draws a solid rectangle at the specified upper-left x- and y-coordinates and of the specified width and height.

  fillOval—Takes four arguments and draws a solid oval inside a bounding rectangular area. The first two arguments are the x- and y-coordinates of the top-left corner of the rectangular area and the second two are the width and height.

  setColor—Sets the color of the Graphics object.

Math   The Math class provides methods to perform different mathematical functions.

- **Methods**

  abs—Returns the absolute value of its argument.

  max—Returns the greater of its two arguments.

  min—Returns the lesser of its two arguments.

Tutorial 28: Phone Book Application (Introducing the Java Speech API)

Central   This class (in the `javax.speech` package) provides access to all speech input and output capabilities, such as the speech synthesizer.

- ■ *Methods*

  `createSynthesizer`—Creates a `Synthesizer` object, which is used to speak text to the users.

Locale   This class represents a specific region of the world.

- ■ *Constants*

  `Locale.US`—Represents a `Locale` object for the United States.

Synthesizer   This class provides speech synthesis capabilities, such as speaking text.

- ■ *Methods*

  `allocate`—Allocates the resources such as the speech synthesizer, required by the speech engine.

  `deallocate`—Frees the resources, such as the speech synthesizer, that are allocated to the speech engine.

  `getSynthesizerProperties`—Used to obtain the `SynthesizerProperties` object associated with the speech synthesizer.

  `resume`—Used to get the speech synthesizer ready to speak.

  `speakPlainText`—Used to speak text to the user.

SynthesizerModeDesc   This class specifies the basic properties of the speech synthesizer.

- ■ *Constructor*

  `SynthesizerModeDesc`—Takes five arguments, each representing a basic property of the speech engine. The first argument (a `String`) specifies the name of the text-to-speech engine. The second argument (a `String`) identifies the mode of operation of the speech engine. The third argument (a `Locale`) specifies the language supported by the speech engine. The fourth argument (a `Boolean`) indicates whether a speech engine is already running. The fifth argument (an array of `Voice` objects).

  ```
  SynthesizerModeDesc descriptor = new SynthesizerModeDesc(
      "Unlimited domain FreeTTS Speech Synthesizer " +
      "from Sun Labs", null, Locale.US, Boolean.FALSE, null );
  ```

SynthesizerProperties   This class contains various properties of a speech synthesizer.

- ■ *Properties*

  `speakingRate`—Specifies the speaking rate in words per minute.

- ■ *Methods*

  `setSpeakingRate`—Sets the *speakingRate* property of the speech synthesizer.

Voice   This class specifies the output voice of a speech synthesizer.

Tutorial 29: Bookstore Web Application (Introducing Web Applications and the Apache Tomcat Web Server)

No new elements.

Tutorial 30: Bookstore Web Application: Client Tier (Introducing HTML

a (anchor)   This element is used to add a hyperlink in an HTML document.

- *Attributes*

  href—Specifies the location of a linked resource.

---

body   This element contains the HTML elements that will be displayed in the Web browser window.

---

form   This element is used to insert a form in an HTML document to collect user inputs.

---

h1   This is the highest-level header element. Typically, an h1 element is rendered by browsers in a large font.

---

head   This element specifies the settings of the document, such as its title.

---

img   This element is used to insert an image in an HTML document.

- *Attributes*

  alt—Specifies the text to display if the browser cannot locate the image.
  src—Specifies the location of the image file.

---

input   This element is used to create a "submit" button.

- *Attributes*

  type—Specifies the type of an input element. Setting the type to "submit" indicates that the input element is a "submit" button.
  value—Sets the text displayed on the "submit" button.

---

p (paragraph)   This element adds a paragraph to a JSP or an HTML document.

---

select   This element is used to create an HTML menu control.

- *Attributes*

  name—This attribute identifies the drop-down list menu control. The identifier used is similar to a variable name in Java.

---

title   This element sets the title displayed in the title bar at the top of the browser window.

Tutorial 31: Bookstore Web Application: Information Tier (Examining the Database and Creating Database Components)

JSP comment   A comment delimited by <%-- and --%>.

---

out   This implicit JSP object is used to write text as a part of the response to a client request.

- *Methods*

  println—Writes text as part of the response to a client request.

request   This implicit JSP object represents the client request. This object can be used to get data that is submitted to a JSP as part of the client request.

- *Methods*

    getParameter—Obtains the value of a request parameter.

scriptlet   A JSP scriptlet enables programmers to insert a block of Java code in a JSP. Scriptlets are delimited by <% and %>.

Tutorial 32: Bookstore Web Application: Middle Tier (form Attributes method/action and Inserting Query Results in a JSP)

option   This HTML element is used inside the select HTML element to add items to the HTML menu control.

form   This HTML element is used to insert a form in an HTML document that will collect user inputs.

- *Attributes*

    action—Specifies where to send form data when the user submits the form by clicking the "submit" button.

    method—Describes how the HTML form's data is sent to the Web server.

JSP expression   An expression used to insert dynamic content (such as information from a database) in the response to a client. JSP expressions are delimited by <%= and %>.

Keyword Chart

The table in Fig. E.1 contains a listing of Java keywords. Many of these keywords are discussed throughout the text.

Java Keywords			
abstract	assert	boolean	break
byte	case	catch	char
class	continue	default	do
double	else	extends	final
finally	float	for	if
implements	import	instanceof	int
interface	long	native	new
package	private	protected	public
return	short	static	strictfp
super	switch	synchronized	this
throw	throws	transient	try
void	volatile	while	

Keywords that are reserved, but not currently used

const	goto

Figure E.1   Java keywords.

Primitive Types

The table in Fig. F.1 contains a complete listing of Java's primitive types, the number of bytes used to store each type and the range of values that each type can represent.

Type	Size in bytes	Values
boolean		false, true
char	2	0 to 65535
byte	1	−128 to +127 (-2^7 to $2^7 - 1$)
short	2	−32,768 to +32,767 (-2^{15} to $2^{15} - 1$)
int	4	−2,147,483,648 to +2,147,483,647 (-2^{31} to $2^{31} - 1$)
long	8	−9,223,372,036,854,775,808 to +9,223,372,036,854,775,807 (-2^{63} to $2^{63} - 1$)
float	4	*Negative range:* −3.4028234663852886e+38 to −1.40129846432481707e−45 *Positive range:* 1.40129846432481707e−45 to 3.4028234663852886e+38
double	8	*Negative range:* −1.7976931348623157e+308 to −4.94065645841246544e−324 *Positive range:* 4.94065645841246544e−324 to 1.7976931348623157e+308

Figure F.1 Java primitive type sizes and value ranges.

A

a (anchor) element in HTML—Used to create a hyperlink.

abs method of the Math class—Returns the absolute value of a given value.

absolute positioning—Specifies the exact size and location of a component in a container.

absolute value—The value of a number without the sign of the number.

abstract class—A class that cannot be instantiated. Often called an abstract superclass because it is usable only as the superclass in an inheritance hierarchy. These classes are incomplete; they are missing pieces necessary for instantiation which concrete subclasses must implement.

abstract keyword—Used to declare that a class or method is abstract.

abstract method—Declares a method header but no method body. Any class with an abstract method must be an abstract class.

access modifier—Keywords public and private are called access modifier.

accessor—A *get* method.

ACE table—A program development tool you can use to relate GUI events with the actions that should be performed in response to those events.

action/decision model of programming—Representing control statements as UML activity diagrams with action-state symbols, indicating *actions* to be performed, and diamond symbols, indicating *decisions* to be made.

ActionEvent—The type of event object generated when an action is performed, such as clicking a JButton. This object is sent to event handler actionPerformed (if one is registered for the component on which the action is performed).

actionPerformed event handler—Method called to handle an ActionEvent.

action attribute of the form HTML element—The attribute that specifies where to send form data when the user submits the form by clicking the "submit" button.

action expression (in the UML)—Used in an action state within a UML activity diagram to specify a particular action to perform.

action state (in the UML)—An action (represented by an action-state symbol) to perform in a UML activity diagram.

action-state symbol (in the UML)—A rectangle with its left and right sides replaced with arcs curving outward that represents an action to perform in a UML activity diagram.

activity diagram (in the UML)—A UML diagram that models the activity (also called the workflow) of a portion of a software system.

Ada—A programming language, named after Lady Ada Lovelace, that was developed under the sponsorship of the U.S. Department of Defense (DOD) in the 1970s and early 1980s.

add method of ButtonGroup—Adds a JRadioButton to the ButtonGroup.

add method of class ArrayList—Adds a specified object at the end of an ArrayList.

add method of JMenu—Adds a JMenu, JMenuItem, JCheckBox-MenuItem or JRadioButtonMenuItem to the JMenu.

add method of JMenuBar—Adds a JMenu to the JMenuBar.

addActionListener method of JButton—Registers an action-Performed event handler with a component. The actionPerformed event handler will then be called if an ActionEvent is generated by a user's interaction with the component.

addChangeListener method of JSpinner—Registers a state-Changed event handler with a component. The stateChanged event handler will then be called if a ChangeEvent is generated by a user's interaction with the component.

addkeyListener method—Registers an event listener with an event source, such as a JTextArea.

addMouseListener method—Registers with a GUI component an event listener object that implements the MouseListener interface. The component can now react to mouse events.

addMouseMotionListener method—Registers with a GUI component an event listener object that implements the MouseMotionListener interface. The component can now react to mouse motion events.

addSeparator method of JMenu—Adds a separator bar to the JMenu.

algorithm—A procedure for solving a problem, specifying the actions to be executed and the order in which these actions are to be executed.

allocate method of Synthesizer—Used to allocate resources required by the speech engine.

alt attribute of HTML img element—Specifies the text to display if the browser cannot locate an image.

anonymous inner class—An unnamed inner class that must be used to instantiate one object at the same time the class is declared. Anonymous inner classes are often used for event handling.

Apache Tomcat—A Web server from the Apache Group that is free and available for many platforms.

append method of JTextArea—Adds text to a JTextArea component.

argument—A value that is passed to a method by being placed in the parentheses that follow the method name in a method call.

argument list—A comma-separated list of the arguments sent to a method. The number, order and type of arguments must agree with the parameters in the method's parameter list.

arithmetic and logic unit (ALU)—The "manufacturing" section of the computer. The ALU performs calculations and makes decisions.

arithmetic operators—The operators +, -, *, / and % used for performing calculations.

array—A data structure containing elements of the same type.

array bounds—Integers that determine what indices can be used to access an element in the array. The lower bound is 0; the upper bound is the length of the array minus one.

array initializer—A comma-separated list of expressions enclosed in braces—{ and }—which is used to initialize the elements in an array. When the initializer is empty, the elements in the array are initialized to the default value for the array type.

ArrayList collection/class—Used to store a group of objects. Unlike arrays, ArrayLists can be dynamically resized and have access to several methods that allow programmers to easily manipulate the contents of the ArrayList.

arrayName.**length expression**—Contains the number of elements in an array.

Arrays.sort—Sorts the elements in its array argument into ascending or alphabetical order.

assembly language—A type of programming language that uses English-like abbreviations to represent the fundamental operations of the computer.

assignment operator—The assignment operator, =, copies the value of the expression on its right side into the variable on its left side.

asterisk (*)—An arithmetic operator that indicates multiplication.

attribute—Another name for a property of an object.

B

background **property**—Property that specifies the background color of a content pane or component.

bandwidth—The information-carrying capacity of communications lines.

BASIC (Beginner's All-Purpose Symbolic Instruction Code)—A programming language that was developed in the mid-1960s by Professors John Kemeny and Thomas Kurtz of Dartmouth College as a language for writing simple programs and its primary purpose was to familiarize novices with programming techniques.

binary digit—A digit that can assume one of two values (0 or 1).

binary operator—An operator that requires two operands.

bit—Short for "binary digit."

block—A group of code statements that are enclosed in curly braces ({ and }).

body—A set of statements that is enclosed in curly braces ({ and }). This is also called a block.

body element in HTML—Contains the HTML elements that will be displayed in the Web browser window.

book-title capitalization—A style that capitalizes the first letter of each significant word in the text (for example, **Calculate the Total**).

boolean logical exclusive OR (^) operator—A logical operator that evaluates to true if and only if one of its operands is true and the other is false.

boolean type—A type that represents the values true and false.

Boolean.FALSE—A constant in class Boolean that represents a false value as a Boolean object. Class Boolean also contains a TRUE constant.

border **property**—Allows a border to be added to some GUI components.

bottom tier—The tier (also known as the information tier, or the data tier) containing the application data of a multi-tier application—typically implemented as a database.

bounding box—A box encompassing an oval or other graphic, that specifies height, width, and location.

bounds **property**—The property that specifies both the location and size of a component.

break mode—Debugger mode the application is in when execution stops at a breakpoint.

break statement—Typically appears at the end of each case. This statement immediately terminates the switch statement, and program control continues with the next statement after the switch.

breakpoint—A marker that can be set in the debugger at any executable line of source code, causing the application to pause when it reaches the specified line of code. One reason to set a breakpoint is to be able to examine the values of variables at that point in the application's execution.

BufferedReader class—Provides the functionality of reading lines of text from a file.

bug—A flaw in an application that prevents the application from executing correctly.

ButtonGroup—A group of any number of JRadioButtons. Only one JRadioButton in the ButtonGroup can be selected at a time. When one JRadioButton is selected, the previously selected JRadioButton is deselected.

byte—A piece of data typically composed of eight bits.

C

callee—The method being called.

caller—The method that calls another method. Also known as the calling method.

case label—Precedes the statements that will execute if the switch's controlling expression matches the expression in the case label.

cast operator—Converts its operand to the type placed within the parentheses of the cast.

cast operator—A type name enclosed in parentheses. A cast operator is used to perform explicit conversions. A

temporary value of the type in the parentheses will be created and used in the expression.

case sensitive—Distinguishes between uppercase and lowercase letters in code. Identifiers with identical spelling are treated differently if the capitalization of the identifiers differs.

catch block—Also called an exception handler, this block executes when the corresponding `try` block in the application detects an exceptional situation and throws an exception of the type the `catch` block declares.

catch-or-declare requirement—The code that generates a checked exception should be wrapped in a `try` block and provide a `catch` block for that checked exception. The method that contains the code that generates a checked exception must provide a `throws` block containing the checked exception unless it provides a handler for it.

Central class—Used to provide access to all speech input and output capabilities, such as speech synthesis. Also used to locate the speech engines, select a matching engine based on the set of properties defined by the descriptor and create speech recognizers and speech synthesizers.

central processing unit (CPU)—The part of the computer's hardware that is responsible for supervising the operation of the other units of the computer.

ChangeEvent class—The type of event object generated when a JSpinner's value is changed by clicking on one of its arrows or entering a value. This object is sent to event handler stateChanged.

char type—Type used to store character values.

character—A digit, letter or special symbol (characters in Java are Unicode characters, which are composed of 2 bytes).

character constant—Another name for a character literal.

character literal—The value of a variable of type char, it is represented by a character within single quotes, such as `'A'`, `'d'`, `'*'`, `'.'` and the like.

character set—The set of all characters used to write applications and represent data items on a particular computer. Java uses the Unicode character set.

charAt method of class String—Returns the character located at a specific index in a String.

checked exception—An exception type that is not a subclass of RuntimeException, which must satisfy the catch-or-declare requirement.

class—The type of a group of similar objects. A class specifies the general format of its objects; the properties and actions available to an object depend on its class. An object is to its class much as a house is to its blueprint.

class's body—Code that is included in the { and } of a class declaration.

Class class—Represents a class in a running Java application.

class declaration—The code that defines a class, beginning with the class keyword.

.class file—The type of file that is executed by the Java Runtime Environment (JRE). A .class file is created by compiling the application's .java file.

class hierarchy—Also known as inheritance hierarchy, this defines the inheritance relationships among classes.

class keyword—The keyword used to begin a class declaration.

class name—The identifier used as the name of a class.

ClassNotFoundException class—An exception thrown by the Class method forName if the class the application is attempting to load cannot be found.

CLASSPATH environment variable—Specifies the location of the class libraries that are required to run an application.

clear debugger command—Command that removes a breakpoint.

clear method of class ArrayList—Removes all elements in an ArrayList.

client—When you create and use an object of a class in an application, your application is known as a client of that class.

client tier—The user interface of a multi-tier application (also called the top tier).

close method of BufferedReader—Closes the file being read.

close method of Connection—Closes a database connection.

close method of PrintWriter—Closes the file to which information is being written.

close method of Statement—Closes a Statement and release its database resources.

close method of ResultSet—Closes a ResultSet and release its database resources.

COBOL (COmmon Business Oriented Language)—A language that was developed in the late 1950s by a group of computer manufacturers in conjunction with government and industrial computer users. This language is used primarily for business applications that manipulate large amounts of data.

code reuse—Using pre-existing code to save time, effort and money.

collection—An object that stores groups of related objects.

column (in an array)—In referring to an element of a two-dimensional array, the second index specifies the column.

column (in a database table)—Represents an individual data attribute.

command-line arguments—Arguments that are supplied to the java interpreter that specify the options to run an application.

comment (//)—Explanatory text that is inserted to improve an application's readability.

comment in HTML—Starting with <!-- and ending with -->, an HTML comment is used to describe portions of an HTML document or JSP. HTML comments support multi-line text. Browsers ignore comments when they render HTML documents.

compiler—A translator program that converts high-level-language programs into machine language.

compiling—The process that converts a source code file (.java) into a .class file.

complex condition—A condition that combines multiple simple conditions.

computer—A device capable of performing computations and making logical decisions at speeds millions and even billions of times faster than the speeds at which human beings carry out those same tasks.

computer program—A set of instructions that guides a computer through an orderly series of actions.

computer programmer—A person who writes computer programs in programming languages.

concrete class—A class that can be instantiated.

conditional AND (&&) operator—A logical operator used to ensure that two conditions are both `true` before choosing a path of execution. Performs short-circuit evaluation.

conditional OR (||) operator—A logical operator used to ensure that either or both of two conditions are `true` before a path of execution is chosen. Performs short-circuit evaluation.

`Connection` object—Manages a connection to a database.

consistent state—A way to maintain the values of an object's instance variables such that those values are always valid.

constant expression—A value that cannot be changed. A case label consists of the keyword `case` followed by a constant expression. This constant expression must be a character literal or an integer literal.

constructor—Initializes a class's variables and has the same name as the class that contains it. They are similar to methods, but do not have a return type.

`cont` debugger command—Command that resumes program execution after a breakpoint is reached while debugging.

container—An object that contains components.

content pane—The portion of a `JFrame` that contains the GUI components.

control variable—A variable used to control the number of iterations of a counter-controlled loop.

controlling expression—The expression in a `switch` statement whose value is compared sequentially with each `case` until either a match occurs, the `default` case is executed or the right brace is reached.

control statement—A program statement (such as `if`, `if...else`, `switch`, `while`, `do...while` or `for`) that specifies the flow of control (that is, the order in which statements execute).

control-statement nesting—Placing one control statement in the body of another control statement.

control-statement stacking—A set of control statements in sequence. The exit point of one control statement is connected to the entry point of the next control statement in sequence.

coordinate pair—Composed of an *x*-coordinate (the horizontal coordinate) and a *y*-coordinate (the vertical coordinate). A coordinate pair can be used to reference a single pixel on a GUI component.

coordinate system—A scheme for identifying every possible point on the computer screen.

counter—A variable often used to determine the number of times a block of statements in a loop will execute.

counter-controlled repetition—A technique that uses a counter variable to determine the number of times that a block of statements will execute. Also called definite repetition.

`createStatement` method of `Connection`—Creates an object that implements interface `Statement` for submitting SQL to a DBMS.

`createSynthesizer` method of `Central`—Used to create a speech synthesizer.

cursor—A pointer to a row in a `ResultSet`.

D

database management system (DBMS)—A collection of programs designed to create and manage databases.

data hierarchy—The collection of data items processed by computers, which become larger and more complex in structure as you progress from bits to characters to fields to files, and so on.

data structure—Groups and organizes related data.

data tier—The tier (also known as the information tier, or the bottom tier) containing the application data of a multi-tier application—typically implemented as a database.

database—An organized collection of information.

`Date` class—Stores date and time information.

`DateFormat` class—Formats date and time information.

`deallocate` method of `Synthesizer`—Frees the resources (such as speech synthesizers) that are allocated to the speech engine.

debugger—Software that allows you to monitor the execution of your applications to locate and remove logic errors.

debugging—The process of locating and removing errors in an application.

decimal digits—The digits 0, 1, 2, 3, 4, 5, 6, 7, 8 and 9.

`DecimalFormat`—The class used to format floating-point numbers (that is, numbers with decimal points).

decision symbol (in the UML)—The diamond-shaped symbol in a UML activity diagram that indicates a decision is to be made.

declare a variable—Specify the type and name of a variable to be used in an application.

declaration—Code that specifies the name and type of a variable.

decrementing—The process of subtracting one from an integer variable.

`default` case—The optional case whose statements execute if the `switch`'s controlling expression does not match any of the cases' values.

definite repetition—See counter-controlled repetition.

destructive—The process of writing to a memory location in which the previous value is overwritten or lost.

`double`—Type that is used to store floating-point numbers.

dialog—A window used to display a message to the user or display various options from which the user can choose.

diamond symbol (in the UML)—The UML symbol that represents the decision symbol or the merge symbol, depending on how it is used.

`dir` command—Command typed in a **Command Prompt** window to list the directory contents.

direct superclass—The superclass from which the subclass inherits.

disabled—A component that has its *enabled* property set to `false`. Such components do not respond to user interactions.

dismiss—A synonym for closing a dialog.

divide-and-conquer technique—The techniques of constructing large applications from small, manageable pieces to make development and maintenance of those applications easier.

DNS lookup—The process that translates fully qualified domain names into IP addresses.

domain—Represents a group of hosts on the Internet.

domain name—Also known as a Web address, which uniquely identifies the location of a business or organization on the Internet.

Domain Name System (DNS) server—Computer that maintains a database of host names and their corresponding IP addresses.

do...while repetition statement—A control statement that executes a set of body statements while the loop-continuation condition is `true`. The condition is tested after the loop body executes, so the body statements always execute at least once.

dot separator—Allows programmers to access members of a class or object.

dotted line (in the UML)—A UML activity diagram symbol that connects each UML-style note with the element that the note describes.

double type—A type that can represent numbers with decimal points.

Double.parseDouble method—A method that converts a `String` containing a floating-point number into a `double` value.

double-selection statement—A statement, such as `if...else`, that selects between two different actions or sequences of actions.

dragging the mouse—Moving the mouse while holding down the mouse button.

drawLine method of the Graphics class—Draws a line using the given *x*- and *y*-coordinates.

drawOval method of the Graphics class—Draws an oval using the bounding box's upper-left *x*- and *y*-coordinates and the width and height.

drawRect method of the Graphics class—Draws a rectangle using the given *x*- and *y*-coordinates and the rectangle's width and height.

DriverManager class—Provides services for managing JDBC drivers. This class also is used to establish a connection to a database.

dynamic content—A type of content that is animated or interactive.

dynamic resizing—Enables an `ArrayList` object to vary its size to meet the storage demands of your application.

E

echo character—Replaces each character displayed in a `JPasswordField`. The default echo character is *, but the programmer can specify the echo character by calling the `JPasswordField`'s `setEchoChar` method.

editable **property**—The property that specifies the appearance and behavior of a `JTextField`, which allows you to distinguish an input `JTextField` (*editable* property is `true`) from an output `JTextField` (*editable* property is `false`).

editable **property of a JPasswordField**—Determines whether the `JPasswordField` will allow user input.

element—An item in an array.

element in HTML—Markup used to specify a document's structure.

empty element—An element that does not place text between the start and end tags.

empty string ("")—A string that does not contain any characters.

enabled **property**—Specifies whether a component, such as a `JButton`, appears enabled (`true`) or disabled (`false`).

end tag in HTML—Consists of the element name preceded by a / in angle brackets, which ends an HTML element.

end-of-line comment—A comment that appears at the end of a code line.

endsWith method of class String—Returns `true` if a `String` ends with a particular substring and `false` otherwise.

entry point—The location in an application's source code where execution begins. In Java, the entry point for an application is the `main` method.

equality operators—Operators `==` (is equal to) and `!=` (is not equal to) that compare two values.

equals method of class String—Returns `true` when `String` contains the same text as the argument to method `equals`.

Error class—The class that represents exceptional situations happening in the Java runtime system that typically should not be caught by an application.

escape character—The backslash (\) character that is used to form escape sequences.

escape sequence—The backslash (\) and the character next to it, when used within a `string`, form an escape sequence to represent a special character such as a newline (\n) or a tab (\t).

event—An action that generates an event object and initiates a call to an appropriate registered event handler.

event-driven programming—The type of programming in which the application waits for certain events to occur, then responds to those events.

event handler—Method that executes when a certain event occurs. Event handlers must be registered with a component.

event listener—The object notified by an event source when an event is generated.

event source—The GUI component the user acts on to generate an event.

event object—An object generated when the user interacts with a component. The event object contains information about the event that occurred.

exception—An indication of a problem that occurs during an application's execution.

Exception class—The class that represents exceptional situations occurring in a Java application that should be caught and handled by the application.

exception handler—A block that executes (in a `catch` block) when the application detects an exceptional situation and throws an exception.

exception handling—Creating applications that can resolve (or handle) problems during application execution.

exception parameter—Identifies the type of exception that an exception handler can process.

executable statement—An action that is performed when the corresponding Java application is run.

executeQuery method of Statement—Used to execute a SQL query. This method returns a ResultSet object containing the results of the query.

executeUpdate method of Statement—Used to execute a SQL statement that modifies database data, such as UPDATE. This method returns an int value that indicates the number of rows that were updated.

explicit conversion—An operation converting a value of one type to a value of another type requiring a cast operator. Also called casting.

extending a class—Creating a new class based on an existing class (also called inheritance).

extends keyword—Specifies that a subclass inherits members (fields and methods) from its superclass.

extensible language—A language that can be "extended" with new classes.

F

false—One of the two possible values for a boolean type; the other is true.

field—A group of characters that conveys some meaning. For example, a field consisting of uppercase and lowercase letters can represent a person's name.

field (of a class)—A variable defined in a class.

file—A group of related records that is assigned a name. Files are used for long-term persistence of data, even after the application that created the data terminates.

File class—Represents a file and can be used to retrieve information about a file, such as the name of the file.

file processing—A capability of Java that includes creating, reading from and writing to files.

FileReader class—Used to read characters from a file.

FileWriter class—Used to write characters from a file.

fillOval method of Graphics—Draws an oval. This method takes as arguments the coordinates of the upper-left corner of the oval's bounding box and the width and height of the bounding box.

fillRect method of class Graphics—A method that draws a filled rectangle defined by the arguments: *x*- and *y*- coordinates of the upper-left corner, the width and the height of the rectangle.

final keyword—Precedes the data type in a declaration of a constant.

final state (in the UML)—A solid circle surrounded by a hollow circle (a "bullseye") in a UML activity diagram. It represents the end of the workflow after an application performs its activities.

final value of a control variable—The last value a control variable will hold before a counter-controlled loop terminates.

finally block—A block that is guaranteed to execute if its corresponding try block executes. Typically, the finally block is used to release resources.

first generation language—Another name for a machine language.

floating-point number—A number with a decimal point such as 2.3456, 0.0 and -845.4680.

focus—When a component is selected, it is said to have the focus of the application. Focus is used to help bring attention to the component that should be used next.

Font class—Creates and manipulates fonts.

font property—The property that specifies the font name (for example, SansSerif, Times, Courier, etc.), style (for instance, Font.PLAIN) and font size in points (for example, 12, 18, 36, etc.) of any displayed text in a JFrame or one of its components.

Font.BOLD constant—Represents the bold font style.

Font.ITALIC constant—Represents the italic font style.

Font.PLAIN constant—Represents the plain font style.

for keyword—The keyword that begins each for statement.

for statement header/for header—The first line in a for statement. The for header specifies all four essential elements for counter-controlled repetition—the name of a control variable, the initial value, the increment or decrement value and the final value.

for repetition statement—A repetition statement that conveniently handles the details of counter-controlled repetition. The for header uses all four elements essential to counter-controlled repetition.

form element in HTML—Used to collect user inputs.

format method of DecimalFormat—Method that returns a String containing a formatted number.

formatting—Modifying the appearance of text for display purposes.

forName method of Class—The method used to load the class for the database driver.

FORTRAN (FORmula TRANslator)—Programming language developed by IBM Corporation in the mid-1950s to create scientific and engineering applications that require complex mathematical computations.

forward slash (/)—An arithmetic operator that indicates division.

forward-slash characters—A comment begins with two forward slashes (//).

fourth generation language (4GL)—A programming language similar to a natural language like English and is primarily used to manipulate information that is stored in databases.

Framework Class Library (FCL)—A powerful library of reusable software components developed for Microsoft's .NET platform. The FCL provides similar capabilities to the Java class library.

FROM SQL keyword—The keyword used with SELECT to specify the table from which to get data.

full-line comment—A comment that appears on a line by itself in source code.

fully qualified domain name (FQDN)—A host name combined with a domain and top-level domain that provides a user-friendly way to identify a site on the Internet.

functionality—The tasks or actions an application can execute.

G

-g compiler option—Causes the compiler to generates debugging information that is used by the debugger to help you debug your applications.

***get* method**—Used to retrieve a value of an instance variable.

get method of class `ArrayList`—Returns a reference to the element in the `ArrayList` at the specified index.

getBackground method of `JPanel`—Returns a `Color` object that is the color of the background.

getConnection method of `DriverManager`—A method that attempts to connect to a database.

getDouble method of `ResultSet`—Method used to get a column value as a double.

getInt method of `ResultSet`—Method used to get a column value as an `int`.

getItemAt method of `JComboBox`—Takes an `int` argument representing an index and returns the object at that index of a `JComboBox`.

getKeyCode method of `KeyEvent`—Returns the virtual key code associated with the key that the user interacted with.

getName method of `File`—Returns the name of the selected file.

getParameter method of the implicit JSP object `request`—Used to obtain the value of a request parameter.

getPassword method—Returns the text in the `JPasswordField`.

getPoint method of class `MouseEvent`—Returns a `Point` object containing the coordinates of the mouse cursor.

getSelectedFile method of `JFileChooser`—Returns `File` object containing the selected file from the `JFileChooser`.

getSelectedIndex method of `JComboBox`—Returns the index of the selected item.

getSize method of `Font`—Returns the size of the `Font`.

getSource method of `ActionEvent`—Returns a reference to the GUI component that raised the event (also called the source of the event).

getString method of `ResultSet`—The method used to get a column value as a `String`.

getStyle method of `Font`—Returns the style of the `Font`.

getSynthesizerProperties method of `Synthesizer`—Used to obtain the `SynthesizerProperties` object associated with the speech synthesizer.

getText method—A method that accesses (or gets) the *text* property of a component such as a `JLabel`, `JTextField` or a `JButton`.

getValue method of class `JSpinner`—Returns the current value displayed in a `JSpinner` component.

graphical user interface (GUI)—The visual part of an application with which users interact.

`Graphics` object—An object that draws pixels on the screen to represent text and other graphical objects (such as lines, ellipses, rectangles and other polygons).

guard condition (in the UML)—A condition contained in square brackets that must be associated with a transition arrow leading from a decision symbol in a UML activity diagram.

The guard condition associated with a particular transition determines whether workflow continues along that path.

GUI component—A reusable component, such as a `JButton` or `JComboBox`, that enables the user to interact with an application.

H

h1 element in HTML—Highest-level header element. Typically, an h1 element is rendered by browsers in a large font.

hardware—The various devices that make up a computer, including the keyboard, screen, mouse, hard drive, memory, CD-ROM and DVD drives and processing units.

***has a* relationship**—A relationship, in which an object contains one or more references to other objects.

hasNext method of class `Iterator`—Tests if there are any remaining elements in the `ArrayList` accessed by this `Iterator` object.

head element in HTML—Specifies various settings of an HTML document, such as its title.

header—A line of text at the top of a `JTextArea` that clarifies the information being displayed.

header element in HTML—Used to specify the relative importance of information.

hidden variable—An instance variable with the same name as a local variable is hidden while the local variable has scope. Hidden variables can lead to logic errors.

high-level language—A type of programming language in which a single program statement accomplishes a substantial task. High-level language instructions look almost like everyday English and contain common mathematical notations.

horizontal coordinate—The horizontal distance moving right from the upper-left corner of a GUI component. Also known as the *x*-coordinate.

***horizontalAlignment* property of `JLabel`**—The property that specifies how text is aligned within a `JLabel`.

***horizontalAlignment* property of `JTextField`**—The property that specifies the text alignment in a `JTextField` (`JTextField.LEFT`, `JTextField.CENTER` or `JTextField.RIGHT`).

host—A computer that stores and maintains resources, such as Web pages, databases and multimedia files.

HTML element—A part of the HTML language, such as h1, select or input, that determines the format of a Web page and the GUI components that appear on a Web page.

HTML markup—Contains text that represents the content of a document and elements that specify a document's structure.

HTML menu control—A drop-down list that is created by an HTML select element.

hyperlink in HTML—Used to reference other resources, such as HTML documents and JSPs.

HyperText Markup Language (HTML)—Language for marking up information to share over the World Wide Web via hyperlinked text documents.

I

***icon* property**—The property that specifies the file name of the image displayed in a `JLabel`.

identifier—A series of characters consisting of letters, digits and underscores used to name application units such as classes and GUI components.

if statement—The `if` single-selection statement performs an action (or sequence of actions) based on a condition.

if...else statement—The `if...else` double-selection statement performs an action (or sequence of actions) if a condition is true and performs a different action (or sequence of actions) if the condition is false.

img element in HTML—Inserts an image in an HTML document.

immutable—`String`s in Java are immutable, meaning that the contents of a `String` cannot be changed after it is created.

implement an interface—Implementing a method body for each method declared in an interface.

implicit conversion—An operation that converts a primitive type to another type without writing code to (explicitly) tell the application to do the conversion.

implicit object—Provides the programmer with access to the request from the client and the response to the client in the context of a JavaServer Page. The programmer does not have to explicitly create the implicit object to use it.

import declaration—Used to import classes or packages.

incrementing—The process of adding one to an integer variable.

increment (or decrement) of a control variable—The amount by which the control variable's value changes during each iteration of the loop.

index—An array element's position number, also called a subscript. An index must be zero, a positive integer or an integer expression that evaluates to zero or a positive integer. If an application uses an expression as an index, the expression is evaluated first to determine the index.

index of an `ArrayList`—The value with which you can refer to a specific element in an `ArrayList`, based on the element's location in that `ArrayList`.

indexed array name—The array name followed by an index enclosed in square brackets. The indexed array name can be used on the left side of an assignment statement to place a new value into an array element. The indexed array name can be used in the right side of an assignment to retrieve the value of that array element.

indexOf method of class `ArrayList`—Returns the index in the `ArrayList` where a specified object is stored. If the object does not exist in the `ArrayList`, `indexOf` returns -1.

indexOf method of class `String`—Returns the index of the first occurrence of a substring in a `String`; returns -1 if the substring is not found.

indirect superclass—A superclass that is two or more levels up the class hierarchy.

infinite loop—A logical error in which a repetition statement never terminates.

information tier—The tier containing the application data of a multi-tier application—typically implemented as a database (also called the bottom tier or database tier).

inheritance—A form of software reuse in which classes are based on an existing class's fields (attributes) and methods (behaviors) and extend them with new or modified capabilities (also called extending a class).

inheritance hierarchy—The inheritance relationships among classes. Also known as the class hierarchy.

initial state (in the UML)—The beginning of the workflow in a UML activity diagram before the application performs the activities.

initial value of a control variable—The value a control variable will hold when counter-controlled repetition begins.

initialization value—The beginning value of a variable.

inner class—A class that is declared completely inside another class. A type of inner class, the anonymous inner class, is often used for event handling.

input dialog—Causes the application to wait for the user to input data. The dialog contains a `JTextField` designed to retrieve user input.

input element in HTML—Creates a "submit" button.

input `JTextField`—A `JTextField` used to get user input. The *editable* property of an input `JTextField` is set to `true`, which is the default.

input unit—The "receiving" section of the computer that obtains information (data and computer programs) from various input devices, such as the keyboard and the mouse.

instance—Also known as an object.

instance variable—Declared inside a class but outside any methods of that class. The scope of an instance variable is its entire class.

instant-access application—An application for which particular information must be located immediately.

instantiate an object—Create an object of a class.

int type—The type that stores integer values.

interface—A way to declare *what* a class does without declaring *how* it does it.

integer—A whole number, such as 919, –11 or 0.

Integer object—An object that contains a single piece of `int` data.

Integer.parseInt method—Returns the integer equivalent of its `String` argument.

Internet—A worldwide computer network. Most people today access the Internet through the World Wide Web.

interpreter—A program that executes high-level language programs directly without the need for compiling those programs into machine language.

intValue method of class `Integer`—Returns the primitive `int` data in an `Integer` object.

invoke a method—Call a method.

IOException—An error that indicates that a problem occurred while opening, reading or writing a file.

IP (Internet Protocol) address—A unique address used to locate a computer on the Internet.

is a relationship—A relationship, in which an object of a subclass also can be treated as an object of its superclass.

isMetaDown method—Returns `true` if the right mouse button is pressed, `false` otherwise.

isSelected method of class JCheckBox—Specifies whether the JCheckBox is selected (true) or deselected (false).

isSelected method of JRadioButton—Returns true if the JRadioButton is selected and false otherwise.

iterator—An object that allows you to loop through each element in a collection.

Iterator interface—Implemented by iterator objects, which allow you to loop through each element in a collection.

iterator method of class ArrayList—Creates a new object of type Iterator used for iterating through each element contained in the ArrayList.

J

Java API (Application Programming Interface)—Collection of existing classes provided as part of the Java programming language.

Java class library—See Java API.

.java file—The type of file in which programmers write the Java code for an application.

Java Runtime Environment (JRE)—A portion of the J2SDK that executes (that is, runs) Java programs.

JavaServer Pages—A technology to develop dynamic Web pages through the use of Java and HTML.

Java Speech API—A technology used to add speech capabilities to applications or Web pages to support new means of human interaction with computers.

Java Speech technology—The use of speech synthesis to produce synthetic speech from text.

java.awt—The package containing classes for graphics and images.

java.awt.event package—Provides interfaces and classes for handling all kinds of events, such as keyboard events and mouse events.

javac command—The command that compiles a source code file (.java) into a .class file.

java.io package—Includes classes that enable you to access and manipulate files.

java.util package—Provides, among other capabilities, random number generation capabilities with class Random.

javax.speech package—The classes and interfaces in the javax.speech package support audio connectivity.

javax.speech.synthesis package—Package of classes and interfaces that support speech synthesis.

jdb—Starts the Java debugger when typed at the **Command Prompt**.

JButton component—A component that, when clicked, commands the application to perform an action.

JCheckBox component—A small gray square GUI element that either is blank or contains a check mark. This component includes the text displayed beside the square.

JCheckBox text—The text that appears alongside a JCheckBox.

JCheckBoxMenuItem component—A specific type of menu item that has a check box to its left, allowing the user to see if the item is currently selected.

JColorChooser component—Displays a dialog containing color options to a user.

JComboBox component—Presents options in a drop-down list.

JDBC API—The part of the Java API that is used to interact with databases.

JDBC driver—A class that enables Java applications to access a particular DBMS.

JDBC URL—An address that directs a JDBC driver to a database location.

JFileChooser component—Allows a user to select a file.

JFileChooser.APPROVE_OPTION constant—A value representing the **OK** JButton being clicked in the JFileChooser.

JFileChooser.CANCEL_OPTION constant—A value representing the **Cancel** JButton being clicked in the JFileChooser.

JFileChooser.ERROR_OPTION constant—A value specifying that an error occurred in a JFileChooser dialog.

JLabel—The component that displays text or an image that the user cannot modify.

JLabel component—A component used to describe another component. This helps users understand a component's purpose.

JMenu component—A menu that can be added to a JMenuBar and can contain other JMenus and JMenuItems.

JMenuBar component—The bar at the top of an application that hold JMenus.

JMenuItem component—An item within a menu.

JOptionPane class—Provides a method for displaying message dialogs and constants for displaying icons in those dialogs.

JOptionPane.showInputDialog method—Displays an input dialog.

JPanel component—Groups related components.

JPasswordField—Displays or inputs a password. The characters displayed in a JPasswordField are replaced with asterisks (*). Users can type passwords into an editable JPassword-Field.

JRadioButtonMenuItem component—A specific type of menu item that has a JRadioButton to its left, allowing the user to see if an item is currently selected.

JScrollPane component—Adds scrollbars to a component. When a component is added to a JScrollPane, the component will display scrollbars as necessary (that is, when more information appears in the added component than can be displayed at once).

JSP comment—Delimited by <%-- and --%>.

JSP expression—An expression delimited by <%= and %>. JSP expressions are used to insert dynamic content (such as information from a database) in the response to a client.

JSpinner component—Limits user input to a specific range of values. The programmer can specify a maximum and minimum for the range, an increment (or decrement) when the user clicks the up (or down) arrow and an initial value to be displayed.

JTextArea component—Allows the user to view multiline text.

JTextField component—A component that can accept user input from the keyboard or display output to the user.

JTextField.CENTER—Used with setHorizontalAlignment to center align the text in a JTextField.

JTextField.LEFT—Used with setHorizontalAlignment to left align the text in a JTextField.

JTextField.RIGHT—Used with setHorizontalAlignment to right align the text in a JTextField.

K

keyboard event—An event raised when a key on the keyboard is pressed or released.

KeyEvent class—Contains information about keyboard events (such as the pressing of a key on the keyboard) and constants that represent each key on the keyboard.

KeyListener interface—Declares event handler headers for keyboard events.

keyPressed event handler—Invoked when a key is pressed.

keyReleased event handler—Invoked when a key is released.

keyTyped event handler—Declared in the KeyListener interface. Invoked when a key is typed.

keyword—A word that is reserved by Java. These words cannot be used as identifiers.

L

Lady Ada Lovelace—The person credited with being the world's first computer programmer, for work she did in the early 1800s.

lastIndexOf method of class String—Returns the index of the last occurrence of a substring in a String; returns -1 if the substring is not found.

layout **property**—Controls how components are arranged in a container (such as the content pane or JPanel).

left brace ({)—Denotes the beginning of a block of code.

left operand—An expression that appears on the left side of a binary operator.

length member of an array—Contains the number of elements in an array.

length method of class String—Returns the number of characters in a String.

letter—An uppercase letter A–Z or a lowercase letter a–z.

literal String objects—A String constant written as a sequence of characters in double quotation marks (also called a string constant or string literal).

local variable—Declared inside a block. The scope of a local variable is from the point at which the declaration appears in the block to the end of that block. Such variables can be used only in the method in which they are declared.

Locale object—Represents a specific region of the world.

Locale.US constant—Represents a Locale object for the United States.

localhost—The host name that identifies the computer you are using.

location **property**—Property that specifies where a component's upper-left corner appears on the JFrame.

logic error—An error that does not prevent the application from compiling successfully, but does cause the application to produce erroneous results when it runs.

logical negation (!) operator—A logical operator that enables a programmer to reverse the meaning of a condition: A true condition, when logically negated, becomes false, and a false condition, when logically negated, becomes true.

logical operators—The operators (&&, ||, &, |, ^ and !) that can be used to form complex conditions by combining simple ones.

loop—Another name for a repetition statement.

loop-continuation condition—The condition used in a repetition statement (such as while) that enables repetition to continue while the condition is true, but that causes repetition to terminate when the condition becomes false.

M

machine dependent—Only one computer platform supports a machine-dependent technology.

machine language—A computer's "natural" language, generally consisting of streams of numbers (1s and 0s) that tell the computer how to perform its most elementary operations.

main method—When an application is run, this is the first method of the application class that is called by Java.

mask character—Another name for an echo character.

Math.max—Returns the maximum of two argument values.

Math.pow method—Performs exponentiation. The first argument specifies the value that will be raised to a power, and the second argument specifies the power to which the first argument will be raised.

Math.sqrt—Returns the square root of the argument value.

m-by-*n* **array**—A two-dimensional array with *m* rows and *n* columns.

members of a class—Methods and variables declared within the body of a class.

memory unit—The rapid-access, relatively low-capacity "warehouse" section of the computer, which stores data temporarily while an application is running.

menu—A component that groups related commands for GUI applications. Menus are an integral part of GUIs, because they organize commands without cluttering the GUI. In Java, a menu is created with a JMenu component.

menu bar—A bar at the top of an application that contains the menus. In Java, a menu is created with a JMenuBar component.

menu item—An item located in a menu that, when selected, causes the application to perform a specific action. In Java, a menu item is created with a JMenuItem component.

merge symbol—A symbol in the UML that joins two flows of activity into one flow of activity.

message dialog—A dialog that displays messages to users.

method—An application block that performs a task. Methods are used to divide an application into smaller, more manageable pieces that can be called from multiple places within an application.

method attribute of the form HTML element—The attribute that describes how the HTML form's data is sent to the Web server.

method body—The declarations and statements that appear between the braces after the method header. The method body contains statements that perform actions, generally by manipulating the parameters from the parameter list.

method call—Invokes a method, by specifying the method name and providing information (arguments) that the callee (the method being called) requires to perform its task.

method declaration—The method header followed by the method body.

method header—The beginning portion of a method (including the keyword `private`, the return type, the method name and the parameter list).

method name—The identifier for a method, which distinguishes one method from another. The method name follows the return type, can be any valid identifier and is used to call the method.

method overloading—Allows several methods to have the same name but different numbers of arguments or different types of arguments.

microprocessor—The chip that makes a computer work (that is, the "brain" of the computer).

middle tier—The tier that controls interaction between the client and information tiers of a multi-tier application. This is sometimes known as the business logic tier.

min method of the Math class—Returns the minimum of two values.

mnemonic—Allows the user to perform an action on a component using the keyboard.

mnemonic property of class JButton—The mnemonic used to perform an action on a JButton.

mouse event—An event that is generated when a user interacts with an application using the computer's mouse.

mouseClicked event handler—Invoked when a mouse button is clicked (pressed and released).

mouseDragged event handler—Invoked when a mouse cursor is moved while one of the mouse buttons is pressed.

mouseEntered event handler—Invoked when a mouse cursor enters the bounds of the component.

MouseEvent—The type of event object generated when the mouse is used to interact with an application.

mouseExited event handler—Invoked when a mouse cursor leaves the bounds of the component.

MouseListener interface—Declares five event handlers for mouse events. These event handlers are: `mouseClicked`, `mouseEntered`, `mouseExited`, `mousePressed` and `mouseReleased`.

MouseMotionListener interface—Declares two event handlers for mouse motion events. These event handlers: `mouseDragged` and `mouseMoved`.

mouseMoved event handler—Invoked when the mouse is moved.

mousePressed event handler—Invoked when a mouse button is pressed.

mouseReleased event handler—Invoked when a mouse button is released.

multiline statement—A statement that is spread over multiple lines of code for readability.

multimedia—The use of various media, such as sound, video and animation, to create content in an application.

multiple-selection statement—A statement, such as a `switch` statement, that selects one of many actions (or sequences of actions), depending on the value of the controlling expression.

multiplication operator—The asterisk (*) used to multiply its two numeric operands, calculating their product as a result.

multi-tier application—Application (sometimes referred to as an *n*-tier application) whose functionality is divided into separate tiers, which can be on the same machine or can be distributed to separate machines across a network. One popular form of multi-tier application has three tiers—the client tier, which contains the application's user interface, the information tier, which maintains the data for the application and the business logic tier, which controls interactions between application clients (such as Web browsers) and application data in the information tier.

mutator—A *set* method.

N

name attribute of HTML select element—Identifies the drop-down list menu control. The identifier specified is similar to a variable name in Java.

name of a variable—The identifier used in an application to access or modify a variable's value.

name of a control variable—Identifier used to reference the control variable of a loop.

narrowing conversion—An operation that converts a "larger" type value to a "smaller" type value. These conversions are dangerous because information about the value can be lost.

nested loop—A loop (such as a `for` statement) which is enclosed inside another control statement.

nested statement—A statement that is placed inside another control statement.

new keyword—Creates an object and assigns it a location in memory.

newline—A character that is inserted in code when you press *Enter*.

next (debugger command)—The debugger command used to execute the next statement in an application. The `next` command executes method calls in their entirety.

next method of interface Iterator—Returns a reference to the next element in the ArrayList.

next method of ResultSet—Moves the ResultSet cursor to the next row in a ResultSet.

nextDouble method of Random—Generates a random positive `double` value that is greater than or equal to 0.0 and less than 1.0.

nextInt method of Random—Generates an `int` value selected from all possible `int` values, when called with no arguments. When called with an `int` argument, it generates an `int` value from 0 to one less than the argument.

nondestructive—The process of reading from a memory location, which does not modify the value in that location.

note (in the UML)—An explanatory remark (represented by a rectangle with a folded upper-right corner) describing the purpose of a symbol in a UML activity diagram.

null keyword—A reference value which indicates that a variable is not currently referring to an object.

NumberFormatException class—A subclass of RuntimeException that is thrown when the application cannot convert a string to a desired numeric type, such as int or double.

O

object—A reusable software component that models a real world entity.

object-oriented, event-driven programming (OOED)—Using objects, such as GUI components, to enable users to interact with an application. Each interaction generates an event, which causes the application to perform an action.

object technology—A packaging scheme for creating meaningful software units that are focused on particular application areas. Examples of objects include date objects, time objects, paycheck objects and file objects.

off-by-one error—The kind of logic error that occurs when a loop executes for one more or one fewer iterations than is intended.

one-dimensional array—An array that uses only one index.

open source software—Software that is freely available for download, both as completed applications for use and source code for reproduction and modification.

operand—An expression that is combined with an operator (and possibly other expressions) to perform a task (such as multiplication).

option HTML element—The element that adds items to the HTML menu control, which is defined by the select HTML element.

out implicit JSP object—Used to write text as a part of the response to a user request.

output device—A device to which information that is processed by the computer can be sent.

output JTextField—A JTextField used to display calculation results. The *editable* property of an output JTextField is set to false with setEditable.

output unit—The section of the computer that takes information the computer has processed and places it on various output devices, making the information available for use outside the computer.

override—Supersedes a superclass method with a new implementation declared in the subclass.

P

p (paragraph) element in HTML—Adds a paragraph to a JSP or an HTML document.

package—A group of related classes. A package can be imported to add functionality to an application.

paintComponent method of class JPanel—Draws graphics on the JPanel.

palette—A set of colors.

parameter—A variable declared in a method's parameter list. Values passed to a method are stored in that method's parameters and can be used within the method body.

parameter list—A comma-separated list in which a method declares each parameter's type and name.

Pascal—A programming language named after the 17th-century mathematician and philosopher Blaise Pascal. This language was designed for teaching structured programming.

pass-by-reference—Arguments in the caller can be accessed and modified by the called method.

pass-by-value—A copy of the caller's argument is passed to the method. Original data cannot be accessed and modified by the called method.

***password* property of a JPasswordField**—Holds text entered in a JPasswordField.

persistent data—Data that exists even after the application that created the data terminates.

pixel—A point on your computer screen. Pixel is short for "picture element."

platform independent—Not dependent on a specific computer system. The Java programming language is platform independent, because Java programs can be created and run on various systems.

Point—This class represents a location in the component.

polymorphism—Concept that allows you to write applications that handle, in a more general manner, a wide variety of classes related by inheritance.

position number—A value that indicates a specific position within an array. Position numbers begin at 0 (zero).

primary key—A column (or combination of columns) in a database table that contains unique values used to distinguish one row from another.

primitive type—A type already defined in Java. The primitive types are boolean, byte, char, short, int, long, float and double.

print debugger command—Command that displays the value of a variable when an application is stopped at a breakpoint during execution in the debugger.

print command (in the debugger)—A debugger command that is used to examine the values of variables and expressions.

println method of the implicit JSP object out—Writes text as part of the response to a user request.

println method of PrintWriter—Takes as an argument a value of any primitive type or Object and writes the String version of that value to the file, followed by a newline.

println method of System.out—The method that displays a line of text in the **Command Prompt** window.

PrintWriter class—Provides the functionality of writing lines of text, but does not know how to open a file for output.

private keyword—Access modifier that makes instance variables or methods accessible only to methods of that class.

procedural programming language—A programming language (such as FORTRAN, Pascal, BASIC and C) that focuses on actions (verbs) rather than things or objects (nouns).

program control—The task of executing an application's statements in the correct order.

programmer-declared class—Class that a programmer declares, as opposed to a class predeclared in the Java class library.

programmer-declared method—Method created by a programmer to meet the unique needs of a particular application.

property—An object attribute, such as size, color or weight.

protocol—A set of rules to define how data is transported between the Java application and the database.

pseudocode—An informal language that helps programmers develop algorithms.

public keyword—The access modifier that allows objects of other classes to call a method.

R

Random class—Contains methods to generate random numbers. Declared in package `java.util`.

readLine method of the BufferedReader class—Reads a line of text from a stream and returns it as a `String`.

record—A collection of related fields. A record is usually represented as a `class` in Java.

record key—A unique field used to identify a record and distinguish that record from all other records.

Rectangle class—Specifies a rectangle defined by the *x*- and the *y*-coordinates of the upper-left corner, the width and the height of a rectangle.

redundant parentheses—Extra parentheses used in calculations to clarify the order in which calculations are performed. Such parentheses can be removed without affecting the results of the calculations.

reference—A variable that refers to an object. A reference specifies the location in the computer's memory of an object.

registering an event handler—Specifying which event handler to call on a component when an event object is generated by the component.

relational database—A database that maintains data in a set of related tables.

relational database management system (RDBMS)—Database management system for relational databases.

relational operators—Operators < (less than), > (greater than), <= (less than or equal to) and >= (greater than or equal to) that compare two values.

relative positioning—Specifies the size and location of components in relation to other components on a container.

relative URL—A relative URL does not contain the protocol of the resource (such as `http`), the domain name of the resource or IP address of the resource. The relative URL contains only the path to the resource.

remainder operator (%)—An arithmetic operator that calculates the remainder of a division.

remove method of class ArrayList—Removes an object at a specified location of an `ArrayList`.

removeAllItems method of JComboBox—Removes all items in the `JComboBox`.

repaint method of class JPanel—Clears all previous drawings and updates any current drawings in the `JPanel`.

repetition statement—A control statement that might cause an application to execute statements multiple times.

repetition statement—Allows the programmer to specify that an action or actions should be repeated, depending on the value of a condition.

request implicit JSP object—Represents the client request. This object can be used to get data that is submitted to a JSP as part of the client request.

requestFocusInWindow method—The method that sets the component to have the focus, attracting the user's attention.

reserved word—A word that is reserved for use by Java and cannot be used to create your own identifiers. See also "keyword."

ResultSet object—A table of data that is generated by executing a query statement.

resume method of Synthesizer—Used to get the speech synthesizer ready to speak.

rethrow the exception—The `catch` block can defer the exception handling (or perhaps a portion of it) to another `catch` block using the `throw` keyword.

return a value from a method—Some methods, when called, return a value to the statement in the application that called the method. The returned value can then be used in that statement.

return statement—The statement that returns a value from a method. A `return` statement begins with the keyword `return`, followed by an expression.

return type—Type of the result returned from a method to its caller.

RGB value—The amount of red, green and blue needed to create a color.

right brace (})—Denotes the end of a block of code.

right operand—An expression that appears on the right side of a binary operator.

row (of an array)—In referring to an element of a two-dimensional array, the first index specifies the row.

row (of a database table)—Uniquely represents a set of values in a relational database.

rules of operator precedence—Rules that determine the precise order in which operators are applied in an expression.

run debugger command—Command to begin executing an application with the Java debugger.

RuntimeException class—The superclass of all unchecked exceptions that can be thrown during application execution.

S

scope—The portion of an application in which an identifier (such as a variable name) can be referenced. Some identifiers can be referenced throughout an application, while others can be referenced only from limited portions of an application (such as within a single method or block).

screen scraping—The process of extracting desired information from the HTML that composes a Web page.

scriptlet—Block of code delimited by <% abd %> that enables programmers to insert Java code in a JSP.

second generation language—Another name for an assembly language.

secondary storage media—Devices such as magnetic disks, optical disks and magnetic tapes on which computers store files.

secondary storage unit—Long-term, high-capacity "warehouse" section of the computer.

select element in HTML—Creates an HTML menu control (also called a drop-down list).

SELECT SQL keyword—The keyword used to specify queries that request information from a database.

selected **property**—Defines if a component has been selected.

selection criteria—Specifies what rows to select.

selection statement—A control statement that selects among alternative courses of action.

semicolon (;)—The character used to indicate the end of a Java statement.

sentence-style capitalization—A style that capitalizes the first letter of the first word in the text (for example, **Cartons per shipment**); other letters in the text are lowercase, unless they are the first letters of proper nouns.

separator bar—A bar placed in a menu to separate related menu items.

sequential-access file—A file that contains data that is read in the order that it was written.

set command (in the debugger)—A debugger command that is used to change the value of a variable.

set **method**—Sets the value of an instance variable. Validates the value to ensure that it is appropriate for the variable that is being set.

setBorder method of JPanel—Sets the border that is displayed around the JPanel.

setColor method of class Graphics—Sets the color of an object to be drawn.

setDialogTitle method of JFileChooser—Changes the text displayed in the title bar of the JFileChooser.

setEchoChar method—Specifies the echo character in a JPass-wordField.

setEditable method of JTextArea—Sets the *editable* property of the JTextArea component to specify whether or not the user can edit the text in the JTextArea.

setEnabled method—Sets the *enabled* property of a component to true or false. Set the *enabled* property to true if the component should react to user interactions. Set the *enabled* property to false if the component should not react to user interactions.

setFont method of JTextArea—Sets the Font of a JTextArea.

setForeground method of JTextArea—Sets the foreground Color of the JTextArea.

setJMenuBar method of JFrame—Sets the JMenuBar of the JFrame.

setLayout method of JPanel—Sets the way components are arranged in the JPanel.

setListData method of class JList—Sets the text to display in a JList.

setMaximumRowCount method of JComboBox—Specifies how many items can be displayed in the drop-down list at once.

setMnemonic method of class JButton—Sets the mnemonic to be used to "press" the JButton.

setMnemonic method of JMenu—Sets the keyboard shortcut of the JMenu.

setMnemonic method of JMenuItem—Sets the keyboard shortcut of a JMenuItem.

setProperty method of System—Sets the system property, such as db2j.system.home.

setSelected method of JRadioButton—Sets the state of the JRadioButton to selected (true) or unselected (false).

setSelectedIndex method of JComboBox—Sets the index of the JComboBox's selected item.

setSpeakingRate method of SynthesizerProperties—Used to set the *speakingRate* property of the speech synthesizer.

setText method—A method that sets the *text* property of a component, such as a JLabel, JTextField, JTextArea or JButton.

setTitle method of TitledBorder—Sets the text displayed in the TitledBorder.

setValue method of JSpinner—Called to change the value in a JSpinner.

showDialog method of JColorChooser—Displays the JColor-Chooser color dialog.

showOpenDialog method of JFileChooser—Displays a dialog allowing a user to select a file or directory.

short-circuit evaluation—The evaluation of the right operand in && and || expressions occurs only if the left condition is true in an expression containing && or false in an expression containing ||.

showMessageDialog method of class JOptionPane—Used to display a message dialog.

simple condition—A condition that contains one expression.

single-entry/single-exit control statement—Control statement with one entry point and one exit point.

single-selection statement—A statement, such as the if statement, that selects or ignores a single action or sequence of actions.

size of a variable—The number of bytes required to store a value of the variable's type. For example, an int is stored in four bytes of memory and a double is stored in eight bytes.

size method of class ArrayList—Returns the number of objects contained in an ArrayList.

size **property**—Property that specifies the width and height, in pixels, of a component.

small circles (in the UML)—The solid circle in an activity diagram represents the activity's initial state and the solid circle surrounded by a hollow circle represents the activity's final state.

software—The programs that run on computers.

software reuse—An approach to software development that enables programmers to develop new applications faster, through the reuse of existing software components.

solid circle (in the UML)—A UML activity diagram symbol that represents the activity's initial state.

sorting—Arranging data into some particular order, such as ascending or descending order.

source code file—A file with the extension .java that stores Java code written by a programmer.

speakingRate **property of the speech synthesizer**—Specifies the speaking rate in words per minute.

speakPlainText method of Synthesizer—Used to speak text to the user.

special character—Characters such as +, -, *, /, $, white space and others. Does not include letters or digits.

speech recognition—A technique that produces text from audio input that contains speech.

speech-recognition engine—An application that translates vocal sound input from a microphone into a language that the computer understands.

speech synthesis—Also known as text-to-speech technology, this produces synthetic speech from text.

SpinnerNumberModel object—The object that specifies that a JSpinner will contain numerical values for its range.

SQLException—An exception that is thrown when an error occurs while accessing a database.

src attribute of HTML img element—Specifies the location of the image file.

standard output object—A System.out object that allows Java applications to display sets of characters in the **Command Prompt** window from which the Java application executes.

start method of class Timer—Starts generating an Action-Event as each interval of time (specified in Timer's constructor) passes.

start tag in HTML—Consists of the element name in angle brackets, which starts an HTML element.

startsWith method of class String—Returns true if a String starts with a particular substring and false otherwise.

state button—A button that can be in the on/off (true/false) state (for example, a JRadioButton or JCheckBox).

stateChanged event handler—Called when a JSpinner's value is changed.

statement—Code that instructs the computer to perform a task. Every statement ends with a semicolon (;) character. Most applications consist of many statements.

Statement object—The object used to execute SQL.

static—Modifier which allows access to a method without requiring an instance of that method's class.

step (debugger command)—The debugger command used in the debugger to execute the next statement in an application. The step command steps into method calls, allowing users to execute the called method's statements line by line.

step size—Specifies by how much the value of a JSpinner component changes when the user clicks the component's up arrow (for incrementing) or down arrow (for decrementing).

step up (debugger command)—The debugger command used to execute the remaining statements in the current method and move control to the location where the method was called.

stop debugger command—Command that sets a breakpoint at the specified line of executable code.

stop method of class Timer—Stops the Timer and prevents further ActionEvents from being generated.

straight-line form—The manner in which arithmetic expressions must be written so they can be typed in Java code.

stream—Object that has access to a sequence of characters.

String—A class that represents a sequence of characters treated as a single unit.

string constant—Another term for string literal or literal String object.

string literal—Another term for string constant or literal String object.

string-concatenation operator—A version of the plus (+) operator that combines its two operands into a single String.

String literal—A sequence of characters within double quotes.

String.valueOf method—A method that converts a numeric value into text.

structured programming—A technique for organizing program control to help you develop applications that are easy to understand, debug and modify.

Structured Query Language (SQL)—A language used by relational databases to perform queries and manipulate data.

subclass—A class that extends (inherits from) another class (called a superclass).

submenu—A menu within another menu.

"submit" button—A button created by setting the type attribute of the input HTML element to "submit".

subprotocol—A set of rules to define how data is transported between the Java application and the database. Typically, the subprotocol contains rules that are specific to a particular DBMS.

subscript—Another name for the term "index."

substring—A sequence of characters that makes up part or all of a String.

substring method of class String—Returns a String that is a specified portion of the original String.

super keyword—The keyword used for accessing the superclass's constructor and members.

superclass—A class that is extended by another class to form a subclass. The subclass inherits from the superclass.

superclass constructor call syntax—Uses the super keyword, followed by a set of parentheses containing the superclass constructor arguments.

supercomputer—A computer that can perform hundreds of billions of calculations per second.

switch statement—The multiple-selection statement used to make a decision by comparing a controlling expression to a series of case values. The algorithm then takes different actions based on those values.

syntax error—An error that occurs when code violates the grammatical rules of a programming language.

Synthesizer object—Provides speech synthesis capabilities, such as speaking text.

SynthesizerModeDesc object—A descriptor that specifies the basic properties of the speech synthesizer.

SynthesizerProperties object—Contains various properties of a speech synthesizer.

System.out object—The object that allows Java applications to display sets of characters in the **Command Prompt** window from which the Java application executes. Also known as the standard output object.

T

table (in arrays)—A two-dimensional array used to contain information arranged in rows and columns.

table (in databases)—Used to store information in rows and columns in a database.

text file—A file containing human-readable characters.

text **property**—The property that specifies the text displayed by a JLabel.

text-to-speech engine—An application that translates typed words into spoken sound that users hear through headphones or speakers connected to a computer.

text-to-speech technology—Produces synthetic speech from text.

third generation language—Another name for a high-level language.

this keyword—Provides a reference to the current object.

Throwable class—The superclass of all exceptions and errors.

throw keyword—The keyword used to rethrow an exception in a catch block.

throws an exception—A method throws an exception if a problem occurs during method execution that the method is unable to handle.

throws clause—The throws clause appears after the parameter list and before the method body. It specifies the exceptions the method throws, but does not handle. The clause contains a comma-separated list of exceptions the method will throw if a problem occurs when the method executes.

tier—Logical groupings of functionality.

Timer class—An object of class Timer can generate an Action-Event as each specified interval of time passes. This is similar to the ticking of a clock in the real world.

title bar—The area at the top of a JFrame where its title appears.

title element in HTML—Sets the title displayed in the title bar at the top of the browser.

title **property of TitledBorder**—Controls the text that is displayed in the border.

TitledBorder class—Allows a component to have a border with a String title.

toArray method of class ArrayList—Converts the ArrayList to a one-dimensional array. This is convenient for cases when the elements of an ArrayList need to be passed to a method that is expecting a one-dimensional array.

toString method of class Date—Returns the current date as a String, in the format Tue Feb 13 16:50:00 EST 2003.

top tier—The tier containing the application's user interface in a multi-tier application—typically implemented as a GUI.

top-level domain (TLD)—The portion of a Web address that usually describes the type of organization that owns the domain name. For example, the com TLD usually refers to a commercial business, the org TLD usually refers to a nonprofit organization and the edu TLD usually refers to an educational institution.

top-level menu—A menu that is added directly to the menu bar.

transferring the focus—Setting a component to have the application's focus. This is implemented by calling the component's requestFocusInWindow method.

transition (in the UML)—A change from one action state to another that is represented by transition arrows in a UML activity diagram.

Transmission Control Protocol/Internet Protocol—TCP/IP for short. Combined set of communications protocols for the Internet.

trim method of class String—Returns a new String object with all white space removed from the beginning and end of a String.

true—One of the two possible values for a boolean type; the other is false.

truncating in integer division—Any fractional part of an integer division result is discarded.

truth table—A table that displays the truth value of a logical operator for all possible combinations of true and false values of its operand(s).

try block—A block that contains statements that might cause exceptions and statements that should not execute if an exception occurs.

try statement—A statement that consists of keyword try, followed by braces ({}) that delimit a try block, followed by one or more catch blocks, optionally followed by a finally block.

two-dimensional array—An array requiring two indices to specify a value. These arrays are often used to represent tables of information with values arranged in rows and columns.

type attribute of HTML input element—Specifies the type of an input element. Setting the type to "submit" indicates that the input element is a "submit" button.

type of a variable—Specifies the kind of data that can be stored in a variable and the range of values that can be stored. For instance, a int variable can store only whole numbers in the range –2,147,483,648 to +2,147,483,647.

U

UML (Unified Modeling Language)—An industry standard for modeling software systems graphically.

unary decrement operator (--)—Subtracts one from an integer variable.

unary increment operator (++)—Adds one to an integer variable.

unary operator—An operator with only one operand (such as unary + or unary -).

uncaught exception—An exception that does not have an exception handler. Uncaught exceptions might terminate application execution.

unchecked exception—An exception type that is a subclass of RuntimeException. Such exceptions are thrown during application execution.

Unicode character—Composed of 2 bytes. Characters are represented in Java using the Unicode character set.

unwatch command (in the debugger)—Removes the watch from a variable.

uneditable JTextField—A JTextField in which the user cannot type values or edit existing text. Such JTextFields are often used to display the results of calculations.

UPDATE SQL keyword—The keyword used in SQL statements that modify data in a database table.

URL (Uniform Resource Locator)—An address that can be used to direct a browser to a resource on the Web.

V

value attribute of HTML input element—Sets the text on a "submit" button.

value of a variable—The piece of data that is stored in a variable's location in memory.

variable—A location in the computer's memory where a value can be stored for use by an application.

vertical coordinate—The vertical distance moving down from the upper-left corner of a GUI component. Also known as the y-coordinate.

virtual key code—A constant that represents a key on the keyboard.

Voice class—Specifies the output voice of a speech synthesizer.

void keyword—A return type that specifies that the method does not return any information.

W

watch command (in the debugger)—Puts a watch on a variable. The debugger then notifies you every time the variable is modified.

Web address—Also known as a domain name, which uniquely identifies the location of a business or organization on the Internet.

Web application—Also known as Web-based application, can use JavaServer Pages (JSP) technology to create Web content.

Web content—Data that can be viewed in a Web browser, such as Internet Explorer or Netscape.

Web server—Specialized software that responds to Web client requests by sending Web pages and other resources back to the client.

WHERE SQL keyword—The keyword that specifies criteria that determine the rows to retrieve or update.

while repetition statement—A control statement that executes a set of body statements while its loop-continuation condition is true.

white space—A tab, space or newline.

widening conversion—An operation that converts a "smaller" type value to a "larger" type value.

workflow—The activity of a portion of a software system.

World Wide Web (WWW)—A collection of hardware and software associated with the Internet that allows computer users to locate and view multimedia-based documents (such as documents with text, graphics, animations, audios and videos).

World Wide Web Consortium (W3C)—A forum through which individuals and companies cooperate to develop and recommend technologies for the World Wide Web.

X

x instance variable of class Point—The instance variable of the Point class that specifies the x-coordinate.

x-axis—Describes every horizontal coordinate.

x-coordinate—The horizontal distance moving right from the upper-left corner of a GUI component.

Y

y instance variable of class Point—The instance variable of the Point class that specifies the y-coordinate.

y-axis—Describes every vertical coordinate.

y-coordinate—Vertical distance moving down from the upper-left corner of a GUI component.

Z

zeroth element—The first element in an array.

INDEX

End User License Agreement

SUN MICROSYSTEMS, INC. BINARY CODE LICENSE AGREEMENT

READ THE TERMS OF THIS AGREEMENT AND ANY PROVIDED SUPPLEMENTAL LICENSE TERMS (COLLECTIVELY "AGREE-MENT") CAREFULLY BEFORE OPENING THE SOFTWARE MEDIA PACKAGE. BY OPENING THE SOFTWARE MEDIA PACKAGE, YOU AGREE TO THE TERMS OF THIS AGREEMENT. IF YOU ARE ACCESSING THE SOFTWARE ELECTRONICALLY, INDICATE YOUR AC-CEPTANCE OF THESE TERMS BY SELECTING THE "ACCEPT" BUTTON AT THE END OF THIS AGREEMENT. IF YOU DO NOT AGREE TO ALL THESE TERMS, PROMPTLY RETURN THE UNUSED SOFTWARE TO YOUR PLACE OF PURCHASE FOR A REFUND OR, IF THE SOFTWARE IS ACCESSED ELECTRONICALLY, SELECT THE "DECLINE" BUTTON AT THE END OF THIS AGREEMENT

1.   LICENSE TO USE. Sun grants you a non-exclusive and non-transferable license for the internal use only of the accompanying software and documentation and any error corrections provided by Sun (collectively "Software"), by the number of users and the class of computer hardware for which the corresponding fee has been paid.

2.   RESTRICTIONS. Software is confidential and copyrighted. Title to Software and all associated intellectual property rights is retained by Sun and/or its licensors. Except as specifically authorized in any Supplemental License Terms, you may not make copies of Software, other than a single copy of Software for archival purposes. Unless enforcement is prohibited by applicable law, you may not modify, decompile, or reverse engineer Software. You acknowledge that Software is not designed, licensed or intended for use in the design, construction, operation or maintenance of any nuclear facility. Sun disclaims any express or implied warranty of fitness for such uses. No right, title or interest in or to any trademark, service mark, logo or trade name of Sun or its licensors is granted under this Agreement.

3.   LIMITED WARRANTY. Sun warrants to you that for a period of ninety (90) days from the date of purchase, as evidenced by a copy of the receipt, the media on which Software is furnished (if any) will be free of defects in materials and workmanship under normal use. Except for the foregoing, Software is provided "AS IS". Your exclusive remedy and Sun's entire liability under this limited warranty will be at Sun's option to replace Software media or refund the fee paid for Software.

4.   DISCLAIMER OF WARRANTY. UNLESS SPECIFIED IN THIS AGREEMENT, ALL EXPRESS OR IMPLIED CONDITIONS, REPRESENTATIONS AND WARRANTIES, INCLUDING ANY IMPLIED WARRANTY OF MERCHANTABILITY, FITNESS FOR A PARTICULAR PURPOSE OR NON-INFRINGEMENT ARE DISCLAIMED, EXCEPT TO THE EXTENT THAT THESE DISCLAIMERS ARE HELD TO BE LEGALLY INVALID.

5.   LIMITATION OF LIABILITY. TO THE EXTENT NOT PROHIBITED BY LAW, IN NO EVENT WILL SUN OR ITS LICENSORS BE LIABLE FOR ANY LOST REVENUE, PROFIT OR DATA, OR FOR SPECIAL, INDIRECT, CONSEQUENTIAL, INCIDENTAL OR PUNITIVE DAMAGES, HOWEVER CAUSED REGARDLESS OF THE THEORY OF LIABILITY, ARISING OUT OF OR RELATED TO THE USE OF OR INABILITY TO USE SOFTWARE, EVEN IF SUN HAS BEEN ADVISED OF THE POSSIBILITY OF SUCH DAMAGES. In no event will Sun's liability to you, whether in contract, tort (including negligence), or otherwise, exceed the amount paid by you for Software under this Agreement. The foregoing limitations will apply even if the above stated warranty fails of its essential purpose.

6.   Termination. This Agreement is effective until terminated. You may terminate this Agreement at any time by destroying all copies of Software. This Agreement will terminate immediately without notice from Sun if you fail to comply with any provision of this Agreement. Upon Termination, you must destroy all copies of Software.

7.   Export Regulations. All Software and technical data delivered under this Agreement are subject to US export control laws and may be subject to export or import regulations in other countries. You agree to comply strictly with all such laws and regulations and acknowledge that you have the responsibility to obtain such licenses to export, re-export, or import as may be required after delivery to you.

8.   U.S. Government Restricted Rights. If Software is being acquired by or on behalf of the U.S. Government or by a U.S. Government prime contractor or subcontractor (at any tier), then the Government's rights in Software and accompanying documentation will be only as set forth in this Agreement; this is in accordance with 48 CFR 227.7201 through 227.7202-4 (for Department of Defense (DOD) acquisitions) and with 48 CFR 2.101 and 12.212 (for non-DOD acquisitions).

9.   Governing Law. Any action related to this Agreement will be governed by California law and controlling U.S. federal law. No choice of law rules of any jurisdiction will apply.

10.   Severability. If any provision of this Agreement is held to be unenforceable, this Agreement will remain in effect with the provision

omitted, unless omission would frustrate the intent of the parties, in which case this Agreement will immediately terminate.

11.   Integration. This Agreement is the entire agreement between you and Sun relating to its subject matter. It supersedes all prior or contemporaneous oral or written communications, proposals, representations and warranties and prevails over any conflicting or additional terms of any quote, order, acknowledgment, or other communication between the parties relating to its subject matter during the term of this Agreement. No modification of this Agreement will be binding, unless in writing and signed by an authorized representative of each party.

JAVA™ 2 SOFTWARE DEVELOPMENT KIT (J2SDK), STANDARD EDITION, VERSION 1.4.1_X SUPPLEMENTAL LICENSE TERMS

These supplemental license terms ("Supplemental Terms") add to or modify the terms of the Binary Code License Agreement (collectively, the "Agreement"). Capitalized terms not defined in these Supplemental Terms shall have the same meanings ascribed to them in the Agreement. These Supplemental Terms shall supersede any inconsistent or conflicting terms in the Agreement, or in any license contained within the Software.

1.   Software Internal Use and Development License Grant. Subject to the terms and conditions of this Agreement, including, but not limited to Section 4 (Java Technology Restrictions) of these Supplemental Terms, Sun grants you a non-exclusive, non-transferable, limited license without fees to reproduce internally and use internally the binary form of the Software complete and unmodified for the sole purpose of designing, developing and testing your Java applets and applications intended to run on the Java platform ("Programs").

2.   License to Distribute Software. Subject to the terms and conditions of this Agreement, including, but not limited to Section 4 (Java Technology Restrictions) of these Supplemental Terms, Sun grants you a non-exclusive, non-transferable, limited license without fees to reproduce and distribute the Software, provided that (i) you distribute the Software complete and unmodified (unless otherwise specified in the applicable README file) and only bundled as part of, and for the sole purpose of running, your Programs, (ii) the Programs add significant and primary functionality to the Software, (iii) you do not distribute additional software intended to replace any component(s) of the Software (unless otherwise specified in the applicable README file), (iv) you do not remove or alter any proprietary legends or notices contained in the Software, (v) you only distribute the Software subject to a license agreement that protects Sun's interests consistent with the terms contained in this Agreement, and (vi) you agree to defend and indemnify Sun and its licensors from and against any damages, costs, liabilities, settlement amounts and/or expenses (including attorneys' fees) incurred in connection with any claim, lawsuit or action by any third party that arises or results from the use or distribution of any and all Programs and/or Software. (vi) include the following statement as part of product documentation (whether hard copy or electronic), as a part of a copyright page or proprietary rights notice page, in an "About" box or in any other form reasonably designed to make the statement visible to users of the Software: "This product includes code licensed from RSA Security, Inc.", and (vii) include the statement, "Some portions licensed from IBM are available at http://oss.software.ibm.com/icu4j/".

3.   License to Distribute Redistributables. Subject to the terms and conditions of this Agreement, including but not limited to Section 4 (Java Technology Restrictions) of these Supplemental Terms, Sun grants you a non-exclusive, non-transferable, limited license without fees to reproduce and distribute those files specifically identified as redistributable in the Software "README" file ("Redistributables") provided that: (i) you distribute the Redistributables complete and unmodified (unless otherwise specified in the applicable README file), and only bundled as part of Programs, (ii) you do not distribute additional software intended to supersede any component(s) of the Redistributables (unless otherwise specified in the applicable README file), (iii) you do not remove or alter any proprietary legends or notices contained in or on the Redistributables, (iv) you only distribute the Redistributables pursuant to a license agreement that protects Sun's interests consistent with the terms contained in the Agreement, (v) you agree to defend and indemnify Sun and its licensors from and against any damages, costs, liabilities, settlement amounts and/or expenses (including attorneys' fees) incurred in connection with any claim, lawsuit or action by any third party that arises or results from the use or distribution of any and all Programs and/or Software, (vi) include the following statement as part of product documentation (whether hard copy or electronic), as a part of a copyright page or proprietary rights notice page, in an "About" box or in any other form reasonably designed to make the statement visible to users of the Software: "This product includes code licensed from RSA Security, Inc.", and (vii) include the statement, "Some portions licensed from IBM are available at http://oss.software.ibm.com/icu4j/".

4.   Java Technology Restrictions. You may not modify the Java Platform Interface ("JPI", identified as classes contained within the "java" package or any subpackages of the "java" package), by creating additional classes within the JPI or otherwise causing the addition to or modification of the classes in the JPI. In the event that you create an additional class and associated API(s) which (i) extends the functionality of the Java platform, and (ii) is exposed to third party software developers for the purpose of developing additional software which invokes such additional API, you must promptly publish broadly an accurate specification for such API for free use by all developers. You may not create, or authorize your licensees to create, additional classes, interfaces, or subpackages that are in any way identified as "java", "javax", "sun" or similar convention as specified by Sun in any naming convention designation.

5.   Notice of Automatic Software Updates from Sun. You acknowledge that the Software may automatically download, install, and execute applets, applications, software extensions, and updated versions of the Software from Sun ("Software Updates"), which may require you to accept updated terms and conditions for installation. If additional terms and conditions are not presented on installation, the Software Updates will be considered part of the Software and subject to the terms and conditions of the Agreement.

6.   Notice of Automatic Downloads. You acknowledge that, by your use of the Software and/or by requesting services that require use of the Software, the Software may automatically download, install, and execute software applications from sources other than Sun ("Other Software"). Sun makes no representations of a relationship of any kind to licensors of Other Software. TO THE EXTENT NOT PROHIBITED BY LAW, IN NO EVENT WILL SUN OR ITS LICENSORS BE LIABLE FOR ANY LOST REVENUE, PROFIT OR DATA, OR FOR SPECIAL, INDIRECT, CONSEQUENTIAL, INCIDENTAL OR PUNITIVE DAMAGES, HOWEVER CAUSED REGARDLESS OF THE THEORY OF LIABILITY, ARISING OUT OF OR RELATED TO THE USE OF OR INABILITY TO USE OTHER SOFTWARE, EVEN IF SUN HAS BEEN ADVISED OF THE POSSIBILITY OF SUCH DAMAGES.

7.   Distribution by Publishers. This section pertains to your distribution of the Software with your printed book or magazine (as those terms are commonly used in the industry) relating to Java technology ("Publication"). Subject to and conditioned upon your compliance with the restrictions and obligations contained in the Agreement, in addition to the license granted in Paragraph 1 above, Sun hereby grants to you a non-exclusive, nontransferable limited right to reproduce complete and unmodified copies of the Software on electronic media (the "Media") for the sole purpose of inclusion and distribution with your Publication(s), subject to the following terms: (i) You may not distribute the Software on a stand-alone basis; it

must be distributed with your Publication(s); (ii) You are responsible for downloading the Software from the applicable Sun web site; (iii) You must refer to the Software as JavaTM 2 Software Development Kit, Standard Edition, Version 1.4.1; (iv) The Software must be reproduced in its entirety and without any modification whatsoever (including, without limitation, the Binary Code License and Supplemental License Terms accompanying the Software and proprietary rights notices contained in the Software); (v) The Media label shall include the following information: Copyright 2002, Sun Microsystems, Inc. All rights reserved. Use is subject to license terms. Sun, Sun Microsystems, the Sun logo, Solaris, Java, the Java Coffee Cup logo, J2SE , and all trademarks and logos based on Java are trademarks or registered trademarks of Sun Microsystems, Inc. in the U.S. and other countries. This information must be placed on the Media label in such a manner as to only apply to the Sun Software; (vi) You must clearly identify the Software as Sun's product on the Media holder or Media label, and you may not state or imply that Sun is responsible for any third-party software contained on the Media; (vii) You may not include any third party software on the Media which is intended to be a replacement or substitute for the Software; (viii) You shall indemnify Sun for all damages arising from your failure to comply with the requirements of this Agreement. In addition, you shall defend, at your expense, any and all claims brought against Sun by third parties, and shall pay all damages awarded by a court of competent jurisdiction, or such settlement amount negotiated by you, arising out of or in connection with your use, reproduction or distribution of the Software and/or the Publication. Your obligation to provide indemnification under this section shall arise provided that Sun: (i) provides you prompt notice of the claim; (ii) gives you sole control of the defense and settlement of the claim; (iii) provides you, at your expense, with all available information, assistance and authority to defend; and (iv) has not compromised or settled such claim without your prior written consent; and (ix) You shall provide Sun with a written notice for each Publication; such notice shall include the following information: (1) title of Publication, (2) author(s), (3) date of Publication, and (4) ISBN or ISSN numbers. Such notice shall be sent to Sun Microsystems, Inc., 4150 Network Circle, M/S USCA12-110, Santa Clara, California 95054, U.S.A , Attention: Contracts Administration.

8.   Trademarks and Logos. You acknowledge and agree as between you and Sun that Sun owns the SUN, SOLARIS, JAVA, JINI, FORTE, and iPLANET trademarks and all SUN, SOLARIS, JAVA, JINI, FORTE, and iPLANET-related trademarks, service marks, logos and other brand designations ("Sun Marks"), and you agree to comply with the Sun Trademark and Logo Usage Requirements currently located at http://www.sun.com/policies/trademarks. Any use you make of the Sun Marks inures to Sun's benefit.

9.   Source Code. Software may contain source code that is provided solely for reference purposes pursuant to the terms of this Agreement. Source code may not be redistributed unless expressly provided for in this Agreement.

10.   Termination for Infringement. Either party may terminate this Agreement immediately should any Software become, or in either party's opinion likely to become, the subject of a claim of infringement of any intellectual property right.

For inquiries please contact: Sun Microsystems, Inc., 4150 Network Circle, Santa Clara, California 95054, U.S.A
(LFI#120080/Form ID#011801)

SUN™ ONE STUDIO 4 UPDATE 1, COMMUNITY EDITION SUPPLEMENTAL LICENSE TERMS

These supplemental license terms ("Supplemental Terms") add to or modify the terms of the Binary Code License Agreement (collectively, the "Agreement"). Capitalized terms not defined in these Supplemental Terms shall have the same meanings ascribed to them in the Agreement. These Supplemental Terms shall supersede any inconsistent or conflicting terms in the Agreement, or in any license contained within the Software.

1.   Software Internal Use and Development License Grant. Subject to the terms and conditions of this Agreement, including, but not limited to Section 4 (Java Technology Restrictions) of these Supplemental Terms, Sun grants you a non-exclusive, non-transferable, limited license to reproduce internally and use internally the binary form of the Software complete and unmodified for the sole purpose of designing, developing and testing your applets and applications ("Programs"). To the extent that you are designing, developing and testing Java applets and applications for a particular version of the Java platform, any executable output generated by a compiler that is contained in the Software must (a) only be compiled from source code that conforms to the corresponding version of the OEM Java Language Specification; (b) be in the class file format defined by the corresponding version of the OEM Java Virtual Machine Specification; and (c) execute properly on a reference runtime, as specified by Sun, associated with such version of the Java platform.

2.   License to Distribute Software. Subject to the terms and conditions of this Agreement, including, but not limited to Section 4 (Java Technology Restrictions) of these Supplemental Terms, Sun grants you a non-exclusive, non-transferable, limited license to reproduce and distribute the Software in binary code form only, provided that (i) you distribute the Software complete and unmodified, (ii) you do not distribute additional software intended to replace any component(s) of the Software, (iii) if you are distributing Java applets and applications for a particular version of the Java platform, any executable output generated by a compiler that is contained in the Software must (a) only be compiled from source code that conforms to the corresponding version of the OEM Java Language Specification; (b) be in the class file format defined by the corresponding version of the OEM Java Virtual Machine Specification; and (c) execute properly on a reference runtime, as specified by Sun, associated with such version of the Java platform, (iv) you do not remove or alter any proprietary legends or notices contained in the Software, (v) you only distribute the Software subject to a license agreement that protects Sun's interests consistent with the terms contained in this Agreement, and (vi) you agree to defend and indemnify Sun and its licensors from and against any damages, costs, liabilities, settlement amounts and/or expenses (including attorneys' fees) incurred in connection with any claim, lawsuit or action by any third party that arises or results from the use or distribution of any and all Programs and/or Software.

3.   License to Distribute Redistributables. Subject to the terms and conditions of this Agreement, including but not limited to Section 4 (Java Technology Restrictions) of these Supplemental Terms, Sun grants you a non-exclusive, non-transferable, limited license to reproduce and distribute the binary form of those files specifically identified as redistributable in the Software "RELEASE NOTES" file ("Redistributables") provided that: (i) you distribute the Redistributables complete and unmodified (unless otherwise specified in the applicable RELEASE NOTES file), and only bundled as part of Programs, (ii) you do not distribute additional software intended to supersede any component(s) of the Redistributables, (iii) you do not remove or alter any proprietary legends or notices contained in or on the Redistributables, (iv) if you are distributing Java applets and applications for a particular version of the Java platform, any executable output generated by a compiler that is contained in the Software must (a) only be compiled from source code that conforms to the corresponding version of the OEM Java Language Specification; (b) be in the class file format defined by the corresponding version of the OEM Java Virtual Machine Specification; and (c) execute properly on a reference runtime, as specified by Sun,

associated with such version of the Java platform, (v) you only distribute the Redistributables pursuant to a license agreement that protects Sun's interests consistent with the terms contained in the Agreement, and (v) you agree to defend and indemnify Sun and its licensors from and against any damages, costs, liabilities, settlement amounts and/or expenses (including attorneys' fees) incurred in connection with any claim, lawsuit or action by any third party that arises or results from the use or distribution of any and all Programs and/or Software.

4.　　　　Java Technology Restrictions. You may not modify the Java Platform Interface ("JPI", identified as classes contained within the "java" package or any subpackages of the "java" package), by creating additional classes within the JPI or otherwise causing the addition to or modification of the classes in the JPI. In the event that you create an additional class and associated API(s) which (i) extends the functionality of the Java platform, and (ii) is exposed to third party software developers for the purpose of developing additional software which invokes such additional API, you must promptly publish broadly an accurate specification for such API for free use by all developers. You may not create, or authorize your licensees to create, additional classes, interfaces, or subpackages that are in any way identified as "java", "javax", "sun" or similar convention as specified by Sun in any naming convention designation.

5.　　　　Java Runtime Availability. Refer to the appropriate version of the Java Runtime Environment binary code license (currently located at http://www.java.sun.com/jdk/index.html) for the availability of runtime code which may be distributed with Java applets and applications.

6.　　　　Distribution by Publishers. This section pertains to your distribution of the Software with your printed book or magazine (as those terms are commonly used in the industry) relating to Java technology ("Publication"). Subject to and conditioned upon your compliance with the restrictions and obligations contained in the Agreement, in addition to the license granted in Paragraph 1 above, Sun hereby grants to you a non-exclusive, nontransferable limited right to reproduce complete and unmodified copies of the Software on electronic media (the "Media") for the sole purpose of inclusion and distribution with your Publication(s), subject to the following terms: (i) you may not distribute the Software on a stand-alone basis; it must be distributed with your Publication(s); (ii) you are responsible for downloading the Software from the applicable Sun web site; (iii) you must refer to the Software as Sun ONE Studio 4, Community Edition; (iv) the Software must be reproduced in its entirety and without any modification whatsoever (including, without limitation, the Binary Code License and Supplemental License Terms accompanying the Software and proprietary rights notices contained in the Software); (v) the Media label shall include the following information: Copyright 2002, Sun Microsystems, Inc., 4150 Network Circle, Santa Clara, CA 95054. Java and SUN One and all trademarks and logos based on Java and SUN One are trademarks or registered trademarks of Sun Microsystems, Inc. in the U.S. and other countries. This information must be placed on the Media label in such a manner as to only apply to the Sun Software; (vi) you must clearly identify the Software as Sun's product on the Media holder or Media label, and you may not state or imply that Sun is responsible for any third-party software contained on the Media; (vii) you may not include any third party software on the Media which is intended to be a replacement or substitute for the Software or which directly competes with the Software; (viii) you shall indemnify Sun for all damages arising from your failure to comply with the requirements of this Agreement. In addition, you shall defend, at your expense, any and all claims brought against Sun by third parties, and shall pay all damages awarded by a court of competent jurisdiction, or such settlement amount negotiated by you, arising out of or in connection with your use, reproduction or distribution of the Software and/or the Publication. Your obligation to provide indemnification under this section shall arise provided that Sun: (i) provides you prompt notice of the claim; (ii) gives you sole control of the defense and settlement of the claim; (iii) provides you, at your expense, with all available information, assistance and authority to defend; and (iv) has not compromised or settled such claim without your prior written consent; (ix) you shall provide Sun with a written notice for each Publication; such notice shall include the following information: (1) title of Publication, (2) author(s), (3) date of Publication, and (4) ISBN or ISSN numbers. Such notice shall be sent to Sun Microsystems, Inc., 4150 Network Circle, M/S USCA12-110, Palo Alto, CA 94303-4900, Attention: Contracts Administration; and (x) you shall provide Sun with quarterly written reports regarding the number of copies of the Software distributed during the prior quarter; such reports shall be sent to Sun Microsystems, Inc., 4150 Network Circle, Santa Clara, CA, 95054, Attn.: Sun ONE Studio Product Management Group, M/S UOAK01.

7.　　　　Trademarks and Logos. You acknowledge and agree as between you and Sun that Sun owns the SUN, SOLARIS, JAVA, JINI, FORTE, and iPLANET trademarks and all SUN, SOLARIS, JAVA, JINI, FORTE, and iPLANET-related trademarks, service marks, logos and other brand designations ("Sun Marks"), and you agree to comply with the Sun Trademark and Logo Usage Requirements currently located at http://www.sun.com/policies/trademarks. Any use you make of the Sun Marks inures to Sun's benefit.

8.　　　　Source Code. Software may contain source code that is provided solely for reference purposes pursuant to the terms of this Agreement. Source code may not be redistributed unless expressly provided for in this Agreement.

9.　　　　Termination for Infringement. Either party may terminate this Agreement immediately should any Software become, or in either party's opinion be likely to become, the subject of a claim of infringement of any intellectual property right.

For inquiries please contact: Sun Microsystems, Inc.
4150 Network Circle, Santa Clara, California 95054.
(LFI#117241/Form ID#011801)

JCREATOR LE LICENSE AGREEMENT

NOTICE TO ALL USERS:CAREFULLY READ THE FOLLOWING LEGAL AGREEMENT, FOR THE LICENSE OF SPECIFIED SOFTWARE BY XINOX SOFTWARE. BY INSTALLING THE SOFTWARE, YOU (EITHER AN INDIVIDUAL OR A SINGLE ENTITY) CONSENT TO BE BOUND BY AND BECOME A PARTY TO THIS AGREEMENT. IF YOU DO NOT AGREE TO ALL OF THE TERMS OF THIS AGREEMENT, CLICK THE BUTTON THAT INDICATES THAT YOU DO NOT ACCEPT THE TERMS OF THIS AGREEMENT AND DO NOT INSTALL THE SOFTWARE.

1. GENERAL

This End-User License Agreement ("EULA") is a legal agreement between you and Xinox Software for the Xinox Software products identified above, which may include computer software and associated media, electronic documentation and printed materials ("The Software"). By installing, copying, distributing or otherwise using The Software you agree to be bound by the terms of this EULA. If you do not agree to the terms of this EULA, you must not install, use or distribute The Software, and you must destroy all copies of The Software that you have.

The Software is protected by copyright laws and international copyright treaties, as well as other intellectual property laws and treaties. The Software is

licensed, not sold and always remains the property of Xinox Software.

2. LICENSE RESTRICTIONS:
YOU MAY NOT: (a) Sublicense, sell, assign, transfer, pledge, distribute, rent or remove any proprietary notices on the Software except as expressly permitted in this Agreement; (b) Use, copy, adapt, disassemble, decompile, reverse engineer or modify the Software, in whole or in part, except as expressly permitted in this Agreement; (c) Take any action designed to unlock or bypass any Company-implemented restrictions on usage, access to, or number of installations of the Software; or (d) Use the Software if you fail to pay any license fee due and the Company notifies you that your license is terminated.
IF YOU DO ANY OF THE FOREGOING, YOUR RIGHTS UNDER THIS LICENSE WILL AUTOMATICALLY TERMINATE. SUCH TERMINATION SHALL BE IN ADDITION TO AND NOT IN LIEU OF ANY CRIMINAL, CIVIL OR OTHER REMEDIES AVAILABLE TO XINOX SOFTWARE.

3. TRANSFER OF RIGHTS
You may permanently transfer all of your rights under this EULA, provided you retain no copies of The Software, you transfer all of The Software (including all component parts, documentation upgrades, and this EULA), and the recipient agrees to the terms of this EULA. If The Software is an upgrade, any transfer must include all prior versions of The Software.

4. TERMINATION
Without prejudice to any other rights, Xinox Software may terminate this EULA if you fail to comply with the terms and conditions of this EULA. In such event, you must destroy all copies of The Software.

5. COPYRIGHT
All title, including but not limited to copyrights, in and to The Software and any copies thereof are owned by Xinox Software. All title and intellectual property rights in and to the content which may be accessed through use of The Software is the property of the respective content owner and may be protected by applicable copyright or other intellectual property laws and treaties. This EULA grants you no rights to use such content. All rights not expressly granted are reserved by Xinox Software.

6. LIMITED WARRANTY
TO THE MAXIMUM EXTENT PERMITTED BY APPLICABLE LAW, XINOX SOFTWARE DISCLAIMS ALL WARRANTIES AND CONDITIONS, EITHER EXPRESS OR IMPLIED, INCLUDING, BUT NOT LIMITED TO, IMPLIED WARRANTIES OF MERCHANTABILITY, FITNESS FOR A PARTICULAR PURPOSE, TITLE, AND NON-INFRINGEMENT, WITH REGARD TO THE SOFTWARE, AND THE PROVISION OF OR FAILURE TO PROVIDE SUPPORT SERVICES.XINOX SOFTWARE DOES NOT WARRANT THAT THE SOFTWARE WILL MEET YOUR REQUIREMENTS OR THAT THE OPERATION OF THE SOFTWARE WILL BE UNINTERRUPTED OR ERROR FREE.THE ENTIRE RISK AS TO SATISFACTORY QUALITY, PERFORMANCE, ACCURACY, AND EFFORT IS WITH YOU, THE USER.

7. LIMITATIONS OF REMEDIES AND LIABILITY
TO THE MAXIMUM EXTENT PERMITTED BY APPLICABLE LAW, IN NO EVENT SHALL XINOX SOFTWARE BE LIABLE FOR ANY SPECIAL, INCIDENTAL, INDIRECT, CONSEQUENTIAL OR OTHER DAMAGES WHATSOEVER (INCLUDING, WITHOUT LIMITATION, DAMAGES FOR LOSS OF PROFITS, BUSINESS INTERRUPTION, LOSS OF INFORMATION, OR ANY OTHER PECUNIARY LOSS) ARISING OUT OF THE USE OF OR INABILITY TO USE THE SOFTWARE PRODUCT OR THE PROVISION OF OR FAILURE TO PROVIDE SUPPORT SERVICES, EVEN IF XINOX SOFTWARE HAS BEEN ADVISED OF THE POSSIBILITY OF SUCH DAMAGES. SOME STATES AND JURISDICTIONS DO NOT ALLOW THE EXCLUSION OR LIMITATION OF LIABILITY, THE ABOVE LIMITATION MAY NOT APPLY TO YOU.

8. DISTRIBUTION
You are hereby licensed to make as many copies of the installation package for The Software as you wish; give exact copies of the original installation package for The Software to anyone; and distribute the original installation package for The Software in its unmodified form via electronic or other means. The Software must be clearly identified as an free version where described.
You are specifically prohibited from charging, or requesting donations, for any such copies, however made; and from distributing The Software including documentation with other products (commercial or otherwise) without prior written permission from Xinox Software. You are also prohibited from distributing components of The Software other than the complete original installation package.

9. FINAL
9.1 This Licence is governed by Dutch Law and is subject to exclusive jurisdiction of the Dutch courts.

9.2 This Licence constitutes the complete and exclusive statement of our agreement with you and supercedes all proposals, representations, understandings and prior agreements whether oral or written and all communications with you relating thereto.

JEDIT LICENSE AGREEMENT

jEdit is released under the terms of the GNU General Public License, and developed by Slava Pestov and others. Please review the GNU General Public License on the CD.

JGRASP™ LICENSE LICENSE AGREEMENT

Software License for jGRASP Version 1.5.3
Copyright 1999-2002 Auburn University

Section 1. License Grant.

Auburn University grants to you a non-exclusive and non-transferable license to use jGRASP and the associated documentation provided in jgrasp/help, collectively "jGRASP". jGRASP may be installed for use on a single computer or on a local area network. The "wedge" source code provided in the jgrasp/src directory is free of license restrictions. It may be used or modified for any purpose. jGRASP is a Trademark of Auburn University.

Section 2. Restrictions

Distribution of jGRASP is not permitted without written permission (see Supplements), except that it may be distributed internally within a single organization. Distribution of components of jGRASP separately from the whole is not permitted, except that the complete associated documentation provided in jgrasp/help may be distributed separately. Reverse engineering of jGRASP is not permitted. Any use of image files, icons, or executable components of jGRASP separately from the whole is prohibited.

Section 3. Disclaimer of Warranty

jGRASP is licensed "as is". There are no express or implied warranties, including, but not limited to, the implied warranties of merchantability and fitness for a particular purpose. Auburn University makes no warranty with respect to the accuracy or completeness of information obtained through the use of this program. Auburn University does not warrant that jGRASP will meet all of your requirements or that its operation will be uninterrupted or error free or that any defect within jGRASP will be corrected. No oral or written information, representation, or advice given by Auburn University or an authorized representative of Auburn University shall create a warranty. Auburn University and its agents shall in no event be held liable to the user for any damages, including direct, indirect, incidental, or consequential damages, lost profits, lost savings, or other such damages arising out of the installation, use, improper use, or inability to use jGRASP, even if Auburn University has been advised of the possibility of such damages, or any claim by any other person or entity related thereto.

Supplements

Distribution for Educational Purposes - Publishers may distribute the jGRASP software and the jGRASP Handbook on CDs that accompany their textbooks provided that (1) the title "jGRASP(TM) 1.5.3 copyright 1999-2002 Auburn University" is included on each CD label, (2) descriptions of the CD indicate that jGRASP is included on the CD, and (3) a list of the textbooks that include jGRASP is provided to Auburn University (cross@eng.auburn.edu). Permission to distribute jGRASP for educational purposes covers all CDs created prior to May 31, 2003 for inclusion in textbooks. While it is anticipated that distribution of jGRASP for educational purposes will remain royalty free, this supplement of the jGRASP license will be re-evaluated on an annual basis.

For additional information, contact James H. Cross II, Computer Science and Software Engineering, 107 Dunstan Hall, Auburn University, AL 36849 (334-844-6315, cross@eng.auburn.edu).

APACHE TOMCAT VERSION 4.1.24 LICENSE AGREEMENT

The Apache Software License, Version 1.1
Copyright (c) 1999-2002 The Apache Software Foundation. All rights reserved.

Redistribution and use in source and binary forms, with or without modification, are permitted provided that the following conditions are met:

1.   Redistributions of source code must retain the above copyright notice, this list of conditions and the following disclaimer.
2.   Redistributions in binary form must reproduce the above copyright notice, this list of conditions and the following disclaimer in the documentation and/or other materials provided with the distribution.
3.   The end-user documentation included with the redistribution, if any, must include the following acknowledgement:

"This product includes software developed by the Apache Software Foundation <http://www.apache.org/>."
Alternately, this acknowledgement may appear in the software itself, if and wherever such third-party acknowledgements normally appear.
4.   The names "The Jakarta Project", "Tomcat", and "Apache Software Foundation" must not be used to endorse or promote products derived from this software without prior written permission. For written permission, please contact <apache@apache.org>.
5.   Products derived from this software may not be called "Apache" nor may "Apache" appear in their names without prior written permission of the Apache Software Foundation.

THIS SOFTWARE IS PROVIDED "AS IS" AND ANY EXPRESSED OR IMPLIED WARRANTIES INCLUDING, BUT NOT LIMITED TO, THE IMPLIED WARRANTIES OF MERCHANTABILITY AND FITNESS FOR A PARTICULAR PURPOSE ARE DISCLAIMED. IN NO EVENT SHALL THE APACHE SOFTWARE FOUNDATION OR ITS CONTRIBUTORS BE LIABLE FOR ANY DIRECT, INDIRECT, INCIDENTAL, SPECIAL, EXEMPLARY, OR CONSEQUENTIAL DAMAGES (INCLUDING, BUT NOT LIMITED TO, PROCUREMENT OF SUBSTITUTE GOODS OR SERVICES; LOSS OF USE, DATA, OR PROFITS; OR BUSINESS INTERRUPTION) HOWEVER CAUSED AND ON ANY

THEORY OF LIABILITY, WHETHER IN CONTRACT, STRICT LIABILITY, OR TORT (INCLUDING NEGLIGENCE OR OTHERWISE) ARISING IN ANY WAY OUT OF THE USE OF THIS SOFTWARE, EVEN IF ADVISED OF THE POSSIBILITY OF SUCH DAMAGE.

This software consists of voluntary contributions made by many individuals on behalf of the Apache Software Foundation. For more information on the Apache Software Foundation, please see <http://www.apache.org/>.

Portions of this software are based upon public domain software originally written at the National Center for Supercomputing Applications, University of Illinois, Urbana-Champaign.

IBM® CLOUDSCAPE™ VERSION 5.1.3 LICENSE AGREEMENT

International License Agreement for Evaluation of Programs

Part 1 - General Terms
PLEASE READ THIS AGREEMENT CAREFULLY BEFORE USING THE PROGRAM. IBM WILL LICENSE THE PROGRAM TO YOU ONLY IF YOU FIRST ACCEPT THE TERMS OF THIS AGREEMENT. BY USING THE PROGRAM YOU AGREE TO THESE TERMS. IF YOU DO NOT AGREE TO THE TERMS OF THIS AGREEMENT, PROMPTLY RETURN THE UNUSED PROGRAM TO IBM.
The Program is owned by International Business Machines Corporation or one of its subsidiaries (IBM) or an IBM supplier, and is copyrighted and licensed, not sold.
The term "Program" means the original program and all whole or partial copies of it. A Program consists of machine-readable instructions, its components, data, audio-visual content (such as images, text, recordings, or pictures), and related licensed materials.
This Agreement includes Part 1 - General Terms and Part 2 - Country-unique Terms and is the complete agreement regarding the use of this Program, and replaces any prior oral or written communications between you and IBM. The terms of Part 2 may replace or modify those of Part 1.

1. License
Use of the Program
IBM grants you a nonexclusive, nontransferable license to use the Program.
You may 1) use the Program only for internal evaluation, testing or demonstration purposes, on a trial or "try-and-buy" basis and 2) make and install a reasonable number of copies of the Program in support of such use, unless IBM identifies a specific number of copies in the documentation accompanying the Program. The terms of this license apply to each copy you make. You will reproduce the copyright notice and any other legends of ownership on each copy, or partial copy, of the Program.
THE PROGRAM MAY CONTAIN A DISABLING DEVICE THAT WILL PREVENT IT FROM BEING USED UPON EXPIRATION OF THIS LICENSE. YOU WILL NOT TAMPER WITH THIS DISABLING DEVICE OR THE PROGRAM. YOU SHOULD TAKE PRECAUTIONS TO AVOID ANY LOSS OF DATA THAT MIGHT RESULT WHEN THE PROGRAM CAN NO LONGER BE USED.
You will 1) maintain a record of all copies of the Program and 2) ensure that anyone who uses the Program does so only for your authorized use and in compliance with the terms of this Agreement.
You may not 1) use, copy, modify or distribute the Program except as provided in this Agreement; 2) reverse assemble, reverse compile, or otherwise translate the Program except as specifically permitted by law without the possibility of contractual waiver; or 3) sublicense, rent, or lease the Program. This license begins with your first use of the Program and ends 1) as of the duration or date specified in the documentation accompanying the Program or 2) when the Program automatically disables itself. Unless IBM specifies in the documentation accompanying the Program that you may retain the Program (in which case, an additional charge may apply), you will destroy the Program and all copies made of it within ten days of when this license ends.

2. No Warranty
SUBJECT TO ANY STATUTORY WARRANTIES WHICH CANNOT BE EXCLUDED, IBM MAKES NO WARRANTIES OR CONDITIONS EITHER EXPRESS OR IMPLIED, INCLUDING WITHOUT LIMITATION, THE WARRANTY OF NON-INFRINGEMENT AND THE IMPLIED WARRANTIES OF MERCHANTABILITY AND FITNESS FOR A PARTICULAR PURPOSE, REGARDING THE PROGRAM OR TECHNICAL SUPPORT, IF ANY. IBM MAKES NO WARRANTY REGARDING THE CAPABILITY OF THE PROGRAM TO CORRECTLY PROCESS, PROVIDE AND/OR RECEIVE DATE DATA WITHIN AND BETWEEN THE 20TH AND 21ST CENTURIES.
This exclusion also applies to any of IBM's subcontractors, suppliers or program developers (collectively called "Suppliers").
Manufacturers, suppliers, or publishers of non-IBM Programs may provide their own warranties.

3. Limitation of Liability
NEITHER IBM NOR ITS SUPPLIERS ARE LIABLE FOR ANY DIRECT OR INDIRECT DAMAGES, INCLUDING WITHOUT LIMITATION, LOST PROFITS, LOST SAVINGS, OR ANY INCIDENTAL, SPECIAL, OR OTHER ECONOMIC CONSEQUENTIAL DAMAGES, EVEN IF IBM IS INFORMED OF THEIR POSSIBILITY. SOME JURISDICTIONS DO NOT ALLOW THE EXCLUSION OR LIMITATION OF INCIDENTAL OR CONSEQUENTIAL DAMAGES, SO THE ABOVE EXCLUSION OR LIMITATION MAY NOT APPLY TO YOU.

PRENTICE HALL LICENSE AGREEMENT AND LIMITED WARRANTY

READ THE FOLLOWING TERMS AND CONDITIONS CAREFULLY BEFORE OPENING THIS SOFTWARE PACKAGE. THIS LEGAL DOCUMENT IS AN AGREEMENT BETWEEN YOU AND PRENTICE-HALL, INC. (THE "COMPANY"). BY OPENING THIS SEALED SOFTWARE PACKAGE, YOU ARE AGREEING TO BE BOUND BY THESE TERMS AND CONDITIONS. IF YOU DO NOT AGREE WITH THESE TERMS

AND CONDITIONS, DO NOT OPEN THE SOFTWARE PACKAGE. PROMPTLY RETURN THE UNOPENED SOFTWARE PACKAGE AND ALL ACCOMPANYING ITEMS TO THE PLACE YOU OBTAINED THEM FOR A FULL REFUND OF ANY SUMS YOU HAVE PAID.

1.   GRANT OF LICENSE: In consideration of your purchase of this book, and your agreement to abide by the terms and conditions of this Agreement, the Company grants to you a nonexclusive right to use and display the copy of the enclosed software program (hereinafter the "SOFTWARE") on a single computer (i.e., with a single CPU) at a single location so long as you comply with the terms of this Agreement. The Company reserves all rights not expressly granted to you under this Agreement.

2.   OWNERSHIP OF SOFTWARE: You own only the magnetic or physical media (the enclosed media) on which the SOFTWARE is recorded or fixed, but the Company and the software developers retain all the rights, title, and ownership to the SOFTWARE recorded on the original media copy(ies) and all subsequent copies of the SOFTWARE, regardless of the form or media on which the original or other copies may exist. This license is not a sale of the original SOFTWARE or any copy to you.

3.   COPY RESTRICTIONS: This SOFTWARE and the accompanying printed materials and user manual (the "Documentation") are the subject of copyright. The individual programs on the media are copyrighted by the authors of each program. Some of the programs on the media include separate licensing agreements. If you intend to use one of these programs, you must read and follow its accompanying license agreement. You may not copy the Documentation or the SOFTWARE, except that you may make a single copy of the SOFTWARE for backup or archival purposes only. You may be held legally responsible for any copying or copyright infringement which is caused or encouraged by your failure to abide by the terms of this restriction.

4.   USE RESTRICTIONS: You may not network the SOFTWARE or otherwise use it on more than one computer or computer terminal at the same time. You may physically transfer the SOFTWARE from one computer to another provided that the SOFTWARE is used on only one computer at a time. You may not distribute copies of the SOFTWARE or Documentation to others. You may not reverse engineer, disassemble, decompile, modify, adapt, translate, or create derivative works based on the SOFTWARE or the Documentation without the prior written consent of the Company.

5.   TRANSFER RESTRICTIONS: The enclosed SOFTWARE is licensed only to you and may not be transferred to any one else without the prior written consent of the Company. Any unauthorized transfer of the SOFTWARE shall result in the immediate termination of this Agreement.

6.   TERMINATION: This license is effective until terminated. This license will terminate automatically without notice from the Company and become null and void if you fail to comply with any provisions or limitations of this license. Upon termination, you shall destroy the Documentation and all copies of the SOFTWARE. All provisions of this Agreement as to warranties, limitation of liability, remedies or damages, and our ownership rights shall survive termination.

7.   MISCELLANEOUS: This Agreement shall be construed in accordance with the laws of the United States of America and the State of New York and shall benefit the Company, its affiliates, and assignees.

8.   LIMITED WARRANTY AND DISCLAIMER OF WARRANTY: The Company warrants that the SOFTWARE, when properly used in accordance with the Documentation, will operate in substantial conformity with the description of the SOFTWARE set forth in the Documentation. The Company does not warrant that the SOFTWARE will meet your requirements or that the operation of the SOFTWARE will be uninterrupted or error-free. The Company warrants that the media on which the SOFTWARE is delivered shall be free from defects in materials and workmanship under normal use for a period of thirty (30) days from the date of your purchase. Your only remedy and the Company's only obligation under these limited warranties is, at the Company's option, return of the warranted item for a refund of any amounts paid by you or replacement of the item. Any replacement of SOFTWARE or media under the warranties shall not extend the original warranty period. The limited warranty set forth above shall not apply to any SOFTWARE which the Company determines in good faith has been subject to misuse, neglect, improper installation, repair, alteration, or damage by you. EXCEPT FOR THE EXPRESSED WARRANTIES SET FORTH ABOVE, THE COMPANY DISCLAIMS ALL WARRANTIES, EXPRESS OR IMPLIED, INCLUDING WITHOUT LIMITATION, THE IMPLIED WARRANTIES OF MERCHANTABILITY AND FITNESS FOR A PARTICULAR PURPOSE. EXCEPT FOR THE EXPRESS WARRANTY SET FORTH ABOVE, THE COMPANY DOES NOT WARRANT, GUARANTEE, OR MAKE ANY REPRESENTATION REGARDING THE USE OR THE RESULTS OF THE USE OF THE SOFTWARE IN TERMS OF ITS CORRECTNESS, ACCURACY, RELIABILITY, CURRENTNESS, OR OTHERWISE.

IN NO EVENT, SHALL THE COMPANY OR ITS EMPLOYEES, AGENTS, SUPPLIERS, OR CONTRACTORS BE LIABLE FOR ANY INCIDENTAL, INDIRECT, SPECIAL, OR CONSEQUENTIAL DAMAGES ARISING OUT OF OR IN CONNECTION WITH THE LICENSE GRANTED UNDER THIS AGREEMENT, OR FOR LOSS OF USE, LOSS OF DATA, LOSS OF INCOME OR PROFIT, OR OTHER LOSSES, SUSTAINED AS A RESULT OF INJURY TO ANY PERSON, OR LOSS OF OR DAMAGE TO PROPERTY, OR CLAIMS OF THIRD PARTIES, EVEN IF THE COMPANY OR AN AUTHORIZED REPRESENTATIVE OF THE COMPANY HAS BEEN ADVISED OF THE POSSIBILITY OF SUCH DAMAGES. IN NO EVENT SHALL LIABILITY OF THE COMPANY FOR DAMAGES WITH RESPECT TO THE SOFTWARE EXCEED THE AMOUNTS ACTUALLY PAID BY YOU, IF ANY, FOR THE SOFTWARE.

SOME JURISDICTIONS DO NOT ALLOW THE LIMITATION OF IMPLIED WARRANTIES OR LIABILITY FOR INCIDENTAL, INDIRECT, SPECIAL, OR CONSEQUENTIAL DAMAGES, SO THE ABOVE LIMITATIONS MAY NOT ALWAYS APPLY. THE WARRANTIES IN THIS AGREEMENT GIVE YOU SPECIFIC LEGAL RIGHTS AND YOU MAY ALSO HAVE OTHER RIGHTS WHICH VARY IN ACCORDANCE WITH LOCAL LAW.

ACKNOWLEDGMENT

YOU ACKNOWLEDGE THAT YOU HAVE READ THIS AGREEMENT, UNDERSTAND IT, AND AGREE TO BE BOUND BY ITS TERMS AND CONDITIONS. YOU ALSO AGREE THAT THIS AGREEMENT IS THE COMPLETE AND EXCLUSIVE STATEMENT OF THE AGREEMENT BETWEEN YOU AND THE COMPANY AND SUPERSEDES ALL PROPOSALS OR PRIOR AGREEMENTS, ORAL, OR WRITTEN, AND ANY OTHER COMMUNICATIONS BETWEEN YOU AND THE COMPANY OR ANY REPRESENTATIVE OF THE COMPANY RELATING TO THE SUBJECT MATTER OF THIS AGREEMENT.

Should you have any questions concerning this Agreement or if you wish to contact the Company for any reason, please contact in writing at the address below.

Robin Short
Prentice Hall PTR
One Lake Street
Upper Saddle River, New Jersey 07458

The DEITEL® Suite of Products...

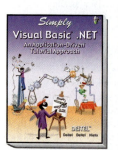

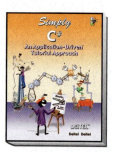
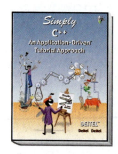

HOW TO PROGRAM BOOKS

The Deitels' acclaimed *How to Program Series* has achieved its success largely due to the innovative pedagogy used to teach key programming concepts. Their signature *LIVE-CODE Approach,* icon-identified programming tips and comprehensive exercises form the backbone of a series of books that has taught over one million students the craft of programming.

C++ How to Program Fourth Edition

BOOK / CD-ROM

©2003, 1400 pp., paper
(0-13-038474-7)

The world's best-selling C++ textbook is now even better! Designed for beginning through intermediate courses, this comprehensive, practical introduction to C++ includes hundreds of hands-on exercises and uses 267 *LIVE-CODE* programs to demonstrate C++'s powerful capabilities. This edition includes a new chapter—Web Programming with CGI—that provides everything readers need to begin developing their own Web-based applications that will run on the Internet!

Java™ How to Program Fifth Edition

BOOK / CD-ROM

©2003, 1500 pp., paper
(0-13-101621-0)

The Deitels' new Fifth Edition of *Java™ How to Program* is now even better! It now includes a tuned treatment of object-oriented programming; coverage of Java 1.4's new I/O APIs; new chapters on JDBC, servlets and JSP; an updated, optional case study on object-oriented design with version 1.4 of the UML; and a new code highlighting feature that makes it easier for readers to locate important program segments.

Visual Basic® .NET How to Program Second Edition

BOOK / CD-ROM

©2002, 1400 pp., paper
(0-13-029363-6)

This book provides a comprehensive introduction to the next version of Visual Basic—Visual Basic .NET—featuring extensive updates and increased functionality. *Visual Basic .NET How to Program, Second Edition* covers introductory programming techniques as well as more advanced topics, featuring ASP .NET, ADO .NET, Web services and developing Web-based applications. This book also includes extensive coverage of XML.

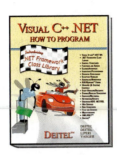

Visual C++ .NET How To Program

BOOK / CD-ROM

©2004, 1400 pp., paper (0-13-437377-4)

Written by the authors of the world's best-selling introductory/intermediate C and C++ textbooks, this comprehensive book thoroughly examines Visual C++® .NET. *Visual C++® .NET How to Program* begins with a strong foundation in the introductory and intermediate programming principles students will need in industry, including fundamental topics such as arrays, functions and control structures. Readers learn the concepts of object-oriented programming, including how to create reusable software components with classes and assemblies. The text then explores such essential topics as networking, databases, XML and multimedia. Graphical user interfaces are also extensively covered, giving students the tools to build compelling and fully interactive programs using the "drag-and-drop" techniques provided by the latest version of Visual Studio .NET.

Advanced Java™ 2 Platform How to Program

BOOK / CD-ROM

©2002, 1811 pp., paper (0-13-089560-1)

Expanding on the world's best-selling Java textbook—*Java™ How to Program*—*Advanced Java™ 2 Platform How To Program* presents advanced Java topics for developing sophisticated, user-friendly GUIs; significant, scalable enterprise applications; wireless applications and distributed systems. Primarily based on Java 2 Enterprise Edition (J2EE), this textbook integrates technologies such as XML, JavaBeans, security, JDBC™, JavaServer Pages (JSP™), servlets, Remote Method Invocation (RMI), Enterprise JavaBeans™ (EJB) and design patterns into a production-quality system that allows developers to benefit from the leverage and platform independence Java 2 Enterprise Edition provides. The book also features the development of a complete, end-to-end e-business solution using advanced Java technologies.

C# How to Program

BOOK / CD-ROM

©2002, 1568 pp., paper (0-13-062221-4)

C# How to Program provides a comprehensive introduction to Microsoft's new object-oriented language. C# builds on the skills already mastered by countless C++ and Java programmers, enabling them to create powerful Web applications and components—ranging from XML-based Web services on Microsoft's .NET platform to middle-tier business objects and system-level applications.

C How to Program Fourth Edition

BOOK / CD-ROM

©2004, 1328 pp., paper (0-13-142644-3)

The Fourth Edition of the world's best-selling C text is designed for introductory through intermediate courses as well as programming languages survey courses. This comprehensive text is aimed at readers with little or no programming experience through intermediate audiences. Highly practical in approach, it introduces fundamental notions of structured programming and software engineering and gets up to speed quickly.

Getting Started with Microsoft® Visual C++™ 6 with an Introduction to MFC

BOOK / CD-ROM

©2000, 163 pp., paper (0-13-016147-0)

Internet & World Wide Web How to Program Second Edition

BOOK / CD-ROM

©2002, 1428 pp., paper (0-13-030897-8)

Internet & World Wide Web How to Program, Second Edition offers a thorough treatment of programming concepts that yield visible or audible results in Web pages and Web-based applications. This book discusses effective Web-based design, server- and client-side scripting, multi-tier Web-based applications development, ActiveX® controls and electronic commerce essentials.

Wireless Internet & Mobile Business How to Program

©2002, 1292 pp., paper (0-13-062226-5)

Wireless Internet & Mobile Business How to Program offers a thorough treatment of both the management and technical aspects of wireless Internet applications development, including coverage of current practices and future trends.

Python How to Program

BOOK / CD-ROM

©2002, 1376 pp., paper (0-13-092361-3)

Python How to Program provides a comprehensive introduction to Python— a powerful object-oriented programming language with clear syntax and the ability to bring together various technologies quickly and easily.

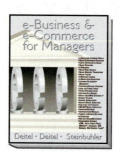

e-Business & e-Commerce for Managers

©2001, 794 pp., cloth (0-13-032364-0)

This comprehensive overview of building and managing e-businesses explores topics such as the decision to bring a business online, choosing a business model, accepting payments, marketing strategies and security, as well as many other important issues (such as career resources).

XML How to Program

BOOK / CD-ROM

©2001, 934 pp., paper (0-13-028417-3)

This book is a comprehensive guide to programming in XML. It teaches how to use XML to create customized tags and includes chapters that adress markup languages for science and technology, multimedia, commerce and many other fields.

Perl How to Program

BOOK / CD-ROM

©2001, 1057 pp., paper (0-13-028418-1)

This comprehensive guide to Perl programming emphasizes the use of the Common Gateway Interface (CGI) with Perl to create powerful, dynamic multi-tier Web-based client/server applications.

e-Business & e-Commerce How to Program

BOOK / CD-ROM

©2001, 1254 pp., paper (0-13-028419-X)

e-Business & e-Commerce How to Program explores programming technologies for developing Web-based e-business and e-commerce solutions, and covers e-business and e-commerce models and business issues.

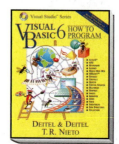

Visual Basic® 6 How to Program

BOOK / CD-ROM

©1999, 1015 pp., paper (0-13-456955-5)

Visual Basic® 6 How to Program was developed in cooperation with Microsoft to cover important topics such as graphical user interfaces (GUIs), multimedia, object-oriented programming, networking, database programming, Script®, COM/DCOM and ActiveX®.

The DEITEL® DEVELOPER SERIES

Deitel & Associates is recognized worldwide for its best-selling *How to Program Series* of books for college and university students and its signature *LIVE-CODE Approach* to teaching programming languages. Now, for the first time, Deitel & Associates brings its proven teaching methods to a new series of books specifically designed for professionals.

THREE TYPES OF BOOKS FOR THREE DISTINCT AUDIENCES:

A Technical Introduction

A Technical Introduction books provide programmers, technical managers, project managers and other technical professionals with introductions to broad new technology areas.

A Programmer's Introduction

A Programmer's Introduction books offer focused treatments of programming fundamentals for practicing programmers. These books are also appropriate for novices.

For Experienced Programmers

For Experienced Programmers books are for experienced programmers who want a detailed treatment of a programming language or technology. These books contain condensed introductions to programming language fundamentals and provide extensive intermediate level coverage of high-end topics.

Java™ Web Services
for Experienced Programmers

©2003, 700 pp., paper (0-13-046134-2)

Java™ Web Services for Experienced Programmers provides the experienced Java programmer with 103 *LIVE-CODE* examples and covers industry standards including XML, SOAP, WSDL and UDDI. Learn how to build and integrate Web services using the Java API for XML RPC, the Java API for XML Messaging, Apache Axis and the Java Web Services Developer Pack.

Web Services
A Technical Introduction

©2003, 400 pp., paper (0-13-046135-0)

Web Services: A Technical Introduction familiarizes programmers, technical managers and project managers with key Web services concepts, including what Web services are and why they are revolutionary. The book covers the business case for Web services, the latest Web-services standards and Web services implementations in .NET and Java.

ORDER INFORMATION

SINGLE COPY SALES:
Visa, Master Card, American Express, Checks, or Money Orders only
Toll-Free: 800-643-5506; Fax: 800-835-5327

GOVERNMENT AGENCIES:
Prentice Hall Customer Service
(#GS-02F-8023A)
Tel: 201-767-5994; Fax: 800-445-6991

COLLEGE PROFESSORS:
For desk or review copies, please visit us on the World Wide Web at www.prenhall.com

CORPORATE ACCOUNTS:
Quantity, Bulk Orders totaling 10 or more books. Purchase orders only — No credit cards.
Tel: 201-236-7156; Fax: 201-236-7141
Toll-Free: 800-382-3419

CANADA:
Pearson Technology Group Canada
10 Alcorn Avenue, suite #300
Toronto, Ontario, Canada M4V 3B2
Tel: 416-925-2249; Fax: 416-925-0068
E-mail: phcinfo.pubcanada@pearsoned.com

UK/IRELAND:
Pearson Education
Edinburgh Gate
Harlow, Essex CM20 2JE UK
Tel: 01279 623928; Fax: 01279 414130
E-mail: enq.orders@pearsoned-ema.com

EUROPE, MIDDLE EAST & AFRICA:
Pearson Education
P.O. Box 75598
1070 AN Amsterdam, The Netherlands
Tel: 31 20 5755 800; Fax: 31 20 664 5334
E-mail: amsterdam@pearsoned-ema.com

ASIA:
Pearson Education Asia
317 Alexandra Road #04-01
IKEA Building
Singapore 159965
Tel: 65 476 4688; Fax: 65 378 0370

JAPAN:
Pearson Education
Nishi-Shinjuku, KF Building 101
8-14-24 Nishi-Shinjuku, Shinjuku-ku
Tokyo, Japan 160-0023
Tel: 81 3 3365 9001; Fax: 81 3 3365 9009

INDIA:
Pearson Education Indian Liaison Office
90 New Raidhani Enclave, Ground Floor
Delhi 110 092, India
Tel: 91 11 2059850 & 2059851
Fax: 91 11 2059852

AUSTRALIA:
Pearson Education Australia
Unit 4, Level 2
14 Aquatic Drive
Frenchs Forest, NSW 2086, Australia
Tel: 61 2 9454 2200; Fax: 61 2 9453 0089
E-mail: marketing@pearsoned.com.au

NEW ZEALAND/FIJI:
Pearson Education
46 Hillside Road
Auckland 10, New Zealand
Tel: 649 444 4968; Fax: 649 444 4957
E-mail: sales@pearsoned.co.nz

SOUTH AFRICA:
Pearson Education
P.O. Box 12122
Mill Street
Cape Town 8010 South Africa
Tel: 27 21 686 6356; Fax: 27 21 686 4590

LATIN AMERICA:
Pearson Education Latinoamerica
815 NW 57th Street Suite 484
Miami, FL 33158
Tel: 305 264 8344; Fax: 305 264 7933

We make it click.

Complete Training Courses

Each complete package includes the corresponding *How to Program Series* textbook and interactive multimedia Windows-based CD-ROM *Cyber Classroom*. *Complete Training Courses* are perfect for anyone interested in Web and e-commerce programming. They are affordable resources for college students and professionals learning programming for the first time or reinforcing their knowledge.

Intuitive Browser-Based Interface

You'll love the *Complete Training Courses'* browser-based interface, designed to be easy and accessible to anyone who's ever used a Web browser. Every *Complete Training Course* features the full text, illustrations and program listings of its corresponding *How to Program* textbook—all in full color—with full-text searching and hyperlinking.

Further Enhancements to the Deitels' Signature LIVE-CODE Approach

Every code sample from the main text can be found in the interactive, multimedia, CD-ROM-based *Cyber Classrooms* included in the *Complete Training Courses*. Syntax coloring of code is included for the *How to Program* books that are published in full color. Even the two-color books use effective syntax shading. The *Cyber Classroom* products are always in full color.

Audio Annotations

Hours of detailed, expert audio descriptions of thousands of lines of code help reinforce concepts.

Easily Executable Code

With one click of the mouse, you can execute the code or save it to your hard drive to manipulate using the programming environment of your choice. With selected *Complete Training Courses*, you can also load all of the code into a development environment such as Microsoft® Visual C++, enabling you to modify and execute the programs with ease.

Abundant Self-Assessment Material

Practice exams test your understanding of key concepts with hundreds of test questions and answers in addition to those found in the main text. The textbook includes hundreds of programming exercises, while the *Cyber Classrooms* include answers to about half the exercises.

www.phptr.com/phptrinteractive

BOOK/MULTIMEDIA PACKAGES

The Complete C++ Training Course, Fourth Edition

(0-13-100252-X)

The Complete e-Business & e-Commerce Programming Training Course

(0-13-089549-0)

The Complete Java™ Training Course, Fifth Edition

(0-13-101766-7)

The Complete Perl Training Course

(0-13-089552-0)

The Complete Visual Basic® .NET Training Course, Second Edition

(0-13-042530-3)

The Complete Visual Basic® 6 Training Course

(0-13-082929-3)

The Complete C# Training Course

(0-13-064584-2)

The Complete Python Training Course

(0-13-067374-9)

The Complete Internet & World Wide Web Programming Training Course, Second Edition

(0-13-089550-4)

The Complete Wireless Internet & Mobile Business Programming Training Course

(0-13-062335-0)

The Complete XML Programming Training Course

(0-13-089557-1)

All of these ISBNs are retail ISBNs. College and university instructors should contact your local Prentice Hall representative or write to cs@prenhall•com for the corresponding student edition ISBNs.

License Agreement and Limited Warranty

Using the CD-ROM

The interface to the contents of this CD is designed to start automatically through the **AUTORUN.EXE** file. If a startup screen does not pop up automatically when you insert the CD into your computer, double click on the welcome.htm file to launch the Student CD or refer to the file **readme.txt** on the CD.

Contents of the CD-ROM

- Java™ 2 Platform, Software Development Kit Standard Edition Version1.4.1_2 for Windows and Linux (32-bit)
- jEdit Version 4.1 for Windows and Linux platforms
- JCreator Lite Version 2.50 build 8 for Windows
- jGRASP Version 1.5.3 for Windows and Linux platforms
- Sun™ ONE Studio 4 update 1, Community Edition for Windows and Linux platforms
- IBM® Cloudscape™ Version 5.1.3, Evaluation Copy (60 Days) for Windows and Linux platforms
- Apache Tomcat Version 4.1.24 for Windows and Linux platforms
- Live code examples from the book Java How to Program 5/e
- Web Resources -- Links to internet sites mentioned in the book Java How to Program, 5/e
- Additional Resources (in the Adobe ® Acrobat ® PDF format) not included in the book

Software and Hardware System Requirements

- 500 MHz (minimum) Pentium III or faster processor
- Microsoft Windows® NT (with Service Pack 6a), Windows 2000 Professional (with Service Pack 3 or greater), Windows XP, or
- Red Hat Linux 7.2
- 256 MB of RAM (minimum), 512 MB of RAM (recommended)
- CD-ROM drive
- Internet connection and web browser
- Adobe® Acrobat® Reader® 4.0 or 5.0